T0180362

Lecture Notes in Computer Science 9057

Commenced Publication in 1973
Founding and Former Series Editors:
Gerhard Goos, Juris Hartmanis, and Jan van Leeuwen

Editorial Board

More information about this series at http://www.springer.com/series/7410

Elisabeth Oswald · Marc Fischlin (Eds.)

Advances in Cryptology – EUROCRYPT 2015

34th Annual International Conference on the Theory
and Applications of Cryptographic Techniques
Sofia, Bulgaria, April 26–30, 2015
Proceedings, Part II

Springer

Editors

Elisabeth Oswald
University of Bristol
Bristol
UK

Marc Fischlin
Technische Universität Darmstadt
Darmstadt
Germany

ISSN 0302-9743
Lecture Notes in Computer Science
ISBN 978-3-662-46802-9
DOI 10.1007/978-3-662-46803-6

ISSN 1611-3349   (electronic)

ISBN 978-3-662-46803-6   (eBook)

Library of Congress Control Number: 2015935614

LNCS Sublibrary: SL4 – Security and Cryptology

Springer Heidelberg New York Dordrecht London

Printed on acid-free paper

Springer-Verlag GmbH Berlin Heidelberg is part of Springer Science+Business Media
(www.springer.com)

Preface

Eurocrypt 2015, the 34th annual International Conference on the Theory and Applications of Cryptographic Techniques, was held during April 26–30, 2015, in Sofia, Bulgaria, and sponsored by the International Association for Cryptologic Research (IACR). Responsible for the local organization were Svetla Nikova, from Katholieke Universiteit Leuven, and Dimitar Jetchev, from EPFL. They were supported by a Local Organizing Committee consisting of Tsonka Baicheva (Institute of Mathematics and Informatics, BAS), Violeta Ducheva (SANS), and Georgi Sharkov (ESI Center Eastern Europe). We are indebted to them for their support.

To accommodate the request by IACR to showcase as many high-quality submissions as possible, the program was organized in two tracks. These tracks ran in parallel with the exception of invited talks, the single best paper, and two papers with honorable mention. Following a popular convention in contemporary cryptography, one track was labeled $\mathcal{R}$ and featured results more closely related to 'real' world cryptography, whereas the second track was labeled $\mathcal{I}$ and featured results in a more abstract or 'ideal' world.

A total of 194 submissions were considered during the review process, many were of high quality. As usual, all reviews were conducted double-blind and we excluded Program Committee members from discussing submissions for which they had a possible conflict of interest. To account for a desire (by authors and the wider community alike) to maintain the high standard of publications, we allowed for longer submissions such that essential elements of proofs or other form of evidence could be included in the body of the submissions (appendices were not scrutinized by reviewers). Furthermore, a more focused review process was used that consisted of two rounds. In the first round of reviews we solicited three independent reviews per submission. After a short discussion phase among the 38 Program Committee members, just over half of the submissions were retained for the second round. Authors of these retained papers were given the opportunity to comment on the reviews so far. After extensive deliberations in a second round, we accepted 57 papers. The revised versions of these papers are included in these two volume proceedings, organized topically within their respective track.

The review process would have been impossible without the hard work of the Program Committee members and over 210 external reviewers, whose effort we would like to commend here. It has been an honor to work with everyone. The process was enabled by the Web Submission and Review Software written by Shai Halevi and the server was hosted by IACR. We would like to thank Shai for setting up the service on the server and for helping us whenever needed.

The Program Committee decided to honor one submission with the Best Paper Award this year. This submission was "Cryptanalysis of the Multilinear Map over the Integers" authored by Junghee Cheo, Kyoohyung Han, Changmin Lee, Hansol Ryu, and

Damien Stehlé. The two runners-up to the award, "Robust Authenticated-Encryption: AEZ and the Problem that it Solves" (by Viet Tung Hoang, Ted Krovetz, and Phillip Rogaway) and "On the behaviors of affine equivalent Sboxes regarding differential and linear attacks" (by Anne Canteaut and Joëlle Roué) received Honorable Mentions and hence also invitations for the Journal of Cryptology.

In addition to the contributed talks, we had three invited speakers: Kristin Lauter, Tal Rabin, and Vincent Rijmen. We would like to thank them for accepting our invitation and thank everyone (speakers, session chairs, and rump session chair) for their contribution to the program of Eurocrypt 2015.

April 2015   Elisabeth Oswald
                                                              Marc Fischlin

EUROCRYPT 2015

The 34th Annual International Conference on the Theory and Applications of Cryptographic Techniques, Track $\mathcal{I}$ Sofia, Bulgaria, April 26–30, 2015

General Chairs

Svetla Nikova — Katholieke Universiteit Leuven, Belgium
Dimitar Jetchev — École Polytechnique Fédérale de Lausanne, Switzerland

Program Co-chairs

Elisabeth Oswald — University of Bristol, UK
Marc Fischlin — Technische Universität Darmstadt, Germany

Program Commitee

Masayuki Abe — NTT, Japan
Gilles Barthe — IMDEA, Spain
Lejla Batina — Radboud University Nijmegen, The Netherlands
Alex Biryukov — University of Luxembourg, Luxembourg
Alexandra Boldyreva — Georgia Institute of Technology, USA
Jan Camenisch — IBM Research – Zurich, Switzerland
Anne Canteaut — Inria, France
Liqun Chen — HP Laboratories, UK
Chen-Mou Cheng — National Taiwan University, Taiwan
Marten van Dijk — University of Connecticut, USA
Jens Groth — University College London, UK
Tetsu Iwata — Nagoya University, Japan
Marc Joye — Technicolor, USA
Charanjit Jutla — IBM Research, USA
Eike Kiltz — Ruhr-Universität Bochum, Germany
Markulf Kohlweiss — Microsoft Research, UK
Gregor Leander — Ruhr-Universität Bochum, Germany
Benoît Libert — ENS Lyon, France
Yehuda Lindell — Bar-Ilan University, Israel
Stefan Mangard — Graz University of Technology, Austria
Steve Myers — Indiana University, USA
Gregory Neven — IBM Research – Zurich, Switzerland

Kaisa Nyberg	Aalto University, Finland
Kenneth G. Paterson	Royal Holloway, University of London, UK
David Pointcheval	École Normale Supérieure Paris, France
Manoj Prabhakaran	University of Illinois at Urbana–Champaign, USA
Emmanuel Prouff	ANSSI, France
Christian Rechberger	Technical University of Denmark, Denmark
Pankaj Rohatgi	Cryptography Research Inc., USA
Alon Rosen	Herzliya Interdisciplinary Center, Herzliya, Israel
Alessandra Scafuro	University of California, Los Angeles, USA
Christian Schaffner	University of Amsterdam, The Netherlands
Dominique Schröder	Saarland University, Germany
Martijn Stam	University of Bristol, UK
François-Xavier Standaert	Université catholique de Louvain, Belgium
Douglas Stebila	Queensland University of Technology, Australia
Frederik Vercauteren	Katholieke Universiteit Leuven, Belgium
Bogdan Warinschi	University of Bristol, UK

External Reviewers

Divesh Aggarwal
Shweta Agrawal
Martin Albrecht
Hiroaki Anada
Prabhanjan Ananth
Elena Andreeva
Benny Applebaum
Srinivasan Arunachalam
Gilad Asharov
Nuttapong Attrapadung
Saikrishna Badrinarayanan
Rachid El Bansarkhani
Manuel Barbosa
Lynn Batten
Amos Beimel
Sonia Belaid
Josh Benaloh
Florian Bergsma
Sanjay Bhattacherjee
Nir Bitansky
Cèline Blondeau
Andrej Bogdanov
Niek Bouman
Colin Boyd
Elette Boyle
Zvika Brakerski

Luís T.A.N. Brandão
Billy Bob Brumley
Christina Brzuska
Claude Carlet
Angelo De Caro
Ignacio Cascudo
David Cash
Andrea Cerulli
Pyrros Chaidos
Yun-An Chang
Jie Chen
Baudoin Collard
Geoffroy Couteau
Edouard Cuvelier
Joan Daemen
Vizár Damian
Jean-Paul Degabriele
Patrick Derbez
David Derler
Christoph Dobraunig
Nico Döttling
Manu Drijvers
Maria Dubovitskaya
Orr Dunkelman
Francois Dupressoir
Stefan Dziembowski

Markus Dürmuth
Robert Enderlein
Chun-I Fan
Edvard Fargerholm
Pooya Farshim
Feng-Hao Liu
Matthieu Finiasz
Dario Fiore
Rob Fitzpatrick
Robert Fitzpatrick
Nils Fleischhacker
Jean-Pierre Flori
Pierre-Alain Fouque
Thomas Fuhr
Eiichiro Fujisaki
Benjamin Fuller
Tommaso Gagliardoni
Steven Galbraith
Nicolas Gama
Praveen Gauravaram
Ran Gelles
Rosario Gennaro
Henri Gilbert
Sergey Gorbunov
Matthew Green
Vincent Grosso

Johann Groszschädl

Sylvain Guilley

Shai Halevi

Michael Hamburg

Mike Hamburg

Fabrice Ben Hamouda

Christian Hanser

Ryan Henry

Jens Hermans

Javier Herranz

Ryo Hiromasa

Shoichi Hirose

Yan Huang

Yuval Ishai

Cess Jansen

Thomas Johansson

Anthony Journault

Antoine Joux

Ali El Kaafarani

Saqib Kakvi

Akshay Kamath

Bhavana Kanukurthi

Carmen Kempka

Dmitry Khovratovich

Dakshita Khurana

Susumu Kiyoshima

Stefan Koelbl

François Koeune

Vlad Kolesnikov

Anna Krasnova

Stephan Krenn

Po-Chun Kuo

Fabien Laguillaumie

Adeline Langlois

Martin M. Laurisden

Jooyoung Lee

Anja Lehmann

Tancrède Lepoint

Reynald Lercier

Gaëtan Leurent

Anthony Leverrier

Huijia Lin

Steve Lu

Atul Luykx

Giulio Malavolta

Mark Marson

Dan Martin

Christian Matt

Ueli Maurer

Ingo von Maurich

Matthew McKague

Marcel Medwed

Florian Mendel

Bart Mennink

Arno Mittelbach

Payman Mohassel

Mridul Nandi

María Naya-Plasencia

Phong Nguyen

Ryo Nishimaki

Kobbi Nissim

Adam O'Neill

Wakaha Ogata

Miyako Ohkubo

Olya Ohrimenko

Tatsuaki Okamoto

Jiaxin Pan

Omkant Pandey

Omer Paneth

Saurabh Panjwani

Louiza Papachristodolou

Anat Paskin-Cherniavsky

Rafael Pass

Chris Peikert

Ludovic Perret

Léo Perrin

Thomas Peters

Christophe Petit

Duong Hieu Phan

Krzysztof Pietrzak

Benny Pinkas

Jérôme Plût

Christopher Portmann

Romain Poussier

Ignacio Cascudo Pueyo

Ivan Pustogarov

Bertram Pöttering

Max Rabkin

Carla Rafols

Somindu Ramanna

Jothi Rangasamy

Alfredo Rial

Vincent Rijmen

Ben Riva

Matthieu Rivain

Thomas Roche

Mike Rosulek

Ron Rothblum

Yannis Rouselakis

Arnab Roy

Atri Rudra

Kai Samelin

Palash Sarkar

Benedikt Schmidt

Peter Scholl

Peter Schwabe

Gil Segev

Nicolas Sendrier

Yannick Seurin

Abhi Shelat

Adam Shull

Jamie Sikora

Mark Simkin

Daniel Slamanig

Hadi Soleimany

Juarj Somorovsky

Florian Speelman

Damien Stehlé

John Steinberger

Noah
    Stephens-Davidowitz

Marc Stevens

Pierre-Yves Strub

Stefano Tessaro

Susan Thomson

Mehdi Tibouchi

Tyge Tiessen

Pei-Yih Ting

Elmar Tischhauser

Mike Tunstall

Dominique Unruh

Vinod Vaikuntanathan

Kerem Varici

Vesselin Velichkov

Muthuramakrishnan
    Venkitasubramaniam

Daniele Venturi

Nicolas Veyrat-Charvillon

Ivan Visconti

David Wagner

Hoeteck Wee

Erich Wenger

Cyrille Wielding

David Wu

Keita Xagawa

Bo-Yin Yang

Shang-Yi Yang

Kazuki Yoneyama

Mark Zhandry

Vassilis Zikas

Contents – Part II, Track I

Crypto Currencies

Secret Sharing

Outsourcing Computations

Obfuscation and E-Voting

Multi-party Computations

Encryption

Resistant Protocols

Key Exchange

Quantum Cryptography

Discrete Logarithms

Contents – Part I, Track R

Masking

Fully Homomorphic Encryption I

Related-Key Attacks

Fully Homomorphic Encryption II

Efficient Two-Party Protocols

Symmetric Cryptanalysis III

Lattices

Signatures

Universal Signature Aggregators

Susan Hohenberger[1]([✉]), Venkata Koppula[2], and Brent Waters[2]

[1] Johns Hopkins University, Baltimore, USA
susan@cs.jhu.edu
[2] University of Texas at Austin, Austin, USA
{kvenkata,bwaters}@cs.utexas.edu

Abstract. We introduce the concept of universal signature aggregators. In a universal signature aggregator system, a third party, using a set of common reference parameters, can aggregate a collection of signatures produced from *any* set of signing algorithms (subject to a chosen length constraint) into one short signature whose length is independent of the number of signatures aggregated. In prior aggregation works, signatures can only be aggregated if all signers use the same signing algorithm (e.g., BLS) and shared parameters. A universal aggregator can aggregate across schemes even in various algebraic settings (e.g., BLS, RSA, ECDSA), thus creating novel opportunities for compressing authentication overhead. It is especially compelling that *existing* public key infrastructures can be used and that the signers do not have to alter their behavior to enable aggregation of their signatures.

We provide multiple constructions and proofs of universal signature aggregators based on indistinguishability obfuscation and other supporting primitives. We detail our techniques as well as the tradeoffs in features and security of our solutions.

1 Introduction

An aggregate signature system, as introduced by Boneh, Gentry, Lynn and Shacham [13], allows a party to bundle a set of signatures together into a single short cryptographic signature. Aggregate signatures are motivated by applications where one needs to simultaneously verify several signatures from different users on different messages in environments with communication or storage resource constraints. For example, Boneh et al. [13] proposed applying aggregate signatures to Secure BGP [34] path authentication; later this idea was empirically evaluated by Zhao et al. [45].

S. Hohenberger—Supported by the National Science Foundation CNS-1228443 and CNS-1414023; the Defense Advanced Research Projects Agency (DARPA) and the Air Force Research Laboratory (AFRL) under contract FA8750-11-C-0080, the Office of Naval Research under contract N00014-14-1-0333, and a Microsoft Faculty Fellowship.
B. Waters—Supported by NSF CNS-1228599 and CNS-1414082, DARPA through the U.S. Office of Naval Research under Contract N00014-11-1-0382, a Google Faculty Research Award, an Alfred P. Sloan Fellowship, a Microsoft Faculty Fellowship, and a Packard Foundation Fellowship.

E. Oswald and M. Fischlin (Eds.): EUROCRYPT 2015, Part II, LNCS 9057, pp. 3–34, 2015.
DOI: 10.1007/978-3-662-46803-6_1

Over the past several years many solutions to aggregate signatures [1,5,11, 13,18,20,22,31,36,37,39,43] have been proposed that have explored tradeoffs regarding computational cost, security models, features (e.g. identity-based), limitations (e.g. sequential signing), and cryptographic assumptions. However, all of these constructions have one thing in common in that they require *all signers to adopt a common signature system and shared parameters*.

In practice, the common scheme and parameter requirements can be a large barrier to adoption. Existing users will already have established signing keys and algorithms which are entrenched in an existing public key infrastructure. The overhead of changing and re-certifying one's public keys may very well overwhelm the perceived benefit of creating signatures that can be aggregated by a third party. Indeed the original signer might not even be incentivized to allow aggregation in the first place when the benefits fall to the aggregating party or verifier of the signatures. Furthermore, even if a user moved from one signature system to an aggregate signature system, all previously created signatures would be unaggregatable.[1]

Universal Signature Aggregators. We introduce the concept of universal signature aggregators. In a universal signature aggregator system, a third party, using a set of common reference parameters, can aggregate a collection of signatures produced from *any* set of signing algorithms (subject to a chosen length constraint) into one short signature whose length is independent of the number of signatures aggregated. A verifier can use the common parameters to verify the aggregate signature. The system will be secure in the sense that it is hard to produce an aggregate signature on a verification algorithm, verification key, message tuple, (Verify, VK, m), unless the holder of the corresponding secret key produced a signature on m. Signers in the system need not do anything special to allow aggregation; indeed they could be unaware of the existence of such a system.

Our central challenge is to create a way to compress many signatures of varying types into one short object. Prior solutions required all signatures to reside in a common (often bilinear) group, where it was possible to leverage homomorphic properties of the group structure. Here we are afforded no such luxury as signatures will reside in different groups or even be based on a scheme with no algebraic structure.

Our approach will be to overcome these limitations by applying the tool of program obfuscation. At the highest level, a trusted setup routine will produce a pair of a global signature verification key for a universal signature aggregator and a shared obfuscated program. The job of the obfuscated program will be to take as input tuples of the form (Verify, VK, m, σ) that respectively represent verification algorithm, verification key, message and signature 4-tuples. The program will first verify using algorithm Verify and key VK that σ is a signature on m. If this check passes, it will produce a signature using a master secret key

---

[1] Integrating "special property"cryptography into existing keys is relatively unexplored, but has been considered in ring signatures [9] and deniable encryption [44].

on the message $\textsc{Msg} = (\text{Verify}, \text{VK}, m)$ — essentially transforming the arbitrary signature into one of an aggregatable form.

At first glance it might appear that obfuscation provides an open and close solution to our problem. Indeed, if we heuristically model the obfuscated program as an oracle to the program, the analysis is relatively straightforward. However, as noted by Hada [27] such a definition is impossible to achieve for any functionality. Our goal is to create probably secure constructions under a realizable definition of obfuscation — ideally indistinguishability obfuscation.

Achieving provable security under indistinguishability obfuscation (and without knowledge assumptions [2]) presents significant challenges. The primary technical challenge is how to design a construction and corresponding reduction that can extract a forgery on an arbitrary input signature scheme from an attacker that forges on the aggregate. We emphasize that without an oracle interface or knowledge assumption a reduction is not afforded the opportunity to simply "look at" the input signatures.

Universally Aggregating Unique Signatures. We begin by exploring how to universally aggregate unique signatures — a unique signature system [25] is one where there is at most one signature that will verify per message. Notably, RSA based full domain hash [6,7] are unique signatures that form the basis of the widely deployed PKCS#1 standard [33]. As evidence of the wide scale deployment, Heninger et al. [28] performed an Internet-wide scan of machines responding on the TLS and SSH ports for IPv4 space and reported 3.9 million distinct RSA keys compared to only 1.9 thousand DSA keys.

Our construction will be parameterized by four polynomial functions over the security parameter: $\ell_{\text{ver}}(\lambda)$, $\ell_{\text{vk}}(\lambda)$, $\ell_{\text{msg}}(\lambda)$, $\ell_{\text{sig}}(\lambda)$. These respectively represent a bound on the size of verification circuits, verification keys, length of messages signed and size of signatures that are aggregated. While we are interested in signatures of arbitrary length messages, in practice almost all signature schemes will apply the "hash and sign" paradigm where a longer message is first hashed down to a fixed size hash value (dependent on the security parameter). The core signature scheme then signs this value.

In our first construction (Sect. 4), the UniversalSetup first chooses an RSA modulus N and exponent $e \leftarrow \mathbb{Z}^*_{\phi(N)}$. Next, it chooses a puncturable PRF [15, 16, 35, 44] key K for a function F that takes inputs of the form $(\text{Verify}, \text{VK}, m) \in \{0,1\}^{\ell_{\text{ver}}} \times \{0,1\}^{\ell_{\text{vk}}} \times \{0,1\}^{\ell_{\text{msg}}}$ (i.e., 3-tuples representing a verification circuit, verification key and message). The puncturable PRF will output into $\mathbb{Z}_N$.

Finally, the setup will publish (indistinguishability) obfuscations of two programs. The first is $\text{Transform}_{N,K}$. This program takes as input a 4-tuple Verify, VK, m, σ. It then computes $\text{Verify}(\text{VK}, m, \sigma)$, which verifies the signature under the algorithm. If the signature verifies, the program outputs $F(K, \text{Verify}, \text{VK}, m) \in \mathbb{Z}_N$. This is a "transformed signature" where the obfuscated program maps the original

---

[2] A different direction is to attempt to build universal aggregation from succinct arguments of knowledge (SNARKs)[10]. We aim to achieve our goals without applying knowledge assumptions.

signature into one over $\mathbb{Z}_N$. The second program is Transform-Image$_{N,K,e}$. On input (Verify, VK, m), it computes $F(K, \text{Verify}, \text{VK}, m)^e \pmod{N}$.

One can now aggregate a sequence of signatures (Verify$_i$, VK$_i$, m_i, σ_i) by transforming each one as[3] $s_i = \text{Transform}_{N,K}(\text{Verify}_i, \text{VK}_i, m_i, \sigma_i)$ and then aggregating into one element of $\mathbb{Z}_N$ as $\sigma_{\text{agg}} = \prod_i s_i$. To verify an aggregate signature, σ_{agg}, on (Verify$_i$, VK$_i$, m_i) compute $t_i = \text{Transform-Image}_{N,K}(\text{Verify}_i, \text{VK}_i, m_i)$ and test whether $\sigma_{\text{agg}}^e \stackrel{?}{=} \prod_i t_i$. [4] Essentially the Transform program maps an arbitrary signature to an RSA FullDomain hash type signature on the "message" (Verify$_i$, VK$_i$, m_i).

We prove selective security where the attacker declares before seeing the public parameters a message m^* that they will forge on.[5] Our security argument is centered around an alternative program Transform-Reject which is programmed to behave the same as Transform except on input $y = (\text{Verify}^*, \text{VK}^*, m^*)$ on which it always outputs $\bot$ *even if it is given a valid signature on m^**. It also uses a PRF key that is punctured at y.

Security follows from two primary arguments about the program. We first establish that if an attack algorithm, Att, is successful when given Transform, it must be almost as successful when given Transform-Reject; otherwise, the underlying unique signature scheme is broken. Suppose that there is an attacker, Att, with a non-negligible difference in advantage between these two games, then we can build a reduction algorithm that extracts the unique signature on m^* in a bit by bit fashion. The reduction algorithm runs as the challenger in the aggregate signature game and receives a challenge verification key from the challenger in the standard signature security game. It runs to the point in the security game where the input public key and parameters are established and saves the state of the game (including the state of Att). Then for each bit of the signature it performs the following process multiple times.[6] It runs a third program TransformAlt$_{y,j}$. This program runs as Transform, but rejects if the j-th bit of the input signature is 1. For each j, it runs the experiment multiple times with fresh randomness. If the measured advantage of the attacker drops when using TransformAlt$_{y,j}$ then it guesses that the j-th bit of the signature is 1; otherwise it guesses that it is 0. It compiles all of these guesses together to output a forgery. (The amount of rewinding needed depends on the difference in advantage. In addition, our actual analysis addresses other technical details.)

---

[3] We slightly abuse notation in the introduction for ease of exposition by using the names Transform and Transform-Image to refer both to the obfuscated and unobfuscated forms of the program. In the main body, we are careful about these distinctions.

[4] We require in verification that no 3-tuples are repeated. I.e., for all $i \neq j$, (Verify$_i$, VK$_i$, m_i,) $\neq$ (Verify$_j$, VK$_j$, m_j).

[5] The usual complexity leveraging arguments for adaptive security can be applied here if we are willing to make sub-exponential hardness assumptions.

[6] In a nutshell, uniqueness is necessary in this construction, because, among other things, our proof extracts the signature bit-by-bit, and so we don't want the signature to "change" during the extraction process.

Since signatures are unique, the program $\mathsf{TransformAlt}_{y,j}$ is functionally equivalent to $\mathsf{Transform}$ if the j-th bit of the unique signature on m^* is 0 and thus by indistinguishability obfuscation the attacker's advantage should be negligibly close in these two cases. Similarly, $\mathsf{TransformAlt}_{y,j}$ is functionally equivalent to $\mathsf{Transform\text{-}Reject}$ if the j-th signature bit is 1 and again by indistinguishability obfuscation the advantage should be close to that of $\mathsf{Transform\text{-}Reject}$.

After we have established that the advantage when given $\mathsf{Transform\text{-}Reject}$ is close to that of $\mathsf{Transform}$, we show that an attacker that can win when given $\mathsf{Transform\text{-}Reject}$ will either break indistinguishability obfuscation, the punctured PRF's security or the RSA assumption and roughly follows [32] using punctured programming [44] techniques. The main proof innovation is combining a rewinding argument with indistinguishability obfuscation to extract a unique signature.

We show a variation of this idea in the full version [30] that is a universal aggregator of unique signatures, but where we avoid using the RSA assumption. (Indistinguishability obfuscation and punctured PRFs are still used.) The tradeoff is that there is an a priori bound n on the number of signatures that can be aggregated. In the construction, the parameters will grow polynomially with n, but the size of the signatures is independent of n. We conjecture that in our main construction the RSA-type transformed signature can be replaced by a BLS [14] type signature (as in [32]), but do not formally show this.

Universal Aggregation of Arbitrary Signatures Using VBB Obfuscation. While covering unique signatures achieves progress, we want to push toward our central goal of aggregating arbitrary signatures. Our next step is to show that a tweak to the previous construction gives us a universal aggregator of arbitrary signatures under a specific virtual black box (VBB) assumption. This appears in Sect. 5.

It might first seem that a solution proven under a VBB assumption is not better than the oracle heuristic outlined earlier. However, achieving a VBB proof provides both a sounder justification and is more technically challenging than the oracle heuristic. First, modeling an obfuscated program as an oracle is a heuristic — a piece of code is clearly a different object than an oracle. In contrast, a VBB assumption could be true for many functionalities even though there exists certain functionalities for which it cannot hold [3].[7]

Proving our construction secure under a VBB definition presents an interesting technical barrier. A natural proof methodology is to first say that an obfuscator for a given circuit cannot be more successful than a simulator with oracle access to the same circuit using VBB. And then making further hybrid security arguments leveraging the fact that the simulator has oracle access. The

---

[7] An iO obfuscator can serve as a candidate for whatever functionalities are possible to VBB obfuscate via the "best possible" obfuscation argument of Goldwasser and Rothblum [26]. So if the functionalities we consider could be VBB obfuscated, any iO candidate for them would suffice, e.g., [21]. However, there does not exist any clean conjecture of what functionalities can be VBB obfuscated. Recent works [2,17] suggest that most "natural" functionalities can be VBB obfuscated; however, it is currently unknown how to turn this intuition into a precise statement.

primary problem with this strategy is that while the universal aggregator security game gives the attacker access to a signing oracle, there is no place to "put" this signing oracle when applying the VBB security game.

We overcome this obstacle by introducing a new technique that we call "oracle assimilation" which we believe might be of independent interest. In our construction, the Transform-VBB program behaves in almost the same way as Transform before except an extra mode bit is added to the input. If this mode bit b is set to 1, it indicates normal input and the Transform-VBB program operates roughly as described above. If the mode bit is set to 0, it indicates query input and the program outputs a rejecting $\perp$ on all inputs of this type. The query type input is only used in the proof and not in the construction.

Our proof of security proceeds by a sequence of games. In the initial security game, all query inputs output a rejecting $\perp$. The proof (in a couple of steps) then moves to a game where the query inputs will take a form of (a, m) and output a signature on m under the challenge input secret signing key if $\mathrm{PRG}(a) = \alpha$ for some value α chosen by the game, but hidden from the attacker. We can argue this change is indiscernable to the attacker by obfuscator and pseudorandom generator security. At this point the security game will use the query interface of the obfuscated program to answer signing queries and we can say that the signing oracle was "assimilated" into the obfuscated program. Next, we can use VBB security to argue that there must exist a simulator with oracle access to the program that outputs 1 with probability close to the same probability that the attacker wins. Now that the input signing algorithm is accessed by an oracle we can use its security to argue that the game is indistinguishable from when the circuit refuses to transform on m^*, the challenge message.[8] Finally, we use VBB again to reason about the attack algorithm's advantage when given this second circuit that will not transform on m^*. From here, the proof follows as in the unique signature case.

Stepping back, the main innovation for this proof is to use punctured programming techniques to subliminally assimilate the signing oracle for one scheme into the obfuscated program, then use the VBB interface to execute the proof. We expect that this technique will be useful in other contexts. One interesting view is that we could apply either this VBB argument for arbitrary signatures or the previous $i\mathcal{O}$ argument for unique signatures to this single construction. So a user with any signature scheme would get VBB based security and if a user had a unique signature scheme, she would get the added benefit of $i\mathcal{O}$ based security.

Aggregating Arbitrary Signatures Using Indistinguishability Obfuscation. Finally, we return to our goal of aggregating arbitrary signatures using indistinguishability obfuscation. Our primary challenge again is how to extract an input forgery from the attacker in a proof. The previous two methods used the structure of a unique signature and an oracle interface, neither of which is available to us now.

---

[8] The proof in the main body proves selective security; however, we show how a minor transformation of the construction using admissible hash functions [12] gives adaptive security in the full version [30].

We overview the main solution ideas and our proof approach. At a high level, we devise a means for being able to extract and check the validity of a single signature (from the aggregate) of our choice in the proof without the adversary being able to know which one we are "looking at". Thus, we build our confidence in the validity of all the signatures by being able to check any given one of them. We call this an "enforce all by one" technique.

To do this, we first use additively (or singly) homomorphic encryption to combine the encryptions of several signatures together into one object t. Then we will have an obfuscated program generate a PRF-type signature component s on a message representing ciphertext tag t along with tuples $\{\text{Verify}_i, \text{VK}_i, m_i\}$ if the input contains valid signatures on each message. The output aggregate signature is $\sigma_{\text{agg}} = (t, s)$. Although the homomorphic ciphertext t will not be large enough to contain all of the input signatures, in the proof it can be used to remember one of the input signatures and thus provide us with an opportunity to extract a forgery on the input signature. The difficulty is in using $i\mathcal{O}$ to ensure that an attacker can only output a verifying $\sigma_{\text{agg}} = (t, s)$ on a ciphertext "tag" t that contains a proper forgery in the proof.

Diving in further, the setup algorithm will be parameterized by a polynominal $n(\cdot)$ that gives an a-priori bound on the number of signatures that can be verified. The size of the parameters will grow polynomially with n, but the signature size will be independent of it. The setup algorithm will output n ciphertexts $\{\text{count}_i \leftarrow \text{HE.enc}(\text{pk}, 0)\}_{i=1,\ldots n}$ each of which is an encryption of 0.

The universal aggregation algorithm takes input $\{\text{Verify}_i, \text{VK}_i, m_i, \sigma_i\}$. It then computes $t = \Sigma_i \text{count}_i \cdot \sigma_i$. Next it will input t and the tuples $\{\text{Verify}_i, \text{VK}_i, m_i, \sigma_i\}$ to an obfuscated program AggSign which will evaluate and output a punctured PRF on t and $\{\text{Verify}_i, \text{VK}_i, m_i\}$ if the input signatures verify. (We will return shortly to where the obfuscated program comes from.)

We use a sequence of hybrids proof, where the first step of the hybrid is to guess an index j (incurring a $1/n$ loss) where the forgery occurs. Next, we change count_j to be an encryption of 1. This causes an honestly computed value t to be an encryption of the j-th signature that we will eventually use for extraction.

The challenge at this point is to come up with a formulation of the program AggSign for which we can prove security using indistinguishability arguments. We provide two approaches. In the first one (see Sect. 6), we allow AggSign to be created by a Universal Sampler (also called a Universal Parameters Scheme) as defined by Hofheinz et al. [29]. A Universal Sampler is allowed to adaptively sample from an arbitrary (efficiently computable) distribution. In this case we sample from an obfuscation of the AggSign_t program that is parameterized to only work with a given tag value t. As noted in [29], Universal Samplers are realizable in the random oracle model from indistinguishability obfuscation. So this solution will exist in the random oracle model as well. An advantage of Universal Samplers is that they can define the AggSign_t program adaptively.

We propose a second variation of this solution in [30] that does not need the random oracle heuristic. Instead, it applies complexity leveraging requiring sub-exponential hardness of some underlying computational assumptions.

1.1 Summary of Our Results

Our results are summarized in the following table. The first column labels the construction. The remaining columns indicate: type of signatures that can be aggregated, selective or adaptive security, standard or random oracle model proofs, whether the aggregator is bounded or not, and finally, the cryptographic assumptions used in the security proof. In our assumptions, we prefix them with "subexp" to indicate if sub-exponential hardness is required for complexity leveraging. Since PRFs, PRGs, and (selectively-secure) puncturable PRFs are constructible from one-way functions, we list OWF as the assumption. UPS stands for a universal parameters scheme [29] (implied by $i\mathcal{O}$ in the random oracle model), HE stands for singly homomorphic encryption, $i\mathcal{O}$ stands for indistinguishability obfuscation, and VBB stands for virtual black-box obfuscation, where we assume that VBB holds only for a certain limited family of circuits.

Construction	Type	Selective/ Adaptive	RO	Bounded Aggregator	Assumptions
Sect. 4	Unique	Selective	No	No	$i\mathcal{O}$, RSA, OWF
Sect. 5	Arbitrary	Selective[9]	No	No	$i\mathcal{O}$, RSA, VBB, OWF
Sect. 6	Arbitrary	Adaptive	Yes	Yes	$i\mathcal{O}$, UPS, HE, OWF
Full version [30]	Arbitrary	Selective	No	Yes	subexp-$i\mathcal{O}$, HE, subexp-OWF

Organization. In Sect. 2, we provide background material. In Sect. 3, we give our security definition of universal signature aggregators. In Sect. 4, we show our first construction, based on indistinguishability obfuscation. Section 5 contains our construction based on VBB obfuscation. In Sect. 6, we describe a construction on indistinguishability obfuscation, but in the random oracle model. A variety of alternate constructions are included in the full version [30].

In all of our constructions, we prove security via a sequence of games argument. Our core proof ideas are mostly captured in the hybrid structure itself. For space reasons, we chose to include the hybrids here and defer the supporting claims to the full version [30].

2 Preliminaries

2.1 Notations

For any set $\mathcal{X}$, $x \leftarrow \mathcal{X}$ denotes a uniformly random element drawn from $\mathcal{X}$. Given integers $\ell_{ckt}, \ell_{inp}, \ell_{out}$, let $\mathcal{C}[\ell_{ckt}, \ell_{inp}, \ell_{out}]$ denote the set of circuits that can be represented using ℓ_{ckt} bits, take ℓ_{inp} bits as input, and output ℓ_{out} bits.

---

[9] In [30], we modify this construction to achieve adaptive security without any additional assumptions.

2.2 Admissible Hash Functions

We recall the notion of *admissible hash functions* due to Boneh and Boyen [12]. Here we state a simplified definition from [32].

Definition 1. *Let l, n and θ be efficiently computable univariate polynomials, $h : \{0,1\}^{l(\lambda)} \to \{0,1\}^{n(\lambda)}$ be an efficiently computable function, and* AdmSample *a PPT algorithm that takes as input 1^λ and an integer q, and outputs $u \in \{0,1,\perp\}^{n(\lambda)}$. For any $u \in \{0,1,\perp\}^{n(\lambda)}$, define $P_u : \{0,1\}^{l(\lambda)} \to \{0,1\}$ as follows: $P_u(x) = 0$ if for all $1 \leq j \leq n(\lambda), h(x)_j \neq u_j$, else $P_u(x) = 1$ (where u_j denotes the jth bit of u).*

We say that $(h, \mathsf{AdmSample})$ is θ-admissible if the following condition holds:

For any efficiently computable polynomial Q, for all $x^1, \ldots, x^{Q(\lambda)}$ and $x^* \in \{0,1\}^{l(\lambda)}$, where $x^* \notin \{x^i\}_i$,

$$Pr[(\forall i \leq Q(\lambda), P_u(x^i) = 1) \wedge P_u(x^*) = 0] \geq \frac{1}{\theta(Q(\lambda))}$$

where the probability is taken over $u \leftarrow \mathsf{AdmSample}(1^\lambda, Q(\lambda))$.

Theorem 1 (Admissible Hash Function Family [12], simplified proof in [20]). *For any efficiently computable polynomial l, there exist efficiently computable polynomials n, θ such that there exist θ-admissible function families mapping l bits to n bits.*

2.3 Signature Schemes

A signature scheme $\mathcal{S}$ with message space $\mathcal{M}(\lambda)$, signature key space $\mathcal{SK}(\lambda)$ and verification key space $\mathcal{VK}(\lambda)$ consists of the standard algorithms: key generation $\mathsf{Gen}(1^\lambda) \to (\mathrm{VK}, \mathrm{SK})$, signing $\mathsf{Sign}(\mathrm{SK}, m) \to \sigma$ and verification $\mathsf{Verify}(\mathrm{VK}, m, \sigma) \to \{0,1\}$. It is said to be *correct* if: For all $\lambda \in \mathbb{N}$, $(\mathrm{SK}, \mathrm{VK}) \leftarrow \mathsf{Gen}(1^\lambda)$, messages $m \in \mathcal{M}(\lambda)$, it holds that $\mathsf{Verify}(\mathrm{VK}, m, \mathsf{Sign}(\mathrm{SK}, m)) = 1$.

Security [24] is based on a game between an adversary $\mathcal{A}$ and a challenger. (**Setup Phase**) Challenger chooses $(\mathrm{SK}, \mathrm{VK}) \leftarrow \mathsf{Gen}(1^\lambda)$. (**Signing Phase**) $\mathcal{A}$ sends signature query $m_i \in \mathcal{M}$ and receives $\sigma_i \leftarrow \mathsf{Sign}(\mathrm{SK}, m_i)$. (**Forgery Phase**) $\mathcal{A}$ outputs a message m and signature σ. $\mathcal{A}$ wins if m was not queried during the Signing Phase and $\mathsf{Verify}(\mathrm{VK}, m, \sigma) = 1$. Let $\mathsf{Adv}_{\mathcal{A}}(\lambda) = \Pr[\mathcal{A} \text{ wins}]$.

Definition 2 (Signature Security [24]). *A signature scheme $\mathcal{S} = (\mathsf{Gen}, \mathsf{Sign}, \mathsf{Verify})$ is* existentially unforgeable under a chosen message attack *if for all PPT adversaries $\mathcal{A}$, $\mathsf{Adv}_{\mathcal{A}}(\lambda)$ is negligible in λ.*

Definition 3 (Unique Signatures [25]). *A signature scheme $\mathcal{S} = (\mathsf{Gen}, \mathsf{Sign}, \mathsf{Verify})$ is said to be* unique *if for all tuples $(\mathrm{VK}, m, \sigma_1, \sigma_2)$, either*

$$\sigma_1 = \sigma_2 \text{ or } \mathsf{Verify}(\mathrm{VK}, m, \sigma_1) = 0 \text{ or } \mathsf{Verify}(\mathrm{VK}, m, \sigma_2) = 0.$$

In this work, we will be considering signature schemes where the messages, signatures and verification keys have bounded length, and the verification algorithm is deterministic. In practice, most signature schemes use a collision resistant hash function to compress an arbitrary length message to bounded length. We will be dealing with these 'post-hash' messages.

Definition 4 (($\ell_{\text{vk}}, \ell_{\text{msg}}, \ell_{\text{sig}}$)-*bounded length* **signature scheme**). *Let ℓ_{vk}, ℓ_{msg} and ℓ_{sig} be fixed polynomials. A signature scheme $\mathcal{S} = (\text{Gen}, \text{Sign}, \text{Verify})$ is said to be ($\ell_{\text{vk}}, \ell_{\text{msg}}, \ell_{\text{sig}}$)-bounded length if all verification keys output by $\text{Gen}(1^\lambda)$ have length at most $\ell_{\text{vk}}(\lambda)$, Sign takes as input messages of length at most $\ell_{\text{msg}}(\lambda)$ and outputs signatures of length bounded by $\ell_{\text{sig}}(\lambda)$.*

Since the verification keys, messages and signatures have bounded length, we can view Verify as a circuit with three inputs- verification key VK, message m and signature σ. We assume every circuit can be represented as a binary string.

Definition 5 (($\ell_{\text{ver}}, \ell_{\text{vk}}, \ell_{\text{msg}}, \ell_{\text{sig}}$)-*length qualified* **signature scheme**). *Let $\ell_{\text{ver}}, \ell_{\text{vk}}, \ell_{\text{msg}}, \ell_{\text{sig}}$ be fixed polynomials. A ($\ell_{\text{vk}}, \ell_{\text{msg}}, \ell_{\text{sig}}$)-bounded length signature scheme $\mathcal{S} = (\text{Gen}, \text{Sign}, \text{Verify})$ is said to be ($\ell_{\text{ver}}, \ell_{\text{vk}}, \ell_{\text{msg}}, \ell_{\text{sig}}$)-length qualified if the verification circuit Verify and signing circuit Sign can be represented as a binary string of length at most $\ell_{\text{ver}}(\lambda)$ bits.*

Abusing notation, we say that a tuple $(\text{Verify}, \text{VK}, m, \sigma)$ is a ($\ell_{\text{ver}}, \ell_{\text{vk}}, \ell_{\text{msg}}, \ell_{\text{sig}}$)-length qualified tuple if Verify is a circuit that can be represented using $\ell_{\text{ver}}(\lambda)$ bits, and VK$, m, \sigma$ are of length at most $\ell_{\text{vk}}(\lambda)$, $\ell_{\text{msg}}(\lambda)$ and $\ell_{\text{sig}}(\lambda)$ respectively. Similarly, a tuple $(\text{Verify}, \text{VK}, m)$ is a ($\ell_{\text{ver}}, \ell_{\text{vk}}, \ell_{\text{msg}}$)-length qualified if Verify, VK and m have length at most $\ell_{\text{ver}}(\lambda)$, $\ell_{\text{vk}}(\lambda)$ and $\ell_{\text{vk}}(\lambda)$ respectively.

2.4   Additively Homomorphic Encryption

In this work, we will be using encryption schemes which allow us to perform additive operations on ciphertexts. Many encryptions schemes [8,19,23,38,40,41] have the 'additive homomorphism' property. We will now define the syntax and security definition for an additively homomorphic encryption scheme.

Let p be a prime[10]. An additively homomorphic encryption scheme $\mathcal{HE}$ with message space $\mathbb{F}_p$ and ciphertext space $\mathcal{C}_{\text{HE}}$ consists of the standard algorithms: $\text{HE.setup}(1^\lambda) \to (\text{pk}, \text{sk})$, $\text{HE.enc}(\text{pk}, m) \to \text{ct}$, $\text{HE.dec}(\text{sk}, \text{ct}) \to$ element in $\mathbb{F}_p$ or $\perp$, $\text{HE.add}(\text{pk}, \text{ct}_1, \text{ct}_2) \to \text{ct}$.

For simplicity of notation, we will represent $\text{HE.add}(\text{pk}, \text{ct}_1, \text{ct}_2)$ as $\text{ct}_1 + \text{ct}_2$.

Correctness. Let p be any prime and q any polynomial in λ. For any $\lambda \in \mathbb{N}$, $(\text{pk}, \text{sk}) \leftarrow \text{HE.setup}(1^\lambda)$, q messages $m_1, \ldots, m_q \in \mathbb{F}_p$, the following must hold:

$$\text{HE.dec}(\text{sk}, \text{HE.enc}(m_1) + \ldots + \text{HE.enc}(m_q)) = m_1 + \ldots + m_q.$$

Given an encryption ct of message $m \in \mathbb{F}_p$ and a plaintext $a \in \mathbb{F}_p$, HE.add can compute an encryption of $m \cdot a$ efficiently. Let $a \cdot \text{ct}$ represent this operation.

For space reasons, we omit the usual IND-CPA security game.

---

[10] The prime p is a property of the encryption scheme.

2.5   Obfuscation

We recall the definition of indistinguishability obfuscation from [21,44].

Definition 6. *(Indistinguishability Obfuscation) Let $\mathcal{C} = \{\mathcal{C}_\lambda\}_{\lambda \in \mathbb{N}}$ be a family of polynomial-size circuits. Let $i\mathcal{O}$ be a uniform PPT algorithm that takes as input the security parameter λ, a circuit $C \in \mathcal{C}_\lambda$ and outputs a circuit C'. $i\mathcal{O}$ is called an indistinguishability obfuscator for a circuit class $\{\mathcal{C}_\lambda\}$ if it satisfies the following conditions:*

- *(Preserving Functionality) For all security parameters $\lambda \in \mathbb{N}$, for all $C \in \mathcal{C}_\lambda$, for all inputs x, we have that $C'(x) = C(x)$ where $C' \leftarrow i\mathcal{O}(1^\lambda, C)$.*
- *(Indistinguishability of Obfuscation) For any (not necessarily uniform) PPT distinguisher $\mathcal{B} = (Samp, \mathcal{D})$, there exists a negligible function $negl(\cdot)$ such that the following holds: if for all security parameters $\lambda \in \mathbb{N}, \Pr[\forall x, C_0(x) = C_1(x) : (C_0; C_1; \sigma) \leftarrow Samp(1^\lambda)] > 1 - negl(\lambda)$, then*

$$| \Pr[\mathcal{D}(\sigma, i\mathcal{O}(1^\lambda, C_0)) = 1 : (C_0; C_1; \sigma) \leftarrow Samp(1^\lambda)] -$$
$$\Pr[\mathcal{D}(\sigma, i\mathcal{O}(1^\lambda, C_1)) = 1 : (C_0; C_1; \sigma) \leftarrow Samp(1^\lambda)]| \leq negl(\lambda).$$

In a recent work, [21] showed how indistinguishability obfuscators can be constructed for the circuit class $P/poly$. We remark that $(Samp, \mathcal{D})$ are two algorithms that pass state, which can be viewed equivalently as a single stateful algorithm $\mathcal{B}$. In our proofs we employ the latter approach, although here we state the definition as it appears in prior work.

A stronger notion of obfuscation is called *virtual black box obfuscation* [4].

Definition 7 (Virtual Black-Box Obfuscator). *Let $\mathcal{C} = \{\mathcal{C}_\lambda\}_{\lambda \in \mathbb{N}}$ be a family of polynomial-size circuits. Let $\mathcal{O}$ be a PPT algorithm that takes as input the security parameter λ, a circuit $C \in \mathcal{C}_\lambda$ and outputs a circuit C'. $\mathcal{O}$ is called a virtual black-box obfuscator for a circuit class $\{\mathcal{C}_\lambda\}_{\lambda \in \mathbb{N}}$ if it satisfies the following:*

- *(Preserving Functionality) For all security parameters $\lambda \in \mathbb{N}$, for all $C \in \mathcal{C}_\lambda$, for all inputs x, we have that $C'(x) = C(x)$ where $C' \leftarrow \mathcal{O}(1^\lambda, C)$.*
- *(Virtual Black-Box) For every (non-uniform) PPT algorithm $\mathcal{A}$, there exists a PPT simulator S such that, for all $C \in \mathcal{C}_\lambda$,*

$$\Pr[\mathcal{A}(\mathcal{O}(1^\lambda, C)) = 1] - \Pr[S^C(1^\lambda, 1^{|C|}) = 1] \leq negl(\lambda)$$

For simplicity of notation, we will drop the dependence of $i\mathcal{O}$ and $\mathcal{O}$ on 1^λ.

2.6   Puncturable Pseudorandom Functions

The notion of constrained PRFs was introduced in [15,16,35]. Punctured PRFs, first termed by [44] are a special class of constrained PRFs.

A PRF $F : \mathcal{K} \times \mathcal{X} \to \mathcal{Y}$ is a puncturable pseudorandom function if there is an additional key space $\mathcal{K}_p$ and three polynomial time algorithms $F.\mathsf{setup}$, $F.\mathsf{eval}$ and $F.\mathsf{puncture}$ as follows:

- F.setup(1^λ) is a randomized algorithm that takes the security parameter λ as input and outputs a description of the key space $\mathcal{K}$, the punctured key space $\mathcal{K}_p$ and the PRF F.
- F.puncture(K, x) is a randomized algorithm that takes as input a PRF key $K \in \mathcal{K}$ and $x \in \mathcal{X}$, and outputs a key $K\{x\} \in \mathcal{K}_p$.
- F.eval($K\{x\}, x'$) is a deterministic algorithm that takes as input a punctured key $K\{x\} \in \mathcal{K}_p$ and $x' \in \mathcal{X}$. Let $K \in \mathcal{K}$, $x \in \mathcal{X}$ and $K\{x\} \leftarrow F$.puncture(K, x). For correctness, we need the following property:

$$F.\text{eval}(K\{x\}, x') = \begin{cases} F(K, x') & \text{if } x \neq x' \\ \perp & \text{otherwise} \end{cases}$$

In this work, we only need selectively secure puncturable PRFs. The selective security game between the challenger and the adversary A consists of:

Challenge Phase. A sends a challenge $x^* \in \mathcal{X}$. The challenger chooses uniformly at random a PRF key $K \leftarrow \mathcal{K}$ and a bit $b \leftarrow \{0, 1\}$. It computes $K\{x^*\} \leftarrow F$.puncture(K, x^*). If $b = 0$, the challenger sets $y = F(K, x^*)$, else $y \leftarrow \mathcal{Y}$. It sends $K\{x^*\}, y$ to A.

Guess. A outputs a guess b' of b.

A wins if $b = b'$. The advantage of A is defined to be $\text{Adv}_A^F(\lambda) = \Pr[A \text{ wins}]$.

Definition 8. *The PRF F is a selectively secure puncturable PRF if for all probabilistic polynomial time adversaries $\mathcal{A}$, $\text{Adv}_A^F(\lambda)$ is negligible in λ.*

2.7   Universal Parameters

In a recent work, Hofheinz et al. [29] introduced the notion of universal parameters. A universal parameters scheme $\mathcal{U}$, parameterized by polynomials $\ell_{\text{ckt}}, \ell_{\text{inp}}$ and ℓ_{out}, consists of algorithms UniversalGen and InduceGen defined below.

- UniversalGen(1^λ) takes as input the security parameter λ and outputs the universal parameters U.
- InduceGen(U, d) takes as input the universal parameters U and a circuit d of size at most ℓ_{ckt} bits. The circuit d takes as input ℓ_{inp} bits and outputs ℓ_{out} bits. As described in the security property, these ℓ_{out} bits output 'look' like the ℓ_{out} bits output by circuit d on uniformly random input.

In this work, we will be using a universal parameter scheme that is adaptively secure in the random oracle model. In order to define adaptive security for universal parameters, let us first define the notion of an admissible adversary $\mathcal{A}$.

An admissible adversary $\mathcal{A}$ is defined to be an efficient interactive Turing Machine that outputs one bit, with the following input/output behavior:

- $\mathcal{A}$ takes as input security parameter λ and a universal parameter U.
- $\mathcal{A}$ can send a random oracle query (RO, x), and receives the output of the random oracle on input x.

- $\mathcal{A}$ can send a message of the form (params, d) where $d \in \mathcal{C}[\ell_{\mathsf{ckt}}, \ell_{\mathsf{inp}}, \ell_{\mathsf{out}}]$. Upon sending this message, $\mathcal{A}$ must honestly compute $p_d = \mathsf{InduceGen}(U, d)$, making use of any additional random oracle queries, and $\mathcal{A}$ appends (d, p_d) to an auxiliary tape.

Let SimUGen and SimRO be PPT algorithms. Consider two experiments:
$\mathsf{Real}^{\mathcal{A}}(1^\lambda)$:

1. The random oracle RO is implemented by assigning random outputs to each unique query made to RO.
2. $U \leftarrow \mathsf{UniversalGen}^{\mathsf{RO}}(1^\lambda)$.
3. $\mathcal{A}(1^\lambda, U)$ is executed, where every message of the form (RO, x) receives the response $\mathsf{RO}(x)$.
4. Upon termination of $\mathcal{A}$, the output of the experiment is the final output of the execution of $\mathcal{A}$.

$\mathsf{Ideal}^{\mathcal{A}}_{\mathsf{SimUGen},\mathsf{SimRO}}(1^\lambda)$:

1. A truly random function F that maps ℓ_{ckt} bits to ℓ_{out} bits is implemented by assigning random ℓ_{out}-bit outputs to each unique query made to F. Throughout this experiment, a Parameters Oracle O is implemented as follows: On input d, where $d \in \mathcal{C}[\ell_{\mathsf{ckt}}, \ell_{\mathsf{inp}}, \ell_{\mathsf{out}}]$, O outputs $d(F(d))$.
2. $(U, \tau) \leftarrow \mathsf{SimUGen}(1^\lambda)$. Here, SimUGen can make arbitrary queries to the Parameters Oracle O.
3. $\mathcal{A}(1^\lambda, U)$ and $\mathsf{SimRO}(\tau)$ begin simultaneous execution.
   - Whenever $\mathcal{A}$ sends a message of the form (RO, x), this is forwarded to SimRO, which produces a response to be sent back to $\mathcal{A}$.
   - SimRO can make any number of queries to the Parameter Oracle O.
   - Finally, after $\mathcal{A}$ sends any message of the form (params, d), the auxiliary tape of $\mathcal{A}$ is examined until an entry of the form (d, p_d) is added to it. At this point, if p_d is not equal to $d(F(d))$, then experiment aborts, resulting in an *Honest Parameter Violation*.
4. Upon termination of $\mathcal{A}$, the output of the experiment is the final output of the execution of $\mathcal{A}$.

Definition 9. *A universal parameters scheme* $\mathcal{U} = (\mathsf{UniversalGen}, \mathsf{InduceGen})$, *parameterized by polynomials* $\ell_{\mathsf{ckt}}, \ell_{\mathsf{inp}}$ *and* ℓ_{out}, *is said to be adaptively secure in the random oracle model if there exist PPT algorithms* SimUGen *and* SimRO *such that for all PPT adversaries* $\mathcal{A}$, *the following hold:*

$$\Pr[\mathsf{Ideal}^{\mathcal{A}}_{\mathsf{SimUGen},\mathsf{SimRO}}(1^\lambda) \ aborts\,] = 0.^{11}$$

$$|\Pr[\mathsf{Real}^{\mathcal{A}}(1^\lambda) = 1] - \Pr[\mathsf{Ideal}^{\mathcal{A}}_{\mathsf{SimUGen},\mathsf{SimRO}}(1^\lambda) = 1]| \leq negl(\lambda)$$

Hofheinz et al. [29] construct a universal parameters scheme that is adaptively secure in the random oracle model assuming an indistinguishability obfuscator, a selectively secure puncturable PRF and an injective one way function.

2.8   RSA Assumption

Assumption 1 (RSA [42])   *Let λ be the security parameter. Let $N = pq$ be the RSA modulus, where p, q are randomly chosen, distinct, λ-bit primes. Let e be a randomly chosen positive integer less than and relatively prime to $\phi(N) = (p-1)(q-1)$ and $y \leftarrow \mathbb{Z}_N$. For any PPT algorithm $\mathcal{A}$, $\Pr[x \leftarrow \mathcal{A}(N, e, y) \text{ and } x^e = y] \leq negl(\lambda)$.*

3   Universal Signature Aggregators

In this section, we define the notion of universal signature aggregators. Let ℓ_{ver}, ℓ_{vk}, ℓ_{msg}, ℓ_{sig} be polynomials. Given any security parameter λ, $\ell_{\text{ver}}(\lambda)$ represents a bound on the size of verification circuits, $\ell_{\text{vk}}(\lambda)$ represents a bound on the size of verification key, $\ell_{\text{msg}}(\lambda)$ is a bound on the length of messages signed and $\ell_{\text{sig}}(\lambda)$ is a bound on the size of signatures. For simplicity of notation, we will drop the dependence on λ when the context is clear.

A universal signature aggregator $(\ell_{\text{ver}}, \ell_{\text{vk}}, \ell_{\text{msg}}, \ell_{\text{sig}})$-UniversalSigAgg consists of three algorithms UniversalSetup, UniversalAgg and UniversalVerify defined as:

- UniversalSetup(1^λ) is a randomized algorithm that takes as input security parameter λ and outputs public parameters PP.
- UniversalAgg(PP, $\{(\text{Verify}_i, \text{VK}_i, m_i, \sigma_i)\}_{i=1}^{t}$) is a deterministic algorithm that takes as input security parameter λ, public parameters PP and t tuples $(\text{Verify}_i, \text{VK}_i, m_i, \sigma_i)$ (for some arbitrary t) where each tuple is $(\ell_{\text{ver}}, \ell_{\text{vk}}, \ell_{\text{msg}}, \ell_{\text{sig}})$-length qualified. It outputs an aggregate signature σ_{agg} whose length is polynomial in λ, but independent of t.
- UniversalVerify(PP, $\{(\text{Verify}_i, \text{VK}_i, m_i)\}_{i=1}^{t}, \sigma_{\text{agg}}$) is a deterministic algorithm that takes as input security parameter λ, public parameters PP, t tuples $(\text{Verify}_i, \text{VK}_i, m_i)$ that are $(\ell_{\text{ver}}, \ell_{\text{vk}}, \ell_{\text{msg}})$-length qualified, and an aggregated signature σ_{agg}. It outputs either 0 or 1.

For our constructions, we will assume that all verification circuits have ℓ_{ver} bit representation, all verification keys have length ℓ_{vk}, all messages signed have length ℓ_{msg} and the corresponding signatures have length ℓ_{sig}.

Correctness.   Let $\{(\text{Verify}_i, \text{VK}_i, m_i, \sigma_i)\}_{i=1}^{t}$ be any t distinct tuples that are $(\ell_{\text{ver}}, \ell_{\text{vk}}, \ell_{\text{msg}}, \ell_{\text{sig}})$-length qualified and for all $i \leq t$, $\text{Verify}_i(\text{VK}_i, m_i, \sigma_i) = 1$. For all $\lambda \in \mathbb{N}$, PP $\leftarrow$ UniversalSetup(1^λ) and $\sigma_{\text{agg}} \leftarrow$ UniversalAgg(1^λ, PP, $\{(\text{Verify}_i, \text{VK}_i, m_i, \sigma_i)\}_i$), UniversalVerify(PP, $\{(\text{Verify}_i, \text{VK}_i, m_i)\}_i, \sigma_{\text{agg}}$) = 1.

3.1   Security of Universal Signature Aggregators

We turn to the formal security definition for universal signature aggregators.

Let $\mathcal{S} = (\mathcal{S}.\text{Gen}, \mathcal{S}.\text{Sign}, \mathcal{S}.\text{Verify})$ be a secure $(\ell_{\text{ver}}, \ell_{\text{vk}}, \ell_{\text{msg}}, \ell_{\text{sig}})$-length qualified signature scheme. Consider the following security game between an adversary $\mathcal{A}$ and the challenger.

$\text{Exp}_{\mathcal{A}, \mathcal{S}}(\lambda)$:

- **Setup Phase** Challenger chooses $(SK, VK) \leftarrow S.\mathsf{Gen}(1^\lambda)$, computes $PP \leftarrow$ UniversalSetup(1^λ) and sends PP, VK to $\mathcal{A}$.
- **Signing Phase** $\mathcal{A}$ sends signing query x_i, and receives $\sigma_i \leftarrow S.\mathsf{Sign}(SK, x_i)$.
- **Forgery** $\mathcal{A}$ finally outputs t tuples $(\mathsf{Verify}_i, VK_i, m_i)$ and an aggregated forgery σ_{agg}.

$\mathcal{A}$ wins if there exists $i^* \in [t]$ such that $\mathsf{Verify}_{i^*} = S.\mathsf{Verify}$, $VK_{i^*} = VK$, message m_{i^*} was not queried during the signing phase and UniversalVerify$(PP, \{(\mathsf{Verify}_i, VK_i, m_i)\}, \sigma_{\mathrm{agg}}) = 1$. Let $\mathsf{Adv}_{\mathcal{A},S}(\lambda) = \Pr[\mathcal{A} \text{ wins } \mathsf{Exp}_{\mathcal{A},S}(\lambda)]$.

Definition 10. *Let S be a $(\ell_{\mathrm{ver}}, \ell_{\mathrm{vk}}, \ell_{\mathrm{msg}}, \ell_{\mathrm{sig}})$- length qualified secure signature scheme. A universal signature aggregator $(\ell_{\mathrm{ver}}, \ell_{\mathrm{vk}}, \ell_{\mathrm{msg}}, \ell_{\mathrm{sig}})$-UniversalSigAgg is secure with respect to scheme S if for all PPT adversaries $\mathcal{A}$, $\mathsf{Adv}_{\mathcal{A},S}(\lambda)$ is negligible in λ.*

We can also define a weaker *selective* notion where the adversary $\mathcal{A}$ chooses the message m corresponding to $(S.\mathsf{Verify}, VK)$ before receiving the public parameters PP. More formally, the selective experiment $\mathsf{Exp}^{\mathrm{sel}}_{\mathcal{A},S}(\lambda)$ is defined as:
$\mathsf{Exp}^{\mathrm{sel}}_{\mathcal{A},S}(\lambda)$:

- $\mathcal{A}$ sends a message m to the challenger.
- **Setup Phase** Challenger computes $(SK, VK) \leftarrow S.\mathsf{Gen}(1^\lambda)$ and $PP \leftarrow$ UniversalSetup(1^λ) and sends PP, VK to $\mathcal{A}$.
- **Signing Phase** $\mathcal{A}$ sends signing query $x_i \neq m$, and gets $\sigma_i \leftarrow S.\mathsf{Sign}(SK, x_i)$.
- **Forgery** $\mathcal{A}$ finally outputs t tuples $(\mathsf{Verify}_i, VK_i, m_i)$ and an aggregated forgery σ_{agg}.

$\mathcal{A}$ wins if there exists an $i^* \in [t]$ such that $\mathsf{Verify}_{i^*} = S.\mathsf{Verify}$, $VK_{i^*} = VK$, $m_{i^*} = m$ and UniversalVerify$(PP, \{(\mathsf{Verify}_i, VK_i, m_i)\}, \sigma_{\mathrm{agg}}) = 1$. Let $\mathsf{Adv}^{\mathrm{sel}}_{\mathcal{A},S}(\lambda) = \Pr[\mathcal{A} \text{ wins } \mathsf{Exp}^{\mathrm{sel}}_{\mathcal{A},S}(\lambda)]$.

Definition 11. *Let S be a $(\ell_{\mathrm{ver}}, \ell_{\mathrm{vk}}, \ell_{\mathrm{msg}}, \ell_{\mathrm{sig}})$- length qualified secure signature scheme. A universal signature aggregator $(\ell_{\mathrm{ver}}, \ell_{\mathrm{vk}}, \ell_{\mathrm{msg}}, \ell_{\mathrm{sig}})$- UniversalSigAgg is selectively secure with respect to scheme S if for all PPT adversaries $\mathcal{A}$, $\mathsf{Adv}^{\mathrm{sel}}_{\mathcal{A},S}(\lambda)$ is negligible in λ.*

In certain situations, it may be possible that the number of signatures to be aggregated is known in advance. In such a scenario, we can use bounded universal signature aggregators (defined below).

Definition 12. *An n-bounded universal signature aggregator scheme $(\ell_{\mathrm{ver}}, \ell_{\mathrm{vk}}, \ell_{\mathrm{msg}}, \ell_{\mathrm{sig}})$-UniversalSigAgg = (UniversalSetup, UniversalAgg, UniversalVerify) is a universal signature aggregator in which UniversalSetup takes an additional input 1^n. The public parameters output by UniversalSetup have size bounded by some polynomial in λ and n. However, the aggregated signature has size bounded by a polynomial in λ, but is independent of n.*

4 Universally Aggregating Unique Signatures

We will now describe our scheme $(\ell_{\text{ver}}, \ell_{\text{vk}}, \ell_{\text{msg}}, \ell_{\text{sig}})$-UniversalSigAgg. Let $i\mathcal{O}$ be a secure indistinguishability obfuscation scheme, F a puncturable PRF with key space $\mathcal{K}$, punctured key space $\mathcal{K}_p$, domain $\mathcal{X} = \{0,1\}^{\ell_{\text{ver}}} \times \{0,1\}^{\ell_{\text{vk}}} \times \{0,1\}^{\ell_{\text{msg}}}$ and range $\mathcal{Y} = \mathbb{Z}_N^*$ for some randomly chosen RSA modulus N, and algorithms F.setup, F.puncture, F.eval. Our scheme consists of the three algorithms UniversalSetup, UniversalAgg and UniversalVerify.

UniversalSetup(1^λ) UniversalSetup chooses an RSA modulus N and $e \leftarrow \mathbb{Z}_{\phi(N)}^*$. Next, it chooses a PRF key $K \leftarrow F$.setup(1^λ) and computes obfuscations of the programs Transform$_{N,K}$[12] and Transform-Image$_{N,K,e}$[13] defined below. It sets the public parameters PP $= (i\mathcal{O}(\text{Transform}_{N,K}), i\mathcal{O}(\text{Transform-Image}_{N,K,e}), N, e)$.

Transform$_{N,K}$:

Inputs: Verify$' \in \{0,1\}^{\ell_{\text{ver}}}$, VK$' \in \{0,1\}^{\ell_{\text{vk}}}$, $m' \in \{0,1\}^{\ell_{\text{msg}}}$, $\sigma' \in \{0,1\}^{\ell_{\text{sig}}}$.
Constants : RSA modulus $N \in \mathbb{N}$, $K \in \mathcal{K}$.

   if Verify$'(\text{VK}', m', \sigma') = 0$ **then**
       Output $\perp$.
   else
       Output $F(K, \text{Verify}'\|\text{VK}'\|m')$.
   end if

Transform-Image$_{N,K,e}$:

Inputs: Verify$' \in \{0,1\}^{\ell_{\text{ver}}}$, VK$' \in \{0,1\}^{\ell_{\text{vk}}}$, $m' \in \{0,1\}^{\ell_{\text{msg}}}$.
Constants : RSA modulus $N \in \mathbb{N}$, $K \in \mathcal{K}$, $e \in \mathbb{Z}_{\phi(N)}$.

   Let $w = F(K, \text{Verify}'\|\text{VK}'\|m')$. Output $w^e \pmod{N}$.

UniversalAgg(PP, $\{(\text{Verify}_i, \text{VK}_i, M_i, \sigma_i)\}_{i=1}^n$): Let PP $= (P_1, P_2, N, e)$. It first checks if the n tuples are distinct. If not, it outputs $\perp$. Else, it computes $t_i = P_1(\text{Verify}_i, \text{VK}_i, m_i, \sigma_i)$ for each $i \leq n$. If $t_i = \perp$ for some i, then UniversalAgg outputs $\perp$, else it outputs $\sigma_{\text{agg}} = \prod_i t_i \pmod{N}$.

UniversalVerify(PP, $\{(\text{Verify}_i, \text{VK}_i, M_i)\}_{i=1}^n, \sigma_{\text{agg}}$): Let PP $= (P_1, P_2, N, e)$. It first checks if all n tuples are distinct. If not, it outputs 0. Else, it computes, for all $i \leq n$, $s_i = P_2(\text{Verify}_i, \text{VK}_i, m_i)$. If $(\prod_i s_i) = \sigma_{\text{agg}}^e \pmod{N}$, it outputs 1, else 0.

---

[12] Padded to be of the same size as TransformAlt and Transform-Reject.
[13] Padded to be of the same size as Transform-Image-1.

Correctness: Let $\{(\mathsf{Verify}_i, \mathrm{VK}_i, m_i, \sigma_i)\}_{i=1}^n$ be n tuples such that they are all distinct and $\mathsf{Verify}_i(\mathrm{VK}_i, m_i, \sigma_i) = 1$ for all $i \leq n$. Fix any $\lambda \in \mathbb{N}$, PP $\leftarrow$ UniversalSetup(1^λ), $(\sigma_{\mathrm{agg}}) \leftarrow$ UniversalAgg$(\mathrm{PP}, \{(\mathsf{Verify}_i, \mathrm{VK}_i, m_i, \sigma_i)\})$. Then,

$$\sigma_{\mathrm{agg}}^e = (\prod \mathsf{Transform}(\mathsf{Verify}_i, \mathrm{VK}_i, m_i, \sigma_i))^e \pmod{N}$$

$$= (\prod F(K, \mathsf{Verify}_i \| \mathrm{VK}_i \| m_i))^e \pmod{N}$$

$$= (\prod F(K, \mathsf{Verify}_i \| \mathrm{VK}_i \| m_i)^e) \pmod{N}$$

$$= (\prod \mathsf{Transform\text{-}Image}_{N,K,e}(\mathsf{Verify}_i, \mathrm{VK}_i, m_i)) \pmod{N}$$

Also, note that the size of the aggregated signature ($\sigma_{\mathrm{agg}} \in \mathbb{Z}_N^*$) depends only on the security parameter λ, but not on the number of signatures aggregated.

4.1 Proof of Security

In this subsection, we will show that our construction from Sect. 4 is selectively secure with respect to secure unique signature schemes.

Theorem 2. *Assuming $i\mathcal{O}$ is a secure indistinguishability obfuscator, F is a selectively secure puncturable PRF and RSA is secure, for all $(\ell_{\mathrm{ver}}, \ell_{\mathrm{vk}}, \ell_{\mathrm{msg}}, \ell_{\mathrm{sig}})$-length qualified secure unique signatures $\mathcal{S}$, the universal signature aggregator $(\ell_{\mathrm{ver}}, \ell_{\mathrm{vk}}, \ell_{\mathrm{msg}}, \ell_{\mathrm{sig}})$-UniversalSigAgg is selectively secure with respect to $\mathcal{S}$.*

Let $\mathcal{S} = (\mathcal{S}.\mathsf{Gen}, \mathcal{S}.\mathsf{Sign}, \mathcal{S}.\mathsf{Verify})$ be a secure $(\ell_{\mathrm{ver}}, \ell_{\mathrm{vk}}, \ell_{\mathrm{msg}}, \ell_{\mathrm{sig}})$-length qualified unique signature scheme, and Att a PPT adversary. To prove this theorem, we define a sequence of experiments Game 0-Game 3, where Game 0 = $\mathsf{Exp}_{\mathrm{Att},\mathcal{S}}^{\mathrm{sel}}$.

Sequence of Games

Game 0: This game corresponds to $\mathsf{Exp}_{\mathrm{Att},\mathcal{S}}^{\mathrm{sel}}$. The adversary Att first sends message m, and then receives the verification key and public parameters for the aggregator. Next, Att makes signing queries, and finally submits the forgery.

1. Att sends message m.
2. Compute $(\mathrm{SK}, \mathrm{VK}) \leftarrow \mathcal{S}.\mathsf{Gen}(1^\lambda)$. Choose an RSA modulus N, $e \leftarrow \mathbb{Z}_{\phi(N)}^*$, $K \leftarrow F.\mathsf{setup}(1^\lambda)$ and set $\mathrm{PP} = (i\mathcal{O}(\mathsf{Transform}_{N,K}), i\mathcal{O}(\mathsf{Transform\text{-}Image}_{N,K,e}), N, e)$. Send PP, VK to Att.
3. For each sign query $x_i \neq m$, run $\sigma_i \leftarrow \mathcal{S}.\mathsf{Sign}(\mathrm{SK}, x_i)$ and send σ_i to Att.
4. Att sends forgery σ_{agg} and n tuples $\{(\mathsf{Verify}_i, \mathrm{VK}_i, m_i)\}$. Att wins if $\exists i^* \in [n]$ such that $\mathsf{Verify}_{i^*} = \mathcal{S}.\mathsf{Verify}$, $\mathrm{VK}_{i^*} = \mathrm{VK}$ and $m_{i^*} = m$ and UniversalVerify(PP, $\{(\mathsf{Verify}_i, \mathrm{VK}_i, m_i)\}, \sigma_{\mathrm{agg}}) = 1$.

Game 1: This game is like the previous one, except that the program Transform is replaced by Transform-Reject[14] which outputs $\perp$ if the input tuple is ($\mathcal{S}.\mathsf{Verify}, \mathrm{VK}, m, \sigma$). Also, it uses a PRF key punctured at $y = \mathcal{S}.\mathsf{Verify} \| \mathrm{VK} \| m$.

---

[14] Padded appropriately to be of the same size as Transform and TransformAlt.

2. Compute $(\mathrm{SK}, \mathrm{VK}) \leftarrow \mathcal{S}.\mathsf{Gen}(1^\lambda)$. Choose an RSA modulus N, $e \leftarrow \mathbb{Z}^*_{\phi(N)}$, $K \leftarrow F.\mathsf{setup}(1^\lambda)$.
   Set $y = \mathcal{S}.\mathsf{Verify}\|\mathrm{VK}\|m$, compute punctured key $K\{y\} \leftarrow F.\mathsf{puncture}(K, y)$ and $\overline{\mathrm{PP} = (i\mathcal{O}(\mathsf{Transform\text{-}Reject}_{y,N,K\{y\}}), i\mathcal{O}(\mathsf{Transform\text{-}Image}_{N,K,e}), N, e)}$.
   Send PP, VK to Att.

$\mathsf{Transform\text{-}Reject}_{y,N,K\{y\}}$:

Inputs: $\mathsf{Verify}' \in \{0,1\}^{\ell_{\mathrm{ver}}}$, $\mathrm{VK}' \in \{0,1\}^{\ell_{\mathrm{vk}}}$, $m' \in \{0,1\}^{\ell_{\mathrm{msg}}}$, $\sigma' \in \{0,1\}^{\ell_{\mathrm{sig}}}$.
Constants : $y \in \{0,1\}^{\ell_{\mathrm{ver}}} \times \{0,1\}^{\ell_{\mathrm{vk}}} \times \{0,1\}^{\ell_{\mathrm{msg}}}$, RSA modulus $N \in \mathbb{N}$, $K\{y\} \in \mathcal{K}_p$.

    if $\mathsf{Verify}'(\mathrm{VK}', m', \sigma') = 0$ **then** output $\perp$.
    else if $\mathsf{Verify}'\|\mathrm{VK}'\|m' = y$ **then** output $\perp$.
    else output $F.\mathsf{eval}(K\{y\}, \mathsf{Verify}'\|\mathrm{VK}'\|m')$.
    end if

Game 2: This game is like previous one, except that the program $\mathsf{Transform\text{-}Image}$ is replaced by $\mathsf{Transform\text{-}Image\text{-}1}$[15]. It uses a PRF key punctured at $y = \mathcal{S}.\mathsf{Verify}\|\mathrm{VK}\|m$. For input y, it outputs a hardwired constant z. In this game, z is set to be $F(K, y)^e$.

2. Compute $(\mathrm{SK}, \mathrm{VK}) \leftarrow \mathcal{S}.\mathsf{Gen}(1^\lambda)$. Choose an RSA modulus N, $e \leftarrow \mathbb{Z}^*_{\phi(N)}$ and $K \leftarrow F.\mathsf{setup}(1^\lambda)$.
   Set $y = \mathcal{S}.\mathsf{Verify}\|\mathrm{VK}\|m$. Compute $K\{y\} \leftarrow F.\mathsf{puncture}(K, y)$, $w = F(K, y)$, $z = w^e \pmod{N}$.
   $\overline{\mathrm{Set}\ \mathrm{PP} = (i\mathcal{O}(\mathsf{Transform\text{-}Reject}_{y,N,K\{y\}}), i\mathcal{O}(\mathsf{Transform\text{-}Image\text{-}1}_{y,N,K\{y\},z,e})}$, $N, e)$ and send PP, VK to Att.

$\mathsf{Transform\text{-}Image\text{-}1}_{y,N,K\{y\},z,e}$:

Inputs: $\mathsf{Verify}' \in \{0,1\}^{\ell_{\mathrm{ver}}}$, $\mathrm{VK}' \in \{0,1\}^{\ell_{\mathrm{vk}}}$, $m' \in \{0,1\}^{\ell_{\mathrm{msg}}}$.
Constants: $y \in \{0,1\}^{\ell_{\mathrm{ver}}} \times \{0,1\}^{\ell_{\mathrm{vk}}} \times \{0,1\}^{\ell_{\mathrm{msg}}}$, RSA modulus $N \in \mathbb{N}$, $K\{y\} \in \mathcal{K}_p$, $z \in \mathbb{Z}^*_N$, $e \in \mathbb{Z}^*_{\phi(N)}$.

    if $\mathsf{Verify}'\|\mathrm{VK}'\|m' = y$ **then** output z.
    else
        Let $w = F.\mathsf{eval}(K\{y\}, \mathsf{Verify}'\|\mathrm{VK}'\|m')$.
        Output w^e.
    end if

---

[15] Padded appropriately to be of the same size as $\mathsf{Transform\text{-}Image}$.

Game 3: In this game, the challenger chooses z at random.

2. Compute $(\text{SK}, \text{VK}) \leftarrow \mathcal{S}.\text{Gen}(1^\lambda)$. Choose an RSA modulus N, $e \leftarrow \mathbb{Z}^*_{\phi(N)}$ and $K \leftarrow F.\text{setup}(1^\lambda)$.
Set $y = \mathcal{S}.\text{Verify}||\text{VK}||m$. Compute $K\{y\} \leftarrow F.\text{puncture}(K, y)$ and $z \leftarrow \mathbb{Z}^*_N$.
Set $\text{PP} = (i\mathcal{O}(\text{Transform-Reject}_{y,N,K\{y\}}), i\mathcal{O}(\text{Transform-Image-1}_{y,N,K\{y\},z,e}),$ $N, e)$ and send PP, VK to Att.

Analysis. Let $\text{Adv}^j_{\text{Att}}$ denote the advantage of adversary Att in Game j. We will state the claims here; the proofs can be found in the full version [30].

Lemma 1. *Assuming $i\mathcal{O}$ is a secure indistinguishability obfuscator and $\mathcal{S}$ is a secure $(\ell_{\text{ver}}, \ell_{\text{vk}}, \ell_{\text{msg}}, \ell_{\text{sig}})$-length qualified unique signature scheme, for any PPT adversary Att, $\text{Adv}^0_{\text{Att}} - \text{Adv}^1_{\text{Att}} \leq negl(\lambda)$.*

Claim 1. *Assuming $i\mathcal{O}$ is a secure indistinguishability obfuscator, for any PPT adversary Att, $\text{Adv}^1_{\text{Att}} - \text{Adv}^2_{\text{Att}} \leq negl(\lambda)$.*

Claim 2. *Assuming F is a selectively secure puncturable PRF, for any PPT adversary Att, $\text{Adv}^2_{\text{Att}} - \text{Adv}^3_{\text{Att}} \leq negl(\lambda)$.*

Claim 3. *Assuming RSA is secure, for any PPT adversary Att, $\text{Adv}^3_{\text{Att}} \leq negl(\lambda)$.*

Using the above claims, it follows that any PPT adversary has negligible advantage in Game 0, assuming $i\mathcal{O}$ is a secure indistinguishability obfuscator, F is a selectively secure puncturable PRF and the RSA assumption holds. Therefore, the construction in Sect. 4 is selectively secure with respect to all secure unique signature schemes.

5 Universal Aggregation of Arbitrary Signatures Using VBB Obfuscation

In this section, we will describe our construction based on *virtual black box* obfuscation. The construction is similar to the one in Sect. 4, the only difference being in program Transform-VBB, which now takes some additional inputs and has additional constants hardwired. The additional inputs/constants are used for "oracle assimilation" (see Sect. 1 for a discussion on this technical issue).

We assume signing algorithms (corresponding to schemes whose signatures need to be aggregated) use at most ℓ_{rnd} random bits to compute signatures, for some polynomial ℓ_{rnd}. We use a pseudorandom generator $\text{PRG} : \{0,1\}^\ell \leftarrow \{0,1\}^{2\ell}$ (where ℓ is some polynomial in λ), a (standard) PRF $\tilde{F}$ with key space $\tilde{\mathcal{K}}$, domain $\tilde{\mathcal{X}}$ and range $\tilde{\mathcal{Y}} = \{0,1\}^{\ell_{\text{rnd}}}$ and a puncturable PRF F as in Sect. 4.

Transform-VBB$_{N,K}$:

Inputs: $b \in \{0,1\}, a \in \{0,1\}^{\ell}$, Verify$' \in \{0,1\}^{\ell_{\text{ver}}}$, VK$' \in \{0,1\}^{\ell_{\text{vk}}}$,
$m' \in \{0,1\}^{\ell_{\text{msg}}}, \sigma' \in \{0,1\}^{\ell_{\text{sig}}}$.
Constants : RSA modulus $N \in \mathbb{N}$, $K \in \mathcal{K}$.

if $b = 0$ **then**
    Output $\perp$.
else if Verify$'($VK$', m', \sigma') = 0$ **then**
    Output $\perp$.
else
    Output $F(K, $Verify$'||VK'||m')$.
end if

Our universal signature aggregator consists of the three algorithms: UniversalSetup, UniversalAgg and UniversalVerify described below.

UniversalSetup(1^{λ}). UniversalSetup first chooses random primes $p, q \in \Theta(2^{\lambda})$, sets the RSA modulus $N = pq$. It chooses $e \leftarrow \mathbb{Z}^*_{\phi(N)}$, PRF key $K \leftarrow F.\text{setup}(1^{\lambda})$ as in Sect. 4. It computes obfuscations of the programs Transform-VBB$_{N,K}$ [16] and Transform-Image$_{N,K,e}$ [17], where Transform-VBB$_{N,K}$ is defined below, while Transform-Image$_{N,K,e}$ is the same as in Sect. 4. It sets the public parameters to be PP $= (\mathcal{O}(\text{Transform-VBB}_{N,K}), \mathcal{O}(\text{Transform-Image}_{N,K,e}), N, e)$.

UniversalAgg(PP, $\{(\text{Verify}_i, \text{VK}_i, M_i, \sigma_i)\}_{i=1}^n$): Let PP $= (P_1, P_2, N, e)$. It first checks that all the n tuples are distinct. If not, it outputs $\perp$. Else, it computes $t_i = P_1(1, 0^{\ell}, \text{Verify}_i, \text{VK}_i, m_i, \sigma_i)$ [18] for each $i \leq n$. If $t_i = \perp$ for some i, then UniversalAgg outputs $\perp$, else it outputs $\sigma_{\text{agg}} = \prod_i t_i \pmod{N}$.

UniversalVerify(PP, $\{(\text{Verify}_i, \text{VK}_i, M_i)\}_{i=1}^n, \sigma_{\text{agg}}$): Let PP $= (P_1, P_2, N, e)$. It first checks that the n tuples are distinct. If not, it outputs 0. Else, it computes for $i \leq n$, $s_i = P_2(\text{Verify}_i, \text{VK}_i, m_i)$. If $(\prod_i s_i) = \sigma^e_{\text{agg}} \pmod{N}$, it outputs 1, else 0.

5.1 Proof of Security

We will now prove that the construction in Sect. 5 is selectively secure with respect to all secure signature schemes. The proof involves a sequence of intermediate hybrid experiments, which are described below.

Theorem 3. *Assuming $\mathcal{O}$ is a secure virtual black-box obfuscator for a class of circuits $\mathcal{C}$ (defined in [30]), F is a selectively secure puncturable PRF, $\tilde{F}$ is a secure PRF, PRG is a secure pseudorandom generator and RSA is secure, for all $(\ell_{\text{ver}}, \ell_{\text{vk}}, \ell_{\text{msg}}, \ell_{\text{sig}})$-length qualified signature schemes $\mathcal{S}$, the universal signature aggregator $(\ell_{\text{ver}}, \ell_{\text{vk}}, \ell_{\text{msg}}, \ell_{\text{sig}})$-UniversalSigAgg is selectively secure w.r.t. $\mathcal{S}$.*

---

[16] Padded appropriately to be of the same size as Transform-VBB-1, Transform-VBB-2, Transform-VBB-3 defined later in this section.

[17] Padded appropriately to be of the same size as Transform-Image-1 as in Sect. 4.

[18] The input $a = 0^{\ell}$ will not be used by the program, since the mode $b = 1$.

It may appear odd that the above theorem statement includes assumptions on primitives (e.g., PRG and the standard PRF) which are *not* used in the protocol itself. However, re-writing the theorem statement to omit these assumptions would require a different proof from the one we are now able to provide.

Sequence of Games

Game 0: This game corresponds to $\mathsf{Exp}^{\mathrm{sel}}_{\mathrm{Att},\mathcal{S}}$.

1. Att sends message m.
2. Compute $(\mathrm{SK}, \mathrm{VK}) \leftarrow \mathcal{S}.\mathsf{Gen}(1^\lambda)$. Choose an RSA modulus N, $e \leftarrow \mathbb{Z}^*_{\phi(N)}$, $K \leftarrow F.\mathsf{setup}(1^\lambda)$. Set $\mathrm{PP} = (\mathcal{O}(\mathsf{Transform\text{-}VBB}_{N,K}), \mathcal{O}(\mathsf{Transform\text{-}Image}_{N,K,e})$, $N, e)$. Send PP, VK to Att.
3. For each signing query $x_i \neq m$, compute $\sigma_i \leftarrow \mathcal{S}.\mathsf{Sign}(\mathrm{SK}, x_i)$ and send σ_i to Att.
4. Att sends forgery σ_{agg} and n tuples $\{(\mathsf{Verify}_i, \mathrm{VK}_i, m_i)\}$. Att wins if $\exists i^* \in [n]$ such that $\mathsf{Verify}_{i^*} = \mathcal{S}.\mathsf{Verify}$, $\mathrm{VK}_{i^*} = \mathrm{VK}$ and $m_{i^*} = m$ and $\mathsf{UniversalVerify}($ PP, $\{(\mathsf{Verify}_i, \mathrm{VK}_i, m_i)\}$, $\sigma_{\mathrm{agg}}) = 1$.

Game 1: In this game, the challenger uses pseudorandomly generated strings as randomness for the signature queries.

2. Compute $(\mathrm{SK}, \mathrm{VK}) \leftarrow \mathcal{S}.\mathsf{Gen}(1^\lambda)$. Choose an RSA modulus N, $e \leftarrow \mathbb{Z}^*_{\phi(N)}$, $K \leftarrow F.\mathsf{setup}(1^\lambda)$. Choose standard PRF key $\tilde{K} \leftarrow \tilde{F}.\mathsf{setup}(1^\lambda)$. Set PP $=$ $(\mathcal{O}(\mathsf{Transform\text{-}VBB}_{N,K}), \mathcal{O}(\mathsf{Transform\text{-}Image}_{N,K,e}), N, e)$. Send PP, VK to Att.
3. For each signing query $x_i \neq m$, choose $r \leftarrow \{0,1\}^{\ell_{\mathrm{sig}}}$, compute $r_i = F(\tilde{K}, r)$, $\sigma_i = \mathcal{S}.\mathsf{Sign}(\mathrm{SK}, x_i; r_i)$ and send σ_i to Att.

Game 2: In this game, the challenger uses the program Transform-VBB-1 instead of Transform-VBB. Unlike Transform-VBB, Transform-VBB-1 uses the input a to check if $\mathrm{PRG}(a)$ is equal to the hardwired α. If the 'mode' bit is 0 and $\mathrm{PRG}(a) = \alpha$, then the program outputs the verification key VK and a signature on the desired message.

2. Compute $(\mathrm{SK}, \mathrm{VK}) \leftarrow \mathcal{S}.\mathsf{Gen}(1^\lambda)$. Choose an RSA modulus N, $e \leftarrow \mathbb{Z}^*_{\phi(N)}$, $K \leftarrow F.\mathsf{setup}(1^\lambda)$. Choose PRF key $\tilde{K} \leftarrow \tilde{F}.\mathsf{setup}(1^\lambda)$, $\alpha \leftarrow \{0,1\}^{2\ell}$. Let Transform-VBB-1[19] be the circuit defined below.
Set PP $=(\mathcal{O}(\mathsf{Transform\text{-}VBB\text{-}1}_{N,K,\alpha,\mathrm{SK},\tilde{K}}), \mathcal{O}(\mathsf{Transform\text{-}Image}_{N,K,e}), N, e)$. Send PP, VK to Att.

---

[19] Padded appropriately to be of the same size as Transform-VBB, Transform-VBB-2 and Transform-VBB-3.

Transform-VBB-1$_{N,K,\alpha,\text{SK},\tilde{K}}$:

Inputs: $b \in \{0,1\}, a \in \{0,1\}^\ell, \text{Verify}' \in \{0,1\}^{\ell_{\text{ver}}}$, VK$' \in \{0,1\}^{\ell_{\text{vk}}}$,
$m' \in \{0,1\}^{\ell_{\text{msg}}}, \sigma' \in \{0,1\}^{\ell_{\text{sig}}}$.
Constants : RSA modulus $N \in \mathbb{N}$, $K \in \mathcal{K}$,
$\alpha \in \{0,1\}^{2\ell}$, SK $\in \mathcal{SK}$, $\tilde{K} \in \tilde{\mathcal{K}}$.

if $b = 0$ **then**
    if $\text{PRG}(a) \neq \alpha$ **then** output $\perp$.
    else output $(\text{VK}, \mathcal{S}.\text{Sign}(\text{SK}, m'; \tilde{F}(\tilde{K}, \sigma')))$.
    end if
else if $\text{Verify}'(\text{VK}', m', \sigma') = 0$ **then** output $\perp$.
else output $F(K, \text{Verify}' \| \text{VK}' \| m')$.
end if

Game 3: Now, α is a pseudorandom string; i.e. $\alpha = \text{PRG}(a)$, where $a \leftarrow \{0,1\}^\ell$.

2. Compute $(\text{SK}, \text{VK}) \leftarrow \mathcal{S}.\text{Gen}(1^\lambda)$. Choose an RSA modulus N, $e \leftarrow \mathbb{Z}^*_{\phi(N)}$, $K \leftarrow F.\text{setup}(1^\lambda)$. Choose $a \leftarrow \{0,1\}^\ell$ and set $\alpha = \text{PRG}(a)$. Choose PRF key $\tilde{K} \leftarrow \tilde{F}.\text{setup}(1^\lambda)$. Set PP $=(\mathcal{O}(\text{Transform-VBB-1}_{N,K,\alpha,\text{SK},\tilde{K}})$, $\mathcal{O}(\text{Transform-Image}_{N,K,e}), N, e)$. Send PP, VK to Att.

Transform-VBB-2$_{y,N,K,\alpha,\text{SK},\tilde{K}}$:

Inputs: $b \in \{0,1\}, a \in \{0,1\}^\ell, \text{Verify}' \in \{0,1\}^{\ell_{\text{ver}}}$, VK$' \in \{0,1\}^{\ell_{\text{vk}}}$,
$m' \in \{0,1\}^{\ell_{\text{msg}}}, \sigma' \in \{0,1\}^{\ell_{\text{sig}}}$.
Constants : $y \in \{0,1\}^{\ell_{\text{ver}}} \times \{0,1\}^{\ell_{\text{vk}}} \times \{0,1\}^{\ell_{\text{msg}}}$,RSA modulus
$N \in \mathbb{N}$, $K \in \mathcal{K}$, $\alpha \in \{0,1\}^{2\ell}$, SK $\in \mathcal{SK}$, $\tilde{K} \in \tilde{\mathcal{K}}$.

if $b = 0$ **then**
    if $\text{PRG}(a) \neq \alpha$ **then** output $\perp$.
    else output $(\text{VK}, \mathcal{S}.\text{Sign}(\text{SK}, m'; \tilde{F}(\tilde{K}, \sigma')))$.
    end if
else if $\text{Verify}'(\text{VK}', m', \sigma') = 0$ **then** output $\perp$.
else if $\text{Verify}' \| \text{VK}' \| m' = y$ **then** output $\perp$.
else output $F(K, \text{Verify}' \| \text{VK}' \| m')$.
end if

Game 4: This experiment is similar to the previous one, except that the challenger uses Transform-VBB-2 instead of Transform-VBB-1.

2. Compute $(\text{SK}, \text{VK}) \leftarrow \mathcal{S}.\text{Gen}(1^\lambda)$. Choose an RSA modulus N, $e \leftarrow \mathbb{Z}^*_{\phi(N)}$, $K \leftarrow F.\text{setup}(1^\lambda)$. Choose $a \leftarrow \{0,1\}^\ell$ and set $\alpha = \text{PRG}(a)$. Choose $\tilde{K} \leftarrow \tilde{F}.\text{setup}(1^\lambda)$. Let Transform-VBB-2[20] be the circuit defined below.

---

[20] Padded appropriately to be of the same size as Transform-VBB, Transform-VBB-1 and Transform-VBB-3.

Set $y = \mathcal{S}.\mathsf{Verify}\|\mathsf{VK}\|m$, parameters $\mathsf{PP} = (\mathcal{O}(\mathsf{Transform\text{-}VBB\text{-}2}_{y,N,K,\alpha,\mathsf{SK},\tilde{K}})$, $\mathcal{O}(\mathsf{Transform\text{-}Image}_{N,K,e}), N, e)$. Send PP, VK to Att.

Game 5: In this experiment, the challenger uses a key punctured at y instead of the master PRF key.

2. Compute $(\mathsf{SK}, \mathsf{VK}) \leftarrow \mathcal{S}.\mathsf{Gen}(1^\lambda)$. Choose an RSA modulus N, $e \leftarrow \mathbb{Z}^*_{\phi(N)}$, $K \leftarrow F.\mathsf{setup}(1^\lambda)$. Choose $a \leftarrow \{0,1\}^\ell$ and set $\alpha = \mathsf{PRG}(a)$. Choose $\tilde{K} \leftarrow \tilde{F}.\mathsf{setup}(1^\lambda)$. Set $y = \mathcal{S}.\mathsf{Verify}\|\mathsf{VK}\|m$, compute $K\{y\} \leftarrow F.\mathsf{puncture}(K, y)$ and $z = F(K, y)^e$. Let $\mathsf{Transform\text{-}VBB\text{-}3}^{21}$ be the circuit defined next, while $\mathsf{Transform\text{-}Image\text{-}1}^{22}, e)$ is the same as Sect. 4.1 Set $\mathsf{PP} = (\mathcal{O}(\mathsf{Transform\text{-}VBB\text{-}3}_{y,N,K\{y\},\alpha,\mathsf{SK},\tilde{K}})$, $\mathcal{O}(\mathsf{Transform\text{-}Image\text{-}1}_{y,N,K\{y\},z,e})$. Send PP, VK to Att.

$\mathsf{Transform\text{-}VBB\text{-}3}_{y,N,K\{y\},\alpha,\mathsf{SK},\tilde{K}}$:

Inputs: $b \in \{0,1\}, a \in \{0,1\}^\ell, \mathsf{Verify}' \in \{0,1\}^{\ell_{\mathrm{ver}}}, \mathsf{VK}' \in \{0,1\}^{\ell_{\mathrm{vk}}}$, $m' \in \{0,1\}^{\ell_{\mathrm{msg}}}, \sigma' \in \{0,1\}^{\ell_{\mathrm{sig}}}$.
Constants : $y \in \{0,1\}^{\ell_{\mathrm{ver}}} \times \{0,1\}^{\ell_{\mathrm{vk}}} \times \{0,1\}^{\ell_{\mathrm{msg}}}$, RSA modulus $N \in \mathbb{N}$, $K\{y\} \in \mathcal{K}_p, \alpha \in \{0,1\}^{2\ell}, \mathsf{SK} \in \mathcal{SK}, \tilde{K} \in \tilde{\mathcal{K}}$.

if $b = 0$ **then**
    if $\mathsf{PRG}(a) \neq \alpha$ **then** output $\bot$.
    else output $(\mathsf{VK}, \mathcal{S}.\mathsf{Sign}(\mathsf{SK}, m'; \tilde{F}(\tilde{K}, \sigma')))$.
    end if
else if $\mathsf{Verify}'(\mathsf{VK}', m', \sigma') = 0$ **then** output $\bot$.
else if $\mathsf{Verify}'\|\mathsf{VK}'\|m' = y$ **then** output $\bot$.
else output $F.\mathsf{eval}(K\{y\}, \mathsf{Verify}'\|\mathsf{VK}'\|m')$.
end if

Game 6: Here the challenger chooses a uniformly random $z \leftarrow \mathbb{Z}^*_N$.

2. Compute $(\mathsf{SK}, \mathsf{VK}) \leftarrow \mathcal{S}.\mathsf{Gen}(1^\lambda)$. Choose an RSA modulus N, $e \leftarrow \mathbb{Z}^*_{\phi(N)}$, $K \leftarrow F.\mathsf{setup}(1^\lambda)$. Choose $a \leftarrow \{0,1\}^\ell$ and set $\alpha = \mathsf{PRG}(a)$. Choose $\tilde{K} \leftarrow \tilde{F}.\mathsf{setup}(1^\lambda)$. Set $y = \mathcal{S}.\mathsf{Verify}\|\mathsf{VK}\|m$, compute $K\{y\} \leftarrow F.\mathsf{puncture}(K, y)$ and $z \leftarrow \mathbb{Z}^*_N$. Set $\mathsf{PP} = (\mathcal{O}(\mathsf{Transform\text{-}VBB\text{-}3}_{y,N,K\{y\},\alpha,\mathsf{SK},\tilde{K}})$, $\mathcal{O}(\mathsf{Transform\text{-}Image\text{-}1}_{y,N,K\{y\},z,e}), e)$. Send PP, VK to Att.

Analysis. We will now show that if a PPT adversary has non negligible advantage in Game i, then it has non-negligible advantage in the next game. Some of the proofs are very similar to the corresponding ones in Sect. 4.1, and hence we

---

[21] Padded appropriately to be of the same size as Transform-VBB, Transform-VBB-1 and Transform-VBB-2.

[22] Padded appropriately to be of the same size as Transform-Image-1.

skip them in this section. Due to limited space, the remaining proofs, including those using the technique of "oracle assimilation", are given in [30]).

Let $\mathsf{Adv}^j_{\mathsf{Att}}$ denote the advantage of adversary Att in Game j.

Claim 4. *Assuming $\tilde{F}$ is a secure PRF, for any PPT adversary Att, $\mathsf{Adv}^0_{\mathsf{Att}} - \mathsf{Adv}^1_{\mathsf{Att}} \leq negl(\lambda)$.*

Claim 5. *Assuming $\mathcal{O}$ is a secure indistinguishability obfuscator, for any PPT adversary Att, $\mathsf{Adv}^1_{\mathsf{Att}} - \mathsf{Adv}^2_{\mathsf{Att}} \leq negl(\lambda)$.*

Claim 6. *Assuming PRG is a secure pseudorandom generator, for any PPT adversary Att, $\mathsf{Adv}^2_{\mathsf{Att}} - \mathsf{Adv}^3_{\mathsf{Att}} \leq negl(\lambda)$.*

Lemma 2. *Assuming $\mathcal{O}$ is a secure virtual black box obfuscator for a class of circuits $\mathcal{C}$ (defined in [30]), $\tilde{F}$ is a secure pseudorandom function, PRG is a secure pseudorandom generator and $\mathcal{S}$ is a $(\ell_{\mathrm{ver}}, \ell_{\mathrm{vk}}, \ell_{\mathrm{msg}}, \ell_{\mathrm{sig}})$-length qualified secure signature scheme, $\mathsf{Adv}^3_{\mathsf{Att}} - \mathsf{Adv}^4_{\mathsf{Att}} \leq negl(\lambda)$.*

Claim 7. *Assuming $\mathcal{O}$ is a secure indistinguishability obfuscator, for any PPT adversary Att, $\mathsf{Adv}^4_{\mathsf{Att}} - \mathsf{Adv}^5_{\mathsf{Att}} \leq negl(\lambda)$.*

Claim 8. *Assuming F is a selectively secure puncturable PRF, for any PPT adversary Att, $\mathsf{Adv}^5_{\mathsf{Att}} - \mathsf{Adv}^6_{\mathsf{Att}} \leq negl(\lambda)$.*

Claim 9. *Assuming RSA is secure, for any PPT adversary Att, $\mathsf{Adv}^6_{\mathsf{Att}} \leq negl(\lambda)$.*

The proof of these last three claims are similar to the corresponding proofs of claims in the previous section.

Using the above claims, we can conclude that any PPT adversary has at most negligible advantage in Game 0, assuming $\mathcal{O}$ is a secure virtual black-box obfuscator for circuit family $\mathcal{C}$, F is a selectively secure puncturable PRF, $\tilde{F}$ is a secure (standard) PRF, PRG is a secure pseudorandom generator, and RSA is secure. Therefore, the construction described in Sect. 5 is selectively secure with respect to all secure length-qualified signature schemes.

6 Universal Aggregation of Arbitrary Signatures from $i\mathcal{O}$ in the Random Oracle Model

Next, we describe our n-bounded scheme $(\ell_{\mathrm{ver}}, \ell_{\mathrm{vk}}, \ell_{\mathrm{msg}}, \ell_{\mathrm{sig}})$-UniversalSigAgg. By n-bounded, we mean that at most n signatures can be aggregated.

We will use a secure $(\ell_{\mathrm{ckt}}, \ell_{\mathrm{inp}}, \ell_{\mathrm{out}})$ universal parameters scheme $\mathcal{U} = $ (UniversalGen, InduceGen) (where the parameters $\ell_{\mathrm{ckt}}, \ell_{\mathrm{inp}}$ and ℓ_{out} will be specified later), an additively homomorphic encryption scheme (HE.setup, HE.enc, HE.dec, HE.add) with message space $\mathbb{F}_p$ for some prime $p > 2^{\ell_{\mathrm{sig}}}$ and ciphertext space $\mathcal{C}_{\mathsf{HE}}$. We will assume each $\mathrm{ct} \in \mathcal{C}_{\mathsf{HE}}$ can be represented using ℓ_{ct} bits. Finally, we will also use a one-way function $f : \{0,1\}^\ell \to \{0,1\}^{2\ell}$ and a secure indistinguishability obfuscator $i\mathcal{O}$.

Our construction consists of three algorithms UniversalSetup, UniversalAgg and UniversalVerify described as follows.

UniversalSetup$(1^\lambda, 1^n)$. Let $(\mathsf{pk}, \mathsf{sk}) \leftarrow \mathsf{HE.setup}(1^\lambda)$. It computes n ciphertexts $\mathsf{ct}_i \leftarrow \mathsf{HE.enc}(\mathsf{pk}, 0)$ and $U \leftarrow \mathsf{UniversalGen}(1^\lambda)$. It sets the public parameters $\mathsf{PP} = (\mathsf{pk}, \mathsf{ct}_1, \ldots, \mathsf{ct}_n, U)$. Let us assume PP can be represented using ℓ_{pp} bits.

$\mathsf{AggSetup}_{t,\mathsf{PP},\{\mathsf{Verify}_i, \mathrm{VK}_i, m_i\}_i}$:

Inputs: Security parameter 1^λ, $r \in \{0,1\}^{\ell_{\mathsf{inp}}}$.
Constants: $t \in \mathcal{C}_{\mathsf{HE}}$, $\mathsf{PP} = (\mathsf{pk}, \mathsf{ct}_1, \ldots, \mathsf{ct}_n, U) \in \{0,1\}^{\ell_{\mathsf{PP}}}$, $\{\mathsf{Verify}_i, \mathrm{VK}_i, m_i\}_i \in (\{0,1\}^{\ell_{\mathsf{ver}}} \times \{0,1\}^{\ell_{\mathsf{vk}}} \times \{0,1\}^{\ell_{\mathsf{msg}}})^n$.

1. Choose $s \leftarrow \{0,1\}^\ell$ using r.
2. Compute $C_{\mathsf{agg}} \leftarrow i\mathcal{O}(\mathsf{AggSign}_{s,t,\mathsf{PP},\{\mathsf{Verify}_i, \mathrm{VK}_i, m_i\}_i})$, where $\mathsf{AggSign}$ is the circuit described below.

> $\mathsf{AggSign}_{s,t,\mathsf{PP},\{\mathsf{Verify}_i, \mathrm{VK}_i, m_i\}_i}$:
>
> Inputs: $\sigma_1, \ldots, \sigma_n$, where $\sigma_i \in \{0,1\}^{\ell_{\mathsf{sig}}}$.
> Constants: $s \in \{0,1\}^\ell$, $t \in \mathcal{C}_{\mathsf{HE}}$, $\mathsf{PP} = (\mathsf{pk}, \mathsf{ct}_1, \ldots, \mathsf{ct}_n, U)$, $\{\mathsf{Verify}_i, \mathrm{VK}_i, m_i\}_i$.
>
> **if** $\exists i$ such that $\mathsf{Verify}_i(\mathrm{VK}_i, m_i, \sigma_i) = 0$ **then**
>   Output $\perp$.
> **end if**
> **if** $t \neq \sigma_1 \cdot \mathsf{ct}_1 + \ldots + \sigma_n \cdot \mathsf{ct}_n$ **then**
>   Output $\perp$.
> **end if**
> Output s.

3. Compute $\tilde{s} = f(s)$.
4. Output $(C_{\mathsf{agg}}, \tilde{s})$.

$\mathsf{UniversalAgg}(\mathsf{PP} = (\mathsf{pk}, \mathsf{ct}_1, \ldots, \mathsf{ct}_n, U), \{\mathsf{Verify}_i, \mathrm{VK}_i, M_i, \sigma_i\}_{i=1}^n)$. We will view each signature σ_i as an integer in $[0, 2^{\ell_{\mathsf{sig}}} - 1]$.

The universal aggregator first checks if all n tuples are distinct. If not, it outputs $\perp$. Else, it computes $t = \sigma_1 \cdot \mathsf{ct}_1 + \ldots + \sigma_n \cdot \mathsf{ct}_n$.[23]

Let $\mathsf{AggSetup}$ be the (randomized) algorithm (defined above) that takes as input security parameter λ, and outputs a program C_{agg} and $\tilde{s} \in \{0,1\}^{2\ell}$. It uses ℓ_{inp} bits of randomness and outputs ℓ_{out} bits. Let $\mathcal{C}\text{-}\mathsf{AggSetup}_{t,\mathsf{PP},\{\mathsf{Verify}_i, \mathrm{VK}_i, m_i\}_i} \in \{0,1\}^{\ell_{\mathsf{ckt}}}$ be the canonical description of $\mathsf{AggSetup}_{t,\mathsf{PP},\{\mathsf{Verify}_i, \mathrm{VK}_i, m_i\}_i}$. We will

---

[23] Recall we are using an additively homomorphic encryption scheme. For simplicity of notation, we use $\mathsf{ct}_1 + \mathsf{ct}_2$ to represent $\mathsf{HE.add}(\mathsf{PP}, \mathsf{ct}_1, \mathsf{ct}_2)$. Also, we can use the additive homomorphism property to perform multiplications with plaintext elements. If $\sigma \in \mathbb{F}_p$ is a plaintext and ct is a ciphertext, then $\sigma \cdot \mathsf{ct}$ represents the multiplication, which can be computed using $\mathsf{HE.add}$.

assume that given C-$\mathsf{AggSetup}_{t,\mathrm{PP},\{\mathsf{Verify}_i,\mathrm{VK}_i,m_i\}_i}$, one can efficiently extract the hardwired constants t, PP and the n tuples $\{\mathsf{Verify}_i, \mathrm{VK}_i, m_i\}_i$.

Let $\tilde{C} = C$-$\mathsf{AggSetup}_{t,\mathrm{PP},\{\mathsf{Verify}_i,\mathrm{VK}_i,m_i\}_i}$. The aggregator algorithm first computes $(C_{\mathrm{agg}}, \tilde{s}) = \mathsf{InduceGen}(U, \tilde{C})$. Next, it computes $s = C_{\mathrm{agg}}(\sigma_1, \ldots, \sigma_n)$ and outputs $\sigma_{\mathrm{agg}} = (t, s)$.

$\mathsf{UniversalVerify}(\mathrm{PP} = (\mathrm{pk}, \mathrm{ct}_1, \ldots, \mathrm{ct}_n, U), \{\mathsf{Verify}_i, \mathrm{VK}_i, M_i\}_{i=1}^n, \sigma_{\mathrm{agg}} = (t, s'))$. The verification algorithm first checks if all n tuples are distinct. If not, it outputs 0. Else, let C-$\mathsf{AggSetup}$ be the canonical description of $\mathsf{AggSetup}$ as defined above. It computes $(C_{\mathrm{agg}}, \tilde{s}) = \mathsf{InduceGen}(U, C$-$\mathsf{AggSetup}_{t,\mathrm{PP},\{\mathsf{Verify}_i,\mathrm{VK}_i,m_i\}_i})$. If $\tilde{s} = f(s')$, output 1, else output 0.

Correctness follows from the fact that $\mathsf{InduceGen}$ is a deterministic algorithm.

6.1   Proof of Security

Theorem 4. *Assuming $i\mathcal{O}$ is a secure indistinguishability obfuscator, ($\mathsf{UniversalGen}, \mathsf{InduceGen}$) is a secure universal parameters scheme in the random oracle model, $\mathcal{HE}$ is a secure additively homomorphic encryption scheme and f is a secure one-way function, for all $(\ell_{\mathrm{ver}}, \ell_{\mathrm{vk}}, \ell_{\mathrm{msg}}, \ell_{\mathrm{sig}})$-length qualified secure signature schemes $\mathcal{S}$, the bounded universal signature aggregator described in Section 6 is adaptively secure in the random oracle model with respect to $\mathcal{S}$.*

We first describe a sequence of intermediate experiments $\mathsf{Game}\ 0, \ldots, \mathsf{Game}\ 5$, where $\mathsf{Game}\ 0$ is the adaptive security game in random oracle model. From $\mathsf{Game}\ 3$ onwards, the challenger starts simulating the universal parameters and the responses to random oracle queries. In order to do so, the challenger implements a parameter oracle O, and the simulation algorithms are allowed to make random oracle queries to O. Let us assume the simulator algorithms $\mathsf{SimUGen}$ and SimRO makes at most q_{par} calls to the Parameters Oracle.

Sequence of Games

$\mathsf{Game}\ 0$: In this game, the challenger first sends PP, VK to the adversary Att. Att then makes polynomially many signature and random oracle queries. Finally, Att outputs forgery σ_{agg} and n tuples $\{\mathsf{Verify}_i, \mathrm{VK}_i, m_i\}_i$.

1. Choose $(\mathrm{SK}, \mathrm{VK}) \leftarrow \mathcal{S}.\mathsf{Gen}(1^\lambda)$, $(\mathrm{pk}, \mathrm{sk}) \leftarrow \mathsf{HE}.\mathsf{setup}(1^\lambda)$ and $U \leftarrow \mathsf{UniversalGen}(1^\lambda)$. Compute $\mathrm{ct}_i \leftarrow \mathsf{HE}.\mathsf{enc}(\mathrm{pk}, 0)$ for all $i \in [n]$ and set $\mathrm{PP} = (\mathrm{pk}, \mathrm{ct}_1, \ldots, \mathrm{ct}_n, U)$. Send PP, VK to Att.
2. For each signature query x_i, compute $\sigma_i = \mathcal{S}.\mathsf{Sign}(\mathrm{SK}, x_i)$, send σ_i to Att.
3. For each random oracle query y_i, check if y_i has already been queried. If yes, let (y_i, α_i) be the tuple corresponding to y_i. Send α_i to Att. If not, choose $\alpha_i \leftarrow \{0,1\}^{\ell_{\mathrm{RO}}}$, send α_i to Att and add (y_i, α_i) to table.
4. Finally, Att sends a forgery $\sigma_{\mathrm{agg}} = (t^*, s^*)$ and n tuples $\{\mathsf{Verify}_i, \mathrm{VK}_i, m_i\}_i$. Att wins if

(a) $\exists i^*$ such that $\mathsf{Verify}_{i^*} = \mathcal{S}.\mathsf{Verify}$ and $\mathrm{VK}_{i^*} = \mathrm{VK}$,

(b) m_{i^*} was not queried during the signing phase,

(c) $f(s^*) = \tilde{s}$ and $\mathsf{InduceGen}(U, \mathcal{C}\text{-}\mathsf{AggSetup}_{t^*, \mathrm{PP}, \{\mathsf{Verify}_i, \mathrm{VK}_i, m_i\}_i}) = (C, \tilde{s})$.

Game 1: This game is exactly similar to the previous one, except that the challenger guesses a position $i^* \in [n]$, and the attacker wins only if the forgery verifies, and the i^*th tuple corresponds to $\mathcal{S}.\mathsf{Verify}, \mathrm{VK}$.

1. Choose $i^* \leftarrow [n]$. Choose $(\mathrm{SK}, \mathrm{VK}) \leftarrow \mathcal{S}.\mathsf{Gen}(1^\lambda)$, $(\mathsf{pk}, \mathsf{sk}) \leftarrow \mathsf{HE}.\mathsf{setup}(1^\lambda)$ and $U \leftarrow \mathsf{UniversalGen}(1^\lambda)$. Compute $\mathsf{ct}_i \leftarrow \mathsf{HE}.\mathsf{enc}(\mathsf{pk}, 0)$ and set $\mathrm{PP} = (\mathsf{pk}, \mathsf{ct}_1, \ldots, \mathsf{ct}_n, U)$. Send PP, VK to Att.

4. Att wins if

(a) $\mathsf{Verify}_{i^*} = \mathcal{S}.\mathsf{Verify}$ and $\mathrm{VK}_{i^*} = \mathrm{VK}$,

(b) m_{i^*} was not queried during the signing phase,

(c) $f(s^*) = \tilde{s}$ and $\mathsf{InduceGen}(U, \mathcal{C}\text{-}\mathsf{AggSetup}_{t^*, \mathrm{PP}, \{\mathsf{Verify}_i, \mathrm{VK}_i, m_i\}_i}) = (C, \tilde{s})$.

Game 2: In this game, the challenger modifies the public parameters PP. Instead of outputting n encryptions of 0, the challenger outputs an encryption of 1 at position i^*.

1. Choose $i^* \leftarrow [n]$. Choose $(\mathrm{SK}, \mathrm{VK}) \leftarrow \mathcal{S}.\mathsf{Gen}(1^\lambda)$, $(\mathsf{pk}, \mathsf{sk}) \leftarrow \mathsf{HE}.\mathsf{setup}(1^\lambda)$ and $U \leftarrow \mathsf{UniversalGen}(1^\lambda)$.
   Compute $\mathsf{ct}_i \leftarrow \mathsf{HE}.\mathsf{enc}(\mathsf{pk}, 0)$ for all $i \in [n], i \neq i^*$. Let $\mathsf{ct}_{i^*} \leftarrow \mathsf{HE}.\mathsf{enc}(\mathsf{pk}, 1)$. Set $\mathrm{PP} = (\mathsf{pk}, \mathsf{ct}_1, \ldots, \mathsf{ct}_n, U)$. Send PP, VK to Att.

Game 3. In this game, the challenger 'simulates' both the universal parameters U and the responses to random oracle queries. Let $\mathsf{SimUGen}$ and SimRO be the simulation algorithms corresponding to the universal parameters scheme $(\mathsf{UniversalGen}, \mathsf{InduceGen})$. The challenger also implements the Parameters Oracle O. O takes as input a circuit $d \in \mathcal{C}[\ell_{\mathrm{ckt}}, \ell_{\mathrm{inp}}, \ell_{\mathrm{out}}]$. If d has already been queried, O returns the same response. Else, it chooses $r \leftarrow \{0,1\}^{\ell_{\mathrm{inp}}}$, outputs $d(r)$, and adds $(d, d(r))$ to its table T. Though the parameters oracle O is described in the Setup Phase, it is used in all the later phases as well.

1. Choose $i^* \leftarrow [n]$. Choose $(\mathrm{SK}, \mathrm{VK}) \leftarrow \mathcal{S}.\mathsf{Gen}(1^\lambda)$, $(\mathsf{pk}, \mathsf{sk}) \leftarrow \mathsf{HE}.\mathsf{setup}(1^\lambda)$.
   Compute $U \leftarrow \mathsf{SimUGen}(1^\lambda)$ and ciphertexts $\mathsf{ct}_i \leftarrow \mathsf{HE}.\mathsf{enc}(\mathsf{pk}, 0)$ for all $i \in [n], i \neq i^*$. Let $\mathsf{ct}_{i^*} \leftarrow \mathsf{HE}.\mathsf{enc}(\mathsf{pk}, 1)$. Set $\mathrm{PP} = (\mathsf{pk}, \mathsf{ct}_1, \ldots, \mathsf{ct}_n, U)$.
   Implement the Parameters Oracle O as follows.
   - Maintain a table T. Initially, T is empty.
   - For the ith query $d \in \mathcal{C}[\ell_{\mathrm{ckt}}, \ell_{\mathrm{inp}}, \ell_{\mathrm{out}}]$, check if T contains an entry for d.
   - If T contains an entry of the form (d, δ), output δ.
   - Else choose $r \leftarrow \{0,1\}^{\ell_{\mathrm{inp}}}$ and output $d(r)$. Add $(d, d(r))$ to T.
   Send PP, VK to Att.

4. For each random oracle query y_i, output $\mathsf{SimRO}(y_i)$.

5. Finally, Att sends a forgery σ_{agg} and n tuples $\{\mathsf{Verify}_i, \mathrm{VK}_i, m_i\}_i$.
   Let O-Queries$_i$ denote the set of first i queries to O. Att wins if

(a) $\mathsf{Verify}_{i^*} = \mathcal{S}.\mathsf{Verify}$ and $\mathrm{VK}_{i^*} = \mathrm{VK}$,

(b) m_{i^*} was not queried during the signing phase,

(c) $f(s^*) = \tilde{s}$ and $\underline{O(\mathcal{C}\text{-}\mathsf{AggSetup}_{t^*,\mathrm{PP},\{\mathsf{Verify}_i,\mathrm{VK}_i,m_i\}_i}) = (C, \tilde{s})}$.

Recall from Section 6 that $\mathcal{C}\text{-}\mathsf{AggSetup}_{t,\mathrm{PP},\{\mathsf{Verify}_i,\mathrm{VK}_i,m_i\}} \in \{0,1\}^{\ell_{\mathrm{ckt}}}$ allows efficient extraction of t, PP and $(\mathsf{Verify}_i, \mathrm{VK}_i, m_i)$ for all $i \leq n$. Without loss of generality, we can assume that if Att outputs $\sigma_{\mathrm{agg}} = (t^*, s^*)$ as forgery, along with n tuples $\{\mathsf{Verify}_i, \mathrm{VK}_i, m_i\}_i$, then the circuit $\mathcal{C}\text{-}\mathsf{AggSetup}_{t^*,\mathrm{PP},\{\mathsf{Verify}_i,\mathrm{VK}_i,m_i\}_i}$ was sent as query to the Parameters Oracle O. We will now define games Game 4-j-a and Game 4-j-b for $j \leq q_{\mathsf{par}}$. Let us first define some notations. Given a canonical circuit $\mathcal{C}\text{-}\mathsf{AggSetup}_{t,\mathrm{PP},\{\mathsf{Verify}_i,\mathrm{VK}_i,m_i\}_i}$, call it (i^*, sk)-rejecting if $\mathsf{Verify}_{i^*}(\mathrm{VK}_{i^*}, m_{i^*}, \mathsf{HE.dec}(\mathsf{sk}, t)) = 0$. Let Reject-ckt be a circuit of size same as AggSign that outputs $\perp$ for all inputs.

Game 4-j-a

1. Choose $i^* \leftarrow [n]$.
   Choose $(\mathrm{SK}, \mathrm{VK}) \leftarrow \mathcal{S}.\mathsf{Gen}(1^\lambda)$, $(\mathsf{pk}, \mathsf{sk}) \leftarrow \mathsf{HE.setup}(1^\lambda)$.
   Compute $U \leftarrow \mathsf{SimUGen}(1^\lambda)$.
   Compute $\mathrm{ct}_i \leftarrow \mathsf{HE.enc}(\mathsf{pk}, 0)$ for all $i \in [n], i \neq i^*$. Let $\mathrm{ct}_{i^*} \leftarrow \mathsf{HE.enc}(\mathsf{pk}, 1)$.
   Set $\mathrm{PP} = (\mathsf{pk}, \mathrm{ct}_1, \ldots, \mathrm{ct}_n, U)$.
   Implement the Parameters Oracle O as follows.
   - Maintain a table T. Initially, T is empty.
   - For the ith query $d \in \mathcal{C}[\ell_{\mathrm{ckt}}, \ell_{\mathrm{inp}}, \ell_{\mathrm{out}}]$, check if T contains an entry corresponding to d.
   - If T contains an entry of the form (d, δ), output δ.
   - Else if $i \leq j$ and $d = \mathcal{C}\text{-}\mathsf{AggSetup}_{t,\mathrm{PP},\{\mathsf{Verify}_i,\mathrm{VK}_i,m_i\}}$ is (i^*, sk)-rejecting, $\underline{\text{output } i\mathcal{O}(\mathsf{Reject\text{-}ckt}) \text{ and } f(s) \text{ for } s \leftarrow \{0,1\}^\ell}$.
   - Else, choose $r \leftarrow \{0,1\}^{\ell_{\mathrm{inp}}}$ and output $d(r)$. Add $(d, d(r))$ to T.
   Send PP, VK to Att.

Game 4-j-b

5. Finally, Att sends a forgery $\sigma_{\mathrm{agg}} = (t^*, s^*)$ and n tuples $\{\mathsf{Verify}_i, \mathrm{VK}_i, m_i\}_i$. Att wins if
   (a) $\mathsf{Verify}_{i^*} = \mathcal{S}.\mathsf{Verify}$ and $\mathrm{VK}_{i^*} = \mathrm{VK}$,
   (b) m_{i^*} was not queried during the signing phase,
   (c) $(\mathcal{C}\text{-}\mathsf{AggSetup}_{t^*,\mathrm{PP},\{\mathsf{Verify}_i,\mathrm{VK}_i,m_i\}}$ is not (i^*, sk)-rejecting) **or** $(\mathcal{C}\text{-}\mathsf{AggSetup}_{t^*,\mathrm{PP},\{\mathsf{Verify}_i,\mathrm{VK}_i,m_i\}} \notin O\text{-Queries}_j)$,
   (d) $\overline{f(s^*) = \tilde{s}}$ and $O(\mathcal{C}\text{-}\mathsf{AggSetup}_{t^*,\mathrm{PP},\{\mathsf{Verify}_i,\mathrm{VK}_i,m_i\}_i}) = (C, \tilde{s})$.

Game 5. This game is exactly Game 4-q_{par}-b.

5. Finally, Att sends a forgery $\sigma_{\mathrm{agg}} = (t^*, s^*)$ and n tuples $\{\mathsf{Verify}_i, \mathrm{VK}_i, m_i\}_i$. Att wins if
   (a) $\mathsf{Verify}_{i^*} = \mathcal{S}.\mathsf{Verify}$ and $\mathrm{VK}_{i^*} = \mathrm{VK}$,

(b) m_{i*} was not queried during the signing phase,

(c) $\mathcal{S}.\mathsf{Verify}(\mathsf{VK}, m_{i*}, \mathsf{HE.dec}(\mathsf{sk}, t^*)) = 1$,

(d) $\overline{f(s^*) = \tilde{s}}$ and $O(\mathcal{C}\text{-}\mathsf{AggSetup}_{t^*, \mathrm{PP}, \{\mathsf{Verify}_i, \mathsf{VK}_i, m_i\}_i}) = (C, \tilde{s})$.

Analysis. Let $\mathsf{Adv}^j_{\mathsf{Att}}$ denote the advantage of Att in $\mathsf{Game}\ j$. Due to space constraints, we state the claims here and the proofs can be found in [30].

Claim 10. *For any adversary* Att, $\mathsf{Adv}^1_{\mathsf{Att}} = \mathsf{Adv}^0_{\mathsf{Att}}/n$.

Claim 11. *Assuming* $(\mathsf{HE.setup}, \mathsf{HE.enc}, \mathsf{HE.dec})$ *is a secure additively homomorphic encryption scheme, for any PPT adversary* Att, $\mathsf{Adv}^1_{\mathsf{Att}} - \mathsf{Adv}^2_{\mathsf{Att}} \leq negl(\lambda)$.

Claim 12. *Assuming* $(\mathsf{UniversalGen}, \mathsf{InduceGen})$ *is a secure* $(\ell_{\mathrm{ckt}}, \ell_{\mathrm{inp}}, \ell_{\mathrm{out}})$ *universal parameters scheme, for any PPT adversary* Att, $\mathsf{Adv}^2_{\mathsf{Att}} - \mathsf{Adv}^3_{\mathsf{Att}} \leq negl(\lambda)$.

Claim 13. *Assuming* $i\mathcal{O}$ *is a secure indistinguishability obfuscator, for any* $j \leq q_{\mathsf{par}}$, *for any PPT adversary* Att, $\mathsf{Adv}^{4-(j-1)-b}_{\mathsf{Att}} - \mathsf{Adv}^{4-j-a}_{\mathsf{Att}} \leq negl(\lambda)$.

Claim 14. *Assuming* f *is a secure one way function, for any* $j \leq q_{\mathsf{par}}$, *for any PPT adversary* Att, $\mathsf{Adv}^{4-j-a}_{\mathsf{Att}} - \mathsf{Adv}^{4-j-b}_{\mathsf{Att}} \leq negl(\lambda)$.

Claim 15. *Assuming* $\mathcal{S}$ *is a* $(\ell_{\mathrm{ver}}, \ell_{\mathrm{vk}}, \ell_{\mathrm{msg}}, \ell_{\mathrm{sig}})$-*length qualified secure signature scheme, for any adversary* Att, $\mathsf{Adv}^5_{\mathsf{Att}} \leq negl(\lambda)$.

Using the above claims, it follows that any PPT adversary has negligible advantage in $\mathsf{Game}\ 0$, assuming the universal parameters scheme is secure, $\mathcal{HE}$ is a secure additively homomorphic encryption scheme and f is a secure one-way function. Therefore, the universal signature aggregator in Section 6 is adaptively secure (in the random oracle model) w.r.t. all secure signature schemes.

References

1. Ahn, J.H., Green, M., Hohenberger, S.: Synchronized aggregate signatures: new definitions, constructions and applications. In: Proceedings of the 17th ACM Conference on Computer and Communications Security, pp. 473–484 (2010)
2. Barak, B., Garg, S., Kalai, Y.T., Paneth, O., Sahai, A.: Protecting obfuscation against algebraic attacks. In: Nguyen, P.Q., Oswald, E. (eds.) EUROCRYPT 2014. LNCS, vol. 8441, pp. 221–238. Springer, Heidelberg (2014)
3. Barak, B., Goldreich, O., Impagliazzo, R., Rudich, S., Sahai, A., Vadhan, S.P., Yang, K.: On the (im)possibility of obfuscating programs. In: Kilian, J. (ed.) CRYPTO 2001. LNCS, vol. 2139, pp. 1–18. Springer, Heidelberg (2001)
4. Barak, B., Goldreich, O., Impagliazzo, R., Rudich, S., Sahai, A., Vadhan, S.P., Yang, K.: On the (im)possibility of obfuscating programs. J. ACM **59**(2), 6 (2012)
5. Bellare, M., Namprempre, C., Neven, G.: Unrestricted aggregate signatures. In: Arge, L., Cachin, C., Jurdziński, T., Tarlecki, A. (eds.) ICALP 2007. LNCS, vol. 4596, pp. 411–422. Springer, Heidelberg (2007)

6. Bellare, M., Rogaway, P.: Random oracles are practical: A paradigm for designing efficient protocols. In: ACM Conference on Computer and Communications Security, pp. 62–73 (1993)

7. Bellare, M., Rogaway, P.: The exact security of digital signatures - How to sign with RSA and Rabin. In: Maurer, U.M. (ed.) EUROCRYPT 1996. LNCS, vol. 1070, pp. 399–416. Springer, Heidelberg (1996)

8. Benaloh, J.D.C.: Verifiable Secret-ballot Elections. Ph.D. thesis, Yale University (1987)

9. Bender, A., Katz, J., Morselli, R.: Ring signatures: Stronger definitions, and constructions without random oracles. J. Cryptol. **22**(1), 114–138 (2008)

10. Bitansky, N., Canetti, R., Chiesa, A., Tromer, E.: Recursive composition and bootstrapping for SNARKS and proof-carrying data. In: STOC, pp. 111–120 (2013)

11. Boldyreva, A., Gentry, C., O'Neill, A., Yum, D.H.: Ordered multisignatures and identity-based sequential aggregate signatures, with applications to secure routing. In: Proceedings of the 2007 ACM Conference on Computer and Communications Security, CCS, pp. 276–285 (2007)

12. Boneh, D., Boyen, X.: Secure identity based encryption without random oracles. In: Franklin, M. (ed.) CRYPTO 2004. LNCS, vol. 3152, pp. 443–459. Springer, Heidelberg (2004)

13. Boneh, D., Gentry, C., Lynn, B., Shacham, H.: Aggregate and verifiably encrypted. In: Biham, E. (ed.) EUROCRYPT 2003. LNCS, vol. 2656, pp. 416–432. Springer, Heidelberg (2003)

14. Boneh, D., Lynn, B., Shacham, H.: Short signatures from the weil pairing. In: Boyd, C. (ed.) ASIACRYPT 2001. LNCS, vol. 2248, pp. 514–532. Springer, Heidelberg (2001)

15. Boneh, D., Waters, B.: Constrained pseudorandom functions and their applications. In: Sako, K., Sarkar, P. (eds.) ASIACRYPT 2013, Part II. LNCS, vol. 8270, pp. 280–300. Springer, Heidelberg (2013)

16. Boyle, E., Goldwasser, S., Ivan, I.: Functional signatures and pseudorandom functions. In: Krawczyk, H. (ed.) PKC 2014. LNCS, vol. 8383, pp. 501–519. Springer, Heidelberg (2014)

17. Brakerski, Z., Rothblum, G.N.: Virtual black-box obfuscation for all circuits via generic graded encoding. In: Lindell, Y. (ed.) TCC 2014. LNCS, vol. 8349, pp. 1–25. Springer, Heidelberg (2014)

18. Brogle, K., Goldberg, S., Reyzin, L.: Sequential aggregate signatures with lazy verification from trapdoor permutations - (extended abstract). In: Wang, X., Sako, K. (eds.) ASIACRYPT 2012. LNCS, vol. 7658, pp. 644–662. Springer, Heidelberg (2012)

19. Damgård, I., Jurik, M.: A length-flexible threshold cryptosystem with applications. In: Safavi-Naini, R., Seberry, J. (eds.) ACISP 2003. LNCS, vol. 2727, pp. 350–364. Springer, Heidelberg (2003)

20. Freire, E.S.V., Hofheinz, D., Paterson, K.G., Striecks, C.: Programmable hash functions in the multilinear setting. In: Canetti, R., Garay, J.A. (eds.) CRYPTO 2013, Part I. LNCS, vol. 8042, pp. 513–530. Springer, Heidelberg (2013)

21. Garg, S., Gentry, C., Halevi, S., Raykova, M., Sahai, A., Waters, B.: Candidate indistinguishability obfuscation and functional encryption for all circuits. In: FOCS (2013)

22. Gentry, C., Ramzan, Z.: Identity-based aggregate signatures. In: Dodis, Y., Kiayias, A., Malkin, T., Yung, M. (eds.) PKC 2006. LNCS, vol. 3958, pp. 257–273. Springer, Heidelberg (2006)

23. Goldwasser, S., Micali, S.: Probabilistic encryption. Jour. of Computer and System Science **28**(2), 270–299 (1984)
24. Goldwasser, S., Micali, S., Rivest, R.L.: A digital signature scheme secure against adaptive chosen-message attacks. SIAM J. Comput. **17**(2), 281–308 (1988)
25. Goldwasser, S., Ostrovsky, R.: Invariant signatures and non-interactive zero-knowledge proofs are equivalent (extended abstract). In: Brickell, E.F. (ed.) CRYPTO 1992. LNCS, vol. 740, pp. 228–245. Springer, Heidelberg (1993)
26. Goldwasser, S., Rothblum, G.N.: On best-possible obfuscation. In: Vadhan, S.P. (ed.) TCC 2007. LNCS, vol. 4392, pp. 194–213. Springer, Heidelberg (2007)
27. Hada, S.: Zero-knowledge and code obfuscation. In: Okamoto, T. (ed.) ASIACRYPT 2000. LNCS, vol. 1976, pp. 443–457. Springer, Heidelberg (2000)
28. Heninger, N., Durumeric, Z., Wustrow, E., Halderman, J.A.: Mining your ps and qs: Detection of widespread weak keys in network devices. In: USENIX Security Symposium, pp. 205–220 (2012)
29. Hofheinz, D., Jager, T., Khurana, D., Sahai, A., Waters, B., Zhandry, M.: How to generate and use universal parameters. Cryptology ePrint Archive, Report 2014/507 (2014). http://eprint.iacr.org/
30. Hohenberger, S., Koppula, V., Waters, B.: Universal signature aggregators. Cryptology ePrint Archive, Report 2014/745 (2014). http://eprint.iacr.org/
31. Hohenberger, S., Sahai, A., Waters, B.: Full domain hash from (leveled) multilinear maps and identity-based aggregate signatures. In: Canetti, R., Garay, J.A. (eds.) CRYPTO 2013, Part I. LNCS, vol. 8042, pp. 494–512. Springer, Heidelberg (2013)
32. Hohenberger, S., Sahai, A., Waters, B.: Replacing a random oracle: Full domain hash from indistinguishability obfuscation. In: Nguyen, P.Q., Oswald, E. (eds.) EUROCRYPT 2014. LNCS, vol. 8441, pp. 201–220. Springer, Heidelberg (2014)
33. Kaliski, B., Staddon, J.: PKCS #1: RSA Cryptography Specifications Version 2.0. In: RFC Editor, United States (1998)
34. Kent, S., Lynn, C., Mikkelson, J., Seo, K.: Secure border gateway protocol (s-bgp). IEEE Journal on Selected Areas in Communications **18**, 103–116 (2000)
35. Kiayias, A., Papadopoulos, S., Triandopoulos, N., Zacharias, T.: Delegatable pseudorandom functions and applications. In: ACM Conference on Computer and Communications Security, pp. 669–684 (2013)
36. Lu, S., Ostrovsky, R., Sahai, A., Shacham, H., Waters, B.: Sequential aggregate signatures and multisignatures without random oracles. In: Vaudenay, S. (ed.) EUROCRYPT 2006. LNCS, vol. 4004, pp. 465–485. Springer, Heidelberg (2006)
37. Lysyanskaya, A., Micali, S., Reyzin, L., Shacham, H.: Sequential aggregate signatures from trapdoor permutations. In: Cachin, C., Camenisch, J.L. (eds.) EUROCRYPT 2004. LNCS, vol. 3027, pp. 74–90. Springer, Heidelberg (2004)
38. Naccache, D., Stern, J.: A new public key cryptosystem based on higher residues. In: Proceedings of the 5th ACM Conference on Computer and Communications Security, CCS 1998, pp. 59–66 (1998)
39. Neven, G.: Efficient sequential aggregate signed data. IEEE Transactions on Information Theory **57**(3), 1803–1815 (2011)
40. Okamoto, T., Uchiyama, S.: A new public-key cryptosystem as secure as factoring. In: Nyberg, K. (ed.) EUROCRYPT 1998. LNCS, vol. 1403, pp. 308–318. Springer, Heidelberg (1998)
41. Paillier, P.: Public-key cryptosystems based on composite degree residuosity classes. In: Stern, J. (ed.) EUROCRYPT 1999. LNCS, vol. 1592, pp. 223–238. Springer, Heidelberg (1999)
42. Rivest, R.L., Shamir, A., Adleman, L.M.: A method for obtaining digital signatures and public-key cryptosystems. Commun. ACM **21**(2), 120–126 (1978)

43. Rückert, M., Schröder, D.: Aggregate and verifiably encrypted signatures from multilinear maps without random oracles. In: Park, J.H., Chen, H.-H., Atiquzzaman, M., Lee, C., Kim, T., Yeo, S.-S. (eds.) ISA 2009. LNCS, vol. 5576, pp. 750–759. Springer, Heidelberg (2009)
44. Sahai, A., Waters, B.: How to use indistinguishability obfuscation: deniable encryption, and more. In: STOC, pp. 475–484 (2014)
45. Zhao, M., Smith, S.W., Nicol, D.M.: Aggregated path authentication for efficient BGP security. In: ACM Conference on Computer and Communications Security, pp. 128–138 (2005)

Fully Structure-Preserving Signatures and Shrinking Commitments

Masayuki Abe[1]([⊠]), Markulf Kohlweiss[2],
Miyako Ohkubo[3], and Mehdi Tibouchi[1]

[1] Secure Platform Laboratories, NTT, Tokyo, Japan
{abe.masayuki,tibouchi.mehdi}@lab.ntt.co.jp
[2] Microsoft Research, Cambridge, UK
markulf@microsoft.com
[3] Security Fundamentals Laboratory, NSR, NICT, Tokyo, Japan
m.ohkubo@nict.go.jp

Abstract. Structure-preserving signatures are schemes in which public keys, messages, and signatures are all collections of source group elements of some bilinear groups. In this paper, we introduce fully structure-preserving signature schemes, with the additional requirement that even secret keys should be group elements. This new type of structure-preserving signatures allows for efficient non-interactive proofs of knowledge of the secret key and is useful in designing cryptographic protocols with strong security guarantees based on the simulation paradigm where the simulator has to extract the secret keys on-line. To gain efficiency, we construct shrinking structure-preserving trapdoor commitments. This is by itself an important primitive and of independent interest as it appears to contradict a known impossibility result. We argue that a relaxed binding property lets us circumvent the impossibility result while still retaining the usefulness of the primitive in important applications as mentioned above.

Keywords: Structure-preserving signatures · Secret key extraction · Structure-preserving commitments

1 Introduction

In pairing-based cryptography, cryptographic primitives are often designed to have algorithms in which messages and public materials consist only of source group elements and correctness can be proved using pairing-product equations to allow smooth coupling with other primitives. This interest in so called structure-preserving primitives [3] led to the study of algebraic algorithms with many positive but also negative results [1, 2, 4–7, 11, 18, 34].

In structure-preserving signature schemes, all components but secret keys are group elements. This raises a natural question: *"Can secret keys consist entirely of source group elements as well?"* Having messages and signatures in the same group prevents us from relying on the one-wayness of exponentiation (or of

© International Association for Cryptologic Research 2015
E. Oswald and M. Fischlin (Eds.): EUROCRYPT 2015, Part II, LNCS 9057, pp. 35–65, 2015.
DOI: 10.1007/978-3-662-46803-6_2

the isomorphism from one source group to the other in the case of asymmetric bilinear groups) to blend messages into signatures, and it is a major difficulty in designing structure-preserving signatures. In existing schemes, this is overcome by having secret keys in the exponent. Thus, it is quite unclear how messages and secret keys can blend into signatures if even secret keys are group elements.

Besides the above question being a fascinating fundamental question in its own right, it is connected to practical protocol design since group secret keys combined with the Groth-Sahai proof system [31] allow straight-line (i.e., no rewinding) extraction of the secret keys when necessary. While there are solutions in the random oracle model, e.g. [19,26], secret key extraction without random oracles is currently prohibitively expensive. Meiklejohn [35] demonstrates how to extract a secret key in the exponent using the Groth-Sahai proofs. It requires bit-by-bit decomposition of secret x, and the proof consists of $20 \log_2 x + 18$ group elements. For instance, applying it to a structure-preserving signature scheme [2] whose secret key consists of $4 + 2\ell$ scalar values for signing messages of ℓ group elements, proving secret keys for signing 10 group elements at 128-bit security, requires more than 61,000 group elements.

Our contribution. This paper contains one main result and one important by-product that is of independent interest. First, we present a *fully structure-preserving signature (FSPS)* scheme all of whose components, including secret keys, consist of source group elements of bilinear groups. This result demonstrates that the paradigm of structure-preserving cryptography can be extended to cover private key material. The security against adaptive chosen message attacks is proved based on static (i.e., not q-type) assumptions. Its secret key consists only of four group elements, and a witness indistinguishable proof of knowledge about the secret key consists of 18 group elements (see Section 5.3). These are huge savings compared to the current solution mentioned above.

A price to pay is the signature size $O(\sqrt{\ell})$ for messages consisting of ℓ elements. A precise performance analysis shows that this remains relatively practical for short messages, e.g., a signature consists of 23 elements for messages of 9 elements (see Table 1). We show a non-trivial trade-off between the size of verification keys and signatures that implies that an order of $\sqrt{\ell}$ elements in signatures is inherent, at least for the type of modular constructions considered in this paper.

The investigation of efficient instantiations lead us to our second contribution: a *shrinking structure-preserving trapdoor commitment scheme* (SPTC). We present an SPTC scheme that produces constant-size commitments consisting of a single group element regardless of the message size. In addition to being an important primitive in itself, it is a remarkable construction in light of the well-known impossibility result [8] stating that SPTC schemes that yield shorter commitments than messages cannot be binding (or collision resistant, equivalently). We get around the impossibility by making two exclusive relaxations in the requirements. One is to weaken the security from collision resistance to what we call chosen-message target collision resistance (CM-TCR). In the proof of impossibility in [8], it is essential that the adversary finding a collision knows the randomness used to create the commitment. In CMTCR, it is still the adversary who chooses the messages to commit to, but it is the challenger who creates the target commitment from the given message. Therefore the random coins used for the target are hidden from the adversary.

Despite the first relaxation, it is still not easy to achieve CMTCR security. As a stepping stone we make the second relaxation and allow the commitment function to take exponents as input while mapping it to group elements for verification. The resulting scheme is no longer structure-preserving but does preserve the group structure with respect to verification. As we require a bijection γ between the message space for commitment and that for verification, we call such schemes γ-binding commitments. Finding a concrete construction satisfying the shrinking property is another challenge. There are commitment schemes whose messages can be scalar values in a bilinear group setting, e.g. [3,22,31,33,38], but none are γ-binding and shrinking. We present a concrete scheme whose commitment consists of a single group element and achieves collision resistance. We then use the shrinking γ-binding commitments to compress verification keys of a (not necessarily fully) structure-preserving partially one-time signature scheme (POS), and prove that it constitutes a shrinking SPTC with the CMTCR property.

Related work. At least one FSPS scheme already exists [2] but with constraints on both security and usability. Namely, it only meets the weak security guarantee (unforgeable against extended random message attacks), and the signing function takes messages of the form (G^m, F^m, U^m) that essentially requires knowledge of m [14,32]. Nevertheless, the UF-XRMA-secure FSPS scheme is a reasonable starting point and we overcome its shortcomings by combining it with structure-preserving trapdoor commitments or one-time structure-preserving signatures.

Regarding SPTC, the study by Abe et al.[8], is an important piece of context. It presents a concrete attack against all shrinking SPTC schemes. In fact, all existing SPTCs, e.g. [3], are rather expanding. The way we circumvent the impossibility, namely the γ-binding property, resembles the F-unforgeability notion [13] for signature schemes.

The use of trapdoor commitments and chameleon hashing has also been explored in the construction of on-line off-line signatures [21,25]. The work of Even, Goldreich, and Micali already formed the basis for the generic construction of SPS [2]. In addition, Catalano et al. [21], and Mohassel [37] observed an interesting relationship between one-time signatures and chameleon hashing.

We discuss potential applications of FSPS in the context of efficient secret key extraction from concrete to more high-level as follows.

Public-key infrastructure. On the very applied side, the question is connected with the timely problem of public-key infrastructures. Few protocols have been designed with the goal of being secure against adversarial keys, and few real-world certificate authorities validate that registrees provide valid public keys or prove knowledge of the corresponding secret keys. The availability of schemes with efficient non-interactive proofs-of-knowledge of secret key possession can only improve this situation. In the provable security literature, this *knowledge of secret key* solution to *rogue-key attacks* appeared early on in the study of multi-signatures by Micali et al. [36, Problem 4 and Fix 4].

Protocol design in strong security model. More generally, these obstacles to secret key extraction have hindered modular composable protocol design. Camenisch et al. [19] developed a framework for practical universally composable (UC) zero-knowledge proofs, in which they identify proofs-of-knowledge of exponents as a major bottleneck. Dubovitskaya [24] constructed unlinkable redactable signatures and anonymous credentials that are UC-secure. Their construction requires proofs-of-knowledge of the signing key of a structure-preserving signature scheme, which in turn, as studied by Chase et al. [23], is an instance of a general transformation for making signature schemes simulatable [10]. Given these examples, we conjecture that fully structure-preserving signature schemes help build UC-secure privacy preserving protocols.

Strengthening privacy in group and ring signatures. In classical group and ring signatures, e.g. [15,17,30,39], the goal of the adversary against privacy is to distinguish signatures from two *honest* members whose keys are actually generated and registered by the challenger. The attack game aborts if either of the targets is a corrupted member registered with an adversarially generated key. Instead of excluding such corrupt members from the scope of security, stronger privacy in the presence of adversarial keys can be guaranteed, if the challenger can extract the secret key to create group or ring signatures on their behalf. Such a model is meaningful when some keys are generated incorrectly, e.g., because of multiple potentially flawed implementations, but their owners nevertheless use them with the correct signing algorithm.

Other applications of FSPS are settings in which the signing keys need to be verifiably encrypted, for instance when extending delegatable anonymous credential systems [12,23,27] with all-or-nothing non-transferability [20].

Organization. After recalling preliminaries and existing building blocks in Sections 2 and 3 we give constructions of shrinking SPTC and FSPS schemes in Sections 4 and 5. We refer to [9] for variations of our FSPS constructions obtained by replacing some building blocks in our construction.

2   Preliminaries

2.1   Notations

By $|X|$ we denote the size of X (in some implicit unit). In particular, if X consists of group elements of some groups, it counts the number of elements in X. For x representing an object, $\boldsymbol{x}$ denotes an ordered set of x and is understood as $\boldsymbol{x} = (x_1, \ldots, x_n)$ for some positive integer n that is limited by a polynomial in the security parameter. The size n will be implicit if it is not very important in the context. By $y \leftarrow A(x)$, we denote that algorithm A takes x as input and outputs y. When it is clear from the context, we abuse notation like $\boldsymbol{y} \leftarrow A(\boldsymbol{x})$ to denote repetition of execution $y_i \leftarrow A(x_i)$ for $x_i \in \boldsymbol{x}$ and $y_i \in \boldsymbol{y}$.

2.2 Bilinear Groups

Let $\mathcal{G}$ be a generator of bilinear groups that takes security parameter 1^λ as input and outputs $\Lambda := (p, \mathbb{G}_1, \mathbb{G}_2, \mathbb{G}_T, e, G, \tilde{G})$, where p is a λ-bit prime, $\mathbb{G}_1, \mathbb{G}_2, \mathbb{G}_T$ are groups of prime order p with efficiently computable group operations, membership tests, and bilinear mapping $e : \mathbb{G}_1 \times \mathbb{G}_2 \to \mathbb{G}_T$. Elements G and $\tilde{G}$ are default random generators of $\mathbb{G}_1$, $\mathbb{G}_2$, and $e(G, \tilde{G})$ generates $\mathbb{G}_T$. We use the multiplicative notation for group operations in $\mathbb{G}_1$, $\mathbb{G}_2$, and $\mathbb{G}_T$. The pairing operation e satisfies that $^\forall A \in \mathbb{G}_1$, $^\forall B \in \mathbb{G}_2$, $^\forall x, y \in \mathbb{Z} : e(A^x, B^y) = e(A, B)^{xy}$. An equation of the form $\prod_i \prod_j e(A_i, B_j)^{a_{ij}} = 1$ for constants $a_{ij} \in \mathbb{Z}_p$, and constants or variables $A_i \in \mathbb{G}_1$, $B_j \in \mathbb{G}_2$ is called a pairing product equation (PPE). By $\mathbb{G}_1^*$, we denote $\mathbb{G}_1 \setminus 1_{\mathbb{G}_1}$, and similar for $\mathbb{G}_2^*$ and $\mathbb{Z}_p^*$.

Throughout the paper, we work over asymmetric bilinear groups (so-called Type-III setting [28]) where no efficient isomorphisms exist between $\mathbb{G}_1$ and $\mathbb{G}_2$. Some building blocks in our construction rely on the double pairing assumption [3].

Assumption 1 (Double Pairing Assumption: DBP). The double pairing assumption holds in $\mathbb{G}_2$ relative to $\mathcal{G}$ if, for all probabilistic polynomial-time algorithms $\mathcal{A}$, probability

$$\Pr \begin{bmatrix} \Lambda \leftarrow \mathcal{G}(1^\lambda); \\ \tilde{G}_z \leftarrow \mathbb{G}_2^*; \\ (Z, R) \leftarrow \mathcal{A}(\Lambda, \tilde{G}_z) \end{bmatrix} : \begin{array}{l} (Z, R) \in \mathbb{G}_1^* \times \mathbb{G}_1^*, \wedge \\ 1 = e(Z, \tilde{G}_z)\, e(R, \tilde{G}) \end{array} \end{bmatrix} \tag{1}$$

is negligible in security parameter λ.

The DBP assumption in $\mathbb{G}_1$ is defined by swapping $\mathbb{G}_1$ and $\mathbb{G}_2$ in the above definition. Note that the DBP assumption (in $\mathbb{G}_1$ and $\mathbb{G}_2$) is implied by the Decision Diffie-Hellman assumption (in $\mathbb{G}_1$ and $\mathbb{G}_2$, respectively) which is often assumed in Type-III setting.

We also use a building block that requires more assumptions such as DDH_2, $XDLIN_1$, and co-CDH that we refer to [2] for definitions.

2.3 Digital Signatures

In this section we recall definitions of digital signatures, one-time signatures and their security notions. On top of the standard notions, we define structure-preserving and fully structure-reserving signatures.

Definition 2 (Digital Signature Scheme). *A digital signature scheme is a set of algorithms {Setup, Key, Sign, Vrf}. Setup(1^λ) $\to$ gk is a setup function that, given a security parameter λ, generates common parameter gk, which defines message space $\mathcal{M}$. Key(gk) $\to$ (vk, sk) is a key generation algorithm that* *takes common parameter gk and generates a verification key vk and a signing key sk. Sign(sk, m) → σ is a signature generation algorithm that computes a signature σ for input message m ∈ M by using signing key sk. Vrf(vk, m, σ) → 1/0 is a verification algorithm that outputs 1 for acceptance or 0 for rejection according to the input.*

For correctness, it must hold that, for any legitimately generated gk, vk, and sk and for any message m ∈ M, 1 = Vrf(vk, m, Sign(sk, m)). A key pair (vk, sk) is correct if it is in the output distribution of the key generation function Key.

Definition 3 (Unforgeability against Adaptive Chosen-Message Attacks). *A signature scheme, SIG = {Setup, Key, Sign, Vrf}, is unforgeable against adaptive chosen message attacks (UF-CMA) if the following advantage function is negligible against any polynomial-time adversary A.*

$$\mathrm{Adv}^{uf\text{-}cma}_{SIG,\mathcal{A}}(\lambda) := \Pr\left[\begin{array}{c} gk \leftarrow Setup(1^\lambda), \\ (vk, sk) \leftarrow Key(gk), \\ (\sigma^\dagger, m^\dagger) \leftarrow \mathcal{A}^{\mathcal{O}_{sk}}(vk) \end{array}\middle|\begin{array}{c} m^\dagger \notin Q_m \wedge \\ 1 = Vrf(vk, m^\dagger, \sigma^\dagger) \end{array}\right], \qquad (2)$$

where $\mathcal{O}_{sk}$ is an oracle that, given m, executes σ ← Sign(sk, m), records m to Q_m, and returns σ.

A non-adaptive chosen message attack is defined by letting adversary $\mathcal{A}$ commit to the messages to query before seeing vk. ($\mathcal{A}$ is given gk that defines the message space.) Existential unforgeability against non-adaptive chosen message attack is denoted by UF-NACMA.

A one-time signature scheme is a digital signature scheme with the limitation that a verification key has to be used only once to retain security. Unforgeability against one-time chosen message attacks is defined as in Definition 3 by restricting the game to answer only a single signing oracle request.

Definition 4 (Structure-Preserving Signature Scheme). *A digital signature scheme is called structure-preserving with respect to bilinear group generator $\mathcal{G}$ if the following conditions are all satisfied. 1) Common parameter gk consists of a group description Λ generated by $\mathcal{G}$ and constants a_{ij} in $\mathbb{Z}_p$. 2) Verification key vk consists of group elements in $\mathbb{G}_1$ and $\mathbb{G}_2$ other than gk. 3) Messages and signatures consist of group elements in $\mathbb{G}_1$ and $\mathbb{G}_2$. 4) Verification algorithm Vrf consists only of evaluating membership in $\mathbb{G}_1$ and $\mathbb{G}_2$ and relations described by paring product equations.*

When messages consist of both source groups, $\mathbb{G}_1$ and $\mathbb{G}_2$, they are called bilateral. They are unilateral, otherwise.

The notion of structure-preserving cryptography requires *public* components to be group elements. We extend it so that *private* components consist of group elements as well.

Definition 5 (Fully Structure-Preserving Signature Schemes). *A structure-preserving signature scheme is fully structure-preserving if the following additional conditions are also satisfied. 5) Signing key sk (other than* *included vk) consists of group elements in* $\mathbb{G}_1$ *and* $\mathbb{G}_2$. *6) Correctness of sk with respect to vk can be verified by evaluating membership in* $\mathbb{G}_1$ *and* $\mathbb{G}_2$ *and relations described by pairing product equations.*

Once conditions 5 and 6 are satisfied, one can construct proof of knowledge about the secret keys by using the Groth-Sahai proof system, which allows one to extract a correct secret key corresponding to the verification key. It is however important to note that there could exist more than one correct secret key for a verification key and they may yield signatures in different distributions. One might need stronger extractability that allows to extract the secret key for a particular distribution of signatures. It is indeed the case for the group signature application mentioned in Section 1.

3   Building Blocks

3.1   Common Setup Function

Building blocks in this paper are defined with individual setup functions. As we work over bilinear groups, an output from a setup function should include a description of bilinear groups Λ. Some random generators specific to the building block may be included as well. Other parameters such as message spaces, are also defined there.

The individual setup functions will be merged into a common setup function, denoted as Setup, when the building blocks are used together in constructing upper-level schemes. By $gk \leftarrow \mathsf{Setup}(1^\lambda)$, we mean that Setup takes security parameter λ and generates a common parameter gk. This formulation is useful to share some domains in the building blocks. For instance, we require the message space of a signature scheme to match the key spaces of another signature scheme. Due to the interdependence between building blocks, it is inherent that Setup is constructed from individual setup algorithms in a non-blackbox manner. Suppose that two building blocks, say A and B, are used together. We say that A and B have common setup function Setup if $gk \leftarrow \mathsf{Setup}(1^\lambda)$ can be simulated whichever of $gk_A \leftarrow \mathsf{A.Setup}(1^\lambda)$ or $gk_B \leftarrow \mathsf{B.Setup}(1^\lambda)$ is given, and both gk_A and gk_B can be recovered from gk in polynomial time. In the rest of the paper, we abuse this property and give common parameter gk to individual functions of A and B.

3.2   Partially One-Time Signatures

When only a part of a verification key of one-time signatures must be updated for every signing, i.e., the remaining part of the verification key can be used an unbounded number of times, the scheme is called partially one-time [2,16].

Definition 6 (Partially One-Time Signature Scheme). *A partially one-time signature scheme is a set of algorithms POS = {Setup, Key, Ovk, Sign, Vrf} that:*

Setup$(1^\lambda) \to gk$: *A setup function that, given a security parameter λ, generates common parameter gk, which defines message space $\mathcal{M}$.*

Key$(gk) \to (vk, sk)$: *A long-term key generation function that takes gk and outputs a long-term key pair (vk, sk).*

Ovk$(gk) \to (ovk, osk)$: *A one-time key generation function that takes gk and outputs a one-time key pair (ovk, osk).*

Sign$(sk, osk, m) \to \sigma$: *A signing function that takes sk, osk and a message m as inputs and issues a signature σ.*

Vrf$(vk, ovk, m, \sigma) \to 1/0$: *A verification function that outputs 1 or 0 according to the validity of the input.*

For any $gk \leftarrow$ Setup(1^λ), $(vk, sk) \leftarrow$ Key(gk), $m \in \mathcal{M}$, and $(ovk, osk) \leftarrow$ Ovk(gk), $\sigma \leftarrow$ Sign(sk, osk, m), it must hold that $1 \leftarrow$ Vrf(vk, ovk, m, σ).

Definition 7 (One-Time Chosen-Message Attack for POS). *A partially one-time signature scheme, POS = {Setup, Key, Ovk, Sign, Vrf}, is unforgeable against non-adaptive partial one-time chosen message attacks (OT-NACMA), if advantage function* $\mathrm{Adv}_{POS,A}^{ot\text{-}nacma}(\lambda)$ *defined by probability*

$$
\Pr \left[
\begin{array}{l}
gk \leftarrow \text{Setup}(1^\lambda), \\
(vk, sk) \leftarrow \text{Key}(gk), \\
(ovk^\dagger, \sigma^\dagger, m^\dagger) \leftarrow \mathcal{A}^{\mathcal{O}_{sk}}(vk)
\end{array}
\left|
\begin{array}{l}
ovk^\dagger \in Q_{mv} \wedge (ovk^\dagger, m^\dagger) \notin Q_{mv} \wedge \\
1 = \text{Vrf}(vk, ovk^\dagger, m^\dagger, \sigma^\dagger)
\end{array}
\right.
\right]
\tag{3}
$$

is negligible against any polynomial-time adversary $\mathcal{A}$. Here $\mathcal{O}_{sk}$ is an oracle that, given $m \in \mathcal{M}$, executes $(ovk, osk) \leftarrow$ Ovk(gk), $\sigma \leftarrow$ Sign(sk, osk, m), records (ovk, m) to Q_{mv}, and returns (σ, ovk). When $\mathcal{O}_{sk}$ allows $\mathcal{A}$ to separately access Ovk and Sign, it is called an adaptive partial one-time chosen message attack (OT-CMA).

Obviously, OT-CMA security implies OT-NACMA security. The following construction taken from [2] with trivial modifications for optimality is OT-CMA secure under the DBP assumption in $\mathbb{G}_1$.

[Partially One-time Signature Scheme: POS]

Setup(1^λ): Run $gk := (p, \mathbb{G}_1, \mathbb{G}_2, \mathbb{G}_T, e, G, \tilde{G}) \leftarrow \mathcal{G}(1^\lambda)$. Set message space $\mathcal{M}$ to $\mathbb{G}_2^\ell$ for preliminary-fixed positive integer ℓ.

Key(gk): Take generators G and $\tilde{G}$ from gk. Choose w_z randomly from $\mathbb{Z}_p^*$, and compute $G_z := G^{w_z}$. For $i = 1, \ldots, \ell$, uniformly choose χ_i from $\mathbb{Z}_p$ and compute $G_i := G^{\chi_i}$. Output $vk := (G_z, G_1, \ldots, G_\ell) \in \mathbb{G}_1^{\ell+1}$ and $sk := (\chi_1, \ldots, \chi_\ell, w_z)$.

Ovk(gk): Choose $a \leftarrow \mathbb{Z}_p$ and output $ovk = A := G^a$, and $osk := a$.

Sign(sk, osk, m): Parse m into $(\tilde{M}_1, \cdots, \tilde{M}_\ell) \in \mathbb{G}_2^\ell$. Take a and w_z from osk and sk, respectively. Choose ζ randomly from $\mathbb{Z}_p^*$ and compute the signature as $(\tilde{Z}, \tilde{R})$ where $\tilde{Z} = \tilde{G}^\zeta, \tilde{R} = \tilde{G}^{a - \zeta w_z} \prod_{i=1}^\ell \tilde{M}_i^{-\chi_i}$.

Vrf(vk, ovk, m, σ): Parse σ as $(\tilde{Z}, \tilde{R}) \in \mathbb{G}_2^2$, m as $(\tilde{M}_1, \ldots, \tilde{M}_\ell) \in \mathbb{G}_2^\ell$, and ovk as A. Return 1, if $e(A, \tilde{G}) = e(G_z, \tilde{Z}) e(G, \tilde{R}) \prod_{i=1}^\ell e(G_i, \tilde{M}_i)$ holds. Return 0, otherwise.

3.3 xRMA-Secure Fully Structure-Preserving Signature Scheme

We follow the notion of extended random message attacks and take a concrete scheme from [2].

Definition 8 (Unforgeability against Extended Random Message Attacks). *A signature scheme, xSIG = {Setup, Key, Sign, Vrf}, is unforgeable against extended random message attacks (UF-XRMA) with respect to message sampler SampleM if probability*

$$
\text{Adv}_{xSIG,\mathcal{A}}^{uf\text{-}xrma}(\lambda) := \Pr \left[\begin{array}{l} gk \leftarrow \textsf{Setup}(1^{\lambda}), \\ (vk, sk) \leftarrow \textsf{Key}(gk), \\ \boldsymbol{m} \leftarrow \textsf{SampleM}(gk; \omega), \\ \boldsymbol{\sigma} \leftarrow \textsf{Sign}(sk, \boldsymbol{m}), \\ (\sigma^{\dagger}, m^{\dagger}) \leftarrow \mathcal{A}(vk, \boldsymbol{\sigma}, \boldsymbol{m}, \omega) \end{array} \middle| \begin{array}{l} m^{\dagger} \notin \boldsymbol{m} \wedge \\ 1 = \textsf{Vrf}(vk, m^{\dagger}, \sigma^{\dagger}) \end{array} \right] \tag{4}
$$

is negligible against any polynomial-time adversary $\mathcal{A}$. Here ω is a uniformly chosen randomness.

[xRMA-secure Signature Scheme: xSIG]

Setup(1^{λ}): Run $(p, \mathbb{G}_1, \mathbb{G}_2, \mathbb{G}_T, e, G, \tilde{G}) \leftarrow \mathcal{G}(1^{\lambda})$. For some fixed $\ell \geq 1$, choose $u_1, \cdots, u_{\ell}, \varrho, \delta$ randomly from $\mathbb{Z}_p^*$ and compute $F_1 := G^{\varrho}$, $F_2 := G^{\delta}$, $\tilde{F}_1 := \tilde{G}^{\varrho}$, $\tilde{F}_2 := \tilde{G}^{\delta}$, $U_i := G^{u_i}$, and $\tilde{U}_i := \tilde{G}^{u_i}$. Output $gk := (p, \mathbb{G}_1, \mathbb{G}_2, \mathbb{G}_T, e, G, \tilde{G}, F_1, F_2, \tilde{F}_1, \tilde{F}_2, \{U_i, \tilde{U}_i\}_{i=1}^{\ell})$. This constitutes the message space $\mathcal{M} = \{(\tilde{M}_{11}, \tilde{M}_{12}, \tilde{M}_{13}), \ldots, (\tilde{M}_{\ell 1}, \tilde{M}_{\ell 2}, \tilde{M}_{\ell 3}) \mid^{\forall i, \exists} m_i \in \mathbb{Z}_p$ s.t. $(\tilde{M}_{i1}, \tilde{M}_{i2}, \tilde{M}_{i3}) = (\tilde{F}_1^{m_i}, \tilde{F}_2^{m_i}, \tilde{U}_i^{m_i})\}$.

Key(gk): On input gk, choose $\tau_1, \tau_2, \tau_3, \rho, a, b, \alpha$ from $\mathbb{Z}_p$, and compute

$$
\begin{array}{llll}
\tilde{V}_1 := \tilde{G}^b, & \tilde{V}_2 := \tilde{G}^a, & \tilde{V}_3 := \tilde{G}^{ba}, & \tilde{V}_4 := \tilde{G}^{\tau_1 + a\tau_2}, \\
\tilde{V}_5 := \tilde{V}_4^b, & \tilde{V}_6 := \tilde{G}^{\tau_3}, & V_7 := G^{\rho}, & \tilde{V}_8 := \tilde{G}^{ab/\rho}, \\
K_1 := G^{\alpha}, & K_2 := G^b, & K_3 := G^{\tau_1}, & K_4 := G^{\tau_2}.
\end{array} \tag{5}
$$

(For completeness of description, pick $\tilde{V}_8$ uniformly from $\mathbb{G}_2$ if $\rho = 0$.) Output $vk := (gk, \tilde{V}_1, \tilde{V}_2, \tilde{V}_3, \tilde{V}_4, \tilde{V}_5, \tilde{V}_6, V_7, \tilde{V}_8)$ and $sk := (vk, K_1, K_2, K_3, K_4)$.

Sign(sk, M): Parse message M into $\{(\tilde{M}_{11}, \tilde{M}_{12}, \tilde{M}_{13}), \cdots, (\tilde{M}_{\ell 1}, \tilde{M}_{\ell 2}, \tilde{M}_{\ell 3})\} \in \mathcal{M}$. Select $r_1, r_2, z \leftarrow \mathbb{Z}_p$, set $r := r_1 + r_2$, compute

$$
\tilde{S}_0 := (\tilde{V}_6 \prod_{i=1}^{\ell} \tilde{M}_{i3})^{r_1}, \qquad S_1 := K_1 K_3^r, \qquad S_2 := K_4^r G^{-z}, \tag{6}
$$

$$
S_3 := K_2^z, \qquad S_4 := K_2^{r_2}, \text{ and} \qquad S_5 := G^{r_1}.
$$

Output $\sigma := (\tilde{S}_0, \ldots, S_5) \in \mathbb{G}_2 \times \mathbb{G}_1^5$.

Vrf(vk, M, σ): Output 1 if the following relations hold:

$$e(S_5, \tilde{V}_6 \prod_{i=1}^{\ell} \tilde{M}_{i3}) = e(G, \tilde{S}_0),$$

$$e(S_1, \tilde{V}_1)e(S_2, \tilde{V}_3)e(S_3, \tilde{V}_2) = e(S_4, \tilde{V}_4)e(S_5, \tilde{V}_5)e(V_7, \tilde{V}_8), \tag{7}$$

$$e(F_1, \tilde{M}_{i3}) = e(U_i, \tilde{M}_{i1}), \quad e(F_2, \tilde{M}_{i3}) = e(U_i, \tilde{M}_{i2}) \quad \text{for } i = 1, \cdots, \ell.$$

Output 0, otherwise.

The above scheme comes with trivial modifications from the original in [2]. First it is extended to sign random messages consisting of $\ell \geq 1$ message blocks, and second it takes randomness from $\mathbb{Z}_p$ rather than $\mathbb{Z}_p^*$ in the key generation. Those changes do not essentially affect to the security that we recall below.

Theorem 9 ([2]). *If the DDH_2, $XDLIN_1$, and co-CDH assumptions hold, then the above xSIG is UF-XRMA with respect to the message sampler that returns $aux = m_i$ for every random message block $(\tilde{F}_1^{m_i}, \tilde{F}_2^{m_i}, \tilde{U}_i^{m_i})$.*

Theorem 10. *The above xSIG is fully structure-preserving.*

Proof. By inspection, it is clear that vk (modulo group description in gk), sk, M, and σ consist of source group elements, and xSIG.Vrf consists of evaluating PPEs.

Next we show that the following PPEs are satisfied if and only if the verification key and the secret key is in the correct distribution.

$$e(K_2, \tilde{G}) = e(G, \tilde{V}_1), \quad e(G, \tilde{V}_3) = e(K_2, \tilde{V}_2), \quad e(K_1, \tilde{V}_1) = e(V_7, \tilde{V}_8),$$
$$e(K_2, \tilde{V}_4) = e(G, \tilde{V}_5), \quad e(K_3, \tilde{G})e(K_4, \tilde{V}_2) = e(G, \tilde{V}_4). \tag{8}$$

Showing correctly generated keys satisfy the above relations is trivial. We argue the other direction as follows. The independent variables that define a key pair are a, b, α, τ_1, τ_2, τ_3 and ρ. They are uniquely determined by $\tilde{V}_2$, $\tilde{V}_1$, K_1, K_3, K_4, $\tilde{V}_6$, and V_7, respectively. We verify that the remaining $\tilde{V}_3$, $\tilde{V}_4$, $\tilde{V}_5$, $\tilde{V}_8$, and K_2 are in the support of the correct distribution if the above relations are satisfied. The first equation is $e(K_2, \tilde{G}) = e(G, \tilde{G})^b$ that defines $K_2 = G^b$. The second equation is $e(G, \tilde{V}_3) = e(G, \tilde{G})^{ba}$ that defines $\tilde{V}_3 = \tilde{G}^{ba}$. The third equation is $e(G, \tilde{G})^{\alpha b} = e(G, \tilde{V}_8)^\rho$ that defines $\tilde{V}_8 = \tilde{G}^{\alpha b / \rho}$ for $\rho \neq 0$. If $\rho = 0$, $\tilde{V}_8$ can be an arbitrary value as prescribed in the key generation. The fourth equation is $e(G, \tilde{V}_4)^b = e(G, \tilde{V}_5)$ that defines $\tilde{V}_5 = \tilde{V}_4^b$. The last equation is $e(G, \tilde{G})^{\tau_1 + a\tau_2} = e(G, \tilde{V}_4)$ that defines $\tilde{V}_4 = \tilde{G}^{\tau_1 + a\tau_2}$ as prescribed. □

4   Trapdoor Commitment Schemes

4.1   Definitions

We adopt the following standard syntax for trapdoor commitment schemes.

Definition 11 (Trapdoor Commitment Scheme). *A trapdoor commitment scheme TC is a tuple of polynomial-time algorithms TC = {Setup, Key, Com, Vrf, SimCom, Equiv} that:*

Setup$(1^\lambda) \to gk$: *A common-parameter generation algorithm that takes security parameter λ and outputs a common parameter, gk. It determines the message space $\mathcal{M}$, the commitment space $\mathcal{C}$, and opening space $\mathcal{I}$.*

Key$(gk) \to (ck, tk)$: *A key generation algorithm that takes gk as input and outputs a commitment key, ck, and a trapdoor key, tk.*

Com$(ck, m) \to (com, open)$: *A commitment algorithm that takes ck and message $m \in \mathcal{M}$ and outputs a commitment, $com \in \mathcal{C}$, and an opening information, $open \in \mathcal{I}$.*

Vrf$(ck, com, m, open) \to 1/0$: *A verification algorithm that takes ck, com, m, and $open$ as input, and outputs 1 or 0 representing acceptance or rejection, respectively.*

SimCom$(gk) \to (com, ek)$: *A sampling algorithm that takes common parameter gk and outputs commitment com and equivocation key ek.*

Equiv$(m, ek, tk) \to open$: *An algorithm that takes ck, ek, tk and $m \in \mathcal{M}$ as input, and returns $open$.*

It is correct if, for all $\lambda \in \mathbb{N}$, $gk \leftarrow$ Setup(1^λ), $(ck, tk) \leftarrow$ Key(gk), $m \leftarrow \mathcal{M}$, $(com, open) \leftarrow$ Com(ck, m), it holds that $1 =$ Vrf$(ck, com, m, open)$. Furthermore, it is statistical trapdoor if, for any $gk \in$ Setup(1^λ), $(ck, tk) \in$ Key(gk), $m \in \mathcal{M}$, $(com, open) \leftarrow$ Com(ck, m), $(com', ek) \leftarrow$ SimCom(gk); $open' \leftarrow$ Equiv(m, ek, tk), two distributions $(ck, m, com, open)$ and $(ck, m, com', open')$ are statistically close.

Definition 12 (Structure-Preserving Trapdoor Commitment Scheme). *A trapdoor commitment scheme is structure-preserving relative to group generator $\mathcal{G}$ if its gk includes a description of bilinear groups generated by $\mathcal{G}$ and its commitment keys, messages, commitments, and opening information consist only of source group elements, and the verification function consists only of evaluating group membership and relations described by pairing product equations.*

We say that a commitment scheme is shrinking if $|com| \le |m|$ where equality holds only for the case of $|m| = 1$.

Trapdoor commitments should be hiding and binding. Since the hiding property follows from the statistical trapdoor property and is not important for our purpose, we focus on the binding property in the rest of this paper.

The standard binding property requires that it is infeasible for any polynomial-time adversary to find two distinct messages and openings for a single commitment value com. It is also referred to as collision resistance. A weaker notion known as target collision resistance asks the adversary to find a collision on a given message. We here introduce a weaker binding notion that lies between collision resistance and target collision resistance. This new notion, which we call *chosen-message target collision resistance* (CMTCR), allows the adversary to choose the message but it is committed to by the challenger. Thus, the adversary does not know the randomness used to create the target commitment.

Definition 13 (Chosen-Message Target Collision Resistance). *For a trapdoor commitment scheme,* TC, *let* $\mathcal{O}_{ck}$ *denote an oracle that, given* $m \in \mathcal{M}$, *executes* $(com, open) \leftarrow$ Com(ck, m), *records* (com, m) *to* Q, *and returns* $(com, open)$. *We say* TC *is chosen-message target collision resistant if advantage* $\mathrm{Adv}_{TC,\mathcal{A}}^{cmtcr}(\lambda)$ *defined by*

$$\Pr \left[\begin{array}{l} gk \leftarrow \mathsf{Setup}(1^\lambda), \\ (ck, tk) \leftarrow \mathsf{Key}(gk), \\ (com^\dagger, m^\dagger, open^\dagger) \leftarrow \mathcal{A}^{\mathcal{O}_{ck}}(ck) \end{array} \middle| \begin{array}{l} com^\dagger \in Q \wedge (com^\dagger, m^\dagger) \notin Q \wedge \\ 1 = \mathsf{Vrf}(ck, com^\dagger, m^\dagger, open^\dagger) \end{array} \right] \quad (9)$$

is negligible in security parameter λ *for any polynomial-time adversary* $\mathcal{A}$.

4.2 γ-Binding Commitment Scheme

This section presents a new primitive we call a γ-binding commitment scheme (TCγ). It has a special property that the message space $\mathcal{M}^{com}$ for creating a commitment and the space $\mathcal{M}^{ver}$ for verification differ and there exists an efficiently computable bijection $\gamma : \mathcal{M}^{com} \rightarrow \mathcal{M}^{ver}$ that computes messages for verification from those for committing. The formal definition is as follows.

Definition 14 (γ-Binding Commitment Scheme). *A γ-binding commitment scheme is a set of algorithms* TCγ = {Setup, Key, Com, Vrf, SimCom, Equiv} *that:*

Setup$(1^\lambda) \rightarrow gk$: *A setup function that, given a security parameter λ, generates common parameter gk, which defines message spaces; $\mathcal{M}^{com}$ for commitment generation and $\mathcal{M}^{ver}$ for verification, and an efficiently computable bijection $\gamma : \mathcal{M}^{com} \rightarrow \mathcal{M}^{ver}$. It also determines the commitment space $\mathcal{C}$, and the opening space $\mathcal{I}$.*

Key$(gk) \rightarrow (ck, tk)$: *A key generation algorithm that takes gk and outputs a public commitment key, ck, and a trapdoor key, tk.*

Com$(ck, m) \rightarrow (com, open)$: *A commitment algorithm that takes ck and message $m \in \mathcal{M}^{com}$ and outputs a commitment, $com \in \mathcal{C}$, and an opening information, $open \in \mathcal{I}$.*

Vrf$(ck, com, M, open) \rightarrow 1/0$: *A verification algorithm that takes ck, com, $M \in \mathcal{M}^{ver}$, and $open$ as inputs, and outputs 1 or 0 representing acceptance or rejection, respectively.*

SimCom$(gk) \rightarrow (com, ek)$: *A sampling algorithm that takes common parameter gk and outputs commitment com and equivocation key ek.*

Equiv$(M, ek, tk) \rightarrow open$: *An algorithm that takes ck, ek, tk, and $M \in \mathcal{M}^{ver}$ as input and returns $open$.*

Correctness, statistical trapdoor, and shrinking property are defined as well as Definition 11.

We say that a γ-binding commitment scheme is structure-preserving with respect to verification if ck, com, $open$, and $\mathcal{M}^{ver}$ consist of source group elements of bilinear groups and the verification function consists only of evaluating group membership and pairing product equations.

Next we formally define the security notions, γ-target collision resistance and γ-collision resistance. As well as ordinary notions of collision resistance, γ-collision resistance implies γ-target collision resistance.

Definition 15 (γ-Target Collision Resistance). *For a γ-binding commitment scheme, $\mathsf{TC}\gamma$, let com and $open$ denote vectors of commitment and openings produced by Com for uniformly sampled messages m. We say $\mathsf{TC}\gamma$ is γ-target collision resistant if advantage function $\mathrm{Adv}^{tcr}_{\mathsf{TC}\gamma,\mathcal{A}}(\lambda)$ defined by*

$$\Pr\left[\begin{array}{l} gk \leftarrow \mathsf{Setup}(1^\lambda), (ck, tk) \leftarrow \mathsf{Key}(gk), \\ m \leftarrow \mathcal{M}^{com}, (com, open) \leftarrow \mathsf{Com}(ck, m), \\ (com, M, open) \leftarrow \mathcal{A}(ck, m, com, open) \end{array} \middle| \begin{array}{l} com \in com \wedge M \notin \gamma(m) \wedge \\ 1 = \mathsf{Vrf}(ck, com, M, open) \end{array} \right]$$

is negligible in security parameter λ for any polynomial-time adversary $\mathcal{A}$.

Definition 16 (γ-Collision Resistance). *A γ-binding commitment scheme, $\mathsf{TC}\gamma$, is γ-collision resistant if advantage $\mathrm{Adv}^{cr}_{\mathsf{TC}\gamma,\mathcal{A}}(\lambda)$ defined by*

$$\Pr\left[\begin{array}{l} gk \leftarrow \mathsf{Setup}(1^\lambda), (ck, tk) \leftarrow \mathsf{Key}(gk), \\ (com, M_1, open_1, M_2, open_2) \leftarrow \mathcal{A}(ck) \end{array} \middle| \begin{array}{l} M_1 \neq M_2 \wedge \\ 1 = \mathsf{Vrf}(ck, com, M_1, open_1) \wedge \\ 1 = \mathsf{Vrf}(ck, com, M_2, open_2) \end{array} \right]$$

is negligible in security parameter λ for any polynomial-time adversary $\mathcal{A}$.

Now we present a concrete scheme for a structure-preserving γ-binding trapdoor commitment scheme for $\gamma : \mathbb{Z}_p \rightarrow \mathbb{G}_1$. For our purpose, we only require target collision resistance but the concrete construction satisfies the stronger notion.

[γ-Binding Trapdoor Commitment Scheme: $\mathsf{TC}\gamma$]

$\mathsf{Setup}(1^\lambda)$: Run $\mathcal{G}(1^\lambda)$ and obtain $gk := (p, \mathbb{G}_1, \mathbb{G}_2, \mathbb{G}_T, e, G, \tilde{G})$. It defines message spaces $\mathcal{M}^{com} := \mathbb{Z}_p^\ell$, $\mathcal{M}^{ver} := \mathbb{G}_1^\ell$ for fixed $\ell \geq 1$ and bijection $\gamma : \mathbb{Z}_p^\ell \rightarrow \mathbb{G}_1^\ell$ by $\gamma(m_1, \ldots, m_\ell) = (G^{m_1}, \ldots, G^{m_\ell})$. Output gk.

$\mathsf{Key}(gk)$: For $i = 1, \ldots, \ell$, choose $\rho_i \leftarrow \mathbb{Z}_p^*$ and compute $\tilde{X}_i := \tilde{G}^{\rho_i}$. Output $ck := (gk, \tilde{X}_1, \ldots, \tilde{X}_\ell)$ and $tk := (gk, \rho_1, \ldots, \rho_\ell)$.

$\mathsf{Com}(ck, m)$: Parse m into $(m_1, \cdots, m_\ell) \in \mathbb{Z}_p^\ell$. Choose $\zeta \leftarrow \mathbb{Z}_p^*$ and compute $\tilde{G}_u := \tilde{G}^\zeta \prod_{i=1}^\ell \tilde{X}_i^{m_i}$ and $R := G^\zeta$. Output $com := \tilde{G}_u$ and $open := R$.

$\mathsf{Vrf}(ck, com, M, open)$: Parse $ck = (gk, \tilde{X}_1, \ldots, \tilde{X}_\ell)$, $open = R$, $M = (M_1, \ldots, M_\ell) \in \mathbb{G}_1^\ell$, and $com = \tilde{G}_u$, respectively. Take generators $(G, \tilde{G})$ from gk. Return 1 if

$$e(G, \tilde{G}_u) = e(R, \tilde{G}) \prod_{i=1}^\ell e(M_i, \tilde{X}_i) \tag{10}$$

holds. Return 0, otherwise.

SimCom(gk): Choose $\omega_u \in \mathbb{Z}_p^*$. Compute $\tilde{G}_u := \tilde{G}^{\omega_u}$ and output $com := \tilde{G}_u$ and $ek := \omega_u$.

Equiv(M, ek, tk): Parse $tk = (gk, \rho_1, \ldots, \rho_\ell)$, $ek = \omega_u$, and $M = (M_1, \ldots, M_\ell)$. Compute $R := G^{\omega_u} \prod_{i=1}^{\ell} M_i^{-\rho_i}$. Then output $open := R$.

Theorem 17. *TCγ is correct, statistical trapdoor, and structure-preserving with respect to verification. It is γ-collision resistant if the DBP assumption holds.*

Proof. Correctness is verified as $e(R, \tilde{G}) \prod_{i=1}^{\ell} e(M_i, \tilde{X}_i) = e(G^\varsigma, \tilde{G}) \prod_{i=1}^{\ell} e(G^{m_i}, \tilde{X}_i) = e(G, \tilde{G}^\varsigma) e(G, \prod_{i=1}^{\ell} \tilde{X}_i^{m_i}) = e(G, \tilde{G}_u)$. To see if it is statistically trapdoor, observe that SimCom outputs $\tilde{G}_u$ uniformly over $\mathbb{G}_2^*$ whereas that from Com distributes statistically close to uniform over $\mathbb{G}_2$. Then R from Equiv is the one that is uniquely determined by the verification equation since it satisfies

$$e(R, \tilde{G}) \prod_{i=1}^{\ell} e(M_i, \tilde{X}_i) = e(G^{\omega_u} \prod_{i=1}^{\ell} M_i^{-x_i}, \tilde{G}) \prod_{i=1}^{\ell} e(M_i, \tilde{G}^{x_i}) = e(G, \tilde{G}_u).$$

Finally, it is obviously structure-preserving with respect to verification due to verification equation (10).

Next we prove the γ-collision resistance. Let $\mathcal{A}$ be an adversary that breaks the CR security of TCγ. We show algorithm $\mathcal{B}$ that attacks the DBP with black-box access to $\mathcal{A}$. Given an instance $(e, \mathbb{G}_1, \mathbb{G}_2, G, \tilde{G}, \tilde{G}_z)$ of the DBP, algorithm $\mathcal{B}$ sets up key ck as follows. Set $gk := (p, \mathbb{G}_1, \mathbb{G}_2, \mathbb{G}_T, e, G, \tilde{G})$. For $i = 1, \ldots, \ell$, choose $\xi_i, \varphi_i \leftarrow (\mathbb{Z}_p^*)^2$ and set $\tilde{X}_i := (\tilde{G}_z)^{\xi_i} \tilde{G}^{\varphi_i}$. Then give $ck := (gk, \tilde{X}_1, \ldots, \tilde{X}_\ell)$ to $\mathcal{A}$.

Suppose that $\mathcal{A}$ outputs $(\tilde{G}_u, R_1, M_1, R_2, M_2)$ that passes the verification as required. $\mathcal{B}$ then outputs $(Z^\star, R^\star)$ where

$$R^\star := \frac{R_1}{R_2} \prod_{i=1}^{\ell} \left(\frac{M_{1i}}{M_{2i}}\right)^{\varphi_i}, \text{ and } Z^\star := \prod_{i=1}^{\ell} \left(\frac{M_{1i}}{M_{2i}}\right)^{\xi_i}, \tag{11}$$

as the answer to the DBP. This completes the description of $\mathcal{B}$.

We first verify that the simulated ck is correctly distributed. In the key generation, gk is set legitimately to the given output of $\mathcal{G}$. Each simulated $\tilde{X}_i$ distributes uniformly over $\mathbb{G}_2$, whereas the real one distributes uniformly over $\mathbb{G}_2^*$. Thus, the simulated ck is statistically close to the real one.

We then argue that the resulting $(Z^\star, R^\star)$ is a valid answer to the given instance of the DBP. Since the output from $\mathcal{A}$ satisfies the verification equation, we have

$$1 = e\left(\frac{R_1}{R_2}, \tilde{G}\right) \prod_{i=1}^{\ell} e\left(\frac{M_{1i}}{M_{2i}}, (\tilde{G}_z)^{\xi_i} \tilde{G}^{\varphi_i}\right) \tag{12}$$

$$= e\left(\prod_{i=1}^{\ell}\left(\frac{M_{1i}}{M_{2i}}\right)^{\xi_i}, \tilde{G}_z^\star\right) e\left(\frac{R_1}{R_2} \prod_{i=1}^{\ell}\left(\frac{M_{1i}}{M_{2i}}\right)^{\varphi_i}, \tilde{G}\right) = e(Z^\star, \tilde{G}_z^\star)\, e(R^\star, \tilde{G}). \tag{13}$$

Observe that every ξ_i is independent of the view of $\mathcal{A}$ as it is information theoretically hidden into $\tilde{X}_i$. Since a valid output from $\mathcal{A}$ satisfies $M_1 \neq M_2$, there exists index $i^\star \in \{1, \ldots, \ell\}$ that $M_{1i^\star} \neq M_{2i^\star}$. Thus $Z^\star$ follows the distribution of $(M_{1i}/M_{2i})^{\xi_i}$ at $i = i^\star$. Since $M_{1i^\star}/M_{2i^\star} \neq 1$ and $\xi_{i^\star}$ is uniform over $\mathbb{Z}_p^*$, we conclude that $Z^\star = 1$ occurs only with negligible probability.

Thus, $\mathcal{B}$ breaks the DBP assumption with almost the same probability and running time of $\mathcal{A}$ breaking the γ-collision resistance of $\mathsf{TC}\gamma$. $\square$

4.3 Structure-Preserving Shrinking Trapdoor Commitment Scheme

Let POS be a partially one-time signature scheme. Let $\mathcal{M}_{\mathsf{pos}}$ be the message space of POS defined with respect to gk. We denote the key spaces as $\mathcal{K}_{\mathsf{pos}}^{vk}$, $\mathcal{K}_{\mathsf{pos}}^{sk}$, $\mathcal{K}_{\mathsf{pos}}^{ovk}$, and $\mathcal{K}_{\mathsf{pos}}^{osk}$ in a self-explanatory manner. Let $\gamma_{sk} : \mathcal{K}_{\mathsf{pos}}^{sk} \to \mathcal{K}_{\mathsf{pos}}^{vk}$ and $\gamma_{osk} : \mathcal{K}_{\mathsf{pos}}^{osk} \to \mathcal{K}_{\mathsf{pos}}^{ovk}$ be efficiently computable bijections. Let γ be $\gamma = \gamma_{sk} \times \gamma_{osk}^{(1)} \times \cdots \times \gamma_{osk}^{(k)}$. Let $\mathsf{TC}\gamma$ be a γ-binding trapdoor commitment scheme for such γ. It is assumed that POS and $\mathsf{TC}\gamma$ have a common setup function, Setup, that outputs gk based on POS.Setup and $\mathsf{TC}\gamma$.Setup, as mentioned in Section 3.1. (When instantiated from POS in Section 3.2 and $\mathsf{TC}\gamma$ from Section 4.2, Setup is as simple as running $gk \leftarrow \mathcal{G}(1^\lambda)$). Using these building blocks, we construct an SPTC scheme, TC, achieving CMTCR security as follows.

[**Trapdoor Commitment Scheme: TC**]

Setup(1^λ): It the same as the common setup function for POS and $\mathsf{TC}\gamma$. The relevant message spaces are set as $\mathcal{M}_{\mathsf{gbc}}^{com} := \mathcal{K}_{\mathsf{pos}}^{sk} \times (\mathcal{K}_{\mathsf{pos}}^{osk})^k$, $\mathcal{M}_{\mathsf{gbc}}^{ver} := \mathcal{K}_{\mathsf{pos}}^{vk} \times (\mathcal{K}_{\mathsf{pos}}^{ovk})^k$, and $\mathcal{M} := (\mathcal{M}_{\mathsf{pos}})^k$ for some integer $k > 0$.

Key(gk): Run $(ck_{\mathsf{gbc}}, tk_{\mathsf{gbc}}) \leftarrow \mathsf{TC}\gamma.\mathsf{Key}(gk)$. Output $ck := ck_{\mathsf{gbc}}$ and $tk := tk_{\mathsf{gbc}}$. It is assumed that gk is included in ck. The message space for TC is set to $\mathcal{M} := (\mathcal{M}_{\mathsf{pos}})^k$.

Com(ck, M): Parse $ck := ck_{\mathsf{gbc}}$ and $M := (M^{(1)}, \cdots, M^{(k)}) \in (\mathcal{M}_{\mathsf{pos}})^k$. Take gk from ck. Run $(vk_{\mathsf{pos}}, sk_{\mathsf{pos}}) \leftarrow \mathsf{POS}.\mathsf{Key}(gk)$. Execute $(ovk_{\mathsf{pos}}^{(i)}, osk_{\mathsf{pos}}^{(i)}) \leftarrow \mathsf{POS}.\mathsf{Ovk}(gk)$ and $\sigma_{\mathsf{pos}}^{(i)} := \mathsf{POS}.\mathsf{Sign}(sk_{\mathsf{pos}}, osk_{\mathsf{pos}}^{(i)}, M^{(i)})$ for $i = 1, \ldots, k$. Then run $(com_{\mathsf{gbc}}, open_{\mathsf{gbc}}) \leftarrow \mathsf{TC}\gamma.\mathsf{Com}(ck_{\mathsf{gbc}}, (sk_{\mathsf{pos}}, osk_{\mathsf{pos}}^{(1)}, \cdots, osk_{\mathsf{pos}}^{(k)}))$. Output $com := com_{\mathsf{gbc}}$ and $open := (open_{\mathsf{gbc}}, vk_{\mathsf{pos}}, ovk_{\mathsf{pos}}^{(1)}, \cdots, ovk_{\mathsf{pos}}^{(k)}, \sigma_{\mathsf{pos}}^{(1)}, \cdots, \sigma_{\mathsf{pos}}^{(k)})$.

Vrf($ck, com, M, open$): Parse $com = com_{\text{gbc}}$, $M = (M^{(1)}, \cdots, M^{(k)}) \in (\mathcal{M}_{\text{pos}})^k$ and $open = (open_{\text{gbc}}, vk_{\text{pos}}, ovk_{\text{pos}}^{(1)}, \cdots, ovk_{\text{pos}}^{(k)}, \sigma_{\text{pos}}^{(1)}, \cdots, \sigma_{\text{pos}}^{(k)})$. Execute $b_0 \leftarrow \text{TC}\gamma.\text{Vrf}(ck_{\text{gbc}}, com_{\text{gbc}}, (vk_{\text{pos}}, ovk_{\text{pos}}^{(1)}, \cdots, ovk_{\text{pos}}^{(k)}), open_{\text{gbc}})$, and $b_i \leftarrow \text{POS.Vrf}(vk_{\text{pos}}, ovk_{\text{pos}}^{(i)}, M^{(i)}, \sigma_{\text{pos}}^{(i)})$ for $i = 1, \ldots, k$. Output 1 if $b_i = 1$ for all $i = 0, \ldots, k$. Output 0, otherwise.

SimCom(gk): Take gk_{gbc} from gk and run $(com_{\text{gbc}}, ek_{\text{gbc}}) \leftarrow \text{TC}\gamma.\text{SimCom}(gk_{\text{gbc}})$ and output $com := com_{\text{gbc}}$ and $ek := (com_{\text{gbc}}, ek_{\text{gbc}})$.

Equiv(M, ek, tk): The same as TC.Com except that, $\text{TC}\gamma.\text{Com}$ is replaced by $open_{\text{gbc}} \leftarrow \text{TC}\gamma.\text{Equiv}((vk_{\text{pos}}, ovk_{\text{pos}}^{(1)}, \cdots, ovk_{\text{pos}}^{(k)}), ek_{\text{gbc}}, tk_{\text{gbc}})$ and com_{gbc} included in ek.

Theorem 18. *The commitment scheme TC described above is CMTCR if POS is OT-NACMA, and $TC\gamma$ is γ-target collision resistant.*

Proof. We follow the game transition framework. Let Game 0 be the CMTCR game launched by adversary $\mathcal{A}$. By $com^\dagger = com_{\text{gbc}}^\dagger$, $open^\dagger = (open_{\text{gbc}}^\dagger, vk_{\text{pos}}^\dagger, ovk_{\text{pos}}^{\dagger\,(1)}, \cdots, ovk_{\text{pos}}^{\dagger\,(k)}, \sigma_{\text{pos}}^{\dagger\,(1)}, \cdots, \sigma_{\text{pos}}^{\dagger\,(k)})$ and $M^\dagger = (M^{\dagger(1)}, \cdots, M^{\dagger(k)})$, we denote the collision $\mathcal{A}$ outputs.

In Game 1, abort if $(vk_{\text{pos}}^\dagger, ovk_{\text{pos}}^{\dagger\,(1)}, \cdots, ovk_{\text{pos}}^{\dagger\,(k)})$ differs from any of $(vk_{\text{pos}}, ovk_{\text{pos}}^{(1)}, \cdots, ovk_{\text{pos}}^{(k)})$ observed by the signing oracle. We show that this occurs only if $\text{TC}\gamma$ is broken by constructing adversary $\mathcal{B}$ attacking the γ-target collision resistance of $\text{TC}\gamma$. Adversary $\mathcal{B}$ is given ck_{gbc} and q_s reference commitments com_{gbc} and opening $open_{\text{gbc}}$ for random messages of the form $(sk_{\text{pos}}, osk_{\text{pos}}^{(1)}, \ldots, osk_{\text{pos}}^{(k)})$. Each message is uniquely mapped to $(vk_{\text{pos}}, ovk_{\text{pos}}^{(1)}, \ldots, ovk_{\text{pos}}^{(k)})$ by bijection γ. Adversary $\mathcal{B}$ invokes $\mathcal{A}$ with $ck := ck_{\text{gbc}}$ as input. For every commitment query M, adversary $\mathcal{B}$ takes a fresh sample $(sk_{\text{pos}}, osk_{\text{pos}}^{(1)}, \ldots, osk_{\text{pos}}^{(k)})$ with its commitment com_{gbc} and opening $open_{\text{gbc}}$, and compute $\sigma_{\text{pos}}^{(j)} \leftarrow \text{POS.Sign}(sk_{\text{pos}}, osk_{\text{pos}}^{(j)}, M^{(j)})$ for $j = 1, \ldots, k$. It then returns $com := com_{\text{gbc}}$ and $open := (open_{\text{gbc}}, vk_{\text{pos}}, ovk_{\text{pos}}^{(1)}, \cdots, ovk_{\text{pos}}^{(k)}, \sigma_{\text{pos}}^{(1)}, \cdots, \sigma_{\text{pos}}^{(k)})$. If $\mathcal{A}$ eventually outputs a collision, $\mathcal{B}$ outputs $com_{\text{gbc}}^\star := com_{\text{gbc}}^\dagger$, $open_{\text{gbc}}^\star := open_{\text{gbc}}^\dagger$ and $M^\star := (vk_{\text{pos}}^\dagger, ovk_{\text{pos}}^{\dagger\,(1)}, \cdots, ovk_{\text{pos}}^{\dagger\,(k)})$. This completes the description of $\mathcal{B}$.

The simulated commitments and openings distribute the same as the real ones since every $osk_{\text{pos}}^{(j)}$ is sampled legitimately by the challenger and the commitment generation procedure is the genuine one. Furthermore, the output of $\mathcal{B}$ is a valid collision against $\text{TC}\gamma$ since $\mathcal{A}$ must have chosen $com^\dagger (= com_{\text{gbc}}^\dagger)$ from once used commitments and $M^\star$ is fresh due to the condition of abort. Accordingly, we have $|\Pr[\text{Game 0}] - \Pr[\text{Game 1}]| \leq \text{Adv}_{\text{TC}\gamma, \mathcal{B}}^{\text{tcr}}(\lambda)$.

We then argue that $\mathcal{A}$ wins in Game 1 only if POS is broken. Let $\mathcal{C}$ be an adversary attacking the OT-NACMA property of POS. Given $vk_{\text{pos}}^\star$ from outside, $\mathcal{C}$ first flips a coin $i^\dagger \leftarrow \{1, \ldots, q_s\}$. It then takes gk from $vk_{\text{pos}}^\star$ and executes $(ck_{\text{gbc}}, tk_{\text{gbc}}) \leftarrow \text{TC}\gamma.\text{Key}(gk)$. Then it invokes $\mathcal{A}$ with input $ck := ck_{\text{gbc}}$. Given j-th query for $j \neq i^\dagger$, $\mathcal{C}$ runs the legitimate procedure of TC.Com and returns obtained $(open, com)$. For the $i^\dagger$-th query $M = (M^{(1)}, \ldots, M^{(k)})$, $\mathcal{C}$ makes a query $M^{(j)}$ to the signing oracle of POS and obtains $ovk_{pos}^{(j)}$ and $\sigma_{pos}^{(j)}$ for $j = 1, \ldots, k$. $\mathcal{C}$ then computes $(com_{gbc}, ek_{gbc}) \leftarrow \mathsf{TC}\gamma.\mathsf{SimCom}(gk)$ and $open_{gbc} \leftarrow \mathsf{TC}\gamma.\mathsf{Equiv}((vk_{pos}^\star, ovk_{pos}^{(1)}, \cdots, ovk_{pos}^{(k)}), ek_{gbc}, tk_{gbc})$ and outputs $com := com_{gbc}$ and $open := (open_{gbc}, vk_{pos}^\star, ovk_{pos}^{(1)}, \cdots, ovk_{pos}^{(k)}, \sigma_{pos}^{(1)}, \cdots, \sigma_{pos}^{(k)})$. On receiving a collision from $\mathcal{A}$, $\mathcal{C}$ aborts if $vk_{pos}^\dagger \neq vk_{pos}^\star$. Otherwise, find $i^\star$ that $M^{\dagger^{(i^\star)}} \neq M^{(i^\star)}$ (such an index must exist since $M^\dagger$ differs from any queried messages) and outputs $ovk_{pos}^\star := ovk_{pos}^{\dagger^{(i^\star)}}$ and $M^\star := M^{\dagger^{(i^\star)}}$. This completes the description of $\mathcal{C}$. The simulated signatures are statistically close to the real ones due to the statistical trapdoor property of $\mathsf{TC}\gamma.\mathsf{SimCom}$ and $\mathsf{TC}\gamma.\mathsf{Equiv}$. Aborting event $vk_{pos}^\dagger \neq vk_{pos}^\star$ does not occur with probability $1/q_s$. Thus, we have $\frac{1}{q_s} \Pr[\text{Game 1}] - \epsilon_{sim} \leq \mathsf{Adv}_{POS,\mathcal{C}}^{\text{ot-nacma}}(\lambda)$, where ϵ_{sim} is the statistical loss by $\mathsf{TC}\gamma.\mathsf{SimCom}$ and $\mathsf{TC}\gamma.\mathsf{Equiv}$.

All in all, we have

$$\mathsf{Adv}_{TC,\mathcal{A}}^{\text{cmtcr}}(\lambda) \leq \mathsf{Adv}_{TC\gamma,\mathcal{B}}^{\text{tcr}}(\lambda) + q_s \cdot \mathsf{Adv}_{POS,\mathcal{C}}^{\text{ot-nacma}}(\lambda) + \epsilon_{sim},$$

which proves the statement. □

The following is immediate from the construction. In particular, Correctness holds due to the correctness of $\mathsf{TC}\gamma$ and POS and the existence of a bijection from the secret keys of POS to the verification keys.

Theorem 19. *Above TC is a structure-preserving trapdoor commitment scheme if TCγ is structure-preserving with respect to verification, and POS is structure-preserving.*

5 Fully Structure-Preserving Signatures

We argue that constructing an FSPS requires a different approach than those for all known constructions of SPSs. The verification equations of existing structure-preserving constant-size signatures on message vectors $(G^{m_1}, \ldots, G^{m_n})$ involve pairings such as $\prod e(G^{x_i}, G^{m_i})$, where G^{x_i} is a public key element and G^{m_i} is a message element. The message is squashed into a signature element, say S, in such a form that $S := A \cdot \prod_{i=1}^n G^{m_i x_i}$ where x_i is a signing key component and A is computed from inputs other than the message. Such a structure requires either m_i or x_i to be detected to the signing algorithm. In FSPS, however, neither is given to the signing function.

Our starting point is the FSPS scheme in Section 3.3. The following sections present constructions that upgrade the security to UF-CMA by incorporating one-time signatures or trapdoor commitments.

5.1 Warm-Up: Based on One-Time Signatures

Our first approach is to take x_i from randomness instead of the signing key. That is, x_i works as a random one-time key and G^{x_i} is regarded as a one-time public key, which is then authenticated by an FSPS that is secure against extended random message attacks. This results in a combination of a weaker signature scheme with OTS, which is well known as a method for upgrading the security of the underlying signature scheme. This in fact can be seen as a special case of the construction of SPS by Abe et al. [2]. We nevertheless work out the scheme in detail to discuss our motivation for our main scheme and settle a basis for comparison. Let OTS and xSIG be a one-time and an ordinary signature scheme that have common setup function Setup. We construct FSP1 as follows.

[**Signature Scheme: FSP1**]

Setup(1^λ): It is the same as Setup for OTS and xSIG. It outputs $gk \leftarrow$ Setup(1^λ), and sets $\mathcal{M}_{xsig} := \mathcal{K}^{vk}_{ots}$ and $\mathcal{M} := \mathcal{M}_{ots}$.

Key(gk): Run (vk_{xsig}, sk_{xsig}) $\leftarrow$ xSIG.Key(gk). (It is assumed that gk is included in vk_{xsig} and sk_{xsig}.) Output (vk, sk) := (vk_{xsig}, sk_{xsig}).

Sign(sk, M): Take sk_{xsig} and gk from sk. Compute (ovk_{ots}, osk_{ots}) $\leftarrow$ OTS.Key(gk), $\sigma_{xsig} \leftarrow$ xSIG.Sign(sk_{xsig}, ovk_{ots}), $\sigma_{ots} \leftarrow$ OTS.Sign(osk_{ots}, M). Output $\sigma := (\sigma_{xsig}, \sigma_{ots}, ovk_{ots})$

Vrf(vk, M, σ): : Take vk_{xsig} and ($\sigma_{xsig}, \sigma_{ots}, ovk_{ots}$) from the input. Output 1 if $1 =$ OTS.Vrf($vk_{ots}, M, \sigma_{ots}$) and $1 =$ xSIG.Vrf($vk_{xsig}, vk_{ots}, \sigma_{xsig}$). Output 0, otherwise.

Theorem 20. *If OTS is a UF-NACMA secure SPS and xSIG is a UF-XRMA secure FSPS, then FSP1 is a UF-CMA secure FSPS scheme.*

Proof. Since the syntactical consistency and correctness are trivial from the construction, we only show that the scheme is fully structure-preserving. The public component of FSP1 is $(vk, \sigma, M) = (vk_{xsig}, (\sigma_{xsig}, \sigma_{ots}, ovk_{ots}), M)$, which consists of public components of xSIG.Key and the OTS. Also, the signing key of FSP1 consists of sk_{xsig}. Thus, both public and private components of FSP1 consist of group elements since xSIG is FSPS and the OTS is SPS. Furthermore, FSP1.Vrf evaluates OTS.Vrf and xSIG.Vrf that evaluate PPEs. Thus, FSP1 is FSPS.

We next prove the UF-CMA security of FSP1 by following the standard game transition technique. Let $\mathcal{A}$ be an adversary against FSP1. By Pr[Game i] we denote probability that $\mathcal{A}$ eventually outputs a valid forgery as defined in Definition 3. Let Game 0 be the UF-CMA game that $\mathcal{A}$ is playing. By definition, Pr[Game 0] = Adv$^{uf\text{-}cma}_{FSP1,\mathcal{A}}(\lambda)$. Let ($\sigma^\dagger, m^\dagger$) be a forgery $\mathcal{A}$ outputs. Let $\sigma^\dagger :=$ ($\sigma^\dagger_{xsig}, \sigma^\dagger_{ots}, vk^\dagger_{ots}$).

In Game 1, abort the game if ($\sigma^\dagger, m^\dagger$) is a valid forgery and $vk^\dagger_{ots}$ is never used by the signing oracle. We show that this event occurs only if the UF-XRMA security of xSIG is broken. Let $\mathcal{B}$ be an adversary against xSIG launching an XRMA attack. $\mathcal{B}$ is given ($vk_{xsig}, (\sigma^{(1)}_{xsig}, vk^{(1)}_{ots}, \omega^{(1)}), \ldots, (\sigma^{(q_s)}_{xsig}, vk^{(q_s)}_{ots}, \omega^{(q_s)})$) where $\omega^{(j)}$ is the randomness used to generate $vk^{(j)}_{ots}$ with OTS.Key. $\mathcal{B}$ first obtains $sk^{(j)}_{ots}$ from $\omega^{(j)}$ by executing OTS.Key by itself. Then it invokes $\mathcal{A}$ with input $vk := vk_{xsig}$. On receiving $m^{(j)}$ for signing, $\mathcal{B}$ computes $\sigma^{(j)}_{ots} \leftarrow$ OTS.Sign($sk_{ots}, m^{(j)}$) and returns $\sigma^{(j)} := (\sigma^{(j)}_{\mathsf{xsig}}, \sigma^{(j)}_{\mathsf{ots}}, vk^{(j)}_{\mathsf{ots}})$. When $\mathcal{A}$ outputs forgery $\sigma^\dagger := (\sigma^\dagger_{\mathsf{xsig}}, \sigma^\dagger_{\mathsf{ots}}, vk^\dagger_{\mathsf{ots}})$, $\mathcal{B}$ outputs $\sigma^\star_{\mathsf{xsig}} := \sigma^\dagger_{\mathsf{xsig}}$ and $m^\star := vk^\dagger_{\mathsf{ots}}$. This is a valid forgery since $vk^\dagger_{\mathsf{ots}} \neq vk^{(j)}_{\mathsf{ots}}$. Thus, we have $|\Pr[\text{Game } 0] - \Pr[\text{Game } 1]| \leq \mathsf{Adv}^{\mathsf{uf\text{-}xrma}}_{\mathsf{xSIG},\mathcal{B}}(\lambda)$.

Next we show that $\mathcal{A}$ wins Game 1 only if OTS is broken. Let $\mathcal{C}$ be an adversary attacking OTS with NACMA. Given gk from outside, $\mathcal{C}$ first flips a coin $i^\dagger \leftarrow \{1, \ldots, q_s\}$. It then executes $(vk, sk) \leftarrow \mathsf{FSP1.Key}(gk)$. Given $m^{(j)}$ for $j \neq i^\dagger$, $\mathcal{C}$ runs $\sigma^{(j)} \leftarrow \mathsf{FSP1.Sign}(sk, m^{(j)})$ and returns $\sigma^{(j)}$ to $\mathcal{A}$. For $j = i^\dagger$, $\mathcal{C}$ forwards $m^{(i^\dagger)}$ to the signing oracle of OTS and receive $\sigma^{(i^\dagger)}_{\mathsf{ots}}$ and $vk^{(i^\dagger)}_{\mathsf{ots}}$. Then $\mathcal{B}$ executes $\sigma^{(i^\dagger)}_{\mathsf{xsig}} \leftarrow \mathsf{xSIG.Sign}(sk_{\mathsf{xsig}}, vk^{(i^\dagger)}_{\mathsf{ots}})$ and returns $\sigma^{(i^\dagger)} := (\sigma^{(i^\dagger)}_{\mathsf{xsig}}, \sigma^{(i^\dagger)}_{\mathsf{ots}}, vk^{(i^\dagger)}_{\mathsf{ots}})$ to $\mathcal{A}$. When $\mathcal{A}$ outputs forgery $\sigma^\dagger := (\sigma^\dagger_{\mathsf{xsig}}, \sigma^\dagger_{\mathsf{ots}}, vk^\dagger_{\mathsf{ots}})$ and $m^\dagger$, $\mathcal{C}$ aborts if $vk^\dagger_{\mathsf{ots}} \neq vk^{(i^\dagger)}_{\mathsf{ots}}$. Otherwise, $\mathcal{C}$ outputs $\sigma^\star_{\mathsf{xsig}} := \sigma^\dagger_{\mathsf{ots}}$ and $m^\star := m^\dagger$. This is a valid forgery since $m^\dagger \neq m^{(i^\dagger)}$. Thus, we have $\frac{1}{q_s}\Pr[\text{Game } 1] \leq \mathsf{Adv}^{\mathsf{uf\text{-}nacma}}_{\mathsf{OTS},\mathcal{C}}(\lambda)$.

In total, we have

$$\mathsf{Adv}^{\mathsf{uf\text{-}cma}}_{\mathsf{FSP1},\mathcal{A}}(\lambda) \leq \mathsf{Adv}^{\mathsf{uf\text{-}xrma}}_{\mathsf{xSIG},\mathcal{B}}(\lambda) + q_s \cdot \mathsf{Adv}^{\mathsf{uf\text{-}nacma}}_{\mathsf{OTS},\mathcal{C}}(\lambda),$$

which proves the statement. □

Though the above reduction involves a loss factor of q_s, it will vanish if OTS is based on a random-self reducible problem like SDP.

The above construction requires $\mathcal{K}^{vk}_{\mathsf{ots}}$ to match $\mathcal{M}_{\mathsf{xsig}}$. When they are instantiated with the concrete schemes from previous sections (using the POS in Section 3.2 as OTS by swapping $\mathbb{G}_1$ and $\mathbb{G}_2$, and using xSIG in Section 3.3), the space adjustment is done as follows.

Setup: It runs xSIG.Setup and sets $(F_1, \tilde{F}_1)$ as default generators $(G, \tilde{G})$ for OTS. It also provide extra generators $(F_2, U_1, \ldots, U_{\ell+2})$ to OTS for the following procedures to work.

OTS.Key: It runs POS.Key and POS.Ovk in sequence and set $vk_{\mathsf{ots}} := (vk_{\mathsf{pos}}, ovk_{\mathsf{pos}})$. The key spaces are adjusted as follows.
  – POS.Key On top of the legitimate procedure with $G := F_1$ to obtain $(G^{w_z}, G^{\chi_1}, \ldots, G^{\chi_\ell})$, it computes the extended part as $G_{i2} := F_2^{\chi_i}$ $G_{i3} := U_i^{\chi_i}$ for $i = 1, \ldots, \ell$, and $G_{z2} := F_2^{w_z}$, $G_{z3} := U_{\ell+1}^{w_z}$, and include all of them to vk_{pos}.
  – POS.Ovk On top of legitimate procedure with $G := F_1$ that computes $A := G^a$, it computes extra parts $A_2 := F_2^a$ and $A_3 := U_{\ell+2}^a$ and includes them to ovk_{pos}.

Then those extended vk_{pos} and ovk_{pos} constitute a message $((G_z, G_{z2}, G_{z3}), (G_1, G_{12}, G_{13}), \ldots, (G_\ell, G_{\ell2}, G_{\ell3}), (A, A_2, A_3))$ given to xSIG to sign.

Below, we present a summary of the resulting instantiation of FSP1.

Common Parameter $(G, \tilde{G}, F_1, F_2, \tilde{F}_1, \tilde{F}_2, \{U_i, \tilde{U}_i\}_{i=1}^{\ell+2})$

Public-key $(\tilde{V}_1, \tilde{V}_2, \tilde{V}_3, \tilde{V}_4, \tilde{V}_5, \tilde{V}_6, V_7, \tilde{V}_8)$

Secret-key (K_1, K_2, K_3, K_4)

Message $(M_1, \ldots, M_\ell)$

Signature $(\tilde{S}_0, S_1, \ldots, S_5, \tilde{A}, \tilde{A}_2, \tilde{A}_3, \tilde{G}_z, \tilde{G}_{z2}, \tilde{G}_{z3}, \{\tilde{G}_i, \tilde{G}_{i2}, \tilde{G}_{i3}\}_{i=1}^\ell,$ $Z, R)$

Verification PPEs $e(G, \tilde{A}) = e(Z, \tilde{G}_z) \, e(R, \tilde{G}) \prod_{i=1}^\ell e(M_i, \tilde{G}_i),$

$e(S_5, \tilde{V}_6 \, \tilde{A}_3 \, \tilde{G}_{z3} \prod_{i=1}^\ell \tilde{G}_{i3}) = e(G, \tilde{S}_0),$

$e(S_1, \tilde{V}_1) \, e(S_2, \tilde{V}_3) \, e(S_3, \tilde{V}_2) = e(S_4, \tilde{V}_4) \, e(S_5, \tilde{V}_5) \, e(V_7, \tilde{V}_8),$

$e(F_1, \tilde{A}_3) = e(U_{\ell+2}, \tilde{A}), \quad e(F_2, \tilde{A}_3) = e(U_{\ell+2}, \tilde{A}_2)$

$e(F_1, \tilde{G}_{z3}) = e(U_{\ell+1}, \tilde{G}_z), \, e(F_2, \tilde{G}_{z3}) = e(U_{\ell+1}, \tilde{G}_{z2})$

For $i = 1, \ldots, \ell$:

$$e(F_1, \tilde{G}_{i3}) = e(U_i, \tilde{G}_i), \; e(F_2, \tilde{G}_{i3}) = e(U_i, \tilde{G}_{i2})$$

Motivation for Improvement. Since an SPS is an OTS, construction FSP1 can be seen as a generic conversion from any SPS to an FSPS. In exchange for the generality, the construction has several shortcomings when instantiated with current building blocks.

- $(O(|m|)$-size signatures) The resulting signature σ includes the one-time verification key ovk_{ots}, which is linear in the size of messages in all current instantiations of OTS.
- (Factor 3 expansion in xSIG) As shown above, the message space of xSIG must cover ovk_{ots}, which is linear in the size of the message. Even worse, the currently known instantiation of xSIG suffers from an expansion factor of $\mu = 3$ for messages. That is, to sign a message consisting of a group element, say G^x, it requires to represent the message with two more extra elements F_2^x and U_i^x for given bases F_2 and U_i. Thus, the size of ovk_{ots} will actually be μ times larger than the one-time verification key that OTS originally requires.

The above shortcomings amplify each other. Finding an instantiation of xSIG with a smaller expansion factor is one direction of improvement. We leave it as an interesting open problem and focus on a generic approach in the next section.

5.2 Main Construction Based on Shrinking Trapdoor Commitments

Our idea is to avoid signing any components whose size grows to that of messages directly with xSIG. We achieve this by committing to the message using a shrinking commitment scheme and signing the commitment with xSIG. Again, combining a trapdoor commitment scheme (or a chameleon hash) and a signature scheme to achieve such an improvement is ultimately a known approach. What is important here is the security required from each building block. We show that chosen-message target collision resistance is sufficient for TC to reach UF-CMA in combination with an XRMA-secure signature scheme.

Let xSIG be a UF-XRMA secure FSPS scheme and TC be a CMTCR secure trapdoor commitment scheme with common setup function Setup. We construct our FSPS scheme FSP2 from xSIG and TC as follows.

[Signature Scheme: FSP2]

Setup(1^λ): Run common setup $gk \leftarrow$ Setup(1^λ) and output gk. Set the message spaces $\mathcal{M}_{\mathsf{xsig}} := \mathcal{C}_{\mathsf{tc}}$ and $\mathcal{M} := \mathcal{M}_{\mathsf{tc}}$.

Key(gk): Run $(vk_{\mathsf{xsig}}, sk_{\mathsf{xsig}}) \leftarrow$ xSIG.Key(gk), and $(ck_{\mathsf{tc}}, tk_{\mathsf{tc}}) \leftarrow$ TC.Key(gk). Set $vk := (vk_{\mathsf{xsig}}, ck_{\mathsf{tc}})$, $sk := sk_{\mathsf{xsig}}$. Output (vk, sk)

Sign(sk, M): Parse sk into sk_{xsig}. Run $(com_{\mathsf{tc}}, open_{\mathsf{tc}}) \leftarrow$ TC.Com(ck_{tc}, M) and $\sigma_{\mathsf{xsig}} \leftarrow$ xSIG.Sign($sk_{\mathsf{xsig}}, com_{\mathsf{tc}}$). Output $\sigma := (\sigma_{\mathsf{xsig}}, open_{\mathsf{tc}}, com_{\mathsf{tc}})$

Vrf(vk, M, σ): Parse $vk = (vk_{\mathsf{xsig}}, ck_{\mathsf{tc}})$ and $\sigma = (\sigma_{\mathsf{xsig}}, open_{\mathsf{tc}}, com_{\mathsf{tc}})$. Output 1 if $1 = $ TC.Vrf($ck_{\mathsf{tc}}, com_{\mathsf{tc}}, M, open_{\mathsf{tc}}$) and $1 = $ xSIG.Vrf($vk_{\mathsf{xsig}}, com_{\mathsf{tc}}, \sigma_{\mathsf{xsig}}$). Output 0, otherwise.

Theorem 21. *If TC is a CMTCR secure SPTC, and xSIG is a UF-XRMA secure FSPS relative to TC.SimCom as a message sampler, then FSP2 is a UF-CMA FSPS.*

Proof. Correctness holds trivially from those of the underlying TC and xSIG. Regarding the full structure-preserving property, observe that sk consists of sk_{xsig}, which that are source group elements since xSIG is fully structure-preserving. The same is true for public components, i.e., public keys, messages, and signatures. The verification only evaluates verification functions of these underlying building blocks, which evaluate PPEs. Thus, FSP2 is FSPS.

We next prove the security property. Let $\mathcal{A}$ be an adversary against FSP2. Let Game 0 be the UF-CMA game that $\mathcal{A}$ is playing. By definition, Pr[Game 0] $=$ Adv$_{\mathsf{FSP2},\mathcal{A}}^{\mathsf{uf\text{-}cma}}(\lambda)$. Let $(\sigma^\dagger, m^\dagger)$ be a forgery $\mathcal{A}$ outputs. Let $\sigma^\dagger := (\sigma_{\mathsf{xsig}}^\dagger, open_{\mathsf{tc}}^\dagger, com_{\mathsf{tc}}^\dagger)$.

In Game 1, abort the game if $(\sigma^\dagger, m^\dagger)$ is a valid forgery and $com_{\mathsf{tc}}^\dagger$ is never viewed by the signing oracle. We show that this event occurs only if the UF-XRMA security of xSIG is broken. Let $\mathcal{B}$ be an adversary against xSIG launching an XRMA attack. The message sampler for XRMA is TC.SimCom. That is, the challenger samples random messages by $(com_{\mathsf{tc}}, ek_{\mathsf{tc}}) \leftarrow$ TC.SimCom($gk; \omega$) with random coin ω and gives com_{tc} and ω with signature σ_{xsig} on com_{tc} as a message. Let $sample^{(j)}$ be the j-th sample, i.e., $sample^{(j)} := (com_{\mathsf{tc}}^{(j)}, \omega^{(j)}, \sigma_{\mathsf{xsig}}^{(j)})$. Given $(vk_{\mathsf{xsig}}, sample^{(1)}, \ldots, sample^{(q_s)})$ as input, $\mathcal{B}$ runs as follows. It first takes gk from vk_{xsig} and recovers every $ek_{\mathsf{tc}}^{(j)}$ from $\omega^{(j)}$ by $(com_{\mathsf{tc}}, ek_{\mathsf{tc}}) \leftarrow$ TC.SimCom($gk; \omega$). It then runs $(ck_{\mathsf{tc}}, tk_{\mathsf{tc}}) \leftarrow$ TC.Key(gk) and invokes $\mathcal{A}$ with input $vk := (vk_{\mathsf{xsig}}, ck_{\mathsf{tc}})$. Given the j-th signing query $m^{(j)}$ from $\mathcal{A}$, it executes $open_{\mathsf{tc}}^{(j)} \leftarrow$

TC.Equiv($m^{(j)}, tk_{tc}, ek_{tc}^{(j)},$) and returns $\sigma := (\sigma_{xsig}^{(j)}, open_{tc}^{(j)}, com_{tc}^{(j)})$ to $\mathcal{A}$. If $\mathcal{A}$ eventually outputs a forgery, $\sigma^{\dagger} = (\sigma_{xsig}^{\dagger}, open_{tc}^{\dagger}, com_{tc}^{\dagger})$ and $m^{\dagger}$, it outputs $\sigma_{xsig}^{\star} := \sigma_{xsig}^{\dagger}$ and $m^{\star} := com_{tc}^{\dagger}$ as a forgery with respect to xSIG.

Correctness of the above reduction holds from statistically close distribution of simulated $com_{tc}^{(j)}$, and $open_{tc}^{(j)}$. The output $(\sigma_{xsig}^{\star}, m^{\star})$ is also a valid forgery since $com_{tc}^{\dagger}$ differs from any $com_{tc}^{(j)}$. Letting ϵ_{sim} denote the statistical distance, we have $|\Pr[\text{Game } 0] - \Pr[\text{Game } 1]| \leq \text{Adv}_{xSIG,\mathcal{B}}^{uf\text{-}xrma}(\lambda) + \epsilon_{sim}$.

Now we claim that $\mathcal{A}$ winning in Game 1 occurs only if the CMTCR security of TC is broken. The reduction from successful $\mathcal{A}$ in Game 1 to adversary $\mathcal{C}$ that breaks TC is straightforward. Given ck_{tc}, $\mathcal{C}$ runs $(vk_{xsig}, sk_{xsig}) \leftarrow \text{xSIG.Key}(gk)$ and invokes $\mathcal{A}$ with $vk := (vk_{xsig}, ck_{tc})$. Then, given message $m^{(j)}$, forward it to the oracle of TC and obtain $(com_{tc}^{(j)}, open_{tc}^{(j)})$. Then sign $com_{tc}^{(j)}$ using sk_{xsig} to obtain $\sigma_{xsig}^{(j)}$ and return $(\sigma_{xsig}^{(j)}, open_{tc}^{(j)}, com_{tc}^{(j)})$ to $\mathcal{A}$. Given a forged signature $(\sigma_{xsig}^{\dagger}, open_{tc}^{\dagger}, com_{tc}^{\dagger})$ and $m^{\dagger}$, output $open_{tc}^{\star} := open_{tc}^{\dagger}$ and $m^{\star} := m^{\dagger}$. It is a valid forgery since $m^{\dagger} \neq m^{(j)}$ for all j. We thus have $\Pr[\text{Game } 1] = \text{Adv}_{TC,\mathcal{C}}^{cmtcr}(\lambda)$.

By summing up the differences, we have

$$\text{Adv}_{FSP2,\mathcal{A}}^{uf\text{-}cma}(\lambda) \leq \text{Adv}_{xSIG,\mathcal{B}}^{uf\text{-}xrma}(\lambda) + \text{Adv}_{TC,\mathcal{C}}^{cmtcr}(\lambda) + \epsilon_{sim}, \tag{14}$$

which proves the statement. □

To instantiate this construction with the building blocks from previous sections, we again need to duplicate $com_{gbc} = \tilde{G}_u = \tilde{G}^{\varsigma} \prod_{i=1}^{\ell} \tilde{X}_i^{m_i}$ to a triple with respect to bases $\tilde{G} = \tilde{F}_2, \tilde{F}_3$ and $\tilde{U}_1$ as follows. To be able to do so without holding the discrete logarithms of the $\tilde{X}_i$'s, we need to duplicate $\tilde{X}$ to the same set of bases as well. Details are shown below.

Setup: It runs xSIG.Setup and sets $(F_1, \tilde{F}_1)$ as default generators $(G, \tilde{G})$ for TCγ with extra generators (F_2, U_1) as well.

TCγ.Key: On top of the legitimate procedure with $G := \tilde{F}_1$ to obtain $\tilde{X}_i := G^{\rho_i}$, additionally compute $\tilde{X}_{i2} := \tilde{F}_2^{\rho_i}$ and $\tilde{X}_{i3} := \tilde{U}_1^{\rho_i}$ for $i = 1, \ldots, \ell$ and include them to ck_{gbc}.

TCγ.Com: On top of the legitimate procedure that computes $\tilde{G}_u = \tilde{G}^{\varsigma} \prod_{i=1}^{\ell} \tilde{X}_i^{m_i}$ for $\tilde{G} := \tilde{F}_1$, compute $\tilde{G}_{u2} := \tilde{F}_2^{\varsigma} \prod_{i=1}^{\ell} \tilde{X}_{i1}^{m_i}$ and $\tilde{G}_{u3} := \tilde{U}_1^{\varsigma} \prod_{i=1}^{\ell} \tilde{X}_{i3}^{m_i}$ and include them to com_{gbc}.

TCγ.SimCom: Compute the above extra components as $\tilde{G}_{u2} := \tilde{F}_2^{\omega_u}$, and $\tilde{G}_{u3} := U_1^{\omega_u}$.

The result is an extended commitment $com_{gbc} = (\tilde{G}_u, \tilde{G}_{u2}, \tilde{G}_{u3})$ that matches to the message space of xSIG with $\ell = 1$. Note that the duplicated keys have no effect on the security of POS nor TCγ since they can be easily simulated when the discrete-logs of the extra bases to the original base $\tilde{G}$ are known.

We summarize the instantiation of FSP2 in the following. Let $k = \lceil \frac{\ell}{\ell_{\mathsf{pos}}} \rceil$ and $\ell_{\mathsf{gbc}} = 1 + k + \ell_{\mathsf{pos}}$.

Common Parameter	$(G, \tilde{G}, F_1, F_2, \tilde{F}_1, \tilde{F}_2, U_1, \tilde{U}_1)$
Public-key	$(\tilde{V}_1, \tilde{V}_2, \tilde{V}_3, \tilde{V}_4, \tilde{V}_5, \tilde{V}_6, V_7, \tilde{V}_8, \{\tilde{X}_i, \tilde{X}_{i2}, \tilde{X}_{i3}\}_{i=1}^{\ell_{\mathsf{gbc}}})$
Secret-key	(K_1, K_2, K_3, K_4)
Message	$(\tilde{M}_1, \ldots, \tilde{M}_\ell)$
Signature	$(\tilde{S}_0, \ldots, S_5, \tilde{G}_u, \tilde{G}_{u2}, \tilde{G}_{u3}, R, G_z, G_1, \ldots, G_{\ell_{\mathsf{pos}}}, \{A_i, \tilde{Z}_i, \tilde{R}_i\}_{i=1}^{k})$
Verification PPEs	Let $(N_1, \ldots, N_{\ell_{\mathsf{gbc}}}) := (G_z, G_1, \ldots, G_{\ell_{\mathsf{pos}}}, A_1, \ldots, A_k)$.

For $j = 1, \ldots, k$:

$$e(A_j, \tilde{G}) = e(G_z, \tilde{Z}_j) \, e(G, \tilde{R}_j) \prod_{i=1}^{\ell_{\mathsf{pos}}} e(G_i, \tilde{M}_{(j-1)\ell_{\mathsf{pos}}+i}),$$

$$e(G, \tilde{G}_u) = e(R, \tilde{G}) \prod_{i=1}^{\ell_{\mathsf{gbc}}} e(N_i, \tilde{X}_i)$$

$$e(S_5, \tilde{V}_6 \, \tilde{G}_{u3}) = e(G, \tilde{S}_0),$$

$$e(S_1, \tilde{V}_1) \, e(S_2, \tilde{V}_3) \, e(S_3, \tilde{V}_2) = e(S_4, \tilde{V}_4) \, e(S_5, \tilde{V}_5) \, e(V_7, \tilde{V}_8),$$

$$e(F_1, \tilde{G}_{u3}) = e(U_1, \tilde{G}_u), \quad e(F_2, \tilde{G}_{u3}) = e(U_1, \tilde{G}_{u2}).$$

5.3 Efficiency

In this section, we assess the efficiency of FSP1 and FSP2 instantiated as described in Section 5.1 and 5.2.

Signature Size and Number of PPEs. Here we assess the sizes of a key and a signature for unilateral messages consisting of ℓ group elements. By $|vk_{\mathsf{x}}|$ for $\mathsf{x} \in \{\mathsf{ots}, \mathsf{xsig}\}$, we denote the number of group elements in vk_{x} except for those in $|gk|$. By the term $\#\mathsf{PPE}_{\mathsf{x}}$ we denote the number of pairing product equations in the corresponding building block x. Table 1 summarizes the comparison with signature length for some concrete message lengths.

Table 1. Size of secret keys, verification keys, signatures, and number of PPEs in verification for unilateral messages of size ℓ

Scheme	$|sk|$	$|vk|$		$|\sigma|$					$\#\mathsf{PPE}$
			ℓ	$\ell = 1$	4	9	25	100	
FSP1	4	$18 + 2\ell$	$14 + 3\ell$	17	26	41	89	314	$7 + 2\ell$
FSP2	4	$19 + 6\lceil \sqrt{\ell} \rceil$	$11 + 4\lceil \sqrt{\ell} \rceil$	15	19	23	31	51	$5 + \lceil \sqrt{\ell} \rceil$

– FSP1. According to the descriptions in Section 3.2 and Section 3.3, we have the following parameters for the building blocks.

- OTS: $|vk_{ots}| = |vk_{pos}| + |ovk_{pos}| = \ell + 2$, $|\sigma_{ots}| = 2$, and $\#\,\mathsf{PPE}_{ots} = 1$.
- xSIG: $|sk_{xsig}| = 4$, $|vk_{xsig}| = 8$, and $\#\,\mathsf{PPE}_{xsig} = 2 + 2\,|vk_{ots}|$.

The common setup function for these building blocks generates bases $(G, \tilde{G}, F_1, F_2, \tilde{F}_1, \tilde{F}_2, \{U_i, \tilde{U}_i\}_{i=1}^{\ell_{xsig}})$ for $\ell_{xsig} = |vk_{ots}|$ to allow xSIG to sign vk_{ots}. (Note that vk_{ots} consists only of group elements from $\mathbb{G}_1$, which xSIG can sign.) Taking the message expansion factor $\mu = 3$ into account, we obtain the following for FSP1:

$$|gk| = 6 + 2\,|vk_{ots}|$$

$$|sk| = |sk_{xsig}| = 4$$

$$|vk| = |gk| + |vk_{xsig}| = 18 + 2\ell$$

$$|\sigma| = |\sigma_{xsig}| + |\sigma_{ots}| + \mu\,|vk_{ots}| = 14 + 3\ell$$

$$\#\,\mathsf{PPE} = \#\,\mathsf{PPE}_{xsig} + \#\,\mathsf{PPE}_{ots} = 7 + 2\,\ell$$

- FSP2. The underlying components are xSIG, TCγ and POS. Since POS is repeatedly used in FSP2, its message size ℓ_{pos} can be set independently from the input message size ℓ. The parameters for these underlying components are:
  - POS: $|vk_{pos}| = \ell_{pos} + 1$, $|ovk_{pos}| = 1$, $|\sigma_{pos}| = 2$, and $\#\,\mathsf{PPE}_{pos} = 1$.
  - TCγ: $|ck_{gbc}| = |vk_{pos}| + \lceil \ell/\ell_{pos} \rceil \cdot |ovk_{pos}| = 1 + \lceil \ell/\ell_{pos} \rceil + \ell_{pos}$, $|com_{gbc}| = 1$, and $|open_{gbc}| = 1$.
  - xSIG: $|sk_{xsig}| = 4$, $|vk_{xsig}| = 8$, and $\#\,\mathsf{PPE}_{xsig} = 2 + 2\,|com_{gbc}|$.

As well as the previous case, the common setup function outputs gk including bases $(G, \tilde{G}, F_1, F_2, \tilde{F}_1, \tilde{F}_2, \{U_i, \tilde{U}_i\}_{i=1}^{\ell_{xsig}})$ for $\ell_{xsig} = |com_{gbc}|$ to allow xSIG to sign com_{gbc}. Based on these parameters, the following evaluation is obtained for FSP2:

$$|sk| = |sk_{xsig}| = 4$$

$$|vk| = |gk| + |vk_{xsig}| + |ck_{gbc}| = 19 + 3\lceil \ell/\ell_{pos} \rceil + 3\,\ell_{pos} = 19 + 6\lceil \sqrt{\ell} \rceil$$

$$|\sigma| = |\sigma_{xsig}| + |open_{gbc}| + |\sigma_{pos}| + \mu|com_{gbc}| + |vk_{pos}| + \lceil \ell/\ell_{pos} \rceil \cdot |ovk_{pos}|$$

$$= 11 + 3\lceil \ell/\ell_{pos} \rceil + \ell_{pos} = 11 + 4\lceil \sqrt{\ell} \rceil$$

$$\#\,\mathsf{PPE} = \#\,\mathsf{PPE}_{xsig} + \#\,\mathsf{PPE}_{gbc} + \lceil \ell/\ell_{pos} \rceil \cdot \#\,\mathsf{PPE}_{pos}$$

$$= 5 + \lceil \ell/\ell_{pos} \rceil = 5 + \lceil \sqrt{\ell} \rceil$$

The last equality in each evaluation is obtained at the optimal setting; $\ell_{pos} = \lceil \ell/\ell_{pos} \rceil = \lceil \sqrt{\ell} \rceil$.

Proof Size for Knowing a Secret Key. Next we assess the cost for proving one's knowledge of a secret key for FSP1 and FSP2 with the Groth-Sahai proof as a non-interactive witness indistinguishable proof (NIWIPoK) or a zero-knowledge proof (NIZKPoK). Results are summarized in Table 2. In either scheme, a secret key comes only from xSIG, which is of the form (K_1, K_2, K_3, K_4).

- NIWIPoK: Relations to prove are in (8) that we recall as

$$
\begin{aligned}
e(\underline{K_2}, \tilde{G}) = e(G, \tilde{V}_1), \quad e(G, \tilde{V}_3) = e(\underline{K_2}, \tilde{V}_2), \quad e(\underline{K_1}, \tilde{V}_1) = e(V_7, \tilde{V}_8), \\
e(\underline{K_2}, \tilde{V}_4) = e(G, \tilde{V}_5), \quad e(\underline{K_3}, \tilde{G}) e(\underline{K_4}, \tilde{V}_2) = e(G, \tilde{V}_4),
\end{aligned} \tag{15}
$$

These are linear relations in $\mathbb{G}_1$ when proved with the Groth-Sahai proofs. Underlined variables are the witnesses the prover commits to. According to [31], committing to a group element in $\mathbb{G}_1$ (or $\mathbb{G}_2$) requires 2 elements in $\mathbb{G}_1$ (or $\mathbb{G}_2$, respectively). Proving a linear relation with a PPE yields a proof consisting of 2 group elements in $\mathbb{G}_2$. Thus, with 4 witnesses, and 5 linear relations, the resulting proof (i.e. commitments and proofs for all relations) consists of $4 \times 2 + 5 \times 2 = 18$ group elements (8 in $\mathbb{G}_1$ and 10 in $\mathbb{G}_2$).

- NIZKPoK: The above witness-indistinguishable proof is turned into zero-knowledge in the following manner. First, the prover commits to public-key elements V_7 and G and proves relations

$$
\underline{W} = V_7 \quad \text{and} \quad \underline{V} = G. \tag{16}
$$

Committing to W and V costs $2 \times 2 = 4$ group elements in $\mathbb{G}_1$, and proving elations in (16) as multiscalar multiplication equations requires $2 \times 2 = 4$ scalar values in $\mathbb{Z}_p$. The prover also proves relations:

$$
\begin{aligned}
e(\underline{K_2}, \tilde{G}) = e(\underline{V}, \tilde{V}_1), \quad e(\underline{V}, \tilde{V}_3) = e(\underline{K_2}, \tilde{V}_2), \quad e(\underline{K_1}, \tilde{V}_1) = e(\underline{W}, \tilde{V}_8), \\
e(\underline{K_2}, \tilde{V}_4) = e(\underline{V}, \tilde{V}_5), \quad e(\underline{K_3}, \tilde{G}) e(\underline{K_4}, \tilde{V}_2) = e(\underline{V}, \tilde{V}_4).
\end{aligned} \tag{17}
$$

Since all witnesses in (17) belong to $\mathbb{G}_1$, the cost for proving the relations is unchanged from that for (15). Thus the total cost is $18 + 4 = 22$ group elements (12 in $\mathbb{G}_1$ and 10 in $\mathbb{G}_2$) and 4 scalar values in $\mathbb{Z}_p$.

Proof Size for Knowing a Valid Signature. Here we assess the cost for proving possession of a valid signature using the Groth-Sahai proofs as NIWIPoK. The result is summarized in Table 2.

Table 2. Number of group elements in the Groth-Sahai proofs for possession of a secret key and a signature for unilateral messages of size ℓ with the optimal parameter setting. For ZK, proofs actually include a small number of elements in $\mathbb{Z}_p$ ignored here.

Scheme	WI (sk)	ZK (sk)	WI (σ)	ZK (σ)
FSP1	18	22	$54 + 10\ell$	$56 + 10\ell$
FSP2	18	22	$44 + 16\lceil\sqrt{\ell}\rceil$	$46 + 16\lceil\sqrt{\ell}\rceil$

– Case of FSP1. According to the descriptions in Section 5.1, a valid signature satisfies the following relations.

$$e(G, \tilde{\underline{A}}) = e(\underline{Z}, \tilde{G}_z)\, e(\underline{R}, \tilde{G}) \prod_{i=1}^{\ell} e(M_i, \tilde{G}_i), \quad e(\underline{S_5}, \tilde{V}_6\, \tilde{\underline{A}}_3\, \tilde{G}_{z3}) \prod_{i=1}^{\ell} \tilde{G}_{i3}) = e(G, \tilde{\underline{S}_0}),$$

$$e(\underline{S_1}, \tilde{V}_1)\, e(\underline{S_2}, \tilde{V}_3)\, e(\underline{S_3}, \tilde{V}_2) = e(\underline{S_4}, \tilde{V}_4)\, e(\underline{S_5}, \tilde{V}_5)\, e(V_7, \tilde{V}_8),$$

$$e(F_1, \tilde{\underline{A}}_3) = e(U_{\ell+2}, \tilde{\underline{A}}), \quad e(F_2, \tilde{\underline{A}}_3) = e(U_{\ell+2}, \tilde{\underline{A}}_2), \quad e(F_1, \tilde{G}_{z3}) = e(U_{\ell+1}, \tilde{\underline{G}}_z),$$

$$e(F_2, \tilde{G}_{z3}) = e(U_{\ell+1}, \tilde{G}_{z2}), \quad e(F_1, \tilde{G}_{i3}) = e(U_i, \tilde{\underline{G}}_i), \quad e(F_2, \tilde{G}_{i3}) = e(U_i, \tilde{G}_{i2})$$

for $i = 1, \ldots, \ell$ for the last two relations. There are 7 underlined witnesses in $\mathbb{G}_1$ and $1 + 3(\ell+2)$ in $\mathbb{G}_2$. Committing to these witnesses requires 14 elements in $\mathbb{G}_1$ and $14 + 6\ell$ elements in $\mathbb{G}_2$. The first two relations involve witnesses in both groups whose proofs require 2×4 elements in $\mathbb{G}_1$ and $\mathbb{G}_2$. The third relation has witnesses only in $\mathbb{G}_1$. Its proof consists of 2 elements in $\mathbb{G}_2$. The remaining $4 + 2\ell$ relations have witnesses only in $\mathbb{G}_2$, and each of their proof costs 2 elements in $\mathbb{G}_1$. In total the proofs and commitments consist of $14 + 4 \times 2 + 2 \times (4 + 2\ell) = 30 + 4\ell$ elements in $\mathbb{G}_1$ and $14 + 6\ell + 4 \times 2 + 2 = 24 + 6\ell$ elements in $\mathbb{G}_2$, which sum up to $54 + 10\ell$ group elements.

– Case of FSP2. As described in Section 5.2, a valid signature satisfies the following relations:

$$e(\underline{A_j}, \tilde{G}) = e(\underline{G_z}, \tilde{Z}_j)\, e(G, \tilde{R}_j) \prod_{i=1}^{\ell_{\mathrm{pos}}} e(\underline{G_i}, \tilde{M}_{(j-1)\ell_{\mathrm{pos}}+i}) \quad (\text{for } j = 1, \ldots, k),$$

$$e(G, \tilde{\underline{G}}_u) = e(\underline{R}, \tilde{G}) \prod_{i=1}^{\ell_{\mathrm{gbc}}} e(\underline{N_i}, \tilde{X}_i), \quad e(\underline{S_5}, \tilde{V}_6\, \tilde{\underline{G}}_{u3}) = e(G, \tilde{\underline{S}_0}),$$

$$e(\underline{S_1}, \tilde{V}_1)\, e(\underline{S_2}, \tilde{V}_3)\, e(\underline{S_3}, \tilde{V}_2) = e(\underline{S_4}, \tilde{V}_4)\, e(\underline{S_5}, \tilde{V}_5)\, e(V_7, \tilde{V}_8),$$

$$e(F_1, \tilde{G}_{u3}) = e(U_1, \tilde{\underline{G}}_u), \quad e(F_2, \tilde{G}_{u3}) = e(U_1, \tilde{G}_{u2}).$$

where $(N_1, \ldots, N_{\ell_{\mathrm{gbc}}})$ is actually $(G_z, G_1, \ldots, G_{\ell_{\mathrm{pos}}}, A_1, \ldots, A_k)$ that are also witnesses. Thus we do not need to count the cost for committing to N_i. We consider $\ell_{\mathrm{gbc}} = k = \lceil\sqrt{\ell}\rceil$. A signature consists of $4 + 2\lceil\sqrt{\ell}\rceil$ elements in $\mathbb{G}_1$ and $7 + 2\lceil\sqrt{\ell}\rceil$ elements in $\mathbb{G}_2$. Thus committing to the signature costs

$2(4+2\lceil\sqrt{\ell}\rceil)$ and $2(7+2\lceil\sqrt{\ell}\rceil)$ elements in $\mathbb{G}_1$ and $\mathbb{G}_2$, respectively. The first three relations (indeed $\lceil\sqrt{\ell}\rceil + 2$ relations) that came from POS and TCγ involve witnesses in both groups. Hence proofs for them cost $4(\lceil\sqrt{\ell}\rceil + 2)$ elements in $\mathbb{G}_1$ and $\mathbb{G}_2$, respectively. The remaining three relations that came from xSIG involves witnesses for either of $\mathbb{G}_1$ or $\mathbb{G}_2$. Proofs for those relations costs 2 group elements in $\mathbb{G}_2$ and 2×2 group elements in $\mathbb{G}_1$. In total the proofs and commitments consists of $2(4+2\lceil\sqrt{\ell}\rceil)+4(\lceil\sqrt{\ell}\rceil+2)+4 = 20 + 8\lceil\sqrt{\ell}\rceil$ and $2(7+2\lceil\sqrt{\ell}\rceil) + 4(\lceil\sqrt{\ell}\rceil + 2) + 2 = 24 + 8\lceil\sqrt{\ell}\rceil$ in $\mathbb{G}_1$ and $\mathbb{G}_2$, respectively. They sum up to $44 + 16\lceil\sqrt{\ell}\rceil$ group elements in total.

For either scheme, proving in zero-knowledge is possible only by additionally committing to V_7 and proving the correctness. It adds 2 elements in $\mathbb{G}_1$ for the commitment of V_7 and 2 $\mathbb{Z}_p$ elements as a proof.

5.4 Lower Bound on Signature Size and Verification Key Size

The signatures of our concrete FSPSs consist of $\Omega(\sqrt{\ell})$ group elements when signing ℓ-element messages. This may seem disappointing compared to previous constructions of SPS, which have generally achieved constant-size signatures, but we argue that, at least for our modular constructions of FSPS, the $\sqrt{\ell}$ factor is unavoidable. This is a consequence of the following new trade-off between signature and verification key size for arbitrary (possibly one-time) SPS schemes.

Theorem 22. *Consider a (possibly one-time) SPS scheme on messages in $\mathbb{G}_2^\ell$ in the asymmetric (Type III) bilinear group setting. Let κ be the number of verification key elements and σ the number of group elements in signatures. If the scheme is existentially unforgeable in a model in which the adversary has access to a valid signature on a known message and the scheme has an algebraic signing algorithm, we have $\kappa + \sigma \geq \sqrt{\ell}$.*

Proof. Denote by $(M_1, \ldots, M_\ell) \in \mathbb{G}_2^\ell$ the message vector, by $(U_1, \ldots, U_{\kappa_1}, V_1, \ldots, V_{\kappa_2}) \in \mathbb{G}_1^{\kappa_1} \times \mathbb{G}_2^{\kappa_2}$ $(\kappa_1 + \kappa_2 = \kappa)$ the verification key elements, and by $(R_1, \ldots, R_{\sigma_1}, S_1, \ldots, S_{\sigma_2}) \in \mathbb{G}_1^{\sigma_1} \times \mathbb{G}_2^{\sigma_2}$ $(\sigma_1 + \sigma_2 = \sigma)$ the signature elements. The corresponding discrete logarithms are written in lowercase letters.

Each verification equation of the scheme can be expressed as a bilinear relation between the discrete logarithms of the group elements in $\mathbb{G}_1$ (namely the U_i's and R_i's) on the one hand, and those of the elements in $\mathbb{G}_2$ (namely the M_i's, V_i's and S_i's) on the other. The i-th pairing product equation can thus be written in matrix form as:

$$X^T E_i Y = 0, \tag{18}$$

where X and Y are the column vectors given by

$$X = (r_1, \ldots, r_{\sigma_1}, u_1, \ldots, u_{\kappa_1}, 1)^T, \text{ and}$$

$$Y = (m_1, \ldots, m_\ell, s_1, \ldots, s_{\sigma_2}, v_1, \ldots, v_{\kappa_2}, 1)^T,$$

and E_i is a public $(\kappa_1 + \sigma_1 + 1) \times (\ell + \kappa_2 + \sigma_2 + 1)$ matrix over $\mathbb{Z}_p$.

Now fix a valid message-signature pair $(M_1, \ldots, M_\ell, R_1, \ldots, R_{\sigma_1}, S_1, \ldots, S_{\sigma_2})$, and suppose that there exists a non-zero tuple $(m_1^*, \ldots, m_\ell^*) \in \mathbb{Z}_p^\ell$ such that

$$E_i(m_1^*, \ldots, m_\ell^*, 0, \ldots, 0)^T = 0$$

for all i. Then, it is clear from the shape (18) of the corresponding verification equations that $(R_1, \ldots, R_{\sigma_1}, S_1, \ldots, S_{\sigma_2})$ is still a valid signature on the distinct message vector $(M_1 \tilde{G}^{m_1^*}, \ldots, M_\ell \tilde{G}^{m_\ell^*})$, which contradicts existential unforgeability.

Therefore, by denoting by n as the number of verification equations, the linear map $\mathbb{Z}_p^\ell \to \mathbb{Z}_p^{n(\kappa_1 + \sigma_1 + 1)}$ mapping $(m_1, \ldots, m_\ell)$ to the concatenation of all vectors $E_i(m_1, \ldots, m_\ell, 0, \ldots, 0)^T$ must be injective. In particular, we have:

$$\ell \leq n \cdot (\kappa_1 + \sigma_1 + 1) \leq n \cdot (\kappa + \sigma),$$

where the second inequality comes from the fact that we must have $\sigma_2 \geq 1$; otherwise, the algebraic signing algorithm would output signatures that cannot depend on the message.

Finally, an argument similar to [6, Theorem 5] shows that we must have $n \leq \sigma$ (after removing possibly redundant verification equations). Indeed, if it were not the case, the quadratic system satisfied by the discrete logarithms of the signature elements would be overdetermined, and a generic message would not admit any valid signature at all. We thus obtain $\ell \leq \sigma \cdot (\kappa + \sigma) \leq (\kappa + \sigma)^2$, which concludes the proof.   □

As a result, we immediately see that an FSPS scheme obtained from construction FSP1 must have signatures of more than $\sqrt{\ell}$ elements. This is because all signatures include as a subset including both the verification key and signature of a structure-preserving OTS scheme signing ℓ-element messages. Similarly, the following result holds with the same proof as above:

Theorem 23. *Consider a structure-preserving commitment scheme on messages in $\mathbb{G}_2^\ell$ in the asymmetric (Type III) bilinear group setting. Assume that the commitment key consists of elements in $\mathbb{G}_2$, and let χ be the number of elements in commitments and o the number of group elements in the opening information. If the scheme is collision resistant and has an algebraic commitment algorithm, we have $\chi + o \geq \sqrt{\ell}$.*

This shows that an FSPS scheme obtained from construction FSP2 must also have signatures of more than $\sqrt{\ell}$ elements, at least when the underlying trapdoor commitment scheme has its key elements on the same side as the resulting signature, which seems necessary with our approach based on TCγ (in particular, this holds for the instantiation above and all the variants in [9]).

References

1. Abe, M., Camenisch, J., Dowsley, R., Dubovitskaya, M.: On the impossibility of structure-preserving deterministic primitives. In: Lindell, Y. (ed.) TCC 2014. LNCS, vol. 8349, pp. 713–738. Springer, Heidelberg (2014)
2. Abe, M., Chase, M., David, B., Kohlweiss, M., Nishimaki, R., Ohkubo, M.: Constant-size structure-preserving signatures: generic constructions and simple assumptions. In: Wang, X., Sako, K. (eds.) ASIACRYPT 2012. LNCS, vol. 7658, pp. 4–24. Springer, Heidelberg (2012)
3. Abe, M., Fuchsbauer, G., Groth, J., Haralambiev, K., Ohkubo, M.: Structure-preserving signatures and commitments to group elements. Journal of Cryptology (2014). doi:10.1007/s00145-014-9196-7
4. Abe, M., Groth, J., Haralambiev, K., Ohkubo, M.: Optimal structure-preserving signatures in asymmetric bilinear groups. In: Rogaway, P. (ed.) CRYPTO 2011. LNCS, vol. 6841, pp. 649–666. Springer, Heidelberg (2011)
5. Abe, M., Groth, J., Ohkubo, M.: Separating short structure-preserving signatures from non-interactive assumptions. In: Lee, D.H., Wang, X. (eds.) ASIACRYPT 2011. LNCS, vol. 7073, pp. 628–646. Springer, Heidelberg (2011)
6. Abe, M., Groth, J., Ohkubo, M., Tibouchi, M.: Structure-preserving signatures from type II pairings. In: Garay, J.A., Gennaro, R. (eds.) CRYPTO 2014, Part I. LNCS, vol. 8616, pp. 390–407. Springer, Heidelberg (2014)
7. Abe, M., Groth, J., Ohkubo, M., Tibouchi, M.: Unified, minimal and selectively randomizable structure-preserving signatures. In: Lindell, Y. (ed.) TCC 2014. LNCS, vol. 8349, pp. 688–712. Springer, Heidelberg (2014)
8. Abe, M., Haralambiev, K.: Group to group commitments do not shrink. In: Pointcheval, D., Johansson, T. (eds.) EUROCRYPT 2012. LNCS, vol. 7237, pp. 301–317. Springer, Heidelberg (2012)
9. Abe, M., Kohlweiss, M., Ohkubo, M., Tibouchi, M.: Fully structure-preserving signatures and shrinking commitments. IACR ePrint Archive, Report 2015/076 (2015). http://eprint.iacr.org
10. Abe, M., Ohkubo, M.: A framework for universally composable non-committing blind signatures. IJACT **2**(3), 229–249 (2012)
11. Barthe, G., Fagerholm, E., Fiore, D., Scedrov, A., Schmidt, B., Tibouchi, M.: Strongly-optimal structure preserving signatures from type II pairings: synthesis and lower bounds. In: Katz, J. (ed.) PKC 2015. LNCS, vol. 9020, pp. 355–376. Springer, Heidelberg (2015)
12. Belenkiy, M., Camenisch, J., Chase, M., Kohlweiss, M., Lysyanskaya, A., Shacham, H.: Randomizable proofs and delegatable anonymous credentials. In: Halevi, S. (ed.) CRYPTO 2009. LNCS, vol. 5677, pp. 108–125. Springer, Heidelberg (2009)
13. Belenkiy, M., Chase, M., Kohlweiss, M., Lysyanskaya, A.: P-signatures and noninteractive anonymous credentials. In: Canetti, R. (ed.) TCC 2008. LNCS, vol. 4948, pp. 356–374. Springer, Heidelberg (2008)
14. Bellare, M., Palacio, A.: The knowledge-of-exponent assumptions and 3-round zero-knowledge protocols. In: Franklin, M. (ed.) CRYPTO 2004. LNCS, vol. 3152, pp. 273–289. Springer, Heidelberg (2004)
15. Bellare, M., Shi, H., Zhang, C.: Foundations of group signatures: the case of dynamic groups. In: Menezes, A. (ed.) CT-RSA 2005. LNCS, vol. 3376, pp. 136–153. Springer, Heidelberg (2005)
16. Bellare, M., Shoup, S.: Two-tier signatures, strongly unforgeable signatures, and fiat-shamir without random oracles. In: Okamoto, T., Wang, X. (eds.) PKC 2007. LNCS, vol. 4450, pp. 201–216. Springer, Heidelberg (2007)

17. Bender, A., Katz, J., Morselli, R.: Ring signatures: Stronger definitions, and constructions without random oracles. J. Cryptology **22**(1), 114–138 (2009)
18. Camenisch, J., Haralambiev, K., Kohlweiss, M., Lapon, J., Naessens, V.: Structure preserving CCA secure encryption and applications. In: Lee, D.H., Wang, X. (eds.) ASIACRYPT 2011. LNCS, vol. 7073, pp. 89–106. Springer, Heidelberg (2011)
19. Camenisch, J., Krenn, S., Shoup, V.: A framework for practical universally composable zero-knowledge protocols. In: Lee, D.H., Wang, X. (eds.) ASIACRYPT 2011. LNCS, vol. 7073, pp. 449–467. Springer, Heidelberg (2011)
20. Camenisch, J.L., Lysyanskaya, A.: An efficient system for non-transferable anonymous credentials with optional anonymity revocation. In: Pfitzmann, B. (ed.) EUROCRYPT 2001. LNCS, vol. 2045, pp. 93–118. Springer, Heidelberg (2001)
21. Catalano, D., Di Raimondo, M., Fiore, D., Gennaro, R.: Off-line/on-line signatures: theoretical aspects and experimental results. In: Cramer, R. (ed.) PKC 2008. LNCS, vol. 4939, pp. 101–120. Springer, Heidelberg (2008)
22. Cathalo, J., Libert, B., Yung, M.: Group encryption: non-interactive realization in the standard model. In: Matsui, M. (ed.) ASIACRYPT 2009. LNCS, vol. 5912, pp. 179–196. Springer, Heidelberg (2009)
23. Chase, M., Kohlweiss, M., Lysyanskaya, A., Meiklejohn, S.: Malleable signatures: New definitions and delegatable anonymous credentials. 2013 IEEE 27th Computer Security Foundations Symposium (2014)
24. Dubovitskaya, M.: Cryptographic Protocols for Privacy-Preserving Access Control in Databases (2014)
25. Even, S., Goldreich, O., Micali, S.: On-line/off-line digital signatures. J. Cryptology **9**(1), 35–67 (1996)
26. Fischlin, M.: Communication-efficient non-interactive proofs of knowledge with online extractors. In: Shoup, V. (ed.) CRYPTO 2005. LNCS, vol. 3621, pp. 152–168. Springer, Heidelberg (2005)
27. Fuchsbauer, G.: Commuting signatures and verifiable encryption. In: Paterson, K.G. (ed.) EUROCRYPT 2011. LNCS, vol. 6632, pp. 224–245. Springer, Heidelberg (2011)
28. Galbraith, S.D., Paterson, K.G., Smart, N.P.: Pairings for cryptographers. Discrete Applied Mathematics **156**(16), 3113–3121 (2008)
29. Goldwasser, S., Micali, S., Rivest, R.: A digital signature scheme secure against adaptive chosen-message attacks. SIAM Journal on Computing **17**(2), 281–308 (1988)
30. Groth, J.: Fully anonymous group signatures without random oracles. In: Kurosawa, K. (ed.) ASIACRYPT 2007. LNCS, vol. 4833, pp. 164–180. Springer, Heidelberg (2007)
31. Groth, J., Sahai, A.: Efficient noninteractive proof systems for bilinear groups. SIAM Journal of Computing **41**(5), 1193–1232 (2012)
32. Hada, S., Tanaka, T.: On the existence of 3-round zero-knowledge protocols. In: Krawczyk, H. (ed.) CRYPTO 1998. LNCS, vol. 1462, pp. 408–423. Springer, Heidelberg (1998)
33. Kate, A., Zaverucha, G.M., Goldberg, I.: Constant-size commitments to polynomials and their applications. In: Abe, M. (ed.) ASIACRYPT 2010. LNCS, vol. 6477, pp. 177–194. Springer, Heidelberg (2010)
34. Libert, B., Peters, T., Joye, M., Yung, M.: Linearly homomorphic structure-preserving signatures and their applications. In: Canetti, R., Garay, J.A. (eds.) CRYPTO 2013, Part II. LNCS, vol. 8043, pp. 289–307. Springer, Heidelberg (2013)
35. Meiklejohn, S.: An extension of the Groth-Sahai proof system. In Brown University Masters thesis (2009)

36. Micali, S., Ohta, K., Reyzin, L.: Accountable-subgroup multisignatures: extended abstract. In: ACM CCS 2001, 245–254 (2001)
37. Mohassel, P.: One-time signatures and chameleon hash functions. In: Biryukov, A., Gong, G., Stinson, D.R. (eds.) SAC 2010. LNCS, vol. 6544, pp. 302–319. Springer, Heidelberg (2011)
38. Pedersen, T.P.: Non-interactive and information-theoretic secure verifiable secret sharing. In: Feigenbaum, J. (ed.) CRYPTO 1991. LNCS, vol. 576, pp. 129–140. Springer, Heidelberg (1992)
39. Rivest, R.L., Shamir, A., Tauman, Y.: How to leak a secret. In: Boyd, C. (ed.) ASIACRYPT 2001. LNCS, vol. 2248, pp. 552–565. Springer, Heidelberg (2001)

Zero-Knowledge Proofs

Disjunctions for Hash Proof Systems: New Constructions and Applications

Michel Abdalla$^{(\boxtimes)}$, Fabrice Benhamouda$^{(\boxtimes)}$, and David Pointcheval$^{(\boxtimes)}$

ENS, CNRS, INRIA, and PSL,
École Normale Supérieure, 45 rue d'Ulm, 75005 Paris, France
{michel.abdalla,fabrice.benhamouda,david.pointcheval}@ens.fr

Abstract. Hash Proof Systems were first introduced by Cramer and Shoup (Eurocrypt'02) as a tool to construct efficient chosen-ciphertext-secure encryption schemes. Since then, they have found many other applications, including password authenticated key exchange, oblivious transfer, and zero-knowledge arguments. One of the aspects that makes hash proof systems so interesting and powerful is that they can be seen as implicit proofs of membership for certain languages. As a result, by extending the family of languages that they can handle, one often obtains new applications or new ways to understand existing schemes. In this paper, we show how to construct hash proof systems for the disjunction of languages defined generically over cyclic, bilinear, and multilinear groups. Among other applications, this enables us to construct the most efficient one-time simulation-sound (quasi-adaptive) non-interactive zero-knowledge arguments for linear languages over cyclic groups, the first one-round group password-authenticated key exchange without random oracles, the most efficient threshold structure-preserving chosen-ciphertext-secure encryption scheme, and the most efficient one-round password authenticated key exchange in the UC framework.

Keywords: Hash proof system · Non-interactive zero-knowledge proof · Group password authenticated key exchange · Threshold encryption · Linearly homomorphic signature · Structure preserving primitive

1 Introduction

Hash Proof Systems or Smooth Projective Hash Functions (SPHFs), which can be seen as a kind of implicit designated-verifier proofs of membership [4,7], were originally introduced by Cramer and Shoup [12] as a way to build efficient chosen-ciphertext-secure (IND-CCA) encryption schemes. Informally speaking, SPHFs are families of pairs of functions (Hash, ProjHash) defined on a language $\mathscr{L} \subset \mathcal{X}$. These functions are indexed by a pair of associated keys (hk, hp), where the hashing key hk and the projection key hp can be seen as the private and public keys, respectively. When computed on a word $C \in \mathscr{L}$, both functions should lead to the same result: $\mathsf{Hash}(\mathsf{hk}, \mathscr{L}, C)$ with the hashing key and $\mathsf{ProjHash}(\mathsf{hp}, \mathscr{L}, C, w)$ with the projection key and a witness w that $C \in \mathscr{L}$. Of course, if $C \notin \mathscr{L}$, such a

© International Association for Cryptologic Research 2015
E. Oswald and M. Fischlin (Eds.): EUROCRYPT 2015, Part II, LNCS 9057, pp. 69–100, 2015.
DOI: 10.1007/978-3-662-46803-6_3

witness does not exist, and the smoothness property states that $\mathsf{Hash}(\mathsf{hk}, \mathscr{L}, C)$ is independent of hp. As a consequence, the value $\mathsf{Hash}(\mathsf{hk}, \mathscr{L}, C)$ cannot be guessed even with the knowledge of hp.

Since their introduction, SPHFs have been used in various applications, including Password Authenticated Key Exchange (PAKE) [23,16,24], Oblivious Transfer [22,1], One-Time Relatively-Sound Non-Interactive Zero-Knowledge Arguments [19], Zero-Knowledge Arguments [6], and Trapdoor Smooth Projective Hash Functions (TSPHFs) [6]. An SPHF for a language $\mathscr{L}$ also directly leads to a witness encryption scheme [15] for the same language $\mathscr{L}$: encrypting a message m for a word C consists in generating an hashing key hk and a projection key hp and outputting hp together with m masked with the hash value $\mathsf{Hash}(\mathsf{hk}, \mathscr{L}, C)$ of C under hk. If we know a witness w for C, we can compute this hash value from hp, while if $C \notin \mathscr{L}$, this hash value statistically masks the message.

As explained in [6], various variants of SPHFs have been proposed over the years, depending on whether the projection key hp is allowed to depend on C and whether the smoothness holds even when C is chosen after having seen hp. For witness encryption, for example, the weakest notion (hp depends on C) is sufficient, while for encryption schemes and one-round PAKE, the strongest notion (hp does not depend on C and C may be chosen after hp in the smoothness property) is required. In this article, we focus on the strongest notion of SPHF, also called KV-SPHF in [6], since it has more applications. However, most parts of the paper could be adapted to use the weaker GL-SPHF notion.

Expressiveness of SPHFs. Due to the wide range of applications of SPHFs, one may wonder what kind of languages can be handled by SPHFs. First, since SPHF implies statistical witness encryption, it is important to remark that it is impossible to construct SPHF for any NP language, unless the polynomial hierarchy collapses [15]. Nevertheless, as the many different applications show, the class of languages supported by SPHFs can be very rich.

Diverse Groups and Diverse Vector Spaces. In [12], Cramer and Shoup showed that SPHFs can handle any language based on what they call a diverse group. Most, if not all, constructions of SPHF are based on diverse groups. However, in the context of languages over cyclic groups, bilinear groups or even multilinear groups, diverse groups may appear slightly too generic. That is why, in [6], Benhamouda et al. introduced a generic framework (later called *diverse vector space*) encompassing most known SPHFs based over these kinds of groups. It can be seen as particular diverse groups with more mathematical structure, namely using vector spaces instead of groups. In this article, we are mainly interested on SPHFs based on diverse vector spaces.

Operations on SPHFs. In order to enrich the class of languages that can be handled by SPHFs, Abdalla, Chevalier, and Pointcheval [4] showed how to build SPHFs for languages that can be described in terms of disjunctions and conjunctions of simpler languages for which SPHFs are known to exist. Let $\mathscr{L}_1$ and $\mathscr{L}_2$ be two such languages. In the particular case of conjunctions, when given

SPHFs for $\mathscr{L}_1$ and $\mathscr{L}_2$, they showed how to build an SPHF for the conjunction $\mathscr{L} = \mathscr{L}_1 \times \mathscr{L}_2$, so that a word $C = (C_1, C_2) \in \mathscr{L}$ if and only if $C_1 \in \mathscr{L}_1$ and $C_2 \in \mathscr{L}_2$. Note that this definition is a generalization of the "classical" conjunction: $C_1 \in \mathscr{L}$ if and only if $C_1 \in \mathscr{L}_1$ and $C_1 \in \mathscr{L}_2$, which we can get by setting $C_1 = C_2$.

In the case of disjunctions, when given SPHFs for $\mathscr{L}_1$ and $\mathscr{L}_2$, Abdalla et al. showed how to build an SPHF for language $\mathscr{L} = (\mathscr{L}_1 \times \mathcal{X}_2) \cup (\mathcal{X}_1 \times \mathscr{L}_2)$, so that $C = (C_1, C_2) \in \mathscr{L}$ if and only if $C_1 \in \mathscr{L}_1$ or $C_2 \in \mathscr{L}_2$. In particular, a witness for $C = (C_1, C_2) \in \mathscr{L}$ can be either a witness w_1 for $C_1 \in \mathscr{L}_1$ or a witness w_2 for $C_2 \in \mathscr{L}_2$. As for conjunctions, by setting $C_1 = C_2$, one gets the "classical" disjunction: $C = (C_1, C_1) \in \mathscr{L}$ if and only if $C_1 \in \mathscr{L}_1$ or $C_1 \in \mathscr{L}_2$.

Unfortunately, while the conjunction of two strong SPHFs in [4] yields a strong SPHF, the same is not true for disjunctions, where the projection key hp necessarily depends on C. And this greatly limits its applications[1].

1.1 Results

Disjunction of SPHFs. Our first main result is to show how to construct the disjunction of two SPHFs for two languages based on diverse vector spaces. Essentially, the only requirement for the construction is that it is possible to compute a pairing between an element of the first language $\mathscr{L}_1$ and an element of the second language $\mathscr{L}_2$. Concretely, if we have a bilinear map $e : \mathbb{G}_1 \times \mathbb{G}_2 \to \mathbb{G}_T$ where $\mathbb{G}_1$, $\mathbb{G}_2$ and $\mathbb{G}_T$ are cyclic groups of some prime order p (we say that $(p, \mathbb{G}_1, \mathbb{G}_2, \mathbb{G}_T, e)$ is a bilinear group), and if $\mathscr{L}_1$ is defined over $\mathbb{G}_1$ and $\mathscr{L}_2$ over $\mathbb{G}_2$, then our construction provides an SPHF for the disjunction of $\mathscr{L}_1$ and $\mathscr{L}_2$. Furthermore, this disjunction can be repeated multiple times, if multilinear maps are available. The only limitation is that the complexity of our constructions grows exponentially with the number of repetitions, therefore limiting the total number of disjunctions that we can compute.

Application: Constant-Size NIZK and One-Time Simulation-Sound NIZK. First, we show how to use disjunctions of SPHFs to create efficient *non-interactive zero-knowledge arguments (NIZK)* and even *one-time simulation-sound NIZK*, i.e., NIZK in which a dishonest (polynomial-time) prover cannot produce a valid proof of a false statement, even when seeing one simulated proof on a statement of its choice (which may be false). The proof size consists of only two group elements, even for the one-time simulation-sound version, assuming the language we are interested in can be handled by an SPHF over some group $\mathbb{G}_1$, where $(p, \mathbb{G}_1, \mathbb{G}_2, \mathbb{G}_T)$ is an asymmetric bilinear group, and assuming DDH is hard in $\mathbb{G}_2$. The languages handled roughly consist of languages defined by "linear" equations over $\mathbb{G}_1$, such as the DDH language, the language of valid Cramer-Shoup [11] ciphertexts and many other useful languages as shown in [6,20].

---

[1] A reader familiar with [17] may wonder why the methods in [17] cannot be applied to provide a form of disjunction, given that SPHFs exist for languages of quadratic pairing equations over commitments [6]. Unfortunately, this technique would not yield a real SPHF, since additional commitments would be required.

Our NIZK is slightly different from a usual NIZK, since the common reference string depends on the language. Jutla and Roy called them quasi-adaptive NIZK in [20], and showed that they can replace NIZK in several applications.

Our one-time simulation-sound NIZK yields a very efficient structure-preserving threshold IND-CCA encryption scheme, with the shortest ciphertext size so far. Threshold means the decryption key can be shared between parties and a ciphertext can be decrypted if and only if enough parties provide a partial decryption of it using their key share, while structure-preserving means it can be used in particular with Groth-Sahai NIZK [18] or our new NIZK construction. In addition, this new encryption can be used in the one-round password authenticated key exchange (PAKE) scheme in the UC model in [6] to obtain an improvement of up to 30% in the communication complexity, under the same assumptions.

Other Applications. Another important application is the first *one-round group password authenticated key exchange (GPAKE)* with n players, assuming the existence of a $(n-1)$-multilinear map and the hardness of the n-linear assumption n-Lin without random oracles[2]. This was an open problem. We remark, however, that our construction only works for small values of n since the overall complexity of the protocol and the gap in the security reduction grows exponentially in n. We note, however, that the tripartite PAKE which only requires pairings is reasonably efficient since it consists of flows with 61 group elements for each user (5 for the Cramer-Shoup ciphertext and 56 for the projection key).

A second application is a new construction for TSPHF, which supports slightly more languages than the original one, but which is slightly less efficient. A TSPHF (Trapdoor Smooth Projective Hash Function [6]) is a variant of an SPHF with a full-fledged zero-knowledge flavor: there exists a trapdoor for computing the hash value of any word $C \in \mathcal{X}$ when only given C and the projection key hp.

Finally, the unforgeability of the one-time linearly homomorphic structure-preserving signature scheme of Libert et al. [25] can be explained by the smoothness of some underlying SPHF, which can be seen as the disjunction of two SPHFs. This new way of seeing their signature scheme directly shows how to extend it to other assumptions, such as SXDH, κ-Lin, or even any MDDH assumption [13] secure in bilinear groups.

Pseudo-Random Projective Hash Functions (PrPHFs) and More Efficient Applications. For our NIZK and our new TSPHF, the construction essentially consists in the disjunction of an SPHF for the language in which we are interested, and another SPHF for a language which is used to provide extra features (zero-knowledge and "public verifiability" for our NIZK and trapdoor for our TSPHF). This second language $\mathcal{L}_2$ is supposed to be a hard subset member-

---

[2] At the time the first version of this paper was made public [2], the multilinear map construction by Coron et al. [10] seemed to be a plausible candidate. However, as recently shown by Cheon et al. [9], this is no longer the case. Unfortunately, no current candidate multilinear map construction is known to work for our framework for $n \geq 3$.

ship one, i.e., it is hard to distinguish a random word $C_2 \in \mathscr{L}_2$ from a random word $C_2 \in \mathcal{X}_2 \setminus \mathscr{L}_2$.

To get more efficient applications, we introduce the notion of pseudo-random projective hash functions (PrPHFs) which are particular SPHFs over trivial languages, i.e., languages $\mathscr{L} = \mathcal{X}$, where all words are in the language. Of course, smoothness becomes trivial, in this case. That is why PrPHFs are supposed to have another property called *pseudo-randomness*, which ensures that if the parameters of the language $\mathscr{L}$ and the word C are chosen at random, given a projection key hp (and no witness for C), the hash value H of C appears random.

We then show that we can replace the second hard subset membership language in our NIZK and our TSPHF by a trivial language with a PrPHF, assuming a certain property over the first language $\mathscr{L}_1$ (which is almost always verified). This conversion yields slightly shorter proofs (for our NIZK and our one-time simulation-sound NIZK) or slightly shorter projection keys (for our TSPHF).

Related Work. Until now, the most efficient NIZK for similar languages was the one of Jutla and Roy [21], and the most efficient *one-time* simulation-sound NIZK was the *unbounded* simulation-sound NIZK of Libert et al. [26]. Even though all these constructions have constant-size proofs, our second NIZK is slightly more efficient for κ-linear assumptions, with $\kappa \geq 2$, while our one-time simulation-sound NIZK is about ten times shorter. Moreover, our construction might be simpler to understand due to its modularity. We provide a detailed comparison in Section 7.3.

1.2   Organization

In the next section, we give the high level intuition for all our constructions and their applications. Then, after recalling some preliminaries in Section 3, we give the details of our construction of disjunctions of SPHFs in Section 4, which is one of our main contributions. We then show how to build efficient NIZK and one-time simulation-sound NIZK from it in Section 5. After that, we introduce the notion of PrPHF in Section 6 and show in Section 7 how this can improve some of our previous applications. These last two sections are much more technical: although the underlying ideas are similar to the ones in previous sections, the proofs are more complex. Due to lack of space, details of our two other applications, namely one-round GPAKE and TSPHF, are presented in the full version, but an overview is available in Section 2.3.

2   Overview of Our Constructions

2.1   Disjunction of Languages

Intuition. From a very high point of view, the generic framework [6] enables us to construct an SPHF for any language $\mathscr{L}$ which is a subspace of the vector space of all words $\mathcal{X}$.

It is therefore possible to do the conjunction of two languages $\mathscr{L}_1$ and $\mathscr{L}_2$ supported by this generic framework by remarking that $\mathscr{L}_1 \times \mathscr{L}_2$ is a subspace of the vector space $\mathcal{X}_1 \times \mathcal{X}_2$. This construction of conjunctions is an "algebraic" version of the conjunction proposed in [4].

Unfortunately, the same approach cannot be directly applied to the case of disjunctions, because $(\mathscr{L}_1 \times \mathcal{X}_2) \cup (\mathcal{X}_1 \times \mathscr{L}_2)$ is not a subspace of $\mathcal{X}_1 \times \mathcal{X}_2$, and the subspace generated by the former union of sets is $\mathcal{X}_1 \times \mathcal{X}_2$. In this article, we solve this issue by observing that, instead of using $\mathcal{X} = \mathcal{X}_1 \times \mathcal{X}_2$, we can consider the tensor product of $\mathcal{X}_1$ and $\mathcal{X}_2$: $\mathcal{X} = \mathcal{X}_1 \otimes \mathcal{X}_2$. Then the disjunction of $\mathscr{L}_1$ and $\mathscr{L}_2$ can be seen as the subspace $\mathscr{L}$ of $\mathcal{X}$ generated by: $\mathscr{L}_1 \otimes \mathcal{X}_2$ and $\mathcal{X}_1 \otimes \mathscr{L}_2$. Notice that $(\mathscr{L}_1 \otimes \mathcal{X}_2) \cup (\mathcal{X}_1 \otimes \mathscr{L}_2)$ is not a subspace and so $\mathscr{L}$ is much larger than this union of sets. But we can prove that if $C_1 \otimes C_2 \in \mathscr{L}$, then $C_1 \in \mathscr{L}_1$ or $C_2 \in \mathscr{L}_2$.

Before providing more details about these constructions, let us first briefly recall the main ideas of the generic framework for constructing SPHFs.

Generic Framework for SPHFs. The generic framework for SPHFs in [6] uses a common formalization for cyclic groups, bilinear groups, and even multilinear groups[3] (of prime order p), called graded rings[4].

Basically, graded rings enable us to use a ring structure over these groups: the addition and the multiplication of two elements u and v, denoted $u + v$ and $u \bullet v$, respectively, correspond to the addition and the multiplication of their discrete logarithms. For example, if g is a generator of a cyclic group $\mathbb{G}$, and a and b are two scalars in $\mathbb{Z}_p$, $a + b = a + b$, $a \bullet b = a \cdot b$ (because the "discrete logarithm" of a scalar is the scalar itself), $g^a + g^b = g^{a+b}$, and $g^a \bullet g^b = g_T^{a \cdot b}$, with g_T a generator of another cyclic group $\mathbb{G}_T$ of order p.

Of course, computing $g^a \bullet g^b = g_T^{a \cdot b}$ requires a bilinear map $e : \mathbb{G} \times \mathbb{G} \to \mathbb{G}_T$, if the discrete logarithms of g^a and g^b are not known. And if such a bilinear map exists, we can compute $g^a \bullet g^b$ as $e(g^a, g^b)$. For a similar reason, the multiplication of three group elements via $\bullet$ would require a trilinear map. Therefore, graded rings can be seen as the ring $\mathbb{Z}_p$ with some limitations on the multiplication. Here, to avoid technicalities, the group of each element is implicit, and we suppose that above constraints on the multiplications are satisfied. Formal details are left to the following sections.

From a high level point of view, in this framework, we suppose there exists a map θ from the set of words $\mathcal{X}$ to a vector space $\hat{\mathcal{X}}$ of dimension n, together with a subspace $\hat{\mathscr{L}}$ of $\hat{\mathcal{X}}$, generated by a family of vectors $(\varGamma_i)_{i=1}^k$, such that $C \in \mathscr{L}$ if and only if $\theta(C) \in \hat{\mathscr{L}}$. When the function θ is clear from context, we often write $\hat{C} := \theta(C)$.

---

[3] In this work, we need a multilinear map for which DDH, κ-Lin, or any MDDH assumption [13] hold in the multilinear groups. Unfortunately, as explained in Footnote 2, no current candidate multilinear map construction is known to work for our framework.

[4] Graded rings were named after graded encodings systems [14] and are unrelated to the mathematical notion of graded rings.

A witness for a word $C \in \mathscr{L}$ is a vector $\boldsymbol{\lambda} = (\lambda_i)_{i=1}^k$ so that $\hat{C} = \theta(C) = \sum_{i=1}^k \lambda_i \bullet \boldsymbol{\Gamma_i}$. In other words, it consists of the coefficients of a linear combination of $(\boldsymbol{\Gamma_i})_{i=1}^k$ equal to $\hat{C}$.

Then, a hashing key hk is just a random linear form $\mathsf{hk} := \alpha \in \hat{\mathscr{X}}^*$ ($\hat{\mathscr{X}}^*$ being the dual vector space of $\hat{\mathscr{X}}$, i.e., the vector space of linear maps from $\hat{\mathscr{X}}$ to $\mathbb{Z}_p$), and the associated projection key is the vector of its values on $\boldsymbol{\Gamma_1}, \ldots, \boldsymbol{\Gamma_k}$:

$$\mathsf{hp} := \boldsymbol{\gamma} = (\gamma_i)_{i=1}^k = (\alpha(\boldsymbol{\Gamma_i}))_{i=1}^k.$$

The hash value of a word C is then $H := \alpha(\hat{C})$. If $\boldsymbol{\lambda}$ is a witness for $C \in \mathscr{L}$, then the latter can also be computed as:

$$H = \alpha(\hat{C}) = \alpha\left(\sum_{i=1}^k \lambda_i \bullet \boldsymbol{\Gamma_i}\right) = \sum_{i=1}^k \lambda_i \bullet \alpha(\boldsymbol{\Gamma_i}) = \sum_{i=1}^k \lambda_i \bullet \gamma_i,$$

which only depends on the witness $\boldsymbol{\lambda}$ and the projection key hp. The smoothness comes from the fact that, if $C \notin \mathscr{L}$, then $\hat{C} \notin \hat{\mathscr{L}}$ and $\hat{C}$ is linearly independent from $(\boldsymbol{\Gamma_i})_{i=1}^k$. Hence, $\alpha(\hat{C})$ looks random even given $\mathsf{hp} = (\alpha(\boldsymbol{\Gamma_i}))_{i=1}^k$.

For a reader familiar with [12], the generic framework is similar to a diverse group, but with more structure: a vector space instead of a simple group. When θ is the identity function, $(\mathscr{X}^*, \mathscr{X}, \mathscr{L}, \mathbb{Z}_p)$ is a diverse group. We remark, however, that one does not need to know diverse groups to understand our paper.

Example 1 (SPHF for DDH). Let us illustrate this framework for the DDH language: let g, h be two generators of a cyclic group $\mathbb{G}$ of prime order p, let $\mathscr{X} = \mathbb{G}^2$ and $\mathscr{L} = \{(g^r, h^r)^\mathsf{T} \in \mathscr{X} \mid r \in \mathbb{Z}_p\}$. We set $\hat{\mathscr{X}} = \mathscr{X}$, $\hat{\mathscr{L}} = \mathscr{L}$ and θ the identify function so that $C = \hat{C} = (u, v)^\mathsf{T}$. $\hat{\mathscr{L}}$ is generated by the column vector $\boldsymbol{\Gamma_1} = (g, h)^\mathsf{T}$. The witness for $C = (g^r, h^r)^\mathsf{T}$ is $\lambda_1 = r$. The hashing key $\mathsf{hk} = \alpha \xleftarrow{\$} \hat{\mathscr{X}}^*$ can be represented by a row vector $\boldsymbol{\alpha} = (\alpha_1, \alpha_2) \in \mathbb{Z}_p^{1 \times 2}$ and

$$\mathsf{hp} = \gamma_1 = \alpha(\boldsymbol{\Gamma_1}) = \boldsymbol{\alpha} \bullet \boldsymbol{\Gamma_1} = g^{\alpha_1} \cdot h^{\alpha_2}$$

$$H = \alpha(\hat{C}) = \boldsymbol{\alpha} \bullet \hat{C} = u^{\alpha_1} \cdot v^{\alpha_2} = \gamma_1 \bullet r = \gamma_1^r.$$

This is exactly the original SPHF of Cramer and Shoup for the DDH language in [12].

Remark on the Notation of Vectors (Transposition) and Link with [13]. Compared to [6], in this paper, we transposed all the vectors and matrices: elements of $\mathscr{X}$ are now column vectors, while hashing keys (elements of $\mathscr{X}^*$) are row vectors. This seems more natural and makes our notation closer to the one of Escala et al. [13].

Warm up: Conjunction of Languages. As a warm up, let us first construct the conjunction $\mathscr{L} = \mathscr{L}_1 \times \mathscr{L}_2$ of two languages $\mathscr{L}_1 \subset \mathscr{X}_1$ and $\mathscr{L}_2 \subset \mathscr{X}_2$ supported by the generic framework, in a more algebraic way than the one in [4]. We can just set:

$$\hat{\mathcal{X}} := \hat{\mathcal{X}}_1 \times \hat{\mathcal{X}}_2 \qquad\qquad n := n_1 + n_2$$

$$\hat{\mathscr{L}} := \hat{\mathscr{L}}_1 \times \hat{\mathscr{L}}_2 \qquad\qquad k := k_1 + k_2$$

$$\theta((C_1, C_2)) = \hat{\boldsymbol{C}} := \begin{pmatrix} \theta_1(C_1) \\ \theta_2(C_2) \end{pmatrix} \qquad (\boldsymbol{\Gamma}_i)_{i=1}^k := \left(\begin{pmatrix} \boldsymbol{\Gamma}_i^{(1)} \\ \boldsymbol{0} \end{pmatrix}_{i=1}^{k_1}, \begin{pmatrix} \boldsymbol{0} \\ \boldsymbol{\Gamma}_i^{(2)} \end{pmatrix}_{i=1}^{k_2} \right)$$

This is what is implicitly done in all conjunctions of SPHFs in [6], for example.

Example 2 (SPHF for Conjunction of DDH). Let g_1, h_1, g_2, h_2 be four generators of a cyclic group $\mathbb{G}$ of prime order p. Let $\mathcal{X}_1 = \mathcal{X}_2 = \mathbb{G}^2$ and $\mathscr{L}_i = \{(g_i^{r_i}, h_i^{r_i})^\mathsf{T} \in \mathcal{X}_i \mid r_i \in \mathbb{Z}_p\}$ for $i = 1, 2$. We set $\hat{\mathcal{X}}_i = \mathcal{X}_i$, $\hat{\mathscr{L}}_i = \mathscr{L}_i$ and θ_i the identify function so that $C_i = \hat{C}_i = (u_i, v_i)^\mathsf{T}$, for $i = 1, 2$. $\hat{\mathscr{L}}_i$ is generated by the column vector $\boldsymbol{\Gamma}_1^{(i)} = (g_i, h_i)^\mathsf{T}$. The witness for $C_i = (g_i^{r_i}, h_i^{r_i})^\mathsf{T}$ is $\lambda_1^{(i)} = r_i$. Then, the SPHF for the conjunction of $\mathscr{L}_1$ and $\mathscr{L}_2$ is defined by:

$$\hat{\mathcal{X}} := \hat{\mathcal{X}}_1 \times \hat{\mathcal{X}}_2 = \mathbb{G}^4 \qquad\qquad n = 4 \quad k = 2$$

$$\hat{\mathscr{L}} := \hat{\mathscr{L}}_1 \times \hat{\mathscr{L}}_2 = \{(g_1^{r_1}, h_1^{r_1}, g_2^{r_2}, h_2^{r_2})^\mathsf{T} \mid r_1, r_2 \in \mathbb{Z}_p\}$$

$$\boldsymbol{\Gamma}_1 := (g_1, h_1, 1, 1)^\mathsf{T} \in \mathbb{G}^4 \qquad\qquad \boldsymbol{\Gamma}_2 := (1, 1, g_2, h_2)^\mathsf{T} \in \mathbb{G}^4$$

$$\theta(C) := \hat{\boldsymbol{C}} := (u_1, v_1, u_2, v_2)^\mathsf{T} \in \mathbb{G}^4 \text{ for } C = (C_1, C_2) = ((u_1, v_1)^\mathsf{T}, (u_2, v_2)^\mathsf{T})$$

The hashing key $\mathsf{hk} = \alpha \xleftarrow{\$} \hat{\mathcal{X}}^*$ can be represented by a row vector $\boldsymbol{\alpha} = (\alpha_1, \alpha_2, \alpha_3, \alpha_4) \in \mathbb{Z}_p^{1 \times 4}$ and

$$\mathsf{hp} = \begin{pmatrix} \gamma_1 \\ \gamma_2 \end{pmatrix} = \begin{pmatrix} \boldsymbol{\alpha} \bullet \boldsymbol{\Gamma}_1 \\ \boldsymbol{\alpha} \bullet \boldsymbol{\Gamma}_2 \end{pmatrix} = \begin{pmatrix} g_1^{\alpha_1} \cdot h_1^{\alpha_2} \\ g_2^{\alpha_3} \cdot h_2^{\alpha_4} \end{pmatrix}$$

$$H = \alpha(\hat{C}) = \boldsymbol{\alpha} \bullet \hat{\boldsymbol{C}} = u_1^{\alpha_1} \cdot v_1^{\alpha_2} \cdot u_2^{\alpha_3} \cdot v_2^{\alpha_4} = \gamma_1 \bullet r_1 + \gamma_2 \bullet r_2 = \gamma_1^{r_1} \cdot \gamma_2^{r_2}.$$

Disjunction of Languages. We first remark we cannot naively extend the previous construction by choosing $\hat{\mathcal{X}} = \hat{\mathcal{X}}_1 \times \hat{\mathcal{X}}_2$ and $\hat{\mathscr{L}} = (\hat{\mathscr{L}}_1 \times \hat{\mathcal{X}}_2) \cup (\hat{\mathcal{X}}_1 \times \hat{\mathscr{L}}_2)$, because, in this case $\hat{\mathscr{L}}$ is not a subspace, and the subspace generated by $\hat{\mathscr{L}}$ is $\hat{\mathcal{X}}_1 \times \hat{\mathcal{X}}_2$. That is why we use tensor products of vector spaces instead of direct product of vector spaces. Concretely, we set

$$\hat{\mathcal{X}} := \hat{\mathcal{X}}_1 \otimes \hat{\mathcal{X}}_2 \qquad\qquad n := n_1 n_2$$

$$\hat{\mathscr{L}} := \langle (\hat{\mathscr{L}}_1 \otimes \hat{\mathcal{X}}_2) \cup (\hat{\mathcal{X}}_1 \otimes \hat{\mathscr{L}}_2) \rangle \qquad\qquad k := k_1 n_2 + n_1 k_2$$

$$\theta(C) = \hat{\boldsymbol{C}} := \hat{\boldsymbol{C}}_1 \otimes \hat{\boldsymbol{C}}_2$$

where the notation $\langle V \rangle$ is the vector space generated by V. The vectors $\boldsymbol{\Gamma}_i$ are described in detail in the core of the paper. This construction works since, if $\hat{\boldsymbol{C}}_1 \otimes \hat{\boldsymbol{C}}_2 \in \hat{\mathscr{L}}$ then, thanks to properties of the tensor product, $\hat{\boldsymbol{C}}_1 \in \hat{\mathscr{L}}_1$ or $\hat{\boldsymbol{C}}_2 \in \hat{\mathscr{L}}_2$.

It is important to remark that computing a tensor product implies computing a multiplication. So if $\hat{C}_1$ in $\hat{\mathcal{X}}_1$ and $\hat{C}_2$ in $\hat{\mathcal{X}}_2$ are over some cyclic groups $\mathbb{G}_1$ and $\mathbb{G}_2$, we need a bilinear map $e : \mathbb{G}_1 \times \mathbb{G}_2 \to \mathbb{G}_T$ to actually be able to compute $\hat{C}_1 \otimes \hat{C}_2$. More generally, doing the disjunction of K languages over cyclic groups requires a K-way multilinear map. This can be seen in the following example and we formally deal with this technicality in the core of the paper.

Example 3 (SPHF for Disjunction of DDH). Let us use the same notation as in Example 2, except that this time $(p, \mathbb{G}_1, \mathbb{G}_2, \mathbb{G}_T, e)$ is an asymmetric bilinear group (e is a bilinear map: $\mathbb{G}_1 \times \mathbb{G}_2 \to \mathbb{G}_T$), g_1, h_1 are generators of $\mathbb{G}_1$, g_2, h_2 are generators of $\mathbb{G}_2$, and $\mathcal{X}_i = \hat{\mathcal{X}}_i = \mathbb{G}_i^2$ (instead of $\mathbb{G}^2$) for $i = 1, 2$.

The disjunction of $\mathscr{L}_1$ and $\mathscr{L}_2$ is defined by

$$\hat{\mathcal{X}} := \hat{\mathcal{X}}_1 \otimes \hat{\mathcal{X}}_2 = \mathbb{G}_T^4 \qquad\qquad n := 4$$

$$\mathscr{L} := \langle (\hat{\mathscr{L}}_1 \otimes \hat{\mathcal{X}}_2) \cup (\hat{\mathcal{X}}_1 \otimes \hat{\mathscr{L}}_2) \rangle \qquad\qquad k := 4$$

$$\Gamma_1 := \begin{pmatrix} g_1 \\ h_1 \end{pmatrix} \otimes \begin{pmatrix} 1 \in \mathbb{Z}_p \\ 0 \in \mathbb{Z}_p \end{pmatrix} = \begin{pmatrix} g_1^1 \\ g_1^0 \\ h_1^1 \\ h_1^0 \end{pmatrix} = \begin{pmatrix} g_1 \\ 1 \\ h_1 \\ 1 \end{pmatrix} \in \mathbb{G}_1^4$$

$$\Gamma_2 := \begin{pmatrix} g_1 \\ h_1 \end{pmatrix} \otimes \begin{pmatrix} 0 \in \mathbb{Z}_p \\ 1 \in \mathbb{Z}_p \end{pmatrix} = \begin{pmatrix} g_1^0 \\ g_1^1 \\ h_1^0 \\ h_1^1 \end{pmatrix} = \begin{pmatrix} 1 \\ g_1 \\ 1 \\ h_1 \end{pmatrix} \in \mathbb{G}_1^4$$

$$\Gamma_3 := \begin{pmatrix} 1 \in \mathbb{Z}_p \\ 0 \in \mathbb{Z}_p \end{pmatrix} \otimes \begin{pmatrix} g_2 \\ h_2 \end{pmatrix} = \begin{pmatrix} g_2^1 \\ h_2^1 \\ g_2^0 \\ h_2^0 \end{pmatrix} = \begin{pmatrix} g_2 \\ h_2 \\ 1 \\ 1 \end{pmatrix} \in \mathbb{G}_2^4$$

$$\Gamma_4 := \begin{pmatrix} 0 \in \mathbb{Z}_p \\ 1 \in \mathbb{Z}_p \end{pmatrix} \otimes \begin{pmatrix} g_2 \\ h_2 \end{pmatrix} = \begin{pmatrix} g_2^0 \\ h_2^0 \\ g_2^1 \\ h_2^1 \end{pmatrix} = \begin{pmatrix} 1 \\ 1 \\ g_2 \\ h_2 \end{pmatrix} \in \mathbb{G}_2^4$$

$$\theta(C) = \hat{C} := \hat{C}_1 \otimes \hat{C}_2 = (u_1 \bullet u_2, u_1 \bullet v_2, v_1 \bullet u_2, v_1 \bullet v_2)^\mathsf{T}$$
$$= (e(u_1, u_2), e(u_1, v_2), e(v_1, u_2), e(v_1, v_2))^\mathsf{T} \in \mathbb{G}_T^4,$$

for $C = (C_1, C_2) = ((u_1, v_1), (u_2, v_2))$. The generating family of $\mathscr{L}$ we used here is $(\Gamma_1, \Gamma_2, \Gamma_3, \Gamma_4)$. As seen after, if we know the witness r_1 for C_1, we can use Γ_1 and Γ_2 to compute the hash value of $C = (C_1, C_2)$, while if we know the witness r_2 for C_2, we can use Γ_3 and Γ_4 to compute the hash value of C. Obviously this generating family is not free, since $\mathscr{L}$ has dimension 3 and this family has cardinality 4.

The witnesses λ for a word $C = (C_1, C_2)$ are

$$\begin{cases} (r_1 \bullet u_2, r_1 \bullet v_2, 0, 0) & \text{if } (u_1, v_1) = (g^{r_1}, h^{r_1}) \quad \text{(i.e., if } r_1 \text{ is a witness for } C_1) \\ (0, 0, r_2 \bullet u_1, r_2 \bullet v_1) & \text{if } (u_2, v_2) = (g^{r_2}, h^{r_2}) \quad \text{(i.e., if } r_2 \text{ is a witness for } C_2), \end{cases}$$

the hashing key $\mathsf{hk} = \alpha \xleftarrow{\$} \hat{\mathcal{X}}^*$ can be represented by a row vector $\alpha = (\alpha_1, \alpha_2, \alpha_3, \alpha_4) \in \mathbb{Z}_p^{1 \times 4}$ and

$$\mathsf{hp} = (\gamma_1, \gamma_2, \gamma_3, \gamma_4)^\mathsf{T} = (g_1^{\alpha_1} \cdot h_1^{\alpha_3}, \ g_1^{\alpha_2} \cdot h_1^{\alpha_4}, \ g_2^{\alpha_1} \cdot h_2^{\alpha_2}, \ g_2^{\alpha_3} \cdot h_2^{\alpha_4})^\mathsf{T} \in \mathbb{G}_1^2 \times \mathbb{G}_2^2$$

$$H = \alpha(\hat{C}) = \hat{C} \bullet \alpha = e(u_1, u_2)^{\alpha_1} \cdot e(u_1, v_2)^{\alpha_2} \cdot e(v_1, u_2)^{\alpha_3} \cdot e(v_1, v_2)^{\alpha_4}$$

$$= \begin{cases} r_1 \bullet u_2 \bullet \gamma_1 + r_1 \bullet v_2 \bullet \gamma_2 = e(\gamma_1, u_2)^{r_1} e(\gamma_2, v_2)^{r_1}, & \text{if } (u_1, v_1) = (g_1^{r_1}, h_1^{r_1}) \\ r_2 \bullet u_1 \bullet \gamma_3 + r_2 \bullet v_1 \bullet \gamma_4 = e(u_1, \gamma_3)^{r_2} e(v_1, \gamma_4)^{r_2}, & \text{if } (u_2, v_2) = (g_2^{r_2}, h_2^{r_2}) \end{cases}$$

The last equalities, which show the way the projection hashing works, explain the choice of the generating family $(\Gamma_i)_i$.

2.2 Main Application: One-Time Simulation-Sound NIZK Arguments

The language of the NIZK is $\mathscr{L}_1$, while $\mathscr{L}_2$ is a hard subset membership language used to build the NIZK. For the sake of simplicity, we suppose that $\mathscr{L}_2 = \hat{\mathscr{L}}_2$, $\mathcal{X}_2 = \hat{\mathcal{X}}_2$, and θ_2 is the identity function. We will consider the SPHF of the disjunction of $\mathscr{L}_1$ and $\mathscr{L}_2$, so we need to suppose that it is possible to build it. For this high level overview, let us just suppose that $(p, \mathbb{G}_1, \mathbb{G}_2, \mathbb{G}_T, e)$ is a bilinear group and that $\mathscr{L}_1$ is defined over $\mathbb{G}_1$, $\mathscr{L}_2$ over $\mathbb{G}_2$. If DDH holds in $\mathbb{G}_2$, $\mathscr{L}_2$ can just be the DDH language in $\mathbb{G}_2$ recalled in Example 1.

The common reference string is a projection key hp for the disjunction of $\mathscr{L}_1$ and $\mathscr{L}_2$, while the trapdoor (to simulate proofs) is the hashing key. Essentially, a proof $\pi = (\pi_{i_2})_{i_2}$ for a statement C_1 is just a vector of the hash values of (C_1, e_{2,i_2}) where $(e_{2,i_2})_{i_2}$ are the scalar vectors of the canonical base of $\hat{\mathcal{X}}_2$. These hash values are $\pi_{i_2} = \alpha(\hat{C}_1 \otimes e_{2,i_2})$, and can also be computed from the projection key hp and a witness for $\hat{C}_1$.

The basic idea is that a valid proof for a word $C_1 \in \mathscr{L}_1$ enables us to compute the hash value H' of (C_1, C_2) for any word $C_2 \in \hat{\mathcal{X}}_2$, by linearly combining elements of the proof, since any word C_2 can be written as a linear combination of $(e_{2,i_2})_{i_2}$:

$$H' := \sum_{i_2} \pi_{i_2} \bullet C_{2,i_2} = \sum_{i_2} \alpha(\hat{C}_1 \otimes (C_{2,i_2} \bullet e_{2,i_2})) = \alpha(\hat{C}_1 \otimes C_2),$$

if $C_2 = \sum_{i_2} C_{2,i_2} \bullet e_{1,i_2}$. Hence, for any word $C_2 \in \mathscr{L}_2$ for which we know a witness, we can compute the hash value of (C_1, C_2), either using a valid proof for C_1 (as H' above), or directly using the witness of C_2 and the projection key hp (as for any SPHF for a disjunction).

To check a proof, we basically check that for any word $C_2 \in \mathscr{L}_2$, these two ways of computing the hash value of (C_1, C_2) yields the same result. Thanks to the linearity of the language $\mathscr{L}_2$, it is sufficient to make this test for a family of words C_2 which generate $\mathscr{L}_2$, such as the words $\Gamma_j^{(2)}$ (for $j = 1, \ldots, k_2$). We recall that the witness for $\Gamma_j^{(2)}$ is the column vector $(0, \ldots, 0, 1, 0, \ldots, 0)^\mathsf{T} \in \mathbb{Z}_p^{k_2}$, where the j-th coordinate is 1.

The trapdoor, i.e., the hashing key, clearly enables us to simulate any proof, and the resulting proofs are perfectly indistinguishable from normal ones, hence the perfect zero-knowledge property. Moreover, the soundness comes from the fact that a proof for a word $C_1 \notin \mathscr{L}_1$ can be used to break the hard subset membership in $\mathscr{L}_2$.

More precisely, let us consider a soundness adversary which takes as input the projection key hp and which outputs a word $C_1 \notin \mathscr{L}_1$ and a valid proof π for C_1. On the one hand, such a valid proof enables us to compute the hash value H' of (C_1, C_2) for any word $C_2 \in \mathscr{L}_2$, by linearly combining elements of the proofs (as seen above), and the validity of the proof ensures the resulting value H' is correct if $C_2 \in \mathscr{L}_2$. On the other hand, we can also compute a hash value H of (C_1, C_2) for any $C_2 \in \mathcal{X}_2$ using the hashing key hk. Then, if $C_2 \in \mathscr{L}_2$, necessarily $H = H'$, while if $C_2 \notin \mathscr{L}_2$, the smoothness ensures that H looks completely random when given only hp. Since H' does not depend on hk but only on hp, it is different from H with overwhelming probability. Therefore, we can use such an adversary to solve the hard subset membership problem in $\mathscr{L}_2$ (namely, the DDH in $\mathbb{G}_2$ in the example below).

Example 4 (NIZK for DDH in $\mathbb{G}_1$, assuming DDH in $\mathbb{G}_2$). Using the SPHF in Example 3, the proof for a word $C_1 = (u_1 = g_1^r, v_1 = h_1^r) \in \mathbb{G}_1^2$ is the vector $\pi = (\pi_1, \pi_2) \in \mathbb{G}_1^2$ where: π_1 is the hash value of $(C_1, (1,0)^\mathsf{T}) \in \mathbb{G}_1^2 \times \mathbb{Z}_p^2$ and π_2 is the hash value of $(C_1, (0,1)^\mathsf{T}) \in \mathbb{G}_1^2 \times \mathbb{Z}_p^2$. Concretely we have:

$$\pi_1 = \gamma_1 \bullet r = \gamma_1^r \in \mathbb{G}_1 \qquad \qquad \pi_2 = \gamma_2 \bullet r = \gamma_2^r \in \mathbb{G}_1.$$

This proof is valid if and only if:

$$e(\pi_1, g_2) \cdot e(\pi_2, h_2) = \pi_1 \bullet g_2 + \pi_2 \bullet h_2 \stackrel{?}{=} u_1 \bullet \gamma_3 + v_1 \bullet \gamma_4 = e(u_1, \gamma_3) \cdot e(v_1, \gamma_4).$$

This check can be done using the common reference string $\mathsf{hp} = (\gamma_1, \gamma_2, \gamma_3, \gamma_4)$.

Finally, to simulate a proof for $C_1 = (u_1, v_1)$ without knowing any witness for C_1 but knowing the trapdoor $\mathsf{hk} = \boldsymbol{\alpha} = (\alpha_1, \alpha_2, \alpha_3, \alpha_4) \in \mathbb{Z}_p^{1 \times 4}$, we compute π_1 and π_2 as follows:

$$\pi_1 := u_1 \bullet \alpha_1 + v_1 \bullet \alpha_3 = u_1^{\alpha_1} \cdot v_1^{\alpha_3} \qquad \pi_2 := u_1 \bullet \alpha_2 + v_1 \bullet \alpha_4 = u_1^{\alpha_2} \cdot v_1^{\alpha_4}.$$

To get a one-time simulation-sound NIZK, we replace the SPHF over $\mathscr{L}_1$ by a stronger kind of SPHF for which, roughly speaking, the hash value of a word $C \notin \mathscr{L}_1$ appears random even if we are given the projection key hp and the hash value of another word $C \in \mathcal{X}_1$ of our choice. We show that it is always possible to transform a normal SPHF into this stronger variant, assuming the existence of collision-resistant hash functions[5].

---

[5] Actually, the use of collision-resistant hash functions could be avoided, but that would make the construction much less efficient.

2.3   Other Applications

TSPHF. A TSPHF is an extension of an SPHF, with an additional CRS and an associated trapdoor, where the latter provides a way to efficiently compute the hash value of any word C knowing only the projection key hp. Since hp now needs to contain enough information to compute the hash value of any word in $\mathcal{X}$, the smoothness property of TSPHFs is no longer statistical but computational. As shown in [6], TSPHFs can be used to construct two-round zero-knowledge protocols and the most efficient one-round PAKE in the standard model.

TSPHF is a direct application of disjunctions of SPHFs: as for NIZK, the language we are interested in is $\mathcal{L}_1$, while $\mathcal{L}_2$ is a hard subset membership language. The common reference string contains a word $C_2 \in \mathcal{L}_2$, and the trapdoor is just a witness w_2 for this word. The hash value of some $C_1 \in \mathcal{X}_1$, is the hash value of (C_1, C_2) for the disjunction of $\mathcal{L}_1$ and $\mathcal{L}_2$, which can be computed in two or three ways: using hk, or using hp and w_1 (classical projection hashing — possible only when $C_1 \in \mathcal{L}_1$ and w_1 is a witness for it), or using hp and w_2 (trapdoor). The smoothness comes from the hard subset membership property of $\mathcal{L}_2$ (which says that this common reference string is indistinguishable from a word $C_2 \notin \mathcal{L}_2$) and the fact that when $C_2 \notin \mathcal{L}_2$, the hash value of (C_1, C_2) appears random by smoothness when $C_1 \notin \mathcal{L}_1$, given only hp.

The resulting TSPHF is slightly less efficient than the construction in [6]: if $\mathcal{L}_2$ corresponds to the DDH language (Example 1), the projection key contains less than twice more elements than the original construction. But it has the advantage of handling more languages, since contrary to the original construction, there is no need to have a trapdoor $\mathcal{T}_{crs}$ for crs which enables us to compute the discrete logarithms of all entries of Γ_1 (a property called witness-samplability in [20])[6].

One-Time Linearly Homomorphic Structure-Preserving Signature. We can obtain the one-time linearly homomorphic structure-preserving signature scheme of messages in $\mathbb{G}_1^{n_1}$ of Libert et al. [25] and extend it to work under any hard-subset membership language assumption, such as the DDH language in Example 1 but also DLin or any MDDH assumption [13] as seen later (instead of just DLin as in the original paper). The construction is very similar to our NIZK construction.

Let $\mathcal{L}_2 = \hat{\mathcal{L}}_2 \subset \mathcal{X}_2 = \hat{\mathcal{X}}_2$ be a hard membership language and $\mathcal{X}_1 = \hat{\mathcal{X}}_1 = \mathbb{G}_1^{n_1}$ (the language $\mathcal{L}_1 = \hat{\mathcal{L}}_1$ will be defined later). The secret key is the hashing key hk $= \alpha$ of the SPHF of the disjunction of $\mathcal{L}_1$ and $\mathcal{L}_2$ (notice that it does not depend on the language $\hat{\mathcal{L}}_1$ but only on $\hat{\mathcal{X}}_1$), while the public key is the associated projection key when $\mathcal{L}_1 = \hat{\mathcal{L}}_1 = \{0\}$. The signature of a message $\boldsymbol{M} \in \hat{\mathcal{X}}_1 = \mathbb{G}_1^{n_1}$ is the vector of the hash values of $(\boldsymbol{M}, \boldsymbol{e}_{2,i_2})$ where $(\boldsymbol{e_{2,i_2}})_{i_2}$

---

[6] However, due to the definition of computational smoothness of TSPHF in [6], it is still required to have such a trapdoor $\mathcal{T}_{crs}$ enabling to check whether a word C_1 is in $\mathcal{L}_1$ or not. It may be possible to change definitions to avoid that, but in all applications we are aware of, this is never a problem.

are the scalar vectors of the canonical base of $\hat{\mathcal{X}}_2$. It can be computed using the secret key hk. Actually, this corresponds to the NIZK proof of M (computed using the trapdoor hk), in our NIZK scheme above. Checking the signature can be done by checking the validity of the proof using the projection key hp when $\hat{\mathcal{L}}_1 = \{0\}$.

Finally, to prove the one-time unforgeability, we just need to remark that knowing signatures of $M_1, \ldots, M_n \in \hat{\mathcal{X}}_1$ actually can be seen as knowing a projection key hp' associated to hk when $\hat{\mathcal{L}}_1$ is the subspace generated by $\Gamma_1 := M_1, \ldots, \Gamma_n := M_n$. Therefore, generating a signature of a message M linearly independent of these messages means generating an NIZK proof for a statement $M \notin \hat{\mathcal{L}}_1$, which has been shown to be hard thanks to the smoothness property of the SPHF and the hard subset membership property of $\mathcal{L}_2$.

One-Round GPAKE. A one-round group password-based authenticated key exchange (GPAKE) is a protocol enabling n users sharing a password pw to establish a common secret key sk in only one round: just by sending one flow. For such protocols, online dictionary attacks, which consist in guessing the password of an honest user and running honestly the protocol with this guessed password, are unavoidable. As a result, the best security that one can hope for is to limit the adversary to at most one password guess per interaction with an honest party. In order to capture this intuition, the formal security model of Abdalla et al. [3], which is recalled in the full version, essentially guarantees that, in a secure GPAKE scheme, no adversary having at most q interactions with honest parties can win with probability higher than q/N, where N is the number of possible passwords. Here, winning means distinguishing a real key (generated by an honest user following the protocol, controlled by the challenger) from a random key sk.

Our construction is a non-trivial extension of the one-round PAKE of Benhamouda et al. in [6], which is an efficient instantiation of the Katz-Vaikuntanathan framework [24]. Basically, a user U_i ($1 \leq i \leq n$) sends an extractable commitment C_i (i.e., an encryption for some public key ek in the common reference string) of his password pw together with a projection key hp_i for the disjunction of $n-1$ languages of valid commitments of pw (words in this disjunction are tuple $C_i = (C_j)_{j \neq i}$ of $n-1$ commitments where at least one of them is a valid commitment of pw). Each partner U_j of this user U_i can compute the hash value H_i of the tuple C_i, with hp_i, just by additionally knowing the witness (the random coins) of his commitment C_j onto pw, while U_i uses hk_i. The resulting secret key K is just the XOR of all these hash values (one per hashing key, i.e., one per user): $\mathsf{sk} = H_1 \,\mathsf{xor}\, \cdots \,\mathsf{xor}\, H_n$.

At a first glance, one may wonder why our construction relies on a disjunction and not on a conjunction: intuitively, as a user, we would like that every other user commits to the same password as ours. Unfortunately, in this case, nobody would be able to compute the hash value of the expected conjunction, except for the user who generated the hashing key. This is because this computation would require the knowledge of all the witnesses and there is no way for a user to know the witness for a commitment of another user. However, by relying on a disjunction, each user is only required to know the witness for his own commitment.

To understand why this is a secure solution, please note that the challenger (in the security game) can make dummy commitments for the honest players he controls. Then, if no corrupted user (controlled by the adversary) commits to a correct password, the tuple of the $n-1$ other commitments would not be a valid word in the disjunction language (no commitment would be valid) for any of the honest users. Hence, the hash value would appear random to the adversary. The complete proof is a very delicate extension of the proof of the one-round PAKE of Katz and Vaikuntanathan in [24], and may be of independent interest.

Due to recent results by Cheon et al. [9], currently no concrete instantiation of our GPAKE is known for $n \geq 4$ (see Footnote 2 on page 72). For $n = 3$, our scheme only relies on bilinear groups and is practical

2.4   Pseudo-Random Projective Hash Functions and More Efficient Applications

Pseudo-Random Projective Hash Functions. As already explained in Section 1.1, for our (one-time simulation-sound) NIZK and our TSPHF, the second language $\mathscr{L}_2$ is used to provide extra features. Security properties come from its hard subset membership property. However, hard subset membership comes at a cost: the dimension k_2 of $\mathscr{L}_2$ has to be at least 1 to be non-trivial, and so the dimension n_2 of $\hat{\mathcal{X}}_2$ is at least 2, otherwise $\mathscr{L}_2 = \hat{\mathcal{X}}_2$. This makes the projection key of the disjunction of $\mathscr{L}_1$ and $\mathscr{L}_2$ of size $k_1 n_2 + n_1 k_2 \geq 2k_1 + n_1$.

Intuitively, what we would like is to be able to have a language $\mathscr{L}_2$ where $n_2 = k_2 = 1$. Such a language would clearly not be hard subset membership, and the smoothness property of SPHF would be completely trivial, since $\hat{\mathcal{X}}_2 \setminus \mathscr{L}_2$ would be empty. That is why we introduce the notion of pseudo-randomness which says that the hash value of a word C_2 chosen at random in $\mathcal{X}_2$ (and for implicit languages parameters crs_2 chosen at random), the hash value of C_2 looks random, given only the projection key.

Under DDH in $\mathbb{G}_2$, we can simply choose $\mathsf{crs}_2 = g_2$ a random generator in $\mathbb{G}_2$, $\mathcal{X}_2 = \hat{\mathcal{X}}_2 = \mathscr{L}_2 = \hat{\mathscr{L}}_2 = \mathbb{G}_2$, and θ_2 the identity function. The witness for a word $C_2 \in \mathbb{G}_2$ is just its discrete logarithm in base g_2, and so $\mathscr{L}_2$ is seen as generated by the vector $\boldsymbol{\Gamma}_1^{(2)} = (g_2)$. An hashing key hk is just a random scalar $\alpha \in \mathbb{Z}_p$, the associated projection key is $\mathsf{hp} = g_2^\alpha$. Finally the hash value is $H = C_2^\alpha$. It can also be computed using hp if we know the discrete logarithm of C_2. The DDH assumption says that if $g_2, \mathsf{hp} = g_2^\alpha, C_2$ are chosen uniformly at random in $\mathbb{G}_2$, it is hard to distinguish $H = C_2^\alpha$ from a random group element $H \in \mathbb{G}_2$; hence the pseudo-randomness.

Mixed Pseudo-Randomness. In all our applications, we are not really interested in the SPHF on $\mathscr{L}_2$ but in the SPHF on the disjunction $\mathscr{L}$ of $\mathscr{L}_1$ and $\mathscr{L}_2$. Of course, this SPHF would be smooth, but that property is again trivial, since all words (C_1, C_2) are in $\mathscr{L}$. We therefore again need a stronger property called *mixed pseudo-randomness* which roughly says that if hk is a random hashing key, if $C_1 \notin \mathscr{L}_1$ and if C_2 is chosen at random, the hash value of $(C_1, C_2) \in \mathscr{L}$ appears random to any polynomial-time adversary, even given access to the projection key hp.

The proof of this property is quite technical and requires that it is possible to generate parameters of $\mathscr{L}_1$ so that we know the discrete logarithm of the generators $(\Gamma_{i_1}^{(1)})_{i_1}$ of $\hat{\mathscr{L}}_1$. This last property is verified by most languages in which we are interested.

Applications. Using the mixed pseudo-randomness property, we easily get more efficient NIZK and TSPHF, just by replacing $\mathscr{L}_2$ by a language $\mathscr{L}_2$ with a pseudo-random Projective Hash Function. Getting a more efficient one-time simulation-sound NIZK is slightly more complex and is only detailed in the core of the paper. The resulting TSPHF construction actually corresponds to the original construction in [6]. But seeing it as a disjunction of an SPHF for the language we are interested in and of a pseudo-random projective hash function sheds new light on the construction and make it easier to understand, in our opinion.

3 Preliminaries

3.1 Notation

As usual, all the players and the algorithms will be possibly probabilistic and stateful. Namely, adversaries can keep a state , during the different phases, and we denote by $\xleftarrow{\$}$ the outcome of a probabilistic algorithm or the sampling from a uniform distribution. The statement $y \xleftarrow{\$} \mathcal{A}(x; r)$ denotes the operation of running $\mathcal{A}$ with input x and random tape r and storing the result in y. For the sake of clarity, we will sometimes omit the random tape r in $\mathcal{A}(x; r)$.

The qualities of adversaries will be measured by their successes and advantages in certain experiments $\mathsf{Exp}^{\mathsf{sec}}$ or $\mathsf{Exp}^{\mathsf{sec}-b}$ (between the cases $b = 0$ and $b = 1$), denoted $\mathsf{Succ}^{\mathsf{sec}}(\mathcal{A}, \mathfrak{K})$ and $\mathsf{Adv}^{\mathsf{sec}}(\mathcal{A}, \mathfrak{K})$ respectively, where $\mathfrak{K}$ is the security parameter. Formal definition of all of this and of statistical distance can be found in the full version.

3.2 Definition of SPHF

Let $(\mathscr{L}_{\mathsf{crs}})_{\mathsf{crs}}$ be a family of NP languages indexed by crs with witness relation $\mathcal{R}_{\mathsf{crs}}$, namely $\mathscr{L}_{\mathsf{crs}} = \{x \in \mathcal{X}_{\mathsf{crs}} \mid \exists w, \ \mathcal{R}_{\mathsf{crs}}(x, w) = 1\}$, where $(\mathcal{X}_{\mathsf{crs}})_{\mathsf{crs}}$ is a family set. The value crs is generated by a polynomial-time algorithm $\mathsf{Setup}_{\mathsf{crs}}$ taking as input the unary representation of the security parameter $\mathfrak{K}$, and is usually a common reference string. The description of the underlying group or graded ring is implicit and not part of crs. We suppose that membership in $\mathcal{X}_{\mathsf{crs}}$ and $\mathcal{R}_{\mathsf{crs}}$ can be checked in polynomial time (in $\mathfrak{K}$).

Finally, we suppose that $\mathsf{Setup}_{\mathsf{crs}}$ also outputs a trapdoor $\mathcal{T}_{\mathsf{crs}}$ associated to crs. This trapdoor is empty $\perp$ in most cases, but for some applications (namely NIZK constructions from Section 7), we require that $\mathcal{T}_{\mathsf{crs}}$ contains enough information to decide whether a word $C \in \mathcal{X}$ is in $\mathscr{L}$ or not (or slightly more information).

We notice that for most, if not all, languages (we are interested in), it is easy to make $\mathsf{Setup_{crs}}$ output such a trapdoor, without changing the distribution of crs. In the sequel, crs is often dropped to simplify notation.

An SPHF over $(\mathscr{L}_{\mathsf{crs}})$ is defined by four polynomial-time algorithms:

- $\mathsf{HashKG(crs)}$ generates a hashing key hk;
- $\mathsf{ProjKG(hk, crs)}$ derives a projection key hp from hk;
- $\mathsf{Hash(hk, crs}, C)$ outputs the hash value from the hashing key, for any crs and for any word $C \in \mathcal{X}$;
- $\mathsf{ProjHash(hp, crs}, C, w)$ outputs the hash value from the projection key hp, and the witness w, for a word $C \in \mathscr{L}_{\mathsf{crs}}$ (i.e., $\mathcal{R}_{\mathsf{crs}}(C, w) = 1$).

The set of hash values is called the *range* and is denoted Π. It is often a cyclic group. We always suppose that its size is super-polynomial in the security parameter $\mathfrak{K}$ so that the probability to guess correctly a uniform hash value is negligible.

An SPHF has to satisfy two properties:

- *Perfect correctness.* For any crs and any word $C \in \mathscr{L}_{\mathsf{crs}}$ with witness w (i.e., such that $\mathcal{R}_{\mathsf{crs}}(C, w) = 1$), for any $\mathsf{hk} \xleftarrow{\$} \mathsf{HashKG(crs)}$ and for $\mathsf{hp} \leftarrow \mathsf{ProjKG(hk, crs)}$, $\mathsf{Hash(hk, crs}, C) = \mathsf{ProjHash(hp, crs}, C, w)$;
- *Perfect smoothness.* The hash value of a word outside the language looks completely random. More precisely, an SPHF is 0-smooth or perfectly smooth if for any crs and any $C \notin \mathscr{L}_{\mathsf{crs}}$, the following two distributions are identical:

$$\left\{ (\mathsf{hp}, H) \mid \mathsf{hk} \xleftarrow{\$} \mathsf{HashKG(crs)}; \mathsf{hp} \leftarrow \mathsf{ProjKG(hk, crs)}; H \leftarrow \mathsf{Hash(hk, crs}, C) \right\}$$

$$\left\{ (\mathsf{hp}, H) \mid \mathsf{hk} \xleftarrow{\$} \mathsf{HashKG(crs)}; \mathsf{hp} \leftarrow \mathsf{ProjKG(hk, crs)}; H \xleftarrow{\$} \Pi \right\}.$$

As shown in the full version, this definition of SPHF actually corresponds to a strong version of KV-SPHF [6] with perfect smoothness[7]. In particular, it is stronger than the definition of SPHF given in [12], where the smoothness is not perfect and is actually defined only for random elements $C \in \mathcal{X} \setminus \mathscr{L}_{\mathsf{crs}}$. This is also slightly stronger than the 1-universal hash proof systems also defined in [12], since the hash value is supposed to look completely random and not just having some minimal entropy.

We restrict ourselves to this very strong form of SPHFs for the sake of simplicity and because most applications we consider require KV-SPHF. However, the construction of disjunctions of SPHFs can still easily be extended to weaker forms of SPHFs.

3.3   Hard Subset Membership Languages

A family of languages $(\mathscr{L}_{\mathsf{crs}} \subseteq \mathcal{X}_{\mathsf{crs}})_{\mathsf{crs}}$ is said to be a hard subset membership family of languages, if it is hard to distinguish between a word randomly drawn

---

[7] The reader familiar with [6] may remark that in our definition, there is no parameter aux in addition to crs. This parameter is indeed useless in the context of KV-SPHFs (contrary to GL-SPHFs), as it can be included in the word C.

from inside $\mathscr{L}_{\mathrm{crs}}$ from a word randomly drawn from outside $\mathscr{L}_{\mathrm{crs}}$ (i.e., from $\mathcal{X}_{\mathrm{crs}} \setminus \mathscr{L}_{\mathrm{crs}}$). This definition implicitly assumes the existence of a distribution over $\mathcal{X}_{\mathrm{crs}}$ and a way to sample efficiently words from $\mathscr{L}_{\mathrm{crs}}$ and from $\mathcal{X}_{\mathrm{crs}} \setminus \mathscr{L}_{\mathrm{crs}}$. This property is formally defined in the full version.

3.4   Bilinear Groups, Graded Rings and Assumptions

All our concrete constructions are based on bilinear groups, which are extensions of cyclic groups. Even though groups should be generated by an appropriate setup algorithm taking the security parameter as input, our definitions below use fixed groups for simplicity.

Cyclic Groups and Bilinear Groups. $(p, \mathbb{G}, g)$ denotes a (multiplicative) cyclic group $\mathbb{G}$ of order p and of generator g. When $(p, \mathbb{G}_1, g_1)$, $(p, \mathbb{G}_2, g_2)$, and $(p, \mathbb{G}_T, g_T)$ are three cyclic groups, $(p, \mathbb{G}_1, \mathbb{G}_2, \mathbb{G}_T, e, g_1, g_2)$ or $(p, \mathbb{G}_1, \mathbb{G}_2, \mathbb{G}_T, e)$ is called a *bilinear group* if $e : \mathbb{G}_1 \times \mathbb{G}_2 \to \mathbb{G}_T$ is a bilinear map (called a *pairing*) efficiently computable and such that $e(g_1, g_2) = g_T$ is a generator of $\mathbb{G}_T$. It is called a *symmetric* bilinear group if $\mathbb{G}_1 = \mathbb{G}_2 = \mathbb{G}$. In this case, we denote it $(p, \mathbb{G}, \mathbb{G}_T, e)$ and we suppose $g = g_1 = g_2$. Otherwise, if $\mathbb{G}_1 \neq \mathbb{G}_2$, it is called an *asymmetric* bilinear group.

Graded Rings. To understand the constructions in the article, it is sufficient to see a graded ring as a way to use ring operations $(+, \bullet)$ over cyclic groups, bilinear groups, or even multilinear groups, as explained at the beginning of Section 2.1. In the sequel, we will often consider two multiplicatively compatible sub-graded rings $\mathfrak{G}_1$ and $\mathfrak{G}_2$ of some graded ring $\mathfrak{G}$: this basically means that it is possible to compute the product $\bullet$ of any element of $\mathfrak{G}_1$ with any element of $\mathfrak{G}_2$, and the result is in $\mathfrak{G}$. Concretely, as a first approach, it is possible to consider that $\mathfrak{G}$ is a bilinear group $(p, \mathbb{G}_1, \mathbb{G}_2, \mathbb{G}_T, e)$, and that $\mathfrak{G}_1$ and $\mathfrak{G}_2$ corresponds to $\mathbb{G}_1$ and $\mathbb{G}_2$: if $u_1 \in \mathbb{G}_1$ and $u_2 \in \mathbb{G}_2$, $u_1 \bullet u_2 = e(u_1, u_2)$. General and formal definitions are given in the full version.

Assumptions. The assumption we use the most is the SXDH assumption The SXDH assumption over a bilinear group $(p, \mathbb{G}_1, \mathbb{G}_2, \mathbb{G}_T, e, g_1, g_2)$ says the DDH assumption holds both in $(p, \mathbb{G}_1, g_1)$ and $(p, \mathbb{G}_2, g_2)$, where the DDH assumption is defined as follows:

Definition 5 (Decisional Diffie-Hellman (DDH)). *The Decisional Diffie-Hellman assumption says that, in a cyclic group $(p, \mathbb{G}, g)$, when we are given (g^a, g^b, g^c) for unknown random $a, b \xleftarrow{\$} \mathbb{Z}_p$, it is hard to decide whether $c = ab \bmod p$ (a DH tuple) or $c \xleftarrow{\$} \mathbb{Z}_p$ (a random tuple).*

We also propose constructions under weaker assumptions than SXDH or DDH, namely κ-Lin, defined as follows:

Definition 6 (κ-Lin). *The κ-Linear assumption says that, in a cyclic group $(p, \mathbb{G}, g)$, when we are given $(g^{a_1}, \dots, g^{a_\kappa}, g^{a_1 b_1}, \dots, g^{a_\kappa b_\kappa}, g^c)$ for unknown $a_1, \dots, a_\kappa, b_1, \dots, b_\kappa \xleftarrow{\$} \mathbb{Z}_p$, it is hard to decide whether $c = b_1 + \cdots + b_\kappa$ (a κ-Lin tuple) or $c \xleftarrow{\$} \mathbb{Z}_p$ (a random tuple).*

The 1-Lin assumption is exactly DDH. One advantage of κ-Lin with $\kappa \geq 2$ is that it can hold even in symmetric bilinear groups (where $\mathbb{G}_1 = \mathbb{G}_2$) while DDH or SXDH do not. 2-Lin is also denoted DLin, and κ-Lin often means κ-Lin in $\mathbb{G}_1$ and in $\mathbb{G}_2$. Actually, our constructions can easily be tweaked to support any MDDH assumption [13]. MDDH assumptions generalize κ-Lin assumptions.

4   Smooth Projective Hash Functions for Disjunctions

4.1   Generic Framework and Diverse Vector Spaces

Let us now recall the generic framework for SPHFs. We have already seen the main ideas of this framework in Section 2.1. These ideas were stated in term of generic vector space. Even though using generic vector spaces facilitates the explanation of high level ideas, it is better to use an explicit basis when it comes to details. As already explained in Section 2.1 on page 75, compared to [6], all vectors and matrices are transposed.

Let $\mathfrak{G}$ be a graded ring. We now set $\hat{\mathcal{X}} = \mathfrak{G}^n$, so that any vector $\hat{C} \in \hat{\mathcal{X}}$ is a n-dimensional *column* vector. We denote by $(e_i)_{i=1}^n$ the canonical basis of $\hat{\mathcal{X}}$. The dual space of $\hat{\mathcal{X}}$ is isomorphic[8] to $\mathbb{Z}_p^{1 \times n}$, and the hashing key $\alpha \in \hat{\mathcal{X}}^*$ corresponds to the *row* vector $\alpha = (\alpha_i)_{i=1}^n$, with $\alpha_i = \alpha(e_i)$. We denote by Γ the matrix with columns $(\Gamma_i)_{i=1}^k$, where the family (Γ_i) generates the subspace $\hat{\mathscr{L}}$ of $\hat{\mathcal{X}}$. Finally, we assume that for each coordinate of the vector $\theta(C) \in \mathfrak{G}^n$, the group in which it is (called the index of the coordinate, in the formal description of graded rings in the full version) is independent of C.

We suppose that, a word $C \in \mathcal{X}$ is in $\mathscr{L}$ if and only if there exists $\lambda \in \mathfrak{G}^k$ such that $\hat{C} := \theta(C) = \Gamma \bullet \lambda$. We also assume the latter equality holds if and only if it would hold by only looking at the discrete logarithms (and not at the groups or indexes of entries or coordinates)[9]. In addition, we suppose that λ can be computed easily from any witness w for C; and in the sequel we often simply consider that $w = \lambda$. By analogy with diverse groups [12], as explained in Section 2.1, we say that a tuple $V = (\mathcal{X}, \mathscr{L}, \mathcal{R}, \mathfrak{G}, n, k, \Gamma, \theta)$ satisfying the above properties is a *diverse vector space*.

A summary of diverse vector spaces and the construction of SPHF over them can be found in Fig. 1. It is straightforward to see (and this is proven in [6]) that any SPHF defined by a discrete vector space V as in Fig. 1 is correct and smooth.

4.2   Disjunctions of SPHFs

As explained in Section 2.1, an SPHF for the disjunction of two languages $\mathscr{L}_1$ and $\mathscr{L}_2$ roughly consists in doing the tensor product of their related vector spaces $\hat{\mathcal{X}}_1$ and $\hat{\mathcal{X}}_2$. However, our vector spaces are not classical vector spaces, since they are

---

[8] Here we consider $\hat{\mathcal{X}}$ as $\mathbb{Z}_p^n$, for the sake of simplicity.
[9] Formal requirements can be found in the full version.

Diverse Vector Space $\mathcal{V}$ = tuple $(\mathcal{X}, \mathcal{L}, \mathcal{R}, \mathfrak{G}, n, k, \Gamma, \theta)$ where

- n, k are two positive integers;
- $\mathcal{L} \subset \mathcal{X}$ is an NP-language, defined by a witness relation $\mathcal{R}$ (and implicitly indexed by crs):

$$\mathcal{L}_{\mathsf{crs}} = \{x \in \mathcal{X}_{\mathsf{crs}} \mid \exists \lambda \in \mathfrak{G}^k, \ \mathcal{R}_{\mathsf{crs}}(x, \lambda) = 1\}$$

- $\mathfrak{G}$ is a graded ring;
- θ is a function from $\mathcal{L}$ to $\mathfrak{G}^n$; *notation:* $\hat{C} := \theta(C)$;
- Γ is a matrix in $\mathfrak{G}^{n \times k}$;

such that for $C \in \mathcal{X}$ and $\lambda \in \mathfrak{G}^k$:

$$\mathcal{R}(x, \lambda) = 1 \quad \Longleftrightarrow \quad \hat{C} := \theta(C) = \Gamma \bullet \lambda,$$

plus some additional technical assumptions on groups or indexes of coefficients of $\theta(C)$ and Γ (see text).
Notation: $\hat{\mathcal{L}}$ is the vector space generated by the columns of Γ;

SPHF for $\mathcal{V} = (\mathcal{X}, \mathcal{L}, \mathcal{R}, \mathfrak{G}, n, k, \Gamma, \theta)$:

HashKG(crs)	outputs a random row vector $\mathsf{hk} := \alpha \xleftarrow{\$} \mathbb{Z}_p^{1 \times n}$
ProjKG(hk, crs)	outputs $\mathsf{hp} := \gamma = \alpha \bullet \Gamma \in \mathfrak{G}^{1 \times k}$
Hash(hk, crs, C)	outputs $H := \alpha \bullet \hat{C} \in \mathfrak{G}$
ProjHash(hp, crs, C, λ)	outputs $H' := \gamma \bullet \lambda \in \mathfrak{G}$

Fig. 1. Diverse Vector Space and Smooth Projective Hash Function (SPHF)

over graded rings. In particular, multiplication of scalars is not always possible, and so tensor product may not be always possible either. That is why we first need to introduce the notion of tensor product of vector spaces over graded rings, before giving the detailed construction of disjunctions of SPHFs.

Tensor Product of Vector Spaces over Graded Rings. Let us very briefly recall notations for tensor product and adapt them to vector spaces over graded rings. Let $\mathfrak{G}_1$ and $\mathfrak{G}_2$ be two multiplicatively compatible sub-graded rings of $\mathfrak{G}$. Let V_1 be a n_1-dimensional vector space over $\mathfrak{G}_1$ and V_2 be a n_2-dimensional vector space over $\mathfrak{G}_2$. Let $(e_{1,i})_{i=1}^{n_1}$ and $(e_{2,i})_{i=1}^{n_2}$ be bases of V_1 and V_2 respectively. Then the *tensor product* V of V_1 and V_2, denoted $V = V_1 \otimes V_2$ is the $n_1 n_2$-dimensional vector space over $\mathfrak{G}$ generated by the free family $(e_{1,i} \otimes e_{2,j})_{\substack{i=1,\dots,n_1 \\ j=1,\dots,n_2}}$. The operator $\otimes$ is bilinear, and if $u = \sum_{i=1}^{n_1} u_i \bullet e_{1,i}$ and $v = \sum_{j=1}^{n_2} v_j \bullet e_{2,j}$, then:

$$u \otimes v = \sum_{i=1}^{n_1} \sum_{j=1}^{n_2} (u_i \bullet v_j) \bullet (e_{1,i} \otimes e_{2,j}).$$

More generally, we can define the tensor product of two matrices $M \in \mathfrak{G}_1^{k \times m}$ and $M' \in \mathfrak{G}_2^{k' \times m'}$, $T = M \otimes M' \in \mathfrak{G}^{kk' \times mm'}$ by

$$T_{(i-1)k'+i',(j-1)m'+j'} = M_{i,j} \bullet M'_{i',j'} \qquad \text{for} \quad \begin{cases} i = 1, \ldots, k, \ i' = 1, \ldots, k', \\ j = 1, \ldots, m, \ j' = 1, \ldots, m'. \end{cases}$$

And if $M \in \mathfrak{G}_1^{k \times m}$, $M' \in \mathfrak{G}_2^{k' \times m'}$, $N \in \mathfrak{G}_1^{m \times n}$ and $N' \in \mathfrak{G}_2^{m' \times n'}$, and if $M \bullet N$ and $M' \bullet N'$ are well-defined (i.e., index of coefficients are "coherent"), then we have

$$(M \otimes M') \bullet (N \otimes N') = (M \bullet N) \otimes (M' \bullet N').$$

Finally, this definition can be extended to more than 2 vector spaces.

Disjunctions of SPHFs. In Fig. 2, we show the construction of the disjunction of two diverse vector spaces, over two multiplicatively sub-graded rings $\mathfrak{G}_1$ and $\mathfrak{G}_2$ of some graded ring $\mathfrak{G}$. In applications, we will often have $\mathfrak{G}_1 = \mathbb{G}_1$ and $\mathfrak{G}_2 = \mathbb{G}_2$ where $(p, \mathbb{G}_1, \mathbb{G}_2, \mathbb{G}_T, e, g_1, g_2)$ is a bilinear group.

Diverse vector space $\mathcal{V} = (\mathcal{X}, \mathcal{L}, \mathcal{R}, \mathfrak{G}, n, k, \Gamma, \theta)$ **disjunction** of diverse vector spaces $\mathcal{V}_1 = (\mathcal{X}_1, \mathcal{L}_1, \mathcal{R}_1, \mathfrak{G}_1, n_1, k_1, \Gamma_1, \theta_1)$ and $\mathcal{V}_2 = (\mathcal{X}_2, \mathcal{L}_2, \mathcal{R}_2, \mathfrak{G}_2, n_2, k_2, \Gamma_2, \theta_2)$:

- $\mathfrak{G}_1$ and $\mathfrak{G}_2$ are two multiplicatively compatible sub-graded rings of $\mathfrak{G}$;
- $n = n_1 n_2$ $k = k_1 n_2 + n_1 k_2$;
- $\mathcal{X} = \mathcal{X}_1 \times \mathcal{X}_2$ $\mathcal{L} = (\mathcal{L}_1 \times \mathcal{X}_2) \cup (\mathcal{X}_1 \times \mathcal{L}_2)$
- $\Gamma = \begin{pmatrix} \Gamma^{(1)} \otimes \mathsf{Id}_{n_2} & \mathsf{Id}_{n_1} \otimes \Gamma^{(2)} \end{pmatrix}$ $\theta((C_1, C_2)) = \hat{C}1 \otimes \hat{C}2$;
- Witnesses λ for $C = (C_1, C_2) \in \mathcal{L}$ (i.e., vectors $\lambda \in \mathfrak{G}^k$ such that $\mathcal{R}(C, \lambda) = 1$) are:

$$\lambda = \begin{cases} \begin{pmatrix} \lambda_1 \otimes \hat{C}_2 \\ 0 \in \mathbb{Z}_p^{n_1 k_2} \end{pmatrix} & \text{when } \mathcal{R}_1(C_1, \lambda_1) = 1 \\[2mm] \begin{pmatrix} 0 \in \mathbb{Z}_p^{k_1 n_2} \\ \hat{C}_1 \otimes \lambda_2 \end{pmatrix} & \text{when } \mathcal{R}_2(C_2, \lambda_2) = 1 \end{cases}$$

for any $C = (C_1, C_2) \in \mathcal{X}$ and any $\lambda \in \mathfrak{G}^n$.

Notation: Due to the form of witnesses, we split γ in two parts: $\gamma^{(1)}$ corresponds to the first $k_1 n_2$ columns of γ, while $\gamma^{(2)}$ corresponds to the last $k_2 n_1$ columns of γ.

Fig. 2. Disjunction of Diverse Vector Spaces

Let us explain this construction. First, the rows of Γ generate the following subspace of $\hat{\mathcal{X}} = \mathfrak{G}^{1 \times n} = \hat{\mathcal{X}}_1 \otimes \hat{\mathcal{X}}_2$:

$$\hat{\mathcal{L}} = \langle (\hat{\mathcal{L}}_1 \otimes \hat{\mathcal{X}}_2) \cup (\hat{\mathcal{X}}_1 \otimes \hat{\mathcal{L}}_2) \rangle,$$

where $\hat{\mathcal{X}}_1 = \mathfrak{G}_1^{n_1}$, $\hat{\mathcal{X}}_2 = \mathfrak{G}_2^{n_2}$, $\hat{\mathcal{L}}_1$ is the subspace of $\hat{\mathcal{X}}_1$ generated by the rows of $\Gamma^{(1)}$ and $\hat{\mathcal{L}}_2$ is the subspace of $\hat{\mathcal{X}}_2$ generated by the rows of $\Gamma^{(2)}$. So this construction corresponds exactly to the one sketched in the Section 2.1.

Then, we need to prove that $\mathcal{V}$ is really a diverse vector space, namely that $C \in \mathcal{L}$ if and only if $\theta(C) \in \hat{\mathcal{L}}$. Clearly, if $C = (C_1, C_2) \in \mathcal{L}$, then $\hat{C}_1 \in \hat{\mathcal{L}}_1$ or $\hat{C}_2 \in \hat{\mathcal{L}}_2$ and so $\hat{C} = \hat{C}_1 \otimes \hat{C}_2 \in \hat{\mathcal{L}}$. Now, let us prove the converse. Let $C = (C_1, C_2) \notin \mathcal{L}$. So, $\hat{C}_1 \notin \hat{\mathcal{L}}_1$ and $\hat{C}_2 \notin \hat{\mathcal{L}}_2$. Let H_1 and H_2 be supplementary vector spaces of $\hat{\mathcal{L}}_1$ and $\hat{\mathcal{L}}_2$ (in $\hat{\mathcal{X}}_1$ and $\hat{\mathcal{X}}_2$, respectively). Then $\hat{\mathcal{X}}_1$ is the direct sum of $\hat{\mathcal{L}}_1$ and H_1, while $\hat{\mathcal{X}}_2$ is the direct sum of $\hat{\mathcal{L}}_2$ and H_2. Therefore, $\hat{\mathcal{L}}_1 \otimes \hat{\mathcal{X}}_2$ is the direct sum of $\hat{\mathcal{L}}_1 \otimes \hat{\mathcal{L}}_2$ and $\hat{\mathcal{L}}_1 \otimes H_2$, while $\hat{\mathcal{X}}_1 \otimes \hat{\mathcal{L}}_2$ is the direct sum of $\hat{\mathcal{L}}_1 \otimes \hat{\mathcal{L}}_2$ and $H_1 \otimes \hat{\mathcal{L}}_2$. So finally, $\hat{\mathcal{L}}$ is the direct sum of $\hat{\mathcal{L}}_1 \otimes \hat{\mathcal{L}}_2$, $\hat{\mathcal{L}}_1 \otimes H_2$ and $H_1 \otimes \hat{\mathcal{L}}_2$; and $H_1 \otimes H_2$ is a supplementary of $\hat{\mathcal{L}}$. Since $0 \neq \hat{C}_1 \otimes \hat{C}_2 \in H_1 \otimes H_2$, $\theta(C) = \hat{C}_1 \otimes \hat{C}_2 \notin \hat{\mathcal{L}}$.

Besides showing the correctness of the construction, this proof helps to better understand the structure of $\hat{\mathcal{L}}$. In particular, it shows that $\hat{\mathcal{L}}$ has dimension $l_1 l_2 + (n_1 - l_1) l_2 + l_1 (n_2 - l_2) = l_1 n_2 + n_1 l_2 - l_1 l_2$, if $\hat{\mathcal{L}}_1$ has dimension l_1 and $\hat{\mathcal{L}}_2$ has dimension l_2. If the rows of $\Gamma^{(1)}$ and $\Gamma^{(2)}$ are linearly independent, $l_1 = k_1$ and $l_2 = k_2$, $\hat{\mathcal{L}}$ has dimension $k_1 n_2 + n_1 k_2 - k_1 k_2$, which is less than $k_1 n_2 + n_1 k_2$, the number of rows of Γ. Therefore the rows of Γ are never linearly independent. Actually, this last result can directly be proven by remarking that if $\hat{C}_1 \in \hat{\mathcal{L}}_1$ and $\hat{C}_2 \in \hat{\mathcal{L}}_2$, then $\hat{C}_1 \otimes \hat{C}_2 \in (\hat{\mathcal{L}}_1 \otimes \hat{\mathcal{X}}_2) \cap (\hat{\mathcal{X}}_1 \otimes \hat{\mathcal{L}}_2)$. For the sake of completeness, detailed and concrete equations are detailed in the full version.

5   One-Time Simulation-Sound NIZK from Disjunctions of SPHFs

In this section, we present our construction of NIZK and one-time simulation-sound NIZK from disjunctions of SPHFs. The latter requires the use of a new notion: 2-smooth projective hash functions. We suppose the reader is familiar with NIZK and one-time simulation-sound NIZK. Formal definitions can be found in the full version.

5.1   NIZK from Disjunctions of SPHFs

Construction. In Fig. 3, we show how to construct a NIZK for any family of languages $\mathcal{L}_1$ such that there exist two diverse vector spaces $\mathcal{V}_1 = (\mathcal{X}_1, \mathcal{L}_1, \mathcal{R}_1, \mathfrak{G}_1, n_1, k_1, \Gamma^{(1)}, \theta_1)$ and $\mathcal{V}_2 = (\mathcal{X}_2, \mathcal{L}_2, \mathcal{R}_2, \mathfrak{G}_2, n_2, k_2, \Gamma^{(2)}, \theta_2)$ over two multiplicatively-compatible sub-graded rings $\mathfrak{G}_1$ and $\mathfrak{G}_2$ of some graded ring $\mathfrak{G}$, such that the second diverse vector space corresponds to a hard subset membership language. In particular, this construction works for any diverse vector space $\mathcal{V}_1$ where $\mathfrak{G}_1 = \mathbb{G}_1$ is a cyclic group of some bilinear group $(p, \mathbb{G}_1, \mathbb{G}_2, \mathbb{G}_T, e)$, where SXDH holds, by using as $\mathcal{V}_2$ the discrete vector space for DDH over $\mathbb{G}_2$ (Example 1).

NIZK for $\mathcal{V}_1 = (\mathcal{X}_1, \mathscr{L}_1, \mathcal{R}_1, \mathfrak{G}_1, n_1, k_1, \Gamma_1, \theta_1)$, using $\mathcal{V}_2 = (\mathcal{X}_2, \mathscr{L}_2, \mathcal{R}_2, \mathfrak{G}_2, n_2, k_2, \Gamma_2, \theta_2)$, with $\mathscr{L}_2$ a hard subset membership language:

- $\mathcal{V} = (\mathcal{X}, \mathscr{L}, \mathcal{R}, \mathfrak{G}, n, k)$ disjunction of $\mathcal{V}_1$ and $\mathcal{V}_2$;
- Setup: computes $\mathsf{hk} = \alpha \xleftarrow{\$} \mathbb{Z}_p^{1 \times n}$, $\mathsf{hp} = \gamma = \Gamma \bullet \alpha$, and outputs trapdoor $\mathcal{T} := \mathsf{hk}$, and CRS $\sigma := (\mathsf{crs}_2, \mathsf{hp})$;
- Proof π of $C_1 \in \mathscr{L}_1$ with witness $\boldsymbol{\lambda_1} \in \mathfrak{G}^{k_1}$:

$$\pi := \gamma^{(1)} \bullet (\boldsymbol{\lambda_1} \otimes \mathsf{Id}_{n_2}) \in \mathfrak{G}_1^{1 \times n_2};$$

- Verification of proof π for C_1:

$$\pi \bullet \Gamma^{(2)} \overset{?}{=} \gamma^{(2)} \bullet (\hat{C}_1 \otimes \mathsf{Id}_{k_2}), \qquad (1)$$

- Simulation of proof π for C_1 knowing $\mathcal{T} = \mathsf{hk}$:

$$\pi := \alpha \bullet (\hat{C}_1 \otimes \mathsf{Id}_{n_2}).$$

Fig. 3. NIZK from Disjunctions of Diverse Spaces

The proof π of a word C_1 can just be seen as the hash values of rows[10] of $\hat{C}_1 \otimes \mathsf{Id}_{n_2}$. Let us now show that our NIZK is complete, zero-knowledge and sound.

Completeness. If the proof π has been generated correctly, the left hand side of the verification equation (Eq. (1)) is equal to

$$\gamma^{(1)} \bullet (\boldsymbol{\lambda_1} \otimes \mathsf{Id}_{n_2}) \bullet \Gamma^{(2)} = (\alpha \bullet (\Gamma^{(1)} \otimes \mathsf{Id}_{n_2})) \bullet (\boldsymbol{\lambda_1} \otimes \mathsf{Id}_{n_2}) \bullet (\mathsf{Id}_1 \otimes \Gamma^{(2)})$$
$$= \alpha \bullet (\Gamma^{(1)} \otimes \mathsf{Id}_{n_2}) \bullet ((\boldsymbol{\lambda_1} \bullet \mathsf{Id}_1) \otimes (\mathsf{Id}_{n_2} \bullet \Gamma^{(2)}))$$
$$= \alpha \bullet (\Gamma^{(1)} \otimes \mathsf{Id}_{n_2}) \bullet (\boldsymbol{\lambda_1} \otimes \Gamma^{(2)})$$
$$= \alpha \bullet ((\Gamma^{(1)} \bullet \boldsymbol{\lambda_1}) \otimes (\mathsf{Id}_{n_2} \bullet \Gamma^{(2)})),$$

while the right hand side is always equal to:

$$\gamma^{(2)} \bullet (\hat{C}_1 \otimes \mathsf{Id}_{k_2}) = \alpha \bullet (\mathsf{Id}_{n_1} \otimes \Gamma^{(2)}) \bullet (\hat{C}_1 \otimes \mathsf{Id}_{k_2}) = \alpha \bullet ((\mathsf{Id}_{n_1} \bullet \hat{C}_1) \otimes (\Gamma^{(2)} \bullet \mathsf{Id}_{k_2})),$$

which is the same as the left hand side, since $\Gamma^{(1)} \bullet \boldsymbol{\lambda_1} = \mathsf{Id}_{n_1} \bullet \hat{C}_1$ and $\mathsf{Id}_{n_2} \bullet \Gamma^{(2)} = \Gamma^{(2)} \bullet \mathsf{Id}_{k_2}$. Hence the *completeness*. Another way to see it, is that the row i_2 of the right hand side is the hash value of "$(\hat{C}_1, \Gamma^{(2)} \bullet e_{2,i_2})$" computed using the witness $\boldsymbol{\lambda_2} = e_{2,i_2}$, while the row i_2 of the left hand side is this hash value computed using the witness $\boldsymbol{\lambda_1}$.

Zero-Knowledge. The (perfect) unbounded *zero-knowledge* property comes from the fact that the normal proof π for $C_1 \in \mathscr{L}_1$ with witness $\boldsymbol{\lambda_1}$ is:

$$\gamma^{(1)} \bullet (\boldsymbol{\lambda_1} \otimes \mathsf{Id}_{n_2}) = \alpha \bullet (\Gamma^{(1)} \otimes \mathsf{Id}_{n_2}) \bullet (\boldsymbol{\lambda_1} \otimes \mathsf{Id}_{n_2}) = \alpha \bullet ((\Gamma^{(1)} \bullet \boldsymbol{\lambda_1}) \otimes (\mathsf{Id}_{n_2} \bullet \mathsf{Id}_{n_2})),$$

---

[10] This is not quite accurate, since rows of $\hat{C}_1 \otimes \mathsf{Id}_{n_1}$ are not words in $\mathcal{X}$ but in $\hat{\mathcal{X}}$. But to give intuition, we will often make this abuse of notation.

which is equal to the simulated proof for C_1, as $\hat{C}_1 = \Gamma^{(1)} \bullet \boldsymbol{\lambda_1}$ and $\mathsf{Id}_{n_2} \bullet \mathsf{Id}_{n_2} = \mathsf{Id}_{n_2}$.

Soundness. It remains to prove the soundness property, under the hard subset membership of $\mathscr{L}_2$. We just need to show that if the adversary is able to generate a valid proof π for a word $C_1 \notin \mathscr{L}_1$, then we can use π to check if a word C_2 is in $\mathscr{L}_2$ or not. More precisely, let $C_2 \in \mathcal{X}_2$, let H be the hash value of (C_1, C_2) computed using hk, and let us define $H' := \pi \bullet \hat{C}_2$.

On the one hand, if $C_2 \in \mathscr{L}_2$, there exists a witness $\boldsymbol{\lambda_2}$ such that $\hat{C}_2 = \Gamma^{(2)} \bullet \boldsymbol{\lambda_2}$ and so, thanks to (1):

$$H' = \pi \bullet \Gamma^{(2)} \bullet \boldsymbol{\lambda_2} = \gamma^{(2)} \bullet (\hat{C}_1 \otimes \mathsf{Id}_{k_2}) \bullet \boldsymbol{\lambda_2} = \gamma^{(2)} \bullet (\hat{C}_1 \otimes \boldsymbol{\lambda_2}) = H,$$

the last equality coming from the correctness of the SPHF and the fact the last-but-one expression is just the hash value of (C_1, C_2) computed using ProjHash and witness $\boldsymbol{\lambda_2}$.

On the other hand, if $C_2 \notin \mathscr{L}_2$, then $(C_1, C_2) \notin \mathscr{L}$. So H looks completely random by smoothness and the probability that $H' = H$ is at most $1/|\Pi|$.

Toward One-Time Simulation Soundness. The previous proof does not work anymore if the adversary is allowed to get even one single simulated proof of a word $C_1 \notin \mathscr{L}_1$. Indeed, in this case, the smoothness does not hold anymore, in the above proof of soundness. That is why we need a stronger form of smoothness for SPHF, called 2-smoothness.

5.2 2-Smooth Projective Hash Functions

Definition. In order to define the notion of 2-smoothness, let us first introduce the notion of tag-SPHF. A *tag-SPHF* is similar to an SPHF except that Hash and ProjHash now take a new input, called a tag $\mathsf{tag} \in \mathsf{Tags}$. Similarly a *tag diverse vector space* is a diverse vector space where the function θ also takes as input a tag $\mathsf{tag} \in \mathbb{Z}_p$. The vector $\boldsymbol{\lambda}$ is now allowed to depend on tag, but the matrix Γ is independent of tag.

A 2-smooth SPHF is a tag-SPHF for which the hash value of a word $C \in \mathcal{X}$ for a tag tag looks random even if we have access to the hash value of another word $C' \in \mathcal{X}$ for a different tag $\mathsf{tag}' \neq \mathsf{tag}$. Formally, a tag-SPHF is perfectly 2-smooth, if for any crs, any $C' \in \mathcal{X}$, any distinct tags $\mathsf{tag}, \mathsf{tag}'$, and any $C \notin \mathscr{L}_{\mathsf{crs}}$, the following two distributions are identical:

$$\left\{ (\mathsf{hp}, H', H) \;\middle|\; \begin{array}{ll} \mathsf{hk} \xleftarrow{\$} \mathsf{HashKG}(\mathsf{crs}); & \mathsf{hp} \leftarrow \mathsf{ProjKG}(\mathsf{hk}, \mathsf{crs}); \\ H' \leftarrow \mathsf{Hash}(\mathsf{hk}, \mathsf{crs}, (C', \mathsf{tag}')); & H \leftarrow \mathsf{Hash}(\mathsf{hk}, \mathsf{crs}, (C, \mathsf{tag})) \end{array} \right\}$$

$$\left\{ (\mathsf{hp}, H', H) \;\middle|\; \begin{array}{ll} \mathsf{hk} \xleftarrow{\$} \mathsf{HashKG}(\mathsf{crs}); & \mathsf{hp} \leftarrow \mathsf{ProjKG}(\mathsf{hk}, \mathsf{crs}); \\ H' \leftarrow \mathsf{Hash}(\mathsf{hk}, \mathsf{crs}, (C', \mathsf{tag}')); & H \xleftarrow{\$} \Pi \end{array} \right\}.$$

A weaker (statistical instead of perfect) definition is proposed in the full version. The 2-smoothness property is similar to the 2-universality property in [12].

There are however two minor differences, the first being the existence of an explicit tag, and the second being that the hash value of a word outside the language is supposed to be uniformly random instead of just having some entropy. This slightly simplifies its usage in our constructions, in our opinion.

Canonical Construction from Diverse Vector Spaces. Let $\mathcal{V} = (\mathcal{X}, \mathcal{L}, \mathcal{R}, \mathfrak{G}, n, k, \Gamma, \theta)$ be a diverse vector space. If we set $\tilde{n} = 2n$, $\tilde{k} = 2k$, and:

$$\tilde{\Gamma} = \begin{pmatrix} \Gamma & 0 \\ 0 & \Gamma \end{pmatrix} \qquad \tilde{\lambda} = \begin{pmatrix} \lambda \\ \mathsf{tag} \bullet \lambda \end{pmatrix} \qquad \tilde{\theta}(C, \mathsf{tag}) = \begin{pmatrix} \hat{C} \\ \mathsf{tag} \bullet \hat{C} \end{pmatrix},$$

where $\tilde{\lambda}$ is the witness for a word $C \in \mathcal{L}$ and a tag tag, then $\tilde{\mathcal{V}} = (\mathcal{X}, \mathcal{L}, \mathcal{R}, \mathfrak{G}, \tilde{n}, \tilde{k}, \tilde{\Gamma}, \tilde{\theta})$ is a 2-smooth diverse vector space. It is clear that $C \in \mathcal{L}$ if and only if $\hat{C} = \tilde{\theta}(C, \mathsf{tag})$ is a linear combination of rows of Γ.

To prove the 2-smoothness property, let $C' \in \mathcal{X}$ and $C \in \mathcal{X} \setminus \mathcal{L}$, and let tag' and tag be two distinct tags. We have

$$\tilde{C}' = \begin{pmatrix} \hat{C}' \\ \mathsf{tag}' \bullet \hat{C}' \end{pmatrix} \qquad \text{and} \qquad \tilde{C} = \begin{pmatrix} \hat{C} \\ \mathsf{tag} \bullet \hat{C} \end{pmatrix}.$$

We just need to prove that $\tilde{C}$ is not in the subspace generated by the rows of Γ and $\tilde{C}'$, or in other words that it is not in $\hat{\mathcal{L}}' = \langle \hat{\mathcal{L}} \cup \{\tilde{C}'\} \rangle$. Indeed, in that case, H' could just be seen as a part of the projection key for the language $\mathcal{L}'$, and by smoothness, we get that H looks uniformly random.

So it remains to prove that linear independence of $\tilde{C}$. By contradiction, let us suppose there exists $\tilde{\lambda} \in \mathbb{Z}_p^{2k}$ and μ such that:

$$\tilde{C} = \begin{pmatrix} \hat{C} \\ \mathsf{tag} \bullet \hat{C} \end{pmatrix} = \tilde{\Gamma} \bullet \tilde{\lambda} + \tilde{C}' \bullet \mu = \begin{pmatrix} \Gamma & 0 \\ 0 & \Gamma \end{pmatrix} \bullet \tilde{\lambda} + \begin{pmatrix} \hat{C}' \\ \mathsf{tag}' \bullet \hat{C}' \end{pmatrix} \bullet \mu.$$

Therefore $\hat{C} + \mu \bullet \hat{C}'$ and $\mathsf{tag} \bullet \hat{C} + \mathsf{tag}' \bullet \mu \bullet \hat{C}'$ are both linear combination of rows of Γ, and so is

$$\mathsf{tag}' \bullet (\hat{C} + \mu \bullet \hat{C}') + (\mathsf{tag} \bullet \hat{C} + \mathsf{tag}' \bullet \mu \bullet \hat{C}') = (\mathsf{tag}' - \mathsf{tag}) \bullet \hat{C}.$$

As $\mathsf{tag}' - \mathsf{tag} \neq 0$, this implies that $\hat{C}$ is also a linear combination of rows of Γ, hence $C \in \mathcal{L}$, which is not the case.

5.3 One-Time Simulation-Sound Zero-Knowledge Arguments from SPHF

Let us now replace the first diverse vector space by its canonical 2-smooth version in the NIZK construction of Section 5.1. The resulting construction is a one-time simulation-sound NIZK, if $\hat{C}_1$ is computed as $\theta_1(C_1, \mathsf{tag})$ where tag is the hash value of (C_1, ℓ) under some collision-resistant hash function $\mathcal{H}$: $\mathsf{tag} = \mathcal{H}((C_1, \ell))$.

Completeness and perfect zero-knowledge can be proven the same way. It remains to prove the one-time simulation soundness. The proof is similar to the one in Section 5.1, except for the final step: proving that the hash value H of (C_1, C_2) with tag $\mathsf{tag} = \mathcal{H}((C_1, \ell))$ looks random even if the adversary sees a simulated NIZK π' for a word $C_1' \in \mathcal{X}_1$ and label ℓ'.

We first remark that the tag tag' can be supposed distinct from the tag tag for the NIZK π created by the adversary, thanks to the collision-resistance of $\mathcal{H}$. We recall that π' is the hash values of the rows of $\hat{C}_1' \otimes \mathsf{Id}_{n_2}$. So to prove that the hash value of (C_1, C_2) with tag tag looks random even with access to π', we just need to remark that $\hat{C}_1 \otimes \hat{C}_2$ is linearly independent of rows of Γ and $\hat{C}_1' \otimes \mathsf{Id}_{n_2}$. The proof is similar to the proof of 2-smoothness.

Remark 7. *It would be easy to extend this construction to handle N-time simulation-sound NIZK, for any constant N. The NIZK CRS σ size would just be N times larger compared to the NIZK construction of Section 5.1, and the proof size would remain constant.*

5.4   Concrete Instantiation

If $\mathcal{V}_1$ is a diverse vector space over $\mathbb{G}_1$ and $\mathcal{V}_2$ is the diverse vector space for DDH in $\mathbb{G}_2$, where $(p, \mathbb{G}_1, \mathbb{G}_2, \mathbb{G}_T, e, g_1, g_2)$ is a bilinear group where DDH is hard in $\mathbb{G}_2$, then we get a NIZK and a one-time simulation sound NIZK whose proof is composed of only $n_2 = 2$ group elements in $\mathbb{G}_1$.

More generally, we can use as $\mathcal{V}_2$, any diverse vector space from any MDDH assumption [13]. Under κ-Lin, we get a proof consisting of only $n_2 = \kappa + 1$ group elements. Details can be found in the full version.

Languages handled are exactly languages for which there exists such a diverse vector space $\mathcal{V}_1$ over $\mathbb{G}_1$. That corresponds to languages handled by Jutla and Roy NIZK [20], which they call linear subspaces (assuming θ is the identity function), if we forget the fact that in [20], it is supposed that crs can be generated in such a way that discrete logarithms of Γ is known (that is what they call *witness-samplable* languages). That encompasses DDH, κ-Lin, and languages of ElGamal, Cramer-Shoup or similar ciphertexts whose plaintexts verify some linear system of equations, as already shown in [6]. Concrete comparison with previous work can be found in Section 7.3.

5.5   Application: Threshold Cramer-Shoup-like Encryption Scheme

The Cramer-Shoup public-key encryption scheme [11] is one of the most efficient IND-CCA encryption schemes with a proof of security in the standard model. We remark here that, if we replace the last part of a Cramer-Shoup ciphertext (the 2-universal projective hash proof) by a one-time simulation-sound NIZK on the DDH language, we can obtain an IND-CCA scheme supporting efficient threshold decryption. Intuitively, this comes from the fact that the resulting scheme becomes "publicly verifiable", in the sense that, after verifying the NIZK (which is publicly verifiable), one can obtain the underlying message via "simple" algebraic operations which can easily be "distributed".

Previous one-time simulation-sound NIZK were quite inefficient and the resulting scheme would have been very inefficient compared to direct constructions of threshold IND-CCA encryption schemes. However, in our case, our new one-time simulation-sound NIZK based on disjunctions of SPHF only adds one group element to the ciphertext (compared to original Cramer-Shoup encryption scheme; see the full version for details). In addition, both the encryption and the decryption algorithms only require to perform operations in the first group $\mathbb{G}_1$. A detailed comparison is given in Section 7.4, where we also introduce a more efficient version of that threshold encryption scheme, for which the ciphertexts have the same size as the ciphertexts of the original Cramer-Shoup encryption scheme.

6 Pseudo-Random Projective Hash Functions and Disjunctions

In this section, we sometimes make explicit use of crs (or crs_1, or crs_2), the language parameters of the diverse vector space $\mathcal{V}$ (respectively of $\mathcal{V}_1$, and $\mathcal{V}_2$), to provide clearer definitions. We recall that we suppose there exists an algorithm Setup$_{crs}$ which can generate crs together with a trapdoor $\mathcal{T}_{crs}$. Contrary to construction in previous sections, where $\mathcal{T}_{crs} = \bot$, the security of the constructions in this section will depend on some properties of $\mathcal{T}_{crs}$.

6.1 Pseudo-Randomness

Definition. An SPHF is said to be *pseudo-random*, if the hash value of a random word C in $\mathscr{L}_{crs}$ looks random to an adversary only knowing the projection key hp and ignoring the hashing key hk and a witness for the word C. More precisely, this property is defined by the experiments $\mathsf{Exp}^{\mathrm{ps-rnd}-b}$ depicted in Fig. 4. Contrary to smoothness, this property is computational. A projective hashing function which is pseudo-random is called a PrPHF. A PrPHF is not necessarily smooth.

Link with Hard Subset Membership Languages. It is easy to see that an SPHF over a hard subset membership family of languages is pseudo-random. This yields a way to create PrPHF under DDH using Example 1. However, this is inefficient since, in this case $\mathcal{X}$ has dimension 2, while we would prefer to have $\mathcal{X}$ of dimension 1. Actually, since for hard subset membership languages, $\mathscr{L}_{crs} \neq \mathcal{X}$, any SPHF based on diverse vector space for these languages is such that $\mathcal{X}$ has dimension at least 2. More generally, as shown in 5.4, for a hard subset membership language based on κ-Lin, $\mathcal{X} = \mathbb{G}^{1 \times (\kappa+1)}$ and $\mathscr{L}_{crs}$ has dimension κ. That is why, we introduce another way to construct PrPHF, still based on diverse vector spaces, but not using hard subset membership languages.

$\mathsf{Exp}^{\mathtt{ps\text{-}rnd\text{-}}b}(\mathcal{A}, \mathfrak{K})$	$\mathsf{Exp}^{\mathtt{mixed\text{-}ps\text{-}rnd\text{-}}b}(\mathcal{A}, \mathfrak{K})$
$(\mathsf{crs}, \mathcal{T}_{\mathsf{crs}}) \xleftarrow{\$} \mathsf{Setup}_{\mathsf{crs}}(1^{\mathfrak{K}})$	$(\mathsf{crs} = (\mathsf{crs}_1, \mathsf{crs}_2), (\mathcal{T}_{\mathsf{crs}_1}, \mathcal{T}_{\mathsf{crs}_2})) \xleftarrow{\$} \mathsf{Setup}_{\mathsf{crs}}(1^{\mathfrak{K}})$
$\mathsf{hk} \xleftarrow{\$} \mathsf{HashKG}(\mathsf{crs})$	$\mathsf{hk} \xleftarrow{\$} \mathsf{HashKG}(\mathsf{crs})$; $\mathsf{hp} \leftarrow \mathsf{ProjKG}(\mathsf{hk}, \mathsf{crs})$
$\mathsf{hp} \leftarrow \mathsf{ProjKG}(\mathsf{hk}, \mathsf{crs})$	$C_2 \xleftarrow{\$} \mathscr{L}_{2,\mathsf{crs}_2}$
$C \xleftarrow{\$} \mathscr{L}_{\mathsf{crs}}$	$(C_1, \mathsf{st}) \xleftarrow{\$} \mathcal{A}(\mathsf{crs}, \mathcal{T}_{\mathsf{crs}_1}, \mathsf{hp}, C_2)$; $C \leftarrow (C_1, C_2)$
if $b = 0$ **then**	**if** $b = 0$ or $C_1 \in \mathscr{L}_{1,\mathsf{crs}_1}$ **then**
$\qquad H \leftarrow \mathsf{Hash}(\mathsf{hk}, \mathsf{crs}, C)$	$\qquad H \leftarrow \mathsf{Hash}(\mathsf{hk}, \mathsf{crs}, C)$
else $H \xleftarrow{\$} \Pi$	**else** $H \xleftarrow{\$} \Pi$
return $\mathcal{A}(\mathsf{crs}, C, \mathsf{hp}, H)$	**return** $\mathcal{A}(\mathsf{st}, H)$

Fig. 4. Experiments $\mathsf{Exp}^{\mathtt{ps\text{-}rnd\text{-}}b}$ and $\mathsf{Exp}^{\mathtt{mixed\text{-}ps\text{-}rnd\text{-}}b}$ for pseudo-randomness and mixed pseudo-randomness

6.2 Canonical PrPHF under κ-Lin

Let us construct a diverse vector space $(\mathcal{X}, \mathscr{L}, \mathcal{R}, \mathbb{G}, n, k, \Gamma, \theta)$ which yields a pseudo-random SPHF under κ-Lin in the cyclic group $\mathbb{G}$.

We set $\mathcal{X} = \mathscr{L}_{\mathsf{crs}} = \{\perp\}$ and $\hat{\mathcal{X}} = \hat{\mathscr{L}}_{\mathsf{crs}} = \mathbb{G}^{\kappa}$. For DDH = 1-Lin, we get a PrPHF with $\mathcal{X}$ of dimension 1, which is the best we can do using diverse vector spaces. Even though the resulting projective hash function will be smooth, the smoothness property is completely trivial, since $\mathscr{L}_{\mathsf{crs}} \setminus \mathcal{X}$ is empty, and does not imply the pseudo-randomness property. We will therefore need to manually prove the pseudo-randomness.

The "language" is defined by $\mathsf{crs} = (\zeta_1, \ldots, \zeta_\kappa) \xleftarrow{\$} \mathbb{G}^\kappa$ and the PrPHF by:

$$\Gamma := \begin{pmatrix} \zeta_1 & 0 & \cdots & 0 \\ 0 & \zeta_2 & \cdots & 0 \\ \vdots & \vdots & \ddots & \vdots \\ 0 & 0 & \cdots & \zeta_\kappa \end{pmatrix} \in \mathbb{G}^{\kappa \times \kappa} \qquad \boldsymbol{\lambda} := \begin{pmatrix} \hat{\zeta}_1 \\ \hat{\zeta}_2 \\ \vdots \\ \hat{\zeta}_\kappa \end{pmatrix} \in \mathbb{Z}_p^\kappa \quad \theta(\perp) := \begin{pmatrix} g \\ g \\ \vdots \\ g \end{pmatrix} \in \mathbb{G}^\kappa$$

$$\mathsf{hk} := \boldsymbol{\alpha} \xleftarrow{\$} \mathbb{Z}_p^{1 \times \kappa} \qquad\qquad \mathsf{hp} := (\gamma_1, \ldots, \gamma_\kappa)^\mathsf{T} = (\zeta_1^{\alpha_1}, \ldots, \zeta_\kappa^{\alpha_\kappa})^\mathsf{T} \in \mathbb{G}^\kappa$$

$$H := \prod_{i=1}^{n} g^{\alpha_i} = g^{\sum_{i=1}^{n} \alpha_i} = \prod_{i=1}^{n} \gamma_i^{\hat{\zeta}_i} =: H',$$

where $\boldsymbol{\lambda}$ is the witness for $C = \perp$, with $\zeta_i = g^{1/\hat{\zeta}_i}$. The pseudo-randomness directly comes from the hardness of κ-Lin.

6.3 Disjunction of an SPHF and a PrPHF

Let $\mathcal{V}_1 = (\mathcal{X}_1, \mathscr{L}_1, \mathcal{R}_1, \mathfrak{G}_1, n_1, k_1, \Gamma^{(1)}, \theta_1)$ and $\mathcal{V}_2 = (\mathcal{X}_2, \mathscr{L}_2, \mathcal{R}_2, \mathfrak{G}_2, n_2, k_2, \Gamma^{(2)}, \theta_2)$ be two diverse vector spaces over two multiplicatively sub-graded rings $\mathfrak{G}_1$ and $\mathfrak{G}_2$ of some graded ring $\mathfrak{G}$. Let $\mathcal{V} = (\mathcal{X}, \mathscr{L}, \mathfrak{G}, n, k, \Gamma, \theta)$ be the vector space corresponding to the disjunction of the two previous languages. We have already seen that this vector space corresponds to a smooth projective hash function.

But, if the second language is the canonical PrPHF under κ-Lin, the smoothness brings nothing, since $\mathcal{X} = \mathcal{L}$. Therefore, we need to prove a stronger property called *mixed pseudo-randomness*.

Definition of Mixed Pseudo-Randomness. The resulting SPHF is said mixed pseudo-random, if the hash value of a word $C = (C_1, C_2)$ looks random to the adversary, when $C_1 \notin \mathcal{L}_1$ is chosen by the adversary, while C_2 is chosen at random in $\mathcal{L}_2$. More precisely, the mixed pseudo-randomness property is defined by the experiments $\mathsf{Exp}^{\mathtt{mixed-ps-rnd-}b}$ depicted in Fig. 4.

Proof of Mixed Pseudo-Randomness. The proof of mixed pseudo-randomness is actually close to the one for computational soundness of trapdoor smooth projective functions in [6]. It requires that $\mathcal{T}_{\mathsf{crs}_1}$ contains enough information to be able to compute the discrete logarithm of elements of $\Gamma^{(1)}$, denoted $\mathfrak{L}(\Gamma^{(1)})$.

The proof reduces the pseudo-randomness property to the mixed pseudo-randomness property. The detailed proof is quite technical and can be found in the full version. Basically, we choose a random hashing key $\boldsymbol{\varepsilon}$ and we randomize it using a basis of the kernel of $\mathfrak{L}(\Gamma^{(1)})$ and projection keys given by the pseudo-randomness game (for some fixed word C_2, using an hybrid method). Then we show how to compute from that, a valid projection key hp for the language of the disjunction together with a hash value H of (C_1, C_2), for $C_1 \notin \mathcal{L}_1$. This value H is the correct hash value, if the hash values of C_2, given by the challenger of the hybrid pseudo-randomness game, were valid; and it is a random value, otherwise. That proves that an adversary able to break the mixed pseudo-randomness property also breaks the pseudo-randomness property.

7   One-Time Simulation-Sound **NIZK** from Disjunctions of an **SPHF** and a **PrPHF**

7.1   **NIZK** from Disjunctions of an **SPHF** and a **PrPHF**

The construction is identical to the one in Section 5.1, except that the second diverse vector space $\mathcal{V}_2$ is just supposed to be a PrPHF, and no more supposed to be related to a hard subset membership language $\mathcal{L}_2$. However, we suppose that the disjunction of $\mathcal{V}_1$ and $\mathcal{V}_2$ yields a mixed pseudo-random SPHF, which is the case if $\mathcal{T}_{\mathsf{crs}}$ contains enough information to compute the discrete logarithm of elements of $\Gamma^{(1)}$.

Completeness and zero-knowledge can be proven exactly in the same way. It remains therefore to prove the soundness property, under the mixed pseudo-randomness. The proof is very similar to the one in Section 5.1: if π is a proof of some word $C_1 \notin \mathcal{L}_1$, then it is possible to compute the hash value of any word (C_1, C_2) with $C_2 \in \mathcal{L}_2$ as $H' := \hat{C}_2 \bullet \pi$. This comes from the fact that if $C_2 \in \mathcal{L}_2$, then there exists $\boldsymbol{\lambda_2}$ such that $\hat{C}_2 = \boldsymbol{\lambda_2} \bullet \Gamma^{(2)}$, hence:

$$H' = \boldsymbol{\lambda_2} \bullet \Gamma^{(2)} \bullet \pi = \boldsymbol{\lambda_2} \bullet (\hat{C}_1 \otimes \mathsf{Id}_{k_2}) \bullet \gamma^{(2)} = (\hat{C}_1 \otimes \boldsymbol{\lambda_2}) \bullet \gamma^{(2)},$$

which is the hash value of (C_1, C_2) computed using ProjHash and witness λ_2. But the mixed pseudo-randomness property ensures that this value looks uniformly random when C_2 is chosen randomly in $\mathscr{L}_2$. That proves the soundness property.

7.2   One-Time Simulation-Sound NIZK

Unfortunately, for the one-time simulation-sound variant, this is not as easy: the construction in Section 5.3 seems difficult (if at all possible) to prove sound. The main problem is that the security proof of mixed pseudo-randomness is not statistical, so we do not know $\mathsf{hk} = \alpha$, but only some representation of α, which does not allow computing the proof π' of a word C_1' for a tag $\mathsf{tag}_{C_1'}$. Directly adapting the proof with a 2-smooth $\mathcal{V}_1$ would require to choose from the beginning π' (as is chosen hp from the beginning), but that is not possible since C_1' and tag' (the tag for C_1') are not known at the beginning of the game.

Our solution is to use the tag bit-by-bit. So we just need to guess which bit is different between tag_{C_1} and $\mathsf{tag}_{C_1'}$. This idea is inspired from [8]. Details can be found in the full version.

7.3   Concrete Instantiation and Comparison with Previous Work

If $\mathcal{V}_1$ is a diverse vector space over $\mathbb{G}_1$ (for which $\mathcal{T}_{\mathsf{crs}_1}$ gives enough information to compute the discrete logarithm of $\Gamma^{(1)}$) and $\mathcal{V}_2$ is the canonical PrPHF under DDH in Section 6.2, where $(p, \mathbb{G}_1, \mathbb{G}_2, \mathbb{G}_T, e)$ is a bilinear group where DDH is hard in $\mathbb{G}_2$, then we get an NIZK and a one-time simulation sound NIZK whose proof is composed of only $n_2 = 1$ group element in $\mathbb{G}_1$. More generally, if $\mathcal{V}_2$ is canonical PrPHF under κ-Lin, then the proof consists of only κ group elements, one less than our first construction in Section 5.4. However, this encompasses slightly fewer languages than this first construction, due to the restriction on $\mathscr{L}_1$ and $\mathcal{T}_{\mathsf{crs}_1}$. More precisely, our NIZK handles the same languages as Jutla-Roy NIZK in [20, 21].

Table 1 compares NIZK for linear subspaces as Jutla and Roy call it in [20], i.e., any language over $\mathbb{G}_1$ (first group of some bilinear group) for which there exists a diverse vector space $\mathcal{V}_1$ (assuming θ is the identity function and a witness is $\lambda \in \mathbb{Z}_p^k$). Some of the entries of this table were derived from [21] and from [26]. The DDH (in $\mathbb{G}_2$) variant requires asymmetric bilinear groups, while the κ-Lin variant for $\kappa \geq 2$ could work on symmetric bilinear groups.

First of all, as far as we know, our one-time simulation-sound NIZK is the most efficient such NIZK with a constant-size proof: the single-theorem relatively-sound construction of Libert et al. [26] is weaker than our one-time simulation-sound NIZK and requires at least one group element more in the proof, while their universal simulation-sound construction is much more inefficient. A direct application of our construction is our efficient structure-preserving threshold IND-CCA encryption scheme, under DDH.

Second, the DLin version of our NIZK in Section 5.1 is similar to the one by Libert et al. [26], but our DLin version of our NIZK in Section 7.1 is more

Table 1. Comparison of NIZK for linear subspaces

		WS	DDH (in $\mathbb{G}_2$) Proof $|\pi|$	Pairings	DLin (in $\mathbb{G}_1 = \mathbb{G}_2 = \mathbb{G}$) Proof $|\pi|$	Pairings
Groth-Sahai [18]			$n+2k$	$2n(k+2)$	$2n+3k$	$3n(k+3)$
Jutla-Roy [20]		✓	$n-k$	$(n-k)(k+2)$	$2n-2k$	$2(n-k)(k+2)$
Libert et al. [26]					3	$2n+4$
Libert et al. [26]	RSS				4	$2n+6$
Libert et al. [26]	USS				20	$2n+30$
Jutla-Roy[21]		✓	1	$n+1$	2	$2(n+2)$
§5.1			2	$n+2$	3	$2n+3$
§7.1		✓	1	$n+1$	2	$2n+2$
§5.3	OTSS		2	$2n+2$	3	$4n+3$
§7.2	OTSS	✓	1	$\nu n+2$	2	$2\nu n+2$

- full table with CRS sizes in the full version;
- $n = n_1$, $k = k_1$, and $\nu = 2\mathfrak{K}$; pairings: number of pairings required to verify the proof;
- sizes $|\cdot|$ are measured in term of group elements ($\mathbb{G}_1$ and $\mathbb{G}_2$, or $\mathbb{G}$ if the bilinear group is symmetric). Generators $g_1 \in \mathbb{G}_1$ and $g_2 \in \mathbb{G}_2$ (for DDH in $\mathbb{G}_2$) or $g \in \mathbb{G}$ (for DLin) are not counted in the CRS;
- *OTSS*: one-time simulation-soundness; *RSS*: single-theorem relative simulation-soundness [19] (weaker than OTSS); *USS*: universal simulation-soundness (stronger than OTSS);
- WS: witness-samplability in [20], generation of crs so that $\mathcal{T}_{crs_1}$ enables us to compute the discrete logarithms of Γ_1. This slightly restricts the set of languages which can be handled.

efficient (the proof has 2 group elements instead of 3). Furthermore, the ideas of the constructions in [26] seem quite different.

Third, our NIZK in Section 7.1 is similar to the one by Jutla and Roy in [21] for DDH. However, in our opinion, our construction seems to be more modular and simpler to understand. In addition, under κ-Lin, with $\kappa \geq 2$, our construction is slightly more efficient in terms of CRS size and verification time.

7.4 Application: Threshold Cramer-Shoup-like Encryption Scheme (Variant)

In the construction of Section 5.5, we can replace the previous one-time simulation-sound NIZK by this new NIZK. This yields a threshold encryption where the ciphertext size only consists of 4 group elements as the original Cramer-Shoup encryption scheme, at the expense of having a public key size linear in the security parameter.

Our two schemes are threshold and *structure-preserving* [5]: they are "compatible" with Groth-Sahai NIZK, in the sense that we can do a Groth-Sahai NIZK to prove that we know the plaintext of a ciphertext for our encryption schemes. In addition, normal decryption does not require any pairings, which still are very costly, compared to exponentiations. A detailed comparison with existing efficient IND-CCA encryption schemes based on cyclic or bilinear groups is given in the full version. To summarize, to the best of our knowledge, our two constructions are the most efficient threshold and structure-preserving IND-CCA encryption schemes.

Acknowledgments. We would like to thank Jens Groth and the anonymous reviewers for detailed comments on a previous version of this paper. This work was supported in part by the French ANR-12-INSE-0014 SIMPATIC Project, the CFM Foundation, the European Commission through the FP7-ICT-2011-EU-Brazil Program under Contract 288349 SecFuNet, and the European Research Council under the European Community's Seventh Framework Programme (FP7/2007-2013 Grant Agreement no. 339563 – CryptoCloud).

References

1. Abdalla, M., Benhamouda, F., Blazy, O., Chevalier, C., Pointcheval, D.: SPHF-friendly non-interactive commitments. In: Sako, K., Sarkar, P. (eds.) ASIACRYPT 2013, Part I. LNCS, vol. 8269, pp. 214–234. Springer, Heidelberg (2013)

2. Abdalla, M., Benhamouda, F., Pointcheval, D.: Disjunctions for hash proof systems: New constructions and applications. Cryptology ePrint Archive, Report 2014/483 (2014). http://eprint.iacr.org/2014/483

3. Abdalla, M., Bresson, E., Chevassut, O., Pointcheval, D.: Password-based group key exchange in a constant number of rounds. In: Yung, M., Dodis, Y., Kiayias, A., Malkin, T. (eds.) PKC 2006. LNCS, vol. 3958, pp. 427–442. Springer, Heidelberg (2006)

4. Abdalla, M., Chevalier, C., Pointcheval, D.: Smooth projective hashing for conditionally extractable commitments. In: Halevi, S. (ed.) CRYPTO 2009. LNCS, vol. 5677, pp. 671–689. Springer, Heidelberg (2009)

5. Abe, M., Fuchsbauer, G., Groth, J., Haralambiev, K., Ohkubo, M.: Structure-preserving signatures and commitments to group elements. In: Rabin, T. (ed.) CRYPTO 2010. LNCS, vol. 6223, pp. 209–236. Springer, Heidelberg (2010)

6. Benhamouda, F., Blazy, O., Chevalier, C., Pointcheval, D., Vergnaud, D.: New techniques for SPHFs and efficient one-round PAKE protocols. In: Canetti, R., Garay, J.A. (eds.) CRYPTO 2013, Part I. LNCS, vol. 8042, pp. 449–475. Springer, Heidelberg (2013)

7. Blazy, O., Pointcheval, D., Vergnaud, D.: Round-optimal privacy-preserving protocols with smooth projective hash functions. In: Cramer, R. (ed.) TCC 2012. LNCS, vol. 7194, pp. 94–111. Springer, Heidelberg (2012)

8. Chen, J., Wee, H.: Fully, (almost) tightly secure IBE and dual system groups. In: Canetti, R., Garay, J.A. (eds.) CRYPTO 2013, Part II. LNCS, vol. 8043, pp. 435–460. Springer, Heidelberg (2013)

9. Cheon, J.H., Han, K., Lee, C., Ryu, H., Stehlé, D.: Cryptanalysis of the multilinear map over the integers. Cryptology ePrint Archive, Report 2014/906 (2014). http://eprint.iacr.org/2014/906

10. Coron, J.-S., Lepoint, T., Tibouchi, M.: Practical multilinear maps over the integers. In: Canetti, R., Garay, J.A. (eds.) CRYPTO 2013, Part I. LNCS, vol. 8042, pp. 476–493. Springer, Heidelberg (2013)

11. Cramer, R., Shoup, V.: A practical public key cryptosystem provably secure against adaptive chosen ciphertext attack. In: Krawczyk, H. (ed.) CRYPTO 1998. LNCS, vol. 1462, pp. 13–25. Springer, Heidelberg (1998)

12. Cramer, R., Shoup, V.: Universal hash proofs and a paradigm for adaptive chosen ciphertext secure public-key encryption. In: Knudsen, L.R. (ed.) EUROCRYPT 2002. LNCS, vol. 2332, pp. 45–64. Springer, Heidelberg (2002)

13. Escala, A., Herold, G., Kiltz, E., Ràfols, C., Villar, J.: An algebraic framework for diffie-hellman assumptions. In: Canetti, R., Garay, J.A. (eds.) CRYPTO 2013, Part II. LNCS, vol. 8043, pp. 129–147. Springer, Heidelberg (2013)
14. Garg, S., Gentry, C., Halevi, S.: Candidate multilinear maps from ideal lattices. In: Johansson, T., Nguyen, P.Q. (eds.) EUROCRYPT 2013. LNCS, vol. 7881, pp. 1–17. Springer, Heidelberg (2013)
15. Garg, S., Gentry, C., Sahai, A., Waters, B.: Witness encryption and its applications. In: Boneh, D., Roughgarden, T., Feigenbaum, J. (eds.) 45th ACM STOC, pp. 467–476. ACM Press, June 2013
16. Gennaro, R., Lindell, Y.: A framework for password-based authenticated key exchange. In: Biham, E. (ed.) EUROCRYPT 2003. LNCS, vol. 2656, pp. 524–543. Springer, Heidelberg (2003). http://eprint.iacr.org/2003/032.ps.gz
17. Groth, J.: Simulation-sound NIZK proofs for a practical language and constant size group signatures. In: Lai, X., Chen, K. (eds.) ASIACRYPT 2006. LNCS, vol. 4284, pp. 444–459. Springer, Heidelberg (2006)
18. Groth, J., Sahai, A.: Efficient non-interactive proof systems for bilinear groups. In: Smart, N.P. (ed.) EUROCRYPT 2008. LNCS, vol. 4965, pp. 415–432. Springer, Heidelberg (2008)
19. Jutla, C., Roy, A.: Relatively-sound NIZKs and password-based key-exchange. In: Fischlin, M., Buchmann, J., Manulis, M. (eds.) PKC 2012. LNCS, vol. 7293, pp. 485–503. Springer, Heidelberg (2012)
20. Jutla, C.S., Roy, A.: Shorter quasi-adaptive NIZK proofs for linear subspaces. In: Sako, K., Sarkar, P. (eds.) ASIACRYPT 2013, Part I. LNCS, vol. 8269, pp. 1–20. Springer, Heidelberg (2013)
21. Jutla, C.S., Roy, A.: Switching lemma for bilinear tests and constant-size NIZK proofs for linear subspaces. In: Garay, J.A., Gennaro, R. (eds.) CRYPTO 2014, Part II. LNCS, vol. 8617, pp. 295–312. Springer, Heidelberg (2014)
22. Kalai, Y.T.: Smooth projective hashing and two-message oblivious transfer. In: Cramer, R. (ed.) EUROCRYPT 2005. LNCS, vol. 3494, pp. 78–95. Springer, Heidelberg (2005)
23. Katz, J., Ostrovsky, R., Yung, M.: Efficient password-authenticated key exchange using human-memorable passwords. In: Pfitzmann, B. (ed.) EUROCRYPT 2001. LNCS, vol. 2045, pp. 475–494. Springer, Heidelberg (2001)
24. Katz, J., Vaikuntanathan, V.: Round-optimal password-based authenticated key exchange. In: Ishai, Y. (ed.) TCC 2011. LNCS, vol. 6597, pp. 293–310. Springer, Heidelberg (2011)
25. Libert, B., Peters, T., Joye, M., Yung, M.: Linearly homomorphic structure-preserving signatures and their applications. In: Canetti, R., Garay, J.A. (eds.) CRYPTO 2013, Part II. LNCS, vol. 8043, pp. 289–307. Springer, Heidelberg (2013)
26. Libert, B., Peters, T., Joye, M., Yung, M.: Non-malleability from malleability: simulation-sound quasi-adaptive NIZK proofs and CCA2-secure encryption from homomorphic signatures. In: Nguyen, P.Q., Oswald, E. (eds.) EUROCRYPT 2014. LNCS, vol. 8441, pp. 514–532. Springer, Heidelberg (2014)

Quasi-Adaptive NIZK
for Linear Subspaces Revisited

Eike Kiltz[1]([✉]) and Hoeteck Wee[2]

[1] Ruhr-Universität Bochum, Bochum, Germany
eike.kiltz@rub.de
[2] ENS, France, Paris
wee@di.ens.fr

Abstract. Non-interactive zero-knowledge (NIZK) proofs for algebraic relations in a group, such as the Groth-Sahai proofs, are an extremely powerful tool in pairing-based cryptography. A series of recent works focused on obtaining very efficient NIZK proofs for linear spaces in a weaker quasi-adaptive model. We revisit recent quasi-adaptive NIZK constructions, providing clean, simple, and improved constructions via a conceptually different approach inspired by recent developments in identity-based encryption. We then extend our techniques also to linearly homomorphic structure-preserving signatures, an object both of independent interest and with many applications.

1 Introduction

Non-interactive zero-knowledge (NIZK) proofs for efficiently proving algebraic relations in a group [14,35,37,38] have had a profound impact on pairing-based cryptography, notably in (i) improving the concrete efficiency of non-interactive cryptography schemes like group signatures [36], (ii) realizing stronger security guarantees in applications like anonymous credentials [9,10,33], and (iii) minimizing interaction in secure computation and two-party protocols [31,44].

A recent fruitful line of works has focused in obtaining very efficient NIZK proofs for proving membership in a linear subspace over a group, which is an important subset of the algebraic relations supported by the Groth-Sahai NIZK [38]. For linear subspaces, the Groth-Sahai proofs were linear in the dimensions of the (sub)space. The first substantial improvement was obtained by Jutla and Roy [42] in a weaker *quasi-adaptive* model, where the CRS may depend on the linear subspace, and the soundness guarantee is computational but adaptive. In addition, they used quasi-adaptive NIZK (QANIZK) for linear subspaces to

---

E. Kiltz—Supported by a Sofja Kovalevskaja Award of the Alexander von Humboldt Foundation, the German Israel Foundation, and ERC Project ERCC (FP7/615074).
H. Wee—CNRS, INRIA and Columbia University. Partially supported by the Alexander von Humboldt Foundation, NSF Award CNS-1445424, ANR-14-CE28-0003 (Project EnBid) and ERC Project CryptoCloud (FP7/2007-2013 Grant Agreement no. 339563).

E. Oswald and M. Fischlin (Eds.): EUROCRYPT 2015, Part II, LNCS 9057, pp. 101–128, 2015.
DOI: 10.1007/978-3-662-46803-6_4

obtain improved KDM-CCA2-secure encryption as well as CCA2-secure IBE scheme with short, publicly verifiable ciphertexts [18,19]. Further efficiency improvements were subsequently obtained in [1,43,48], leading to constant-size proofs, independent of the dimensions of space and subspace; several of these constructions also realized stronger notions of soundness like one-time simulation soundness and unbounded simulation soundness [27,51], which in turn enable new applications.

1.1 Our Results and Techniques: QANIZK

We present clean, simple, and improved constructions of QANIZK protocols via a conceptually novel approach. Previous constructions use fairly distinct techniques, resulting in a large family of schemes with incomparable efficiency and security guarantees. We obtain a family of schemes that simultaneously match – and in many settings, improve upon – the efficiency, assumptions, and security guarantees of all of the previous constructions. Figure 1 summarizes the efficiency of our constructions. Like the earliest Jutla-Roy scheme [42], our schemes are fully explicit and simple to describe: the prover and verifier carry out simple matrix-vector products in the exponent, and both correctness and zero-knowledge follow readily from one simple equation. Furthermore, our schemes have a natural derivation from a symmetric-key setting, and the derivation even extends to a modular and intuitive proof of security. Finally, in all but the settings with unbounded security, we obtain a qualitative improvement in the underlying assumptions from decisional to computational (search) assumptions; specifically, security relies on a natural computational analogue of the decisional k-Lin assumption.

Our constructions and techniques are inspired by recent developments in obtaining adaptively secure identity-based encryption schemes, notably the use of pairing groups to "compile" a symmetric-key primitive into an asymmetric-key primitive [13,23,54], and the dual system encryption methodology for achieving adaptive security against unbounded collusions [46,52]. We then extend our techniques to linearly homomorphic structure-preserving signatures [47,48], an object both of independent interest and with many applications.

Overview of Our Constructions. Fix a pairing group $(\mathbb{G}_1, \mathbb{G}_2, \mathbb{G}_T)$ with $e : \mathbb{G}_1 \times \mathbb{G}_2 \to \mathbb{G}_T$. We present a very simple non-interactive argument system for linear subspaces over $\mathbb{G}_1$ as defined by a matrix[1] $[\mathbf{M}]_1 := g_1^{\mathbf{M}} \in \mathbb{G}_1^{n \times t}$ $(n > t)$ and captured by the language:

$$\mathcal{L}_\mathbf{M} = \left\{ [\mathbf{y}]_1 \in \mathbb{G}_1^n : \exists\, \mathbf{x} \in \mathbb{Z}_q^t \text{ s.t. } \mathbf{y} = \mathbf{M}\mathbf{x} \right\}.$$

The starting point of our construction is a hash proof system [26] for the language, which is essentially a symmetric-key analogue of NIZK with a

---

[1] We use implicit representation notation for group elements, as explained in Section 2.1.

designated verifier. Namely, we pick a secret hash key $\mathbf{K} \leftarrow_R \mathbb{Z}_q^{n \times (k+1)}$ known to the verifier ($k \geq 1$ is a parameter of the security assumption) and publish the projection $[\mathbf{P}]_1 := [\mathbf{M}^\top \mathbf{K}]_1$ in the CRS. The proof is given by $[\pi]_1 := [\mathbf{x}^\top \mathbf{P}]_1$, and verification works by checking whether $\pi \overset{?}{=} \mathbf{y}^\top \mathbf{K}$. Completeness and perfect zero-knowledge follow readily from the fact that for all $\mathbf{y} = \mathbf{M}\mathbf{x}$ and $\mathbf{P} = \mathbf{M}^\top \mathbf{K}$:

$$\mathbf{x}^\top \mathbf{P} = \mathbf{x}^\top (\mathbf{M}^\top \mathbf{K}) = \mathbf{y}^\top \mathbf{K}.$$

Next, observe that if $\mathbf{y}$ is outside the span of $\mathbf{M}$, then $\mathbf{y}^\top \mathbf{K}$ is completely random given $\mathbf{M}^\top \mathbf{K}$; this is the case even if such a $\mathbf{y}$ is adaptively chosen after seeing $\mathbf{M}^\top \mathbf{K}$. Thus, the construction achieves statistical adaptive soundness: namely, a computationally unbounded cheating prover, upon seeing $\mathbf{P}$, still cannot produce a vector outside $\mathcal{L}_\mathbf{M}$ along with an accepting proof.

To achieve public verifiability, we carry out the hash proof system in $\mathbb{G}_1$ and publish a "partial commitment" to $\mathbf{K}$ in $\mathbb{G}_2$ as given by $[\mathbf{A}]_2, [\mathbf{K}\mathbf{A}]_2$, where the choice of $\mathbf{A} \in \mathbb{Z}_q^{(k+1) \times k}$ is defined by the security assumption. Instead of checking whether $\pi \overset{?}{=} \mathbf{y}^\top \mathbf{K}$ as before, anyone can now publicly check whether $\pi \mathbf{A} \overset{?}{=} \mathbf{y}^\top \mathbf{K}\mathbf{A}$ via a pairing. As $[\mathbf{A}]_2, [\mathbf{K}\mathbf{A}]_2$ leaks additional information about the secret hash key $\mathbf{K}$, we can only prove computational adaptive soundness. In particular, we rely on the $\mathcal{D}_k$-KerMDH Assumption [49], which stipulates that given a random $[\mathbf{A}]_2$ drawn from a matrix distribution $\mathcal{D}_k$, it is hard to find a non-zero $[\mathbf{s}]_1 \in \mathbb{G}_1^{k+1}$ such that $\mathbf{s}^\top \mathbf{A} = \mathbf{0}$; this is implied by the $\mathcal{D}_k$-MDDH Assumption [30], a generalization of the k-Lin Assumption.[2] Therefore, for any $([\mathbf{y}]_1, [\pi]_1)$ produced by an efficient adversary,

$$\pi \mathbf{A} = \mathbf{y}^\top \mathbf{K}\mathbf{A} \implies (\pi - \mathbf{y}^\top \mathbf{K})\mathbf{A} = \mathbf{0} \overset{\text{using assumption}}{\implies} \pi - \mathbf{y}^\top \mathbf{K} = \mathbf{0} \implies \pi = \mathbf{y}^\top \mathbf{K},$$

upon which we are back in the symmetric-key setting, with a little more work to account for the leakage from $\mathbf{K}\mathbf{A}$. Moreover, adaptive security in the symmetric-key setting (which is easy to analyze via a purely information-theoretic argument) carries over to adaptive security in the public-key setting.

Two Simple Extensions. We extend this simple construction in two simple ways:

- First, we show that we can use $\mathbf{A}$ with the bottom row deleted, which saves one element to obtain proofs of size k, albeit at the cost of a more intricate security reduction and a restriction to witness-sampleable (WS) distributions for $[\mathbf{M}]_1$ [42]. The latter means that we are given an explicit description of $\mathbf{M}$ in the security reduction, which we need to program the CRS as with prior works [1,43] that achieve the same proof size. In the case $k = 1$, the proof consists of 1 element and the CRS only contains $n + t$ group elements, which seems optimal.

---

[2] That is, $\mathcal{D}_k$-MDDH $\Rightarrow \mathcal{D}_k$-KerMDH; for the specific linear distribution $\mathcal{D}_k = \mathcal{L}_k$ we have k-Lin $:= \mathcal{L}_k$-MDDH $\Rightarrow \mathcal{L}_k$-KerMDH $=: k$-KerLin. We refer the reader to Section 2.2 for a more detailed treatment of the assumptions.

	Soundness	WS?	Assumption	Proof	CRS
GS08 [38]	AS		2-Lin ($\mathbb{G}_2$)	$2n+3t$	6
LPJY14 [48]	AS		2-KerLin ($\mathbb{G}_2$)	3	$2n+3t+3$
ABP14 [1]	AS		k-Lin ($\mathbb{G}_2$)	$k+1$	$kn+(k+1)t+k$
Π_{as} (Fig 4)	AS		$\mathcal{D}_k$-KerMDH ($\mathbb{G}_2$) ✓	$k+1$	$kn+(k+1)t+\mathsf{RE}(\mathbf{A})$
JR13 [42]	AS	yes	k-KerLin ($\mathbb{G}_2$)	$k(n-t)$	$2kt(n-t)+k+1$
JR14 [43]	AS	yes	k-Lin ($\mathbb{G}_2$)	k	$kn+kt+k^2$
ABP14 [1]	AS	yes	k-Lin ($\mathbb{G}_2$)	k	$kn+kt+k$
Π'_{as} (Fig 5)	AS	yes	$\mathcal{D}_k$-KerMDH ($\mathbb{G}_2$) ✓	k	$kn+kt+\overline{\mathsf{RE}}(\overline{\mathbf{A}})$ ✓
ABP14 [1]	OTSS		k-Lin ($\mathbb{G}_2$)	$k+1$	$2kn+2(k+1)t+k$
$\Pi_{\mathsf{ot\text{-}ss}}$ (Fig 6)	OTSS		$\mathcal{D}_k$-KerMDH ($\mathbb{G}_2$) ✓	$k+1$	$2kn+2(k+1)t+\mathsf{RE}(\mathbf{A})$
ABP14 [1]	OTSS	yes	k-Lin ($\mathbb{G}_2$)	k	$2\lambda(kn+(k+1)t)+k$
$\Pi'_{\mathsf{ot\text{-}ss}}$ (Fig 9)	OTSS	yes	$\mathcal{D}_k$-KerMDH ($\mathbb{G}_2$) ✓	k	$2\lambda(kn+(k+1)t)+\overline{\mathsf{RE}}(\overline{\mathbf{A}})$ ✓
CCS09 [18]	USS		2-Lin ($\mathbb{G}_2,\mathbb{G}_2$)	$2n+6t+52$	18
LPJY14 [48]	USS	yes	2-Lin ($\mathbb{G}_1,\mathbb{G}_2$)	20	$2n+3t+3\lambda+10$
Π_{uss} (Fig 7)	USS	yes	$\mathcal{D}_k$-MDDH ($\mathbb{G}_1,\mathbb{G}_2$) ✓	$2k+2$ ✓	$kn+4(k+t+1)k+2\mathsf{RE}(\mathbf{A})$ ✓

Fig. 1. QANIZK for linear subspaces of $\mathbb{Z}_q^n$ of dimension t and tag-space $\mathcal{T}=\{0,1\}^\lambda$. For the soundness column we use AS for adaptive soundness, OTSS for one-time simulation soundness, and USS for unbounded simulation soundness. WS stands for witness sampleability [42] and slightly restricts the class of languages, cf. Section 3.2. We omit the generators for the group when computing the CRS size. $\mathsf{RE}(\mathbf{A})$ and $\overline{\mathsf{RE}}(\overline{\mathbf{A}})$ depend on the assumption and denote the number of group elements needed to represent $[\mathbf{A}]$ and $[\overline{\mathbf{A}}]$ (the top k rows of $[\mathbf{A}]$), respectively. In case of k-Lin, we have $\mathsf{RE}(\mathbf{A})=k$ and $\overline{\mathsf{RE}}(\overline{\mathbf{A}})=k-1$. Recall that k-Lin is a special case of $\mathcal{D}_k$-MDDH (decisional assumptions) and k-KerLin is a special case of $\mathcal{D}_k$-KerMDH (search assumptions), for $\mathcal{D}_k=\mathcal{L}_k$, the linear distribution. In all settings, we improve upon either the assumption (c.f. Figure 3), the CRS size, or # pairings used in verification (which can be further reduced using randomized verification), as indicated by a ✓.

- Second, we show how to achieve one-time simulation soundness, by replacing $\mathbf{K}$ with 2-wise independent hash function $\mathbf{K}_0+\tau\mathbf{K}_1$ where τ is a tag, and we publish $[\mathbf{A}]_2,[\mathbf{K}_0\mathbf{A}]_2,[\mathbf{K}_1\mathbf{A}]_2$ for public verification. A single simulated proof reveals only an evaluation of the hash function at a single point, while its evaluation at every other point remains hidden, upon which we are back in the setting of standard adaptive soundness.

Unbounded Simulation-Soundness. To achieve unbounded simulation-soundness, we move from a 2-wise independent hash function to an affine pseudo-random MAC (or, a randomized PRF) [13,25,29], which guarantees pseudorandomness at a single point even upon giving out evaluations for polynomially many other points. Here, we require a decisional assumption over $\mathbb{G}_1$. Our construction may also be viewed as an instantiation of the dual system encryption methodology, whereas prior constructions in [47,48] rely on the random partitioning technique in [12,53]. This allows us to immediately bypass two of the main limitations of random partitioning: long public parameters and a polynomial-time but inefficient security reduction.

1.2   Extension: Linearly Homomorphic Structure Preserving Signatures

Linearly homomorphic signatures (LHS) [15,28,40] are signatures where the messages consist of vectors over group $\mathbb{G}_1$ such that from any set of signatures on $[\mathbf{m}_i]_1 \in \mathbb{G}_1^n$, one can efficiently derives a signature σ on any element message $[\mathbf{m}]_1 := [\sum \omega_i \mathbf{m}_i]_1$ in the span of $\mathbf{m}_1, \ldots, \mathbf{m}_q$. For security, one requires that it is infeasible to produce a signature on a message outside of the span of all previously signed messages. In recent years, LHS have drawn considerable attentions from the community with a wide range of constructions under different assumptions [6–8,16,17,20,32,34]. Linearly homomorphic structure preserving signatures (LHSPS) [47] have the additional property that signatures and public keys are all elements of the groups $\mathbb{G}_1, \mathbb{G}_2, \mathbb{G}_T$. This is a useful property when combined with other algebraic tools such as Groth-Sahai NIZK systems. Applications beyond the algebraic compatibility include IND-CCA1-secure encryption with publicly verifiable ciphertexts and verifiable computation for encrypted cloud storage [4,47], non-malleable trapdoor commitments to group elements [47] and QANIZK [48]. The first constructions of LHSPS were given in [21,47].

We show how to extend our QANIZK techniques to LHSPS. Concretely, for our one-time secure LHSPS, we define a signature σ on message $[\mathbf{m}]_1 \in \mathbb{G}_1^n$ as

$$\sigma = [\mathbf{m}^\top \mathbf{K}]_1,$$

and publish $[\mathbf{A}]_2, [\mathbf{K}\mathbf{A}]_2$ for verification. Security follows by the same argument as in our QANIZK construction. Our construction can also be seen as a generalization of a 2-KerLin based scheme from [47] to $\mathcal{D}_k$-KerMDH. Similarly, the construction of unbounded simulation-sound QANIZK gives rise to a fully secure LHSPS scheme. In the latter, the signatures on previously signed messages $([\mathbf{m}_i]_1)_{1 \le i \le q}$ reveal $\mathbf{M}^\top \mathbf{K}$ to the adversary, where $\mathbf{M} = (\mathbf{m}_1, \ldots, \mathbf{m}_q)$. The winning condition of LHSPS is to produce a valid signature on a message outside of the language $\mathcal{L}_\mathbf{M}$, which corresponds to breaking simulation-soundness in the QANIZK. Here, we do have to address an additional complication arising from the fact that the LHSPS adversary is allowed to have previously requested signatures for the challenge tag. Our constructions improve upon the efficiency of the prior schemes; see Figure 2. Moreover, our techniques also offer two qualitative advantages over those in [48]: first, they immediately yield fully randomizable linearly homomorphic signatures, which means they are strongly context-hiding [4,7], and second, we completely eliminate the additional restriction that adversary only query linearly independent vectors on each tag [47, §2.1].

In fact, our constructions follow a more general and natural (in hindsight) methodology for constructing LHSPS from any QANIZK: the signing key is the simulation trapdoor; a signature on $[\mathbf{m}]_1$ is a simulated proof on the vector $[\mathbf{m}]_1$; verifying a signature is the same as verifying a proof. The proof of LHSPS security uses the honest prover to simulate signatures. When a LHSPS adversary requests signatures on $([\mathbf{m}_i]_1)_{1 \le i \le q}$, it gets QANIZK proofs for the vectors lying

	Security	Restrictions on adv.	Assumption	signature	pk
LPJY13 [47, §3.1]:	OT	none	2-KerLin ($\mathbb{G}_2$)	3	$2n+3$
LPJY14 [48, §D]:	OT	none	$\mathcal{L}_k$-KerMDH ($\mathbb{G}_2$)	$k+1$	$kn+2k-1$
LHSPS$_{ot}$ (Fig 10)	OT	none	$\mathcal{D}_k$-KerMDH ($\mathbb{G}_2$)	$k+1$	$kn+\mathsf{RE}(\mathcal{D}_k)$
LPJY13 [47, §3.2]:	full	indep.	2-KerLin ($\mathbb{G}_1=\mathbb{G}_2$)	4	$2n+\lambda+5$
LPJY13 [47, §B.2]:	full, randindep., targeting		2-Lin ($\mathbb{G}_1=\mathbb{G}_2$)	15	$2n+\lambda+7$
LHSPS$_{full}$ (Fig 8)	full, randtargeting		$\mathcal{D}_k$-MDDH ($\mathbb{G}_1,\mathbb{G}_2$)	$2k+2$	$kn+4(k+1)k+2\mathsf{RE}(\mathcal{D}_k)$

Fig. 2. Linearly homomorphic structure-preserving signatures for $\mathcal{M} = \mathbb{G}_1^n$ and tag-space $\mathcal{T} = \{0,1\}^\lambda$. In the security column, OT stands for one-time security and full for full security; rand stands for full randomizability. The restrictions column describes the restrictions required on the adversary. An independent adversary is restricted to querying linearly independent vectors on each tag; a targeting adversary is required to provide a certificate that its output vector is outside the span of previous queried messages.

in the span of the matrix $\mathbf{M} := (\mathbf{m}_1, \ldots, \mathbf{m}_q)$. Soundness for QANIZK tells us that it is infeasible to produce an accepting proof for a vector outside the span of $\mathbf{M}$; this means that it is infeasible to produce a valid signature for a vector outside the span of $([\mathbf{m}_i]_1)_{1 \leq i \leq q}$. For the above construction to work, we require that proof verification does not depend on $\mathbf{M}$, which is indeed satisfied by all of our QANIZK protocols. The main qualitative difference between QANIZK and LHSPS security is that in QANIZK, the entire $\mathbf{M}$ is fixed in advance, whereas in signatures, the corresponding matrix is chosen adaptively and incrementally row by row. This means that QANIZK proof techniques that require WS and that program an explicit description of $\mathbf{M}$ into the CRS (which is the case for the QANIZK schemes with the shortest proofs) do not yield LHSPS schemes.

1.3   Discussion

Comparison with Previous Approaches. We briefly outline previous approaches for obtaining constant-size QANIZK proofs for linear subspaces. The constructions in [1, 43] both derive their basic QANIZK with adaptive soundness from a more general framework: a switching lemma in [43] and hash proof system for disjunctions in [1]. Both frameworks seem inherently limited to decisional assumptions, whereas our constructions enable the use of computational search assumptions. Moreover, the switching lemma framework appears to be limited to applications where the adversary's winning condition is efficiently checkable, and therefore seems unlikely to extend beyond WS distributions or to LHSPS even in the one-time setting. On the other hand, these more general frameworks could enable other new applications.

Previous QANIZK constructions achieving one-time simulation-soundness as well as the weaker notion of single-theorem relatively soundness [41] proceed by combining a basic adaptively secure QANIZK scheme with either a hash proof system [42, 43, 48] or some strengthening thereof [1]. Our approach for one-time simulation-soundness by replacing a single key with the output of a 2-wise independent hash function is arguably simpler and more natural.

The constructions of Libert et al. in [48] used LHSPS in the constructions of QANIZK. Interestingly, while this prior work [48] used LHSPS to build QANIZK, we reverse the connection in this work, and as a result, obtained even more efficient QANIZK and LHSPS. Their basic QANIZK with adaptive soundness builds upon on an existing one-time structure-preserving signature in [2,3]. Their QANIZK scheme with unbounded simulation-soundness as well as the fully secure LHSPS in [47] relies on Waters' random partitioning technique [12,53], which originated in the context of adaptively secure IBE; the final QANIZK scheme is fairly complex, require a long CRS, an inefficient security reduction, and in addition the use of Groth-Sahai NIWI proofs. Our schemes for unbounded simulation-soundness and full security rely on the more powerful dual system encryption methodology [52] for building adaptively secure IBE, and are largely self-contained.

Other Related Work. The idea of compiling symmetric to asymmetric cryptography also appeared in several prior works. In 1989, Bellare and Goldwasser [11] gave a transformation from a message authentication code (originally, a PRF) and a NIZK to a signature scheme; interestingly, their transformation requires NIZK as a building block, whereas NIZK is the target of our compiler. To the best of our knowledge, the first works to explicitly point out that we can directly compile a symmetric primitive into an asymmetric one in pairing groups came from the literature on attribute-based and identity-based encryption [5,13,24,54]. These latter works can be viewed as an instantiation of the dual system encryption methodology [46,52]. In the specific case of (H)IBE, they can also be viewed as an algebraic MAC plus a Groth-Sahai NIZK [13].

Perspective. As noted at the beginning of the introduction, Groth-Sahai NIZK have been widely used in many cryptographic applications in recent years. We presented a conceptually different yet very simple approach for building NIZK with extremely short proofs for linear subspaces, and also to improve one of the applications. We are optimistic that our approach will yield concrete improvements to many constructions that currently rely on Groth-Sahai proofs.

2 Definitions

Notation. If $\mathbf{x} \in \mathcal{B}^n$, then $|\mathbf{x}|$ denotes the length n of the vector. Further, $x \leftarrow_{\mathrm{R}} \mathcal{B}$ denotes the process of sampling an element x from set $\mathcal{B}$ uniformly at random. If $\mathbf{A} \in \mathbb{Z}_q^{n \times k}$ is a matrix with $n > k$, then $\overline{\mathbf{A}} \in \mathbb{Z}_q^{k \times k}$ denotes the upper square matrix of $\mathbf{A}$ and then $\underline{\mathbf{A}} \in \mathbb{Z}_q^{(n-k) \times k}$ denotes the remaining $n - k$ rows of $\mathbf{A}$. We use $span()$ to denote the column span of a matrix.

2.1 Pairing Groups

Let GGen be a probabilistic polynomial time (PPT) algorithm that on input 1^λ returns a description $\mathcal{PG} = (\mathbb{G}_1, \mathbb{G}_2, \mathbb{G}_T, q, g_1, g_2, e)$ of asymmetric pairing groups where $\mathbb{G}_1, \mathbb{G}_2, \mathbb{G}_T$ are cyclic groups of order q for a λ-bit prime q, g_1 and

g_2 are generators of $\mathbb{G}_1$ and $\mathbb{G}_2$, respectively, and $e : \mathbb{G}_1 \times \mathbb{G}_2$ is an efficiently computable (non-degenerate) bilinear map. Define $g_T := e(g_1, g_2)$, which is a generator in $\mathbb{G}_T$.

We use implicit representation of group elements as introduced in [30]. For $s \in \{1, 2, T\}$ and $a \in \mathbb{Z}_q$, define $[a]_s = g_s^a \in \mathbb{G}_s$ as the *implicit representation* of a in $\mathbb{G}_s$. More generally, for a matrix $\mathbf{A} = (a_{ij}) \in \mathbb{Z}_q^{n \times m}$ we define $[\mathbf{A}]_s$ as the implicit representation of $\mathbf{A}$ in $\mathbb{G}_s$:

$$[\mathbf{A}]_s := \begin{pmatrix} g_s^{a_{11}} & \cdots & g_s^{a_{1m}} \\ & & \\ g_s^{a_{n1}} & \cdots & g_s^{a_{nm}} \end{pmatrix} \in \mathbb{G}_s^{n \times m}$$

We will always use this implicit notation of elements in $\mathbb{G}_s$, i.e., we let $[a]_s \in \mathbb{G}_s$ be an element in $\mathbb{G}_s$. Note that from $[a]_s \in \mathbb{G}_s$ it is generally hard to compute the value a (discrete logarithm problem in $\mathbb{G}_s$). Further, from $[b]_T \in \mathbb{G}_T$ it is hard to compute the value $[b]_1 \in \mathbb{G}_1$ and $[b]_2 \in \mathbb{G}_2$ (pairing inversion problem). Obviously, given $[a]_s \in \mathbb{G}_s$ and a scalar $x \in \mathbb{Z}_q$, one can efficiently compute $[ax]_s \in \mathbb{G}_s$. Further, given $[a]_1, [a]_2$ one can efficiently compute $[ab]_T$ using the pairing e. For two matrices $\mathbf{A}, \mathbf{B}$ with matching dimensions define $e([\mathbf{A}]_1, [\mathbf{B}]_2) := [\mathbf{AB}]_T \in \mathbb{G}_T$.

2.2 Matrix Diffie-Hellman Assumption

We recall the definitions of the Matrix Decision Diffie-Hellman (MDDH) and the Kernel Diffie-Hellman assumptions [30, 49].

Definition 1 (Matrix Distribution). *Let $k \in \mathbb{N}$. We call $\mathcal{D}_k$ a matrix distribution if it outputs matrices in $\mathbb{Z}_q^{(k+1) \times k}$ of full rank k in polynomial time.*

Without loss of generality, we assume the first k rows of $\mathbf{A} \leftarrow_R \mathcal{D}_k$ form an invertible matrix. The $\mathcal{D}_k$-Matrix Diffie-Hellman problem is to distinguish the two distributions $([\mathbf{A}], [\mathbf{Aw}])$ and $([\mathbf{A}], [\mathbf{u}])$ where $\mathbf{A} \leftarrow_R \mathcal{D}_k$, $\mathbf{w} \leftarrow_R \mathbb{Z}_q^k$ and $\mathbf{u} \leftarrow_R \mathbb{Z}_q^{k+1}$.

Definition 2 ($\mathcal{D}_k$-Matrix Diffie-Hellman Assumption $\mathcal{D}_k$-MDDH). *Let $\mathcal{D}_k$ be a matrix distribution and $s \in \{1, 2, T\}$. We say that the $\mathcal{D}_k$-Matrix Diffie-Hellman ($\mathcal{D}_k$-MDDH) Assumption holds relative to GGen in group $\mathbb{G}_s$ if for all PPT adversaries $\mathcal{A}$,*

$$\mathbf{Adv}_{\mathcal{D}_k, \mathsf{GGen}}^{\mathrm{mddh}}(\mathcal{A}) := |\Pr[\mathcal{A}(\mathcal{G}, [\mathbf{A}]_s, [\mathbf{Aw}]_s) = 1] - \Pr[\mathcal{A}(\mathcal{G}, [\mathbf{A}]_s, [\mathbf{u}]_s) = 1]| = \mathrm{negl}(\lambda),$$

where the probability is taken over $\mathcal{G} \leftarrow_R \mathsf{GGen}(1^\lambda)$, $\mathbf{A} \leftarrow_R \mathcal{D}_k, \mathbf{w} \leftarrow_R \mathbb{Z}_q^k, \mathbf{u} \leftarrow_R \mathbb{Z}_q^{k+1}$.

The Kernel-Diffie-Hellman assumption $\mathcal{D}_k$-KerMDH [49] is a natural *computational analogue* of the $\mathcal{D}_k$-MDDH Assumption.

Definition 3 ($\mathcal{D}_k$-Kernel Diffie-Hellman Assumption $\mathcal{D}_k$-KerMDH). *Let $\mathcal{D}_k$ be a matrix distribution and $s \in \{1, 2\}$. We say that the $\mathcal{D}_k$-Kernel Diffie-Hellman ($\mathcal{D}_k$-KerMDH) Assumption holds relative to GGen in group $\mathbb{G}_s$ if for all PPT adversaries $\mathcal{A}$,*

$$\mathbf{Adv}^{\mathrm{kmdh}}_{\mathcal{D}_k,\mathsf{GGen}}(\mathcal{A}) := \Pr[\mathbf{c}^\top \mathbf{A} = \mathbf{0} \wedge \mathbf{c} \neq \mathbf{0} \mid [\mathbf{c}]_{3-s} \leftarrow_{\mathrm{R}} \mathcal{A}(\mathcal{G}, [\mathbf{A}]_s)] = \mathrm{negl}(\lambda),$$

where the probability is taken over $\mathcal{G} \leftarrow_{\mathrm{R}} \mathsf{GGen}(1^\lambda)$, $\mathbf{A} \leftarrow_{\mathrm{R}} \mathcal{D}_k$.

Note that we can use a non-zero vector in the kernel of $\mathbf{A}$ to test membership in the column space of $\mathbf{A}$. This means that the $\mathcal{D}_k$-KerMDH assumption is a relaxation of the $\mathcal{D}_k$-MDDH assumption, as captured in the following lemma from [49].

Lemma 1. *For any matrix distribution $\mathcal{D}_k$, $\mathcal{D}_k$-MDDH $\Rightarrow \mathcal{D}_k$-KerMDH.*

For each $k \geq 1$, [30,49] specify distributions $\mathcal{L}_k$, $\mathcal{SC}_k$, $\mathcal{U}_k$ (and others) such that the corresponding $\mathcal{D}_k$-MDDH and $\mathcal{D}_k$-KerMDH assumptions are generically secure in bilinear groups and form a hierarchy of increasingly weaker assumptions.

$$\mathcal{SC}_k : \mathbf{A} = \begin{pmatrix} 1 & 0 & 0 & \cdots & 0 \\ a & 1 & 0 & \cdots & 0 \\ 0 & a & 1 & & 0 \\ 0 & 0 & a & & 0 \\ & & & \ddots & \\ 0 & 0 & 0 & \cdots & a \end{pmatrix}, \ \mathcal{L}_k : \mathbf{A} = \begin{pmatrix} 1 & 1 & 1 & \cdots & 1 \\ a_1 & 0 & 0 & \cdots & 0 \\ 0 & a_2 & 0 & \cdots & 0 \\ 0 & 0 & a_3 & & 0 \\ \vdots & & & \ddots & \\ 0 & 0 & 0 & \cdots & a_k \end{pmatrix}, \ \mathcal{U}_k : \mathbf{A} = \begin{pmatrix} a_{1,1} & \cdots & a_{1,k} \\ \vdots & \ddots & \vdots \\ a_{k+1,1} & \cdots & a_{k+1,k} \end{pmatrix},$$

where $a, a_i, a_{i,j} \leftarrow \mathbb{Z}_q$. We define $\mathsf{Lin}_k := \mathcal{L}_k$-MDDH ($k$-Linear Assumption of [39]) and $\mathsf{KerLin}_k := \mathcal{L}_k$-KerMDH. Note that $\mathsf{KerLin}_2 = \mathsf{SDP}$ (Simultaneous Double Pairing Assumption of [22]). The relations between the different assumptions for $\mathcal{D}_k = \mathcal{L}_k$ are as follows:

$$\begin{array}{ccccc}
\mathsf{DDH} & \Longrightarrow & 2\text{-}\mathsf{Lin} & \Longrightarrow & 3\text{-}\mathsf{Lin} \Longrightarrow \cdots \\
\Downarrow & & \Downarrow & & \Downarrow \\
1\text{-}\mathsf{KerLin} & \Rightarrow & 2\text{-}\mathsf{KerLin} & \Rightarrow & 3\text{-}\mathsf{KerLin} \Rightarrow \cdots \quad \Rightarrow \mathsf{CDH} \\
& & \| & & \\
& & \mathsf{SDP} & &
\end{array}$$

Fig. 3. The relation between k-KerLin and k-Lin

2.3 Quasi-Adaptive Non-Interactive Zero-Knowledge

Quasi-Adaptive NIZK (QA-NIZK) proofs are NIZK proofs where the CRS is allowed to depend on the specific language for which proofs have to be generated [42]. The common reference string crs is generated in a specific way and contains a fixed part par, produced by an algorithm $\mathsf{Gen}_{\mathsf{par}}$, and a language-dependent part crs_l. However, for the zero-knowledge property there should be a single simulator for the entire class of languages.

For public parameters par produced by $\mathsf{Gen}_{\mathsf{par}}$, let $\mathcal{D}_{\mathsf{par}}$ be a probability distribution over a collection of relations $R = \{R_\rho\}$ parametrized by a string ρ with an associated language $\mathcal{L}_\rho = \{y : \exists x \text{ s.t. } R_\rho(y, x) = 1\}$.

We now give a formal definition of QANIZK for $\mathcal{D}_{\mathsf{par}}$ in its tag-based variant.

Definition 4 (Quasi-Adaptive Non-Interactive Zero Knowledge Argument).
A Quasi-adaptive Non-Interactive Zero Knowledege Argument (QANIZK) Π for a language distribution $\mathcal{D}_{\mathsf{par}}$ consists of five PPT algorithms $\Pi = (\mathsf{Gen}_{\mathsf{par}}, \mathsf{Gen}_{\mathsf{crs}}, \mathsf{Prove}, \mathsf{Sim}_\pi, \mathsf{Verify})$:

- *The probabilistic key generation algorithm $\mathsf{Gen}_{\mathsf{par}}(\lambda)$ returns the public parameters* par.
- *The probabilistic algorithm $\mathsf{Gen}_{\mathsf{crs}}(\mathsf{par}, \rho)$ returns a common reference string crs and a trapdoor trap. We assume that crs implicitly contains par and ρ and that it defines a tag-space $\mathcal{T}$. (This is the classical QANIZK setting.) If $\mathcal{T}$ is not specified then $\mathcal{T} = \{\varepsilon\}$ and tags can be ignored in all algorithms.*
- *The probabilistic proving algorithm $\mathsf{Prove}(\mathsf{crs}, \tau, x, y)$ returns a proof π with respect to tag $\tau \in \mathcal{T}$.*
- *The deterministic verification algorithm $\mathsf{Verify}(\mathsf{crs}, \tau, y, \pi)$ returns 1 or 0, where 1 means that π is a valid proof of $y \in \mathcal{L}_\rho$.*
- *The probabilistic proving algorithm $\mathsf{Sim}_\pi(\mathsf{crs}, \mathsf{trap}, \tau, y)$ returns a proof π for some y (not necessarily in $\mathcal{L}_\rho$) with respect to tag $\tau \in \mathcal{T}$.*

We require that the algorithms satisfy the following properties:

(Perfect completeness). *For all λ, all* par *output by $\mathsf{Gen}_{\mathsf{par}}(\lambda)$, all ρ output by $\mathcal{D}_{\mathsf{par}}$, all (x, y) with $R_\rho(y, x) = 1$, all $\tau \in \mathcal{T}$, we have*

$$\Pr\left[\mathsf{Verify}(\mathsf{crs}, \tau, y, \pi) = 1 \,\middle|\, \begin{array}{l} (\mathsf{crs}, \mathsf{trap}) \leftarrow_{\mathrm{R}} \mathsf{Gen}_{\mathsf{crs}}(\mathsf{par}, \rho) \\ \pi \leftarrow_{\mathrm{R}} \mathsf{Prove}(\mathsf{crs}, \tau, x, y) \end{array}\right] = 1.$$

(Perfect zero-knowledge). *For all λ, all* par *output by $\mathsf{Gen}_{\mathsf{par}}(\lambda)$, all ρ output by $\mathcal{D}_{\mathsf{par}}$, all $(\mathsf{crs}, \mathsf{trap})$ output by $\mathsf{Gen}_{\mathsf{crs}}(\mathsf{par}, \rho)$, all (x, y) with $R_\rho(y, x) = 1$, all $\tau \in \mathcal{T}$, the distributions*

$$\mathsf{Prove}(\mathsf{crs}, \tau, x, y) \text{ and } \mathsf{Sim}_\pi(\mathsf{crs}, \mathsf{trap}, \tau, y)$$

are the same (where the coin tosses are taken over $\mathsf{Prove}, \mathsf{Sim}_\pi$).

(Computational adaptive soundness). *For all PPT adversaries $\mathcal{A}$, $\mathbf{Adv}_\Pi^{\mathrm{as}}(\mathcal{A}) :=$*

$$\Pr\left[\begin{array}{l} y^\star \notin \mathcal{L}_\rho \\ \wedge \mathsf{Verify}(\mathsf{crs}, \tau^\star, y^\star, \pi^\star) = 1 \end{array} \,\middle|\, \begin{array}{l} \mathsf{par} \leftarrow_{\mathrm{R}} \mathsf{Gen}_{\mathsf{par}}(\lambda); \rho \leftarrow_{\mathrm{R}} \mathcal{D}_{\mathsf{par}} \\ (\mathsf{crs}, \mathsf{trap}) \leftarrow_{\mathrm{R}} \mathsf{Sim}_{\mathsf{crs}}(\mathsf{par}, \rho) \\ (\tau^\star, y^\star, \pi^\star) \leftarrow_{\mathrm{R}} \mathcal{A}(\mathsf{par}, \mathsf{crs}, \rho) \end{array}\right]$$

is negligible.

Note that our formalization of perfect knowledge is similar to that of composable zero knowledge in [38] and requires indistinguishability even for adversaries that get access to $(\mathsf{crs}, \mathsf{trap})$. In particular, the formalization implies composability (namely, the adversary may see multiple proofs for many adaptively chosen instances in the language). We also consider simulation soundness [27,51], which is a strengthening of adaptive soundness, and stipulates that an adversary cannot prove a false statement, even if it can see simulated proofs for instances y of its choice.

Definition 5 (Simulation Soundness). *A QANIZK system Π is said to be (unbounded) simulation-sound if for all PPT adversaries $\mathcal{A}$, $\mathbf{Adv}_\Pi^{\mathrm{uss}}(\mathcal{A}) :=$*

$$\Pr\left[\begin{array}{l} y^\star \notin \mathcal{L}_\rho \wedge \tau^\star \notin \mathcal{Q}_{\mathrm{tags}} \\ \wedge \mathsf{Verify}(\mathsf{crs}, \tau^\star, y^\star, \pi^\star) = 1 \end{array} \,\middle|\, \begin{array}{l} \mathsf{par} \leftarrow_{\mathrm{R}} \mathsf{Gen}_{\mathsf{par}}(\lambda); \rho \leftarrow_{\mathrm{R}} \mathcal{D}_{\mathsf{par}} \\ (\mathsf{crs}, \mathsf{trap}) \leftarrow_{\mathrm{R}} \mathsf{Sim}_{\mathsf{crs}}(\mathsf{par}, \rho) \\ (\tau^\star, y^\star, \pi^\star) \leftarrow_{\mathrm{R}} \mathcal{A}^{\mathsf{ProveO}(\cdot, \cdot)}(\mathsf{par}, \mathsf{crs}, \rho) \end{array}\right]$$

is negligible, where ProveO(τ, y) *returns* Sim$_\pi$(crs, trap, τ, y) *and adds* τ *to the set* $\mathcal{Q}_{\text{tags}}$. Π *is said to be* one-time simulation-sound *with corresponding advantage function* **Adv**$_\Pi^{\text{ot-ss}}(\mathcal{A})$, *if* $\mathcal{A}$ *is restricted to make at most one query to the oracle* ProveO.

We remark that a QANIZK with exponential tag-space can be transformed into a classical QANIZK with $\mathcal{T} = \{\varepsilon\}$ using a one-time signature scheme or a MAC. Other security properties remain the same.

2.4 Linearly Homomorphic Structure-Preserving Signatures

We now define syntax and security of a linearly homomorphic structure-preserving signature (LHSPS) scheme [15,32,47], where the signatures are fully randomizable and also strongly context-hiding [4,7]. We assume the existence of Gen$_{\text{par}}(\lambda)$, a probabilistic key generation algorithm that returns public parameters par containing the description of a group $\mathbb{G}$.

Definition 6 (Linearly Homomorphic Structure-Preserving Signature). *A* linearly homomorphic structure-preserving signature *(LHSPS) scheme* LHSPS *consists of four PPT algorithms* LHSPS $=$ (Gen, Sign, SignDerive, Verify) *with the following properties.*

- *The probabilistic key generation algorithm* Gen(par) *returns the (master) public/secret key* (pk, sk), *where* pk $\in \mathbb{G}^{n_{\text{pk}}}$ *for some* $n_{\text{pk}} \in \text{poly}(\lambda)$. *We assume that* pk *implicitly defines a message space* $\mathcal{M} = \mathbb{G}^n$, *for some* $n \in \text{poly}(\lambda)$, *and a tag space* $\mathcal{T}$.
- *The probabilistic signing algorithm* Sign(sk, τ, [**m**]) *returns a signature* $\sigma \in \mathbb{G}^{n_\sigma}$ *on message* [**m**] $\in \mathbb{G}^n$ *with respect to tag* τ.
- *The probabilistic signature derivation algorithm* SignDerive(pk, τ, $(\omega_i, \sigma_i)_{1 \leq i \leq \ell}$) *returns a signature* $\sigma \in \mathbb{G}^{n_\sigma}$ *on the vector* $[\sum \omega_i \mathbf{m}_i]$, *where* $\omega_i \in \mathbb{Z}_q$ *and* σ_i *is a valid signature on* [$\mathbf{m}_i$] *with respect to tag* τ.
- *The deterministic verification algorithm* Verify(pk, τ, [**m**], σ) *returns 1 or 0, where 1 means that* σ *is a valid signature in* [**m**].

We require that for all $\lambda \in \mathbb{N}$, *all pairs* (pk, sk) *generated by* Gen(par), *all tags* $\tau \in \mathcal{T}$, *the following holds:*

(Perfect correctness.) *for all messages* [**m**] $\in \mathbb{G}^n$, *all* σ *generated by* Sign(sk, τ, [**m**]) *we have*

$$\text{Ver}(\text{pk}, \tau, [\mathbf{m}], \sigma) = 1.$$

(Full randomizability.) *for all messages* [$\mathbf{m}_1$], ..., [$\mathbf{m}_\ell$] $\in \mathbb{G}^n$, *all* $\omega_1, ..., \omega_\ell \in \mathbb{Z}_q$, *for all* $\sigma_1, ..., \sigma_\ell$ *where* $\sigma_i \leftarrow$ Sign(sk, τ, [$\mathbf{m}_i$]), *the distributions*

$$\text{Sign}(\text{sk}, \tau, [\sum \omega_i \mathbf{m}_i]) \text{ and } \text{SignDerive}(\text{pk}, \tau, (\omega_i, \sigma_i)_{1 \leq i \leq \ell})$$

are the same.

Note that our requirement of full randomizability implies strongly context hiding as considered in [4,7]. We now define security for LHSPS schemes.

Definition 7. *To an adversary* $\mathcal{A}$ *and* LHSPS *we associate the advantage function* **Adv**$_{\text{LHSPS}}^{\text{ufcma}}(\mathcal{A}) :=$

$$\text{Pr}\left[\begin{array}{c|c} \mathbf{m}^* \notin span(\mathbf{M}_{\tau^*}) & (\text{pk}, \text{sk}) \leftarrow_{\text{R}} \text{Gen}(\text{par}) \\ \wedge \text{Verify}(\text{pk}, \tau^*, [\mathbf{m}^*], \sigma^*) = 1 & (\tau^*, [\mathbf{m}^*], \sigma^*) \leftarrow_{\text{R}} \mathcal{A}^{\text{SignO}(\cdot, \cdot)}(\text{pk}) \end{array}\right],$$

where $\mathsf{SignO}(\tau, [\mathbf{m}])$ *runs* $\sigma \leftarrow_{\mathrm{R}} \mathsf{Sign}(\mathsf{sk}, \tau, [\mathbf{m}])$, *appends the vector* $\mathbf{m}$ *(as a new column) to the matrix* $\mathbf{M}_\tau$ *(initialized with* $\mathbf{0}$*) and returns* σ *to* $\mathcal{A}$.

Note that the winning condition $\mathbf{m}^* \notin span(\mathbf{M}_{\tau^*})$ may not be efficiently verifiable. We will also consider security against a restricted class of "targeting adveraries" [47] which provide a certificate $\mathbf{c}^*$ for $\mathbf{m}^* \notin span(\mathbf{M}_{\tau^*})$.

Definition 8. *To an adversary* $\mathcal{A}$ *and* LHSPS *we associate the advantage function* $\mathbf{Adv}_{\mathsf{LHSPS}}^{\mathsf{ufcma-t}}(\mathcal{A}) :=$

$$\Pr\left[\begin{array}{l} \mathbf{c}^{*\top}\mathbf{m}^* \neq 0 \wedge \mathbf{c}^{*\top}\mathbf{M}_{\tau^*} = \mathbf{0} \\ \wedge \mathsf{Verify}(\mathsf{pk}, \tau^*, [\mathbf{m}^*], \sigma^*) = 1 \end{array} \middle| \begin{array}{l} (\mathsf{pk}, \mathsf{sk}) \leftarrow_{\mathrm{R}} \mathsf{Gen}(\mathsf{par}) \\ (\tau^*, [\mathbf{m}^*], \sigma^*, [\mathbf{c}^*]) \leftarrow_{\mathrm{R}} \mathcal{A}^{\mathsf{SignO}(\cdot,\cdot)}(\mathsf{pk}) \end{array}\right],$$

where $\mathsf{SignO}(\tau, [\mathbf{m}])$ *runs* $\sigma \leftarrow_{\mathrm{R}} \mathsf{Sign}(\mathsf{sk}, \tau, [\mathbf{m}])$, *appends the vector* $\mathbf{m}$ *(as a new column) to the matrix* $\mathbf{M}_\tau$ *(initialized with* $\mathbf{0}$*) and returns* σ *to* $\mathcal{A}$.

Observe that $\mathbf{c}^{*\top}\mathbf{m}^* \neq 0 \wedge \mathbf{c}^{*\top}\mathbf{M}_{\tau^*} = \mathbf{0}$ (which we can check via the pairing) implies $\mathbf{m}^* \notin span(\mathbf{M}_{\tau^*})$.

3   Quasi-Adaptive Zero Knowledge for Linear Spaces

In this section we will describe a number of Quasi-Adaptive Zero Knowledge Proofs for linear spaces. From now on and for the rest of this paper we will use $\mathsf{Gen}_{\mathsf{par}} = \mathsf{GGen}$. That is, $\mathsf{Gen}_{\mathsf{par}}(1^\lambda)$ returns $\mathsf{par} = \mathcal{PG}$, where $\mathcal{PG} = (\mathbb{G}_1, \mathbb{G}_2, \mathbb{G}_T, q, g_1, g_2, e)$ is a pairing group. The probability distribution $\mathcal{D}_{\mathsf{par}}$ returns a matrix $\rho = [\mathbf{M}]_1 \in \mathbb{G}_1^{n \times t}$, for integers $n > t$. Given par and ρ, the language $\mathcal{L}_\mathbf{M}$ is defined as

$$\mathcal{L}_\mathbf{M} = \left\{ [\mathbf{y}]_1 \in \mathbb{G}_1^n : \exists\, \mathbf{x} \in \mathbb{Z}_q^t \text{ s.t. } \mathbf{y} = \mathbf{M}\mathbf{x} \right\}.$$

Lemma 2 (core lemma for adaptive soundness). *Let* n, t, k *be integers. For any* $\mathbf{M} \in \mathbb{Z}_q^{n \times t}, \mathbf{A} \in \mathbb{Z}_q^{(k+1) \times k}$ *and any (possibly unbounded) adversary* $\mathcal{A}$,

$$\Pr\left[\mathbf{y} \notin span(\mathbf{M}) \wedge \mathbf{z}^\top = \mathbf{y}^\top \mathbf{K} \middle| \begin{array}{l} \mathbf{K} \leftarrow_{\mathrm{R}} \mathbb{Z}_q^{n \times (k+1)} \\ (\mathbf{z}, \mathbf{y}) \leftarrow \mathcal{A}(\mathbf{M}^\top \mathbf{K}, \mathbf{K}\mathbf{A}) \end{array} \right] \leq \frac{1}{q}$$

$$\Pr\left[\begin{array}{l} \mathbf{y} \notin span(\mathbf{M}) \wedge \tau \neq \hat{\tau} \\ \wedge\, \mathbf{z}^\top = \mathbf{y}^\top (\mathbf{K}_0 + \hat{\tau}\mathbf{K}_1) \end{array} \middle| \begin{array}{l} \mathbf{K}_0, \mathbf{K}_1 \leftarrow_{\mathrm{R}} \mathbb{Z}_q^{n \times (k+1)}; \\ (\mathbf{z}, \mathbf{y}, \tau) \leftarrow \mathcal{A}^{\mathcal{O}(\cdot)}(\mathbf{M}^\top \mathbf{K}_0, \mathbf{M}^\top \mathbf{K}_1, \mathbf{K}_0 \mathbf{A}, \mathbf{K}_1 \mathbf{A}) \end{array} \right] \leq \frac{1}{q},$$

where $\mathcal{O}(\hat{\tau})$ *may only be called one time and returns* $\mathbf{K}_0 + \hat{\tau}\mathbf{K}_1$.

Proof. To prove the first equation of the lemma, fix $\mathbf{M} \in \mathbb{Z}_q^{n \times t}, \mathbf{A} \in \mathbb{Z}_q^{(k+1) \times k}$, and fix a non-zero vector $\hat{\mathbf{a}} \notin span(\mathbf{A})$. Then, for any $\mathbf{y} \notin span(\mathbf{M})$, the following distributions

$$(\mathbf{M}^\top \mathbf{K}, \mathbf{K}\mathbf{A}, \mathbf{y}^\top \mathbf{K}\hat{\mathbf{a}}) \quad \text{and} \quad (\mathbf{M}^\top \mathbf{K}, \mathbf{K}\mathbf{A}, u) \tag{1}$$

are the same, where $\mathbf{K} \leftarrow_{\mathrm{R}} \mathbb{Z}_q^{n \times (k+1)}, u \leftarrow_{\mathrm{R}} \mathbb{Z}_q$. By a standard argument (e.g. complexity leveraging[3]), this means that the two distributions are the same even if $\mathbf{y} \notin span(\mathbf{M})$ is adaptively chosen after seeing $(\mathbf{M}^\top \mathbf{K}, \mathbf{K}\mathbf{A})$. Therefore, for any adversary $\mathcal{A}$, we have

$$\Pr_{\mathbf{K} \leftarrow_{\mathrm{R}} \mathbb{Z}_q^{n \times (k+1)}}[\mathbf{y} \notin span(\mathbf{M}) \wedge \mathbf{z}^\top \hat{\mathbf{a}} = \mathbf{y}^\top \mathbf{K}\hat{\mathbf{a}} \mid (\mathbf{z}, \mathbf{y}) \leftarrow_{\mathrm{R}} \mathcal{A}(\mathbf{M}^\top \mathbf{K}, \mathbf{K}\mathbf{A})] \leq 1/q$$

---

[3] Using complexity leveraging, we can transform any adaptive distinguisher into a non-adaptive one with an exponential loss in the distinguishing advantage. If the optimal non-adaptive distinguishing advantage is 0 as is the case for two identical distributions, then the optimal adaptive distinguishing advantage must also be 0.

since $\mathbf{y}^\top \mathbf{K}\hat{\mathbf{a}}$ is uniformly random from the adversary's view-point. The lemma then follows from the fact that $\mathbf{z}^\top = \mathbf{y}^\top \mathbf{K}$ implies $\mathbf{z}^\top \hat{\mathbf{a}} = \mathbf{y}^\top \mathbf{K}\hat{\mathbf{a}}$.

To prove the second equation of the lemma, observe that $(\mathbf{K}_0 + \tau\mathbf{K}_1, \mathbf{K}_0 + \hat{\tau}\mathbf{K}_1)$ are pairwise-independent, so we can essentially give away $\mathbf{K}_0 + \tau\mathbf{K}_1$ to $\mathcal{A}$ and still carry out the preceding proof with $\mathbf{K}_0 + \hat{\tau}\mathbf{K}_1$ in place of $\mathbf{K}$. More formally, for any $\tau \neq \hat{\tau}$ and any $\mathbf{y} \notin span(\mathbf{M})$, the following distributions

$$(\mathbf{M}^\top \mathbf{K}_0, \mathbf{M}^\top \mathbf{K}_1, \mathbf{K}_0\mathbf{A}, \mathbf{K}_1\mathbf{A}, \mathbf{K}_0 + \tau\mathbf{K}_1, \mathbf{y}^\top(\mathbf{K}_0 + \hat{\tau}\mathbf{K}_1)\hat{\mathbf{a}})$$

$$\text{and} \quad (\mathbf{M}^\top \mathbf{K}_0, \mathbf{M}^\top \mathbf{K}_1, \mathbf{K}_0\mathbf{A}, \mathbf{K}_1\mathbf{A}, \mathbf{K}_0 + \tau\mathbf{K}_1, u)$$

are the same, where $\mathbf{K}_0, \mathbf{K}_1 \leftarrow_\text{R} \mathbb{Z}_q^{n \times (k+1)}, u \leftarrow_\text{R} \mathbb{Z}_q$. Upon eliminating the terms involving $\mathbf{K}_0 + \tau\mathbf{K}_1$, the preceding claim follows from the fact that the following distributions

$$(\mathbf{M}^\top \mathbf{K}_1, \mathbf{K}_1\mathbf{A}, (\hat{\tau} - \tau)\mathbf{y}^\top \mathbf{K}_1\hat{\mathbf{a}}) \text{ and } (\mathbf{M}^\top \mathbf{K}_1, \mathbf{K}_1\mathbf{A}, u)$$

are the same, where $\mathbf{K}_1 \leftarrow_\text{R} \mathbb{Z}_q^{n \times (k+1)}, u \leftarrow_\text{R} \mathbb{Z}_q$, as considered earlier in (1). The proof then proceeds as before.

3.1 Simple QANIZK with Adaptive Soundness

Let $\mathcal{D}_k$ be any matrix distribution from Definition 1. Consider protocol Π_as from Figure 4.

Gen(par, $[\mathbf{M}]_1 \in \mathbb{G}_1^{n \times t}$):	Prove(crs, $[\mathbf{y}]_1, \mathbf{x}$): // $\mathbf{y} = \mathbf{Mx}$
$\mathbf{A} \leftarrow_\text{R} \mathcal{D}_k; \mathbf{K} \leftarrow_\text{R} \mathbb{Z}_q^{n \times (k+1)}$ $\mathbf{P} := \mathbf{M}^\top\mathbf{K}; \mathbf{C} := \mathbf{KA}$ crs $:= ([\mathbf{P}]_1, [\mathbf{C}]_2, [\mathbf{A}]_2)$ Return (crs, trap $= \mathbf{K}$)	Return $\pi := ([\mathbf{x}^\top \mathbf{P}]_1) \in \mathbb{G}_1^{k+1}$ Sim(crs, trap $= \mathbf{K}, [\mathbf{y}]_1$): Return $\pi := ([\mathbf{y}^\top \mathbf{K}]_1)$ Verify(crs, $[\mathbf{y}]_1, \pi$): Check: $e(\pi, [\mathbf{A}]_2) = e([\mathbf{y}^\top]_1, [\mathbf{C}]_2)$

Fig. 4. QANIZK Π_as with adaptive soundness under $\mathcal{D}_k$-KerMDH Assumption

Theorem 1. *Protocol Π_as from Figure 4 is a Quasi-adaptive Non-Interactive Zero Knowledege Argument. Furthermore, under the $\mathcal{D}_k$-KerMDH Assumption in $\mathbb{G}_2$, it has adaptive soundness.*

Proof. Perfect completeness and perfect zero-knowledge follow readily from the fact that for all $\mathbf{y} = \mathbf{Mx}$ and $\mathbf{P} = \mathbf{M}^\top\mathbf{K}$:

$$\mathbf{x}^\top\mathbf{P} = \mathbf{x}^\top(\mathbf{M}^\top\mathbf{K}) = \mathbf{y}^\top\mathbf{K}.$$

We proceed to establish adaptive soundness based on the $\mathcal{D}_k$-KerMDH assumption. We will show that for all adversaries $\mathcal{A}$, there exists an adversary $\mathcal{B}$ with $\mathbf{T}(\mathcal{A}) \approx \mathbf{T}(\mathcal{B})$ and

$$\mathbf{Adv}_{\Pi_\text{as}}^\text{as}(\mathcal{A}) \leq \mathbf{Adv}_{\mathcal{D}_k,\text{GGen}}^\text{kmdh}(\mathcal{B}) + 1/q. \tag{2}$$

Adversary $\mathcal{B}(\mathcal{PG}, [\mathbf{A}]_2 \in \mathbb{G}_2^{(k+1)\times k})$ generates $[\mathbf{M}]_1 \leftarrow_\mathrm{R} \mathcal{D}_\mathrm{par}$, and the rest of the CRS as in the real scheme by picking $\mathbf{K} \in \mathbb{Z}_q^{n\times(k+1)}$ and computing

$$\mathsf{crs} = ([\mathbf{P}]_1 = \left[\mathbf{M}^\top\mathbf{K}\right]_1 \in \mathbb{G}_1^{t\times k},\quad [\mathbf{C}]_2 = [\mathbf{K}\cdot\mathbf{A}]_2 \in \mathbb{G}_2^{n\times k},\quad [\mathbf{A}]_2 \in \mathbb{G}_2^{(k+1)\times k}).$$

Next, $\mathcal{B}$ runs $\mathcal{A}$ on crs and obtains a proof $\pi = [\mathbf{z}^\top]_1 \in \mathbb{G}_1^{1\times k}$ and $[\mathbf{y}]_1 \in \mathbb{G}_1^n$ satisfying $\mathbf{y} \notin span(\mathbf{M})$ and $\mathbf{z}^\top\cdot\mathbf{A} = \mathbf{y}^\top\cdot\mathbf{C} = \mathbf{y}^\top\mathbf{K}\cdot\mathbf{A}$ with probability $\mathbf{Adv}_{\Pi_\mathrm{as}}^\mathrm{as}(\mathcal{A})$. Finally, $\mathcal{B}$ returns $[\mathbf{s}]_1$ computed as

$$\mathbf{s}^\top = \mathbf{z}^\top - \mathbf{y}^\top\mathbf{K}.$$

Clearly, $\mathbf{s}^\top\mathbf{A} = \mathbf{0}$ and $\Pr[\mathbf{s} = \mathbf{0}] \leq 1/q$ by Lemma 2. This proves equation (2).

3.2   More Efficient QANIZK with Adaptive Soundness for WS Distributions

Recall that we are considering a probability distribution $\mathcal{D}_\mathrm{par}$ that outputs a matrix $[\mathbf{M}]_1 \in \mathbb{G}_1^{n\times t}$. Such distributions are called *witness sampleable* (WS) [42] if there exist an efficiently sampleable distribution $\mathcal{D}_\mathrm{par}'$ that outputs $\mathbf{M}' \in \mathbb{Z}_q^{n\times t}$ such that $[\mathbf{M}']_1$ has the same distribution as $[\mathbf{M}]_1$. Note that this slightly restricts the set of languages which can be handled. Whereas the techniques used in QANIZK protocols for WS distributions pose no restrictions for most applications, are not applicable to structure-preserving signatures (for the latter, $[\mathbf{M}]_1$ is chosen adaptively by an adversary).

In Figure 5 we give an efficiency improvement of Π_as from Figure 4 which only works for WS distributions.

$\mathsf{Gen}(\mathsf{par}, [\mathbf{M}]_1 \in \mathbb{G}_1^{n\times t})$:	$\mathsf{Prove}(\mathsf{crs}, [\mathbf{y}]_1, \mathbf{x})$: // $\mathbf{y} = \mathbf{Mx}$
$\mathbf{A} \leftarrow_\mathrm{R} \mathcal{D}_k; \mathbf{K} \leftarrow_\mathrm{R} \mathbb{Z}_q^{n\times k}$	Return $\pi := \left[\mathbf{x}^\top\mathbf{P}\right]_1 \in \mathbb{G}_1^{1\times k}$
$\mathbf{P} := \mathbf{M}^\top\mathbf{K}; \mathbf{C} := \mathbf{K}\overline{\mathbf{A}}$	
$\mathsf{crs} := ([\mathbf{P}]_1, [\mathbf{C}]_2, [\overline{\mathbf{A}}]_2)$	$\mathsf{Sim}_\pi(\mathsf{crs}, \mathsf{trap} = \mathbf{K}, [\mathbf{y}]_1)$:
Return $(\mathsf{crs}, \mathsf{trap} = \mathbf{K})$	Return $\pi := \left[\mathbf{y}^\top\mathbf{K}\right]_1$
	$\mathsf{Verify}(\mathsf{crs}, [\mathbf{y}]_1, \pi)$:
	Check: $e(\pi, [\overline{\mathbf{A}}]_2) = e(\left[\mathbf{y}^\top\right]_1, [\mathbf{C}]_2)$

Fig. 5. More efficient QANIZK Π_as' with adaptive soundness for WS distributions under $\mathcal{D}_k$-KerMDH Assumption. Recall that $\overline{\mathbf{A}} \in \mathbb{Z}_q^{k\times k}$ denotes the upper square matrix of $\mathbf{A} \in \mathbb{Z}_q^{(k+1)\times k}$.

Theorem 2. *Protocol Π_as' from Figure 5 is a Quasi-adaptive Non-Interactive Zero Knowledege Argument. Suppose in addition that $\mathcal{D}_\mathrm{par}$ is a witness sampleable distribution. Then, under the $\mathcal{D}_k$-KerMDH Assumption in $\mathbb{G}_2$, the protocol has adaptive soundness.*

Proof. Perfect completeness and perfect zero-knowledge follow readily from the fact that for all $\mathbf{y} = \mathbf{Mx}$ and $\mathbf{P} = \mathbf{M}^\top\mathbf{K}$:

$$\mathbf{x}^\top\mathbf{P} = \mathbf{x}^\top(\mathbf{M}^\top\mathbf{K}) = \mathbf{y}^\top\mathbf{K}.$$

We proceed to establish adaptive soundness based on the $\mathcal{D}_k$-KerMDH assumption. We will show that for all adversaries $\mathcal{A}$, there exists an adversary $\mathcal{B}$ with $\mathbf{T}(\mathcal{A}) \approx \mathbf{T}(\mathcal{B})$ and

$$\mathbf{Adv}_{\Pi'_{as}}^{as}(\mathcal{A}) \leq \mathbf{Adv}_{\mathcal{D}_k,\mathsf{GGen}}^{kmdh}(\mathcal{B}) + 1/q. \tag{3}$$

Adversary $\mathcal{B}(\mathcal{PG}, [\mathbf{A}]_2 \in \mathbb{G}_2^{(k+1)\times k})$ generates $\mathbf{M} \leftarrow_R \mathcal{D}'_{par}$. (The latter algorithm exists since $\mathcal{D}_{par}$ is witness sampleable.) Let $\mathbf{M}^\perp \in \mathbb{Z}_q^{n\times(n-t)}$ be a basis for the kernel of $\mathbf{M}^\top$, that is, $\mathbf{M}^\perp$ is a full-rank matrix such that $\mathbf{M}^\top \mathbf{M}^\perp = \mathbf{0}$. Next, it picks $\mathbf{K}' \in \mathbb{Z}_q^{n\times k}, \mathbf{R} \in \mathbb{Z}_q^{(n-t-1)\times(k+1)}$ and defines

$$\mathbf{A}' := \begin{pmatrix} \mathbf{A} \\ \mathbf{R}\cdot\mathbf{A} \end{pmatrix} \in \mathbb{Z}_q^{(k+n-t)\times k}.$$

Let $\mathbf{T}_{\mathbf{A}'} \in \mathbb{Z}_q^{(n-t)\times k}$ be such that $\mathbf{T}_{\mathbf{A}'}\overline{\mathbf{A}'} = \underline{\mathbf{A}'}$. By implicitly defining $\mathbf{K} = \mathbf{K}' + \mathbf{M}^\perp \mathbf{T}_{\mathbf{A}'}$, $\mathcal{B}$ can compute

$$[\mathbf{C}]_2 = [\mathbf{K}\overline{\mathbf{A}}]_2 = [(\mathbf{K}' + \mathbf{M}^\perp\mathbf{T}_{\mathbf{A}'})\overline{\mathbf{A}}]_2 = [\mathbf{K}'\overline{\mathbf{A}} + \mathbf{M}^\perp\underline{\mathbf{A}'}]_2 = [(\mathbf{K}'\|\mathbf{M}^\perp)\cdot\mathbf{A}']_2$$
$$[\mathbf{P}]_1 = [\mathbf{M}^\top\mathbf{K}]_1 = [\mathbf{M}^\top\mathbf{K}']_1.$$

(The way we program the CRS is similar to that in [43, Theorem 13].)

Next, $\mathcal{B}$ runs $\mathcal{A}$ on $\mathsf{crs} := ([\mathbf{P}]_1, [\mathbf{C}]_2, [\overline{\mathbf{A}}]_2)$ and obtains a proof $\pi = [\mathbf{z}^\top]_1 \in \mathbb{G}_1^{1\times k}$ and $[\mathbf{y}]_1 \in \mathbb{G}_1^n$ satisfying $\mathbf{y}^\top\mathbf{M}^\perp \neq \mathbf{0}$ and

$$\mathbf{z}^\top\cdot\overline{\mathbf{A}} = \mathbf{y}^\top\cdot\mathbf{C}. \tag{4}$$

By the definitions of $\mathbf{C}$ and $\mathbf{A}'$,

$$\mathbf{z}^\top\overline{\mathbf{A}} = (\mathbf{z}^\top\|0)\mathbf{A}' = \mathbf{y}^\top\cdot\mathbf{C} = \mathbf{y}^\top(\mathbf{K}'\|\mathbf{M}^\perp)\cdot\mathbf{A}'$$

such that $[\mathbf{c}]_1$ with

$$\mathbf{c}^\top = ((\mathbf{z}^\top - \mathbf{y}^\top\mathbf{K}')\| - \mathbf{y}^\top\mathbf{M}^\perp) \neq \mathbf{0}$$

satisfies $\mathbf{c}^\top\mathbf{A}' = \mathbf{0}$. From $\mathbf{c}^\top = (\mathbf{c}_1^\top\|\mathbf{c}_2^\top) \in \mathbb{Z}_q^{1\times(k+1)} \times \mathbb{Z}_q^{1\times(n-t-1)}$ we will now extract a solution $\mathbf{s}$ to the $\mathcal{D}_k$-KerMDH problem. Define $\mathbf{s}^\top = \mathbf{c}_1^\top + \mathbf{c}_2^\top\mathbf{R}$ such that $\mathbf{s}^\top\mathbf{A} = \mathbf{c}_1^\top\mathbf{A} + \mathbf{c}_2^\top\mathbf{R}\mathbf{A} = \mathbf{c}^\top\mathbf{A}' = \mathbf{0}$. Since $\mathbf{c} \neq \mathbf{0}$ and matrix $\mathbf{R}$ only leaks through $\mathbf{A}'$ as $\mathbf{R}\mathbf{A}$,

$$\Pr_{\mathbf{R}\leftarrow_R\mathbb{Z}_q^{(n-t-1)\times(k+1)}}[\mathbf{c}_1^\top + \mathbf{c}_2^\top\mathbf{R} = \mathbf{0} \mid \mathbf{R}\mathbf{A}] \leq 1/q.$$

This proves equation (3).

3.3 Simple QANIZK with Adaptive One-Time Simulation Soundness

Protocol $\Pi_{\mathsf{ot\text{-}ss}}$ from Figure 6 with one-time simulation soundness is based on Π_{as} from Figure 4 with the hash key $\mathbf{K}$ replaced by the 2-wise independent hash function $h(\tau) := \mathbf{K}_0 + \tau\mathbf{K}_1$. This allows arguing for one-time simulation soundness. We remark that the protocol can be easily extending to ℓ-time simulation soundness by using the ℓ-wise independent hash function $h(\tau) = \sum_{i=0}^{\ell} \tau^i\mathbf{K}_i$. The size of crs would grow with ℓ, but the proof size remains the same.

Gen(par, $[\mathbf{M}]_1 \in \mathbb{G}_1^{n \times t}$):	Prove(crs, τ, $[\mathbf{y}]_1$, $\mathbf{x}$): $// \mathbf{y} = \mathbf{Mx}$
$\mathbf{A} \leftarrow_R \mathcal{D}_k; \mathbf{K}_0, \mathbf{K}_1 \leftarrow_R \mathbb{Z}_q^{n \times (k+1)}$	Return $\pi := \left[\mathbf{x}^\top (\mathbf{P}_0 + \tau \mathbf{P}_1)\right]_1 \in \mathbb{G}_1^{k+1}$
$(\mathbf{P}_0, \mathbf{P}_1) := (\mathbf{M}^\top \mathbf{K}_0, \mathbf{M}^\top \mathbf{K}_1)$	
$(\mathbf{C}_0, \mathbf{C}_1) := (\mathbf{K}_0 \mathbf{A}, \mathbf{K}_1 \mathbf{A})$	Sim$_\pi$(crs, trap $= (\mathbf{K}_0, \mathbf{K}_1), \tau, [\mathbf{y}]_1$):
crs := $([\mathbf{P}_0]_1, [\mathbf{P}_1]_1, [\mathbf{C}_0]_2, [\mathbf{C}_1]_2, [\mathbf{A}]_2)$	Return $\pi := \left[\mathbf{y}^\top (\mathbf{K}_0 + \tau \mathbf{K}_1)\right]_1$
Return (crs, trap $= (\mathbf{K}_0, \mathbf{K}_1)$)	
//crs defines tag-space $\mathcal{T} = \mathbb{Z}_q$	Verify(crs, τ, $[\mathbf{y}]_1$, π):
	Check: $e(\pi, [\mathbf{A}]_2) = e(\left[\mathbf{y}^\top\right]_1, [\mathbf{C}_0 + \tau \mathbf{C}_1]_2)$

Fig. 6. QANIZK $\Pi_{\text{ot-ss}}$ protocol with adaptive one-time simulation-soundness under $\mathcal{D}_k$-KerMDH Assumption

Theorem 3. *Protocol $\Pi_{\text{ot-ss}}$ from Figure 6 is a Quasi-adaptive Non-Interactive Zero Knowledge Argument. Furthermore, under the $\mathcal{D}_k$-KerMDH Assumption in $\mathbb{G}_2$, it has adaptive one-time simulation soundness.*

The proof of Theorem 3 is the same as that for Theorem 1 instantiated with the second part of Lemma 2.

Proof. Perfect completeness and perfect zero-knowledge follow readily from the fact that for all $\mathbf{y} = \mathbf{Mx}$ and $(\mathbf{P}_0, \mathbf{P}_1) = (\mathbf{M}^\top \mathbf{K}_0, \mathbf{M}^\top \mathbf{K}_1)$ and all τ:

$$\mathbf{x}^\top (\mathbf{P}_0 + \tau P_1) = \mathbf{x}^\top (\mathbf{M}^\top \mathbf{K}_0 + \tau \mathbf{M}^\top \mathbf{K}_1) = \mathbf{y}^\top (\mathbf{K}_0 + \tau \mathbf{K}_1).$$

We proceed to establish adaptive soundness based on the $\mathcal{D}_k$-KerMDH assumption. We will show that for all adversaries $\mathcal{A}$, there exists an adversary $\mathcal{B}$ with $\mathbf{T}(\mathcal{A}) \approx \mathbf{T}(\mathcal{B})$ and

$$\mathbf{Adv}_{\Pi_{\text{ot-ss}}}^{\text{ot-ss}}(\mathcal{A}) \leq \mathbf{Adv}_{\mathcal{D}_k, \text{GGen}}^{\text{kmdh}}(\mathcal{B}) + 1/q. \tag{5}$$

Adversary $\mathcal{B}(\mathcal{PG}, [\mathbf{A}]_2 \in \mathbb{G}_2^{(k+1) \times k})$ generates $[\mathbf{M}]_1 \leftarrow_R \mathcal{D}_{\text{par}}$, and the rest of the CRS as in the real scheme by picking $\mathbf{K}_0, \mathbf{K}_1 \in \mathbb{Z}_q^{n \times (k+1)}$ and computing crs as before. Next, $\mathcal{B}$ runs $\mathcal{A}$ on crs, simulates Sim$_\pi$ once using $(\mathbf{K}_0, \mathbf{K}_1)$, and obtains a tag τ, a proof $\pi = [\mathbf{z}^\top]_1 \in \mathbb{G}_1^{1 \times k}$ and $[\mathbf{y}]_1 \in \mathbb{G}_1^n$ satisfying $\mathbf{y} \notin span(\mathbf{M})$ and $\mathbf{z}^\top \cdot \mathbf{A} = \mathbf{y}^\top \cdot (\mathbf{C}_0 + \tau \mathbf{C}_1) = \mathbf{y}^\top (\mathbf{K}_0 + \tau \mathbf{K}_1) \cdot \mathbf{A}$. Finally, $\mathcal{B}$ returns $[\mathbf{s}]_1$ computed as

$$\mathbf{s}^\top = \mathbf{z}^\top - \mathbf{y}^\top (\mathbf{K}_0 + \tau \mathbf{K}_1).$$

Clearly, $\mathbf{s}^\top \mathbf{A} = \mathbf{0}$ and $\Pr[\mathbf{s} = \mathbf{0}] \leq 1/q$ by the second part of Lemma 2. This proves equation (5).

4   QANIZK with Unbounded Simulation Soundness for WS Distributions

In this section, we present a QANIZK with unbounded simulation soundness. For unbounded simulation-soundness, we can no longer rely on information-theoretic techniques for the core lemma (Lemma 2) as in the previous section. Instead, we introduce a computational variant of the core lemma based on the $\mathcal{D}_k$-MDDH assumption in $\mathbb{G}_1$, which we will use again for the fully secure LHSPS in Section 5.

4.1   Computational Core Lemma

In the computational core lemma, instead of giving out zero/one copy of $\mathbf{K}_0 + \tau\mathbf{K}_1$ to the adversary as in Lemma 2, we give out unbounded copies of

$$([\mathbf{r}^\top\mathbf{B}^\top(\mathbf{K}_0 + \tau\mathbf{K}_1)]_1, [\mathbf{r}^\top\mathbf{B}^\top]_1) \in (\mathbb{G}_1^{1\times(k+1)})^2 \tag{6}$$

where $\mathbf{B} \leftarrow_{\mathrm{R}} \mathcal{D}_k, \mathbf{K}_0, \mathbf{K}_1 \leftarrow_{\mathrm{R}} \mathbb{Z}_q^{(k+1)\times(k+1)}$ are fixed and a fresh $\mathbf{r} \leftarrow_{\mathrm{R}} \mathbb{Z}_q^k$ is chosen for each sample. Under the $\mathcal{D}_k$-MDDH assumption in $\mathbb{G}_1$ w.r.t. the matrix $\mathbf{B}$, this essentially yields a pseudorandom MAC (or randomized PRF) [13,23,25,29]. Note that we can verify these pairs given $(\mathbf{K}_0, \mathbf{K}_1)$. As before, we then publish $[\mathbf{A}]_2, [\mathbf{K}_0\mathbf{A}]_2, [\mathbf{K}_1\mathbf{A}]_2$ for public verification. For completeness, we use the fact that for all $\mathbf{A}, \mathbf{B}, \mathbf{r}, \mathbf{K}_0, \mathbf{K}_1$:

$$e([\mathbf{r}^\top\mathbf{B}^\top(\mathbf{K}_0 + \tau\mathbf{K}_1)]_1, [\mathbf{A}]_2) = e([\mathbf{r}^\top\mathbf{B}^\top]_1, [\mathbf{K}_0\mathbf{A} + \tau\mathbf{K}_1\mathbf{A}]_2). \tag{7}$$

The computational core lemma says that random samples in (6) are pseudorandom subject to the preceding verification equation, in the sense that the first component hides any vector in the kernel of $\mathbf{A}$. The construction and proof strategy build upon those used in recent $\mathcal{D}_k$-MDDH-based fully secure IBE schemes in [13,23], which in turn build upon earlier dual system IBE schemes in [24,45,50,52].

Lemma 3 (computational core lemma for unbounded adaptive soundness).
For all adversaries $\mathcal{A}$, there exists an adversary $\mathcal{B}$ with $\mathbf{T}(\mathcal{A}) \approx \mathbf{T}(\mathcal{B})$ and

$$\Pr\left[\begin{array}{c|c} \tau^* \notin \mathcal{Q}_{\text{tags}} \\ \wedge\, b' = b \end{array} \begin{array}{l} \mathbf{A}, \mathbf{B} \leftarrow_{\mathrm{R}} \mathcal{D}_k \\ \mathbf{K}_0, \mathbf{K}_1 \leftarrow_{\mathrm{R}} \mathbb{Z}_q^{(k+1)\times(k+1)} \\ (\mathbf{P}_0, \mathbf{P}_1) := (\mathbf{B}^\top\mathbf{K}_0, \mathbf{B}^\top\mathbf{K}_1) \\ \mathsf{pk} := ([\mathbf{P}_0]_1, [\mathbf{P}_1]_1, [\mathbf{B}]_1, \mathbf{K}_0\mathbf{A}, \mathbf{K}_1\mathbf{A}, \mathbf{A}) \\ b \leftarrow_{\mathrm{R}} \{0,1\}; b' \leftarrow_{\mathrm{R}} \mathcal{A}^{\mathcal{O}_b(\cdot), \mathcal{O}^*(\cdot)}(\mathsf{pk}) \end{array}\right]$$
$$\leq \frac{1}{2} + 2Q \cdot \mathbf{Adv}_{\mathcal{D}_k,\mathsf{GGen}}^{\mathrm{mddh}}(\mathcal{B}) + Q/q,$$

where

- $\mathcal{O}_b(\tau)$ *returns* $([b\mu\mathbf{a}^\perp + \mathbf{r}^\top(\mathbf{P}_0 + \tau\mathbf{P}_1)]_1, [\mathbf{r}^\top\mathbf{B}^\top]_1) \in (\mathbb{G}_1^{1\times(k+1)})^2$ *with* $\mu \leftarrow_{\mathrm{R}}$ $\mathbb{Z}_q, \mathbf{r} \leftarrow_{\mathrm{R}} \mathbb{Z}_q^k$ *and adds τ to $\mathcal{Q}_{\text{tags}}$. Here, $\mathbf{a}^\perp \neq \mathbf{0}$ satisfies $\mathbf{a}^\perp\mathbf{A} = \mathbf{0}$.*
- $\mathcal{O}^*(\tau^*)$ *returns $\mathbf{K}_0 + \tau^*\mathbf{K}_1$. $\mathcal{A}$ only gets a single call τ^* to $\mathcal{O}^*$.*
- *Q is the number of queries $\mathcal{A}$ makes to $\mathcal{O}_b$.*

Proof. We proceed via a series of games. For $i = 0, 1, \ldots, Q$, in Game i, we answer the first i queries to $\mathcal{O}_b$ using $\mathcal{O}_0$, and the last $Q - i$ queries using $\mathcal{O}_1$. Let $\mathbf{Adv}_i$ denote the probability that $\mathcal{A}$ wins the game, that is, $\tau^* \notin \mathcal{Q}_{\text{tags}} \wedge b' = b$. It suffices to show that for all $i = 0, 1, \ldots, Q - 1$,

$$|\mathbf{Adv}_i - \mathbf{Adv}_{i+1}| \leq 2\mathbf{Adv}_{\mathcal{D}_k,\mathsf{GGen}}^{\mathrm{mddh}}(\mathcal{B}) + 1/q.$$

The main difference between Game i and Game $i + 1$ is that we answer the i'th query τ to $\mathcal{O}_b$ using $\mathcal{O}_0$ in Game i and $\mathcal{O}_1$ in Game $i + 1$, where $\mathcal{O}_b$ returns:

$$\left([b\mu\mathbf{a}^\perp + \mathbf{r}^\top\mathbf{B}^\top(\mathbf{K}_0 + \tau\mathbf{K}_1)]_1, [\mathbf{r}^\top\mathbf{B}^\top]_1\right), \text{where } \mu \leftarrow_{\mathrm{R}} \mathbb{Z}_q, \mathbf{r} \leftarrow_{\mathrm{R}} \mathbb{Z}_q^k.$$

Using the MDDH assumption twice, we may switch $[\mathbf{Br}]_1$ with $[\mathbf{w}]_1 \leftarrow_{\mathrm{R}} \mathbb{G}_1^{k+1}$ and then reverse the switch. Then, we just need to bound the advantage of $\mathcal{A}$ in an experiment where we answer the i'th query τ to $\mathcal{O}_b$ with

$$\left(\left[b\mu \mathbf{a}^\perp + \mathbf{w}^\top (\mathbf{K}_0 + \tau \mathbf{K}_1) \right]_1, [\mathbf{w}^\top]_1 \right), \text{ where } \mu \leftarrow_{\mathrm{R}} \mathbb{Z}_q, \mathbf{w} \leftarrow_{\mathrm{R}} \mathbb{Z}_q^{k+1};$$

and the remaining $q-1$ queries are handled using the normal $\mathcal{O}_0, \mathcal{O}_1$ as before. We may then proceed via an information-theoretic argument (similar to that used in Lemma 2) to bound the advantage for this experiment. Specifically, it suffices to show that for all $\mathbf{A}, \mathbf{B} \leftarrow \mathcal{D}_k$, with probability $1 - 1/q$ over $\mathbf{w} \leftarrow_{\mathrm{R}} \mathbb{Z}_q^{k+1}$: for all $\tau \neq \tau^*$, the following distributions

$$(\mathsf{pk}, \mathbf{w}^\top (\mathbf{K}_0 + \tau \mathbf{K}_1), \mathbf{K}_0 + \tau^* \mathbf{K}_1) \text{ and } (\mathsf{pk}, \mu \mathbf{a}^\perp + \mathbf{w}^\top (\mathbf{K}_0 + \tau \mathbf{K}_1), \mathbf{K}_0 + \tau^* \mathbf{K}_1) \quad (8)$$

are the same, where $\mathbf{K}_0, \mathbf{K}_1 \leftarrow_{\mathrm{R}} \mathbb{Z}_q^{(k+1) \times (k+1)}$. (As in Lemma 2, we may use complexity leveraging to handle adaptive choices of τ, τ^*.) The quantities in the distributions above correspond to the answers for the i'th query to $\mathcal{O}_b$ and the query to $\mathcal{O}^*$; moreover, given pk, we can compute $\mathbf{a}^\perp$ and simulate the remaining $q-1$ queries to $\mathcal{O}_0$ and $\mathcal{O}_1$. Upon eliminating the terms involving $\mathbf{K}_0 + \tau^* \mathbf{K}_1$, it suffices to show that with probability $1 - 1/q$ over $\mathbf{w} \leftarrow_{\mathrm{R}} \mathbb{Z}_q^{k+1}$, the following distributions

$$((\tau - \tau^*) \mathbf{w}^\top \mathbf{K}_1, \mathbf{K}_1 \mathbf{A}, \mathbf{B}^\top \mathbf{K}_1) \text{ and } (\mu \mathbf{a}^\perp + (\tau - \tau^*) \mathbf{w}^\top \mathbf{K}_1, \mathbf{K}_1 \mathbf{A}, \mathbf{B}^\top \mathbf{K}_1)$$

where $\mathbf{K}_1 \leftarrow_{\mathrm{R}} \mathbb{Z}_q^{(k+1) \times (k+1)}$ are the same. To establish the last statement, let us sample $\mathbf{K}_1$ as $\mathbf{K}' + \mu' \mathbf{b}^{\perp\top} \mathbf{a}^\perp$ where $\mathbf{K}' \leftarrow_{\mathrm{R}} \mathbb{Z}_q^{(k+1) \times (k+1)}, \mu' \leftarrow_{\mathrm{R}} \mathbb{Z}_q$ and $\mathbf{b}^\perp \neq \mathbf{0}$ satisfies $\mathbf{b}^\perp \mathbf{B} = \mathbf{0}$. Observe that $(\mathbf{K}_1 \mathbf{A}, \mathbf{B}^\top \mathbf{K}_1) = (\mathbf{K}' \mathbf{A}, \mathbf{B}^\top \mathbf{K}')$ and that with probability $1 - 1/q$ over $\mathbf{w}$, we have $\mathbf{b}^\perp \mathbf{w} \neq 0$. Fix such a $\mathbf{w}$, and the last statement follows from the fact that for all μ, the following distributions

$$((\tau - \tau^*) \mu' \mathbf{w}^\top \mathbf{b}^{\perp\top} \mathbf{a}^\perp) \text{ and } (\mu \mathbf{a}^\perp + (\tau - \tau^*) \mu' \mathbf{w}^\top \mathbf{b}^{\perp\top} \mathbf{a}^\perp)$$

are the same, where $\mu' \leftarrow_{\mathrm{R}} \mathbb{Z}_q$.

4.2   Our QANIZK Construction

Our protocol Π_{uss} with unbounded simulation soundness for witness sampleable distributions (c.f. Section 3.2) is given in Figure 7. We basically combine Π_{as} with the pseudorandom MAC given in the computational core lemma. The (simulated) proofs, instead of being $[\mathbf{y}^\top \mathbf{K}]_1$ as in Π_{as}, are now given by

$$([\mathbf{y}^\top \mathbf{K} + \mathbf{r}^\top \mathbf{B}^\top (\mathbf{K}_0 + \tau \mathbf{K}_1)]_1, [\mathbf{r}^\top \mathbf{B}^\top]_1)$$

Roughly speaking, the pseudo-random MAC allows us to hide partial information about $\mathbf{K}$ across all the simulated proofs, upon which we can use an information-theoretic argument as before.

The WS requirement basically means that we may assume that we know an explicit representation of the matrix $\mathbf{M}$ in the proof of security. For the protocol in Section 3.2, we need an explicit representation of $\mathbf{M}^\perp$ (a basis for the kernel of $\mathbf{M}$) in the proof of security. For the protocol in this section, it suffices to know $[\mathbf{M}^\perp]_2$, with which we can efficiently verify the winning condition for (simulation) soundness; the latter is necessary in order to build a distinguisher for the pseudorandom MAC.

$\mathsf{Gen}(\mathsf{par}, [\mathbf{M}]_1 \in \mathbb{G}_1^{n \times t})$:	$\mathsf{Prove}(\mathsf{crs}, \tau, [\mathbf{y}]_1, \mathbf{x})$: // $\mathbf{y} = \mathbf{Mx}$
$\mathbf{A}, \mathbf{B} \leftarrow_{\text{R}} \mathcal{D}_k$	$\mathbf{r} \leftarrow_{\text{R}} \mathbb{Z}_q^k$
$\mathbf{K} \leftarrow_{\text{R}} \mathbb{Z}_q^{n \times (k+1)}$;	$\pi := \left([\mathbf{x}^\top \mathbf{P} + \mathbf{r}^\top (\mathbf{P}_0 + \tau \mathbf{P}_1)]_1, [\mathbf{r}^\top \mathbf{B}^\top]_1 \right)$
$\mathbf{K}_0, \mathbf{K}_1 \leftarrow_{\text{R}} \mathbb{Z}_q^{(k+1) \times (k+1)}$	Return π
$\mathbf{P} := \mathbf{M}^\top \mathbf{K}; \mathbf{C} := \mathbf{KA}$	
$(\mathbf{C}_0, \mathbf{C}_1) := (\mathbf{K}_0 \mathbf{A}, \mathbf{K}_1 \mathbf{A})$	$\mathsf{Verify}(\mathsf{crs}, \tau, [\mathbf{y}]_1, \pi)$:
$(\mathbf{P}_0, \mathbf{P}_1) := (\mathbf{B}^\top \mathbf{K}_0, \mathbf{B}^\top \mathbf{K}_1)$	Parse $\pi = (\pi_1, \pi_2)$
$\mathsf{crs} := ([\mathbf{P}]_1, [\mathbf{C}]_2, [\mathbf{A}]_2, [\mathbf{B}]_1,$	Check: $e(\pi_1, [\mathbf{A}]_2)$ $=$ $e([\mathbf{y}^\top]_1, [\mathbf{C}]_2)$ ·
$[\mathbf{C}_0]_2, [\mathbf{C}_1]_2, [\mathbf{P}_0]_1, [\mathbf{P}_1]_1)$	$e(\pi_2, [\mathbf{C}_0 + \tau \mathbf{C}_1]_2)$
$\mathsf{trap} := \mathbf{K}$	
Return $(\mathsf{crs}, \mathsf{trap})$	$\mathsf{Sim}_\pi(\mathsf{crs}, \mathsf{trap} = \mathbf{K}, \tau, [\mathbf{y}]_1)$:
//crs defines tag-space $\mathcal{T} = \mathbb{Z}_q$	$\mathbf{r} \leftarrow_{\text{R}} \mathbb{Z}_q^k$
	Return $\pi :=$
	$\left([\mathbf{y}^\top \mathbf{K} + \mathbf{r}^\top (\mathbf{P}_0 + \tau \mathbf{P}_1)]_1, [\mathbf{r}^\top \mathbf{B}^\top]_1 \right)$

Fig. 7. QANIZK Π_{uss} protocol with (adaptive) unbounded simulation-soundness for WS distributions under $\mathcal{D}_k$-MDDH Assumption

Theorem 4. *Protocol Π_{uss} from Figure 7 is a Quasi-adaptive Non-Interactive Zero Knowledege Argument. Suppose in addition that $\mathcal{D}_{\mathsf{par}}$ is a witness sampleable distribution. Then, under the $\mathcal{D}_k$-MDDH Assumption in $\mathbb{G}_1$ and $\mathcal{D}_k$-KerMDH Assumption in $\mathbb{G}_2$, the protocol has adaptive unbounded simulation soundness.*

Proof. Perfect completeness and perfect zero-knowledge follow readily from the fact that for all $\mathbf{y} = \mathbf{Mx}$ and $\mathbf{P} = \mathbf{M}^\top \mathbf{K}$:

$$\mathbf{x}^\top \mathbf{P} = \mathbf{x}^\top (\mathbf{M}^\top \mathbf{K}) = \mathbf{y}^\top \mathbf{K},$$

along with (7).

We proceed to establish adaptive unbounded simulation soundness. We will show that for any adversary $\mathcal{A}$ that makes at most Q queries to Sim_π, there exists adversaries $\mathcal{B}_0, \mathcal{B}_1$ with $\mathbf{T}(\mathcal{A}) \approx \mathbf{T}(\mathcal{B}_0) \approx \mathbf{T}(\mathcal{B}_1)$ and

$$\mathbf{Adv}_{\Pi_{\mathsf{uss}}}^{\mathsf{uss}}(\mathcal{A}) \leq \mathbf{Adv}_{\mathcal{D}_k, \mathsf{GGen}}^{\mathsf{kmdh}}(\mathcal{B}_0) + 2Q \cdot \mathbf{Adv}_{\mathcal{D}_k, \mathsf{GGen}}^{\mathsf{mddh}}(\mathcal{B}_1) + (Q + 1)/q. \tag{9}$$

We proceed via a series of games and we use $\mathbf{Adv}_i$ to denote the advantage of $\mathcal{A}$ in Game i.

Game 0. This is the real experiment from Definition 5.

Game 1. Switch Verify to Verify*:

$\mathsf{Verify}^*(\mathsf{crs}, \tau, [\mathbf{y}]_1, \pi)$:
Parse $\pi = (\pi_1, \pi_2)$
Check: $\pi_1 = [\mathbf{y}]_1^\top \mathbf{K} + \pi_2 (\mathbf{K}_0 + \tau \mathbf{K}_1)$

To bound $|\mathbf{Adv}_0 - \mathbf{Adv}_1|$, it suffices to bound the probability that $\mathcal{A}$ produces $([\mathbf{y}]_1, \pi_1, \pi_2)$ that passes Verify but not Verify*. We may rewrite the verification equation in Verify as

$$e(\pi_1, [\mathbf{A}]_2) = e([\mathbf{y}]_1^\top \mathbf{K}, [\mathbf{A}]_2) \cdot e(\pi_2 (\mathbf{K}_0 + \tau \mathbf{K}_1), [\mathbf{A}]_2)$$
$$\iff e(\pi_1 - [\mathbf{y}]_1^\top \mathbf{K} + \pi_2 (\mathbf{K}_0 + \tau \mathbf{K}_1), [\mathbf{A}]_2) = 0$$

Observe that for any $([\mathbf{y}]_1, \pi_1, \pi_2)$ that passes Verify but not Verify*, the value

$$\pi_1 - [\mathbf{y}]_1^\top \mathbf{K} + \pi_2(\mathbf{K}_0 + \tau \mathbf{K}_1) \in \mathbb{G}_1^{1 \times (k+1)}$$

is a non-zero vector in the kernel of $\mathbf{A}$, which is hard to sample under the $\mathcal{D}$-KerMDH assumption. This means that

$$|\mathbf{Adv}_0 - \mathbf{Adv}_1| \leq \mathbf{Adv}_{\mathcal{D}_k, \mathsf{GGen}}^{\mathrm{kmdh}}(\mathcal{B}_0).$$

Game 2. Let $\mathbf{a}^\perp$ be an element from the kernel of $\mathbf{A}$. Switch Sim_π to Sim_π^* where

$\mathsf{Sim}_\pi^*(\mathsf{crs}, \mathsf{trap} = \mathbf{K}, \tau, [\mathbf{y}]_1)$:   // adds $\mu \mathbf{a}^\perp$
$\mathbf{r} \leftarrow_{\mathrm{R}} \mathbb{Z}_q^k; \mu \leftarrow_{\mathrm{R}} \mathbb{Z}_q$
Return $\pi := \left([\mathbf{y}^\top \mathbf{K} + \mu \mathbf{a}^\perp + \mathbf{r}^\top (\mathbf{P}_0 + \tau \mathbf{P}_1)]_1, [\mathbf{r}^\top \mathbf{B}^\top]_1\right)$

It follows readily from Lemma 3 and the fact that we can efficiently verify the winning condition for $\mathcal{A}$ that

$$|\mathbf{Adv}_1 - \mathbf{Adv}_2| \leq 2Q\mathbf{Adv}_{\mathcal{D}_k, \mathsf{GGen}}^{\mathrm{mddh}}(\mathcal{B}_1) + Q/q.$$

Basically, we pick $\mathbf{K}$ ourselves and proceed as follows:

- when $\mathcal{A}$ makes a query $(\tau, [\mathbf{y}]_1)$ and $\tau \neq \tau^*$, query $\mathcal{O}_b$ at τ to simulate either Sim_π or Sim_π^*, where $b = 0$ corresponds to Sim_π and $b = 1$ to Sim_π^*;
- when $\mathcal{A}$ makes a query $(\tau, [\mathbf{y}]_1)$ and $\tau = \tau^*$, pick $\mathbf{r} \leftarrow \mathbb{Z}_q^k$, return $\left([\mathbf{y}^\top \mathbf{K} + \mathbf{r}^\top (\mathbf{P}_0 + \tau \mathbf{P}_1)]_1, [\mathbf{r}^\top \mathbf{B}^\top]_1\right)$;
- we query $\mathcal{O}^*$ at τ^* to simulate Verify*.

The winning condition of $\mathcal{A}$ can be efficiently verified because $\mathcal{D}_{\mathrm{par}}$ is a witness sampleable distribution: given $[\mathbf{y}]_1$ and $\mathbf{M} \in \mathbb{Z}_q^{n \times t}$ we can verify $[\mathbf{y}]_1 \in \mathcal{L}_\mathbf{M} \Leftrightarrow [\mathbf{y}^\top]_1 \mathbf{M}^\perp \neq [\mathbf{0}]_1$.

Game 3. Switch $\mathbf{K} \leftarrow_{\mathrm{R}} \mathbb{Z}_q^{n \times (k+1)}$ in Gen to $\mathbf{K} := \mathbf{K}' + \mathbf{u} \mathbf{a}^\perp$, where $\mathbf{K}' \leftarrow_{\mathrm{R}} \mathbb{Z}_q^{n \times (k+1)}, \mathbf{u} \leftarrow_{\mathrm{R}} \mathbb{Z}_q^n$.

We will bound the advantage of the adversary $\mathcal{A}$ in Game 3 via an information-theoretic argument. We first look at what the adversary's view together with $\mathbf{K}'$ leaks about $\mathbf{u}$:

- $\mathbf{C} = (\mathbf{K}' + \mathbf{u} \mathbf{a}^\perp)\mathbf{A} = \mathbf{K}' \mathbf{A}$ completely hides $\mathbf{u}$;
- $\mathbf{P} = \mathbf{M}^\top (\mathbf{K}' + \mathbf{u} \mathbf{a}^\perp)$ leaks $\mathbf{M}^\top \mathbf{u}$;
- the output of Sim_π^* completely hides $\mathbf{u}$, since $\mathbf{y}^\top (\mathbf{K}' + \mathbf{u} \mathbf{a}^\perp) + \mu \mathbf{a}^\perp$ is identically distributed to $\mathbf{y}^\top \mathbf{K}' + \mu \mathbf{a}^\perp$ (namely, $\mathbf{y}^\top \mathbf{u}$ is masked by $\mu \leftarrow_{\mathrm{R}} \mathbb{Z}_q$).

To convince Verify* to accept a proof (π_1, π_2) on $\mathbf{y}^*$, the adversary must correctly compute

$$\mathbf{y}^{*\top} (\mathbf{K}' + \mathbf{u} \mathbf{a}^\perp)$$

and thus $(\mathbf{y}^*)^\top \mathbf{u} \in \mathbb{Z}_q$. Given $\mathbf{M}^\top \mathbf{u}$, for any adaptively chosen $\mathbf{y}^*$ not in the span of $\mathbf{M}$, we have that $(\mathbf{y}^*)^\top \mathbf{u}$ is uniformly random over $\mathbb{Z}_q$ from the adversary's view-point. Therefore, $\mathbf{Adv}_3 \leq 1/q$.

5   Linearly Homomorphic Structure-Preserving Signatures

We show how to extend our QANIZK techniques to LHSPS (linearly homomorphic structure-preserving signature), via a general methodology outlined in Section 1.2.

The simplest example of our techniques as applied to the QANIZK protocol Π_{as} from Figure 4 yields a one-time LHSPS, presented in Section A.2. Next, we modify the QANIZK protocol Π_{uss} from Figure 7 into a fully secure LHSPS: we use $\mathsf{sk} = \mathsf{trap}$ and define a signature on $[\mathbf{m}]_1$ as the "simulated proof" $\mathsf{Sim}_\pi(\mathsf{trap}, [\mathbf{m}]_1)$. We only achieve security against targeting adversaries (c.f. Definition 8), namely adversaries for which the winning condition is efficiently verifiable; the latter is necessary in order to build a distinguisher for the pseudorandom MAC in the security proof.

Gen(par):	Sign(pk, sk, τ, $[\mathbf{m}]_1$):
$\mathbf{A}, \mathbf{B} \leftarrow_R \mathcal{D}_k; \mathbf{K} \leftarrow_R \mathbb{Z}_q^{n \times (k+1)}$	$\mathbf{r} \leftarrow_R \mathbb{Z}_q^k;$
$\mathbf{K}_0, \mathbf{K}_1 \leftarrow_R \mathbb{Z}_q^{(k+1) \times (k+1)}$	$\sigma := \left([\mathbf{m}^\top \mathbf{K} + \mathbf{r}^\top (\mathbf{P}_0 + \tau \mathbf{P}_1)]_1, [\mathbf{r}^\top \mathbf{B}^\top]_1 \right)$
$\mathbf{C} := \mathbf{K}\mathbf{A} \in \mathbb{Z}_q^{n \times k}$	Return $\sigma \in (\mathbb{G}_1^{1 \times (k+1)})^2$
$(\mathbf{C}_0, \mathbf{C}_1) := (\mathbf{K}_0 \mathbf{A}, \mathbf{K}_1 \mathbf{A})$	
$(\mathbf{P}_0, \mathbf{P}_1) := (\mathbf{B}^\top \mathbf{K}_0, \mathbf{B}^\top \mathbf{K}_1)$	SignDerive(pk, τ, $(\omega_i, \sigma_i)_{1 \le i \le \ell}$):
$\mathsf{sk} := \mathbf{K}$	$\mathbf{r} \leftarrow_R \mathbb{Z}_q^k;$
$\mathsf{pk} := ([\mathbf{C}_0]_2, [\mathbf{C}_1]_2, [\mathbf{P}_0]_1, [\mathbf{P}_1]_1,$	Parse $\sigma_i = ([\mathbf{s}_i], [\mathbf{t}_i])$
$[\mathbf{C}]_2, [\mathbf{A}]_2, [\mathbf{B}]_1)$	$\sigma := \left(\left[\mathbf{r}^\top (\mathbf{P}_0 + \tau \mathbf{P}_1) + \sum_{i=1}^\ell \omega_i \mathbf{s}_i \right]_1, \right.$
Return (pk, sk)	$\left. \left[\mathbf{r}^\top \mathbf{B}^\top + \sum_{i=1}^\ell \omega_i \mathbf{t}_i \right]_1 \right)$
	Return $\sigma \in (\mathbb{G}_1^{1 \times (k+1)})^2$
	Verify(pk, τ, $[\mathbf{m}]_1$, σ):
	Parse $\sigma = (\sigma_1, \sigma_2)$
	Check:
	$e(\sigma_1, [\mathbf{A}]_2) = e([\mathbf{m}^\top]_1, [\mathbf{C}]_2) \cdot e(\sigma_2, [\mathbf{C}_0 + \tau \mathbf{C}_1]_2)$

Fig. 8. Linearly homomorphic structure-preserving signature LHSPS_{full} with message-space $\mathcal{M} = \mathbb{G}_1^n$ and tag-space $\mathcal{T} = \mathbb{Z}_q$

Theorem 5. *Under the $\mathcal{D}_k$-MDDH Assumption in $\mathbb{G}_1$ and $\mathcal{D}_k$-KerMDH Assumption in $\mathbb{G}_2$, LHSPS_{full} from Figure 8 is a linearly homomorphic structure-preserving signature scheme secure against targeting adversaries.*

The proof is similar to that in Theorem 4, with a complication and an additional $1/(Q+1)$ factor security loss arising from the fact that the adversary is allowed to have previously requested signatures for the challenge tag τ^*.

Proof. Perfect correctness and full randomizability are straight-forward. We proceed to establish security against targeting adversaries. We will show that for any adversary $\mathcal{A}$ that makes at most Q signing queries, there exists adversaries $\mathcal{B}_0, \mathcal{B}_1$ with $\mathbf{T}(\mathcal{A}) \approx \mathbf{T}(\mathcal{B}_0) \approx \mathbf{T}(\mathcal{B}_1)$ and

$$\mathbf{Adv}_{\mathsf{LHSPS}_{full}}^{\mathrm{ufcma-t}}(\mathcal{A}) \le (Q+1)(\mathbf{Adv}_{\mathcal{D}_k, \mathsf{GGen}}^{\mathrm{kmdh}}(\mathcal{B}_0) + 2Q\mathbf{Adv}_{\mathcal{D}_k, \mathsf{GGen}}^{\mathrm{mddh}}(\mathcal{B}_1) + \frac{Q+1}{q}). \quad (10)$$

We proceed via a series of games and we use $\mathbf{Adv}_i$ to denote the advantage of $\mathcal{A}$ in Game i.

Game 0. This is the real experiment from Definition 8.

Game 1. Suppose the adversary makes at most Q queries to SignO with tags $\tau_1, \ldots, \tau_Q$. In addition, we define $\tau_{Q+1} := \tau^*$. Now, pick $i^* \leftarrow_R [Q+1]$ and abort if i^* is not the smallest index i for which $\tau^* = \tau_i$. In the rest of the proof, we focus on the case we do not abort, which means that $\tau^* = \tau_{i^*}$ and $\tau_1, \ldots, \tau_{i^*-1}$ are all different from τ^*. This means that given τ, SignO can check whether τ^* equals τ: for the rest $i^* - 1$ queries, answer NO, and starting from the i^*'th query, we know τ^*. It is easy to see that

$$\mathbf{Adv}_1 \geq \frac{1}{Q+1}\mathbf{Adv}_0.$$

Game 2. Switch Verify to Verify*:

Verify$^*(\mathsf{pk}, \tau, [\mathbf{m}]_1, \sigma)$:

Parse $\sigma = (\sigma_1, \sigma_2)$

Check: $\sigma_1 = [\mathbf{m}]_1^\top \mathbf{K} + \sigma_2(\mathbf{K}_0 + \tau \mathbf{K}_1)$

As in the proof of Theorem 4, observe that for any $([\mathbf{m}]_1, \sigma_1, \sigma_2)$ that passes Verify but not Verify*, the value

$$\sigma_1 - [\mathbf{m}]_1^\top \mathbf{K} - \sigma_2(\mathbf{K}_0 + \tau \mathbf{K}_1) \in \mathbb{G}_1^{1 \times (k+1)}$$

is a non-zero vector in the kernel of $\mathbf{A}$, which is hard to sample under the $\mathcal{D}$-KerMDH assumption. This means that

$$|\mathbf{Adv}_1 - \mathbf{Adv}_2| \leq \mathbf{Adv}_{\mathcal{D}_k, \mathsf{GGen}}^{\mathrm{kmdh}}(\mathcal{B}_0).$$

Game 3. Switch Sign to Sign* where

Sign$^*(\mathsf{pk}, \mathsf{sk}, \tau, [\mathbf{m}]_1)$:   // adds $\mu \mathbf{a}^\perp$ for $\tau \neq \tau^*$

$\mathbf{r} \leftarrow_R \mathbb{Z}_q^k; \mu \leftarrow_R \mathbb{Z}_q$

if $\tau = \tau^*$, $\mu := 0$

Return $\sigma := \left([\mathbf{m}^\top \mathbf{K} + \mu \mathbf{a}^\perp + \mathbf{r}^\top(\mathbf{P}_0 + \tau \mathbf{P}_1)]_1, [\mathbf{r}^\top \mathbf{B}^\top]_1\right)$

As in the proof of Theorem 4, it follows readily from Lemma 3 and the fact that the adversary is targeting that

$$|\mathbf{Adv}_2 - \mathbf{Adv}_3| \leq 2Q\mathbf{Adv}_{\mathcal{D}_k, \mathsf{GGen}}^{\mathrm{mddh}}(\mathcal{B}_1) + Q/q$$

Basically, we pick $\mathbf{K}$ ourselves and use $\mathcal{O}_b$ to simulate either Sign or Sign* for $\tau \neq \tau^*$; compute the signature directly to simulate Sign or Sign* for $\tau = \tau^*$; and $\mathcal{O}^*$ to simulate Verify*. The winning condition of $\mathcal{A}$ can be efficiently verified since $\mathcal{A}$ is a targeting adversary.

Game 4. Switch $\mathbf{K} \leftarrow_R \mathbb{Z}_q^{n \times (k+1)}$ in Gen to $\mathbf{K} := \mathbf{K}' + \mathbf{u}\mathbf{a}^\perp$, where $\mathbf{K}' \leftarrow_R \mathbb{Z}_q^{n \times (k+1)}, \mathbf{u} \leftarrow_R \mathbb{Z}_q^n$.

We will bound the advantage of the adversary in Game 4 via an information-theoretic argument, similar to that in Theorem 4. We first look at what the adversary's view together with $\mathbf{K}'$ leaks about $\mathbf{u}$:

- $\mathbf{C} = (\mathbf{K}' + \mathbf{u}\mathbf{a}^\perp)\mathbf{A} = \mathbf{K}'\mathbf{A}$ completely hides $\mathbf{u}$;

- the output of SignO^* on $(\mathbf{m}, \tau)$ for $\tau \neq \tau^*$ completely hides $\mathbf{u}$, since $\mathbf{m}^\top(\mathbf{K}' + \mathbf{u}\mathbf{a}^\perp) + \mu\mathbf{a}^\perp$ is identically distributed to $\mathbf{m}^\top\mathbf{K}' + \mu\mathbf{a}^\perp$ (namely, $\mathbf{m}^\top\mathbf{u}$ is masked by $\mu \leftarrow_{\mathrm{R}} \mathbb{Z}_q$).
- the output of SignO^* on τ^* leaks $\mathbf{M}_{\tau^*}^\top(\mathbf{K}' + \mathbf{u}\mathbf{a}^\perp)$, which is captured by $\mathbf{M}_{\tau^*}^\top\mathbf{u}$;

To convince Verify^* to accept a signature (σ_1, σ_2) on $\mathbf{m}^*$, the adversary must correctly compute

$$\mathbf{m}^{*\top}(\mathbf{K}' + \mathbf{u}\mathbf{a}^\perp)$$

and thus $(\mathbf{m}^*)^\top\mathbf{u} \in \mathbb{Z}_q$. Given $\mathbf{M}_{\tau^*}^\top\mathbf{u}$, for any adaptively chosen $\mathbf{m}^*$ not in the span of $\mathbf{M}_{\tau^*}$, we have that $(\mathbf{m}^*)^\top\mathbf{u}$ is uniformly random over $\mathbb{Z}_q$ from the adversary's viewpoint. Therefore, $\mathbf{Adv}_4 \leq 1/q$.

Acknowledgments. We thank Fabrice Benhamouda and Olivier Blazy for helpful discussions on prior works and the reviewers for detailed and constructive feedback.

A   Appendix

A.1   More Efficient QANIZK with One-Time Simulation Soundness for WS Distributions

In Figure 9 we give a one-time simulation-sound QANIZK for WS distributions. It is a variant of $\Pi_{\text{ot-ss}}$ from Figure 9 with shorter proofs as with Π'_{as}. The result is inspired by the prior construction in [1]. Recall that in $\Pi_{\text{ot-ss}}$, we replaced $\mathbf{K}$ in Π_{as} with a 2-wise independent hash function $\mathbf{K}_0 + \tau\mathbf{K}_1$, which serves also as a one-time MAC. Unfortunately, we cannot apply the same modification to Π'_{as}. Roughly speaking, in the proof of security for Π'_{as}, we need to program $\mathbf{K}$. In the setting for one-time simulation soundness, we would need to program $\mathbf{K}_0 + \tau^*\mathbf{K}_1$, which we cannot do since τ^* is adaptively chosen.

Instead, we replace $\mathbf{K}$ in Π'_{as} with a different 2-wise independent hash function

$$\tau \mapsto \sum_{i=1}^{\ell} \mathbf{K}_{i,\tau_i}$$

as in Lamport's one-time signature. As in the security proof for Lamport's one-time signature, we would guess $i' \leftarrow_{\mathrm{R}} [\lambda], b' \leftarrow_{\mathrm{R}} \{0,1\}$ so that $\tau^*_{i'} \neq \tau_{i'}$ and $\tau^*_{i'} = b'$ (such a (i', b') exists since $\tau \neq \tau^*$) and then program $\mathbf{K}_{i',b'}$.

Theorem 6. *The protocol from Figure 9 is a Quasi-adaptive Non-Interactive Zero Knowledge Argument. Suppose in addition that $\mathcal{D}_{\text{par}}$ is a witness sampleable distribution. Then, under the $\mathcal{D}_k$-KerMDH Assumption in $\mathbb{G}_2$, the protocol has adaptive one-time simulation soundness.*

The proof is similar to that for Theorem 2, along with ideas from the security proof for Lamport's one-time signature scheme.

Proof. Perfect completeness and perfect zero-knowledge are straight-forward as before. We proceed to establish adaptive soundness based on the $\mathcal{D}_k$-KerMDH assumption. We will show that for all adversaries $\mathcal{A}$, there exists an adversary $\mathcal{B}$ with $\mathbf{T}(\mathcal{A}) \approx \mathbf{T}(\mathcal{B})$ and

$$\mathbf{Adv}_{\Pi'_{\text{ot-ss}}}^{\text{ot-ss}}(\mathcal{A}) \leq \frac{1}{2\lambda}(\mathbf{Adv}_{\mathcal{D}_k, \mathsf{GGen}}^{\text{kmdh}}(\mathcal{B}) + 1/q).$$

$\mathcal{B}$ begins by choosing $i' \leftarrow_{\mathrm{R}} [\lambda], b' \leftarrow_{\mathrm{R}} \{0,1\}$ and abort later if it is not the case that $\tau^*_{i'} \neq \tau_{i'}$ and $\tau^*_{i'} = b'$. $\mathcal{B}$ then selects $(\mathbf{K}_{i,b})_{1 \leq i \leq \ell, 0 \leq b \leq 1}$ as follows:

Gen(par, $[\mathbf{M}]_1 \in \mathbb{G}_1^{n \times t}$):	Prove(crs, τ, $[\mathbf{y}]_1$, $\mathbf{x}$): // $\mathbf{y} = \mathbf{Mx}$
$\mathbf{A} \leftarrow_R \mathcal{D}_k$; $\mathbf{K}_{i,b} \leftarrow_R \mathbb{Z}_q^{n \times k}, i = 1, \ldots, \lambda, b = 0, 1$ $\mathbf{P}_{i,b} := \mathbf{M}^\top \mathbf{K}_{i,b}$; $\mathbf{C}_{i,b} := \mathbf{K}_{i,b} \bar{\mathbf{A}}$ crs := $([\mathbf{P}_{i,b}]_1, [\mathbf{C}_{i,b}]_2, [\bar{\mathbf{A}}]_2)$ Return (crs, trap = $(\mathbf{K}_{i,b})_{1 \le i \le \ell, 0 \le b \le 1}$) //crs defines tag-space $\mathcal{T} = \{0,1\}^\lambda$	Return $\pi := \left[\mathbf{x}^\top \sum_{i=1}^{\ell} \mathbf{P}_{i,\tau_i} \right]_1$ Sim$_\pi$(crs, trap = $(\mathbf{K})_{i,b}, \tau, [\mathbf{y}]_1$): Return $\pi := \left[\mathbf{y}^\top \sum_{i=1}^{\ell} \mathbf{K}_{i,\tau_i} \right]_1$ Verify(crs, τ, $[\mathbf{y}]_1$, π): Check: $e(\pi, [\bar{\mathbf{A}}]_2)$ = $e([\mathbf{y}^\top]_1, [\sum_{i=1}^{\ell} \mathbf{C}_{i,\tau_i}]_2)$

Fig. 9. QANIZK $\Pi'_{\text{ot-ss}}$ protocol with adaptive one-time simulation-soundness for WS distributions under $\mathcal{D}_k$-KerMDH Assumption

- if $(i, b) \neq (i', b')$, pick $\mathbf{K}_{i,b} \leftarrow_R \mathbb{Z}_q^{n \times k}$;
- if $(i, b) = (i', b')$, pick $\mathbf{K}' \leftarrow_R \mathbb{Z}_q^{n \times k}$ and implicitly define $\mathbf{K}_{i',b'} = \mathbf{K}' + \mathbf{M}^\perp \mathbf{T}_{\mathbf{A}'}$ (as in the proof of Theorem 2). This yields $[\mathbf{C}_{i',b'}]_2 = [(\mathbf{K}' \| \mathbf{M}^\perp) \cdot \mathbf{A}']_2$.

Suppose $\tau_{i'}^* \neq \tau_{i'}$ and $\tau_{i'}^* = b'$, which happens with probability $\frac{1}{2\lambda}$. Then, $\mathcal{B}$ can simulate Sim$_\pi$ on τ since it knows $(\mathbf{K}_{i,\tau_i})_{1 \le i \le \lambda}$ explicitly. In addition, upon obtaining from $\mathcal{A}$ an accepting proof $\pi = [\mathbf{z}^\top]_1 \in \mathbb{G}_1^{1 \times k}$ for τ^* and $[\mathbf{y}]_1 \in \mathbb{G}_1^n$ satisfying $\mathbf{y}^\top \mathbf{M}^\perp \neq 0$, we have

$$(\mathbf{z}^\top - \sum_{i \neq i'} \mathbf{K}_{i,\tau_i^*}) \cdot \bar{\mathbf{A}} = \mathbf{y}^\top \cdot \mathbf{C}_{i',b'} = \mathbf{y}^\top (\mathbf{K}' \| \mathbf{M}^\perp) \cdot \mathbf{A}'.$$

We may then proceed as in Theorem 2 to extract a solution to the $\mathcal{D}_k$-KerMDH problem.

A.2 One-Time Linearly Homomorphic Structure-Preserving Signatures

We now modify the QANIZK protocol Π_{as} from Figure 4 into a one-time structure-preserving linearly homomorphic signature scheme. One-time basically means that the tag space is a singleton set, upon which we may omit the tag from the signature algorithms. Following the general methodology outlined in Section 1.2, we use sk = trap and define a signature on $[\mathbf{m}]_1$ as the "simulated proof" Sim$_\pi$(trap, $[\mathbf{m}]_1$). The scheme can also be seen as a generalization of the one-time LHSPS scheme from [47] from $\mathcal{D}_k = \mathcal{L}_2$ to arbitrary matrix distributions. It serves as a warm-up for our unbounded construction in the next section.

Theorem 7. *Under the $\mathcal{D}_k$-KerMDH Assumption in $\mathbb{G}_2$, LHSPS$_{\text{ot}}$ from Figure 10 is a one-time linearly homomorphic structure-preserving signature scheme.*

The proof of Theorem 7 is essentially the same as the one of Theorem 1 with the difference that $[\mathbf{P}]_1 = [\mathbf{M}^\top \mathbf{K}]_1$ from crs of Π_{as} is being constructed adaptively "on the fly", where $\mathbf{M} = (\mathbf{m}_1, \ldots, \mathbf{m}_q) \in \mathbb{Z}_q^{n \times q}$ and $[\mathbf{m}_i]_1 \in \mathbb{Z}_q^n$ is the message of the i-th signing query. (This adaptivity is also the reason why one cannot use the more efficient QANIZK protocol Π'_{as} from Figure 5.)

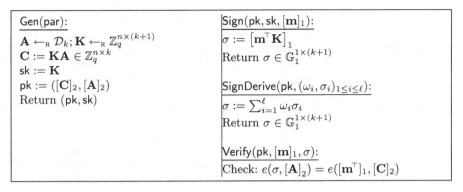

Fig. 10. One-time linearly homomorphic structure-preserving signature LHSPS$_{ot}$ with message-space $\mathcal{M} = \mathbb{G}_1^n$

Proof. Perfect correctness and full randomizability are straight-forward. We proceed to establish security based on the $\mathcal{D}_k$-KerMDH assumption. We will show that for all adversaries $\mathcal{A}$, there exists an adversary $\mathcal{B}$ with $\mathbf{T}(\mathcal{A}) \approx \mathbf{T}(\mathcal{B})$ and

$$\mathbf{Adv}_{\mathsf{LHSPS}_{ot}}^{\mathrm{ufcma}}(\mathcal{A}) \leq \mathbf{Adv}_{\mathcal{D}_k,\mathsf{GGen}}^{\mathrm{kmdh}}(\mathcal{B}) + 1/q. \tag{11}$$

Adversary $\mathcal{B}(\mathcal{PG}, [\mathbf{A}]_2 \in \mathbb{G}_2^{(k+1)\times k})$ generates pk as in the real scheme by picking $\mathbf{K} \in \mathbb{Z}_q^{n\times(k+1)}$. Next, $\mathcal{B}$ runs $\mathcal{A}$ on pk, answers signing queries on messages $[\mathbf{m}_1]_1, \ldots, [\mathbf{m}_Q]_1$ as in the real scheme using $\mathbf{K}$, and obtains a signature $\sigma = [\mathbf{z}^\top]_1 \in \mathbb{G}_1^{1\times k}$ on $[\mathbf{m}^*]_1 \in \mathbb{G}_1^n$ such that $\mathbf{m}^* \notin span(\mathbf{M})$, where $\mathbf{M} = (\mathbf{m}_1, \ldots, \mathbf{m}_Q) \in \mathbb{Z}_q^{n\times Q}$. Finally, $\mathcal{B}$ returns $[\mathbf{s}]_1$ computed as

$$\mathbf{s}^\top = \mathbf{z}^\top - \mathbf{m}^{*\top}\mathbf{K}.$$

As before in Theorem 7, $\mathbf{s}^\top \mathbf{A} = \mathbf{0}$ and $\Pr[\mathbf{s} = \mathbf{0}] \leq 1/q$ by Lemma 2, since the signing queries only leak $\mathbf{M}^\top\mathbf{K}$. This proves equation (11). $\quad\square$

References

1. Abdalla, M., Benhamouda, F., Pointcheval, D.: Disjunctions for hash proof systems: New constructions and applications. In: Eurocrypt, Also, Cryptology ePrint Archive, Report 2014/483 (2015)
2. Abe, M., Chase, M., David, B., Kohlweiss, M., Nishimaki, R., Ohkubo, M.: Constant-size structure-preserving signatures: Generic constructions and simple assumptions. In: Wang, X., Sako, K. (eds.) ASIACRYPT 2012. LNCS, vol. 7658, pp. 4–24. Springer, Heidelberg (2012)
3. Abe, M., David, B., Kohlweiss, M., Nishimaki, R., Ohkubo, M.: Tagged one-time signatures: Tight security and optimal tag size. In: Kurosawa, K., Hanaoka, G. (eds.) PKC 2013. LNCS, vol. 7778, pp. 312–331. Springer, Heidelberg (2013)
4. Ahn, J.H., Boneh, D., Camenisch, J., Hohenberger, S., Shelat, A., Waters, B.: Computing on authenticated data. In: Cramer, R. (ed.) TCC 2012. LNCS, vol. 7194, pp. 1–20. Springer, Heidelberg (2012)
5. Attrapadung, N.: Dual system encryption via doubly selective security: Framework, fully secure functional encryption for regular languages, and more. In: Nguyen, P.Q., Oswald, E. (eds.) EUROCRYPT 2014. LNCS, vol. 8441, pp. 557–577. Springer, Heidelberg (2014)

6. Attrapadung, N., Libert, B.: Homomorphic network coding signatures in the standard model. In: Catalano, D., Fazio, N., Gennaro, R., Nicolosi, A. (eds.) PKC 2011. LNCS, vol. 6571, pp. 17–34. Springer, Heidelberg (2011)

7. Attrapadung, N., Libert, B., Peters, T.: Computing on authenticated data: New privacy definitions and constructions. In: Wang, X., Sako, K. (eds.) ASIACRYPT 2012. LNCS, vol. 7658, pp. 367–385. Springer, Heidelberg (2012)

8. Attrapadung, N., Libert, B., Peters, T.: Efficient completely context-hiding quotable and linearly homomorphic signatures. In: Kurosawa, K., Hanaoka, G. (eds.) PKC 2013. LNCS, vol. 7778, pp. 386–404. Springer, Heidelberg (2013)

9. Belenkiy, M., Camenisch, J., Chase, M., Kohlweiss, M., Lysyanskaya, A., Shacham, H.: Randomizable proofs and delegatable anonymous credentials. In: Halevi, S. (ed.) CRYPTO 2009. LNCS, vol. 5677, pp. 108–125. Springer, Heidelberg (2009)

10. Belenkiy, M., Chase, M., Kohlweiss, M., Lysyanskaya, A.: P-signatures and noninteractive anonymous credentials. In: Canetti, R. (ed.) TCC 2008. LNCS, vol. 4948, pp. 356–374. Springer, Heidelberg (2008)

11. Bellare, Mihir, Goldwasser, Shafi: New Paradigms for Digital Signatures and Message Authentication Based on Non-interactive Zero Knowledge Proofs. In: Brassard, Gilles (ed.) CRYPTO 1989. LNCS, vol. 435, pp. 194–211. Springer, Heidelberg (1990)

12. Bellare, M., Ristenpart, T.: Simulation without the artificial abort: Simplified proof and improved concrete security for Waters' IBE scheme. In: Joux, A. (ed.) EUROCRYPT 2009. LNCS, vol. 5479, pp. 407–424. Springer, Heidelberg (2009)

13. Blazy, O., Kiltz, E., Pan, J.: (hierarchical) identity-based encryption from affine message authentication. In: Garay, J.A., Gennaro, R. (eds.) CRYPTO 2014, Part I. LNCS, vol. 8616, pp. 408–425. Springer, Heidelberg (2014)

14. Blum, M., Feldman, P., Micali, S.: Non-interactive zero-knowledge and its applications (extended abstract). In: 20th ACM STOC, pp. 103–112. ACM Press, May 1988

15. Boneh, D., Freeman, D., Katz, J., Waters, B.: Signing a linear subspace: Signature schemes for network coding. In: Jarecki, S., Tsudik, G. (eds.) PKC 2009. LNCS, vol. 5443, pp. 68–87. Springer, Heidelberg (2009)

16. Boneh, D., Freeman, D.M.: Homomorphic signatures for polynomial functions. In: Paterson, K.G. (ed.) EUROCRYPT 2011. LNCS, vol. 6632, pp. 149–168. Springer, Heidelberg (2011)

17. Boneh, D., Freeman, D.M.: Linearly homomorphic signatures over binary fields and new tools for lattice-based signatures. In: Catalano, D., Fazio, N., Gennaro, R., Nicolosi, A. (eds.) PKC 2011. LNCS, vol. 6571, pp. 1–16. Springer, Heidelberg (2011)

18. Camenisch, J., Chandran, N., Shoup, V.: A public key encryption scheme secure against key dependent chosen plaintext and adaptive chosen ciphertext attacks. In: Joux, A. (ed.) EUROCRYPT 2009. LNCS, vol. 5479, pp. 351–368. Springer, Heidelberg (2009)

19. Canetti, R., Halevi, S., Katz, J.: Chosen-ciphertext security from identity-based encryption. In: Cachin, C., Camenisch, J.L. (eds.) EUROCRYPT 2004. LNCS, vol. 3027, pp. 207–222. Springer, Heidelberg (2004)

20. Catalano, D., Fiore, D., Warinschi, B.: Efficient network coding signatures in the standard model. In: Fischlin, M., Buchmann, J., Manulis, M. (eds.) PKC 2012. LNCS, vol. 7293, pp. 680–696. Springer, Heidelberg (2012)

21. Catalano, D., Marcedone, A., Puglisi, O.: Authenticating computation on groups: New homomorphic primitives and applications. In: Asiacrypt, pp. 193–212 (2014)

22. Cathalo, J., Libert, B., Yung, M.: Group encryption: Non-interactive realization in the standard model. In: Matsui, M. (ed.) ASIACRYPT 2009. LNCS, vol. 5912, pp. 179–196. Springer, Heidelberg (2009)

23. Chen, J., Gay, R., Wee, H.: Improved dual system ABE in prime-order groups via predicate encodings. In: Eurocrypt (2015). To appear

24. Chen, J., Wee, H.: Fully, (almost) tightly secure IBE and dual system groups. In: Canetti, R., Garay, J.A. (eds.) CRYPTO 2013, Part II. LNCS, vol. 8043, pp. 435–460. Springer, Heidelberg (2013)

25. Cramer, R., Shoup, V.: A practical public key cryptosystem provably secure against adaptive chosen ciphertext attack. In: Krawczyk, H. (ed.) CRYPTO 1998. LNCS, vol. 1462, p. 13. Springer, Heidelberg (1998)

26. Cramer, R., Shoup, V.: Universal hash proofs and a paradigm for adaptive chosen ciphertext secure public-key encryption. In: Knudsen, L.R. (ed.) EUROCRYPT 2002. LNCS, vol. 2332, p. 45. Springer, Heidelberg (2002)

27. De Santis, A., Di Crescenzo, G., Ostrovsky, R., Persiano, G., Sahai, A.: Robust non-interactive zero knowledge. In: Kilian, J. (ed.) CRYPTO 2001. LNCS, vol. 2139, p. 566. Springer, Heidelberg (2001)

28. Desmedt, Y.: Computer security by redefining what a computer is. In: New Security Paradigms Workshop (NSPW) (1993)

29. Dodis, Y., Kiltz, E., Pietrzak, K., Wichs, D.: Message authentication, revisited. In: Pointcheval, D., Johansson, T. (eds.) EUROCRYPT 2012. LNCS, vol. 7237, pp. 355–374. Springer, Heidelberg (2012)

30. Escala, A., Herold, G., Kiltz, E., Ràfols, C., Villar, J.: An algebraic framework for Diffie-Hellman assumptions. In: Canetti, R., Garay, J.A. (eds.) CRYPTO 2013, Part II. LNCS, vol. 8043, pp. 129–147. Springer, Heidelberg (2013)

31. Fischlin, M., Libert, B., Manulis, M.: Non-interactive and re-usable universally composable string commitments with adaptive security. In: Lee, D.H., Wang, X. (eds.) ASIACRYPT 2011. LNCS, vol. 7073, pp. 468–485. Springer, Heidelberg (2011)

32. Freeman, D.M.: Improved security for linearly homomorphic signatures: A generic framework. In: Fischlin, M., Buchmann, J., Manulis, M. (eds.) PKC 2012. LNCS, vol. 7293, pp. 697–714. Springer, Heidelberg (2012)

33. Fuchsbauer, G.: Commuting signatures and verifiable encryption. In: Paterson, K.G. (ed.) EUROCRYPT 2011. LNCS, vol. 6632, pp. 224–245. Springer, Heidelberg (2011)

34. Gennaro, R., Katz, J., Krawczyk, H., Rabin, T.: Secure network coding over the integers. In: Nguyen, P.Q., Pointcheval, D. (eds.) PKC 2010. LNCS, vol. 6056, pp. 142–160. Springer, Heidelberg (2010)

35. Groth, J.: Simulation-sound NIZK proofs for a practical language and constant size group signatures. In: Lai, X., Chen, K. (eds.) ASIACRYPT 2006. LNCS, vol. 4284, pp. 444–459. Springer, Heidelberg (2006)

36. Groth, J.: Fully anonymous group signatures without random oracles. In: Kurosawa, K. (ed.) ASIACRYPT 2007. LNCS, vol. 4833, pp. 164–180. Springer, Heidelberg (2007)

37. Groth, J., Ostrovsky, R., Sahai, A.: Perfect non-interactive zero knowledge for NP. In: Vaudenay, S. (ed.) EUROCRYPT 2006. LNCS, vol. 4004, pp. 339–358. Springer, Heidelberg (2006)

38. Groth, J., Sahai, A.: Efficient non-interactive proof systems for bilinear groups. In: Smart, N.P. (ed.) EUROCRYPT 2008. LNCS, vol. 4965, pp. 415–432. Springer, Heidelberg (2008)

39. Hofheinz, D., Kiltz, E.: Secure hybrid encryption from weakened key encapsulation. In: Menezes, A. (ed.) CRYPTO 2007. LNCS, vol. 4622, pp. 553–571. Springer, Heidelberg (2007)

40. Johnson, R., Molnar, D., Song, D., Wagner, D.: Homomorphic signature schemes. In: Preneel, B. (ed.) CT-RSA 2002. LNCS, vol. 2271, p. 244. Springer, Heidelberg (2002)

41. Jutla, C., Roy, A.: Relatively-sound NIZKs and password-based key-exchange. In: Fischlin, M., Buchmann, J., Manulis, M. (eds.) PKC 2012. LNCS, vol. 7293, pp. 485–503. Springer, Heidelberg (2012)

42. Jutla, C.S., Roy, A.: Shorter quasi-adaptive NIZK proofs for linear subspaces. In: Sako, K., Sarkar, P. (eds.) ASIACRYPT 2013, Part I. LNCS, vol. 8269, pp. 1–20. Springer, Heidelberg (2013)

43. Jutla, C.S., Roy, A.: Switching lemma for bilinear tests and constant-size NIZK proofs for linear subspaces. In: Garay, J.A., Gennaro, R. (eds.) CRYPTO 2014, Part II. LNCS, vol. 8617, pp. 295–312. Springer, Heidelberg (2014)

44. Katz, J., Vaikuntanathan, V.: Round-optimal password-based authenticated key exchange. In: Ishai, Y. (ed.) TCC 2011. LNCS, vol. 6597, pp. 293–310. Springer, Heidelberg (2011)

45. Lewko, A.: Tools for simulating features of composite order bilinear groups in the prime order setting. In: Pointcheval, D., Johansson, T. (eds.) EUROCRYPT 2012. LNCS, vol. 7237, pp. 318–335. Springer, Heidelberg (2012)

46. Lewko, A., Waters, B.: New techniques for dual system encryption and fully secure HIBE with short ciphertexts. In: Micciancio, D. (ed.) TCC 2010. LNCS, vol. 5978, pp. 455–479. Springer, Heidelberg (2010)

47. Libert, B., Peters, T., Joye, M., Yung, M.: Linearly homomorphic structure-preserving signatures and their applications. In: Canetti, R., Garay, J.A. (eds.) CRYPTO 2013, Part II. LNCS, vol. 8043, pp. 289–307. Springer, Heidelberg (2013)

48. Libert, B., Peters, T., Joye, M., Yung, M.: Non-malleability from malleability: Simulation-sound quasi-adaptive NIZK proofs and CCA2-secure encryption from homomorphic signatures. In: Nguyen, P.Q., Oswald, E. (eds.) EUROCRYPT 2014. LNCS, vol. 8441, pp. 514–532. Springer, Heidelberg (2014)

49. Morillo, P., Ràfols, C., Villar, J.L.: Matrix computational assumptions in multilinear groups. Manuscript (2015)

50. Okamoto, T., Takashima, K.: Fully secure functional encryption with general relations from the decisional linear assumption. In: Rabin, T. (ed.) CRYPTO 2010. LNCS, vol. 6223, pp. 191–208. Springer, Heidelberg (2010)

51. Sahai, A.: Non-malleable non-interactive zero knowledge and adaptive chosen-ciphertext security. In: 40th FOCS, pp. 543–553. IEEE Computer Society Press, October 1999

52. Waters, B.: Dual system encryption: Realizing fully secure IBE and HIBE under simple assumptions. In: Halevi, S. (ed.) CRYPTO 2009. LNCS, vol. 5677, pp. 619–636. Springer, Heidelberg (2009)

53. Waters, B.: Efficient identity-based encryption without random oracles. In: Cramer, R. (ed.) EUROCRYPT 2005. LNCS, vol. 3494, pp. 114–127. Springer, Heidelberg (2005)

54. Wee, H.: Dual system encryption via predicate encodings. In: Lindell, Y. (ed.) TCC 2014. LNCS, vol. 8349, pp. 616–637. Springer, Heidelberg (2014)

Leakage-Resilient Cryptography

Leakage-Resilient Circuits Revisited – Optimal Number of Computing Components Without Leak-Free Hardware

Dana Dachman-Soled[1]($\boxtimes$), Feng-Hao Liu[1], and Hong-Sheng Zhou[2]

[1] University of Maryland, College Park, USA
danadach@ece.umd.edu, fenghao@cs.umd.edu
[2] Virginia Commonwealth University, Richmond, USA
hszhou@vcu.edu

Abstract. Side channel attacks – attacks that exploit implementation-dependent information of a cryptosystem – have been shown to be highly detrimental, and the cryptographic community has recently focused on developing techniques for securing implementations against such attacks. An important model called *Only Computation Leaks* (OCL) [Micali and Reyzin, TCC '04] and its stronger variants were proposed to model a broad class of leakage attacks (a type of side-channel attack). These models allow for unbounded, arbitrary leakage as long as (1) information in each leakage observation is bounded, and (2) different parts of the computation leak independently. Various results and techniques have been developed for these models and we continue this line of research in the current work.

We address the problem of compiling any circuit into a circuit secure against OCL attacks. In order to leverage the OCL assumption, the resulting circuit will be split into components, where at any point in time only a single component is active. Optimally, we would like to output a circuit that has only one component, and no part of the computation needs to be leak-free. However, this task is impossible due to the result of Barak et al. [JACM '12]. The current state-of-the-art constructions achieve either two components with additional leak-free hardware, or many components without leak-free hardware.

In this work, we show how to achieve the best of both worlds: We construct two-component OCL schemes without relying on leak-free components. Our approach is general and modular – we develop generic techniques to remove the hardware component from hardware-based constructions, when the functionality provided by the hardware satisfies some properties. Our techniques use universal deniable encryption (recently constructed by Sahai and Water [STOC '14] using indistinguishable obfuscation) and non-committing encryption in a novel way. Then, we observe that the functionalities of the hardware used in previous two-component constructions of Juma and Vahlis [Crypto '10], and Dziembowski and Faust [TCC '12] satisfy the required properties.

The techniques developed in this paper have deep connections with adaptively secure and leakage tolerant multi-party computation (MPC). Our constructions immediately yield adaptively secure and leakage tolerant MPC protocols for any no-input randomized functionality in the

© International Association for Cryptologic Research 2015
E. Oswald and M. Fischlin (Eds.): EUROCRYPT 2015, Part II, LNCS 9057, pp. 131–158, 2015.
DOI: 10.1007/978-3-662-46803-6_5

semi-honest model. The result holds in the CRS model, without pre-processing. Our results also have implications to two-party leakage tolerant computation for arbitrary functionalities, which we obtain by combining our constructions with a recent result of Bitansky, Dachman-Soled, and Lin [Crypto '14].

1   Introduction

Side-channel attacks are attacks that exploit implementation-dependent information of a cryptosystem. Passive side-channel attacks, or *leakage attacks*, such as timing attacks, power analysis attacks, acoustic attacks, and more [1,6,28,33, 39,40], have proven highly detrimental. Indeed, it has been shown that leakage attacks can be used to recover the entire secret key in common implementations of the RSA [29], AES [48] and DES [38] cryptosystems. These attacks are not just theoretical, and can be launched in complex, real-life settings, e.g. Boneh and Brumley [12] launched a practical network-based timing attack on SSL-enabled web servers.

In recent years, the cryptographic community has been devoted to developing adversarial models for side-channel attacks and constructing provably secure cryptosystems in these models. An important framework of this approach is to construct efficient *compilers* which take any circuit C (which may have a secret s hardcoded) and convert it to a new circuit $\tilde{C}$ that is secure against *leakage* attacks, where the adversarial model allows the attacker to adaptively choose inputs x and observe outputs $y = \tilde{C}(x)$ as well as adaptively obtaining leakage functions $\ell(\tilde{C})$ on the state of the circuit. Unfortunately, achieving security against adversaries who obtain even a *single bit* of arbitrary leakage is impossible since it implies *virtual black box* obfuscation, which was ruled out by the work of Barak et al. [4,5][1].

Thus, the community turned to study reasonable ways to restrict the leakage function ℓ the adversary may leak on the internal state of the circuit. An important restricted class of leakage attacks was suggested by Micali and Reyzin [42], called the only computation leaks (OCL) model. In this model, throughout the computation, devices can have active states and inactive states, and at any point in time, information can only be leaked on the currently active state. This assumption is meant to capture a large class of attacks such as timing attacks, power analysis attacks and acoustic attacks, which only leak information on data this is currently being computed on.

Subsequently, various works have constructed so-called OCL compilers, which take any circuit C as input and convert it onto a new circuit $\tilde{C}$ such that $\tilde{C}$ is not only functionally equivalent, but also secure against OCL attacks. The way these compilers work is by splitting the computation into *components*, where during any time period only a single component is active. Specifically, consider an n-component circuit $\tilde{C} = \{\tilde{C}_1, \ldots, \tilde{C}_n\}$. At time period i where some component $\tilde{C}_j$ is active, the adversary may obtain some leakage $\ell_i(\tilde{C}_j)$ for some *bounded*

---

[1] This argument was explicitly stated in the work [32].

output length function ℓ_i he chose. We say the scheme secure against *continual* OCL attacks if the adversary may run the circuit many times and obtain an unbounded total amount of leakage, as long as its leakage per time period is bounded. As noted previously, due to the impossibility result of Barak et al. [4], the minimal number of components required is two.

The first OCL compiler constructions were by Juma and Vahlis [37] and Goldwasser and Rothblum [31]. Both of these constructions require a secure hardware component to achieve security against OCL attacks; the construction of [37] requires only two components, and that of [31] requires many. Subsequently, Dziembowski and Faust [24] presented an alternative two-component OCL construction which achieves information-theoretic security, but also requires secure hardware. Although these works had argued that the hardware functionalities required are simple and independent of the circuit C,[2] it is still unsatisfactory if we need additional trusted assumptions on top of the existing one (the OCL assumption), especially when they are not necessary.

To date, the only known OCL compiler which does not require secure hardware is the information-theoretic construction of Goldwasser and Rothblum [32]. However, their OCL scheme requires a large number of OCL components[3]. We note that in works concurrent with this work [16,21,27], indirect constructions of 2-component OCL via leakage tolerant computation were constructed by applying Theorem 1 of [10], which shows an equivalence between 2-party leakage tolerant computation and 2-componenet OCL. For direct constructions, the state-of-the art previous to this work was to either rely on secure hardware to achieve OCL with optimal number of components, or to achieve OCL without secure hardware, but with a large number of components. A major open question left along this line is:

> *Can we construct two-component OCL compilers without relying on secure hardware?*

Beyond the fact that the question of optimal component OCL is of theoretical interest, OCL with minimal components has implications for the strength of the adversary we can tolerate, the hardware required by the OCL scheme, and for settings such as leakage-tolerant two-party computation. We discuss some of these implications below:

- **Strength of adversary.** Instead of characterizing a result as an OCL result, OCL results can be alternatively described as a class of leakage functions (out of all possible functions) that we provide security for. It is not hard to see that the fewer OCL components are, the larger the class of leakage functions we can handle.

---

[2] This is to avoid the trivial solution that the hardware does all the computation of C.

[3] The original result of [32] requires $|C|$ components, where $|C|$ is the size of the original circuit. It was shown by [10] that the "ciphertext bank" of [32] can be combined with the construction of [24] to achieve an OCL compiler without secure hardware. The number of components required by this modification is a large constant, approximated by [10] as 20.

- **Hardware.** Although OCL is an attractive assumption, it is not always clear whether the assumption holds universally under all environments. For example, the cold boot attacks by Halderman et al. [33] that showed memory can be leaky even if they are not active[4]. In order to implement an OCL scheme, we need an underlying hardware design that supports the OCL feature. The more components we need, the harder the design can be. Moreover, the overhead becomes larger with the number of components, so a large number of components, even though it is a constant such as twenty in the work [10], may be prohibitive.
- **Leakage tolerant computation.** As will be discussed in the sequel, two-component OCL without hardware has implications for leakage tolerant two-party computation. Loosely speaking, this is two-party secure computation where, in addition to corrupting parties, the adversary may ask for leakage on honest parties.

Model in This Paper. In the literature, there are several strengthening OCL models, such as OCL^+ or a closely related model LDS (leaky distributed system) proposed by Bitansky et al. [7][5]. Unlike the OCL assumption where the adversary can only get leakage of components that follow a *particular* order (the order of activation), OCL^+ and LDS allow the adversary to leak component of an *arbitrary* order he likes. In these models, the adversary cannot leak on joint states of components, which is similar to the concept of split-state leakage (c.f. see the work of [34,41] for further discussions). These models capture some memory attacks (such as some cold boot attacks [33]) beyond the traditional OCL model, as long as the leakage does not apply on joint states and are bounded per time period. Since the restrictions are weaker, it is easier to design hardware that achieves the requirements. Thus security guaranteed by these models is stronger.

It is not hard to see that the scheme JV [37] also achieves the notion of security under these models. It was observed [10] that the previous schemes GR [32] and DF [24] also achieve these stronger security notions. We remark that the above motivations for minimizing the number of components also hold for the OCL^+ and LDS settings. Throughout the whole paper, we consider the stronger OCL^+ model where the adversary can leak on any arbitrary order of the component. To avoid unnecessary complications, we will still call our model OCL, but the reader should keep in mind that the leakage can be obtained on any order of the components.

---

[4] Some cold boot attacks can be captured by some strengthened OCL models as discussed later; yet we have the same motivation for reducing the number of components – the less the components, the more plausible the assumption can be.

[5] Bitansky et al. [7] showed that an LDS scheme is also an OCL^+ scheme; on the other hand, one can construct an LDS scheme from an OCL^+ scheme using non-committing encryption. Therefore, the two models are essentially equivalent.

1.1   Our Results

In this work, we answer the question above affirmatively. We present two constructions of two-component OCL compilers from different assumptions. We take a modular approach with the following steps:

- First we establish a technique of how to get rid of hardware used in an OCL scheme – that is, given any secure hardware-based OCL scheme, suppose there exists a two-party protocol that realizes the functionality provided by the hardware with some strong property (defined later), then we can replace the hardware with the two-party protocol, resulting in a secure OCL scheme without hardware. The result can be summarized (informally) as Theorem 1.
- Then we consider how to construct a protocol that meets the requirements above. We show that under the existence of universal deniable encryption schemes (which can be constructed from indistinguishable obfuscation by Sahai and Waters [47]) and non-committing encryption schemes [15], for any *simple* randomized functionality that takes no inputs, we can construct a protocol that achieves the goal (the strong property). The result can be summarized (informally) as Theorem 2.
- Finally, we look into the two currently known two-component hardware-based schemes with hardware, i.e. the JV scheme [37] and the DF scheme [24]. We observe that in both cases, the functionalities of the hardwares in both bases are "simple" in the sense that they can be expressed as no-input two-party randomized functionalities. Therefore, we can apply the theorems above to achieve two-component schemes that do not require secure hardware, by simply replacing the hardwares of JV or DF with the corresponding two-party protocols. We summarize the results as Corollary 3.

Our results are general and can be viewed as a design paradigm for OCL schemes: we can first construct a scheme that uses some simple hardware, which is presumably much easier to construct and to analyze. Then we can apply the generic tool to get rid of the hardware while preserving security. We state the two informal theorems below.

Theorem 1 (Hardware replacement theorem (Informal)). *Let $\Lambda^{\mathcal{F}}$ be some two-component OCL scheme with secure hardware implementing some two-party functionality $\mathcal{F}$. Assume there exists a two-party protocol ρ that realizes $\mathcal{F}$ (with some strong oblivious property), then there exists a two-component OCL scheme Λ' without hardware.*

Theorem 2 (Two-party protocol for simple hardware (Informal)). *Assume the existence of universal deniable encryption schemes and non-committing encryption schemes, then for any no-input two-party randomized functionality $\mathcal{F}$, there exists a two-party protocol ρ that realizes $\mathcal{F}$ with the strong oblivious property.*

By applying the theorems above to the hardware-based constructions of JV [37] and DF [24], we achieve the following corollary.

Corollary 3 *Assume the existence of universal deniable encryption schemes and non-committing encryption schemes. Then we achieve:*

- **(JV + Theorems 1, 2).** *If there further exists a fully homomorphic encryption (with cipher refreshing) that is secure against $2^{O(\ell(\lambda))}$ adversaries, the there exists a two-component OCL scheme that is $O(\ell)$ continual leakage resilient, where λ is the security parameter.*
- **(DF + Theorems 1, 2).** *There exists a two-component OCL scheme that is ℓ continual leakage resilient, for $\ell(\lambda) = m(\lambda)/10, m(\lambda) = \omega(\log(\lambda))$, where λ is the security parameter.*

Furthermore, both constructions do not require secure hardware.

We remark that our results rely on the existence of universal deniable encryption. This can be constructed from indistinguishable obfuscation for general circuits by Sahai and Waters [47]. Indistinguishable obfuscation for general circuits was constructed in the breakthrough result of Garg et al. [26] and followup work [2,3,11,30,45]; please refer to [49,50] for more applications of indistinguishable obfuscation. Our constructions use universal deniable encryption in a black-box way, so they do not depend on a particular construction of universal deniable encryption nor indistinguishable obfuscation. Our results can be understood without the context of indistinguishable obfuscation, so we do not further discuss the notion to avoid digression.

1.2 Connections with Multi-Party Computation

Our results have deep connections with multi-party computation (MPC) constructions that achieve different levels of security. In particular, we consider MPC for the following two classes of functionalities.

No-Input Randomized Functionalities. The strong oblivions simulation property in Theorem 2 actually implies a stronger notion of adaptive security (against semi-honest corruption), called corruption-oblivious simulation by Bitansky et al. [8]. As shown in the work [8], such notion also implies leakage tolerance (against semi-honest corruptions). We will further discuss the strong oblivious property after Definition 3.

Thus, as an implication of the theorem, for any two-party no-input randomized functionalities, we are able to construct a two-party protocol (in the CRS model) that is simultaneously leakage tolerant, and adaptively secure (against semi-honest corruptions). In Section 5, we show how to generalize the construction to the setting of N-party no-input randomized functionalities.

Moreover, our protocols can implement randomized functionalities beyond "adaptively well-formed" ones according to Canetti et al. [18] – the functionalities do *not* need to leak its internal randomness to the adversary when all parties are corrupted. Additionally our protocols only need *two* rounds. To our knowledge, these are the *first* constructions that achieve adaptive security beyond the well-formed constraints; they are also the first constant-round protocols that are adaptively secure and leakage tolerant (against semi-honest corruptions) for this class of functionalities. We further elaborate on this in Remark 3.

General Two-Party Functionalities. We observe that both the two-component constructions (JV-based and DF-based) are in fact of so-called *strong* OCL compilers (as introduced by Bitansky et al. [10]), where a strong OCL compiler is an OCL compiler with some enhanced simulation properties. Leveraging a recent result of Bitanksy et al. [10], which shows an *equivalence* between two-component strong OCL and two-party leakage tolerant computation in the input-independent preprocessing model (when no parties are corrupted), we obtain the following corollary:

Corollary 4 (Informal) *Assume the existence of universal deniable encryption schemes and non-committing encryption schemes, Then for every function f, there exists a two-party leakage tolerant protocol which UC-emulates f in the input-indepdendent preprocessing model when no parties are corrupted.*

We note that constructions of leakage tolerant 2-party computation secure under *semi-honest* corruptions were presented in the concurrent works of [16, 21, 27]. Very recently, it was shown that based on standard cryptographic assumptions, the equivalence between two-component strong OCL and two-party leakage tolerant computation in the input-independent preprocessing model can be extended to the case where one or both parties are *actively* corrupted [9]. Combining this result with our two-component strong OCL constructions, we then obtain, for every function f, a two-party leakage tolerant protocol which UC-emulates f in the input-independent preprocessing model under static, *active* corruption of parties.

1.3   Techniques

In this section, we highlight some of our techniques to achieve our two main theorems.

Hardware Replacement Theorem. Let $\Lambda^{\mathcal{F}}$ be some secure hardware-based two-component OCL scheme where the hardware implements some functionality $\mathcal{F}$. Similar to the spirit of the Universal Composability framework [13,14], our goal is to replace the hardware by a two-party protocol ρ while preserving OCL security.[6] Clearly the theorem cannot work with any arbitrary two-party protocol – we argue that the protocol ρ at least needs to be somewhat leakage resilient to the OCL leakage (independent leakage on each party), since the replacement theorem should also work for the trivial case where $\mathcal{F}$ is a secure hardware that computes the circuit we want to protect.

In this work, we identified a strong oblivious simulation property that captures the spirit of the corruption-oblivious simulation defined by Bitansky et al. [8] in a compact and simple way. Then we show suppose ρ realizes $\mathcal{F}$ with such strong oblivious simulation, then we can replace the hardware by the protocol ρ while preserving the security. We note that since the syntaxes of

---

[6] We do not use the term of "composability" to avoid confusion since OCL schemes, through related, are different from protocols in syntax and many other properties.

OCL compilers and leakage tolerant protocols are quite different, it is not clear whether the hardware replacement theorem can be implied by the composition theorem by Bitansky et al. [8].

Informally, the strong oblivious simulation requires that there exist independent simulators $(\mathcal{S}_{\mathrm{tr}}, \mathcal{S}_1, \mathcal{S}_2)$ such that the simulator $\mathcal{S}_{\mathrm{tr}}$ can generate an indistinguishable transcript τ, and for $b = \{1, 2\}$, $\mathcal{S}_b(x_b, y_b, \tau)$ can generate an indistinguishable view (or state) of the party P_b, where x_1, x_2, y_1, y_2 are the inputs/outputs to the ideal functionality, i.e. $(y_1, y_2) \leftarrow \mathcal{F}(x_1, x_2)$. This means, any leakage function g on P_b's state can be simulated by $g(\mathcal{S}_b(x_b, y_b, \tau))$. Therefore, any leakage attack at the state of party P_b (the real world) can be translated to a leakage attack at the input/output of the party P_b in the ideal world. Using the idea, we can further show that any OCL leakage attack at the scheme Λ^ρ (a scheme where we replace the hardware functionality by ρ) can be translated to an OCL leakage attack at the scheme $\Lambda^\mathcal{F}$. Thus, the security of Λ^ρ is guaranteed by the security of $\Lambda^\mathcal{F}$.

Constructing Protocols for Simple Functionalities. The next part of our main contribution is to construct protocols that achieve the strong oblivious simulation property. We note that this property is very strong that we do not know how to construct protocols for general functionalities. However, for a restricted but still very useful class of functionalities – no-input randomized functionalities, we show how to construct protocols that achieve the strong obvious simulation property, using deniable encryptions (recently constructed by Sahai and Waters [47] with indistinguishable obfuscation). Then we observe that the "simple" hardwares used in the literature [24, 37] can be captured by such class.

We use a (universal) deniable encryption and a receiver non-committing encryption as our building blocks. Informally, a deniable encryption allows a sender to come up with a message and randomness that explain a ciphertext. That is, given any ciphertext c^* and a message m, the sender can come up with (indistinguishable) randomness r such that $\mathsf{Enc}(m; r) = c^*$; a receiver non-committing encryption allows a simulator to first generate a pair of simulated public-key and ciphertext (without knowing what the underlying message was), and later to come up with consistent random coins that explain the key generation, and decrypt the ciphertext to an arbitrary message m. By combining the two in a novel way, we show how to design protocols that achieve the strong oblivious simulation for no-input randomized functionalities. We give further overviews in Section 3.

1.4 Related Work

In this section, we compare our two-component OCL compilers with previous results from the literature. OCL compilers which require secure hardware were constructed by [24, 31, 37]. These OCL compilers all require two components; the compiler of [24] is information theoretic; the compiler of [31] relies on the DDH assumption and the compiler of [37] requires fully homomorphic encryption with a ciphertext refreshing property. An OCL compiler which does not require secure hardware was first constructed by [32]; moreover, theire construction is information theoretic. The compiler of [32] is described as requiring $O(|C|)$ components, where $|C|$ is the size of the underlying circuit. However, it was shown in [10] how to combine techniques from [32] and [24] to achieve an OCL compiler without secure hardware and a large constant number of components, approximated by [10] as 20.

In the following table, we present a comparison of the assumptions, number of components and leakage rates achieved by best known previous work [10,24,32,37], as well our JV-based and DF-based schemes. Let ℓ be some parameter. The following table presents parameters for different schemes in order to construct an OCL compiler that tolerates ℓ-bit leakage per time.

Table 1. Comparison of various OCL schemes in the literature

Scheme	Hardware	Assumption	Components	Leakage rate (Asymptotically)
JV	Yes	2^ℓ-secure FHE	2	$\ell/w|C|$
DF	Yes	None	2	$1/\ell|C|$
GR12	No	None	$O(|C|)$	$1/\ell^{O(1)}$
BDL14	No	None	20	$1/\ell^{O(1)} \cdot |C|$
Ours (JV-based)	No	2^ℓ-secure FHE, Deniable Enc, NCE	2	$\ell/w|C|$
Ours (DF-based)	No	Deniable Enc, NCE	2	$1/\ell|C|$
Ours (DF + FHE based)	No	Deniable Enc, NCE + FHE	2	$1/\ell^{1+o(1)}$

w corresponds to the length of the FHE ciphertext, $|C|$ corresponds to the size of the underlying circuit. NCE stands for non-committing encryption. We note that the ciphertext length w must be at least as large as ℓ; otherwise it is easy to break the FHE scheme in time 2^ℓ. The constant of $O(1)$ depends on the best algorithm of matrix multiplication. Both constants are greater than 1.37 under the best known algorithm by Williams [51].

We remark that even though the leakage rate of the previous constant-component constructions depends on the circuit size $|C|$, there is a generic way to get rid of the dependency by using FHE. We can first encrypt the circuit C (keep it public) by the FHE, and then apply the OCL compiler only on the decryption circuit, which has size λ (can be re-parameterized as the security parameter) and is independent of the circuit C. This idea is generic and can be applied to all OCL constructions. We only state one example in the last row of the table, but note that the rates for other constructions can be also improved in this way.

Alternative *Leakage on Computation* Models and Compilers in These Models. Ishai et al. [35] suggested a leakage model which captures wire probing attacks where the adversary may leak the value of individual wires during the computation. Note that the OCL model subsumes this model. Additional models for leakage on computation were introduced by [19], and [25] . These models allow unbounded-length "noisy" leakage (leakage that does not reduce the entropy of the circuit's secret state by too much) and leakage under restricted classes of leakage functions (such as $\mathcal{AC}^0$ leakage), respectively. Compilers for the wire probing model were constructed by [35]; compilers for the noisy leakage model were constructed by [23,25]; compilers for restricted classes of leakage functions were constructed by [25,43,44,46].

2   Two-Component OCL Schemes and Hardware Replacement Theorem

A two-component OCL scheme for a (private) circuit $C(\cdot)$, consists of an efficient compiler Comp and a two-party protocol $\Pi = (P_1, P_2)$. To compute $C(\cdot)$ in a leakage-resilient way, the circuit is *compiled* ahead of time by $\mathsf{Comp}(C(\cdot))$ that produces a public parameter pp, and initial states $(\mathsf{intl}_1, \mathsf{intl}_2)$ for each party. This compilation is done "in the dark" without any leakage. Afterwards, the public parameter pp will be given to the two parties and the adversary (at all time), and then, the parties can compute together $y = C(x)$ for any input x by running the protocol Π for an arbitrary polynomial number of inputs.

Below we provide the formal definition and security requirements of OCL schemes. Here the adversaries are allowed to continually leak on the internal state during each iteration. As discussed in the introduction, here we consider a stronger adversary that he can leak on *any* arbitrary order of the components. Additionally, we consider a further stronger security notion where we require the simulator to be oblivious of the leakage queries from the adversaries.

Definition 1. *Two-component OCL schemes]* *We say that* $\Lambda = (\mathsf{Comp}, \Pi = \langle P_1, P_2 \rangle)$ *is a continual, two-component OCL scheme if it satisfies the following properties.*

Initialization: *For every security parameter* $\lambda \in \mathbb{N}$, *polynomial-sized circuit family* $\mathcal{C} = \{C_\lambda\}_{\lambda \in \mathbb{N}}$, *the compiler* $\mathsf{Comp}(1^\lambda, C_\lambda)$ *runs in time* $\mathrm{poly}(\lambda)$ *and outputs a public parameter* pp *and 2 initial states* $\mathsf{intl}_1, \mathsf{intl}_2$. *Note that* pp *will be kept the same during all evaluations, and given to all parties.*

Unbounded-time evaluation: *The evaluation procedure invokes the protocol* Π *between the components* $P_1(\mathsf{pp}, \mathsf{intl}_1)$, $P_2(\mathsf{pp}, \mathsf{intl}_2)$, *which interact in an arbitrary polynomial number of iterations: In the* i^{th} *iteration,* P_1 *receives an input* $x_i \in \{0,1\}^{|C_\lambda|}$ *and* P_2 *produces an output* y_i[7]. *At the end of the evaluation, an update procedure is carried out, producing the new initial states for the next iteration; then all information other than the new initial states are erased. Note that* pp *will not be erased and will be reused in the next iteration.*

For each component $b \in \{1, 2\}$, *denote by* $\mathsf{intl}_{i,b}$ *the initial states of component* b *at the onset of the* i^{th} *iteration (in the first iteration,* $\mathsf{intl}_{1,b} = \mathsf{intl}_b$), *and* $\mathsf{evl}_{i,b}$ *the random coins tossed and messages exchanged by each* P_b *during the* i^{th} *iteration, including its state during the update phase.*

---

[7] It is without loss of generality that P_1 receives inputs and P_2 produces an output. We can always achieve this by sending one more round of message.

Correctness with adaptive input selection: *For every* $\lambda \in \mathbb{N}$, *polynomial-sized circuit family* $\mathcal{C} = \{C_\lambda\}_{\lambda \in \mathbb{N}}$, *auxiliary input* $z \in \{0,1\}^{\text{poly}(\lambda)}$, *and* PPT *adversary* $\mathcal{A}$, *in the following real experiment* $\mathbf{Real}_\mathcal{A}(1^\lambda, C_\lambda, z)$ *where* $\mathcal{A}$ *initiates an arbitrary number of evaluations with adaptively chosen inputs, it holds that with all but negligible probability, the outputs of all evaluations are correct.*
We say that an OCL scheme has perfect correctness if the above holds with probability 1.

2.1   Security Model

We now describe the security experiments of OCL schemes. A scheme $\varLambda$ is said to be ℓ-leakage-resilient with oblivious simulation if there is a simulator $\mathcal{S}$, such that, for every $\lambda \in \mathbb{N}$, polynomial-sized family $\mathcal{C}$, and auxiliary input $z \in \{0,1\}^{\text{poly}(\lambda)}$, the views of the adversary in the following real and ideal experiments are indistinguishable. In the real world, the adversary has the power of obtaining leakage independently from each component in honest OCL evaluations over inputs chosen adaptively by the adversary, whereas in the ideal world, it obtains leakage from states of the components simulated by an oblivious simulator, given oracle access to the circuit $C_\lambda(\cdot)$. More formally,

Experiment $\mathbf{Real}_\mathcal{A}(1^\lambda, C_\lambda, z)$: The adversary $\mathcal{A}(1^\lambda, |C_\lambda|, z)$ proceeds as follows:

1. The initial states $(\mathsf{pp}, \mathsf{intl}_1, \mathsf{intl}_2) \leftarrow \mathsf{Comp}(1^\lambda, C_\lambda)$ are sampled.
2. $\mathcal{A}$ gets the public parameter pp and launches ℓ-bounded leakage attacks on an unbounded polynomial number of evaluations of its choice. In the ith iteration, $\mathcal{A}$ works as follows:
   (a) $\mathcal{A}$ submits an input $x_i \in \{0,1\}^{|C_\lambda|}$, which is evaluated on C_λ by resuming the protocol execution of $\varPi$ between the components $P_1(\mathsf{pp}, \mathsf{intl}_{i,1})$, $P_2(\mathsf{pp}, \mathsf{intl}_{i,2})$ with input x_i to the first component P_1.
   (b) $\mathcal{A}$ launches an ℓ-bounded leakage attack on the ith evaluation. It issues leakage queries
   $(G_{1,b_1}, G_{2,b_2}, \ldots,)$, where each $b_k \in \{1,2\}$ to the two components (adaptively), and obtain leakage answers of all queries, i.e., $G_{k,b_k}(\mathsf{intl}_{i,b_k}, \mathsf{evl}_{i,b_k})$, as long as the total amount of leakage on each component in this iteration is smaller than $\ell(\lambda)$ bits. Denote $L_i \in \{0,1\}^{\leq \ell}$ be the leakage observed in the ith round.
   (c) $\mathcal{A}$ obtains the output of the evaluation, which is the output of P_2.

Denote $\text{VIEW}_\mathcal{A}^\ell(1^\lambda, C_\lambda, z) = (\mathsf{pp}, x_1, y_1, L_1, x_2, y_2, L_2, \ldots,)$ as the view of $\mathcal{A}$ in the above experiment.

Experiment $\mathbf{Ideal}_{\mathcal{S}, \mathcal{A}}(1^\lambda, C_\lambda, z)$: In the ideal experiment, the simulator $\mathcal{S}^{\mathcal{A}(1^\lambda, |C_\lambda|, z), C_\lambda(\cdot)}$ gets oracle access to the adversary $\mathcal{A}$ and oracle access to the circuit $C_\lambda(\cdot)$. His task is to produce an indistinguishable view of the adversary.

Furthermore, we say the simulator is oblivious, if it uses the following strategy to interact with the adversary: let the adversary $\mathcal{A}(1^\lambda, |C_\lambda|, z)$ participate in the same experiment as above. The simulator at the beginning generates a public parameter $\widetilde{pp}$ and gives it to the adversary $\mathcal{A}$. Then at each round i, the simulator works as follows.

(a) Let x_i be the input $\mathcal{A}$ submits in this iteration, and $y_i = C_\lambda(x_i)$ be the answer obtained by the oracle query. $\mathcal{S}(1^\lambda, i, x_i, y_i; \mathbf{w}_i)$ is invoked, producing simulated states $(\widetilde{\mathsf{intl}}_{i,1}, \widetilde{\mathsf{intl}}_{i,2}, \widetilde{\mathsf{evl}}_{i,1}, \widetilde{\mathsf{evl}}_{i,2})$, where w_i is the fresh random coins tossed for the simulation in iteration i and $\mathbf{w}_i = w_1, \cdots, w_i$ is all the random coins that have been tossed for simulation in the first i iterations.

(b) Let $(G_{1,b_1}, G_{2,b_2}, \dots,)$ where $b_k \in \{1, 2\}$, be the leakage queries $\mathcal{A}$ makes (perhaps in an adaptive way) in this round. Then $\mathcal{S}$ returns $G_{k,b_k}(\widetilde{\mathsf{intl}}_{i,b_k}, \widetilde{\mathsf{evl}}_{i,b_k})$ for all these queries, as long as the total amount of leakage on each component in this iteration is smaller than $\ell(\lambda)$ bits.

(c) $\mathcal{S}$ sends y_i to the adversary.

Denote $\widetilde{\mathrm{VIEW}}^\ell_{\mathcal{S},\mathcal{A}}(1^\lambda, C_\lambda, z)$ as the (simulated) view of $\mathcal{A}$ in the above experiment.

Definition 2 (Continual ℓ-leakage-resilience with oblivious simulation). *We say that a continual OCL scheme OCL is continually ℓ-leakage-resilient with oblivious simulation if there is a PPT simulator $\mathcal{S}$, such that, for every PPT adversary $\mathcal{A}$, every polynomial-sized circuit family $\mathcal{C}$, the following two ensembles are indistinguishable.*

- $\{\mathrm{VIEW}^\ell_{\mathcal{A}}(1^\lambda, C_\lambda, z)\}_{\lambda \in \mathbb{N}, C_\lambda \in \mathcal{C}, z \in \{0,1\}^{\mathrm{poly}(\lambda)}}$
- $\{\widetilde{\mathrm{VIEW}}^\ell_{\mathcal{S},\mathcal{A}}(1^\lambda, C_\lambda, z)\}_{\lambda \in \mathbb{N}, C_\lambda \in \mathcal{C}, z \in \{0,1\}^{\mathrm{poly}(\lambda)}}$

$\mathcal{F}$-hybrid OCL schemes. A two-component OCL scheme may use subroutines during its execution. Let $\mathcal{F}$ denote a two-party functionality. We say a two-component OCL scheme $\Lambda = (\mathsf{Comp}, \Pi = \langle P_1, P_2 \rangle)$ is an $\mathcal{F}$-hybrid OCL scheme if Λ completes its execution by calling $\mathcal{F}$ (probably multiple times). Often we write it as $\Lambda^\mathcal{F} = (\mathsf{Comp}, \Pi^\mathcal{F})$. If the OCL scheme Λ calls $\mathcal{F}$ at a round i, and let (x_1, x_2) be the values provided by P_1, P_2 and (y_1, y_2) be the values $\mathcal{F}$ returns to P_1, P_2 respectively, then the states $\mathsf{evl}_{i,1}, \mathsf{evl}_{i,2}$ will include (x_1, y_1) and (x_2, y_2), respectively. The adversary can obtain leakage of (x_1, y_1), (x_2, y_2) (perhaps adaptively but not jointly) via (adaptive) leakage queries.

Usually, we can think of $\mathcal{F}$ as some hardware that generates messages securely, i.e. there is no leakage on the internal states. We next consider how to *replace* such $\mathcal{F}$ with a two-party protocol. Intuitively, suppose there is a two-party protocol ρ that "realizes" $\mathcal{F}$, then we have a two-component OCL scheme where we can replace the calls to $\mathcal{F}$ by running the protocol ρ. We denote the scheme as $\Lambda' = (\mathsf{Comp}, \Pi^\rho)$. We also consider the case where ρ realizes $\mathcal{F}$ in a setting that a common reference string (CRS) crs is always available. In this case, we can combine the CRS generation into the compilation: Comp may generate a certain pubic parameter pp, and we can simply augment Comp into Comp' that generates $\mathsf{pp}' = \mathsf{pp} \| \mathsf{crs}$. This is denoted as $\Lambda' = (\mathsf{Comp}', \Pi^\rho)$.

However, standard simulation based security is not sufficient for the argument of the hardware replacement as above because the simulation (of ρ) could be a *joint* simulation for both participants. This is inconsistent with the security requirement of OCL scheme where the emulation for one component is oblivious to the emulation of the other component. In the following, we define a stronger version of realization, and prove that if ρ realizes $\mathcal{F}$ in this sense, then we can replace $\mathcal{F}$ with ρ and the OCL scheme remains secure. The definition we present is a compact and simplified version that captures the notion of "security under adaptive corruptions with a corruption-oblivious simulator" defined by [8]. We consider the semi-honest case only.

Definition 3 (Strong oblivious simulation for protocols). *Let* crs $\leftarrow$ CRS.Gen(1^λ), *and let* $\pi = (P_1, P_2)$ *be a two-party protocol using such common reference string* crs. *Let* $\mathcal{F}$ *be a two-input (perhaps randomized) ideal functionality. We say* π *realizes the functionality* $\mathcal{F}$ *with strong oblivious simulation, if there exists a* PPT *simulator* $\mathcal{S} = (\mathcal{S}_1, \mathcal{S}_2, \mathcal{S}_{tr})$ *for all (non-uniform)* PPT *adversary* $\mathcal{A}$ *such that the following distributions are computationally indistinguishable:*

$$\left\{ \begin{array}{c} \mathsf{crs} \leftarrow \mathsf{CRS.Gen}(1^\lambda); \\ (x_1, x_2) \leftarrow \mathcal{A}(\mathsf{crs}); \\ (r_1, r_2) \leftarrow U_\lambda \times U_\lambda; \\ \tau = \langle P_1(\mathsf{crs}, x_1; r_1), P_2(\mathsf{crs}, x_2; r_2) \rangle \\ : (\mathsf{crs}, x_1, r_1, \tau, x_2, r_2) \end{array} \right\} \approx \left\{ \begin{array}{c} \mathsf{crs} \leftarrow \mathsf{CRS.Gen}(1^\lambda); \\ (x_1, x_2) \leftarrow \mathcal{A}(\mathsf{crs}); \\ (y_1, y_2) \leftarrow \mathcal{F}(x_1, x_2); \\ \tilde{\tau} \leftarrow \mathcal{S}_{tr}(\mathsf{crs}); \\ \tilde{r}_1 \leftarrow \mathcal{S}_1(\mathsf{crs}, x_1, y_1, \tilde{\tau}); \\ \tilde{r}_2 \leftarrow \mathcal{S}_2(\mathsf{crs}, x_2, y_2, \tilde{\tau}) \\ : (\mathsf{crs}, x_1, \tilde{r}_1, \tilde{\tau}, x_2, \tilde{r}_2) \end{array} \right\} .$$

Note that r_1, r_2 *are the random coins of the parties, and* τ *is the transcript (i.e. message exchanges) by running the protocol* $\langle P_1(\mathsf{crs}, x_1; r_1), P_2(\mathsf{crs}, x_2; r_2) \rangle$.

Remark 1. The notion above is related to the notion of security under adaptive corruptions with a corruption-oblivious simulator defined by Bitansky et al. [8]. We elaborate further below.

- Our notion implies adaptive security where the simulator uses a universal strategy that is independent of the order of corruption, i.e. $\mathcal{S}_1$ and $\mathcal{S}_2$ simulate independently (with a joint transcript $\tilde{\tau}$ that is independent of the inputs/outputs). In contrast, in the adaptive security case, the simulator is allowed to see the already corrupted party's input/output, i.e. if the adversary first corrupts P_1 and then P_2, then the simulator can see both (x_1, y_1) and (x_2, y_2) when simulating the view of P_2. Known constructions of adaptively secure two party computation for all functionalities, such as [18], do not admit such simulators.

- Following the approach of [8], our notion implies a strong notion of leakage tolerant two-party computation in the semi-honest setting where any t-bit leakage function in the real world can be translated to a t-bit leakage function in the ideal world. There is no prior bound on t. Moreover, if the leakage function in the real world does not leak on the joint states, then the ideal leakage function does not, either.

Theorem 5 (OCL hardware replacement theorem). *Let $\mathcal{F}$ be some two-party functionality, and $\Lambda^{\mathcal{F}} = (\mathsf{Comp}, \Pi^{\mathcal{F}})$ be an $\mathcal{F}$-hybrid two-component OCL scheme that is ℓ-leakage-resilient with oblivious simulation. Suppose there exists a two-party protocol ρ using a common reference string crs, that realizes $\mathcal{F}$ with strong oblivious simulation as Definition 3. Then there exists a two-component OCL scheme $\Lambda' = (\mathsf{Comp}', \Pi^{\rho})$ that is ℓ-leakage-resilient with oblivious simulation.*

The intuition of the proof of Theorem 5 is the following: The two-component OCL scheme Λ' will simply replace each call to the ideal functionality $\mathcal{F}$ with an execution of the two-party protocol ρ, where each component plays the part of one of the parties in ρ. To obtain an oblivious simulator for the composed execution Λ', we must reconstruct the entire state of each component. Note that the state of each component in Λ' simply consists of its state in Λ, concatenated with its state in ρ. Thus, a natural approach is to reconstruct each party's state by concatenating the output of the simulator $\widehat{\mathcal{S}}$ for Λ and the output of the simulator $\widetilde{\mathcal{S}}$ for ρ. Indeed, this approach does in fact work since the only shared information between the component's simulated state in Λ and its simulated state in ρ is the input/output of the ideal functionality $\mathcal{F}$. Therefore, conditioned on the input/output of $\mathcal{F}$, each component's state in ρ can be reconstructed entirely independently of its state in Λ. We note that the bound in Λ' inherits from the underlying scheme Λ. By the security of the protocol ρ as discussed above, any leakage to the evaluation states of ρ can be translated to leakage of the input/output of $\mathcal{F}$. For this part we do not need a prior bound. We defer the formal proof to the full version of this paper [22].

Remark 2. Very recently, Bitansky et al. [10] defined a notion of *strong* two-component OCL schemes. They showed this notion has implications to two-party leakage tolerant protocols as discussed in the introduction. We note that the previous schemes [24,37] satisfy this stronger notion, and a similar hardware replacement theorem can be achieved. Please refer to the full version of this paper [22] for more details.

3   How to Implement Simple Functionalities

In this section, we construct two-party protocols to realize functionalities that provided by hardware components in previous schemes (with strong oblivious simulation). However, the requirement is very strong as we discussed in the previous section, and it is not clear how to construct protocols for general functionalities. Fortunately, the functionalities used in the previous constructions by Juma and Vahlis, and by Dziembowski and Faust [24,37] (and in all the other known constructions) are "simple". We show how to construct protocols for certain simple functionalities.

3.1   Ideal Functionality

Here we define a functionality $\mathcal{F}^{\Delta}_{\text{sampling}}$ which samples correlated randomness (according to some distributions) for both parties *without* taking any inputs. This functionality captures the hardwares used in the previous schemes of Juma-Vahlis and Dziembowski-Faust.

The ideal functionality $\mathcal{F}^{\Delta}_{\text{sampling}}$ is parametrized by an efficiently samplable distribution Δ that outputs correlated random coins $(\gamma_1, \gamma_2) \leftarrow \Delta(1^{\lambda})$.

Functionality $\mathcal{F}^{\Delta}_{\text{sampling}}$

$\mathcal{F}^{\Delta}_{\text{sampling}}$, parameterized with a distribution Δ, a variable done with initial value 0, running with parties (P_1, P_2) and an adversary $\mathcal{A}$, operates as follows:

- Upon receiving request from P_i, if done $= 0$, then sample $(\gamma_1, \gamma_2) \leftarrow \Delta(1^{\lambda})$, and set done $:= 1$. Return γ_i to party P_i, and ignore future request from P_i.

Fig. 1. The ideal functionality for sampling correlated randomness

3.2   Building Blocks

In this section, we present two building blocks for our construction – receiver non-committing encryption, and universal deniable encryption transformation. Basically, a receiver non-committing public key encryption allows a simulator to first generate a pair of simulated public-key and ciphertext (without knowing what the underlying message was), and later to come up with consistent random coins that explain the key generation, and decrypt the ciphertext to an arbitrary message m. This notion is weaker than standard non-committing public key encryption [15], which can be constructed from *trapdoor simulatable public key encryption* [20], which in turn can be instantiated under standard assumptions such as CDH, RSA, DDH, LWE and factoring Blum integers.

Universal Deniable Encryption is a new notion proposed by Sahai and Waters [47]. Here we paraphrase the ideas as Definition 5: given any encryption scheme E = {Gen, Enc, Dec}, there is a one-time setup UniGen that takes input the encryption algorithm E.Enc and generates two programs $C_{\text{encrypt}}, C_{\text{explain}}$, an encryption program and an explanation program. The one-time setup is generated by some trusted party.

Basically, the encryption program C_{encrypt} takes inputs a public key pk and a message m, outputs a ciphertext. The explanation program C_{explain} takes inputs a public key pk, a ciphertext c, and a message m outputs random coins r to "explain" that c is an encryption of m. That is, running the encryption program with input pk, m and randomness r, it will output c, i.e. $c = C_{\text{encrypt}}(\text{pk}, m; r)$. The security requires that (1) the distribution of $\{C_{\text{encrypt}}(\text{pk}, m)\}$ is statistically close to that of $\{\mathsf{E.Enc}(\mathsf{pk}, m)\}$. In other words, using C_{encrypt} is essentially the same as using the encryption algorithm. (2) It is computationally hard to distinguish the real random coins from the explained random coins (by C_{explain}). Note that since $C_{\mathsf{encrypt}}, C_{\mathsf{explain}}$ can be generated without knowing any secret information, the semantic security of E preserves even given these two programs.

Actually, the universal deniable encryption in the work of Sahai and Waters [47] is more general: it allows $C_{\mathsf{encrypt}}, C_{\mathsf{explain}}$ to take public keys from different encryption schemes. In our application, this slightly restricted version already suffices. So for clarity of exposition, we present this simpler version.

Definition 4 (Receiver non-committing encryption [17,36]). *A one-sided non-committing encryption scheme (for the receiver) consists of a tuple* $(\mathsf{NCGen}, \mathsf{NCEnc}, \mathsf{NCDec}, \mathsf{NCSim})$ *such that* $(\mathsf{NCGen}, \mathsf{NCEnc}, \mathsf{NCDec})$ *is an encryption scheme and* $\mathsf{NCSim} = (\mathsf{NCSim}_1, \mathsf{NCSim}_2)$ *is a tuple of two simulation algorithms. On input* 1^λ, $\mathsf{NCSim}_1(1^\lambda)$ *outputs a simulated public key* $\widetilde{\mathsf{pk}}$ *and a simulated ciphertext* $\widetilde{c}$; *on inputs a simulated public key,* $\widetilde{\mathsf{pk}}$, *a simulated ciphertext* $\widetilde{c}$, *and a message* m, $\mathsf{NCSim}_2(\widetilde{\mathsf{pk}}, \widetilde{c}, m)$ *outputs random coins* $\widetilde{\sigma}$ *(for the key generation,* NCGen*). We say the scheme is secure if for all messages* m, *the following two distributions are indistinguishable:*

- *the view of honest decryptor in a normal encryption of* m:

$$\{(\mathsf{pk}, c, \sigma) : (\mathsf{pk}, \mathsf{sk}) \leftarrow \mathsf{NCGen}(\sigma), c \leftarrow \mathsf{NCEnc}(\mathsf{pk}, m)\},$$

- *simulated view of an encryption of* m:

$$\left\{(\widetilde{\mathsf{pk}}, \widetilde{c}, \widetilde{\sigma}) : (\widetilde{\mathsf{pk}}, \widetilde{c}) \leftarrow \mathsf{NCSim}_1(1^\lambda), \widetilde{\sigma} \leftarrow \mathsf{NCSim}_2(\widetilde{\mathsf{pk}}, \widetilde{c}, m)\right\}.$$

Definition 5 (Universal deniable encryption transformation for an encryption scheme). *Let* $\mathsf{E} = \{\mathsf{Gen}, \mathsf{Enc}, \mathsf{Dec}\}$ *be a (bit) encryption scheme. A universal deniable encryption transformation for* E *is a* PPT *algorithm* UniGen *that takes input security parameter* 1^λ, *an encryption circuit that implements the encryption algorithm* $\mathsf{E.Enc}(1^\lambda, \cdot; \cdot)$ *and outputs two programs* $C_{\mathsf{encrypt}}, C_{\mathsf{explain}}$ *with the following syntax: let* pk *be a public key,* m *be a message,* c *be a ciphertext.*

- C_{encrypt} *takes inputs* pk, m, *random coins* r, *and* $C_{\mathsf{encrypt}}(\mathsf{pk}, m; r)$ *outputs a ciphertext* c;
- C_{explain} *takes inputs* pk, c, m, *random coins* $\bar{v}$, *and* $C_{\mathsf{explain}}(\mathsf{pk}, c, m; \bar{v})$ *outputs a string* r.

We say the transformation is secure if:

(a) *For all* $\mathsf{pk} \in \mathsf{E}.\mathsf{Gen}(1^\lambda)$, *messages* $m \in \{0,1\}$, *and any* $C_{\mathsf{encrypt}} \in \mathsf{UniGen}(1^\lambda)$, *the following two distributions are statistically close:* $\{C_{\mathsf{encrypt}}(\mathsf{pk}, m)\} \approx \{\mathsf{E}.\mathsf{Enc}(\mathsf{pk}, m)\}$. *Note that the circuit* C_{encrypt} *and the encryption algorithm* $\mathsf{E}.\mathsf{Enc}$ *might have different spaces for random coins, but the distributions can still be statistically close.*

(b) *For any message* $m \in \{0,1\}$, *the following two distributions are computationally indistinguishable:*

$$\{(C_{\mathsf{encrypt}}, C_{\mathsf{explain}}, \mathsf{pk}, c, r)\} \approx \{(C_{\mathsf{encrypt}}, C_{\mathsf{explain}}, \mathsf{pk}, c, r')\},$$

where $(C_{\mathsf{encrypt}}, C_{\mathsf{explain}}) \leftarrow \mathsf{UniGen}(1^\lambda)$, $\mathsf{pk} \leftarrow \mathsf{E}.\mathsf{Gen}(1^\lambda)$, $r \leftarrow U_{\mathrm{poly}(\lambda)}, c = C_{\mathsf{encrypt}}(\mathsf{pk}, m; r)$, $r' \leftarrow C_{\mathsf{explain}}(\mathsf{pk}, c, m)$, *and* $U_{\mathrm{poly}(\lambda)}$ *denotes the uniform distribution over a polynomial number of bits.*

Theorem 6 ([47]). *Assume there exist indistinguishable obfuscation for general circuits and one way functions. Then there exists a secure universal deniable encryption transformation for any encryption scheme.*

As pointed out in the introduction, our constructions only use universal deniable encryption and non-committing encryption in a black-box way. We do not explicitly use indistinguishable obfuscation so we do not present the syntax here.

3.3 Our Construction

Now we are ready to describe our protocol. Let $\mathsf{E} = \{\mathsf{NCGen}, \mathsf{NCEnc}, \mathsf{NCDec}, \mathsf{NCSim}\}$ be a receiver non-committing encryption, Δ be the (efficiently samplable) distribution that the ideal functionality wants to sample, and UniGen is a secure universal deniable encryption transformation. First we consider a bit encryption $\mathsf{E}' = \{\mathsf{Gen}, \mathsf{Enc}, \mathsf{Dec}\}$ that works as follows:

– $\mathsf{E}'.\mathsf{Gen}(1^\lambda)$: run $(\mathsf{pk}, \mathsf{sk}) \leftarrow \mathsf{E}.\mathsf{NCGen}(1^\lambda)$. Output $(\mathsf{pk}, \mathsf{sk})$ as the public and secret keys.

$$\boxed{\begin{array}{ll}
\multicolumn{2}{c}{\mathsf{crs} = (C_{\mathsf{encrypt}}, C_{\mathsf{explain}})} \\
\quad P_1(\mathsf{crs}) & \qquad\qquad P_2(\mathsf{crs}) \\[1ex]
r_1 \leftarrow U_{\mathrm{poly}(\lambda)} & r_2 \leftarrow U_{\mathrm{poly}(\lambda)} \\
& \xleftarrow{\quad\mathsf{pk}\quad} (\mathsf{pk}, \mathsf{sk}) \leftarrow \mathsf{E}.\mathsf{NCGen}(1^\lambda; r_2) \\
(\gamma_1, c_2) \leftarrow C_{\mathsf{encrypt}}(\mathsf{pk}, 0; r_1) & \\
& \xrightarrow{\quad c_2\quad} \gamma_2 \leftarrow \mathsf{E}.\mathsf{NCDec}(\mathsf{sk}, c_2) \\[1ex]
\text{output: } \gamma_1 & \text{output: } \gamma_2
\end{array}}$$

Fig. 2. A protocol for $\mathcal{F}_{\mathsf{sampling}}$

- $\mathsf{E'.Enc}(1^\lambda, \mathsf{pk}, b)$: sample $(\gamma_1, \gamma_2) \leftarrow \Delta(1^\lambda)$. Then output $c \leftarrow (\gamma_1, \mathsf{E.NCEnc}(\mathsf{pk}, \gamma_2 \| b))$ as the ciphertext. The random coins of this process consist of the randomness used for sampling Δ, and that for encryption algorithm $\mathsf{E.NCEnc}$.
- $\mathsf{E'.Dec}(1^\lambda, \mathsf{sk}, c)$: parse $c = (c_1, c_2)$. Run $\gamma_2 \| b := \mathsf{E.NCDec}(\mathsf{sk}, c_2)$, and output b.

The CRS sampling. Let C be a circuit that implements $\mathsf{E'.Enc}(1^\lambda)$. The sampling algorithm runs
$(C_{\mathsf{encrypt}}, C_{\mathsf{explain}}) \leftarrow \mathsf{UniGen}(C)$, and outputs $\mathsf{crs} = (C_{\mathsf{encrypt}}, C_{\mathsf{explain}})$ as the CRS.

The protocol. The parties upon receiving $\mathsf{crs} = (C_{\mathsf{encrypt}}, C_{\mathsf{explain}})$ do the following:

- P_2 first samples a random string r_2 and runs $(\mathsf{pk}, \mathsf{sk}) \leftarrow \mathsf{E.NCGen}(1^\lambda; r_2)$ and sends pk to P_1.
- P_1 then samples a random string r_1, and runs $(\gamma_1, c_2) \leftarrow C_{\mathsf{encrypt}}(\mathsf{pk}, 0; r_1)$. Then P_1 locally outputs γ_1 and then sends c_2 to P_2.
- P_2 runs $\gamma_2 \| 0 := \mathsf{E.NCDec}(\mathsf{sk}, c_2)$ and then outputs γ_2.

The transcript of the protocol is (pk, c_2).

Here it is important that P_1 does not directly use $\mathsf{E'.Enc}$ to generate the ciphertext. Suppose he used $\mathsf{E'.Enc}$ directly, then his random coins r_1 must contain information about the underlying message of $c_2 = \mathsf{E.Enc}(\mathsf{pk}, \gamma_2 \| 0)$. We argue that it is impossible to satisfy our security requirement as follows.

Let us recall the security definition (Definition 3): to prove security, we need to construct a simulator $\mathcal{S} = (\mathcal{S}_{\mathsf{tr}}, \mathcal{S}_1, \mathcal{S}_2)$ such that we require $\mathcal{S}_1$ to simulate the view of P_1 without knowing γ_2, and similarly $\mathcal{S}_2$ to simulate the view of P_2 without knowing γ_1. Therefore, a secure protocol cannot allow one to derive γ_2 from P_1's random coins r_1; otherwise, it is impossible for $\mathcal{S}_1$ (who does not know γ_2) to simulate such view of P_1.

To tackle such challenge, we use the universal deniable encryption transformation as Definition 5: to generate ciphertext of $\mathsf{E'}$, we use the program C_{encrypt}. Note that even if the randomness spaces for C_{encrypt} and $\mathsf{E'.Enc}$ are different, the output distributions are statistically close, so using C_{encrypt} is essentially the same as using $\mathsf{E'.Enc}$. More importantly, by the property of randomness explainability and the security of E, we can argue that the random coins r_1 (of the program C_{encrypt}) is only linked to the ciphertext (γ_1, c_2), but not the message γ_2 under c_2. More formally, we can argue that (r_1, γ_1, c_2) is indistinguishable from $(\tilde{r}_1, \gamma_1, \tilde{c}_2)$, where $\tilde{c}_2$ is a simulated ciphertext that does not contain information about γ_2, and $\tilde{r}_1$ is explained randomness by C_{explain}.

Using the ideas above, we are able to establish the following theorem:

Theorem 7. *Assume that* E *is a secure receiver non-committing encryption,* Δ *is an efficiently samplable distribution, and* UniGen *is a secure universal deniable transformation for the encryption scheme* $\mathsf{E'}$ *defined as above. Then the protocol described above realizes* $\mathcal{F}^\Delta_{\mathsf{sampling}}$ *with strong oblivious simulation, using the common reference string* crs.

Before proving the theorem, we give an *interesting* remarks about implications of our protocols to adaptive security in the MPC setting.

Remark 3. The protocol above allows us to realize randomized functionalities beyond "adaptively well-formed" ones as discussed in the introduction. Recall that for an adaptively well-formed randomized functionality, the adversary gets the random coins of the functionality when all parties are corrupted. We go beyond this restriction. In our protocol above, the sampling is done in the C_{encrypt}, and we can simply use the C_{explain} to reconstruct the randomness. Essentially this gives the ideal functionality a way to erase the internal randomness after generating the outputs!

For further exposition, we take the example from the work [18, Section 3.3]. Consider the randomized functionality that outputs a value N to both P_1 and P_2 where $N = p \cdot q$ and p, q are randomly chosen (large) primes. To handle the case that all parties are corrupted without revealing the random coins of the functionality (i.e. p, q) to the adversary, essentially we need to be able to sample the domain $\{N | N = pq\}$ (or a domain that is computationally indistinguishable from it) without knowing p or q. The work [18] explicitly pointed out that this task may be possible, though the paper did not know how to do it.

In this paper, we show that this task is exactly what universal deniable encryption can achieve! In our protocol above, by using C_{encrypt} and some random coins r, P_1 is able to sample N without knowing the (p, q). Then the simulator in the ideal world, via C_{explain} can come up with consistent and indistinguishable random coins r' that explains that N *is* computed based on C_{encrypt} and r', even though the simulator is not able to learn such p, q.

How is this possible? For readers who are familiar with the Sahai-Waters instantiation [47], we further elaborate on how things work with their concrete scheme: recall that C_{encrypt} is an obfuscated circuit that contains some keys of (three) puncturable pseudo-random functions, say one of them is $F_1(K_1, \cdot)$ (consistent with the notation in [47]). When a user inputs some random coins r, if r does not hit some hidden trigger (the hitting probability is negligible), then the program will use $u = F_1(K_1, r)$ as the random coins to sample N. Since the whole process (i.e. the key K_1 and the computation of u) is inside the obfuscation (i.e. C_{encrypt}), thus the user can only obtain the output N without learning the underlying coins u (that may contain information about p, q).

Proof. To prove the theorem, we need to construct a simulator $\mathcal{S} = (\mathcal{S}_{\text{tr}}, \mathcal{S}_1, \mathcal{S}_2)$ such that the distribution of the real experiment **Real** $= (\text{crs}, r_1, \tau, r_2)$ is indistinguishable from that of the simulation experiment **Ideal** $= (\text{crs}, \tilde{r}_1, \tilde{\tau}, \tilde{r}_2)$ according to Definition 3.

Now, we describe the simulators. Let (γ_1, γ_2) be the output of the functionality $\mathcal{F}^{\Delta}_{\text{sampling}}$, $\text{NCSim} = (\text{NCSim}_1, \text{NCSim}_2)$ be the simulator(s) of the non-committing encryption scheme E, $\text{crs} = (C_{\text{encrypt}}, C_{\text{explain}})$ be the CRS sampled as described above.

- $\mathcal{S}_{\text{tr}}(\text{crs})$ samples $(\tilde{pk}, \tilde{c}_2) \leftarrow \text{NCSim}_1(1^\lambda)$ and then outputs $\tilde{\tau} = (\tilde{pk}, \tilde{c}_2)$.

- $S_1(\text{crs}, \tilde{\tau}, \gamma_1)$ runs $\tilde{r}_1 \leftarrow C_{\text{explain}}(\tilde{\text{pk}}, (\gamma_1, \tilde{c}_2), 0)$. That is, S_1 interprets $(\gamma_1, \tilde{c}_2)$ as a ciphertext of the scheme E', and uses C_{explain} to explain the randomness (for a ciphertext $E'.\text{Enc}(\text{pk}, 0)$).
- $S_2(\text{crs}, \tilde{\tau}, \gamma_2)$ runs $\tilde{r}_2 \leftarrow \text{NCSim}_2(\tilde{\text{pk}}, \tilde{c}_2, \gamma_2 || 0)$. That is, S_2 uses the simulator of the non-committing encryption to generate random coins that decrypt $\tilde{c}_2$ to $\gamma_2 || 0$.

Then we will establish the following claim, and the proof of the theorem follows directly from the claim.

Claim. The following two distributions are computationally indistinguishable: **Real** $= (\text{crs}, r_1, \tau, r_2) \approx$ **Ideal** $= (\text{crs}, \tilde{r}_1, \tilde{\tau}, \tilde{r}_2)$, where the experiments are sampled as the protocol and the simulation described above. Recall that r_2 is P_2's randomness that generates pk, and r_1 is P_1's randomness that is used for $C_{\text{encrypt}}(\text{pk}, 0)$.

Proof. To prove the claim, we consider the following hybrids:

The Real experiment. Real $= (\text{crs}, r_1, \tau = (\text{pk}, c_2), r_2)$: recall that in the real experiment, the transcript $\tau = (\text{pk}, c_2)$ is generated as follows. pk is generated by P_2, and c_2 is one part of a ciphertext of E' generated by P_1, i.e. $(\gamma_1, c_2) = C_{\text{encrypt}}(\text{pk}, 0; r_1)$.

Hybrid 1. $H_1 = (\text{crs}, \tilde{r}_1, \tau = (\text{pk}, c_2), r_2)$: this experiment is the same as the real experiment except instead of outputting r_1 as the randomness of P_1, we use $\tilde{r}_1 \leftarrow C_{\text{explain}}(\text{pk}, (\gamma_1, c_2), 0)$. More precisely, H_1 first samples $(\text{crs}, r_1, \tau, r_2)$ as the experiment **Real** (then γ_1, c_2 are defined), and replaces the r_1 with $\tilde{r}_1$ as described.

Hybrid 2. $H_2 = (\text{crs}, \tilde{r}_1, \tau' = (\text{pk}, c_2), r_2)$: this experiment is the same as H_1 except it does not use $C_{\text{encrypt}}(\text{pk}, 0)$ to generate the transcript. Instead, it samples $E'.\text{Enc}(\text{pk}, 0)$ as follows: first it samples $(\gamma_1, \gamma_2) \leftarrow \Delta(1^\lambda)$, and then generates $c_2 \leftarrow E.\text{Enc}(\text{pk}, \gamma_2)$. Then the experiment generates $\tilde{r}_1 \leftarrow C_{\text{explain}}(\text{pk}, (\gamma_1, c_2), 0)$ as H_1. Basically, this experiment runs $E'.\text{Enc}$ on its own to replace $C_{\text{encrypt}}(\text{pk}, 0)$.

Hybrid 3. $H_3 = \left(\text{crs}, \tilde{r}_1, \tilde{\tau} = (\tilde{\text{pk}}, \tilde{c}_2), \tilde{r}_2\right)$: this experiment is the same as H_2 except it runs $(\tilde{\text{pk}}, \tilde{c}_2) \leftarrow \text{NCSim}_1(1^\lambda)$ to generate the transcript. Finally, it runs $\tilde{r}_2 \leftarrow \text{NCSim}_2(\tilde{\text{pk}}, \tilde{c}_2, \gamma_2)$ to explain the randomness of P_2. Note that this experiment is identical to the simulation experiment **Ideal**.

Then we prove the adjacent hybrids are computationally indistinguishable by the following claims:

Claim. **Real** $\approx H_1$.

This is by the security of the universal deniable encryption transformation (property (b) of Definition 5). Suppose there exists a PPT distinguisher D that can distinguish **Real** from H_1 (with non-negligible probability), then we can construct a PPT distinguisher D' that breaks the property (b) as follows: D' takes input $(C_{\text{encrypt}}, C_{\text{explain}}, \text{pk}, (\gamma^*, c^*), r^*)$ where $C_{\text{encrypt}}, C_{\text{explain}}$ are generated as the universal deniable encryption transformation setup, (i.e. $\text{UniGen}(E'.\text{Enc}(1^\lambda, \cdot, \cdot)))$,

$(\gamma^*, c^*) \leftarrow C_{\text{encrypt}}(\text{pk}, 0)$, and r^* is either the one that generated (γ^*, c^*) or sampled by $C_{\text{explain}}(\text{pk}, (\gamma^*, c^*), 0)$.

Then $\mathcal{D}'$ interprets $\text{crs} = (C_{\text{encrypt}}, C_{\text{explain}})$, samples a random string r_2, and runs $\mathcal{D}(\text{crs}, r^*, (\text{pk}, c^*), r_2)$ and outputs whatever $\mathcal{D}$ outputs. Suppose r^* is distributed according to the former, then the input to $\mathcal{D}$ is distributed identical to **Real**. On the other hand, suppose r^* is distributed as the latter, then the input to $\mathcal{D}$ is distributed identical to H_1. Thus suppose $\mathcal{D}$ can distinguish **Real** from H_1, $\mathcal{D}'$ break security of the property (b).

Then we are going to show:

Claim. $H_1 \approx H_2$.

This is by the security property (a) of Definition 5), which says that $\{C_{\text{encrypt}}(\text{pk}, 0)\}$ is statistically close to $\{\text{E}'.\text{Enc}(\text{pk}, 0)\}$. The only difference between H_1 and H_2 is the generation of the (γ_1, c_2). In H_1 it was generated by $C_{\text{encrypt}}(\text{pk}, 0)$, and in H_2 it was generated by $\text{E}'.\text{Enc}(\text{pk}, 0)$. By the property (a), we know that the distributions of generating (γ_1, c_2) in both ways are statistically close. Thus H_1 is statistically close to H_2.

Then we are going to show:

Claim. $H_2 \approx H_3$.

This is by the security of the non-committing encryption E (as Definition 4). That is, suppose there exists a PPT distinguisher that can distinguish H_2 from H_3 (with non-negligible probability), then there exists a PPT distinguisher $\mathcal{D}'$ that breaks the non-committing encryption E as follows:

- $\mathcal{D}'$ first samples $(\gamma_1, \gamma_2) \leftarrow \Delta(1^\lambda)$ and sets $m = \gamma_2 \| 0$.
- $\mathcal{D}'$ takes input $(\text{pk}^*, c^*, \sigma^*)$ (from the challenger), which is distributed according to either the honest view of encryption of m or the simulated view as Definition 4.
- It samples $\text{crs} = (C_{\text{encrypt}}, C_{\text{explain}}) \leftarrow \text{UniGen}(C)$ where C is an encryption circuit of E'. This step is independent of the input.
- It generates $\tilde{r}_1 \leftarrow C_{\text{explain}}(\text{pk}^*, (\gamma_1, c^*), 0)$.
- It runs $\mathcal{D}(\text{crs}, \tilde{r}_1, (\text{pk}^*, c^*), \sigma^*)$, and outputs whatever $\mathcal{D}$ outputs.

It is clear that if the input $(\text{pk}^*, c^*, \sigma^*)$ is distributed as the honest view of encryption of m, then $(\text{crs}, \tilde{r}_1, (\text{pk}^*, c^*), \sigma^*)$ is distributed identicalyl to H_2. On the other hand, if that is distributed as the simulated view, then $(\text{crs}, \tilde{r}_1, (\text{pk}^*, c^*), \sigma^*)$ is distributed identically to H_3. Thus, suppose $\mathcal{D}$ distinguishes H_2 from H_3 with a non-negligible probability, $\mathcal{D}'$ breaks the receiver non-committing encryption scheme E. This completes the proof of the claimx.

Finally, we observe that the experiment H_3 is identical to the experiment **Ideal** output by the simulator. Thus by Claims 3.3, 3.3, 3.3, we prove Claim 3.3, i.e. **Real** $\approx$ **Ideal**. This completes the proof of Theorem 7.

4   Hardwares in JV and DF Schemes

In this section, we present concretely how to express the hardwares in the previous hardware-based schemes of Juma and Vahlis [37] and Dziembowski and

Faust [24] as the ideal functionality $\mathcal{F}^{\Delta}_{\text{sampling}}$. Thus, we can instantiate the hardware of the JV (resp. DF) two-component OCL scheme with the two-party protocol in Theorem 7 and apply Theorem 5 to obtain the first two-component OCL schemes without secure hardware.

4.1 Sampling Distribution for the Juma-Vahlis Compiler

We define the sampling distribution Δ_{JV} for functionality $\mathcal{F}^{\Delta_{\text{JV}}}_{\text{sampling}}$ that provided by the trusted hardware of the Juma-Vahlis compiler (a description of the compiler can be found in the full version of this paper [22]). Let FHE = FHE.{Gen, Enc, Dec, Eval} be a fully homomorphic encryption scheme with the additional cipher refreshing properties required by the JV construction. The distribution $\Delta_{\text{JV}}(1^\lambda)$ is defined as follows:

- Sample $(\text{pk}, \text{sk}) \leftarrow \text{Gen}(1^\lambda)$; and then sample $\text{ct}_0 \leftarrow \text{Enc}_{\text{pk}}(0)$ and $\text{ct}'_0 \leftarrow \text{Enc}_{\text{pk}}(0)$.
- Output (γ_1, γ_2), where $\gamma_1 = (\text{pk}, \text{ct}_0, \text{ct}'_0)$, adn $\gamma_2 = (\text{pk}, \text{sk})$.

Juma and Vahlis [37] showed that assuming FHE is a fully homomorphic encryption (with cipher refreshing) that is secure against $2^{O(\ell(\lambda))}$ adversaries, then there exists a two-component OCL scheme in the $\mathcal{F}^{\Delta_{\text{JV}}}_{\text{sampling}}$ hybrid world that is $O(\ell)$-leakage resilient. We denote the scheme as $\Lambda^{\mathcal{F}}_{\text{JV}} = (\text{Comp}_{\text{JV}}, \Pi^{\mathcal{F}}_{\text{JV}})$ where $\mathcal{F} = \mathcal{F}^{\Delta_{\text{JV}}}_{\text{sampling}}$. By our Theorem 7, we can realize the functionality that provided by the trusted hardware with a protocol φ_{JV} with strong oblivious simulation. Leveraging our OCL Hardware Replacement Theorem (Theorem 5), we can obtain an OCL scheme $\Lambda'_{\text{JV}} = (\text{Comp}'_{\text{JV}}, \Pi^{\varphi_{\text{JV}}}_{\text{JV}})$ that does not require any secure hardware. Formally, we obtain the following theorem:

Theorem 8. *Assume there exist a secure receiver non-committing encryption scheme and a secure universal deniable encryption transformation for any encryption scheme,[8] and* FHE *is a fully homomorphic encryption (with cipher refreshing) that is secure against $2^{O(\ell(\lambda))}$ adversaries. Then Λ'_{JV} is $O(\ell)$-leakage resilient, where λ is security parameter.*

4.2 Sampling Distribution for the Dziembowski-Faust Compiler

Here we define the distribution Δ_{DF} for functionality $\mathcal{F}^{\Delta_{\text{DF}}}_{\text{sampling}}$ that provided by the trusted hardware of the Dziembowski-Faust compiler. In the initialization stage of the DF compiler, a private circuit C is compiled. Afterwards, in each evaluation when P_1 obtains an input x, the parties then jointly compute the universal boolean circuit $U(\cdot, \cdot)$ on the underlying input (C, x), and eventually P_2 returns output $y = C(x)$. Please refer to the full version of this paper [22] for a description of the DF compiler[9]. Let $\mathbb{F}_2$ be binary field, and each share used in

---

[8] This can be implied by the existence of indistinguishable obfuscation and one-way functions (Theorem 6).

[9] Our presentation of the DF scheme adapts from the simplified version of the DF scheme presented in the work [9].

DF compiler be of length m. Note that the length m is related to the amount of leakage that can be tolerated as described in the following theorem statement. Let $\mathcal{O}_b^n$ be the uniform distribution on $(L, R) \in \mathbb{F}_2^{n \times n}$ conditioned on $\langle L, R \rangle = b$. Without loss of generality, assume the universal boolean circuit $U(\cdot, \cdot)$ consists of T number of NAND gates, labeled with a set $G = \{1, \ldots, T\}$. The distribution $\Delta_{\text{DF}}(1^\lambda)$ is defined as follows:

- For $g \in G$, sample vectors $(L_g'\|L_g'', R_g'\|R_g'') \leftarrow \mathcal{O}_0^{2m^2}$;
  for $j \leq |C|$, sample vectors $(A_j'\|A_j'', B_j'\|B_j'') \leftarrow \mathcal{O}_0^{2m}$,
- Output (γ_1, γ_2), where $\gamma_1 = \left(\{L_g'\|L_g''\}_{g \in G}, \{A_j'\|A_j''\}_{j \leq |C|}\right)$
  and $\gamma_2 = \left(\{R_g'\|R_g''\}_{g \in G}, \{B_j'\|B_j''\}_{j \leq |C|}\right)$.

Dziembowski and Faust [24] showed that (without any cryptographic assumption) there exists a two-component OCL scheme in the $\mathcal{F}_{\text{sampling}}^{\Delta_{\text{DF}}}$ hybrid world, denoted as $\Lambda_{\text{DF}}^{\mathcal{F}} = (\text{Comp}_{\text{DF}}, \Pi_{\text{DF}}^{\mathcal{F}})$ where $\mathcal{F} = \mathcal{F}_{\text{sampling}}^{\Delta_{\text{DF}}}$. By our Theorem 7, we can realize the functionality that provided by the hardware with a protocol φ_{DF} with strong oblivious simulation. Leveraging our OCL Hardware Replacement Theorem (Theorem 5), we can obtain an OCL scheme $\Lambda_{\text{DF}}' = (\text{Comp}_{\text{DF}}', \Pi_{\text{DF}}^{\varphi_{\text{DF}}})$ that does not require any secure hardware. Formally, we obtain the following theorem:

Theorem 9. *Assume there exist a secure receiver non-committing encryption scheme and a secure universal deniable encryption transformation for any encryption scheme. Then Λ_{DF}' is ℓ-leakage resilient for $\ell(\lambda) = m(\lambda)/10$, $m(\lambda) = \omega(\log(\lambda))$, where λ is the security parameter.*

5 Extension: Multi-component OCL Schemes

In this section, we discuss some extensions of our main results. First we note that the hardware replacement theorem (Theorem 5) also holds for any N-component OCL schemes. Even if we have two-component constructions (in this paper), still potentially, there can be other more-component constructions that are more efficient or achieve better leakage rate. As we emphasize before, this can be viewed as a general design paradigm of OCL constructions. The definition of N-component OCL can be found in the work of Bitansky et al. [10], and the corresponding hybrid schemes can be defined analogously. A natural extension of strong oblivious simulation (Definition 3) for N-party protocols can be defined as follow:

Definition 6 (Strong oblivious simulation for N-party protocols). *Let* crs $\leftarrow$ CRS.Gen(1^λ), *and let* $\pi = (P_1, \ldots, P_N)$ *be an N-party protocol using such common reference string* crs. *Let $\mathcal{F}$ be an N-input (perhaps randomized) ideal functionality. We say π realizes the functionality $\mathcal{F}$ with strong oblivious simulation, if there exists a PPT simulator $\mathcal{S} = (\mathcal{S}_1, \ldots, \mathcal{S}_N, \mathcal{S}_{\text{tr}})$ for all (non-uniform)*

PPT *adversary $\mathcal{A}$ such that the following distributions are computationally indistinguishable:*

$$
\left\{
\begin{array}{c}
\mathsf{crs} \leftarrow \mathsf{CRS.Gen}(1^\lambda); \\
(x_1, \ldots, x_N) \leftarrow \mathcal{A}(\mathsf{crs}); \\
(r_1, \ldots, r_N) \leftarrow (U_\lambda)^N; \\
\tau = \langle P_1(\mathsf{crs}, x_1; r_1), \ldots, P_N(\mathsf{crs}, x_N; r_N) \rangle \\
: (\mathsf{crs}, \{x_i, r_i\}_{i \in [N]}, \tau)
\end{array}
\right\}
\approx
\left\{
\begin{array}{c}
\mathsf{crs} \leftarrow \mathsf{CRS.Gen}(1^\lambda); \\
(x_1, \ldots, x_N) \leftarrow \mathcal{A}(\mathsf{crs}); \\
(y_1, \ldots, y_N) \leftarrow \mathcal{F}(x_1, \ldots, x_N); \\
\tilde{\tau} \leftarrow \mathcal{S}_{\mathsf{tr}}(\mathsf{crs}); \\
\forall i \in [N], \ \ \tilde{r}_i \leftarrow \mathcal{S}_i(\mathsf{crs}, x_i, y_i, \tilde{\tau}); \\
: (\mathsf{crs}, \{x_i, \tilde{r}_i\}_{i \in [N]}, \tilde{\tau})
\end{array}
\right\}.
$$

Note that r_i's *are the random coins of the parties, and τ is the transcript (i.e. message exchanges) by running the N-party protocol .*

A similar OCL hardware replacement theorem can be obtained for N-component OCL scheme. Since the proof is essentially the same as that of Theorem 5, we only state the theorem but omit the proof.

Theorem 10 (N-component OCL hardware replacement theorem). *Let $\mathcal{F}$ be some N-party functionality, and $\Lambda^{\mathcal{F}} = (\mathsf{Comp}, \Pi^{\mathcal{F}})$ be a $\mathcal{F}$-hybrid N-component OCL scheme that is ℓ-leakage-resilient with oblivious simulation. Suppose there exists an N-party protocol ρ using a common reference string crs, that realizes $\mathcal{F}$ with strong oblivious simulation as above. Then there exists an N-component OCL scheme $\Lambda' = (\mathsf{Comp}', \Pi^\rho)$ that is ℓ-leakage-resilient with oblivious simulation.*

Our construction in Section 3.3 can be extended to any N-output $\mathcal{F}^\Delta_{\mathrm{sampling}}$ functionality for any N-output distribution Δ. Let $\mathsf{E} = \{\mathsf{NCGen}, \mathsf{NCEnc}, \mathsf{NCDec}, \mathsf{NCSim}\}$ be a receiver non-committing encryption, Δ be an N-output distribution that the ideal functionality wants to sample, and UniGen is a secure universal deniable encryption transformation. Similarly we consider a bit encryption $\mathsf{E}' = \{\mathsf{Gen}, \mathsf{Enc}, \mathsf{Dec}\}$ that works as follows:

- $\mathsf{E}'.\mathsf{Gen}(1^\lambda)$: run $(\mathsf{pk}_2, \mathsf{sk}_2, \ldots, \mathsf{pk}_N, \mathsf{sk}_N) \leftarrow \mathsf{E}.\mathsf{NCGen}(1^\lambda)$ (running the generation $N - 1$ times. Here we deliberately start the index with 2.). Set the public key to be $\mathsf{pk} = (\mathsf{pk}_2, \ldots, \mathsf{pk}_N)$, and $\mathsf{sk} = (\mathsf{sk}_2, \ldots, \mathsf{sk}_N)$.
- $\mathsf{E}'.\mathsf{Enc}(1^\lambda, \mathsf{pk}, b)$: sample $(\gamma_1, \ldots, \gamma_N) \leftarrow \Delta(1^\lambda)$. Then output

$$c \leftarrow (\gamma_1, \mathsf{E}.\mathsf{NCEnc}(\mathsf{pk}_2, \gamma_2 || b), \ldots, \mathsf{E}.\mathsf{NCEnc}(\mathsf{pk}_N, \gamma_N || b))$$

as the ciphertext. The random coins of this process consist of the randomness used for sampling Δ, and that for encryption algorithm $\mathsf{E}.\mathsf{NCEnc}$.

- $\mathsf{E}'.\mathsf{Dec}(1^\lambda, \mathsf{sk}, c)$: parse $c = (\gamma_1, c_2, \ldots, c_N)$. Run $\gamma_2 || b := \mathsf{E}.\mathsf{NCDec}(\mathsf{sk}, c_2)$, and output b.

The CRS sampling. Let C be a circuit that implements $\mathsf{E}'.\mathsf{Enc}(1^\lambda)$. The sampling algorithm runs $(C_{\mathsf{encrypt}}, C_{\mathsf{explain}}) \leftarrow \mathsf{UniGen}(C)$, and outputs $\mathsf{crs} = (C_{\mathsf{encrypt}}, C_{\mathsf{explain}})$ as the CRS.

The protocol. The parties upon receiving $\mathsf{crs} = (C_{\mathsf{encrypt}}, C_{\mathsf{explain}})$ do the following:

- For $i \in [N] \setminus \{1\}$, P_i first samples a random string r_i and runs $(\mathsf{pk}_i, \mathsf{sk}_i) \leftarrow$ $\mathsf{E.NCGen}(1^\lambda; r_i)$ and sends pk_i to P_1.
- P_1 then samples a random string r_1, and runs $(\gamma_1, c_2, \ldots, c_N) \leftarrow C_{\mathsf{encrypt}}(\mathsf{pk}, 0;$ $r_1)$. Then P_1 locally outputs γ_1 and then sends c_i to P_i for all $i \in [N] \setminus \{1\}$.
- For $i \in [N] \setminus \{1\}$, P_i runs $\gamma_i \| 0 := \mathsf{E.NCDec}(\mathsf{sk}_i, c_i)$ and then outputs γ_i.

The analysis of the protocol is essentially the same the previous one. For succinctness of presentation, we only state the theorem below, but omit the details to avoid repetition.

Theorem 11. *Assume that* E *is a secure receiver non-committing encryption,* Δ *is an efficiently samplable N-output distribution, and* UniGen *is a secure universal deniable transformation for the encryption scheme* E' *defined as above. Then the N-party protocol described above realizes* $\mathcal{F}^\Delta_{\mathsf{sampling}}$ *with strong oblivious simulation, using the common reference string* crs.

Similar to the two-party case, the connection between the above protocol and MPC was already discussed in the introduction and Definition 3. We restate the implication: for any N-party randomized functionality (even beyond the adaptively well-formed ones [18]; the discussions in Remark 3 also apply to the N-party setting), we are able to construct a protocol that is adaptively secure and leakage tolerance, using the above construction.

Acknowledgments. We thank Dov Gordon and Adam O'Neill for many insightful discussions at the early stage of this work. We also thank Nir Bitansky and Rachel Lin for sharing the draft of paper [9].

References

1. Agrawal, D., Archambeault, B., Rao, J.R., Rohatgi, P.: The EM side-channel(s). In: Kaliski Jr., B.S., Koç, Ç.K., Paar, C. (eds.) CHES 2002. LNCS, vol. 2523, pp. 29–45. Springer, Heidelberg (2003)

2. Ananth, P., Gupta, D., Ishai, Y., Sahai, A.: Optimizing obfuscation: Avoiding barrington's theorem. Cryptology ePrint Archive, Report 2014/222 (2014). http://eprint.iacr.org/2014/222

3. Barak, B., Garg, S., Kalai, Y.T., Paneth, O., Sahai, A.: Protecting obfuscation against algebraic attacks. In: Nguyen, P.Q., Oswald, E. (eds.) EUROCRYPT 2014. LNCS, vol. 8441, pp. 221–238. Springer, Heidelberg (2014)

4. Barak, B., Goldreich, O., Impagliazzo, R., Rudich, S., Sahai, A., Vadhan, S.P., Yang, K.: On the (im)possibility of obfuscating programs. In: Kilian, J. (ed.) CRYPTO 2001. LNCS, vol. 2139, pp. 1–18. Springer, Heidelberg (2001)

5. Barak, B., Goldreich, O., Impagliazzo, R., Rudich, S., Sahai, A., Vadhan, S.P., Yang, K.: On the (im)possibility of obfuscating programs. Journal of the ACM **59**(2), 6 (2012)

6. Biham, E., Shamir, A.: Differential fault analysis of secret key cryptosystems. In: Kaliski Jr., B.S. (ed.) CRYPTO 1997. LNCS, vol. 1294, pp. 513–525. Springer, Heidelberg (1997)

7. Bitansky, N., Canetti, R., Goldwasser, S., Halevi, S., Kalai, Y.T., Rothblum, G.N.: Program obfuscation with leaky hardware. In: Lee, D.H., Wang, X. (eds.) ASIACRYPT 2011. LNCS, vol. 7073, pp. 722–739. Springer, Heidelberg (2011)

8. Bitansky, N., Canetti, R., Halevi, S.: Leakage-tolerant interactive protocols. In: Cramer, R. (ed.) TCC 2012. LNCS, vol. 7194, pp. 266–284. Springer, Heidelberg (2012)

9. Bitansky, N., Dachman-Soled, D., Lin, H.: Personal communication (2014)

10. Bitansky, N., Dachman-Soled, D., Lin, H.: Leakage-tolerant computation with input-independent preprocessing. In: Garay, J.A., Gennaro, R. (eds.) CRYPTO 2014, Part II. LNCS, vol. 8617, pp. 146–163. Springer, Heidelberg (2014)

11. Brakerski, Z., Rothblum, G.N.: Virtual black-box obfuscation for all circuits via generic graded encoding. In: Lindell, Y. (ed.) TCC 2014. LNCS, vol. 8349, pp. 1–25. Springer, Heidelberg (2014)

12. Brumley, D., Boneh, D.: Remote timing attacks are practical. Computer Networks **48**(5), 701–716 (2005)

13. Canetti, R.: Universally composable security: A new paradigm for cryptographic protocols. Cryptology ePrint Archive, Report 2000/067 (2000). http://eprint.iacr.org/2000/067

14. Canetti, R.: Universally composable security: a new paradigm for cryptographic protocols. In: 42nd FOCS, pp. 136–145. IEEE Computer Society Press, October 2001

15. Canetti, R., Feige, U., Goldreich, O., Naor, M.: Adaptively secure multi-party computation. In: 28th ACM STOC, pp. 639–648. ACM Press, May 1996

16. Canetti, R., Goldwasser, S., Poburinnaya, O.: Adaptively secure two-party computation from indistinguishability obfuscation. IACR Cryptology ePrint Archive, 2014:845 (2014)

17. Canetti, R., Halevi, S., Katz, J.: Adaptively-secure, non-interactive public-key encryption. In: Kilian, J. (ed.) TCC 2005. LNCS, vol. 3378, pp. 150–168. Springer, Heidelberg (2005)

18. Canetti, R., Lindell, Y., Ostrovsky, R., Sahai, A.: Universally composable two-party and multi-party secure computation. In: 34th ACM STOC, pp. 494–503. ACM Press, May 2002

19. Chari, S., Jutla, C.S., Rao, J.R., Rohatgi, P.: Towards sound approaches to counteract power-analysis attacks. In: Wiener, M. (ed.) CRYPTO 1999. LNCS, vol. 1666, pp. 398–412. Springer, Heidelberg (1999)

20. Choi, S.G., Dachman-Soled, D., Malkin, T., Wee, H.: Improved non-committing encryption with applications to adaptively secure protocols. In: Matsui, M. (ed.) ASIACRYPT 2009. LNCS, vol. 5912, pp. 287–302. Springer, Heidelberg (2009)

21. Dachman-Soled, D., Katz, J., Rao, V.: Adaptively secure, universally composable, multi-party computation in constant rounds. IACR Cryptology ePrint Archive, 2014:858 (2014)

22. Dachman-Soled, D., Liu, F.-H., Zhou, H.-S.: Leakage-resilient circuits revisited - optimal number of computing components without leak-free hardware. Cryptology ePrint Archive, Report 2014/856 (2014). http://eprint.iacr.org/

23. Duc, A., Dziembowski, S., Faust, S.: Unifying leakage models: from probing attacks to noisy leakage. In: Nguyen, P.Q., Oswald, E. (eds.) EUROCRYPT 2014. LNCS, vol. 8441, pp. 423–440. Springer, Heidelberg (2014)

24. Dziembowski, S., Faust, S.: Leakage-resilient circuits without computational assumptions. In: Cramer, R. (ed.) TCC 2012. LNCS, vol. 7194, pp. 230–247. Springer, Heidelberg (2012)

25. Faust, S., Rabin, T., Reyzin, L., Tromer, E., Vaikuntanathan, V.: Protecting circuits from leakage: the computationally-bounded and noisy cases. In: Gilbert, H. (ed.) EUROCRYPT 2010. LNCS, vol. 6110, pp. 135–156. Springer, Heidelberg (2010)

26. Garg, S., Gentry, C., Halevi, S., Raykova, M., Sahai, A., Waters, B.: Candidate indistinguishability obfuscation and functional encryption for all circuits. In: 54th FOCS, pp. 40–49. IEEE Computer Society Press, October 2013

27. Garg, S., Polychroniadou, A.: Two-round adaptively secure MPC from indistinguishability obfuscation. IACR Cryptology ePrint Archive, 2014:844 (2014)

28. Genkin, D., Pipman, I., Tromer, E.: Get your hands off my laptop: physical side-channel key-extraction attacks on PCs. In: Batina, L., Robshaw, M. (eds.) CHES 2014. LNCS, vol. 8731, pp. 242–260. Springer, Heidelberg (2014)

29. Genkin, D., Shamir, A., Tromer, E.: RSA key extraction via low-bandwidth acoustic cryptanalysis. In: Garay, J.A., Gennaro, R. (eds.) CRYPTO 2014, Part I. LNCS, vol. 8616, pp. 444–461. Springer, Heidelberg (2014)

30. Gentry, C., Lewko, A., Sahai, A., Waters, B.: Indistinguishability obfuscation from the multilinear subgroup elimination assumption. Cryptology ePrint Archive, Report 2014/309 (2014). http://eprint.iacr.org/2014/309

31. Goldwasser, S., Rothblum, G.N.: Securing computation against continuous leakage. In: Rabin, T. (ed.) CRYPTO 2010. LNCS, vol. 6223, pp. 59–79. Springer, Heidelberg (2010)

32. Goldwasser, S., Rothblum, G.N.: How to compute in the presence of leakage. In: 53rd FOCS, pp. 31–40. IEEE Computer Society Press, October 2012

33. Alex Halderman, J., Schoen, S.D., Heninger, N., Clarkson, W., Paul, W., Calandrino, J.A., Feldman, A.J., Appelbaum, J., Felten, E.W.: Lest we remember: cold boot attacks on encryption keys. In: USENIX Security Symposium, pp. 45–60 (2008)

34. Halevi, S., Lin, H.: After-the-fact leakage in public-key encryption. In: Ishai, Y. (ed.) TCC 2011. LNCS, vol. 6597, pp. 107–124. Springer, Heidelberg (2011)

35. Ishai, Y., Sahai, A., Wagner, D.: Private circuits: securing hardware against probing attacks. In: Boneh, D. (ed.) CRYPTO 2003. LNCS, vol. 2729, pp. 463–481. Springer, Heidelberg (2003)

36. Jarecki, S., Lysyanskaya, A.: Adaptively secure threshold cryptography: introducing concurrency, removing erasures (extended abstract). In: Preneel, B. (ed.) EUROCRYPT 2000. LNCS, vol. 1807, pp. 221–242. Springer, Heidelberg (2000)

37. Juma, A., Vahlis, Y.: Protecting cryptographic keys against continual leakage. In: Rabin, T. (ed.) CRYPTO 2010. LNCS, vol. 6223, pp. 41–58. Springer, Heidelberg (2010)

38. Kelsey, J., Schneier, B., Wagner, D., Hall, C.: Side channel cryptanalysis of product ciphers. Journal of Computer Security 8(2/3), 141–158 (2000)

39. Kocher, P.C.: Timing attacks on implementations of diffie-hellman, RSA, DSS, and other systems. In: Koblitz, N. (ed.) CRYPTO 1996. LNCS, vol. 1109, pp. 104–113. Springer, Heidelberg (1996)

40. Kocher, P.C., Jaffe, J., Jun, B.: Differential power analysis. In: Wiener, M. (ed.) CRYPTO 1999. LNCS, vol. 1666, p. 388. Springer, Heidelberg (1999)

41. Liu, F.-H., Lysyanskaya, A.: Tamper and leakage resilience in the split-state model. In: Safavi-Naini, R., Canetti, R. (eds.) CRYPTO 2012. LNCS, vol. 7417, pp. 517–532. Springer, Heidelberg (2012)

42. Micali, S., Reyzin, L.: Physically observable cryptography (extended abstract). In: Naor, M. (ed.) TCC 2004. LNCS, vol. 2951, pp. 278–296. Springer, Heidelberg (2004)

43. Miles, E.: Iterated group products and leakage resilience against NC1. In: Naor, M. (ed.) ITCS 2014, pp. 261–268. ACM, January 2014

44. Miles, E., Viola, E.: Shielding circuits with groups. In: Boneh, D., Roughgarden, T., Feigenbaum, J. (eds.) 45th ACM STOC, pp. 251–260. ACM Press, June 2013

45. Pass, R., Seth, K., Telang, S.: Indistinguishability obfuscation from semantically-secure multilinear encodings. In: Garay, J.A., Gennaro, R. (eds.) CRYPTO 2014, Part I. LNCS, vol. 8616, pp. 500–517. Springer, Heidelberg (2014)

46. Rothblum, G.N.: How to compute under $\mathcal{AC}^0$ leakage without secure hardware. In: Safavi-Naini, R., Canetti, R. (eds.) CRYPTO 2012. LNCS, vol. 7417, pp. 552–569. Springer, Heidelberg (2012)

47. Sahai, A., Waters, B.: How to use indistinguishability obfuscation: deniable encryption, and more. In: Shmoys, D.B. (ed.) 46th ACM STOC, pp. 475–484. ACM Press, May/June 2014

48. Tromer, E., Osvik, D.A., Shamir, A.: Efficient cache attacks on aes, and countermeasures. J. Cryptology $23(1)$, 37–71 (2010)

49. Waters, B.: CS 395T Special Topic: Obfuscation in Cryptography (2014). http://www.cs.utexas.edu/~bwaters/classes/CS395T-Fall-14/outline.html

50. Waters, B.: How to use indistinguishability obfuscation. In: Visions of Cryptography, (2014). http://www.cs.utexas.edu/~bwaters/presentations/files/how-to-use-IO.ppt

51. Williams, V.V.: Multiplying matrices faster than coppersmith-winograd. In: Karloff, H.J., Pitassi, T. (eds.) 44th ACM STOC, pp. 887–898. ACM Press, May 2012

Noisy Leakage Revisited

Stefan Dziembowski[1]([✉]), Sebastian Faust[2,3], and Maciej Skorski[1]

[1] Warsaw University, Warszawa, Poland
stefan@dziembowski.net
[2] EPFL Lausanne, Lausanne, Switzerland
sebastian.faust@gmail.com
[3] Ruhr-University Bochum, Bochum, Germany
m.skorski@mimuw.edu.pl

Abstract. Physical side-channel leakages are an important threat for cryptographic implementations. One of the most prominent countermeasures against such leakage attacks is the use of a masking scheme. A masking scheme conceals the sensitive information by randomizing intermediate values thereby making the physical leakage independent of the secret. An important practical leakage model to analyze the security of a masking scheme is the so-called noisy leakage model of Prouff and Rivain (Eurocrypt'13). Unfortunately, security proofs in the noisy leakage model require a technically involved information theoretic argument. Very recently, Duc et al. (Eurocrypt'14) showed that security in the probing model of Ishai et al. (Crypto'03) implies security in the noisy leakage model. Unfortunately, the reduction to the probing model is non-tight and requires a rather counter-intuitive growth of the amount of noise, i.e., the Prouff-Rivain bias parameter decreases proportional to the size of the set $\mathcal{X}$ of the elements that are leaking (e.g., if the leaking elements are bytes, then $|\mathcal{X}| = 256$). The main contribution of our work is to eliminate this non-optimality in the reduction by introducing an alternative leakage model, that we call the *average probing model*. We show a tight reduction between the noisy leakage model and the much simpler average random probing model; in fact, we show that these two models are essentially equivalent. We demonstrate the potential of this equivalence by two applications:

- We show security of the additive masking scheme used in many previous works for a constant bias parameter.
- We show that the compiler of Ishai et al. (Crypto'03) is secure in the average probing model (assuming a simple leak free component). This results into security with an *optimal bias parameter* of the noisy leakage for the ISW construction.

S. Dziembowski and M. Skorski—Supported by the WELCOME/2010-4/2 grant founded within the framework of the EU Innovative Economy (National Cohesion Strategy) Operational Programme.
S. Faust—Received funding from the Marie Curie IEF/FP7 project GAPS, grant number: 626467.

E. Oswald and M. Fischlin (Eds.): EUROCRYPT 2015, Part II, LNCS 9057, pp. 159–188, 2015.
DOI: 10.1007/978-3-662-46803-6_6

1   Introduction

Side-channel attacks break cryptographic implementations by exploiting physical observations of, e.g., the power consumption [18] or running time [17] of a cryptographic device. One of the most well-studied and widely used side-channel attacks are power analysis techniques (see, e.g., [18,13,3,20] and many more). In a power analysis attack the adversary exploits the instantaneous power consumption of a physical cryptographic device, e.g., of a smart card, with the goal to extract sensitive information and breaking the cryptographic implementation. One of the most prominent countermeasures against power analysis attacks are masking schemes [2,13]. The basic idea of a masking scheme is to secretly share all sensitive information, including the secret key and all intermediate values that depend on it, thereby making the leakage independent of the secret data. The most prominent masking scheme is the Boolean masking: a secret bit X is encoded by random bits $(X_1, \ldots, X_n)$ such that $X = X_1 \oplus \ldots \oplus X_n$. It is easy to extend the Boolean masking to work over larger fields $\mathcal{X}$ with $|\mathcal{X}| > 1$. In this case the shares X_i are random elements in $\mathcal{X}$ and $\oplus$ denotes addition in $\mathcal{X}$.

Amplifying Noise with Masking. As physical measurements are inherently noisy, one main challenge for a side-channel adversary is to isolate the relevant sensitive information from the noise in the measurement. Indeed, an attack is more likely to succeed if the adversary obtains less noisy measurements. Moreover, in practice noise can be relatively easily amplified using practical techniques [3,5,20,2], where one particular example to amplify noise is the masking countermeasure. The fact that masking amplifies noise in measurements was first formally studied in the the pioneering work of Chari et al. [2]. In particular, their main result considers shares X_i of the binary field and shows that if the adversary observes a noisy version $\nu(X_i)$ for each share X_i, he will need an exponential number (in n) of measurements to recover the secret bit X.

Noisy Leakage Models for Masking. The noisy leakage model of Chari et al. assumes a specific noise model, where the noise χ is assumed to be sampled from a Gaussian distribution and the adversary obtains $X + \chi$ as the noisy leakage. The recent work of Prouff and Rivain [25] generalizes the definition of noise by introducing the concept of a noisy leakage function $\nu(.)$. Informally speaking, a function $\nu(.)$ is δ-noisy if the statistical distance between the uniform distribution X and the conditional distribution $X|\nu(X)$ is bounded by some parameter $\delta \in [0, 1]$. To give a better understanding of the Prouff-Rivain noise model, consider the example when δ is close to 0. In this case the function ν is assumed to be very noisy, i.e., the leakage is non-informative as the noise dominates the signal. On the other extreme, when δ is close to 1 then the noisy component of the leakage $\nu(.)$ is close to deterministic.

The way in which Prouff and Rivain model the noisy leakage has two important advantages over the work of Chari et al.: first, the noise is neither assumed to be sampled from some fixed Gaussian distribution nor is it required to be of an additive nature. Instead, in [25] *any* type of noisy leakage is allowed as long as it satisfies the proposed statistical measure. Second, the noisy leakage model of [25] provides a meaningful and natural interpretation of what it means to obtain noisy leakage from values of larger sets (e.g., leakage from a byte). For instance, $\nu(.)$ may take as input a byte X and first computes the Hamming weight of X before perturbing the result by a noisy component.

While the model of Prouff and Rivain provides a first good approximation of physical side-channel leakage, which is generally applicable in practice, it is very involved to work in. In particular, in [25] the authors prove the security of the masking scheme of [14] against noisy leakage by going through a technical information theoretic argument. This situation is unsatisfying as proving the security of new masking schemes requires to redo the involved analysis of Prouff and Rivain.

Leakage Reductions. The recent work of Duc, Dziembowski and Faust [7] reconsiders the notion of noisy leakages. Their main result is a simple reduction from the noisy leakage model to the much simpler and cleaner random probing model. The ϵ-random probing model – first introduced by Ishai et al. [14] – considers only a single simple noisy leakage function φ, where $\varphi(X) = X$ with probability ϵ, and $\perp$ otherwise. Notice that in case when φ outputs $\perp$ the adversary learns nothing about the underlying secret value X. The consequence of this reduction are twofold: first, it significantly simplifies security proofs in the noisy leakage model as one only needs to analyze the security of the masking scheme in the random probing model. Second, Duc et al. [7] show by a simple Chernoff argument that any scheme that is secure in the t-probing model of Ishai, Sahai and Wagner [14] is secure in the random probing model, which by their reduction also implies security in the noisy leakage model of Prouff and Rivain. Recall that in the t-probing model the leakage is bounded to t-bits and hence eventually the noisy leakage is reduced to the much simpler and cleaner *deterministic* bounded leakage model.

While Duc et al. [7] provide a first step towards a better understanding of the noisy leakage model, one main drawback of their analysis is the fact that the reduction between the noisy leakage model and the random probing model is not tight. More precisely, when one extends the Boolean masking to work over larger fields, i.e., when the shares X_i of the encoding are from a larger field $\mathcal{X}$ with $|\mathcal{X}| > 1$, then ϵ-random probing security implies "only" $\delta := \epsilon/|\mathcal{X}|$ noisy resilience in the Prouff-Rivain model. Recall that in the Prouff-Rivain noise model a smaller value for δ results into a weaker result as the leakage is required to be "more noisy". For instance, consider the situation where the shares X_i of the encoding $(X_1, \ldots, X_n)$ are bytes or words as it would be the case on many standard hardware architectures. In this case, as an artefact of the proof the requirement on the noise needs to take into account an additional factor of 2^8 or 2^{32} in order to compensate for the $1/|\mathcal{X}|$ loss.

The main contribution of our work is to eliminate this unnatural loss in the reduction by developing a tight characterization of the noisy leakage model of

Prouff and Rivain. Our main new technique to achieve this goal is to show a tight (up to a constant 2) equivalence between the noisy leakage model and a new leakage model that we call the *average probing model*.

We emphasize that the equivalence between these two models allows us to significantly improve the formally verifiable security guarantees of common masking schemes (see below) when the noisy component of the leakage is small. Moreover, our improved reduction is of particular importance for applications that work with fields of super-polynomial size, e.g, when we use blinding in a discrete-log based scheme. In this case, the reduction of Duc et al. looses a factor that is super-polynomial in the security parameter and hence results into meaningless security guarantees due to requiring almost uniform noise.

1.1   Our Contribution

The main contribution of our work is to introduce a new noisy leakage model that we name the ϵ-*average probing model* that provides a much tighter (and essentially optimal) equivalence to the leakage model of Prouff and Rivain. Our approach is in spirit of the recent work of Duc et al. [7] who show that t-probing security implies security in the noisy leakage model. In contrast to [7], however, our reduction does not result in the $1/|\mathcal{X}|$ loss that occurs in the reduction of Duc et al. We demonstrate how to use the new leakage model by two applications that result due to the tightness of the reduction to the noisy leakage model to significantly improved security statements compared to earlier works; namely, we show that using the natural noise model of Prouff and Rivain [25] the additive masking is secure with a δ-noise parameter that is independent of the size of the underlying field. As a second important application, we show that masking schemes based on the ISW construction [14] are secure in the average probing model (under the assumption of a leak-free component). Our analysis results in an asymptotically optimal δ-noise parameter for the ISW construction as for asymptotically higher values of δ the ISW construction can be broken. We provide more details on our contributions below. A summary of our contributions are given in Figure 2 and Figure 1.

The ϵ-average Probing Model. The definition of the ϵ-*average probing model*, described formally in Section 5, can be viewed as a relaxation of the definition of the random probing model of Ishai et al. [14] and Duc et al. [7] . Intuitively, it comes from a different interpretation of an informal statement "probability of $\varphi(x) \neq \perp$ is equal to ϵ" (where φ is the leakage function). Recall that in [7] it was required that it holds for *every* $x \in \mathcal{X}$, and the randomness in the probability came only from the internal random choices[1] made by φ. In contrast, in the ϵ-average probing model we require that $\mathbb{P}(\varphi(X) \neq \perp)$ is equal to ϵ when the probability is taken *also over* X. This seemingly small change has huge implications. In particular, it allows us to show a tight (up to a factor 2) equivalence between our new probing model and the model of [25]. This, in turn, permits

---

[1] In the sequel we will often make this internal randomness of φ explicit.

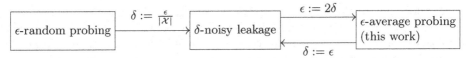

Fig. 1. The figure illustrates the connection between the noisy leakage model of [25], the ϵ-random probing model of [14] and the new average probing model introduced in this work. As shown in the figure, the average probing model is equivalent to the noisy leakage model.

us to obtain much better parameters for the security of additive masking. We elaborate on these points below.

New Characterization of Noisy Leakage Functions. We show that the leakage model of Prouff-Rivain is essentially equivalent to the average probing model described above. More concretely, we show (cf. Lemma 7) that every ϵ-noisy adversary can be perfectly simulated by an ϵ-average-probing adversary. We also show the reduction in the other direction (cf. Lemma 8), namely that every ϵ-average-probing adversary can be perfectly simulated by a 2ϵ-noisy adversary. This means that instead of analyzing security against noisy leakage (in the [25] sense) one can use the ϵ-average-probing model. Moreover, we show two important applications of the average probing model that improve the earlier works of [25,7] when δ is large (i.e., the noise component is rather small compared to the sensitive information). A summary of known reductions between leakage models is given in Figure 1.

Application to Masking Function. As a first application of our new techniques we show that the additive masking function used in many works [2,14, 28,4] is secure for a δ-noise parameter which is independent of the size of the underlying field. Security of the encoding function here means that if the adversary obtains a noisy version $\nu(X_i)$ of each share X_i of an encoding $(X_1, \ldots, X_n)$ he cannot distinguish between an encoding of any two messages. While earlier works showed feasibility with weak bounds [25,7], i.e., when $\delta < \frac{1}{c|\mathcal{X}|}$ for some constant $c < 1/2$, we are able for the first time to show security of the additive masking function for a constant $\delta < 1/16$ – in particular, δ is independent of $\mathcal{X}$.

Our result also can be viewed as an answer to a question raised in the original work of Chari et al. [2]. In this work (Section 3.7) the authors ask for an extension of the security analysis when leakage is not on bits but from bytes. Unfortunately [2] does not precisely define what "noisy leakage of a byte value" means (e.g., noisy version of each byte share, noisy HW, do we use bit-strings or decimals to represent bytes,...). We believe that a very appealing noise model for bytes is given by the noisy leakage model of Prouff and Rivain [25]. Using the Prouff-Rivain interpretation of a noisy leakage from a byte value, we can provide an answer to the question of Chari et al. [2], namely, we show that security of the encoding can be achieved for a constant δ-noise parameter (which is optimal for the model of [25]). We remark that a constant δ-noise parameter in the model of [25] does not imply that we can show security for a constant noise level in the common leakage model of additive Gaussian noise with a *constant* standard deviation. For instance, if the leakage from the byte is the Hamming weight perturbed by additive Gaussian noise with a constant standard deviation, it is easy to see that the encoding cannot achieve a strong distance-based security notion when the underlying field size grows. In particular, for the additive Gaussian noise and the Hamming weight leakage function the standard deviation of the noise distribution has to grow at least logarithmically with the size of the field in order to achieve security.

Application to Masked Computation. While our improvement of the δ-noise parameter for the encoding scheme provides a first indication of the usefulness of the average probing model, we provide a second – practically more relevant – application of the average probing model. Consider the situation where a side-channel adversary attacks a masked implementation of an AES. Of course, in this setting the adversary can target any intermediate value of the computation (e.g., the masked input of an AES S-Box), and hence clearly it does not suffice to only analyze the security of the encoding scheme. Recent works, [25, 7] overcome this restriction and provide the first security analysis of masked computation in the noisy leakage model; in particular, [25, 7] show security of the ISW-construction [14] in the noisy leakage model. Unfortunately, in both cases the requirement on the δ-noise parameter is rather strong: δ decreases linearly with the size of the field $|\mathcal{X}|$ *and* the security parameter n (cf. Figure 2). While the loss in the security parameter is necessary (i.e., one can show easy attacks if the noise is independent of n), there is no fundamental reason why δ has to decrease linearly with the size of the field. We prove that indeed the later loss is unnecessary and show that the ISW construction is secure for noise levels that *only* depend on the necessary factor n – leading to an asymptotically optimal noise rate for the ISW construction. To achieve this goal, we apply the framework of reconstructors introduced by Faust et al. [10]. Quite surprisingly, while at first sight proofs in the average probing model seem more involved as the leakage can implicitly depend on all intermediate values (which is in contrast to the much simpler random probing model), the notion of reconstructors allows for a rather simple security proof. Hence, our analysis of the ISW construction can be seen as a basic *tool box* for proving security of different masking schemes against noisy leakages with tight security bounds. We notice that – similar to the work of Prouff and Rivain [25] – our analysis requires simple leak free components. We leave it as an important direction for future work whether this assumption can be eliminated.

Adaptive Noisy Leakages. In our proofs we assume that the leakage functions are chosen adaptively, i.e. if the adversary attacks a sequence $X_1, \ldots, X_\ell$ of variables, then his choice of the leakage function φ_i that will be applied to X_i depends on the leakage information that he obtained from $X_1, \ldots, X_{i-1}$. This is in contrast with the proofs in [25, 7]. We believe that in our case assuming the adaptiveness of the adversary makes particular sense, since the adversary in our

Author	Proof technique	Noise for Encoding	Noise for any computation	Leak-free gates
Prouff/Rivain [25]	Direct analysis	$O(1/\sqrt{|\mathcal{X}|})$	$O(1/d|\mathcal{X}|)$	yes
Duc et al. [7]	Random probing	$O(1/|\mathcal{X}|)$	$O(1/d|\mathcal{X}|)$	no
Our work	Average probing	$O(1/16)$	$O(1/d)$	yes

Fig. 2. The second column shows the proof technique with which the results are achieved. The third column shows the noise rate that is required for security of encoding. The fourth column shows the noise rate for arbitrary computation. The last column shows under which assumption we can achieve security for arbitrary computation.

model has a much bigger choice of leakage functions than in [7] (where his only choice was the ϵ parameter and clearly the best choice for him is to take the maximal ϵ he was allowed to). On a technical level, the only price for going to the adaptive case is that instead of relying on the Chernoff's bound we need to use the theory of martingales and the Azuma-Hoeffding inequality.

Additional Facts About the [25] Leakage Model. We also show some simple facts about the [25] leakage model. Although they are not directly needed for our main technical result we believe that they help in understanding this model (this is why we placed it relatively early in the paper, in Section 4), and provide an additional justification why the Prouff-Rivain model is natural. In particular, we show an alternative (but equivalent) definition of the [25] leakage in spirit of the definition of semantic security, and show by a simple hybrid argument how the amount of noise needs to grow when the adversary obtains multiple noisy measurements of the same value X.

1.2   Other Related Works

Masking and Leakage Resilient Circuits. A large body of work has proposed various masking schemes and studies their security in different security models (see, e.g., [13,1,24,31,28,4]). The already mentioned t-probing model has been considered in the work of Rivain and Prouff [28], who show how to extend the work of Ishai et al. to larger fields and propose efficiency improvements. With the emerge of leakage resilient cryptography several works have proposed new security models and alternative masking schemes [10,29,15,11,8,12]. The main difference between these security models and the noisy leakage model is that these works typically put a quantitative bound on the amount of leakage – so-called "bounded leakages". While from a theoretical point of view the bounded leakage model offers a beautiful abstraction to analyze the security of cryptographic schemes with weak secrets, it has been questioned [30,19,25] whether it models physical leakages in an appropriate way. For instance, a power measurement can typically not be described by a few bits of information but instead requires megabytes if not even gigabytes of information for its description. The noisy leakage model studied in our work more realistically models practical side-channel leakages.

Noisy Leakage Models. The work of Faust et al. [10] also considers circuit compilers for noisy leakages. Specifically, they propose a construction with security in the binomial noise model, where each value on a wire is flipped independently with probability $p \in (0, 1/2)$. Besides these works on circuit compilers, several works consider noisy leakages for concrete cryptographic schemes [9,23,16]. Typically, the noise model considered in these works is significantly more general than the noise model that is considered for masking schemes. In particular, no strong assumption about the independency of the noise is made.

2 Preliminaries

We start with some standard definitions and lemmas about the statistical distance. If $\mathcal{A}$ is a set then $U \leftarrow \mathcal{A}$ denotes a random variable sampled uniformly from $\mathcal{A}$. Recall that if A and B are random variables over the same set $\mathcal{A}$ then the *statistical distance between A and B* is denoted as $\Delta(A; B)$, and defined as $\Delta(A; B) := \frac{1}{2} \sum_{a \in \mathcal{A}} |\mathbb{P}(A = a) - \mathbb{P}(B = a)|$. It is easy to see that $\Delta(A; B)$ can be also defined in the following alternative ways:

$$\Delta(A; B) = \sum_{a \in \mathcal{A}} \max(0, \mathbb{P}(A = a) - \mathbb{P}(B = a)) \tag{1}$$

$$= 1 - \sum_{a \in \mathcal{A}} \min(\mathbb{P}(A = a), \mathbb{P}(B = a)) \tag{2}$$

$$= \sum_{a : \mathbb{P}(A=a) \geq \mathbb{P}(B=a)} \mathbb{P}(A = a) - \mathbb{P}(B = a). \tag{3}$$

Moreover, Δ satisfies the triangle inequality, i.e. for every A, B and C we have $\Delta(A; B) \leq \Delta(A; C) + \Delta(C; B)$. If $\mathcal{X}, \mathcal{Y}$ are some events then by $\Delta((A|\mathcal{X}) ; (B|\mathcal{Y}))$ we will mean the distance between variables A' and B', distributed according to the conditional distributions $P_{A|\mathcal{X}}$ and $P_{B|\mathcal{Y}}$. If $\mathcal{X}$ is an event of probability 1 then we also write $\Delta(A ; (B|\mathcal{Y}))$ instead of $\Delta((A|\mathcal{X}) ; (B|\mathcal{Y}))$. If C is a random variable then by $\Delta(A ; (B|C))$ we mean $\sum_c \mathbb{P}(C = c) \cdot \Delta(A ; (B|(C = c)))$.

If A, B, and C are random variables and $\mathcal{X}$ is an event then $\Delta((B; C) \mid A)$ denotes $\Delta((BA); (CA))$ (where AB denotes the joint distribution of A and B) and $\Delta((B; C) \mid A, \mathcal{X})$ denotes $\Delta((BA)|\mathcal{X}; (CA)|\mathcal{X})$. It is easy to see that it is equal to $\Delta((B; C) \mid A, \mathcal{X}) = \sum_a \mathbb{P}(A = a|\mathcal{X}) \cdot \Delta((B|A = a, \mathcal{X}) ; (C|A = a, \mathcal{X}))$. If $\Delta(A; B) \leq \epsilon$ then we say that A and B are *ϵ-close*. The "$\overset{d}{=}$" symbol denotes the equality of distributions, i.e., $A \overset{d}{=} B$ if and only if $\Delta(A; B) = 0$. For A distributed over $\mathcal{A}$ by $d(A)$ we will mean the distance of A from the uniform distribution over $\mathcal{A}$, i.e. $\Delta(A; U)$, where $U \leftarrow \mathcal{A}$. This notation extended to the conditional case in the natural way, e.g. $d(A|\mathcal{X}) := \Delta((A|\mathcal{X}); U)$. The following lemma was proven in [22] (Lemma 1)[2].

---

[2] In [22] it was shown for the quasi-groups, but we do not need this generalization in our paper.

Lemma 1 ([22]). *For any two independent random variables A and B over an additive finite group we have $d(A + B) \leq 2d(A)d(B)$*

It is easy to see that the constant 2 in the lemma above cannot be replaced by a smaller number, at least as long as we quantify over all finite groups. To see why, consider the group $(Z_2^n, \oplus)$, where $n > 1$ and $(x_1, \ldots, x_n) \oplus (y_1, \ldots, y_n) = (x_1 + y_1, \ldots, x_n + y_n)$. Let A and B be uniformly distributed over the set of all elements $x \in Z_2^n$ such that $x_0 = 0$. Then it is easy to verify that $d(A) = d(B) = d(A + B) = 1/2$, and hence $d(A + B)/(d(A)d(B)) = 2$.

The following lemmata are standard information theoretic facts whose proofs are omitted.

Lemma 2. *For any two independent random variables A and B over an additive finite group we have*

$$d(A + B) \leq d(A)$$

Lemma 3. *For any random variables A, B and C that takes values over some set $\mathcal{C}$, and any event $\mathcal{W}$ we have*

$$d(A|B, \mathcal{W}) \leq \sum_{c \in \mathcal{C}} d(A|B, C = c, \mathcal{W}) \cdot \mathbb{P}(C = c|\mathcal{W})$$

3   Previous Noisy Leakage Models

In this section we review the most relevant noisy leakage models that have been used to analyze the security of masking schemes. For the lack of space we do not cover several other models used in the literature and refer the reader for some important references to the introduction.

Noisy Model of Prouff and Rivain. As discussed in the introduction the noisy model of Prouff and Rivain [25] is a generalization of the model of Chari et al. [2]. In particular, it introduces the notion of a noisy leakage function which is formally defined below.

Definition 1 ([25]). *We say that a function $\nu : \mathcal{X} \times \mathcal{R} \to \mathcal{Y}$ is δ-noisy if*

$$\Delta((\nu(X, R); \nu(X', R)) \mid X) \leq \delta \tag{4}$$

where X and X' are uniform over $\mathcal{X}$ and R is uniform over $\mathcal{R}$.

Some explanations are needed here, since the definition from [25] may appear different from Definition 1 at first sight. First, to make the notation consistent with the rest of this paper, we decided to keep the internal randomness of ν explicit. Secondly, instead of having a bound on "$\Delta((\nu(X, R); \nu(X', R)) \mid X)$" (as in Definition 1)) in the work of [25] the authors impose an upper bound on "$\Delta(X; (X|\nu(X, R)))$" (cf. Eq. (2) in [25]). This is not a problem since as shown by Duc et al. [7] both definitions are equivalent. Finally, the definition in [25] uses as the distance measure the Euclidean norm, while we follow [7] and use the total variation. We refer the reader to [7] for further motivation on this choice and only emphasize here that it corresponds to the maximum distinguishing advantage of the best possible adversary. This intuitively matches with our understanding of security and is standard in cryptographic research.

Let us now define a notion of an adversary that adaptively attacks a sequence of field elements using the noisy functions. For $\delta \geq 0$ a δ-*noisy adversary on* $\mathcal{X}^\ell$ (or *on* $\mathcal{X}$ if $\ell = 1$) is a machine $\mathcal{A}$ that, for $i = 1, \ldots, \ell$ plays the following game against an oracle that knows $(x_1, \ldots, x_\ell) \in \mathcal{X}^\ell$.

1. $\mathcal{A}$ specifies a δ_i-noisy function $\nu_i : \mathcal{X} \times \mathcal{R} \to \mathcal{Y}$ such that $\delta_i \leq \delta$.
2. $\mathcal{A}$ receives $\nu_i(x_i, R_i)$, where each R_i is sampled uniformly at random from $\mathcal{R}$.

At the end of the execution $\mathcal{A}$ outputs a value that we denote $out_\mathcal{A}(x_1, \ldots, x_\ell)$. We say that $\mathcal{A}$ is *non-adaptive* if he has to specify the functions $\nu_1, \ldots, \nu_\ell$ in advance. If $\mathcal{A}$ works in polynomial time and the noise functions specified by $\mathcal{A}$ are efficiently decidable then we say that $\mathcal{A}$ *is poly-time-noisy* [7].

Random Probing Model. The following model has been introduced in [14] and used in [7]. Here, we follow the formalism of [7]. We start with the following definition.

Definition 2 ([7]). *A function* $\varphi : \mathcal{X} \times \mathcal{R} \to \mathcal{X} \cup \{\perp\}$ *is an ϵ-identity if for every x and r we have that either* $\varphi(x, r) = x$ *or* $\varphi(x, r) = \perp$ *and*

$$\text{for every } x \quad \mathbb{P}_{R \leftarrow \mathcal{R}} (\varphi(x, R) \neq \perp) = \epsilon.$$

For $\epsilon \leq 1$ an ϵ-*probing adversary on* $\mathcal{X}^\ell$ (or *on* $\mathcal{X}$ if $\ell = 1$) is a machine $\mathcal{A}$ that, for $i = 1, \ldots, \ell$ plays the following game against an oracle that knows $(x_1, \ldots, x_\ell) \in \mathcal{X}^\ell$:

1. $\mathcal{A}$ specifies an ϵ_i-identity function $\varphi_i : \mathcal{X} \times \mathcal{R} \to \mathcal{X} \cup \{\perp\}$ where each $\epsilon_i \leq \epsilon$.
2. $\mathcal{A}$ receives $\varphi_i(x_i, R_i)$, where each R_i is sampled uniformly at random from $\mathcal{R}$.

At the end of the execution $\mathcal{A}$ outputs a value that we denote $out_\mathcal{A}(x_1, \ldots, x_\ell)$. We say that $\mathcal{A}$ in *non-adaptive* if he has to specify the functions $\varphi_1, \ldots, \varphi_\ell$ in advance.

4   Useful Facts About the Prouff and Rivain Noise Model

In this section we show some basic facts about the noise model of [25] that, to the best of our knowledge, have not been shown before. We do it because, first of all, we believe that they are of general interests, and may be useful in some future work in the noisy leakage model. Secondly, we think that they may serve as an additional justification why Prouff-Rivain noisy leakage model is natural. This is in particular the case with Lemma 4 below, that essentially provides an alternative and very intuitive interpretation of the [25] noise definition. The proofs are deferred to the full version of this paper.

Lemma 4. *For every δ-noisy function $\nu : \mathcal{X} \times \mathcal{R} \to \mathcal{Y}$ we have*

$$2\delta \geq \Delta((\nu(X_0); \nu(X_1)) \mid X_0, X_1) \geq \delta,$$

where X_0, X_1 are two independent uniform random variables distributed over $\mathcal{X}$.

Let us now argue why this lemma is interesting, by showing a natural interpretation of the "$\Delta((\nu(X_0); \nu(X_1)) \mid X_0, X_1)$" formula. To this end, consider the following game played by any adversary $\mathcal{A}$:

1. X_0, X_1 are chosen uniform at random from $\mathcal{X}$ and sent to the adversary,
2. the adversary receives $\nu(X_b)$ for a random $b \leftarrow \{0, 1\}$,
3. the adversary has to guess b (if he does it correctly then we say that he *won the game*).

Note that this game can be essentially summarized as "$\mathcal{A}$ has to distinguish noisy leakage from two random elements X_0 and X_1", and of course it closely resembles a "random message attack" used in defining security of the encryption schemes. Using Lemma 4 it is easy to show the following lemma, which upper bounds the success probability of an adversary in the above game.

Lemma 5. *The probability of any $\mathcal{A}$ winning the game above is upper-bounded by $\Delta((\nu(X_0); \nu(X_1)) \mid X_0, X_1)/2 + 1/2$.*

When considering noisy leakage it is also natural to ask how this notion behaves when the adversary obtains several independent noisy leakage information from the same given element. It turns out that the characterization of noise shown in Lemma 4 is also useful to prove that the success probability of the adversary only increases linearly with the number of measurements. The proof is by a simple hybrid argument.

Lemma 6. *Let $\nu_1, \ldots, \nu_n : \mathcal{X} \to \mathcal{Y}$ be such that for every i and $X_0, X_1 \leftarrow \mathcal{X}$ we have $\Delta((\nu_i(X_0); \nu_i(X_1)) \mid X_0, X_1) \leq \delta$. Then*

$$\Delta((\nu_1(X_0), \ldots, \nu_n(X_0)); (\nu_1(X_1), \ldots, \nu_n(X_1)) \mid X_0, X_1) \leq n\delta.$$

5   Epsilon-Average Probing Model

The main contribution of [7] is a reduction from the noisy leakage to the probing model (cf. Lemma 2 of [7]). Although their reduction suffices for improving the results of [25], it suffers from one important weakness which is a significant loss in the error parameter. Namely, in order to "simulate" a δ-noisy function (defined over set $\mathcal{X}$), they need an ϵ-random probing function with $\epsilon = \delta \cdot |\mathcal{X}|$, a consequence of this being that in order to hope for any security one needs to assume that $\delta < 1/|\mathcal{X}|$.

It is relatively straightforward to see that this loss is inherent for this reduction (i.e. Lemma 2 of [7] cannot be improved using better proof techniques). To see why it is the case, consider the following noisy function (let x_0 be some fixed element of $\mathcal{X}$, and let $\alpha \in [0, 1]$):

$$\nu(x) := \begin{cases} x_0 \text{ with probability } \alpha \text{ if } x = x_0 \\ \bot \text{ otherwise.} \end{cases}$$

The following calculation shows that ν defined above is approximately $2\alpha/|\mathcal{X}|$-noisy for large $\mathcal{X}$ (let X, X' and R be uniformly random):

$$\Delta((\nu(X); \nu(X')) \mid X) = \frac{1}{|\mathcal{X}|} \left(\Delta(\nu(x_0); \nu(X')) + \sum_{x \neq x_0} \Delta(\nu(x, R); \nu(X', R)) \right)$$

$$= \frac{1}{|\mathcal{X}|} \left(\alpha - \frac{\alpha}{|\mathcal{X}|} + \frac{(|\mathcal{X}| - 1) \cdot \alpha}{|\mathcal{X}|} \right)$$

$$= \frac{2\alpha}{|\mathcal{X}|} \left(1 - \frac{1}{|\mathcal{X}|} \right) \approx 2\alpha/|\mathcal{X}|.$$

On the other hand it is clear that to simulate ν any probing function φ on input x_0 needs to output x_0 with probability at least α. Hence the $|\mathcal{X}|^{-1}$ factor in the security loss is unavoidable.

Our main insight is that this problem can be bypassed by slightly relaxing the definition of the "random probing". Recall that in Definition 2 we had a universal quantifier over all x's from $\mathcal{X}$. In particular, this meant that the probing probability of φ had to depend on the "worst-case" (over all $x \in \mathcal{X}$) behavior of the noisy function ν. This was particularly visible in the example above, where the "worst case" was $x = x_0$ (and the reduction could not take into account that such x occurs with very low probability). Instead, our new definition will look at the *average* $x \in \mathcal{X}$. In other words: it will be possible that φ outputs $\bot$ with a different probability for each x, and the only thing that we will require is that the probability (over both X and R) of receiving $\bot$ is high. A formal definition follows.

Definition 3. *A function $\varphi : \mathcal{X} \times \mathcal{R} \to \mathcal{X} \cup \{\bot\}$ is an ϵ-average-identity if for every $x \in \mathcal{X}$ and every $r \in \mathcal{R}$ we have that either $\varphi(x, r) = x$ or $\varphi(x, r) = \bot$ and*

$$\mathbb{P}_{\substack{X \leftarrow \mathcal{X} \\ R \leftarrow \mathcal{R}}} (\varphi(X, R) \neq \bot) = \epsilon. \tag{5}$$

Typically in our applications an adversary will obtain not only $\varphi(X, R)$ but also the randomness R. One way to interpret this situation is as follows: (a) the adversary chooses a set of functions $\{\varphi(\cdot, r) : \mathcal{X} \to \mathcal{X} \cup \{\bot\}\}_{r \in \mathcal{R}}$ (such that (5) holds), then (b) a function $\varphi(\cdot, r)$ is chosen randomly from this set, and finally (c) he learns this function together with $\varphi(x, r)$. Observe that it is enough to restrict ourselves to deterministic functions $\varphi(\cdot, r)$ since anyway a clever adversary will always prefer to make the whole randomness explicit (i.e. to encode it into r), as later he learns it for free.

We will later show (cf. Lemma 7) that the relaxation from Definition 3 allows us to get rid of the $|\mathcal{X}|^{-1}$ factor in the reduction from noisy to probing leakage. Moreover we show that Lemma 7 is essentially optimal, by proving a reduction in the opposite direction (Lemma 8), that looses only factor 2 in the error parameter. Altogether these lemmas provide an alternative but (essentially) equivalent definition of the [25] noise that may be easier to reason about. As an evidence to support this belief we show how Lemma 7 can be used to obtain better error parameters (that do not deepened on $|\mathcal{X}|$) for the additive masking scheme and how it can be used to reason about the ISW masking scheme. This is done in Section 6.

We are now ready to define the ϵ-average probing adversaries (analogously to the ϵ-probing adversaries in Section 3). Let ℓ be some natural parameter and $\mathcal{X}$ be a finite set. For $\epsilon \le 1$ an ϵ-average-probing adversary on $\mathcal{X}^\ell$ (or on $\mathcal{X}$ if $\ell = 1$) is a randomized machine $\mathcal{A}$ that for $i = 1, \ldots, \ell$ plays the following game against an oracle that knows $(x_1, \ldots, x_\ell) \in \mathcal{X}^\ell$:

1. $\mathcal{A}$ specifies an ϵ_i-average-identity function φ_i, where each ϵ_i is at most ϵ.
2. $\mathcal{A}$ receives $(\varphi_i(x_i, R_i), R_i)$, where each R_i is sampled uniformly at random from $\mathcal{R}$.

At the end of the execution $\mathcal{A}$ outputs a value that we denote $out_\mathcal{A}(x_1, \ldots, x_\ell)$. We say that $\mathcal{A}$ in *non-adaptive* if he has to specify the functions $\varphi_1, \ldots, \varphi_\ell$ in advance.

5.1   Connection to the Noisy Leakage

In this section we show a reduction form the δ-noisy model to the δ-average-probing (Lemma 7) and vice versa (Lemma 8), establishing an equivalence between these two models (except of the factor 2 loss in the second reduction). Applications of this equivalence are discussed further in Section 6.

Lemma 7. *For any δ let $\mathcal{A}$ be a δ-noisy adversary on some $\mathcal{X}^\ell$. Then there exists a δ-average-probing adversary $\mathcal{S}$ on $\mathcal{X}^\ell$ such that for every $(x_1, \ldots, x_\ell) \in \mathcal{X}^\ell$ we have*

$$out_\mathcal{A}(x_1, \ldots, x_\ell) \overset{d}{=} out_\mathcal{S}(x_1, \ldots, x_\ell). \tag{6}$$

Moreover if $\mathcal{A}$ is non-adaptive then so is $\mathcal{S}$, and if the noise functions issued by $\mathcal{A}$ are poly-time-decidable then $\mathcal{S}$ works in polynomial time.

Proof. Let the $\nu_1, \ldots, \nu_\ell$ be the functions chosen by $\mathcal{A}$. Each ν_i is δ_i'-noisy (for some $\delta_i' \le \delta$). Clearly we can assume that $\mathcal{A}$ simply outputs all the values $\nu_1(x_1, R_\nu^1), \ldots, \nu_\ell(x_\ell, R_\nu^\ell)$ that it receives (where the R_ν^ν's are uniform over $\mathcal{R}^\nu$ and independent). We construct an adversary $\mathcal{S}$ that for each ν_i chooses a δ_i'-average-identity function φ_i, receives $(\varphi(x_i, R_i^\varphi), R_i^\varphi)$ from the oracle (where R_i^φ is uniform over $\mathcal{R}^\varphi$), and computes a value out_i that is distributed identically to $\nu_i(x_i, R_i^\nu)$. Since these experiments are independent for each i it suffices to consider each i separately. To ease the notation we drop the subscript i in $x_i, \nu_i, R_i^\nu, R_i^\varphi, out_i$ and φ_i. We also assume that $\delta_i = \delta$.

Hence, what we have to show is that for every δ-noisy function $\nu : \mathcal{X} \times \mathcal{R}^\nu \to \mathcal{Y}$ there exists a randomized machine $\mathcal{S}$ that (1) specifies a δ-average-identity function $\varphi : \mathcal{X} \times \mathcal{R}^\varphi \to \mathcal{Y}$, and (2) after receiving $(\varphi(x, R^\varphi), R^\varphi)$ outputs $out_\mathcal{S}(x)$ such that for every x we have

$$\nu(x, R^\nu) \overset{d}{=} out_\mathcal{S}(x), \tag{7}$$

for $R^\nu \leftarrow \mathcal{R}^\nu$ and $R^\varphi \leftarrow \mathcal{R}^\varphi$. We now show how to construct such $\mathcal{S}$. The set $\mathcal{R}^\varphi$ from which the function φ draws its random inputs will be defined as a product of $\mathcal{X}$ and the set $\mathcal{R}^\nu$ of random inputs of ν, i.e: $\mathcal{R}^\varphi := \mathcal{X} \times \mathcal{R}^\nu$. Informally speaking this random input will be used to sample "offline" (i.e. independently of the "real" x) a value y according to the distribution $\nu(X', R^\nu)$ (where $X' \leftarrow \mathcal{X}$ and $R^\nu \leftarrow \mathcal{R}^\nu$).[3] (One can think of such y as a "guess" of the noise value, performed by someone who has no idea about the "real" x.) More precisely the adversary $\mathcal{S}$ constructs the function $\varphi : \mathcal{X} \times \mathcal{R}^\varphi \to \mathcal{X} \cup \{\bot\}$ in the following way. On input $(x, (x', r^\nu))$ the function computes $y = \nu(x', r^\nu)$, and then it outputs[4]

$$\varphi(x, (x', r^\nu)) := \begin{cases} \bot \text{ with probability min} \left(1, \frac{\mathbb{P}(\nu(x, R^\nu) = y)}{\mathbb{P}(\nu(X, R^\nu) = y)}\right) \\ x \text{ otherwise,} \end{cases} \tag{8}$$

Informally, $w = \bot$ indicates that the function φ (whose input is the "real" x) is happy with the value y that was sampled "off-line". To get some intuitions about (8) consider two extreme cases. First suppose that $\mathbb{P}(\nu(x, R^\nu) = y) \geq \mathbb{P}(\nu(X, R^\nu) = y)$. This means that the value y is at least as likely to happen with the "real" x as it is with a uniformly random X (i.e. when it is sampled "off-line"). Hence intuitively φ is "happy" with this y and wants to communicate to the adversary a message "just output y", which is technically done by outputting $\bot$.

Now, consider the other extreme case, i.e.: $\mathbb{P}(\nu(x, R^\nu) = y) = 0$. Here, in some sense, the value of y is "totally wrong", i.e., it is never going to occur as a noise value for this particular x. Hence the function φ sends a message "wrong y, please resample the noise using x", which is technically done by outputting x. The cases when $0 < \mathbb{P}(\nu(x, R^\nu) = y) < \mathbb{P}(\nu(X, R^\nu) = y)$ are somewhere in between these two extremes and hence φ can either output $\bot$ or x with probability depending on the ratio $\mathbb{P}(\nu(x, R^\nu) = y) / \mathbb{P}(\nu(X, R^\nu) = y)$.

Now, let $(w, (x', r^\nu))$ be the value that $\mathcal{S}$ receives from the oracle. Since $w = \bot$ indicates that y sampled from (x', r^ν) is "correct for the real x" in this

---

[3] We could also assume that the random input of φ is simply Y that is distributed according to $\nu(X', R^\nu)$, this, however, would lead to more complicated definitions, as in this case we would need to consider randomized functions that take non-uniform random inputs.

[4] A careful reader may notice that φ defined this way is randomized, which seemingly contradicts the definition of the average-identity (where it is required to be deterministic). This is not a problem since we can always extend $\mathcal{R}^\varphi$ to include also the "internal" randomness needed to compute φ. We decided to keep this additional randomness implicit, for the sake of the clarity of the proof (cf. also remarks after Definition 3).

case simply $\mathcal{S}$ outputs y. Otherwise $w = x$. In this case the adversary $\mathcal{S}$ outputs a value z according to the distribution in which every $z \in \mathcal{Y}$ has probability[5]

$$\max \left(0, \frac{\mathbb{P}\left(\nu(x, R^\nu) = z \right) - \mathbb{P}\left(\nu(X, R^\nu) = z \right)}{\Delta(\nu(x, R^\nu); \nu(X, R^\nu))} \right). \tag{9}$$

This distribution is chosen in such a way that it will "compensate" the fact that y's chosen "off-line" have sometimes lower probability than they should have in the "real" distribution.

We first show that $\mathcal{S}$ is δ-average-probing, i.e. that the expected probability of not receiving $\perp$ in the above experiment is equal to δ, more formally:

$$\mathbb{P}\left(\varphi(X, (X', R^\nu)) \neq \perp \right) = \delta \tag{10}$$

(where the variables X, X' and R^ν are uniform and independent). We have

$$\mathbb{P}\left(\varphi(X, (X', R^\nu)) = \perp \right)$$

$$= \sum_{x \in \mathcal{X}} \mathbb{P}\left(X = x \right) \cdot \mathbb{P}\left(\varphi(x, (X', R^\nu)) = \perp \right)$$

$$= \sum_{x \in \mathcal{X}} \mathbb{P}\left(X = x \right) \cdot \sum_{y \in \mathcal{Y}} \mathbb{P}\left(\nu(X', R^\nu) = y \right) \mathbb{P}\left(\varphi(x, (X', R^\nu)) = \perp \mid \nu(X', R^\nu) = y \right)$$

$$= \sum_{x \in \mathcal{X}} \mathbb{P}\left(X = x \right) \cdot \sum_{y \in \mathcal{Y}} \mathbb{P}\left(\nu(X', R^\nu) = y \right) \cdot \min \left(1, \frac{\mathbb{P}\left(\nu(x, R^\nu) = y \right)}{\mathbb{P}\left(\nu(X', R^\nu) = y \right)} \right)$$

$$= \sum_{\substack{x \in \mathcal{X} \\ y \in \mathcal{Y}}} \mathbb{P}\left(X = x \right) \cdot \mathbb{P}\left(\nu(X', R^\nu) = y \right) \cdot \min \left(1, \frac{\mathbb{P}\left(\nu(x, R^\nu) = y \right)}{\mathbb{P}\left(\nu(X', R^\nu) = y \right)} \right)$$

$$= \sum_{\substack{x \in \mathcal{X} \\ y \in \mathcal{Y}}} \min \left(\mathbb{P}\left(X = x \right) \cdot \mathbb{P}\left(\nu(X', R^\nu) = y \right) , \mathbb{P}\left(X = x \right) \cdot \mathbb{P}\left(\nu(x, R^\nu) = y \right) \right)$$

$$= \sum_{\substack{x \in \mathcal{X} \\ y \in \mathcal{Y}}} \min \left(\mathbb{P}\left((X, \nu(X', R^\nu)) = (x, y) \right) , \mathbb{P}\left((X, \nu(X, R^\nu)) = (x, y) \right) \right) \tag{11}$$

$$= 1 - \Delta((X, \nu(X', R^\nu)); (X, \nu(X, R^\nu))) = 1 - \delta \tag{12}$$

where in (11) we used the independence of the variables, and (12) follows from Eq. (2). What remains is to show (7). Take some $x \in \mathcal{X}$ and $y \in \mathcal{Y}$. We have

$$\mathbb{P}\left(out_{\mathcal{S}}(x) = y \right) = \tag{13}$$

$$\mathbb{P}\left(\varphi(x, (X', R^\nu)) = \perp \wedge out_{\mathcal{S}}(x) = y \right) + \tag{14}$$

$$\mathbb{P}\left(\varphi(x, (X', R^\nu)) \neq \perp \wedge out_{\mathcal{S}}(x) = y \right) \tag{15}$$

---

[5] Eq. (9) defines a probability distribution, since the values in (9) are clearly non-negative and they sum up to 1 (when the sum is computed over all $z \in \mathcal{Y}$), which follows from the fact that $\sum_{z \in \mathcal{Y}} \max(0, \mathbb{P}\left(\nu(x, R^\nu) = z \right) - \mathbb{P}\left(\nu(X, R^\nu) = z \right)) = \Delta(\nu(x, R^\nu); \nu(X, R^\nu))$ (cf. (1)).

It is easy to see that (14) is equal to

$$
\mathbb{P}\left(\varphi(x,(X',R^\nu))=\perp \wedge \nu(X',R^\nu)=y\right)
$$
$$
\mathbb{P}\left(\nu(X',R^\nu)=y\right)\cdot \mathbb{P}\left(\varphi(x,(X',R^\nu))=\perp \mid \nu(X',R^\nu)=y\right)
$$
$$
=\mathbb{P}\left(\nu(X',R^\nu)=y\right)\cdot \mathbb{P}\left(\varphi(x,(X',R^\nu))=\perp \mid \nu(X',R^\nu)=y\right)
$$
$$
=\mathbb{P}\left(\nu(X',R^\nu)=y\right)\cdot \min\left(1,\frac{\mathbb{P}\left(\nu(x,R^\nu)=y\right)}{\mathbb{P}\left(\nu(X,R^\nu)=y\right)}\right)
$$
$$
=\min\left(\mathbb{P}\left(\nu(X',R^\nu)=y\right),\ \frac{\mathbb{P}\left(\nu(X',R^\nu)=y\right)\cdot \mathbb{P}\left(\nu(x,R^\nu)=y\right)}{\mathbb{P}\left(\nu(X,R^\nu)=y\right)}\right)
$$

which, since (X,R^ν) and (X',R^ν) have identical distributions is equal to

$$
\min\left(\mathbb{P}\left(\nu(X',R^\nu)=y\right),\mathbb{P}\left(\nu(x,R^\nu)=y\right)\right).
$$

On the other hand (15) is equal to the product of

$$
\mathbb{P}\left(\varphi(x,(X',R^\nu))\neq \perp\right) \tag{16}
$$

and

$$
\mathbb{P}\left(out_S(x)=y \mid \varphi(x,(X',R^\nu))\neq \perp\right). \tag{17}
$$

Clearly (16) is equal to

$$
\sum_{z\in \mathcal{Y}}\mathbb{P}\left(\nu(X',R^\nu)=z\right)\cdot \mathbb{P}\left(\varphi(x,(X',R^\nu))\neq \perp \mid \mathbb{P}\left(\nu(X',R^\nu)=z\right)\right)
$$
$$
=\sum_{z\in \mathcal{Y}}\mathbb{P}\left(\nu(X',R^\nu)=z\right)\cdot \left(1-\min\left(1,\frac{\mathbb{P}\left(\nu(x,R^\nu)=z\right)}{\mathbb{P}\left(\nu(X,R^\nu)=z\right)}\right)\right)
$$
$$
=\sum_{z\in \mathcal{Y}}\mathbb{P}\left(\nu(X',R^\nu)=z\right)\cdot \max\left(0,\frac{\mathbb{P}\left(\nu(X,R^\nu)=z\right)-\mathbb{P}\left(\nu(x,R^\nu)=z\right)}{\mathbb{P}\left(\nu(X,R^\nu)=z\right)}\right) \tag{18}
$$
$$
=\sum_{z\in \mathcal{Y}}\left(\max\left(0,\mathbb{P}\left(\nu(X,R^\nu)=z\right)-\mathbb{P}\left(\nu(x,R^\nu)=z\right)\right)\right) \tag{19}
$$
$$
=\Delta(\nu(x,R^\nu);\nu(X,R^\nu)), \tag{20}
$$

where in (18) we used the fact that for any $0\leq c\leq 1$ we have $1-\min(1,c)=\max(0,1-c)$, in (19) we used $(X,\mathcal{R}^\nu)$ and $(X',\mathcal{R}^\nu)$ are identically distributed, and in (20) we used Eq. (1). In turn, from the construction of S it is clear that Eq. (17) is equal to

$$
\max\left(0,\frac{\mathbb{P}\left(\nu(x,R^\nu)=y\right)-\mathbb{P}\left(\nu(X,R^\nu)=y\right)}{\Delta(\nu(x,R^\nu);\nu(X,R^\nu))}\right). \tag{21}
$$

Since (15) is equal to the product of (20) and (21), thus it is equal to

$$
\max\left(0,\mathbb{P}\left(\nu(x,R^\nu)=y\right)-\mathbb{P}\left(\nu(X,R^\nu)=y\right)\right),
$$

and therefore (13) is equal to

$$\overbrace{\min\left(\mathbb{P}\left(\nu(X',R^\nu)=y\right),\mathbb{P}\left(\nu(x,R^\nu)=y\right)\right)}^{=(14)} \tag{22}$$

$$+\overbrace{\max\left(0,\mathbb{P}\left(\nu(x,R^\nu)=y\right)-\mathbb{P}\left(\nu(X,R^\nu)=y\right)\right)}^{=(15)}$$

$$=\mathbb{P}\left(\nu(x,R^\nu)=y\right), \tag{23}$$

where (23) comes from a simple calculation[6]. In this way we have shown that

$$\mathbb{P}\left(out_S(x)=y\right)=\mathbb{P}\left(\nu(x,R^\nu)=y\right),$$

which implies (7). This finishes the proof of (6). It is also clear from the construction of S that if A is non-adaptive then so is S, and that S works in polynomial time provided the noise functions issued by A are poly-time-decidable.   □

The opposite direction, namely the reduction from the average probing leakage model to the noisy leakage model is given in the lemma below. For space limitations the proof is referred to the full version of this paper.

Lemma 8. *For any ϵ let A be a ϵ-average-probing adversary on some $\mathcal{X}^\ell$. Then there exists a 2ϵ-noisy adversary S on $\mathcal{X}^\ell$ such that for a every $(x_1,\dots,x_\ell)\in\mathcal{X}^\ell$ we have*

$$A(x_1,\dots,x_\ell)\overset{d}{=}S(x_1,\dots,x_\ell). \tag{24}$$

6   Applications of the Average Probing Model

In this section, we present some applications of the average probing model and the reduction to the noisy leakage model of Prouff and Rivain. We first show in Section 6.1 that the standard additive masking function used in numerous works [26,28,14,4] as a building block for masked computation is secure in the ϵ-average probing model. As a second application, we prove in Section 6.2 that the masking scheme of ISW (or rather its extension to larger fields by Rivain and Prouff [28]) is secure in the average probing model using leak-free gates similar to [25,10]. We emphasize that in both cases we can achieve security with significantly improved δ-noise parameter – in particular, in contrast to earlier works [25,7] we improve the δ parameter by a factor $|\mathcal{X}|$.

6.1   Security of the Additive Masking

In this section we show the security of the additive masking scheme over a finite group in the average probing model. Let n be a natural number and $(\mathcal{X},+)$ be

---

[6] More precisely we use the fact that for every two real numbers A and B we have $\min(A,B)+\max(0,A-B)=A$, with $A:=\mathbb{P}\left(\nu(x,R^\nu)=y\right)$ and $B:=\mathbb{P}\left(\nu(x,R^\nu)=y\right)$.

a finite group. Define an *encoding function* $Enc_{\mathcal{X}}^n : \mathcal{X} \to \mathcal{X}^n$ and a *decoding function* $Dec_{\mathcal{X}}^n : \mathcal{X}^n \to \mathcal{X}$ as follows. Let

$$Enc_{\mathcal{X}}^n(x) = (X_1, \ldots, X_n), \tag{25}$$

where $(X_1, \ldots, X_{n-1}) \leftarrow \mathcal{X}^{n-1}$ and $X_n := x - (X_1 + \cdots + X_{n-1})$ and let $Dec_{\mathcal{X}}^n(X_1, \ldots, X_n) = X_1 + \cdots + X_n$.

Proof of Security. Before we show the security of the encoding scheme, we provide some technical lemmata for the average probing model. The main technical challenge we are facing when applying the average probing model to masking schemes is the fact that average probing leakage reveals non-trivial information about X to an adversary even in the case when $\varphi(X, R) = \bot$, which was not the case in the random probing model. This is because $\varphi(x, R) = \bot$ may be more likely for some x's than for the other (as an example think of φ defined identically to ν in the example at the beginning of Section 5). This technicality makes security proofs in the average probing model more involved than security proofs in the random probing model. Fortunately, in this paper we develop a set of tools that enables us to deal with this technicality of the model. We start by giving some technical lemmata, whose proofs appears in the full version of this paper.

Lemma 9. *Let X and R be random variables with uniform distribution over $\mathcal{X}$ and $\mathcal{R}$, respectively. For any ϵ-average-identity function φ we have*

$$d(X \mid \varphi(X, R) = \bot, R) = \epsilon.$$

The problem with Lemma 9 above is that it only gives information about the expected value (over $r \leftarrow R$) of $d(X \mid \varphi(X, R) = \bot, R = r)$. Hence, for certain r's this value can be very large – or in other words $\varphi(X, R) = \bot$ and $R = r$ can reveal some significant information about X. We deal with this problem by using a Markov-style argument: if the expected value of some term is small, then with good probability this term is small. More precisely, let φ be an ϵ-average-identity function, and for every $\xi \in [0, 1]$ define a function $f : \mathcal{R} \to [0, 1]$ as

$$f(r) := d(X | \varphi(X, r) = \bot, R = r).$$

and let[7]

$$Probe_{\varphi}^{\xi}(x, r) := \begin{cases} ? & \text{if } \varphi(x, r) = \bot \text{ and } f(r) \leq \epsilon/\xi \\ x & \text{otherwise.} \end{cases}$$

In some sense $Probe_{\varphi}^{\xi}$ is more "generous" to the adversary than φ since it outputs x also in cases when φ outputs $\bot$. Clearly $\varphi(x, r)$ can be easily computed from $(Probe_{\varphi}^{\xi}(x, r), r)$, and hence any adversary that learns $(Probe_{\varphi}^{\xi}(X, R), R)$ is at least as powerful as an adversary that learns $(\varphi(X, R), R))$. We will use this fact later. First, we show some useful properties of $Probe_{\varphi}^{\xi}(x, r)$.

---

[7] The "?" symbol is used in a similar way as "$\bot$". We chosen to use "?" in order to avoid confusion in the notation.

Lemma 10. *Let φ be an ϵ-average-identity function. For every $\xi \in [0,1]$ we have that*

$$\underset{r}{\forall}\ d(X | Probe_{\varphi}^{\xi}(X,r) = ?, R = r) \leq \epsilon/\xi \tag{26}$$

and

$$\mathbb{P}\left(Probe_{\varphi}^{\xi}(X,R) \neq ?\right) \leq \xi + \epsilon. \tag{27}$$

The next lemma shows that if we obtain ℓ times the value ? from $Probe_{\varphi}^{\xi}(X_i)$, then the distance of $X_1 + \ldots + X_\ell$ decreases exponentially, and exhibits the first step to show the security of the encoding function.

Lemma 11. *Let $\varphi_1, \ldots, \varphi_\ell$ be ϵ-average-identity functions. Suppose $\mathcal{X}$ is an additive group. Let $(X_1, \ldots, X_\ell) \leftarrow \mathcal{X}^\ell$ and $(R_1, \ldots, R_\ell) \leftarrow \mathcal{R}^\ell$ be uniform and independent random variables and set $X := X_1 + \cdots + X_\ell$. Then for every $(r_1, \ldots, r_\ell)$ we have*

$$d(X \mid \forall_{i=1}^{\ell} Probe_{\varphi}^{\xi}(X_i, r_i) = ?, R_1 = r_1, \ldots, R_\ell = r_\ell) \leq (2\epsilon/\xi)^\ell, \tag{28}$$

and hence

$$d(X \mid \forall_{i=1}^{\ell} Probe_{\varphi}^{\xi}(X_i, R_i) = ?, R_1, \ldots, R_\ell) \leq (2\epsilon/\xi)^\ell. \tag{29}$$

The above already shows that conditioned on the auxiliary information the distance of X from uniform decreases exponentially in ℓ. We start by showing how to translate this into showing security of the encoding scheme $(Enc_{\mathcal{X}}^n, Dec_{\mathcal{X}}^n)$, when X is uniform. Later (cf. Corollary 1) we show how to translate this result into one where x is chosen by the adversary, which is the standard indistinguishability-based security definition of leakage resilient encoding schemes. Notice that the lemma below is fully adaptive, i.e., we allow the adversary to obtain $\varphi_i(X_i, R_i)$ and only afterwards he has to decide on which noisy leakage function φ_{i+1} he wants to observe. As such strengthening of the model comes essentially without any additional loss in the parameters (i.e., it comes for free) using the theory of martingales and Azuma inequality, we chose to present the most general version of the fully adaptive adversary below.

Lemma 12. *For every $\epsilon, \lambda, \xi \in [0,1]$ and an ϵ-average-probing adversary $\mathcal{A}$ on $\mathcal{X}^\ell$ and a uniform $X \leftarrow \mathcal{X}$ we have*

$$d(X | out_{\mathcal{A}}(Enc_{\mathcal{X}}^n(X))) \leq (2\epsilon/\xi)^{\lceil(1-\xi-\epsilon-\lambda)n\rceil} + e^{-2\lambda^2 n}. \tag{30}$$

Before we present the proof let us state the basic facts from the theory of martingales (more on this subject can be found, e.g., in [6]). Recall that a sequence $Y_0, Y_1, \ldots$ of random variables is a *submartingale* with respect to a sequence $W_0, W_1, \ldots$ of random variables if every Y_i is a function of $W_0, \ldots, W_{i-1}$ and $\mathbb{E}(Y_i | W_0, \ldots, W_{i-1}) \geq Y_{i-1}$ for every i. The sequence $\{X_i = Y_i - Y_{i-1}\}_{i \geq 1}$ is called a *submartingale difference sequence* (w.r.t. $W_0, W_1, \ldots$). A submartingale $Y_0, Y_1, \ldots$ satisfies the *bounded difference condition with parameters A and B* if for every i it is the case that $X_i \in [A, B]$. We have the following fact (see, e.g., [6], Section 5.3)

Lemma 13 (Azuma-Hoeffding inequality). *Let $Y_0, Y_1, \ldots$ be a submartingale (w.r.t. some other sequence) satisfying the bounded difference condition with parameters A and B. Then for any $t > 0$ we have*

$$\mathbb{P}\left(Y_n < Y_0 - t\right) \leq \exp\left(-\frac{2t^2}{n(B-A)^2}\right).$$

We are now ready for the proof of the lemma.

Proof (of Lemma 12). Let $(X_1, \ldots, X_n) = \text{Enc}_{\mathcal{X}}^n(X)$. Since X is uniform thus $X_1, \ldots, X_n$ are independent. Let $\varphi_1, \ldots, \varphi_n$ be functions specified by $\mathcal{A}$. Since $\mathcal{A}$ is ϵ-average-probing thus each φ_i is an ϵ_i-average identity, where $\epsilon_i \leq \epsilon$. Let, for each i, the function $Probe_{\varphi_i}^{\xi} : \mathcal{X} \times \mathcal{R} \to \mathcal{X} \cup \{?\}$ be defined as above. To simplify notation for each i let $W_i = Probe_{\varphi_i}^{\xi}(X_i, R_i)$ (where $R_i \leftarrow \mathcal{R}$). For each $i = 1, \ldots, n$ define a variable Y_i as

$$Y_i := \begin{cases} 1 \text{ if } W_i = ? \\ 0 \text{ otherwise.} \end{cases}$$

Since the adversary is adaptive, thus his choice of each φ_i can depend on the values $W_1, \ldots, W_{i-1}$. On the other hand, no matter how he behaves, from Lemma 10 we are guaranteed that $\mathbb{P}\left(W_i = ?\right) \geq 1 - \xi - \epsilon$ and hence $\mathbb{E}\left(Y_i | W_1, \ldots, W_{i-1}\right) \geq 1 - \xi - \epsilon$. Define Y_i' as $Y_i - (1 - \xi - \epsilon)$. Obviously then $\mathbb{E}\left(Y_i' | W_1, \ldots, W_{i-1}\right) \geq 0$. Hence $Y_0', Y_1', \ldots$ is a submartingale difference sequence w.r.t. $W_0, W_1, \ldots$. Moreover for each i we have

$$-(1 - \xi - \epsilon) \leq Y_i' \leq 1 - (1 - \xi - \epsilon).$$

Hence, if for every $j = 0, \ldots, n$ we let $Z^j := \sum_{i=1}^{j} Y_i'$ then $Z^0, \ldots, Z^n$ is a submartingale[8] w.r.t. $W_0, W_1, \ldots$ satisfying bounded difference condition with parameters $-(1 - \xi - \epsilon)$ and $1 - (1 - \xi - \epsilon)$. Therefore from Azuma-Hoeffding inequality (Lemma 13) we get that

$$\mathbb{P}\left(Z^n < -\lambda n\right) \leq \exp\left(-\frac{2(\lambda n)^2}{n}\right)$$

$$= \exp\left(-2\lambda^2 n\right).$$

Of course $\sum_{i=1}^{n} Y_i = Z^n + n(1 - \xi - \epsilon)$. Therefore

$$\exp\left(-2\lambda^2 n\right) \geq \mathbb{P}\left(\sum_{i=1}^{n} Y_i < -\lambda n + n(1 - \xi - \epsilon)\right)$$

$$= \mathbb{P}\left(\sum_{i=1}^{n} Y_i < n(1 - \xi - \epsilon - \lambda)\right) \tag{31}$$

---

[8] It is easy to see that if the adversary was non-adaptive then we could also use Chernoff inequality, instead of the Azuma-Hoeffding inequality and martingales.

For every set $\mathcal{I} \subseteq \{1, \ldots, n\}$ such that $|\mathcal{I}| \geq n(1 - \xi - \epsilon - \lambda)$ let $\mathcal{W}^{\mathcal{I}}$ denote the event defined as a following conjunction of events:

$$\mathcal{W}^{\mathcal{I}} := \left(\bigwedge_{j \in \mathcal{I}} Probe_{\varphi_j}^{\xi}(X_j, r_j) = ? \right) \wedge \left(\bigwedge_{j \notin \mathcal{I}} Probe_{\varphi}^{\xi}(X_j, r_j) \neq ? \right)$$

And let: $\mathcal{W} := \bigvee_{\mathcal{I}:|\mathcal{I}| \geq n(1 - \xi - \epsilon - \lambda)} \mathcal{W}^{\mathcal{I}}$. From (31) we clearly have

$$\mathbb{P}(\mathcal{W}) \geq 1 - e^{-2\lambda^2 n}. \tag{32}$$

Suppose that $\mathcal{W}^{\mathcal{I}}$ occurred for some $\mathcal{I}$ and let $m = |\mathcal{I}|$. Denote $X^{\mathcal{I}} := X_{i_1} + \cdots + X_{i_m}$. By Lemma 11 we have

$$(2\epsilon/\xi)^{\lceil n(1 - \xi - \epsilon - \lambda) \rceil}$$
$$\geq d(X^{\mathcal{I}} | R_{i_1}, \ldots, R_{i_m}, \mathcal{W}^{\mathcal{I}})$$
$$\geq d(X^{\mathcal{I}} | \varphi_{i_1}(X_{i_1}, R_{i_1}), \ldots, \varphi_{i_m}(X_{i_m}, R_{i_m}), R_{i_1}, \ldots, R_{i_m}, \mathcal{W}^{\mathcal{I}}) \tag{33}$$
$$\geq d(X^{\mathcal{I}} | \varphi_1(X_1, R_1), \ldots, \varphi_m(X_n, R_n), R_1, \ldots, R_n, \mathcal{W}^{\mathcal{I}}) \tag{34}$$
$$\geq d(X | \varphi_1(X_1, R_1), \ldots, \varphi_n(X_n, R_n), R_1, \ldots, R_n, \mathcal{W}^{\mathcal{I}}). \tag{35}$$

where (33) comes from the fact that, as observed in Section 5, $\varphi(x, r)$ is a function of $(Probe_{\varphi}^{\xi}(x, r), r)$. Eq. (34) holds because obviously for $i \notin \mathcal{I}$ the value of $(\varphi_i(X_i, R_i), R_i)$ does not bring any additional information about $X^{\mathcal{I}}$. Eq. (35) holds because of Lemma 2 with $A := X^{\mathcal{I}}$ and B equal to the sum of all X_i's with indices not in $\mathcal{I}$. We now have that

$$d(X | \varphi_1(X_1, R_1), \ldots, \varphi_n(X_n, R_n), R_1, \ldots, R_n, \mathcal{W})$$
$$\leq \sum_{\mathcal{I}:|\mathcal{I}| \geq n(1 - \xi - \epsilon - \lambda)} d(X | \varphi_1(X_1, R_1), \ldots, \varphi_n(X_n, R_n), R_1, \ldots, R_n, \mathcal{W}^{\mathcal{I}}) \cdot \mathbb{P}(\mathcal{W}^{\mathcal{I}})$$
$$\leq (2\epsilon/\xi)^{\lceil n(1 - \xi - \epsilon - \lambda) \rceil} \cdot \overbrace{\sum_{\mathcal{I}} \mathbb{P}(\mathcal{W}^{\mathcal{I}})}^{\leq 1}, \tag{36}$$

where the first inequality comes from the fact that the events $\mathcal{W}^{\mathcal{I}}$ are pairwise disjoint and hence we can use Lemma 3 (interpreting C as a variable that indicates which $\mathcal{W}^{\mathcal{I}}$ occurred). We therefore obtain that

$$d(X | out_{\mathcal{A}}(Enc_{\mathcal{X}}^n(X)), \mathcal{W}) \leq (2\epsilon/\xi)^{\lceil n(1 - \xi - \epsilon - \lambda) \rceil}. \tag{37}$$

We now have

$$d(X | out_{\mathcal{A}}(Enc_{\mathcal{X}}^n(X))) \leq d(X | out_{\mathcal{A}}(Enc_{\mathcal{X}}^n(X)), \mathcal{W}) + \mathbb{P}(\neg \mathcal{W})$$
$$\leq (2\epsilon/\xi)^{\lceil n(1 - \xi - \epsilon - \lambda) \rceil} + e^{-2\lambda^2 n},$$

where in the last inequality we used (37) and (32). This finishes the proof. $\square$

Of course, in practice it makes more sense to have the security even if the adversary picks up the encoded element x himself. This is shown in the corollary below. The price is that the error parameter get multiplied by the group size (and a constant). What is important is that this factor simply multiplies the total error, which is much better than in [25,7], where ϵ was multiplied by $|\mathcal{X}|$. As a consequence, even for very large fields this error can be made negligible by increasing n (which was not the case in [25,7]). The following is a simple consequence of Lemma 12 (the formal derivation of this corollary appears in the extended version of this paper).

Corollary 1. *For every $\epsilon, \lambda, \xi \in [0, 1]$ and an ϵ-average-probing adversary (or equivalently: ϵ-noisy adversary) $\mathcal{A}$ on $\mathcal{X}^\ell$ the information that $\mathcal{A}$ receives about any encoded element x can be "simulated" without access to x, up to a small error. More precisely there exists a random variable Y such that for every $x \in \mathcal{X}$ we have*

$$\Delta(out_{\mathcal{A}}(Enc_{\mathcal{X}}^n(x)) \; ; \; Y) \le 2\,|\mathcal{X}| \cdot \left((2\epsilon/\xi)^{\lceil (1-\xi-\epsilon-\lambda)(n-1) \rceil} + e^{-2\lambda^2(n-1)} \right) (38)$$

Moreover for any $x_0, x_1 \in \mathcal{X}$ we have

$$\Delta(out_{\mathcal{A}}(Enc_{\mathcal{X}}^n(x_0)) \; ; \; out_{\mathcal{A}}(Enc_{\mathcal{X}}^n(x_1)))$$
$$\le 4\,|\mathcal{X}| \cdot \left((2\epsilon/\xi)^{\lceil (1-\xi-\epsilon-\lambda)(n-1) \rceil} + e^{-2\lambda^2(n-1)} \right), \qquad (39)$$

and in particular (by setting $\xi = \sqrt{\epsilon}$ and $\lambda = 1/2$) we have

$$\Delta(out_{\mathcal{A}}(Enc_{\mathcal{X}}^n(x_0)) \; ; \; out_{\mathcal{A}}(Enc_{\mathcal{X}}^n(x_1)))$$
$$\le 4\,|\mathcal{X}| \cdot \left((4\epsilon)^{\lceil (1/4-\sqrt{\epsilon}/2-\epsilon/2)(n-1) \rceil} + e^{-(n-1)/2} \right). \qquad (40)$$

Moreover fixing $\epsilon = 1/16$ we get that this last term is at most

$$4\,|\mathcal{X}| \cdot \left(e^{-0.13\cdot(n-1)} + e^{-(n-1)/2} \right) \le 8\,|\mathcal{X}| \cdot e^{-0.13\cdot(n-1)}.$$

From Eq. (39) in the above corollary it is easy to see that with increasing number of shares n and a decreasing ϵ (i.e., more noise) the statistical distance decreases. We notice that the second term of the addition, i.e., $e^{-2\lambda^2(n-1)}$ only gets negligible if n increases, and in particular will dominate the first term when ϵ is negligible. While the same additional error term appeared in the work of Duc et al. [7] (due to the use of a Chernoff bound), the result of Prouff and Rivain [25] did not had this additional error term. We emphasize, however, that this additional error term only becomes relevant when we consider very small values for the δ-bias of the Prouff-Rivain model, i.e., for very noisy leakage functions. In the full version of this paper we show how to eliminate this additional error term using an alternative argument.

Finally, we emphasize that for the noise level in the last part of Corollary 1 ($\epsilon = 1/16$) neither the work of Prouff and Rivain [25], nor the work of Duc et al. [7] gives meaningful bounds unless the field is of a constant size.

6.2   Security of the ISW Compiler with Leak-Free Gates

As a second application, we demonstrate that also more complicated masked computation can be proven secure in the average probing model. To this end, we show that the ISW compiler (or rather its extension to larger fields by Prouff and Rivain [25]), which has been widely used as building block for masking schemes [25,4,7] is secure in the average · probing model assuming leak-free gates. As our reduction from the average probing model to the noisy leakage model of Prouff and Rivain is tight, we improve the noise rate of the work of Prouff and Rivain and Duc et al. [25,7] significantly – in particular, we are able to eliminate the factor $|\mathcal{X}|$ from the bounds in [7,25]. We note that compared to the recent work of Duc et al. [7] our analysis of the ISW compiler has one important drawback, namely, that we rely on the assumption that certain parts of the computation are leak-free. We will discuss this assumption in more detail below.

The Original Circuit Γ. Following the description of [14], we model computation as an arithmetic circuit Γ carrying values from an (arbitrary) finite field $\mathcal{X}$ on their wires and using the following gates to carry out computation in $\mathcal{X}$:

- $+, -$, and $\cdot$, which compute, respectively, the sum, difference, and product in $\mathcal{X}$, of their two inputs,
- the "coin flip" gate coin, which has no inputs and produces a random independently chosen element of $\mathcal{X}$,
- and for every $\alpha \in \mathcal{X}$, the constant gate const_α, which has no inputs and simply outputs α.

Fanout in Γ is handled by a special copy gate that takes as input a single value and outputs two copies. Circuits that only contain the above types of gates are called *stateless*.

Ishai et al. also consider the notion of *stateful circuits*. In addition to the gates described above, stateful circuits also contain memory gates, each of which has a single incoming and a single outgoing wire. Memory gates maintain state: at any round, a memory gate sends its current state down its outgoing wire and updates it according to the value of its incoming wire. The state of all memory gates at clock cycle i is denoted by m_{i-1}, with m_0 denoting the initial state. For instance, the state m_0 of an AES circuit may be its secret key.

The computation of a stateful circuit is performed in several rounds $i = 1, 2, \ldots$. In each of the rounds the circuit will take some public input x, its current internal state m_{i-1} and produces an output y and potentially updates its state to m_i. The evaluation of the circuit proceeds in a straightforward way: when all the input wires of a given gate are known, then the value on the output wire can be computed naturally, i.e., for a multiplication gate with inputs a, b the output wire becomes $c = a \cdot b$. An execution of the circuit Γ with state m_{i-1} on input x is denoted by $(y, m_i) \leftarrow \Gamma(m_{i-1}, x)$. The values that are carried on the wires of the circuit when run on input (m_{i-1}, x) conditioned on the output being (y, m_i) are denoted by the random variable $\mathcal{W}_\Gamma((m_{i-1}, x)|(y, m_i))$.

The Protected Circuit Γ'. The compiler takes as input the description of the circuit Γ and outputs Γ'. The main building block of Γ' is the encoding scheme $\mathrm{Enc}_{\mathcal{X}}^n$. The initial state m_0 is represented in Γ' in encoded form, i.e., as $M_0 \leftarrow \mathrm{Enc}_{\mathcal{X}}^n(m_0)$. Notice that if m_0 consists of multiple field elements, then we apply the encoding function to each element of m_0 individually. Next, we consider the wires that connect individual gates. In Γ' such wires are represented by *wire bundles* that carry the value of the wire in encoded form. The main difficulty to compile Γ into Γ' is to describe how to transform the gates, i.e., the basic operations described in the last paragraph. For each gate in Γ we have a a sub-circuit – so-called *gadget* – that represents the computation in Γ' and carries out the computation in encoded form. For instance, for a multiplication operation in Γ that takes as input two field elements a, b and outputs $c = a \cdot b$, in Γ' we use a gadget that takes as input two encodings of a (resp.) b and outputs an encoding of c. We emphasize that the computation in the gadgets uses the standard operations defined above and additionally a leak-free gate $\mathcal{O}$. We now provide some details about the most important algorithm of Γ' – the multiplication gadget Mult. The remaining operations, i.e., in particular the addition gadget is done as in the work of Faust et al. (see Figure 3 in [10]) and omitted for space reasons.

The construction of Mult is essentially the construction of Faust et al. [10] from Eurocrypt 2010 (which is essentially the transformation of ISW with leak-free gates) for AC0 leakage functions. In particular, we use their leak-free gate $\mathcal{O}$, which sample from $\mathrm{Enc}_{\mathcal{X}}^n(0)$, i.e., $X \leftarrow \mathcal{O}(1^n)$, where X is a random encoding of 0. We refer to the motivation of this leak-free component to the work of [10] or the work of Prouff and Rivain [25]. The later uses a similar component for their security proof in the noisy leakage model. We only notice that the computation of $\mathcal{O}(1^n)$ can be implemented in a very simple way, namely, sample random field elements $X_1, \ldots, X_{n-1}$ uniformly at random and compute $X_n = -X_1 - \ldots - X_{n-1}$. The output of $\mathcal{O}(1^n)$ is $(X_1, \ldots, X_n)$.

For some finite field $\mathcal{X}$ the multiplication gadget Mult takes as input two vectors $A \leftarrow \mathrm{Enc}_{\mathcal{X}}^n(a)$ and $B \leftarrow \mathrm{Enc}_{\mathcal{X}}^n(b)$, and produces $C \leftarrow \mathrm{Enc}_{\mathcal{X}}^n(c)$, where $c = a \cdot b$. To this end it performs the operations shown in Figure 3. To make the algorithm easier to read, we use small letters to denote elements in $\mathcal{X}$. Vectors over $\mathcal{X}$ will be denoted by capital letters, and matrices are denoted with a "hat" symbol.

The basic property that we require from the protected circuit Γ' is *correctness*. That is, we want that for any input x and any initial state m_0 the circuit Γ and Γ' with initial state $M_0 \leftarrow \mathrm{Enc}_{\mathcal{X}}^n(m_0)$ produce the same output distribution. In addition to correctness, Γ' shall be secure against certain classes of leakages, which we discuss next.

Security Definition. Informally, security means that an adversary that obtains leakage from the execution of the protected circuit shall not have any advantage over an adversary that attacks the original circuit with just black-box access. To describe this formally, we use the standard simulation-based paradigm. We start by introducing some different types of adversaries. In the following, we assume

---

The multiplication gadget Mult

1. Compute the $n \times n$ matrix $\hat{T} = (a_i \cdot b_j)_{i,j \in [n]}$, where a_i, b_j are the elements of the vector A and B, respectively.
2. Compute the $n \times n$ matrix $\hat{S}$ where the i-th column of $\hat{S}$ is sampled as $S_i \leftarrow \mathcal{O}(1^n)$.
3. Compute $\hat{U} = \hat{T} + \hat{S}$ using matrix addition.
4. Sum the values in each row of $\hat{U}$, i.e., for each $i \in [n]$ compute $q_i = \sum_j u_{i,j}$, where q_i denotes the i-th element of the vector Q.
5. Sample $O \leftarrow \mathcal{O}(1^n)$ and compute the output as $C = Q + O$.

Fig. 3. The multiplication operation takes as input (A, B) and produces the encoding C of ab. The leak-free component $\mathcal{O}(1^n)$ samples from the distribution $\mathrm{Enc}_{\mathcal{X}}^n(0)$ and can be implemented as described in the text above.

that the adversary chooses his leakage functions in each round non-adaptively. This can be extended to the adaptive case by making the description of the model more involved and we omit details for space reasons.

A *black-box circuit adversary* $\mathcal{A}$ is a machine that interacts with a circuit Γ via the input and output interface. We denote by $out\left(\mathcal{A} \overset{bb}{\leftrightarrows} \Gamma(m_0)\right)$ the output of $\mathcal{A}$ after interacting with Γ whose initial memory state is m_0. A δ-*noisy circuit adversary* $\mathcal{A}$ is an adversary that has the following additional ability: after each ith round, $\mathcal{A}$ obtains some partial information about the internal state of the computation via the noisy leakage functions. More precisely: let $\mathcal{W}_{\Gamma'}((x, M_{i-1})|(y, M_i))$ be the random variable denoting the values on the wires of $\Gamma'(M_0)$ in the ith round when run on input x and outputting y. Then $\mathcal{A}$ plays the role of a δ-noisy adversary in a game against $\mathcal{W}_{\Gamma'}((x, M_{i-1})|(y, M_i))$ (cf. Section 3), namely: he chooses a sequence $\{\nu_i : \mathcal{X} \times \mathcal{R} \to \mathcal{Y}\}_{i=1}^{\ell}$ of functions such that every ν_i is δ_i-noisy for some $\delta_i \leq \delta$ and he receives $\nu_1(V_1), \ldots, \nu_\ell(V_\ell)$, where V_i denotes a random variable that is part of the wire assignment $\mathcal{W}_{\Gamma'}((x, M_{i-1})|(y, M_i))$. The adversary can repeat this process multiple times for chosen inputs x and we denote the output of $\mathcal{A}$ at the end of this experiment by $out\left(\mathcal{A} \overset{noisy}{\leftrightarrows} \Gamma'(M_0)\right)$.

We can also replace, in the above definition, the "δ-noisy adversary" with the "ϵ-average probing adversary". In this case, after each ith round $\mathcal{A}$ chooses a sequence $(\epsilon_1, \ldots, \epsilon_\ell)$ such that each $\epsilon_i \leq \epsilon$ and he learns $\varphi_1(V_1), \ldots, \varphi_\ell(V_\ell)$, where each φ_i is the ϵ_i-average identity function. Let $out\left(\mathcal{A} \overset{avg}{\leftrightarrows} \Gamma'(M_0)\right)$ denote the output of such $\mathcal{A}$ after interacting with Γ whose initial memory state is M_0. We are now ready to define security of a transformed circuit Γ'.

Definition 4. *Consider a stateful circuit Γ and its transformation Γ' (over some field $\mathcal{X}$) and a randomized encoding function $\mathrm{Enc}_{\mathcal{X}}^n$. We say that Γ' is a (δ, γ)-noise resilient implementation of a circuit Γ w.r.t. $\mathrm{Enc}_{\mathcal{X}}^n$ if for every δ-noisy circuit adversary $\mathcal{A}$ there exists a black-box circuit adversary $\mathcal{S}$ such that* *for every $m \in \mathcal{X}^\ell$ (for $\ell \in \mathbb{N}$), we have:*

$$\Delta \left(out \left(\mathcal{S} \overset{bb}{\leftrightarrows} \Gamma(m) \right) \; ; \; out \left(\mathcal{A} \overset{noisy}{\leftrightarrows} \Gamma'(Enc_{\mathcal{X}}^n(m)) \right) \right) \leq \gamma. \qquad (41)$$

The definition of Γ' being a (ϵ, γ)-average-probing resilient implementation of a circuit Γ is identical to the one above, except that we let $\mathcal{A}$ be an ϵ-average-probing circuit adversary $\mathcal{A}$ and Equation 41 is replaced with:

$$\Delta \left(out \left(\mathcal{S} \overset{bb}{\leftrightarrows} \Gamma(m) \right) \; ; \; out \left(\mathcal{A} \overset{avg}{\leftrightarrows} \Gamma'(Enc_{\mathcal{X}}^n(m)) \right) \right) \leq \gamma.$$

In all cases above we will say that Γ' is an implementation of Γ with efficient simulation if the simulator $\mathcal{S}$ works in time polynomial in $\Gamma' \cdot |\mathcal{X}|$ as long as $\mathcal{A}$ is poly-time and the noise functions specified by $\mathcal{A}$ are efficiently decidable, which will be the case for all our results.

Security of Γ' Against Noisy Leakages. In contrast to Section 6.1, where we show the security of the additive encoding function in the average probing model, the security analysis of computation is more involved. The reason is that now we have multiple intermediate values that may depend in some predictable way on each other. Intuitively, noise will cancel out the sensitive information in the intermediate values if the sensitive information does not influence too many other intermediate values in the computation, and hence its value is not leaked too many times with independent noise. A similar approach was already exploited in the analysis of Duc et al. [7] – though there the situation was considerably simpler as in the ϵ-probing model the leakage is independent of most of the computation (i.e., large parts of the computation do not leak at all!). In contrast in the average probing model considered in this work, the leakage depends implicitly on *all* intermediate values as even in the case when the leakage function outputs $\perp$ the adversary may learn non-trivial information about the value probed.

To overcome these difficulties we use the framework of *reconstructors* introduced by Faust et al. [10] to argue about the security of masked gadgets. Informally, we give a simulator that just has leakage access to the inputs and outputs of the gadget and from that can simulate the entire leakage from the intermediate values of the gadget. We say that a simulation is good if the simulated leakage is indistinguishable from the real leakage of the intermediate values, when the leakage is assumed to be an ϵ-average probing leakage function. Moreover, we will require the simulator to be from some restricted class of functions. This is important since eventually we want to reduce the security of the protected circuit to the security of the underlying encoding scheme. We here strongly rely on the formalization given in [10] who consider such restricted simulators to achieve security against noisy leakages (albeit in a different noise model).

At a very informal level, we show that the internal values of a gadget can be simulated by a function REC that takes as input X (which is an encoded input of the gadget) and returns two types of values to simulate the internals of the gadget: (i) either constant values that are independent of the input X, or (ii) values that depend in a very restricted way on REC's input, namely for an input X they have the form $cX + C$, where c and C are constants in $\mathcal{X}$ and $\mathcal{X}^n$ respectively. Now, clearly (i) does not reveal any sensitive information about X (since it is independent of relevant information), and (ii) can essentially be reduced to just (multiple) noisy leakages from the encoding. As the security proof is very similar to [10], and in our work the circuit compiler is merely an application to show how to carry out security proofs of masked computation in the average probing model, we refer the reader to the full version of [10] for further details on the formalization of reconstructors.

To formalize the above informal description of what an admissible simulator REC shall look like, we recall the definition of the function class $\mathsf{LOCAL}(\ell)$ introduced by [10]. Function ins $\mathsf{LOCAL}(\ell)$ depend only in a very restricted way on their inputs, and are hence useful to simulate noisy leakage without revealing too much sensitive information. For some $\ell, n, t, k \in \mathbb{N}$, a function $f : \mathcal{X}^{tn} \to \mathcal{X}^k$ with inputs $X^{(1)}, \ldots, X^{(t)} \in \mathcal{X}^n$ is said to be in $\mathsf{LOCAL}(\ell)$ if the following holds for each $i \in [1, t]$:

> For any fixed $t - 1$ inputs $X^{(1)}, \ldots, X^{(i-1)}, X^{(i+1)}, \ldots, X^{(t)}$, all but at most $n\ell$ output values (from $\mathcal{X}$) of the function $f(X^{(1)}, \ldots, X^{(t)})$ (as a function of $X^{(i)}$) are constant (i.e., do not depend on $X^{(i)}$); the remaining outputs are computed as $cX^{(i)} + C$, for some constant $C \in \mathcal{X}^n$ and $c \in \mathcal{X}$.

The identity function, for instance, is in $\mathsf{LOCAL}(1)$, while a function that outputs ℓ copies of its inputs is in $\mathsf{LOCAL}(\ell)$.

We now give a formal definition of efficient simulators (aka reconstructors) tailored to our setting of ϵ average probing leakage functions and for the masked multiplication operation. It is straightforward to generalize the notion to arbitrary masked computation. We then show that the multiplication gadget satisfies the notion. Given that the multiplication gadget is reconstructible, Faust et al. [10] show that security according to Definition 4 can be achieved (cf. Theorem 1 below).

Definition 5 $((\epsilon, \gamma, \ell)$-reconstructors [10]). *Let* Mult *be the masked multiplication with encoded inputs* $X := (A, B)$ *and encoded outputs* $Y := C$. *We say that a pair of strings* (X, Y) *is* plausible *for* Mult *if* Mult *might output* Y *on input* X, *i.e., if* $\Pr[\mathsf{Mult}(X) = Y] > 0$.

Consider a distribution $\mathsf{REC}_{\mathsf{Mult}}$ *over the functions whose input is a plausible pair* (X, Y), *and whose output is an assignment to the wires of* Mult. *Define* $\mathsf{REC}_{\mathsf{Mult}}(X, Y)$ *as the distribution obtained by sampling a function* R_{Mult} *from* $\mathsf{REC}_{\mathsf{Mult}}$ *and computing* $R_{\mathsf{Mult}}(X, Y)$. *Such a distribution is called a* (ϵ, γ, ℓ)-reconstructor *for* Mult *if for any plausible* (X, Y) *and any* ϵ-average probing *adversary* $\mathcal{A}$, *the following two distributions are* γ-close:

- $out_{\mathcal{A}}(\mathcal{W}_{\mathsf{Mult}}(X|Y))$,
- $out_{\mathcal{A}}(\mathsf{REC}_{\mathsf{Mult}}(X, Y))$.

If the support of the distribution $\mathsf{REC}_{\mathsf{Mult}}$ *is in some set of functions* $\mathsf{LOCAL}(\ell)$, *we say that* Mult *is* (ϵ, γ, ℓ)-*reconstructible.*

Besides the reconstructibility property, we also require that the gadgets of Γ' are *re-randomizing*. We only state it in an informal way here and refer the reader to Definition 3 in [10]. Informally, we say that the masked multiplication operation is re-randomizing if the output of the multiplication is distributed as $\mathsf{Enc}_{\mathcal{X}}^n(c)$ for $c = a \cdot b$ even given the input encoding $A := \mathsf{Enc}_{\mathcal{X}}^n(a)$ and $B := \mathsf{Enc}_{\mathcal{X}}^n(b)$.

It is easy to see that the masked multiplication Mult is re-randomizing. What is more challenging to prove is the fact that Mult is (ϵ, γ, ℓ)-reconstructible, which is shown in the lemma below. The proof of the lemma is very similar to the proof of Lemma 9 in [10], and is deferred to the full version of the paper. To simply notation the lemma below uses the particular parameter setting of Eq. (40) from Corollary 1. It is easy to generalize the lemma for other settings of the parameters.

Lemma 14. *Let n be the security parameter and $\mathcal{X}$ be some finite field. Let ϵ be a function in n defining the noise parameter of the average probing model. The Mult operation is $(\epsilon, \gamma, 2n)$-reconstructible for:*

$$\gamma := 4\,|\mathcal{X}|\,n \cdot \left((4(n+1)\epsilon)^{\lceil (1/4 - \sqrt{((n+1)\epsilon}/2 - (n+1)\epsilon/2)(n-1))\rceil} + e^{-(n-1)/2} \right).$$

Given the above lemma we are now ready to apply the framework of Faust et al. [10] and prove that Γ' is secure according to Definition 4. The proof is straightforward and merely puts the different parameters together.

Theorem 1. *Let $n > 1$ be the security parameter. Let Γ be an arbitrary stateful arithmetic circuit over some field $\mathcal{X}$. Let Γ' be the circuit that results from the transformation procedure described above. Let q be the number of observations, then Γ' is a (δ, γ)-noise resilient implementation of Γ (with efficient simulation), where*

$$\gamma = 4\,|\mathcal{X}|\,q\,|\Gamma|\,(n+3) \cdot \left((4(n+1)\delta)^{\lceil (1/4 - \sqrt{((n+1)\delta}/2 - (n+1)\delta/2)(n-1))\rceil} + e^{-(n-1)/2} \right)$$

For concreteness, when we plug-in for $\delta := (24n)^{-1}$ we get for $n > 4$:

$$\gamma := 4\,|\mathcal{X}|\,q\,|\Gamma|\,(n+3) \cdot \exp(-n/12) \tag{42}$$

We notice that the number of measurements/observations (i.e., the number of times the adversary can apply a noisy leakage attack on the implementation Γ') was ignored in the work of [7]. In case we do not consider multiple measurements, we can eliminate the factor q from the above bound. Moreover, if we compare the above concrete bound from Eq. (42) with the bound that was achieved by Duc et al. (see Theorem 1 in [7]), then we see that we improve the noise level not only by a factor $|\mathcal{X}|$ but also the constant is increased from $1/28$ to $1/24$ in our work while achieving (asymptotically for large n) the same bound on the statistical distance.

Acknowledgments. We thank the anonymous reviewers of Eurocrypt 2015 for improving the presentation of our result.

References

1. Blömer, J., Guajardo, J., Krummel, V.: Provably secure masking of AES. In: Handschuh, H., Hasan, M.A. (eds.) SAC 2004. LNCS, vol. 3357, pp. 69–83. Springer, Heidelberg (2004)
2. Chari, S., Jutla, C.S., Rao, J.R., Rohatgi, P.: Towards sound approaches to counteract power-analysis attacks. In: Wiener, M. (ed.) CRYPTO 1999. LNCS, vol. 1666, pp. 398–412. Springer, Heidelberg (1999)
3. Clavier, C., Coron, J.-S., Dabbous, N.: Differential power analysis in the presence of hardware countermeasures. In: Koç, Ç.K., Paar, C. (eds.) CHES 2000. LNCS, vol. 1965, pp. 252–263. Springer, Heidelberg (2000)
4. Coron, J.-S.: Higher order masking of look-up tables. In: Nguyen, P.Q., Oswald, E. (eds.) EUROCRYPT 2014. LNCS, vol. 8441, pp. 441–458. Springer, Heidelberg (2014)
5. Coron, J.-S., Kizhvatov, I.: Analysis and improvement of the random delay countermeasure of CHES 2009. In: Mangard, S., Standaert, F.-X. (eds.) [21], pp. 95–109
6. Dubhashi, D.P., Panconesi, A.: Concentration of Measure for the Analysis of Randomized Algorithms. Cambridge University Press (2009)
7. Duc, A., Dziembowski, S., Faust, S.: Unifying leakage models: from probing attacks to noisy leakage. In: Nguyen, P.Q., Oswald, E. (eds.) EUROCRYPT 2014. LNCS, vol. 8441, pp. 423–440. Springer, Heidelberg (2014)
8. Dziembowski, S., Faust, S.: Leakage-resilient circuits without computational assumptions. In: Cramer, R. (ed.) TCC 2012. LNCS, vol. 7194, pp. 230–247. Springer, Heidelberg (2012)
9. Dziembowski, S., Pietrzak, K.: Leakage-resilient cryptography in the standard model. IACR Cryptology ePrint Archive, 2008:240 (2008)
10. Faust, S., Rabin, T., Reyzin, L., Tromer, E., Vaikuntanathan, V.: Protecting circuits from leakage: the computationally-bounded and noisy cases. In: Gilbert, H. (ed.) EUROCRYPT 2010. LNCS, vol. 6110, pp. 135–156. Springer, Heidelberg (2010)
11. Goldwasser, S., Rothblum, G.N.: Securing computation against continuous leakage. In: Rabin, T. (ed.) [27], pp. 59–79
12. Goldwasser, S., Rothblum, G.N.: How to compute in the presence of leakage. In: FOCS, pp. 31–40. IEEE Computer Society (2012)
13. Goubin, L., Patarin, J.: DES and differential power analysis the "Duplication" method. In: Koç, Ç.K., Paar, C. (eds.) CHES 1999. LNCS, vol. 1717, pp. 158–172. Springer, Heidelberg (1999)
14. Ishai, Y., Sahai, A., Wagner, D.: Private circuits: securing hardware against probing attacks. In: Boneh, D. (ed.) CRYPTO 2003. LNCS, vol. 2729, pp. 463–481. Springer, Heidelberg (2003)
15. Juma, A., Vahlis, Y.: Protecting cryptographic keys against continual leakage. In: Rabin, T. (ed.) [27], pp. 41–58
16. Katz, J., Vaikuntanathan, V.: Signature schemes with bounded leakage resilience. In: Matsui, M. (ed.) ASIACRYPT 2009. LNCS, vol. 5912, pp. 703–720. Springer, Heidelberg (2009)
17. Kocher, P.C.: Timing attacks on implementations of diffie-hellman, RSA, DSS, and other systems. In: Koblitz, N. (ed.) CRYPTO 1996. LNCS, vol. 1109, pp. 104–113. Springer, Heidelberg (1996)
18. Kocher, P.C., Jaffe, J., Jun, B.: Differential power analysis. In: Wiener, M. (ed.) CRYPTO 1999. LNCS, vol. 1666, pp. 388–397. Springer, Heidelberg (1999)

19. Kocher, P.C., Jaffe, J., Jun, B., Rohatgi, P.: Introduction to differential power analysis. J. Cryptographic Engineering **1**(1), 5–27 (2011)
20. Mangard, S., Oswald, E., Popp, T.: Power Analysis Attacks: Revealing the Secrets of Smart Cards (Advances in Information Security). Springer-Verlag New York, Inc., Secaucus (2007)
21. Mangard, S., Standaert, F.-X. (eds.): CHES 2010. LNCS, vol. 6225. Springer, Heidelberg (2010)
22. Maurer, U., Pietrzak, K., Renner, R.: Indistinguishability amplification. In: Menezes, A. (ed.) CRYPTO 2007. LNCS, vol. 4622, pp. 130–149. Springer, Heidelberg (2007)
23. Naor, M., Segev, G.: Public-key cryptosystems resilient to key leakage. In: Halevi, S. (ed.) CRYPTO 2009. LNCS, vol. 5677, pp. 18–35. Springer, Heidelberg (2009)
24. Oswald, E., Mangard, S., Pramstaller, N., Rijmen, V.: A side-channel analysis resistant description of the AES S-box. In: Gilbert, H., Handschuh, H. (eds.) FSE 2005. LNCS, vol. 3557, pp. 413–423. Springer, Heidelberg (2005)
25. Prouff, E., Rivain, M.: Masking against side-channel attacks: a formal security proof. In: Johansson, T., Nguyen, P.Q. (eds.) EUROCRYPT 2013. LNCS, vol. 7881, pp. 142–159. Springer, Heidelberg (2013)
26. Prouff, E., Roche, T.: Higher-order glitches free implementation of the AES using secure multi-party computation protocols. In: Preneel, B., Takagi, T. (eds.) CHES 2011. LNCS, vol. 6917, pp. 63–78. Springer, Heidelberg (2011)
27. Rabin, T. (ed.): CRYPTO 2010. LNCS, vol. 6223. Springer, Heidelberg (2010)
28. Rivain, M., Prouff, E.: Provably secure higher-order masking of AES. In: Mangard, S., Standaert, F.-X. (eds.) [21], pp. 413–427
29. Rothblum, G.N.: How to compute under $\mathcal{AC}^0$ leakage without secure hardware. In: Safavi-Naini, R., Canetti, R. (eds.) CRYPTO 2012. LNCS, vol. 7417, pp. 552–569. Springer, Heidelberg (2012)
30. Standaert, F.-X., Pereira, O., Yu, Y., Yung, M., Oswald, E.: Leakage resilient cryptography in practice. In: Towards Hardware Intrinsic Security Foundation and Practice (book chapter) (2010)
31. Standaert, F.-X., Veyrat-Charvillon, N., Oswald, E., Gierlichs, B., Medwed, M., Kasper, M., Mangard, S.: The world is not enough: another look on second-order DPA. In: Abe, M. (ed.) ASIACRYPT 2010. LNCS, vol. 6477, pp. 112–129. Springer, Heidelberg (2010)

Garbled Circuits

Privacy-Free Garbled Circuits
with Applications to Efficient Zero-Knowledge

Tore Kasper Frederiksen[(✉)], Jesper Buus Nielsen[(✉)],
and Claudio Orlandi[(✉)]

Department of Computer Science, Aarhus University, Aarhus, Denmark
{jot2re,jbn,orlandi}@cs.au.dk

Abstract. In the last few years garbled circuits (GC) have been
elevated from being merely a component in Yao's protocol for secure two-
party computation, to a cryptographic primitive in its own right, following the growing number of applications that use GCs. Zero-Knowledge
(ZK) protocols is one of these examples: In a recent paper Jawurek
et al. [JKO13] showed that GCs can be used to construct efficient ZK
proofs for unstructured languages. In this work we show that due to
the property of this particular scenario (i.e., one of the parties knows
all the secret input bits, and therefore all intermediate values in the
computation), we can construct more efficient garbling schemes specifically tailored to this goal. As a highlight of our result, in one of our
constructions only *one ciphertext* per gate needs to be communicated
and XOR gates never require any cryptographic operations. In addition
to making a step forward towards more practical ZK, we believe that
our contribution is also interesting from a conceptual point of view: in
the terminology of Bellare *et al.* [BHR12] our garbling schemes achieve
authenticity, but no privacy nor obliviousness, therefore representing the
first *natural* separation between those notions.

1 Introduction

A garbled circuit (GC) is a cryptographic tool that allows one to evaluate
"encrypted" circuits on "encrypted" inputs. Garbled circuits were introduced
by Yao in the 80's in the context of secure two-party computation [Yao86], and
they owe their name to Beaver *et al.* [BMR90].

Since then, garbled circuits have been used in a number of different contexts
such as two- and multi-party secure computation [Yao86,GMW87], verifiable

Partially supported by the European Research Commission Starting Grant 279447
and the Danish National Research Foundation and The National Science Foundation of China (grant 61361136003) for the Sino-Danish Center for the Theory of
Interactive Computation and from the Center for Research in Foundations of Electronic Markets (CFEM), supported by the Danish Strategic Research Council. Tore
is supported by Danish Council for Independent Research Starting Grant 10-081612.
The research leading to these results has received funding from the European Union
Seventh Framework Programme ([FP7/2007-2013]) under grant agreement number
ICT-609611 (PRACTICE).

© International Association for Cryptologic Research 2015
E. Oswald and M. Fischlin (Eds.): EUROCRYPT 2015, Part II, LNCS 9057, pp. 191–219, 2015.
DOI: 10.1007/978-3-662-46803-6_7

outsourcing of computation [GGP10], key-dependent message security [BHHI10], efficient zero-knowledge [JKO13], functional encryption [SS10] etc. However, it is not until recently that a formal treatment of garbled circuits appeared in the literature. The first proof of security of Yao's celebrated protocol for two-party computation, to the best of our knowledge, only appeared a few years ago in [LP09], and it is not until [BHR12] that garbled circuits were elevated from a technique to be used in other protocols, to a cryptographic primitive in their own right.

Different applications of GC often use different properties of the garbling scheme: In some applications we need GCs to protect the privacy of encrypted inputs, in others we need GCs to hide partial information about the encrypted function, while in yet others we ask GCs to ensure that even a malicious evaluator cannot tamper with the output of the GC. In their foundational work, Bellare *et al.* [BHR12] formally defined the different security properties that different applications require from GCs, showed separations between them, and showed that the original garbling scheme proposed by Yao satisfies all of the above properties. This raises a natural question:

Can we construct garbling schemes tailored to specific applications, which are more efficient than Yao's original construction?

In this work we give the first such example, namely a garbling scheme which only satisfies *authenticity* (in the terminology of Bellare *et al.*) but not *privacy*: One of the main properties of Yao's garbling scheme is that the circuit evaluator cannot learn the values associated to the internal wires during the evaluation of the garbled circuit. This implies that the evaluation of each garbled gate must be *oblivious* (it must be the same for each input combination). In this work we give up on this property and we construct a scheme where the evaluator learns the values associated which each wire in the circuit, and explicitly uses this knowledge to perform *non-oblivious* garbled gate evaluation. This allows us to significantly reduce the size of a garbled circuit and the computational overhead for the circuit constructor. We show that this does not have any impact on *authenticity*, i.e., the only thing that a malicious evaluator can do with a garbled input and a garbled circuit is to use them in the intended way, that is to evaluate the garbled circuit on the garbled input and produce the (correct) garbled output.

Our new garbling schemes can be immediately plugged-in in Jawurek *et al.* [JKO13] efficient zero-knowledge protocol for non-algebraic languages, and therefore we believe that our results have both practical and conceptual value. It is an interesting future direction to investigate which other applications could benefit significantly from our new garbling scheme (natural candidates include verifiable outsourcing of computation, functional encryption etc.).

1.1 Other Garbling Schemes

Since the introduction of GCs by Yao, a number of optimizations have been proposed to increase their efficiency. Some of the most significant optimizations include *point-and-permute* [Rog91, MNPS04] (which reduces the work of the circuit evaluator from 4 to 1 decryption per garbled gate) the *row-reduction technique* [NPS99, PSSW09] (which reduces the number of ciphertexts per garbled gate, by fixing some of them to be constant values), the *free-XOR* and *fleXOR* techniques [KS08, KMR14] (which allows to garble/evaluate XOR gates using none/less cryptographic operations). In [BHR12, BHKR13] efficient garbling schemes, which only use one call to a block-cipher for each row in a garbled gate, are presented. Information theoretic garbling schemes can efficiently be constructed [IK02, Kol05, KK12] for low-depth circuits. All these techniques lead to very efficient garbling schemes that are used today in practical implementation of secure two-party computation. Our optimization is conceptually different from all of the above, as our schemes are not "general purpose" since they do not satisfy privacy.

LEGO GCs [NO09, FJN+13] are different from Yao GCs as they allow one to generate garbled gates independently of each other and then, at a later time, to solder them together into a functional garbled circuit. LEGO GCs can be used for secure two-party computation in the presence of active corruptions.

The size of garbled input in Yao-style GCs grows linearly in the security parameter. In [AIKW13] a garbling scheme where the garbled input grows only by a constant factor is presented at the price of using public-key primitives (traditional GCs only use symmetric key operations). Traditional GCs only work on Boolean circuits, while [AIK11] presents a way of garbling arithmetic circuits directly.

All previously discussed garbling schemes are *one-time*, meaning that no security is guaranteed against an adversary that receives the garbling of two different inputs for the same garbled circuit. A recent line of work considers *reusable garbled circuits* [GKP+13] and their (asymptotic) overhead [GGH+13]. While the concept of reusable garbled circuits has numerous applications in establishing important theoretical feasibility result, their use of heavy crypto machinery makes them (still) far from being practical. Finally, there exist garbling schemes tailored for other models of computation [KW13] including RAM programs [LO13, GHL+14].

Independently from us Ishai and Wee [IW14] defined the notion of *partial garbling*: like us, they noticed that in some applications one of the parties controls all the inputs and therefore it is possible to construct garbling schemes which are more efficient than traditional ones. However they develop this observation in a very different direction compared to us: the two works use different abstraction models (*garbling schemes* vs. *randomized encodings*), are useful for different tasks, and use completely different techniques.

Finally, Zahur *et al.* [ZRE15] extended our work to the two-party case, demonstrating that it is possible to combine (in a very clever way) two privacy-free garbling schemes – where each party knows all of the inputs for one of the two garblings – into a garbling scheme which guarantees privacy and is more efficient than existing ones, in terms of communication complexity.

1.2 Our Contributions

We propose some novel garbling schemes which satisfy authenticity only and are more efficient than general purpose garbling schemes[1]:

Privacy Free GRR1 with cheap XOR: In this garbling scheme we only send one ciphertext for each encrypted gate (both XOR and non-XOR). The circuit evaluator uses 3 calls to a *Key Derivation Function* (KDF) for each non-XOR gate, and none for each XOR gate (so from a computational point of view XOR gates are free). The scheme combines the row reduction technique with non-oblivious gate evaluation.

Privacy Free GRR2 with free-XOR: In this garbling scheme we send two ciphertexts for each encrypted non-XOR gate, and XOR gates are "for free". The circuit evaluator uses 3 calls to a KDF for each non-XOR gate (and none for XOR gates). The scheme is similar to GRR1, but using the free-XOR technique reduces the degrees of freedom we have in choosing the output keys and therefore require higher communication complexity for non-XOR gates.

Privacy Free fleXOR: In this garbling scheme we combine either our GRR1 or GRR2 scheme with the fleXOR technique of [KMR14]. The cost of non-XOR gates is unchanged from the previous scheme, i.e. one or two ciphertexts per gate respectively, but now the cost of XOR gate depends on the structure of the circuit: XOR gates require no cryptographic operations, while for communication, depending on the circuit structure, XOR gates require communication of 2, 1 or 0 ciphertexts. Also note that our fleXOR variant, being tailored for privacy-free garbled circuits, performs better than the original.

Furthermore, we present a formal generalization of garbling schemes with gates with arbitrary fan-in and show how to construct each of our privacy-free schemes in such a setting. It turns our that all types of our privacy-free garbled gates yield even more significant improvements in computation (and in some settings also communication) over general garbled garbles when fan-in is larger than two.

1.3 Overview of Our Schemes

In a nutshell, our garbling schemes work as follows: Consider a NAND gate, with associate input keys L^0, L^1, R^0, R^1 for the left and right wire respectively, and output keys O^0, O^1. The circuit constructor needs to provide the evaluator with a cryptographic gadget that, on input L^a, R^b, outputs the corresponding output key $O^{a \wedge b}$. Remember that our goal is not privacy, but only authenticity, meaning that the evaluator is allowed to learn a and b but even a corrupted evaluator should not learn $O^{1-(a \wedge b)}$. In particular, this means that the evaluator should learn O^0 if and only if (iff) he holds both L^1 and R^1. This can be ensured by encrypting O^0 under *both* L^1 and R^1.

---

[1] The naming convention here follows [PSSW09], where GRR stands for *garbled row reductions*.

On the other hand, it is enough that one of the inputs is 0 for the output to be 1, so it "should be enough" to hold L^0 or R^0 to learn O^1. In standard Yao GCs we do not want the evaluator to learn which of the three possible combinations of input keys he owns (nor the output of the gate) and therefore we encrypt O^1 under all the three possibilities in the same way as we encrypt the 0 key. But if the evaluator is allowed to know which bits keys correspond to, we can simply encrypt O^1 separately under L^0 and R^0, thus saving one encryption.

Note that, using the row-reduction technique, we can instead derive O^0 as $O^0 = \mathsf{KDF}(L^1, R^1)$ and therefore we can remove one ciphertext from the garbled table. We now have two-choices:

- If we want to be compatible with the free-XOR technique the value O^1 is already determined by O^0 and the global difference Δ, and thus no more row-reduction is possible.
- Alternatively we can decide to give up on free-XOR and derive O^1 as $O^1 = \mathsf{KDF}(L^0)$, thus removing yet another ciphertext from the garbled table, that now contains only the ciphertext $C = O^1 \oplus \mathsf{KDF}(R^0)$.

"Almost" free-XOR. If we choose the second path, we need an efficient way of garbling the XOR gates: we do so by defining the output keys O^0 and O^1 respectively as $O^0 = L^0 \oplus R^0$ and $O^1 = L^0 \oplus R^1$. Of course, it might be that at evaluation time the evaluator holds L^1 instead of L^0, and thus we provide him with an "advice" to compute the correct output key in this case. It turns out that it suffices to reveal the value $C = L^0 \oplus R^0 \oplus L^1 \oplus R^1$. Due to the symmetry of the XOR gate, now the evaluator can always derive the correct output key. Note that now XOR gates do not require any cryptographic operation but only the communication of a k-bit string (k being the security parameter), and therefore are "almost" for free.

The paranoid reader might now worry on whether revealing the XOR of all input keys affects the security of our scheme, and the impatient reader might not want to wait for the formal proof, which appears later in the paper: Intuitively revealing C does not represent a problem because, if it did, then the free-XOR technique would be insecure as well: In (standard) free-XOR the value C is always 0, as $L^0 \oplus L^1 = R^0 \oplus R^1$, and therefore known to the adversary already.

Privacy free fleXOR. Finally we combine our technique with the recent fleXOR garbling scheme [KMR14]. A central concept in fleXOR is to look, for each wire, at the XOR between the two keys associated to that wire, or the *offset* of that wire. While in freeXOR the offset is a constant for the whole circuit (therefore fixing half of the keys in the circuit), in fleXOR wires are ordered in a way to maximize the number of offsets which are the same, while at the same time leaving the circuit garbler the ability to choose freely the output keys for the non-XOR gates.

The fleXOR wire ordering induces a partitioning of the wires for each XOR gates. In particular, each XOR gates is assigned a parameter t which denotes how many input wires have offset *different* than the output wire. Then a 0-XOR gate can be garbled exactly like in free-XOR, while for t-XORs (with $t > 0$) the garbler sends t ciphertexts to the evaluator, which are used to "adjust" the offsets of those input wires. In the privacy-free case, exploiting non-oblivious gate evaluation, we can simply reveal the XOR of the offsets instead, exactly like in our GRR1 scheme. So, while the original fleXOR requires the garbler and the evaluator to perform $2t$ and t calls respectively to the KDF, we do not require any cryptographic operations for fleXOR gates.

Garbling XORs. To conclude this technical introduction, we would like to present the reader with a recap of the different ways in which XOR gates are garbled in this paper. Like before, let L^0, L^1, R^0, R^1, and O^0, O^1 be the keys for the left, right and output wire, and let Δ_L, Δ_R and Δ_O be their differences, the offsets associated to the wires. Now, the "baseline" garbling of a XOR gate is done as follows: the garbler sets $O^0 = L^0 \oplus R^0$, then computes and send to the evaluator the following values:

$$C_L = \Delta_L \oplus \Delta_O \text{ and } C_R = \Delta_R \oplus \Delta_O$$

Now, on input keys L_a, R_b, the evaluator retrieves

$$O^{a \oplus b} = L^a \oplus R^b \oplus a \cdot C_L \oplus b \cdot C_R$$

The baseline garbling transmits 2 ciphertexts, but in most cases we can do better.

GRR1: In this case the garbler can freely choose both Δ_O, which is set to be equal to Δ_L (so that $O^1 = L^1 \oplus R^0$) and therefore we do not need to communicate C_L, saving one ciphertexts w.r.t. the baseline.

free-XOR: Here it holds that $\Delta_L = \Delta_R = \Delta_O$, therefore both $C_L = C_R = 0$ and no ciphertexts need to be transfered.

fleXOR: a t-XOR gate is garbled like in the baseline garbling when $t = 2$, like in GRR1 when $t = 1$ and like free-XOR when $t = 0$.

1.4   Efficiency Improvements

Our garbling schemes offer different performances in terms of communication and computation overhead. It is natural to ask which one is the most efficient one. Like most interesting questions, the answer is not as simple as one might want, and to answer which garbling scheme offers the best performances one must define the price of communication vs. computation. The ultimate answer depends on the actual hardware setting (CPU, network) on which the protocol is to be run and can only be determined empirically.

In Table 1 and Table 2 we benchmark our garbling scheme against the best previous garbling schemes, on a number of circuits that we believe relevant for the zero-knowledge application that we have in mind e.g., proving "I know a secret x s.t., $y = \text{SHA}(x)$" for a y known to both the prover and the verifier.

Table 1. Comparison with other garbling schemes on some circuit examples from [ST12] in terms of communication complexity. The fleXOR scheme used is based on GRR1 and thus a "safe" topological ordering is assumed (see [KMR14]). The number in each cell shows the amortized number of ciphertext per gate that need to be sent. We ignore the inversion gates, as they can be pulled inside other kind of gates. The "Saving" column is computed against the previously best solution.

Circuit	Communication (amortized # of ciphertexts per gate)								
	# of Gates		Private			Privacy-free			Saving
	AND	XOR	GRR2	free-XOR	fleXOR	GRR1	free-XOR	fleXOR	
DES	18124	1340	2.0	2.79	1.89	1.0	1.86	**0.96**	49%
AES	6800	25124	2.0	0.64	0.72	1.0	**0.43**	0.51	33%
SHA-1	37300	24166	2.0	1.82	1.39	1.0	1.21	**0.78**	44%
SHA-256	90825	42029	2.0	2.05	1.56	1.0	1.37	**0.87**	44%

Table 2. Comparison with other garbling schemes on some circuit examples from [ST12] in terms of computational overhead. The fleXOR scheme used is based on a "safe" topological ordering (see [KMR14]). The number in each cell shows the amortized number of calls to a KDF per gate that the constructor/evaluator need to perform. (The evaluator always performs 1 KDF evaluation for non-free gates.) Note that we do not count the non cryptographic operations in this table (polynomial interpolation in GRR2, XOR of strings in all others). The "Saving" column is computed against the previously best solution.

Circuit	Computation (amortized # of encryptions per gate for garbler/evaluator)						
	# of Gates		Private			Privacy-free	Saving
	AND	XOR	GRR2	free-XOR	fleXOR	-	
DES	18124	1340	4.0/1.0	3.72/0.93	3.78/0.96	**2.79/0.93**	25%/0%
AES	6800	25124	4.0/1.0	0.85/0.21	1.44/0.51	**0.64/0.21**	25%/0%
SHA-1	37300	24166	4.0/1.0	2.43/0.61	2.78/0.78	**1.82/0.61**	25%/0%
SHA-256	90825	42029	4.0/1.0	2.73/0.68	3.11/0.87	**2.05/0.68**	25%/0%

The circuits used are due to Smart and Tillich and are publicly available [ST12]. Note however that the numbers in our tables depend on the actual circuits being used, meaning that it might be possible to find different circuits that compute the same functions but that are more favorable to one or another garbling scheme. Finding such circuits requires non-trivial heuristics and manual work (e.g., [BP12]), as there is evidence that finding such circuits is computationally hard [Fin14,KMR14].

Still, no previous garbling scheme performs better than *all* of our proposed schemes, therefore while the actual saving factor might change, one of our schemes will always outperforms the rest.

2 Preliminaries and Definitions

To keep the paper self-contained, we include the definitions for garbling schemes from [BHR12,BHKR13] in this section.

2.1 Notation

Let $\mathbb{N} = \{1, 2, \dots\}$ be the natural numbers, excluding 0. We write $[x, y]$ (with $x < y \in \mathbb{N}$) for $\{x, x+1, \dots, y\}$ and $[x]$ for $[1, x]$. We use $|\cdot|$ as a shorthand for the cardinality of a set or amount of bits in a string. If S is a set we use $x \in_R S$ to denote that x is a uniformly random sampled element from S. We let $\mathrm{poly}(\cdot)$ denote any polynomial of the argument.

Regarding variable names we let $k \in \mathbb{N}$ be the security parameter and call a function $\mathrm{negl} : \mathbb{N} \to \mathbb{R}^+$ negligible if for a big enough k it holds that $\mathrm{negl}(k) < 1/\mathrm{poly}(k)$. In general we use $\mathrm{negl}(\cdot)$ to denote any negligible function.

We let $L \subset \{0, 1\}^*$ be an arbitrary language in NP and M_L be the language verification function, i.e., for all $y \in L$ there exists a string $x \in \{0, 1\}^{\mathrm{poly}(|y|)}$ s.t. $M_L(x, y) = \texttt{accept}$ and for all $y \notin L$ and $x \in \{0, 1\}^*$ we have $M_L(x, y) = \texttt{reject}$.

2.2 Defining Our Garbling Scheme

We start by considering a plain description of a Boolean circuit with a single output bit, consisting of Boolean gates having arbitrary fan-in. This can be used to compute a Boolean function. The description is closely related to the ones in [BHR12,JKO13], but generalized to support gates with arbitrary fan-in along with non-oblivious gate evaluation.

Let f be a description of such a circuit, taking $n \in \mathbb{N}$ bits as input and consisting of $q \in \mathbb{N}$ internal gates. We let $r = n+q$ be the number of wires in the circuit and specifically define inputWires $= [n]$, Wires $= [n+q]$, outputWire $= n+q$ and Gates $= [n + 1, n + q]$, where inputWires represent the set of input wires, outputWire represents the output wire, Gates represents the set of Boolean gates of arbitrary fan-in and Wires the set of all wires in the circuit.

Next we let I be a function mapping each element of Gates to an integer describing the fan-in of that gate, i.e., $I : \mathsf{Gates} \to \mathbb{N}$. We let W be a function mapping an element of Gates, along with an integer i (representing a gate's i'th input wire) to an element in Wires. When calling W on some $g \in$ Gates we require that the i'th input wire is in $[I(g)]$, otherwise we return $\perp$. Thus, the signature for the method is $W : \mathsf{Gates} \times \mathbb{N} \to \{\mathsf{Wires} \backslash \mathsf{outputWire}\}^* \cup \{\perp\}$. We further require that $W(g, i) < W(g, i+1) < g$ for all $g \in$ Gates and $i \in [I(g) - 1]$ in order to avoid circularities in the circuit description.

Finally, we let G be a function taking as input an element of Gates along with an array of bits and returning a single bit or $\perp$. That is, $G : \mathsf{Gates} \times \{0, 1\}^* \to \{0, 1\} \cup \{\perp\}$. Specifically G is a description of the functionality of each gate in the circuit along with a short-circuit features such that $\perp$ is returned if the amount of elements in the binary input vector is not equal to the integer returned by I

when queried on the same gate index. More formally $G\left(g, \{b_i\}_{i \in [I(g)]}\right) \in \{0,1\}$ for all $g \in$ Gates, $b_i \in \{0,1\}$ and $\perp$ otherwise. Sometimes we abuse notation and simply write $G(g, b)$ if $g \in$ Gates and $b \in \{0,1\}^m$ when $I(g) = m$. We also say $G(g, \cdot) = $ NAND or $G(g, \cdot) = $ XOR if the truth table constructed from G is the truth table of a NAND, respectively, XOR gate.

Finally we combine all these functions and variables in f by letting $f = (n, q, I, W, G)$. However, we sometimes abuse notation and view f as a black box Boolean function, i.e., $f : \{0,1\}^n \to \{0,1\}$.

With this plain description of a Boolean circuit in hand we define a *verifiable* projective garbling scheme by a tuple

$$\mathcal{G} = (\mathsf{Gb}, \mathsf{En}, \mathsf{De}, \mathsf{Ev}, \mathsf{ev}, \mathsf{Ve})$$

such that:

- $\mathsf{Gb}(1^k, f) \to (F, e, d)$ is the *garbling function*, a randomized algorithm that takes as input a security parameter 1^k and a description of a Boolean function $(n, q, I, W, G) \leftarrow f$ under the constraint that $n = \mathrm{poly}(k)$, $n \geq k$ and $|f| = \mathrm{poly}(k)$. The function outputs a triple (F, e, d) representing a garbled circuit (F), input encoding information (e) and output decoding information (d).
- $\mathsf{En}(e, x) \to X$ is the *encoding function*, a deterministic function that uses the input encoding information e to map an input x to a *garbled input* X. We say a scheme is *projective* if $e = \left(\{X_i^0, X_i^1\}_{i \in [n]}\right)$ and the garbled input X is simply $\{X_i^{x_i}\}_{i \in [n]}$. In this paper we are only interested in projective schemes and therefore we do not use the En function explicitly.
- $\mathsf{Ev}(F, X, x) \to Z$ is the *evaluation function*, a deterministic functionality that produces an encoded output Z by evaluating a garbled circuit F on an encoded input X. We assume that for fixed F, the evaluation can output at most two values Z^0 and Z^1.
- $\mathsf{De}(d, Z) \to z$ is the *decoding function*, a deterministic functionality that, using the string d, decodes the encoded output Z into a plaintext bit, z. We are only interested in whether $z = 1$ (e.g., the NP relation accepts in the ZK setting), therefore we let $d = Z^1$ and $\mathsf{De}(d, Z)$ outputs $z = 1$ if $Z \stackrel{?}{=} Z^1$ and $z = 0$ otherwise.
- $\mathsf{ev}(f, x) \to b$ is the *plaintext evaluation function*, a deterministic functionality that evaluates the plain function described by f on some input x, i.e., $\mathsf{ev}(f, x) = f(x)$.
- $\mathsf{Ve}(F, f, e) \to b$ is the *verification function*, a deterministic functionality that on input a garbled circuit F, a description of a Boolean function f and the input encoding information $e = \{X_i^0, X_i^1\}_{i \in [n]}$ outputs 1 if the garbled circuit F computes the functionality f. Otherwise the functionality outputs 0.

We now list a number of properties that we require from a garbling scheme and refer to [BHR12, JKO13] for a detailed explanation of these definitions.

The following definition says that a correct evaluation of a correct garbling gives the right output.

Definition 1 (Correctness). *Let $\mathcal{G}$ be a verifiable projective garbling scheme described as above. We say that $\mathcal{G}$ enjoys* correctness *if for all $n = \text{poly}(k), f : \{0,1\}^n \to \{0,1\}$ and all $x \in \{0,1\}^n$ s.t. $f(x) = 1$ the following probability*

$$\Pr\left(\mathsf{Ev}\left(F, \{X_i^{x_i}\}_{i \in [n]}, x\right) \neq Z^1 : \left(F, \{X_i^0, X_i^1\}_{i \in [n]}, Z^1\right) \leftarrow \mathsf{Gb}\left(1^k, f\right)\right)$$

is negligible in k.

The following definition says that from a correct garbling of an input and a function outputting 0 on that input, you cannot find the decoding information for output 1, i.e., Z^1.

Definition 2 (Authenticity). *Let $\mathcal{G}$ be a verifiable projective garbling scheme described as above. We say that $\mathcal{G}$ enjoys* authenticity *if for all $n = \text{poly}(k), f : \{0,1\}^n \to \{0,1\}$ and all inputs $x \in \{0,1\}^n$ s.t. $f(x) = 0$ and for any probabilistic polynomial time (PPT) $\mathcal{A}$, the following probability:*

$$\Pr\left(\mathcal{A}\left(f, x, F, \{X_i^{x_i}\}_{i \in [n]}\right) = Z^1 : \left(F, \{X_i^0, X_i^1\}_{i \in [n]}, Z^1\right) \leftarrow \mathsf{Gb}\left(1^k, f\right)\right)$$

is negligible in k.

The following definition says that there is a unique garbled outputs corresponding to the output value 1, and that this unique value can be efficiently extracted given all the input labels. This holds also for maliciously generated circuits, as long as they pass the verification procedure. This implies that the garbled output value Z^1 leaks no information about the original input x except for the fact that $f(x) = 1$.

Definition 3 (Verifiability). *Let $\mathcal{G}$ be a verifiable projective garbling scheme described as above. We say that $\mathcal{G}$ enjoys* verifiability *if for all $n = \text{poly}(k), f : \{0,1\}^n \to \{0,1\}$ and all $x \in \{0,1\}^n$ with $f(x) = 1$ and for all PPT $\mathcal{A}$ there exists an expected polynomial time algorithm* Ext *such that*

$$\Pr\left(\mathrm{Ext}\left(F, \{X_i^0, X_i^1\}_{i \in [n]}\right) = \mathsf{Ev}\left(F, \{X_i^{x_i}\}_{i \in [n]}, x\right)\right) > 1 - \text{negl}(k)$$

when $\mathsf{Ve}\left(F, f, \{X_i^0, X_i^1\}_{i \in [n]}\right) = 1$ *and* $\left(F, \{X_i^0, X_i^1\}_{i \in [n]}\right) \leftarrow \mathcal{A}(1^k, f)$.

Finally, combining these definitions we get a definition of a secure verifiable, projective and privacy-free garbling scheme.

Definition 4 (Privacy-free Garbling Scheme). *Let $\mathcal{G}$ be a verifiable projective garbling scheme described as above. If this scheme enjoys* correctness, authenticity *and* verifiability *in accordance with Def. 1, Def. 2 and Def. 3 respectively, then $\mathcal{G}$ is a secure privacy-free garbling scheme.*

2.3   Key Derivation Function

We are going to use a "compressing" key derivation function $\mathsf{KDF} : \{0,1\}^* \to \{0,1\}^k$ mapping an arbitrary binary string to a pseudorandom string of k bits. The applications of the function will be of the form $K = \mathsf{KDF}(K_1, \ldots, K_m; id)$ for some $m \in \mathbb{N}$, where $K_i \in \{0,1\}^k$ is a wire key and $id \in \{0,1\}^*$ is a unique label or tweak.

We need a notion of security where the adversary cannot compute the output of the key derivation function except if he can do so trivially because he knows the entire input. Specifically we let keys be fresh uniformly random values, derived or linear combinations of other keys, and id be publicly known. We require that the adversary cannot guess a key derived from at least one uniformly random key, "uncompromised" derived key or linear combination of keys where at least one is "uncompromised". An uncompromised derived key is one that was derived from at least one uniformly random key, uncompromised derived key or linear combination where at least one key in the combination was uncompromised. We allow the adversary to compromise keys by leaking them and construct new keys through linear combinations or key derivations. Furthermore, we call a (potential) key compromised if the leaked keys allow to determine the key, in which case the adversary can trivially compute it. More precisely:

Definition 5 (Game KDF). *Let $\mathcal{A}$ be any PPT adversary and consider the following game:*

Initialize: *Let* $\mathsf{ID} \leftarrow \emptyset$ *be a set of identifiers used by the adversary and let* $\mathsf{LEAK} \leftarrow \emptyset$ *be the set of identifiers that should be leaked.*

Query: *Let $\mathcal{A}$ make an arbitrary amount of calls, in any combination, to the following methods:*

Fresh key: *If $\mathcal{A}$ outputs (**fresh key**, $id \notin \mathsf{ID}$), then sample $K_{id} \in_R \{0,1\}^k$ and store (id, K_{id}) and let $\mathsf{ID} \leftarrow \mathsf{ID} \cup \{id\}$.*

Linear: *If $\mathcal{A}$ outputs (**linear**, $id_0 \notin \mathsf{ID}, id_1, \ldots, id_m$) where $id_i \in \mathsf{ID}$ for all $i \in [m]$, then compute $K_{id_0} \leftarrow \bigoplus_{i=1}^m K_{id_i}$, store (id_0, K_{id_0}), and let $\mathsf{ID} \leftarrow \mathsf{ID} \cup \{id_0\}$.*

Derive: *If $\mathcal{A}$ outputs (**derive**, $id_0 \notin \mathsf{ID}, id_1, \ldots, id_m$) where $id_i \in \mathsf{ID}$ for all $i \in [m]$, then compute $K_{id_0} \leftarrow \mathsf{KDF}(K_{id_1}, \ldots, K_{id_m}; id_0)$, store (id_0, K_{id_0}) and let $\mathsf{ID} \leftarrow \mathsf{ID} \cup \{id_0\}$.*

Leak: *If $\mathcal{A}$ outputs (**leak**, $id \in \mathsf{ID}$) set $\mathsf{LEAK} = \mathsf{LEAK} \cup \{id\}$.*

End: *When $\mathcal{A}$ outputs (**end**) then return the set $\{K_i\}_{i \in \mathsf{LEAK}}$ to $\mathcal{A}$.*

Guess: *When $\mathcal{A}$ outputs (**guess**, id^*, K^*) for $id^* \in \mathsf{ID}$, then the adversary wins if $K^* = K_{id^*}$ and id^* was not compromised, i.e., if $id^* \notin \mathsf{COMP}$, see below.*

*We define the set COMP of IDs of compromised keys iteratively as follows: Define a linear system LIN over formal variables X_{id} and c_{id} for $id \in \mathsf{ID}$. For each linear query (**linear**, $id_0, id_1, \ldots, id_m$) add the equation $\bigoplus_{i=1}^m X_{id_i} = X_{id_0}$ to LIN. For each leakage command (**leak**, $id \in \mathsf{ID}$), add the equation $X_{id} = c_{id}$ to LIN. In the following we call an identifier id^* determined in LIN if the linear system LIN allows to write X_{id^*} as a linear combination of the variables c_{id} for $id \in \mathsf{ID}$.*

We use Det(LIN) *to denote the set of identifiers that are determined in* LIN. *We call id* derivable in* LIN *if there was a command* (**derive**, $id^*, id_1, \ldots, id_m$) *and* $id_i \in$ Det(LIN) *for each* $i \in [m]$. *We use* Der(LIN) *to denote the set of identifiers that are derivable in* LIN. *We define an extension* LIN' = Ext(LIN) *by letting* LIN' *be* LIN *but with the equation* $X_{id^*} = c_{id^*}$ *added for each id* $\in$* Der(LIN). *Define* $\text{LIN}_0 = \text{LIN}$ *and* $\text{LIN}_{i+1} = \text{Ext}(\text{LIN}_i)$. *There are finitely many variables, so this has a fixed index j such that* $\text{LIN}_{j+1} = \text{Ext}(\text{LIN}_j)$. *We let* COMP = LIN_j.

We use $\text{GUESS}_{\text{KDF},\mathcal{A}}(1^k)$ to denote the probability that $\mathcal{A}$ wins the game. Using this game we define the notion of a secure key derivation function.

Definition 6 (Secure Key Derivation Function). *We say that a* KDF($\cdot$) *is secure if the advantage of any PPT adversary $\mathcal{A}$ playing the* KDF *game is negligible in k, i.e.*

$$\text{GUESS}_{\text{KDF},\mathcal{A}}(1^k) \leq \text{negl}(k)$$

for some negligible function negl($\cdot$).

It can be proven using standard techniques that a (non-programmable, non-extractable) random oracle is a secure KDF in the above sense. More precisely:

Theorem 1. *If* KDF($\cdot$) *is modeled by a non-programmable, non- extractable random oracle with k bits output then for any PPT $\mathcal{A}$ it holds that* $\text{GUESS}_{\text{KDF},\mathcal{A}}(1^k) \leq$ negl(k) *for some negligible function* negl($\cdot$).

The proof appears in the full version [FNO14].

We leave as future work the investigation of which exact computational assumptions are required for implementing our different garbling schemes: while it is clear that the freeXOR and fleXOR variant require strong notion of security (security under related-key attack and a flavor of circular security), it seems that the GRR1 variant could be instantiated using standard security notions.

3   Our Privacy-Free Garbling Schemes

In this section we present our novel garbling schemes. Our schemes support gates with arbitrary fan-in, but as a warm-up we first present the garbling schemes for gates with fan-in 2 using GRR1 or GRR2 with free-XOR. Both allow to garble every Boolean gate with fan-in 2 using only 3 calls to the KDF for non-XOR gates and require no calls to the KDF for XOR gates.

Our first scheme has communication complexity of k bits per gate while our second garbling scheme is compatible with "free-XOR", but requires communication complexity of $2k$ bits for non-XOR gates.

Afterwards we present our two schemes for gates with arbitrary fan-in and in Section 4 a scheme that supports the recent fleXOR approach [KMR14].

Table 3. Exact performances of our privacy-free garbling scheme. The "Garb." and "Eval." column state the number of calls to a KDF required for garbling and evaluation respectively, as a function of the gate fan-in m. The column "Size" states the number of bits added to the garbled circuit for each gate. We only report the fleXOR variant based on "Safe" wire ordering.

		Garb.	Eval.	Size
GRR1	NAND	$m + 1$	1	$k(m - 1)$
	XOR	0	0	$k(m - 1)$
Free-XOR	NAND	$m + 1$	1	km
	XOR	0	0	0
FleXOR	NAND	$m + 1$	1	$k(m - 1)$
	t-XOR	0	0	kt

3.1   Warm-Up

To simplify notation and give the intuition of our scheme we here only describe how to garble/evaluate a single NAND or XOR gate. We call the input keys to the left wire of a gate L^0, L^1, the input keys to the right wire R^0, R^1 and the output keys O^0, O^1. All these values are elements of $\{0, 1\}^k$.

Again we point out that in contrast with general garbled circuits, in our case if the circuit evaluator has two keys L^a, R^b, he knows the corresponding bits a, b.

First consider a NAND gate with GRR1:

Garbling a GRR1 NAND Gate: Let $O^0 = \mathsf{KDF}\left(L^1, R^1\right)$ and $O^1 = \mathsf{KDF}\left(L^0\right)$. Compute $C = \mathsf{KDF}\left(R^0\right) \oplus O^1$ and output C.

Evaluating a GRR1 NAND Gate: To evaluate on input L^a, R^b, if $a = b = 1$ then output $O^0 = \mathsf{KDF}\left(L^1, R^1\right)$ otherwise, if $a = 0$ compute $O^1 = \mathsf{KDF}\left(L^0\right)$. Otherwise, if $b = 0$ compute $O^1 = C \oplus \mathsf{KDF}\left(R^0\right)$.

It should be clear that the scheme is correct. The intuition of authenticity is that if the evaluator only knows one input key for each wire, he can only learn one output key unless he can guess the output of KDF on an input he does not know. Next consider a XOR gate:

Garbling a GRR1 XOR Gate: Let $O^0 = L^0 \oplus R^0$ along with $O^1 = L^0 \oplus R^1$. Finally output $C = L^0 \oplus L^1 \oplus R^0 \oplus R^1$.

Evaluating a GRR1 XOR Gate: On input L^a, R^b if $a = 0$ then output $O^{a \oplus b} = L^a \oplus R^b$. Otherwise compute and return $O^{a \oplus b} = C \oplus L^a \oplus R^b$.

Again, it should be clear that the scheme is correct. The authenticity intuitively follows from the fact that the evaluator can only learn the XOR of two unknown keys which will not help decrypting the next gate.

Now consider how to achieve the same, while allowing support for free-XOR gates (and in turn GRR2). In this scheme there is a global difference Δ s.t., for all wires w in a garbled circuit, the key pair X_w^0, X_w^1 satisfies $X_w^0 \oplus X_w^1 = \Delta$.

Garbling a GRR2 NAND Gate: Let $O^0 = \mathsf{KDF}\left(L^1, R^1\right)$. This defines $O^1 = O^0 \oplus \Delta$ as well. Let $C_L = \mathsf{KDF}\left(L^0\right) \oplus O^1$ and $C_R = \mathsf{KDF}\left(R^0\right) \oplus O^1$. Finally output $\{C_L, C_R\}$.

Evaluating a GRR2 NAND Gate: To evaluate on input L^a, R^b, if $a = b = 1$ then output $O^0 = \mathsf{KDF}\left(L^1, R^1\right)$ otherwise, if $a = 0$ output $O^1 = \mathsf{KDF}\left(L^0\right) \oplus C_L$ otherwise output $O^1 = \mathsf{KDF}(R^0) \oplus C_R$.

Next consider a XOR gate:

Garbling a free-XOR Gate: Let $O^0 = L^0 \oplus R^0$. This defines $O^1 = O^0 \oplus \Delta$ as well. Output nothing.

Evaluating a free-XOR Gate: On input L^a, R^b, output $O^{a \oplus b} = L^a \oplus R^b$.

Again correctness should be clear and authenticity for NAND gates follow from the same argument as for GRR1 NAND gates, whereas authenticity follows from the security of free-XOR, i.e. that it is hard to learn Δ, unless one is given both keys on some wire.

3.2   Generalization Intuition

We now consider how our approaches generalizes to gates with arbitrary fan-in.

NAND gates. Consider a NAND gate with fan-in m, call this gate g. Recall that for this gate the output bit $b_g = 0$ should occur exactly if all the input bits are equal to 1, $b_1 = b_2 = \ldots = b_m = 1$. This means that we can define the output key representing bit 0 directly from these: If we denote the key on input wire i by $X_i^{b_i}$, then the output 0-key is computed as

$$X_g^0 = \mathsf{KDF}\left(X_1^1, X_2^1, \ldots, X_m^1\right) \ .$$

Now, if we are not using a free-XOR scheme we define the 1-output key to be $X_g^1 = \mathsf{KDF}\left(X_1^0\right)$. Then the entries in the garbled computation table is as follows:

$$\left\{C_i = X_g^1 \oplus \mathsf{KDF}\left(X_i^0\right)\right\}_{i=2}^m \ .$$

When we are using a free-XOR scheme we have another entry in the garbled computation table since the output key X_g^1 needs to meet the constraint $X_g^1 = X_g^0 \oplus \Delta$ and thus we cannot define it to simply be $\mathsf{KDF}\left(X_1^0\right)$. However, similarly to the scheme above that does not use free-XOR we use the KDF applied to the first input key (which we have not used to hide anything in the scheme above) to hide X_g^1. We let the rest of the table remain as before and thus the whole garbled computation table is computed as follows:

$$\left\{C_i = X_g^1 \oplus \mathsf{KDF}\left(X_i^0\right)\right\}_{i=1}^m \ .$$

We describe the evaluation: Call the input keys $X_1^{b_1'}, X_2^{b_2'}, \ldots, X_m^{b_m'}$. If $b_i' = 1$ for all $i \in [m]$ then the output is $X_g^0 = \mathsf{KDF}\left(X_1^1, X_2^1, \ldots, X_m^1\right)$. Otherwise find the first value of i for which $b_i' \neq 1$ and output $X_g^1 = C_i \oplus \mathsf{KDF}\left(X_i^0\right)$, except if $i = 1$ and we do not use a free-XOR garbling scheme, in which case the output is $X_g^1 = \mathsf{KDF}\left(X_1^0\right)$.

XOR gates. To garble XOR gates (when we are not using the free-XOR method), we define the output 0-key from information based on all the input 0-keys. Specifically as

$$X_g^0 = X_1^0 \oplus X_2^0 \oplus \cdots \oplus X_m^0 = \bigoplus_{i=1}^{m} X_i^0 \ .$$

In a similar manner we define the output 1-key from information based on the first input 1-key and all the other input 0-keys, that is

$$X_g^1 = X_1^1 \oplus X_2^0 \oplus \cdots \oplus X_{m-1}^0 \oplus X_m^0 = X_1^1 \oplus \left(\bigoplus_{i=2}^{m} X_i^0 \right) \ .$$

Let b_i, for all $i \in [m]$ be the input bits at evaluation time and $b_g = b_1 \oplus \ldots \oplus b_m$ be the output of that gate. It might be the case that $b_1 \neq 1$ or that there are other j s.t., $b_j = 1$. So we let the garbled computation table consist of information which makes it possible for the evaluator to compute the right output key in any such situation. Specifically we define the table as the following set:

$$\{ C_i = X_i^0 \oplus X_i^1 \oplus X_1^0 \oplus X_1^1 \}_{i=2}^{m} \ .$$

It is clear that, for any $j \neq 1$

$$\left(\bigoplus_{i \in [m]} X_i^{b_i} \right) \oplus C_j = X_1^{b_1 \oplus 1} \oplus X_j^{b_j \oplus 1} \bigoplus_{j \neq i > 2} X_i^{b_i}$$

Thus by XORing all the C_i's for which $b_i = 1$ we obtain

$$\left(\bigoplus_{i \in [m]} X_i^{b_i} \right) \oplus \left(\bigoplus_{i : b_i = 1} C_i \right) = X_1^{b_1 \oplus \ldots \oplus b_m} \oplus \left(\bigoplus_{i : b_i = 0} X_i^0 \right) \oplus \left(\bigoplus_{i : b_i = 1} X_i^{1 \oplus 1} \right) = X_g^{b_g}$$

Other gates. It is easy to see that our garbling scheme can be applied also to few other kind of gates such as AND, (N)OR, XNOR etc., also in the case of high fan-in (by using a different partitioning of the inputs and relabeling the outputs) but it cannot be used in for generic, "unstructured" gates of high fan-in.

Using high fan-in gates. Note that our garbling scheme is favorable for gates with high fan-in, since the complexity shown in Table 3 (both in terms of communication and computational complexity) only grows linearly with the gate fan-in, while a straightforward use of standard garbled circuit leads in a exponential blow-up in the gate fan-in. Even when comparing the garbling of a gate with fan-in m to a circuit implementing the same functionality (e.g., a tree of fan-in 2 NANDs to implement a NAND with fan-in m) our scheme is still favorable. Depending on the garbling scheme we can save a factor 2-3 in terms of computation for the garbler and also save in communication. In addition, the evaluator has an overhead of $\log(m)$ when evaluating the circuit (versus a single call to the KDF in our case).

3.3 Formal Specification

We describe our gate garbling schemes in the same notation as [BHR12], but with some changes in order to reflect that we only require privacy, only assume one bit output and that we support gates of arbitrary fan-in. The specification of the garbling scheme is given in Fig. 1 and the realizations for individual gate garbling is given in Fig. 2 and Fig. 3, depending on whether or not one uses free-XOR or GRR1.

To enhance understanding we describe each step of these procedures.

The Garbling Scheme. The first method, Gb, constructs a garbled circuit, F, along with information, e, to encode a binary string as garbled input to this garbled circuit and information, d, to check if the output of an evaluation of the garbled circuit has the semantic value 1. The method takes as input a security parameter 1^k and a description of the Boolean function to be computed, f. The format of the function description should be in accordance with the description given in Section 2.2, and thus can be viewed directly as a Boolean circuit. In step 1 the algorithm chooses two keys for each of the n input bits to f, in accordance with the specific type of garbling scheme used. These are the 0-, respectively, 1-input keys. Step 2 involves iteratively constructing each of the q garbled gates of the circuit, along with the two output keys needed for each of these gates. It is done by first using I to decide the fan-in of a given gate, then using G to find the specific functionality of the given gate. Finally the input keys for that gate (which have already been constructed) are loaded using W and all the information is passed to the gate garbling method Garb. In step 3 the garbled circuit, F, is set to include all the information of f along with the garbled computation table returned by Garb in the previous step for all the gates in the circuit. These tables are called P. Furthermore, the encoding information e is set to be the two keys for each input wire and the decoding information d is set to be the output 1-key of the final gate in the circuit. In the last step, the garbled circuit F, the input encoding information, e, and decoding information, d, is returned.

The second method, En, constructs an ordered set of input keys to a garbled circuit, X. It takes as input the encoding information e (along with a binary string x of length n) representing the input to the garbled circuit. In the first step the method parses e as n ordered pairs of keys. In step 2 the functionality returns an ordered subset of the keys. In particular if the i'th bit of x is 0 then the i'th element in the ordered set is the i'th 0-key, otherwise it is the i'th 1-key.

The third method, De, evaluates whether some value, Z, is equal to the output 1-key of a garbled circuit, d. It takes as input the decoding information of a garbled circuit, d, along with a potential output key, Z. The method only has one step which checks if $d = Z$ and returns 1 if that is true, otherwise it returns 0.

The fourth method, Ev, evaluates a garbled circuit, F, and returns the output key of the final gate as a result of this evaluation, Z. It takes as input a garbled circuit F, and an ordered set of input keys, X, along with a binary vector x

$\mathsf{Gb}\left(1^k, f\right) \rightarrow (F, e, d)$

   1. Set $(n, q, I, W, G) \leftarrow f$ and $\left\{X_i^0, X_i^1\right\}_{i \in [n]} \leftarrow \mathsf{InKeys}(n, k)$.

   2. For each $g \in [n+1, n+q]$ set $m = I(g)$ and define $G' : \{0, 1\}^m \rightarrow \{0, 1\}$ s.t. $G'(i) = G(g, i)$ for all $i \in \{0, 1\}^m$ and set $\left\{\left(X_g^0, X_g^1\right), P[g]\right\} \leftarrow \mathsf{Garb}\left(g, G', \left\{X_{W(g,i)}^0, X_{W(g,i)}^1\right\}_{i \in [m]}\right)$.

   3. Set $F \leftarrow (n, q, I, W, G, P)$, $e \leftarrow \left\{X_i^0, X_i^1\right\}_{i \in [n]}$ and $d \leftarrow X_{n+q}^1$.

   4. Finally return (F, e, d).

$\mathsf{En}(e, x) \rightarrow X$

   1. Set $\left\{X_i^0, X_i^1\right\}_{i \in [n]} \leftarrow e$.

   2. Then set $X \leftarrow \left\{X_i^{x_i}\right\}_{i \in [n]}$ and return X.

$\mathsf{De}(d, Z) \rightarrow b$

   1. If $d = Z$ then output 1 otherwise output 0.

$\mathsf{Ev}(F, X, x) \rightarrow Z$

   1. Set $(n, q, I, W, G, P) \leftarrow F$ and for all $i \in [n]$ set $w_i = x_i$ and define $Q = \{w_i\}_{i \in [n]}$.

   2. For each $g \in [n+1, n+q]$ let $m = I(g)$ and add $w_g = G\left(g, \{w_{W(g,i)}\}_{i \in [m]}\right)$ to the set Q.

   3. Now for each $g \in [n+1, n+q]$ let $m = I(g)$ and define $G' : \{0, 1\}^m \rightarrow \{0, 1\}$ s.t. $G'(i) = G(g, i)$ and $w' \in \{0, 1\}^m$ s.t. $w'_i = w_{W(g,i)}$ for all $i \in [m]$ and set $X_g \leftarrow \mathsf{Eval}\left(g, G', w', \{X_{W(g,i)}\}_{i \in [m]}, P[g]\right)$.

   4. Return X_{n+q}.

$\mathsf{ev}(f, x) \rightarrow b$

   1. Set $(n, q, I, W, G) \leftarrow f$ and for all $i \in [n]$ set $w_i = x_i$ and define $Q \leftarrow \{w_i\}_{i \in [n]}$.

   2. For each $g \in [n+1, n+q]$ let $m = I(g)$ and add $w_g = G\left(g, \{w_{W(g,i)}\}_{i \in [m]}\right)$ to the set Q.

   3. Finally return w_{n+q}.

$\mathsf{Ve}(F, f, e) \rightarrow b$

   1. Set $(n, q, I, W, G, P) \leftarrow F$, $(n', q', I', W', G') \leftarrow f$ and $\left\{X_i^0, X_i^1\right\}_{i \in [n]} \leftarrow e$.

   2. If $n \neq n'$, $q \neq q'$, $I \neq I'$, $W \neq W'$ or $G \neq G'$ output 0.

   3. For each $g \in [n+1, n+q]$ let $m = I(g)$ and define $G' : \{0, 1\}^m \rightarrow \{0, 1\}$ s.t. $G'(i) = G(g, i)$ for all $i \in \{0, 1\}^m$ and set $\left\{\left(X_g^0, X_g^1\right), \bar{P}[g]\right\} \leftarrow \mathsf{Garb}\left(g, G', \left\{X_{W(g,i)}^0, X_{W(g,i)}^1\right\}_{i \in [m]}\right)$.

   4. If for any $g \in [n+1, n+q]$ we have $\bar{P}[g] \neq P[q]$ output 0, otherwise output 1.

Fig. 1. Privacy-free Garbling

where the i'th bit represents the semantic value of the i'th input key. In step 1 the method parses the information stored in the garbled circuit F and defines an ordered set of bits, Q, which represents the bits on each each wire in the garbled circuit. Initially this set only includes the bits of the input wires. Step 2 iteratively evaluates the garbled circuit one gate at a time. It first finds the fan-in of a given gate using I and then evaluates the gate in plain using the set Q along with the gate description G. After evaluating the gate in plain it updates

Q to contain the output bit of the given gate. Thus at the end Q contains the expected bit on each wire given the garbled circuit F and the binary input x. In step 3 the method proceeds to evaluate each garbled gate iteratively. Again it uses I to learn the fan-in for a given gate, it uses G to decode the specific functionality of the gate and the elements of Q to find the semantic meaning of the keys supposed to be input to the garbled gate. Using this information, along with the garbled computation table of the gate, P, it calls Eval to evaluate the garbled gate and stores the output key which the method returns. Finally in step 4 it returns the output key of the final gate in the garbled circuit.

The fifth method, ev, evaluates the Boolean functionality f in plain using a binary input vector x. It returns a bit being the value $f(x)$. In Step 1 it parses the functionality f and constructs a set Q which represents the bit on each wire in the circuit. Initially this set only contains the bits on the input wires, exactly as specified by x. In step 2 it iteratively evaluates each gate of the functionality. It does so by first learning the fan-in of the give gate using I and then using G with the given gate index and bits already stored in Q. It updates the set Q with the result. Finally it returns the result of evaluating the final gate in the circuit.

The sixth and last method, Ve, checks whether a garbled circuit, F, evaluates the same as some plain circuit, f, given both pairs of input keys for all wires of the garbled circuit, e. The method returns either 1 (for accept) or 0 (for reject). It takes as input a garbled circuit F, a plain description of the circuit functionality f along with the ordered set of input keys, e. In the first step it parses the garbled circuit F and the plain function description f. Step 2 is a sanity check which verifies that the "meta" data of F and f is the same, i.e., same amount of input bits, n, the same amount of gates q, each with the same fan-in I, using the same wires, W, and computing the same functionality, G. If any of these checks fail the method outputs reject. Then step 3 iteratively constructs a new garbled circuit using Garb in the same manner as in Gb, based on the information in f. Finally in step 4 the method checks equality of each garbled computation table given in F with each of the tables generated in the previous step. If any are not equal then the method outputs reject, otherwise it outputs accept.

Gate Garbling. All of our garbling schemes have two methods: Garb and Eval. The first constructs a garbled gate, $\tilde{g}$, and two keys, (X_g^0, X_g^1). It takes as input a nonce, g (gate ID), a function mapping a binary vector to a bit, G', along with a pair of input keys for each input wire to the gate. The second method reconstructs a single output key. It takes as input a nonce, g (gate ID), a function mapping a binary vector to a bit, G', a binary vector describing the bits on the input wires to the gate, w', an ordered set of input keys $\{X_i\}_{i \in [m]}$ along with an ordered set which is the garbled computation table $\tilde{g}$.[2] Two concrete schemes are shown in Fig. 2 and Fig. 3.

---

[2] Note that, as it is described, the running time of Eval depends on the particular input used. To prevent leakage of the input based on timing attacks, any implementation of Eval would need to take appropriate countermeasures, and ensure that the running time does not depend on the input used.

$\mathsf{InKeys}(n, k) \rightarrow \left\{ X_i^0, X_i^1 \right\}_{i \in [n]}$

    1. For each $i \in [n]$ sample uniformly random $X_i^0, X_i^1 \in_R \{0,1\}^k$ and return the set $\left\{ X_i^0, X_i^1 \right\}_{i \in [n]}$.

$\mathsf{Garb}\left(g, G', \left\{ \left(X_i^0, X_i^1 \right) \right\}_{i \in [m]} \right) \rightarrow \left\{ \left(X_g^0, X_g^1 \right), \tilde{g} \right\}$

    1. If $G'(\cdot) = \mathrm{NAND}$

        do as follows:

        (a) Let $X_g^0 = \mathsf{KDF}\left(X_1^1, X_2^1, \ldots, X_m^1; (\mathbf{key}, g, 0) \right)$ and $X_g^1 = \mathsf{KDF}\left(X_1^0; (\mathbf{key}, g, 1) \right)$.

        (b) Next let $C_i = X_g^1 \oplus \mathsf{KDF}\left(X_i^0; (\mathbf{inte}, g, i) \right)$ for all $i \in [2, m]$ and set $\tilde{g} = \{C_i\}_{i=2}^m$.

        (c) Return $\left\{ \left(X_g^0, X_g^1 \right), \tilde{g} \right\}$.

    2. If instead $G'(\cdot) = \mathrm{XOR}$ do as follows:

        (a) Let $X_g^0 = \bigoplus_{i=1}^m X_i^0$ and $X_g^1 = X_1^1 \oplus \left(\bigoplus_{i=2}^m X_i^0 \right)$.

        (b) Next let $C_i = X_1^0 \oplus X_1^1 \oplus X_i^0 \oplus X_i^1$ for all $i \in [2, m]$ and set $\tilde{g} = \{C_i\}_{i=2}^m$.

        (c) Return $\left\{ \left(X_g^0, X_g^1 \right), \tilde{g} \right\}$.

$\mathsf{Eval}\left(g, G', w', \{X_i\}_{i \in [m]}, \tilde{g} \right) \rightarrow \{X_g\}$

    1. If $G'(\cdot) = \mathrm{NAND}$ do as follows:

        (a) If $w' = 1^m$ then set $X_g = \mathsf{KDF}\left(X_1, X_2, \ldots, X_m; (\mathbf{key}, g, 0) \right)$. If instead $w_1' = 0$ then set $X_g = \mathsf{KDF}\left(X_1; (\mathbf{key}, g, 1) \right)$. Otherwise find the first $i \in [2, m]$ s.t. $w_i' = 0$, parse $\{C_i\}_{i=2}^m \leftarrow \tilde{g}$ and set $X_g = C_i \oplus \mathsf{KDF}\left(X_i; (\mathbf{inte}, g, i) \right)$.

        (b) Return X_g.

    2. If instead $G'(\cdot) = \mathrm{XOR}$ do as follows:

        (a) Parse $\{C_i\}_{i=2}^m \leftarrow \tilde{g}$.

        (b) Let S be the set of $i \in \{2, m\}$ for which it is true that $w_i' = 1$.

        (c) Return $X_g = \left(\bigoplus_{i \in [m]} X_i \right) \oplus \left(\bigoplus_{i \in S} C_i \right)$.

Fig. 2. Garbling GRR1 - Without free-XOR

3.4 Security

The scheme presented in Fig. 1 composed with Fig. 2 and Fig. 3 respectively are clearly correct. In fact, any correctly generated scheme evaluates to the correct output key with probability 1. From this it also follows that the schemes have verifiability, as we verify by regenerating each garbled gate, and hence a verified garbled gate is correctly generated. This takes care of the demands of correctness (Def. 1) and verifiability (Def. 3) of a secure privacy-free garbling scheme, as defined in Def. 4. What remains is authenticity (Def. 2): In the following we reduce this to the security of the KDF used.

Theorem 2. *If the* KDF *used in the garbling scheme of Fig. 1 composed with Fig. 2 is secure according to Def. 6, then the composed scheme enjoys authenticity according to Def. 2.*

Proof. For notational convenience we are going to focus on the case with fan-in 2. The proof idea generalizes immediately.

$\mathsf{InKeys}(n,k) \rightarrow \left\{ X_i^0, X_i^1 \right\}_{i \in [n]}$

   1. Sample a uniformly random difference $\Delta \in \{0,1\}^k$.
   2. Then for each $i \in [n]$ sample uniformly random $X_i^0 \in_R \{0,1\}^k$ and return
      the set $\left\{ X_i^0, X_i^0 \oplus \Delta \right\}_{i \in [n]}$.

$\mathsf{Garb}\left(g, G', \left\{ \left(X_i^0, X_i^1 \right) \right\}_{i \in [m]} \right) \rightarrow \left\{ \left(X_g^0, X_g^1 \right), \tilde{g} \right\}$

   1. Set $\Delta = X_1^0 \oplus X_1^1$.
   2. If $G'(\cdot) = \mathrm{NAND}$ do as follows:
     (a) Let $X_g^0 = \mathsf{KDF}\left(X_1^1, X_2^1, \ldots, X_m^1; (\mathtt{key}, g, 0) \right)$ and $X_g^1 = X_g^0 \oplus \Delta$.
     (b) Next let $C_i = X_g^1 \oplus \mathsf{KDF}\left(X_i^0; (\mathtt{inte}, g, i) \right)$ for all $i \in [m]$ and set
        $\tilde{g} = \{C_i\}_{i=1}^m$.
     (c) Return $\left\{ \left(X_g^0, X_g^1 \right), \tilde{g} \right\}$.
   3. If instead $G'(\cdot) = \mathrm{XOR}$ set $X_g^0 = \bigoplus_{i=1}^m X_i^0$, $X_g^1 = X_g^0 \oplus \Delta$ and return
     $\left\{ \left(X_g^0, X_g^1 \right), \perp \right\}$.

$\mathsf{Eval}\left(g, G', w', \{X_i\}_{i \in [m]}, \tilde{g} \right) \rightarrow \{X_g\}$

   1. If $G'(\cdot) = \mathrm{NAND}$ do as follows: If $w' = 1^m$ then set $X_g = \mathsf{KDF}\left(X_1, X_2, \ldots, X_m; (\mathtt{key}, g, 0) \right)$. Otherwise find the first $i \in [m]$ s.t. $w_i' = 0$, parse $\{C_i\}_{i=1}^m \leftarrow \tilde{g}$ and compute and return $X_g = C_i \oplus \mathsf{KDF}\left(X_i; (\mathtt{inte}, g, i) \right)$.
   2. If instead $G'(\cdot) = \mathrm{XOR}$ return $X_g = \bigoplus_{i=1}^m X_i$.

Fig. 3. Garbling GRR2 - With free-XOR

A NAND gate with input keys L^0, L^1 for the left wire and R^0, R^1 for the right wire and gate identifier g is garbled as follows:

$$O^1 \leftarrow \mathsf{KDF}(L^0; (\mathtt{key}, g, 1)) , \tag{1}$$

$$O^0 \leftarrow \mathsf{KDF}(L^1, R^1; (\mathtt{key}, g, 0)) , \tag{2}$$

$$A \leftarrow \mathsf{KDF}(R^0; (\mathtt{inte}, g)) , \tag{3}$$

$$C \leftarrow A \oplus O^1 (\text{with label } (\mathtt{garb}, g)) . \tag{4}$$

The output keys are (O^0, O^1). The garbled gate is just C.

An XOR gate with input keys L^0, L^1 for the left wire and R^0, R^1 for the right wire and gate identifier g is garbled as follows:

$$O^0 \leftarrow L^0 \oplus R^0 \text{ (with label } (\mathtt{key}, g, 0)) , \tag{5}$$

$$O^1 \leftarrow L^0 \oplus R^1 \text{ (with label } (\mathtt{key}, g, 1)) , \tag{6}$$

$$C \leftarrow L^0 \oplus L^1 \oplus R^0 \oplus R^1 \text{ (with label } (\mathtt{garb}, g)) . \tag{7}$$

The output keys are (O^0, O^1). The garbled gate is just C.

Besides this, the circuit garbling just consist of reusing the appropriate output keys as input keys to later gates. A garbled circuit F consists of, amongst other, a garbled gate for each of the q internal wires, $P = (C_{n+1}, \ldots, C_{n+q})$, in an order in which they can be evaluated. For each garbled gate C_i, let L_i^0 and L_i^1 be the corresponding keys on the left input wire, let R_i^0 and R_i^1 be the corresponding keys on the right input wire, and let O_i^0 and O_i^1 be the output keys.

We can assume without loss of generality that the last gate is the output gate. For a garbled input $X = \{(X_i^0, X_i^1)\}_{i=1}^{n}$ and a plaintext input $x \in \{0,1\}^n$, let $X^x = \{X_i^{x_i}\}_{i \in [n]}$ be the garbled version of x. For $i = n+1, \ldots, n+q$, let w_i be the bit we get by computing plaintext gate number i on the bits for its input wires, that is $w_i = G(i, \{W(i,1), W(i,2)\})$ in accordance with Fig. 1. This defines a *plaintext evaluation* $w = (w_1, \ldots, w_n, w_{n+1}, \ldots, w_{n+q})$. For $i = n+1, \ldots, n+q$, let $K_i = O_i^{w_i}$. This defines a *garbled evaluation* $K^x = (K_1, \ldots, K_n, K_{n+1}, \ldots, K_{n+q})$. The scheme is constructed such that from a correct garbled circuit F and X^x one can efficiently compute K^x, which in particular allows one to compute $K_{n+q} = O_{n+q}^{f(x)}$. We have to prove that from a randomly generated P and X^x one cannot also efficiently compute $O_{n+q}^{1-f(x)}$. For this, it is sufficient to prove that one cannot efficiently compute $(i, O_i^{1-w_i})$ for any $i \in [n+q]$ with non-negligible probability.

We do the proof by a simple reduction to the game KDF in Def. 5. It is easy to see that the garbling and the keys learned by the evaluator in the scheme can be computed by queries to the game KDF in such a way that all the keys $O_i^{1-w_i}$ are uncompromised. In more detail, the reduction runs as follows:

Input keys: For each $i \in [n]$ and $b \in \{0,1\}$, output $(\texttt{fresh key}, (\texttt{key}, i, b))$ to define a fresh random key $X_i^b \in_R \{0,1\}^k$. Then for each $i \in [n]$, output $(\texttt{leak}, (\texttt{key}, i, x_i))$ to add $X_i^{x_i}$ to the set of values to leak. Let $X^x = \{X_i^{x_i}\}_{i=1}^{n}$. Now for each input wire, both keys are defined in the game KDF.

Internal gates: Iteratively go through all the gates. Specifically for each $i \in [n+1, q]$ we do as follows, depending on whether or not gate i is a NAND or XOR gate:

NAND gate: Call the plaintext value on the left input wire $l_i = w_{W(i,1)}$, call the plaintext value on the right input wire $r_i = w_{W(i,2)}$, and call the plaintext value on the output wire w_i. Call the keys on these wires (L_i^0, L_i^1), (R_i^0, R_i^1) and (O_i^0, O_i^1) respectively. Thus $(L_i^0, L_i^1) = (X_{W(i,1)}^0, X_{W(i,1)}^1)$, $(R_i^0, R_i^1) = (X_{W(i,2)}^0, X_{W(i,2)}^1)$ and $(O_i^0, O_i^1) = (X_i^0, X_i^1)$. The first four of these keys are defined in the game KDF and we are given $L_i^{l_i}$ and $R_i^{r_i}$ before our guess. We should define (O_i^0, O_i^1) in the game and make sure we learn $O_i^{w_i}$ before our guess. We use $\texttt{derive}$-commands to define $O_i^1 = \mathsf{KDF}(L_i^0; (\texttt{key}, i, 1))$, $O_i^0 = \mathsf{KDF}(L_i^1, R_i^1; (\texttt{key}, i, 0))$, and $A_i = \mathsf{KDF}(R_i^0; (\texttt{inte}, i))$. Then we use a $\texttt{linear}$-command to define $C_i = A_i \oplus O_i^1$ (with label $(\texttt{garb}, i)$). Then we add C_i to the set of values to leak by outputting $(\texttt{leak}, (\texttt{garb}, i))$. This is a correct garbling, so when we are later given $L_i^{l_i}$ and $R_i^{r_i}$, we can use them to compute $O_i^{w_i}$ by computing the garbled gate on $(L_i^{l_i}, R_i^{r_i})$.

XOR gate: We proceed as for NAND gates, except for the specific commands issued: We use $\texttt{linear}$-commands to define $O_i^0 = L_i^0 \oplus R_i^0$ (under identifier $(\texttt{key}, i, 0)$), $O_i^1 = L_i^1 \oplus R_i^0$ (under identifier $(\texttt{key}, i, 1)$) and $C_i = L_i^0 \oplus L_i^1 \oplus R_i^0 \oplus R_i^1$ (under identifier $(\texttt{garb}, i)$). Then we add C_i to the set of values to leak by outputting $(\texttt{leak}, (\texttt{garb}, i))$. This is a correct garbling, so we later use it to compute $O_i^{w_i}$ by computing the garbled gate on $(L_i^{l_i}, R_i^{r_i})$.

End: After having handled all the gates, we issue the **end**-command and learn the input keys $K_i = X_i^{x_i}$ for $i \in [n]$, along with the garbled gates C_i for $i \in [n+1; n+q]$. Using these we can evaluate the garbled circuit and thus learn the value $K_i = O_i^{w_i}$ for all $i \in [n+1; q]$. We then give $K^x = \{K_i, \ldots, K_{n+q}\}$ to the adversary.

Guess: If the adversary outputs $(i, O_i^{1-w_i})$ for any $i \in [n+q]$, then we output $(\mathsf{guess}, (\mathsf{key}, i, 1 - w_i), O_i^{1-w_i})$.

It is clear that we win the guessing game exactly when $(\mathsf{key}, i, 1 - w_i)$ is uncompromised and $O_i^{1-w_i}$ is the correct "other" key for wire i supplied by the adversary – we call $O_i^{w_i}$ the *known key* and we call $O_i^{1-w_i}$ the *other key*. We call a key O_i^b *compromised* if the label (key, i, b) is compromised as defined by the KDF game. We call gate C_i *compromised* if *the other key* $O_i^{1-w_i}$ is compromised as defined by the KDF game.

It is sufficient to prove that $(\mathsf{key}, i, 1 - w_i)$ is uncompromised for all i. It is clear that whether $(\mathsf{key}, i, 1 - w_i)$ is uncompromised does not depend on the strategy of the adversary, only the structure of the circuit, the nature of our garbling scheme and the input x. Hence, if for a fixed circuit and fixed input x some $(\mathsf{key}, i, 1 - w_i)$ is sometimes compromised, then it is always compromised. Hence, if any $(\mathsf{key}, i, 1 - w_i)$ can be compromised, then there exists a first gate j such that before executing the commands corresponding to gate j, no identifier $(\mathsf{key}, i, 1 - w_i)$ was compromised, and after executing the commands corresponding to gate j, some identifier $(\mathsf{key}, i, 1 - w_i)$ is compromised, where $i \leq j$. Consider this gate C_j. Furthermore, among the commands executed for gate j there is a first command that leads to a compromise of a gate. We call this command *patient zero*. We first show that patient zero is not a key derivation command. Then we show that it is not a linear command followed by a leak command. And then we are done.

Assume first that patient zero is a key derivation command. We use several times that a key derivation command, when it is the last command to have been executed, cannot compromise any other key than its output key. When patient zero is a key derivation command, then gate j must be a NAND gate, as there are no key derivation commands in XOR gates. Recall that we issue the key derivation commands (1), (2) and (3), as part of a NAND gate, and then we leak C_j. Assume that $l_j = 0$. In that case $O_j^1 = \mathsf{KDF}\left(L_j^0; (\mathsf{key}, j, 1)\right)$ is a known key and hence cannot be a compromised *other* key. We can also assume that L_j^1 is uncompromised (as it is an *other* key and we are at patient zero), and hence the *other* output key $O_j^0 = \mathsf{KDF}\left(L_j^1, R_j^1; (\mathsf{key}, j, 0)\right)$ will clearly be uncompromised after executing the command. Assume then that $r_j = 0$. In that case the other output key is again $O_j^0 = \mathsf{KDF}\left(L_j^1, R_j^1; (\mathsf{key}, j, 0)\right)$, and now R_j^1 is uncompromised. The command $A_j = \mathsf{KDF}\left(R_j^0; (\mathsf{inte}, j)\right)$ can therefore never be the patient zero compromising an output key, as A_j is not an output key.

Before we prove that patient zero cannot be a linear command we change the system that we analyze by replacing the processing of all NAND gates by the following commands: First we execute $(\texttt{fresh key}, (\texttt{key}, j, 0))$, $(\texttt{fresh key}, (\texttt{key}, j, 1))$ and $(\texttt{fresh key}, (\texttt{inte}, j))$ to define the values O_j^0, O_j^1 and A_j respectively. Then we compute $C_j = A_j \oplus O_j^1$, and leak C_j by issuing the commands $(\texttt{linear}, (\texttt{garb}, j), (\texttt{inte}, j), (\texttt{key}, j, 0))$ and $(\texttt{leak}, (\texttt{garb}, j))$ in that order. In addition we leak $O_j^{w_j}$. If $r_j = 0$ such that R_j^0 is a known key, then we also leak A_j. So, we essentially skip all key derivation commands and simulate their effect on the system by leaking the produced known keys. Since we could compute $O_j^{w_j}$ before the change, it was compromised before the change. It is also compromised after the change, as we now leak it. Similarly for A_j. Hence, the set of compromised identifiers is the same before and after the introduced changes, *at least right after the gate has been handled.* As a consequence, we have not changed whether or not some *other* key later gets compromised.[3] Furthermore, notice that since we have already showed that patient zero could not be a key derivation command this change does not affect the adversary's advantage. We therefore just have to prove that in the modified system, no *other* key gets compromised. Since there are no key derivation commands left, this is simple linear algebra.

Assume that patient zero is $C_j = A_j \oplus O_j^1$. Since A_j is a fresh key and only occurs in this equation, if A_j is uncompromised, adding this equation cannot change whether an output key is compromised or not.[4] Hence it must be the case that A_j is compromised. Since A_j is fresh and occurs in no other equation, this can only have happened because we leaked it earlier. Hence R_j^0 is a known key. So, $l_j = 0$ and hence $w_j = 1$. Therefore O_j^1 is a known key and hence already compromised. Hence $C_j = A_j \oplus O_j^1$ will compromise A_j, but since A_j occurs in no other equation, this does not further change the status of any variable. We can therefore assume in the following that we process all NAND gates, with index i, as follows: Call $(\texttt{fresh key}, (\texttt{key}, i, 0))$, $(\texttt{fresh key}, (\texttt{key}, i, 1))$ and $(\texttt{leak}, (\texttt{key}, i, w_i))$ to first define the key O_i^0, O_i^1 and then leak $O_i^{w_i}$. This does not change whether or not there will be a patient zero. We can even make further changes. We once and for all create a global key Δ through the call $(\texttt{fresh key}, \texttt{delta})$. Then we execute each NAND gate as follows: Call $(\texttt{fresh key}, (\texttt{key}, i, 0))$, $(\texttt{linear}, (\texttt{key}, i, 1), (\texttt{key}, i, 0), \texttt{delta})$ and $(\texttt{leak}, (\texttt{key}, i, w_i))$ to define the key O_i^0 and O_i^1 respectively and leak $O_i^{w_i}$. Similarly we can create the input keys X_i^0 and $X_i^1 = X_i^0 \oplus \Delta$ by calling $(\texttt{fresh key}, (\texttt{key}, i, 0))$ and $(\texttt{linear}, (\texttt{key}, i, 1), (\texttt{key}, i, 0), \texttt{delta})$ respectively for $i \in [n]$. This will only *add* equations to the system, and hence if there was a patient

---

[3] Note that if eventually an *other* key gets compromised, then the introduced changes *will* have an effect. When we use key derivation commands, one compromised *other* key leads to many compromised *other* keys. When we use fresh key commands, a compromised *other* key might not have an avalanche effect. However, we are proving that the number of compromised *other* keys is 0, and hence using one system or the other is equally good.

[4] If O_j^1 is uncompromised then A_j goes from uncompromised to compromised, but A_j is not an output key, and clearly no other key than A_j can change status by this equation.

zero in the system before the change there will also be a patient zero in the system after the change.

Assume then that patient zero is a linear command from an XOR gate, again with index j. We process such a gate as follows: Compute $O_j^0 \leftarrow L_j^0 \oplus R_j^0$ (with label $(\text{key}, j, 0)$), $O_j^1 \leftarrow L_j^1 \oplus R_j^0$ (with label $(\text{key}, j, 1)$) and $C_j \leftarrow L_j^0 \oplus L_j^1 \oplus R_j^0 \oplus R_j^1$ (with label (garb, j)) using the $\texttt{linear}$ command, and leak C_j using the $\texttt{leak}$ command. Notice that $L_j^0 \oplus L_j^1 \oplus R_j^0 \oplus R_j^1 = \Delta \oplus \Delta = 0$. Hence leaking C_j does not change the status of any key. We can therefore assume that we process XOR gates as follows: Compute $O_j^0 \leftarrow L_j^0 \oplus R_j^0$ and $O_j^1 \leftarrow L_j^1 \oplus R_j^0$ using the $\texttt{linear}$ command.

After all the changes to the system, we now "garble" as follows: First call $\Delta \leftarrow (\texttt{fresh key}, \texttt{delta})$ Then for each input key, $i \in [n]$, do:

$$X_i^0 \leftarrow (\texttt{fresh key}, (\text{key}, i, 0)) \; ,$$
$$X_i^1 \leftarrow (\texttt{linear}, (\text{key}, i, 1), (\text{key}, i, 0), \texttt{delta}) \; ,$$
$$X_i^{x_i} \leftarrow (\texttt{leak}, (\text{key}, i, x_i)) \; .$$

For each NAND gate, with index i, do:

$$O_i^0 \leftarrow (\texttt{fresh key}, (\text{key}, i, 0)) \; ,$$
$$O_i^1 \leftarrow (\texttt{linear}, (\text{key}, i, 1), (\text{key}, i, 0), \texttt{delta}) \; ,$$
$$O_i^{w_i} \leftarrow (\texttt{leak}, (\text{key}, i, w_i)) \; .$$

Finally, for each XOR gate, with index i, do:

$$O_i^0 \leftarrow (\texttt{linear}, (\text{key}, i, 0), (\text{key}, l_i, 0), (\text{key}, r_i, 0)) \; ,$$
$$O_i^1 \leftarrow (\texttt{linear}, (\text{key}, i, 0), (\text{key}, l_i, 0), (\text{key}, r_i, 1)) \; ,$$
$$O_i^{w_i} \leftarrow (\texttt{leak}, (\text{key}, i, w_i)) \; .$$

It is then fairly straight-forward to see that there are no compromised *other* key. In particular, it is trivial to see that if an other key would be compromised in this system, then the free-XOR scheme from [KS08] would trivially be insecure, as the system of equations created by the free-XOR scheme is a super set of the system created by the above commands. We therefore refer to [KS08] for the details of why the free-XOR trick is secure.

Notice that we can use a subset of this proof to prove security of our free-XOR privacy-free garbling scheme, since the free-XOR already implements the global difference Δ. Specifically we have the following theorem: □

Theorem 3. *If the KDF used in the garbling scheme of Fig. 1 composed with Fig. 3 is secure according to Def. 6, then the composed scheme enjoys authenticity according to Def. 2.*

$\mathsf{Gb}\left(1^k, f, \mathcal{L}\right) \to (F, e, d)$

1. Set $(n, q, I, W, G) \leftarrow f$ and $\left\{X_i^0, X_i^1, \{\Delta_i\}_{i\in[L]}\right\}_{i\in[n]} \leftarrow \mathsf{InKeys}(n, k, \mathcal{L})$.

2. For each $g \in [n+1, n+q]$ set $m = I(g)$ and define $G' : \{0,1\}^m \to \{0,1\}$ s.t. $G'(i) = G(g, i)$ for all $i \in \{0,1\}^m$ and set $\left\{(X_g^0, X_g^1), P[g]\right\} \leftarrow \mathsf{Garb}\left(g, G', \mathcal{L}, \{X_{W(g,i)}^0, X_{W(g,i)}^1\}_{i\in[m]}, \Delta_{\mathcal{L}(g)}\right)$.

3. Set $F \leftarrow (n, q, I, W, G, \mathcal{L}, P)$, $e \leftarrow \left\{X_i^0, X_i^1\right\}_{i\in[n]}$ and $d \leftarrow X_{n+q}^1$.

4. Finally return (F, e, d).

$\mathsf{En}(e, x) \to X$

Like in Fig. 1.

$\mathsf{De}(d, Z) \to b$

Like in Fig. 1.

$\mathsf{Ev}(F, X, x) \to Z$

1. Set $(n, q, I, W, G, \mathcal{L}, P) \leftarrow F$ and for all $i \in [n]$ set $w_i = x_i$ and define $Q = \{w_i\}_{i\in[n]}$.

2. For each $g \in [n+1, n+q]$ let $m = I(g)$ and add $w_g = G\left(g, \{w_{W(g,i)}\}_{i\in[m]}\right)$ to the set Q.

3. Now for each $g \in [n+1, n+q]$ let $m = I(g)$ and define $G' : \{0,1\}^m \to \{0,1\}$ s.t. $G'(i) = G(g, i)$ and $w' \in \{0,1\}^m$ s.t. $w_i' = w_{W(g,i)}$ for all $i \in [m]$ and set $X_g \leftarrow \mathsf{Eval}\left(g, G', \mathcal{L}, w', \{X_{W(g,i)}\}_{i\in[m]}, P[g]\right)$.

4. Return X_{n+q}.

$\mathsf{ev}(f, x) \to b$

Like in Fig. 1.

$\mathsf{Ve}(F, f, e) \to b$

1. Set $(n, q, I, W, G, \mathcal{L}, P) \leftarrow F$, $(n', q', I', W', G') \leftarrow f$ and $\left\{X_i^0, X_i^1\right\}_{i\in[n]} \leftarrow e$.

2. If $n \neq n'$, $q \neq q'$, $I \neq I'$, $W \neq W'$ or $G \neq G'$ output 0.

3. For each $g \in [n+1, n+q]$ let $m = I(g)$ and define $G' : \{0,1\}^m \to \{0,1\}$ s.t. $G'(i) = G(g, i)$ for all $i \in \{0,1\}^m$ and set $\left\{(X_g^0, X_g^1), \bar{P}[g]\right\} \leftarrow \mathsf{Garb}\left(g, G', \mathcal{L}, \{X_{W(g,i)}^0, X_{W(g,i)}^1\}_{i\in[m]}, \Delta_{\mathcal{L}(g)}\right)$.

4. If for any $g \in [n+1, n+q]$ we have $\bar{P}[g] \neq P[g]$ output 0, otherwise output 1.

Fig. 4. Privacy-free FleXOR Garbling

4 Privacy-Free FleXOR

In [KMR14] Kolesnikov *et al.* introduced a generalization and optimization of the free-XOR approach which allows to weaken the security assumption needed for free-XOR and/or limit the amount of ciphertexts used to garble non-XOR gates. In their schemes (only considering fan-in 2 gates) non-XOR gates are constructed exactly as one would in a regular garbling scheme, but XOR gates are constructed differently and, depending on a wire ordering of the circuit, consists of either 0, 1 or 2 ciphertexts. When the garbling scheme used implements aggressive row reduction (i.e., GRR1) this yields an overall smaller size for most garbled circuits compared the size of garbled circuits constructed using the free-XOR approach.

$\mathsf{InKeys}(n, k, \mathcal{L}) \to \left\{ \left(X_i^0, X_i^1 \right)_{i \in [n]}, \{\Delta_i\}_{i \in [L]} \right\}$

1. For each $i \in [L]$ sample uniformly random differences $\Delta_i \in \{0, 1\}^k$.
2. Then for each $i \in [n]$ sample uniformly random $X_i^0 \in_R \{0, 1\}^k$ and return the set $\left\{ \left(X_i^0, X_i^0 \oplus \Delta_{\mathcal{L}(i)} \right)_{i \in [n]}, \{\Delta_i\}_{i \in [L]} \right\}$.

$\mathsf{Garb}\left(g, G', \mathcal{L}, \left\{ \left(X_i^0, X_i^1 \right) \right\}_{i \in [m]}, \Delta_{\mathcal{L}(g)} \right) \to \left\{ \left(X_g^0, X_g^1 \right), \tilde{g} \right\}$

1. If $G'(\cdot) = \text{NAND}$ do garbling as described in Fig. 2 if $\mathcal{L}$ is *safe*, otherwise as described in Fig. 3.
2. If instead $G'(\cdot) = \text{XOR}$ do as follows:
   (a) Let T be the set of integers $i \in [m]$ for which $\mathcal{L}(i) \neq \mathcal{L}(g)$.
   (b) Let $X_g^0 = \bigoplus_{i=1}^m X_i^0$ and $X_g^1 = X_g^0 \oplus \Delta_{\mathcal{L}(g)}$.
   (c) Next let $C_i = \Delta_{\mathcal{L}(g)} \oplus \Delta_{\mathcal{L}(i)}$ for all $i \in T$ and set $\tilde{g} = \{C_i\}_{i \in T}$.
   (d) Return $\left\{ \left(X_g^0, X_g^1 \right), \tilde{g} \right\}$.

$\mathsf{Eval}\left(g, G', \mathcal{L}, w', \{X_i\}_{i \in [m]}, \tilde{g} \right) \to \{X_g\}$

1. If $G'(\cdot) = \text{NAND}$ do evaluation as described in Fig. 2 if $\mathcal{L}$ is *safe*, otherwise as described in Fig. 3.
2. If instead $G'(\cdot) = \text{XOR}$ do as follows:
   (a) Let T be the set of integers $i \in [m]$ for which $\mathcal{L}(i) \neq \mathcal{L}(g)$ and parse $\{C_i\}_{i \in T} \leftarrow \tilde{g}$.
   (b) Parse $\{C_i\}_{i \in T} \leftarrow \tilde{g}$.
   (c) Let S be the subset of T for which it is true that $w_i' = 1$.
   (d) Return $X_g = \left(\bigoplus_{i \in [m]} X_i \right) \oplus \left(\bigoplus_{i \in S} C_i \right)$.

Fig. 5. Garbling - Using fleXOR

Here we propose a variant of fleXOR which combines their ideas with non-oblivious gate evaluation, leading to a significant improvements in terms of computation complexity. Before we can describe our privacy-free fleXOR construction we need a few definitions. These are taken almost verbatim from [KMR14]. We assume familiarity with their construction and direct the reader to their paper if that is not the case.

Definition 7 (Wire Ordering). *A wire ordering for a Boolean circuit f is a function $\mathcal{L}$ that assigns an integer to each wire in f. Without loss of generality, we assume that $im(\mathcal{L}) = \{1, \dots, L\}$ for some integer L, and we denote $|\mathcal{L}| = L$. We say a wire ordering $\mathcal{L}$ is safe if:*

- *For each non-XOR gate with output wire i, and each wire j where there exists a directed path in the circuit that contains wire j before wire i, we have $\mathcal{L}(i) > \mathcal{L}(j)$.*
- *For each value $\ell \in im(\mathcal{L})$, there is at most one non-XOR gate whose output wire i satisfies $\mathcal{L}(i) = \ell$.*

We say that a topological ordering of gates in a circuit f is safety-respecting of $\mathcal{L}$ if for every non-XOR gate g with output wire i, g appears earlier in the ordering than any other gate g' with output wire i' satisfying $\mathcal{L}(i) = \mathcal{L}(i')$.

Formal Description. We describe the privacy-free fleXOR protocol for gates of fan-in m in Fig. 4 and Fig. 5. Notice that the description in Fig. 4 is essentially the same as the one for the general privacy-free scheme we described in Fig. 1, except for the fact that we include the wire ordering $\mathcal{L}$ needed in order for the garbling scheme to know which Δ's should be used for which wires. Regarding the specificities of the garbling, described in Fig. 5, see that the garbling of NAND gates is exactly the same as in Fig. 2 and Fig. 3, depending on whether or not the wire ordering is safe. That is, the scheme first checks whether or not a gate is an XOR or NAND gate. If it is a NAND gate then the garbling is the same as in Fig. 2 if $\mathcal{L}$ is *safe*, and the same as in Fig. 3 if $\mathcal{L}$ is not safe.

Regarding XOR gates, we garble them essentially as in Fig. 2 but, since the offsets of the wires are chosen during the InKeys procedure, the Garb procedure can only define the 0-key corresponding to the output wire. Then, as in Fig. 2, the Garb procedure computes and outputs the XOR of the offsets between the inputs and output wire, but only for the wires that belong to the set T, that is those for which $\mathcal{L}(i) \neq \mathcal{L}(g)$, which means that the Δ used for the 1-key on wire i is different from the Δ used on the output wire of the gate g. This in turn means that we must associate a ciphertext in order to "adjust" the key on wire i.

Regarding evaluation: for NAND gates the scheme again does the same as in Fig. 2 and Fig. 3 depending on whether or not the wire ordering is safe or not, respectively. For XOR gates the scheme first defines (in step a) the set of input wires for which $\mathcal{L}(i) \neq \mathcal{L}(g)$, T, and parses the garbled gate $\tilde{g}$ to its ciphertexts, $\{C_i\}_{i \in T}$. Then in step c the scheme identifies the subset $S \subset T$ of the input wires for which it is true that the input value for wire i is equal to 1 and finally, in step d it computes the output key by XORing all input keys and the adjustments for all the wires belonging to the set S.

Security. Like for our other privacy-free garbling schemes, correctness and verifiability follows relatively straightforwards from the constructions. The proof of authenticity follows from the one for the scheme in Fig. 2 (since the fleXOR variant is a generalization of the schemes described in Fig. 2, for which some input wires happen to the same offset as the output wire) and from the assumption on the wire ordering. We refer to [KMR14] for more details.

Acknowledgments. We would like to thank Payman Mohassel and Benny Pinkas (for useful discussions), the authors of [KMR14] (for sharing with us an early copy of their manuscript and the result of their "safe ordering" heuristics that were used for compiling Table 1 and 2), and Helene Flyvholm Haag (for valuable editorial comments).

References

[AIK11] Applebaum, B., Ishai, Y., Kushilevitz, E.: How to garble arithmetic circuits. In: FOCS, pp. 120–129 (2011)

[AIKW13] Applebaum, B., Ishai, Y., Kushilevitz, E., Waters, B.: Encoding functions with constant online rate or how to compress garbled circuits keys. In: Canetti, R., Garay, J.A. (eds.) CRYPTO 2013, Part II. LNCS, vol. 8043, pp. 166–184. Springer, Heidelberg (2013)

[BHHI10] Barak, B., Haitner, I., Hofheinz, D., Ishai, Y.: Bounded key-dependent message security. In: Gilbert, H. (ed.) EUROCRYPT 2010. LNCS, vol. 6110, pp. 423–444. Springer, Heidelberg (2010)

[BHKR13] Bellare, M., Hoang, V.T., Keelveedhi, S., Rogaway, P.: Efficient garbling from a fixed-key blockcipher. In: IEEE Symposium on Security and Privacy, pp. 478–492. IEEE Computer Society (2013). http://eprint.iacr.org/2013/426

[BHR12] Bellare, M., Hoang, V.T., Rogaway, P.: Foundations of garbled circuits. In: ACM Conference on Computer and Communications Security, pp. 784–796 (2012). http://eprint.iacr.org/2012/265

[BMR90] Beaver, D., Micali, S., Rogaway, P.: The round complexity of secure protocols (extended abstract). In: STOC, pp. 503–513 (1990)

[BP12] Boyar, J., Peralta, R.: A small depth-16 circuit for the AES S-Box. In: Gritzalis, D., Furnell, S., Theoharidou, M. (eds.) SEC 2012. IFIP AICT, vol. 376, pp. 287–298. Springer, Heidelberg (2012)

[Fin14] Find, M.G.: On the complexity of computing two nonlinearity measures. In: Hirsch, E.A., Kuznetsov, S.O., Pin, J.É., Vereshchagin, N.K. (eds.) CSR 2014. LNCS, vol. 8476, pp. 167–175. Springer, Heidelberg (2014)

[FJN+13] Frederiksen, T.K., Jakobsen, T.P., Nielsen, J.B., Nordholt, P.S., Orlandi, C.: MiniLEGO: efficient secure two-party computation from general assumptions. In: Johansson, T., Nguyen, P.Q. (eds.) EUROCRYPT 2013. LNCS, vol. 7881, pp. 537–556. Springer, Heidelberg (2013)

[FNO14] Frederiksen, T.K., Nielsen, J.B., Orlandi, C.: Privacy-free garbled circuits with applications to efficient zero-knowledge. IACR Cryptology ePrint Arch. **2014**, 598 (2014)

[GGH+13] Gentry, C., Gorbunov, S., Halevi, S., Vaikuntanathan, V., Vinayagamurthy, D.: How to compress (reusable) garbled circuits. IACR Cryptology ePrint Arch. **2013**, 687 (2013)

[GGP10] Gennaro, R., Gentry, C., Parno, B.: Non-interactive verifiable computing: outsourcing computation to untrusted workers. In: Rabin, T. (ed.) CRYPTO 2010. LNCS, vol. 6223, pp. 465–482. Springer, Heidelberg (2010)

[GHL+14] Gentry, C., Halevi, S., Lu, S., Ostrovsky, R., Raykova, M., Wichs, D.: Garbled RAM revisited. In: Nguyen, P.Q., Oswald, E. (eds.) EUROCRYPT 2014. LNCS, vol. 8441, pp. 405–422. Springer, Heidelberg (2014)

[GKP+13] Goldwasser, S., Kalai, Y.T., Popa, R.A., Vaikuntanathan, V., Zeldovich, N.: Reusable garbled circuits and succinct functional encryption. In: STOC, pp. 555–564 (2013)

[GMW87] Goldreich, O., Micali, S., Wigderson, A.: How to play any mental game or a completeness theorem for protocols with honest majority. In: STOC, pp. 218–229 (1987)

[IK02] Ishai, Y., Kushilevitz, E.: Perfect constant-round secure computation via perfect randomizing polynomials. In: Widmayer, P., Triguero, F., Morales, R., Hennessy, M., Eidenbenz, S., Conejo, R. (eds.) ICALP 2002. LNCS, vol. 2380, pp. 244–256. Springer, Heidelberg (2002)

[IW14] Ishai, Y., Wee, H.: Partial garbling schemes and their applications. In: Esparza, J., Fraigniaud, P., Husfeldt, T., Koutsoupias, E. (eds.) ICALP 2014. LNCS, vol. 8572, pp. 650–662. Springer, Heidelberg (2014). http://eprint.iacr.org/2014/995

[JKO13] Jawurek, M., Kerschbaum, F., Orlandi, C.: Zero-knowledge using garbled circuits: how to prove non-algebraic statements efficiently. In: ACM Conference on Computer and Communications Security, pp. 955–966 (2013)

[KK12] Kolesnikov, V., Kumaresan, R.: Improved secure two-party computation via information-theoretic garbled circuits. In: Visconti, I., De Prisco, R. (eds.) SCN 2012. LNCS, vol. 7485, pp. 205–221. Springer, Heidelberg (2012)

[KMR14] Kolesnikov, V., Mohassel, P., Rosulek, M.: FleXOR: flexible garbling for XOR gates that beats free-XOR. In: Garay, J.A., Gennaro, R. (eds.) CRYPTO 2014, Part II. LNCS, vol. 8617, pp. 440–457. Springer, Heidelberg (2014)

[Kol05] Kolesnikov, V.: Gate evaluation secret sharing and secure one-round two-party computation. In: Roy, B. (ed.) ASIACRYPT 2005. LNCS, vol. 3788, pp. 136–155. Springer, Heidelberg (2005)

[KS08] Kolesnikov, V., Schneider, T.: Improved garbled circuit: free XOR gates and applications. In: Aceto, L., Damgård, I., Goldberg, L.A., Halldórsson, M.M., Ingólfsdóttir, A., Walukiewicz, I. (eds.) ICALP 2008, Part II. LNCS, vol. 5126, pp. 486–498. Springer, Heidelberg (2008)

[KW13] Kamara, S., Wei, L.: Garbled circuits via structured encryption. In: Adams, A.A., Brenner, M., Smith, M. (eds.) FC 2013. LNCS, vol. 7862, pp. 177–188. Springer, Heidelberg (2013)

[LO13] Lu, S., Ostrovsky, R.: How to garble ram programs? In: Johansson, T., Nguyen, P.Q. (eds.) EUROCRYPT 2013. LNCS, vol. 7881, pp. 719–734. Springer, Heidelberg (2013)

[LP09] Lindell, Y., Pinkas, B.: A proof of security of Yao's protocol for two-party computation. J. Cryptology 22(2), 161–188 (2009)

[MNPS04] Malkhi, D., Nisan, N., Pinkas, B., Sella, Y.: Fairplay - secure two-party computation system. In: USENIX Security Symposium, pp. 287–302 (2004)

[NO09] Nielsen, J.B., Orlandi, C.: LEGO for two-party secure computation. In: Reingold, O. (ed.) TCC 2009. LNCS, vol. 5444, pp. 368–386. Springer, Heidelberg (2009)

[NPS99] Naor, M., Pinkas, B., Sumner, R.: Privacy preserving auctions and mechanism design. In: ACM Conference on Electronic Commerce, pp. 129–139 (1999)

[PSSW09] Pinkas, B., Schneider, T., Smart, N.P., Williams, S.C.: Secure two-party computation is practical. In: Matsui, M. (ed.) ASIACRYPT 2009. LNCS, vol. 5912, pp. 250–267. Springer, Heidelberg (2009)

[Rog91] Rogaway, P.: The round complexity of secure protocols. Ph.D thesis, Massachusetts Institute of Technology (1991)

[SS10] Sahai, A., Seyalioglu, H.: Worry-free encryption: functional encryption with public keys. In: ACM Conference on Computer and Communications Security, pp. 463–472 (2010)

[ST12] Smart, N., Tillich, S.: Circuits of basic functions suitable for MPC and FHE (2012). http://www.cs.bris.ac.uk/Research/CryptographySecurity/MPC/

[Yao86] Yao, A.C.-C.: How to generate and exchange secrets (extended abstract). In: FOCS, pp. 162–167 (1986)

[ZRE15] Zahur, S., Rosulek, M., Evans, D.: Two halves make a whole: reducing data transfer in garbled circuits using half gates. In: These proceedings (2015). http://eprint.iacr.org/2014/756

Two Halves Make a Whole
Reducing Data Transfer in Garbled Circuits Using Half Gates

Samee Zahur[1]($\boxtimes$), Mike Rosulek[2], and David Evans[1]

[1] University of Virginia, Charlottesville, USA
{samee,evans}@virginia.edu
[2] Oregon State University, Corvallis, OR, USA
rosulekm@eecs.oregonstate.edu
http://MightBeEvil.com/halfgates

Abstract. The well-known classical constructions of garbled circuits use four ciphertexts per gate, although various methods have been proposed to reduce this cost. The best previously known methods for optimizing AND gates (two ciphertexts; Pinkas et al., ASIACRYPT 2009) and XOR gates (zero ciphertexts; Kolesnikov and Schneider, ICALP 2008) were incompatible, so most implementations used the best known method compatible with free-XOR gates (three ciphertexts; Kolesnikov and Schneider, ICALP 2008). In this work we show how to simultaneously garble AND gates using two ciphertexts and XOR gates using zero ciphertexts, resulting in smaller garbled circuits than any prior scheme. The main idea behind our construction is to break an AND gate into two *half-gates* — AND gates for which one party knows one input. Each half-gate can be garbled with a single ciphertext, so our construction uses two ciphertexts for each AND gate while being compatible with free-XOR gates. The price for the reduction in size is that the evaluator must perform two cryptographic operations per AND gate, rather than one as in previous schemes. We experimentally demonstrate that our garbling scheme leads to an overall decrease in time (up to 25%), bandwidth (up to 33%), and energy use (up to 20%) over several benchmark applications. We show that our construction is optimal for a large class of garbling schemes encompassing all known practical garbling techniques.

1 Introduction

Yao's garbled circuit technique remains one of the most promising and actively studied methods for secure multi-party computation. The first implementation of secure two-party computation (2PC) [26] used Yao's basic garbled circuit approach, and it remains the primary (but not only) paradigm for the many 2PC implementations that have been developed over the past ten years [10,12,14,21, 25,28]. Because the generation and execution of gates benefits from advances in processor speed (in particular, hardware support for cryptographic operations) as well as the increasing availability of large numbers of cores, the computation time

© International Association for Cryptologic Research 2015
E. Oswald and M. Fischlin (Eds.): EUROCRYPT 2015, Part II, LNCS 9057, pp. 220–250, 2015.
DOI: 10.1007/978-3-662-46803-6_8

and cost for garbled circuit protocols has dropped dramatically. Thus, the main bottleneck for 2PC protocols is network bandwidth which is predominantly due to the transmission of garbled gates. Many optimizations in 2PC have focused on reducing the size of the garbled circuits themselves [19,20,27] and reducing the number of circuits required (in the case of malicious security) [6,15,22,24,29]. Our work reduces the overall size of garbled circuits by reducing the amount of data that needs to be transferred for each garbled gate.

1.1 Background

We assume some familiarity with garbled circuit constructions (for a comprehensive treatment of Yao's classical construction see Lindell and Pinkas [23]). In a garbled gate, each wire of the (Boolean) circuit is associated with two random strings/keys called *wire labels* which encode TRUE and FALSE. In the "classical" construction of garbled circuits, the sender provides a garbled truth table for each gate, where each combination of input wire labels is used to encrypt the appropriate output wire label. Hence, there are four "ciphertexts" per gate — one for each input combination to the gate — and the evaluator who only knows one label for each input wire can only open one of them. In general, we will measure the size of a garbled gate in units of such "ciphertexts."

We now give a brief history of work reducing the data needed to transmit a garbled gate, summarized in Table 1. In the **point-and-permute** optimization, introduced by Beaver, Micali and Rogaway [3], a *select bit* is appended to each wire label, so that the two labels on each wire have opposite select bits. The association between select bits and logical truth values is random and secret, but the garbled truth table can be arranged by these public select bits. While the result is still four ciphertexts per gate, the ciphertexts no longer need to be from a CPA-secure encryption scheme (and this indeed leads to a reduction in concrete size). Rather, they can be of the form $H(A\|B) \oplus C$, where A, B,

Table 1. Optimizations of garbled circuits. Size is number of "ciphertexts" (multiples of k bits)

| | size per gate | | calls to H per gate | | | |
| | | | generator | | evaluator | |
technique	XOR	AND	XOR	AND	XOR	AND
classical [31]	4	4	4	4	4	4
point-permute [3]	4	4	4	4	1	1
row reduction (GRR3) [27]	3	3	4	4	1	1
row reduction (GRR2) [28]	2	2	4	4	1	1
free XOR + GRR3 [20]	0	3	0	4	0	1
fleXOR [19]	$\{0,1,2\}$	2	$\{0,2,4\}$	4	$\{0,1,2\}$	1
half gates [this work]	0	2	0	4	0	2

and C are wire labels, and H is a hash function or key-derivation function. Further, instead of trying all four ciphertexts, the evaluator can simply select the appropriate one based on the select bits of visible wire labels.

Naor, Pinkas and Sumner introduced **garbled row-reduction** as a way to reduce the number of ciphertexts per gate [27]. Instead of choosing random wire labels for each wire, one of the wire labels is chosen as $H(A\|B)$, where A and B are labels of the input wires. Thus, one of the four ciphertexts in each gate (say, the first one) will always be the all-zeroes string and does not need to be sent. We call this method *GRR3* since only three ciphertexts need to be transmitted for each gate. Going even further, Pinkas et al. [28] describe a way, which we denote *GRR2*, to further reduce each gate to 2 ciphertexts, applying a polynomial interpolation at each gate.

Kolesnikov and Schneider [20] introduced the **free-XOR** technique. The idea is to choose all wire labels of the form $(A, A \oplus R)$, where R is secret and common to all wires. An evaluator who has one of $(A, A \oplus R)$ and one of $(B, B \oplus R)$, can perform the XOR operation simply by XORing the two wire labels. The result will be either C or $C \oplus R$ (where $C = A \oplus B$), which correctly represents the result. Hence, no ciphertexts are required at all for an XOR gate. This technique is compatible with GRR3 for AND gates, but not GRR2. The reason is that the GRR2 technique chooses both output wire labels of a gate as fixed pseudorandom functions of the input wire labels. Hence, it is not possible to guarantee that the output wire labels are of the form $(C, C \oplus R)$ for some pre-specified R.

Kolesnikov, Mohassel, and Rosulek [19] proposed a generalization of free-XOR caled *fleXOR*. In fleXOR, an XOR gate can be garbled using 0, 1, or 2 ciphertexts, depending on structural and combinatorial properties of the circuit. However, fleXOR can be made compatible with GRR2 applied to the AND gates. For circuits with many AND gates, this method results in smaller circuits than with free-XOR (while the construction can actually collapse to free-XOR in other cases).

1.2   Our Contributions

Half-gates. We present a method for garbling AND gates that requires only two ciphertexts. However, unlike the GRR2 method, our method is compatible with free-XOR. That is, our method can guarantee that the output wires of an AND gate are indeed of the form $(C, C \oplus R)$, when the input wires are also of this form.

The main insight is to employ what we call **half-gates**: AND gates for which one party knows one of the inputs. We show how to garble *generator half-gates* and *evaluator half-gates* using one ciphertext each, in a way that is compatible with free-XOR. We then show how an AND gate can be written as a combination of XORs and two half-gates of opposite orientations. Hence, the resulting AND gate uses only two ciphertexts in combination with free-XOR. We prove the security of our scheme in Section 4.

For *all* circuits, our half-gate technique leads to smaller garbled circuits than *all* previous methods (i.e., our row of Table 1 dominates all other rows). For many

Table 2. Optimizations of **privacy-free** garbled circuits. Size is number of cipher-texts (multiples of k bits). The three prior schemes are from Frederiksen, Nielsen, and Orlandi [8].

| | size per gate | | calls to H per gate | | | |
| | | | sender | | receiver | |
technique	XOR	AND	XOR	AND	XOR	AND
row reduction (GRR1)	1	1	0	3	0	1
free XOR + GRR2	0	2	0	3	0	1
fleXOR	$\{0,1,2\}$	1	0	3	0	1
half gates [this work]	0	1	0	2	0	1

circuits (i.e., those for which free-XOR previously gave the smallest garbled circuits), our work gives a 33% reduction in garbled circuit size (and thus a similar reduction in cost for most protocols that rely on garbled circuits). This leads to reductions in overall latency (up to 25% in our benchmarks), as well as energy (which is the primary concern for data centers as well as mobile devices) since the extra computation required to compute the hash function twice is more than offset by the energy savings of reduced bandwidth. We provide experimental results in Section 5.

Privacy-free garbling. Frederiksen, Nielsen, and Orlandi [8] showed that garbling schemes that satisfy only the *authenticity* security property (i.e., not the *privacy* property) can be significantly smaller than their fully-secure counterparts. These privacy-free schemes are useful in settings where the evaluator knows the entire (cleartext) input to the garbled circuit, as in the highly efficient zero-knowledge proof protocol of Jawurek, Kerschbaum and Orlandi [18].

Table 2 summarizes the three privacy-free garbling schemes introduced by Frederiksen, Nielsen, and Orlandi [8], which are adaptations of fully-secure schemes. Their GRR1 construction garbles all gates at a cost of one ciphertext each. Their free-XOR adaptation garbles AND gates at a cost of two ciphertexts each (with XOR gates free). Their fleXOR adaptation garbles AND gates using one ciphertext each, with XOR gates costing 0, 1, or 2 ciphertexts each.

In Section 6, we show that our approach with half-gates also gives a similar improvement in this setting. We can simply garble all AND gates using our evaluator half-gate. In this setting, the evaluator knows both inputs to all gates, but we only need to take advantage of its knowledge of one of the inputs to reduce the size of garbled AND gates to one ciphertext. Overall, we achieve a privacy-free garbled circuit containing one ciphertext per AND gate, and no ciphertexts for XOR gates. As for standard grabled circuits, our half-gates app-roach is strictly better than all previous constructions. For example, we reduce the size of a privacy-free garbled circuit for AES by 50%.

Optimality. For prior garbling schemes that we described above, it was always possible to reduce the size of garbled AND gates by one ciphertext by sacrificing compatibility with free-XOR. Given that we can now garble AND gates with two ciphertexts in a way that is compatible with free-XOR, one might wonder whether it is possible to garble an AND gate with just one ciphertext, in a way that is incompatible with free-XOR.

In Section 7, we show that in a reasonable model that captures all existing techniques, it is not possible to garble an AND gate (with privacy) using just one ciphertext, even if compatibility with free-XOR is sacrificed. Hence, our construction gives **optimally-sized garbled circuits**, among garbling schemes whose gate-by-gate operations fall within our model.

To show optimality, we introduce a new methodology for stating and proving such quantitative lower bounds on the size of garbled gates. We observe that all existing techniques for practical garbling (including our own) are *linear* in a certain sense. We formalize these techniques in a linear class of garbling schemes, and show that these schemes require two ciphertexts for a single AND gate. These lower bounds suggest that any practical improvement over our scheme will require a dramatically different approach to garbled circuits in general.

2   Preliminaries

We use the *garbling schemes* abstraction introduced by Bellare, Hoang, and Rogaway [5]. Roughly speaking, a garbling scheme consist of the following algorithms:[1]

Gb: On input 1^k and a boolean circuit f, outputs (F, e, d), where F is a **garbled circuit**, e is encoding information, and d is decoding information.

En: On input (e, x), where e is as above and x is an input suitable for f, outputs a **garbled input** X.

Ev: On input (F, X) as above, outputs a **garbled output** Y.

De: On input (d, Y) as above, outputs a plain output y.

The correctness property is that, if $(F, e, d) \leftarrow \mathsf{Gb}(1^k, f)$ then for all x:

$$\mathsf{De}(d, \mathsf{Ev}(F, \mathsf{En}(e, x))) = f(x)$$

Additionally, several security properties are described:

Privacy ($\mathsf{prv.sim}_{\mathcal{S}}$): Intuitively, the collection (F, X, d) should not reveal any more information about x than $f(x)$. More concretely, there must exist a simulator $\mathcal{S}$ that takes input $(1^k, f, f(x))$ and whose output is indistinguishable from (F, X, d) generated the usual way.

---

[1] The formalization of [5] allows for garbling of any form of computation. Here we specialize the notation for garbling *circuits*, as this is all that is required in our work.

Obliviousness (obv.sim$_\mathcal{S}$): Intuitively, (F, X) should reveal no information about x. More concretely, there must exist a simulator $\mathcal{S}$ that takes input $(1^k, f)$ and whose output is indistinguishable from (F, X) generated the usual way.

Authenticity (aut): Given input (F, X) alone, no adversary should be able to produce $\tilde{Y} \neq \mathsf{Ev}(F, X)$ such that $\mathsf{De}(d, \tilde{Y}) \neq \perp$, except with negligible probability.

A garbling scheme may satisfy any combination of these security properties. See Bellare, Hoang, and Rogaway [5] for the complete treatment of garbling schemes and further relations among the security properties.

3 Half-Gates Garbling Scheme

First, we give a high-level and self-contained overview of our construction of *half-gates*, which form the basis of our improved garbling schemes. Then, we present the details more formally.

3.1 Approach

Recall that a half-gate is a garbled AND gate for which one of the parties knows one of the inputs (in the clear). Let's say we want to compute the gate $c = a \wedge b$. We are in the free-XOR setting, so let $(A, A \oplus R)$ and $(B, B \oplus R)$ denote the input wire labels to this gate, and $(C, C \oplus R)$ denote the output wire labels, with A, B, and C each encoding FALSE. R is the free-XOR offset common to all wires. Finally, H will denote a hash (or key derivation) function.

We describe how to construct half-gates for two cases: when the garbled-circuit generator knows one of the inputs, and when the evaluator knows one of the inputs.

Generator half-gate. We consider the case of an AND gate $c = a \wedge b$, where a and b are intermediate wires in the circuit and the generator somehow knows in advance what the value a will be. Conceptually, when $a = 0$, the generator will garble a unary gate that always outputs false; when $a = 1$, the generator will garble a unary identity gate. This idea was also used implicitly by Kolesnikov and Schneider [20, Fig. 2], in the context of programming components of a universal circuit.

Hence, the generator produces the two ciphertexts:

$$H(B) \oplus C$$
$$H(B \oplus R) \oplus C \oplus aR$$

These are then suitably permuted according to the select bits of B. The evaluator takes a hash of its wire label for B and decrypts the appropriate ciphertext. If $a = 0$, it obtains output wire label C in both values of b. If $a = 1$, the evaluator obtains either C or $C \oplus R$, depending on the bit b. Intuitively, the evaluator will never know both B and $B \oplus R$, hence the other ciphertext appears completely random.

Next, we eliminate one of the ciphertexts by applying a standard idea of garbled row-reduction [27]. Instead of choosing C uniformly, we choose C so that the first of the two ciphertexts is the all-zeroes ciphertext (we choose C as $H(B)$, $H(B \oplus R)$, or $H(B \oplus R) \oplus R$, depending on the select bits and the value a). As such, the first ciphertext does not actually need to be sent; in the case where the evaluator would have decrypted the first ciphertext, it infers it to be the all-zeroes string. Overall, this garbled half-gate consists of one ciphertext (k bits). The generator calls H twice; the evaluator calls H once.

Evaluator half-gate. We now consider the case of an AND gate $c = a \wedge b$, where a and b are intermediate wires in the circuit and the evaluator will somehow already know the value of a at the time of evaluation.

We exploit the fact that the evaluator can behave differently based on the truth value of a. Intuitively, when $a = 0$ the evaluator should always obtain output wire label C; when $a = 1$, it is enough for the evaluator to obtain $\Delta = C \oplus B$. It can then XOR Δ with the other wire label (either B or $B \oplus R$) to obtain either C or $C \oplus R$ appropriately.

Hence, the generator provides the two ciphertexts:

$$H(A) \oplus C$$
$$H(A \oplus R) \oplus C \oplus B$$

The ciphertexts do not have to be permuted here. They can be arranged according to the truth value of a as shown here, since the evaluator already knows a. If $a = 0$, the evaluator uses wire label A to decrypt the first ciphertext. If $a = 1$, the evaluator uses wire label $A \oplus R$ to decrypt the second ciphertext and XORs the result with the wire label for b.

Again, we can remove the first ciphertext using garbled row-reduction. We choose $C = H(A)$ so that the first ciphertext becomes all-zeroes and is not sent. Overall, the cost of this garbled half-gate is the same as above: it consists of one ciphertext (k bits). The generator calls H twice; the evaluator calls H once.

Two halves make a whole. Now consider the case where we want to garble an AND gate $c = a \wedge b$ where both inputs are secret. Consider:

$$\begin{aligned} c &= a \wedge b \\ &= a \wedge (r \oplus r \oplus b) \\ &= (a \wedge r) \oplus (a \wedge (r \oplus b)) \end{aligned}$$

Suppose the generator chooses a uniformly random bit r. In that case, the first AND gate $(a \wedge r)$ can be garbled with a generator-half-gate. If we further arrange for the evaluator to learn the value $r \oplus b$, then the second AND gate $(a \wedge (r \oplus b))$ can be garbled with an evaluator-half-gate. Leaking this extra bit $r \oplus b$ to the evaluator is safe, as it carries no information about the sensitive value b. The remaining XOR is free, and the total cost is two ciphertexts.

We can actually convey $r \oplus b$ to the evaluator without any overhead. The generator will choose r to be the select bit of the false wire label on wire b. For security, select bits of wires are chosen (pseudo)randomly already. Then when a particular value b is on that wire, the evaluator will hold a wire label whose select bit is $b \oplus r$.

Thus, we garble a (full) AND gate with two ciphertexts, taking the XOR of two half-gates. The generator calls H four times; the evaluator calls H twice.

3.2 Details of Our Scheme

We now give a formal description of our garbling scheme, following the basic approach outlined above.

Notation and concepts. For a boolean circuit f, we associate each wire in the circuit with a numeric index. We let $\mathsf{Inputs}(f)$, $\mathsf{Outputs}(f)$, and $\mathsf{XorGates}(f)$ denote the set of wire indices of the input wires, output wires, xor gate output wires, respectively, in f. We abuse notation slightly and extend these functions as $\mathsf{Inputs}(\hat{F})$, $\mathsf{Outputs}(\hat{F})$ and $\mathsf{XorGates}(\hat{F})$, where $\hat{F}$ is a garbled version of f. We use v_i to denote the single-bit plaintext value of the ith wire in a circuit, when the input is understood from context. For non-input wires, we also refer to the *ith gate* to mean the logic gate whose output wire has index i.

Our garbling scheme follows standard paradigms of the free-XOR & point-and-permute optimizations. We use $W_i^0, W_i^1 \in \{0,1\}^k$ to denote the wire labels for FALSE and TRUE, respectively, on the ith wire. Here, and throughout the paper, k denotes the scheme's security parameter. For each wire label W, its least significant bit $\mathsf{lsb}\, W$ is reserved as a **select bit** that is used as in the point-and-permute technique. For the ith wire, define $p_i = \mathsf{lsb}\, W_i^0$. This value, which we call the *permute bit* of the wire, is a secret known only to the generator. Intuitively, when the evaulator holds a wire label for wire i whose select bit is s_i, that wire label is $W_i^{s_i \oplus p_i}$, corresponding to truth value $v_i = s_i \oplus p_i$. In the context of evaluating a garbled circuit, we typically omit the superscript from the wire label notation and write just W_i to indicate the fact that the evaluator indeed does not know v_i.

The value $R \in \{0,1\}^{k-1}1$ is a circuit-global, randomly chosen *free-XOR offset*; hence, $W_i^0 \oplus W_i^1 = R$ holds for each i in the circuit. We have $\mathsf{lsb}\, R = 1$ so that $\mathsf{lsb}\, W_i^0 \neq \mathsf{lsb}\, W_i^1$ and complementary wires have opposite select bits.

Frequently, we will omit $\wedge$ and just juxtapose two symbols to indicate logical AND. So $ab = a \wedge b$. When a is a single bit and R is a long string, we write aR to mean R when $a = 1$ and $0^{|R|}$ when $a = 0$. We write sequences or tuples with a 'hat'; for example, $\hat{F} = (F_1, F_2, \ldots)$ or $\hat{X} = (X_1, X_2, \ldots)$.

Finally, we will use $H : \{0,1\}^k \times \mathbb{Z} \mapsto \{0,1\}^k$ to indicate a hash-function suitable for use in garbled circuits (see Section 4 for suitability criteria). In informal discussions, we will often shorten $H(W_i^b, j)$ to just $H(W_i^b)$, and it will

Computes: $f_G(v_a, p_b) :=$ $(v_a \oplus \alpha_a)(p_b \oplus \alpha_b) \oplus \alpha_c$	Computes: $f_E(v_a, v_b \oplus p_b) :=$ $(v_a \oplus \alpha_a)(v_b \oplus p_b)$
Before GRR and permutation: $H(W_a^0) \oplus f_G(0, p_b)R \oplus W_{Gc}^0$ $H(W_a^1) \oplus f_G(1, p_b)R \oplus W_{Gc}^0$	Before GRR: $H(W_b^{p_b}) \oplus W_{Ec}^0$ $H(W_b^{p_b \oplus 1}) \oplus W_{Ec}^0 \oplus W_a^{\alpha_a}$
After GRR and permutation: $T_{Gc} \leftarrow H(W_a^0) \oplus H(W_a^1) \oplus (p_b \oplus \alpha_b)R$ $W_{Gc}^0 \leftarrow H(W_a^{p_a}) \oplus f_G(p_a, p_b)R$	After GRR (permutation not needed): $T_{Ec} \leftarrow H(W_b^0) \oplus H(W_b^1) \oplus W_a^{\alpha_a}$ $W_{Ec}^0 \leftarrow H(W_b^{p_b})$
Generator sends T_{Gc}	Generator sends T_{Ec}

(a) Generator half-gate: v_a known to generator.

(b) Evaluator half-gate: $v_b \oplus p_b$ known to evaluator.

Fig. 1. The construction of a non-free binary gate for computing $(v_a, v_b) \mapsto (v_a \oplus \alpha_a)(v_b \oplus \alpha_b) \oplus \alpha_c$, where $\alpha_a, \alpha_b, \alpha_c$ determines the type of the gate. After the two half-gates are evaluated, output label is obtained by computing $W_c = W_{Gc} \oplus W_{Ec}$

be implicitly understood that we are using unique, but public, j for different groups of calls to H. In the formal descriptions, the value of j is always explicit.

Arbitrary gates. The approach just described can be used to garble any gate whose truth table contains an odd number of ones (e.g., AND, NAND, OR, NOR, etc.). All such gates can be expressed as the form

$$(v_a, v_b) \mapsto (\alpha_a \oplus v_a) \wedge (\alpha_b \oplus v_b) \oplus \alpha_c$$

for constants $\alpha_a, \alpha_b, \alpha_c$. For example, setting all to 0 results in an AND gate; setting all to 1 results in an OR gate. These α values need not (but can) be secret. We describe the general construction of these gates in Figure 1. We note that the evaluator's logic does not depend on the α values.

Following the description in Section 3.1, we garble each gate using a composition of two half-gates. Conceptually, W_{Gi}^b and W_{Ei}^b denote the output wire labels for these two half-gates (generator-side and evaluator-side, respectively) that comprise the ith gate. The final logical output wire label for the ith gate is then set to be $W_i^0 = W_{Gi}^0 \oplus W_{Ei}^0$. Similarly, we use T_{Gi} and T_{Ei} to denote the single garbled row transmitted for each half gate used in the ith gate.

The first rows of Figure 1 show the function being computed by each half gate. In (a), generator knows p_b while in (b) the evaluator knows $v_b \oplus p_b = \mathsf{lsb}\, W_b$. The second rows show the two ciphertexts of each half-gate, before they are permuted according to their select bits (in case of (a)) and before garbled row reduction (GRR) is applied. Here, we have expanded $W_{Gc}^{f(x,p_b)}$ to $W_{Gc}^0 \oplus f(x, p_b)R$ to make the row reduction clearer in the next step. The third rows show the final result.

The complete scheme. The full garbling procedure for an entire circuit is shown in Figure 2. The scheme works for any binary gate, but for simplicity of discussion and proof we assume all gates are either AND or XOR.

---

procedure Gb($1^k, f$):
  $R \leftarrow \{0,1\}^{k-1}1$
  for $i \in$ Inputs(f) **do**
    $W_i^0 \leftarrow \{0,1\}^k$
    $W_i^1 \leftarrow W_i^0 \oplus R$
    $e_i \leftarrow W_i^0$
  for $i \notin$ Inputs(f) {*in topo. order*} **do**
    $\{a,b\} \leftarrow$ GateInputs(f, i)
    if $i \in$ XorGates(f) **then**
      $W_i^0 \leftarrow W_a^0 \oplus W_b^0$
    else
      $(W_i^0, T_{Gi}, T_{Ei}) \leftarrow$ GbAnd(W_a^0, W_b^0)
      $F_i \leftarrow (T_{Gi}, T_{Ei})$
    end if
    $W_i^1 \leftarrow W_i^0 \oplus R$
  for $i \in$ Outputs(f) **do**
    $d_i \leftarrow$ lsb(W_i^0)
  return ($\hat{F}, \hat{e}, \hat{d}$)

private procedure GbAnd(W_a^0, W_b^0):
  $p_a \leftarrow$ lsb W_a^0; $p_b \leftarrow$ lsb W_b^0
  $j \leftarrow$ NextIndex(); $j' \leftarrow$ NextIndex()
  {*First half gate*}
  $T_G \leftarrow H(W_a^0, j) \oplus H(W_a^1, j) \oplus p_b R$
  $W_G^0 \leftarrow H(W_a^0, j) \oplus p_a T_G$
  {*Second half gate*}
  $T_E \leftarrow H(W_b^0, j') \oplus H(W_b^1, j') \oplus W_a^0$
  $W_E^0 \leftarrow H(W_b^0, j') \oplus p_b(T_E \oplus W_a^0)$
  {*Combine halves*}
  $W^0 \leftarrow W_G^0 \oplus W_E^0$
  return (W^0, T_G, T_E)

procedure En($\hat{e}, \hat{x}$):
  for $e_i \in \hat{e}$ **do**
    $X_i \leftarrow e_i \oplus x_i R$
  return $\hat{X}$

procedure De($\hat{d}, \hat{Y}$):
  for $d_i \in \hat{d}$ **do**
    $y_i \leftarrow d_i \oplus$ lsb Y_i
  return $\hat{y}$

procedure Ev($\hat{F}, \hat{X}$):
  for $i \in$ Inputs($\hat{F}$) **do**
    $W_i \leftarrow X_i$
  for $i \notin$ Inputs($\hat{F}$) {*in topo. order*} **do**
    $\{a,b\} \leftarrow$ GateInputs($\hat{F}, i$)
    if $i \in$ XorGates($\hat{F}$) **then**
      $W_i \leftarrow W_a \oplus W_b$
    else
      $s_a \leftarrow$ lsb W_a; $s_b \leftarrow$ lsb W_b
      $j \leftarrow$ NextIndex(); $j' \leftarrow$ NextIndex()
      $(T_{Gi}, T_{Ei}) \leftarrow F_i$
      $W_{Gi} \leftarrow H(W_a, j) \oplus s_a T_{Gi}$
      $W_{Ei} \leftarrow H(W_b, j') \oplus s_b(T_{Ei} \oplus W_a)$
      $W_i \leftarrow W_{Gi} \oplus W_{Ei}$
    end if
  for $i \in$ Outputs($\hat{F}$) **do**
    $Y_i \leftarrow W_i$
  return $\hat{Y}$

Fig. 2. Our complete garbling scheme. NextIndex is a stateful procedure that simply increments an internal counter.

4 Security

We now prove the security of our scheme, using the $\mathsf{prv.sim}_\mathcal{S}$ and $\mathsf{obv.sim}_\mathcal{S}$ security definitions of Bellare, Hoang, and Rogaway [5]. The scheme shown in Figure 2 does not provide authenticity, simply because authenticity is not required in many use cases including semi-honest Yao's circuits. However, there are well-known, standard modifications to the decoding procedure that can add authenticity, which we describe separately in Section 4.3. Finally, since we only consider circuits with just AND and XOR gates, everything about the function f is public and we do not define a separate function $\Phi(f)$ to extract public information about f.

4.1 Circular Correlation Robustness for Naturally Derived Keys

We first describe the security property required of the hash/key-derivation function H. Roughly speaking, we can use either a circular-correlation-robust hash function, as defined by Choi et al. [7], or a Davis-Meyer construction in the ideal random permutation model [4]. Note that a result of using half gates is we need arguably simpler single-key functions instead of the previously proposed dual-key ones. So, we first present the single-key analogs of these two definitions. Then we define a weaker notion of security that is satisfied by both these classes of hash functions. Functions satisfying this new notion of security will be said to have circular correlation robustness *for naturally derived keys*. Finally we show that our garbling scheme is secure given any hash function that satisfies this new, weaker notion of security.

Circular correlation robustness. We revisit the definition of circular correlation robustness. The definition is the same as the one introduced in [7], except that we are able to simplify the notation for H that takes only one wire label / key. Given a hash function H, we define two oracles:

– $\mathsf{Circ}_R(x, i, b) = H(x \oplus R, i) \oplus bR$, where $R \in \{0, 1\}^{k-1}1$
– $\mathsf{Rand}(x, i, b)$: random function with k-bit output.

Definition 1. *Say that a sequence of oracle queries of the form (x, i, b) is legal if the same value of (x, i) is never queried with different values of b. Then H is circular correlation robust if, for all all polynomial-time adversaries $\mathcal{A}$ making legal queries,*

$$\left| \Pr_R[\mathcal{A}^{\mathsf{Circ}_R}(1^k) = 1] - \Pr_{\mathsf{Rand}}[\mathcal{A}^{\mathsf{Rand}}(1^k) = 1] \right| \text{ is negligible.}$$

The restriction to *legal* queries prevents the adversary from trivially finding R. Note that for the single-key version here we do not need an extra parameter a to produce values of the form $H(x \oplus aR, i) \oplus bR$, since the definitions in Choi et al. [7] would have made it illegal to use $a = 0$ anyway.

Finally, we emphasize that the adversary is allowed unrestricted access to H. Thus, modeling H as a random oracle, the adversary has oracle access to H in addition to the oracle in the experiment. In the standard model, the adversary is allowed to depend arbitrarily on H.

Constructions from ideal permutations. Bellare et al. [4] construct a gate-level cipher in the ideal random permutation model. In this model, all parties have access to a randomly chosen permutation $\pi : \{0, 1\}^k \to \{0, 1\}^k$ and its inverse π^{-1}. This is meant to model a setting where a garbling scheme is based on AES with a (public) fixed key, which can be implemented very efficiently with AES-NI instructions.

Bellare et al. [4] do not abstract a concrete security property that their hash function must satisfy. Instead, they describe how to construct their hash function, and prove security of the entire garbling scheme directly from the underlying assumption of a random permutation. Our ultimate abstraction (robustness for naturally derived keys) can be seen as a formalization of the properties of H actually used in their proofs.

We first describe the hash function of [4], altered for our single-key setting:

Definition 2. *For a random permutation* $\pi : \{0,1\}^k \mapsto \{0,1\}^k$, *we define the hash function* $H_\pi(x,i)$ *to be* $\pi(K) \oplus K$ *where* $K = 2x \oplus i$.

For concreteness, $2x$ refers to doubling in $\mathrm{GF}(2^k)$. However, there are many alternative ways of constructing H_π from π, which do not affect our proof. We refer the reader to Bellare et al. [4] for these alternate constructions and how they affect the exact constants on the security bounds. We also point out that in the following, the adversary is assumed to have access to π and π^{-1}.

Our abstraction. We now define a security notion that is satisfied by both of the above constructions.

Definition 3. *Say that a sequence of queries of the form* (x,i,b) *to an oracle* $\mathcal{O}$ *are* natural *if they satisfy the following:*

- *for the qth query, we have* $i = q$.
- $b \in \{0,1\}$
- x *is* naturally derived, *meaning that it is obtained from one of these operations:*
    - $x \leftarrow \{0,1\}^k$
    - $x \leftarrow x_1 \oplus x_2$, *where* x_1 *and* x_2 *are naturally derived*
    - $x \leftarrow H(x_1, i)$, *where* x_1 *is naturally derived and* $i \in \mathbb{Z}$
    - $x \leftarrow \mathcal{O}(x_1, i, b)$ *where* x_1 *is naturally derived.*

Then H *is* circular correlation robust for natural keys *if, for all all polynomial-time adversaries* $\mathcal{A}$ *making natural queries,*

$$\left| \Pr_R[\mathcal{A}^{\mathsf{Circ}_R}(1^k) = 1] - \Pr_{\mathsf{Rand}}[\mathcal{A}^{\mathsf{Rand}}(1^k) = 1] \right| \text{ is negligible.}$$

Note that these restrictions only apply when querying $\mathcal{O}$ — the adversary is still allowed to make unrestricted queries to H directly (and π, π^{-1} in the ideal permutation model). While it is a weak notion of security (since the adversary is very restricted), it turns out to be enough to prove security of our garbling scheme (Section 4.2).

Achieving the definition. While it is evident that circular correlation robustness against naturally derived keys is a restricted version of circular correlation robustness defined in Definition 1, it may not be as obvious that the H_π ideal permutation construction satisfies this notion.

Intuitively, the purpose of the naturally-derived restrictions is to make it unlikely that the adversary can ever query $\mathcal{O}$ with both (x, i, b) and (x', i', b') where $2x \oplus i = 2x' \oplus i'$ even though $(x, i) \neq (x', i')$. That would have created a problem in the case where $\mathcal{O}$ uses H_π. This would in turn invoke $\pi(2x \oplus 2R \oplus i) = \pi(2x' \oplus 2R \oplus i')$. If the adversary uses $b \neq b'$ then the responses to these queries reveal R.

The proof that the H_π construction achieves our definition in the ideal permutation model basically follows directly from the security proofs in Bellare et al. [4]. There, the bulk of the proofs are devoted to bounding the probability of the adversary making a query of the above form. They use only the fact that wire labels in their constructions are naturally derived, in our terminology (or, at least, the obvious generalization of naturally-derived to the two-key setting).

Following their proofs, one can work out the advantage of an adversary that makes q queries to the oracle $\mathcal{O}$ and Q queries to π, π^{-1}, in our security game. The advantage comes out to be $O((qQ + q^2)/2^k)$. The quadratic terms in that expression come from the birthday bounds of hash functions with k-bit output. We did not derive the exact constants since, in practice, much larger constants are likely to arise when π is replaced by a concrete function (e.g. AES). In any case, it is negligible in k, and therefore satisfies our notion of security.

4.2   Proof of Privacy and Obliviousness

The first thing to note is that we can easily rewrite the scheme in Figure 2 such that it only uses R through the oracle Circ_R. In particular, we can rewrite the assignments to T_{Gi} and T_{Ei} as:

$$T_{Gi} \leftarrow H(W_a^0, j) \oplus \mathsf{Circ}_R(W_a^0, j, p_b)$$
$$T_{Ei} \leftarrow H(W_b^0, j') \oplus \mathsf{Circ}_R(W_b^0, j', 0) \oplus W_a^0$$

Moreover, observe that we are only ever invoking Circ_R with naturally derived keys, assuming NextIndex returns sequential integers. This is partly why we did not write the assignments to W_{Gi}^0 and W_{Ei}^0 in Figure 2 more naturally using if statements conditioned on p_a and p_b — we did not want to repeat j values between oracle calls. Second, we no longer need to explicitly use R anywhere in Gb outside of the oracle (W_i^1 values are no longer needed).

Theorem 1. *Our scheme satisfies the security notion of* obv.sim$_\mathcal{S}$ *and* prv.sim$_\mathcal{S}$ *with any H that has correlation robustness for naturally derived keys.*

Proof. The proof for obv.sim$_\mathcal{S}$ is identical to that of prv.sim$_\mathcal{S}$, except that the simulator does not receive $\hat{y}$ and does not need to compute $\hat{d}$. So we will only provide the proof for prv.sim$_\mathcal{S}$. To prove indistinguishability between the simulator (Figure 3) and the real protocol (Figure 1) we use the following chain of hybrids:

procedure $\mathcal{S}(1^k, f, \hat{y})$:
  for $i \in \mathsf{Inputs}(f)$ **do**
    $W_i^0 \twoheadleftarrow \{0,1\}^k$
    $X_i \leftarrow W_i^0$
  for $i \notin \mathsf{Inputs}(f)$ {*in topo. order*} **do**
    $\{a,b\} \leftarrow \mathsf{GateInputs}(f,i)$
    if $i \in \mathsf{XorGates}(f)$ **then**
      $W_i^0 \leftarrow W_a^0 \oplus W_b^0$
    else
      $(W_i^0, T_{Gi}, T_{Ei}) \leftarrow \mathsf{SimAnd}(W_a^0, W_b^0)$
      $F_i \leftarrow (T_{Gi}, T_{Ei})$
    end if
  for $i \in \mathsf{Outputs}(f)$ **do**
    $d_i \leftarrow \mathsf{lsb}(W_i^0) \oplus y_i$
  return $(\hat{F}, \hat{X}, \hat{d})$

private procedure $\mathsf{SimAnd}(W_a^0, W_b^0)$:
  $p_a \leftarrow \mathsf{lsb}\, W_a^0;\; p_b \leftarrow \mathsf{lsb}\, W_b^0$
  $j \leftarrow \mathsf{NextIndex}();\; j' \leftarrow \mathsf{NextIndex}()$
  $T_G \leftarrow H(W_a^0, j) \oplus \mathsf{Rand}(W_a^0, j, p_b)$
  $W_G^0 \leftarrow H(W_a^0, j) \oplus p_a T_G$
  $T_E \leftarrow H(W_b^0, j') \oplus \mathsf{Rand}(W_b^0, j', 0) \oplus W_a^0$
  $W_E^0 \leftarrow H(W_b^0, j') \oplus p_b(T_E \oplus W_a^0)$
  $W^0 \leftarrow W_G^0 \oplus W_E^0$
  return (W^0, T_G, T_E)

---

procedure $\mathcal{G}_1^{\mathcal{O}}(1^k, f, \hat{x})$: // $\boxed{\mathcal{G}_2^{\mathsf{Circ}} R}$

$\hat{v} \leftarrow \mathsf{evalWires}(f, \hat{x})$
for $i \in \mathsf{Inputs}(f)$ **do**
  $W_i^{v_i} \twoheadleftarrow \{0,1\}^k;\; \boxed{W_i^{\overline{v_i}} \leftarrow W_i^{v_i} \oplus R}$
  $X_i \leftarrow W_i^{v_i}$
for $i \notin \mathsf{Inputs}(f)$ {*in topo. order*} **do**
  $\{a,b\} \leftarrow \mathsf{GateInputs}(f,i)$
  if $i \in \mathsf{XorGates}(f)$ **then**
    $W_i^{v_i} \leftarrow W_a^{v_a} \oplus W_b^{v_b}$
  else
    $(W_i^{v_i}, T_{Gi}, T_{Ei}) \leftarrow \mathsf{SimAnd}_1^{\mathcal{O}}(W_a^{v_a}, W_b^{v_b}, v_a, v_b)$
    $F_i \leftarrow (T_{Gi}, T_{Ei})$
  end if
  $\boxed{W_i^{\overline{v_i}} \leftarrow W_i^{v_i} \oplus R}$
for $i \in \mathsf{Outputs}(f)$ **do**
  $d_i \leftarrow \mathsf{lsb}(W_i^{v_i}) \oplus v_i$
return $(\hat{F}, \hat{X}, \hat{d})$

private procedure $\mathsf{SimAnd}_1^{\mathcal{O}}(W_a^{v_a}, W_b^{v_b}, v_a, v_b)$:
  $s_a \leftarrow \mathsf{lsb}\, W_a^{v_a};\; s_b \leftarrow \mathsf{lsb}\, W_b^{v_b}$
  $j \leftarrow \mathsf{NextIndex}();\; j' \leftarrow \mathsf{NextIndex}()$
  $T_G \leftarrow H(W_a^{v_a}, j) \oplus \mathcal{O}(W_a^{v_a}, j, v_b \oplus s_b)$
  $W_G^{v_a(v_b \oplus s_b)} \leftarrow H(W_a^{v_a}, j) \oplus s_a T_G$
  $T_E \leftarrow H(W_b^{v_b}, j') \oplus \mathcal{O}(W_b^{v_b}, j', v_a) \oplus W_a^{v_a}$
  $W_E^{v_a s_b} \leftarrow H(W_b^{v_b}, j') \oplus s_b(T_E \oplus W_a^{v_a})$
  $W^{v_a v_b} \leftarrow W_G^{v_a(v_b \oplus s_b)} \oplus W_E^{v_a s_b}$
  return $(W^{v_a v_b}, T_G, T_E)$

private procedure $\mathsf{evalWires}(f, \hat{x})$:
  for $i \in \mathsf{Inputs}(f)$ **do** $v_i \leftarrow x_i$
  for $i \notin \mathsf{Inputs}(f)$ **do**
    $\{a,b\} \leftarrow \mathsf{GateInputs}(f,i)$
    if $i \in \mathsf{XorGates}(f)$ **then**
      $v_i \leftarrow v_a \oplus v_b$
    else $v_i \leftarrow v_a \wedge v_b$
  return $\hat{v}$

---

procedure $\mathcal{G}_3(1^k, f, \hat{x})$:
$R \twoheadleftarrow \{0,1\}^{k-1} 1$
for $i \in \mathsf{Inputs}(f)$ **do**
  $W_i^0 \twoheadleftarrow \{0,1\}^k$
  $W_i^1 \leftarrow W_i^0 \oplus R$
  $X_i \leftarrow W_i^{x_i}$
for $i \notin \mathsf{Inputs}(f)$ {*in topo. order*} **do**
  $\{a,b\} \leftarrow \mathsf{GateInputs}(f,i)$
  if $i \in \mathsf{XorGates}(f)$ **then**
    $W_i^0 \leftarrow W_a^0 \oplus W_b^0$
  else
    $(W_i^0, T_{Gi}, T_{Ei}) \leftarrow \mathsf{SimAnd}_3(W_a^0, W_b^0)$
    $F_i \leftarrow (T_{Gi}, T_{Ei})$
  end if
  $W_i^1 \leftarrow W_i^0 \oplus R$
for $i \in \mathsf{Outputs}(f)$ **do**
  $d_i \leftarrow \mathsf{lsb}(W_i^0)$
return $(\hat{F}, \hat{X}, \hat{d})$

private procedure $\mathsf{SimAnd}_3(W_a^0, W_b^0)$:
  $p_a \leftarrow \mathsf{lsb}\, W_a^0;\; p_b \leftarrow \mathsf{lsb}\, W_b^0$
  $j \leftarrow \mathsf{NextIndex}();\; j' \leftarrow \mathsf{NextIndex}()$
  $T_G \leftarrow H(W_a^0, j) \oplus H(W_a^1, j) \oplus p_b R$
  $W_G^0 \leftarrow H(W_a^0, j) \oplus p_a T_G$
  $T_E \leftarrow H(W_b^0, j') \oplus H(W_b^1, j') \oplus W_a^0$
  $W_E^0 \leftarrow H(W_b^0, j') \oplus p_b(T_E \oplus W_a^0)$
  $W^0 \leftarrow W_G^0 \oplus W_E^0$
  return (W^0, T_G, T_E)

Fig. 3. The simulator for $\mathsf{prv.sim}_{\mathcal{S}}$ security, and the hybrids used in the proof

1. $\mathcal{S} \equiv \mathcal{G}_1^{\mathsf{Rand}}$: Both generate uniformly random values for each of the components in $(\hat{F}, \hat{X}, \hat{d})$, and are therefore identically distributed. More concretely, $\mathcal{G}_1$ uses $\hat{x}$ to determine a truth value v_i on each wire (via evalWires). Yet these truth values $\hat{v}$ are used only as a superscript for W_i^v. We could have obtained the same result if we had named these variables W_i^0 for all i instead of $W_i^{v_i}$. In Figure 3, $\mathcal{G}_1$ does *not* include the boxed statements.

2. $\mathcal{G}_1^{\mathsf{Rand}} \approx \mathcal{G}_1^{\mathsf{Circ}_R}$: We have just changed the oracle $\mathcal{O}$ from Rand to Circ_R. These two hybrids are indistinguishable simply by our assumption about the hash function.

3. $\mathcal{G}_1^{\mathsf{Circ}_R} \equiv \mathcal{G}_2^{\mathsf{Circ}_R}$: In Figure 3, we obtain $\mathcal{G}_2$ by adding the boxed statements to $\mathcal{G}_1$. We let the variable R in $\mathcal{G}_2$ refer to the R of the oracle Circ_R.

   The only difference between these two is that $\mathcal{G}_2$ computes some extra values that are never used (they will be used in $\mathcal{G}_3$). We couldn't compute these earlier since we couldn't use R while performing the previous step of the hybrid.

4. $\mathcal{G}_2^{\mathsf{Circ}_R} \equiv \mathcal{G}_3$: $\mathcal{G}_3$ induces identical distributions on all of the variables (W_i^0, W_i^1, T_{Gi}, and T_{Ei}), but does so without explicitly having to compute v_i for non-input wires. For example, instead of randomly sampling $W_i^{v_i}$ and then setting $W_i^{\overline{v_i}} \leftarrow W_i^{v_i} \oplus R$, $\mathcal{G}_3$ randomly samples W_i^0 and then sets $W_i^1 \leftarrow W_i^0 \oplus R$. The algebraic relationships between each variable are still unchanged. We have also expanded the oracle calls in SimAnd_3 to correspond to $\mathcal{O} = \mathsf{Circ}_R$.

Finally, $\mathcal{G}_3$ computes $(\hat{F}, \hat{X}, \hat{d})$ as $(\hat{F}, \hat{e}, \hat{d}) \leftarrow \mathsf{Gb}(1^k, f)$; $\hat{X} \leftarrow \mathsf{En}(\hat{e}, x)$. This is precisely how these values are computed in the real interaction in the $\mathsf{prv.sim}_{\mathcal{S}}$ game. This completes our proof.

4.3 Obtaining Authenticity

In the aut security game defined by Bellare et al. [5], an adversary is given $(\hat{F}, \hat{X})$. It is necessary to show that the adversary cannot produce $\tilde{Y} \neq \mathsf{Ev}(\hat{F}, \hat{X})$ such that $\mathsf{De}(\hat{d}, \tilde{Y}) \neq \bot$, except with negligible probability. This is clearly not the case for the scheme as we present it in Figure 2; in fact, De never returns $\bot$.

To achieve authenticity, we modify the scheme as described in Figure 4.

Theorem 2. *Our modified scheme (Figure 4) satisfies the security notion of* aut *with any H that has correlation robustness for naturally derived keys.*

Proof (Proof Sketch). Consider an interaction in which we run the prv.sim-simulator $\mathcal{S}$ (with the change described in Figure 4) to generate $(\hat{F}, \hat{X}, \hat{d})$. We give $(\hat{F}, \hat{X})$ to the adversary and use $\hat{d}$ to run De and check whether the adversary succeeded in violating authenticity. In order to do so, the adversary would have to guess a value h that was chosen in the final loop of $\mathcal{S}$. But these values are independent of the adversary's view, so this can happen with probability at most $1/2^k$. The rest of the proof follows an identical sequence of hybrids as the proof of Theorem 1. Eventually, we reach an interaction that is identical to the aut game played against the adversary. By the indistinguishability of

	procedure $\mathsf{De}(\hat{d}, \hat{Y})$:	
	for $d_i \in \hat{d}$ **do**	{*modify final loop of $\mathcal{S}$:*}
{*modify final loop of Gb:*}	$\quad j \leftarrow \mathsf{NextIndex}()$	**for** $i \in \mathsf{Outputs}(f)$ **do**
for $i \in \mathsf{Outputs}(f)$ **do**	$\quad$ parse $(h_0, h_1) \leftarrow d_i$	$\quad j \leftarrow \mathsf{NextIndex}(); h \leftarrow \{0,1\}^k$
$\quad j \leftarrow \mathsf{NextIndex}()$	$\quad$ **if** $H(Y_i, j) = h_0$ **then** $y_i \leftarrow 0$	$\quad$ **if** $y_i = 0$
$\quad d_i \leftarrow (H(W_i^0, j), H(W_i^1, j))$	$\quad$ **else if** $H(Y_i, j) = h_1$ **then** $y_i \leftarrow 1$	$\quad\quad$ **then** $d_i \leftarrow (H(W_i^0, j), h)$
	$\quad$ **else return** $\perp$	$\quad\quad$ **else** $d_i \leftarrow (h, H(W_i^0, j))$
	return $\hat{y}$	

Fig. 4. Changes to our scheme required to achieve authenticity

the hybrids, the adversary's success probability must be negligible. Note that the changes we have made to the scheme and simulator still allow the steps in the proof to retain *naturally derived* accesses to the oracles.

5   Performance Comparison

We evaluate the performance of our scheme in comparison to previous garbling schemes using both analytical and experimental measurements.

Table 3 shows computations of the raw garbled circuit size in our scheme, calculated for several circuit designs. The table is derived from the one provided with fleXOR [19]; the circuits were obtained from [11,30]. Our technique outperforms all previous garbling schemes in this metric, achieving the expected maximum of 33% gain for most circuits. There are some AND-intensive circuits (e.g., the DES circuit used here) for which the previous fleXOR technique already does well, but we manage to improve a little upon that as well.

We selected a smaller, well-studied set of benchmark circuits for experimental evaluation. The aim here was to understand the cost tradeoffs for our scheme more clearly, in the context of a secure two-party computation protocol. In our scheme the evaluator performs one extra hash operation per gate while reducing network usage. Therefore, it is possible that we end up paying more in terms of computational resources, such as energy used.

Table 3. Comparison of garbled circuit size, for selected circuits of interest. Size measured in average number of ciphertexts per gate.

circuit	GRR2 [28]	free-XOR [20]	fleXOR [19]	**this work**	$\downarrow$%
DES	2.0	2.79	1.89	1.86	1%
AES	2.0	0.64	0.72	0.42	33%
SHA-1	2.0	1.82	1.39	1.21	12%
SHA-256	2.0	2.05	1.56	1.37	12%
Hamming distance	2.0	0.50	0.50	0.33	33%
minimum in set	2.0	0.87	0.87	0.58	33%
32 × 32 fast mult	2.0	0.90	0.94	0.60	33%
1024-bit millionaires	2.0	1.00	1.00	0.67	33%

Table 4. Resource usage for three common programs. Edit distance refers to the Levenstein distance between two 200-byte strings. AES refers to 1 block of encryption and key expansion, iterated 10 times. Set intersection is performed on set of 1024, 32-bit integers, iterated 10 times. Each of these 3 jobs were in turn executed 5 times and measured separately, and the numbers are averages over these 5 runs. Whole denotes experimental setup using free-XOR with GRR2, while Half denotes a setup using our half-gates construction.

Benchmark	Time (s)			Bandwidth (MB)			Energy (kJ)		
	Whole	Half	↓%	Whole	Half	↓%	Whole	Half	↓%
Edit distance [14]	17.8	13.2	25.7%	200.4	133.6	33.3%	1.13	0.89	21.0%
AES [14]	18.2	17.0	7.0%	115.6	77.1	33.3%	1.25	1.18	5.3%
Set intersection [13]	37.0	29.7	19.7%	324.5	219.9	32.2%	2.41	2.03	15.5%

Table 4 shows our measurements. Details of our experimental setup are provided below. We see that our scheme significantly reduces the total time and energy used by the evaluator in every test of the protocol. In our tests, we found that our scheme actually *increased* the power usage (i.e., higher wattage), but the increase was more than offset by the reduced runtime (i.e., lower total energy). It is conceivable that a very slow evaluator connected to a very fast LAN may not enjoy the same reduction in energy usage, but we did not have the equipment to run such a test and such a scenario seems unlikely to occur in practice. If the two parties have symmetric computational power, however, our protocol should always be better since the computational bottleneck would be the generator, who is performing four calls to H per AND gate in all schemes.

Experimental Setup. The experiments were performed using the Obliv-C system [32], where we hooked into the protocol execution to implement our own garbling scheme. This allowed us to easily reuse the exact same benchmark programs for both schemes. We executed Yao's standard semi-honest protocol for 2PC, with a security of 80-bit keys, and compared our scheme to Free-XOR with GRR3 AND gates. In both experimental setups, we used pipelining optimizations [14] and instantiated the H hash function in the garbling scheme using the fixed-key AES construction of [4] (described in Section 4). All measurements (time, network and energy) include the time for performing oblivious transfers and output sharing (which are not affected by the garbling scheme), hence the overall reductions support the argument that bulk of the bandwidth and computation is due to the garbled circuit execution.

The compilation was done using GCC 4.8.2, linked with libgcrypt 1.6.1 (older versions are much slower). We executed the protocol between an Intel Core i7-2600S at 2.8 GHz, running Ubuntu 14.04, and an i7-2600 at 3.4 GHz running Ubuntu 13.10, connected over a LAN. Energy consumption was measured by using an electrical meter plugged in to the wall power outlet for one of the machines — the power meter had an USB interface that allowed us to measure power only for the duration of the job. For all jobs we report the average (time/energy) measurement over five runs, which was more than enough for obtaining statistically significant results (at $p < 0.05$).

6   Privacy-Free Garbling

Jawurek, Kerschbaum, and Orlandi [18] described an elegant and practical zero-knowledge protocol based on garbled circuits. It allows a prover to prove statements of the form "$\exists x : C(x) = 1$", at a cost of just one garbled circuit for C.

In their protocol, the garbled circuit is evaluated by a prover who knows the entire input to the garbled circuit and the truth value along each wire. Hence, only the *authenticity* property of garbled circuits is required, and not the *privacy* property (in the terminology of Bellare et al. [5]). We call a garbling scheme *privacy-free* if it only satisfies the authenticity property. Frederiksen, Nielsen, and Orlandi [8] showed that privacy-free garbled circuits can be significantly smaller than their full-fledged counterparts.

Very roughly speaking, removing the privacy requirement saves one ciphertext per gate. Frederiksen et al. [8] adapt three garbling schemes to the privacy-free setting: GRR2, free-XOR, and fleXOR. Mirroring the situation with full-fledged garbled circuits, they showed how to garble an AND gate using just one ciphertext (i.e., *GRR1*), but in a way that is incompatible with free-XOR. When using free-XOR, it was necessary to garble AND gates using two ciphertexts.

Our approach using half-gates can also give a direct improvement in this privacy-free setting. Namely, one can garble a circuit with free-XOR gates, and garble AND gates using our evaluator-half-gate construction. In this setting, the evaluator knows *both* inputs to every AND gate, though our half-gate only takes advantage of the evaluator's knowledge of one input. Overall, we can perform privacy-free garbling at a cost of only one ciphertext per AND gate, and no cost for XOR gates. Interestingly, our construction of privacy-free garbling also results in less overall computation than the previous schemes — only two calls to H instead of three.

A summary of our results for privacy-free garbling is given in Table 5. As before, our best improvements in this setting are on circuits for which free-XOR was previously the best approach. Here, the relative improvement is more

Table 5. Comparison of **privacy-free** garbled circuit size, for selected circuits of interest. Previous constructions and their statistics are from Frederiksen, Nielsen, and Orlandi [8]. Size measured in average number of ciphertexts per gate.

circuit	GRR1	free-XOR	fleXOR	this work	↓%
DES	1.0	1.86	0.96	0.93	3%
AES	1.0	0.43	0.51	0.21	50%
SHA-1	1.0	1.21	0.78	0.61	22%
SHA-256	1.0	1.37	0.87	0.68	22%

dramatic: we cut the size of the garbled circuit in half. Concretely, using the protocol of Jawurek, Kerschbaum, and Orlandi [18], it is possible to prove in zero knowledge a statement of the form "I know k such that $\text{AES}(k, m) = c$" (for public m, c) by sending only 108 kilobytes of garbled circuit (using 128-bit wire labels; for 80-bit wire labels, the garbled circuit is 68 kilobytes).

7   Lower Bounds on Garbled Circuits

This section introduces a methodology for reasoning about lower bounds on the size of garbled gates and shows that our construction is size-optimal for a large class of garbling schemes, which encompasses all known practical techniques.

When thinking about the size of garbled gates, instead of thinking about free-XOR compatibility, it turns out to be more instructive to think about the degrees of freedom available for choosing a gate's output wire labels. In the classical scheme that uses four ciphertexts, both output wire labels can be arbitrary; there are two degrees of freedom. In the GRR3 scheme that uses three ciphertexts, one of the output wire labels is fixed as soon as the input wire labels are fixed (since one output wire label is a hash of some input wire labels). Hence there is just one degree of freedom, for choosing the other wire label, and this is typically exploited to ensure free-XOR compatibility. In the GRR2 scheme that uses two ciphertexts, both output wire labels are fixed as soon as the input wire labels are fixed; there are no degrees of freedom. In our construction also, there are no degrees of freedom on the output wire labels. One is chosen as a hash of input wire labels, and, furthermore, the two output wire labels must have the same offset as one of the input wires.

7.1   Basic Methodology

There are many techniques that fall under the category of garbling schemes. We wish to focus on techniques based on (fast, practical) symmetric-key primitives only. Hence, in this section we model parties as computationally unbounded entities that can make polynomially many queries to a random oracle. This is the standard setting (initiated by Impagliazzo and Rudich [17]) for proving lower bounds about Minicrypt.[2]

We wish to prove lower bounds relating to *concrete efficiency*; for example, prove that it is possible to garble an AND-gate with $2k$ bits of ciphertext but not with k bits. We say that a garbling scheme has **ideal security** if no adversary of the above form (computationally unbounded, with bounded queries to a random oracle) has advantage better than $\text{poly}(k)/2^k$ (rather than negligible) in the

---

[2] Minicrypt is one of Impagliazzo's hypothetical worlds [16] in which one-way functions exist but no stronger cryptography (in particular, public-key cryptography) exists. Since a random oracle models an ideal one-way function, we can model a world without cryptography beyond one-way functions as a world with computationally-unbounded entities that have access to a random oracle.

security games, where k is the security parameter and output length of the random oracle.

To see why it makes sense to restrict to ideal security in our setting, consider a garbling scheme where, with security parameter k, we apply our "two-ciphertext" construction for AND gates but with a $k/2$-bit random oracle. The resulting garbled gate is then only k bits, and indeed, no adversary has better than negligible advantage in the appropriate security games. However, it is possible to achieve advantage $\text{poly}(k)/2^{k/2}$.

Intuitively, a random oracle with security parameter (output length) k is an object that gives security $\text{poly}(k)/2^k$. We wish to consider only garbling schemes which do not "cheat" the size of the garbled gates by artificially degrading the security parameter of the random oracle relative to the security parameter of the garbling scheme.

Still, consider a garbling scheme that on security parameter k instantiates an ideally secure garbling scheme on security parameter $k - O(\log k)$. The result yields security $\text{poly}(k)/2^{k-O(\log k)} = \text{poly}(k)/2^k$, satisfying our ideal security definition as well. Hence, even with our model one cannot prove a clean lower bound of the form "$2k$ bits are required for an AND gate." Rather, one must prove something like "$2k - O(\log k)$ bits are required for an AND gate."[3] The special case we consider below, however, is already restricted to schemes whose gates are an integer multiple of k bits.

7.2   Linear Garbling Schemes

We first observe that, to the best of our knowledge, all techniques for practical garbling schemes share certain features. Roughly speaking, the Gb and Ev procedures use only *linear* operations apart from queries to the random oracle (in this setting, we assume a random-oracle instantiation of the scheme), and choosing which linear operation to apply based on select bits of given wire labels (in the case of Ev) or on the association of select bits to TRUE/FALSE (in the case of Gb).

For example:

- In the classical garbling scheme, ciphertexts that comprise the garbled gate are all formed by taking an XOR of oracle responses with wire labels. Similarly, in most other schemes the garbled gate consists of values of the form $H(A\|B) \oplus C$, $H(A) \oplus C$, where A, B, and C are wire labels. The select bits and permute bits are used to decide which linear operations to apply (which ciphertext to decrypt in Ev).
- When using GRR3 row-reduction, one output wire label is chosen as $H(A\|B)$, hence linearly in the sense described above. Then behavior in Ev depends on the select bits of the given wire labels (i.e., whether to decrypt a ciphertext or simply take a hash of the input wire labels as the output), but in each case the resulting behavior is linear.

---

[3] Indeed, constructions that use the point-and-permute optimization degrade (by just one bit) the security of the underlying block cipher / hash function by using the least significant bit in a structured way.

- In the GRR2 construction [28], generating and evaluating a gate involves interpolating polynomials that pass through points of the form $(t, H(A\|B))$. Since the values t are fixed, interpolation is a linear operation on outputs of H. Both the garbled gate itself and the output wire labels are the result of such interpolation. In Gb, the choice of which points to interpolate (hence, the choice of which linear operation to perform) depends on the assocation of select bits to TRUE/FALSE.
- In our scheme, Ev performs an additional XOR depending on the select bits of wire labels.
- When using free-XOR, wire labels are chosen subject to a linear relation $A_0 \oplus A_1 = B_0 \oplus B_1$.

We also observe the following properties common to existing garbling techniques:

- When garbling a circuit, the gates are processed in topological order. At the time a gate is processed, the labels of its input wires have already been determined, but the output wire labels may be determined as a result of garbling this gate.
- When restricted to operate on a **single gate**, the queries to the random oracle are made statically. That is, neither Ev nor Gb ever use the result of an oracle query to determine a future oracle query. For many schemes, this property is not true when garbling a larger circuit (an oracle query is used to determine an output wire label, which is then used to determine another oracle query in a downstream gate).

We argue that restrictions of this form capture **all existing practical approaches for garbled circuits**. Of course, we exclude techniques based on specific algebraic assumptions (e.g., [1,2]) or more exotic tools like multilinear maps (e.g., [9]) which are arguably impractical and already ruled out by restricting our focus to Minicrypt.

The model. We formalize the observations above as follows. We restrict our focus to garbling schemes that garble a single AND gate. We say that a garbling scheme is **linear** if its procedures have the following form:

Gb: Parameterized by integers m, r, q and vectors $\boldsymbol{A}_0$, $\boldsymbol{A}_1$, $\boldsymbol{B}_0$, $\boldsymbol{B}_1$, $\{\boldsymbol{C}_{a,b,0} \mid a, b \in \{0,1\}\}$, $\{\boldsymbol{C}_{a,b,1} \mid a, b \in \{0,1\}\}$, and $\{\boldsymbol{G}_{a,b}^{(i)} \mid a, b \in \{0,1\}, i \in [m]\}$. Each vector is of length $r + q$, with entries in $GF(2^k)$.

1. For $i \in [r]$, choose $R_i \leftarrow GF(2^k)$.
2. Make q distinct queries to the random oracle (which can be chosen as a deterministic function of the R_i values). Let $Q_1, \ldots, Q_q$ denote the responses to these queries. Define $\boldsymbol{S} = (R_1, \ldots, R_r, Q_1, \ldots, Q_q)$. These are the values on which the algorithm acts linearly.
3. Choose random permute bits $a, b \leftarrow \{0,1\}$ for the two input wires.
4. For $i \in \{0,1\}$, compute $A_i = \langle \boldsymbol{A}_i, \boldsymbol{S} \rangle$; $B_i = \langle \boldsymbol{B}_i, \boldsymbol{S} \rangle$; $C_i = \langle \boldsymbol{C}_{a,b,i}, \boldsymbol{S} \rangle$. Then $(A_0\|0, A_1\|1)$ and $(B_0\|0, B_1\|1)$ are taken as the input wire labels to the gate (i.e., the subscripts denote the public select bits), with A_a

and B_b corresponding to FALSE. (C_0, C_1) are the output wire labels with C_1 corresponding to TRUE.

5. For $i \in [m]$, compute $G_i = \langle \boldsymbol{G}_{a,b}^{(i)}, \boldsymbol{S} \rangle$. The values $G_1, \ldots, G_m$ comprise the garbled circuit.

En: On input $x_a, x_b \in \{0, 1\}$, set $\alpha = x_a \oplus a$ and $\beta = x_b \oplus b$, where a and b are the permute bits chosen above. Output $A_\alpha \| \alpha$ and $B_\beta \| \beta$.

Ev: Parameterized by integer q and vectors $\{\boldsymbol{V}_{\alpha,\beta} \mid \alpha, \beta \in \{0, 1\}\}$, where each vector is of length $q + m + 2$.

1. The input are wire labels $A_\alpha \| \alpha, B_\beta \| \beta$, tagged with their corresponding select bits, and the garbled circuit $G_1, \ldots, G_m$.

2. Make q distinct queries to the random oracle (which can be chosen as a deterministic function of the input wire labels). Let $Q'_1, \ldots, Q'_q$ denote the responses to these queries, and define $\boldsymbol{T} = (A_\alpha, B_\beta, Q'_1, \ldots, Q'_q, G_1, \ldots, G_m)$. These are the values on which Ev acts linearly.

3. Output the inner product $\langle \boldsymbol{V}_{\alpha,\beta}, \boldsymbol{T} \rangle$.

In Appendix A we show how well-known previous practical garbling schemes are linear in the above sense.

Limitations. We emphasize that our linear model of garbling schemes is most meaningful when garbling a single *atomic* gate. This is due to the issue regarding adaptive queries to the random oracle that happen when combining several garbled gates in a larger circuit.

For example, the best known way to garble an N-input AND gate is to garble it as a circuit of $N - 1$, 2-input AND gates, for a total cost of $2N - 2$ ciphertexts. But garbling in this way results in adaptive oracle queries, and the resulting scheme is not covered by our current model.

We suspect that it may be possible to augment our proof techniques for larger garbled circuits while accounting for adaptive oracle queries, but we leave this investigation to future work.

7.3 Lower Bound

Theorem 3. *Every ideally secure garbling scheme for AND gates that is linear in the above sense must have $m \geq 2$. That is, the garbled gate consists of at least $2k$ bits.*

Proof. From the correctness of the scheme, we must have $C_{(a \oplus \alpha) \wedge (b \oplus \beta)} = \langle \boldsymbol{V}_{\alpha,\beta}, \boldsymbol{T} \rangle$. Let us divide the vector $\boldsymbol{T}$ into a *public* and *private* part:

- The public part $\boldsymbol{T}^{pub}$ of $\boldsymbol{T}$ consists of the wire labels and oracle responses. Without loss of generality, the oracle queries made by Ev are a subset of the queries made by Gb. Any query made by Ev but not Gb will have an answer that is independent of all the activity of Gb. As such, correctness is violated if this oracle response is actually used in the evaluator's inner product. Hence the public portion of T is linear function of S, and that linear function depends only on α, β, and not the secret permute bits a, b. We write $T^{pub} = \mathbb{M}_{\alpha,\beta} \times S^{\top}$.

- The private part T^{prv} of T consists of the garbled circuit components G_i. These are a linear function of S that can depend on the secret permute bits a, b. In particular, let $\mathbb{G}_{a,b}$ denote the matrix whose rows are $G_{a,b}^{(1)}, \ldots, G_{a,b}^{(m)}$. Then $T^{prv} = \mathbb{G}_{a,b} \times S^{\top}$. Our goal is to show that $\mathbb{G}_{a,b}$ must have at least 2 rows.

Let us also divide $V_{\alpha,\beta}$ into a public and private portion, in an analogous way. We may thus rewrite the correctness condition as follows:

$$
\begin{aligned}
\langle C_{a,b,(a\oplus\alpha)\wedge(b\oplus\beta)}, S \rangle = C_{(a\oplus\alpha)\wedge(b\oplus\beta)} &= \langle V_{\alpha,\beta}, T \rangle \\
&= \langle V_{\alpha,\beta}^{pub}, T^{pub} \rangle + \langle V_{\alpha,\beta}^{prv}, T^{prv} \rangle \\
&= \langle V_{\alpha,\beta}^{pub}, \mathbb{M}_{\alpha,\beta} \times S^{\top} \rangle + \langle V_{\alpha,\beta}^{prv}, \mathbb{G}_{a,b} \times S^{\top} \rangle \\
&= \langle Z_{\alpha,\beta}, S \rangle + \langle V_{\alpha,\beta}^{prv} \times \mathbb{G}_{a,b}, S \rangle
\end{aligned}
$$

where $Z_{\alpha,\beta} = V_{\alpha,\beta}^{pub} \times \mathbb{M}_{\alpha,\beta}$ is a vector that depends only on α, β.

Now, the vector S is uniformly distributed. For this correctness probability to hold with probability 1 (or even noticeable probability) over the choice of S, we must have the following equality of *vectors*:

$$
C_{a,b,(a\oplus\alpha)\wedge(b\oplus\beta)} = Z_{\alpha,\beta} + V_{\alpha,\beta}^{prv} \times \mathbb{G}_{a,b}
$$

Claim: Matrices $\{\mathbb{G}_{a,b} \mid a, b \in \{0,1\}\}$ are all distinct. Fix some permute bits a, b, then by the correctness condition, the values $\{Z_{\alpha,\beta} + V_{\alpha,\beta}^{prv} \times \mathbb{G}_{a,b}\}$ form a multi-set in which one element has multiplicity 3 and the other element has multiplicity 1. The element of multiplicity 1 is associated with a unique pair α, β. Changing the permute bits (and thus changing $\mathbb{G}_{a,b}$) must change which α, β is associated with the multiplicity-1 element. Hence the matrices $\mathbb{G}_{a,b}$ must be distinct.

Claim: Vectors $\{Z_{\alpha,\beta} \mid \alpha, \beta \in \{0,1\}\}$ are pairwise linearly independent. To see why, suppose to the contrary that (by symmetry) $Z_{0,1} = \sigma Z_{0,0}$ for some scalar σ. Then consider an adversary given input wire labels corresponding to $\alpha = \beta = 0$. Instead of computing $\langle V_{0,0}, T \rangle$ as instructed, she can compute $\underline{\sigma} \cdot \langle V_{0,0}^{pub}, T^{pub} \rangle + \langle V_{0,1}^{prv}, T^{prv} \rangle = \langle V_{0,1}, T \rangle$. The result will reveal what the output of the garbled circuit would be if she had instead had input wires $\alpha = 0, \beta = 1$. For an AND gate, this is a violation of the privacy property (the output changes if and only if A_α encodes true).[4]

Claim: Vectors $\{V_{\alpha,\beta}^{prv} \mid \alpha, \beta \in \{0,1\}\}$ are all distinct. To see why, consider the example of $V_{0,0}^{prv}$ and $V_{0,1}^{prv}$. With select bits either $(0,0)$ or $(0,1)$, and permute

---

[4] Note that this scenario does not violate security for an XOR gate. No matter what inputs the evaluator holds, she already knows that flipping one input bit always flips the output.

bits $(0,0)$, the garbled gate should evaluate to false. Hence:

$$Z_{0,0} + V_{0,0}^{prv} \times \mathbb{G}_{0,0} = C_{0,0,0}$$

$$Z_{0,1} + V_{0,1}^{prv} \times \mathbb{G}_{0,0} = C_{0,0,0}$$

$$\implies (Z_{0,0} - Z_{0,1}) + (V_{0,0}^{prv} - V_{0,1}^{prv})\mathbb{G}_{0,0} = 0$$

Since $Z_{0,0} - Z_{0,1}$ is nonzero, $V_{0,0}^{prv} - V_{0,1}^{prv}$ must also be nonzero. More generally, for any two elements of $\{V_{\alpha,\beta}^{prv} \mid \alpha, \beta \in \{0,1\}\}$, one can choose permute bits a, b that cause those two input combinations to give the same output to the garbled gate.[5]

We now prove the theorem. Consider two choices of select bits $(\alpha, \beta) \in \{(0,0), (0,1)\}$, and two choices of permute bits $(a,b) \in \{(0,0), (0,1)\}$. For all such combinations, the garbled gate must evaluate to false. Hence, we have:

$$C_{0,0,0} = Z_{0,0} + V_{0,0}^{prv} \times \mathbb{G}_{0,0} \qquad (a)$$

$$C_{0,0,0} = Z_{0,1} + V_{0,1}^{prv} \times \mathbb{G}_{0,0} \qquad (b)$$

$$C_{0,1,0} = Z_{0,0} + V_{0,0}^{prv} \times \mathbb{G}_{0,1} \qquad (c)$$

$$C_{0,1,0} = Z_{0,1} + V_{0,1}^{prv} \times \mathbb{G}_{0,1} \qquad (d)$$

If we combine these four equations as (a)-(b)-(c)+(d), we obtain:

$$0 = 0 + (V_{0,0}^{prv} - V_{0,1}^{prv}) \times \mathbb{G}_{0,0} - (V_{0,0}^{prv} - V_{0,1}^{prv}) \times \mathbb{G}_{0,1}$$

$$= (V_{0,0}^{prv} - V_{0,1}^{prv}) \times (\mathbb{G}_{0,0} - \mathbb{G}_{0,1})$$

We see that $V_{0,0}^{prv} - V_{0,1}^{prv}$ is a *nonzero* vector in the left kernel of the *nonzero* matrix $\mathbb{G}_{0,0} - \mathbb{G}_{0,1}$. This implies that $\mathbb{G}_{0,0} - \mathbb{G}_{0,1}$ must have at least 2 rows. Hence, each $\mathbb{G}_{a,b}$ has at least 2 rows, and garbled gates consist of at least $2k$ bits, as desired.

Discussion. Let us define the *parity* of a binary boolean gate as the number of 1s in its truth table. XOR, for instance, has even parity, while AND has odd parity. The proof of Theorem 3 applies to any odd-parity gate. We frequently used the facts that (a) the gate has one output with multiplicity 3 and another with multiplicity 1, and (b) depending on the permute bits, the output with multiplicity 1 could be associated with any of the 4 possible input combinations.

We are currently unable to prove a lower bound for completely arbitrary garbling schemes. As such, we cannot rule out the possibility of garbling an AND gate with only k bits. Yet, our lower bound shows that if such a method exists, then it must use (expensive) public-key primitives or be significantly non-linear

---

[5] This is another step of the proof that does not apply to XOR gates. Consider input wires with select bits $(0,0)$ or $(0,1)$. There is no choice of permute bits that could cause an XOR gate to give the same output for both.

in how it uses wire labels and outputs from the random oracle. Any non-linearity outside our model would represent an entirely new technical approach for garbled circuits.

What about the privacy-free setting? In arguing that the $\mathbb{G}_{a,b}$ matrices were distinct, we did not use the privacy property of the scheme. Privacy was only used to establish the other claims. Hence, for privacy-free garbled circuits we still have that the $\mathbb{G}_{a,b}$ matrices are distinct. As such, these cannot all be the empty matrix; they must contain at least one row. So for privacy-free garbling on an AND gate, we must have $m \geq 1$ (as in our construction); in other words, the garbled gate must contain at least k bits.

Availability

The source code for our half gates implementation and the benchmarks used in this paper is available under an open source license at http://MightBeEvil.com/halfgates.

Acknowledgments. We thank Jonathan Dorn for providing the energy usage metering apparatus for our experiments and helping us use it. Mike Rosulek was supported by NSF Award 1149647. David Evans and Samee Zahur were supported by NSF Award 1111781.

References

1. Applebaum, B.: Garbling XOR gates "For Free" in the standard model. In: Sahai, A. (ed.) TCC 2013. LNCS, vol. 7785, pp. 162–181. Springer, Heidelberg (2013)
2. Applebaum, B., Ishai, Y., Kushilevitz, E.: How to garble arithmetic circuits. In: 52nd Symposium on Foundations of Computer Science (2011)
3. Beaver, D., Micali, S., Rogaway, P.: The round complexity of secure protocols. In: 22nd Symposium on Theory of Computing (1990)
4. Bellare, M., Hoang, V.T., Keelveedhi, S., Rogaway, P.: Efficient garbling from a fixed-key blockcipher. In: 34th IEEE Symposium on Security and Privacy (2013)
5. Bellare, M., Hoang, V.T., Rogaway, P.: Foundations of garbled circuits. In: 19th ACM Conference on Computer and Communications Security (2012)
6. Brandão, L.T.A.N.: Secure two-party computation with reusable bit-commitments, via a cut-and-choose with forge-and-lose technique. In: Sako, K., Sarkar, P. (eds.) ASIACRYPT 2013, Part II. LNCS, vol. 8270, pp. 441–463. Springer, Heidelberg (2013)
7. Choi, S.G., Katz, J., Kumaresan, R., Zhou, H.-S.: On the security of the "Free-XOR" technique. In: Cramer, R. (ed.) TCC 2012. LNCS, vol. 7194, pp. 39–53. Springer, Heidelberg (2012)
8. Frederiksen, T.K., Nielsen, J.B., Orlandi, C.: Privacy-free garbled circuits with applications to efficient zero-knowledge. In: EUROCRYPT (2014)

9. Goldwasser, S., Kalai, Y.T., Popa, R.A., Vaikuntanathan, V., Zeldovich, N.: Reusable garbled circuits and succinct functional encryption. In: 45th ACM STOC (2013)

10. Henecka, W., Kögl, S., Sadeghi, A.R., Schneider, T., Wehrenberg, I.: TASTY: tool for automating secure two-party computations. In: 17th ACM Conference on Computer and Communications Security (2010)

11. Henecka, W., Schneider, T.: Memory efficient secure function evaluation. https://code.google.com/p/me-sfe/

12. Holzer, A., Franz, M., Katzenbeisser, S., Veith, H.: Secure two-party computations in ANSI C. In: 19th ACM Conference on Computer and Communications Security (2012)

13. Huang, Y., Evans, D., Katz, J.: Private set intersection: are garbled circuits better than custom protocols? In: 19th Network and Distributed System Security Symposium (2012)

14. Huang, Y., Evans, D., Katz, J., Malka, L.: Faster secure two-party computation using garbled circuits. In: 20th USENIX Security Symposium (2011)

15. Huang, Y., Katz, J., Evans, D.: Efficient secure two-party computation using symmetric cut-and-choose. In: Canetti, R., Garay, J.A. (eds.) CRYPTO 2013, Part II. LNCS, vol. 8043, pp. 18–35. Springer, Heidelberg (2013)

16. Impagliazzo, R.: A personal view of average-case complexity. In: 10th Structure in Complexity Theory Conference (1995)

17. Impagliazzo, R., Rudich, S.: Limits on the provable consequences of one-way permutations. In: Goldwasser, S. (ed.) CRYPTO 1988. LNCS, vol. 403, pp. 8–26. Springer, Heidelberg (1990)

18. Jawurek, M., Kerschbaum, F., Orlandi, C.: Zero-knowledge using garbled circuits: how to prove non-algebraic statements efficiently. In: ACM CCS 13 (2013)

19. Kolesnikov, V., Mohassel, P., Rosulek, M.: FleXOR: flexible garbling for XOR gates that beats free-XOR. In: Garay, J.A., Gennaro, R. (eds.) CRYPTO 2014, Part II. LNCS, vol. 8617, pp. 440–457. Springer, Heidelberg (2014)

20. Kolesnikov, V., Schneider, T.: Improved garbled circuit: free XOR gates and applications. In: Aceto, L., Damgård, I., Goldberg, L.A., Halldórsson, M.M., Ingólfsdóttir, A., Walukiewicz, I. (eds.) ICALP 2008, Part II. LNCS, vol. 5126, pp. 486–498. Springer, Heidelberg (2008)

21. Kreuter, B., Shelat, A., Shen, C.: Billion-gate secure computation with malicious adversaries. In: 21st USENIX Security Symposium (2012)

22. Lindell, Y.: Fast cut-and-choose based protocols for malicious and covert adversaries. In: Canetti, R., Garay, J.A. (eds.) CRYPTO 2013, Part II. LNCS, vol. 8043, pp. 1–17. Springer, Heidelberg (2013)

23. Lindell, Y., Pinkas, B.: A proof of security of Yao's protocol for two-party computation. Journal of Cryptology 22(2) (2009)

24. Lindell, Y., Pinkas, B.: Secure two-party computation via cut-and-choose oblivious transfer. In: Ishai, Y. (ed.) TCC 2011. LNCS, vol. 6597, pp. 329–346. Springer, Heidelberg (2011)

25. Lindell, Y., Pinkas, B., Smart, N.P.: Implementing two-party computation efficiently with security against malicious adversaries. In: Ostrovsky, R., De Prisco, R., Visconti, I. (eds.) SCN 2008. LNCS, vol. 5229, pp. 2–20. Springer, Heidelberg (2008)

26. Malkhi, D., Nisan, N., Pinkas, B., Sella, Y.: Fairplay - secure two-party computation system. In: 13th USENIX Security Symposium (2004)
27. Naor, M., Pinkas, B., Sumner, R.: Privacy preserving auctions and mechanism design. In: 1st ACM Conference on Electronic Commerce (1999)
28. Pinkas, B., Schneider, T., Smart, N.P., Williams, S.C.: Secure two-party computation is practical. In: Matsui, M. (ed.) ASIACRYPT 2009. LNCS, vol. 5912, pp. 250–267. Springer, Heidelberg (2009)
29. shelat, A., Shen, C.: Two-output secure computation with malicious adversaries. In: Paterson, K.G. (ed.) EUROCRYPT 2011. LNCS, vol. 6632, pp. 386–405. Springer, Heidelberg (2011)
30. Tillich, S., Smart, N.: Circuits of basic functions suitable for MPC and FHE. http://www.cs.bris.ac.uk/Research/CryptographySecurity/MPC/
31. Yao, A.C.C.: How to generate and exchange secrets. In: 27th FOCS (1986)
32. Zahur, S.: Obliv-C: A lightweight compiler for data-oblivious computation (2014). https://github.com/samee/obliv-c

A   Linear Garbling Schemes

In this section we show that all existing garbling schemes are **linear** in the sense of Section 7.2. We show only the garbling procedure for AND gates, and use the notation of Section 7: (A_0, A_1) and (B_0, B_1) are the input wire labels, and (C_0, C_1) are the output wire labels. Bits a and b are secret so that A_a and B_b encode false. C_0 always encodes false.

Classical garbling: In a "classical" garbled circuit (with point-and-permute) optimization, the four ciphertexts comprising a garbled gate have the form $H(A\|B) \oplus C$, where the choice of C_0 or C_1 depends on the association between select bits and truth values. Below is an example of the linear operation of the scheme's operations. Highlighted entries are the positions that will vary based on a, b in Gb, or α, β in Ev.

$$
\mathsf{Gb}: \quad
\begin{bmatrix} A_0 \\ A_1 \\ B_0 \\ B_1 \\ C_0 \\ C_1 \\ G_1 \\ G_2 \\ G_3 \\ G_4 \end{bmatrix}
=
\begin{bmatrix}
1 & 0 & 0 & 0 & 0 & 0 & 0 & 0 & 0 & 0 \\
0 & 1 & 0 & 0 & 0 & 0 & 0 & 0 & 0 & 0 \\
0 & 0 & 1 & 0 & 0 & 0 & 0 & 0 & 0 & 0 \\
0 & 0 & 0 & 1 & 0 & 0 & 0 & 0 & 0 & 0 \\
0 & 0 & 0 & 0 & 1 & 0 & 0 & 0 & 0 & 0 \\
0 & 0 & 0 & 0 & 0 & 1 & 0 & 0 & 0 & 0 \\
0 & 0 & 0 & 0 & 1 & 0 & 1 & 0 & 0 & 0 \\
0 & 0 & 0 & 0 & 1 & 0 & 0 & 1 & 0 & 0 \\
0 & 0 & 0 & 0 & 1 & 0 & 0 & 0 & 1 & 0 \\
0 & 0 & 0 & 0 & 0 & 1 & 0 & 0 & 0 & 1
\end{bmatrix}
\begin{bmatrix} A_0 \\ A_1 \\ B_0 \\ B_1 \\ C_0 \\ C_1 \\ H(A_0\|B_0) \\ H(A_0\|B_1) \\ H(A_1\|B_0) \\ H(A_1\|B_1) \end{bmatrix}
\qquad \text{for } a = b = 0
$$

$$
\mathsf{Ev}: \quad C = \begin{bmatrix} 0 & 0 & 1 & 0 & 1 & 0 & 0 \end{bmatrix}
\begin{bmatrix} A_\alpha \\ B_\beta \\ H(A_\alpha\|B_\beta) \\ G_1 \\ G_2 \\ G_3 \\ G_4 \end{bmatrix}
\qquad \text{for } \alpha = 0, \beta = 1
$$

Row-reduction (GRR3). The row-reduction optimization of [27] sets one of the output wire labels to be $H(A\|B)$, so that one of the ciphertexts is no longer required (it becomes the all-zeroes string). Modifying the example from above, we have:

$$
\mathsf{Gb}: \quad
\begin{bmatrix} A_0 \\ A_1 \\ B_0 \\ B_1 \\ C_0 \\ C_1 \\ G_2 \\ G_3 \\ G_4 \end{bmatrix}
=
\begin{bmatrix}
1 & 0 & 0 & 0 & 0 & 0 & 0 & 0 & 0 \\
0 & 1 & 0 & 0 & 0 & 0 & 0 & 0 & 0 \\
0 & 0 & 1 & 0 & 0 & 0 & 0 & 0 & 0 \\
0 & 0 & 0 & 1 & 0 & 0 & 0 & 0 & 0 \\
0 & 0 & 0 & 0 & 0 & 1 & 0 & 0 & 0 \\
0 & 0 & 0 & 0 & 1 & 0 & 0 & 0 & 0 \\
0 & 0 & 0 & 0 & 0 & 1 & 1 & 0 & 0 \\
0 & 0 & 0 & 0 & 0 & 1 & 0 & 1 & 0 \\
0 & 0 & 0 & 0 & 1 & 0 & 0 & 0 & 1
\end{bmatrix}
\begin{bmatrix} A_0 \\ A_1 \\ B_0 \\ B_1 \\ C \\ H(A_0\|B_0) \\ H(A_0\|B_1) \\ H(A_1\|B_0) \\ H(A_1\|B_1) \end{bmatrix}
\qquad \text{for } a = b = 0
$$

$$
\mathsf{Ev}: \quad C = \begin{bmatrix} 0 & 0 & 1 & 1 & 0 & 0 \end{bmatrix}
\begin{bmatrix} A_\alpha \\ B_\beta \\ H(A_\alpha\|B_\beta) \\ G_2 \\ G_3 \\ G_4 \end{bmatrix}
\qquad \text{for } \alpha = 0, \beta = 1
$$

$$
\mathsf{Ev}: \quad C = \begin{bmatrix} 0 & 0 & 1 & 0 & 0 & 0 \end{bmatrix}
\begin{bmatrix} A_\alpha \\ B_\beta \\ H(A_\alpha\|B_\beta) \\ G_2 \\ G_3 \\ G_4 \end{bmatrix}
\qquad \text{for } \alpha = \beta = 0
$$

In this example, output wire label C_0 is chosen as $H(A_0\|B_0)$ because input combination A_0, B_0 should lead to the false wire label in this case ($a = b = 0$). The other output wire label C_1 is chosen randomly. In the case that $a = b = 1$, the two darkly shaded rows would be exchanged (and the three rows below would be changed accordingly).

In Ev, we compute the output wire label as $H(A_\alpha\|B_\beta)$ directly, when $\alpha = \beta = 0$. In other cases, we compute $H(A_\beta\|B_\beta)$ and use it to unmask one of the 3 ciphertexts.

Free-XOR + GRR3. In the free-XOR optimization [20], all wire label pairs are chosen as $(X, X \oplus R)$, where R is common to all wires. To achieve this, Gb is modified (from the previous example) as follows:

$$
\text{Gb}:
\begin{bmatrix}
A_0 \\
A_1 \\
B_0 \\
B_1 \\
C_0 \\
C_1 \\
G_2 \\
G_3 \\
G_4
\end{bmatrix}
=
\begin{bmatrix}
1\,0\,0\,0\,0\,0\,0 \\
1\,0\,1\,0\,0\,0\,0 \\
0\,1\,0\,0\,0\,0\,0 \\
0\,1\,1\,0\,0\,0\,0 \\
0\,0\,0\,1\,0\,0\,0 \\
0\,0\,1\,1\,0\,0\,0 \\
0\,0\,0\,1\,1\,0\,0 \\
0\,0\,0\,1\,0\,1\,0 \\
0\,0\,1\,1\,0\,0\,1
\end{bmatrix}
\begin{bmatrix}
A_0 \\
B_0 \\
R \\
H(A_0\|B_0) \\
H(A_0\|B_1) \\
H(A_1\|B_0) \\
H(A_1\|B_1)
\end{bmatrix}
\qquad \text{for } a = b = 0
$$

Advanced row-reduction (GRR2). The garbled row-reduction optimization of [28] results in only 2 ciphertexts per AND gate. The idea is the following. For simplicity, assume $a = b = 0$, so that A_0, B_0 represent false. Then the evaluator should be able to obtain C_0 if he obtains any of $\{K_1 = H(A_0\|B_0), K_2 = H(A_0\|B_1), K_3 = H(A_1\|B_0)\}$, and obtain C_1 if he obtains $K_4 = H(A_1\|B_1)$.

We let P denote the unique degree-3 polynomial (over $GF(2^k)$) passing through points $\{(1, K_1), (2, K_2), (3, K_3)\}$. We then let Q denote the unique degree-3 polynomial passing through points $\{(4, K_4), (5, P(5)), (6, P(6))\}$. We give out values $P(5)$ and $P(6)$. Then if the evaluator who has input wire labels A_α, B_β interpolates a polynomial through $\{(2\alpha + \beta + 1, H(A_\alpha\|B_\beta)), (5, P(5)), (6, P(6))\}$, she will obtain either P or Q depending on the logic of the AND gate. Hence, we can set output wire labels $C_0 = P(0)$ and $C_1 = Q(0)$.

Let $V_{x,y,z}$ denote the 3×3 Vandermonde matrix that evaluates a polynomial-coefficient vector on points x, y, and z. Then $V_{x,y,z}^{-1}$ is the matrix that interpolates a polynomial's coefficients given its value at points x, y, and z. Hence, we have:

$$
\text{Gb}: \quad
\begin{bmatrix} C_0 \\ P_5 \\ P_6 \end{bmatrix}
= V_{0,5,6} \times V_{1,2,3}^{-1} \times
\begin{bmatrix} H(A_0\|B_0) \\ H(A_0\|B_1) \\ H(A_1\|B_0) \end{bmatrix}
\qquad \text{for } a = b = 0
$$

$$
[C_1] = \begin{bmatrix} 1 & 0 & 0 \end{bmatrix} \times V_{4,5,6}^{-1} \times
\begin{bmatrix} H(A_1\|B_1) \\ P_5 \\ P_6 \end{bmatrix}
$$

$$
\text{Ev}: \quad
C = \begin{bmatrix} 1 & 0 & 0 \end{bmatrix} \times V_{2\alpha+\beta+1,5,6}^{-1} \times
\begin{bmatrix} H(A_\alpha\|B_\beta) \\ P_5 \\ P_6 \end{bmatrix}
$$

For different choices of a, b, different corresponding Vandermonde matrices are used in Gb.

For simplicity in Gb, we have written C_1 as a linear function of P_5, P_6. Clearly the linear operations compose, but we have not written out the tedious full expression for C_1 in terms of the $H(A_\alpha\|B_\beta)$ values.

Our scheme. In our scheme, the output wires of an AND gate will be $H(A_0) \oplus H(B_0)$ and $H(A_0) \oplus H(B_0) \oplus R$. The first (sender)half-gate is garbled as $H(A_0) \oplus H(A_1) \oplus bR$. The second (receiver)half-gate is garbled as $H(B_0) \oplus H(B_1) \oplus A_0 \oplus aR$.

$$
\text{Gb}: \quad
\begin{bmatrix} A_0 \\ A_1 \\ B_0 \\ B_1 \\ C_0 \\ C_1 \\ G_1 \\ G_2 \end{bmatrix}
=
\begin{bmatrix}
1 & 0 & 0 & 0 & 0 & 0 & 0 \\
1 & 0 & 1 & 0 & 0 & 0 & 0 \\
0 & 1 & 0 & 0 & 0 & 0 & 0 \\
0 & 1 & 1 & 0 & 0 & 0 & 0 \\
0 & 0 & ab & 1 & 0 & 1 & 0 \\
0 & 0 & 1-ab & 1 & 0 & 1 & 0 \\
0 & 0 & b & 1 & 1 & 0 & 0 \\
1 & 0 & a & 0 & 0 & 1 & 1
\end{bmatrix}
\begin{bmatrix} A_0 \\ B_0 \\ R \\ H(A_0) \\ H(A_1) \\ H(B_0) \\ H(B_1) \end{bmatrix}
$$

$$
\text{Ev}: \quad
C = \begin{bmatrix} \beta & 0 & 1 & 1 & \alpha & \beta \end{bmatrix}
\begin{bmatrix} A_\alpha \\ B_\beta \\ H(A_\alpha) \\ H(B_\beta) \\ G_1 \\ G_2 \end{bmatrix}
$$

We can show the correctness of the scheme as follows. Recall that the result of evaluation should be $\gamma = (\alpha \oplus a) \wedge (\beta \oplus b)$. Since we are working in a field of characteristic 2, we have:

$$
[\beta\,0\,1\,1\,\alpha\,\beta]
\begin{bmatrix}
A_\alpha \\
B_\beta \\
H(A_\alpha) \\
H(B_\beta) \\
G_1 \\
G_2
\end{bmatrix}
=
\begin{pmatrix}
\beta\,[1\,0\,\alpha & 0 & 0 & 0 & 0] \\
+\quad [0\,0\,0 & 1-\alpha & \alpha & 0 & 0] \\
+\quad [0\,0\,0 & 0 & 0 & 1-\beta & \beta] \\
+\alpha\,[0\,0\,b & 1 & 1 & 0 & 0] \\
+\beta\,[1\,0\,a & 0 & 0 & 1 & 1]
\end{pmatrix}
\begin{bmatrix}
A_0 \\
B_0 \\
R \\
H(A_0) \\
H(A_1) \\
H(B_0) \\
H(B_1)
\end{bmatrix}
$$

$$
= [0\,0\,\alpha\beta+\alpha b+\beta a\,1\,0\,1\,0]
\begin{bmatrix}
A_0 \\
B_0 \\
R \\
H(A_0) \\
H(A_1) \\
H(B_0) \\
H(B_1)
\end{bmatrix}
$$

$$
= [0\,0\,\underbrace{(\alpha+a)(\beta+b)}_{\gamma}+ab\,1\,0\,1\,0]
\begin{bmatrix}
A_0 \\
B_0 \\
R \\
H(A_0) \\
H(A_1) \\
H(B_0) \\
H(B_1)
\end{bmatrix}
= C_\gamma
$$

Crypto Currencies

One-Out-of-Many Proofs:
Or How to Leak a Secret and Spend a Coin

Jens Groth[1]([⊠]) and Markulf Kohlweiss[2]

[1] University College London, London, UK
j.groth@ucl.ac.uk
[2] Microsoft Research, Cambridge, UK

Abstract. We construct a 3-move public coin special honest verifier zero-knowledge proof, a so-called Sigma-protocol, for a list of commitments having at least one commitment that opens to 0. It is not required for the prover to know openings of the other commitments. The proof system is efficient, in particular in terms of communication requiring only the transmission of a logarithmic number of commitments.

We use our proof system to instantiate both ring signatures and zerocoin, a novel mechanism for bitcoin privacy. We use our Sigma-protocol as a (linkable) ad-hoc group identification scheme where the users have public keys that are commitments and demonstrate knowledge of an opening for one of the commitments to unlinkably identify themselves (once) as belonging to the group. Applying the Fiat-Shamir transform on the group identification scheme gives rise to ring signatures, applying it to the linkable group identification scheme gives rise to zerocoin.

Our ring signatures are very small compared to other ring signature schemes and we only assume the users' secret keys to be the discrete logarithms of single group elements so the setup is quite realistic. Similarly, compared with the original zerocoin protocol we only rely on a weak cryptographic assumption and do not require a trusted setup.

A third application of our Sigma protocol is an efficient proof of membership of a secret committed value belonging to a public list of values.

Keywords: Sigma-protocol · Zero-knowledge · Disjunctive proof · Ring signature · Zerocoin · Membership proof

1 Introduction

A large fraction of deployed cryptographic schemes rely either on cryptographic hash-functions or the discrete logarithm assumption for their security. As a consequence their underlying mathematical structures, compression functions and cyclic prime-order groups respectively, has undergone a lot of cryptanalytic

J. Groth—The research leading to these results has received funding from the European Research Council under the European Union's Seventh Framework Programme (FP/2007-2013) / ERC Grant Agreement n. 307937.

E. Oswald and M. Fischlin (Eds.): EUROCRYPT 2015, Part II, LNCS 9057, pp. 253–280, 2015.
DOI: 10.1007/978-3-662-46803-6_9

scrutiny. This makes them attractive building-blocks for peer-to-peer applications that operate in a world in which no-one is trusted and everyone is potentially malicious. We revisit two such applications, ring signatures and zerocoin, and show how to construct both of them using a Σ-protocol that relies only on the security of a homomorphic commitment scheme. When instantiated with Pedersen commitments it is computationally sound, relying only on the discrete logarithm assumption. This results in very efficient instantiations under a weak cryptographic assumption for both ring signatures and zerocoin and reveals a striking connection between the two schemes.

Σ-protocols are 3-move interactive protocols that allow a prover to convince a verifier that a statement is true. The prover sends an initial message, the verifier responds with a random challenge, and the prover sends a response. At the end of the interaction, the verifier looks at the transcript and decides whether to accept or reject the proof that the statement is true. A Σ-protocol should be complete, sound and zero-knowledge in the following sense:

Complete: If the prover knows a witness w for the statement u then she should be able to convince the verifier.

Special sound: If the prover does not know a witness w for the statement, she should not be able to convince the verifier. This is formalized as saying that if the prover can answer several different challenges satisfactorily, then it is possible to extract a witness from the accepting transcripts.

Special honest verifier zero-knowledge: The Σ-protocol should not reveal anything about the prover's witness. This is formalized as saying that given any verifier challenge it is possible to simulate a protocol transcript.

Σ-protocols are widely used. When working in cyclic prime-order groups or RSA-type groups there are very efficient Σ-protocols such as the identification schemes of Schnorr [Sch91] and Guillou-Quisquater [GQ88]. An advantage of Σ-protocols is that they are easy to make non-interactive by using the Fiat-Shamir heuristic [FS86] where a cryptographic hash-function is used to compute the challenge instead of having an online verifier. It can be argued in the random oracle model [BR93] where the hash-function is modeled as a truly random function that this gives us secure non-interactive zero-knowledge proofs. This makes Σ-protocols very useful in the construction of digital signature schemes and encryption schemes, which are non-interactive in nature.

1.1   Our Contribution

It is well-known that there are efficient Σ-protocols with linear complexity for NP-complete languages such as circuit satisfiability. We consider statements consisting of N commitments $c_0, \ldots, c_{N-1}$. The prover's claim is that she knows an opening of one of the commitments c_ℓ to the value 0. Our main contribution is a new Σ-protocol for this type of statement that has logarithmic communication complexity.

Our construction works for any additively homomorphic non-interactive commitment scheme (see Sect. 2.1) over $\mathbb{Z}_q$, where q is a large prime. Examples of such commitment schemes include Pedersen commitments [Ped91] and variants of ElGamal encryption [ElG85] where the message is encoded as an exponent. These commitment schemes specify a commitment key ck, which in the case of Pedersen commitments specifies a prime-order group $\mathbb{G}$ and two group elements g, h. Given a value $m \in \mathbb{Z}_q$ and perhaps some randomness $r \in \mathbb{Z}_q$ it is then possible to compute a commitment, which in the case of Pedersen commitments is computed as $c = g^m h^r$.

Given a commitment key ck and a statement of the form $(c_0, \ldots, c_{N-1})$ the prover who knows an opening $(0, r)$ of one of the commitments $c_\ell = \text{Com}_{ck}(m; r)$ with $m = 0$ can use our Σ-protocol to convince the verifier of having this knowledge. Our Σ-protocol has perfect completeness, i.e., the verifier can always convince the verifier when she has a witness $(0, r)$. It has $(\log N + 1)$-special soundness, which means given $\log N + 1$ accepting transcripts for the statement with distinct challenges $x_0, \ldots, x_{\log N}$ from the verifier, it is possible to compute an opening $(0, r)$ of one of the commitments. Finally, it has special honest verifier zero-knowledge such that for any given challenge x from the verifier it is possible to simulate a transcript without knowing an opening of any of the commitments. When instantiated with the Pedersen commitment scheme our Σ-protocol has perfect special honest verifier zero-knowledge, since the Pedersen commitment scheme is perfectly hiding.

Our Σ-protocol requires the prover to send $4 \log N$ commitments and $3 \log N + 1$ elements in $\mathbb{Z}_q$. When instantiated with Pedersen commitments the prover has to compute roughly $N \log N$ exponentiations and the verifier has to compute roughly N exponentiations. Multi-exponentiation techniques and batching techniques can be used to reduce the computational cost.

If the prover knows the openings of all the commitments its computation can be faster and is determined by the cost of approximately $3N \log N$ multiplications in $\mathbb{Z}_q$ and making $4 \log N$ commitments. This is a huge improvement over existing protocols in the literature like those employed by [DMV13] for rate-limited function evaluation.

Another example where the prover knows the openings is in a membership proof. Here the prover has a commitment c and wants to prove knowledge of an opening to a value u that belongs to a list $\mathcal{L} = \{\lambda_0, \ldots, \lambda_{N-1}\}$. This can be done by forming commitments $c_0 = c \cdot \text{Com}_{ck}(-\lambda_0), \ldots, c_{N-1} = c \cdot \text{Com}_{ck}(-\lambda_{N-1})$ and proving knowledge of an opening of one of the commitments to 0. Due to the special structure of the commitments $c_0, \ldots, c_{N-1}$ this only costs $2N \log N$ multiplications in $\mathbb{Z}_q$ for the prover and $2N$ multiplications in $\mathbb{Z}_q$ for the verifier. This is an improvement over the membership proofs of Bayer and Groth [BG13] that use $O(N \log^2 N)$ multiplications for both the prover and verifier.[1]

1.2   Applications to Ring Signatures and Zerocoin

Ring signatures enable a signer to include herself in an ad-hoc group, a *ring*, and sign a message as a user in the ring without disclosing which one of them

---

[1] Bayer and Groth's technique also yields a non-membership proof with the same complexity. Our techniques do not provide non-membership proofs.

is the signer. A ring signature scheme can for instance be used by a whistle blower that wants to assure the recipient that the message has been signed by a knowledgeable source, e.g., an employee of a company laundering money, yet at the same time wishes to remain anonymous, such that the company does not fire her when she tells the world about their misdeeds.

Our Σ-protocol gives rise to a natural ad-hoc group identification scheme. All users have a commitment that they know how to open to 0. When a user wants to identify herself as a member of an ad-hoc group, she forms the statement consisting of the commitments $c_0, \ldots, c_{N-1}$ of the users in the group and uses the Σ-protocol to prove she knows an opening of one of the commitments.

By applying the Fiat-Shamir heuristic, i.e., by computing the challenge as a hash of the initial message and the message to be signed, we can convert the group identification scheme into a ring signature scheme. The ring signature scheme inherits the properties of the Σ-protocol. Completeness implies that it is possible for users in the ring to sign messages since they know an opening of one of the commitments to 0. Special soundness implies that ring signatures can only be generated by somebody in the ring, since they imply knowledge of an opening of at least one of the commitments to 0. Special honest verifier zero-knowledge implies that one cannot tell which commitment the signer can open, so the signer remains anonymous within the ring.

Specifying the ring in a ring signature may in the worst case require linear communication but can be amortized over many ring signatures when the same ring is used repeatedly or the ring can be specified indirectly, e.g., by saying the ring is all employees of a particular company. Decreasing the cost of ring signatures has therefore received attention in the cryptographic literature (see related work in Sect. 1.3). Our construction gives rise to a communication-efficient ring signature scheme, where the signature size grows logarithmically in the number of users in the ring. If we use the Pedersen commitment scheme, the ring signature only relies on the discrete logarithm assumption in the random oracle model. Furthermore, the users' keys are just single group elements for which the users know the discrete logarithms. This makes it easy to make ring signatures on top of a pre-existing setup in an organization that has a PKI where users have been assigned public keys consisting of group elements of which they know the discrete logarithms.

Zerocoin, also known as decentralized e-cash, enables users to generate their own coins. Coins become valuable once they are accepted on a public *bulletin board*. These coins can then be anonymously spent by their respective owners without disclosing which coin they are spending. To prevent double spending a secret serial number is revealed during the spending protocol. Zerocoin was proposed as an add on, or decentralized mix, to provide strong anonymity guarantees for bitcoin.

Our Σ-protocol gives rise to a natural one-time ad-hoc group identification scheme. Each user has a commitment c_i to a secret random serial number S that only she knows the opening of. When a user wants to identify herself as a member of an ad-hoc group, she reveals her serial-number S and forms a statement for the Σ-protocol consisting of the commitments $c_0 \cdot \mathrm{Com}_{ck}(S)^{-1}, \ldots, c_{N-1} \cdot \mathrm{Com}_{ck}(S)^{-1}$ and proves that she knows an opening to zero for one of these commitments. To enforce the one-time property, the verifier accepts the proof only if S has not previously been recorded. By applying the Fiat-Shamir heuristic to this adapted identification scheme one obtains a zerocoin protocol. An important benefit of our construction is that in contrast to existing zerocoin instantiations it does not rely on a trusted setup process assuming the commitment parameters ck have been generated in a way that is publicly verifiable and excludes trapdoors, e.g., using hash functions.

1.3 Related Work

There has been a significant amount of research on efficient zero-knowledge proofs. An important early work in this direction was by Kilian [Kil92] that used probabilistically checkable proofs and hash-trees to create an interactive argument for circuit satisfiability with polylogarithmic communication complexity. Kilian's argument has computational soundness; if we require unconditional soundness the communication complexity grows linearly in the witness size as is for instance the case in Ishai et al. [IKOS09]. Using fully homomorphic encryption it is possible to get unconditionally sound proofs of size $|w| + \mathrm{poly}(\lambda)$ [GGI+14], where w is the witness and λ is the security parameter, although this comes at a huge computational cost. There has also been works targeting specifically the discrete logarithm setting such as Cramer and Damgård [CD98] getting linear communication complexity and Groth [Gro09] that gives computationally sound arguments for circuit satisfiability with communication that is proportional to the square root of the circuit size. Our Σ-protocol is much more efficient than these works since it is fine-tuned for a specific language.

Our Σ-protocol can be used to prove that one out of many commitments can be opened to 0, which can be seen as a large disjunctive statement. Cramer, Damgård and Schoenmakers [CDS94] gave a general method to construct Σ-protocols for disjunctive statements. Their technique leads to a Σ-protocol with linear communication complexity. There has been works on related types of statements to the one we consider, i.e., proving something about one out of N elements [Gro09, CGS07, BDD07] that could be potentially be used to get a square root complexity although we are not aware of this actually having been done.

Bayer and Groth [BG13] give logarithmic size arguments for proving membership in a list, i.e., having values $\lambda_0, \ldots, \lambda_{N-1}$ and commitment c to a value λ_ℓ in the list. This can be seen as a dual to our type of disjunctive statement, we in contrast have many commitments $c_0, \ldots, c_{N-1}$ but just a single value $\lambda_\ell = 0$ and want to prove one of the commitments c_ℓ contains this value. The membership proofs of Bayer and Groth rely on an efficient proof of correct polynomial evaluation in a a secret committed value.

The strategy both here and in [BG13] is to construct polynomials of degree $\log N$ in a random challenge chosen by the verifier. In both cases, we can see the constructed polynomials as arising from a weighted sum or product (with weights depending on the statement) over the vertices of a hypercube of dimension $\log N$ but the papers differ in the weights at the vertices of the hypercube and how they are used. In [BG13] the weights are the coefficients of the polynomial P and the vertices in the hypercube contain N powers u^i of a point u where the polynomial is evaluated. In our paper the weights are the commitments and the hypercube has a single non-zero vertex corresponding to the commitment (out of N) that we are interested in. The correct evaluation of the hypercube is built and verified using polynomials of degree $\log N$ in a challenge x.

Ring signatures were introduced by Rivest, Shamir and Tauman [RST01] and Bender, Katz and Morselli [BKM09] provide rigorous security definitions for ring signatures and generic constructions based on trapdoor permutations. The idea of using Σ-protocol for anonymous identification within a group has been proposed before, see e.g. [CDS94, Cam97], and has found use in the constructions of ring signatures based on non-interactive zero-knowledge proofs in the random oracle model or using pairings. Courtois [Cou01] constructs a ring signature scheme based on a Σ-protocol for the MinRank problem. Abe et al. [AOS04] use disjunctive proofs to demonstrate possession of one out of N secret keys to construct ring signatures. The instantiation of their scheme based on the discrete logarithm assumption and using the same group for all users is similar to our ring signature except their Σ-protocol based on techniques from [CDS94] give signatures that grow linearly in the size of the ring. Herranz and Sáez [HS03] also give a linear size ring signature based on the discrete logarithm problem in the random oracle model. There are also several pairing-based constructions of ring signatures including [BGLS03, CWLY06, SW07, Boy07, CGS07]. The most efficient without random oracles is by Chandran, Groth and Sahai [CGS07] who exhibit square root size ring signatures using pairing based non-interactive zero-knowledge proofs.

The smallest ring signatures are by Dodis et al. [DKNS04] who use accumulators based on the strong RSA assumption [CL02] to get ring signatures consisting of a constant number of group elements in the random oracle model. Their construction, however, requires a setup that includes an RSA modulus, which may not be readily available. Furthermore, since RSA moduli have to be of size $\frac{\lambda^3}{\text{polylog}\lambda}$ bits to resist factorization attacks they end up with ring signatures where the size has cubic growth in the security parameter. Nguyen [Ngu05] also give constant size ring signatures in the random oracle model, but requires a linear size public key and relies on pairing-based cryptography, which also leads to a ring signature size of $\frac{\lambda^3}{\text{polylog}\lambda}$ bits. In contrast, our construction is based on the discrete logarithm assumption and if we use elliptic curve groups with group elements of size $O(\lambda)$ bits, we end up with an asymptotic quasilinear complexity of $O(\lambda \log N) = O(\lambda \log \lambda)$ bits for our ring signatures when the ring size N is polynomial in the security parameter.

Zerocoin was introduced by Miers et al. [MGGR13]. Their construction is in the random oracle model and uses an accumulator based on the strong RSA assumption together with cut-and-choose techniques to prove group representations in the exponent. The cut-and-choose technique results in their proofs of spending having quintic growth in the security parameter. Danezis et al. [DFKP13] show how to efficiently construct zerocoin using succinct arguments of knowledge (SNARKs). Ben-Sasson et al. [BSCG+14] extend zerocoin with secret balances to build a SNARK-based alternative currency. All known zerocoin constructions rely on a common reference string with a specific probability distribution, except for the original zerocoin protocol when used together with the techniques of Sander [San99] to construct theoretically efficient RSA UFOs[2]

While existing constructions are constant in the number of coins on the bulletin board, RSA accumulator based zerocoin proofs consist of $\sim 50,000$ bytes, compared with $32(7 \log N + 1)$ bytes in our construction using 256-bit elliptic curve groups. This means that for all practical purposes the logarithmic size will be preferable. The constant size of SNARK based constructions, usually below a dozen group elements, is hard to beat, and indeed these constructions pay for this by having to rely on knowledge of exponent assumptions.

2   Preliminaries

We write $y = A(x; r)$ when the algorithm A on input x and randomness r, outputs y. We write $y \leftarrow A(x)$ for the process of picking randomness r at random and setting $y = A(x; r)$. We also write $y \leftarrow S$ for sampling y uniformly at random from a set S.

All algorithms in our schemes get a security parameter $\lambda \in \mathbb{N}$ as input written in unary 1^λ. The intuition is that the higher the security parameter, the greater security we get.

Given two functions $f, g : \mathbb{N} \to [0,1]$ we write $f(\lambda) \approx g(\lambda)$ if $|f(\lambda) - g(\lambda)| = \lambda^{-\omega(1)}$. We say f is negligible if $f(\lambda) \approx 0$ and that f is overwhelming if $f(\lambda) \approx 1$.

2.1   Homomorphic Commitment Schemes

A non-interactive commitment scheme allows a sender to construct a commitment to a value. The sender may later open the commitment and reveal the value. The receiver of the commitment can then verify the opening and check that indeed it was this particular value that was committed in the first place. A commitment scheme must be hiding and binding. Hiding means that the commitment does not reveal the committed value. Binding means that the sender cannot open the commitment to two different values.

Formally, a non-interactive commitment scheme is a pair of probabilistic polynomial time algorithms $(\mathcal{G}, \mathsf{Com})$. The setup algorithm $ck \leftarrow \mathcal{G}(1^\lambda)$ generates a

---

[2] An RSA UFO is a large integer generated in a specific way from a source of uniformly random bits such that there is overwhelming probability that there are two large random primes that cannot be split from each other in a factorization of the integer. Known constructions of RSA UFOs yield integers much larger than standard RSA moduli, so in practice protocols built on RSA UFOs are inefficient.

commitment key ck. The commitment key specifies a message space $\mathcal{M}_{ck}$, a randomness space $\mathcal{R}_{ck}$ and a commitment space $\mathcal{C}_{ck}$. The commitment algorithm combined with the commitment key specifies a function $\text{Com}_{ck} : \mathcal{M}_{ck} \times \mathcal{R}_{ck} \rightarrow \mathcal{C}_{ck}$. Given a message $m \in \mathcal{M}_{ck}$ the sender picks uniformly at random $r \leftarrow \mathcal{R}_{ck}$ and computes the commitment $c = \text{Com}_{ck}(m; r)$.

Definition 1 (Hiding). *A non-interactive commitment scheme $(\mathcal{G}, \text{Com})$ is hiding if a commitment does not reveal the value. For all probabilistic polynomial time stateful adversaries $\mathcal{A}$*

$$\Pr\left[ck \leftarrow \mathcal{G}(1^{\lambda}); (m_0, m_1) \leftarrow \mathcal{A}(ck); b \leftarrow \{0,1\}; c \leftarrow \text{Com}_{ck}(m_b) : \mathcal{A}(c) = b\right] \approx \frac{1}{2},$$

where $\mathcal{A}$ outputs $m_0, m_1 \in \mathcal{M}_{ck}$. If the probability is exactly $\frac{1}{2}$ we say the commitment scheme is perfectly *hiding.*

Definition 2 (Binding). *A non-interactive commitment scheme $(\mathcal{G}, \text{Com})$ is binding if a commitment can only be opened to one value. For all probabilistic polynomial time adversaries $\mathcal{A}$*

$$\Pr\left[\begin{matrix} ck \leftarrow \mathcal{G}(1^{\lambda}) \\ (m_0, r_0, m_1, r_1) \leftarrow \mathcal{A}(ck) \end{matrix} : \begin{matrix} m_0 \neq m_1 \\ \text{Com}_{ck}(m_0; r_0) = \text{Com}_{ck}(m_1; r_1) \end{matrix}\right] \approx 0,$$

where $\mathcal{A}$ outputs $m_0, m_1 \in \mathcal{M}_{ck}$ and $r_0, r_1 \in \mathcal{R}_{ck}$. If the probability is exactly 0 we say the commitment scheme is perfectly *binding.*

Definition 3 (Strongly binding). *A non-interactive commitment scheme $(\mathcal{G}, \text{Com})$ is strongly binding if a commitment can only be opened in one way, i.e., not even the randomness can change. For all probabilistic polynomial time adversaries $\mathcal{A}$*

$$\Pr\left[\begin{matrix} ck \leftarrow \mathcal{G}(1^{\lambda}) \\ (m_0, r_0, m_1, r_1) \leftarrow \mathcal{A}(ck) \end{matrix} : \begin{matrix} (m_0, r_0) \neq (m_1, r_1) \\ \text{Com}_{ck}(m_0; r_0) = \text{Com}_{ck}(m_1; r_1) \end{matrix}\right] \approx 0,$$

where $\mathcal{A}$ outputs $m_0, m_1 \in \mathcal{M}_{ck}$ and $r_0, r_1 \in \mathcal{R}_{ck}$.

We will focus on the case where the message and randomness spaces are $\mathbb{Z}_q$ for a prime $q > 2^{\lambda}$ specified in the commitment key ck. Furthermore, we require the commitment scheme to be homomorphic, which means that the commitment space is also a group (written multiplicatively) and we have for all well-formed commitment keys ck and $m_0, m_1 \in \mathcal{M}_{ck}$ and $r_0, r_1 \in \mathcal{R}_{ck}$ that

$$\text{Com}_{ck}(m_0; r_0) \cdot \text{Com}_{ck}(m_1; r_1) = \text{Com}_{ck}(m_0 + m_1; r_0 + r_1).$$

Pedersen commitments. The Pedersen commitment scheme [Ped91] is a natural example of a homomorphic commitment scheme with the desired properties. The key generation algorithm $\mathcal{G}$ outputs a description of a cyclic group $\mathbb{G}$ of prime order q and random generators g, h. The commitment key is $ck = (\mathbb{G}, q, g, h)$. To commit to $m \in \mathbb{Z}_q$ the committer picks randomness $r \in \mathbb{Z}_q$ and computes $\text{Com}_{ck}(m; r) = g^m h^r$. The commitment scheme is perfectly hiding and computationally strongly binding under the discrete logarithm assumption.

2.2 Σ-Protocols

A Σ-protocol is a special type of 3-move interactive proof system that allows a prover to convince a verifier that a statement is true. The prover sends an initial message to the verifier, the verifier picks a random *public coin* challenge $x \leftarrow \{0,1\}^\lambda$, and the prover responds to the challenge. Finally the verifier checks the transcript of the interaction and decides whether the proof should be accepted or rejected.

We assume the existence of a probabilistic polynomial time setup algorithm $\mathcal{G}$ that generates a common reference string ck that is available to all parties. In this paper the common reference string will be a public key ck for a homomorphic non-interactive commitment scheme. It is worth noting that such keys may be set up using prime order groups based on the discrete logarithm problem, which makes it possible to sample them from uniformly random bits. So at the cost of a small overhead stemming from the use of uniformly random bits, we could set our schemes up in the common *random* string model.

Let R be a polynomial time decidable ternary relation, we call w a witness for a statement u if $(ck, u, w) \in R$. We define the CRS-dependent language

$$L_{ck} = \{u \mid \exists w : (ck, u, w) \in R\}$$

as the set of statements u that have a witness w in the relation R.

A Σ-protocol for R is a triple of probabilistic polynomial time stateful interactive algorithms $(\mathcal{G}, \mathcal{P}, \mathcal{V})$. The following run of a Σ-protocol describes the interaction of the algorithms

$ck \leftarrow \mathcal{G}(1^\lambda)$: Generates the common reference string.

$a \leftarrow \mathcal{P}(ck, u, w)$: Given $(ck, u, w) \in R$ the prover generates an initial message a.

$x \leftarrow \{0,1\}^\lambda$: The verifier's challenge x is chosen uniformly at random.

$z \leftarrow \mathcal{P}(x)$: The prover responds to the challenge x.

$b \leftarrow \mathcal{V}(ck, u, a, x, z)$: The verifier algorithm, which will always be deterministic in this paper, returns 1 if accepting the proof and 0 if rejecting the proof.

The triple $(\mathcal{G}, \mathcal{P}, \mathcal{V})$ is called a Σ-protocol for R if it is complete, special sound and special honest verifier zero-knowledge as defined below.

Definition 4 (Perfect completeness). *$(\mathcal{G}, \mathcal{P}, \mathcal{V})$ is perfectly complete if for all $\lambda \in \mathbb{N}, ck \leftarrow \mathcal{G}(1^\lambda)$ and (u, w) such that $(ck, u, w) \in R$*

$$\Pr\left[a \leftarrow \mathcal{P}(ck, u, w); x \leftarrow \{0,1\}^\lambda; z \leftarrow \mathcal{P}(x) : \mathcal{V}(ck, u, a, x, z) = 1\right] = 1.$$

A Σ-protocol should be a proof of knowledge; a prover should only be able to respond to a random challenge if the prover "knows" a witness for the statement u. We define this in the form of special soundness, which says that given responses to a number of different challenges it is possible to compute a witness for the statement.

Definition 5 (n-special soundness). $(\mathcal{G}, \mathcal{P}, \mathcal{V})$ *is n-special sound if there is an efficient extraction algorithm $\mathcal{X}$ that can compute the witness given n accepting transcripts with the same initial message. Formally, for all probabilistic polynomial time adversaries $\mathcal{A}$*

$$\Pr\left[\begin{array}{l} ck \leftarrow \mathcal{G}(1^\lambda); (u, a, x_1, z_1, \ldots, x_n, z_n) \leftarrow \mathcal{A}(ck) \\ w \leftarrow \mathcal{X}(ck, u, a, x_1, z_1, \ldots, x_n, z_n) \end{array} : (ck, u, w) \in R \right] \approx 1,$$

where $\mathcal{A}$ outputs distinct $x_1, \ldots, x_n \in \{0,1\}^\lambda$ and for all $i \in \{1, \ldots, n\}$ the transcript is accepting, i.e., $\mathcal{V}(ck, u, a, x_i, z_i) = 1$.

We say the proof is perfect n-special sound *if the probability is exactly 1.*

A non-standard requirement that many Σ-protocols satisfy is that responses are unique, or at least quasi unique, i.e. given an accepting proof an adversary cannot find a new valid response for the challenge in the proof. This non-malleability property is important to achieve simulation soundness [Fis05, FKMV12].

Definition 6 (Quasi unique response). $(\mathcal{G}, \mathcal{P}, \mathcal{V})$ *has quasi unique responses if for all probabilistic polynomial time adversaries $\mathcal{A}$*

$$\Pr\left[\begin{array}{l} ck \leftarrow \mathcal{G}(1^\lambda) \\ (u, a, x, z, z') \leftarrow \mathcal{A}(ck) \end{array} : \begin{array}{l} z \neq z' \\ \mathcal{V}(ck, u, a, x, z) = \mathcal{V}(ck, u, a, x, z') = 1 \end{array} \right] \approx 1.$$

A Σ-protocol is zero-knowledge if it does not leak information about the witness beyond what can be inferred from the truth of the statement. We will present Σ-protocols that are special honest verifier zero-knowledge in the sense that if the verifier's challenge is known in advance, then it is possible to simulate the entire argument without knowing the witness.

Definition 7 (Special honest verifier zero-knowledge (SHVZK)). $(\mathcal{G}, \mathcal{P}, \mathcal{V})$ *is special honest verifier zero knowledge if there exists a probabilistic polynomial time simulator $\mathcal{S}$ such that for all interactive probabilistic polynomial time adversaries $\mathcal{A}$*

$$\Pr\left[ck \leftarrow \mathcal{G}(1^\lambda); (u, w, x) \leftarrow \mathcal{A}(ck); a \leftarrow \mathcal{P}(ck, u, w); z \leftarrow \mathcal{P}(x) : \mathcal{A}(a, z) = 1\right]$$

$$\approx \Pr\left[ck \leftarrow \mathcal{G}(1^\lambda); (u, w, x) \leftarrow \mathcal{A}(ck); (a, z) \leftarrow \mathcal{S}(ck, u, x) : \mathcal{A}(a, z) = 1\right],$$

where $\mathcal{A}$ outputs (u, w, x) such that $(ck, u, w) \in R$ and $x \in \{0,1\}^\lambda$.

The Σ-protocol is said to be perfect special honest verifier zero-knowledge *if the two probabilities are exactly equal to each other.*

In real life applications, special honest verifier zero-knowledge may not suffice since a malicious verifier may give non-random challenges. However, it is easy to convert an SHVZK argument into a full zero-knowledge argument secure against *arbitrary* verifiers in the common reference string model using standard techniques (see e.g. [Dam00]). The conversion can be very efficient and only incur a small additive overhead, so we will in the paper without loss of generality just focus on building efficient SHVZK arguments.

For our application to ring signatures and zerocoin we do not need full zero-knowledge. It suffices to have have witness-indistinguishability, which is implied by perfect special honest verifier zero-knowledge. A Σ-protocol is witness indistinguishable if it is infeasible to distinguish which of several possible witnesses the prover uses.

Definition 8 (Witness-indistinguishability). $(\mathcal{G}, \mathcal{P}, \mathcal{V})$ *is witness indistinguishable if for all interactive polynomial time adversaries* $\mathcal{A}$

$$\Pr\left[\begin{matrix} ck \leftarrow \mathcal{G}(1^\lambda); (u, w_0, w_1) \leftarrow \mathcal{A}(ck); b \leftarrow \{0,1\} \\ a \leftarrow \mathcal{P}(ck, u, w_b); x \leftarrow \mathcal{A}(a); z \leftarrow \mathcal{P}(x) \end{matrix} : \mathcal{A}(z) = b\right] \approx \frac{1}{2},$$

where $\mathcal{A}$ *outputs* (u, w_0, w_1) *such that* $(ck, u, w_0) \in R$ *and* $(ck, u, w_1) \in R$ *and* $x \in \{0,1\}^\lambda$.

The Σ-*protocol is* perfectly *witness-indistinguishable if the probability is exactly half.*

Theorem 1 ([CDS94]). *A perfect SHVZK* Σ-*protocol is perfectly witness-indistinguishable.*

Proof. Perfect special honest verifier zero-knowledge implies the existence of a simulator that for any $x \in \{0,1\}^\lambda$ simulates (a, z) that is perfectly indistinguishable from a real proof. This means that conditioned on any particular $x \in \{0,1\}^\lambda$, two different witnesses w_0 and w_1 both lead to proofs with the same probability distribution as the simulation. This implies that conditioned on a, x we get the same probability distribution of the response z regardless of which witness was used. Moreover, the perfect special honest verifier zero-knowledge property also guarantees that the initial messages a are distributed identically regardless of the witness used. $\square$

2.3 Σ-Protocol for Commitment to 0 or 1

We will now give a well-known example of a Σ-protocol for knowledge of a committed value being 0 or 1, which will be useful later. Let ck be a commitment key for a homomorphic commitment scheme as described in Sect. 2.1 and let R be the relation consisting of commitments to 0 or 1, with the witnesses being openings of the commitment, i.e.,

$$R = \left\{ \big(ck, c, (m, r)\big) \mid c = \mathrm{Com}_{ck}(m; r) \text{ and } m \in \{0,1\} \text{ and } r \in \mathbb{Z}_q \right\}.$$

Fig. 1 gives a Σ-protocol $(\mathcal{G}, \mathcal{P}, \mathcal{V})$ for R, where $\mathcal{G}$ is the key generation algorithm for the commitment scheme, and where $\mathcal{P}, \mathcal{V}$ are running on $ck \leftarrow \mathcal{G}(1^\lambda)$, $m \in \{0,1\}$ and $r \in \mathbb{Z}_q$.

Theorem 2. *The* Σ-*protocol in Fig. 1 for commitment to* $m \in \{0,1\}$ *is perfectly complete, perfect 2-special sound and perfect SHVZK.*

$\mathcal{P}(ck, c, (m, r))$ $\qquad\qquad\qquad\qquad\qquad$ $\mathcal{V}(ck, c)$

$a, s, t \leftarrow \mathbb{Z}_q$ $\qquad\xrightarrow{\quad c_a, c_b \quad}$
$c_a = \mathrm{Com}_{ck}(a; s)$
$c_b = \mathrm{Com}_{ck}(am; t)$ $\qquad\xleftarrow{\quad x \leftarrow \{0,1\}^\lambda \quad}$

$\qquad\qquad\qquad\qquad\qquad\qquad\qquad$ Accept if and only if
$f = mx + a$ $\qquad\xrightarrow{\quad f, z_a, z_b \quad}$ $c_a, c_b \in \mathcal{C}_{ck}, f, z_a, z_b \in \mathbb{Z}_q$
$z_a = rx + s$ $\qquad\qquad\qquad\qquad\qquad\qquad\quad$ $c^x c_a = \mathrm{Com}_{ck}(f; z_a)$
$z_b = r(x - f) + t$ $\qquad\qquad\qquad\qquad\qquad\quad$ $c^{x-f} c_b = \mathrm{Com}_{ck}(0; z_b)$

Fig. 1. Σ-protocol for commitment to $m \in \{0, 1\}$

Proof. By the homomorphic property of the commitment scheme $c^{x-f} c_b$ is a commitment to $m(x - f) + am = m(1 - m)x - ma + am = x(1 - m)m$, which is 0 if $m \in \{0, 1\}$. With this in mind, it is straightforward to verify that the Σ-protocol is perfectly complete.

We will now show that the Σ-protocol is perfect 2-special sound. Given responses f, z_a, z_b and f', z_a', z_b' to two different challenges x and x' on the same initial commitments c_a, c_b we get by combining the verification equations that $c^{x-x'} = \mathrm{Com}_{ck}(f - f'; z_a - z_a')$ and $c^{x-f-x'+f'} = \mathrm{Com}_{ck}(0; z_b - z_b')$. Defining $m = \frac{f-f'}{x-x'}$ and $r = \frac{z_a - z_a'}{x-x'}$ we extract an opening of $c = \mathrm{Com}_{ck}(m; r)$. Furthermore, since $c^{x-x'+f'-f} = c^{(1-m)(x-x')} = \mathrm{Com}_{ck}(m(1 - m)(x - x'); r(1 - m)(x - x')) = \mathrm{Com}_{ck}(0; z_b - z_b')$ we either get a breach of the binding property of the commitment scheme (in which case the opening of c can be modified into an opening to $m \in \{0, 1\}$) or we have $m(1 - m) = 0$, which implies $m \in \{0, 1\}$.

Finally, let us prove that the protocol is perfect special honest verifier zero-knowledge. The simulator given ck, c and x first chooses $f, z_a, z_b \leftarrow \mathbb{Z}_q$. It then computes $c_a = c^{-x}\mathrm{Com}_{ck}(f; z_a)$ and $c_b = c^{f-x}\mathrm{Com}_{ck}(0; z_b)$. Both in a real proof and in the simulation this gives independent and uniformly random $f, z_a, z_b \in \mathbb{Z}_q$. Conditioned on these values and x the verification equations uniquely determine c_a, c_b in both real proofs and simulated proofs. This shows that real proofs and simulated proofs have identical probability distributions. $\qquad\square$

3 Σ-Protocol for One Out of N Commitments Containing 0

We will now give a Σ-protocol for knowledge of one out of N commitments $c_0, \ldots, c_{N-1}$ being a commitment to 0. More precisely, we will give a Σ-protocol for the relation

$$R = \left\{ (ck, (c_0, \ldots, c_{N-1}), (\ell, r)) \ \middle| \ \begin{array}{l} c_0, \ldots, c_{N-1} \in \mathcal{C}_{ck} \text{ and } \ell \in \{0, \ldots, N - 1\} \\ \text{and } r \in \mathbb{Z}_q \text{ and } c_\ell = \mathrm{Com}_{ck}(0; r) \end{array} \right\}.$$

To explain the idea behind the Σ-protocol let us for simplicity assume the commitment scheme is perfectly binding such that each commitment has a unique committed value. Saying that one of the commitments contains 0 is equivalent to saying there exists an index ℓ such that $\prod_{i=0}^{N-1} c_i^{\delta_{i\ell}}$ is a commitment to 0, where $\delta_{i\ell}$ is Kronecker's delta, i.e., $\delta_{\ell\ell} = 1$ and $\delta_{i\ell} = 0$ for $i \neq \ell$. We can always copy some commitments in the statement, so let us without loss of generality assume $N = 2^n$. Writing $i = i_1 \ldots i_n$ and $\ell = \ell_1 \ldots \ell_n$ in binary, we have $\delta_{i\ell} = \prod_{j=1}^n \delta_{i_j \ell_j}$ so we can reformulate what we want to prove as $\prod_{i=0}^{N-1} c_i^{\prod_{j=1}^n \delta_{i_j \ell_j}}$ being a commitment to 0.

The prover will start by making commitments $c_{\ell_1}, \ldots, c_{\ell_n}$ to the bits $\ell_1, \ldots, \ell_n$. She then engages in n parallel Σ-protocols as described in Sect. 2.3 to demonstrate knowledge of openings of these commitments to values $\ell_j \in \{0, 1\}$. In the Σ-protocols for $\ell_j \in \{0, 1\}$ the prover reveals $f_1, \ldots, f_n$ of the form $f_j = \ell_j x + a_j$. Let $f_{j,1} = f_j = \ell_j x + a_j = \delta_{1\ell_j} x + a_j$ and $f_{j,0} = x - f_j = (1 - \ell_j)x - a_j = \delta_{0\ell_j} x - a_j$. Then we have for each i that the product $\prod_{j=1}^n f_{j,i_j}$ is a polynomial of the form

$$p_i(x) = \prod_{j=1}^n (\delta_{i_j \ell_j} x) + \sum_{k=0}^{n-1} p_{i,k} x^k = \delta_{i\ell} x^n + \sum_{k=0}^{n-1} p_{i,k} x^k. \qquad (1)$$

The idea is now that the prover in the initial message will send commitments $c_{d_0}, \ldots, c_{d_{n-1}}$ that will be used to cancel out the low order coefficients corresponding to $x^0, \ldots, x^{n-1}$. Meanwhile the high order coefficient for x^n will guarantee the commitment c_ℓ can be opened to 0. More precisely, the verifier will at the end check that

$$\prod_{i=0}^{N-1} c_i^{\prod_{j=1}^n f_{j,i_j}} \cdot \prod_{k=0}^{n-1} c_{d_k}^{-x^k}$$

is a commitment to 0, which by the Schwartz-Zippel lemma has negligible probability of being true unless indeed c_ℓ is a commitment to 0.

Fig. 2 gives the full Σ-protocol $(\mathcal{G}, \mathcal{P}, \mathcal{V})$ for R with $\mathcal{G}$ being the key generation algorithm for the commitment scheme and $\mathcal{P}, \mathcal{V}$ running on $ck \leftarrow \mathcal{G}(1^\lambda)$, $c_0, \ldots, c_{N-1} \in \mathcal{C}_{ck}$, $\ell \in \{0, \ldots, N-1\}$ and $r \in \mathbb{Z}_q$ such that $c_\ell = \text{Com}_{ck}(0; r)$. Without loss of generality we assume $N = 2^n$.

Theorem 3. *The Σ-protocol in Fig. 2 for knowledge of one out of N commitments opening to 0 is perfectly complete. It is (perfect) $(n + 1)$-special sound if the commitment scheme is (perfectly) binding. It is (perfect) special honest verifier zero-knowledge if the commitment scheme is (perfectly) hiding.*

Proof. To see that the Σ-protocol is complete observe that $\prod_{j=1}^n f_{j,i_j}$ is a polynomial in the challenge x of the form $p_i(x) = \delta_{i\ell} x^n + \sum_{k=0}^{n-1} p_{i,k} x^k$. When c_ℓ is a commitment to 0 we therefore get that $c_\ell^{\prod_{j=1}^n f_{j,\ell_j}}$ in the verification equation is a commitment to 0, while the other commitments c_i get raised to polynomials

$$\boxed{\begin{array}{ll}
\mathcal{P}(ck,(c_0,\ldots,c_{N-1}),(\ell,r)) & \mathcal{V}(ck,(c_0,\ldots,c_{N-1}))) \\
\end{array}}$$

For $j = 1,\ldots,n$

$r_j, a_j, s_j, t_j, \rho_k \leftarrow \mathbb{Z}_q$

$c_{\ell_j} = \mathrm{Com}_{ck}(\ell_j; r_j)$

$c_{a_j} = \mathrm{Com}_{ck}(a_j; s_j)$

$c_{b_j} = \mathrm{Com}_{ck}(\ell_j a_j; t_j)$

$c_{d_k} = \prod_i c_i^{p_{i,k}} \mathrm{Com}_{ck}(0; \rho_k)$

using $k = j - 1$

and $p_{i,k}$ from (1)

$\xrightarrow{\quad c_{\ell_1}, c_{a_1}, c_{b_1}, c_{d_0}, \ldots, \quad}$
$\xrightarrow{\quad c_{\ell_n}, c_{a_n}, c_{b_n}, c_{d_{n-1}} \quad}$ Accept if and only if

$c_{\ell_1},\ldots,c_{d_{n-1}} \in \mathcal{C}_{ck}$

$f_1,\ldots,z_d \in \mathbb{Z}_q$

$\xleftarrow{\quad x \leftarrow \{0,1\}^\lambda \quad}$ For all $j \in \{1,\ldots,n\}$

$c_{\ell_j}^x c_{a_j} = \mathrm{Com}_{ck}(f_j; z_{a_j})$

For $j = 1,\ldots,n$

$\xrightarrow{\quad f_1, z_{a_1}, z_{b_1}, \ldots, \quad}$

$f_j = \ell_j x + a_j$

$z_{a_j} = r_j x + s_j$

$z_{b_j} = r_j(x - f_j) + t_j$

$z_d = r x^n - \sum_{k=0}^{n-1} \rho_k x^k$

$\xrightarrow{\quad f_n, z_{a_n}, z_{b_n}, z_d \quad}$

$c_{\ell_j}^{x-f_j} c_{b_j} = \mathrm{Com}_{ck}(0; z_{b_j})$

$\prod_i c_i^{\prod_{j=1}^n f_{j,i_j}} \cdot \prod_{k=0}^{n-1} c_{d_k}^{-x^k}$

$= \mathrm{Com}_{ck}(0; z_d)$

using $f_{j,1} = f_j$

and $f_{j,0} = x - f_j$

Fig. 2. Σ-protocol for commitment to $m = 0$ in list $c_0,\ldots,c_{N-1}$

of degree $n - 1$ in x as $c_i^{\prod_{j=1}^n f_{j,i_j}}$ in the verification equation. With this in mind straightforward verification shows that the Σ-protocol is perfectly complete.

We will now show how to convert an adversary with probability ε of breaking $(n+1)$-soundness, into an adversary with approximately the same runtime that has probability ε of breaking the binding property of the commitment scheme.

Suppose the adversary creates $n + 1$ accepting responses $f_1^{(0)},\ldots,z_d^{(0)},\ldots,f_1^{(n)},\ldots,z_d^{(n)}$ to $n + 1$ different challenges $x^{(0)},\ldots,x^{(n)}$ on the same initial message $c_{\ell_1},\ldots,c_{d_{n-1}}$.

The 2-special soundness of the Σ-protocol from Sect. 2.3 gives us openings of $c_{\ell_1},\ldots,c_{\ell_n}$ of the form $c_{\ell_j} = \mathrm{Com}_{ck}(\ell_j; r_j)$ with $\ell_j \in \{0,1\}$. From the verification equations it is then easy to get openings of $c_{a_j} = \mathrm{Com}_{ck}(a_j; s_j)$. Unless the adversary breaks the binding property of the commitment scheme, it must hold for all challenges that $f_j^{(0)} = \ell_j x^{(0)} + a_j, \ldots, f_j^{(n)} = \ell_j x^{(n)} + a_j$ for all $j = 1,\ldots,n$.

The form of the f_j's gives us that $f_{j,1} = \ell_j x + a_j$ and $f_{j,0} = (1 - \ell_j)x - a_j$. For $i \neq \ell$ we therefore get that $\prod_{j=1}^n f_{j,i_j}$ is a degree $n - 1$ polynomial $p_i(x)$ and for $i = \ell$ it is a polynomial of the form $p_\ell(x) = x^n + \ldots$. This means we can rewrite the last verification as

$$c_\ell^{x^n} \cdot \prod_{k=0}^{n-1} c_{*k}^{x^k} = \mathrm{Com}_{ck}(0; z_d)$$

for some fixed $c_{*0},\ldots,c_{*n-1}$ that can be computed from commitments in the statement and the initial message.

Observe that the vectors $(1, x^{(e)}, \ldots, (x^{(e)})^n)$ can be viewed as rows in a Vandermonde matrix and since $x^{(0)}, \ldots, x^{(n)}$ are all different the matrix is invertible and we can therefore find a linear combination $(\alpha_0, \ldots, \alpha_n)$ of the rows that gives us the vector $(0, \ldots, 0, 1)$. Combining the $n + 1$ accepting verification equations we therefore get

$$c_\ell = \prod_{e=0}^{n} \left(c_\ell^{(x^{(e)})^n} \cdot \prod_{k=0}^{n-1} c_{*k}^{(x^{(e)})^k} \right)^{\alpha_e} = \mathrm{Com}_{ck}(0; \sum_{e=0}^{n} \alpha_e z_d^{(e)}).$$

This gives us an extracted opening of c_ℓ to 0 with randomness $r = \sum_{e=0}^{n} \alpha_e z_d^{(e)}$.

Finally, let us describe a special honest verifier zero-knowledge simulator that is given a challenge $x \in \{0,1\}^\lambda$. It starts by picking the elements of the response uniformly at random as $f_1, \ldots, z_d \leftarrow \mathbb{Z}_q$. It then chooses $c_{\ell_1}, \ldots, c_{\ell_n}, c_{d_1}, \ldots, c_{d_{n-1}} \leftarrow \mathrm{Com}_{ck}(0)$ as random commitments to 0. Finally, it computes $c_{a_j} = c_{\ell_j}^{-x} \mathrm{Com}_{ck}(f_j; z_{a_j})$ and $c_{b_j} = c_{\ell_j}^{x-f} \mathrm{Com}_{ck}(0; z_{b_j})$ to finish the simulation of the proofs that $c_{\ell_1}, \ldots, c_{\ell_n}$ contain 0 and $c_{d_0} = \prod_{i=0}^{N-1} c_i^{\prod_{j=1}^{n} f_{j,i_j}} \cdot \prod_{k=1}^{n-1} c_{d_k}^{-x^k} \cdot \mathrm{Com}_{ck}(0; -z_d)$ to satisfy the last verification equation. It returns the simulated initial message and response $(c_{\ell_1}, \ldots, c_{d_{n-1}}, f_1, \ldots, z_d)$.

We will now argue that an adversary that distinguishes the simulation from a real argument with ε advantage can be turned into an adversary that breaks the hiding property of the commitment scheme with $\frac{\varepsilon}{2n-1}$ advantage. First, we observe that in both real proofs and simulated proofs $f_1, \ldots, z_d$ are uniformly random in $\mathbb{Z}_q$. Furthermore, the verification equations uniquely determine $c_{a_1}, c_{b_1}, \ldots, c_{a_n}, c_{b_n}$ and c_{d_0} conditioned on $f_1, \ldots, z_d$ and $c_{\ell_1}, \ldots, c_{d_{n-1}}$ both in real and in simulated proofs. The adversary's advantage of ε must therefore come from being able to distinguish real and simulated commitments $c_{\ell_1}, \ldots, c_{\ell_n}, c_{d_1}, \ldots, c_{d_{n-1}}$. A standard hybrid argument gives us a $\frac{\varepsilon}{2n-1}$ advantage in breaking the hiding property of the commitment scheme. $\square$

We state in the following two lemmas a couple of additional properties that will be useful later.

Lemma 1. *If the commitment scheme is strongly binding, the Σ-protocol in Fig. 2 has quasi unique responses.*

Lemma 2. *For each possible initial message in the Σ-protocol in Fig. 2 there is negligible probability that it will be chosen by the SHVZK simulator.*

Proof. The simulator picks c_{ℓ_1} as a random commitment to 0. We will now argue that c_{ℓ_1} has negligible probability of matching a fixed value c. We have by the hiding and binding properties

$$\Pr\left[ck \leftarrow \mathcal{G}(1^\lambda); c \leftarrow \mathrm{Com}_{ck}(0); c_{\ell_1} \leftarrow \mathrm{Com}_{ck}(0) : c_{\ell_1} = c \right]$$
$$\approx \Pr\left[ck \leftarrow \mathcal{G}(1^\lambda); c \leftarrow \mathrm{Com}_{ck}(0); c_{\ell_1} \leftarrow \mathrm{Com}_{ck}(1) : c_{\ell_1} = c \right] \approx 0.$$

$\square$

Efficiency. The prover sends $4 \log N$ commitments and $3 \log N + 1$ field elements. With N being polynomial in the security parameter the prover therefore only sends $O(\log \lambda)$ commitments and field elements. If we use the Pedersen commitment scheme in an elliptic curve based group where the group elements are of size $O(\lambda)$ bits the total communication cost is just $O(\lambda \log \lambda)$ bits.

If we are using the Pedersen commitment scheme the prover's cost is dominated by n multi-exponentiations of N group elements when computing $c_{d_0}, \ldots, c_{d_{n-1}}$. Using multi-exponentiation techniques [Lim00] we can reduce the cost of computing $c_{d_0}, \ldots, c_{d_{n-1}}$ to roughly N single exponentiations. Computing the commitments is more efficient than this once pre-computation techniques are factored in; and the polynomial coefficients $p_{i,k}$ can be computed by fast polynomial multiplication techniques, which will have significantly smaller cost than the exponentiations because they are done over $\mathbb{Z}_q$.

The verifier's computation is dominated by the multi-exponentiation $\prod_{i=0}^{N-1} c_i^{\prod_{j=1}^n f_{j,i_j}}$. If we are using Pedersen commitments this can be done at a cost that is not much higher than $\frac{N}{\log N}$ single exponentiations.

When prover knows openings of all commitments. If the prover knows openings of all commitments $c_0, \ldots, c_{N-1}$ she can reduce her computation significantly. Observe that if $c_i = \mathrm{Com}_{ck}(m_i; \gamma_i)$ then $c_{d_k} = \prod_{i=0}^{N-1} c_i^{p_{i,k}} \mathrm{Com}_{ck}(0; \rho_k) = \mathrm{Com}_{ck}(d_k, \phi_k + \rho_k)$ where $d_0, \phi_0, \ldots, d_{n-1}, \phi_{n-1}$ are coefficients in the two polynomials

$$d(x) = \sum_{k=0}^{n-1} d_k x^k = \sum_{i=0}^{N-1} m_i p_i(x) \qquad \phi(x) = \sum_{k=0}^{n-1} \phi_k x^k = \sum_{i=0}^{N-1} \gamma_i p_i(x) - \gamma_\ell x^n,$$

where the latter holds because $p_i(x) = \delta_{i\ell} x^n + \sum_{k=0}^{n-1} p_{i,k} x^k$, so $p_\ell(x)$ is the only polynomial with a non-zero coefficient for x^n.

The two polynomials $d(x)$ and $\phi(x)$ can be efficiently computed using Lagrange interpolation. Picks n distinct elements $\omega_1, \ldots, \omega_n \in \mathbb{Z}_q$ and evaluate $d(\omega_1), \phi(\omega_1), \ldots, d(\omega_n), \phi(\omega_n)$ from which the coefficients $d_0, \phi_0, \ldots, d_{n-1}, \phi_{n-1}$ can be computed in time depending only on $n = \log N$.

We will now show that given $\omega \in \mathbb{Z}_q$ it is possible to compute both $d(\omega)$ and $\phi(\omega)$ using $3N$ multiplications in $\mathbb{Z}_q$. Each $f_{j,0}$ and $f_{j,1}$ is a degree 1 polynomial in x and we can compute all $f_{j,0}(\omega), f_{j,1}(\omega)$ for $j = 1, \ldots, n$ using a few modular additions for each of them. Now, $p_i(\omega) = \prod_{j=1}^n f_{j,i_j}(\omega)$, so we can view $p_0(\omega), \ldots, p_{N-1}(\omega)$ as leaves on a binary tree, where the root is $\prod_{j=1}^n f_{j,0}(\omega)$ and for each parent at level $j - 1$ we let the left child be the same as the parent and the right child be the parent multiplied by $\frac{f_{j,1}(\omega)}{f_{j,0}(\omega)}$. The leaves can be computed using roughly $N = 2^n$ multiplications, which gives us $p_0(\omega), \ldots, p_{N-1}(\omega)$. Computing the sums $d(\omega) = \sum_{i=0}^{N-1} m_i p_i(\omega)$ and $\phi(\omega) = \sum_{i=0}^{N-1} \gamma_i p_i(\omega) - \gamma_\ell \omega^n$ costs an additional $2N$ multiplications, for a total of $3N + o(N)$ multiplications to compute $d(\omega), \phi(\omega)$. Doing this for n distinct elements $\omega_1, \ldots, \omega_n$ costs roughly $3N \log N$ multiplications. Once we have the evaluations in the n elements, we can at moderate cost compute $d_0, \phi_0, \ldots, d_{n-1}, \phi_{n-1}$ using Lagrange interpolation.

The prover's computation when she knows the openings of all the commitments is therefore determined by the cost of approximately $3N \log N$ multiplications in $\mathbb{Z}_q$ and making $4 \log N$ commitments.

Membership proof. The Σ-protocol in Fig. 2 can be used to construct a membership proof. We are given a commitment c and a set of values $\lambda_0, \ldots, \lambda_{N-1}$ and want to prove that we know an opening of the commitment c to one of the values λ_ℓ. This can be done using our 1-out-of-N Σ-protocol by defining $c_0 = c \cdot \mathrm{Com}_{ck}(-\lambda_0; 0), \ldots, c_{N-1} = c \cdot \mathrm{Com}_{ck}(-\lambda_{N-1}; 0)$ and proving there is a c_ℓ with an opening to 0.

From the prover's perspective this is a case where all the commitments have known openings $(\lambda_\ell - \lambda_i, \gamma_\ell)$ of commitment c_i. Observe that all the commitments have the same randomness, which implies $\phi(x) = 0$ and reduces the computation to $2N \log N$ multiplications for the prover. To see that $\phi(x) = 0$ recall that $\phi(x) = \gamma_\ell \sum_{i=0}^{N-1} p_i(x) - \gamma_\ell x^n$ and

$$\sum_{i=0}^{N-1} p_i(x) = \sum_{i=0}^{N-1} \prod_{j=1}^{n} f_{j,i_j}(x) = \prod_{j=1}^{n} (f_{j,0}(x) + f_{j,1}(x)) = \prod_{j=1}^{n} x = x^n.$$

The verifier is also very efficient, he can compute the product

$$\prod_{i=0}^{N-1} c_i^{\prod_{j=1}^{n} f_{j,i_j}} = \prod_{i=0}^{N-1} (c \cdot \mathrm{Com}_{ck}(-\lambda_i; 0))^{p_i(x)}$$

$$= c^{\sum_{i=0}^{N-1} p_i(x)} \cdot \mathrm{Com}_{ck}\Big(-\sum_{i=0}^{N-1} \lambda_i p_i(x); 0\Big)$$

$$= c^{x^n} \cdot \mathrm{Com}_{ck}\Big(-\sum_{i=0}^{N-1} \lambda_i p_i(x); 0\Big)$$

using $2N$ multiplications, which dominates the computation for large N.

This efficiency compares favorably with the membership proof in Bayer and Groth [BG13]. They prove membership by demonstrating the committed value is a root in the polynomial $P(u) = \prod_{i=0}^{N-1}(u - \lambda_i)$, but the initial step of computing the coefficients of the polynomial requires $O(N \log^2 N)$ multiplications (and only if the modulus q is of a form suitable for using the Fast Fourier Transform).

Bayer and Groth's method also gives rise to a non-membership proof: prove that the polynomial $P(u)$ does not evaluate to 0 to show the committed value u does not belong to the list. Our Σ-protocol does not appear to yield a non-membership proof.

4   Ring Signature

Ring signatures allow users to sign messages on behalf of ad-hoc groups that include themselves. The ad-hoc groups are called rings and contain public keys for the signer and the other users that the signer has chosen to include to include. We formally define ring-signatures in the following section.

Our Σ-protocol for one out of N commitments containing 0 can be used as an ad-hoc group identification scheme. Each user has a commitment to 0 with the private key being the randomness used. To identify yourself as a member of a group you prove that you know the opening of one of the commitments to 0. We can use the Fiat-Shamir heuristic to transform the ad-hoc group identification scheme into a ring signature scheme.

4.1   Definitions

A ring signature scheme consists of a quadruple of PPT algorithms (Setup, KGen, Sign, Vfy) for generating a common key available to all users, generating keys for users, signing messages and verifying ring signatures.

$pp \leftarrow$ Setup(1^λ): Generates and outputs public parameters pp available to all users.

$(vk, sk) \leftarrow$ KGen(pp): Generates a public verification key vk and a private signing key sk.

$\sigma \leftarrow$ Sign$_{pp,sk}(M, R)$: Outputs a signature σ on the message $M \in \{0,1\}^*$ with respect to the ring $R = (vk_1, \ldots, vk_N)$. We require that there is a $vk \in R$ such that (vk, sk) is a valid key pair output by KGen(pp).

$b \leftarrow$ Vfy$_{pp}(M, R, \sigma)$: Verifies a purported ring signature σ on a message M with respect to the ring of public keys R. It outputs 1 if accepting and 0 if rejecting the ring signature.

The quadruple (Setup, KGen, Sign, Vfy) is a ring signature scheme with perfect anonymity if it is correct, unforgeable and anonymous as defined below.

Definition 9 (Perfect correctness). *We require that a user can sign any message on behalf of a ring where she is a member. A ring signature scheme* (Setup, KGen, Sign, Vfy) *has perfect correctness if for all adversaries* $\mathcal{A}$

$$\Pr\left[\begin{array}{c} pp \leftarrow \text{Setup}(1^\lambda); (vk, sk) \leftarrow \text{KGen}(pp) \\ (M, R) \leftarrow \mathcal{A}(pp, vk, sk); \sigma \leftarrow \text{Sign}_{pp,sk}(M, R) \end{array} : \begin{array}{c} \text{Vfy}_{pp}(M, R, \sigma) = 1 \\ \text{or } vk \notin R \end{array}\right] = 1.$$

Definition 10 (Unforgeability). *A ring signature scheme* (Setup, KGen, Sign, Vfy) *is unforgeable (with respect to insider corruption) if it is infeasible to forge a ring signature on a message without controlling one of the members in the ring. Formally, it is unforgeable when for all probabilistic polynomial time adversaries* $\mathcal{A}$

$$\Pr\left[pp \leftarrow \text{Setup}(1^\lambda); (M, R, \sigma) \leftarrow \mathcal{A}^{\text{VKGen,Sign,Corrupt}}(pp) : \text{Vfy}_{pp}(M, R, \sigma) = 1\right] \approx 0,$$

- VKGen *on the ith query picks randomness r_i, runs* $(vk_i, sk_i) \leftarrow$ KGen($pp; r_i$) *and returns vk_i.*

- Sign(i, M, R) returns $\sigma \leftarrow \text{Sign}_{pp,sk_i}(M, R)$, provided (vk_i, sk_i) has been generated by VKGen and $vk_i \in R$.
- Corrupt(i) returns r_i (from which sk_i can be computed) provided (vk_i, sk_i) has been generated by VKGen.
- $\mathcal{A}$ outputs (M, R, σ) such that Sign has not been queried with $(*, M, R)$ and R only contains keys vk_i generated by VKGen where i has not been corrupted.

Definition 11 (Perfect anonymity). *A ring signature scheme* (Setup, KGen, Sign, Vfy) *has perfect anonymity, if a signature on a message M under a ring R and key vk_{i_0} looks exactly the same as a signature on the message M under the ring R and key vk_{i_1}. This means that the signer's key is hidden among all the honestly generated keys in the ring. Formally, we require that for any adversary $\mathcal{A}$*

$$\Pr\left[\begin{array}{l} pp \leftarrow \text{Setup}(1^\lambda); (M, i_0, i_1, R) \leftarrow \mathcal{A}^{\text{KGen}(pp)}(pp) \\ b \leftarrow \{0, 1\}; \sigma \leftarrow \text{Sign}_{pp,sk_{i_b}}(M, R) \end{array} : \mathcal{A}(\sigma) = b \right] = \frac{1}{2},$$

where $\mathcal{A}$ chooses i_0, i_1 such that $(vk_{i_0}, sk_{i_0}), (vk_{i_1}, sk_{i_1})$ have been generated by the key generation oracle KGen(pp) and $vk_{i_0}, vk_{i_1} \in R$.

We remark that perfect anonymity implies anonymity against full key exposure, which is the strongest definition of anonymity of ring signatures in [BKM09].

4.2 Construction

An additively homomorphic commitment perfectly hiding scheme $(\mathcal{G}, \text{Com})$ as defined in Sect. 2.1 and the Σ-protocol $(\mathcal{G}, \mathcal{P}, \mathcal{V})$ in Fig. 2 for one out of N commitments being a commitment to 0 can be combined to build an ad-hoc group identification scheme. We generate a commitment key as setup and let the users' verification keys be commitments to 0. In order to identify herself as a member of an ad-hoc group with N members, the user uses the Σ-protocol to prove that she knows an opening of one of the commitments. If her commitment is among the commitments in the ad-hoc group the correctness of the Σ-protocol guarantees that she manages to identify herself as a member. If on the other hand her commitment is not among the commitments in the group, then the $(\lceil \log N \rceil + 1)$-special soundness of the Σ-protocol guarantees that she has negligible chance of answering a challenge and being accepted. Finally, the special honest verifier zero-knowledge property of the Σ-protocol implies that it is witness-indistinguishable, i.e., even a malicious verifier cannot tell which commitment opening it is that she knows how to open.

We will use the Fiat-Shamir heuristic to make the ad-hoc group identification scheme non-interactive. Let $\mathcal{H}$ be a hash-function generator such that $H \leftarrow \mathcal{H}(1^\lambda)$ returns a hash-function $H : \{0, 1\}^* \to \{0, 1\}^\lambda$. By computing the challenge x in the Σ-protocol using the hash function on the initial message in the Σ-protocol and the message to be signed, we get a transformation of the ad-hoc group identification protocol to a ring signature scheme. Modeling the hash-function H as a random oracle allows us to give a heuristic proof that the ring signature scheme is unforgeable. The ring signature scheme is described in Fig. 3

Setup(1^λ)	Sign$_{pp,sk}(M,R)$	Vfy$_{pp}(M,R,\sigma)$
$ck \leftarrow \mathcal{G}(1^\lambda)$	Parse $R = (c_0, \ldots, c_{N-1})$	Parse $R = (c_0, \ldots, c_{N-1})$
$H \leftarrow \mathcal{H}(1^\lambda)$	with $c_\ell = \text{Com}_{ck}(0; sk)$	Parse $\sigma = (a, z)$
Return $pp = (ck, H)$		
	$a \leftarrow \mathcal{P}(ck, R, (\ell, sk))$	
KGen(pp)	$x = H(ck, M, R, a)$	$x = H(ck, M, R, a)$
	$z \leftarrow \mathcal{P}(x)$	
$r \leftarrow \mathbb{Z}_q$		
$c = \text{Com}_{ck}(0; r)$		
Return $(vk, sk) = (c, r)$	Return $\sigma = (a, z)$	Return $\mathcal{V}(ck, R, a, x, z)$

Fig. 3. Ring signature based on Σ-protocol $(\mathcal{G}, \mathcal{P}, \mathcal{V})$ for 1-out-of-N commitments containing 0

Theorem 4. *The scheme* (Setup, KGen, Sign, Vfy) *is a ring signature scheme with perfect correctness. It has perfect anonymity if the commitment scheme is perfectly hiding. It is unforgeable in the random oracle model if the commitment scheme is perfectly hiding and computationally binding.*

Proof. Perfect correctness follows from the perfect completeness of the Σ-protocol. Perfect anonymity follows from the perfect witness indistinguishability of the Σ-protocol, which guarantees that it is impossible to distinguish which secret key has been used to generate the ring signature.

To see that the ring signature scheme is unforgeable we will rely on the $(n+1)$-special soundness of the Σ-protocol in Fig. 2 and model the hash-function H as a random oracle. Consider a polynomial time adversary $\mathcal{A}$ that makes at most $q_V(\lambda), q_S(\lambda)$ and $q_H(\lambda)$ queries to VKGen, Sign and the random oracle, respectively, and for infinitely many $\lambda \in \mathbb{N}$ has at least $\frac{1}{p(\lambda)}$ probability of breaking the unforgeability property for a positive polynomial p. We will show that it can be used to construct a polynomial time attack that breaks the binding property of the commitment scheme with approximately $\frac{1}{2q_V(\lambda)p(\lambda)}$ chance on infinitely many $\lambda \in \mathbb{N}$. We will without loss of generality assume the adversary checks that it has made a successful forgery, which simplifies the proof since it guarantees the adversary does at some point call the random oracle on a query (ck, M, R, a) corresponding to the forged ring signature.

Given the public parameters we first pick at random $j \in \{1, \ldots, q_V\}$ and set $vk_j = \text{Com}_{ck}(1; r_j)$ for $r_j \leftarrow \mathbb{Z}_q$. Our goal is to run $\mathcal{A}$ using this key for user j and hoping to use rewinding to get $n + 1$ forgeries with a ring R that includes vk_j. The $(n+1)$-soundness of the SHVZK argument may permit extraction of an opening of some vk_i to $(0, r_i)$. By the perfect hiding property of the commitment scheme, with probability $\frac{1}{q_V}$ we have $i = j$ giving us a breach of the commitment scheme's binding property.

Let us now give more details of how the attack works. Whenever $\mathcal{A}$ queries VKGen we run as in a real ring signature scheme, except on the jth query where we return vk_j. If $\mathcal{A}$ ever queries Corrupt(j) we abort (type I). If $\mathcal{A}$ queries Sign(j, M, R) we pick $x \leftarrow \{0, 1\}^\lambda$ at random and use the special honest verifier zero-knowledge simulator to simulate the proof (a, z). We then program the random oracle $H(\cdot)$ to have $H(ck, M, R, a) = x$, except if (ck, M, R, a) has already been queried before in which case we abort (type II).

In the end, $\mathcal{A}$ tries to create a forged ring signature with uncorrupted users in the ring and where the signature does not come from the signing oracle. If $\mathcal{A}$ fails to create a forgery we halt. Otherwise, we get a successful forged ring signature $\sigma = (a, z)$ on M using ring R coming from a random oracle query $H(ck, M, R, a)$ used to get a challenge $x^{(0)}$. We now rewind the adversary to the point where it made the query $H(ck, M, R, a)$ used in the forged signature and give it random answers to the oracle query until it has produced n additional forged ring signatures with challenges $x^{(1)}, \ldots, x^{(n)}$ using the same query. As above, in each rewinding, if the simulation of a signature leads to reuse of a query to the oracle we abort (type II). Furthermore, if the number of rewindings exceed $2p(\lambda)n$ we halt.

If the adversary after rewinding gave us answers to a total of $n + 1$ distinct challenges, we can now use the $(n+1)$-special soundness property to either break the binding property of the commitment scheme or to get an opening $(0, r_i)$ of some $vk_i = \text{Com}_{ck}(0; r_i)$. With probability $\frac{1}{q_V}$ we have $vk_i = vk_j$, giving us a breach of the binding property of the commitment scheme.

Let us analyze the attack described above. A useful starting point is running the real unforgeability experiment, i.e., instead of picking $vk_j = \text{Com}_{ck}(1; r_j)$ we pick $vk_j = \text{Com}_{ck}(0; r_j)$ as a correctly generated key and answer all queries honestly (so we do not have type I or II aborts). Let us consider some $\lambda \in \mathbb{N}$ where $\mathcal{A}$ has at least $\frac{1}{p(\lambda)}$ chance of creating a successful forgery. Observe that an adversary that has probability γ of using a specific random oracle query in a successful forgery will be rewound $n = \gamma \cdot \frac{n}{\gamma}$ times on average on this query to sample n additional forgeries. The probability of the attack entering the rewinding stage and exceeding $2p(\lambda)n$ rewindings will therefore be at most $\frac{1}{2p(\lambda)}$, since otherwise we would exceed the expected number of rewindings. This means we have at least $\frac{1}{p(\lambda)} - \frac{1}{2p(\lambda)} = \frac{1}{2p(\lambda)}$ chance of getting $n + 1$ successful forgeries using a specific oracle query (ck, M, R, a).

Switching to simulation of ring signatures instead of giving real ring signatures may result in type II aborts when the simulation accidentally results in an oracle query $H(ck, M, R, a)$ that has been used before, but with a different challenge. However, Lemma 2 tells us that the simulator has negligible probability of colliding with another oracle query: the probability of a single simulation hitting a specific oracle query is a negligible function $\nu(\lambda)$ and with a maximum of $q_S(\lambda)$ signing queries in each run of the adversary, and a total of $q_H(\lambda) + q_S(\lambda)$ random oracle queries in each run of the adversary we get an upper bound of $(2p(\lambda)n + 1)q_S(\lambda)(q_H(\lambda) + q_S(\lambda)\nu(\lambda)$ for the probability of running into a type II abort.

Another problem that can arise is a collision in the $n + 1$ challenges we get after rewinding. With a maximum of $q_S(\lambda) + q_H(\lambda)$ queries to the random oracle in each run of $\mathcal{A}$ we get a total risk of $\frac{2((1+2p(\lambda)n)(q_S(\lambda)+q_H(\lambda)))^2}{2^\lambda}$ of having a collision in any random oracle outputs. Avoiding type II aborts and collisions leaves us with $\frac{1}{2p(\lambda)} - (2p(\lambda)n+1)q_S(\lambda)(q_H(\lambda)+q_S(\lambda)\nu(\lambda) - \frac{2((1+2p(\lambda)n)(q_S(\lambda)+q_H(\lambda)))^2}{2^\lambda} \approx \frac{1}{2p(\lambda)}$ chance of being able to use $(n+1)$-special soundness to break the commitment scheme or extract an opening $(0, r_i)$ of some vk_i in the ring of a ring signature forgery.

If we extract an opening $(0, r_i)$ of some vk_i in the ring of a ring signature forgery there is $\frac{1}{q_V(\lambda)}$ chance that $i = j$. If $i = j$ we observe as a part of this being a successful forgery, the adversary never queried $\mathrm{Corrupt}(j)$, so we do not have any type I aborts. Since the commitment scheme is perfectly hiding, the switch to using $vk_j = \mathrm{Com}_{ck}(1; r'_j)$ does not change the success probability of the attack. But now an opening of $vk_i = vk_j$ to $vk_i = \mathrm{Com}_{ck}(0; r_i)$ corresponds to a breach of the binding property of the commitment scheme. So for infinitely many $\lambda \in \mathbb{N}$ our attack has close to or higher than $\frac{1}{2q_V(\lambda)p(\lambda)}$ chance of breaking the binding property of the commitment scheme. The attack runs in polynomial time since it will make at most $1 + 2p(\lambda)n$ runs of the polynomial time adversary $\mathcal{A}$.   □

Instantiation with Pedersen commitments. The Pedersen commitment scheme is a natural candidate for the commitment scheme. When our ring signature scheme is instantiated with the Pedersen commitment scheme, the public keys are of the form $c = h^r$, i.e., they are single group elements and the corresponding secret keys are the discrete logarithms.

The instantiation with Pedersen commitments requires a simple setup that is realistic in many settings. Consider any organization where a standard group $\mathbb{G}$ is used for all users and their secret keys are discrete logarithms of public group elements. The ring signature easily fits on top of this setup.

The ring signature scheme yields small signatures. The signature size is logarithmic in the number of ring members and instantiated over a compact group where elements have size $O(\lambda)$ it is $O(\lambda \log N) = O(\lambda \log \lambda)$ bits. This compares favorably with all previous ring signature schemes.

The signer computes $\log N$ multi-exponentiations of N elements to generate a ring signature and the verifier uses a multi-exponentiation of N elements to verify a ring signature. However, when the same ring is used many times or there is significant overlap between different rings, the cost of verification can be reduced to $O(N)$ multiplications in $\mathbb{Z}_q$ by batching the verification of many signatures.

5   Zerocoin

Zerocoin enables users to generate their own coins which become valuable by public consensus by being included on a bulletin board. These coins can then be spent anonymously with double spending being prevented by a secret serial number encoded in each coin which is revealed during the spend protocol.

5.1   Definition

A zerocoin scheme consists of a quadruple of PPT algorithms (Setup, Mint, Spend, Vfy) for generating a common setup available to all users, generating coins, generating proofs that a coin was spend to pay for a transaction and verifying proofs of spending.

- $pp \leftarrow$ Setup(1^λ). Generates public parameters available to all users.
- $(c, skc) \leftarrow$ Mint(pp). Mints a coin c together with a key skc used to authorize its spending.
- $(\pi, S) \leftarrow$ Spend$_{pp,skc}(M, c, C)$. On input some transaction string $M \in \{0,1\}^*$ and an arbitrary set of coins C containing c, the algorithm outputs a proof π and a serial number S. We require that skc is a valid key for coin c as produced by Mint(pp) and that $c \in C$.
- $b \leftarrow$ Vfy$_{pp}(M, S, C, \pi)$. Verifies a purported proof π of a spend transaction with string M of a coin with serial number S from the set of coins C.

The transaction string M in the call to Spend is intended, e.g., for the identity of the transaction recipient, or the terms of a contract.

The quadruple (Setup, Mint, Spend, Vfy) is a zerocoin scheme with perfect anonymity if it is correct, balanced and anonymous as defined next.

Definition 12 (Perfect correctness). *We require that a user can spend any coin with respect to any set of coins. A zerocoin scheme* (Setup, Mint, Spend, Vfy) *has perfect correctness if for all adversaries $\mathcal{A}$*

$$\Pr \left[\begin{array}{l} pp \leftarrow \text{Setup}(1^\lambda); (c, skc) \leftarrow \text{Mint}(pp) \\ (M, C) \leftarrow \mathcal{A}(pp, c, skc) \\ (\pi, S) \leftarrow \text{Spend}_{pp,skc}(M, c, C \cup \{c\}) \end{array} : \text{Vfy}_{pp}(M, S, C \cup \{c\}, \pi) = 1 \right] = 1.$$

Our balance definition is a strengthening of the original zero-coin definition. As for ring signature unforgeability, we allow for Corrupt queries that give the adversary access to the randomness of coins.

Definition 13 (Balance). *A zerocoin scheme* (Setup, Mint, Spend, Vfy) *is balanced (with respect to insider corruption) if an adversary cannot spend more coins than he controls. Formally, it is balanced when for all probabilistic polynomial time adversaries $\mathcal{A}$*

$$\Pr \left[\begin{array}{l} pp \leftarrow \text{Setup}(1^\lambda) \\ (\tilde{c}_1, \ldots, \tilde{c}_m, S_1, \ldots, S_m, S_{m+1}) \leftarrow \mathcal{A}^{\text{CoinGen,Spend,Corrupt}}(pp) \end{array} : \forall_i.\text{Vfy}_{pp}(S_i) = 1 \right] \approx 0,$$

- CoinGen *on query number i selects randomness r_i, runs $(c_i, skc_i) \leftarrow$ Mint($pp; r_i$) and returns c_i after adding c_i to a set $\mathcal{C}$.*
- Spend(i, M, C) *returns $(\pi, S) \leftarrow$ Spend$_{pp,skc_i}(M, c_i, C)$, provided (c_i, skc_i) has been generated by* CoinGen *and was not leaked using* Corrupt(i). *The oracle records (M, S, C, π) in a set $\mathcal{T}$.*
- Corrupt(i) *provided (c_i, skc_i) has been generated by* CoinGen *runs $(\pi, S) \leftarrow$ Spend$_{pp,skc_i}(``$ $", c_i, \{c_i\})$ to determine the serial number of the coin and then returns r_i (from which skc_i can be computed). The oracle removes any tuple matching the pattern $(*, S, *, *)$ from $\mathcal{T}$ and records $(*, S, *, *)$ in $\mathcal{T}$.*

- $\mathcal{A}$ outputs $\tilde{c}_1, \ldots, \tilde{c}_m, \mathcal{S}_1, \ldots, \mathcal{S}_m, \mathcal{S}_{m+1}$ such that $\mathcal{S}_i = (M_i, S_i, C_i, \pi_i)$, $C_i \subset C \cup \{\tilde{c}_1, \ldots, \tilde{c}_m\}$, no $\mathcal{S}_i$ matches a pattern in $\mathcal{T}$, and all $\mathcal{S}_i$ are distinct.

Definition 14 (Perfect anonymity). (Setup, Mint, Spend, Vfy) *has perfect anonymity if a proof of spending with transaction string M for a set of coins C and coin c_{i_0} looks exactly the same as a proof of spending with transaction string M for the set C and coin c_{i_1}. This means that the spender's coin is hidden among all the honestly generated coins in the set. Formally, we require that for any adversary $\mathcal{A}$*

$$\Pr\left[\begin{array}{l} pp \leftarrow \text{Setup}(1^\lambda); (M, i_0, i_1, C) \leftarrow \mathcal{A}^{\text{Mint}(pp)}(pp) \\ b \leftarrow \{0,1\}; (\pi, S) \leftarrow \text{Spend}_{pp, skc_{i_b}}(M, c, C) \end{array} : \mathcal{A}(\pi, S) = b\right] = \frac{1}{2},$$

where $\mathcal{A}$ chooses i_0, i_1 such that $(c_{i_0}, skc_{i_0}), (c_{i_1}, skc_{i_1})$ have been generated by the minting oracle $\text{Mint}(pp)$ and $c_{i_0}, c_{i_1} \in C$.

5.2 Construction

While a ring-signature scheme can be constructed from an ad-hoc group identification scheme using the Fiat-Shamir heuristic, a zerocoin scheme can be obtained from a *linkable* ad-hoc group identification scheme. In particular, almost the same construction can be used to construct zerocoin schemes from a Σ-protocol for 1-out-of-N commitments containing 0. Instead of public keys that are commitments to 0 we now employ coins that are commitments to serial numbers. We homomorphically subtract a serial number S from all coins used in a statement by multiplying them with $\text{Com}_{ck}(S; 0)^{-1}$ before computing the proof, such that the commitment with this serial number turns into a commitment to 0. The zerocoin scheme is described in Fig. 4.

Setup(1^λ)	Spend$_{pp, skc}(M, c, C)$	Vfy$_{pp}(M, S, C, \pi)$
$ck \leftarrow \mathcal{G}(1^\lambda)$	Parse $C = (c_0, \ldots, c_{N-1})$	Parse $C = (c_0, \ldots, c_{N-1})$
$H \leftarrow \mathcal{H}(1^\lambda)$	and $skc = (r, S)$	Parse $\pi = (a, z)$
Return $pp = (ck, H)$	with $c_\ell = c = \text{Com}_{ck}(S; r)$	
Mint(pp)	$c_i' \leftarrow c_i \cdot \text{Com}_{ck}(S; 0)^{-1}$	$c_i' \leftarrow c_i \cdot \text{Com}_{ck}(S; 0)^{-1}$
$r \leftarrow \mathbb{Z}_q$	$a \leftarrow \mathcal{P}(ck, (c_0', \ldots, c_{N-1}'), (\ell, r))$	$x = H(ck, M, S, a)$
$S \leftarrow \mathbb{Z}_q$	$x = H(ck, M, S, a)$	
$c \leftarrow \text{Com}_{ck}(S; r)$	$z \leftarrow \mathcal{P}(x)$	
$skc \leftarrow (r, S)$		Return
Return (c, skc)	Return $\pi = (a, z)$ and S	$\mathcal{V}(ck, (c_0', \ldots, c_{N-1}'), a, x, z)$

Fig. 4. Zerocoin protocol based on Σ-protocol $(\mathcal{G}, \mathcal{P}, \mathcal{V})$ for 1-out-of-N commitments containing 0

Theorem 5. *The scheme* (Setup, Mint, Spend, Vfy) *is a zerocoin scheme with perfect correctness. It has perfect anonymity if the commitment scheme is perfectly hiding. It is balanced in the random oracle model if the commitment scheme is perfectly hiding and strongly binding.*

Proof. Perfect correctness follows from the perfect completeness of the Σ-protocol. Perfect anonymity follows from the perfect witness indistinguishability of the Σ-protocol, which guarantees that it is impossible to distinguish which coin has been used to generate a proof of spending.

To see that the zerocoin scheme is balanced we will rely on the $(n+1)$-special soundness of the Σ-protocol and model the hash-function H as a random oracle. We will show that a zerocoin adversary $\mathcal{A}$, which for a positive polynomial p and an infinite number of $\lambda \in \mathbb{N}$ has more than $\frac{1}{p(\lambda)}$ chance of forging more spending proofs than controlled coins can be used to construct an attack on the strong binding property of the commitment scheme.

Given the public parameters pp we start by forwarding them to $\mathcal{A}$. We simulate the random oracle and the CoinGen, and Corrupt oracles honestly. We use the SHVZK simulator and the random oracle programmability to answer Spend queries with fresh random serial numbers. If this fails because the pre-image is already in the oracle list we abort with "Error 1". Finally $\mathcal{A}$ outputs m coins $(\tilde{c}_1, \ldots, \tilde{c}_m)$ and $m + 1$ valid spending proofs $(\mathcal{S}_1, \ldots, \mathcal{S}_m, \mathcal{S}_{m+1})$. We will for simplicity assume in the proof that $\mathcal{A}$ checks that all its spendings are valid such that for each spent coin the random oracle has been queried on $H(ck, M, S, C, a)$.

For each $1 \leq i \leq m + 1$ we do the following. We find the first entry on the oracle list where $\mathcal{A}$ asked (ck, M_i, S_i, C_i, a_i) to the random oracle; if we created the entry ourselves during the simulation of a Spend query we abort with "Error 2". We then simulate a fresh copy of $\mathcal{A}$ identically up to the point where the above query was asked and answer with a different uniformly random value from the oracle. We repeat this process until we obtain $n_i = \lceil \log |C_i| \rceil + 1$ proofs with the same a_i. If the total number of rewindings exceeds $2p(\lambda) \sum_{i=1}^{m+1} n_i$ we halt. Since the expected number of rewindings for each query is n_i, we have at least $\frac{1}{2p(\lambda)}$ chance of getting the desired number of proofs for each i before running out of time.

If we end up with a collision in the oracle answers such that for any query i there are two rewindings that yield the same uniformly random challenge x we abort. However, since we run in polynomial time such collisions happen with negligible probability, so let us analyze the case where we have $n_i + 1$ distinct challenges for each proof. We can now use the $(n_i + 1)$-special soundness property to break the binding property of the commitment scheme or to get an opening $\mathrm{Com}_{ck}(0; r)$ for one of the commitments in the statement, which translates into an opening $\mathrm{Com}_{ck}(S_i; r)$ for one of the commitments in C_i.

Let us now consider the probability of "Error 1" and "Error 2". "Error 1" occurs if $\mathcal{A}$ already queried (ck, M, S, C, a) before the simulation of a spend query but this happens with negligible probability. "Error 2" occurs if the adversary finds a different answer to a challenge than we used in the simulation, since a successful attack on the balance property implies one of the spending proofs $\mathcal{S}_i$

does not match with a pattern in $\mathcal{T}$. By Lemma 1 this happens with negligible probability. We will now proceed under the assumption that such errors did not happen.

Consider the serial numbers of coins in $\mathcal{C}$. As commitments are perfectly hiding and as we revealed freshly sampled random serial numbers in the simulation of Spend an attacker that uses an honest coin to win the game will with high probability also use a different serial number. In case of corrupted coins he is forced by the rules of the security game to always use a different serial number. This yields a break of the binding property of the commitment scheme.

From now on we assume that $\mathcal{A}$ did not use an honest coin. Then there are m different adversary controlled coins and thus commitments but $m + 1$ verifying proofs with distinct serial numbers. By extracting from all $m + 1$ proofs we are guaranteed that one commitment is opened twice to different serial numbers, which yields a break of the binding property of the commitment scheme.   □

Further applications. One-out-of-many proofs are compatible with extended Pedersen commitments, where there is one commitment for a vector of values. They can thus also be employed in the construction of decentralized anonymous credentials [GGM14] and zero-cash protocols [BSCG+14].

References

[AOS04] Abe, M., Ohkubo, M., Suzuki, K.: 1-out-of-n signatures from a variety of keys. IEICE Transactions, 87-A(1), 131–140 (2004)

[BDD07] Brands, S., Demuynck, L., De Decker, B.: A Practical System for Globally Revoking the Unlinkable Pseudonyms of Unknown Users. In: Pieprzyk, J., Ghodosi, H., Dawson, E. (eds.) ACISP 2007. LNCS, vol. 4586, pp. 400–415. Springer, Heidelberg (2007)

[BG13] Bayer, S., Groth, J.: Zero-Knowledge Argument for Polynomial Evaluation with Application to Blacklists. In: Johansson, T., Nguyen, P.Q. (eds.) EUROCRYPT 2013. LNCS, vol. 7881, pp. 646–663. Springer, Heidelberg (2013)

[BGLS03] Boneh, D., Gentry, C., Lynn, B., Shacham, H.: Aggregate and verifiably encrypted signatures from bilinear maps. In: Biham, E. (ed.) EUROCRYPT 2003. LNCS, vol. 2656, pp. 416–432. Springer, Heidelberg (2003)

[BKM09] Bender, A.: Katz, Jonathan, Morselli, Ruggero: Ring signatures: Stronger definitions, and constructions without random oracles. Journal of Cryptology **22**(1), 114–138 (2009)

[Boy07] Boyen, X.: Mesh Signatures. In: Naor, M. (ed.) EUROCRYPT 2007. LNCS, vol. 4515, pp. 210–227. Springer, Heidelberg (2007)

[BR93] Bellare, M., Rogaway, P.: Random oracles are practical: A paradigm for designing efficient protocols. In: ACM CCS, pp. 62–73 (1993)

[BSCG+14] Ben-Sasson, E., Chiesa, A., Garman, C., Green, M., Miers, I., Tromer, E., Virza, M.: Zerocash: Decentralized anonymous payments from bitcoin. In: IEEE Symposium on Security and Privacy (2014)

[Cam97] Camenisch, J.L.: Efficient and Generalized Group Signatures. In: Fumy, W. (ed.) EUROCRYPT 1997. LNCS, vol. 1233, pp. 465–479. Springer, Heidelberg (1997)

[CD98]   Cramer, R., Damgård, I.B.: Zero-Knowledge Proofs for Finite Field Arithmetic or: Can Zero-Knowledge Be for Free? In: Krawczyk, H. (ed.) CRYPTO 1998. LNCS, vol. 1462, pp. 424–441. Springer, Heidelberg (1998)

[CDS94]   Cramer, R., Damgård, I.B., Schoenmakers, B.: Proof of Partial Knowledge and Simplified Design of Witness Hiding Protocols. In: Desmedt, Y.G. (ed.) CRYPTO 1994. LNCS, vol. 839, pp. 174–187. Springer, Heidelberg (1994)

[CGS07]   Chandran, N., Groth, J., Sahai, A.: Ring Signatures of Sub-linear Size Without Random Oracles. In: Arge, L., Cachin, C., Jurdziński, T., Tarlecki, A. (eds.) ICALP 2007. LNCS, vol. 4596, pp. 423–434. Springer, Heidelberg (2007)

[CL02]   Camenisch, J.L., Lysyanskaya, A.: Dynamic Accumulators and Application to Efficient Revocation of Anonymous Credentials. In: Yung, M. (ed.) CRYPTO 2002. LNCS, vol. 2442, pp. 61–76. Springer, Heidelberg (2002)

[Cou01]   Courtois, N.T.: Efficient Zero-Knowledge Authentication Based on a Linear Algebra Problem MinRank. In: Boyd, C. (ed.) ASIACRYPT 2001. LNCS, vol. 2248, pp. 402–421. Springer, Heidelberg (2001)

[CWLY06] Chow, S.S.M., Wei, V.K.-W., Liu, J.K., Yuen, T.H.: Ring signatures without random oracles. In: ASIACCS, pp. 297–302 (2006)

[Dam00]   Damgård, I.B.: Efficient Concurrent Zero-Knowledge in the Auxiliary String Model. In: Preneel, B. (ed.) EUROCRYPT 2000. LNCS, vol. 1807, pp. 418–430. Springer, Heidelberg (2000)

[DFKP13] Danezis, G., Fournet, C., Kohlweiss, M., Parno, B.: Pinocchio coin: building zerocoin from a succinct pairing-based proof system. In: PETShop at CCS (2013)

[DKNS04] Dodis, Y., Kiayias, A., Nicolosi, A., Shoup, V.: Anonymous Identification in *Ad Hoc* Groups. In: Cachin, C., Camenisch, J.L. (eds.) EUROCRYPT 2004. LNCS, vol. 3027, pp. 609–626. Springer, Heidelberg (2004)

[DMV13]   Dagdelen, Ö., Mohassel, P., Venturi, D.: Rate-Limited Secure Function Evaluation: Definitions and Constructions. In: Kurosawa, K., Hanaoka, G. (eds.) PKC 2013. LNCS, vol. 7778, pp. 461–478. Springer, Heidelberg (2013)

[ElG85]   ElGamal, T.: A public key cryptosystem and a signature scheme based on discrete logarithms. IEEE Transactions on Information Theory **31**(4), 469–472 (1985)

[Fis05]   Fischlin, M.: Communication-Efficient Non-interactive Proofs of Knowledge with Online Extractors. In: Shoup, V. (ed.) CRYPTO 2005. LNCS, vol. 3621, pp. 152–168. Springer, Heidelberg (2005)

[FKMV12] Faust, S., Kohlweiss, M., Marson, G.A., Venturi, D.: On the Non-malleability of the Fiat-Shamir Transform. In: Galbraith, S., Nandi, M. (eds.) INDOCRYPT 2012. LNCS, vol. 7668, pp. 60–79. Springer, Heidelberg (2012)

[FS86]   Fiat, A., Shamir, A.: How to Prove Yourself: Practical Solutions to Identification and Signature Problems. In: Odlyzko, A.M. (ed.) CRYPTO 1986. LNCS, vol. 263, pp. 186–194. Springer, Heidelberg (1987)

[GGI+14] Gentry, C., Groth, J., Ishai, Y., Peikert, C., Sahai, A., Smith, A.: Using fully homomorphic hybrid encryption to minimize non-interactive zero-knowledge proofs. Journal of Cryptology, pp. 1–24 (2014)

[GGM14] Garman, C., Green, M., Miers, I.: Decentralized anonymous credentials. In: 21st Annual Network and Distributed System Security Symposium, NDSS 2014, San Diego, California, USA, February 23–26, 2013 (2014)

[GQ88] Guillou, L.C., Quisquater, J.-J.: A Practical Zero-Knowledge Protocol Fitted to Security Microprocessor Minimizing Both Transmission and Memory. In: Günther, C.G. (ed.) EUROCRYPT 1988. LNCS, vol. 330, pp. 123–128. Springer, Heidelberg (1988)

[Gro09] Groth, J.: Linear Algebra with Sub-linear Zero-Knowledge Arguments. In: Halevi, S. (ed.) CRYPTO 2009. LNCS, vol. 5677, pp. 192–208. Springer, Heidelberg (2009)

[HS03] Herranz, J., Sáez, G.: Forking Lemmas for Ring Signature Schemes. In: Johansson, T., Maitra, S. (eds.) INDOCRYPT 2003. LNCS, vol. 2904, pp. 266–279. Springer, Heidelberg (2003)

[IKOS09] Ishai, Y.: Kushilevitz, Eyal, Ostrovsky, Rafail, Sahai, Amit: Zero-knowledge proofs from secure multiparty computation. SIAM Journal on Computing **39**(3), 1121–1152 (2009)

[Kil92] Kilian, J.: A note on efficient zero-knowledge proofs and arguments. In: STOC, pp. 723–732 (1992)

[Lim00] Lim, C.H.: Efficient multi-exponentiation and application to batch verification of digital signatures (2000). Manuscript available at http://dasan.sejong.ac.kr/chlim/pub/multi_exp.ps

[MGGR13] Miers, I., Garman, C., Green, M., Rubin, A.D.: Zerocoin: Anonymous distributed e-cash from bitcoin. In: IEEE Symposium on Security and Privacy (2013)

[Ngu05] Nguyen, L.: Accumulators from Bilinear Pairings and Applications. In: Menezes, A. (ed.) CT-RSA 2005. LNCS, vol. 3376, pp. 275–292. Springer, Heidelberg (2005)

[Ped91] Pedersen, T.P.: Non-interactive and Information-Theoretic Secure Verifiable Secret Sharing. In: Feigenbaum, J. (ed.) CRYPTO 1991. LNCS, vol. 576, pp. 129–140. Springer, Heidelberg (1992)

[RST01] Rivest, R.L., Shamir, A., Tauman, Y.: How to Leak a Secret. In: Boyd, C. (ed.) ASIACRYPT 2001. LNCS, vol. 2248, pp. 552–565. Springer, Heidelberg (2001)

[San99] Sander, T.: Efficient Accumulators without Trapdoor Extended Abstract. In: Varadharajan, V., Mu, Y. (eds.) ICICS 1999. LNCS, vol. 1726, pp. 252–262. Springer, Heidelberg (1999)

[Sch91] Schnorr, C.-P.: Efficient signature generation by smart cards. Journal of Cryptology **4**(3), 161–174 (1991)

[SW07] Shacham, H., Waters, B.: Efficient Ring Signatures Without Random Oracles. In: Okamoto, T., Wang, X. (eds.) PKC 2007. LNCS, vol. 4450, pp. 166–180. Springer, Heidelberg (2007)

The Bitcoin Backbone Protocol:
Analysis and Applications

Juan Garay[1], Aggelos Kiayias[2]([⊠]), and Nikos Leonardos[3]

[1] Yahoo Labs, Sunnyvale, CA, USA
garay@yahoo-inc.com
[2] Department of Informatics and Telecommunications,
University of Athens, Athens, Greece
aggelos@di.uoa.gr
[3] LIAFA, Université Paris Diderot–Paris 7, Paris, France
nikos.leonardos@gmail.com

Abstract. Bitcoin is the first and most popular decentralized cryptocurrency to date. In this work, we extract and analyze the core of the Bitcoin protocol, which we term the Bitcoin *backbone*, and prove two of its fundamental properties which we call *common prefix* and *chain quality* in the static setting where the number of players remains fixed. Our proofs hinge on appropriate and novel assumptions on the "hashing power" of the adversary relative to network synchronicity; we show our results to be tight under high synchronization.

Next, we propose and analyze applications that can be built "on top" of the backbone protocol, specifically focusing on Byzantine agreement (BA) and on the notion of a public transaction ledger. Regarding BA, we observe that Nakamoto's suggestion falls short of solving it, and present a simple alternative which works assuming that the adversary's hashing power is bounded by 1/3. The public transaction ledger captures the essence of Bitcoin's operation as a cryptocurrency, in the sense that it guarantees the liveness and persistence of committed transactions. Based on this notion we describe and analyze the Bitcoin system as well as a more elaborate BA protocol, proving them secure assuming high network synchronicity and that the adversary's hashing power is strictly less than 1/2, while the adversarial bound needed for security decreases as the network desynchronizes.

1 Introduction

Bitcoin, introduced in [29], is a decentralized payment system that is based on maintaining a public transaction ledger in a distributed manner. The ledger is maintained by anonymous participants ("players") called *miners*, executing

A. Kiayias and N. Leonardos—Research supported by ERC project CODAMODA.
N. Leonardos—Work completed while at the National and Kapodistrian University of Athens.
The full version of this paper can be found at the Cryptology ePrint Archive [22].

International Association for Cryptologic Research 2015
E. Oswald and M. Fischlin (Eds.): EUROCRYPT 2015, Part II, LNCS 9057, pp. 281–310, 2015.
DOI: 10.1007/978-3-662-46803-6_10

a protocol that maintains and extends a distributed data structure called the *blockchain*. The protocol requires from miners to solve a "proof of work" (POW, aka "cryptographic puzzle" — see, e.g., [4,16,24,38]), which essentially amounts to brute-forcing a hash inequality based on SHA-256, in order to generate new blocks for the blockchain. The blocks that comprise the blockchain contain sets of transactions that are generated at will by owners of bitcoins, who issue transactions that credit any entity of their choice who accepts payments in bitcoin. Payers broadcast transactions and miners include the transactions they receive into the blocks they generate. Miners are rewarded for maintaining the blockchain by receiving bitcoins; it is in this manner bitcoins are created and distributed among the miners who are the first recipients of newly minted bitcoins.

An important concern in Bitcoin (or any e-payment system for that matter) is the prevention of *double-spending* attacks. Specifically, in the context of Bitcoin, a double-spending attack can occur when the attacker initially credits an account, receives service or goods by the account holder, but then manages to reorganize the transaction ledger so that the transaction that credits the account holder is reverted. In this way, the attacker keeps her bitcoin while receiving services and thus she is able to spend it again somewhere else.

In [29], Nakamoto provides an initial set of arguments of why the Bitcoin system will prevent double-spending attacks. Specifically, he argues that if a payee waits for the transaction that gives her credit to advance into the blockchain a number of k blocks, then the probability that an attacker can build an alternative blockchain that "reorganizes" the public blockchain (which contains the credit transaction) drops exponentially with k. Nakamoto argues this by modeling the attacker and the set of honest players as two competing actors performing a random walk moving toward a single direction with probabilistic steps. He demonstrates that the k blocks the payee waits are enough to ensure a negligible (in k) probability of the attacker catching up with the honest players.

Nevertheless, the above analysis can be easily seen to be oversimplified: in particular, it does not account for the fact that in Bitcoin's decentralized setting the attacker may attempt to introduce disagreement between the honest miners, thus splitting their hashing power on different POW instances. Nakamoto himself appeared to recognize the relevance of agreement in the context of Bitcoin, arguing in a forum post [30] that actually "Bitcoin's basic concept" of building and exchanging a blockchain is capable of solving Byzantine agreement (BA) [27,36] in the presence of an actively malicious adversary.[1] However a thorough analysis establishing the exact security properties of the Bitcoin system has yet to appear.

---

[1] In [30] Nakamoto refers to the problem as "Byzantine Generals," which is often used to refer to the single-source version of the problem, while in fact he is referring to the case where every party has an input value (Byzantine agreement). In the cryptographic setting, the problems are not equivalent in terms of the number of tolerated misbehaving parties t ($t < n$ vs. $t < n/2$, respectively).

Our Results. In this paper we extract, formally describe, and analyze the core of the Bitcoin protocol. We call this protocol the *Bitcoin backbone*, as we describe it in a way that is versatile and extensible and can be used to solve other problems as well — not just the problem of maintaining a public transaction ledger. The Bitcoin backbone protocol is executed by players that build a blockchain following the Bitcoin source code [31] and allows a set of players to maintain a blockchain in a distributed fashion. The protocol is parameterized by three external functions $V(\cdot), I(\cdot), R(\cdot)$ which we call the *input validation predicate*, the *input contribution function*, and the *chain reading function*, respectively. At a high level, $V(\cdot)$ determines the proper structure of the information that is stored into the blockchain, $I(\cdot)$ specifies how the contents of the blocks are formed by the players, and $R(\cdot)$ determines how a blockchain is supposed to be interpreted in the context of the application. Note that the structure, contents, and interpretation of the blockchain are not important for the description of the backbone protocol and are left to be specified by the three external functions above, which are application-specific (we provide examples of these functions in Section 5).

We analyze the Bitcoin backbone protocol in a static setting when the participants operate in a synchronous communication network (more details below and in Section 2) in the presence of an adversary that controls a subset of the players. We assume that the protocol is executed by a fixed number n of players; note, however, that this number is not necessarily known to the protocol participants. The players themselves *cannot* authenticate each other and therefore there is no way to know the source of a message; we capture this by allowing the adversary to "spoof" the source address of any message that is delivered. We assume that messages are eventually delivered and all parties in the network are able to synchronize in the course of a "round." The notion of round is not important for the description of the backbone protocol (which can also be executed in a loose and asynchronous fashion in the same way that Bitcoin works), however, it is important in terms of Bitcoin's inherent computational assumption regarding the players' ability to produce POWs.

Specifically, we assume that in a single round, all parties involved are allowed the same number of queries to a cryptographic hash function, as well as to communicate with the other participants. The hash function is modeled as a random oracle [6]. For simplicity we assume a "flat model," where all parties have the same quota of hashing queries per round, say q; the non-flat model where parties have differing hashing power capabilities can be easily captured by clustering the flat-model parties into larger virtual entities that are comprised by more than one flat-model player. In fact "mining pools" in Bitcoin can be thought of such aggregations of flat-model players. The adversary itself represents such pool as it controls $t < n$ players; for this reason, the adversary's quota per round is $t \cdot q$ hashing queries. Note that in this setting, the fact $t < n/2$ directly corresponds to the adversary controlling strictly less than half of the system's total "hashing power" that all players collectively harness, thus, we will use terms such as "honest majority" and "(1/2)-bounded adversary" interchangeably.

In our analysis of the Bitcoin backbone protocol we formalize and prove two fundamental properties it possesses. The properties are quantified by three parameters γ, β and f; γ and β roughly correspond to the collective hashing power per round of the honest players and the adversary, respectively, while f represents the expected number of POWs that may be found per round by the Bitcoin network participants as a whole.

- The *common prefix property*. We prove that if $\gamma > \lambda\beta$ for some $\lambda \in [1, \infty)$ that satisfies $\lambda^2 - f\lambda + 1 \geq 0$, then the blockchains maintained by the honest players will possess a large common prefix. More specifically, if two honest parties "prune" (i.e., cut off) k blocks from the end of their local chains, the probability that the resulting pruned chains will not be mutual prefixes of each other drops exponentially in k (see Definition 2 for the precise formulation). Provided that f is very close to 0 this enables us to choose λ very close to 1 and thus establish the common prefix property as long as an honest majority of participants in the flat-model setting is guaranteed (equivalently, when the adversary controls strictly less than 50% of the hashing power). On the other hand, when the network "desynchronizes" and f gets closer to 1, achieving a common prefix requires $\lambda \rightarrow \phi$, where ϕ is the golden ratio, which in turn suggests much stricter bounds on the adversarial behavior (in fact, the upper bound on the adversary for our analysis approaches 0).

- The *chain-quality property*. We prove that if $\gamma > \lambda\beta$, for some $\lambda \in [1, \infty)$, then the ratio of blocks in the chain of any honest player that are contributed by honest players is at least $(1 - \frac{1}{\lambda})$. Again observe that if λ is close to 1, we obtain that the blockchain maintained by honest players is guaranteed to have few, but still some, blocks contributed by honest players; a higher λ would be necessary to guarantee bigger percentages of blocks contributed by honest players in the blockchain. We also observe that this result is basically tight, i.e., that the adversary is capable of following a strategy (that deviates from the strategy of honest players) that enables the introduction of that many blocks in the blockchain, under a favorable (for the adversary) assumption on the propagation of adversarial blocks in the network.

While the above two security properties may seem rather abstract since they refer to properties of the data structure that is maintained distributively by the parties, we demonstrate that they are in fact quite powerful and show that the Bitcoin backbone protocol armed with the above properties can be used as a basis for solving other problems, including the problem of distributively maintaining a "robust" public transaction ledger. In Figure 1 we show how the two properties imply the properties of the applications that are explained below.

Byzantine agreement for (1/3)-bounded adversaries. As a first application, we show how a randomized BA protocol can be built on top of the Bitcoin backbone protocol more or less directly, and based solely on the POW assumption. We instantiate the $V(\cdot), I(\cdot), R(\cdot)$ functions so that parties form blockchains and act according to the following rules: each party i attempts to insert its own input $v_i \in \{0, 1\}$ into the blockchain; a blockchain is valid only if blocks contain elements in $\{0, 1\}$; the protocol terminates when the blockchain has reached

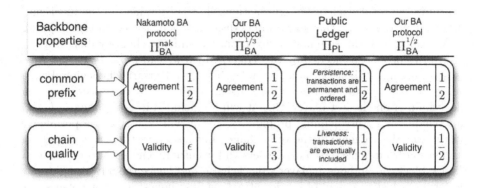

Fig. 1. An overview of the backbone protocol's applications: Nakamoto's BA protocol Π_{BA}^{nak}, our BA protocols $\Pi_{BA}^{1/3}$ and $\Pi_{BA}^{1/2}$, and the public ledger protocol Π_{PL}. All properties must be satisfied with overwhelming probability. In each box we state the name of the property as well as the maximum ratio of the adversarial hashing power that we can prove the protocol withstands (based on the corresponding backbone property). The value ϵ stands for a negligible quantity.

a sufficient length; and, the blockchain is read by the honest parties by pruning k elements from its end and returning the majority bit appearing in the resulting blockchain's prefix. We show how the common prefix property and the chain-quality property of the backbone protocol ensure Agreement and Validity (BA's basic properties; see Section 2) with high probability, thus turning the Bitcoin backbone protocol into a probabilistic BA protocol.

Observe that for the above protocol to work the chain-quality property should ensure that a majority of blocks in the blockchain originate from the honest players (otherwise Validity is lost). Our chain quality property enables this with overwhelming probability assuming the adversarial power is bounded by 1/3. This approach is different from Nakamoto's proposal [30] for BA, which, as we also show, only guarantees Validity with overwhelming probability if the adversary has a negligible amount of hashing power. On the positive side, we stress that Nakamoto's protocol fails gracefully when the adversarial power gets close to 50% as Validity can be shown with constant probability (but not overwhelming).

Public transaction ledgers and BA for honest majority. Next, we focus on how a "robust public transaction ledger" can be built on top of the Bitcoin backbone. We instantiate the $V(\cdot), I(\cdot), R(\cdot)$ functions so that parties form blockchains and act according to the following rules: each party (which in this context is called a "miner") receives a set S of transactions on its input tape and attempts to insert those in its blockchain, omitting any transactions in S that are already included in it. (A Bitcoin transaction is, for example, a statement of the type "account A credits account B a z number of bitcoins," which is signed using the secret key that corresponds to account A's Bitcoin address; each account has a unique Bitcoin address.) Reading a blockchain, on the other hand, amounts to returning the total sequence of transactions that is contained in the blockchain of the miner (and note that miners may disagree about the chain they report).

We show how the common prefix property and the chain-quality property ensure two properties needed by the ledger, which we call *Persistence* and *Liveness*, assuming an honest majority and arbitrary adversarial behavior. Persistence states that once a transaction goes more than k blocks "deep" into the blockchain of one honest player, then it will be included in *every honest player's* blockchain with overwhelming probability, and it will be assigned a permanent position in the ledger. On the other hand, Liveness says that all transactions originating from honest account holders will eventually end up at a depth more than k blocks in an honest player's blockchain, and hence the adversary cannot perform a selective denial of service attack against honest account holders. For both properties to hold we require an honest majority (i.e., that the adversary's hashing power is strictly less than 50%) assuming high network synchronicity (i.e., that the expected number of POW solutions per round satisfies[2] $f \to 0$). If this is violated, Persistence requires stricter bounds on adversarial hashing power in order to be preserved following the bounds of the common prefix property.

In the context of Bitcoin, our analysis implies that the Bitcoin backbone provides an operational transaction ledger under the assumptions: (i) the adversary controls less than half of the total hashing power, and (ii) the network synchronizes much faster relative to the POW solution rate, (iii) digital signatures cannot be forged. On the other hand, when the network desynchronizes our results cannot support that the ledger is maintained by assuming an honest majority. This negative result is consistent with the experimental analysis provided by Decker and Wattenhoffer [15], who predicted a drop below 50% in the required adversarial bound for any setting when information propagation is problematic. Our result also provides some justification for the "slow" rate of 10-minute increments used in Bitcoin block generation. Specifically, information propagation in the Bitcoin network is on the order of seconds[3] so the ratio (essentially f) of this time window over the average 10-minute period is reasonably close to "small" and thus transaction persistence can be shown for roughly an honest majority. On the other hand, cryptocurrencies including Litecoin, Primecoin and others, reacting to the demand to offer faster transaction processing, opted for a faster response rate (some as small as 1 minute), which results in more precarious situations, e.g., $f > 0.1$, which is far from being "negligible" and thus cannot support our analysis that a common prefix would be guaranteed by merely assuming an honest majority. We finally note that the Persistence and Liveness properties we put forth and prove should not be interpreted as proofs that all Bitcoin's objectives are met. In particular, they do not guarantee that miners are properly incentivized to carry out the backbone protocol, and they can only offer guarantees in a setting of an *honest majority* amongst a fixed number of players as opposed to a setting where there is an ever changing pop-

---

[2] Note that we use the notation $f \to 0$ to mean that "f is close to 0" since f will be a constant in our analysis.

[3] See, for example, http://bitcoinstats.com/network/propagation/.

ulation of parties acting rationally; see related work below as well as Section 6 for further discussion.

Finally, we present a BA protocol assuming an honest majority, by suitably exploiting the properties of the robust transaction ledger above. The protocol substitutes Bitcoin's transactions with a type of transactions that are themselves based on POWs, and hence uses POWs in two distinct ways: for the maintenance of the ledger and for the generation of the transactions. We show that the ledger's Persistence implies Agreement, and that Liveness implies Validity, because assuming the ledger is maintained for long enough, a majority of transactions originating from the honest parties will be included (despite the fact that honest parties may control a minority of blocks in the blockchain). The protocol requires special care in the way it employs POWs since the adversary should be incapable of "shifting" work between the two POW tasks that it faces in each round. To solve this problem, we introduce a special strategy for POW-based protocol composition which we call "2-for-1 POWs."

Related Work. Realizing a digital currency with a centralized entity but while achieving strong privacy was proposed early on by Chaum in [13]. A number of other works improved various aspects of this concept, however the approach remained centralized. Nakamoto [29] proposed the first decentralized currency system based on POWs while relaxing the anonymity property of the payment system to mere pseudonymity. This work was followed by a multitude of other related proposals including Litecoin[4], Primecoin [26], and Zerocash [8], to mention a few. Our analysis of the Bitcoin backbone covers all these works as well, since they are based on exactly the same protocol.

It is interesting to juxtapose our positive results to the results of Eyal and Sirer [17], who introduce an attack strategy called "selfish mining" that shows how the number of blocks contributed to the blockchain by an adversary can exceed the percentage of the hashing power the adversary possesses. Their results are consistent and complementary to ours. The crux of the issue is (in our terminology) in terms of the chain-quality property, as its formulation is quite permissive: in particular we show that if the adversary controls a suitably bounded amount of hashing power, then it is also suitably bounded in terms of the number of blocks it has managed to insert in the blockchain that honest players maintain. Specifically, recall that we prove that if the hashing power of the adversary satisfies $\beta < \frac{1}{\lambda}\gamma$ (where γ roughly corresponds to the hashing power of the honest players), then the adversary may control at most a $\frac{1}{\lambda}$ percentage of the blocks in the chain. For instance, if the adversary controls up to 1/3 of the hashing power (i.e., $\lambda = 2$), then it will provably control less than 50% of the blocks in the honest players' blockchain. As it can be easily seen, this does not guarantee that the rate of a party's hashing power translates to an equal rate of rewards (recall that in Bitcoin the rewards are linearly proportional to the number of blocks that a party contributes in the chain). We define as *ideal chain quality* the property that for any coalition of parties (following any mining strategy) the percentage of blocks in the blockchain is exactly proportional to their collective

---

[4] http://www.litecoin.com.

hashing power. The chain quality property that we prove is not ideal and the results of [17] show that in fact there is a strategy that magnifies the percentage of a malicious coalition. Still, their mining attack does much worse than our bound. To close the gap, in the full version of the paper [22] we sketch a simple selfish mining strategy that matches our upper bound and hence our chain quality result is tight in our model[5] assuming the number of honest parties is large.

Byzantine agreement (BA, aka distributed consensus) [27,36] considers a set of n parties connected by reliable and authenticated pair-wise communication links and with possible conflicting initial inputs that wish to agree on a common output in the presence of the disruptive (even malicious) behavior of some of them. The problem has received a considerable amount of attention under various models. In this paper we are interested in randomized solutions to the problem (e.g., [7,11,18,20,25,37])[6] as in the particular setting we are in, deterministic BA algorithms are not possible. In more detail, we consider BA in the *anonymous synchronous setting*, i.e., when processors do not have identifiers and cannot correlate messages to their sources, even across rounds. This model for BA was considered by Okun, who classified it as "anonymous model without port awareness," and proved the aforementioned impossibility result, that deterministic algorithms are impossible for even a single failure [33,34]. In addition, Okun showed that probabilistic BA is feasible by suitably adapting Ben-Or's protocol [7] for the standard, non-anonymous setting (cf. [34])[7]; the protocol, however, takes exponentially many rounds. It turns out that by additionally assuming that the parties are "port-aware" (i.e., they can correlate messages to sources across rounds), deterministic protocols are possible and some more efficient solutions were proposed in [35].

The anonymous synchronous setting was also considered by Aspnes *et al.* [2] who pointed to the potential usefulness of proofs of work (e.g., [4,16,24,38]) as an identity assignment tool, in such a way that the number of identities assigned to the honest and adversarial parties can be made proportional to their aggregate computational power, respectively. For example, by assuming that the adversary's computational power is less than 50%, one of the algorithms in [2] results in a number of adversarial identities less than half of that obtained by the honest parties. By running this procedure in a pre-processing stage, it is then suggested that a standard authenticated BA protocol could be run. Such

---

[5] Our model allows the unfavorable event of adversarial messages winning all head-to-head races in terms of delivery with honestly generated messages in any given round.

[6] We remark that, in contrast to the approach used in typical randomized solutions to the problem, where achieving BA is reduced to (the construction of) a shared random coin, the probabilistic aspect here stems from the parties' likelihood of being able to provide proofs of work. In addition, as our analysis relies on the random oracle model [6], we are interested in computational/cryptographic solutions to the problem.

[7] Hence, BA in this setting shares a similar profile with BA in the asynchronous setting [19].

protocols, however, would require the establishment of a consistent PKI (as well as of digital signatures), details of which are not laid out in [2].

In contrast, and as mentioned above, building on our analysis of the Bitcoin backbone protocol, we propose two BA protocols solely based on POWs that operate in $O(k)$ rounds with error probability $e^{-\Omega(k)}$. The protocols solve BA with overwhelming probability under the assumption that the adversary controls less than $1/3$ and $1/2$ of the computational power, respectively.

The connection between Bitcoin and probabilistic BA was also considered by Miller and LaViola in [28] where they take a different approach compared to ours, by not formalizing how Bitcoin works, but rather only focusing on Nakamoto's suggestion for BA [30] as a standalone protocol. As we observe here, and also recognized in [28], Nakamoto's protocol does not quite solve BA since it does not satisfy Validity with overwhelming probability. The exact repercussions of this fact are left open in [28], while with our analysis, we provide explicit answers regarding the transaction ledger's actual properties and the level of security that the backbone realization can offer.

Finally, related to the anonymous setting, the feasibility of secure computation without authenticated links was considered by Barak *et al.* in [5] in a more extreme model where all messages sent by the parties are controlled by the adversary and can be tampered with and modified (i.e., not only source addresses can be "spoofed," but also messages' contents can be altered and messages may not be delivered). It is shown in [5] that it is possible to limit the adversary so that all he can do is to partition the network into disjoint sets, where in each set the computation is secure, and also independent of the computation in the other sets. Evidently, in such system, one cannot hope to build a global ledger.

Organization of the Paper. The rest of the paper is organized as follows. In Section 2 we present our model within which we formally express the Bitcoin backbone protocol and prove its basic properties. The backbone protocol builds "blockchains" based on a cryptographic hash function; we introduce notation for this data structure as well as the backbone protocol itself in Section 3, followed by its analysis in Section 4. Section 5 is dedicated to applications. In the full version we analyze two simple POW-based BA protocols: Nakamoto's attempt to BA and our protocol tolerating $1/3$ adversarial power. We present the robust public ledger application (Bitcoin's essential task — Section 5.1) and our BA protocol for $1/2$ adversarial power (Section 5.2). Due to space limitations, some of the detailed constructions, various useful remarks, and proofs, can be found in the full version of this paper [22].

2   Model and Definitions

We describe our protocols in a standard multiparty synchronous communication setting (e.g., Canetti's formulation of "real world" execution [12]) with the relaxation that the underlying communication graph is not fully connected and messages are delivered through a "diffusion" mechanism that reflects Bitcoin's peer-to-peer structure. Our adversarial model in the network is "adaptive," meaning that the adversary is allowed to take control of parties on the fly, and "rushing," meaning that in any given round the adversary gets to see all honest players' messages before deciding his strategy, and, furthermore, also allows the adversary to change the source information on every message. Note that the adversary cannot change the contents of the messages nor prevent them from being delivered. Effectively, this parallels communication over TCP/IP in the Internet where messages between parties are delivered reliably, but nevertheless malicious parties may "spoof" the source of a message they transmit and make it appear as originating from an arbitrary party (including another honest party) in the view of the receiver. This aspect of the communication model, where processors cannot correlate messages to their sources, even across arounds, was considered by Okun [33], who classified it as "anonymous model without port awareness." In this setting we use BROADCAST as the message transmission command that captures the "send-to-all" functionality allowed by our communication model. Note that an adversarial sender may abuse BROADCAST and attempt to confuse honest parties by sending and delivering inconsistent messages to them.

The parties' inputs are provided by the environment $\mathcal{Z}$ which also receives the parties' outputs. Parties that receive no input from the environment remain inactive, in the sense that they will not act when their turn comes in each round. The environment may provide input to a party at any round and may also modify that input from round to round. We denote by INPUT() the input tape of each party.

In each round, parties are able to read their input tape INPUT() and communication tape RECEIVE(), perform some computation that will be suitably restricted (see below) and issue[8] a BROADCAST message that is guaranteed to be delivered to all parties in the beginning of the next round. As stated above the adversary can do multiple broadcasts per round and in fact deliver to each honest party a different message or even multiple messages.

The term $\{\text{VIEW}^P_{\Pi,\mathcal{A},\mathcal{Z}}(\kappa, z)\}_{\kappa\in\mathbb{N}, z\in\{0,1\}^*}$ denotes the random variable ensemble describing the view of party P after the completion of an execution with environment $\mathcal{Z}$, running protocol Π, and adversary $\mathcal{A}$, on auxiliary input $z \in \{0,1\}^*$. We often drop the parameters κ and z and simply refer to the ensemble by $\text{VIEW}^P_{\Pi,\mathcal{A},\mathcal{Z}}$ if the meaning is clear from the context. If n parties $P_1, \ldots, P_n$ execute Π, the concatenation of the view of all parties $\langle\text{VIEW}^{P_i}_{\Pi,\mathcal{A},\mathcal{Z}}\rangle_{i=1,\ldots,n}$ is denoted by $\text{VIEW}_{\Pi,\mathcal{A},\mathcal{Z}}$. With foresight, we note that, in contrast to the standard setting where parties are aware of the number of parties executing the protocol, we are interested in protocols Π that do not make explicit use of the number of parties n or their identities. Further, note that because of the unauthenticated nature of the communication model the parties may never be certain about the number of participants in a protocol execution. Nonetheless note that the number of parties is fixed during the course of the protocol execution.

---

[8] For simplicity, we assume that the broadcast operation is atomic and hence the corruption of a party may not happen while the operation is taking place (cf. [21, 23]).

In order to capture the parties' limited ability to produce POWs, we assume that all parties may have access to an oracle $H(\cdot)$ and allowed to perform a number of queries q *per round*, where q is a function of the security parameter κ; we refer to such parties as *q-bounded*. Note that this is a "flat-model" interpretation of the parties' computation power, where all parties are assumed equal. In the real world, different honest parties may have different "hashing power;" nevertheless, our flat-model does not sacrifice generality since one can imagine that real honest parties are simply clusters of some arbitrary number of honest flat-model parties. The adversary $\mathcal{A}$ is allowed to perform $t \cdot q$ queries per round, where $t \leq n$ is the number of corrupted parties. The environment $\mathcal{Z}$, on the other hand, is not permitted any queries to $H(\cdot)$. The rationale for this is that we would like to bound the "CPU power" [29] of the adversary to be proportionate to the number of parties it controls while making it infeasible for them to be aided by external sources or by transferring the hashing power potentially invested in concurrent or previous protocol executions. It follows that in our analysis we will focus on the "standalone" setting, where a single protocol instance is executed in isolation.

We refer to the above restrictions on the environment, the parties and the adversary as the *q-bounded synchronous setting*. The view of the parties participating in the protocol will be denoted by $\text{VIEW}_{\Pi,\mathcal{A},\mathcal{Z}}^{P,H(\cdot)}(\kappa, q, z)$ and the concatenation of all parties' views by $\text{VIEW}_{\Pi,\mathcal{A},\mathcal{Z}}^{H(\cdot)}(\kappa, q, z)$.

In our theorems we will be concerned with *properties* of protocols Π in the q-bounded synchronous setting. Such properties will be defined as predicates over the random variable $\text{VIEW}_{\Pi,\mathcal{A},\mathcal{Z}}^{H(\cdot)}(\kappa, q, z)$ by quantifying over all possible adversaries $\mathcal{A}$ and environments $\mathcal{Z}$. Note that all our protocols will only satisfy properties with a small probability of error in κ as well as in a parameter k that can be freely selected in $\{1, \ldots, \kappa\}$. The probability space is determined by the oracle $H(\cdot)$ as well as any random choices made by the protocol itself (if any). Further details about the model are given in [22].

Byzantine Agreement. As a simple illustration of the formulation above we define the properties of a Byzantine agreement (BA) protocol.

Definition 1. *A protocol Π solves BA in the q-bounded synchronous setting provided it satisfies the following two properties:*
- Agreement. *There is a round after which all honest parties return the same output if queried by the environment.*
- Validity. *The output returned by an honest party P equals the input of some party P' that is honest at the round P's output is produced.*

We note that in our protocols, the participants are capable of detecting agreement and furthermore they can also detect whether other parties detect agreement, thus *termination* can be easily achieved by all honest parties. The formulation of Validity above is intended to capture security/correctness against adaptive adversaries. The notion (specifically, the requirement that the output value be one of the honest parties' inputs) has also been called "Strong Validity" [32], but the distinction is only important in the case of non-binary inputs.

In either case, it is known that in the synchronous cryptographic setting the problem has a solution if and only if $n > |V|t$, where V is the input/decision domain [20]. Our POW-based protocols work for both versions of the problem.

3   The Bitcoin Backbone Protocol

We start by introducing blockchain notation. Let $G(\cdot), H(\cdot)$ be cryptographic hash functions with output in $\{0,1\}^\kappa$. A *block* is any triple of the form $B = \langle s, x, ctr \rangle$ where $s \in \{0,1\}^\kappa, x \in \{0,1\}^*, ctr \in \mathbb{N}$ are such that satisfy predicate validblock$_q^D(B)$ defined as $(H(ctr, G(s,x)) < D) \wedge (ctr \leq q)$.

The parameter $D \in \mathbb{N}$ is also called the block's *difficulty level*. The parameter $q \in \mathbb{N}$ is a bound that in the Bitcoin implementation determines the size of the register ctr; in our treatment we allow this to be arbitrary, and use it to denote the maximum allowed number of hash queries in a round. We do this for convenience and our analysis applies in a straightforward manner to the case that ctr is restricted to the range $0 \leq ctr < 2^{32}$ and q is independent of ctr.

A *blockchain*, or simply a *chain* is a sequence of *blocks*. The rightmost block is the *head* of the chain, denoted head($\mathcal{C}$). Note that the empty string ε is also a chain; by convention we set head(ε) = ε. A chain $\mathcal{C}$ with head($\mathcal{C}$) = $\langle s', x', ctr' \rangle$ can be extended to a longer chain by appending a valid block $B = \langle s, x, ctr \rangle$ that satisfies $s = H(ctr', G(s', x'))$. In case $\mathcal{C} = \varepsilon$, by convention any valid block of the form $\langle s, x, ctr \rangle$ may extend it. In either case we have an extended chain $\mathcal{C}_{new} = \mathcal{C}B$ that satisfies head($\mathcal{C}_{new}$) = B.

The *length* of a chain len($\mathcal{C}$) is its number of blocks. Given a chain $\mathcal{C}$ that has length len($\mathcal{C}$) = $n > 0$ we can define a vector $\mathbf{x}_\mathcal{C} = \langle x_1, \ldots, x_n \rangle$ that contains all the x-values that are stored in the chain such that x_i is the value of the i-th block.

Consider a chain $\mathcal{C}$ of length m and any nonnegative integer k. We denote by $\mathcal{C}^{\lceil k}$ the chain resulting from the "pruning" the k rightmost blocks. Note that for $k \geq$ len($\mathcal{C}$), $\mathcal{C}^{\lceil k} = \varepsilon$. If $\mathcal{C}_1$ is a prefix of $\mathcal{C}_2$ we write $\mathcal{C}_1 \preceq \mathcal{C}_2$.

We note that Bitcoin uses chains of variable difficulty, i.e., the value D may change across different blocks within the same chain according to some rule that is determined by the x values stored in the chain[9]. This is done to account for the fact that the number of parties (and hence the total hashing power of the system) is variable from round to round (as opposed to the unknown but fixed number of parties n we assume). See Section 6 for further discussion. We are now ready to describe the protocol.

3.1   The Backbone Protocol

The Bitcoin backbone protocol is executed by an arbitrary number of parties over an unauthenticated network. For concreteness, we assume that the number of parties running the protocol is n; however, parties need not be aware of

---

[9] In Bitcoin every 2016 blocks the difficulty is recalibrated according to the timestamps stored in the blocks so that the block generation rate remains at approximately 10 minutes per block.

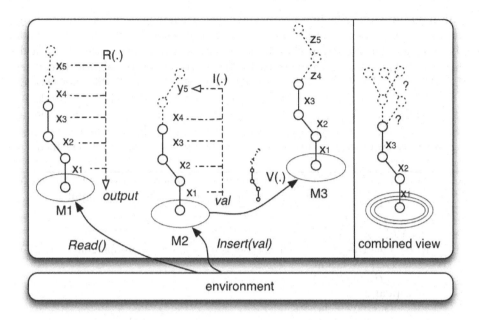

Fig. 2. Overview of the basic operation of the Bitcoin backbone protocol. Miner M_1 receives from the environment a READ instruction that results in the application of the $R(\cdot)$ function on the contents of its chain which are equal to the vector $\langle x_1, x_2, x_3, x_4, x_5 \rangle$. Miner M_2 receives from the environment an INSERT instruction and uses the function $I(\cdot)$ to determine the value y_5 that it subsequently successfully inserts in its local block chain by solving a proof of work; this results in a broadcast of the newly extended chain. Finally miner M_3 receives the newly extended chain and validates it both structurally as well as using the input validation predicate $V(\cdot)$. M_3 will adopt this chain if M_3 deems it better than its local chain as specified by the backbone protocol. Note that the joint view of M_1, M_2, M_3 is inconsistent but there is agreement on the prefix $\langle x_1, x_2, x_3 \rangle$.

this number when they execute the protocol. As mentioned in Section 2, communication over the network is achieved by utilizing a send-to-all BROADCAST functionality that is available to all parties (and maybe abused by the adversary in the sense of delivering different messages to different parties). Each party maintains a blockchain, as defined above. Each party's chain may be different, but, as we will prove, under certain well-defined conditions, the chains of honest parties will share a large common prefix. (Figure 2 depicts the local view of each party as well as the shared portion of their chains.)

In the protocol description we intentionally avoid specifying the type of values that parties try to insert in the chain, the type of chain validation they perform (beyond checking for its structural properties with respect to the hash functions $G(\cdot), H(\cdot)$), and the way they interpret the chain. These functions are handled by the external functions $V(\cdot), I(\cdot), R(\cdot)$ which are specified by the application that runs "on top" of the backbone protocol.

Chain Validation. The first algorithm, called validate performs a validation of the structural properties of a given chain $\mathcal{C}$. It is given as input the values q and D, as well as a hash function $H(\cdot)$. It is parameterized by a predicate $V(\cdot)$, called the *input validation predicate*. For each block of the chain, the algorithm checks that the proof of work is properly solved, that the counter ctr does not exceed q and that the hash of the previous block is properly included in the block. It further collects all the inputs from the chain's blocks and assembles them into a vector $\mathbf{x}_{\mathcal{C}}$. If all blocks verify and $V(\mathbf{x}_{\mathcal{C}})$ is true then the chain is valid; otherwise it is rejected. Note that we purposely leave the predicate $V(\cdot)$ undetermined.

Algorithm 1 The *chain validation predicate*, parameterized by q, D, the hash functions $G(\cdot), H(\cdot)$, and the *input validation predicate* $V(\cdot)$. The input is $\mathcal{C}$.

```
 1: function validate(C)
 2:      b ← V(x_C) ∧ (C ≠ ε)
 3:      if b = True then              ▷ The chain is non-empty and meaningful w.r.t. V(·)
 4:          ⟨s, x, ctr⟩ ← head(C)
 5:          s' ← H(ctr, G(s, x))
 6:          repeat
 7:              ⟨s, x, ctr⟩ ← head(C)
 8:              if validblock_q^D(⟨s, x, ctr⟩) ∧ (H(ctr, G(s, x)) = s') then
 9:                  s' ← s                         ▷ Retain hash value
10:                  C ← C^⌈1                       ▷ Remove the head from C
11:              else
12:                  b ← False
13:              end if
14:          until (C = ε) ∨ (b = False)
15:      end if
16:      return (b)
17: end function
```

Chain Comparison. The objective of the second algorithm, called maxvalid, is to find the "best possible" chain when given a set of chains. The algorithm is straightforward and is parameterized by a $\max(\cdot)$ function that applies some ordering in the space of chains. The most important aspect is the chains' length, in which case $\max(\mathcal{C}_1, \mathcal{C}_2)$ will return the longest of the two. In case $\text{len}(\mathcal{C}_1) = \text{len}(\mathcal{C}_2)$, some other characteristic can be used to break the tie. In our case, $\max(\cdot, \cdot)$ will always return the first operand[10]; alternatively, other options exist, such as lexicographic order or picking a chain at random. The analysis we will perform will essentially be independent of the tie-breaking rule[11].

---

[10] Note that the way we deploy maxvalid, amounts to parties always giving preference to their local chain as opposed to any incoming chain. This is consistent with current Bitcoin operation; however, some debate about alternate tie-breaking rules has ensued in Bitcoin forums, e.g., see [14].

[11] It is worth to point out that the behavior of maxvalid($\cdot$) is associated with some stability aspects of the backbone protocol and currently there are proposals to modify

---

Algorithm 2 The function that finds the "best" chain, parameterized by function $\max(\cdot)$. The input is $\{\mathcal{C}_1, \ldots, \mathcal{C}_k\}$.

1: **function** maxvalid($\mathcal{C}_1, \ldots, \mathcal{C}_k$)
2:     $temp \leftarrow \varepsilon$
3:     **for** $i = 1$ to k **do**
4:         **if** validate($\mathcal{C}_i$) **then**
5:             $temp \leftarrow \max(\mathcal{C}, temp)$
6:         **end if**
7:     **end for**
8:     **return** $temp$
9: **end function**

Algorithm 3 The *proof of work* function, parameterized by q, D and hash functions $H(\cdot), G(\cdot)$. The input is $(x, \mathcal{C})$.

1: **function** pow($x, \mathcal{C}$)
2:     **if** $\mathcal{C} = \varepsilon$ **then**   ▷ Determine proof of work instance
3:         $s \leftarrow 0$
4:     **else**
5:         $\langle s', x', ctr' \rangle \leftarrow \text{head}(\mathcal{C})$
6:         $s \leftarrow H(ctr', G(s', x'))$
7:     **end if**
8:     $ctr \leftarrow 1$
9:     $B \leftarrow \varepsilon$
10:     $h \leftarrow G(s, x)$
11:     **while** ($ctr \leq q$) **do**
12:         **if** ($H(ctr, h) < D$) **then**   ▷ Proof of work succeeded
13:             $B \leftarrow \langle s, x, ctr \rangle$
14:             **break**
15:         **end if**
16:         $ctr \leftarrow ctr + 1$
17:     **end while**
18:     $\mathcal{C} \leftarrow \mathcal{C}B$ ▷ Extend chain
19:     **return** $\mathcal{C}$
20: **end function**

Proof of Work. The third algorithm, called pow, is the main "workhorse" of the backbone protocol. It takes as input a chain and attempts to extend it via solving a proof of work. This algorithm is parameterized by two hash functions $H(\cdot), G(\cdot)$ (which in our analysis will be modeled as random oracles)[12], as well

---

it (e.g., by randomizing it — cf. [17]). It is an interesting question whether any improvement in our results can be achieved by randomizing the maxvalid operation.

[12] In reality the same hash function (SHA-256) instantiates both G and H; however, it is notationally more convenient to consider them as distinct.

as two positive integers q, D; q represents the number of times the algorithm is going to attempt to brute-force the hash function inequality that determines the POW instance, and D determines the "difficulty" of the POW. The algorithm works as follows. Given a chain C and a value x to be inserted in the chain, it hashes these values to obtain h and initializes a counter ctr. Subsequently, it increments ctr and checks to see whether $H(ctr, h) \leq D$; if a suitable ctr is found then the algorithm succeeds in solving the POW and extends chain C by one block inserting x as well as ctr (which serves as the POW). If no suitable ctr is found, the algorithm simply returns the chain unaltered. (See Algorithm 3.)

The Backbone Protocol. Given the three algorithms above, we are now ready to describe the Bitcoin backbone protocol. This is the protocol that is executed by the miners and which is assumed to run "indefinitely" (our security analysis will apply when the total running time is polynomial in κ). It is parameterized by two functions, the input contribution function $I(\cdot)$ and the chain reading function $R(\cdot)$, which is applied to the values stored in the chain.

Each miner maintains a local chain C, attempting to extend it by invoking the POW algorithm pow described above. Prior to updating the chain, the miner checks its communication tape RECEIVE() to see whether a "better" chain has been received. This is done using the maxvalid function, depending on which the local chain is substituted.

The value that the miner attempts to insert in the chain is determined by function $I(\cdot)$. The input to $I(\cdot)$ is the state st, the current chain C, the contents of the miner's input tape INPUT() (recall that they can be written by the environment $\mathcal{Z}$ at the beginning of any round) and communication tape RECEIVE(), as well as the current round number $round$. The protocol expects two types of entries in the input tape, READ and (INSERT, $value$); other inputs are ignored.

We purposely leave the functions $I(\cdot), R(\cdot)$ undetermined in the description of the backbone protocol, as their specifics will vary according to the application. One may choose, for example, $I(\cdot)$ to be as simple as copying the contents of the INSERT input symbols from Input() into x and keeping $st = \epsilon$, or performing a complex operation parsing C and maintaining old inputs in st. We provide explicit examples of $I(\cdot)$ and $R(\cdot)$ in Section 5. When the input x is determined, the protocol attempts to insert it into the chain C by invoking pow. In case the local chain C is modified during the above steps, the protocol transmits ("broadcasts") the new chain to the other parties. Finally, in case a READ symbol is present in the communication tape, the protocol applies function $R(\cdot)$ to its current chain and writes the result onto the output tape OUTPUT(). This way, the round ends and a new round begins, continuing indefinitely.

3.2 (Desired) Properties of the Backbone Protocol

We next define the two main properties of the backbone protocol that we will prove. The first property is called the *common prefix property* and is parameterized by a value $k \in \mathbb{N}$. It considers an arbitrary environment and adversary in the q-bounded setting, and it holds as long as any two honest parties' chains are different only in its most recent k blocks.

Algorithm 4 The Bitcoin backbone protocol, parameterized by the *input contribution function* $I(\cdot)$ and the *chain reading function* $R(\cdot)$.

1: $\mathcal{C} \leftarrow \varepsilon$
2: $st \leftarrow \varepsilon$
3: $round \leftarrow 0$
4: **while** TRUE **do**
5:      $\tilde{\mathcal{C}} \leftarrow \mathsf{maxvalid}(\mathcal{C}, \text{any chain } \mathcal{C}' \text{ found in } \text{RECEIVE}())$
6:      $\langle st, x \rangle \leftarrow I(st, \tilde{\mathcal{C}}, round, \text{INPUT}(), \text{RECEIVE}())$ ▷ Determine the x-value.
7:      $\mathcal{C}_{\mathsf{new}} \leftarrow \mathsf{pow}(x, \tilde{\mathcal{C}})$
8:      **if** $\mathcal{C} \neq \mathcal{C}_{\mathsf{new}}$ **then**
9:          $\mathcal{C} \leftarrow \mathcal{C}_{\mathsf{new}}$
10:          BROADCAST($\mathcal{C}$)
11:      **end if**
12:      $round \leftarrow round + 1$
13:      **if** INPUT() contains READ **then**
14:          **write** $R(\mathbf{x}_{\mathcal{C}})$ to OUTPUT()
15:      **end if**
16: **end while**

Definition 2 (Common Prefix Property). *The common prefix property* Q_{cp} *with parameter* $k \in \mathbb{N}$ *states that for any pair of honest players* P_1, P_2 *maintaining the chains* $\mathcal{C}_1, \mathcal{C}_2$ *in* $\text{VIEW}_{\Pi, \mathcal{A}, \mathcal{Z}}^{H(\cdot)}(\kappa, q, z)$, *it holds that*

$$\mathcal{C}_1^{\lceil k} \preceq \mathcal{C}_2 \text{ and } \mathcal{C}_2^{\lceil k} \preceq \mathcal{C}_1.$$

The second property, which we call the *chain quality property*, aims at expressing the number of honest-player contributions that are contained in a sufficiently long and continuous part of an honest player's chain. Specifically, for parameters $k \in \mathbb{N}$ and $\mu \in (0, 1)$, the rate of adversarial input contributions in a continuous part of an honest party's chain is bounded by μ. This is intended to capture that at any moment that an honest player looks at a sufficiently long part of its blockchain, that part will be of sufficient "quality," i.e., the number of adversarial blocks present in that portion of the chain will be suitably bounded.

Definition 3 (Chain Quality Property). *The chain quality property* Q_{cq} *with parameters* $\mu \in \mathbb{R}$ *and* $\ell \in \mathbb{N}$ *states that for any honest party* P *with chain* $\mathcal{C}$ *in* $\text{VIEW}_{\Pi, \mathcal{A}, \mathcal{Z}}^{H(\cdot)}(\kappa, q, z)$, *it holds that for any* ℓ *consecutive blocks of* $\mathcal{C}$ *the ratio of adversarial blocks is at most* μ.

It is easy to see that any set of, say, h honest parties, obtain as many blocks as their proportion of the total hashing power, i.e., h/n. We say that a protocol Π satisfies *ideal chain quality* if this is the case for adversarial parties as well, i.e., $\mu = t/n$ with respect to those parties. The ideal chain quality is not achieved by the Bitcoin backbone protocol (see [22]).

4   Analysis of the Bitcoin Backbone

We now proceed to the analysis of the protocol presented in the previous section. Let $\{0,1\}^\kappa$ be the range of $H(\cdot)$. Each party tries to provide a POW by issuing queries to $H(\cdot)$, which succeed with probability $p = D/2^\kappa$, where D is the difficulty level. By the properties of the random oracle $H(\cdot)$, any collection of queries will be treated as a collection of independent Bernoulli trials with success probability p. In order to support this we will assume that the function $I(\cdot)$ (which determines the input of the players that is to be inserted in the blockchain) ensures (at least with overwhelming probability) that the inputs are unique. There are two simple ways to enforce this: either have $I(\cdot)$ add a sufficiently long random nonce to x, or, in case parties have unique identities, it may be parameterized by it and introduce it as part of x. In either case, this value will be ignored by the other functions $V(\cdot), R(\cdot)$ as it need not be useful in the application. It is easy to see that if a κ-long nonce is used the output will be unique except for probability at most $\bar{q}^2 \cdot 2^{-\kappa}$ where $\bar{q}$ is the total number of queries submitted to the random oracle; we will ignore this small term in our analysis.

Definitions and Preliminary Lemmas. Recall that n is the number of parties, t of which can be corrupted by the adversary. We introduce the following parameters for notational convenience:

$$\alpha = pq(n-t), \quad \beta = pqt, \quad \gamma = \alpha - \alpha^2, \quad f = \alpha + \beta.$$

The first parameter, α, reflects the hashing power of the honest parties. It is an upper bound on the expected number of solutions that the honest parties compute in one round. Similarly, β, is the expected number of solutions that the corrupted parties compute in one round. Notice the asymmetry that while the honest parties will not compute more than one solution per round, a corrupted party may use all its q queries and potentially compute more than one solution. The parameter γ will serve as a lower bound on the following two probabilities. The first one is that at least one honest party computes a solution in a round:

$$1 - (1-p)^{q(n-t)} \geq 1 - e^{-\alpha} \geq \gamma;$$

we will call such round a *successful round*. The second one is the probability that exactly one honest party does so; we will call such round a *uniquely successful* round. We lower bound the probability of such a round by the probability that out of $q(n-t)$ coin tosses exactly one comes up heads. Thus, the probability is at least:

$$(n-t)qp(1-p)^{q(n-t)-1} \geq \alpha(1 - \alpha + p) \geq \gamma.$$

The ratio $\alpha/\beta = (n-t)/t$ will be of interest for the analysis. When α is small (as it will be when f is small), then $\gamma \approx \alpha$ and we will be justified to concentrate on the ratio γ/β. To understand how well γ estimates the probability of a uniquely successful round, call it γ', we observe the following upper bound:

$$\gamma' = (n-t)(1-(1-p)^q)(1-p)^{q(n-t-1)} \le (n-t)pqe^{-\alpha+pq}$$

$$\le \alpha(1-\alpha+pq+(\alpha-pq)^2/2) = \alpha-\alpha^2(1-\tfrac{1}{n-t})+\tfrac{\alpha^3}{2}(1-\tfrac{1}{n-t})^2,$$

where we use Bernoulli's inequality (see [22]). From this it follows that $\gamma' \le \alpha - \alpha^2 + \alpha^3/2 + O(1/(n-t))$.

The following definition will be crucial in the analysis of the common-prefix property.

Definition 4 (Uniform rounds). *We call a round uniform if, at that round, every honest party invokes the* $\mathrm{pow}(\cdot)$ *algorithm with a chain of the same length (i.e.,* $\mathrm{len}(\tilde{C})$ *at line 7 of Algorithm 4 is the same for all honest parties).*

We will call a query of a party *successful* if it submits a pair (ctr, h) such that $H(ctr, h) \le D$. Without loss of generality, let $P_1, \ldots, P_t$ be the set of corrupted parties (knowledge of this set will not be used in any argument). For each round $i, j \in [q]$, and $k \in [t]$, we define Boolean random variables X_i and $Z_{ijk} \in \{0,1\}$ as follows. If at round i an honest party obtains a POW, then $X_i = 1$, otherwise $X_i = 0$. Regarding the adversary, if at round i, the j-th query of the k-th corrupted party is successful, then $Z_{ijk} = 1$, otherwise $Z_{ijk} = 0$. Further, if $X_i = 1$, we call i a *successful round*. If a round is uniform (Def. 4) and uniquely successful, we say it is a *uniquely successful uniform round*.

Next, we will prove two preliminary lemmas that will be helpful in our analysis. The first one states that, at any round, the length of any honest party's chain will be at least as large as the number of successful rounds. As a consequence, the chain of honest parties will grow at least at the rate of successful rounds. The second lemma is a simple application of Chernoff bounds and states that, with high probability, the honest parties will have, at any round, at least λ as many successful rounds as the adversary has. The usefulness of this lemma will be in showing that honest parties will be building a blockchain at a rate the adversary will find it hard to overcome.

Lemma 1. *Suppose that at round r the chain of an honest party is of length ℓ. Then, after round $s \ge r$, the chain of any honest party will have length at least $\ell + \sum_{i=r}^{s} X_i$.*

Lemma 2. *Assume $\gamma \ge (1+\delta)\lambda\beta$ for some $\delta \in (0,1)$ and $\lambda \ge 1$. The probability that during s rounds the number of successful rounds exceeds by a factor $(1+\frac{\delta}{2})\lambda$ the number of solutions computed by the adversary is at least $1 - e^{-\Omega(\delta^2 s)}$.*

We are now ready for the treatment of the protocol's properties outlined in Section 3.2.

The Common-Prefix Property. This property is established in Theorem 1, whose main argument is in turn given in Lemma 4. We start with a lemma leading to that argument. The lemma will be used to argue that uniform rounds favor the honest parties. Informally, the idea is that a uniquely successful uniform round forces an adversary trying to make honest parties' chains "diverge" to produce POWs. In the second lemma we take advantage of this, to show that if the adversary has appropriately bounded computational power, then there will be enough uniquely successful uniform rounds to prevent him from mounting a successful attack on the common-prefix property.

Lemma 3. *Consider a uniquely successful uniform round where the honest parties have chains of length $\ell - 1$. Then, in any subsequent round, there can be at most one chain C where the ℓ-th block was contributed by an honest party.*

Note that in order for the common-prefix property to be violated at round r, at least two honest parties should have chains C_1 and C_2 such that $C_1^{\lceil k} \npreceq C_2$ or $C_2^{\lceil k} \npreceq C_1$. Therefore, the existence of many blocks computed at uniform rounds forces the adversary to provide as many blocks of its own. We need to show that, with high probability the adversary will fail to collect as many solutions by round r.

We say that two chains *diverge* at a given round, if the last block of their common prefix was computed before that round.

Our main lemma below asserts the following. Suppose the protocol is halted at round r and two honest parties have distinct chains C_1 and C_2. Then, for s large enough, the probability that C_1 and C_2 diverge at round $r - s$ is negligible. The idea of the proof is to upper bound the number of (valid) broadcasts that the adversary can perform during these last s rounds. Note that they are in the order of βs in expectation. The crucial observation here is that if at a given round the adversary is silent, then a uniform round follows. Therefore we expect about $(1 - \beta)s$ uniform rounds, and consequently $\gamma(1 - \beta)s$ uniquely-successful uniform rounds. Recalling Lemma 3, the adversary needs to collect $\gamma(1 - \beta)s$ POWs. Thus, in the lemma's condition we choose the relation between β and γ suitably so that the adversary is incapable of accomplishing this task, except with probability exponentially decreasing in s.

Lemma 4. *Assume $f < 1$ and $\gamma \geq (1+\delta)\lambda\beta$, for some real $\delta \in (0,1)$ and $\lambda \geq 1$ such that $\lambda^2 - f\lambda - 1 \geq 0$. Suppose C_1 and C_2 are the chains of two honest parties at round r. Then, for any $s \leq r$, the probability that C_1 and C_2 diverge at round $r - s$ is at most $e^{-\Omega(\delta^3 s)}$.*

The above lemma is almost what we need, except that it refers to number of rounds instead of number of blocks. In order to obtain the common-prefix property we should use the properties of the blockchains of the parties themselves as the sole measure of divergence. The next theorem establishes the connection.

Theorem 1. *Assume $f < 1$ and $\gamma \geq (1 + \delta)\lambda\beta$, for some real $\delta \in (0,1)$ and $\lambda \geq 1$ such that $\lambda^2 - f\lambda - 1 \geq 0$. Let S be the set of the chains of the honest parties at a given round of the backbone protocol. Then the probability that S does not satisfy the common-prefix property with parameter k is at most $e^{-\Omega(\delta^3 k)}$.*

The Chain-Quality Property. We now turn to the chain-quality property (Definition 3), which the theorem below establishes for a suitable bound on the number of blocks introduced by the adversary. In [22] we argue that the theorem is tight via a "selfish mining"-type strategy.

Theorem 2. *Assume $f < 1$ and $\gamma \geq (1 + \delta)\lambda\beta$ for some $\delta \in (0,1)$. Suppose $\mathcal{C}$ belongs to an honest party and consider any ℓ consecutive blocks of $\mathcal{C}$. The probability that the adversary has contributed more than $(1 - \frac{\delta}{3})\frac{1}{\lambda}\ell$ of these blocks is less than $e^{-\Omega(\delta^2 \ell)}$.*

From the above theorem, it follows immediately that the chain quality is satisfied with parameter $\mu = \frac{1}{\lambda}$ for any segment length ℓ and probability that drops exponentially in ℓ.

5   Applications

We now show how the Bitcoin backbone protocol armed with the above properties can be used as a basis for solving other problems. We start with Byzantine agreement, as suggested by Nakamoto in a forum post [30][13]. Having defined the backbone protocol, this attempt is quite straightforward, and, at a high level, amounts to parties inserting their input values into blocks, and the validation predicate requiring that all valid chains contain the same input value, after running the protocol for a given number of rounds (alternatively, chains acquiring a certain length). However, we observe that Nakamoto's suggestion falls short of satisfying Definition 1, as Validity cannot be guaranteed with high probability, and present an alternative approach solving BA with an error that decreases exponentially in the length of the chain. Besides a change in the decision function, the most important difference is that parties build chains where they insist on inserting their local inputs, which results in a chain that contains inputs contributed by all parties. As long as the majority of blocks are contributed by honest parties one can derive Validity; this happens however provided that the adversary's power is bounded by 1/3. Due to space limitations, these protocols are presented in [22].

Next, we focus on how a "robust public transaction ledger," Bitcoin's essential task, can be built on top of the backbone protocol, followed by a more elaborate POW-based BA protocol assuming an honest majority. (Recall Figure 1.)

5.1   Robust Public Transaction Ledgers

A *public transaction ledger* is defined with respect to a set of valid ledgers $\mathcal{L}$ and a set of valid transactions $\mathcal{T}$, each one possessing an efficient membership test. A ledger $\mathbf{x} \in \mathcal{L}$ is a vector of sequences of transactions $\text{tx} \in \mathcal{T}$. Each transaction tx may be associated with one or more *accounts*, denoted $a_1, a_2, \ldots$ (Here we

---

[13] We note that Nakamoto's description is quite informal. Here we make the most plausible interpretation of it in our framework.

will be treating transactions and accounts rather abstractly; see [22] for more concrete, Bitcoin-like notions.)

The backbone protocol parties, called *miners* in the context of this section, process sequences of transactions of the form $x = \mathsf{tx}_1 \ldots \mathsf{tx}_e$ that are supposed to be incorporated into their local chain $\mathcal{C}$. The input inserted at each block of the chain $\mathcal{C}$ is the sequence x of transactions. Thus, a ledger is a vector of transaction sequences $\langle x_1, \ldots, x_m \rangle$, and a chain $\mathcal{C}$ of length m contains the ledger $\mathbf{x}_{\mathcal{C}} = \langle x_1, \ldots, x_m \rangle$ if the input of the j-th block in $\mathcal{C}$ is x_j.

The description and properties of the ledger protocol will be expressed relative to an oracle Txgen which will control a set of accounts by creating them and issuing transactions on their behalf. In an execution of the backbone protocol, the environment $\mathcal{Z}$ as well as the miners will have access to Txgen. Specifically, Txgen is a stateful oracle that responds to two types of queries (which we purposely only describe at a high level):

– GenAccount(1^{κ}): It generates an account a.
– IssueTrans($1^{\kappa}, \tilde{\mathsf{tx}}$): It returns a transaction tx provided that $\tilde{\mathsf{tx}}$ is some suitably formed string, or $\perp$.

We also consider a symmetric relation on $\mathcal{T}$, denoted by $C(\cdot, \cdot)$, which indicates when two transactions $\mathsf{tx}_1, \mathsf{tx}_2$ are conflicting. Valid ledgers $\mathbf{x} \in \mathcal{L}$ can never contain two conflicting transactions. We call oracle Txgen *unambiguous* if it holds that for all PPT $\mathcal{A}$, the probability that $\mathcal{A}^{\mathsf{Txgen}}$ produces a transaction tx' such that $C(\mathsf{tx}', \mathsf{tx}) = 1$, for tx issued by Txgen, is negligible in κ.

Finally, a transaction tx is called *neutral* if $C(\mathsf{tx}, \mathsf{tx}') = 0$ for any other transaction tx'. The presence of neutral transactions in the ledger can be helpful for a variety of purposes, as we will see next and in the BA protocol that we build on top of the ledger. For convenience we will assume that a single random nonce $\rho \in \{0, 1\}^{\kappa}$ is also a valid transaction. Nonces will be neutral transactions and may be included in the ledger for the sole purpose of ensuring independence between the POW instances solved by the honest parties.

Next, we determine the three functions $V(\cdot), I(\cdot), R(\cdot)$ that will turn the backbone protocol into Π_{PL}, a protocol realizing a public transaction ledger.

We now introduce two essential properties for a protocol maintaning a public transaction ledger: (i) *Persistence* and (ii) *Liveness*. In a nutshell, Persistence states that once an honest player reports a transaction "deep enough" in the ledger, then all other honest players will report it indefinitely whenever they are asked, and at exactly the same position in the ledger (essentially, this means that all honest players agree on all the transactions that took place and in what order). In a more concrete Bitcoin-like setting (see [22]), Persistence is essential to ensure that credits are final and that they happened at a certain "time" in the system's timeline (which is implicitly defined by the ledger itself).

Note that Persistence is useful but not enough to ensure that the ledger makes progress, i.e., that transactions are eventually inserted in a chain. This is captured by the Liveness property, which states that as long as a transaction comes from an honest account holder and is provided by the environment to all honest players, then it will be inserted into the honest players' ledgers,

Input validation predicate $V(\cdot)$	$V(\langle x_1, \ldots, x_m \rangle)$ is true if and only if the vector $\langle x_1, \ldots, x_m \rangle$ is a valid ledger, i.e., $\langle x_1, \ldots, x_m \rangle \in \mathcal{L}$.
Chain reading function $R(\cdot)$	If $V(\langle x_1, \ldots, x_m \rangle)$ = True, the value $R(\mathbf{x}_\mathcal{C})$ is equal to $\langle x_1, \ldots, x_m \rangle$; undefined otherwise.
Input contribution function $I(\cdot)$	$I(st, \mathcal{C}, round, \text{INPUT}())$ operates as follows: if the input tape contains (INSERT, v), it parses v as a sequence of transactions and retains the largest subsequence $x' \preceq v$ that is valid with respect to $\mathbf{x}_\mathcal{C}$ (and whose transactions are not already included in $\mathbf{x}_\mathcal{C}$). Finally, $x = \text{tx}_0 x'$ where tx_0 is a neutral random nonce transaction.

Fig. 3. The public transaction ledger protocol Π_{PL}, built on the Bitcoin backbone

assuming the environment keeps providing it as an input for a sufficient number of rounds[14].

Definition 5. *A protocol Π implements a robust public transaction ledger in the q-bounded synchronous setting if it satisfies the following two properties:*

- Persistence: *Parameterized by $k \in \mathbb{N}$ (the "depth" parameter), if in a certain round an honest player reports a ledger that contains a transaction* tx *in a block more than k blocks away from the end of the ledger, then* tx *will always be reported in the same position in the ledger by any honest player from this round on.*

- Liveness: *Parameterized by $u, k \in \mathbb{N}$ (the "wait time" and "depth" parameters, resp.), provided that a transaction either (i) issued by* Txgen, *or (ii) is neutral, is given as input to all honest players continuously for u consecutive rounds, then there exists an honest party who will report this transaction at a block more than k blocks from the end of the ledger.*

We prove the two properties separately, starting with Persistence. The proof is based on the common prefix property of the backbone protocol (recall Definition 2 and Theorem 1).

Lemma 5 (Persistence). *Suppose $f < 1$ and $\gamma \geq (1 + \delta)\lambda\beta$, for some real $\delta \in (0, 1)$ and $\lambda \geq 1$ such that $\lambda^2 - f\lambda - 1 \geq 0$. Protocol Π_{PL} satisfies Persistence with probability $1 - e^{-\Omega(\delta^3 k)}$, where k is the depth parameter.*

We next prove Liveness, which is based on the chain-quality property (recall Definition 3 and Theorem 2).

---

[14] Observe that here we take the view that new transactions are available to all honest players and the way they are propagated is handled by the environment that feeds the backbone protocol. While this makes sense in the honest/malicious cryptographic model, it has been challenged in a model where all players are rational [3]. Analysis of the backbone protocol in a setting where transaction propagation is governed by rational players is beyond the scope of our paper.

Lemma 6 (Liveness). *Assume $f < 1$ and $\gamma \geq (1 + \delta)\lambda\beta$, for some $\delta \in (0,1)$, $\lambda \in [1,\infty)$ and let $k \in \mathbb{N}$. Further, assume oracle Txgen is unambiguous. Then protocol Π_{PL} satisfies Liveness with wait time $u = 2k/(1 - \delta)\gamma$ and depth parameter k with probability at least $1 - e^{-\Omega(\delta^2 k)}$.*

In [22] we show how to instantiate the public transaction ledger for Bitcoin, by defining the specific sets of accounts, transactions and valid ledgers.

5.2 Byzantine Agreement for Honest Majority

We now use the public transaction ledger formulation to achieve POW-based BA for an honest majority by properly instantiating the notion of a transaction, thus improving on the simple BA protocol tolerating a $(1/3)$-bounded adversary presented in the full version [22].

Here we consider a set of valid ledgers $\mathcal{L}$ that contain sequences of transactions of the form $\langle nonce, v, ctr \rangle$, and satisfy the predicate:

$$(H_1(ctr, G(nonce, v)) < D) \wedge (ctr \leq q), \tag{1}$$

where $H_1(\cdot), G(\cdot)$ are two hash functions as in the definition of the backbone protocol, and $v \in \{0,1\}$ is a party's input. (Recall that D is the difficulty level and q determines how many calls to $H_1(\cdot)$ a party is allowed to make per round.) To distinguish the oracles, in this section we will use $H_0(\cdot)$ to refer to the oracle used in the backbone protocol.

For the ledger we consider in this section, there will be no accounts and all transactions will be neutral — i.e., the conflict predicate $C(\cdot, \cdot)$ will be false for all pairs of transactions.

We first provide a high level description of the BA protocol assuming parties have q queries per round to each oracle $H_0(\cdot), H_1(\cdot)$. We then show how to use a single oracle $H(\cdot)$ to achieve the combined functionality of both of them while only using q queries per round.

At a high level, the protocol, $\Pi_{\mathsf{BA}}^{1/2}$, works as follows:

- *Operation:* In each round, parties run two protocols in parallel. The first protocol is protocol Π_{PL} (Fig. 3), which maintains the transaction ledger and requires q queries to the oracle $H_0(\cdot)$. The second process is a "transaction production" protocol Π_{tx}, which continuously generates transactions satisfying predicate (1).[15] The protocol makes q queries to the $H_1(\cdot)$ oracle.
- *Termination:* When the ledger reaches $2k$ blocks, a party prunes the last k blocks, collects all the unique POW transactions that are present in the ledger and returns the majority bit from the bits occuring in these transactions (note that uniqueness takes also the *nonce* of each transaction into account).

As described, protocol $\Pi_{\mathsf{BA}}^{1/2}$ does not conform to the q-bounded setting since parties require q queries to oracle $H_0(\cdot)$ and q queries to oracle $H_1(\cdot)$ to perform the computation of a single round (the setting imposes a bound of q queries to

---

[15] See [22] for detailed specification.

a single oracle for all parties). Note that a naïve simulation of $H_0(\cdot), H_1(\cdot)$ by a single oracle $H(\cdot)$ in the $(2q)$-bounded setting (e.g., by setting $H_b(x) = H(b, x)$) would violate the restriction imposed on each oracle individually, since nothing would prevent the adversary, for example, from querying $H_0(\cdot)$ $2q$ times. Next, we show how we can combine the two protocols into a single protocol that utilizes at most q queries to a single random oracle in a way that the adversary will remain q-bounded for each oracle. This transformation, explained below, completes the description of $\Pi_{\mathsf{BA}}^{1/2}$.

2-for-1 POWs. We now tackle the problem of how to turn a protocol operation that uses two separate POW subprocedures involving two distinct and independent oracles $H_0(\cdot), H_1(\cdot)$ into a protocol that utilizes a single oracle $H(\cdot)$ for a total number of q queries per round. Our transformation is general and works for any pair of protocols that utilize $H_0(\cdot), H_1(\cdot)$, provided that certain conditions are met (which are satisfied by protocol $\Pi_{\mathsf{BA}}^{1/2}$ above). In more detail, we consider two protocols Π_0, Π_1 that utilize a POW step as shown in Algorithm 5 in Figure 4.

Algorithm 5 POW-based protocol fragment of Π_b, $b \in \{0, 1\}$ parameterized by q, D and hash functions $H_b(\cdot), G(\cdot)$, $b \in \{0, 1\}$. The value w_b is determined from the protocol's context.

```
1: ...                    ▷ Value w_b is determined
2: ctr ← 1
3: B ← ε
4: h_b ← G(w_b)
5: while (ctr ≤ q) do
6:     if (H(ctr, h_b) < D) then
7:         B_b ← ⟨w_b, ctr⟩
8:         break
9:     end if
10:    ctr ← ctr + 1
11: end while
12: ...              ▷ The POW B is exploited here
```

Algorithm 6 The *double proof of work* function, parameterized by q, D and hash functions $H(\cdot), G(\cdot)$ that substitutes steps 2-11 of two POW-based protocols.

```
1: function double-pow(w_0, w_1)
2:     B_0, B_1 ← ε
3:     ctr ← 1
4:     h ← ⟨G(w_0), G(w_1)⟩
5:     while (ctr ≤ q) do
6:         u ← H(ctr, h)
7:         if (u < D) ∧ (B_0 = ε) then
8:             B_0 ← ⟨w_0, ctr, G(w_1)⟩
9:         end if
10:        if ([u]^R < D) ∧ (B_1 = ε) then
11:            B_1 ← ⟨w_1, ctr, G(w_0)⟩
12:        end if
13:        ctr ← ctr + 1
14:    end while
15:    return ⟨B_0, B_1⟩
16: end function
```

Fig. 4. The 2-for-1 POW transformation

In order to achieve composition of the two protocols Π_0, Π_1 in the q-bounded setting with access to a single oracle $H(\cdot)$, we will substitute steps 2-11 in both protocols with a call to a new function, double-pow, defined below. First, observe that in Π_b, $b \in \{0, 1\}$, the POW steps 2-11 operate with input w_b and produce output in B_b if the POW succeeds. The probability of obtaining a solution is $D \cdot 2^{-\kappa}$.

The modification consists in changing the structure of the POWs from pairs of the form (w, ctr) to triples of the form $(w, ctr, label)$, where $label$ is a κ-bit string that is neutral from the point of view of the proof. This will further require the modification of the verification step for POWs in both protocols Π_0, Π_1 in the following manner.

- Any verification step in Π_0 of a POW $\langle w_0, ctr \rangle$ which is of the form $H(ctr, G(w_0)) < D$, will now operate with a POW of the form $\langle w_0, ctr, label \rangle$ and will verify the relation

$$H(ctr, \langle G(w_0), label \rangle) < D.$$

- Similarly for Π_1: it will now verify the relation

$$[H(ctr, \langle label, G(w_1) \rangle)]^{\mathsf{R}} < D,$$

where $[a]^{\mathsf{R}}$ denotes the reverse of the bitstring a.

This parallel composition strategy in the form of function double-pow is shown in Algorithm 6. Either or both the solutions it returns, B_0, B_1, may be empty if no solution is found.

Protocol $\Pi_{\mathsf{BA}}^{1/2}$ will employ double-pow, which will substitute the individual POW operation of the two underlying protocols Π_0, Π_1 as defined in lines 2-11 of Algorithm 5. The correctness of the above composition strategy follows from the following simple observation.

Lemma 7. *Consider a uniform random variable U over the integers in $[0, 2^{\kappa})$ and an integer D such that $D = 2^t$ for some positive integer $t < \kappa/2$. Then, the events $(U < D)$ and $([U]^{\mathsf{R}} < D)$ are independent and they both occur with probability $D \cdot 2^{-\kappa}$.*

Theorem 3. *Assume $f < 1$ and $\gamma \geq (1 + \delta)\lambda\beta$, for some real $\delta \in (0, 1)$ and $\lambda \geq 1$ such that $\lambda^2 - f\lambda - 1 \geq 0$. Protocol $\Pi_{\mathsf{BA}}^{1/2}$ solves BA in $O(k)$ rounds with probability at least $1 - e^{-\Omega(\delta^3 k)}$.*

6   Summary and Directions for Future Work

In this paper we presented a formal treatment of the Bitcoin backbone, the protocol used at the core of Bitcoin's transaction ledger. We expressed and proved two properties of the backbone protocol — "common prefix" and "chain quality" — and showed how they can be used as foundations for designing Byzantine agreement and robust public transaction ledger protocols. Our results show that an honest majority among the (equally equipped) participants suffices, assuming the network synchronizes much faster than the proof of work rate ($f \to 0$ in our notation) and the proper inputs (e.g., transactions) are available to the honest majority[16], while the bound on the adversary for honest parties to reach agreement degenerates as f gets larger.

While these are encouraging results, we have demonstrated deviations that are of concern for the proper operation of Bitcoin. Importantly, we show that as the network ceases to synchronize fast enough compared to the proof-of-work rate (i.e., the worst-case time that takes honest players to "hear" each other becomes substantial compared to the time it takes to solve a proof of work), the honest majority property ceases to hold and the bound offered by our analysis that is required to obtain a robust transaction ledger approaches 0 as f approaches 1. Note that the effects of bad synchronization is in the maintenance of the common prefix property, which is the critical property for showing agreement.

A second important concern is regarding the chain quality property, where our results show that if an adversary controls a hashing power corresponding to β then the ratio of the blocks it can contribute to the blockchain is bounded but can be strictly bigger than β. When β gets close to $1/2$, our bounds show that the honest players' contributions approach 0 in our security model.

The above caveats in the two basic properties of the backbone have repercussions on the Persistence and Liveness properties of the Bitcoin ledger. Firstly, they illustrate that fast information propagation amongst honest players is essential for transaction persistence. Secondly, they show that transaction liveness becomes more fragile as the adversarial power gets close to $1/2$. Note that we achieve Liveness for any adversarial bound less than $1/2$ but we do not assume any upper bound on the number of transactions that may be inserted in a block[17]; it is obvious that the fewer blocks the honest miners get into the blockchain the harder may be for a transaction to get through. Furthermore, the fact that chain quality demonstrably fails to preserve a one-to-one correspondence between a party's hashing power and the ratio of its contributions to the ledger point to the fact that Bitcoin's rewarding mechanism is not incentive compatible (cf. [17]). Assuming the hashing power of the honest parties γ exceeds the adversary's hashing power β by a factor λ, we show that the adversary's contributions to the ledger are bounded by $1/\lambda$ — a result we show to be tight in our rushing adversary model. In this way our results flesh out the incentive compatibility problems of the Bitcoin backbone, but (on a more positive note) they also point to the fact that honest hashing-power majority is sufficient to maintain the public ledger (under favorable network conditions), and hence suggest that the Bitcoin protocol can work as long as the majority of the miners *want it to work* (without taking into account the rationality of their decision).

The above observations apply to the setting where the number of participants is fixed. In the dynamic setting (where the number of parties running the protocol may change from round to round), given the flat model that we consider, the

---

[16] Our formalization is a way to formally express what perhaps was Nakamoto's intuition when he wrote about Bitcoin that "it takes advantage of the nature of information being easy to spread but hard to stifle" [31].

[17] In the current Bitcoin implementation there is an upper bound of 1MB for blocks, hence the number transactions per block is limited.

difficulty D of the blockchain may be calibrated according to the number of players n that are active in the system. If D is set by an omniscient trusted party then the analysis carries in a straightforward way but otherwise, if D is somehow calculated by the parties themselves, the adversary can try to exploit its calculation. Note that in this case the maxvalid function would need to take the difficulty's variability into account and thus choose the "most difficult" chain (as opposed to the longest). Comparing chains based on difficulty is simply done by computing the length of a chain by counting blocks proportionally to how difficult they are (for example, a block whose difficulty is two times larger than a given difficulty value would contribute twice as much in "length").

Interesting open questions include the security analysis of the Bitcoin backbone protocol in a rational setting as opposed to honest/malicious, in the dynamic setting where the parties themselves attempt to recalibrate the difficulty based on some metric (e.g., the time that has passed during the generation of a certain number of blocks), and in a concurrent/universal composition setting as opposed to standalone. Furthermore, the substitution of the random oracle assumption with a suitable computational assumption, as well as the development of backbone modifications that improve its characteristics in terms of common prefix and chain quality. In terms of the ledger application, transaction processing times (i.e., reducing the wait time parameter u in the Liveness property) is also an interesting question with implications to practice (since real world payment systems benefit greatly from fast transaction confirmation and verification). In all these cases, our work offers a formal foundation that allows analyzing the security properties of "tweaks" on the backbone protocol (such as the randomization rule of [17] or the "GHOST" rule in [39] used in ethereum[18]) towards meeting the above goals.

Another set of interesting directions include the development of other applications that may be built on top of the backbone protocol such as secure multiparty computation with properties such as fairness and guaranteed output delivery (current works in this direction, e.g., [1,9,10], assume an idealized version of the Bitcoin system).

References

1. Andrychowicz, M., Dziembowski, S., Malinowski, D., Mazurek, Ł.: Secure multiparty computations on bitcoin. IEEE Security and Privacy (2014)
2. Aspnes, J., Jackson, C., Krishnamurthy, A.: Exposing computationally-challenged Byzantine impostors. Technical Report YALEU/DCS/TR-1332, Yale University Department of Computer Science (July 2005)
3. Babaioff, M., Dobzinski, S., Oren, S., Zohar, A.: On bitcoin and red balloons. In: Faltings, B., Leyton-Brown, K., Ipeirotis, P. (eds.) EC, pp. 56–73. ACM (2012)
4. Back, A.: Hashcash (1997). http://www.cypherspace.org/hashcash
5. Barak, B., Canetti, R., Lindell, Y., Pass, R., Rabin, T.: Secure computation without authentication. J. Cryptology **24**(4), 720–760 (2011)

---

[18] https://www.ethereum.org/

6. Bellare, M., Rogaway, P.: Random oracles are practical: A paradigm for design-ing efficient protocols. In: CCS 1993, Proceedings of the 1st ACM Conference on Computer and Communications Security, Fairfax, Virginia, USA, November 3–5, pp. 62–73 (1993)

7. Ben-Or, M.: Another advantage of free choice: Completely asynchronous agreement protocols (extended abstract). In: Probert, R.L., Lynch, N.A., Santoro, N. (eds.) PODC, pp. 27–30. ACM (1983)

8. Ben-Sasson, E., Chiesa, A., Garman, C., Green, M., Miers, I., Tromer, E., Virza, M.: Zerocash: Decentralized anonymous payments from bitcoin. IACR Cryptology ePrint Archive **2014**, 349 (2014)

9. Bentov, I., Kumaresan, R.: How to Use Bitcoin to Design Fair Protocols. In: Garay, J.A., Gennaro, R. (eds.) CRYPTO 2014, Part II. LNCS, vol. 8617, pp. 421–439. Springer, Heidelberg (2014)

10. Bentov, I., Kumaresan, R.: How to use bitcoin to incentivize correct computations. ACM CCS **2014**, (2014)

11. Berman, P., Garay, J.A.: Randomized distributed agreement revisited. In: Digest of Papers: FTCS-23, The Twenty-Third Annual International Symposium on Fault-Tolerant Computing, Toulouse, France, June 22–24, pp. 412–419. IEEE Computer Society (1993)

12. Canetti, R.: Security and composition of multiparty cryptographic protocols. J. Cryptology **13**(1), 143–202 (2000)

13. Chaum, D.: Blind signatures for untraceable payments, pp. 199–203 (1982)

14. Cunicula. Why doesn't bitcoin use a tiebreaking rule when comparing chains of equal length? (2013) https://bitcointalk.org/index.php?topic=355644.0

15. Decker, C., Wattenhofer, R.: Information propagation in the bitcoin network. In: P2P, pp. 1–10. IEEE (2013)

16. Dwork, C., Naor, M.: Pricing via Processing or Combatting Junk Mail. In: Brickell, E.F. (ed.) CRYPTO 1992. LNCS, vol. 740, pp. 139–147. Springer, Heidelberg (1993)

17. Eyal, I., Sirer, E.G.: Majority is not enough: Bitcoin mining is vulnerable. In: Financial Cryptography (2014)

18. Feldman, P., Micali, S.: An optimal probabilistic protocol for synchronous byzan-tine agreement. SIAM J. Comput. **26**(4), 873–933 (1997)

19. Fischer, M.J., Lynch, N.A., Paterson, M.: Impossibility of distributed consensus with one faulty process. J. ACM **32**(2), 374–382 (1985)

20. Fitzi, M., Garay, J.A.: Efficient player-optimal protocols for strong and differential consensus. In: Borowsky, E., Rajsbaum, S. (eds.) PODC, pp. 211–220. ACM (2003)

21. Garay, J.A., Katz, J., Kumaresan, R., Zhou, H.: Adaptively secure broadcast, revisited. In: Gavoille, C., Fraigniaud, P., (eds.) Proceedings of the 30th Annual ACM Symposium on Principles of Distributed Computing, PODC 2011, San Jose, CA, USA, June 6–8, pp. 179–186. ACM (2011)

22. Garay, J.A., Kiayias, A., Leonardos, N.: The Bitcoin Backbone Protocol: Analysis and Applications. IACR Cryptology ePrint Archive **2014**, 765 (2014)

23. Hirt, M., Zikas, V.: Adaptively Secure Broadcast. In: Gilbert, H. (ed.) EURO-CRYPT 2010. LNCS, vol. 6110, pp. 466–485. Springer, Heidelberg (2010)

24. Juels, A., Brainard, J.G.: Client puzzles: A cryptographic countermeasure against connection depletion attacks. In: NDSS. The Internet Society (1999)

25. Katz, J., Koo, C.-Y.: On expected constant-round protocols for byzantine agree-ment. Journal of Computer and System Sciences **75**(2), 91–112 (2009)

26. King, S.: Primecoin: Cryptocurrency with prime number proof-of-work (July 2013). http://primecoin.io/bin/primecoin-paper.pdf

27. Lamport, L., Shostak, R.E., Pease, M.C.: The byzantine generals problem. ACM Trans. Program. Lang. Syst. **4**(3), 382–401 (1982)
28. Miller, A., LaViola, J.J.: Anonymous byzantine consensus from moderately-hard puzzles: A model for bitcoin. University of Central Florida. Tech Report, CS-TR-14-01 (April 2014)
29. Nakamoto, S.: Bitcoin: A peer-to-peer electronic cash system. (2008) http://bitcoin.org/bitcoin.pdf
30. Nakamoto, S.: The proof-of-work chain is a solution to the byzantine generals' problem. The Cryptography Mailing List (November 2008). https://www.mail-archive.com/cryptography@metzdowd.com/msg09997.html
31. Nakamoto, S.: Bitcoin open source implementation of p2p currency (February 2009). http://p2pfoundation.ning.com/forum/topics/bitcoin-open-source
32. Neiger, G.: Distributed consensus revisited. Inf. Process. Lett. **49**(4), 195–201 (1994)
33. Okun, M.: Agreement Among Unacquainted Byzantine Generals. In: Fraigniaud, P. (ed.) DISC 2005. LNCS, vol. 3724, pp. 499–500. Springer, Heidelberg (2005)
34. Okun, M.: Distributed computing among unacquainted processors in the presence of byzantine distributed computing among unacquainted processors in the presence of byzantine failures. Ph.D. Thesis Hebrew University of Jerusalem (2005)
35. Okun, M., Barak, A.: Efficient algorithms for anonymous byzantine agreement. Theor. Comp. Sys. **42**(2), 222–238 (2008)
36. Pease, M.C., Shostak, R.E., Lamport, L.: Reaching agreement in the presence of faults. J. ACM **27**(2), 228–234 (1980)
37. Rabin, M.O.: Randomized byzantine generals. In: FOCS, pp. 403–409. IEEE Computer Society (1983)
38. Rivest, R.L., Shamir, A., Wagner, D.A.: Time-lock puzzles and timed-release crypto. Technical report, Cambridge, MA, USA (1996)
39. Sompolinsky, Y., Zohar, A.: Accelerating bitcoin's transaction processing. fast money grows on trees, not chains. IACR Cryptology ePrint Archive, 2013:881 (2013)

Secret Sharing

Linear Secret Sharing Schemes from Error Correcting Codes and Universal Hash Functions

Ronald Cramer[1,2]([✉]), Ivan Bjerre Damgård[3],
Nico Döttling[3], Serge Fehr[1], and Gabriele Spini[1,2,4]

[1] CWI, Amsterdam, Netherlands
{Ronald.Cramer,Serge.Fehr}@cwi.nl
[2] Mathematical Institute, Leiden University, Leiden, Netherlands
cramer@math.leidenuniv.nl
[3] Department of Computer Science, Aarhus University, Aarhus C, Denmark
{ivan,nico.doettling}@cs.au.dk
[4] Institut de Mathématiques de Bordeaux, University of Bordeaux,
UMR 5251 Talence, France
G.Spini@cwi.nl

Abstract. We present a novel method for constructing linear secret sharing schemes (LSSS) from linear error correcting codes and linear universal hash functions in a blackbox way. The main advantage of this new construction is that the privacy property of the resulting secret sharing scheme essentially becomes independent of the code we use, only depending on its rate. This allows us to fully harness the algorithmic properties of recent code constructions such as efficient encoding and decoding or efficient list-decoding. Choosing the error correcting codes and universal hash functions involved carefully, we obtain solutions to the following open problems:

- A linear near-threshold secret sharing scheme with both linear time sharing and reconstruction algorithms and large secrets (i.e. secrets of size $\Omega(n)$). Thus, the computational overhead per shared bit in this scheme is *constant*.
- An efficiently reconstructible robust secret sharing scheme for $n/3 \leq t < (1-\epsilon) \cdot n/2$ corrupted players (for any constant $\epsilon > 0$) with shares of optimal size $O(1 + \lambda/n)$ and secrets of size $\Omega(n + \lambda)$, where λ is the security parameter.

Keywords: Linear Secret Sharing Schemes · Linear Time Sharing · Robust Secret Sharing

I.B. Damgård—The authors acknowledge support from the Danish National Research Foundation and The National Science Foundation of China (under the grant 61061130540) for the Sino-Danish Center for the Theory of Interactive Computation, within which part of this work was performed; and also from the CFEM research center (supported by the Danish Strategic Research Council) within which part of this work was performed.

N. Döttling—Supported by European Research Commission Starting Grant no. 279447.

G. Spini—Supported by the Algant-Doc doctoral program.

E. Oswald and M. Fischlin (Eds.): EUROCRYPT 2015, Part II, LNCS 9057, pp. 313–336, 2015.
DOI: 10.1007/978-3-662-46803-6_11

1   Introduction

Linear secret sharing schemes (LSSS) are the central building block for informat-ion-theoretically secure cryptographic primitives such as multiparty computa-tion, robust secret sharing, as well as for two-party primitives via the so-called MPC-in-the-head paradigm [16,18]. Naturally, the computational efficiency of the LSSS directly influences the efficiency of the implied primitive, so it is inter-esting to construct schemes where both sharing a secret and reconstruction is as efficient as possible.

It is well known that there is a natural correspondence between linear codes and LSSS [4,21]. Since there is a rich body of literature about codes with efficient encoding and decoding, one might hope that this would lead to very efficient secret sharing schemes, ideally with linear time (in the number of players) to share and reconstruct a secret. However, for applications, one typically needs an LSSS where both the privacy and reconstruction thresholds are constant frac-tions of the number of players. If we try to reach this goal using the standard method for going from codes to LSSSs, we will need (a family of) codes where both the code itself and its dual are (asymptotically) good codes. But unfortu-nately, the known codes that are efficiently (linear time) en- and decodable have very bad dual codes. Therefore it was previously an open problem to construct LSSSs with linear time sharing and reconstruction.

In this paper, we suggest a new paradigm for constructing LSSSs based on linear codes and linear universal hash functions. The main advantage of this approach is that it gives us a good privacy threshold *no matter which code we start from*. We can therefore use the full power of the known constructions of linear codes with efficient encoding and (list) decoding. We also suggest several applications of the technique. We remark however that there is no obvious way to obtain multiplicative secret sharing schemes via our construction paradigm. But constructions of general MPC protocols such as [4,6] require multiplicative secret sharing schemes. Thus, we consider it an interesting open problem to extend our construction paradigm to multiplicative secret sharing schemes.

A paradigm for building LSSS. First we note that any LSSS can be seen as being derived from a linear code C of length n and a linear function $h : \mathbb{F}^k \mapsto \mathbb{F}^\ell$. We obtain an LSSS as follows: to share a secret $s \in \mathbb{F}^\ell$ we choose at random $\mathbf{x} \in \mathbb{F}^k$ subject to $h(\mathbf{x}) = s$, encode $\mathbf{x}$ in C, and give each entry in the resulting codeword to a player, where in the most general case, each player may receive more than one value.

We can now say which player subsets can reconstruct the secret and which sets have no information: Let A be a player subset and let $\Pi_A : \mathbb{F}^k \mapsto \mathbb{F}^{|A|}$ be the linear mapping that on input $\mathbf{x}$ outputs the shares given to A when $\mathbf{x}$ is the randomness used in the LSSS. Then A can reconstruct the secret if and only if $\dim(h(\ker(\Pi_A))) = 0$, and A has no information on the secret if and only if $\dim(h(\ker(\Pi_A))) = \ell$, i.e., h is surjective on $\ker(\Pi_A)$. This characterisation was first given in Theorem 10 of [4], which we have rephrased here to match our notation (see also Lemma 3 below). It was noted already in [4] that the privacy threshold can be estimated via the dual distance, but that this bound is not sharp. Nevertheless, previous works have often established privacy for LSSS schemes from the dual distance. A notable exception of this is [2], where large privacy of certain secret sharing schemes is established via a field descent technique, but the dual distance of the corresponding code is merely constant. Thus [2] uses the characterization of [4] in its full generality, however for a very special class of codes. As we shall see, the dual distance bound is generally very far from being sharp, and there is great potential in avoiding the dual distance approach.

We now explain our construction of an LSSS from a code C, such that some constant fraction of the players can reconstruct and any set smaller than some (other) constant fraction has no information. Reconstruction is easy to handle: if we have at least r shares, then we can compute the secret if C allows decoding from $n - r$ erasures, and r can be $\Theta(n)$ if C is (asymptotically) good. However, it much less clear what we can say about privacy in general (e.g., if C has a bad dual distance).

Our main idea for solving this is to notice that a player set A has partial information on $\mathbf{x}$ from its shares, namely $\mathbf{x}$ must be in some subspace defined by the shares known to A. Now, suppose we choose h at random from a universal family of linear hash functions. It is well known that such a random function acts as a good randomness extractor, so we may hope that A has little or no information on $h(\mathbf{x})$, at least if A is small enough.

In the following, we show how this intuition can be formalised. It turns out that because the hash functions are linear and the partially unknown string resides in a subspace, things are even better than what the general theory of extractors would predict: fix any small enough corrupted set A and choose h at random from the family. Then with very high probability, the h we have chosen will satisfy that $h(\mathbf{x})$ is uniform in the view of the adversary. We can then simply apply a union bound over all the desired privacy sets to conclude that a random choice of h yields an LSSS with privacy threshold a constant fraction of the number of players. For constant rate (family of) codes, this fraction can be chosen as a constant arbitrarily close to the rate.

We emphasise that the random choice of h only needs to be done once and for all when the LSSS is set up. Then, with overwhelming probability, the LSSS we have constructed has perfect privacy and reconstruction as required for an LSSS. If we were willing to spend a very long (exponential) time in the set-up phase we could verify that a candidate h indeed gives us privacy for all the desired player sets, and this way remove the probabilistic aspect from the construction.

1.1   Applications

Linear time LSSS Clearly, for any linear secret sharing scheme a secret can be shared using a quadratic amount (in the number of players) of field operations. In the light of the above mentioned linear time encodable codes, the question arises whether secret sharing schemes with a linear time sharing phase can be constructed. Recently, Druk and Ishai [9] provided a construction of a linear time near-threshold linear secret sharing scheme. For a near-threshold scheme, one can choose the (relative) privacy and reconstruction thresholds as arbitrarily close constants. Their main tool for this construction is a family of linear time encodable linear codes with good distance and good dual distance. Their construction of linear secret sharing schemes follows Massey's blueprint [21], i.e. exploiting the dual distance to establish privacy. The codes constructed in [9] are not known to be linear time erasure decodable. While their construction allows to compute shares in linear time, reconstruction is more expensive for their scheme, i.e. it requires quadratic time with preprocessing. However more importantly, the secret space of their scheme is limited to a constant number of bits. But this means that in their scheme the computational overhead per shared bit is linear, rather than constant.

Following the paradigm sketched in the last paragraph, we obtain a linear time near-threshold LSSS with secrets of size $\Omega(n)$. In particular, the computational overhead per shared bit in this scheme is constant. Just like in the scheme of Druk and Ishai [9], we can choose the (relative) privacy and reconstruction thresholds as arbitrarily close constants. Our construction uses the following ideas. First, we construct a linear secret sharing scheme where sharing and reconstruction of *random* secrets can be performed in linear time. We do this by plugging a linear time computable linear hash function and linear time en- and decodable code C into our basic construction. We can then choose a random $\mathbf{x}$ and compute a (random) secret $\mathbf{s} = h(\mathbf{x})$ and a share vector $\mathbf{c}$ by encoding $\mathbf{x}$ in C. Note that this can be done without having to invert the hash function which would be too inefficient with known constructions.

We bootstrap this into a standard secret sharing scheme by the following trick. To share a given secret $\mathbf{s}$, first compute a random secret $\mathbf{s}'$ together with corresponding shares $\mathbf{c}$. We can now use $\mathbf{s}'$ to one-time-pad encrypt $\mathbf{s}$, i.e. compute a ciphertext $\mathbf{y} = \mathbf{s} + \mathbf{s}'$. To distribute $\mathbf{y}$ to the players, we *disperse* $\mathbf{y}$, i.e. we encode $\mathbf{y}$ using a linear time encodable erasure correcting code and share the codeword symbols among the players. Note that we have effectively shared $\mathbf{y}$ non-privately, but this is not a problem as $\mathbf{y}$ is not private anyway. Thus, the overall overhead to share the secret $\mathbf{s}$ is linear. To reconstruct, we can use linear time erasure correction algorithms (provided by the codes). Therefore, both sharing and reconstruction can be performed in linear time.

Linear time UC commitments. In a commitment scheme, a prover commits to a bit string towards a verifier who does not learn the string at commitment time, yet the prover is committed to his choice and can later reveal it to the verifier in a convincing way. Universally composable (UC) commitments provide the strongest possible security for commitments schemes, guaranteeing security in any context. Until recently, we only knew UC commitments based on expensive public-key primitives. In [8] (see also [10]), Damgård et al. propose a general scheme that constructs UC commitments with small amortised overhead from any sufficiently good LSSS, assuming a once-and-for-all preprocessing phase where some oblivious transfers are executed. They show how to get UC commitments with linear complexity for the verifier (linear in the size of the string committed to), but left it as an open problem to get linear complexity also for the prover. This problem was solved very recently by Cascudo et al. in [1] using a new construction of a non-threshold LSSS and a new variant of the MPC-in-the-head paradigm.

Our results can be used to give an alternative and simpler solution: since the efficiency of the original construction in [8] is inherited directly from the underlying LSSS, we immediately get linear complexity for both parties by simply plugging in our linear time LSSS. It is also interesting to note that if our scheme can be made multiplicative, then this and another result from [8] would immediately imply non-interactive UC Zero-Knowledge proofs with linear complexity for both prover and verifier.

Robust secret sharing with constant size shares. A *robust* secret sharing scheme is a secret sharing scheme with the additional property that reconstruction of the secret is possible (and, ideally, computationally feasible) even if some of the shares are incorrect. More concretely, a robust secret sharing scheme satisfies standard t-privacy as well as robust-reconstructability, where the latter means that given all n shares, the secret can be reconstructed even if t of them come from dishonest players and may be incorrect. In this work, we consider robust secret sharing in the setting of a non-rushing adversary; this means that the dishonest players have to announce their incorrect shares *before* getting to see the shares of the honest players.

If $t < n/3$ then standard error correction provides robustness for free. On the other extreme, if $t \geq n/2$ then robust secret sharing is not possible. Thus, the interesting range is $n/3 \leq t < n/2$. Here, robust secret sharing is possible, but we have to allow a small error probability of $2^{-\lambda}$, and additional "checking data" needs to be appended to the actual shares. The goal is to optimize the tradeoff between error probability and the increase in share size.

Cramer, Damgård and Fehr [5] gave a construction of a robust secret sharing scheme based on so-called *Algebraic Manipulation Detection* (AMD) codes (even though the terms robust secret sharing and AMD codes were not used there). Roughly speaking, an AMD code enables to detect certain manipulations — namely *algebraic* manipulations — of encoded messages. The robust secret sharing scheme then simply works by sharing an AMD encoding of the secret (using a standard linear secret sharing scheme), and the robust reconstruction is by going through all sets of possibly honest players, reconstruct from their shares, and verify correctness of the reconstructed AMD encoding. By making the AMD codeword large enough, resulting in an overhead in the share size of $O(\lambda + n)$, this procedure finds the correct secret except with probability $2^{-\lambda}$. An obvious downside of this scheme is that the robust reconstruction procedure is not efficient, as there is an exponential number of sets of possibly honest players to be considered.

In [3], based on very different techniques, Cevallos, Fehr, Ostrovsky and Rabani proposed a robust secret sharing scheme, with similar parameters: overhead $O(\lambda + n \log n)$ for an error probability of $2^{-\lambda}$, but which offers an *efficient* robust reconstruction. Both these schemes work for any fraction $t/n < \frac{1}{2}$, and neither becomes significantly better in terms of this error probability versus the size of the checking data if we bound t/n away from $\frac{1}{2}$ by a small constant.

Based on our new paradigm for building LSSSs, we construct a new robust secret sharing scheme. Our construction works when t/n is bounded away from $\frac{1}{2}$ by an arbitrary small positive constant. In this regime, we can consider *ramp* schemes, for which there is a gap between the privacy threshold t and the standard reconstruction threshold r, while still allowing for robust reconstruction in the presence of t faulty shares. In ramp schemes, the (actual) shares may be *smaller* than the secret (by a factor $r - t$). In our construction, we can additionally reduce the size of the checking data per share; this is in contrast to the above mentioned constructions when generalized to ramp schemes where the size of the checking data stays $O(\lambda)$.

Our construction can be seen as an efficient variant of the approach from [5]. We will secret share an AMD codeword, but this time using our construction of LSSS from above and choosing the underlying code C to be one that allows efficient *list decoding*. This means that we can consider the contributed shares as a codeword with errors and apply the list decoding algorithm. This will return a small (i.e., polynomial size) list of possible code words from C, each of these will suggest a possible AMD codeword. Thus, we only have a small number of candidates to check for correctness of the AMD encoding. This not only provides efficiency of the reconstruction (in contrast to the scheme of [5]), but also allows better parameters: using a highly list-decodable code as underlying code in our construction, we obtain that for every constant $\tau < \frac{1}{2}$ there exists a robust secret sharing scheme for threshold $t = \tau n$ that supports secrets of size linear in $n + \lambda$ and has shares of size $O(1 + \lambda/n)$, i.e. the size of the shares actually *decreases* in n.

2   Preliminaries

We will assume basic concepts from linear algebra such as linear maps and their kernels. For any prime power q, we will denote the finite field with q elements by $\mathbb{F}_q$. We will denote vectors $\mathbf{x}$ with boldface letters. We will also consider vectors whose components are vectors, e.g. a vector $\mathbf{x} \in (\mathbb{F}_q^m)^n$ whose components are $\mathbb{F}_q^m$ vectors. For a set $A \subseteq \{1, \ldots, n\}$ we will use $\Pi_A : (\mathbb{F}_q^m)^n \rightarrow (\mathbb{F}_q^m)^{|A|}$ to denote the projection onto the components in A. For a vector $\mathbf{x} \in (\mathbb{F}_q^m)^n$ and a set $A \subseteq \{1, \ldots, n\}$ we will also use the notation $\mathbf{x}_A = \Pi_A(\mathbf{x})$.

2.1   Probability

The binary entropy function $H : [0, 1/2] \rightarrow [0, 1]$ is given by $H(0) := 0$ and $H(x) := -x \cdot \log(x) - (1 - x) \cdot \log(1 - x)$ for $x \in (0, 1/2]$. For $0 \leq t/n \leq 1/2$ we can upper bound binomial coefficients by $\binom{n}{t} \leq 2^{H(t/n) \cdot n}$, for a proof see e.g. [22]. We will also use the Markov inequality (see also [22]).

Lemma 1 (Markov Inequality). *Let X be a non-negative random variable defined on $\mathbb{R}$ for which $\mathsf{E}[X]$ exists. Then it holds for every $x > 0$ that*

$$\Pr[X \geq x] \leq \frac{\mathsf{E}[X]}{x}.$$

Corollary 1. *Let X be a random variable with finite support $\mathcal{X} \subseteq \mathbb{R}$ which assumes its minimum at x_0 and its second smallest value at $x_1 > x_0$. Then it holds that*

$$\mathsf{E}[X] \geq x_0 + (x_1 - x_0) \cdot \Pr[X \neq x_0].$$

Proof. The expectation $\mathsf{E}[X]$ exists as X has a finite support. Since X assumes its minimum at x_0 it holds that $X - x_0$ is non-negative. By the Markov inequality it holds that

$$\Pr[X \neq x_0] = \Pr[X \geq x_1] = \Pr[X - x_0 \geq x_1 - x_0] \leq \frac{\mathsf{E}[X] - x_0}{x_1 - x_0},$$

as $\mathsf{E}[X - x_0] = \mathsf{E}[X] - x_0$ by linearity of expectation. Thus the claim follows.

2.2 Universal Hashing

Universal hash functions are a central tool in information-theoretically secure cryptography.

Definition 1 (Universal Hash Functions). *Let $\mathcal{X}$ and $\mathcal{Y}$ be finite sets. A family $\mathcal{H}$ of functions $\mathcal{X} \to \mathcal{Y}$ is called* family of universal hash functions *if it holds for all distinct $x, x' \in \mathcal{X}$ that*

$$\Pr_{\mathsf{H} \leftarrow_\$ \mathcal{H}}[\mathsf{H}(x) = \mathsf{H}(x')] \leq \frac{1}{|\mathcal{Y}|},$$

where H is chosen uniformly from $\mathcal{H}$.

For families $\mathcal{H}$ of $\mathbb{F}_q$-*linear* functions, meaning that both $\mathcal{X}$ and $\mathcal{Y}$ are $\mathbb{F}_q$-vector spaces and each $\mathsf{h} \in \mathcal{H}$ is a $\mathbb{F}_q$-linear function, the condition of Definition 1 can be rephrased as follows: $\mathcal{H}$ is a family of universal hash functions if and only if for all $\mathbf{x} \in \mathcal{X} \setminus \{\mathbf{0}\}$

$$\Pr_{\mathsf{H} \leftarrow_\$ \mathcal{H}}[\mathsf{H}(\mathbf{x}) = \mathbf{0}] \leq \frac{1}{|\mathcal{Y}|}.$$

We then naturally refer to $\mathcal{H}$ as a *family of $\mathbb{F}_q$-linear universal hash functions*.

There are various efficient families of linear universal hash functions, such random matrices or random Toeplitz matrices (see e.g. [20]). Ishai et al. [16] constructed a linear time computable family of linear universal hash functions, c.f. Section 5.

2.3   Error Correcting Codes

We assume basic concepts from coding theory. Error correcting codes are used to encode messages in such a way that the encoding is resilient against certain types of errors. Formally, a $\mathbb{F}_q$-linear error correcting code C of length n and dimension k is a k-dimensional subspace of $\mathbb{F}_q^n$. We say that C is an $m-folded\ code$, if C is a k-dimensional subspace of $(\mathbb{F}_q^m)^n$. This basically means that the alphabet of C is $\mathbb{F}_q^m$ rather than $\mathbb{F}_q$. An m-folded code C of length n can be naturally interpreted as a code of length $m \cdot n$. In this view, the possible error patterns in a folded code are $burst\ errors$ rather than symbol errors. The rate R of an m-folded $[n,k]$ code is defined by $R = \frac{k}{mn}$, i.e. $1/R$ is the factor by which the code expands messages. We will denote distinguished encoding and decoding algorithms[1] for a linear code C by C.Encode and C.Decode. We will denote the (generalized) Hamming distance for vectors $\mathbf{x}, \mathbf{y} \in (\mathbb{F}_q^m)^n$ by $\mathsf{d}(\mathbf{x}, \mathbf{y}) = |\{i \mid \mathbf{x}_i \neq \mathbf{y}_i\}|$, i.e. $\mathsf{d}(\mathbf{x}, \mathbf{y})$ counts in how many blocks $\mathbf{x}_i, \mathbf{y}_i \in \mathbb{F}_q^m$ the vectors $\mathbf{x}$ and $\mathbf{y}$ differ.

2.4   Secret Sharing Schemes

A secret sharing scheme allows a dealer to distribute a secret to n players in such a way that the players of any large enough set of players can jointly reconstruct the secret from their shares, whereas small coalitions of players have no information on the secret. A secret sharing scheme is called $linear$, if any linear combination of valid share vectors results in a valid share vector of the linear combination applied to the respective secrets. This is summarized in the following definition.

Definition 2. *Let $\mathbb{F}_q$ be a finite field, and let l, m and $t < r \leq n$ be positive integers. A linear secret sharing scheme LSSS consists of two algorithms LSSS.Share($\cdot$) and LSSS.Reconstruct($\cdot$). For every $\mathbf{s} \in \mathbb{F}_q^l$, LSSS.Share($\mathbf{s}$) outputs a vector of shares $\mathbf{c} = (\mathbf{c}_1, \ldots, \mathbf{c}_n) \in (\mathbb{F}_q^m)^n$. We require the following three properties.*

- *t-privacy: for all $\mathbf{s}, \mathbf{s}' \in \mathbb{F}_q^l$ and every $A \in \{1, \ldots, n\}$ of size $|A| = t$, the restrictions $\mathbf{c}_A$ and $\mathbf{c}'_A$ of $\mathbf{c} = $ LSSS.Share($\mathbf{s}$) and $\mathbf{c}' = $ LSSS.Share($\mathbf{s}'$) to the coordinates in A have the same probability distribution.*
- *r-reconstructability: for every $\mathbf{s} \in \mathbb{F}_q^l$ and every $Q \in \{1, \ldots, n\}$ of size $|Q| = r$, it holds for $\mathbf{c} = $ LSSS.Share($\mathbf{s}$) that LSSS.Reconstruct($\tilde{\mathbf{c}}$) = $\mathbf{s}$, where $\tilde{\mathbf{c}}$ is a vector with $\tilde{\mathbf{c}}_Q = \mathbf{c}_Q$ and $\tilde{\mathbf{c}}_{\bar{Q}}$ only contains erasure symbols, i.e. $\tilde{\mathbf{c}}_{\bar{Q}} = \perp^{|\bar{Q}|}$.*
- *Linearity: If $\mathbf{c}_1$ and $\mathbf{c}_2$ are respective sharings of $\mathbf{s}_1$ and $\mathbf{s}_2$, then $\alpha \mathbf{c}_1 + \beta \mathbf{c}_2$ is a sharing of $\alpha \mathbf{s}_1 + \beta \mathbf{s}_2$.*

We emphasize that we do not require $r = t + 1$; secret sharing schemes with $r > t+1$ are sometimes referred to as $ramp$ schemes. We may use this terminology sometimes to emphasize that we allow $r > t+1$. For schemes with $r = t+1$, it is well known that the size of the secret cannot be bigger than the size of a share,

---

[1] such as linear time algorithms for these tasks

i.e., $l \le m$. For a ramp schemes, this generalizes to $l \le (r - t) \cdot m$. The *rate* of a secret sharing scheme is given by $\rho = \frac{l}{mn}$. Using this terminology, the above can be expressed as follows. For any n-player ramp scheme that satisfies τn-privacy and σn-reconstructability, the rate of the scheme can be at most $\rho \le \sigma - \tau$.

3 Subspace Surjectivity of Linear Universal Hash Functions

In this section, we provide a general theorem about universal hash functions. The theorem states that if we fix an r-dimensional subspace V of $\mathbb{F}_q^k$, then a randomly chosen *linear* universal hash function H from a family which maps $\mathbb{F}_q^k$ to $\mathbb{F}_q^l$ is surjective on V, except with probability $q^{-(r-l)}$. By saying that H is surjective on V, we mean that $H(V) = \mathbb{F}_q^l$.

This theorem can be interpreted in information theoretic terms. We can identify a subspace V with the uniform distribution $\mathbf{v}$ on V and consider $\mathbf{v}$ as a *linear source of randomness*. Since V has dimension l, the q-ary min-entropy of $\mathbf{v}$ is at least l. From this point of view, the theorem states that universal hash functions are good extractors for linear sources, i.e. they extract such sources *perfectly*, except with probability $q^{-(r-l)}$. Perfect extraction in this context means that $H(\mathbf{v})$ is exactly the uniform distribution. The leftover hash lemma [15] states that universal hash functions yield good extractors for sources with a sufficient amount of min-entropy. We can actually establish a weaker version of this theorem based on the leftover hash lemma. However, the parameters obtained by our theorem are tighter than parameters obtainable by the leftover hash lemma. The best probability of failure obtainable via the leftover hash lemma is $q^{-(r-l)/2}$, which is worse than the bound given in the theorem.

Theorem 1. *Let $\mathcal{H}$ be a family of linear universal hash functions $\mathbb{F}_q^k \rightarrow \mathbb{F}_q^l$. Further let V be a subspace of $\mathbb{F}_q^k$ of dimension at least r. Let $H \leftarrow_\$ \mathcal{H}$ be chosen uniformly at random and then fixed. Then it holds that $H(V) = \mathbb{F}_q^l$ (i.e. H is surjective on V), except with probability $q^{-(r-l)}$ over the choice of H.*

Proof. For any linear function $h \in \mathcal{H}$, it holds that $h(V) = \mathbb{F}_q^l$ if and only if $\dim(V \cap \ker(h)) = \dim(V) - l$, which is equivalent to $|V \cap \ker(h)| = \frac{|V|}{q^l}$. Now, let $H \leftarrow_\$ \mathcal{H}$ and define the random variable $X = |V \cap \ker(H)|$ (depending on H). By the above it holds that H is surjective on V if and only if $X = |V|/q^l$. For each $\mathbf{v} \in V$, define the random variable

$$X_\mathbf{v} = \begin{cases} 1 & \text{if } H(\mathbf{v}) = 0 \\ 0 & \text{otherwise} \end{cases}$$

Clearly, it holds that $X = \sum_{\mathbf{v} \in V} X_\mathbf{v}$. Since $X_0 = 1$, we have that $X = 1 + \sum_{\mathbf{v} \in V \setminus \{0\}} X_\mathbf{v}$. Moreover, X assumes its minimum at $x_0 = \frac{|V|}{q^l}$ and its second smallest value at $x_1 = \frac{|V|}{q^l-1}$. We will now compute the expectation of X. For each $\mathbf{v} \in V\backslash\{\mathbf{0}\}$ it holds that

$$E[X_\mathbf{v}] = \Pr_{H \leftarrow_{\$} \mathcal{H}}[H(\mathbf{v}) = \mathbf{0}] \leq q^{-l},$$

as $\mathcal{H}$ is a family of universal hash functions. By linearity of expectation, it holds that

$$E[X] = 1 + \sum_{\mathbf{v}\in V\backslash\{\mathbf{0}\}} E[X_\mathbf{v}] = 1 + \frac{|V|-1}{q^l}.$$

By Corollary 1 and the fact that $|V| \geq q^r$ it holds that

$$\Pr\left[X \neq \frac{|V|}{q^l}\right] \leq \frac{1 + \frac{|V|-1}{q^l} - \frac{|V|}{q^l}}{\frac{|V|}{q^{l-1}} - \frac{|V|}{q^l}}$$

$$= \frac{q^l - 1}{|V| \cdot (q-1)}$$

$$\leq \frac{q^l}{|V|} \leq q^{-(r-l)}.$$

Consequently, it holds that $H(V) = \mathbb{F}_q^l$, except with probability $q^{-(k-l)}$.

Given a collection $\mathcal{V}$ of at most r-dimensional subspaces of $\mathbb{F}^k$, taking a union bound over all $V \in \mathcal{V}$ and applying Theorem 1 yields that it holds for all $V \in \mathcal{V}$ that $H(V) = \mathbb{F}_q^l$, except with probability $|\mathcal{V}| \cdot q^{-(r-l)}$. This is summarized in Corollary 2.

Corollary 2. *Let $\mathcal{H}$ be a family of linear universal hash functions $\mathbb{F}_q^k \to \mathbb{F}_q^l$ and $\mathcal{V}$ be a collection of subspaces of $\mathbb{F}_q^k$, each of dimension at least r. Let $H \leftarrow_{\$} \mathcal{H}$ be chosen uniformly at random and then fixed. Then it holds for all $V \in \mathcal{V}$ that $H(V) = \mathbb{F}_q^l$ (i.e. H is surjective on V), except with probability $|\mathcal{V}| \cdot q^{-(r-l)}$ over the choice of H.*

4   Linear Secret Sharing Schemes from Codes and Universal Hash Functions

In this section, we will provide our basic LSSS construction. In the following sections, we will provide applications based on this scheme. The scheme $\mathsf{LSSS}_{C,h}$ is defined by an m-folded $\mathbb{F}_q$-linear code C and an $\mathbb{F}_q$-linear surjective function h. A secret $\mathbf{s}$ is shared by first sampling a random preimage $\mathbf{x}$ of $\mathbf{s}$ under the function h, and then encoding $\mathbf{x}$ using the (folded) code C, obtaining a share vector $\mathbf{c} \in (\mathbb{F}_q^m)^n$. Each share $\mathbf{c}_i$ is a vector in $\mathbb{F}_q^m$. Notice that we can efficiently sample a preimage $\mathbf{x}$ of $\mathbf{s}$ under the function h by using basic linear algebra, since the function h is linear. More specifically, we can sample such an $\mathbf{x}$ by first computing any preimage $\mathbf{x}_1$ of $\mathbf{s}$ and then randomize $\mathbf{x}_1$ by adding a uniformly random

$x_2 \leftarrow_\$ \ker(h)$ to x_1, i.e. setting $\mathbf{x} \leftarrow x_1 + x_2$. Though this sharing algorithm Share is efficient, it still involves a rather costly inversion of h, which has overhead $O(n^3)$ when implemented naively. Thus, even if both h and C.Encode can be computed *super-efficiently* (e.g. in linear time), Share does not achieve the same efficiency.

In order to take full advantage of super-efficient h and C.Encode, we will provide an alternative sharing algorithm ShareRandom which computes both h and ShareRandom only in forward direction. Thus, if both h and C.Encode are super-efficient, then so is ShareRandom. However, ShareRandom only generates shares for randomly chosen secrets. In Section 5 we show how a secret sharing scheme with super-efficient random sharing algorithm can be bootstrapped into a secret sharing scheme with super-efficient standard sharing algorithm Share. We will now provide our construction.

Construction 1. *Let* C *be an* m*-folded* $\mathbb{F}_q$*-linear* $[n, k]$ *code with encoding and decoding procedures* C.Encode *and* C.Decode *and let* $h : \mathbb{F}_q^k \to \mathbb{F}_q^l$ *be a surjective* $\mathbb{F}_q$*-linear function. The secret sharing scheme* $\mathsf{LSSS}_{C,h}$ *is given by the following sharing and reconstruction procedures.*

Share($\mathbf{s}$):	Reconstruct($\tilde{\mathbf{c}}$):	ShareRandom():
$\mathbf{x} \leftarrow_\$ h^{-1}(\mathbf{s})$	$\mathbf{x} \leftarrow$ C.Decode($\tilde{\mathbf{c}}$)	$\mathbf{x} \leftarrow_\$ \mathbb{F}_q^k$
$\mathbf{c} \leftarrow$ C.Encode($\mathbf{x}$)	If $\mathbf{x} = \bot$	$\mathbf{c} \leftarrow$ C.Encode($\mathbf{x}$)
Output share vector $\mathbf{c}$	Output $\bot$	$\mathbf{s} \leftarrow h(\mathbf{x})$
	$\mathbf{s} \leftarrow h(\mathbf{x})$	Output secret $\mathbf{s}$
	Output $\mathbf{s}$	and share vector $\mathbf{c}$

First observe that the linearity of $\mathsf{LSSS}_{C,h}$ follows straightforwardly from the linearity of the code C and the function h. Moreover, all reconstruction properties of $\mathsf{LSSS}_{C,h}$ follow from corresponding properties of the code C.

Lemma 2. *Let* C *be an* m*-folded* $\mathbb{F}_q$*-linear* $[n, k]$ *code and* $h : \mathbb{F}_q^k \to \mathbb{F}_q^l$ *be a surjective* $\mathbb{F}_q$*-linear function. Secrets are elements of* $\mathbb{F}_q^l$*, whereas (single) shares are elements of* $\mathbb{F}_q^m$*. Assume that* C.Decode *can correct* $n - r$ *erasures. Then* $\mathsf{LSSS}_{C,h}$ *is an* n*-player LSSS which fulfills the linearity and* r*-reconstructability properties. Moreover,* ShareRandom *implements the same functionality as choosing* $\mathbf{s}$ *at random, computing* $\mathbf{c} \leftarrow$ Share(s) *and outputting* $(\mathbf{s}, \mathbf{c})$.

Proof. First notice that since h is surjective, the sharing algorithm Share can compute a share vector $\mathbf{c}$ for every message $\mathbf{s} \in \mathbb{F}_q^l$. The $\mathbb{F}_q$-linearity property follows directly from the $\mathbb{F}_q$-linearity if C and h. If r shares are given, we can assemble a vector $\tilde{\mathbf{c}}$ that has at most $n - r$ erasures. Consequently, C.Decode($\tilde{\mathbf{c}}$) will recover the correct $\mathbf{x}$ and we can compute the secret $\mathbf{s} = h(\mathbf{x})$. To see that ShareRandom computes the same functionality as choosing $\mathbf{s}$ uniformly at random and computing $\mathbf{c} \leftarrow \mathsf{Share}(\mathbf{s})$, notice that the $\mathbf{x}$ computed by $\mathsf{Share}(\mathbf{s})$ can be written as $\mathbf{x} = \mathbf{x}_1 + \mathbf{x}_2$, where $\mathbf{x}_1$ is a vector uniquely determined by $\mathbf{s}$ in an l-dimensional subspace W of $\mathbb{F}_q^k$ with $\mathsf{h}(W) = \mathbb{F}_q^l$ and $\mathbf{x}_2$ is chosen uniformly at random from $\ker(\mathbf{h})$. Thus if $\mathbf{s}$ is chosen uniformly at random, then $\mathbf{x}$ is also distributed uniformly at random in $\mathbb{F}_q^k$, just as the $\mathbf{x}$ computed by $\mathsf{ShareRandom}()$. The claim follows.

We will now determine under which conditions $\mathsf{LSSS}_{\mathsf{C},\mathsf{h}}$ fulfills the privacy property. In the first step, we first derive a general condition on the function h which is actually a necessary and sufficient requirement. In the second step, we will show that this requirement is met with overwhelming probability when the function h is chosen randomly from a family of universal hash functions. To simplify the analysis, we will identify the linear function $\mathsf{h} : \mathbb{F}_q^k \rightarrow \mathbb{F}_q^l$ with another linear function $\Phi : \mathsf{C} \rightarrow \mathbb{F}_q^l$. This is always possible as C is a k-dimensional $\mathbb{F}_q$-vectorspace and thus isomorphic to $\mathbb{F}_q^k$. In fact, we can basically define the function Φ by $\Phi(\mathbf{c}) = \mathsf{h}(\mathsf{C}.\mathsf{Decode}(\mathbf{c}))$ for all $\mathbf{c} \in \mathsf{C}$. We will denote projections of shares to a subset A of players by $\Pi_A : \mathsf{C} \rightarrow (\mathbb{F}_q^m)^{|A|}$.

Lemma 3. *A set $A \subseteq \{1, \ldots, n\}$ has privacy if and only if $\Phi(\ker(\Pi_A)) = \mathbb{F}_q^l$, where $\ker(\Pi_A) = \{\mathbf{x} \in \mathsf{C} \mid \Pi_A(\mathbf{x}) = \mathbf{0}\}$.*

Proof. First assume that $\Phi(\ker(\Pi_A)) = \mathbb{F}_q^l$. Fix a subspace $W \subseteq \ker(\Pi_A)$ of dimension l such that $\Phi(W) = \mathbb{F}_q^l$. As $W \cap \ker(\Phi) = \{\mathbf{0}\}$, it holds that $\mathsf{C} = W \oplus \ker(\Phi)$, i.e. we can write every $\mathbf{c} \in \mathsf{C}$ as $\mathbf{c} = \mathbf{c}_s + \mathbf{c}_r$, for unique $\mathbf{c}_s \in W$ and $\mathbf{c}_r \in \ker(\Phi)$. Now, let $\mathbf{c} = \mathsf{Share}(\mathbf{s})$. As $\mathbf{c} \in \mathsf{C}$, we can write $\mathbf{c}$ as

$$\mathbf{c} = \mathbf{c}_s + \mathbf{c}_r,$$

where $\mathbf{c}_s \in W$ is a unique vector such that $\Phi(\mathbf{c}_s) = \mathbf{s}$ and $\mathbf{c}_r$ is chosen uniformly at random from $\ker(\Phi)$. Now, it holds that

$$\Pi_A(\mathbf{c}) = \Pi_A(\mathbf{c}_s + \mathbf{c}_r) = \Pi_A(\mathbf{c}_s) + \Pi_A(\mathbf{c}_r) = \Pi_A(\mathbf{c}_r),$$

as $\mathbf{c}_s \in W \subseteq \ker(\Pi_A)$. Thus, $\Pi_A(\mathbf{c}) = \Pi_A(\mathbf{c}_r)$ is distributed independently of $\mathbf{s}$ and we can conclude that privacy holds.

For the converse direction, assume that $\Phi(\ker(\Pi_A)) \subsetneq \mathbb{F}_q^l$, i.e. there exists an $\mathbf{s}^* \in \mathbb{F}_q^l \setminus \Phi(\ker(\Pi_A))$. We will now show that if $\mathbf{c} = \mathsf{Share}(\mathbf{0})$ and $\mathbf{c}^* = \mathsf{Share}(\mathbf{s}^*)$, then the projections $\Pi_A(\mathbf{c})$ and $\Pi_A(\mathbf{c}^*)$ can always be distinguished. We claim that $\Pi_A(\mathbf{c}^*) \notin \Pi_A(\ker(\Phi))$. To see this, assume towards contradiction that $\Pi_A(\mathbf{c}^*) \in \Pi_A(\ker(\Phi))$. Then there exists a $\mathbf{h} \in \ker(\Phi)$ such that $\Pi_A(\mathbf{c}^*) = \Pi_A(\mathbf{h})$. Since Π_A is linear, it holds that $\Pi_A(\mathbf{c}^* - \mathbf{h}) = \mathbf{0}$ and consequently $\mathbf{c}^* - \mathbf{h} \in \ker(\Pi_A)$. From this, however follows

$$\Phi(\mathbf{c}^*) = \Phi(\mathbf{c}^* - \mathbf{h}) \in \Phi(\ker(\Pi_A)),$$

as $\mathbf{h} \in \ker(\Phi)$. This however contradicts $\mathbf{s}^* = \Phi(\mathbf{c}^*) \notin \Phi(\ker(\Pi_A))$ and we conclude that it must hold that $\Pi_A(\mathbf{c}^*) \notin \Pi_A(\ker(\Phi))$. Finally, notice that $\mathbf{c} \in \ker(\Phi)$ as

$c = \mathsf{Share}(0)$. Thus it holds that $\Pi_A(\mathbf{c}) \in \Pi_A(\ker(\Phi))$. We can therefore easily (and perfectly) distinguish $\Pi_A(\mathbf{c})$ from $\Pi_A(\mathbf{c}^*)$ by checking whether it is in $\Pi_A(\ker(\Phi))$. This contradicts the privacy property and we can conclude the proof.

We will now use the characterization of Lemma 3 and Corollary 2 to show that if we instantiate h with a randomly chosen linear universal hash function, then we obtain a good linear secret sharing scheme.

Lemma 4. *Let* C *be a* m-folded $\mathbb{F}_q$-linear $[n,k]$ code and let $\mathcal{H}$ be a family of $\mathbb{F}_q$-linear universal hash functions $\mathbb{F}_q^k \to \mathbb{F}_q^l$. Let $R = \frac{k}{mn}$ be the rate of C, let $\rho = \frac{l}{nm}$ and let $\tau > 0$ and $\eta > 0$ be constants. Given that $R \geq \rho + \eta + \tau + H(\tau)/(m \cdot \log(q))$, then there exists a $h \in \mathcal{H}$ such that $\mathsf{LSSS}_{C,h}$ has τn-privacy. Moreover, such a function h can be chosen randomly with success-probability $1 - q^{-\eta nm}$.*

Proof. Let $\Psi : C \to \mathbb{F}_q^k$ be the isomorphism that corresponds to the function $C.\mathsf{Decode}(\cdot)$. For each set $A \subseteq \{1, \ldots, n\}$ of size at most $t = \tau n$, it holds that $\ker(\Pi_A) \subseteq C$ is a subspace of dimension at least $k - mt$, as C has dimension k and the image of Π_A has dimension at most mt. Thus, $\Psi(\ker(\Pi_A)) \subseteq \mathbb{F}_q^k$ also has dimension at least $k - mt$, as Ψ is an isomorphism. Consequently $\mathcal{V} = \{\Psi(\ker(\Pi_A)) \mid A \in \{1, \ldots, n\}, |A| = t\}$ is a collection of subspaces of dimension at least $k - mt$. Moreover, as A is taken over all subsets of $\{1, \ldots, n\}$ of size t, it holds that

$$|\mathcal{V}| \leq \binom{n}{t} \leq 2^{H(t/n) \cdot n} = 2^{H(\tau) \cdot n} = q^{\frac{H(\tau)}{m \log(q)} \cdot mn}.$$

By Lemma 3, $\mathsf{LSSS}_{C,h}$ has privacy for all A with $|A| \leq t$ if it holds that $h(V) = \mathbb{F}_q^l$ for each $V \in \mathcal{V}$. By Corollary 2, it holds for all $V \in \mathcal{V}$ that $\mathsf{H}(V) = \mathbb{F}_q^l$, except with probability

$$|\mathcal{V}| \cdot q^{-(k-mt-l)} \leq q^{-(k-mt-l-\frac{H(\tau)}{m \log(q)} \cdot mn)} = q^{-(R-\rho-\tau-\frac{H(\tau)}{m \log(q)}) \cdot mn} \leq q^{-\eta mn},$$

over the choice of $\mathsf{H} \leftarrow_\$ \mathcal{H}$, as $R \geq \rho + \eta + \tau + H(\tau)/(m \cdot \log(q))$. Thus, $\mathsf{LSSS}_{C,H}$ has t-privacy, except with probability $q^{-\eta mn}$ over the choice of $\mathsf{H} \leftarrow_\$ \mathcal{H}$. This concludes the proof.

Remark 1. It can be seen rather easily that the function H in Lemma 4 must either be chosen randomly or depending on the code C, i.e. for any fixed function h we can find a code C^* such that $\mathsf{LSSS}_{C^*,h}$ does not provide any privacy. Thus, to obtain a construction that is oblivious of the specific code we use, randomization is strictly necessary.

5   Linear Time Sharing and Reconstruction

As our first application, we will show how to construct a linear secret sharing scheme with linear time sharing and reconstruction phase. Choosing a linear time encodable code C and a linear time computable function h yields that the sharing procedure $\mathsf{ShareRandom}$ of Construction 1 is also linear time computable.

This is, in turn, not true for the sharing procedure Share of Construction 1. We circumvent this issue by providing a sharing algorithm that first computes shares of a random secret s' using ShareRandom, then uses s' to one-time-pad encrypt the actual secret s. The ciphertext s + s' is then distributed by applying a standard information dispersal technique, i.e. we encode s + s' using an erasure correcting code and append the codeword symbols to the shares. This basically results in a doubling of the share size. This technique bears resemblance to the construction of Krawczyk [19]. However, while in [19] information dispersal is applied to reduce the share size (using a computationally secure encryption scheme), we use this technique to salvage the linear time computability of the (non-random) sharing algorithm.

We will start by providing an instantiation of Construction 1 with linear time random sharing and reconstruction algorithms. Moreover, the scheme we provide will be *near*-threshold. We need both a family of linear time computable universal hash functions and linear time en- and decodable codes. Ishai et al. [17] construct a family of $\mathbb{F}_2$-linear universal hash functions which can be computed in linear time. This result has recently been generalized by Druk and Ishai [9] to any finite field, but the binary case of [17] is sufficient for our application.

Theorem 2 (Ishai et al. [17]). *For every $l < k$, there exists a family $\mathbb{F}_2$-linear universal hash functions $\mathcal{H}$ mapping $\mathbb{F}_2^k$ to $\mathbb{F}_2^l$ which can be computed in time linear in k.*

There is a large corpus of work dealing with linear time encodable codes, starting with the seminal work of Spielman [24]. To the best of our knowledge, the currently best known parameters can be obtained using a family of codes by Guruswami and Indyk [11].

Theorem 3 (Guruswami-Indyk [11]). *For every rate R and every sufficiently small ϵ (depending on R) there exists an infinite family of m-folded $\mathbb{F}_2$-linear codes $\{C_n\}$ of rate R, where $m = O\left(\frac{\log(1/\epsilon)}{\epsilon^4 R}\right)$, such that the codes from the family can be encoded in linear time and also decoded in linear time from an $1 - R - \epsilon$ fraction of erasures.*

We will now instantiate the the linear secret sharing scheme $\mathsf{LSSS}_{C,h}$ of Construction 1 with the codes from Theorem 3 and universal hash functions from Theorem 2.

Lemma 5. *For all constants $0 < \tau < \sigma < 1$ and every rate $\rho < \sigma - \tau$ there exists an infinite family of $\mathbb{F}_2$-linear secret schemes $\{\mathsf{LSSS}_n^1\}$ with τn-privacy, σn-reconstructability and rate ρ. The shares of LSSS_n^1 have size m bits, where $m > 0$ is a constant. Furthermore, LSSS_n^1.ShareRandom and LSSS_n^1.Reconstruct can be computed in linear time. Moreover, such a scheme LSSS_n^1 can be constructed randomly with success-probability $1 - 2^{-\eta mn}$ (for some constant $\eta > 0$ depending on τ, σ and ρ).*

Proof. We will instantiate the linear secret sharing scheme $\mathsf{LSSS}_{C,h}$ from Construction 1 with a linear code C_n from the family $\{C_n\}$ of $\mathbb{F}_2$-linear codes from

Theorem 3 and a function h from the family $\mathcal{H}$ of $\mathbb{F}_2$-linear universal hash functions from Theorem 2. We now show how to choose the parameters for this instantiation.

By Lemma 4, in order to obtain a secret sharing scheme with τn privacy, we need to select an m-folded code C_n from the above family of length n and rate R such that $R \geq \rho + \eta + \tau + H(\tau)/m$ for an arbitrarily small constant η. Moreover, as by Lemma 2 we ne need to be able to correct a $1 - \sigma$ fraction of erasures to have σn reconstruction, we need to choose C_n such that $1 - \sigma \leq 1 - R - \epsilon$, equivalently $R \leq \sigma - \epsilon$. Both constraints together yield

$$\sigma - \tau - \rho \geq \epsilon + \eta + \frac{H(\tau)}{m}. \tag{1}$$

Since $\sigma > \tau$ and $\sigma - \tau > \rho$, the left hand side of Inequality 1 is a constant greater than 0. It is clear from Theorem 3 that we can choose the folding parameter m as an arbitrarily large constant, thereby also decreasing ϵ. Consequently, the terms ϵ and $\frac{H(\tau)}{m}$ become arbitrarily small and we can choose a sufficiently small $\eta > 0$ such that the inequality is satisfied. Setting $R = \sigma - \epsilon$ we found admissible constants $R, m, \eta, \epsilon > 0$ such that $R \geq \rho + \eta + \tau + H(\tau)/m$. Now let C_n be a code of length n from the above family that matches these constants. By Theorem 3 such a code exists for all constants $R, m, \epsilon > 0$. Now let $\mathcal{H}$ be a the family of universal hash functions from 2 mapping $\mathbb{F}_2^{Rmn}$ to $\mathbb{F}_2^{\rho mn}$ obtained by Theorem 2. By Lemma 4, choosing the universal hash function H randomly from $\mathcal{H}$ yields that $LSSS_{C,H}$ has τ privacy, except with probability $2^{-\eta mn}$.

Notice that the computational overhead per shared bit in $LSSS_n^1$ is constant for ShareRandom. We will now bootstrap the scheme $LSSS_n^1$ given by Lemma 5 into a secret sharing scheme with linear time sharing and reconstruction algorithms.

Construction 2. *Let C' be a (folded) $\mathbb{F}_q$-linear $[n, l]$ code with encoding and decoding procedures $C'.Encode$ and $C'.Decode$ and let $LSSS^1$ be a $\mathbb{F}_q$-linear secret sharing scheme with a sharing procedure $LSSS_1.ShareRandom()$ for random secrets. The secret sharing scheme $LSSS^2$ is given by the following sharing and reconstruction procedures.*

Share(s):
    $(s', c) \leftarrow LSSS^1.ShareRandom()$
    $d \leftarrow C'.Encode(s' + s)$
    Parse $c = (c_1, \dots, c_n)$
        and $d = (d_1, \dots, d_n)$
    Output $z = ((c_1, d_1), \dots, (c_n, d_n))$

Reconstruct($\tilde{z}$):
    Parse $\tilde{z} = ((\tilde{c}_1, \tilde{d}_1), \dots, (\tilde{c}_n, \tilde{d}_n))$
    $\tilde{c} \leftarrow (\tilde{c}_1, \dots, \tilde{c}_n)$
    $\tilde{d} \leftarrow (\tilde{d}_1, \dots, \tilde{d}_n)$
    $s' \leftarrow LSSS^1.Reconstruct(\tilde{c})$
    $y \leftarrow C'.Decode(\tilde{d})$
    If $s' = \perp$ or $y = \perp$
        Output $\perp$
    Otherwise
        Output $y - s'$

Lemma 6. *Assume that* LSSS^1 *provides* t-*privacy and* r-*reconstructability, and* LSSS^1.ShareRandom *is linear time computable. Assume further that* C' *is linear time encodable and that* C'.Decode *can decode from* r-*erasures. Then* LSSS^2 *also has* t-*privacy and* r-*reconstructability and* LSSS^2.Share *is linear time computable. Furthermore, if both* LSSS^1.Reconstruct *and* C'.Decode *are linear time computable, then* LSSS^2.Reconstruct *is also linear time computable.*

Proof. Linear time computability of LSSS^2.Share and LSSS^2.Reconstruct follows straightforwardly from the linear time computability of LSSS^1.ShareRandom and C'.Encode as well as LSSS^1.Reconstruct and C'.Decode respectively.

To see that LSSS^2 has r-reconstructability, observe that LSSS^1.Reconstruct($\tilde{\mathbf{c}}$) recovers $\mathbf{s}'$ from t as long as $\tilde{\mathbf{c}}$ contains at most r erasures. Likewise, C'.Decode($\tilde{\mathbf{d}}$) recovers $\mathbf{x} = \mathbf{s} + \mathbf{s}'$ from $\tilde{\mathbf{d}}$ as long as $\tilde{\mathbf{d}}$ contains at most r erasures. r-reconstructability of LSSS^2 follows.

To see that LSSS^2 has t-privacy, let $\mathbf{z} = ((\mathbf{c}_1, \mathbf{d}_1), \ldots, (\mathbf{c}_n, \mathbf{d}_n))$ be a vector of shares generated by LSSS^2.Share($\mathbf{s}$). For any $A \subseteq \{1, \ldots, n\}$ of size at most t, it holds by the t-privacy of LSSS^1 that $\mathbf{s}'$ is distributed uniformly at random given the shares $\mathbf{c}_A$. Thus, the $(\mathbf{c}_A, \mathbf{s} + \mathbf{s}')$ is distributed independently of $\mathbf{s}$. But the same holds for $(\mathbf{c}_A, \mathbf{d}_A)$, as $\mathbf{d}_A$ can be computed from $\mathbf{s} + \mathbf{s}'$. Consequently, t-privacy of LSSS^2 follows.

Finally, plugging the linear secret sharing scheme LSSS_n^1 obtained in Lemma 5 into Construction 2, we obtain the main result for this section. For the sake of simplicity, as code C' in Construction 2 we can choose the same code C as in Lemma 5 and match its rate to the rate of LSSS_n^1. We conclude the following theorem.

Theorem 4. *For all constants* $0 < \tau < \sigma < 1$ *and every rate* $\rho < \sigma - \tau$ *there exists an infinite family of* $\mathbb{F}_2$-*linear secret scheme* $\{\mathsf{LSSS}_n^2\}$ *with* τn-*privacy,* σn-*reconstructability and rate* ρ. *The shares of* LSSS_n^2 *have size* m, *where* $m > 0$ *is a constant.* LSSS_n^2.Share *and* LSSS_n^2.Reconstruct *can be computed in linear time. Moreover, such a scheme* LSSS_n^2 *can be constructed randomly with success-probability* $1 - 2^{-\eta m n}$ *(for some constant* $\eta > 0$ *depending on* τ, σ *and* ρ).

6   Robust Secret Sharing with Constant Size Shares

In this section, we show how our generic construction of LSSSs from codes gives rise to new *robust* secret sharing schemes, i.e., to schemes where the secret can be correctly reconstructed even if some of the shares provided are incorrect.

The idea behind our new scheme is to instantiate Construction 1 with a *highly list-decodable* code C. When confronted with the task of reconstructing the secret in the presence of faulty shares, this allows us to narrow down the list of candidate secrets to a small set. To single out the right secret, we will *precode* it using an AMD code, as introduced in [7]. Informally, an AMD code is a (keyless) code that is resilient towards certain — namely algebraic — manipulations.

This construction is similar to the construction of Cramer, Damgård and Fehr [5]. However, the fact that our construction allows us to use a list-decodable code (whereas [5] uses standard Shamir secret sharing [23]) makes our scheme computationally efficient, in contrast to the robust reconstruction procedure of [5], which involves a brute-force search over all subsets of size t. Furthermore, in the regime we consider, namely when t/n is bounded away from $\frac{1}{2}$, we get better parameters than previous work.

6.1 Formal Definitions and Building Blocks

We start by formalizing the notion of a robust secret sharing scheme.

Definition 3. *A linear secret sharing scheme* LSSS *is* (t, δ)*-robust if there exists an additional algorithm* LSSS.RobustReconstruct *with the property that for every secret* **s** *and for every subset* $A \subset \{1, \ldots, n\}$ *of size* $|A| = t$, *the following holds. If* **c** = LSSS.Share(**s**), *and* $\tilde{\mathbf{c}}$ *is such that* $\tilde{\mathbf{c}}_{\bar{A}} = \mathbf{c}_{\bar{A}}$ *and* $\tilde{\mathbf{c}}_A$ *only depends on* $\mathbf{c}_A$, *then* LSSS.RobustReconstruct($\tilde{\mathbf{c}}$) = **s** *except with probability* δ.

In the range $n/3 \leq t < n/2$, robust secret sharing is only possible if we allow a non-zero error probability δ, and we append some additional "checking data" to the actual shares. The goal is to optimize the trade-off between this overhead in the share size and δ. As outlined above, our construction is based on using a list-decodable code in our general construction of LSSS from codes.

Definition 4. *An* m*-folded* $\mathbb{F}_q$*-linear* $[n, k]$ *code* C *is said to be* (t, ℓ)*-list decodable if there exists an efficient algorithm* C.ListDecode *such that for any codeword* $\mathbf{c} \in C$ *and any error pattern* $\mathbf{e} \in (\mathbb{F}_q^m)^n$ *of weight at most* t, C.ListDecode($\mathbf{c} + \mathbf{e}$) *produces a list of all elements* $\mathbf{x} \in \mathbb{F}_q^k$ *with* d(C.Encode($\mathbf{x}$), $\mathbf{c} + \mathbf{e}$) $\leq t$. *Furthermore, the size of the list is at most* ℓ.

We will now state two results for highly list-decodable codes. The first one is due to Guruswami and Rudra [12] as well as Guruswami and Wang [13] and states that m-folded Reed Solomon codes are highly list-decodable. The second result, due to Guruswami and Xing [14], states that certain m-folded algebraic geometric codes are highly list-decodable.

Theorem 5 (List-decodability of Folded Reed Solomon Codes [12, 13]). *For any rate* $0 < R < 1$ *and* $\epsilon > 0$, *any large enough integer* $m > 0$ *(depending on* R *and* ϵ*) and for any integer* $n > 0$ *there exist a prime power* $q = q(n) = O(n)$ *and an* m*-folded* $\mathbb{F}_q$*-linear code* C *of length* n *and rate* R, *such that* C *is efficiently* $(\tau n, \ell)$*-list decodable with* $\tau = 1 - R - \epsilon$ *and* $\ell = \mathsf{poly}(n)$. *The list decoder has runtime* $\mathsf{poly}(n, m)$.

Theorem 6 (List-decodability of Folded Algebraic Geometric Codes [14]). *For any rate* $0 < R < 1$ *and* $\epsilon > 0$, *and for any large enough integer* $m > 0$ *(depending on* R *and* ϵ*) there exist a constant prime power* q *and an infinite family of* m*-folded* $\mathbb{F}_q$*-linear codes* $\{C_n\}$, *such that the rate of* C_n *is* R, *and* C_n *is efficiently* $(\tau n, \ell)$*-list decodable with* $\tau = 1 - R - \epsilon$ *and* $\ell = \mathsf{poly}(n)$. *The list decoder has runtime* $\mathsf{poly}(n, m)$.

Notice that in both constructions the runtime of the list decoder is polynomial in both the code length n and the folding parameter m. This means that we can choose the folding parameter super constant and still have efficient list decodability. Additionally, we make use of AMD codes (restricting ourselves to $\mathbb{F}_q$-linear spaces for simplicity).

Definition 5 (Algebraic Manipulation Detection Codes [7]). *Let q be a prime-power, $l > k$ be integers and $\delta > 0$. A (q^k, q^l, δ)-AMD code AMD consists of a probabilistic encoding algorithm AMD.Encode : $\mathbb{F}_q^k \to \mathbb{F}_q^l$ and a (deterministic) decoding algorithm AMD.Decode : $\mathbb{F}_q^l \to \mathbb{F}_q^k \sqcup \{\bot\}$, such that the following holds for every $\mathbf{x} \in \mathbb{F}_q^l$.*

- *Correctness:* AMD.Decode(AMD.Encode($\mathbf{x}$)) = $\mathbf{x}$ *with probability 1.*
- *Manipulation detection: for every offset $\boldsymbol{\Delta} \in \mathbb{F}_q^l$, and for $\mathbf{c}$ generated as $\mathbf{c} \leftarrow$ AMD.Encode($\mathbf{x}$), it holds that AMD.Decode($\mathbf{c} + \boldsymbol{\Delta}$) $\in \{\bot, \mathbf{x}\}$ except with probability at most δ.*

A simple example AMD code is given by AMD.Encode : $\mathbb{F}_q^k \to \mathbb{F}_q^k \times \mathbb{F}_q^k \times \mathbb{F}_q^k$, $s \mapsto (s, r, sr)$, where r is uniformly random from $\mathbb{F}_q^k$, and the multiplication sr is given by fixing an isomorphism of $\mathbb{F}_q$-vector spaces $\mathbb{F}_q^k \to \mathbb{F}_{q^k}$, and with the obvious decoding: checking the multiplicative relation. It is not hard to show that this AMD code has error probability $\delta = q^{-k}$. In our construction, we use a slightly more sophisticated AMD code, due to [7], given by

$$\text{AMD.Encode} : \mathbb{F}_q^d \to \mathbb{F}_q^d \times \mathbb{F}_q \times \mathbb{F}_q, \ s \mapsto \left(s, r, r^{d+2} + \sum_{i=1}^{d} s_i r^i\right)$$

where r is uniformly random from $\mathbb{F}_q^k$, char($\mathbb{F}_q) \nmid d + 2$, and with the obvious decoding. This construction gives rise to the following claim.

Lemma 7 ([7]). *For any prime power q and integers $l > 2\kappa > 0$, there exists a $\left(q^{l-2\kappa}, q^l, (l - 2\kappa + 1)/q^\kappa\right)$-AMD code.*

6.2 The Construction

In order to have a modular exposition, we first introduce the notion of a list reconstructible secret sharing scheme. In a nutshell, list reconstructible secret sharing is a weak version of robust secret sharing. Instead of requiring reconstruction of the correct secret (in the presence of faulty shares), we merely require reconstruction of a short *list* of possible candidates of which one is the correct secret. In addition to that, we require some linearity property.

Definition 6. *We say that a linear secret sharing scheme LSSS is (t, ℓ)-list reconstructible, if there exists an efficient algorithm LSSS.ListReconstruct(), such* *that for all* **e** *of weight at most* t, *the following holds.* LSSS.ListReconstruct(**e**) *outputs a list of length* ℓ *containing* **0**, *and for any secret* **s** *and its share vector* **c** *we have*

$$\text{LSSS.ListReconstruct}(\mathbf{c} + \mathbf{e}) = \mathbf{s} + \text{LSSS.ListReconstruct}(\mathbf{e})$$
$$= \{\mathbf{s} + \mathbf{w} \mid \mathbf{w} \in \text{LSSS.ListReconstruct}(\mathbf{e})\},$$

We now show that, not very surprisingly, using a list-decodable code in Construction 1 results in a list reconstructable secret sharing scheme.

Lemma 8. *Let* C *be an* m-folded $\mathbb{F}_q$-*linear* $[n, k]$ *code and* h $: \mathbb{F}_q^k \to \mathbb{F}_q^l$ *an* $\mathbb{F}_q$-*linear function, and let* LSSS$_{\mathsf{C},\mathsf{h}}$ *be the linear secret sharing scheme resulting from Construction 1. If* C *is* (t, ℓ)-*list-decodable then* LSSS$_{\mathsf{C},\mathsf{h}}$ *is* (t, ℓ)-*list reconstructible.*

Proof. ListReconstruct simply works by running C.ListDecode and applying h to all the elements in the list output by C.ListDecode. In order to show that Definition 6 is satisfied, due to the linearity of h it is sufficient to show that

$$\text{C.ListDecode}(\mathbf{c} + \mathbf{e}) = \mathbf{m} + \text{C.ListDecode}(\mathbf{e}),$$

for any $\mathbf{m} \in \mathbb{F}_q^k$, $\mathbf{c} = \text{C.Encode}(\mathbf{m})$, and any error vector **e** of weight at most t.

First of all, the bound on the size of the list, and that it contains **0**, are obvious. For any $\mathbf{w} \in \text{C.ListDecode}(\mathbf{e})$, we have that $d(\text{C.Encode}(\mathbf{w}), \mathbf{e}) \leq t$. By linearity, it holds that

$$\text{C.Encode}(\mathbf{m} + \mathbf{w}) = \mathbf{c} + \text{C.Encode}(\mathbf{w}).$$

Therefore,

$$\text{C.Encode}(\mathbf{m} + \mathbf{w}) - (\mathbf{c} + \mathbf{e}) = \text{C.Encode}(\mathbf{w}) - \mathbf{e}$$

from which follows that

$$d(\text{C.Encode}(\mathbf{m} + \mathbf{w}), \mathbf{c} + \mathbf{e}) = d(\text{C.Encode}(\mathbf{w}), \mathbf{e}) \leq t,$$

i.e. $\mathbf{m} + \mathbf{w} \in \text{C.ListDecode}(\mathbf{c} + \mathbf{e})$. Similarly, for any $\mathbf{w} \in \text{C.ListDecode}(\mathbf{c} + \mathbf{e})$, we have that

$$\text{C.Encode}(\mathbf{w} - \mathbf{m}) = \text{C.Encode}(\mathbf{w}) - \mathbf{c},$$

and consequently

$$\mathbf{e} - \text{C.Encode}(\mathbf{w} - \mathbf{m}) = (\mathbf{c} + \mathbf{e}) - \text{C.Encode}(\mathbf{w}).$$

This proves that the two lists, C.ListDecode($\mathbf{c} + \mathbf{e}$) and $\mathbf{m} + $ C.ListDecode($\mathbf{e}$), contain exactly the same elements, which was to be proven.

Instantiating the above with the list decodable codes from Theorem 5 and Theorem 6 respectively yields the following Lemma.

Lemma 9. *For any $\tau < \frac{1}{2}$, any $\tau < \sigma < 1-\tau$, any $\rho < \sigma - \tau$ and any sufficiently large $m > 0$ we have that:*

- *For every integer $n > 0$ there exists a $q = O(n)$ and an n-player $\mathbb{F}_q$-linear secret sharing scheme LSSS_n with τn-privacy, σn-reconstruction and $(\tau n, \mathsf{poly}(n))$-list reconstruction. Furthermore, the rate of LSSS_n is ρ and the shares of LSSS_n are elements of $\mathbb{F}_q^m$. The list reconstruction algorithm has runtime $\mathsf{poly}(n,m)$.*
- *There exists a constant prime power q and an infinite family of $\mathbb{F}_q$-linear secret sharing schemes $\{\mathsf{LSSS}_n\}$, such that LSSS_n is an n-player scheme with τn-privacy, σn-reconstruction and $(\tau n, \mathsf{poly}(n))$-list reconstruction. Furthermore, the rate of LSSS_n is ρ and the shares of LSSS_n are elements of $\mathbb{F}_q^m$. The list reconstruction algorithm has runtime $\mathsf{poly}(n,m)$.*

Proof. We will instantiate the scheme $\mathsf{LSSS}_{\mathsf{C},\mathsf{h}}$ from Construction 1 enhanced to a list-reconstructible scheme by Lemma 8 with either the codes from Theorem 5 or Theorem 6 respectively and a suitable family $\mathcal{H}$ of universal hash functions.

By Lemma 4, in order to obtain a secret sharing scheme with τn privacy and rate ρ, we need to select an m-folded code C from one of the above families with rate R such that

$$R \geq \rho + \eta + \tau + \frac{H(\tau)}{m\log(q)}$$

for an arbitrarily small constant η. To get list reconstructability, we need to be able to list-decode a τ fraction of errors. Thus, we need to choose the constants R and ϵ for the above families such that $\tau \leq 1 - R - \epsilon$, which is equivalent to $R \leq 1 - \tau - \epsilon$. Together, these two constraints yield a new constraint

$$1 - 2\tau - \rho \geq \epsilon + \eta + \frac{H(\tau)}{m\log(q)}. \tag{2}$$

The left-hand side of Inequality 2 is a constant greater than 0, as $\rho < \sigma - \tau < 1 - 2\tau$ and $1 - 2\tau > 0$, as $\tau < \frac{1}{2}$. Thus, we can fulfill the constraints by choosing sufficiently small constants $\epsilon > 0$ and $\eta > 0$ and an m greater than a sufficiently large constant and setting $R = 1 - \tau - \epsilon$.

- Using the folded RS codes provided by Theorem 5 in Construction 1, we can conclude that for every $n > 0$ there exist a prime power $q = O(n)$ and an n-player $\mathbb{F}_q$-linear secret sharing scheme $\mathsf{LSSS}_{\mathsf{C},\mathsf{h}}$ with τn-privacy, σn-reconstruction, rate ρ, shares from $\mathbb{F}_q^m$ and which is $(\tau n, \mathsf{poly}(n))$-list reconstructible. Here, we use a linear universal hash function h chosen from a family $\mathcal{H}$ of $\mathbb{F}_q$-linear universal hash functions which maps $\mathbb{F}_q^{Rmn}$ to $\mathbb{F}_q^{\rho mn}$.
- Using the folded AG codes provided by Theorem 6 in Construction 1, we can conclude that there exists a constant prime power q and an infinite family of $\mathbb{F}_q$-linear secret sharing schemes $\{\mathsf{LSSS}_n\}$, such that LSSS_n is an n-player $\mathbb{F}_q$-linear secret sharing scheme $\mathsf{LSSS}_{\mathsf{C},\mathsf{h}}$ with τn-privacy, σn-reconstruction, rate ρ, shares from $\mathbb{F}_q^m$ and which is $(\tau n, \mathsf{poly}(n))$-list reconstructible. Here, we use a linear universal hash function h chosen from a family $\mathcal{H}$ of $\mathbb{F}_q$-linear universal hash functions which maps $\mathbb{F}_q^{Rmn}$ to $\mathbb{F}_q^{\rho mn}$.

This concludes the proof.

Construction 3. *Let* LSSS_1 *be an* n-*player linear secret sharing scheme with secret space* $\mathbb{F}_q^l$, *and say that it has* t-*privacy and* r-*reconstructability, as well as* (t, ℓ)-*list reconstructability. Let further* AMD *be a* (q^k, q^l, δ)-*AMD code. We define the secret sharing scheme* LSSS_3, *having message space* $\mathbb{F}_q^k$ *and share spaces equal to those of* LSSS_1, *by the following sharing and reconstruction procedures:*

Share(s):	RobustReconstruct($\tilde{\mathbf{c}}$):
$\quad \mathbf{z} \leftarrow \mathsf{AMD.Encode}(\mathbf{s})$	$\quad L \leftarrow \mathsf{LSSS}_1.\mathsf{ListReconstruct}(\tilde{\mathbf{c}})$
$\quad \mathbf{c} \leftarrow \mathsf{LSSS}_1.\mathsf{Share}(\mathbf{z})$	$\quad$ For $\bar{\mathbf{z}} \in L$:
$\quad$ Output $\mathbf{c} = (c_1, \ldots c_n)$	$\quad\quad \bar{\mathbf{s}} \leftarrow \mathsf{AMD.Decode}(\bar{\mathbf{z}})$
	$\quad\quad$ If $\bar{\mathbf{s}} \neq \perp$
	$\quad\quad\quad$ Output $\bar{\mathbf{s}}$
	$\quad$ Output $\perp$

Lemma 10. *The scheme* LSSS_3 *given above is a* $(t, \ell\delta)$-*robust linear secret sharing scheme with* t-*privacy and* r-*reconstructability.*

As for efficiency, the running time of Share is equal to the sum of the running times of AMD.Encode and $\mathsf{LSSS}_1.\mathsf{Share}$; the running time of RobustReconstruct is equal to he sum of the running time of $\mathsf{LSSS}_1.\mathsf{ListReconstruct}$ and ℓ times the running time of AMD.Decode.

Proof. The fact that LSSS_3 has t-privacy and r-reconstruction follows immediately from the t-privacy and r-reconstruction of LSSS_1. We will now show that LSSS_3 can correctly reconstruct a secret from n shares where up to t are incorrect, except with probability at most $\ell\delta$. Let $\mathbf{c} = \mathsf{LSSS}_3.\mathsf{Share}(\mathbf{s})$ for some adversarially chosen secret $\mathbf{s}$. Assume the adversary $\mathcal{A}$ corrupts a set A of players, where $|A| \leq t$. Thus the corrupted share vector $\tilde{\mathbf{c}}$ can be written as

$$\tilde{\mathbf{c}} = \mathbf{c} + \mathbf{e},$$

where $\mathbf{e}$ is an additive error with support A. Since $\mathcal{A}$ computes $\tilde{\mathbf{c}}_A$ from $\mathbf{c}_A$, which is independent of $\mathbf{z} = \mathsf{AMD.Encode}(\mathbf{s})$ by the t-privacy of LSSS_1, $\mathbf{e}$ is independent of $\mathbf{z}$ (given $\mathbf{s}$). We will consider the error-probability of RobustReconstruct, i.e. the probability that RobustReconstruct($\tilde{\mathbf{c}}$) outputs something different from $\mathbf{s}$.

Consider the list $E = \mathsf{LSSS}_1.\mathsf{ListReconstruct}(\mathbf{e})$. As the weight of $\mathbf{e}$ is at most t, it holds that $\mathbf{0} \in E$ and

$$L = \mathsf{LSSS}_1.\mathsf{ListReconstruct}(\tilde{\mathbf{c}}) = \mathbf{z} + E,$$

and thus in particular that $\mathbf{z} \in L$. Moreover, as the error $\mathbf{e}$ is independent of $\mathbf{z}$, it also holds that E is independent of $\mathbf{z}$. Hence, it holds for each $\mathbf{r} \in E$ that $\mathbf{r}$ is independent of $\mathbf{z}$. By the AMD property it thus holds for each $\mathbf{r} \in E \backslash \{\mathbf{0}\}$ that

$$\Pr[\mathsf{AMD.Decode}(\mathbf{z} + \mathbf{r}) \neq \perp] \leq \delta.$$

A union bound yields that

$$\Pr[\exists \mathbf{r} \in E \backslash \{\mathbf{0}\} : \mathsf{AMD.Decode}(\mathbf{z} + \mathbf{r}) \neq \bot] \leq \ell\delta.$$

Doing a change of variable, namely setting $\bar{\mathbf{z}} = \mathbf{z} + \mathbf{r}$, such that the quantification over $\mathbf{r} \in E \backslash \{\mathbf{0}\}$ becomes a quantification over $\bar{\mathbf{z}} \in \mathbf{z} + E \backslash \{\mathbf{0}\} = L \backslash \{\mathbf{z}\}$, gives us

$$\Pr[\exists \bar{\mathbf{z}} \in L \backslash \{\mathbf{z}\} : \mathsf{AMD.Decode}(\bar{\mathbf{z}}) \neq \bot] \leq \ell\delta.$$

Thus, every $\bar{\mathbf{z}} \in L \backslash \{\mathbf{z}\}$ will be rejected by AMD.Decode, except with probability $\ell\delta$. Furthermore, $\mathbf{z} \in L$ will be accepted. Therefore, we can conclude that $\mathsf{LSSS}_3.\mathsf{RobustReconstruct}(\tilde{\mathbf{c}}) = \mathbf{s}$, except with probability $\ell\delta$. Consequently, LSSS_3 is $(t, \ell\delta)$-robust, which concludes the proof. $\square$

We will now state our main result for this section.

Theorem 7. *For any $\tau < \frac{1}{2}$, any $\tau < \sigma < 1 - \tau$, any $\rho < \sigma - \tau$ and any integer $\lambda > 0$ (the security parameter), we have that:*

- *For every $n > 0$ there exists an efficient n-player $(\tau n, 2^{-\lambda})$-robust secret sharing scheme LSSS with τn-privacy, σn-reconstructability and with rate ρ. The shares have size $\Theta(\log(n) + \lambda/n)$ and the secret has size $\Theta(n \cdot \log(n) + \lambda)$.*
- *There exists an infinite family $\{\mathsf{LSSS}_n\}$ of efficient n-player $(\tau n, 2^{-\lambda})$-robust secret sharing schemes with τn-privacy, σn-reconstructability and with rate ρ. The shares have size $\Theta(1 + \lambda/n)$ and the secret has size $\Theta(n + \lambda)$.*

We emphasize that even for non-robust ramp schemes, the rate ρ cannot be bigger than $\sigma - \tau$.

Proof. We shall instantiate Construction 3 with the list reconstructible secret sharing schemes provided by Lemma 9 and the AMD code given by Lemma 7. Let LSSS be an n-player $\mathbb{F}_q$-linear secret sharing scheme (from one of the two families in Lemma 9) with τn-privacy, σn-reconstructability and $(\tau n, \mathsf{poly}(n))$-list reconstructability, shares in $\mathbb{F}_q^m$ and rate ρ' with $\rho < \rho' < \sigma - \tau$. Recall that both constructions in Lemma 9 allow us to choose the parameter m arbitrarily large.

Now, we consider a $(q^{\rho' mn - 2\kappa}, q^{\rho' mn}, \delta')$-AMD code AMD, as provided by Lemma 7, with $\delta' = (\rho' mn - 2\kappa + 1)/q^{\kappa}$, where κ is to be determined later. By Theorem 7, this gives $(\tau n, \delta)$-robustness for

$$\delta \leq \mathsf{poly}(n) \cdot \delta' \leq \mathsf{poly}(n) \frac{\rho' mn}{q^{\kappa}} = \frac{m \cdot \mathsf{poly}(n)}{q^{\kappa}}.$$

Setting $\kappa = \lambda / \log(q) + \log(m \cdot \mathsf{poly}(n))$ gives $\delta \leq 2^{-\lambda}$. Finally, the rate of the scheme is given by

$$\frac{\rho' mn - 2\kappa}{mn} = \rho' - 2\frac{\lambda}{mn \log(q)} - 2 \cdot \frac{\log(\mathsf{poly}(n))}{mn} - 2\frac{\log(m)}{mn}.$$

By choosing the parameter m large enough, i.e. $m = \Omega(1 + \lambda/(n \cdot \log(q)))$, this becomes bigger than ρ. Finally, for the first family provided in Lemma 9, such an LSSS exists for every length n and we have $q = O(n)$. Thus we can choose the parameter m as $m = \Theta(1 + \lambda/(n \cdot \log(n)))$ and the shares for this instantiation have size $m \cdot \log(q) = \Theta(\log(n) + \lambda/n)$, whereas the secret has size $\rho m n \cdot \log(q) = \Theta(n \cdot \log(n) + \lambda)$. The second family provided by Lemma 9 is an infinite family for a constant q. Thus, for this instantiation the shares have size $m \cdot \log(q) = \Theta(1 + \lambda/n)$, whereas the secret has size $\rho m n \cdot \log(q) = \Theta(n + \lambda)$. This concludes the proof.

Acknowledgments. We would like to thank the anonymous reviewers of Eurocrypt 2015 for their helpful comments on this work. We would also like to thank Ignacio Cascudo and Irene Giacomelli for helpful discussions and comments.

References

1. Cascudo, I., Damgård, I., David, B., Giacomelli, I., Nielsen, J.B., Trifiletti, R.: Additively homomorphic uc commitments with optimal computational overhead (2014) (manuscript)
2. Cascudo, I., Chen, H., Cramer, R., Xing, C.: Asymptotically Good Ideal Linear Secret Sharing with Strong Multiplication over *Any* Fixed Finite Field. In: Halevi, S. (ed.) CRYPTO 2009. LNCS, vol. 5677, pp. 466–486. Springer, Heidelberg (2009)
3. Cevallos, A., Fehr, S., Ostrovsky, R., Rabani, Y.: Unconditionally-Secure Robust Secret Sharing with Compact Shares. In: Pointcheval, D., Johansson, T. (eds.) EUROCRYPT 2012. LNCS, vol. 7237, pp. 195–208. Springer, Heidelberg (2012)
4. Chen, H., Cramer, R., Goldwasser, S., de Haan, R., Vaikuntanathan, V.: Secure Computation from Random Error Correcting Codes. In: Naor, M. (ed.) EURO-CRYPT 2007. LNCS, vol. 4515, pp. 291–310. Springer, Heidelberg (2007)
5. Cramer, R., Damgård, I.B., Fehr, S.: On the Cost of Reconstructing a Secret, or VSS with Optimal Reconstruction Phase. In: Kilian, J. (ed.) CRYPTO 2001. LNCS, vol. 2139, pp. 503–523. Springer, Heidelberg (2001)
6. Cramer, R., Damgård, I.B., Maurer, U.M.: General Secure Multi-party Computation from any Linear Secret-Sharing Scheme. In: Preneel, B. (ed.) EUROCRYPT 2000. LNCS, vol. 1807, pp. 316–334. Springer, Heidelberg (2000)
7. Cramer, R., Dodis, Y., Fehr, S., Padró, C., Wichs, D.: Detection of Algebraic Manipulation with Applications to Robust Secret Sharing and Fuzzy Extractors. In: Smart, N.P. (ed.) EUROCRYPT 2008. LNCS, vol. 4965, pp. 471–488. Springer, Heidelberg (2008)
8. Damgård, I., David, B., Giacomelli, I., Nielsen, J.B.: Compact vss and efficient homomorphic uc commitments. Cryptology ePrint Archive, Report 2014/370 (2014) (to appear in AsiaCrypt 2014)
9. Druk, E., Ishai, Y.: Linear-time encodable codes meeting the gilbert-varshamov bound and their cryptographic applications. In: ITCS, pp. 169–182 (2014)
10. Garay, J.A., Ishai, Y., Kumaresan, R., Wee, H.: On the Complexity of UC Commitments. In: Nguyen, P.Q., Oswald, E. (eds.) EUROCRYPT 2014. LNCS, vol. 8441, pp. 677–694. Springer, Heidelberg (2014)
11. Guruswami, V., Indyk, P.: Linear-time encodable/decodable codes with near-optimal rate. IEEE Transactions on Information Theory **51**(10), 3393–3400 (2005)

12. Guruswami, V., Rudra, A.: Explicit capacity-achieving list-decodable codes. In: STOC, pp. 1–10 (2006)
13. Guruswami, V., Wang, C.: Linear-algebraic list decoding for variants of reed-solomon codes. IEEE Transactions on Information Theory **59**(6), 3257–3268 (2013)
14. Guruswami, V., Xing, C.: Optimal rate list decoding of folded algebraic-geometric codes over constant-sized alphabets. In: SODA, pp. 1858–1866 (2014)
15. Impagliazzo, R., Levin, L.A., Luby, M.: Pseudo-random generation from one-way functions (extended abstracts). In: Proceedings of the 21st Annual ACM Symposium on Theory of Computing, Seattle, Washigton, USA, May 14–17, pp. 12–24 (1989)
16. Ishai, Y., Kushilevitz, E., Ostrovsky, R., Sahai, A.: Zero-knowledge from secure multiparty computation. In: Proceedings of the 39th Annual ACM Symposium on Theory of Computing, San Diego, California, USA, June 11–13, pp. 21–30 (2007)
17. Ishai, Y., Kushilevitz, E., Ostrovsky, R., Sahai, A.: Cryptography with constant computational overhead. In: STOC, pp. 433–442 (2008)
18. Ishai, Y., Prabhakaran, M., Sahai, A.: Founding Cryptography on Oblivious Transfer – Efficiently. In: Wagner, D. (ed.) CRYPTO 2008. LNCS, vol. 5157, pp. 572–591. Springer, Heidelberg (2008)
19. Krawczyk, H.: Secret Sharing Made Short. In: Stinson, D.R. (ed.) CRYPTO 1993. LNCS, vol. 773, pp. 136–146. Springer, Heidelberg (1994)
20. Mansour, Y., Nisan, N., Tiwari, P.: The computational complexity of universal hashing. In: Proceedings: Fifth Annual Structure in Complexity Theory Conference, Universitat Politècnica de Catalunya, Barcelona, Spain, July 8–11, p. 90 (1990)
21. Massey, J.L.: Some applications of coding theory in cryptography. In: Codes and Ciphers: Cryptography and Coding IV, pp. 33–47 (1995)
22. Mitzenmacher, M., Upfal, E.: Probability and Computing: Randomized Algorithms and Probabilistic Analysis. Cambridge University Press, New York (2005)
23. Shamir, A.: How to share a secret. Commun. ACM **22**(11), 612–613 (1979)
24. Spielman, D.A.: Linear-time encodable and decodable error-correcting codes. In: Proceedings of the Twenty-Seventh Annual ACM Symposium on Theory of Computing, Las Vegas, Nevada, USA, 29 May-1 June, pp. 388–397 (1995)

Function Secret Sharing

Elette Boyle[1]([✉]), Niv Gilboa[2], and Yuval Ishai[1]

[1] Computer Science Department, Technion, Haifa, Israel
eboyle@alum.mit.edu, yuvali@cs.technion.ac.il
[2] Department of Communication Systems Engineering, Ben Gurion University,
Beersheba, Israel
gilboan@bgu.ac.il

Abstract. Motivated by the goal of securely searching and updating distributed data, we introduce and study the notion of *function secret sharing* (FSS). This new notion is a natural generalization of distributed point functions (DPF), a primitive that was recently introduced by Gilboa and Ishai (Eurocrypt 2014). Given a positive integer $p \geq 2$ and a class $\mathcal{F}$ of functions $f : \{0,1\}^n \to \mathbb{G}$, where $\mathbb{G}$ is an Abelian group, a p-party FSS scheme for $\mathcal{F}$ allows one to split each $f \in \mathcal{F}$ into p succinctly described functions $f_i : \{0,1\}^n \to \mathbb{G}$, $1 \leq i \leq p$, such that: (1) $\sum_{i=1}^p f_i = f$, and (2) any strict subset of the f_i hides f. Thus, an FSS for $\mathcal{F}$ can be thought of as method for succinctly performing an "additive secret sharing" of functions from $\mathcal{F}$. The original definition of DPF coincides with a two-party FSS for the class of point functions, namely the class of functions that have a nonzero output on at most one input.

We present two types of results. First, we obtain efficiency improvements and extensions of the original DPF construction. Then, we initiate a systematic study of general FSS, providing some constructions and establishing relations with other cryptographic primitives. More concretely, we obtain the following main results:

- IMPROVED DPF. We present an improved (two-party) DPF construction from a pseudorandom generator (PRG), reducing the length of the key describing each f_i from $O(\lambda \cdot n^{\log_2 3})$ to $O(\lambda n)$, where λ is the PRG seed length.
- MULTI-PARTY DPF. We present the first nontrivial construction of a p-party DPF for $p \geq 3$, obtaining a near-quadratic improvement over a naive construction that additively shares the truth-table of f. This constrcution too can be based on any PRG.
- FSS FOR SIMPLE FUNCTIONS. We present efficient PRG-based FSS constructions for natural function classes that extend point functions, including interval functions and partial matching functions.
- A STUDY OF GENERAL FSS. We show several relations between general FSS and other cryptographic primitives. These include a construction of general FSS via obfuscation, an indication for the

Research supported by the European Union's Tenth Framework Programme (FP10/2010-2016) under grant agreement no. 259426 ERC-CaC. The first and third authors were additionally supported by ISF grants 1361/10 and 1709/14 and BSF grant 2012378.

E. Oswald and M. Fischlin (Eds.): EUROCRYPT 2015, Part II, LNCS 9057, pp. 337–367, 2015.
DOI: 10.1007/978-3-662-46803-6_12

implausibility of constructing general FSS from weak cryptographic assumptions such as the existence of one-way functions, a completeness result, and a relation with pseudorandom functions.

1   Introduction

A secret sharing scheme [44] allows a dealer to randomly split a secret s into p shares, such that certain subsets of the shares can be used to reconstruct the secret and others reveal nothing about it. The simplest type of secret sharing is *additive secret sharing*, where the secret is an element of an Abelian group $\mathbb{G}$, it can be reconstructed by adding all p shares, and every subset of $p-1$ shares reveals nothing about the secret. A useful feature of this secret sharing scheme is that it is *homomorphic* in the sense that if p parties hold shares of many secrets, they can locally compute shares of the sum of all secrets. This feature of additive secret sharing (more generally, linear secret sharing) is useful for many cryptographic applications.

In this work we study the following natural extension of additive secret sharing. Suppose we are given a class $\mathcal{F}$ of efficiently computable and succinctly described functions $f : \{0,1\}^n \rightarrow \mathbb{G}$. Is it possible to split an arbitrary $f \in \mathcal{F}$ into p functions $f_1, \ldots, f_p$ such that: (1) $f(x) = \sum_{i=1}^p f_i(x)$ (on every input x), (2) each f_i is described by a short key k_i that enables its efficient evaluation, yet (3) any strict subset of the keys completely hides f? We refer to a solution to this problem as a *function secret sharing* (FSS) scheme for $\mathcal{F}$.

If one insists on perfectly hiding f, then it can be shown that, even for very simple classes $\mathcal{F}$, the best possible solution is to additively share the truthtable representation of f, whose shares consist of 2^n group elements. But if one considers the computational notion of hiding, then there are no apparent limitations to what can be done for polynomial-time computable f. The power of such computationally hiding FSS schemes is the main question considered in this work.

We note that other types of secret sharing of functions have been considered in the literature, mostly in the context of threshold cryptography (cf. [16,18]). However, these other notions either apply only to very specific function classes that enjoy homomorphism properties compatible with the secret sharing, or alternatively they do not require an additive (or homomorphic) representation of the output which is essential for the applications we consider.

A useful instance of FSS, recently introduced by Gilboa and Ishai [26], is a *distributed point function* (DPF). A DPF can be viewed as a 2-party FSS for the function class $\mathcal{F}$ consisting of all point functions, namely all functions $f : \{0,1\}^n \rightarrow \mathbb{G}$ that evaluate to 0 on all but at most one input. For $x \in \{0,1\}^n$ and $y \in \mathbb{G}$, we denote by $f_{x,y}$ the point function that evaluates to y on input x and to 0 on all other inputs. The main result of [26] was an efficient construction of a DPF from any pseudorandom generator (PRG), or equivalently any one-way function [34].[1] More concretely, given a PRG with seed length λ, the length of each key k_i is $O(\lambda \cdot n^{\log_2 3})$.

The DPF problem was motivated in [26] by applications to improving the communication and computation complexity of 2-server private information retrieval (PIR) [14,15,38] and related problems, as well as by the complexity theoretic problem of worst-case to average-case reductions. To further motivate the questions considered in this work, we discuss two typical application scenarios for DPF and the benefits that could be gained by extending DPF to more general instances of FSS.

MULTI-SERVER PIR AND SECURE KEYWORD SEARCH. Suppose that each of p servers holds a database D of m keywords $w_j \in \{0,1\}^n$. A client wants to count the number of occurrences of a given keyword w without revealing w to any strict subset of the servers. Letting $\mathbb{G} = \mathbb{Z}_{m+1}$ and $f = f_{w,1}$, the client splits f into p additive shares and sends to server i the key k_i describing f_i. Server i computes and sends back to the client $\sum_{w_j \in D} f_i(w_j)$. The client can find the number of matches by adding the p group elements received from the servers. In this application, FSS for other classes $\mathcal{F}$ can be used to accommodate richer types of search queries, such as counting the number of keywords that lie in an interval, satisfy a fuzzy match criterion, etc. We note that by using standard randomized sketching techniques, one can obtain similar solutions that do not only count the number of matches but also return the payloads associated with a bounded number of matches (see, e.g., [41]).

INCREMENTAL SECRET SHARING. Suppose that we want to collect statistics about web usage of mobile devices without compromising the privacy of individual users, and while allowing fast collection of real-time aggregate usage data. A natural solution is to maintain a large secret-shared array of group elements between p servers, where each entry in the array is initialized to 0 and is incremented whenever the corresponding web site is visited. A client who visits URL u can now secret-share the point function $f = f_{u,1}$, and each server i updates its shared entry of each URL u_j by locally adding $f_i(u_j)$ to this share. The end result is that only position u_j in the shared array is incremented, while no collusions involving strict subsets of servers learn which entry was incremented.[2] Here too, applying general FSS can allow for more general "attribute-based" writing patterns, such as secretly incrementing all entries whose public attributes satisfy some secret predicate. The above incremental secret sharing primitive can be used to obtain low-communication solutions to the problem of private information storage [40], the "writing" analogue of PIR.

---

[1] The construction from [26] is described for the special case where $\mathbb{G} = \mathbb{Z}_2^m$, but it can be easily extended to the case of a general Abelian $\mathbb{G}$.

[2] Handling malicious clients who may try to tamper with this process is beyond the scope of this work; we note, however, that due to the succinctness and simple structure of FSS shares one could employ general techniques for secure multiparty computation for this purpose without a major toll on efficiency.

1.1 Our Contribution

In this work we improve and extend the work of [26], presenting two types of results. First, we improve the efficiency of the previous DPF construction and obtain the first nontrivial p-party DPF constructions for $p \geq 3$. Second, we initiate a systematic study of general FSS, providing some constructions and establishing relations with other cryptographic primitives. More concretely, we obtain the following main results:

IMPROVED DPF. We present an improved (two-party) DPF construction from one-way functions, reducing the length of the key describing each f_i from $O(\lambda \cdot n^{\log_2 3})$ to $O(\lambda n)$, where λ is a security parameter (that can be thought of as the seed length of a PRG) and n is the input and output length. We also obtain a similar improvement in the evaluation time. This improvement can have relevance to the practical efficiency of 2-server PIR and related primitives.

MULTI-PARTY DPF. We provide the first nontrivial construction of a p-party DPF for $p \geq 3$, obtaining a near-quadratic improvement over a naive construction that additively shares the truth-table of f. This construction too can be based on the (necessary) assumption that a one-way function exists. More concretely, letting $N = 2^n$ denote the input domain size and λ a PRG seed length, the length of each DPF key k_i is $O(\lambda \cdot 2^{p/2} \cdot N^{1/2})$. Improving the asymptotic dependence on N (without relying on stronger assumptions) is one of the main questions left open by this work. For $p \geq 3$, our p-party DPF implies the first p-server, $(p-1)$-private PIR protocols with sublinear query length and constant answer length, as well as the first $(p-1)$-private sublinear-communication storage schemes in the model of [40].

FSS FOR SIMPLE FUNCTIONS. We present efficient PRG-based FSS constructions for natural function classes that go beyond point functions. These include interval functions and instances of partial matching functions. As illustrated above, such extensions can be used to support more general search queries or selection criteria.

A STUDY OF GENERAL FSS. We initiate a study of general FSS by showing several relations between FSS and other primitives. In particular, we obtain the following results:

– We observe that FSS for general polynomial-time computable functions can be obtained from an ideal obfuscation and one-way functions. This implies (using [2]) a provable construction in the generic multilinear map model, as well as a heuristic construction using existing candidates. Furthermore, building on a recent work of Canetti et al. [13], we obtain a similar result based on Indistinguishability Obfuscation (iO) with sub-exponential security.
– Complementing the above, we give evidence against the possibility of constructing general FSS from weak cryptographic assumptions such as the existence of one-way functions or even oblivious transfer. We do this by showing that general FSS implies low-communication protocols for secure

two-party computation that rely on a *reusable* source of correlated randomness (that can be realized via one-time offline preprocessing). Currently all known approaches for obtaining such protocols rely on fully homomorphic encryption or related primitives. We show that a similar "barrier" applies even to FSS for the complexity class AC^0. This should be contrasted with our PRG-based positive results, which apply to strict sub-classes of AC^0.

- We prove the following completeness result: assuming the hardness of LWE, there is a class $\mathcal{F}$ of functions in NC^1 such that an efficient FSS for $\mathcal{F}$ implies an efficient FSS for arbitrary polynomial-time computable functions.

- We show that in an FSS scheme for any "sufficiently rich" function class $\mathcal{F}$ (which covers point functions as a special case), each share f_i must define a pseudorandom function. Note that this is not a-priori clear from the security definition, which only requires that the shares hide f.

1.2 Related Work

In this section we discuss alternative approaches for tackling the motivating applications for DPF and FSS discussed above. Compared to our PRG-based constructions, all of these approaches have significant limitations in efficiency or security.

INFORMATION-THEORETIC MULTI-SERVER PIR. The notion of p-party DPF roughly corresponds to a p-server PIR protocol with 1-bit answers and computational privacy against any $p-1$ servers. In this setting, insisting on information-theoretic privacy implies that the length of the query sent to each server must be linear in the database size [5,45]. This barrier can be overcome by either settling for a lower privacy threshold $t < p-1$ or allowing for longer answers. (The latter relaxation is not suitable for applications that involve "writing," and results in PIR? protocols that have poor information rate when applied to databases with long records.) Even with the above relaxations, the asymptotic communication complexity of the best known information-theoretic PIR protocols [4,6,15,19,21,47] is worse than that of DPF-based protocols.

SINGLE-SERVER PIR. Single-server, computationally-private PIR protocols [12, 38,39] can achieve similar communication complexity to DPF-based 2-server protocols, and moreover they have the advantages of requiring only one server and not being vulnerable to colluding servers. However, they are not suitable for applications that involve writing, they cannot support constant-size answers, and they do not extend to the richer type of queries supported by our PRG-based FSS constructions (except when using fully homomorphic encryption, discussed below). Perhaps most importantly, single-server PIR protocols make an intensive (and in some sense inherent [20]) use of public-key cryptography, compared to our PRG-based constructions for DPF and simple instances of FSS. Thus, the computational overhead on the server side, which typically forms the practical efficiency bottleneck, can be much lower in DPF-based protocols.

FHE AND TFHE. Fully homomorphic encryption (FHE) [23] can be used to accommodate the richer query types implied by general FSS. However, the other limitations of PIR discussed above apply also to FHE-based protocols, and moreover the concrete computational cost of current implementations is even worse. Constructions of a threshold variant of FHE (TFHE) from [1] can be used to realize a relaxed form of FSS, where the output of the function f is secret-shared in a more redundant way that nevertheless still supports homomorphic additions and allows for efficient decoding of the output from the shares without the knowledge of a secret key. However, TFHE is a stronger primitive than standard FHE and its implementations are even less efficient. We note that our barriers for general FSS from weak assumptions do not apply to FHE-based constructions, leaving open the possibility of realizing our general notion of FSS from FHE or specific assumptions such as LWE.

OBLIVIOUS RAM. Oblivious RAM (ORAM) [31] allows a client to efficiently access data stored on a remote server while hiding the contents of the data and the locations being accessed. However, despite the superficial similarity to the PIR scenario considered here, ORAM addresses a very different problem. In particular, ORAM requires that the client "own" the data and does not directly apply in the case where the data to be accessed comes from other sources, nor does it scale efficiently in the case of read and write operations by many clients who do not trust each other.

Organization. In Sect. 2 we formally define our notion of FSS and discuss several variants and relaxations of this notion. In Sect. 3 we describe new PRG-based constructions of DPF schemes and FSS schemes for simple function classes, as well as a general FSS construction via general-purpose obfuscation. Finally, in Sect. 4 we relate the FSS primitive to other cryptographic primitives and present some barriers to basing general FSS on weak primitives such as a one-way function.

2   Function Secret Sharing

We now formally define our notion of a function secret sharing (FSS) scheme. Recall that, unlike "standard" secret sharing for individual elements, we begin with the description of a *function* f that we wish to share among parties. The FSS scheme provides a means to split this function into separate keys, where each party's key enables him to efficiently generate a standard secret share of the evaluation $f(x)$, and yet each key individually does not reveal information about which function f has been shared.

Note that FSS schemes can differ in the underlying procedure for recovering $f(x)$ from the parties' key-computed shares (including the number of shares), and also in the relevant function class $\mathcal{F}$ for which correctness and security are supported. In what follows, we present a general version of this definition, allowing arbitrary output decoding procedures; however, in this work we focus on the setting in which the output decoder is a fixed *linear function* of parties' output shares. Namely, decoding will correspond to taking the sum of the output shares over an Abelian group structure. We discuss this choice of decoding structures below.

Definition 1 (Output Decoder). *A p-party share output decoder* DEC *is a tuple* $(S_1, \ldots, S_p, R, \mathsf{Dec})$ *specifying: share spaces* $S_1, \ldots, S_p$ *for each of the p parties; output space R; and a decoder function* $\mathsf{Dec} : S_1 \times \cdots \times S_p \to R$ *taking parties' shares to an output.*

We define the p-party additive output decoder for an Abelian group $\mathbb{G}$ *to be the tuple* $\mathsf{DEC} = ((\mathbb{G}, \cdots, \mathbb{G}), \mathbb{G}, \mathsf{Dec}^+)$, *where* $\mathsf{Dec}^+(g_1, \ldots, g_p) = \sum_{i=1}^p g_i$ *computes the sum of elements w.r.t. the group operator of* $\mathbb{G}$.

Remark 1 (Modeling Function Families). We model a function family $\mathcal{F}$ as an infinite collection of bit strings f ("functions"), together with efficient procedures IdentifyDomain and Evaluate, such that the procedure $D_f \leftarrow \mathsf{IdentifyDomain}(1^\lambda, f)$ interprets from the string f its corresponding input domain space, and $y \leftarrow \mathsf{Evaluate}(f, x)$, for any input $x \in D_f$, defines the "output" of f at x. By convention, we assume the description of f includes also the input length and output length of f. We refer the reader to e.g. [36] for a complete formal description of this model.

For simplicity of notation, in this work we will refer to the domain D_f of f without making explicit reference to the corresponding call to IdentifyDomain, and will denote an evaluation $\mathsf{Evaluate}(f, x)$ by shorthand notation "$f(x)$."

Definition 2 (Function Secret Sharing). *For* $p \in \mathbb{N}, T \subseteq [p]$, *a p-party, T-secure function secret sharing (FSS) scheme with respect to share output decoder* $\mathsf{DEC} = (S_1, \ldots, S_p, R, \mathsf{Dec})$ *and function class* $\mathcal{F}$ *is a pair of PPT algorithms* (Gen, Eval) *with the following syntax:*

- Gen$(1^\lambda, f)$: *On input the security parameter* 1^λ *and function description* $f \in \mathcal{F}$, *the key generation algorithm outputs p keys,* $(k_1, \ldots, k_p)$.
- Eval(i, k_i, x): *On input a party index i, key* k_i *(which we assume to encode the input and output domains* D, R *of the shared function) and input string* $x \in D$, *the evaluation algorithm outputs a value* $y_i \in S_i$, *corresponding to this party's share of* $f(x)$.

satisfying the following correctness and secrecy requirements:

- **Correctness:** *For all* $f \in \mathcal{F}, x \in D_f$,

$$\Pr\left[(k_1, \ldots, k_p) \leftarrow \mathsf{Gen}(1^\lambda, f)\right.$$
$$\left. : \mathsf{Dec}\big(\mathsf{Eval}(1, k_1, x), \ldots, \mathsf{Eval}(p, k_p, x)\big) = f(x)\right] = 1.$$

- **Security:** *Consider the following indistinguishability challenge experiment for corrupted parties* $T \subset [p]$:
    1: *The adversary outputs* $(f_0, f_1, ,) \leftarrow \mathcal{A}(1^\lambda)$, *where* $f_0, f_1 \in \mathcal{F}$ *with* $D_{f_0} = D_{f_1}$.
    2: *The challenger samples* $b \leftarrow \{0, 1\}$ *and* $(k_1, \ldots, k_p) \leftarrow \mathsf{Gen}(1^\lambda, f_b)$.
    3: *The adversary outputs a guess* $b' \leftarrow \mathcal{A}((k_i)_{i \in T}, ,)$, *given the keys for corrupted T.*

Denote by $\mathsf{Adv}(1^\lambda, \mathcal{A}) := \Pr[b = b'] - 1/2$ *as the advantage of $\mathcal{A}$ in guessing b in the above experiment, where probability is taken over the randomness of the challenger and of $\mathcal{A}$. We say the scheme* $(\mathsf{Gen}, \mathsf{Eval})$ *is T-secure if there exists a negligible function ν such that for all non-uniform PPT adversaries $\mathcal{A}$, it holds that* $\mathsf{Adv}(1^\lambda, \mathcal{A}) \le \nu(\lambda)$.

Unless otherwise specified, we naturally interpret the output domain of the function f as an Abelian group $\mathbb{G}$ (in particular, $\{0, 1\}^n$ is interpreted as an Abelian group with respect to the xor group operator $\oplus$), and DEC *is the corresponding additive output decoder as specified in Definition 1.*

Remark 2. A few remarks about our definition.

1. (Adversary Structure). We say an FSS scheme is *t-secure* for threshold $t < p$ if it is T-secure for all $T \subset [p]$ of size $|T| \le t$. By default, when not otherwise specified, "secure FSS" will refer to $(p-1)$-security, in which any strict subset of parties may be corrupted.
2. (Variable Output Domains). For simplicity, we take the convention that all functions within a class $\mathcal{F}$ share the same output domain (i.e., $f : D_f \to R$ for shared R). We may also extend in a straightforward way to the setting in which each function f has a possibly different output domain R_f. The corresponding security will be required to hold with respect to pairs of functions $f_0, f_1 \in \mathcal{F}$ with both matching domains ($D_{f_0} = D_{f_1}$) *and* ranges ($R_{f_0} = R_{f_1}$).
3. (Simulation-Based Security). Our game-based security definition mirrors that of semantic security, where the shares of corrupted parties play the role of an "encryption" of f. As with semantic security, our game-based indistinguishability security definition can equivalently be expressed as a *simulation-based* definition, where one must be able to simulate the distribution of corrupted parties' shares without knowledge of the shared function f (*cf.* [28,32]).

Output Decoding Schemes. The FSS definition above is presented with respect to an arbitrary choice of output decoding function Dec. Based on the structure of the chosen decoding process, the corresponding FSS scheme will have very different properties. For example, more complex decoding procedures Dec open the possibility of achieving FSS for more general classes of functions $\mathcal{F}$, but place limits on the applicability of the resulting scheme. Many choices for the structure of the output decoding function yield uninteresting notions, as we now discuss.

Arbitrary Reconstruction. Consider, for example, the FSS notion as defined, but with *no restriction* on the reconstruction procedure for parties' output shares. Such wide freedom will render the notion non-meaningful, as it gives rise to trivial constructions. Indeed, for any efficient function family $\mathcal{F}$, one can generate FSS keys for a secret function $f \in \mathcal{F}$ simply by sharing a description of f interpreted as a string, using a standard secret sharing scheme. The evaluation procedure on any input x will simply output x together with the party's share of f, and the decoding procedure Dec will first reconstruct the description of f, and then compute and output the value $f(x)$.

This construction satisfies correctness and security as specified above (indeed, each party's key individually reveals no information on f). But, the scheme clearly leaves much to be desired in terms of utility: From just one evaluation, the entire function f is revealed to whichever party receives and reconstructs these output shares. At such point, the whole notion of function secret sharing becomes moot.

"Function-Private" Output Shares. Instead, from a function secret sharing scheme, one would hope that parties' output shares (resulting from executing Eval) for input x do not reveal more about the secret function f than is necessary to determine $f(x)$. That is, we may impose a "function privacy" requirement on the reconstruction scheme, requiring that pairs of parties' output shares for each input x can be simulated given just the corresponding outputs $f(x)$.

This requirement is both natural and beneficial, but by itself still allows for undesired constructions. For example, given a secret function f, take one FSS key to be a *garbled circuit* of f, and the second key as the information that enables translating inputs x to garbled input labels. This provides a straightforward function-private solution for one output evaluation, and can easily be extended to the many-output case by adding shared secret randomness to the parties' keys.[3] Yet this construction (and thus definition) is unsatisfying: although the output shares now hide f, their size is massive—for every output, comparable to a copy of f itself.

Succinct, Function-Private Output Shares. We thus further restrict the scheme, demanding additionally that output shares be *succinct*: i.e., comparable in size to the function output. This definition already captures a strong, interesting primitive. For example, as shown in Section 4.2, achieving such an FSS scheme for general functions implies a form of communication-efficient secure multi-party computation that is currently only achievable using advanced cryptographic machinery (i.e., fully homomorphic encryption or reusable garbled circuits). However, there is one final property that enables an important class of applications, but which is not yet guaranteed: a notion of *share compressibility*.

Let us explore this property. Recall that one of the exciting application regimes of distributed point functions (DPF) [26] was enabling communication-efficient secure (2-server) Private Information Retrieval (PIR). Intuitively, to privately recover an item x_i from a database held by both servers, one can generate and distribute a pair of DPF keys encoding a point function f_i whose only nonzero output is at secret location i. Each server then responds with a *single* element, computed as the weighted sum of each data item x_j with the server's output share of the evaluation $f_i(x_j)$. Correctness of the DPF scheme implies that the xor of the two servers' replies is precisely the desired data item x_i,

---

[3] Namely, for each new x, the parties will first use their shared randomness to coordinately rerandomize the garbled circuit of f and input labels, respectively.

while security guarantees the servers learn nothing about the index i. But most importantly, the linear structure of the DPF reconstruction enabled the output shares pertaining to all the different elements of the database to be *compressed* into a single short response.

On the other hand, consider, for example, the PIR scenario but where the servers instead hold shares of the function f_i with respect to a *bitwise AND* reconstruction of output shares in the place of xor/addition. Recovery of the requested data item x_i now implies computing set intersection—and thus requires communication complexity equal to the size of the database [37]! In extending the DPF notion to more general FSS primitives, we wish to preserve and extend this class of applications. We thus maintain the crucial property that output shares can be combined and compressed in a meaningful way. To do so, we remain in stride with the *linearity* of output share decoding.

Our setting: Linear share decoding. In this work, we focus purely on the setting of FSS where the output decoder is a *linear function* of parties' shares: specifically, the additive output decoder as in Definition 1. This clean, intuitive structure in fact provides the desired properties discussed above: Linearity of reconstruction provides convenient share *compressibility*. Output shares must themselves be elements of the function output space, immediately guaranteeing share *succinctness*. And as we show in Section 4.1, the linear reconstruction in conjunction with basic key security directly implies *function privacy*.

We hence restrict our attention to this setting, and unless otherwise specified will implicitly take an "FSS scheme" to be one with a linear reconstruction procedure DEC defined above.

2.1 Preliminaries

In this work, we make use of several cryptographic tools. For formal definitions of the notions of *computational indistinguishability, pseudorandom generators,* and *pseudorandom functions,* we refer the reader to [28]. For *fully homomorphic encryption* definitions and constructions, see, e.g., [10,23,25]. And, for program obfuscation, see *virtual black-box* [3], *indistinguishability obfuscation (iO)* [3,22], and *probabilistic iO* [13].

3　New Constructions

In the following section, we present several new constructions of FSS schemes for various function families.

We begin in Section 3.1 by showing two new constructions for the family of *point functions*. The first is a two-key construction that significantly reduces the key size and computational complexity compared to all previous constructions. The second is the first p-key construction, secure against coalitions of up to $p-1$ key holders, with key size a square root of what a trivial construction achieves.

In Section 3.2, we go beyond the family of point functions in several ways. We identify general low-level transformations that modify an existing FSS scheme into one for a modified function class. We combine some of these general transformations, in addition to existing FSS schemes, to yield constructions for more expressive function families. In addition, we extend the previous results for point functions to include the family of interval functions with minimal overhead.

In Section 3.3, we show that FSS for *general efficient functionalities* is implied by certain forms of program obfuscation (namely, virtual black-box or subexponentially secure indistinguishability obfuscation).

3.1 Point Functions

Definition 3. *For $a, b \in \{0, 1\}^n$, the* point function $P_{a,b} : \{0, 1\}^n \to \{0, 1\}^m$ *is defined by $P_{a,b}(a) = b$ and $P_{a,b}(a') = 0^m$ for all $a' \neq a$.*

We begin by describing a construction for the class of two-party point functions $P_{a,b}(x) : \{0, 1\}^n \to \{0, 1\}^m$. The scheme we show, $(\mathsf{Gen}^\bullet, \mathsf{Eval}^\bullet)$, reduces the key size and the computational complexity compared to the construction of distributed point functions in [26], from $O(\lambda n^{\log 3})$ to $O(\lambda n)$, making use of a pseudorandom generator with seed length λ. $(\mathsf{Gen}^\bullet, \mathsf{Eval}^\bullet)$ are given by Algorithms 1 and 2.

At a high level, the scheme works as follows. Each party's key, k_0 and k_1, defines a binary tree of depth n with a pseudo-random string at each node (the strings are the $S\|T$'s defined in lines 9 and 10 of Algorithm 2). The binary trees defined by k_0 and k_1 are identical except for the path from the root to the target point $a = a_1, \ldots, a_n$. On this path, the strings in the two trees are chosen pseudo-randomly and independently of each other.

$\mathsf{Eval}^\bullet(\beta, k_\beta, x)$ traverses a path in the tree that k_β defines from the root to $x = x_1, \ldots, x_n$, computing the strings along the path. At each node with string $S_0^\beta[i]\|S_1^\beta[i]\|T_0^\beta[i]\|T_1^\beta[i]$, $\mathsf{Eval}^\bullet$ computes the corresponding strings for its x_ith child (left or right) by expanding either the left or right seed $S_{x_i}^\beta[i]$ using the pseudo-random generator $G(S_{x_i}^\beta[i])$, and adding in "correction" strings cs, ct (from the key k_β) to the corresponding "s" and "t" portions of the expanded output, as dictated by the bit $T_{x_i}^\beta[i]$.

The function of $\mathsf{Gen}^\bullet(1^\lambda, a, b)$ is to ensure the correct creation of the two trees. Specifically, it ensures that at the exact point that a prefix of x diverges from the path to a, $\mathsf{Eval}^\bullet(0, k_0, x)$ and $\mathsf{Eval}^\bullet(1, k_1, x)$ compute the *same* strings S, T. (Then, for any path continuing from this point, the values will always remain equal). For prefixes that diverge at the root (i.e., $a_1 \neq x_1$), each key includes the same string since lines 2, 3 sets $S_{\neg a_1}^1[1] = S_{\neg a_1}^0[1]$ and $T_{\neg a_1}^1[1] = T_{\neg a_1}^0[1]$ (superscript here is party id). Any other location of diverging prefixes is resolved by setting the correct strings cs, ct in lines 6-9 of Algorithm 1.

$\mathsf{Gen}^\bullet$ has a negligble probability of failure (expressed by setting $w \leftarrow 0$), which is a result of generating equal random values for $S_{a_n}^0[n] = S_{a_n}^1[n]$. It is always possible to run $\mathsf{Gen}^\bullet$ again if it fails. In Algorithm 5 we show how to obtain a scheme without any error.

Intuitively, security holds for (Gen$^\bullet$, Eval$^\bullet$) because all information related to the point function $f_{a,b}$ is encoded in the strings $cs, ct, masked$ by pseudorandom strings whose seeds appear only in the other party's key. Note that the original values S, T in lines 2,3 are completely independent of the point function.

Due to space limitations, we refer the reader to the full version of this work for a complete proof of correctness and security of (Gen$^\bullet$, Eval$^\bullet$).

Notation 1. *We use the following notational conventions in Algorithms 1 and 2. Superscripts denote the party id, and are used for strings appearing in the tree defined by this party's key. Square brackets denote the depth of a node in the tree, ranging from 1 to n. One or two binary-valued subscripts are used to distinguish between strings that are associated with a specific node in the tree (e.g., to be used when continuing to the left or right from this node). For example $S_\alpha^\beta[i]$ is in the tree defined by party β's key k_β at depth i, and is one of two strings (the other is $S_{\neg\alpha}^\beta[i]$) at a specific node in the tree.*

Algorithm 1. Gen$^\bullet$($1^\lambda, a, b$)

1: Let $G : \{0,1\}^\lambda \longrightarrow \{0,1\}^{\max\{2\lambda+2,m\}}$ be a PRG.
2: Choose three random seeds $S_{a_1}^0[1], S_{a_1}^1[1], S_{\neg a_1}^0[1] \in \{0,1\}^\lambda$ and set $S_{\neg a_1}^1[1] \leftarrow S_{\neg a_1}^0[1]$.
3: Choose four random bits $T_\alpha^\beta[1]$, for $\alpha, \beta \in \{0,1\}$, subject to $T_{a_1}^0[1] \neq T_{a_1}^1[1]$ and $T_{\neg a_1}^0[1] = T_{\neg a_1}^1[1]$.
4: **for** $i = 1$ to $n-1$ **do**
5:     Let $G(S_{a_i}^\beta[i]) = s_0^\beta \| s_1^\beta \| t_0^\beta \| t_1^\beta$, where $s_\alpha^\beta \in \{0,1\}^\lambda$, $t_\alpha^\beta \in \{0,1\}$ for $\alpha, \beta \in \{0,1\}$.
6:     Randomly choose $cs_{0,a_{i+1}}, cs_{1,a_{i+1}} \in \{0,1\}^\lambda$.
7:     Randomly choose $cs_{0,\neg a_{i+1}}, cs_{1,\neg a_{i+1}} \in \{0,1\}^\lambda$ subject to $\bigoplus_{\beta=0}^1 (cs_{\beta,\neg a_{i+1}} \oplus s_{\neg a_{i+1}}^\beta) = 0$.
8:     Randomly choose $ct_{0,a_{i+1}}, ct_{1,a_{i+1}} \in \{0,1\}$ subject to $\bigoplus_{\beta=0}^1 (ct_{\beta,a_{i+1}} \oplus t_{a_{i+1}}^\beta) = 1$.
9:     Randomly choose $ct_{0,\neg a_{i+1}}, ct_{1,\neg a_{i+1}} \in \{0,1\}$ subject to $\bigoplus_{\beta=0}^1 (ct_{\beta,\neg a_{i+1}} \oplus t_{\neg a_{i+1}}^\beta) = 0$.
10:    Set $CW_\beta[i] \leftarrow cs_{\beta,0} \| cs_{\beta,1} \| ct_{\beta,0} \| ct_{\beta,1}$ for $\beta = 0, 1$.
11:    Set $S_\alpha^\beta[i+1] \leftarrow s_\alpha^\beta \oplus cs_{\tau,\alpha}$ for $\tau = T_{a_i}^\beta[i]$ and $\alpha, \beta \in \{0,1\}$.
12:    Set $T_\alpha^\beta[i+1] \leftarrow t_\alpha^\beta \oplus ct_{\tau,\alpha}$ for $\tau = T_{a_i}^\beta[i]$ and $\alpha, \beta \in \{0,1\}$.
13: **end for**
14: **if** $G(S_{a_n}^0[n]) \neq G(S_{a_n}^1[n])$ **then**
15:    Set $w \leftarrow (G(S_{a_n}^0[n]) + G(S_{a_n}^1[n]))^{-1} \cdot b$ with arithmetic over $\mathbb{F}_{2^m}$.
16: **else**
17:    Set $w \leftarrow 0$.
18: **end if**
19: Set $k_\beta \leftarrow ((S_0^\beta[1], S_1^\beta[1], T_0^\beta[1], T_1^\beta[1]), (CW_0[1], CW_1[1], \ldots, CW_0[n-1], CW_1[n-1]), w)$.
20: Return (k_0, k_1).

Algorithm 2. Eval$^\bullet(\beta, k_\beta, x)$

1: Let $G : \{0,1\}^\lambda \longrightarrow \{0,1\}^{\max\{2\lambda+2,m\}}$ be a PRG.
2: Let the binary representation of x be $x = x_1, \ldots, x_n$.
3: Parse k_β as $k_\beta = ((S_0^\beta[1], S_1^\beta[1], T_0^\beta[1], T_1^\beta[1]), (CW_0[1], CW_1[1], \ldots, CW_0[n-1], CW_1[n-1]), w)$.
4: Set $S \leftarrow S_{x_1}^\beta[1]$.
5: Set $T \leftarrow T_{x_1}^\beta[1]$.
6: **for** $i = 2$ to n **do**
7:     Parse $G(S)$ as $G(S) = s_0 || s_1 || t_0 || t_1$.
8:     Parse $CW_T[i-1]$ as $CW_T[i-1] = cs_{T,0} || cs_{T,1} || ct_{T,0} || ct_{T,1}$.
9:     Set $S \leftarrow s_{x_i} \oplus cs_{T,x_i}$.
10:    Set $T \leftarrow t_{x_i} \oplus ct_{T,x_i}$.
11: **end for**
12: Return $G(S) \cdot w$ with arithmetic over $\mathbb{F}_{2^m}$.

A p-party protocol. For some applications, one may wish to share a function f among *several parties*. In this setting, there is an additional challenge in maintaining security against collusions of corrupted parties. Note that for any family of functions $\mathcal{F} : \{0,1\}^n \to \{0,1\}^m$, we can trivially support secret sharing of $\mathcal{F}$ across p parties with security against coalitions of up to $p-1$ keys, with key size $2^n \cdot m$. Indeed, this amounts to simply secret sharing the entire evaluation table of the function f among parties as a string: $\mathsf{Gen}(1^\lambda, f)$ chooses p random strings $k_1, \ldots, k_p \in \{0,1\}^{2^n \cdot m}$ such that $\bigoplus_{i=1}^p k_i[x] = f(x)$ for all $x \in \{0,1\}^n$.

We now present a scheme $(\mathsf{Gen}^{p_0}, \mathsf{Eval}^{p_0})$ sharing a DPF $P_{a,b} : \{0,1\}^n \to \{0,1\}^m$, secure against any coalition of at most $p-1$ key holders, and with key length $O(2^{n/2} \cdot 2^{p/2} \cdot m)$. For a constant number of parties $p \in O(1)$, this corresponds to a square root of the key length in the trivial solution. At a high level, the scheme $(\mathsf{Gen}^{p_0}, \mathsf{Eval}^{p_0})$ works as follows. Consider the 2^n-entry evaluation table of the secret function $f_{a,b}$ as a $2^{n/2} \times 2^{n/2}$ grid[4], where rows and columns are indexed by the first and second $n/2$ bits of the input. The algorithm Gen^{p_0} generates the following values: For each row $\gamma' \in \{0,1\}^{n/2}$ in this table, it samples 2^{p-1} random λ-bit strings $s_{\gamma',1}, \ldots, s_{\gamma',2^{p-1}} \in \{0,1\}^\lambda$ to be used as seeds for a pseudorandom generator (PRG) G. In addition, it generates 2^{p-1} total (not per row) "correction words" $cw_1, \ldots, cw_{2^{p-1}} \in (\{0,1\}^m)^{2^{n/2}}$, as a function of the strings $s_{\gamma',\ell}$ and the secret function $P_{a,b}$. Each party i receives as its key the collection of all 2^{p-1} correction words and some subset of the PRG seeds. The algorithm Eval^{p_0}, given a party's key and input x, parses $x = (\gamma', \delta') \in \{0,1\}^{n/2} \times \{0,1\}^{n/2}$, takes its set of PRG seeds corresponding to the row γ', expands each via G to a vector $(\{0,1\}^m)^{2^{n/2}}$ which matches the form of a row in the function evaluation table, takes the exclusive-or of all the expanded vectors together with the corresponding subset of correction words

---

[4] The dimensions of the table in the algorithm are slightly different, which results in reducing the key size by a factor of $2^{p/2}$.

(i.e. the subset of $\{cw_j : j \in [2^{p-1}]\}$ for which its key contained the jth row-γ' seed $s_{\gamma',j}$), and outputs the (δ')th component of this row vector. Collectively, this description corresponds to Step 6 of Algorithm 4.

The subset of seeds, and the generation of the correction words is chosen by Gen^{Po} so as to ensure the following properties:

1. For each row γ' *not* equal to the special row γ, and for each of the 2^{p-1} PRG seeds $s_{\gamma',j}$ corresponding to this row, it will hold that the number of parties holding $s_{\gamma',j}$ in their key is *even*. Thus, during the evaluation phase, all contributions from $G(s_{\gamma',j})$ and from its corresponding jth correction word cw_j will cancel out, leaving the desired 0 evaluation.

2. For the special row γ, each $s_{\gamma,j}$ will appear in an *odd* number of parties' keys. This means there will be exactly one copy of each $G(s_{\gamma,j})$ and each cw_j remaining in the combined evaluation xor from all parties. Further, for each party i, there is at least one seed $s_{\gamma,j}$ (in our construction, exactly one) for which party i is the *only* party given $s_{\gamma,j}$. This will be important for security, as $G(s_{\gamma,j})$ for the uncorrupted party will serve as a mask to hide information on $P_{a,b}$ in the correction words.

3. Given any $p-1$ keys, Case (1) and (2) are indistinguishable.

4. The correction words $cw_j, j \in [2^{p-1}]$ are chosen randomly subject to the constraint $\bigoplus_{j=1}^{2^{p-1}} (cw_j \oplus G(s_{\gamma,j})) = e_\delta \cdot b$, where e_δ denotes the unit vector whose δth component is equal to 1. From Property (2), this constraint exactly yields the required correctness guarantee. And, since the cw_j are random up to this condition, then even given any $(2^{p-1} - 1)$ of the seeds $s_{\gamma,j}$ (but with one missing), the distribution of these seeds together with all the cw_j's is computationally indistinguishable from random.

We now proceed to describe the scheme with these properties.

Given natural numbers p and q, it is readily apparent that for exactly q^{p-1} of the sequences of length p over the set $\{0, \ldots, q-1\}$ the sum of the p elements modulo q is 0 and for exactly q^{p-1} of these sequences the sum of all the elements modulo q is 1. (One way to deduce this statement is that given any choice of the first $p-1$ elements in $\{0, \ldots, q-1\}$ there is a single choice for the last element that makes the sum of the whole sequence 1 and a single choice that makes the sum 0). For the special case of $q = 2$ we introduce the following useful notation.

Notation 2. *Given $p \in \mathbb{N}$, let E_p and O_p denote subsets of binary arrays of size $p \times 2^{p-1}$. Let E_p denote the set of all arrays such that the columns of each array are all the p-bit strings with an even number of 1 bits and let O_p denote the set of all arrays such that the columns of each array are all the p-bit strings with an odd number of 1 bits. We use $A \in_R E_p$ (or $A \in_R O_p$) to denote that A is randomly sampled from E_p (O_p). We use $e_a \cdot b$ to denote a vector of length $2^{|a|}$ with b in location a and 0 in all other locations.*

We present the p-party FSS scheme for point functions $(\mathsf{Gen}^{Po}, \mathsf{Eval}^{Po})$ in Algorithms 3 and 4.

Algorithm 3. $\text{Gen}^{p_0}(1^\lambda, a, b)$

1: Let $G : \{0,1\}^\lambda \longrightarrow \{0,1\}^{m\mu}$ be a PRG (μ is defined in line 2).
2: Let $\mu \leftarrow \lceil 2^{n/2} \cdot 2^{(p-1)/2} \rceil$ and let $\nu \leftarrow \lceil 2^n/\mu \rceil$.
3: Regard a as a pair $a = (\gamma, \delta)$, $\gamma \in [\nu], \delta \in [\mu]$.
4: Choose ν arrays $A_1, \ldots, A_\nu$, s.t. $A_\gamma \in_R O_p$ and $A_{\gamma'} \in_R E_p$ for all $\gamma' \neq \gamma$.
5: Choose randomly and independently $\nu \cdot 2^{p-1}$ seeds $s_{1,1}, \ldots, s_{\nu,2^{p-1}} \in \{0,1\}^\lambda$.
6: Choose 2^{p-1} random strings $cw_1, \ldots, cw_{2^{p-1}} \in \{0,1\}^{m\mu}$ s.t. $\bigoplus_{j=1}^{2^{p-1}}(cw_j \oplus G(s_{\gamma,j})) = e_\delta \cdot b$.
7: Set $\sigma_{i,\gamma'} \leftarrow (s_{\gamma',1} \cdot A_{\gamma'}[i,1]) || \ldots || (s_{\gamma',2^{p-1}} \cdot A_{\gamma'}[i,2^{p-1}])$ for all $1 \leq i \leq p, 1 \leq \gamma' \leq \nu$.
8: Set $\sigma_i = \sigma_{i,1} || \ldots || \sigma_{i,\nu}$ for $1 \leq i \leq p$.
9: Let $k_i = (\sigma_i || cw_1 || \ldots || cw_{2^{p-1}})$ for $1 \leq i \leq p$.
10: Return $(k_1, \ldots, k_p)$.

Algorithm 4. $\text{Eval}^{p_0}(i, k_i, x)$

1: Let $G : \{0,1\}^\lambda \longrightarrow \{0,1\}^{m\mu}$ be a PRG (μ is defined in line 2).
2: Let $\mu \leftarrow \lceil 2^{n/2} \cdot 2^{(p-1)/2} \rceil$ and let $\nu \leftarrow \lceil 2^n/\mu \rceil$.
3: Regard x as a pair $x = (\gamma', \delta')$, $\gamma' \in [\nu], \delta' \in [\mu]$.
4: Parse k_i as $k_i = (\sigma_i, cw_1, \ldots, cw_{2^{p-1}})$.
5: Parse σ_i as $\sigma_i = s_{1,1} || \ldots || s_{1,2^{p-1}} || \ldots || s_{\nu,2^{p-1}}$.
6: Let $y_i \leftarrow \bigoplus_{\substack{1 \leq j \leq 2^{p-1} \\ s_{\gamma',j} \neq 0}}(cw_j \oplus G(s_{\gamma',j}))$.
7: Return $y_i[\delta']$.

We informally argue that $(\text{Gen}^{p_0}, \text{Eval}^{p_0})$ is an FSS scheme for point functions. The scheme is correct because of the following. If $\text{Gen}^{p_0}(k_i, x)$ outputs $(k_1, \ldots, k_p)$ then $\bigoplus_{i=1}^p \text{Eval}^{p_0}(i, k_i, x) = \bigoplus_{i=1}^p y_i[\delta']$. If $\gamma' \neq \gamma$ then $A_{\gamma'} \in E_p$ and hence each of the terms $cw_j \oplus G(s_{\gamma',j})$ appears an even number of times in $\bigoplus_{i=1}^p y_i$, therefore canceling out and ensuring that $\bigoplus_{i=1}^p y = 0$. However, if $\gamma' = \gamma$ then $\bigoplus_{i=1}^p y_i = \sum_{j=1}^{2^{p-1}} cw_j \oplus G(s_{\gamma,j})$. By the definition of the correction words $cw_1, \ldots, cw_{2^{p-1}}$ we have that $\bigoplus_{i=1}^p y_i[\delta'] = 0$ if $\delta' \neq \delta$ while $\bigoplus_{i=1}^p y_i[\delta'] = b$ if $\delta' = \delta$, i.e. if $x = a$.

The scheme $(\text{Gen}^{p_0}, \text{Eval}^{p_0})$ is secret because each subset of at most $p-1$ keys k_i includes $p-1$ strings $\sigma_i = \sigma_{i,1}, \ldots, \sigma_{i,\nu}$. The distribution of seeds in $\sigma_{i,\gamma'}$ reflects the distribution of 1 bits in the i-th row of $A_{\gamma'}$. However, any $p-1$ rows of $A_{\gamma'}$ are distributed identically, regardless of whether $A_{\gamma'}$ is sampled randomly from E_p or it is sampled randomly from O_p. Therefore, the view of the strings σ_i does not give any information on γ. In addition, $cw_1, \ldots, cw_{2^{p-1}}$ are masked by $\bigoplus_{j=1}^{2^{p-1}} G(s_{\gamma,j})$ and there is at least one seed $s_{\gamma,j}$ which is not included in any of the keys in the subset. Therefore, all the correction words together cannot be distinguished from random strings of the appropriate length.

The length of a key k_i that Gen^{p_0} outputs is a sum of the length of σ_i, which is $\nu\lambda \cdot 2^{p-1}$ and the length of the correction words, which is $\mu m \cdot 2^{p-1}$. The key size is therefore $O(2^{n/2} 2^{(p-1)/2}(\lambda + m))$.

3.2 Supporting New Function Classes

In Sections 3.2, 3.2, and 3.2, we (1) present general transformations for obtaining FSS for new function classes from existing ones, (2) provide an extension of the improved DPF construction from the previous section to support the more general class of interval functions with minimal increase in key size, and (3) extend further to the case of *many* parties, where security is required to hold against coalitions of parties.

General Transformations. We begin by describing a number of general transformations to convert one or more existing function secret sharing schemes into a new FSS scheme supporting a modified class of functions. The important metrics to maintain are the key size and computation time of the modified scheme, as a function of the original(s). Slightly abusing notation, we denote by $\mathsf{size}(\mathcal{F})$ and $\mathsf{time}(\mathcal{F})$ the corresponding values for the key size and computation time for the FSS scheme for $\mathcal{F}$ (where the FSS scheme being referred to is clear from context).

Due to space constraints, we provide here only a brief summary of the relevant closure properties, and defer their corresponding constructions and proofs to the full version of the paper.

1. **Including the Zero Function:** $\mathcal{F} \to \mathcal{F} \cup \{0\}$.
   For any FSS scheme for class $\mathcal{F}$, there exists a FSS scheme for the class $\mathcal{F}$ together with the all 0s function, $0(x) = 0 \; \forall x$. It holds that $\mathsf{size}(\mathcal{F} \cup \{0\}) = \mathsf{size}(\mathcal{F})$, $\mathsf{time}(\mathcal{F} \cup \{0\}) = \mathsf{time}(\mathcal{F})$.

2. **Pre-composition with Arbitrary Function:** $(\mathcal{F}, g) \to \mathcal{F} \circ g$.
   For any FSS scheme for function class $\mathcal{F} = \{f : \mathbb{G}_1 \to \mathbb{G}\}$, and arbitrary fixed public function $g : \mathbb{G}_2 \to \mathbb{G}_1$, there exists an FSS scheme for class $\mathcal{F} \circ g := \{f \circ g : \mathbb{G}_2 \to \mathbb{G} | f \in \mathcal{F}\}$, (where functions in $\mathcal{F} \circ g$ are described as the pair (f, g)). The resulting key size is equal to $|g| + \mathsf{size}(\mathcal{F})$, and the computation time is $|g| + \mathsf{time}(\mathcal{F})$.

   This transformation extends to the case where the choice of function g may be made *dependent* on the secret function f, as long as the corresponding distribution of g is computationally indistinguishable from one independent of f. For example, g may consist of an encryption of some portion of f; indeed, such an approach can be used to bootstrap an FSS scheme for NC^1 to one supporting all $P/poly$, making use of fully homomorphic encryption (see Section 4.3).

3. **Post-composition with Linear Function:** $(\mathcal{F}, L) \to L \circ \mathcal{F}$.
   For any FSS for function class $\mathcal{F} = \{f : \mathbb{G}_1 \to \mathbb{G}\}$ and for any fixed linear function $L : \mathbb{G} \to \mathbb{G}_0$, there exists a FSS scheme for class $L \circ \mathcal{F} := \{L \circ f | f \in \mathcal{F}\}$ of functions from $\mathbb{G} \to \mathbb{G}_0$ (where functions $(L \circ f) \in L \circ \mathcal{F}$ are described by the pair (L, f)). The resulting scheme satisfies $\mathsf{size}(L \circ \mathcal{F}) = \mathsf{size}(\mathcal{F}) + |L|$ and $\mathsf{time}(L \circ \mathcal{F}) = \mathsf{time}(\mathcal{F}) + |L|$.

4. **Linear Combination of FSSes:** $(\mathcal{F}, \mathcal{G}) \to \mathcal{F} + \mathcal{G}$.
   Given FSS schemes for families $\mathcal{F}, \mathcal{G}$ taking $\mathbb{G}_1 \to \mathbb{G}$, there exists an FSS

scheme for class $\mathcal{F} + \mathcal{G} := \{f \oplus g | f \in \mathcal{F}, g \in \mathcal{G}\}$, with key size equal to $\mathsf{size}(\mathcal{F}+\mathcal{G}) = \mathsf{size}(\mathcal{F}) + \mathsf{size}(\mathcal{G})$ and evaluation time $\mathsf{time}(\mathcal{F}+\mathcal{G}) = \mathsf{time}(\mathcal{F}) + \mathsf{time}(\mathcal{G})$.

5. **Union of Function Families:** $(\mathcal{F}_1, \mathcal{F}_2) \to \mathcal{F}_1 \cup \mathcal{F}_2$.
   Given FSS schemes for families $\mathcal{F}, \mathcal{G}$, there exists an FSS scheme for the class $\mathcal{F} \cup \mathcal{G}$, with key size and time complexities as in Transformation 4 (combining with Transformation 1).

6. **FSS for Small Function Classes:** Arbitrary $\mathcal{F}$, with $\mathsf{time}(\mathcal{F}) \sim |\mathcal{F}|$, but short keys. For *any* class of functions $\mathcal{F}$ with some canonical indexing, and a DPF (i.e., FSS for class of point functions) with domain size $|\mathcal{F}|$, there exists an FSS scheme for $\mathcal{F}$ with computation time $O\left(|\mathcal{F}| \cdot \mathsf{time}(DPF) \cdot \max_{f \in \mathcal{F}} |f|\right)$ and key size $\mathsf{size}(DPF)$.

We describe useful function classes supported via combinations of the above transformations.

1. NC^0 functions
For each constant depth $d \in \mathbb{N}$ and input/output bit-lengths n, m, by Transformation 6, we obtain an FSS scheme supporting the class $\mathcal{C}_d$ of depth-d boolean circuits with input $\{0,1\}^n$, output $\{0,1\}^m$, and fan-in 2. The important observation is that we may secret share the entire circuit C by independently sharing m separate 1-bit-output sub-circuits (which each has $O(n^{2^d})$ possibilities) instead of separately treating all possible $m^{O(n^{2^d})}$ values for all of C.

Plugging in the state-of-the-art DPF instantiations (as given in Section 3.1), the resulting (server-side) runtime of the scheme is $\mathsf{time}(\mathcal{C}_d) \in O(\lambda n^{2^d} m)$, and the key size is $O(\lambda m \log n)$, where λ is the seed length for the underlying pseudorandom generator, and the hidden constants include a factor of 2^d.

2. Constant-conjunction search queries
As a consequence of Transformation 6, together with the best known DPF instantiations (given in Section 3.1) with key size $O(\lambda n)$ for domain size 2^n and PRG seed length λ, we obtain an FSS scheme for the class $Match_\ell$ of data-matching functions, for a constant number of data entries ℓ, where each of which may take one of polynomially many $|\mathbb{G}_1| \in n^{O(1)}$ possible values. That is, for canonical nonzero element $g \in \mathbb{G}$,

$$Match_\ell = \left\{f_{S,v} : \mathbb{G}_1^n \to \mathbb{G}\right\}_{\substack{S \subset [n], \\ |S| \leq \ell, \\ v \in \mathbb{G}_1^\ell}}, \quad \text{s.t.} \quad f_{S,v}(x) = \begin{cases} g & \text{if } x_i = v_i \ \forall i \in S \\ 0 & \text{else} \end{cases}.$$

Indeed, the class $Match_\ell$ contains $\binom{n}{\ell} |\mathbb{G}_1|^\ell \in O(n^\ell |\mathbb{G}_1|^\ell)$ different functions. Thus, for $N := (n|\mathbb{G}_1|)^\ell$, we obtain a FSS scheme supporting $Match_\ell$ with evaluation time $O(\lambda N \log N)$ and key size $O(\lambda \log N)$. For the case of $|\mathbb{G}_1| \in O(1)$, these correspond to runtime $O(\lambda n^\ell \ell \log n)$ and key size $O(\lambda \ell \log n)$.

3. Interval functions: Black-box from DPF

The class of interval functions consists of those functions $f_{a,b}$ which output a fixed element $g \in \mathbb{G}$ precisely for inputs x that lie within the interval $a < x < b$, and $0 \in \mathbb{G}$ otherwise.

$$\mathcal{F}_n^{int} = \left\{ f_{(a,b)} : \{0,1\}^n \to \mathbb{G} \right\}_{\substack{0 \leq a \\ \leq b < 2^n}}, \text{ where } f_{(a,b)}(x) = \begin{cases} g & a < x < b \\ 0 & \text{else} \end{cases}.$$

Lemma 1. *Based on any DPF (i.e., FSS scheme for the class of multi-bit point functions) with key size s, there exists an FSS scheme for family $\mathcal{F}_n^{int}$, with key sizes $O(sn)$.*

Intuitively, we express the condition $x < a$ as the disjunction of (up to) n mutually inconsistent exact *prefix-matching* conditions, such that an element x is less than a precisely if it contains exactly one the prefixes. (Viewing the target value a as a path down a binary tree, this amounts to the sequence of (up to) n prefixes that agree with a up to some level i, but then continue to 0 at level $i + 1$ whereas a continues to 1). We thus attain the desired FSS as a linear combination of n DPFs, each acting on a *prefix* of the input x (using Transformations 2 and 4).

Two-Key FSS for Comparison and Interval Functions. We show efficient constructions of FSS for the family $\mathcal{F}_n^<$ of all comparison functions from $\{0,1\}^n$ to some finite group $\mathbb{G}$. The class of comparison functions consists of those functions $f_{a,g}$ which output a fixed element $g \in \mathbb{G}$ for inputs x that lie within the interval $0 \leq x < a$, and $0 \in \mathbb{G}$ otherwise.

$$\mathcal{F}_n^< = \left\{ f_{a,g} : \{0,1\}^n \to \mathbb{G} \right\}_{0 \leq a < 2^n}, \text{ where } f_{a,g}(x) = \begin{cases} g & x < a \\ 0 & \text{else} \end{cases}.$$

Note that (by Transformation 4 above), supporting comparison functions also directly yields FSS for interval functions, with a factor of 2 overhead. We describe a two-key construction which is a natural extension of the two-party DPF construction in Algorithms 1 and 2. The key size of this construction is larger by an additive factor of $n \log |\mathbb{G}|$ compared to the key size of the DPF construction.

The scheme for comparison functions has a similar structure to the scheme for DPF. Again, each of the keys k_0, k_1 generated by $\mathsf{Gen}^<(1^\lambda, a, g)$ represents a binary tree of depth n, and $\mathsf{Eval}^<(\beta, k_\beta, x)$ traverses the tree defined by k_β to the leaf $x = x_1, \ldots, x_n$.

However, there are several key differences between the scheme for comparison functions and the DPF scheme. First, the objects in each node of the tree are *group elements*, generalizing the approach in the DPF scheme. In addition, similarly to the DPF scheme, when the path to x diverges from the path to a, if $x \geq a$ then the sum of the two group elements generated by $\mathsf{Eval}^<(0, k_0, x)$ and $\mathsf{Eval}^<(1, k_1, x)$ is 0 for any node from the point of divergence to the leaf.

However, if $x < a$ then the sum of the two group elements in every node is g. Finally, the current Gen algorithm returns correct keys with probability 1.

Notation 3. *Let $\mathbb{G}$ be an abelian group with group operation $+$ (while $\oplus$ denotes the exclusive-or of bits), let $0 \in \mathbb{G}$ denote the identity element, let $g \in \mathbb{G}$ and let $-g$ denote the inverse of g in the group. Let $e_a \cdot g$ denote a sequence of $2^{|a|}$ elements in $\mathbb{G}$ such that the element at location a is g and all other elements in the sequence are the identity element. We assume that the length of e_a is determined by the domain of a.*

Notation 4. *Let $\mathbb{G}$ be a group, let $g \in \mathbb{G}$ and let $b \in -1, 0, 1$. We denote by $g \cdot b$ a group element that is the identity unit 0 if $b = 0$, is equal to g if $b = 1$ and is equal to $-g$ if $b = -1$. Let $c_a \cdot g$ be a sequence in of $2^{|a|}$ elements with g in every location a' such that $a' < a$ and 0 in every other location. We assume that the length of $c_a \cdot g$ is determined by the domain of a.*

Notation 5. *Let $E_{p,q}$ ($O_{p,q}$) be the set of all $p \times q^{p-1}$ arrays over the set $\{0, \ldots, q - 1\}$ such that the sum of elements in every column is 0 modulo q (1 modulo q) and every column appears exactly once in the array.*

We prove the correctness and security of $(\mathsf{Gen}^<, \mathsf{Eval}^<)$ via the following sequence of claims. Due to space limitations, we omit proofs of these claims, and refer the reader to the full version of this paper.

Lemma 2. *For every $n \in \mathbb{N}$, every $a, x \in \{0, 1\}^n$, every finite abelian group $\mathbb{G}$, every $g \in \mathbb{G}$ and every $i, 1 \leq i \leq n$,*

1. *If $(x_1, \ldots, x_i) = (a_1, \ldots, a_i)$ then for $\beta = 0, 1$, the values S^β and T^β that $\mathsf{Eval}^<(\beta, k_\beta, x)$ computes are equal to the values $S^\beta_{a_i}[i]$ and $T^\beta_{a_i}[i]$ (respectively) that $\mathsf{Gen}^<(1^\lambda, a, g)$ computes; in addition, $T^0 \oplus T^1 = 1$.*
2. *If $(x_1, \ldots, x_i) \neq (a_1, \ldots, a_i)$ then $S^0 = S^1$ and $T^0 = T^1$.*

Building atop Lemma 2, we arrive at the desired correctness guarantee:

Proposition 1 (Correctness). *For every $n \in \mathbb{N}$, every $a, x \in \{0, 1\}^n$, every finite abelian group $\mathbb{G}$ and every $g \in \mathbb{G}$, if $(k_0, k_1) \leftarrow \mathsf{Gen}^<(1^\lambda, a, g)$ then $\mathsf{Eval}^<(0, k_0, x) \oplus \mathsf{Eval}^<(1, k_1, x) = f^<_{a,g}(x)$.*

Theorem 6. *For every $n \in \mathbb{N}$, $a \in \{0, 1\}^n$, every security parameter $\lambda \in \mathbb{N}$ and every finite abelian group $\mathbb{G}$, $(\mathsf{Gen}^<, \mathsf{Eval}^<)$ is a two-key FSS scheme for the family of comparison functions from $\{0, 1\}^n$ to $\mathbb{G}$, with key size $O(n(\lambda + \log |\mathbb{G}|))$.*

We remark that, via a simple transformation, the constructed FSS for comparison functions also directly yields an FSS scheme for point functions over a general abelian group $\mathbb{G}$.

Corollary 1. *For every $n \in \mathbb{N}$, every security parameter $\lambda \in \mathbb{N}$ and every finite abelian group $\mathbb{G}$ there exists a two-key scheme for the family of point functions from $\{0, 1\}^n$ to $\mathbb{G}$, without errors and with key size $O(n(\lambda + \log |\mathbb{G}|))$.*

Algorithm 5. $\mathsf{Gen}^<(1^\lambda, a, g)$

1: Let $G : \{0,1\}^\lambda \longrightarrow \{0,1\}^{2\lambda + 2\log|\mathbb{G}|+2}$ be a PRG.
2: Choose three random seeds $S^0_{a_1}[1], S^1_{a_1}[1], S^0_{\neg a_1}[1] \in \{0,1\}^\lambda$ and set $S^1_{\neg a_1}[1] \leftarrow S^0_{\neg a_1}[1]$.
3: Choose random bits $T^\beta_\alpha[1]$, $\alpha, \beta \in \{0,1\}$, subject to $T^0_{a_1}[1] \neq T^1_{a_1}[1]$ and $T^0_{\neg a_1}[1] = T^1_{\neg a_1}[1]$.
4: Choose random elements $V^\beta_\alpha[1] \in \mathbb{G}$, $\alpha, \beta \in \{0,1\}$, subject to $V^0_{a_1}[1] + (-V^1_{a_1}[1]) = 0$ and $V^0_{\neg a_1}[1] + (-V^1_{\neg a_1}[1]) = g \cdot a_1$.
5: **for** $i = 1$ to $n - 1$ **do**
6:     Let $G(S^\beta_{a_i}[i]) = s^\beta_0 || s^\beta_1 || t^\beta_0 || t^\beta_1 || v^\beta_0 || v^\beta_1$, where $s^\beta_\alpha \in \{0,1\}^\lambda$, $t^\beta_\alpha \in \{0,1\}$ and $v^\beta_\alpha \in \mathbb{G}$ for $\alpha, \beta = 0, 1$.
7:     Randomly choose $cs_{0,a_{i+1}}, cs_{1,a_{i+1}} \in \{0,1\}^\lambda$.
8:     Randomly choose $cs_{0,\neg a_{i+1}}, cs_{1,\neg a_{i+1}} \in \{0,1\}^\lambda$ s.t. $\bigoplus^1_{\beta=0}(cs_{\beta,\neg a_{i+1}} \oplus s^\beta_{\neg a_{i+1}}) = 0$.
9:     Randomly choose $ct_{0,a_{i+1}}, ct_{1,a_{i+1}} \in \{0,1\}$ s.t. $\bigoplus^1_{\beta=0}(ct_{\beta,a_{i+1}} \oplus t^\beta_{a_{i+1}}) = 1$.
10:     Randomly choose $ct_{0,\neg a_{i+1}}, ct_{1,\neg a_{i+1}} \in \{0,1\}$ s.t. $\bigoplus^1_{\beta=0}(ct_{\beta,\neg a_{i+1}} \oplus t^\beta_{\neg a_{i+1}}) = 0$.
11:     Randomly choose $cv_{0,a_{i+1}}, cv_{1,a_{i+1}} \in \mathbb{G}$ s.t. $\sum^1_{\beta=0}(cv_{\tau,a_{i+1}} + v^\beta_{a_{i+1}}) \cdot (-1)^\beta = 0$, for $\tau = T^\beta_{a_i}[i]$.
12:     Randomly choose $cv_{0,\neg a_{i+1}}, cv_{1,\neg a_{i+1}} \in \mathbb{G}$ s.t. $\sum^1_{\beta=0}(cv_{\tau,\neg a_{i+1}} + v^\beta_{\neg a_{i+1}}) \cdot (-1)^\beta = g \cdot a_{i+1}$, for $\tau = T^\beta_{\neg a_i}[i]$.
13:     Set $CW_\beta[i] \leftarrow cs_{\beta,0} || cs_{\beta,1} || ct_{\beta,0} || ct_{\beta,1} || cv_{\beta,0} || cv_{\beta,1}$ for $\beta = 0, 1$.
14:     Set $S^\beta_\alpha[i+1] \leftarrow s^\beta_\alpha \oplus cs_{\tau,\alpha}$ for $\tau = T^\beta_{a_i}[i]$ and $\alpha, \beta \in \{0,1\}$.
15:     Set $T^\beta_\alpha[i+1] \leftarrow t^\beta_\alpha \oplus ct_{\tau,\alpha}$ for $\tau = T^\beta_{a_i}[i]$ and $\alpha, \beta \in \{0,1\}$.
16: **end for**
17: Set $k_\beta \leftarrow ((S^\beta_0[1], S^\beta_1[1], T^\beta_0[1], T^\beta_1[1], V^\beta_0[1], V^\beta_1[1]), (CW_0[1], CW_1[1], \ldots, CW_0[n-1], CW_1[n-1]))$.
18: Return (k_0, k_1).

Algorithm 6. $\mathsf{Eval}^<(\beta, k_\beta, x)$

1: Let $G : \{0,1\}^\lambda \longrightarrow \{0,1\}^{2\lambda + 2\log|\mathbb{G}|+2}$ be a PRG.
2: Let the binary representation of x be $x = x_1, \ldots, x_n$.
3: Let $k_\beta = ((S^\beta_0[1], S^\beta_1[1], T^\beta_0[1], T^\beta_1[1], V^\beta_0[1], V^\beta_1[1]), (CW_0[1], CW_1[1], \ldots, CW_0[n-1], CW_1[n-1]))$.
4: Set $S^\beta \leftarrow S^\beta_{x_1}[1]$.
5: Set $T^\beta \leftarrow T^\beta_{x_1}[1]$.
6: Set $V^\beta \leftarrow V^\beta_{x_1}[1]$.
7: **for** $i = 2$ to n **do**
8:     Parse $G(S^\beta)$ as $G(S^\beta) = s_0 || s_1 || t_0 || t_1 || v_0 || v_1$.
9:     Let $CW_{T^\beta}[i-1] = cs_{T^\beta,0} || cs_{T^\beta,1} || ct_{T^\beta,0} || ct_{T^\beta,1} || cv_{T^\beta,0} || cv_{T^\beta,1}$.
10:     Set $S^\beta \leftarrow s_{x_i} \oplus cs_{T^\beta,x_i}$.
11:     Set $T^\beta \leftarrow t_{x_i} \oplus ct_{T^\beta,x_i}$.
12:     Set $V^\beta \leftarrow V^\beta + (v_{x_i} + cv_{T^\beta,x_i})$.
13: **end for**
14: Return $V^\beta \cdot (-1)^\beta$.

Proof. A point function is a linear combination of two comparison functions. Specifically, $P_{a,g}(x) = f_{a+1}^<(x) + (-f_a^<(x))$, where $-f_a^<(x)$ is the inverse of $f_a^<(x)$ in $\mathbb{G}$. The corollary follows from Theorem 6 and the linear combination of FSS schemes in Section 3.2.

Extending to the Many-Party Setting. We construct a scheme for the family of comparison functions from $\{0,1\}^n$ to an abelian group $\mathbb{G}$ that is secure against coalitions of all but one of the keys. The scheme, defined in Algorithms 7 and 8, has a similar structure to Algorithms 3 and 4.

There are several differences between the current scheme and the DPF scheme. The scheme for comparison functions is over $\mathbb{G}$ and the choice of arrays $A_{\gamma'}$ is from the sets $E_{p,q}$ and $O_{p,q}$, for $q = |\mathbb{G}|$, instead of choosing the arrays from E_p or O_p. The correction words, $cw_1, \ldots, cw_\nu$, are chosen in a different way in line 6 of Algorithm 7 and additional group elements, $v_1, \ldots, v_\nu$, are used in line 7 of Algorithm 7 and line 6 of Algorithm 8. The reason for the differences in $cw_1, \ldots, cw_\nu$ and $v_1, \ldots, v_\nu$ is that $f_{a,g}^<(x) = g$ for any $x < a$, while $P_{a,b}(x) = 0$ for any $x < a$.

Theorem 7. *For every security parameter $\lambda \in \mathbb{N}$, every $n, p \in \mathbb{N}$, every abelian group $\mathbb{G}$, $|\mathbb{G}| = q$, every $a, x \in \{0,1\}^n$ and every $g \in \mathbb{G}$, the pair of algorithms $(\mathsf{Gen}^p, \mathsf{Eval}^p)$ is an FSS scheme for the family of all comparison functions from $\{0,1\}^n$ to $\mathbb{G}$, such that Gen outputs p keys $(k_1, \ldots, k_p)$, the scheme is secure against any coalition of at most $p - 1$ keys and the key size is $O(2^{n/2} \cdot q^{(p-1)/2} \log q)$.*

Corollary 2. *For any abelian group $\mathbb{G} = \mathbb{G}_1 \times \ldots \times \mathbb{G}_r$, such that $|\mathbb{G}_i| = q_i$ for $i = 1, \ldots, r$, there exists an FSS scheme for the family of comparison functions from $\{0,1\}^n$ to $\mathbb{G}$ that generates p keys and is secure against coalitions of up to $p - 1$ keys with key size $O(2^{n/2} \cdot q^{(p-1)/2} \sum_{i=1}^{p} \log q_i)$. This result is obtained by running $(\mathsf{Gen}^p, \mathsf{Eval}^p)$ separately on each component $\mathbb{G}_i$.*

Proposition 2 (Correctness). *For every security parameter $\lambda \in \mathbb{N}$, every $n, p \in \mathbb{N}$, every abelian group $\mathbb{G}$, every $a, x \in \{0,1\}^n$ and every $g \in \mathbb{G}$, if $(k_1, \ldots, k_p) \leftarrow \mathsf{Gen}^p(1^\lambda, a, g)$ then $\sum_{i=1}^{p} \mathsf{Eval}^p(i, k_i, x) = f_{a,g}^<(x)$.*

3.3 General FSS from Obfuscation

In this section, we provide general positive constructions of FSS based on program obfuscation. We first obtain FSS schemes for *P/poly* given access to a program obfuscator that satisfies a *virtual black-box (VBB)* notion of security [3]. We then build on top of recent advances in *indistinguishability obfuscation (iO)* [3,22] to demonstrate a similar conclusion from $i\mathcal{O}$ with sub-exponential hardness.

In particular, building atop recent candidate obfuscation constructions, these provide us with heuristic constructions of FSS for any efficiently computable function class of choice. Further, it yields provably secure solutions within idealized models, for which secure constructions of VBB obfuscation have been

---

Algorithm 7. $\mathsf{Gen}^p(1^\lambda, a, g)$

1: Let $G : \{0,1\}^\lambda \longrightarrow \mathbb{G}^\mu$ be a PRG (μ is defined in line 2).
2: Let $\mu \leftarrow \lceil 2^{n/2} \cdot q^{(p-1)/2} \rceil$ and let $\nu \leftarrow \lceil 2^n/\mu \rceil$.
3: Regard a as a pair $a = (\gamma, \delta)$, $\gamma \in \{0,1\}^\nu$, $\delta \in \{0,1\}^\mu$.
4: Choose ν random arrays $A_1, \ldots, A_\nu$, s.t. $A_\gamma \in O_{p,q}$ and $A_{\gamma'} \in E_{p,q}$ for all $\gamma' \neq \gamma$.
5: Choose $\nu \cdot q^{p-1}$ random seeds $s_{1,1}, \ldots, s_{\nu,q^{p-1}} \in \{0,1\}^\lambda$.
6: Randomly choose $cw_1, \ldots, cw_{q^{p-1}} \in \mathbb{G}^\mu$ s.t. $\sum_{j=1}^{q^{p-1}} (cw_j + G(s_{\gamma,j})) = c_\delta$.
7: Select $v_1, \ldots, v_p \in \mathbb{G}^\nu$ randomly s.t. $\sum_{i=1}^p v_i = c_\gamma \cdot g$.
8: If $A_{\gamma'}[i,j] \neq 0$ set $\sigma_{i,\gamma',j} \leftarrow (s_{\gamma',j}, A_{\gamma'}[i,j])$, otherwise $\sigma_{i,\gamma',j} \leftarrow (0,0)$, for all $1 \leq i \leq p, 1 \leq \gamma' \leq \nu, 1 \leq j \leq q^{p-1}$.
9: Set $\sigma_{i,\gamma'} \leftarrow (\sigma_{i,\gamma',1}||\ldots||\sigma_{i,\gamma',q^{p-1}})$, for all $1 \leq i \leq p, 1 \leq \gamma' \leq \nu$.
10: Set $\sigma_i = \sigma_{i,1}||\ldots||\sigma_{i,\nu}$ for $1 \leq i \leq p$.
11: Let $k_i = (\sigma_i, v_i, cw_1, \ldots, cw_{q^{p-1}})$ for $1 \leq i \leq p$.
12: Return $(k_1, \ldots, k_p)$.

Algorithm 8. $\mathsf{Eval}^p(i, k_i, x)$

1: Let $G : \{0,1\}^\lambda \longrightarrow \mathbb{G}^\mu$ be a PRG (μ is defined in line 2).
2: Let $\mu \leftarrow \lceil 2^{n/2} \cdot q^{(p-1)/2} \rceil$ and let $\nu \leftarrow \lceil 2^n/\mu \rceil$.
3: Regard x as a pair $x = (\gamma', \delta')$, $\gamma' \in \{0,1\}^\nu$, $\delta' \in \{0,1\}^\mu$.
4: Parse k_i as $k_i = (\sigma_i, v_i, cw_1, \ldots, cw_{q^{p-1}})$.
5: Parse σ_i as $\sigma_i = (s_{1,1}, A_1[i,1])||\ldots||(s_{1,q^{p-1}}, A_1[i, q^{p-1}])||\ldots||(s_{\nu,q^{p-1}}, A_\nu[\nu, q^{p-1}])$.
6: Let $y_i \leftarrow v_i[\gamma'] + \sum_{\substack{1 \leq j \leq q^{p-1} \\ A_{\gamma'}[i,j] \neq 0}} A_{\gamma'}[i,j] \cdot (cw_j + G(s_{\gamma',j}))$.
7: Return $y_i[\delta']$.

---

constructed [2,9], e.g. in the generic multilinear map model, or in settings with secure hardware.

For purposes of space limits, we describe only the high-level intuition and defer complete constructions and proofs of security to the full version.

General FSS from Virtual Black Box (VBB) Obfuscation

Proposition 3. *Assume the existence of an ideal virtual black-box obfuscation oracle for P/poly, and the existence of one-way functions. Then there exists an FSS scheme supporting P/poly.*

Intuitively, the FSS construction works by obfuscating (1) a pseudorandom function (PRF) F_s for one party, and (2) $(C - F_s)$ for the desired circuit C for the second party. The VBB property enables a party's key to be simulated given black-box access to the underlying program, which can in turn be simulated (by the security of the PRF) by a truly random sequence of outputs.

General FSS From Sub-Exponential $i\mathcal{O}$. Our construction relies on a recent work of Canetti *et al.* [13] which demonstrates that sub-exponential $i\mathcal{O}$ implies a notion of *probabilistic iO* (*piO*). Loosely, *piO* converts a randomized program into a deterministic obfuscated program, and provides the guarantee that it is hard to distinguish obfuscations of two (randomized) circuits whose output distributions at each input are computationally indistinguishable, possibly in the presence of auxiliary input. We refer the reader to [13] for a full definition.

Theorem 8. *Assume the existence of sub-exponentially secure indistinguishability obfuscation and sub-exponentially secure one-way functions. Then there exists an FSS scheme supporting P/poly.*

The construction makes use of a *piO*-obfuscated (randomized) program P that takes as input x, samples a random value R, and outputs *encryptions* of the values R and $f(x) - R$ for the secret function f, under two different hardcoded public keys (i.e., $\mathsf{Enc}_{\mathsf{pk}_A}(R)$ and $\mathsf{Enc}_{\mathsf{pk}_B}(f(x) - R)$), as described in Figure 1. Recall that while this program P is randomized, its *piO*-obfuscation $\tilde{P}$ is a *deterministic* circuit. A party's FSS key for $f \in \mathcal{F}$ will consist of this obfuscated program $\tilde{P}$, together with *one* of the secret keys sk_A or sk_B. To evaluate his FSS share on an input x, the party runs $\tilde{P}(x)$, and decrypts his corresponding output. We remark that (sub-exponentially) secure public-key encryption (PKE) is implied by (sub-exponentially) secure indistinguishability obfuscation together with (sub-exponentially) secure one-way functions [43].

Program FSS$_{f,\mathsf{pk}_A,\mathsf{pk}_B}$
Hardcoded: $f \in \mathcal{F}$, public keys $\mathsf{pk}_A, \mathsf{pk}_B$.
Input: $x \in \{0,1\}^n$. Randomness: R, r_A, r_B.

 1. Encrypt R under pk_A, as $\hat{y}_A \leftarrow \mathsf{Enc}_{\mathsf{pk}_A}(R; r_A)$.
 2. Encrypt $f(x) - R$ under pk_B, as $\hat{y}_B \leftarrow \mathsf{Enc}_{\mathsf{pk}_B}(f(x) - R; r_B)$.
 3. Output $(\hat{y}_A, \hat{y}_B)$.

Fig. 1. Real program obfuscated in $\mathsf{Gen}(1^\lambda, f)$

Correctness of the scheme follows by the correctness of the encryption and the *piO*: since the original program P outputs value pairs $(\hat{y}_A, \hat{y}_B)$ for which $\mathsf{Dec}_{\mathsf{sk}_A}(\hat{y}_A) + \mathsf{Dec}_{\mathsf{sk}_B}(\hat{y}_B) = f(x)$, the same property (which is efficiently testable given auxiliary input $\mathsf{sk}_A, \mathsf{sk}_B$) must hold for the outputs of $\tilde{P}$. By the security of the PKE, a party learns nothing from the second encrypted output, and thus his own decrypted shares (either R or $f(x) - R$) appear indistinguishable from random values. This is formalized in the proof by replacing the obfuscated program $\tilde{P}$ with an obfuscation of a fake program which instead outputs $\mathsf{Enc}_{\mathsf{pk}_A}(R)$ and $\mathsf{Enc}_{\mathsf{pk}_B}(R')$ for a second *independent* random value R'.

4 Relation to Other Primitives

In this section, we explore the relation between FSS and other cryptographic primitives. We first demonstrate in Section 4.1 that once the supported function class $\mathcal{F}$ becomes reasonably rich, each share of function $f \in \mathcal{F}$ must be a *pseudorandom function*. This holds in particular for the special case of point functions. We next provide evidence in Section 4.2 that achieving FSS for certain function classes (beginning as low as AC^0) is likely to require cryptographic tools heavier than one-way functions or even oblivious transfer. This is done by showing that such FSS schemes imply low-communication general secure computation protocols that rely on *reusable* preprocessing. Such protocols are currently only achievable using stronger cryptographic primitives, namely somewhat-homomorphic encryption or reusable garbled circuits. Finally, in Section 4.3 we show that, assuming fully homomorphic encryption (FHE) with decryption in NC^1 (as is the case for nearly all existing constructions, e.g. [8,10,25]), FSS for general functions is implied by the existence of FSS for NC^1.

4.1   Key Functions Are Pseudorandom Functions

Parties' keys in the FSS each define their own *function*, taking inputs x to output shares $\mathsf{Eval}(b, k_b, x)$. This function serves as one piece of the secret function being shared. A natural question is: what can we say about these functions? Can they have any sort of structure? Or, does the security property of the FSS together with the linearity of the output decoding procedure directly enforce a particular structure on the output share functions themselves?

We show that, in fact, if the supported class $\mathcal{F}$ is sufficiently rich, in the sense that it "efficiently spans" the whole function space, then it must be that the parties' output share functions $\mathsf{Eval}(b, k_b, x)$ themselves are *pseudorandom functions (PRFs)*. We formalize this condition on $\mathcal{F}$ as "poly-spanning."

Definition 4. *A family of functions* $\mathcal{F} = \{f : \mathbb{G}_n \to \mathbb{G}_m\}$ *is said to be* poly-spanning *if for each polynomial* $p(n)$ *there exists a polynomial* $q(n)$ *and efficient procedure* $P : (\{0,1\}^n \times \{0,1\}^m)^{p(n)} \to \mathcal{F}^{q(n)}$ *mapping* $p(n)$ *pairs of input-output assignments to a collection of* $q(n)$ *functions from* $\mathcal{F}$, *with* $P\big((x_i, y_i)_{i \in [p(n)]}\big) = (f_j)_{j \in [q(n)]}$ *such that the function* $f' := \sum_{j \in [q(n)]} f_j$ *satisfies* $f'(x_i) = y_i$ *for every* $i \in [p(n)]$.

Remark 3 (Examples of poly-spanning function families).

- **Multi-bit Point Functions.** The class of functions $\{f_{x^*, y^*}\}$ over $x^* \in \{0,1\}^n, y^* \in \{0,1\}^m$ where $f_{x^*, y^*}(x) = y^*$ if $x = x^*$ and 0 otherwise. Indeed, the desired procedure P is simply given by $P\big((x_i, y_i)_{i \in [p(n)]}\big) = (f_{x_i, y_i})_{i \in [p(n)]}$.
- **Comparison Functions.** The class of comparison functions $\mathcal{F}_n^{\leq}$. Indeed, the desired procedure P is given as follows:
  1: Initialize $S \leftarrow \emptyset$.
  2: Sort inputs $x_1, \ldots, x_{p(n)} \in [2^n]$ as $x_1' \leq \ldots \leq x_{p(n)}'$. Denote their outputs as y_i'.
  3: **for** $i = p(n)$ to 1 **do**
  4:     **if** $y_i' \neq y_{i+1}'$ (where $y_{p(n)+1}' := 0$) **then**

5:          Include the new function $f_{x_i'}^{\leq}$ (to flip the output of the sum):
$$S \leftarrow S \cup \{f_{x_i'}^{\leq}\}$$
6:      **end if**
7: **end for**
8: **return** S

We now introduce notation for the output share function that we study.

Definition 5. *Let* $(\mathsf{Gen}, \mathsf{Eval})$ *be an FSS scheme w.r.t. function class* $\mathcal{F}$. *Then for each* $f \in \mathcal{F}$ *and* $b \in \{0,1\}$, *we denote by* $\mathsf{OutputShare}_{f,b}$ *the function family* $\{\mathsf{Eval}(b, k_b, \cdot)\}_{k_b}$ *defined by sampling and evaluation procedures:*

- *Sample: Outputs a key* k_b, *where* $(k_0, k_1) \leftarrow \mathsf{Gen}(1^\lambda, f)$.
- *Evaluate: On input* x, *computes* $\mathsf{Eval}(b, k_b, x)$.

Theorem 9. *Let* $(\mathsf{Gen}, \mathsf{Eval})$ *be a FSS scheme (as per Definition 2) w.r.t. a poly-spanning function class* $\mathcal{F}$. *Then for every* $f \in \mathcal{F}$ *and every* $b \in \{0,1\}$, *the function family* $\mathsf{OutputShare}_{f,b}$ *as given in Definition 5 is a PRF family (against nonuniform adversaries).*

Proof. Intuitively, we first show that oracle access to a randomly sampled party key function $\mathsf{OutputShare}_{f,b}$ (over the randomness of Gen) must be computationally indistinguishable from oracle access to the distribution ($\mathsf{OutputShare}_{f,b} + \sum_{i \in S} f_i$) for any fixed polynomial-size subset S of functions $f_i \in \mathcal{F}$ in the supported function class. Then, we show that if $\mathcal{F}$ is poly-spanning, then for any possible PRF distinguishing adversary $\mathcal{A}$, we can fool this $\mathcal{A}$, guaranteeing that he *cannot* succeed in distinguishing from a random function, with an appropriate carefully tailored choice of functions $\{f_i\}_{i \in S} \subset \mathcal{F}$.

We defer the full proof of Theorem 9 to the full version of this paper.

4.2   Barriers Toward FSS for Expressive Function Classes

We now turn to exploring likely *barriers* in constructing FSS for certain function classes based on lightweight cryptographic tools. Our results in this section take the following form: Assume there exists FSS for a class of functions containing $\mathcal{F} \circ \mathsf{Dec}$, where $\mathcal{F}$ is some function class and Dec corresponds to the complexity of decryption of a symmetric-key encryption scheme. Then there exists a particular form of highly communication-efficient secure computation for functions in $\mathcal{F}$, which is currently only known to exist based on $\mathcal{F}$-*homomorphic encryption*[5] or *reusable garbled circuits for* $\mathcal{F}$. In particular:

- At the high end, FSS for $P/poly$ implies a form of secure computation whose only known constructions rely on *fully homomorphic* encryption or *reusable* garbled circuits for $P/poly$. We conclude that FSS for $P/poly$ is likely to require heavy cryptographic machinery.

---

[5] That is, semantically secure encryption supporting *compact* homomorphic evaluation of the function class $\mathcal{F}$.

– At the low end, FSS for AC^0 in combination with any symmetric-key encryption scheme with decryption in AC^0 together imply a form of secure computation only currently known to exist based on existence of AC^0-homomorphic encryption or reusable garbled circuits for AC^0.

In particular, symmetric-key encryption with decryption in AC^0 is implied by sub-exponential hardness of Learning Parity with Noise (LPN) [7]. However, despite significant efforts in the cryptographic community, it is unknown even how to build from this assumption collision resistant hashing, much less stronger primitives like homomorphic encryption that imply them [35]. Indeed, all proposed constructions to date of homomorphic encryption and reusable garbled circuits (even for the restricted class AC^0), such as those from [10,11,33], rely on Learning With Errors (LWE) [42] or similar lattice-based assumptions; a construction under weaker or significantly different assumptions such as LPN would be considered a major result. We conclude that FSS for AC^0 is unlikely to be achieved based on sub-exponential LPN (or any weaker) assumption alone.

We contrast this conclusion with our construction of FSS for various strict subclasses of AC^0 in Section 3.2 based on *one-way functions*.

We now formalize the above discussion. Concretely, we demonstrate that FSS for a function class $\mathcal{F} \circ \mathsf{Dec}$ (formally defined below) yields a construction of exceedingly communication-efficient (semi-honest) secure multiparty computation (MPC) in the preprocessing model, for the function class $\mathcal{F}$. That is, given an offline setup phase independent of parties' inputs, the parties A, B can reuse this setup to achieve secure evaluation of a fixed $f \in \mathcal{F}$ on arbitrarily many input pairs $(x_1^A, x_1^B), (x_2^A, x_2^B), \ldots$ in the online phase with communication that depends *only on the size of the inputs and outputs* of f, and not on the size of f itself. To date, the only other known approaches to achieving MPC with this efficiency feature (even when allowing reusable preprocessing) rely on strong cryptographic tools: either fully *homomorphic encryption for $\mathcal{F}$* (as in [1,23]) or *reusable* garbled circuits for $\mathcal{F}$ (as in [33].[6])

Intuitively, the FSS enables communication efficiency as follows. Suppose we wish to achieve secure computation of a function $f \in \mathcal{F}$. In the offline phase, the parties A, B will each receive[7] a secret key $\mathsf{sk}_A, \mathsf{sk}_B$ for the symmetric key encryption scheme, and FSS keys of a function $\hat{f}_{\mathsf{sk}} \in \mathcal{F} \circ \mathsf{Dec}$ that depends on both sk_A and sk_B. This function $\hat{f}_{\mathsf{sk}}$ will take as input a pair of ciphertexts $(\hat{x}^A, \hat{x}^B)$, decrypts each with respect to the corresponding hardcoded secret key sk_A or sk_B, and then evaluates the function f on the resulting values. In the online phase,

---

[6] Loosely, the offline phase will result in one party receiving a reusable garbled circuit of f and the second will receive the information to generate garbled input labels; the offline phase will only require communication on order the size of the garbled input and output labels, and not the size of f itself.

[7] For simplicity, we treat the offline setup phase as correlated randomness generated and given to the two parties by some trusted source; in practice, this can be implemented by running a standard MPC protocol between the two parties to securely generate these values.

for each desired input pair (x_i^A, x_i^B), the parties exchange *encryptions* of their private inputs under their respective secret keys. They then use their FSS keys to compute output shares of $\hat{f}_{\mathsf{sk}}$ evaluated on input this pair of ciphertexts $(\hat{x}_i^A, \hat{x}_i^B)$. Finally, the computed output shares are exchanged, and the value of $\hat{f}_{\mathsf{sk}}(\hat{x}_i^A, \hat{x}_i^B)$ is reconstructed. By the correctness of the FSS scheme and the choice of $\hat{f}_{\mathsf{sk}}$, this will exactly allow the parties to compute the desired value $f(x_i^A, f_i^B)$. And by the security of the FSS and the encryption scheme, no additional information on the inputs will be revealed.

We now formalize these intuitions.

Remark 4 (MPC Security). Recall that MPC security is defined with respect to the real/ideal world paradigm. Very loosely, for every PPT adversary $\mathcal{A}$ in a real-world execution of the protocol, there exists a PPT simulator in the ideal-world execution (receiving only the function output(s)) who can consistently simulate the experiment output. We refer the reader to e.g. [30,46] for a formal definition.

Definition 6 (Communication-Efficient Online MPC for $\mathcal{F}$). *It is said that communication-efficient online MPC for the function class $\mathcal{F}$ exists if for any $f \in \mathcal{F}$, there exists a distribution of correlated randomness (D_A, D_B), polynomial p, and a two-party protocol Π in the correlated randomness model such that, for any $\ell \in \mathbb{N}$, and any sequence of (possibly adaptively chosen) inputs $(x_1^A, x_1^B), \ldots, (x_\ell^A, x_\ell^B)$, the protocol Π achieves secure evaluation of f on the input pairs in the semi-honest model, with (online) communication complexity $O\big(\sum_{i=1}^{\ell} \big(|x_i^A| + |x_i^B| + |f(x_i^A, x_i^B)|\big) \cdot p(\lambda)\big)$, where λ is the security parameter. In particular, the online communication complexity is independent of the size of the description of f.*

Definition 7. *For a given symmetric encryption scheme* (Gen, Enc, Dec) *and function class $\mathcal{F}$, we define the function class $\mathcal{F} \circ \mathsf{Dec} := \{ f \circ (\mathsf{Dec}_{\mathsf{sk}_A} \times \mathsf{Dec}_{\mathsf{sk}_B}) : f \in \mathcal{F}, \mathsf{sk}_A, \mathsf{sk}_B \in Supp(\mathsf{Gen}(1^k)) \}$.*

Theorem 10. *Assume the existence of symmetric-key encryption with decryption* Dec, *and FSS for $\mathcal{F} \circ$ Dec (as in Definition 7). Then there exists communication-efficient online MPC for the class $\mathcal{F}$, as in Definition 6.*

Due to space limitations, we defer the proof of Theorem 10 to the full version of this paper.

Remark 5. We note that the proof of Theorem 10 does not rely directly on the linearity of the output decoding procedure of the FSS scheme. Rather, the same result holds identically for any output decoding function that still guarantees *function privacy* (to preserve security of the MPC) and *succinctness* (to maintain communication efficiency in the online phase).

We now address the implications of Theorem 10 to two specific function classes $F \circ$ Dec.

Corollary 3 (FSS for $P/poly$**).** *Assuming FSS for* $P/poly$*, there exists communication-efficient online MPC for all* $P/poly$*.*

Proof. By Theorem 9, FSS for $P/poly$ implies the existence of pseudorandom functions, which thus implies secure symmetric-key encryption with decryption in $P/poly$. The corollary hence follows directly from Theorem 10.

Corollary 4 (FSS for AC^0**).** *Assuming FSS for* AC^0 *and sub-exponential hardness of LPN, there exists communication-efficient online MPC for* AC^0*.*

Proof. Follows from Theorem 10 and [7].

4.3 Bootstrapping with Fully Homomorphic Encryption

We show that FSS schemes enjoy a convenient bootstrapping property, when paired with fully homomorphic encryption (FHE). Namely, assuming the existence of FHE with decryption in NC^1 (as is the case for essentially all existing constructions, e.g. [8,10,25]), then any FSS scheme supporting the class NC^1 directly implies an FSS for the class of *all* circuits, where the FSS key size grows with the size of the circuit being secret shared.[8]

Proposition 4. *Assuming the existence of fully homomorphic encryption with perfect correctness and decryption in* NC^1*, and FSS for* NC^1*, then there exists a secure FSS scheme for* $P/poly$*.*

Proof. Intuitively, the new FSS construction will work by sampling FSS keys in the underlying NC^1-supported scheme for the FHE *decryption* function $\mathsf{Dec}_{\mathsf{sk}}$ for random, secret sk, and additionally providing an *encryption* $\hat{C}$ of a description of the desired circuit $C \in P/poly$. To evaluate, the parties first homomorphically evaluate C on their input x using $\hat{C}$, and then use this evaluated ciphertext as the input to the FSS for $\mathsf{Dec}_{\mathsf{sk}}$.

We defer the full proof of Proposition 4 to the full version of this paper.

Acknowledgments. We thank Nir Bitansky and Vinod Vaikuntanathan for helpful discussions and for pointing out the relevance of [13].

References

1. Asharov, G., Jain, A., López-Alt, A., Tromer, E., Vaikuntanathan, V., Wichs, D.: Multiparty computation with low communication, computation and interaction via threshold FHE. In: Pointcheval, D., Johansson, T. (eds.) EUROCRYPT 2012. LNCS, vol. 7237, pp. 483–501. Springer, Heidelberg (2012)

[8] Note that this growth in key size is necessary, as the size of the two parties' keys together with the complexity of the Eval' must match or exceed the circuit description size; thus circuits of arbitrary polynomial size cannot be supported by a fixed polynomial size key and Eval algorithm.

2. Barak, B., Garg, S., Kalai, Y.T., Paneth, O., Sahai, A.: Protecting obfuscation against algebraic attacks. In: Nguyen, P.Q., Oswald, E. (eds.) EUROCRYPT 2014. LNCS, vol. 8441, pp. 221–238. Springer, Heidelberg (2014)
3. Barak, B., Goldreich, O., Impagliazzo, R., Rudich, S., Sahai, A., Vadhan, S.P., Yang, K.: On the (im)possibility of obfuscating programs. J. ACM 59(2), 6 (2012)
4. Barkol, O., Ishai, Y., Weinreb, E.: On Locally Decodable Codes, Self-Correctable Codes, and t-Private PIR. Algorithmica 58(4), 831–859 (2010)
5. Beigel, R., Fortnow, L., Gasarch, W.I.: A tight lower bound for restricted PIR protocols. Computational Complexity 15(1), 82–91 (2006)
6. Beimel, A., Ishai, Y., Kushilevitz, E., Orlov, I.: Share conversion and private information retrieval. In: IEEE Conference on Computational Complexity 2012, pp. 258–268 (2012)
7. Bogdanov, A., Lee, C.H.: On the depth complexity of homomorphic encryption schemes. Electronic Colloquium on Computational Complexity (ECCC) 2012/157 (2012)
8. Brakerski, Z., Gentry, C., Vaikuntanathan, V.: (Leveled) fully homomorphic encryption without bootstrapping. In: ITCS 2012, pp. 309–325 (2012)
9. Brakerski, Z., Rothblum, G.N.: Virtual black-box obfuscation for all circuits via generic graded encoding. In: Lindell, Y. (ed.) TCC 2014. LNCS, vol. 8349, pp. 1–25. Springer, Heidelberg (2014)
10. Brakerski, Z., Vaikuntanathan, V.: Lattice-based FHE as secure as PKE. In: ITCS 2014, pp. 1–12 (2014)
11. Brakerski, Z., Vaikuntanathan, V.: Efficient fully homomorphic encryption from (standard) LWE. In: FOCS 2011, pp. 97–106 (2011)
12. Cachin, C., Micali, S., Stadler, M.A.: Computationally private information retrieval with polylogarithmic communication. In: Stern, J. (ed.) EUROCRYPT 1999. LNCS, vol. 1592, pp. 402–414. Springer, Heidelberg (1999)
13. Canetti, R., Lin, H., Tessaro, S., Vaikuntanathan, V.: Obfuscation of Probabilistic Circuits and Applications. Cryptology ePrint Archive, Report 2014/882 (2014)
14. Chor, B., Gilboa, N.: Computationally private information retrieval. In: STOC 1997, pp. 304–313 (1997)
15. Chor, B., Goldreich, O., Kushilevitz, E., Sudan, M.: Private Information Retrieval. Journal of the ACM (JACM) 45(6), 965–981 (1998)
16. De Santis, A., Desmedt, Y., Frankel, Y., Yung, M.: How to share a function securely. In: STOC 1994, pp. 522–533 (1994)
17. Desmedt, Y.G.: Society and group oriented cryptography: a new concept. In: Pomerance, C. (ed.) CRYPTO 1987. LNCS, vol. 293, pp. 120–127. Springer, Heidelberg (1988)
18. Desmedt, Y.G., Frankel, Y.: Threshold cryptosystems. In: Brassard, G. (ed.) CRYPTO 1989. LNCS, vol. 435, pp. 307–315. Springer, Heidelberg (1990)
19. Dvir, Z., Gopi, S.: 2-Server PIR with sub-polynomial communication. Electronic Colloquium on Computational Complexity (ECCC) 21, 94 (2014)
20. Di Crescenzo, G., Malkin, T., Ostrovsky, R.: Single database private information retrieval implies oblivious transfer. In: Preneel, B. (ed.) EUROCRYPT 2000. LNCS, vol. 1807, pp. 122–138. Springer, Heidelberg (2000)
21. Efremenko, K.: 3-query locally decodable codes of subexponential length. In: STOC 2009, pp. 39–44 (2009)
22. Garg, S., Gentry, C., Halevi, S., Raykova, M., Sahai, A., Waters, B.: Candidate indistinguishability obfuscation and functional encryption for all circuits. In: FOCS 2013, pp. 40–49 (2013)

23. Gentry, C.: Fully homomorphic encryption using ideal lattices. In: STOC 2009, pp. 169–178 (2009)
24. Gentry, C., Ramzan, Z.: Single-database private information retrieval with constant communication rate. In: Caires, L., Italiano, G.F., Monteiro, L., Palamidessi, C., Yung, M. (eds.) ICALP 2005. LNCS, vol. 3580, pp. 803–815. Springer, Heidelberg (2005)
25. Gentry, C., Sahai, A., Waters, B.: Homomorphic encryption from learning with errors: conceptually-simpler, asymptotically-faster, attribute-based. In: Canetti, R., Garay, J.A. (eds.) CRYPTO 2013, Part I. LNCS, vol. 8042, pp. 75–92. Springer, Heidelberg (2013)
26. Gilboa, N., Ishai, Y.: Distributed point functions and their applications. In: Nguyen, P.Q., Oswald, E. (eds.) EUROCRYPT 2014. LNCS, vol. 8441, pp. 640–658. Springer, Heidelberg (2014)
27. Goldreich, O.: A Note on Computational Indistinguishability. Inf. Process. Lett. **34**(6), 277–281 (1990)
28. Goldreich, O.: Foundations of Cryptography: Basic Tools. Cambridge University Press (2000)
29. Goldreich, O., Goldwasser, S., Micali, S.: How to construct random functions. Journal of the ACM (JACM) **33**(4), 792–807 (1986)
30. Goldreich, O., Micali, S., Wigderson, A.: How to play any mental game or a completeness theorem for protocols with honest majority. In: STOC 1987, pp. 218–229 (1987)
31. Goldreich, O., Ostrovsky, R.: Software Protection and Simulation on Oblivious RAMs. J. ACM **43**(3), 431–473 (1996)
32. Goldwasser, S., Micali, S.: Probabilistic Encryption. J. Comput. Syst. Sci. **28**(2), 270–299 (1984)
33. Goldwasser, S., Kalai, Y.T., Popa, R.A., Vaikuntanathan, V., Zeldovich, N.: Reusable garbled circuits and succinct functional encryption. In: STOC 2013, pp. 555–564 (2013)
34. Hastad, J., Impagliazzo, R., Levin, L., Luby, M.: A Pseudorandom Generator from any One-way Function. SIAM J. Comput. **28**(4), 1364–1396 (1999)
35. Ishai, Y., Kushilevitz, E., Ostrovsky, R.: Sufficient conditions for collision-resistant hashing. In: Kilian, J. (ed.) TCC 2005. LNCS, vol. 3378, pp. 445–456. Springer, Heidelberg (2005)
36. Ishai, Y., Paskin, A.: Evaluating branching programs on encrypted data. In: Vadhan, S.P. (ed.) TCC 2007. LNCS, vol. 4392, pp. 575–594. Springer, Heidelberg (2007)
37. Kalyanasundaram, B., Schnitger, G.: The Probabilistic Communication Complexity of Set Intersection. SIAM J. Discrete Math. **5**(4), 545–557 (1992)
38. Kushilevitz, E., Ostrovsky, R.: Replication is NOT needed: SINGLE database, computationally-private information retrieval. In: FOCS 1997, pp. 364–373 (1997)
39. Lipmaa, H.: An oblivious transfer protocol with log-squared communication. In: Zhou, J., López, J., Deng, R.H., Bao, F. (eds.) ISC 2005. LNCS, vol. 3650, pp. 314–328. Springer, Heidelberg (2005)
40. Ostrovsky, R., Shoup, V.: Private information storage. In: STOC 1997, pp. 294–303. ACM (1997)
41. Ostrovsky, R., Skeith III, W.E.: Private Searching on Streaming Data. J. Cryptology **20**(4), 397–430 (2007)
42. Regev, O.: On lattices, learning with errors, random linear codes, and cryptography. In: STOC 2005, pp. 84–93 (2005)

43. Sahai, A., Waters, B.: How to use indistinguishability obfuscation: deniable encryption, and more. In: STOC 2014, pp. 475–484 (2014)
44. Shamir, A.: How to Share a Secret. CACM **22**(11), 612–613 (1979)
45. Wehner, S., de Wolf, R.: Improved lower bounds for locally decodable codes and private information retrieval. In: Caires, L., Italiano, G.F., Monteiro, L., Palamidessi, C., Yung, M. (eds.) ICALP 2005. LNCS, vol. 3580, pp. 1424–1436. Springer, Heidelberg (2005)
46. Yao, A.C.-C.: Protocols for secure computations (extended abstract). In: FOCS 1982, pp. 160–164 (1982)
47. Yekhanin, S.: Towards 3-query locally decodable codes of subexponential length. STOC 2007, pp. 266–274 (2007)

Outsourcing Computations

Cluster Computing in Zero Knowledge

Alessandro Chiesa[1]($\boxtimes$), Eran Tromer[3], and Madars Virza[2]

[1] ETH Zurich, Zürich, Switzerland
`alessandro.chiesa@inf.ethz.ch`
[2] MIT, Cambridge, USA
`madars@csail.mit.edu`
[3] Tel Aviv University, Tel Aviv, Israel
`tromer@cs.tau.ac.il`

Abstract. Large computations, when amenable to distributed parallel execution, are often executed on computer clusters, for scalability and cost reasons. Such computations are used in many applications, including, to name but a few, machine learning, webgraph mining, and statistical machine translation. Oftentimes, though, the input data is private and only the result of the computation can be published. Zero-knowledge proofs would allow, in such settings, to verify correctness of the output without leaking (additional) information about the input.

In this work, we investigate theoretical and practical aspects of *zero-knowledge proofs for cluster computations*. We design, build, and evaluate zero-knowledge proof systems for which: (i) a proof attests to the correct execution of a cluster computation; and (ii) generating the proof is itself a cluster computation that is similar in structure and complexity to the original one. Concretely, we focus on MapReduce, an elegant and popular form of cluster computing.

Previous zero-knowledge proof systems can in principle prove a MapReduce computation's correctness, via a monolithic NP statement that reasons about all mappers, all reducers, and shuffling. However, it is not clear how to generate the proof for such monolithic statements via parallel execution by a distributed system. Our work demonstrates, by theory and implementation, that proof generation can be similar in structure and complexity to the original cluster computation.

Our main technique is a bootstrapping theorem for succinct non-interactive arguments of knowledge (SNARKs) that shows how, via recursive proof composition and Proof-Carrying Data, it is possible to transform any SNARK into a *distributed SNARK for MapReduce* which proves, piecewise and in a distributed way, the correctness of every step in the original MapReduce computation as well as their global consistency.

Keywords: Computationally-sound proofs · Proof-carrying data · Zero knowledge · Cluster computing · MapReduce

© International Association for Cryptologic Research 2015
E. Oswald and M. Fischlin (Eds.): EUROCRYPT 2015, Part II, LNCS 9057, pp. 371–403, 2015.
DOI: 10.1007/978-3-662-46803-6_13

1   Introduction

We study theoretical and concrete aspects of *zero-knowledge proofs for cluster computations*, seeking proofs for which: (i) the output of the cluster computation carries a zero-knowledge proof of its correctness; and (ii) generating a proof is itself a cluster computation that is similar in structure and complexity to the original one.

1.1   Motivation

Consider the following motivating example. A server owns a private database x, and a client wishes to learn $y := F(x)$ for a public function F, selected either by himself or someone else. A (hiding) commitment cm to x is known publicly. For example, x may be a database containing genetic data, and F may be a machine-learning algorithm that uses the genetic data to compute a classifier y. On the one hand, the client seeks *integrity of computation*: he wants to ensure that the server reports the correct output y (because the classifier y may be used for critical medical decisions). On the other hand, the server seeks *confidentiality* of his own input: he is willing to disclose y to the client, but no additional information about x beyond y (because the genetic data x may contain sensitive personal information).

Zero-knowledge proofs.   Achieving the combination of the aforementioned security requirements seems paradoxical; after all, the client does not have the input x, and the server is not willing to share it. Nevertheless, cryptography offers a powerful tool that is able to do just that: *zero-knowledge proofs* [48]. More precisely, the server, acting as the prover, attempts to convince the client, acting as the verifier, that the following NP statement is true: "there exists $\tilde{x}$ such that $y = F(\tilde{x})$ and $\tilde{x}$ is a decommitment of cm". Indeed: (a) the proof system's *soundness* property addresses the client's integrity concern, because it guarantees that, if the NP statement is false, the prover cannot convince the verifier (with high probability);[1] and (b) the proof system's *zero-knowledge* property addresses the server's confidentiality concern, because it guarantees that, if the NP statement is true, the prover can convince the verifier without leaking any information about x (beyond was is leaked by the output y).

Cluster computations.   When F is amenable to parallel execution by a distributed system, it is often desirable, for scalability and cost reasons, to compute $y := F(x)$ on a *computer cluster*. A computer cluster consists of nodes (e.g., commodity machines) connected via a network, and each node performs local computations as coordinated via messages with other nodes. Thus, to compute $F(x)$, a cluster may break x down into chunks and use these to assign sub-tasks to different nodes; the results of these sub-tasks may require further computation, so that nodes further coordinate, deduce more sub-tasks, and so on, until

---

[1] Sometimes a property stronger than soundness is required: *proof of knowledge* [4,48], which guarantees that, whenever the client is convinced, not only can he deduce that a witness exists, but also that the prover *knows* one such witness.

the final result y can be collected. Parallel execution by a distributed system is possible in many settings, including the aforementioned one of running machine-learning algorithms on private genetic data. Indeed, "cloud" service providers do offer users distributed programming interfaces (e.g., Amazon's "EMR" and Rackspace's "Big Data", both of which use the Hadoop framework).

The problem: how to do cluster computing in zero knowledge? In principle, any zero-knowledge proof system for NP can be used to express an NP statement that captures F's correct execution. However, while F may have been efficient to execute on a computer cluster, the process of generating a proof attesting to its correctness may not be. Suppose, for example, that the NP statement to be proved must be expressed as an instance of circuit satisfiability. Then, one would have to construct a single circuit that expresses the correctness of the computation of every node in the cluster, as well as the correctness of communication among them. Proving the satisfiability of the resulting monolithic circuit via off-the-shelf zero-knowledge proof systems is a computation that looks nothing like the original one and, moreover, may not be suitable for efficient execution on a cluster. Ideally, the proving process should be a distributed computation that is similar to the original one, in that the complexity of producing the proof is not much larger than that of the original computation and, likewise, has a cluster-friendly communication structure. In sum: To what extent can one efficiently perform cluster computing in zero knowledge?

1.2 Our Focus: MapReduce

Cluster computing is a hypernym that encompasses numerous forms of distributed computing, as determined by the cluster's architecture (i.e., its programming model and its execution framework). Indeed, a cluster's architecture often depends on the class of envisioned applications (e.g., indexing the World Wide Web, performing astrophysical N-body simulations, executing machine-learning algorithms on genetic data, and so on).

In this work, we focus on a concrete, yet elegant and powerful, distributed architecture: *MapReduce* [35]. We review MapReduce later (in Section 2), and now only say that MapReduce can express many useful computations, including ones used for machine learning [26,67,82], graph mining and processing [52,58], statistical machine translation [20,38,57,70], document similarity [56], and bioinformatics [54,71]. For concreteness, we specialize to MapReduce the question raised in Section 1.1:

> Can one obtain zero-knowledge proofs attesting to the correctness of MapReduce computations, in which the proving process is itself distributed and can be efficiently expressed via MapReduce computations?

1.3 Our Contributions

In this paper we present two main results, both contributing to the feasibility of cluster computing in zero knowledge.

1. **MapReduce in zero knowledge.** Under knowledge-of-exponent assumptions [5,31,50], we construct a zero-knowledge proof system in which: (i) a proof attests to the correct execution of a MapReduce computation; and (ii) generating a proof consists of MapReduce computations with similar complexity as the original one. Moreover, the proof system is succinct and non-interactive, i.e., is a *zk-SNARK* [12,15,44].
2. **A working prototype.** We design, build, and evaluate a working prototype for the aforementioned construction.

At the heart of our construction (and implementation) lies a **new bootstrapping theorem** for zk-SNARKs. Informally:

> Assuming collision-resistant hashing, there is an efficient transformation that takes as input a zk-SNARK (even one with expensive preprocessing) and outputs a *distributed zk-SNARK for MapReduce*, i.e., a zk-SNARK for MapReduce where the prover can be efficiently implemented via MapReduce.

The transformation consists of the following two steps.

- **Step I:** use a given (non-distributed) zk-SNARK to obtain a *proof-carrying data* (PCD) system [24,25], a cryptographic primitive that enforces local invariants, the *compliance predicates*, in distributed computations.
- **Step II:** use the PCD system on a specially-crafted predicate to obtain a distributed zk-SNARK for MapReduce.

The theory for the first step is due to [13]; a special case was implemented in [8], and our implementation generalizes it to support the MapReduce application. The second step is novel and is an example of using "compliance engineering" to conduct and prove correctness of non-trivial distributed computations. From an implementation standpoint, both steps require significant and careful engineering, as we explain later.

1.4 Prior Work

zk-SNARKs. We study zero-knowledge proofs [48] that are non-interactive [16,17,66]. Specifically, we study non-interactive zero-knowledge proofs that are *succinct*, i.e., short and easy to verify [63]; these are known as *zk-SNARKs* [12, 15,44].

There are many zk-SNARK constructions in the literature, with different properties in efficiency and supported languages. In *preprocessing zk-SNARKs*, the complexity of the setup of public parameters grows with the size of the computation being proved [3,7,9,15,30,33,39,43,49,53,59–61,69,81,83]; in *fully-succinct zk-SNARKs*, that complexity is independent of computation size [8,11–14,32,36, 47,63,64,79]. Working prototypes have been achieved both for preprocessing zk-SNARKs [7,9,30,53,69,83] and for fully-succinct ones [8]. Several works have also explored more in depth various applications of zk-SNARKs [6,21,23,34,41].

Prior work has not sought (or achieved) distributed zk-SNARKs for MapReduce. Of course, non-distributed zk-SNARKs for MapReduce (i.e., where the prover is not amenable to parallel distributed execution) can be achieved, trivially, via any zk-SNARK for NP: (a) express (the correctness of) the MapReduce computation via a suitable NP statement; then (b) prove satisfiability of that NP statement by using the zk-SNARK.

Proof-carrying data. *Proof-Carrying Data* (PCD) [24,25] is a framework for enforcing local invariants in distributed computations; it is captured via a cryptographic primitive called *PCD system*. Proof-Carrying Data covers, as special examples, incrementally-verifiable computation [79] and targeted malleability [19]. Its role in bootstrapping zk-SNARKs was shown in [13], and an implementation of it was achieved in [8].

Outsourcing MapReduce computations. Braun et al. [21] construct (and implement) an interactive protocol for verifiably outsourcing MapReduce computations to untrusted servers. While interacting with the prover, the client has to perform himself the MapReduce shuffling phase; hence, their protocol is neither succinct nor zero knowledge. (In particular, their protocol is not a zk-SNARK and, a fortiori, nor a distributed zk-SNARK.)

Other works on outsourcing computations. Numerous works [2,10,18,21, 22,27–29,40,42,46,51,68,73–78,80] seek to verifiably outsource various classes of computation to untrusted powerful servers, e.g., in order to leverage cheaper cycles or storage. Some of these works have achieved working prototypes of their protocols.

Verifiable outsourcing of computations *is not our goal*. Rather, we study theoretical and practical aspects of zero-knowledge proofs for cluster computations. Zero-knowledge proofs are useful even when applied to relatively-small computations, and even with high overheads (e.g., see [65] for a recent example).[2]

1.5   Summary of Challenges and Techniques

Our construction (and implementation) rely on a new bootstrapping theorem for zk-SNARKs: any zk-SNARK can be transformed into a distributed zk-SNARK for MapReduce. The transformation is done in two steps, as follows.

From the zk-SNARK to a Multi-predicate PCD System The transformation's first step uses the given zk-SNARK to construct a *PCD system* [24,25], a cryptographic primitive that enforces a given local invariant, known as the *compliance predicate*, in distributed computations. Such a transformation was described by [13], following [79] and [24]. It was implemented by [8], and

---

[2] In this paper's setting, the client does not have the server's input, and so cannot conduct the computation on his own. It is thus *not meaningful* to compare "efficiency of outsourced computation at the server" and "efficiency of native execution at the client", since the latter was never an option.

used for obtaining scalable zero-knowledge proofs for random-access machine executions.

These prior works are constrained to enforcing a single compliance predicate at all nodes in the distributed computation. However, in MapReduce computations (as in many others), different nodes are subject to different requirements. In principle one can create a single compliance predicate expressing the disjunction of all these requirements; but the resulting predicate is large (its size is the sum of each requirement's size) and entails a large cost in proving time.

We thus extend [8] to define, construct, and implement a *multi-predicate PCD system*, where different nodes may be subject to different compliance predicates, and yet the cost of producing the proof, at each node, depends merely on the compliance predicate to which this particular node is subject. The presence of multiple compliance predicates complicates the construction of the arithmetic circuits for performing recursive proof composition, as these must now verify a zk-SNARK proof relative to one out of a (potentially large) number of compliance predicates, each with its own verification key, at a cost that is essentially independent of the predicates that are not locally relevant.

Additional restrictions in the prior works, which we also relax, are that node arity (the number of input messages to a node) was fixed, and that a node's input lengths had to equal its output length. While not fundamental, these limitations cause sizable overheads in heterogenous distributed computations (of which MapReduce is an example).

From a Multi-predicate PCD System to a Distributed zk-SNARK for MapReduce The transformation's second step uses the aforementioned multi-predicate PCD system to construct a distributed zk-SNARK for MapReduce.

For each individual map node or reduce node, correctness of the local computation is independent of other computations; so it is fairly straightforward to distill local "map" and "reduce" compliance predicates. However, the shuffle phase of the MapReduce computation is a global computation that involves all of the mappers' outputs. We wish to ensure *globally* correct shuffling, while only enforcing (via the PCD system) the preservation of a compliance predicate, *locally* at each node. (Of course, one could always consider a big shuffler node that takes all the shuffled messages as inputs, but doing so would prevent the proof generation from being distributed.)

We thus show how to decompose correct shuffling into a collection of simple local predicates, while preserving zero knowledge (which introduces subtleties). Roughly, we show that there is a parallel distributed algorithm to simultaneously compute, for each unique key k, a proof attesting that the list of values associated to k in the output of the shuffling process contains all the those values, and only those, that were paired with k by some mapper.

Subsequently, we use the map and reduce compliance predicates, along with those used to prove correct shuffling, and obtain a collection of compliance predicates with the property that any distributed computation that is complaint with these corresponds to a correct MapReduce computation.

Note how the extensions to basic PCD, mentioned in Section 1.5, come into play. First, we specify multiple compliance predicate, for the different stages of the computation, and only pay for the applicable one at every point. Second, because MapReduce computation has a communication pattern that is input-dependent and not very homogenous, we require PCD to support (directly and thus more efficiently) flexible communication patterns, with variable node arity and varying input and output message lengths.

2   Preliminaries

We give notations and definitions needed for this paper's technical discussions.

We denote by λ the security parameter. We write $f = O_\lambda(g)$ to mean that there is $c > 0$ such that $f = O(\lambda^c g)$. We write $|a|$ to denote the number of bits needed to store a (whether a be a vector, a circuit, and so on). Finally, to simplify notation, we do not make explicit adversaries' auxiliary inputs.

2.1   Commitments

A *commitment scheme* is a pair COMM = (COMM.Gen, COMM.Ver) with the following syntax:

- COMM.Gen(z) → (cm, trp). On input data z, the *commitment generator* COMM.Gen probabilistically samples a commitment cm of z and a corresponding trapdoor trp.
- COMM.Ver(z, cm, trp) → b. On input data z, commitment cm, and trapdoor trp, the *commitment verifier* COMM.Ver outputs $b = 1$ if cm is a valid commitment of z with respect to the trapdoor trp (and $b = 0$ otherwise).

The scheme COMM satisfies the natural completeness, (computational) binding, and (statistical) hiding properties. We assume that cm does not even leak $|z|$, and thus $|cm|$ is a fixed polynomial in the security parameter.

2.2   Merkle Trees

We use Merkle trees [62] (based on some collision-resistant function) as non-hiding succinct commitments to lists of values, in the familiar way. A *Merkle-tree scheme* is a tuple MERKLE = (MERKLE.GetRoot, MERKLE.GetPath,) MERKLE.CheckPath with the following syntax:

- MERKLE.GetRoot(z) → rt. Given list $z = (z_i)_{i=1}^n$, the *root generator* MERKLE.GetRoot deterministically computes a root rt of the Merkle tree with the list z at its leaves.
- MERKLE.GetPath(z, i) → ap. Given input list z and index i, the *authentication path generator* MERKLE.GetPath deterministically computes the authentication path ap for z_i.
- MERKLE.CheckPath(rt, i, z_i, ap) → b. Given root rt, input data z_i, index i, and authentication path ap, the *path checker* MERKLE.CheckPath outputs $b = 1$ if ap is a valid path for z_i as the i-th leaf in a Merkle tree with root rt.

The scheme MERKLE satisfies the natural completeness and (computational) binding properties.

2.3 MapReduce

Overview of MapReduce MapReduce is a programming model for describing data-parallel computations to be run on computer clusters [35]. A *MapReduce job* consists of two functions, Map and Reduce, and an input, $\mathbf{x}$, which is a list of key-value pairs; executing the job results into an output, $\mathbf{y}$, which also is a list of key-value pairs. Computing $\mathbf{y}$ requires three phases: (i) *Map phase:* the function Map is separately invoked on each key-value pair in the list $\mathbf{x}$; each such invocation produces an intermediate sub-list of key-value pairs. (ii) *Shuffle phase:* all the intermediate sub-lists of key-value pairs are jointly shuffled so that pairs that share the same key are gathered together into groups. (iii) *Reduce phase:* the function Reduce is separately invoked on each group of key-value pairs; each such invocation produces an output key-value pair; all these pairs are concatenated (in some order) to form $\mathbf{y}$.

Naturally, efficiently computing the three phases on a computer cluster requires a suitable framework to assign computers to Map tasks, implement the distributed shuffle of intermediate key-value pairs, assign computers to Reduce tasks, and collect the various outputs; this is typically orchestrated by a master node. For now, we focus on the definition of the programming model and not the details of a framework that implements it.

Notation for MapReduce We introduce notation that enables us to discuss MapReduce in more detail.

Keys, values, and records. First, we discuss the data associated to a MapReduce job. The main "unit of data" is a *record*, which is a pair (k, v) where k is its *key* and v is its *value*. We distinguish between different kinds of records, depending on which phase they belong to: input records are of *phase* 1 and lie in $\mathcal{K}^1 \times \mathcal{V}^1$; intermediate records are of *phase* 2 and lie in $\mathcal{K}^2 \times \mathcal{V}^2$; and output records are of *phase* 3 lie in $\mathcal{K}^3 \times \mathcal{V}^3$.

MapReduce pairs. Next, we discuss the functions associated to a MapReduce job. A *MapReduce pair* is a pair (Map, Reduce) where Map: $\mathcal{K}^1 \times \mathcal{V}^1 \to (\mathcal{K}^2 \times \mathcal{V}^2)^*$ is its *Map function* and Reduce: $\mathcal{K}^2 \times (\mathcal{V}^2)^* \to (\mathcal{K}^3 \times \mathcal{V}^3)$ is its *Reduce function*; both must run in polynomial time. In other words, on input a phase-1 record $(k^1, v^1) \in (\mathcal{K}^1 \times \mathcal{V}^1)$, Map outputs a list of phase-2 records $((k_i^2, v_i^2))_i \in (\mathcal{K}^2 \times \mathcal{V}^2)^*$. Instead, on input a phase-2 key $k^2 \in \mathcal{K}^2$ and a list of phase-2 values $(v_i^2)_i \in (\mathcal{V}^2)^*$, Reduce outputs a phase-3 record $(k^3, v^3) \in (\mathcal{K}^3 \times \mathcal{V}^3)$.

MapReduce executions. Finally, we discuss how functions operate on data so to *execute* a MapReduce job. Given a MapReduce pair (Map, Reduce) and an input $\mathbf{x} \in (\mathcal{K}^1 \times \mathcal{V}^1)^*$, the output of the execution of (Map, Reduce) on $\mathbf{x}$, denoted $[\mathsf{Map}, \mathsf{Reduce}](\mathbf{x})$, is the result $\mathbf{y} \in (\mathcal{K}^3 \times \mathcal{V}^3)^*$ of the following (abstract) computation.

1. **Map step.** For each $i \in \{1, \ldots, |\mathbf{x}|\}$, letting (k_i^1, v_i^1) be the i-th phase-1 record in $\mathbf{x}$, compute the list of phase-2 records $((k_{i,j}^2, v_{i,j}^2))_j := \mathsf{Map}(k_i^1, v_i^1)$. This step produces a list of intermediate records $\mathbf{z} = ((k_{i,j}^2, v_{i,j}^2))_{i,j}$.

2. **Shuffle step.** Shuffle the list $\mathbf{z}$ so that records with the same key are grouped together. This step induces, for each unique key k^2 appearing in $\mathbf{z}$, a corresponding list $\mathbf{v}^2$ of values paired with k^2.

3. **Reduce step.** For each unique phase-2 key k^2 in $\mathbf{z}$ and its corresponding list of phase-2 values $\mathbf{v}^2$, compute the phase-3 record $(k^3, v^3) = \mathsf{Reduce}(k^2, \mathbf{v}^2)$. The output $\mathbf{y}$ equals the concatenation of all of these phase-3 records.

We note that MapReduce jobs enjoy certain "symmetries" (which simplify the task of execution on clusters): the order of records in $\mathbf{x}$ or in $\mathbf{y}$ is irrelevant.[3] In terms of complexity measures, we say that the execution of $(\mathsf{Map}, \mathsf{Reduce})$ on $\mathbf{x}$ is (m, r, p)-*bounded* if each individual execution of Map takes at most m time, each individual execution of Reduce takes at most r time, and $|\mathbf{x}| \cdot m + |\mathbf{y}| \cdot r \leq p$ (where $\mathbf{y} := [\mathsf{Map}, \mathsf{Reduce}](\mathbf{x})$).[4]

The MapReduce language. We express, via a suitable language, the notion of "correct" MapReduce executions:

Definition 1. *For a MapReduce pair* $(\mathsf{Map}, \mathsf{Reduce})$, *the language* $\mathscr{L}_{(\mathsf{Map},\mathsf{Reduce})}$ *consists of the tuples* $(\mathbf{x}, \mathbf{y})$ *for which* $\mathbf{y} = [\mathsf{Map}, \mathsf{Reduce}](\mathbf{x})$.[5]

In this work, we consider the setting where an input $\mathbf{x}$ is not known to the user, but only its commitment cm is (as $\mathbf{x}$ is private). Thus, we work with a related relation, $\mathscr{R}^{\mathsf{COMM}}_{(\mathsf{Map},\mathsf{Reduce})}$, derived from $\mathscr{L}_{(\mathsf{Map},\mathsf{Reduce})}$ and a commitment scheme $\mathsf{COMM} = (\mathsf{COMM.Gen}, \mathsf{COMM.Ver})$ (using the syntax introduced in Section 2.1). In contrast to $\mathscr{L}_{(\mathsf{Map},\mathsf{Reduce})}$, instances in $\mathscr{R}^{\mathsf{COMM}}_{(\mathsf{Map},\mathsf{Reduce})}$ contain cm instead of $\mathbf{x}$, and witnesses are extended to contain decommitment information (i.e., the input and commitment trapdoor). More precisely, we define the relation $\mathscr{R}^{\mathsf{COMM}}_{(\mathsf{Map},\mathsf{Reduce})}$ as follows.

Definition 2. *For a MapReduce pair* $(\mathsf{Map}, \mathsf{Reduce})$ *and commitment scheme* COMM, *the relation* $\mathscr{R}^{\mathsf{COMM}}_{(\mathsf{Map},\mathsf{Reduce})}$ *consists of instance-witness pairs* $\big((\mathsf{cm}, \mathbf{y}), (\mathbf{x}, \mathsf{trp})\big)$ *such that* $\mathsf{COMM.Ver}(\mathbf{x}, \mathsf{cm}, \mathsf{trp}) = 1$ *and* $(\mathbf{x}, \mathbf{y}) \in \mathscr{L}_{(\mathsf{Map},\mathsf{Reduce})}$.

MapReduce sequences. A single MapReduce execution is at times insufficient to run an algorithm. In such cases, instead of a single MapReduce pair, we consider a *MapReduce sequence* $\mathbf{S}$: a list $\big((I_i, \mathsf{Map}_i, \mathsf{Reduce}_i)\big)_{i=1}^{d}$ such that, for each i, $I_i \subseteq \{0, \ldots, i-1\}$ and $(\mathsf{Map}_i, \mathsf{Reduce}_i)$ is a MapReduce pair. We call d the *depth of* $\mathbf{S}$. The output of the execution of $\mathbf{S}$ on an input $\mathbf{x}$, denoted $\mathbf{S}(\mathbf{x})$, is the result $\mathbf{y}$ obtained as follows: (1) set $\mathbf{y}^{(0)} := \mathbf{x}$; (2) for $i = 1, \ldots, d$, compute $\mathbf{y}^{(i)} := [\mathsf{Map}_i, \mathsf{Reduce}_i](\mathbf{x}^{(i)})$ where $\mathbf{x}^{(i)}$ is the concatenation of all $\mathbf{y}^{(j)}$ with $j \in I_i$; (3) output $\mathbf{y} := \mathbf{y}^{(d)}$. In terms of complexity measures, similarly to above, we say that the execution of $\mathbf{S}$ on $\mathbf{x}$ is (m, r, p)-*bounded* if each individual execution of

---

[3] One only considers Map and Reduce functions that do not introduce asymmetries (by, e.g., leveraging the order of elements in a list).

[4] For simplicity, we ignore the cost of shuffling because it is typically on the order of the input and output sizes [45].

[5] Due to symmetry, $(\mathbf{x}, \mathbf{y}) \in \mathscr{L}_{(\mathsf{Map},\mathsf{Reduce})}$ if and only if $(\pi(\mathbf{x}), \pi'(\mathbf{y})) \in \mathscr{L}_{(\mathsf{Map},\mathsf{Reduce})}$ for any two permutations π and π' (of records).

any Map_i takes at most m time, each individual execution of any Reduce_i takes at most r time, and $\sum_{i=1}^{d}(|\mathbf{x}^{(i-1)}| \cdot m + |\mathbf{x}^{(i)}| \cdot r) \leq p$.

Family of MapReduce sequences. A *family of MapReduce sequences* is a family $(\mathbf{S}_N)_{N \in \mathbb{N}}$ where each $\mathbf{S}_N$ is a MapReduce sequence $\big((I_{N,i}, \mathsf{Map}_{N,i}, \mathsf{Reduce}_{N,i})\big)_{i=1}^{d_N}$.

3   Definition of Distributed zk-SNARKs for MapReduce

We (informally) define non-distributed zk-SNARKs for MapReduce, and then distributed zk-SNARKs for MapReduce. Throughout, we assume familiarity with the notations and definitions for MapReduce introduced in Section 2.3.

3.1   Non-distributed zk-SNARKs for MapReduce

A (non-distributed) *zk-SNARK for MapReduce* is a zk-SNARK for proving knowledge of witnesses in $\mathscr{R}^{\mathsf{COMM}}_{(\mathsf{Map},\mathsf{Reduce})}$, for a user-specified MapReduce pair $(\mathsf{Map}, \mathsf{Reduce})$ and a fixed choice of commitment scheme COMM. That is, it is a cryptographic primitive that provides short and easy-to-verify non-interactive zero-knowledge proofs of knowledge for the relation $\mathscr{R}^{\mathsf{COMM}}_{(\mathsf{Map},\mathsf{Reduce})}$. Concretely, the primitive consists of a tuple $(\mathsf{COMM}, \mathsf{MR.KeyGen}, \mathsf{MR.Prove}, \mathsf{MR.Verify})$ with the following syntax.

- $\mathsf{MR.KeyGen}(1^\lambda, \mathsf{Map}, \mathsf{Reduce}) \rightarrow (\mathsf{pk}, \mathsf{vk})$. On input a security parameter λ (presented in unary) and a MapReduce pair $(\mathsf{Map}, \mathsf{Reduce})$, the *key generator* $\mathsf{MR.KeyGen}$ probabilistically samples a proving key pk and a verification key vk. We assume, without loss of generality, that pk contains (a description of) the MapReduce pair $(\mathsf{Map}, \mathsf{Reduce})$.

The keys pk and vk are published as public parameters and can be used, any number of times, to prove/verify knowledge of witnesses in the relation $\mathscr{R}^{\mathsf{COMM}}_{(\mathsf{Map},\mathsf{Reduce})}$, as follows.

- $\mathsf{MR.Prove}(\mathsf{pk}, \mathsf{cm}, \mathsf{y}, \mathsf{x}, \mathsf{trp}) \rightarrow \pi_{\mathsf{MR}}$. On input a proving key pk, instance $(\mathsf{cm}, \mathsf{y})$, and witness $(\mathsf{x}, \mathsf{trp})$, the *prover* $\mathsf{MR.Prove}$ outputs a proof π_{MR} for the statement "there is $(\mathsf{x}, \mathsf{trp})$ such that $\big((\mathsf{cm}, \mathsf{y}), (\mathsf{x}, \mathsf{trp})\big) \in \mathscr{R}^{\mathsf{COMM}}_{(\mathsf{Map},\mathsf{Reduce})}$."
- $\mathsf{MR.Verify}(\mathsf{vk}, \mathsf{cm}, \mathsf{y}, \pi_{\mathsf{MR}}) \rightarrow b$. On input a verification key vk, commitment cm, output y, and proof π_{MR}, the *verifier* $\mathsf{MR.Verify}$ outputs $b = 1$ if he is convinced that there is $(\mathsf{x}, \mathsf{trp})$ such that $\big((\mathsf{cm}, \mathsf{y}), (\mathsf{x}, \mathsf{trp})\big) \in \mathscr{R}^{\mathsf{COMM}}_{(\mathsf{Map},\mathsf{Reduce})}$.

As in other zk-SNARKs, the above tuple satisfies (variants of) the properties of completeness, succinctness, (computational) proof of knowledge, and (statistical) zero knowledge; we describe these in the full version. Here we recall succinctness: an honestly-generated proof π_{MR} has $O_\lambda(1)$ bits, and $\mathsf{MR.Verify}(\mathsf{vk}, \mathsf{cm}, \mathsf{y}, \pi_{\mathsf{MR}})$ runs in time $O_\lambda(|\mathsf{y}|)$.

Costs of key generation. The above implies that $(\mathsf{pk}, \mathsf{vk})$ is generated in time $O_\lambda(1) \cdot \mathrm{poly}(|\mathsf{Map}| + |\mathsf{Reduce}|)$, that $|\mathsf{pk}| = O_\lambda(1) \cdot \mathrm{poly}(|\mathsf{Map}| + |\mathsf{Reduce}|)$, and that $|vk| = O_\lambda(1)$ (since MR.Verify runs in time $O_\lambda(|y|)$ for any y). These key-generation costs are between those of a preprocessing zk-SNARK (where key generation costs as much as the *entire* computation being proved) and a fully-succinct zk-SNARK (where key generation costs only a fixed polynomial in λ), because they do not depend on the number of mappers and reducers in the MapReduce computation.

One could strengthen the definition above to require "full succinctness", i.e., to further require that key generation depends polynomially on the security parameter only (and, in particular, that the MapReduce pair is not hard-coded into the keys). The results presented in this paper extend to achieve this stronger definition.

3.2 Distributed zk-SNARKs for MapReduce

A *distributed zk-SNARK for MapReduce* is a zk-SNARK for MapReduce where the prover consists of few MapReduce computations whose overall complexity is similar to the MapReduce computation being proved. More precisely, when producing proofs for the relation $\mathscr{R}^{\text{COMM}}_{(\text{Map},\text{Reduce})}$, MR.Prove$(pk, \cdot, \cdot, \cdot, \cdot)$ is a family of MapReduce sequences that is $(\text{Map}, \text{Reduce})$-*faithful*, a property defined below.

Definition 3. *Given a MapReduce pair* $(\text{Map}, \text{Reduce})$, *a family of MapReduce sequences* $(\mathbf{S}_N)_{N \in \mathbb{N}}$ *is* $(\text{Map}, \text{Reduce})$-*faithful if, for all* $N \in \mathbb{N}$ *and* $((\text{cm}, y), (x, trp)) \in \mathscr{R}^{\text{COMM}}_{(\text{Map},\text{Reduce})}$ *with* $|x| + |y| \leq N$:
- *the depth of* $\mathbf{S}_N$ *is logarithmic in* N, *i.e.,* $d_N = O(\log N)$; *and*
- $\mathbf{S}_N$ *has a linear overhead compared to* $(\text{Map}, \text{Reduce})$, *i.e., for all* $m, r, p \in \mathbb{N}$, *if* x *is* (m, r, p)-*bounded then the execution of* $\mathbf{S}_N$ *on* (cm, y, x, trp) *is* $(O_\lambda(m), O_\lambda (r), O_\lambda(p))$-*bounded.*

4 Definition of Multi-predicate PCD

Proof-carrying data (PCD) [24,25] is a cryptographic primitive that encapsulates the security guarantees achievable via recursive composition of proofs. Since recursive proof composition naturally involves multiple (physical or virtual) parties, PCD is phrased in the language of a *distributed computation* among computing nodes, who perform local computations, based on local data and input messages, and then produce output messages. Given a *compliance predicate* Π to express local checks, the goal of PCD is to ensure that any given message msg in the distributed computation is Π-*compliant*, i.e., is consistent with a history in which each node's local computation satisfies Π. This formulation covers, as special cases, incrementally-verifiable computation [79] and targeted malleability [19].

Extending PCD to multiple predicates. The definition of PCD naturally generalizes to compliance with respect to a *vector* $\boldsymbol{\Pi}$ of compliance predicates (rather than a single predicate). Namely, a msg is $\boldsymbol{\Pi}$-*compliant* if it is consistent with a history in which each node's local computation satisfies some predicate Π

in the vector $\boldsymbol{\Pi}$. Moreover, a message msg comprises two parts: the *type*, which records what kind of node output msg, and the *payload*, which is the rest.

The above *multi-predicate PCD* can be "simulated" via a *single-predicate PCD*, by folding all the predicates in the vector $\boldsymbol{\Pi}$ into a single predicate $\Pi^\star$ that (a) reasons about which predicate in $\boldsymbol{\Pi}$ to use at a give node, and (b) enforces a message's type and payload separation. However, this simulation incurs a significant overhead: the size of $\Pi^\star$ is the sum of the sizes of all the predicates in $\boldsymbol{\Pi}$, and this cost is incurred at every node regardless of which predicate is actually used to check compliance at a node. In contrast, in our construction of multi-predicate PCD (see Section 6), we incur, at each node, only the cost of the predicate that is actually used to check compliance.

Implications for MapReduce. As we discuss in Section 5, reducing the correctness of MapReduce computations to compliance of distributed computations involves multiple predicates that perform checks with different semantics: a predicate for mapper nodes, a predicate for reducer nodes, and various other predicates for other nodes that reason about shuffling. These predicates have different sizes and, thus, it is crucial to leverage the flexibility offered by multi-predicate PCD (so to then obtain a distributed zk-SNARK for MapReduce).

Next, we define distributed-computation transcripts (our formal notion of distributed computations), compliance of a transcript T with respect to a given vector $\boldsymbol{\Pi}$ of compliance predicates, and multi-predicate PCD.

Transcripts. A *(distributed-computation) transcript* is a tuple T = $(G, \text{TYPE}, \text{LOC}, \text{PAYLOAD})$, where:
- $G = (V, E)$ is a directed acyclic graph with node set V and edge set $E \subseteq V \times V$;
- TYPE: $V \to \mathbb{N}$ are node labels;
- LOC: $V \to \{0, 1\}^*$ are (another kind of) node labels; and
- PAYLOAD: $E \to \{0, 1\}^*$ are edge labels.

The *message* of an edge $(u, v) \in E$ is the pair $\text{MSG}(u, v) := (\text{TYPE}(u), \text{PAYLOAD}(u, v))$. The *outputs* of the transcript T, denoted OUTS(T), is the set of messages $\text{MSG}(\tilde{u}, \tilde{v})$ where $(\tilde{u}, \tilde{v}) \in E$ and $\tilde{v}$ is a sink. Typically, we denote a message by msg, and its type and payload by msg.type and msg.payload.

Compliant transcripts and messages. A *compliance predicate* Π is a function with a *type*, denoted type(Π). Given a vector $\boldsymbol{\Pi}$ of compliance predicates, we say that:
- a transcript T = $(G, \text{LOC}, \text{TYPE}, \text{PAYLOAD})$ is $\boldsymbol{\Pi}$**-compliant**, denoted $\boldsymbol{\Pi}(\mathsf{T})$
  = OK, if:
    (i) for each $v \in V$, $\text{TYPE}(v) = 0$ if and only if v is a source; and
    (ii) for each non-source $v \in V$ and each $w \in \text{children}(v)$, there is $\Pi \in \boldsymbol{\Pi}$ with $\text{TYPE}(v) = \text{type}(\Pi)$ such that
    $$\Pi\left(\text{MSG}(v, w), \text{LOC}(v), \big(\text{MSG}(u, v)\big)_{u \in \text{parents}(v)}\right) \text{ accepts.}$$
- a message msg is $\boldsymbol{\Pi}$**-compliant** if there is a transcript T such that $\boldsymbol{\Pi}(\mathsf{T}) = \text{OK}$ and msg $\in$ OUTS(T).

A transcript T thus represents a distributed computation, in the following sense. For each node $v \in V$, the function LOC specifies the *local data* used at v; and, for each edge $(u, v) \in E$, the function MSG specifies the *message* sent from node u to node v. A node v with parent nodes parents(v) and children nodes children(v) uses the local data LOC(v) and the *input messages* $\big(\mathrm{MSG}(u, v)\big)_{u \in \mathsf{parents}(v)}$ to compute the *output message* MSG(v, w) for each child $w \in$ children(v). As for the function TYPE, it assigns to each node $v \in V$ a quantity that determines the type of every message output by v; this quantity also determines which compliance predicates can be used to verify compliance of those messages (specifically, the type of the predicate and message must equal).

Multi-predicate PCD systems. A *multi-predicate PCD system* is a triple of polynomial-time algorithms $(\mathbb{G}, \mathbb{P}, \mathbb{V})$, called *key generator, prover,* and *verifier*. The key generator $\mathbb{G}$ is given as input a vector of predicates $\boldsymbol{\Pi}$, and outputs a proving key pk and a verification key vk; these keys allow anyone to prove/verify that a message msg is $\boldsymbol{\Pi}$-compliant. This is achieved by attaching a short and easy-to-verify proof to each message: given pk, input messages $\mathbf{msg_{in}}$ with proofs $\boldsymbol{\pi_{in}}$, local data loc, and an output message msg (allegedly, $\boldsymbol{\Pi}$-compliant), the prover $\mathbb{P}$ computes a new proof π to attach to msg; the verifier $\mathbb{V}(\mathsf{vk}, \mathsf{msg}, \pi)$ checks that msg is $\boldsymbol{\Pi}$-compliant. The triple $(\mathbb{G}, \mathbb{P}, \mathbb{V})$ must satisfy completeness, succinctness, (computational) proof of knowledge, and (statistical) zero knowledge; we describe these in the full version. Here we recall succinctness: an honestly-generated proof π has $O_\lambda(1)$ bits, and $\mathbb{V}(\mathsf{vk}, \mathsf{msg}, \pi)$ runs in time $O_\lambda(|\mathsf{msg}|)$.

5 Step II: from Multi-predicate PCD to Distributed zk-SNARKs

We discuss Step II of our bootstrapping theorem: constructing a distributed zk-SNARK for MapReduce from a multi-predicate PCD system. This step itself consists of two main parts.

- **Compliance engineering** (Section 5.1): a reduction from the correctness of MapReduce computations to a question about the compliance of distributed computations with respect to a certain vector $\boldsymbol{\Pi}^{\mathsf{MR}}$ of predicates.
- **Construction of the proof system** (Section 5.2): suitably invoke the multi-predicate PCD system on the vector $\boldsymbol{\Pi}^{\mathsf{MR}}$ in order to construct a distributed zk-SNARK for MapReduce.

5.1 Compliance Engineering for MapReduce

We show how, given any MapReduce pair (Map, Reduce), one can efficiently construct a vector $\boldsymbol{\Pi}^{\mathsf{MR}}$ of compliance predicates for which "suitable" $\boldsymbol{\Pi}^{\mathsf{MR}}$-compliant transcripts correspond to instance-witness pairs in the relation $\mathscr{R}^{\mathsf{COMM}}_{(\mathsf{Map},\mathsf{Reduce})}$. First, we clarify what "suitable" means, via the following definition.

Definition 4. *For an instance* (cm, y), *a transcript* T *is* (cm, y)-*compatible if* $OUTS(T)$ *contains a message with type 1 and payload* $(cm, |y|)$ *and, for each* $i \in \{1, \ldots, |y|\}$, *a message with type 2 and payload* (cm, y_i).

Next, via the following theorem, we show how one can translate a question of the form

"Given an instance (cm, y), is there a witness (x, trp) such that
$$((cm, y), (x, trp)) \text{ is in } \mathscr{R}^{COMM}_{(Map, Reduce)} ?"$$

to a question of the form

"Given an instance (cm, y), is there a $\mathbf{\Pi}^{MR}$-compliant (cm, y)-compatible
transcript T?"

More precisely:

Theorem 1. *There exists a commitment scheme* COMM *such that, for every* *MapReduce pair* (Map, Reduce), *there exist a vector* $\mathbf{\Pi}^{MR}$ *of compliance predicates and two algorithms* Eval, Ext *satisfying the following properties.*
- EFFICIENCY.
  - *The vector* $\mathbf{\Pi}^{MR}$ *consists of 7 predicates, with the following sizes:*
  $$|\mathbf{\Pi}^{MR}[1]| = O_\lambda(|Map|), \ |\mathbf{\Pi}^{MR}[2]| = O_\lambda(|Reduce|), \ and$$
  $$|\mathbf{\Pi}^{MR}[3]|, \ldots, |\mathbf{\Pi}^{MR}[7]| = O_\lambda(1),$$
  where, above, $|\cdot|$ *denotes per-input running time of the underlying algorithm.*
  - *The algorithm* Eval *is* (Map, Reduce)-*faithful.*
  - *The algorithm* Ext *is linear time.*
- COMPLETENESS. *For any instance* (cm, y), *if there is* (x, trp) *such that* $((cm, y), (x, trp))$ *is in* $\mathscr{R}^{COMM}_{(Map, Reduce)}$, *then there is a* $\mathbf{\Pi}^{MR}$-*compliant* (cm, y)-*compatible transcript* T; *moreover,* Eval(cm, y, x, trp) *outputs* $OUTS(T)$ *by dynamically generating* T *"node by node".*
- PROOF OF KNOWLEDGE. *For any instance* (cm, y), *if there is a* $\mathbf{\Pi}^{MR}$-*compliant* (cm, y)-*compatible transcript* T, *then* Ext(T) *outputs* (x, trp) *such that* $((cm, y), (x, trp))$ *is in* $\mathscr{R}^{COMM}_{(Map, Reduce)}$.

We now sketch a proof of the theorem. Recall proof of knowledge: we must construct a vector $\mathbf{\Pi}^{MR}$ of predicates with the property that, given (cm, y), if there is a distributed-computation transcript T that is both $\mathbf{\Pi}^{MR}$-compliant and (cm, y)-compatible, then we can find (x, trp) for which COMM.Ver$(x, cm, trp) = 1$ and $y = [Map, Reduce](x)$. Intuitively, we achieve proof of knowledge by engineering the predicates in $\mathbf{\Pi}^{MR}$ so that the transcript T is forced to encode within it a history of a correct MapReduce execution. Technically, the main challenge is that we are restricted to local checks: each predicate only sees input and output messages of a single node; in contrast, correct execution of a MapReduce computation (also) involves global properties, such as correct shuffling.

We introduce our approach in steps, by first describing two "failed attempts". For simplicity, we focus on the (artificial) case where each mapper outputs a *single* phase-2 record; later, we explain how this restriction can be lifted.

Failed Attempt #1 It is natural to begin by designing two predicates $\Pi_{\mathsf{exe}}^{\mathsf{Map}}$ and $\Pi_{\mathsf{exe}}^{\mathsf{Reduce}}$ that simply capture the correct execution of a mapper and reduce node, respectively, as in Figure 2.

Now suppose that we see a $(\Pi_{\mathsf{exe}}^{\mathsf{Map}}, \Pi_{\mathsf{exe}}^{\mathsf{Reduce}})$-compliant message msg. What can we deduce about the history of computations that led to msg? If msg.type $=$ type$(\Pi_{\mathsf{exe}}^{\mathsf{Map}})$, then msg was output by a node at which the predicate $\Pi_{\mathsf{exe}}^{\mathsf{Map}}$ was checked; conversely, if msg.type $=$ type$(\Pi_{\mathsf{exe}}^{\mathsf{Reduce}})$, then msg was output by a node at which the predicate $\Pi_{\mathsf{exe}}^{\mathsf{Reduce}}$ was checked. Suppose, for example, that msg.type $=$ type$(\Pi_{\mathsf{exe}}^{\mathsf{Reduce}})$. By construction of $\Pi_{\mathsf{exe}}^{\mathsf{Reduce}}$, we deduce that: (i) msg.payload is a phase-3 record (k^3, v^3), and (ii) there is a list of input messages $\mathsf{msg}_{\mathsf{in}}$ whose payloads contain phase-2 records $((k_j^2, v_j^2))_j$ that all share the same key and, moreover, result in (k^3, v^3) when given as input to Reduce. However, as soon as we try to "dig further into the past", to see what properties each phase-2 record (k_j^2, v_j^2) satisfies, we run into issues not addressed by the above construction of $\Pi_{\mathsf{exe}}^{\mathsf{Map}}$ and $\Pi_{\mathsf{exe}}^{\mathsf{Reduce}}$. Namely,

- **Issue I:** How can we ascertain that each phase-2 record (k_i^2, v_i^2) was the correct output of some mapper node?
- **Issue II:** Even if so, where did that mapper obtain its input phase-1 record?

Failed Attempt #2 We augment $\Pi_{\mathsf{exe}}^{\mathsf{Map}}$ and $\Pi_{\mathsf{exe}}^{\mathsf{Reduce}}$ to address these issues. Roughly, we address Issue I by inspecting message types: $\Pi_{\mathsf{exe}}^{\mathsf{Map}}$ ensures that its input messages have type 0 (i.e., are not output by previous nodes); while $\Pi_{\mathsf{exe}}^{\mathsf{Reduce}}$ ensures that they have type type$(\Pi_{\mathsf{exe}}^{\mathsf{Map}})$. As for Issue II, we augment all messages with a commitment cm to the (overall) input x and extend $\Pi_{\mathsf{exe}}^{\mathsf{Map}}$ to authenticate the phase-1 record it receives. We now describe these ideas.

First, we describe the commitment scheme COMM that we use to create cm. Essentially, COMM consists of (i) a Merkle-tree followed by a commitment to the resulting root, and also (ii) a commitment to the size of the committed data. See Figure 1 for more details; we denote the underlying commitment scheme by COMM$'$ and the Merkle-tree scheme by MERKLE (and use notation introduced in Section 2.1 and Section 2.2).

Fig. 1. Choice of commitment scheme COMM (obtained from MERKLE and COMM$'$)

COMM.Gen(z)	COMM.Ver(z, cm, trp)
1. Compute rt := MERKLE.GetRoot(z). 2. Compute $n := \|z\|$. 3. Compute $(\mathsf{cm}_{\mathsf{rt}}, \mathsf{trap}_{\mathsf{rt}}) \leftarrow$ COMM$'$.Gen(rt). 4. Compute $(\mathsf{cm}_n, \mathsf{trap}_n) \leftarrow$ COMM$'$.Gen(n). 5. Set cm := $(\mathsf{cm}_{\mathsf{rt}}, \mathsf{cm}_n)$. 6. Set trp := $(\mathsf{trap}_{\mathsf{rt}}, \mathsf{trap}_n)$. 7. Output (cm, trp).	1. Compute rt := MERKLE.GetRoot(z). 2. Compute $n := \|z\|$. 3. Parse cm as a pair $(\mathsf{cm}_{\mathsf{rt}}, \mathsf{cm}_n)$. 4. Parse trp as a pair $(\mathsf{trap}_{\mathsf{rt}}, \mathsf{trap}_n)$. 5. Check that COMM$'$.Ver(rt, $\mathsf{cm}_{\mathsf{rt}}, \mathsf{trap}_{\mathsf{rt}}) = 1$. 6. Check that COMM$'$.Ver($n$, $\mathsf{cm}_n, \mathsf{trap}_n) = 1$. 7. Output 1 if the above checks succeeded (else, 0).

Next, in Figure 3, we describe the two (updated) predicates $\Pi_{\mathsf{exe}}^{\mathsf{Map}}$ and $\Pi_{\mathsf{exe}}^{\mathsf{Reduce}}$.

Now suppose that we see a $(\Pi_{\mathsf{exe}}^{\mathsf{Map}}, \Pi_{\mathsf{exe}}^{\mathsf{Reduce}})$-compliant message msg with msg.type $=$ type$(\Pi_{\mathsf{exe}}^{\mathsf{Reduce}})$. By (the new) construction of $\Pi_{\mathsf{exe}}^{\mathsf{Reduce}}$, we know that msg.payload $= (\mathsf{cm}, k^3, v^3)$, where cm is a commitment and (k^3, v^3) is a phase-3 record; moreover, we also know that there is a list of messages $\mathbf{msg}_{\mathsf{in}}$ such that: (i) for each j, $\mathbf{msg}_{\mathsf{in}}[j]$.type $= \mathsf{type}(\Pi_{\mathsf{exe}}^{\mathsf{Map}})$ and $\mathbf{msg}_{\mathsf{in}}[j]$.payload $= (\mathsf{cm}, k^2, v_j^2)$, where (k^2, v_j^2) is a phase-2 record; (ii) $(k^3, v^3) = \mathsf{Reduce}(k^2, (v_j^2)_j)$. In turn, each message $\mathbf{msg}_{\mathsf{in}}[j]$ is $(\Pi_{\mathsf{exe}}^{\mathsf{Map}}, \Pi_{\mathsf{exe}}^{\mathsf{Reduce}})$-compliant and, by (the new) construction of $\Pi_{\mathsf{exe}}^{\mathsf{Map}}$, we know that (k^2, v_j^2) is the result of running Map on some phase-1 record authenticated with respect to cm.

Overall, each $(\Pi_{\mathsf{exe}}^{\mathsf{Map}}, \Pi_{\mathsf{exe}}^{\mathsf{Reduce}})$-compliant message msg with msg.type $= \mathsf{type}(\Pi_{\mathsf{exe}}^{\mathsf{Reduce}})$ and msg.payload $= (\mathsf{cm}, k^3, v^3)$ is the result of applying Reduce to some phase-2 records sharing the same key, each of which is in turn the result of applying Map to some phase-1 record authenticated relative to cm. However, these guarantees are not enough to imply a correct MapReduce computation, as we still need to tackle the following issue.

- **Issue III:** How do we ascertain the correctness of the shuffling phase? Namely, how do we ascertain that each list of phase-2 records (received by a particular reducer node) contains *all* the records having that same key?

Indeed, in principle, some phase-2 records may have been duplicated, dropped, or sent to the wrong reducer node (e.g., to different reducer nodes even if sharing the same key).

Our Approach Unlike previous ones, the above issue is conceptually more complex: tackling it requires ensuring correct shuffling, which is a global computation involving all of the phase-2 (all the mappers' outputs); in contrast, we are restricted to only perform local checks encoded in compliance predicates. Nevertheless, we show how we can further extend $\Pi_{\mathsf{exe}}^{\mathsf{Map}}$ and $\Pi_{\mathsf{exe}}^{\mathsf{Reduce}}$, and also introduce other compliance predicates, to ensure correct shuffling in a distributed way.

Further extending $\Pi_{\mathsf{exe}}^{\mathsf{Map}}$ and $\Pi_{\mathsf{exe}}^{\mathsf{Reduce}}$. Roughly, we extend $\Pi_{\mathsf{exe}}^{\mathsf{Map}}$ to store, in the output message, the index i relative to which the phase-1 record, contained in the input message, was authenticated. Subsequently, when receiving several input messages, $\Pi_{\mathsf{exe}}^{\mathsf{Reduce}}$ verifies that all the indices contained in them are distinct. This additional check prevents duplicate messages from being sent to the same reduce node. However, the check does not prevent the same message from being sent to two different reducer nodes, a message from being dropped altogether, or messages with the same key from being sent to two different reducer nodes. Additional "distributed bookkeeping" is required.

We thus further extend $\Pi_{\mathsf{exe}}^{\mathsf{Reduce}}$ to store in its output message two additional pieces of information: the phase-2 key k^2 shared among its input messages and the number d_{in} of these input messages. More precisely, only commitments $\mathsf{cm}_{k^2}, \mathsf{cm}_{d_{\mathsf{in}}}$ to these are stored, to not violate zero knowledge (by storing information about the internals of the computation in final outputs of the distributed computation). As we now explain, other compliance predicates use the underlying values k^2, d_{in}; for now, in Figure 4, we summarize the changes to $\Pi_{\mathsf{exe}}^{\mathsf{Map}}$ and $\Pi_{\mathsf{exe}}^{\mathsf{Reduce}}$ (highlighted in blue).

$\underline{\Pi_{\text{exe}}^{\text{Map}}(\text{msg}, \text{loc}, \text{msg}_{\text{in}})}$

1. Parse $\text{msg}_{\text{in}}[1].\text{payload}$ as a phase-1 record (k^1, v^1).
2. Parse $\text{msg}.\text{payload}$ as a phase-2 record (k^2, v^2).
3. Check that $((k^2, v^2)) = \text{Map}(k^1, v^1)$.

$\underline{\Pi_{\text{exe}}^{\text{Reduce}}(\text{msg}, \text{loc}, \text{msg}_{\text{in}})}$

1. Parse each $\text{msg}_{\text{in}}[j].\text{payload}$ as a phase-2 record (k_j^2, v_j^2).
2. Parse $\text{msg}.\text{payload}$ as a phase-3 record (k^3, v^3).
3. Check that all the k_j^2's are equal, and let $\boldsymbol{v}^2 := (v_j^2)_j$
4. Check that $(k^3, v^3) = \text{Reduce}(k_1^2, \boldsymbol{v}^2)$.

Fig. 2. Summary of the construction of $\Pi_{\text{exe}}^{\text{Map}}$ and $\Pi_{\text{exe}}^{\text{Reduce}}$ for "Failed attempt #1" (see Section 5.1)

$\underline{\Pi_{\text{exe}}^{\text{Map}}(\text{msg}, \text{loc}, \text{msg}_{\text{in}})}$

1. Check that $\text{msg}_{\text{in}}[1].\text{type} = 0$.
2. Parse $\text{msg}_{\text{in}}[1].\text{payload}$ as a tuple (cm, i, k^1, v^1) where:
   - cm is a commitment (for the scheme COMM);
   - i is an index;
   - (k^1, v^1) is a phase-1 record.
3. Parse $\text{msg}.\text{payload}$ as a tuple (cm', k^2, v^2) where:
   - cm′ is a commitment (for the scheme COMM);
   - (k^2, v^2) is a phase-2 record.
4. Parse loc as a tuple $(\text{rt}, M, \text{trp}_{\text{rt}}, \text{trp}_M, \text{ap})$ where:
   - rt is a commitment (for the scheme MERKLE);
   - M is a positive integer;
   - $\text{trp}_{\text{rt}}, \text{trp}_M$ are trapdoors (for the scheme COMM);
   - ap is an authentication path (for the scheme MERKLE).
5. Parse cm as a pair $(\text{cm}_{\text{rt}}, \text{cm}_M)$ where both components are commitments for the scheme COMM′.
6. Check that $\text{COMM}'.\text{Ver}(\text{rt}, \text{cm}_{\text{rt}}, \text{trp}_{\text{rt}}) = 1$.
7. Check that $\text{COMM}'.\text{Ver}(M, \text{cm}_M, \text{trp}_M) = 1$.
8. Check that $0 \leq i < M$.
9. Check that $\text{MERKLE}.\text{CheckPath}(\text{rt}, i, (k^1, v^1), \text{ap}) = 1$.
10. Check that $\text{cm}' = \text{cm}$.
11. Check that $((k^2, v^2)) = \text{Map}(k^1, v^1)$.

$\underline{\Pi_{\text{exe}}^{\text{Reduce}}(\text{msg}, \text{loc}, \text{msg}_{\text{in}})}$

1. Check that $\text{msg}_{\text{in}}[j].\text{type} = \text{type}(\Pi_{\text{exe}}^{\text{Map}})$ for each j.
2. Parse each $\text{msg}_{\text{in}}[j].\text{payload}$ as a tuple $(\text{cm}_j', k_j^2, v_j^2)$ where:
   - cm′$_j$ is a commitment (for the scheme COMM);
   - (k_j^2, v_j^2) is a phase-2 record.
3. Parse $\text{msg}.\text{payload}$ as a tuple (cm'', k^3, v^3) where:
   - cm″ is a commitment (for the scheme COMM);
   - (k^3, v^3) is a phase-3 record.
4. Check that $\text{cm}'' = \text{cm}_j'$ for each j.
5. Check that all the k_i^2's are equal, and let $\boldsymbol{v}^2 := (v_i^2)_i$.
6. Check that $(k^3, v^3) = \text{Reduce}(k_1^2, \boldsymbol{v}^2)$.

Fig. 3. Summary of the construction of $\Pi_{\text{exe}}^{\text{Map}}$ and $\Pi_{\text{exe}}^{\text{Reduce}}$ for "Failed attempt #2"

We now explain how we leverage, and verify, the messages' new information maintained by $\Pi_{\text{exe}}^{\text{Map}}$ and $\Pi_{\text{exe}}^{\text{Reduce}}$. At high level, we introduce new compliance predicates, called $\Pi_{\text{fmt}}^{\text{Map}}$, $\Pi_{\text{fmt}}^{\text{Reduce}}$, $\Pi_{\text{sum}}^{\text{Map}}$, $\Pi_{\text{sum}}^{\text{Reduce}}$, and Π_{fin}, for checking two main distributed computations: a tree-like distributed computation that aggregates information stored by all the messages output by mapper nodes, and another tree-like distributed computation that aggregates information stored by all the messages output by reducer nodes. By comparing the final outputs of these two tree-like distributed computations, we can check if correct shuffling occurred.

$\Pi_{\mathsf{exe}}^{\mathsf{Map}}(\mathsf{msg}, \mathsf{loc}, \mathbf{msg_{in}})$

1. Check that $\mathsf{msg_{in}}[1].\mathsf{type} = 0$.
2. Parse $\mathsf{msg_{in}}[1].\mathsf{payload}$ as a tuple $(\mathsf{cm}, i, k^1, v^1)$ where:
   - cm is a commitment (for the scheme COMM);
   - i is an index;
   - (k^1, v^1) is a phase-1 record.
3. Parse $\mathsf{msg.payload}$ as a tuple $(\mathsf{cm}', i', k^2, v^2)$ where:
   - cm' is a commitment (for the scheme COMM);
   - i' is an index;
   - (k^2, v^2) is a phase-2 record.
4. Parse loc as a tuple $(\mathsf{rt}, M, \mathsf{trp_{rt}}, \mathsf{trp}_M, \mathsf{ap})$ where:
   - rt is a commitment (for the scheme MERKLE);
   - M is a positive integer;
   - $\mathsf{trp_{rt}}, \mathsf{trp}_M$ are trapdoors (for the scheme COMM);
   - ap is an authentication path (for the scheme MERKLE).
5. Parse cm as a pair $(\mathsf{cm_{rt}}, \mathsf{cm}_M)$ where both components are commitments for the scheme COMM'.
6. Check that $\mathsf{COMM}'.\mathsf{Ver}(\mathsf{rt}, \mathsf{cm_{rt}}, \mathsf{trp_{rt}}) = 1$.
7. Check that $\mathsf{COMM}'.\mathsf{Ver}(M, \mathsf{cm}_M, \mathsf{trp}_M) = 1$.
8. Check that $0 \le i < M$.
9. Check that $\mathsf{MERKLE.CheckPath}(\mathsf{rt}, i, (k^1, v^1), \mathsf{ap}) = 1$.
10. Check that $\mathsf{cm}' = \mathsf{cm}$ and $i' = i$.
11. Check that $((k^2, v^2)) = \mathsf{Map}(k^1, v^1)$.

16

$\Pi_{\mathsf{exe}}^{\mathsf{Reduce}}(\mathsf{msg}, \mathsf{loc}, \mathbf{msg_{in}})$

1. Check that $\mathsf{msg_{in}}[j].\mathsf{type} = \mathsf{type}(\Pi_{\mathsf{exe}}^{\mathsf{Map}})$ for each j.
2. Parse each $\mathsf{msg_{in}}[j].\mathsf{payload}$ as a tuple $(\mathsf{cm}'_j, i'_j, k^2_j, v^2_j)$ where:
   - cm'_j is a commitment (for the scheme COMM);
   - i'_j is an index;
   - (k^2_j, v^2_j) is a phase-2 record.
3. Parse $\mathsf{msg.payload}$ as a tuple $(\mathsf{cm}'', k^3, v^3, \mathsf{cm}_{k^2}, \mathsf{cm}_{d_{in}})$ where:
   - cm'' is a commitment (for the scheme COMM);
   - (k^3, v^3) is a phase-3 record;
   - $\mathsf{cm}_{k^2}, \mathsf{cm}_{d_{in}}$ are commitments (for the scheme COMM').
4. Parse loc as a tuple $(\mathsf{trap}_{k^2}, \mathsf{trap}_{d_{in}})$ where:
   - $\mathsf{trap}_{k^2}, \mathsf{trap}_{d_{in}}$ are trapdoors (for the scheme COMM').
5. Check that $\mathsf{cm}'' = \mathsf{cm}'_j$ for each j.
6. Check that the i'_j are distinct, and let d_{in} be their number.
7. Check that all the k^2_i's are equal, and let $v^2 := (v^2_i)_i$.
8. Check that $\mathsf{COMM}'.\mathsf{Ver}(k^2_1, \mathsf{cm}_{k^2}, \mathsf{trap}_{k^2}) = 1$.
9. Check that $\mathsf{COMM}'.\mathsf{Ver}(d_{in}, \mathsf{cm}_{d_{in}}, \mathsf{trap}_{d_{in}}) = 1$.
10. Check that $(k^3, v^3) = \mathsf{Reduce}(k^2_1, v^2)$.

Fig. 4. Summary of the construction of $\Pi_{\mathsf{exe}}^{\mathsf{Map}}$ and $\Pi_{\mathsf{exe}}^{\mathsf{Reduce}}$ for "Our approach" (see Section 5.1). The text that is highlighted in blue denotes the differences from the construction in Figure 3.

Aggregating mappers' outputs. We describe each of these tree-like distributed computations, starting with the one for messages output by mapper nodes. Each message output by a mapper node has a payload that looks like $(\mathsf{cm}, i, k^2, v^2)$. We use, for each such message, a node to reformat the message into a new with payload $(\mathsf{cm}, a^\perp, a^\top, b, c)$ where $a^\perp = a^\top = i$ and $b = c = 1$. Afterwards, we use a tree of nodes to aggregate all the resulting messages into a final single one, by pairwise transforming two input messages $(\mathsf{cm}, a_1^\perp, a_1^\top, b_1, c_2)$ and $(\mathsf{cm}, a_2^\perp, a_2^\top, b_2, c_2)$ into the new message $(\mathsf{cm}, a_1^\perp, a_2^\top, b_1 + b_2, c_1 + c_2)$, provided that $a_1^\top < a_2^\perp$. Intuitively, the second and third components of a message denote the least and largest index seen so far, the fourth component counts the number of mappers, and the fifth counts the number of mapper outputs. If M denotes the number of mappers, the final message, output by the "root node" has payload $(\mathsf{cm}, 1, M, M, M)$. If, however, some messages are either duplicated or dropped, then at least one node will not satisfy its compliance predicate. We realize this idea by designing two new compliance predicates, $\Pi_{\mathsf{fmt}}^{\mathsf{Map}}$ and $\Pi_{\mathsf{sum}}^{\mathsf{Map}}$, respectively for enforcing the reformatting and aggregation of mapper nodes' output messages.

Aggregating reducers' outputs. We now turn to the tree-like distributed computation to aggregate outputs of reducer nodes. Each message output by a reducer node has a payload that looks like $(\mathsf{cm}, k^3, v^3, \mathsf{cm}_{k^2}, \mathsf{cm}_{d_{in}})$. Similarly to (but not exactly equal to) above, we use a node to reformat the message into a new with payload $(\mathsf{cm}, a^{\perp}, a^{\top}, b, c)$ where $a^{\perp} = a^{\top} = k^2$, $b = 1$ $c = d_{\mathsf{in}}$ (note that the values k^2 and d_{in} can be obtained by receiving decommitment information as part of the node's local data loc). Afterwards, again similarly to above, we use a tree of nodes to aggregate all the resulting messages into a final single one, by pairwise transforming two input messages $(\mathsf{cm}, a_1^{\perp}, a_1^{\top}, b_1, c_1)$ and $(\mathsf{cm}, a_2^{\perp}, a_2^{\top}, b_2, c_2)$ into a new message $(\mathsf{cm}, a_1^{\perp}, a_2^{\top}, b_1 + b_2, c_1 + c_2)$, provided that $a_1^{\top} < a_2^{\perp}$. The final message, output by the root node, looks like $(\mathsf{cm}, k_{\mathsf{min}}^2, k_{\mathsf{max}}^2, R, M)$, where k_{min}^2 and k_{max}^2 are respectively the least and largest keys encountered, R is the total number of reducer nodes, and M is the total number of inputs received by reducer nodes. Again, we concretely realize the above strategy by designing two new predicates, $\Pi_{\mathsf{fmt}}^{\mathsf{Reduce}}$ and $\Pi_{\mathsf{sum}}^{\mathsf{Reduce}}$, respectively for enforcing the reformatting and aggregation of reducer nodes' output messages; both take $O_{\lambda}(1)$ to execute.

Consistency between aggregations. After both aggregations have taken place, we are left with two messages $\mathsf{msg}_{\mathsf{sum}}^{\mathsf{Map}}$ and $\mathsf{msg}_{\mathsf{sum}}^{\mathsf{Reduce}}$, respectively with payloads $(\mathsf{cm}, 1, M, M, M)$ and $(\mathsf{cm}, k_{\mathsf{min}}^2, k_{\mathsf{max}}^2, R, M)$, resulting in an output message $\mathsf{msg}_{\mathsf{fin}}$ with payload (cm, R). A simple predicate Π_{fin} performs consistency checks, such as ensuring that the value of M is actually equal between the two messages (and consistency with the commitment cm_M stored in cm). The message $\mathsf{msg}_{\mathsf{fin}}$ that the two messages $\mathsf{msg}_{\mathsf{sum}}^{\mathsf{Map}}$ and $\mathsf{msg}_{\mathsf{sum}}^{\mathsf{Reduce}}$ have been successfully compared, which demonstrates that the outputs of all M mapper nodes were correctly shuffled to R reducer nodes. (We exclude M from $\mathsf{msg}_{\mathsf{fin}}$, for zero-knowledge reasons.)

Throughout, we leverage message types to enforce communication flow between nodes subject to different compliance predicates.

From sketch to proof. The above sketches how the Eval algorithm produces a suitable graph of nodes, culminating in the transcript's output, as stated in Theorem 1. It skims over many details, some of which are provided in the full version. For example, above we have not explained how to handle the case where a mapper node (or even a reducer node) outputs more than one record. Moreover, not only do we work out the details of a solution, but we also bring the solution to efficient implementations of arithmetic circuits for each of the seven compliance predicates.

5.2 Construction of Distributed zk-SNARKs for MapReduce

We give the construction of our distributed zk-SNARK for MapReduce, by describing its key generator MR.KeyGen, prover MR.Prove, and verifier MR.Verify. (We describe the commitment scheme COMM in Figure 1.)

The key generator MR.KeyGen(1^{λ}, Map, Reduce) $\rightarrow$ (pk, vk). On input a security parameter λ (presented in unary) and a MapReduce pair (Map, Reduce), the key generator MR.KeyGen computes a key pair (pk, vk) as follows.

1. Use Theorem 1 to deduce, from (Map, Reduce), the vector $\boldsymbol{\Pi}^{\mathsf{MR}}$ of compliance predicates.
2. Use the PCD key generator $\mathbb{G}$ to compute a PCD key pair for $\boldsymbol{\Pi}^{\mathsf{MR}}$: (pk, vk) := $\mathbb{G}(1^{\lambda}, \boldsymbol{\Pi}^{\mathsf{MR}})$.

3. Set pk := (Map, Reduce, pk) and vk := (vk); output (pk, vk).

The prover MR.Prove(pk, cm, y, x, trp) → π_{MR}. On input a proving key pk, an instance (cm, y), and a witness (x, trp), the prover MR.Prove computes a non-interactive proof π_{MR} for the statement "I know (x, trp) such that $((cm, y), (x, trp))$ $\in \mathscr{R}^{COMM}_{(Map, Reduce)}$" as follows. By Theorem 1, we know that there is a $\mathit{\Pi}^{MR}$-compliant (cm, y)-compatible transcript T and, moreover, that OUTS(T) can be obtained via a (Map, Reduce)-faithful evaluator Eval, which takes as input the the instance (cm, y) and its witness (x, trp). Thus, the prover MR.Prove computes π_{MR} by recursively invoking the PCD prover $\mathbb{P}$ on T, following Eval as it computes new nodes of T, by providing to $\mathbb{P}$, at each node, the relevant input messages and their proofs, local data, and output message. At the end of this process, itself (Map, Reduce)-faithful, MR.Prove sets π_{MR} equal to the concatenation of the proofs of all messages in OUTS(T).

The verifier MR.Verify(vk, cm, y, π_{MR}) → b. On input a verification key vk, commitment cm, output y, and proof π_{MR}, the verifier MR.Verify computes a decision bit b as follows.

1. Parse vk as a PCD verification key vk.
2. Use the instance (cm, y) to construct the following output messages (recall Definition 4):

$$msg_0 \begin{cases} .type := 1 \\ .payload := (cm, |y|) \end{cases} \quad \text{and, for each } i \in \{1, \ldots, |y|\},$$

$$msg_i \begin{cases} .type := 2 \\ .payload := (cm, y_i) \end{cases}.$$

3. Parse π_{MR} a vector of PCD proofs $(\pi_0, \pi_1, \ldots, \pi_{|\ |})$.
4. For each $i \in \{0, 1, \ldots, |y|\}$, check that the i-th output message is $\mathit{\Pi}^{MR}$-compliant: $\mathbb{V}(vk, msg_i, \pi_i) = 1$.
5. If all the above steps succeeded, output $b := 1$; otherwise output $b := 0$.

Indeed, if MR.Verify outputs 1, then we know that the prover that produced π_{MR} knows a $\mathit{\Pi}^{MR}$-compliant (cm, y)-compatible transcript T (by the proof-of-knowledge property of the PCD system), and thus also knows a witness (x, trp) for the instance (cm, y) (by Theorem 1).

As seen above, the combination of compliance engineering and PCD systems provides a powerful tool for constructing zero-knowledge proofs for distributed computations: compliance engineering allows us to express the desired properties as the compliance of distributed computations, while PCD systems allow us to prove, in a distributed way (and in zero knowledge), the compliance of such distributed computations.

Turning to security, we recall that, when invoking a PCD system to produce proofs along a distributed computation, proof of knowledge is achieved by recursively extracting "past proofs" from known ones. This process is technically quite delicate, and a formal treatment of it is in [13]. Here we only note that the distributed computations considered in this paper are shallow (of logarithmic depth) and are thus easily amenable to recursive proof extraction.

6   Step I: Construction of Multi-predicate PCD

We discuss Step I of our bootstrapping theorem: constructing multi-predicate PCD from (preprocessing) zk-SNARKs. As in [8], we consider compliance predicates Π expressed as $\mathbb{F}$-arithmetic circuits, where $\mathbb{F}$ is a certain field of cryptograph-

ically-large prime size (determined by the underlying zk-SNARK). Throughout this section, $\mathbb{F}_n$ denotes the field of size n, and we assume familiarity with finite fields (and, for background on these, see [55]).

6.1   Arithmetic Circuits and Preprocessing zk-SNARKs

Arithmetic circuits.   As mentioned, we work with circuits that are arithmetic, rather than boolean. Given a finite field $\mathbb{F}$, an $\mathbb{F}$-*arithmetic circuit* takes inputs that are elements in $\mathbb{F}$, and its gates output elements in $\mathbb{F}$; the circuits we consider only have *bilinear gates*. The *circuit satisfaction problem* of an $\mathbb{F}$-arithmetic circuit $C \colon \mathbb{F}^n \times \mathbb{F}^h \to \mathbb{F}^l$ is defined by the relation $\mathscr{R}_C = \{(x, a) \in \mathbb{F}^n \times \mathbb{F}^h : C(x, a) = 0^l\}$.

Preprocessing zk-SNARKs.   As in [9], a *preprocessing zk-SNARK* [13,15] for $\mathbb{F}$-arithmetic circuit satisfiability is a triple of polynomial-time algorithms (G, P, V), called *key generator, prover,* and *verifier.* The key generator G, given a security parameter λ and an $\mathbb{F}$-arithmetic circuit $C \colon \mathbb{F}^n \times \mathbb{F}^h \to \mathbb{F}^l$, samples a *proving key* pk and a *verification key* vk; these are the proof system's public parameters, and are generated only once per circuit. After that, anyone can use pk to generate non-interactive proofs of knowledge for witnesses in the relation $\mathscr{R}_C$, and anyone can use the vk to check these proofs. Namely, given pk and any $(x, a) \in \mathscr{R}_C$, the honest prover $P(\mathsf{pk}, x, a)$ produces a proof π for the statement "there is a such that $(x, a) \in \mathscr{R}_C$"; the verifier $V(\mathsf{vk}, x, \pi)$ checks that π is a convincing proof for this statement. A proof π is a (computational) proof of knowledge, and a (statistical) zero-knowledge proof. The succinctness property requires that π has length $O_\lambda(1)$ and V runs in time $O_\lambda(|x|)$.

6.2   Review of the [8] Construction

For efficiency reasons, Ben-Sasson et al. [8] construct a PCD system via *two* (pre-processing) zk-SNARKs, $(G_\alpha, P_\alpha, V_\alpha)$ and $(G_\beta, P_\beta, V_\beta)$, that satisfy the following. For two primes q_α and q_β: (a) $(G_\alpha, P_\alpha, V_\alpha)$ proves/verifies satisfiability of $\mathbb{F}_{q_\beta}$-arithmetic circuits, while V_α is an $\mathbb{F}_{q_\alpha}$-arithmetic circuit; instead, (b) $(G_\beta, P_\beta, V_\beta)$ proves/verifies satisfiability of $\mathbb{F}_{q_\alpha}$-arithmetic circuits, while V_β is an $\mathbb{F}_{q_\beta}$-arithmetic circuit. This property is achieved by instantiating the two zk-SNARKs via a *PCD-friendly 2-cycle of elliptic curves* (see [8] for details on how to obtain these), and facilitates recursive proof composition.

Specifically, the core of the PCD system construction is the design of two *PCD circuits*: $C_{\mathsf{pcd},\alpha}$ over the field $\mathbb{F}_{q_\beta}$ and $C_{\mathsf{pcd},\beta}$ over the field $\mathbb{F}_{q_\alpha}$. For a given compliance predicate Π, the two circuits work roughly as follows.

- $C_{\mathsf{pcd},\alpha}$: given input $x_\alpha = \mathsf{msg}$ and witness $a_\alpha = (\mathsf{loc}, \mathbf{msg}_{\mathsf{in}}, \boldsymbol{\pi}_{\mathsf{in}})$, use V_β to verify that each input message $\mathbf{msg}_{\mathsf{in}}[j]$ has a valid proof $\boldsymbol{\pi}_{\mathsf{in}}[j]$, and check that Π accepts the output message msg, local data loc, and input messages $\mathbf{msg}_{\mathsf{in}}$.
- $C_{\mathsf{pcd},\beta}$: given input $x_\beta = \mathsf{msg}$ and witness $a_\beta = (\pi_\alpha)$, uses V_α to verify that the message msg has a valid proof π_α.

The aforementioned property ensures that fields "match up": $C_{\mathsf{pcd},\alpha}$ is defined over the same field as V_β, and similarly for $C_{\mathsf{pcd},\beta}$ and V_α. (Such field matching is not possible when using a single elliptic curve.) The two PCD circuits are used as follows: P_α proves satisfiability of $C_{\mathsf{pcd},\alpha}$, and the resulting proof π_α attests to the compliance of msg; and P_β proves the satisfiability of $C_{\mathsf{pcd},\beta}$, and the resulting proof π_β provides a "translation" of π_α so that π_β can in turn be used as part of a witness to $C_{\mathsf{pcd},\alpha}$. We refer to $C_{\mathsf{pcd},\alpha}$ as the *compliance circuit*, and $C_{\mathsf{pcd},\beta}$ as the *translation* circuit.

The above description omits several details (relevant to later discussions): to reduce the size of the PCD circuits $C_{\mathsf{pcd},\alpha}$ and $C_{\mathsf{pcd},\beta}$, [8] additionally use hashing, pre-computation, and hardcoding. First, the input x_α to $C_{\mathsf{pcd},\alpha}$ is $H(\mathsf{bits}(\mathsf{vk}_\beta)\|\mathsf{bits}(\mathsf{msg}))$, where H is a collision-resistant function mapping $\{0,1\}$-vectors to $\mathbb{F}_{q_\beta}$-vectors, vk_β is the verification key for $C_{\mathsf{pcd},\beta}$, and msg is the output message to be checked by Π. This ensures that x_α's length equals H's output length, which only depends on λ. However, H's output is an $\mathbb{F}_{q_\beta}$-vector, and thus cannot be passed as input to $C_{\mathsf{pcd},\beta}$, which is an $\mathbb{F}_{q_\alpha}$-arithmetic circuit. This issue is addressed via two "repacking circuits" that map information content from elements in $\mathbb{F}_{q_\beta}$ to ones in $\mathbb{F}_{q_\alpha}$ and back, respectively. Second, a zk-SNARK verifier V can be viewed as two functions, i.e., an "offline" function V^{offline} (given the verification key vk, compute a *processed verification key* pvk) and an "online" function V^{online} (given pvk, an input x, and proof π, compute the decision bit); the tradeoff between V and V^{online} can be exploited. Finally, vk_α, the verification key for $C_{\mathsf{pcd},\alpha}$, is hardcoded in $C_{\mathsf{pcd},\beta}$. See [8] for more details.

From the point of view of this paper, the construction of [8] in insufficient, because: (i) it supports a single compliance predicate at a time, while our setting calls for multiple ones; and (ii) it requires the compliance predicate to be "rigid" (i.e., accept a fixed number of messages and have input lengths equal output length), while our setting calls for "flexible" predicates.

6.3 Overview of Our Construction

We overview the construction of our PCD system, which extends [8]'s so to achieve native (and thus more efficient) support for multiple compliance predicates, variable message arity, and varying message lengths.

At high level, our construction consists of the following two parts.

- **Part 1:** given a vector of compliance predicates $\boldsymbol{\Pi}$, construct a vector C_{pcd} of PCD circuits. Roughly, for each $\boldsymbol{\Pi}[i]$ in $\boldsymbol{\Pi}$, we construct two circuits, $C_{\mathsf{pcd},\alpha,i}$ and $C_{\mathsf{pcd},\beta,i}$, tasked with recursive proof composition relative to $\boldsymbol{\Pi}[i]$.
- **Part 2:** construct the PCD generator, prover, and verifier. Roughly, the PCD generator $\mathbb{G}$ produces a zk-SNARK key pair for each circuit in C_{pcd}; the PCD prover $\mathbb{P}$, to prove compliance relative to $\boldsymbol{\Pi}[i]$, produces a zk-SNARK proof of

satisfiability for $C_{\mathsf{pcd},\alpha,i}$ and then uses it to produce one for $C_{\mathsf{pcd},\beta,i}$; the PCD verifier $\mathbb{V}$ verifies a zk-SNARK proof by using the appropriate verification key. Below, we elaborate on these two parts. We also note that the above separation is only conceptual, because the two parts are procedurally entangled (due to hard-coding of certain values).

Part 1: the PCD circuits. For each compliance predicate $\Pi[i]$ in Π, we construct two PCD circuits: a *compliance circuit* $C_{\mathsf{pcd},\alpha,i}$, tasked with checking compliance with $\Pi[i]$; and a *translation circuit* $C_{\mathsf{pcd},\beta,i}$, tasked with checking proofs attesting to the satisfiability of $C_{\mathsf{pcd},\alpha,i}$.

The design of $C_{\mathsf{pcd},\beta,i}$ is similar to [8]'s translation circuit. Namely, $C_{\mathsf{pcd},\beta,i}$ provides a way to translate a zk-SNARK proof relative to the verification key $\mathsf{vk}_\alpha[i]$ (generated for $C_{\mathsf{pcd},\alpha,i}$ and hardcoded in $C_{\mathsf{pcd},\beta,i}$) to one relative to the verification key $\mathsf{vk}_\beta[i]$ (generated for $C_{\mathsf{pcd},\beta,i}$); the translation has the only goal of matching fields up.

The design of $C_{\mathsf{pcd},\alpha,i}$ extends [8]'s compliance circuit, so to take into account the fact that input messages may carry proofs relative to different verification keys (depending on which compliance predicate was used to reason about their compliance). So, while the input x_α to [8]'s compliance circuit was $H(\mathsf{bits}(\mathsf{vk}_\beta)\|\mathsf{bits}(\mathsf{msg}))$, we now take the input to $C_{\mathsf{pcd},\alpha,i}$ to be $H(\mathsf{bits}(\mathsf{rt})\|\mathsf{bits}(\mathsf{msg}))$ where rt is the root of the Merkle tree whose leaves consist of the vector vk_β.[6] The circuit $C_{\mathsf{pcd},\alpha,i}$ then receives, as part of the witness, an authentication path for the verification key required of each input message, and checks this authentication path against rt. Additional details of the construction (e.g., checking that the type of the output message equals $\mathsf{type}(\Pi[i])$) are discussed later.

Part 2: the PCD generator, prover, and verifier. Next, we outline below the PCD generator, prover, and verifier.

- The PCD generator $\mathbb{G}$, given a vector Π of compliance predicates, works as follows.
  1. For each i, construct:
     (a) the compliance circuit $C_{\mathsf{pcd},\alpha,i}$ and generate a zk-SNARK key pair $(\mathsf{pk}_\alpha[i], \mathsf{vk}_\alpha[i])$ for it, and then
     (b) the translation circuit $C_{\mathsf{pcd},\beta,i}$ (hardcoding $\mathsf{vk}_\alpha[i]$) and generate a zk-SNARK key pair $(\mathsf{pk}_\beta[i], \mathsf{vk}_\beta[i])$ for it.
  2. Compute rt, the root of the Merkle tree whose leaves consist of the vector vk_β.
  3. Output the key pair $(\mathsf{pk}, \mathsf{vk})$, where $\mathsf{pk} := (\mathsf{pk}_\alpha, \mathsf{vk}_\alpha, \mathsf{pk}_\beta, \mathsf{vk}_\beta, \mathsf{rt})$ and $\mathsf{vk} = (\mathsf{vk}_\beta, \mathsf{rt})$.
- The PCD prover $\mathbb{P}$, given a proving key pk, output message msg, local data loc, and input messages $\mathsf{msg}_{\mathsf{in}}$ with proofs π_{in}, works as follows.
  1. Parse pk as a tuple $(\mathsf{pk}_\alpha, \mathsf{vk}_\alpha, \mathsf{pk}_\beta, \mathsf{vk}_\beta, \mathsf{rt})$.
  2. Let $i^\star$ be the index of the compliance predicate $\Pi[i^\star]$ in Π that is satisfied by $(\mathsf{msg}, \mathsf{loc}, \mathsf{msg}_{\mathsf{in}})$.

---

[6] Merely taking x_α to be $H(\mathsf{bits}(\mathsf{vk}_\beta)\|\mathsf{bits}(\mathsf{msg}))$ would cause $C_{\mathsf{pcd},\alpha,i}$'s to be linear, instead of logarithmic, in the number of predicates.

3. Construct a vector **ap** of authentication paths, where each **ap**$[j]$ is the authentication path, relative to the root rt, for the leaf $\mathbf{vk}_\beta[\boldsymbol{\pi}_{\mathsf{in}}[j].\mathsf{idx}]$.
4. Use rt, $(\mathsf{msg}, \mathsf{loc}, \mathbf{msg}_{\mathsf{in}})$, and **ap** to construct an input x_α and a witness a_α for $C_{\mathsf{pcd},\alpha,i}$.
5. Use $\mathbf{pk}_\alpha[i^\star]$ to generate a zk-SNARK proof π_α attesting that the compliance circuit $C_{\mathsf{pcd},\alpha,i}$ accepts (x_α, a_α).
6. Use rt and msg to construct an input x_β and a witness a_β for $C_{\mathsf{pcd},\beta,i}$.
7. Use $\mathbf{pk}_\beta[i^\star]$ to generate a zk-SNARK proof π_β attesting that the translation circuit $C_{\mathsf{pcd},\beta,i}$ accepts (x_β, a_β).
8. Output the proof π, where $\pi.\mathsf{idx} := i^\star$ and $\pi.\mathsf{proof} := \pi_\beta$.
- The PCD verifier $\mathbb{V}$, given a verification key vk, a message msg, and a proof π, works as follows.
  1. Parse vk as a tuple $(\mathbf{vk}_\beta, \mathsf{rt})$.
  2. Set $i^\star := \pi.\mathsf{idx}$ and $\pi_\beta := \pi.\mathsf{proof}$.
  3. Use rt and msg to construct the input x_β for $C_{\mathsf{pcd},\beta,i^\star}$.
  4. Use $\mathbf{vk}_\beta[i^\star]$ to check that π_β is a valid zk-SNARK proof for x_β.

6.4   Details of Our Construction

We provide more details about the construction of our PCD system.

Representation of a compliance predicate.   The choice of representation of a compliance predicate (e.g., whether the predicate is expressed via a machine or a circuit) does not impact the main ideas behind the construction of multi-predicate PCD (see Section 6.3). Yet, some efficiency optimizations depend on this choice, and so henceforth we make it explicit: a compliance predicate Π is represented as an arithmetic circuit. As in [8], this choice is not arbitrary but, rather, is inherited from the "native" model of computation supported by the underlying zk-SNARK.

Notation for predicates as circuits.   Arithmetic circuits are a "rigid" computation model, so we introduce additional notation to support a detailed description of our construction. To each $\mathbb{F}$-arithmetic compliance predicate Π, we associate several quantities: (i) $\mathsf{outlen}(\Pi)$, the payload length of an output message; (ii) $\mathsf{loclen}(\Pi)$, the length of local data; (iii) $\mathsf{max\text{-}arity}(\Pi)$, the maximum number of input messages; and (iv) $\mathbf{inlen}(\Pi)$, the vector for which $\mathbf{inlen}(\Pi)[j]$ is the payload length for the j-th input message. As for the type of a message (which is merely an integer), it will suffice to use a single element of $\mathbb{F}$ to represent it. Moreover, in order for Π (which is a circuit) to "know" the number $d \in \{0, \ldots, \mathsf{max\text{-}arity}(\Pi)\}$ of input messages, we let Π receive d explicitly (encoded as a single field element).

In sum, if we view Π as a function, we can write that, for some $l \in \mathbb{N}$,

$$\Pi : \mathbb{F}^{(1+\mathsf{outlen}(\Pi))} \times \mathbb{F}^{\mathsf{loclen}(\Pi)} \times \mathbb{F}^{\sum_{j=1}^{\mathsf{max\text{-}arity}(\Pi)}(1+\mathbf{inlen}(\Pi)[j])} \times \mathbb{F} \to \mathbb{F}^l.$$

Indeed, Π receives an output message msg of length $(1 + \mathsf{outlen}(\Pi))$; local data loc of length $\mathsf{loclen}(\Pi)$; $\mathsf{max\text{-}arity}(\Pi)$ input messages, where the j-th input message has length $(1 + \mathbf{inlen}(\Pi)[j])$; and the arity d. For notational convenience, we write $\Pi(\mathsf{msg}, \mathsf{loc}, \mathbf{msg}_{\mathsf{in}}, d)$ even when $\mathbf{msg}_{\mathsf{in}}$ contains less than $\mathsf{max\text{-}arity}(\Pi)$ messages (and assume that $\mathbf{msg}_{\mathsf{in}}$ is extended with arbitrary padding to the correct length).

Ingredients. In addition to the two (preprocessing) zk-SNARKs $(G_\alpha, P_\alpha, V_\alpha)$ and $(G_\beta, P_\beta, V_\beta)$ (see Section 6.2), in the construction we make use of certain arithmetic circuits that we now describe. All all of these circuits are discussed in [8] in more detail, so here we review them only at high level.

We use n_α and n_β to denote the size (number of field elements) of an input to the PCD circuits $C_{\mathsf{pcd},\alpha,i}$ and $C_{\mathsf{pcd},\beta,i}$ (for any i), respectively; these two sizes are fixed, and they equal $n_\alpha := d_{H,\alpha}$ and $n_\beta := \lceil \frac{n_\alpha \cdot \lceil \log r_\alpha \rceil}{\lfloor \log r_\beta \rfloor} \rceil$, where $d_{H,\alpha}$ is the number of elements output by the collision-resistant function H; n_β is the number of elements in $\mathbb{F}_{r_\beta}$ needed to encode n_α elements in $\mathbb{F}_{r_\alpha}$. We use bits_α to denote a function that, given an input y in $\mathbb{F}_{r_\alpha}^\ell$ (for some ℓ), outputs y's binary representation; the corresponding $\mathbb{F}_{r_\alpha}$-arithmetic circuit is denoted $C_{\mathsf{bits},\alpha}$ and has $\ell \cdot \lceil \log r_\alpha \rceil$ gates.

We use the following circuits. An $\mathbb{F}_{r_\alpha}$-arithmetic circuit $C_{S,\alpha\to\beta}$ implementing $S_{\alpha\to\beta} \colon \mathbb{F}_{r_\alpha}^{n_\alpha} \to \mathbb{F}_{r_\alpha}^{n_\beta \cdot \lceil \log r_\beta \rceil}$, the re-packing function from $\mathbb{F}_{r_\alpha}$ to $\mathbb{F}_{r_\beta}$; and an $\mathbb{F}_{r_\beta}$-arithmetic circuit $C_{S,\alpha\leftarrow\beta}$ implementing $S_{\alpha\leftarrow\beta} \colon \mathbb{F}_{r_\beta}^{n_\beta} \to \mathbb{F}_{r_\beta}^{n_\alpha \cdot \lceil \log r_\alpha \rceil}$, the inverse of $S_{\alpha\to\beta}$. An $\mathbb{F}_{r_\alpha}$-arithmetic circuit $C_{V,\alpha}^{\mathsf{online}}$ implementing $V_\alpha^{\mathsf{online}}$ for inputs of n_α elements in $\mathbb{F}_{r_\alpha}$ (an input $x_\alpha \in \mathbb{F}_{r_\alpha}^{n_\alpha}$ is given to $C_{V,\alpha}^{\mathsf{online}}$ as a string of $n_\alpha \cdot \lceil \log r_\alpha \rceil$ elements in $\mathbb{F}_{r_\beta}$, each carrying a bit of x_α). An $\mathbb{F}_{r_\alpha}$-arithmetic circuit $C_{V,\beta}$ implementing V_β for inputs of n_β elements in $\mathbb{F}_{r_\beta}$ (an input $x_\beta \in \mathbb{F}_{r_\beta}^{n_\beta}$ is given to $C_{V,\beta}$ as a string of $n_\beta \cdot \lceil \log r_\beta \rceil$ elements in $\mathbb{F}_{r_\alpha}$, each carrying a bit of x_β).

Moreover, for a given compliance predicate Π, we use various $\mathbb{F}_{r_\alpha}$-arithmetic circuits for hashing: $C_{H,\alpha}^{\mathsf{out}}$ implements a collision-resistant function $H_\alpha^{\mathsf{out}} \colon \{0,1\}^{m_{H,\alpha}^{\mathsf{out}}} \to \mathbb{F}_{r_\alpha}^{d_{H,\alpha}}$, and $\boldsymbol{C}_{H,\alpha}^{\mathsf{in}}$ is a vector such that each $\boldsymbol{C}_{H,\alpha}^{\mathsf{in}}[j]$ implements a collision-resistant function $\boldsymbol{H}_\alpha^{\mathsf{in}}[j] \colon \{0,1\}^{m_{H,\alpha,j}} \to \mathbb{F}_{r_\alpha}^{d_{H,\alpha}}$; parameters are such that $m_{H,\alpha}^{\mathsf{out}} = (d_{H,\alpha} + 1 + \mathsf{outlen}(\Pi)) \cdot \lceil \log r_\alpha \rceil$ and $m_{H,\alpha,j} = (d_{H,\alpha} + 1 + \mathsf{inlen}(\Pi)[j]) \cdot \lceil \log r_\alpha \rceil$.

Finally, we use an $\mathbb{F}_{r_\alpha}$-arithmetic circuit for verification of Merkle-tree authentication paths: $C_{\mathsf{CheckPath},\alpha,p}$ implements the function $\mathsf{MERKLE.CheckPath}$ (see Section 2.2) for paths of length $\lceil \log p \rceil$.

Construction of the PCD circuits. In Figure 5 we provide pseudocode for MakePCDCircuitA and MakePCDCircuitB, the two functions that we use to construct the compliance and translation PCD circuits (i.e., $C_{\mathsf{pcd},\alpha,i}$ and $C_{\mathsf{pcd},\beta,i}$).

Construction of the PCD generator, prover, and verifier. In Figure 6 we provide pseudocode for the PCD generator $\mathbb{G}$, prover $\mathbb{P}$, and verifier $\mathbb{V}$. The construction works for a vector $\boldsymbol{\Pi}$ of $\mathbb{F}_{r_\alpha}$-arithmetic compliance predicates $\boldsymbol{\Pi}$.[7] For convenience, we export $i^\star$, the index of the predicate with respect to which compliance is proved, to $\mathbb{P}$'s interface.

---

[7] For comparison, [8] consider the following special case: $\boldsymbol{\Pi} = (\Pi)$, $\mathsf{inlen}(\Pi)[j] = \mathsf{outlen}(\Pi)$ for all j, and $d = \mathsf{max\text{-}arity}(\Pi)$. Also note that, in this case, there are only two message types (namely, 0 and $\mathsf{type}(\Pi)$), which is why [8] do not discuss message types, and instead only distinguish between messages that are "base case" or not.

MakePCDCircuitA($C^{\text{in}}_{H,\alpha}, C^{\text{out}}_{H,\alpha}, C_{S,\alpha\to\beta}, C_{V,\beta}, C_{\text{CheckPath},\alpha,p}, \Pi$)

Set:
- the input size $n_\alpha := d_{H,\alpha}$; and
- the witness size $h_\alpha := (1 + \text{outlen}(\Pi)) + \text{loclen}(\Pi) + 1 + \sum_{j=1}^{\text{max-arity}(\Pi)} ((1 + \text{inlen}(\Pi)[j]) + |\pi| + |\text{vk}_\beta(n_\beta)| + \ell_{\text{ap}} + 1)$.

Output the $\mathbb{F}_{r_\alpha}$-arithmetic circuit $C_{\text{pcd},\alpha}$ that, given input $x_\alpha \in \mathbb{F}_{r_\alpha}^{n_\alpha}$ and witness $a_\alpha \in \mathbb{F}_{r_\alpha}^{h_\alpha}$, works as follows:
1. Parse the witness a_α as ($\text{msg}, \text{loc}, \textbf{msg}_{\text{in}}, d, \textbf{vk}_\beta, \text{rt}, \textbf{ap}, \boldsymbol{\pi}_{\text{in}}, \textbf{b}_{\text{res}}$).
2. Check that $\text{msg.type} = \text{type}(\Pi)$.
3. Check that $0 \leq d \leq \text{max-arity}(\Pi)$.
4. For $j = 1, \ldots, d$:
   (a) Compute $\sigma_{\text{vk},\beta,j} := C_{\text{bits},\alpha}(\textbf{vk}_\beta[j])$.
   (b) Check that $C_{\text{CheckPath},\alpha,p}(\text{rt}, \boldsymbol{\pi}_{\text{in}}[j].\text{idx}, \sigma_{\text{vk},\beta,j}, \textbf{ap}[j]) = \textbf{b}_{\text{res}}[j]$.
   (c) Compute $x_{\text{in},\alpha,j} := C^{\text{in}}_{H,\alpha}[j](C_{\text{bits},\alpha}(\text{rt}\|\textbf{msg}_{\text{in}}[j].\text{type}\|\textbf{msg}_{\text{in}}[j].\text{payload})) \in \mathbb{F}_{r_\alpha}^{n_\alpha}$.
   (d) Compute $x_{\text{in},\beta,j} := C_{S,\alpha\to\beta}(x_{\text{in},\alpha,j}) \in \mathbb{F}_{r_\alpha}^{n_\beta \cdot \lceil \log r_\beta \rceil}$.
   (e) Check that $C_{V,\beta}(\textbf{vk}_\beta[j], x_{\text{in},\beta,j}, \boldsymbol{\pi}_{\text{in}}[j].\text{proof}) = \textbf{b}_{\text{res}}[j]$.
   (f) Check that $\textbf{b}_{\text{res}}[j] \in \{0,1\}$ and $\textbf{msg}_{\text{in}}[j].\text{type} \cdot (1 - \textbf{b}_{\text{res}}[j]) = 0$ (that is, either $\textbf{msg}_{\text{in}}[j]$ is a base-case message or its proof verified).
5. Check that $x_\alpha = C^{\text{out}}_{H,\alpha}(C_{\text{bits},\alpha}(\text{rt}\|\text{msg.type}\|\text{msg.payload}))$.
6. Check that $\Pi(\text{msg}, \text{loc}, \textbf{msg}_{\text{in}}, d)$ accepts.

MakePCDCircuitB($\text{pvk}_\alpha, C_{S,\alpha\leftarrow\beta}, C^{\text{online}}_{V,\alpha}$)

Set:
- the input size $n_\beta := \left\lceil \frac{n_\alpha \cdot \lceil \log r_\alpha \rceil}{\lfloor \log r_\beta \rfloor} \right\rceil$; and
- the witness size $h_\beta := |\pi_\alpha|$.

Output the $\mathbb{F}_{r_\beta}$-arithmetic circuit $C_{\text{pcd},\beta}$ that, given input $x_\beta \in \mathbb{F}_{r_\beta}^{n_\beta}$ and witness $a_\beta \in \mathbb{F}_{r_\beta}^{h_\beta}$, works as follows:
1. Parse the witness a_β as a zk-SNARK proof π_α.
2. Compute $x_\alpha := C_{S,\alpha\leftarrow\beta}(x_\beta) \in \mathbb{F}_{r_\beta}^{n_\alpha \cdot \lceil \log r_\alpha \rceil}$.
3. Check that $C^{\text{online}}_{V,\alpha}(\text{pvk}_\alpha, x_\alpha, \pi_\alpha) = 1$.

Fig. 5. Construction of PCD circuits for our multi-predicate PCD system

7 Implementation

Our system. We built a system that implements our constructions. First, we implemented multi-predicate PCD, providing interfaces for the PCD generator $\mathbb{G}$, prover $\mathbb{P}$, and verifier $\mathbb{V}$; this realizes Step I (see Section 6). Next, we used multi-predicate PCD to implement a distributed zk-SNARK for MapReduce, providing interfaces for the zk-SNARK generator MR.KeyGen, prover MR.Prove, and verifier MR.Verify; this realizes Step II (see Section 5).

The prover in our implementation is itself a MapReduce computation, currently running on an ad-hoc MapReduce implementation; integration with Hadoop [1], an open-source MapReduce framework, is ongoing.

Integration with libsnark. We have integrated our code with libsnark [72], a C++ library for zk-SNARKs.

PCD generator $\mathbb{G}$

– INPUTS: a vector of p compliance predicates $\boldsymbol{\Pi} = (\boldsymbol{\Pi}[1], \ldots, \boldsymbol{\Pi}[p])$, where each compliance predicate $\boldsymbol{\Pi}[i]$ is a $\mathbb{F}_{r_\alpha}$-arithmetic circuit
– OUTPUTS: a proving key pk and a verification key vk

1. Set $n_\alpha := d_{H,\alpha}$ and $n_\beta := \left\lceil \frac{n_\alpha \cdot \lceil \log r_\alpha \rceil}{\lceil \log r_\beta \rceil} \right\rceil$.

2. Construct $C_{S,\alpha \to \beta}$, the $\mathbb{F}_{r_\alpha}$-arithmetic circuit implementing $S_{\alpha \to \beta} \colon \mathbb{F}_{r_\alpha}^{n_\alpha} \to \mathbb{F}_{r_\alpha}^{n_\beta \cdot \lceil \log r_\beta \rceil}$.

3. Construct $C_{S,\alpha \leftarrow \beta}$, the $\mathbb{F}_{r_\beta}$-arithmetic circuit implementing $S_{\alpha \leftarrow \beta} \colon \mathbb{F}_{r_\beta}^{n_\beta} \to \mathbb{F}_{r_\beta}^{n_\alpha \cdot \lceil \log r_\alpha \rceil}$.

4. Construct $C_{V,\beta}$, the $\mathbb{F}_{r_\alpha}$-arithmetic circuit implementing V_β for inputs of n_β elements in $\mathbb{F}_{r_\beta}$.

5. Construct $C_{V,\alpha}^{\mathsf{online}}$, the $\mathbb{F}_{r_\beta}$-arithmetic circuit implementing $V_\alpha^{\mathsf{online}}$ for inputs of n_α elements in $\mathbb{F}_{r_\alpha}$.

6. Construct $C_{\mathsf{CheckPath},\alpha,p}$, the $\mathbb{F}_{r_\alpha}$-arithmetic circuit implementing MERKLE.CheckPath for depth $\lceil \log p \rceil$.

7. Allocate the proving key pk, consisting of:
    (a) a Merkle tree root $\mathsf{pk.rt}$; and
    (b) four vectors of size p: $\mathsf{pk.pk}_\alpha$, $\mathsf{pk.pk}_\beta$, $\mathsf{pk.vk}_\alpha$, $\mathsf{pk.vk}_\beta$.

8. Allocate the verification key vk, consisting of:
    (a) a Merkle tree root $\mathsf{vk.rt}$; and
    (b) one vector of size p: $\mathsf{vk.vk}_\beta$.

9. For $i = 1, \ldots, p$, compute proving and verification keys for $\boldsymbol{\Pi}[i]$ as follows:
    (a) Construct $C_{H,\alpha}^{\mathsf{out}}$, the $\mathbb{F}_{r_\alpha}$-arithmetic circuit implementing $H_\alpha^{\mathsf{out}} \colon \{0,1\}^{m_{H,\alpha}^{\mathsf{out}}} \to \mathbb{F}_{r_\alpha}^{d_{H,\alpha}}$ for $\boldsymbol{\Pi}[i]$.
    (b) Construct $\boldsymbol{C}_{H,\alpha}^{\mathsf{in}}$, the vector of $\mathbb{F}_{r_\alpha}$-arithmetic circuits such that $\boldsymbol{C}_{H,\alpha}^{\mathsf{in}}[j]$ implements $H_\alpha^{\mathsf{in}}[j] \colon \{0,1\}^{m_{H,\alpha,j}} \to \mathbb{F}_{r_\alpha}^{d_{H,\alpha}}$ for $\boldsymbol{\Pi}[i]$.
    (c) Compute $C_{\mathsf{pcd},\alpha,i} := \mathsf{MakePCDCircuitA}(\boldsymbol{C}_{H,\alpha}^{\mathsf{in}}, C_{H,\alpha}^{\mathsf{out}}, C_{S,\alpha \to \beta}, C_{V,\beta}, C_{\mathsf{CheckPath},\alpha,p}, \boldsymbol{\Pi}[i])$.
    (d) Compute $(\mathsf{pk}_{\alpha,i}, \mathsf{vk}_{\alpha,i}) := G_\alpha(C_{\mathsf{pcd},\alpha,i})$.
    (e) Compute $\mathsf{pvk}_{\alpha,i} := V_\alpha^{\mathsf{offline}}(\mathsf{pk}_{\alpha,i})$.
    (f) Compute $C_{\mathsf{pcd},\beta,i} := \mathsf{MakePCDCircuitB}(\mathsf{pvk}_{\alpha,i}, C_{S,\alpha \leftarrow \beta}, C_{V,\alpha}^{\mathsf{online}})$.
    (g) Compute $(\mathsf{pk}_{\beta,i}, \mathsf{vk}_{\beta,i}) := G_\beta(C_{\mathsf{pcd},\beta,i})$.
    (h) Set $\mathsf{pk.pk}_\alpha[i] := \mathsf{pk}_{\alpha,i}$, $\mathsf{pk.pk}_\beta[i] := \mathsf{pk}_{\beta,i}$, $\mathsf{pk.vk}_\alpha[i] := \mathsf{vk}_{\alpha,i}$, $\mathsf{pk.vk}_\beta[i] := \mathsf{vk}_{\beta,i}$, $\mathsf{vk.vk}_\beta[i] := \mathsf{vk}_{\beta,i}$.

10. Compute $\mathsf{rt} := \mathsf{MERKLE.GetRoot}(\mathsf{vk}_\beta)$ and set $\mathsf{pk.rt} := \mathsf{rt}$, $\mathsf{vk.rt} := \mathsf{rt}$.

11. Output $(\mathsf{pk}, \mathsf{vk})$.

PCD prover $\mathbb{P}$

– INPUTS:
    • proving key pk
    • index $i^\star$ of the compliance predicate $\boldsymbol{\Pi}[i^\star]$ in $\boldsymbol{\Pi}$, with respect to which compliance is proved
    • output message $\mathsf{msg} \in \mathbb{F}_{r_\alpha}^{1+\mathsf{outlen}(\boldsymbol{\Pi}[i^\star])}$
    • local data $\mathsf{loc} \in \mathbb{F}_{r_\alpha}^{\mathsf{loclen}(\boldsymbol{\Pi}[i^\star])}$
    • arity $d \in \{0, \ldots, \mathsf{max\text{-}arity}(\boldsymbol{\Pi}[i^\star])\}$
    • d input messages $\mathsf{msg}_{\mathsf{in}}$, each $\mathsf{msg}_{\mathsf{in}}[j] \in \mathbb{F}_{r_\alpha}^{1+\mathsf{inlen}(\boldsymbol{\Pi}[i^\star])[j]}$
    • d corresponding proofs π_{in} (some entries may equal $\bot$, denoting that there is no prior proof)
– OUTPUTS: a PCD proof π for the output message msg as attested by $\boldsymbol{\Pi}[i^\star]$

1. Compute $x_\alpha := H_\alpha(\mathsf{bits}_\alpha(\mathsf{pk.rt}\|\mathsf{msg.type}\|\mathsf{msg.payload})) \in \mathbb{F}_{r_\alpha}^{n_\alpha}$ and $x_\beta := S_{\alpha \to \beta}(x_\alpha) \in \mathbb{F}_{r_\alpha}^{n_\beta \cdot \lceil \log r_\beta \rceil}$, and parse x_β as lying in $\mathbb{F}_{r_\beta}^{n_\beta}$.

2. Let vk_β, ap and b_{res} be three vectors of size d. For $j = 1, \ldots, d$, do the following:
    (a) If $\mathsf{msg}_{\mathsf{in}}[j].\mathsf{type} \neq 0$, set $b_{\mathsf{res}}[j] := 1$, set $\mathsf{vk}_\beta[j] := \mathsf{pk.vk}_\beta[\pi_{\mathsf{in}}[j].\mathsf{idx}]$, and compute $\mathsf{ap}[j] := \mathsf{MERKLE.GetPath}(\mathsf{pk.vk}_\beta, \pi_{\mathsf{in}}[j].\mathsf{idx})$.
    (b) If $\mathsf{msg}_{\mathsf{in}}[j].\mathsf{type} = 0$, set $b_{\mathsf{res}}[j] := 0$, and let $\mathsf{vk}_\beta[j]$ and $\mathsf{ap}[j]$ have arbitrary contents of the correct length.

3. Extend $\mathsf{msg}_{\mathsf{in}}$ from a vector of size d to a vector of size $\mathsf{max\text{-}arity}(\boldsymbol{\Pi}[i^\star])$ using arbitrary padding. Do the same for π_{in}, vk_β, ap, and b_{res}. For simplicity we denote the padded vectors also by $\mathsf{msg}_{\mathsf{in}}$, π_{in}, vk_β, ap, and b_{res}.

4. Set $a_\alpha := (\mathsf{msg}, \mathsf{loc}, \mathsf{msg}_{\mathsf{in}}, d, \mathsf{vk}_\beta, \mathsf{rt}, \mathsf{ap}, \pi_{\mathsf{in}}, b_{\mathsf{res}})$ and compute $\pi_\alpha := P_\alpha(\mathsf{pk.pk}_\alpha[i^\star], x_\alpha, a_\alpha)$.

5. Set $a_\beta := (\pi_\alpha)$ and compute $\pi_\beta := P_\beta(\mathsf{pk.pk}_\beta[i^\star], x_\beta, a_\beta)$.

6. Output a PCD proof π with $\pi.\mathsf{idx} := i^\star$, $\pi.\mathsf{proof} := \pi_\beta$.

PCD verifier $\mathbb{V}$

– INPUTS:
    • verification key vk
    • message $\mathsf{msg} \in \mathbb{F}_{r_\alpha}^\star$
    • proof π
– OUTPUTS: decision bit

1. Interpret π as a PCD proof with $i := \pi.\mathsf{idx}$ and $\pi_\beta := \pi.\mathsf{proof}$.

2. Compute $x_\alpha := H_\alpha(\mathsf{bits}_\alpha(\mathsf{vk.rt}\|\mathsf{msg.type}\|\mathsf{msg.payload})) \in \mathbb{F}_{r_\alpha}^{n_\alpha}$ and $x_\beta := S_{\alpha \to \beta}(x_\alpha) \in \mathbb{F}_{r_\alpha}^{n_\beta \cdot \lceil \log r_\beta \rceil}$, and parse x_β as lying in $\mathbb{F}_{r_\beta}^{n_\beta}$.

3. Compute $b := V_\beta(\mathsf{vk.vk}_\beta[i], x_\beta, \pi_\beta)$ and output b.

25

Fig. 6. Construction of a multi-predicate PCD system

Our multi-predicate PCD provides an alternative to the single-predicate PCD that was already part of libsnark. In fact, we have harmonized the two PCD interfaces: the object classes for a compliance predicate, messages, and local data are shared across the two. In terms of concrete parameter choices, our multi-predicate PCD uses the two zk-SNARKs (based on PCD-friendly 2-cycles of elliptic curves) that are also used in the single-predicate PCD.

Our distributed zk-SNARK for MapReduce provides an additional choice of proof system in libsnark. A MapReduce pair (Map, Reduce) can be specified via the same "constraint formalism" used throughout libsnark (i.e., *rank-1 constraint systems*), thereby facilitating the re-using and sharing of useful constraint systems.

Prototypical MapReduce example: word counting. For evaluation purposes (see Section 8), we wrote a MapReduce pair (Map, Reduce) that implements the prototypical MapReduce application of *word counting* [35], whose goal is to count the number of occurrences of each word in a text (or a collection of texts). Word counting can be cast in the MapReduce framework, e.g., as follows. Each input record (k^1, v^1) represents a slice of, say, 100 words of the document: the key k^1 is the position of the slice in the document, and the value v^1 is the list of words in the slice. The mapper $\mathsf{Map}_{\mathsf{wordcount}}$, when invoked on an input record (k^1, v^1), emits a list of intermediate records $\big((k_1^2, v_1^2), \ldots, (k_\ell^2, v_\ell^2)\big)$, with $\ell \leq 100$, denoting that the word k_i^2 appears v_i^2 times among the words in the slice v^1. The reducer $\mathsf{Reduce}_{\mathsf{wordcount}}$, when invoked on a particular word k^2 and the vector of counts v^2 for k^2, emits the output record $(k^3, v^3) = (k^2, \sum_i v^2[i])$, which reports the total number of occurrences of k^2 in the collection of input records.

8 Evaluation

We evaluated our system by using it to execute the MapReduce application of word counting (see Section 7).

Experimental results. We ran our system on the word counting example, on our benchmarking system. Each of the reported times is relative to a commodity compute node with a 3.40 GHz Intel Core i7-4770 CPU and 16 GB of RAM available and utilizing all 4 cores. We chose the immortal introduction of Diffie and Hellman's pioneering paper "New directions in cryptography" [37], divided into slices of 100 words each, as the input to the MapReduce computation.

By analyzing our system's components, we deduced a cost model of the prover's runtime as a function of M, the number of slices the document was divided into, and R, the number of distinct words in the document:

$$M \cdot \big(\mathsf{cost}(\varPi_{\mathsf{exe}}^{\mathsf{Map}}) + \mathsf{cost}(\varPi_{\mathsf{fmt}}^{\mathsf{Map}}) + 2 \cdot \mathsf{cost}(\varPi_{\mathsf{sum}}^{\mathsf{Map}})\big) + R \cdot \big(\mathsf{cost}(\varPi_{\mathsf{exe}}^{\mathsf{Reduce}}) + \\ \mathsf{cost}(\varPi_{\mathsf{fmt}}^{\mathsf{Reduce}}) + 2 \cdot \mathsf{cost}(\varPi_{\mathsf{sum}}^{\mathsf{Reduce}})\big) + \mathsf{cost}(\varPi_{\mathsf{fin}}).$$

The above costs have the following meaning, and the following measured values on our reference node: $\mathsf{cost}(\varPi_{\mathsf{exe}}^{\mathsf{Map}}) \approx 9.3\,\mathrm{s}$ is the cost of proving execution of a mapper node; $\mathsf{cost}(\varPi_{\mathsf{exe}}^{\mathsf{Reduce}}) \approx 45.2\,\mathrm{s}$ is the cost of proving execution of a reducer node; $\mathsf{cost}(\varPi_{\mathsf{fmt}}^{\mathsf{Map}}) \approx 13.6\,\mathrm{s}$ and $\mathsf{cost}(\varPi_{\mathsf{sum}}^{\mathsf{Map}}) \approx 14.2\,\mathrm{s}$, as well as $\mathsf{cost}(\varPi_{\mathsf{fmt}}^{\mathsf{Reduce}}) \approx 13.8\,\mathrm{s}$

and $\text{cost}(\varPi_{\text{sum}}^{\text{Reduce}}) \approx 14.3\,\text{s}$ denote the individual costs in proving the correctness of aggregation of mapper nodes' outputs and reducer nodes' inputs, respectively; and $\text{cost}(\varPi_{\text{fin}}) \approx 14.3\,\text{s}$ is the cost of producing the final proof.

Extrapolating the cost model. Our cost model accurately characterizes the prover's runtime for the word counting example. When changing the input, the costs change as follows: (a) the costs of $\varPi_{\text{fmt}}^{\text{Map}}$ and $\varPi_{\text{sum}}^{\text{Map}}$ remain fixed for all MapReduce computations; (b) the costs of $\varPi_{\text{fmt}}^{\text{Reduce}}$, $\varPi_{\text{sum}}^{\text{Reduce}}$ and $\varPi_{\text{fin}}$ remain stable as they only exhibit a slight dependency on the length of k^2, but do not otherwise depend on the specific MapReduce computation; (c) the cost of $\varPi_{\text{exe}}^{\text{Map}}$ changes depending on $N^{\max}$, the maximum number of mapper outputs, and Map's running time. The cost of $\varPi_{\text{exe}}^{\text{Reduce}}$ is dominated by the cost incurred by performing $d_{\text{in}}^{\max}$ proof verifications, each costing $\approx 90,000$ gates.

References

1. Apache Hadoop
2. Applebaum, B., Ishai, Y., Kushilevitz, E.: From secrecy to soundness: efficient verification via secure computation. In: Abramsky, S., Gavoille, C., Kirchner, C., Meyer auf der Heide, F., Spirakis, P.G. (eds.) ICALP 2010. LNCS, vol. 6198, pp. 152–163. Springer, Heidelberg (2010)
3. Backes, M., Fiore, D., Reischuk, R.M.: Nearly practical and privacy-preserving proofs on authenticated data (2014)
4. Bellare, M., Goldreich, O.: On defining proofs of knowledge. In: Brickell, E.F. (ed.) CRYPTO 1992. LNCS, vol. 740, pp. 390–420. Springer, Heidelberg (1993)
5. Bellare, M., Palacio, A.: The knowledge-of-exponent assumptions and 3-round zero-knowledge protocols. In: Franklin, M. (ed.) CRYPTO 2004. LNCS, vol. 3152, pp. 273–289. Springer, Heidelberg (2004)
6. Ben-Sasson, E., Chiesa, A., Garman, C., Green, M., Miers, I., Tromer, E., Virza, M.: Zerocash: decentralized anonymous payments from bitcoin. In: SP 2014 (2014)
7. Ben-Sasson, E., Chiesa, A., Genkin, D., Tromer, E., Virza, M.: SNARKs for C: verifying program executions succinctly and in zero knowledge. In: Canetti, R., Garay, J.A. (eds.) CRYPTO 2013, Part II. LNCS, vol. 8043, pp. 90–108. Springer, Heidelberg (2013)
8. Ben-Sasson, E., Chiesa, A., Tromer, E., Virza, M.: Scalable zero knowledge via cycles of elliptic curves. In: Garay, J.A., Gennaro, R. (eds.) CRYPTO 2014, Part II. LNCS, vol. 8617, pp. 276–294. Springer, Heidelberg (2014). http://eprint.iacr.org/2014/595
9. Ben-Sasson, E., Chiesa, A., Tromer, E., Virza, M.: Succinct non-interactive zero knowledge for a von neumann architecture. In: USENIX Security 2014 (2014). http://eprint.iacr.org/2013/879
10. Benabbas, S., Gennaro, R., Vahlis, Y.: Verifiable delegation of computation over large datasets. In: Rogaway, P. (ed.) CRYPTO 2011. LNCS, vol. 6841, pp. 111–131. Springer, Heidelberg (2011)
11. Bitansky, N., Canetti, R., Chiesa, A., Goldwasser, S., Lin, H., Rubinstein, A., Tromer, E.: The hunting of the SNARK. ePrint 2014/580 (2014)
12. Bitansky, N., Canetti, R., Chiesa, A., Tromer, E.: From extractable collision resistance to succinct non-interactive arguments of knowledge, and back again. In: ITCS 2012 (2012)

13. Bitansky, N., Canetti, R., Chiesa, A., Tromer, E.: Recursive composition and bootstrapping for SNARKs and proof-carrying data. In: STOC 2013 (2013)
14. Bitansky, N., Chiesa, A.: Succinct arguments from multi-prover interactive proofs and their efficiency benefits. In: Safavi-Naini, R., Canetti, R. (eds.) CRYPTO 2012. LNCS, vol. 7417, pp. 255–272. Springer, Heidelberg (2012)
15. Bitansky, N., Chiesa, A., Ishai, Y., Ostrovsky, R., Paneth, O.: Succinct non-interactive arguments via linear interactive proofs. In: Sahai, A. (ed.) TCC 2013. LNCS, vol. 7785, pp. 315–333. Springer, Heidelberg (2013)
16. Blum, M., De Santis, A., Micali, S., Persiano, G.: Non-interactive zero-knowledge. SIAM J. Comp. (1991)
17. Blum, M., Feldman, P., Micali, S.: Non-interactive zero-knowledge and its applications. In: STOC 1988 (1988)
18. Blumberg, A.J., Thaler, J., Vu, V., Walfish, M.: Verifiable computation using multiple provers. ePrint 2014/846 (2014)
19. Boneh, D., Segev, G., Waters, B.: Targeted malleability: homomorphic encryption for restricted computations. In: ITCS 2012 (2012)
20. Brants, T., Popat, A.C., Xu, P., Och, F.J., Dean, J.: Large language models in machine translation. In: EMNLP-CoNLL 2007 (2007)
21. Braun, B., Feldman, A.J., Ren, Z., Setty, S., Blumberg, A.J., Walfish, M.: Verifying computations with state. In: SOSP 2013 (2013)
22. Canetti, R., Riva, B., Rothblum, G.N.: Two protocols for delegation of computation. In: Smith, A. (ed.) ICITS 2012. LNCS, vol. 7412, pp. 37–61. Springer, Heidelberg (2012)
23. Chase, M., Kohlweiss, M., Lysyanskaya, A., Meiklejohn, S.: Succinct malleable NIZKs and an application to compact shuffles. In: Sahai, A. (ed.) TCC 2013. LNCS, vol. 7785, pp. 100–119. Springer, Heidelberg (2013)
24. Chiesa, A., Tromer, E.: Proof-carrying data and hearsay arguments from signature cards. In: ICS 2010 (2010)
25. Chiesa, A., Tromer, E.: Proof-carrying data: Secure computation on untrusted platforms (high-level description). The Next Wave: The National Security Agency's review of emerging technologies (2012)
26. Chu, C., Kim, S.K., Lin, Y., Yu, Y., Bradski, G.R., Ng, A.Y., Olukotun, K.: MapReduce for machine learning on multicore. In: NIPS 2004 (2006)
27. Chung, K.-M., Kalai, Y., Vadhan, S.: Improved delegation of computation using fully homomorphic encryption. In: Rabin, T. (ed.) CRYPTO 2010. LNCS, vol. 6223, pp. 483–501. Springer, Heidelberg (2010)
28. Cormode, G., Mitzenmacher, M., Thaler, J.: Practical verified computation with streaming interactive proofs. In: ITCS 2012 (2012)
29. Cormode, G., Thaler, J., Yi, K.: Verifying computations with streaming interactive proofs. In: Proceedings of the VLDB Endowment (2011)
30. Costello, C., Fournet, C., Howell, J., Kohlweiss, M., Kreuter, B., Naehrig, M., Parno, B., Zahur, S.: Geppetto: Versatile verifiable computation. ePrint 2014/976 (2014)
31. Damgård, I.: Towards practical public key systems secure against chosen ciphertext attacks. In: Feigenbaum, J. (ed.) CRYPTO 1991. LNCS, vol. 576, pp. 445–456. Springer, Heidelberg (1992)
32. Damgård, I., Faust, S., Hazay, C.: Secure two-party computation with low communication. In: Cramer, R. (ed.) TCC 2012. LNCS, vol. 7194, pp. 54–74. Springer, Heidelberg (2012)
33. Danezis, G., Fournet, C., Groth, J., Kohlweiss, M.: Square span programs with applications to succinct NIZK arguments. In: Sarkar, P., Iwata, T. (eds.) ASIACRYPT 2014. LNCS, vol. 8873, pp. 532–550. Springer, Heidelberg (2014)

34. Danezis, G., Fournet, C., Kohlweiss, M., Parno, B.: Pinocchio coin: building zerocoin from a succinct pairing-based proof system. In: PETShop 2013 (2013)
35. Dean, J., Ghemawat, S.: MapReduce: simplified data processing on large clusters. In: OSDI 2014 (2004)
36. Di Crescenzo, G., Lipmaa, H.: Succinct NP proofs from an extractability assumption. In: Beckmann, A., Dimitracopoulos, C., Löwe, B. (eds.) CiE 2008. LNCS, vol. 5028, pp. 175–185. Springer, Heidelberg (2008)
37. Diffie, W., Hellman, M.: New directions in cryptography. IEEE Trans. on Inf. Theory (1976)
38. Dyer, C., Cordova, A., Mont, A., Lin, J.: Fast, easy, and cheap: construction of statistical machine translation models with MapReduce. In: StatMT 2008 (2008)
39. Fauzi, P., Lipmaa, H., Zhang, B.: Efficient modular NIZK arguments from shift and product. In: Abdalla, M., Nita-Rotaru, C., Dahab, R. (eds.) CANS 2013. LNCS, vol. 8257, pp. 92–121. Springer, Heidelberg (2013)
40. Fiore, D., Gennaro, R.: Publicly verifiable delegation of large polynomials and matrix computations, with applications. ePrint 2012/281 (2012)
41. Fredrikson, M., Livshits, B.: Zø: an optimizing distributing zero-knowledge compiler. In: USENIX Security 2014 (2014)
42. Gennaro, R., Gentry, C., Parno, B.: Non-interactive verifiable computing: outsourcing computation to untrusted workers. In: Rabin, T. (ed.) CRYPTO 2010. LNCS, vol. 6223, pp. 465–482. Springer, Heidelberg (2010)
43. Gennaro, R., Gentry, C., Parno, B., Raykova, M.: Quadratic span programs and succinct NIZKs without PCPs. In: Johansson, T., Nguyen, P.Q. (eds.) EUROCRYPT 2013. LNCS, vol. 7881, pp. 626–645. Springer, Heidelberg (2013)
44. Gentry, C., Wichs, D.: Separating succinct non-interactive arguments from all falsifiable assumptions. In: STOC 2011 (2011)
45. Goel, A., Munagala, K.: Complexity measures for Map-Reduce, and comparison to parallel computing. ArXiv abs/1211.6526 (2012)
46. Goldwasser, S., Kalai, Y.T., Rothblum, G.N.: Delegating computation: interactive proofs for muggles. In: STOC 2008 (2008)
47. Goldwasser, S., Lin, H., Rubinstein, A.: Delegation of computation without rejection problem from designated verifier CS-proofs. ePrint 2011/456 (2011)
48. Goldwasser, S., Micali, S., Rackoff, C.: The knowledge complexity of interactive proof systems. SIAM J. Comp. (1989)
49. Groth, J.: Short pairing-based non-interactive zero-knowledge arguments. In: Abe, M. (ed.) ASIACRYPT 2010. LNCS, vol. 6477, pp. 321–340. Springer, Heidelberg (2010)
50. Hada, S., Tanaka, T.: On the existence of 3-round zero-knowledge protocols. In: Krawczyk, H. (ed.) CRYPTO 1998. LNCS, vol. 1462, pp. 408–423. Springer, Heidelberg (1998)
51. Kalai, Y.T., Raz, R.: Probabilistically checkable arguments. In: Halevi, S. (ed.) CRYPTO 2009. LNCS, vol. 5677, pp. 143–159. Springer, Heidelberg (2009)
52. Kang, U., Chau, D.H., Faloutsos, C.: Pegasus: mining billion-scale graphs in the cloud. In: ICASSP 2012 (2012)
53. Kosba, A.E., Papadopoulos, D., Papamanthou, C., Sayed, M.F., Shi, E., Triandopoulos, N.: TRUESET: faster verifiable set computations. In: USENIX Security 2014 (2014)
54. Langmead, B., Schatz, M.C., Lin, J., Pop, M., Salzberg, S.: Searching for SNPs with cloud computing. Genome Biology (2009)
55. Lidl, R., Niederreiter, H.: Finite Fields. Cambridge University Press, second (edn.) (1997)

56. Lin, J.: Brute force and indexed approaches to pairwise document similarity comparisons with mapreduce. In: SIGIR 2009 (2009)
57. Lin, J., Dyer, C.: Data-Intensive Text Processing with MapReduce. Morgan and Claypool Publishers (2010)
58. Lin, J., Schatz, M.C.: Design patterns for efficient graph algorithms in mapreduce. In: MLG 2010 (2010)
59. Lipmaa, H.: Progression-free sets and sublinear pairing-based non-interactive zero-knowledge arguments. In: Cramer, R. (ed.) TCC 2012. LNCS, vol. 7194, pp. 169–189. Springer, Heidelberg (2012)
60. Lipmaa, H.: Succinct non-interactive zero knowledge arguments from span programs and linear error-correcting codes. In: Sako, K., Sarkar, P. (eds.) ASIACRYPT 2013, Part I. LNCS, vol. 8269, pp. 41–60. Springer, Heidelberg (2013)
61. Lipmaa, H.: Efficient NIZK arguments via parallel verification of benes networks. In: Abdalla, M., De Prisco, R. (eds.) SCN 2014. LNCS, vol. 8642, pp. 416–434. Springer, Heidelberg (2014)
62. Merkle, R.C.: A certified digital signature. In: Brassard, G. (ed.) CRYPTO 1989. LNCS, vol. 435, pp. 218–238. Springer, Heidelberg (1990)
63. Micali, S.: Computationally sound proofs. SIAM J. Comp. (2000)
64. Mie, T.: Polylogarithmic two-round argument systems. Journal of Mathematical Cryptology (2008)
65. Miers, I., Garman, C., Green, M., Rubin, A.D.: Zerocoin: anonymous distributed e-cash from bitcoin. In: SP 2013 (2013)
66. Naor, M., Yung, M.: Public-key cryptosystems provably secure against chosen ciphertext attacks. In: STOC 1990 (1990)
67. Panda, B., Herbach, J., Basu, S., Bayardo, R.J.: PLANET: massively parallel learning of tree ensembles with MapReduce. In: Proceedings of the VLDB Endowment (2009)
68. Paneth, O., Rothblum, G.N.: Publicly verifiable non-interactive arguments for delegating computation. ePrint 2014/981 (2014)
69. Parno, B., Gentry, C., Howell, J., Raykova, M.: Pinocchio: nearly practical verifiable computation. In: Oakland 2013 (2013)
70. Pino, J., Waite, A., Byrne, W.: Simple and efficient model filtering in statistical machine translation. Prague Bulletin of Mathematical Linguistics (2012)
71. Schatz, M.C.: CloudBurst: highly sensitive read mapping with MapReduce. Bioinformatics (2009)
72. SCIPR Lab. libsnark: a C++ library for zkSNARK proofs
73. Setty, S., Blumberg, A.J., Walfish, M.: Toward practical and unconditional verification of remote computations. In: HotOS 2011 (2011)
74. Setty, S., Braun, B., Vu, V., Blumberg, A.J., Parno, B., Walfish, M.: Resolving the conflict between generality and plausibility in verified computation. In: EuroSys 2013 (2013)
75. Setty, S., McPherson, M., Blumberg, A.J., Walfish, M.: Making argument systems for outsourced computation practical (sometimes). In: NDSS 2012 (2012)
76. Setty, S., Vu, V., Panpalia, N., Braun, B., Blumberg, A.J., Walfish, M.: Taking proof-based verified computation a few steps closer to practicality. In: USENIX Security 2012 (2012)
77. Thaler, J.: Time-optimal interactive proofs for circuit evaluation. In: Canetti, R., Garay, J.A. (eds.) CRYPTO 2013, Part II. LNCS, vol. 8043, pp. 71–89. Springer, Heidelberg (2013)
78. Thaler, J., Roberts, M., Mitzenmacher, M., Pfister, H.: Verifiable computation with massively parallel interactive proofs. CoRR (2012)

79. Valiant, P.: Incrementally verifiable computation or proofs of knowledge imply time/space efficiency. In: Canetti, R. (ed.) TCC 2008. LNCS, vol. 4948, pp. 1–18. Springer, Heidelberg (2008)

80. Vu, V., Setty, S., Blumberg, A.J., Walfish, M.: A hybrid architecture for interactive verifiable computation. In: Oakland 2013 (2013)

81. Wahby, R.S., Setty, S., Ren, Z., Blumberg, A.J., Walfish, M.: Efficient RAM and control flow in verifiable outsourced computation. ePrint 2014/674 (2014)

82. Wolfe, J., Haghighi, A., Klein, D.: Fully distributed EM for very large datasets. In: ICML 2008 (2008)

83. Zhang, Y., Papamanthou, C., Katz, J.: Alitheia: towards practical verifiable graph processing. In: CCS 2014 (2014)

Hosting Services on an Untrusted Cloud

Dan Boneh[1]([✉]), Divya Gupta[2], Ilya Mironov[3], and Amit Sahai[2]

[1] Stanford University, Stanford, CA, USA
dabo@cs.stanford.edu
[2] UCLA and Center for Encrypted Functionalities, Los Angeles, CA, USA
{divyag,asahai}@cs.ucla.edu
[3] Google, Mountain View, CA, USA
mironov@gmail.com

Abstract. We consider a scenario where a service provider has created a software service S and desires to outsource the execution of this service to an untrusted cloud. The software service contains secrets that the provider would like to keep hidden from the cloud. For example, the software might contain a secret database, and the service could allow users to make queries to different slices of this database depending on the user's identity.

This setting presents significant challenges not present in previous works on outsourcing or secure computation. Because secrets in the software itself must be protected against an adversary that has full control over the cloud that is executing this software, our notion implies indistinguishability obfuscation. Furthermore, we seek to protect knowledge of the software S to the maximum extent possible even if the cloud can collude with several corrupted users.

In this work, we provide the first formalizations of security for this setting, yielding our definition of a *secure cloud service scheme*. We provide constructions of secure cloud service schemes assuming indistinguishability obfuscation, one-way functions, and non-interactive zero-knowledge proofs.

At the heart of our paper are novel techniques to allow parties to simultaneously authenticate and securely communicate with an obfuscated program, while hiding this authentication and communication from the entity in possession of the obfuscated program.

D. Boneh—Supported by NSF and DARPA.
D. Gupta and A. Sahai—Research supported in part from a DARPA/ONR PRO-CEED award, NSF Frontier Award 1413955, NSF grants 1228984, 1136174, 1118096, and 1065276, a Xerox Faculty Research Award, a Google Faculty Research Award, an equipment grant from Intel, and an Okawa Foundation Research Grant. This material is based upon work supported by the Defense Advanced Research Projects Agency through the U.S. Office of Naval Research under Contract N00014-11-1-0389. The views expressed are those of the author and do not reflect the official policy or position of the Department of Defense, the NSF, or the U.S. Government.
I. Mironov—Work done in Microsoft Research.

E. Oswald and M. Fischlin (Eds.): EUROCRYPT 2015, Part II, LNCS 9057, pp. 404–436, 2015.
DOI: 10.1007/978-3-662-46803-6_14

1   Introduction

Consider a service provider that has created some software service S that he wants to make accessible to a collection of users. However, the service provider is computationally weak and wants to outsource the computation of S to an untrusted cloud. Nevertheless, the software is greatly valuable and he does not want the cloud to learn what secrets are embedded in the software S. There are many concrete examples of such a scenario; for example, the software could contain a secret database, and the service could allow users to make queries to different slices of this database depending on the user's identity.

At first glance, such a scenario seems like a perfect application of obfuscation and can be thought to be solved as follows: The provider could obfuscate the software $O(S)$ and send this directly to the cloud. Now, the cloud could receive an input (id, x) directly from a user with identity id, and respond with the computed output $O(S)(\mathsf{id}, x) = S(\mathsf{id}, x)$. Secure obfuscation would ensure that the cloud would never learn the secrets built inside the software, *except* for what is efficiently revealed by the input-output behavior of the software. But this approach does not provide any privacy to the users. In such a setting, the cloud will be able to learn the inputs x and the outputs $S(\mathsf{id}, x)$ of the multitude of users which use this service. This is clearly undesirable in most applications. Worse still, the cloud will be able to query the software on arbitrary inputs and identities of its choice. In our scheme, we want to guarantee input and output privacy for the users. Moreover, we want that only a user who pays for and subscribes to the service is able to access the functionality that the service provides for that particular user.

Ideally, we would like that, first, a user with identity id performs some simple one-time set-up interaction with the service provider to obtain a key K_{id}. This key K_{id} would also serve as authentication information for the user. Later, in order to run the software on input x of his choice, he would encrypt x to $Enc_{K_{\mathsf{id}}}(x)$ and send it to the cloud. The cloud would run the software to obtain an encryption of $S(\mathsf{id}, x)$, which is sent back to the user while still in encrypted form. Finally, the user can decrypt in order to obtain its output.

Let us step back and specify a bit more precisely the security properties we desire from such a secure cloud service.

1. **Security against malicious cloud.** In our setting, if the cloud is the only malicious party, then we require that it cannot learn anything about the nature of the computation except a bound on the running time. In particular, it learns nothing about the code of the software or the input/output of users.
2. **Security against malicious clients.** If a collection of users is malicious, they cannot learn anything beyond what is learnable via specific input/output that the malicious users see. Furthermore, if a client is not authenticated by the service provider, it cannot learn anything at all.
3. **Security against a malicious cloud and clients.** Moreover, even when a malicious cloud colludes with a collection of malicious users, the adversary

cannot learn anything beyond the functionality provided to the malicious users. That is, the adversary does not learn anything about the input/output of the honest users or the slice of service provided to them. More precisely, consider two software services S and S' which are functionally equivalent when restricted to corrupt users. Then the adversary cannot distinguish between the instantiations of the scheme with S and S'.

4. **Efficiency.** Since the service provider and the users are computationally weak parties, we want to make their online computation highly efficient. The interaction in the set-up phase between the provider and a user should be independent of the complexity of the service being provided. For the provider, only its one-time encoding of the software service should depend polynomially on the complexity of the software. The work of the client in encrypting his inputs should only depend polynomially on the size of his inputs and a security parameter. And finally, the running time of the encoded software on the cloud should be bounded by a fixed polynomial of the running time of the software.

Note that since the scheme is for the benefit of the service provider, who could choose to provide whatever service it desires, we assume that the service provider itself is uncompromised.

We call a scheme that satisfies the above listed properties, a *Secure Cloud Service Scheme* (SCSS). In this work, we provide the first construction of a secure cloud service scheme, based on indistinguishability obfuscation, one-way functions, and non-interactive zero-knowledge proofs. At the heart of our paper are novel techniques to allow parties to simultaneously authenticate and securely communicate with an obfuscated program, while hiding this authentication and communication from the entity in possession of the obfuscated program.

Relationships to Other Models. At first glance, the setting we consider may seem similar to notions considered in earlier works. However, as we describe below, there are substantial gaps between these notions and our setting. As an initial observation, we note that a secure cloud service scheme is fundamentally about protecting secrets within software run by a single entity (the cloud), and therefore is intimately tied to obfuscation. Indeed, our definition of a secure cloud service scheme immediately implies indistinguishability obfuscation. Thus, our notion is separated from notions that do not imply obfuscation. We now elaborate further, comparing our setting to two prominent previously considered notions.

○ **Delegation of Computation.** A widely studied topic in cryptography is secure delegation or outsourcing of computation (e.g., [7,11,14,16]), where a *single user* wishes to delegate a computation to the cloud. The most significant difference between delegation and our scheme is that in delegation the role of the provider and the user is combined into a single entity. In contrast, in our setting the entity that decides the function S is the provider, and this entity is completely separate from the entities (users) that receive outputs. Indeed, a user should learn nothing about the function being computed by the cloud beyond what the specific input/output pairs that the user sees. Moreover, the vast majority of delegation notions in literature do not require any kind of obfuscation.

Furthermore, we consider a setting where multiple unique users have access to a different slice of service on the cloud (based on their identities), whereas in standard formulations of delegation, only one computation is outsourced from client to the cloud. There is a recent work on delegation that does consider multiple users: the work of [8] on outsourcing RAM computations goes beyond the standard setting of delegation to consider a multi-user setting. But as pointed out by the authors themselves, in this setting, the cloud can learn arbitrary information about the description of the software. Their notion of privacy only guarantees that the cloud learns nothing about the inputs and outputs of the users, but not about the nature of the computation – which is the focus of our work. Moreover, in their setting, no security is promised in the case of a collusion between a malicious cloud and a malicious client. The primary technical contributions of our work revolve around guaranteeing security in this challenging setting.

o **Multi-Input Functional Encryption (MIFE).** Recently, the work of [10] introduced the extremely general notion of multi-input functional encryption (MIFE), whose setting can capture a vast range of scenarios. Nevertheless, MIFE does not directly apply to our scenario: In our setting, there are an unbounded number of possible clients, each of which gets a unique *encryption* key that is used to prepare its input for the cloud. MIFE has been defined with respect to a fixed number of possible encryption keys [10], but even if it were extended to an unbounded number of encryption keys, each function evaluation key in an MIFE would necessarily be bound to a fixed number of encryption keys. This would lead to a combinatorial explosion of exponentially many function evaluation keys needed for the cloud.

Alternatively, one could try to build a secure cloud service scheme by "jury-rigging" MIFE to nevertheless apply to our scenario. Fundamentally, because MIFE does imply indistinguishability obfuscation [10], this must be possible. But, as far we know, the only way to use MIFE to build a secure cloud service scheme is by essentially carrying out our entire construction, but replacing our use of indistinguishability obfuscation with calls to MIFE. At a very high level, the key challenges in applying MIFE to our setting arise from the IND-definition of MIFE security [10], which largely mirrors the definition of indistinguishability obfuscation security. We elaborate on these challenges below, when we discuss our techniques.

1.1 Our Results

In this work, we formalize the notion of secure cloud service scheme (Section 3) and give the first scheme which achieves this notion. In our formal notion, we consider potential collusions involving the cloud and up to k corrupt users, where

k is a bound fixed in advance. (Note again that even with a single corrupt user, our notion implies indistinguishability obfuscation.) We then give a protocol which implements a secure cloud service scheme. More formally,

Theorem 1. *Assuming the existence of indistinguishability obfuscation, statistically simulation-sound non-interactive zero-knowledge proof systems and one-way functions, for any bound k on the number of corrupt users that is polynomially related to the security parameter, there exists a secure cloud service scheme.*

Note that we only require a bound on the number of corrupt clients, and not on the total number of users in the system. Our scheme provides an exponential space of possible identities for users. We note that the need to bound the number of corrupt users when using indistinguishability obfuscation is related to several other such bounds that are needed in other applications of indistinguishability obfuscation, such as the number of adversarial ciphertexts in functional encryption [6] and multi-input functional encryption [10] schemes. We consider the removal of such a bound using indistinguishability obfuscation to be a major open problem posed by our work.

Furthermore, we also consider the case when the software service takes two inputs: one from the user and other from the cloud. We call this setting a secure cloud service scheme with cloud inputs. This setting presents an interesting technical challenge because it opens up exponential number of possible functions that could have been provided to a client. We resolve this issue using a technically interesting sequence of 2^ℓ hybrids, where ℓ is the length of the cloud's input (see Our Techniques below for further details). To prove security, we need to assume sub-exponential hardness of indistinguishability obfuscation. More formally, we have the following result.

Theorem 2. *Assuming the existence of sub-exponentially hard indistinguishability obfuscation, statistically simulation-sound non-interactive zero-knowledge proof systems and sub-exponentially hard one-way functions, for any bound k on the number of corrupt users that is polynomially related to the security parameter, there exists a secure cloud service scheme with cloud inputs.*

1.2   Our Techniques

Since a secure cloud service scheme implies indistinguishability obfuscation ($i\mathcal{O}$), let us begin by considering how we may apply obfuscation to solve our problem, and use this to identify the technical obstacles that we will face.

The central goal of a secure cloud service scheme is to hide the nature of the service software S from the cloud. Thus, we would certainly use $i\mathcal{O}$ to obfuscate the software S before providing it to the cloud. However, as we have already mentioned, this is not enough, as we also want to provide privacy to honest users. Our scheme must also give a user the ability to encrypt its input x in such a way that the cloud cannot decrypt it, but the obfuscated software can. After choosing a public key PK and decryption key SK for a public-key encryption scheme, we could provide PK to the user, and build SK into the obfuscated software to decrypt inputs. Finally, each user should obtain its output in encrypted form, so that the cloud cannot decrypt it. In particular, each user can choose a secret key K_{id}, and then to issue a query, it can create the ciphertext $c = Enc_{PK}(x, K_{id})$. Thus, we need to build a program $\hat{S}$ that does the following: It takes as input the user id id and a ciphertext c. It then decrypts c using SK to yield (x, K_{id}). It then computes the output $y = S(id, x)$. Finally, it outputs the ciphertext $d = Enc(K_{id}, y)$. The user can decrypt this to obtain y. The cloud should obtain an obfuscated version of this software $\hat{S}$.

At first glance, it may appear that this scheme would already be secure, at least if given an "ideal obfuscation" akin to Virtual Black-Box obfuscation [1]. However, this is not true. In particular, there is a malleability attack that arises: Consider the scenario where the cloud can malleate the ciphertext sent by the user, which contains his input x and key K_{id}, to an encryption of x and K^*, where K^* is maliciously chosen by the cloud. If this were possible, the cloud could use its knowledge of K^* to decrypt the output $d = Enc(K_{id}, y)$ produced by the obfuscated version of $\hat{S}$. But this is not all. Another problem we have not yet handled is authentication: a malicious user could pretend to have a different identity id than the one that it is actually given, thereby obtaining outputs from S that it is not allowed to access. We must address both the malleability concern and the authentication concern, but also do this in a way that works with indistinguishability obfuscation, not just an ideal obfuscation.

Indeed, once we constrain ourselves to only using indistinguishability obfuscation, additional concerns arise. Here, we will describe the two most prominent issues, and describe how we deal with them.

Recall that our security notion requires that if an adversary corrupts the cloud and a user id*, then the view of the adversary is indistinguishable for any two softwares S and S' such that $S(id^*, x) = S'(id^*, x)$ for all possible inputs x. However, S and S' could differ completely on inputs for several other identities id. Ideally, in our proof, we would like to use the security of $i\mathcal{O}$ while making the change from S to S' in the obfuscated program. In order to use the security of $i\mathcal{O}$, the two programs being obfuscated must be equivalent for all inputs, and not just the inputs of the malicious client with identity id*. However, we are given no such guarantee for S and S'. So in our proof of security, we have to construct a hybrid (indistinguishable from real execution on S) in which S can only be invoked for the malicious client identity id*. Since we have functional equivalence for this client, we will then be able to make the switch from $\hat{S}$ to $\hat{S}'$ by security of $i\mathcal{O}$. We stress that the requirement to make this switch is that there does not exist any input to the obfuscated program which give different outputs for $\hat{S}$ and $\hat{S}'$. It does not suffice to ensure that a differing input cannot be computed efficiently. To achieve this, in this hybrid, we must ensure that there does not exist any valid authentication for all the honest users. Thus, since no honest user can actually get a useful output from $\hat{S}$ or $\hat{S}'$, they will be functionally equivalent. In contrast, all the malicious users should still be able to get authenticated and obtain outputs from the cloud; otherwise the adversary would notice that something is wrong. We achieve this using a carefully designed authentication scheme that we describe next.

At a high level, we require the following: Let k be the bound on the number of malicious clients. The authentication scheme should be such that in the "fake mode" it is possible to authenticate the k corrupt user identities and there does not exist (even information-theoretically) any valid authentication for any other identity. We achieve this notion by leveraging k-cover-free sets of [4,13] where there are a super-polynomial number of sets over a polynomial sized universe such that the union of *any* k sets does not cover any other set. We use these sets along with length doubling PRGs to build our authentication scheme.

Another problem that arises with the use of indistinguishability obfuscation concerns how outputs are encrypted within $\hat{S}$. The output of the obfuscated program is a ciphertext which encrypts the actual output of the software. We are guaranteed that the outputs of S and S' are identical for the corrupt clients, but we still need to ensure that the corresponding encryptions are also identical (in order to apply the security of $i\mathcal{O}$.) We ensure this by using an encryption scheme which satisfies the following: If two obfuscated programs using S and S', respectively, are given a ciphertext as input, then if S and S' produce the same output, then the obfuscated programs will produce *identical* encryptions as output. In particular, our scheme works as follows: the user sends a pseudo-random function (PRF) key K_{id} and the program outputs $y = \mathsf{PRF}(K_{\mathsf{id}}, r) \oplus S(x, \mathsf{id})$, where the r value is computed using another PRF applied to the ciphertext c itself. Thus we ensure that for identical ciphertexts as inputs, both programs produce the same r, and hence the same y. This method allows us to switch S to S', but the new challenge then becomes how to argue the *security* of this encryption scheme. To accomplish this, we use the punctured programming paradigm of [18] to build a careful sequence of hybrids using punctured PRF keys to argue security.

We need several other technical ideas to make the security proof work. Please see our protocol in Section 4 and proof in Section 4.1 for details.

When considering the case where the cloud can also provide an input to the computation, the analysis becomes significantly more complex because of a new attack: The cloud can take an input from an honest party, and then try to vary the cloud's own input, and observe the impact this has on the output of the computation. Recall that in our proof of security, in one hybrid, we will need to "cut off" honest parties from the computation – but we need to do this in a way that is indistinguishable from the cloud's point of view. But an honest party that has been cut off will no longer have an output that can depend on the cloud's input. If the cloud can detect this, the proof of security fails. In order to deal with this, we must change the way that our encryption of the output works, in order to include the cloud input in the computation of the r value. But once we do this, the punctured programming methods of [18] become problematic. To deal with this issue, we create a sequence of exponentially many hybrids, where we puncture out exactly one possible cloud input at a time. This lets us avoid a situation where the direct punctured programming approach would have required an exponential amount of puncturing, which would cause the programs being obfuscated to blow up to an exponential size.

2 Prelims

Let λ be the security parameter. Below, we describe the primitives used in our scheme.

2.1 Public Key Encryption Scheme

A public key encryption scheme pke over a message space $\mathcal{M} = \mathcal{M}_\lambda$ consists of three algorithms PKGen, PKEnc, PKDec. The algorithm PKGen takes security parameter 1^λ and outputs the public key pk and secret key sk. The algorithm PKEnc takes public key pk and a message $\mu \in \mathcal{M}$ as input and outputs the ciphertext c that encrypts μ. The algorithm PKDec takes the secret key sk and ciphertext c and outputs a message μ.

A public key encryption scheme pke is said to be correct if for all messages $\mu \in \mathcal{M}$:

$$\Pr[(\mathsf{pk}, \mathsf{sk}) \leftarrow \mathsf{PKGen}(1^\lambda); \mathsf{PKDec}(\mathsf{sk}, \mathsf{PKEnc}(\mathsf{pk}, \mu; u)) \neq \mu] \leqslant \mathsf{negl}(\lambda)$$

A public key encryption scheme pke is said to be IND-CPA secure if for all PPT adversaries $\mathcal{A}$ following holds:

$$\Pr\left[b = b' \;\middle|\; \begin{array}{l} (\mathsf{pk}, \mathsf{sk}) \leftarrow \mathsf{PKGen}(1^\lambda); (\mu_0, \mu_1, \mathsf{st}) \leftarrow \mathcal{A}(1^\lambda, \mathsf{pk}); \\ b \xleftarrow{\$} \{0, 1\}; c = \mathsf{PKEnc}(\mathsf{pk}, \mu_b; u); b' \leftarrow \mathcal{A}(c, \mathsf{st}) \end{array}\right] \leqslant \frac{1}{2} + \mathsf{negl}(\lambda)$$

2.2 Indistinguishability Obfuscation

The definition below is from [6]; there it is called a "family-indistinguishable obfuscator", however they show that this notion follows immediately from their standard definition of indistinguishability obfuscator using a non-uniform argument.

Definition 1 (Indistinguishability Obfuscator $(i\mathcal{O})$). *A uniform PPT machine $i\mathcal{O}$ is called an* indistinguishability obfuscator *for acircuit class $\{\mathcal{C}_\lambda\}$ if the following conditions are satisfied:*

○ *For all security parameters $\lambda \in \mathbb{N}$, for all $C \in \mathcal{C}_\lambda$, for all inputs x, we have that*
$$\Pr[C'(x) = C(x) : C' \leftarrow i\mathcal{O}(\lambda, C)] = 1$$

o *For any (not necessarily uniform) PPT adversaries Samp, D, there exists a negligible function α such that the following holds: if $\Pr[\forall x, C_0(x) = C_1(x) : (C_0, C_1, \sigma) \leftarrow Samp(1^\lambda)] > 1 - \alpha(\lambda)$, then we have:*

$$\Big| \Pr\big[D(\sigma, i\mathcal{O}(\lambda, C_0)) = 1 : (C_0, C_1, \sigma) \leftarrow Samp(1^\lambda)\big]$$
$$- \Pr\big[D(\sigma, i\mathcal{O}(\lambda, C_1)) = 1 : (C_0, C_1, \sigma) \leftarrow Samp(1^\lambda)\big] \Big| \leq \alpha(\lambda)$$

In this paper, we will make use of such indistinguishability obfuscators for all polynomial-size circuits:

Definition 2 (Indistinguishability Obfuscator for $P/poly$). *A uniform PPT machine $i\mathcal{O}$ is called an* indistinguishability obfuscator *for $P/poly$ if the following holds: Let C_λ be the class of circuits of size at most λ. Then $i\mathcal{O}$ is an indistinguishability obfuscator for the class $\{C_\lambda\}$.*

Such indistinguishability obfuscators for all polynomial-size circuits were constructed under novel algebraic hardness assumptions in [6].

2.3   Puncturable PRF

Puncturable PRFs are a simple types of constrained PRFs [2,3,12]. These are PRFs that can be defined on all bit strings of a certain length, except for any polynomial-size set of inputs. Following definition has been taken verbatim from [18].

Definition 3. *A puncturable family of PRFs F is given by a triple of turing machines $\mathsf{PRFKey_F}, \mathsf{Puncture_F}, \mathsf{Eval_F}$, and a pair of computable functions $n(\cdot)$ and $m(\cdot)$, satisfying the following conditions.*

o **Functionality preserved under puncturing.** *For every PPT adversary $\mathcal{A}$ such that $\mathcal{A}(1^\lambda)$ outputs a set $S \subseteq \{0,1\}^{n(\lambda)}$, then for all $x \in \{0,1\}^{n(\lambda)}$ where $x \notin S$, we have that:*

$$\Pr\big[\mathsf{Eval_F}(K, x) = \mathsf{Eval_F}(K_S, x) : K \leftarrow \mathsf{PRFKey_F}(1^\lambda), K_S = \mathsf{Puncture_F}(K, S)\big] = 1$$

o **Pseudorandom at punctured points.** *For every PPT adversary $(\mathcal{A}_1, \mathcal{A}_2)$ such that $\mathcal{A}_1(1^\lambda)$ outputs a set $S \subseteq \{0,1\}^{n(\lambda)}$ and state st, consider an experiment where $K \leftarrow \mathsf{PRFKey_F}(1^\lambda)$ and $K_S = \mathsf{Puncture_F}(K, S)$. Then we have*

$$\Big| \Pr\big[\mathcal{A}_2(\sigma, K_S, S, \mathsf{Eval_F}(K, S)) = 1\big] - \Pr\big[\mathcal{A}_2(\mathsf{st}, K_S, S, U_{m(\lambda)\cdot|S|}) = 1\big] \Big| = \mathsf{negl}(\lambda)$$

where $\mathsf{Eval_F}(K, S)$ *denotes the concatenation of* $\mathsf{Eval_F}(K, x_1)), \ldots,$ $\mathsf{Eval_F}(K, x_k))$ *where* $S = \{x_1, \ldots, x_k\}$ *is the enumeration of the elements of* S *in lexicographic order,* $\mathsf{negl}(\cdot)$ *is a negligible function, and* U_ℓ *denotes the uniform distribution over* ℓ *bits.*

For ease of notation, we write $\mathsf{PRF}(K, x)$ *to represent* $\mathsf{Eval_F}(K, x)$. *We also represent the punctured key* $\mathsf{Puncture_F}(K, S)$ *by* $K(S)$.

The GGM tree-based construction of PRFs [9] from one-way functions are easily seen to yield puncturable PRFs, as recently observed by [2,3,12]. Thus we have:

Theorem 3. *[2, 3, 9, 12] If one-way functions exist, then for all efficiently computable functions* $n(\lambda)$ *and* $m(\lambda)$, *there exists a puncturable PRF family that maps* $n(\lambda)$ *bits to* $m(\lambda)$ *bits.*

2.4   Statistical Simulation-Sound Non-Interactive Zero-Knowledge

This primitive was introduced in [6] and was constructed from standard NIZKs using a commitment scheme. A statistically simulation-sound NIZK proof system for a relation R consists of three algorithms: NIZKSetup, NIZKProve, and NIZKVerify and satisfies the following properties.

Perfect completeness. An honest prover holding a valid witness can always convince an honest verifier. Formally,

$$\Pr\left[\mathsf{NIZKVerify}(\mathsf{crs}, x, \pi) = 1 \,\middle|\, \begin{array}{l} \mathsf{crs} \leftarrow \mathsf{NIZKSetup}(1^\lambda); (x, w) \in R; \\ \pi \leftarrow \mathsf{NIZKProve}(\mathsf{crs}, x, w) \end{array}\right] = 1$$

Statistical soundness. A proof system is sound if it is infeasible to convince an honest verifier when the statement is false. Formally, for all (even unbounded) adversaries $\mathcal{A}$,

$$\Pr\left[\mathsf{NIZKVerify}(\mathsf{crs}, x, \pi) = 1 \,\middle|\, \begin{array}{l} \mathsf{crs} \leftarrow \mathsf{NIZKSetup}(1^\lambda); \\ (x, \pi) \leftarrow \mathcal{A}(\mathsf{crs}); x \notin L \end{array}\right] \leqslant \mathsf{negl}(\lambda)$$

Computational zero-knowledge [5]. A proof system is zero-knowledge if a proof does not reveal anything beyond the validity of the statement. In particular, it does not reveal anything about the witness used by an honest prover. We say that a non-interactive proof system is zero-knowledge if there exists a PPT simulator $\mathcal{S} = (\mathsf{S_1}, \mathsf{S_2})$ such that $\mathsf{S_1}$ outputs a simulated CRS and a trapdoor τ for proving x and $\mathsf{S_2}$ produces a simulated proof which is indistinguishable from an honest proof. Formally, for all PPT adversaries $\mathcal{A}$, for all $x \in L$ such w is witness, following holds.

$$\Pr\left[\mathcal{A}(\text{crs}, x, \pi) = 1 \,\middle|\, \begin{array}{l} \text{crs} \leftarrow \text{NIZKSetup}(1^\lambda); \\ \pi \leftarrow \text{NIZKProve}(\text{crs}, x, w) \end{array}\right] \approx$$

$$\Pr\left[\mathcal{A}(\text{crs}, x, \pi) = 1 \,\middle|\, \begin{array}{l} (\text{crs}, \tau) \leftarrow \mathsf{S}_1(1^\lambda, x); \\ \pi \leftarrow \mathsf{S}_2(\text{crs}, \tau, x) \end{array}\right]$$

Statistical simulation-soundness. A proof system is said to be statistical simulation sound if is infeasible to convince an honest verifier when the statement is false even when the adversary is provided with a simulated proof (of a possibly false statement.) Formally, for all (even unbounded) adversaries $\mathcal{A}$, for all statements x, following holds.

$$\Pr\left[\text{NIZKVerify}(\text{crs}, x', \pi') = 1 \,\middle|\, \begin{array}{l} (\text{crs}, \tau) \leftarrow \mathsf{S}_1(1^\lambda, x); \pi \leftarrow \mathsf{S}_2(\text{crs}, \tau, x); \\ (x', \pi') \leftarrow \mathcal{A}(\text{crs}, x, \pi); x' \notin L \end{array}\right] \leqslant \text{negl}(\lambda)$$

2.5   Cover-Free Set Systems and Authentication Schemes

The authentication system we will use in our scheme will crucially use the notion of a cover-free set systems. Such systems were considered and build in [4,13]. Our definitions and constructions are inspired by those in [13].

Definition 4 (k-cover-free set system). *Let U be the universe and $n := |U|$. A family of sets $\mathcal{T} = \{T_1, \ldots, T_N\}$, where each $T_i \subseteq U$ is a k-cover-free set family if for all $T_1, \ldots, T_k \in \mathcal{T}$ and $T \in \mathcal{T}$ such that $T \neq T_i$ for all $i \in [k]$ following holds: $T \setminus \cup_{i \in [k]} T_i \neq \emptyset$.*

[13] constructed such a set system using Reed-Solomon codes. We define these next. Let $\mathbb{F}_q$ be a finite field of size q. Let $F_{q,k}$ denote the set of polynomials on $\mathbb{F}_q$ of degree at most k.

Definition 5 (Reed-Solomon code). *Let $x_1, \ldots, x_n \in \mathbb{F}_q$ be distinct and $k > 0$. The $(n, k)_q$-Reed-Solomon code is given by the subspace $\{\langle f(x_1), \ldots, f(x_n) \rangle \mid f \in F_{q,k}\}$.*

It is well-known that any two distinct polynomials of degree at most k can agree on at most k points.

Construction of k-cover-free sets. Let $\mathbb{F}_q = \{x_1, \ldots, x_q\}$ be a finite field of size q. We will set q in terms of security parameter λ and k later. Let universe be $U = \mathbb{F}_q \times \mathbb{F}_q$. Define $d := \frac{q-1}{k}$. The k-cover-free set system is as follows: $\mathcal{T} = \{T_f \mid f \in F_{q,d}\}$, where $T_f = \{\langle x_1, f(x_1) \rangle, \ldots \langle x_q, f(x_q) \rangle\} \subset U$.

Note that $N := |\mathcal{T}| = q^{d+1}$. For example, by putting $q = k \log \lambda$, we get $N = \lambda^{\omega(1)}$. In our scheme, we will set $q = k\lambda$ to obtain $N \geqslant 2^\lambda$.

Claim. The set system $\mathcal{T}$ is k-cover-free.

Proof. Note that each set T_f is a $(q,d)_q$-Reed-Solomon code. As pointed out earlier, any two distinct Reed-Solomon codes of degree d can agree on at most d points. Hence, $|T_i \cap T_j| \leqslant d$ for all $T_i, T_j \in \mathcal{T}$. Using this we get, for any $T, T_1, \ldots, T_k \in \mathcal{T}$ such that $T \neq T_i$ for all $i \in [k]$,

$$|T \setminus \cup_{i \in [k]} T_i| \geqslant q - kd = 1$$

Authentication Scheme Based on k-Cover-Free Sets. At a high level, there is an honest authenticator $\mathcal{H}$ who posses a secret authentication key ask and announces the public verification key avk. There are (possibly unbounded) polynomial number of users and each user has an identity. We want to design a primitive such that $\mathcal{H}$ can authenticate a user depending on his identity. The authentication t_{id} can be publicly verified using the public verification key.

Let $\mathsf{PRG} : Y \to Z$ be a pseudorandom generator. with $Y = \{0,1\}^\lambda$ and $Z = \{0,1\}^{2\lambda}$. Let the number of corrupted users be bounded by k. Let $\mathbb{F}_q = \{x_1, \ldots, x_q\}$ be a finite field with $q \geqslant k\lambda$. In the scheme below we will use the k-cover-free sets described above. Let $d = \frac{q-1}{k}$. Let $\mathcal{T}$ be the family of cover-free sets over the universe $\mathbb{F}_q^2$ such that each set is indexed by an element in $\mathbb{F}_q^{d+1}$.

The authentication schemes has three algorithms AuthGen, AuthProve and Authverify described as follows.

- Setup: The algorithm $\mathsf{AuthGen}(1^\lambda)$ works follows: For all $i, j \in [q]$, picks $s_{ij} \xleftarrow{\$} Y$. Set $\mathsf{ask} = \{s_{ij}\}_{i,j \in [q]}$ and $\mathsf{avk} = \{\mathsf{PRG}(s_{ij})\}_{i,j \in [q]} = \{z_{ij}\}_{i,j \in [q]}$. Returns (avk, ask). The keys will also contain the set-system $\mathcal{T}$. We assume this implicitly, and omit writing it.
- Authentication: The algorithm $\mathsf{AuthProve}(\mathsf{ask}, \mathsf{id})$ works as follows for a user id. Interpret id as a polynomial in $F_{q,d}$ for $d = \frac{q-1}{k}$, i.e., $\mathsf{id} \in \mathbb{F}_q^{d+1}$. Let T_{id} be the corresponding set in $\mathcal{T}$. For all $i \in [q]$, if $\mathsf{id}(x_i) = x_j$ for some $j \in [q]$, then set $y_i = s_{ij}$. It returns $t_{id} = \{y_i\}$ for all $i \in [q]$.
- Verification: The algorithm $\mathsf{Authverify}(\mathsf{avk}, \mathsf{id}, t_{id})$ works as follows: Interpret id as a polynomial in $F_{q,d}$ for $d = \frac{q-1}{k}$, i.e., $\mathsf{id} \in \mathbb{F}_q^{d+1}$. Let T_{id} be the corresponding set in $\mathcal{T}$. Let $t_{id} = \{y_1, \ldots, y_q\}$. For all $i \in [q]$, if $\mathsf{id}(x_i) = x_j$ for some $j \in [q]$, then check whether $\mathsf{PRG}(y_i) = z_{ij}$. Accept t_{id} if and only if all the checks pass.

The security properties this scheme satisfies are as follows:

Correctness. Honestly generated authentications always verify under the verification key. Formally, for any id, following holds.

$$\Pr[\mathsf{Authverify}(\mathsf{avk}, \mathsf{id}, t_{id}) = 1 \mid (\mathsf{avk}, \mathsf{ask}) \leftarrow \mathsf{AuthGen}(1^\lambda); t_{id} \leftarrow \mathsf{AuthProve}(\mathsf{ask}, \mathsf{id})] = 1$$

k-Unforgeability. Given authentication of any k users $\{\mathsf{id}_1, \ldots, \mathsf{id}_k\}$, for any PPT adversary $\mathcal{A}$, it is infeasible to compute t_{id^*} for any $\mathsf{id}^* \neq \mathsf{id}_i$ for all $i \in [k]$.

More formally, we have that for PPT adversary $\mathcal{A}$ and any set of at most k corrupt ids $\mathcal{I}$ such that $|\mathcal{I}| \leqslant k$, following holds.

$$\Pr\left[\begin{array}{c|c} \mathsf{id}^* \notin \mathcal{I} \wedge & (\mathsf{ask}, \mathsf{avk}) \leftarrow \mathsf{AuthGen}(1^\lambda); \\ \mathsf{Authverify}(\mathsf{avk}, \mathsf{id}^*, t_{\mathsf{id}^*}) = 1 & t_{\mathsf{id}_i} \leftarrow \mathsf{AuthProve}(\mathsf{ask}, \mathsf{id}_i) \forall \mathsf{id}_i \in \mathcal{I}; \\ & (\mathsf{id}^*, t_{\mathsf{id}^*}) \leftarrow \mathcal{A}(\mathsf{avk}, \{\mathsf{id}_i, t_{\mathsf{id}_i}\}_{\mathsf{id}_i \in \mathcal{I}}) \end{array}\right] \leqslant \mathsf{negl}(\lambda)$$

Our scheme satisfies unforgeability as follows: Since $\mathcal{T}$ is a k-cover-free set system, there exists an element in T_{id^*} which is not present in $\cup_{\mathsf{id}_i \in \mathcal{I}} T_{\mathsf{id}_i}$. Hence, we can use an adversary $\mathcal{A}$ who breaks unforgeability to break the pseudorandomness of PRG.

Fake Setup: In our hybrids, we will also use a fake algorithm of setup. Consider a scenario where a PPT adversary $\mathcal{A}$ controls k corrupt users with identities $\mathsf{id}_1, \ldots, \mathsf{id}_k$, without loss of generality. The fake setup algorithm we describe below will generate keys $(\mathsf{ask}, \mathsf{avk})$ such that it is only possible to authenticate the corrupt users and there does not exist any authentication which verifies under avk for honest users. Moreover, these two settings should be indistinguishable to the adversary. Below, we describe this setup procedure and then state and prove the security property.

The algorithm $\mathsf{FakeAuthGen}(1^\lambda, \mathsf{id}_1, \ldots, \mathsf{id}_k)$ works follows: For each $i \in [k]$, interpret id_i as a polynomial in $F_{q,d}$ for $d = \frac{q-1}{k}$, i.e., $\mathsf{id}_i \in \mathbb{F}_q^{d+1}$. Let T_{id_i} be the corresponding set in $\mathcal{T}$. Define $T^* = \cup_i T_{\mathsf{id}_i}$. Recall that the universe is $\mathbb{F}_q^2$.

Start with $\mathsf{ask} = \emptyset$. For all $i, j \in [q]$, if $(x_i, x_j) \in T^*$, pick $s_{ij} \xleftarrow{\$} Y$ and add (i, j, s_{ij}) to ask. For all $i, j \in [q]$, if $(x_i, x_j) \in T^*$, set $z_{ij} = \mathsf{PRG}(s_{ij})$ else set $z_{ij} \xleftarrow{\$} Z$. Define $\mathsf{avk} = \{\mathsf{PRG}(s_{ij})\}_{i,j \in [q]}$. Return $(\mathsf{avk}, \mathsf{ask})$.

Let $\mathcal{I} = \{\mathsf{id}_1, \ldots, \mathsf{id}_k\}$. The security properties of algorithm $\mathsf{FakeAuthGen}$ are:

○ Correct authentication for all $\mathsf{id} \in \mathcal{I}$: It is easy to see that for any corrupt user $\mathsf{id} \in \mathcal{I}$, $\mathsf{AuthProve}$ will produce a t_{id} which will verify under avk.

○ No authentication for all $\mathsf{id} \notin \mathcal{I}$: For any $\mathsf{id} \notin \mathcal{I}$, by property of k-cover-free sets, there exists a $(x_i, x_j) \in T_{\mathsf{id}}$ such that $(x_i, x_j) \notin T^*$. Moreover, a random element $z \xleftarrow{\$} Z$ does not lie in $\mathsf{im}(\mathsf{PRG})$ with probability $1 - \mathsf{negl}(\lambda)$. Hence, with probability $1 - \mathsf{negl}(\lambda)$, z_{ij} has no pre-image under PRG. This ensures that no t_{id} can verify under avk using algorithm $\mathsf{Authverify}$.

○ Indistinguishability: This implies that any PPT adversary given avk and t_{id} for all corrupt users cannot distinguish between real setup and fake setup. More formally, we have that for any PPT adversary $\mathcal{A}$, and any set of at most k corrupt ids $\mathcal{I} = \{\mathsf{id}_i\}_{i \in [k]}$, following holds.

$$\Pr\left[\mathcal{A}(\mathsf{avk},\{t_{\mathsf{id}_i}\}_{i\in[k]})=1 \left| \begin{array}{l}(\mathsf{ask},\mathsf{avk})\leftarrow\mathsf{AuthGen}(1^\lambda);\\ t_{\mathsf{id}_i}\leftarrow\mathsf{AuthProve}(\mathsf{ask},\mathsf{id}_i)\\ \forall i\in[k]\end{array}\right.\right]\approx$$

$$\Pr\left[\mathcal{A}(\mathsf{avk},\{t_{\mathsf{id}_i}\}_{i\in[k]})=1 \left| \begin{array}{l}(\mathsf{ask},\mathsf{avk})\leftarrow\mathsf{AuthGen}(1^\lambda,\mathcal{I});\\ t_{\mathsf{id}_i}\leftarrow\mathsf{AuthProve}(\mathsf{ask},\mathsf{id}_i)\\ \forall i\in[k]\end{array}\right.\right]$$

We can prove this via a sequence of $q^2-|T^*|$ hybrids. In the first hybrid, we use the algorithm AuthGen to produce the keys. In each subsequent hybrid, we pick a new i,j such that $(x_i,x_j)\notin T^*$ and change z_{ij} to a random element in Z instead of $\mathsf{PRG}(s_{ij}$. Indistinguishability of any two consecutive hybrids can be reduced to the pseudorandomness of PRG.

3   Secure Cloud Service Scheme (SCSS) Model

In this section, we first describe the setting of the secure cloud service, followed by various algorithms associated with the scheme and finally the desired security properties.

In this setting, we have three parties: *The provider*, who owns a program P, the *cloud*, where the program is hosted, and arbitrary many collection of *users*. At a very high level, the provider wants to hosts the program P on a cloud. Additionally, it wants to authenticate users who pay for the service. This authentication should allow a legitimate user to access the program hosted on the cloud and compute output on inputs of his choice. To be useful, we require the scheme to satisfy the following efficiency properties:

Weak Client. The amount of work done by the client should depend only on the size of the input and the security parameter and should be completely independent of the running time of the program P. In other words, the client should perform significantly less work than executing the program himself. This implies that both the initial set up phase with the provider and the subsequent encoding of inputs to the cloud are both highly efficient.

Delegation. The one-time work done by the provider in hosting the program should be bounded by a fixed polynomial in the program size. But, henceforth, we can assume that the work load of the provider in authenticating users only depends on the security parameter.

Polynomial Slowdown. The running time of the cloud on encoded program is bounded by a fixed polynomial in the running time of the actual program.

Next, we describe the different procedures associated with the scheme formally.

Definition 6 (Secure Cloud Service Scheme (SCSS)). *A secure cloud service scheme consists of following procedures* SCSS = (SCSS.prog, SCSS.auth, SCSS.inp, SCSS.eval):

○ $(\tilde{P}, \sigma) \leftarrow$ SCSS.prog$(1^\lambda, P, k)$: *Takes as input security parameter λ, program P and a bound k on the number of corrupt users and returns encoded program $\tilde{P}$ and a secret σ to be useful in authentication.*

○ $\mathsf{auth}_{\mathsf{id}} \leftarrow$ SCSS.auth(id, σ): *Takes the identity of a client and the secret σ and produces an authentication $\mathsf{auth}_{\mathsf{id}}$ for the client.*

○ $(\tilde{x}, \alpha) \leftarrow$ SCSS.inp$(1^\lambda, \mathsf{auth}_{\mathsf{id}}, x)$: *Takes as input the security parameter, authentication for the identity and the input x to produce encoded input $\tilde{x}$. It also outputs α which is used by the client later to decode the output obtained.*

○ $\tilde{y} \leftarrow$ SCSS.eval$(\tilde{P}, \tilde{x})$: *Takes as input encoded program and encoded input and produces encoded output. This can be later decoded by the client using α produced in the previous phase.*

In our scheme, the provider will run the procedure SCSS.prog to obtain the encoded program $\tilde{P}$ and the secret σ. It will then send $\tilde{P}$ to the cloud. Later, it will authenticate users using σ. A user with identity id who has a authentication $\mathsf{auth}_{\mathsf{id}}$, will encode his input x using procedure SCSS.inp to produce encoded input $\tilde{x}$ and secret α. He will send $\tilde{x}$ to the cloud. The cloud will evaluate the encoded program $\tilde{P}$ on encoded input $\tilde{x}$ and return encoded output $\tilde{y}$ to the user. The user can now decode the output using α.

Security Properties. Our scheme is for the benefit of the provider and hence we assume that the provider is uncompromised. The various security properties desired are as follows:

Definition 7 (Untrusted Cloud Security). *Let SCSS be the secure cloud service scheme as described above. This scheme satisfies untrusted cloud security if the following holds. We consider an adversary who corrupts the cloud as well as k clients $\mathcal{I}' = \{\mathsf{id}'_1, \ldots, \mathsf{id}'_k\}$. Consider two programs P and P' such that $P(\mathsf{id}'_i, x) = P'(\mathsf{id}'_i, x)$ for all $i \in [k]$ and all inputs x. Let $m(\lambda)$ be an efficiently computable polynomial. For any m honest users identities $\mathcal{I} = \{\mathsf{id}_1, \ldots, \mathsf{id}_m\}$ such that $\mathcal{I} \cap \mathcal{I}' = \emptyset$ and for any sequence of pairs of inputs for honest users $\{(x_1, x'_1), \ldots, (x_m, x'_m)\}$, consider the following two experiments:*

The experiment Real(1^λ) *is as follows:*

1. $(\tilde{P}, \sigma) \leftarrow$ SCSS.prog$(1^\lambda, P, k)$.
2. *For all $i \in [m]$,* $\mathsf{auth}_{\mathsf{id}_i} \leftarrow$ SCSS.auth(id_i, σ).
3. *For all $i \in [m]$,* $(\tilde{x}_i, \alpha_i) \leftarrow$ SCSS.inp$(1^\lambda, \mathsf{id}_i, \mathsf{auth}_{\mathsf{id}_i}, x_i)$.
4. *For all $j \in [k]$,* $\mathsf{auth}_{\mathsf{id}'_j} \leftarrow$ SCSS.auth(id'_j, σ).
5. *Output* $(\tilde{P}, \{\mathsf{auth}_{\mathsf{id}'_j}\}_{j \in [k]}, \{\tilde{x}_i\}_{i \in [m]})$.

The experiment Real$'(1^\lambda)$ *is as follows:*

1. $(\tilde{P}', \sigma) \leftarrow$ SCSS.prog$(1^\lambda, P', k)$.
2. *For all $i \in [m]$,* $\mathsf{auth}_{\mathsf{id}_i} \leftarrow$ SCSS.auth(id_i, σ).
3. *For all $i \in [m]$,* $(\tilde{x}'_i, \alpha_i) \leftarrow$ SCSS.inp$(1^\lambda, \mathsf{id}_i, \mathsf{auth}_{\mathsf{id}_i}, x'_i)$.
4. *For all $j \in [k]$,* $\mathsf{auth}_{\mathsf{id}'_j} \leftarrow$ SCSS.auth(id'_j, σ).
5. *Output* $(\tilde{P}', \{\mathsf{auth}_{\mathsf{id}'_j}\}_{j \in [k]}, \{\tilde{x}'_i\}_{i \in [m]})$.

Then we have,

$$\mathsf{Real}(1^\lambda) \approx_c \mathsf{Real}'(1^\lambda)$$

Remark: In the above definition, the only difference between two experiments is that Real uses the program P and honest users inputs $\{x_1, \ldots, x_m\}$ and Real$'$ uses program P' and honest users inputs $\{x'_1, \ldots, x'_m\}$. Note that no relationship is required to exist between the set of inputs $\{x_1, \ldots, x_m\}$ and the set of inputs $\{x'_1, \ldots, x'_m\}$.

Definition 8 (Untrusted Client Security). *Let* SCSS *be the secure cloud service scheme as described above. This scheme satisfies untrusted client security if the following holds. Let $\mathcal{A}$ be a PPT adversary who corrupts at most k clients $\mathcal{I}' = \{\mathsf{id}'_1, \ldots, \mathsf{id}'_k\}$. Consider any program P. Let $n(\lambda)$ be an efficiently computable polynomial. Consider the following two experiments:*

The experiment $\mathsf{Real}(1^\lambda)$ *is as follows:*

1. $(\tilde{P}, \sigma) \leftarrow \mathsf{SCSS.prog}(1^\lambda, P, k)$.
2. *For all $i \in [k]$,* $\mathsf{auth}_{\mathsf{id}'_i} \leftarrow \mathsf{SCSS.auth}(\mathsf{id}'_i, \sigma)$. *Send* $\{\mathsf{auth}_{\mathsf{id}'_i}\}_{i \in [k]}$ *to $\mathcal{A}$.*
3. *For each $i \in [n]$,*
   - $\mathcal{A}$ *(adaptively) sends an encoding $\tilde{x}_i$ using identity* id.
   - *Run* $\mathsf{SCSS.eval}(\tilde{P}, \tilde{x}_i)$ *to compute $\tilde{y}_i$. Send this to $\mathcal{A}$.*
4. *Output* $(\{\mathsf{auth}_{\mathsf{id}'_i}\}_{i \in [k]}, \{\tilde{y}_i\}_{i \in [n]})$.

We require that there The definition requires that there exist two procedures decode *and* response. *Based on these procedures, we define* $\mathsf{Sim}^P(1^\lambda)$ *w.r.t. an oracle for the program P. Below,* dummy *is any program of the same size as P.*

1. $(\widetilde{\mathsf{dummy}}, \sigma) \leftarrow \mathsf{SCSS.prog}(1^\lambda, \mathsf{dummy}, k)$.
2. *For all $i \in [k]$,* $\mathsf{auth}_{\mathsf{id}'_i} \leftarrow \mathsf{SCSS.auth}(\mathsf{id}'_i, \sigma)$. *Send* $\{\mathsf{auth}_{\mathsf{id}'_i}\}_{i \in [k]}$ *to $\mathcal{A}$.*
3. *For each $i \in [n]$,*
   - $\mathcal{A}$ *(adaptively) sends an encoding $\tilde{x}_i$ using some identity* id.
   - *If* id $\notin \mathcal{I}'$ *set $\tilde{y} = \bot$. Otherwise, run* $\mathsf{decode}(\sigma, \tilde{x}_i)$ *which either outputs (x_i, τ_i) or $\bot$. If it outputs $\bot$, set $\tilde{y} = \bot$. Else, the simulator sends* (id, x_i) *to the oracle and obtains $y_i = P(\mathsf{id}, x_i)$. Finally, it computes $\tilde{y}_i \leftarrow \mathsf{response}(y_i, \tau_i, \sigma)$. Send $\tilde{y}_i$ to $\mathcal{A}$.*
4. *Output* $(\{\mathsf{auth}_{\mathsf{id}'_i}\}_{i \in [k]}, \{\tilde{y}_i\}_{i \in [n]})$.

Then we have,

$$\mathsf{Real}(1^\lambda) \approx_c \mathsf{Sim}^P(1^\lambda)$$

Intuitively, the above security definition says that a collection of corrupt clients do not learn anything beyond the program's output w.r.t. to their identities on certain inputs of their choice. Moreover, it says that if a client is not authenticated, it learns nothing.

We describe a scheme which is a secure cloud service scheme in Section 4 and prove its security in Section 4.1.

3.1   Additional Properties

We believe our scheme can also be modified to achieve some additional properties which are not the focus of this work. We use this section to mention them below.

Verifiability. In the above scenario, where the cloud outputs $\tilde{y}$ intended for the client, we may also want to add verifiability, where the client is sure that the received output $\tilde{y}$ is indeed the correct output of the computation. We stress that verifiability is not the focus of this work. The scheme we present in Section 4 can be augmented with known techniques to get verifiability. One such method is to use one-time MACs as suggested in [8].

Persistent Memory. An interesting setting to consider is the one where the the cloud also holds a user-specific persistent memory that maintains state across different invocations of the service by the user. In this setting we must ensure that for each invocation of the functionality by a user, there only exists one valid state for the persistent memory that can be used for computing the user's output and the next state for the persistent memory. Such a result would only require the assumptions present in Theorem 2, and would not require any complexity leveraging. We believe that techniques developed in this paper along with those in [8] should be helpful to realize this setting as well.

3.2   Secure Cloud Service Scheme with Cloud Inputs

Here we consider a more general scenario, where the program takes two inputs: one from the user and another from the cloud.

This setting is technically more challenging since the cloud can use any input in each invocation of the program. In particular, it allows users to access super-polynomially potentially different functionalities on the cloud based on cloud's input.

Notationally, this scheme is same as the previous scheme except that the procedure $\mathsf{SCSS.eval}(\tilde{P}, \tilde{x}, z) \to \tilde{y}$ takes additional input z from the cloud. The efficiency and security requirements for this scheme are essentially the same as the simple scheme without the cloud inputs.

There is absolutely no change required in Definition 7. This is because it talks about the view of a malicious cloud. There is a minor change in untrusted client security (Definition 8). The oracle on query (id, x_i), returns $P(\mathsf{id}'_i, x_i, z_i)$, where $z_1, \ldots, z_n$ are arbitrarily chosen choice for cloud's inputs. Note that the security guarantee for an honest cloud is captured in this definition.

We provide a scheme which is secure cloud service scheme with cloud inputs in Section 5.

4   Our Secure Cloud Service Scheme

In this section, we describe our scheme for hosting on the cloud. We have three different parties: The provider who owns the program, the cloud where the program is hosted, and the users. Recall that we assume that the provider of the service is honest.

Let λ be the security parameter. Note that the number of users can be any (unbounded) polynomial in λ. Let k be the bound on the number of corrupt users. In our security game, we allow the cloud as well as any subset of users to be controlled by the adversary as long as the number of such users is at most k.

In order to describe our construction, we first recall the primitives and their notation that we use in our protocol. Let $\mathcal{T}$ be a k-cover-free set system using a finite field $\mathbb{F}_q$ and polynomials of degree $d = (q-1)/k$ described in Section 2.5. Let (AuthGen, AuthProve, Authverify) be the authentication scheme based on this k-cover-free set system. As mentioned before, we will use $q = k\lambda$, so that the number of sets/users is at least 2^λ. We will interpret the user's identity id as the coefficients of a polynomial over $\mathbb{F}_q$ of degree at most d. Let the length of the identity be $\ell_{\mathsf{id}} := (d+1) \lg q$ and length of the authentication be ℓ_{auth}. Note that in our scheme $\ell_{\mathsf{auth}} = 2\lambda q$.

Let $\mathsf{pke} = (\mathsf{PKGen}, \mathsf{PKEnc}, \mathsf{PKDec})$ be public key encryption scheme which accepts messages of length $\ell_e = (\ell_{\mathsf{id}} + \ell_{\mathsf{in}} + \ell_{\mathsf{auth}} + \ell_{\mathsf{kout}} + 1)$ and returns ciphertexts of length ℓ_c. Here ℓ_{in} is the length of the input of the user and ℓ_{kout} is the length of the key for PRF_2 described below.

Let (NIZKSetup, NIZKProve, NIZKVerify) be the statistical simulation-sound non-interactive zero-knowledge proof system with simulator $(\mathsf{S}_1, \mathsf{S}_2)$. In our scheme we use the two-key paradigm along with statistically simulation-sound non-interactive zero-knowledge for non-malleability inspired from [6,15,17].

We will make use of two different family of puncturable PRFs. a) $\mathsf{PRF}_1(K, \cdot)$ that accepts inputs of length $(\ell_{\mathsf{id}} + \ell_c)$ and returns strings of length ℓ_r. b) $\mathsf{PRF}_2(K_{\mathsf{id}}, \cdot)$ that accepts inputs of length ℓ_r and returns strings of length ℓ_{out}, where ℓ_{out} is the length of the output of program. Such PRFs exist by Theorem 3.

Now we describe our scheme.

Consider an honest provider $\mathcal{H}$ who holds a program F which he wants to hosts on the cloud $\mathcal{C}$. Also, there will be a collection of users who will interact with the provider to obtain authentication which will enable them to run the program stored on the cloud. We first describe the procedure $\mathsf{SCSS.prog}(1^\lambda, \mathsf{F}, k)$ run by the provider.

1. Chooses PRF key K at random for PRF_1.
2. Picks $(\mathsf{pk}_1, \mathsf{sk}_1) \leftarrow \mathsf{PKGen}(1^\lambda)$, $(\mathsf{pk}_2, \mathsf{sk}_2) \leftarrow \mathsf{PKGen}(1^\lambda)$.
3. Picks $(\mathsf{avk}, \mathsf{ask}) \leftarrow \mathsf{AuthGen}(1^\lambda)$ with respect to k-cover-free set system $\mathcal{T}$ and pseudorandom generator $\mathsf{PRG} : \{0,1\}^\lambda \rightarrow \{0,1\}^{2\lambda}$.
4. Picks $\mathsf{crs} \leftarrow \mathsf{NIZKSetup}(1^\lambda)$.
5. Creates an indistinguishability obfuscation $P_{comp} = i\mathcal{O}(\mathsf{Compute})$, where Compute is the program described in Figure 1.

Here $\tilde{F} = P_{comp}$ and $\sigma = (\mathsf{ask}, \mathsf{pk}_1, \mathsf{pk}_2, \mathsf{crs}, K)$. Note that K is not used by the honest provider in any of the future steps, but we include it as part of secret for completion. This would be useful in proving untrusted client security later.

Compute

Constants: Secret key sk_1, puncturable PRF key K, verification key avk and common reference string crs.
Input: Identity id and ciphertext $c = (c_1, c_2, \pi)$.

1. If $\mathsf{NIZKVerify}(\mathsf{crs}, (c_1, c_2), \pi) = 0$, output $\perp$ and end.
2. Let $(\mathsf{id}'\|x\|t_{\mathsf{id}}\|K_{\mathsf{id},\mathsf{out}}\|\mathsf{flag}) = \mathsf{PKDec}(\mathsf{sk}_1, c_1)$ for appropriate length strings. If $\mathsf{id} \neq \mathsf{id}'$, output $\perp$ and end.
3. Compute $r = \mathsf{PRF}_1(K, (\mathsf{id}, c))$.
4. If $\mathsf{flag} = 1$, output $y = (r, \mathsf{PRF}_2(K_{\mathsf{id},\mathsf{out}}, r))$ and end.
5. Else if $\mathsf{flag} = 0$, and $\mathsf{Authverify}(\mathsf{avk}, \mathsf{id}, t_{\mathsf{id}}) = 1$, output $y = (r, \mathsf{PRF}_2(K_{\mathsf{id},\mathsf{out}}, r) \oplus \mathsf{F}(\mathsf{id}, x))$ and end.
6. Output $y = \perp$ and end.

Fig. 1. Program Compute

Next, we describe the procedure $\mathsf{SCSS.auth}(\mathsf{id}, \sigma = (\mathsf{ask}, \mathsf{pk}_1, \mathsf{pk}_2, \mathsf{crs}))$, where a user sends his id to the provider for authentication. The provider sends back $\mathsf{auth}_{\mathsf{id}} = (t_{\mathsf{id}}, \mathsf{pk}_1, \mathsf{pk}_2, \mathsf{crs})$, where $t_{\mathsf{id}} = \mathsf{AuthProve}(\mathsf{ask}, \mathsf{id})$. We also describe this interaction in Figure 2.

Provider and User

Inputs: Let the user's identity be id. The provider has two public keys $\mathsf{pk}_1, \mathsf{pk}_2$, common reference string crs and secret key ask for authentication.

1. The user sends his identity id to the provider.
2. The provider computes $t_{\mathsf{id}} \leftarrow \mathsf{AuthProve}(\mathsf{ask}, \mathsf{id})$ and sends $\mathsf{auth}_{\mathsf{id}} = (t_{\mathsf{id}}, \mathsf{pk}_1, \mathsf{pk}_2, \mathsf{crs})$ to the user.

Fig. 2. Authentication phase between the provider and the user

Finally, we describe the procedures $\mathsf{SCSS.inp}$ and $\mathsf{SCSS.eval}$. This interaction between the user and the cloud is also described in Figure 3.

Procedure $\mathsf{SCSS.inp}(1^\lambda, \mathsf{auth}_{\mathsf{id}} = (t_{\mathsf{id}}, \mathsf{pk}_1, \mathsf{pk}_2, \mathsf{crs}), x)$: The user chooses a key $K_{\mathsf{id},\mathsf{out}}$ for PRF_2. Let $m = (\mathsf{id}\|x\|t_{\mathsf{id}}\|K_{\mathsf{id},\mathsf{out}}\|0)$. It then computes $c_1 = \mathsf{PKEnc}(\mathsf{pk}_1, m; r_1)$, $c_2 = \mathsf{PKEnc}(\mathsf{pk}_2, m; r_2)$ and a SSS-NIZK proof π for

$$\exists m, t_1, t_2 \text{ s.t. } (c_1 = \mathsf{PKEnc}(\mathsf{pk}_1, m; t_1) \wedge c_2 = \mathsf{PKEnc}(\mathsf{pk}_2, m; t_2))$$

It outputs $\tilde{x} = (\mathsf{id}, c = (c_1, c_2, \pi))$ and $\alpha = K_{\mathsf{id},\mathsf{out}}$.

Procedure $\mathsf{SCSS.eval}(\tilde{F} = P_{comp}, \tilde{x})$: Run $\tilde{F}$ on $\tilde{x}$ to obtain $\tilde{y}$. The user parses $\tilde{y}$ as $\tilde{y}_1, \tilde{y}_2$ and computes $y = \mathsf{PRF}_2(\alpha, \tilde{y}_1) \oplus \tilde{y}_2$.

User and Cloud

Inputs: Let the user's identity be id. Let the user's input to the function be x. An authenticated user has the authentication $\mathsf{auth_{id}} = (t_{id}, \mathsf{pk}_1, \mathsf{pk}_2, \mathsf{crs})$ obtained from the provider. The cloud has obfuscated program P_{comp}. The user encodes his input for the cloud using $\mathsf{SCSS.inp}(1^\lambda, \mathsf{auth_{id}}, x)$ as follows:

1. Pick a key $K_{id,out}$ for PRF_2. Set $\mathsf{flag} = 0$.
2. Let $m = (\mathsf{id}||x||t_{id}||K_{id,out}||\mathsf{flag})$. Compute $c_1 = \mathsf{PKEnc}(\mathsf{pk}_1, m; r_1)$,
   $c_2 = \mathsf{PKEnc}(\mathsf{pk}_2, m; r_2)$ and a SSS-NIZK proof
   $\pi = \mathsf{NIZKProve}(\mathsf{crs}, \mathsf{stmt}, (m, r_1, r_2))$, where stmt is

   $$\exists m, t_1, t_2 \text{ s.t. } (c_1 = \mathsf{PKEnc}(\mathsf{pk}_1, m; t_1) \land c_2 = \mathsf{PKEnc}(\mathsf{pk}_2, m; t_2))$$

3. $\tilde{x} = (\mathsf{id}, c = (c_1, c_2, \pi))$ and $\alpha = K_{id,out}$.

The cloud runs the program P_{comp} on the input $\tilde{x}$ and obtains output $\tilde{y}$. It sends $\tilde{y}$ to the user.
The user parses $\tilde{y}$ as $\tilde{y}_1, \tilde{y}_2$ and computes $y = \mathsf{PRF}_2(\alpha, \tilde{y}_1) \oplus \tilde{y}_2$.

Fig. 3. Encoding and evaluation phase between an authenticated user and the cloud

4.1 Security Proof

In this section, we give a proof overview for Theorem 1 for the scheme described above.

Untrusted Client Security. In our scheme, the secret information σ created after running the procedure $\mathsf{SCSS.prog}$ is $\sigma = (\mathsf{ask}, \mathsf{pk}_1, \mathsf{pk}_2, \mathsf{crs}, K)$. Hence, on obtaining a encoded $\tilde{x}$ from the adversary the decode procedure can work identically to the program Compute to extract an input x, authentication t_{id}, a key $K_{id,out}$, and flag from $\tilde{x}$. If $\mathsf{flag} = 1$, it gives $y = 0$ to response procedure. Else, if authentication t_{id} verifies using avk, it sends the (id, x) to the oracle implementing P and obtains y which is sent to response. The response procedure finally encodes the output y using $\tau = K_{id,out}$ and $K \in \sigma$ and sends it to the corrupt client. if $\mathsf{flag} = 0$ and t_{id} is invalid, send $\perp$ to the client. This is exactly what the obfuscated program would have done. Hence, the real and simulated experiments are indistinguishable as is required by this security property.

To prove security against unauthenticated clients, we need to prove the following: Any PPT malicious client id who has not done the set up phase to obtain $\mathsf{auth_{id}}$ should not be able to learn the output of F on any input using interaction with the honest cloud. Note that in our scheme F is invoked only if the authentication extracted by the program verifies under avk. Hence, the security will follow from the k-unforgeability property of our scheme (see Section 2.5).

Untrusted Cloud Security. Consider a PPT adversary $\mathcal{A}$ who controls the cloud and a collection of at most k users. Let F and G be two functions such that F and G are functionally equivalent for corrupt users. Then, we will prove that $\mathcal{A}$ can not distinguish between the cases when the provider uses the function F or G. We will prove this via a sequence of hybrids. Below, we first give a high level overview of these hybrids.

Let m be the number of honest users in the scheme. Without loss of generality, let their identities be $\mathsf{id}_1, \ldots, \mathsf{id}_m$ and inputs be $x_1, \ldots, x_m$. In the first sequence of hybrids, we will change the interaction of the honest users with the cloud such that all honest user queries will use $\mathsf{flag} = 1$ and input $0^{\ell_{\mathsf{in}}}$. This will ensure that in the final hybrid of this sequence, function F is not being invoked for any of the honest users.

In the next sequence of hybrids, we will change the output of the procedure AuthGen such that there does not exist any valid authentication for honest users. Now, we can be absolutely certain that the program does not invoke the function F on any of the honest ids. We also know that the functions F and G are functionally equivalent for all the corrupt ids. At this point, we can rely on the indistinguishability of obfuscations of program Compute using F and program Compute using G.

Finally, we can reverse the sequence of all the hybrids used so far so that the final hybrid is the real execution with G with honest user inputs $x'_1, \ldots, x'_m$.

Overview of Hybrids. Below we describe the important steps in the hybrid arguments. For detailed and formal security proof, refer to the full version. We denote changes between subsequent hybrids using underlined font.

Each hybrid below is an experiment that takes as input 1^λ. The final output of each hybrid experiment is the output produced by the adversary when it terminates. Moreover, in each of these hybrids, note that the adversary also receives authentication identities for all the corrupt users.

The first hybrid Hyb_0 is the real execution with F.

1. Choose PRF key K at random for PRF_1.
2. Pick $(\mathsf{pk}_1, \mathsf{sk}_1) \leftarrow \mathsf{PKGen}(1^\lambda)$, $(\mathsf{pk}_2, \mathsf{sk}_2) \leftarrow \mathsf{PKGen}(1^\lambda)$.
3. Pick $(\mathsf{avk}, \mathsf{ask}) \leftarrow \mathsf{AuthGen}(1^\lambda)$ with respect to cover-free set system $\mathcal{T}$ and pseudorandom generator PRG.
4. Pick $\mathsf{crs} \leftarrow \mathsf{NIZKSetup}(1^\lambda)$.
5. Let $P_{comp} = i\mathcal{O}(\mathsf{Compute})$.
6. On receiving a corrupt user's identity id, return the authentication as in real execution. That is, compute $t_{\mathsf{id}} \leftarrow \mathsf{AuthProve}(\mathsf{ask}, \mathsf{id})$ and send $(t_{\mathsf{id}}, \mathsf{pk}_1, \mathsf{pk}_2, \mathsf{crs})$ to the user.
7. Authentication for honest users and queries of honest users are also computed as in real execution. See Figure 3 for details.
8. Output P_{comp} and queries of all honest users $\mathsf{id}_1, \ldots, \mathsf{id}_m$.

Compute

Constants: Secret key sk_1, puncturable PRF key K, verification key avk and common reference string crs.
Input: Identity id and ciphertext $c = (c_1, c_2, \pi)$.

1. If $\mathsf{NIZKVerify}(crs, (c_1, c_2), \pi) = 0$, output $\perp$ and end.
2. Let $(id' || x || t_{id} || K_{id,out} || flag) = \mathsf{PKDec}(sk_1, c_1)$ for appropriate length strings. If $id \neq id'$, output $\perp$ and end.
3. Compute $r = \mathsf{PRF}_1(K, (id, c))$.
4. If $flag = 1$, output $y = (r, \mathsf{PRF}_2(K_{id,out}, r))$ and end.
5. Else if $flag = 0$, and $\mathsf{Authverify}(avk, id, t_{id}) = 1$, output $y = (r, \mathsf{PRF}_2(K_{id,out}, r) \oplus \mathsf{F}(id, x))$ and end.
6. Output $y = \perp$ and end.

Fig. 4. Program Compute

Next we describe the first sequence of hybrids $\mathsf{Hyb}_{1:1}, \ldots, \mathsf{Hyb}_{1:6}, \ldots$, $\mathsf{Hyb}_{m:1}, \ldots, \mathsf{Hyb}_{m:6}$. In the sub-sequence of hybrids $\mathsf{Hyb}_{i:1}, \ldots, \mathsf{Hyb}_{i:6}$, we only change the behavior of the honest user id_i. All the other honest users id_j such that $j \neq i$ behave identically as in $\mathsf{Hyb}_{i-1:6}$. Hence, we omit their behavior from the description of the hybrids for ease of notation.

Also, we denote id_i by id^*.

Let $\mathsf{Hyb}_{0:6} = \mathsf{Hyb}_0$.

$\mathsf{Hyb}_{i:1}$. This is same as $\mathsf{Hyb}_{i-1:6}$. We use this hybrid as a way to write how the user id^* behaves in the real execution explicitly. This would make it easier to describe the changes next.

It is obvious that the output of the adversary in $\mathsf{Hyb}_{i-1:6}$ and $\mathsf{Hyb}_{i:1}$ is identical.

1. Choose PRF key K at random for PRF_1.
2. Pick $(pk_1, sk_1) \leftarrow \mathsf{PKGen}(1^\lambda)$, $(pk_2, sk_2) \leftarrow \mathsf{PKGen}(1^\lambda)$.
3. Pick $(avk, ask) \leftarrow \mathsf{AuthGen}(1^\lambda)$ with respect to cover-free set system $\mathcal{T}$ and PRG.
4. On receiving a corrupt user's identity id, return the authentication as in real execution. That is, compute $t_{id} \leftarrow \mathsf{AuthProve}(ask, id)$ and send $(t_{id}, pk_1, pk_2, crs)$ to the user.
5. Set $t_{id^*} = \mathsf{AuthGen}(ask, id^*)$.
6. Set $flag^* = 0$.
7. Choose a random PRF key $K_{id^*,out}$ for PRF_2.
8. Let x^* be the input. Let $m_1^* = (id^* || x^* || t_{id^*} || K_{id^*,out} || flag^*)$ and $m_2^* = (id^* || x^* || t_{id^*} || K_{id^*,out} || flag^*)$.
9. Compute c_1^*, c_2^* as follows: $c_1^* = \mathsf{PKEnc}(pk_1, m_1^*; r_1)$, $c_2^* = \mathsf{PKEnc}(pk_2, m_2^*; r_2)$.
10. Pick $crs \leftarrow \mathsf{NIZKSetup}(1^\lambda)$.
11. Compute $\pi^* = \mathsf{NIZKProve}(crs, stmt, (m_1^*, r_1, r_2))$.

12. Set $c^* = (c_1^*, c_2^*, \pi^*)$.
13. Let $r^* = \mathsf{PRF}_1(K, (\mathrm{id}^*, c^*))$.
14. Let $y^* = (r^*, \mathsf{PRF}_2(K_{\mathrm{id}^*, \mathrm{out}}, r^*) \oplus \mathsf{F}(\mathrm{id}^*, x^*))$.
15. Let $P_{comp} = i\mathcal{O}(\mathrm{Compute})$.
16. Output $(P_{comp}, (\mathrm{id}^*, c^*))$ and the queries of other honest users.

Compute

Constants: Secret key sk_1, puncturable PRF key K, verification key avk and common reference string crs.
Input: Identity id and ciphertext $c = (c_1, c_2, \pi)$.

1. If $\mathsf{NIZKVerify}(\mathrm{crs}, (c_1, c_2), \pi) = 0$, output $\bot$ and end.
2. Let $(\mathrm{id}' || x || t_{\mathrm{id}} || K_{\mathrm{id}, \mathrm{out}} || \mathrm{flag}) = \mathsf{PKDec}(\mathsf{sk}_1, c_1)$. If $\mathrm{id} \neq \mathrm{id}'$, output $\bot$.
3. Compute $r = \mathsf{PRF}_1(K, (\mathrm{id}, c))$.
4. If $\mathrm{flag} = 1$, output $y = (r, \mathsf{PRF}_2(K_{\mathrm{id}, \mathrm{out}}, r))$ and end.
5. Else if $\mathrm{flag} = 0$, and $\mathsf{Authverify}(\mathrm{avk}, \mathrm{id}, t_{\mathrm{id}}) = 1$, output $y = (r, \mathsf{PRF}_2(K_{\mathrm{id}, \mathrm{out}}, r) \oplus \mathsf{F}(\mathrm{id}, x))$ and end.
6. Output $y = \bot$ and end.

Fig. 5. Program Compute

$\mathsf{Hyb}_{i:2}$. We modify the Compute program as follows. First, we add the constants id^*, c^*, y^* to the program and add an if statement that outputs y^* if the input is (id^*, c^*). Now, because the "if" statement is in place, we know that $\mathsf{PRF}_1(K, \cdot)$ cannot be evaluated at (id^*, c^*) within the program. Hence, we can safely puncture key K at this point. By construction, the Compute program in this hybrid is functionally equivalent to the Compute program in the previous hybrid. Hence, indistinguishability follows by the $i\mathcal{O}$ security.

Next, the value r^* is chosen randomly (at the beginning), instead of as the output of $\mathsf{PRF}_1(K, (\mathrm{id}^*, c^*))$. The indistinguishability of two hybrids follows by pseudorandomness property of the punctured PRF PRF_1.

1. Choose PRF key K at random for PRF_1.
2. Pick $(\mathsf{pk}_1, \mathsf{sk}_1) \leftarrow \mathsf{PKGen}(1^\lambda)$, $(\mathsf{pk}_2, \mathsf{sk}_2) \leftarrow \mathsf{PKGen}(1^\lambda)$.
3. Pick $(\mathrm{avk}, \mathrm{ask}) \leftarrow \mathsf{AuthGen}(1^\lambda)$ with respect to cover-free set system $\mathcal{T}$ and PRG.
4. On receiving a corrupt user's identity id, return the authentication as in real execution. That is, compute $t_{\mathrm{id}} \leftarrow \mathsf{AuthProve}(\mathrm{ask}, \mathrm{id})$ and send $(t_{\mathrm{id}}, \mathsf{pk}_1, \mathsf{pk}_2, \mathrm{crs})$.
5. Set $t_{\mathrm{id}^*} = \mathsf{AuthGen}(\mathrm{ask}, \mathrm{id}^*)$.
6. Set $\mathrm{flag}^* = 0$.
7. Let $\underline{r^* \text{ be chosen randomly}}$.

8. Choose a random PRF key $K_{\text{id}^*,\text{out}}$ for PRF_2.
9. Let x^* be the input. Let $m_1^* = (\text{id}^*||x^*||t_{\text{id}^*}||K_{\text{id}^*,\text{out}}||\text{flag}^*)$ and $m_2^* = (\text{id}^*||x^*||t_{\text{id}^*}||K_{\text{id}^*,\text{out}}||\text{flag}^*)$.
10. Compute c_1^*, c_2^* as follows: $c_1^* = \text{PKEnc}(\text{pk}_1, m_1^*; r_1)$, $c_2^* = \text{PKEnc}(\text{pk}_2, m_2^*; r_2)$.
11. Pick $\text{crs} \leftarrow \text{NIZKSetup}(1^\lambda)$.
12. Compute $\pi^* = \text{NIZKProve}(\text{crs}, \text{stmt}, (m_1^*, r_1, r_2))$.
13. Set $c^* = (c_1^*, c_2^*, \pi^*)$.
14. Let $y^* = (r^*, \text{PRF}_2(K_{\text{id}^*,\text{out}}, r^*) \oplus \text{F}(\text{id}^*, x^*))$.
15. Let $P_{comp} = i\mathcal{O}(\text{Compute})$.
16. Output $(P_{comp}, (\text{id}^*, c^*))$ and the queries of other honest users.

Compute

Constants: (id^*, c^*, y^*), Secret key sk_1, puncturable PRF key $K(\{(\text{id}^*, c^*)\})$, verification key avk and common reference string crs.
Input: Identity id and ciphertext $c = (c_1, c_2, \pi)$.

1. If $(\text{id}, c) = (\text{id}^*, c^*)$ output y^* and end.
2. If $\text{NIZKVerify}(\text{crs}, (c_1, c_2), \pi) = 0$, output $\bot$ and end.
3. Let $(\text{id}'||x||t_{\text{id}}||K_{\text{id},\text{out}}||\text{flag}) = \text{PKDec}(\text{sk}_1, c_1)$. If $\text{id} \neq \text{id}'$, output $\bot$.
4. Compute $r = \text{PRF}_1(K, (\text{id}, c))$.
5. If $\text{flag} = 1$, output $y = (r, \text{PRF}_2(K_{\text{id},\text{out}}, r))$ and end.
6. Else if $\text{flag} = 0$, and $\text{Authverify}(\text{avk}, \text{id}, t_{\text{id}}) = 1$, output $y = (r, \text{PRF}_2(K_{\text{id},\text{out}}, r) \oplus \text{F}(\text{id}, x))$ and end.
7. Output $y = \bot$ and end.

Fig. 6. Program Compute

$\text{Hyb}_{i:3}$. In this sequence of hybrids, first, instead of generating crs honestly, we generate it using the simulator S_1 and also simulate the proof π^* using S_2. The two hybrids are indistinguishable by computational zero-knowledge property of NIZK used.

Next, using a sequence of hybrids, using the two-key switching technique we change both m_1^* and m_2^* to include a punctured key $K_{\text{id}^*,\text{out}}(\{r^*\})$ instead of original key $K_{\text{id}^*,\text{out}}$. In these hybrids we will be relying on $i\mathcal{O}$ as well as $\text{IND} - \text{CPA}$ security of public key encryption scheme pke. For details, refer to the full version.

1. Choose PRF key K at random for PRF_1.
2. Pick $(\text{pk}_1, \text{sk}_1) \leftarrow \text{PKGen}(1^\lambda)$, $(\text{pk}_2, \text{sk}_2) \leftarrow \text{PKGen}(1^\lambda)$.
3. Pick $(\text{avk}, \text{ask}) \leftarrow \text{AuthGen}(1^\lambda)$ with respect to cover-free set system $\mathcal{T}$ and PRG.

4. On receiving a corrupt user's identity id, return the authentication as in real execution. That is, compute $t_{id} \leftarrow \mathsf{AuthProve}(\mathsf{ask}, \mathsf{id})$ and send $(t_{id}, \mathsf{pk}_1, \mathsf{pk}_2, \mathsf{crs})$.
5. Set $t_{id^*} = \mathsf{AuthGen}(\mathsf{ask}, id^*)$.
6. Set $\mathsf{flag}^* = 0$.
7. Let r^* be chosen randomly.
8. Choose a random PRF key $K_{id^*, \mathsf{out}}$ for PRF_2.
9. Let x^* be the input. Let $m_1^* = (id^* || x^* || t_{id^*} || K_{id^*, \mathsf{out}}(\{r^*\}) || \mathsf{flag}^*)$ and $m_2^* = (id^* || x^* || t_{id^*} || K_{id^*, \mathsf{out}}(\{r^*\}) || \mathsf{flag}^*)$.
10. Compute c_1^*, c_2^* as follows: $c_1^* = \mathsf{PKEnc}(\mathsf{pk}_1, m_1^*; r_1)$, $c_2^* = \mathsf{PKEnc}(\mathsf{pk}_2, m_2^*; r_2)$.
11. Pick $(\mathsf{crs}, \tau) \leftarrow \mathsf{S}_1(1^\lambda, \mathsf{stmt})$.
12. Compute $\pi^* = \mathsf{S}_2(\mathsf{crs}, \tau, \mathsf{stmt})$.
13. Set $c^* = (c_1^*, c_2^*, \pi^*)$.
14. Let $y^* = (r^*, \mathsf{PRF}_2(K_{id^*, \mathsf{out}}, r^*) \oplus F(id^*, x^*))$.
15. Let $P_{comp} = i\mathcal{O}(\mathsf{Compute})$.
16. Output $(P_{comp}, (id^*, c^*))$ and the queries of other honest users.

Compute

Constants: (id^*, c^*, y^*), Secret key sk_1, puncturable PRF key $K(\{(id^*, c^*)\})$, verification key avk and common reference string crs.
Input: Identity id and ciphertext $c = (c_1, c_2, \pi)$.

1. If $(id, c) = (id^*, c^*)$ output y^* and end.
2. If $\mathsf{NIZKVerify}(\mathsf{crs}, (c_1, c_2), \pi) = 0$, output $\perp$ and end.
3. Let $(id' || x || t_{id} || K_{id, \mathsf{out}} || \mathsf{flag}) = \mathsf{PKDec}(\mathsf{sk}_1, c_1)$. If $id \neq id'$, output $\perp$.
4. Compute $r = \mathsf{PRF}_1(K, (id, c))$.
5. If $\mathsf{flag} = 1$, output $y = (r, \mathsf{PRF}_2(K_{id, \mathsf{out}}, r))$ and end.
6. Else if $\mathsf{flag} = 0$, and $\mathsf{Authverify}(\mathsf{avk}, id, t_{id}) = 1$, output $y = (r, \mathsf{PRF}_2(K_{id, \mathsf{out}}, r) \oplus F(id, x))$ and end.
7. Output $y = \perp$ and end.

Fig. 7. Program Compute

$\mathsf{Hyb}_{i:4}$. Here, first we change the value of $y^* = (r^*, u^*)$ where u^* is a uniformly random string of appropriate length. By pseudorandomness property of punctured key $K_{id^*, \mathsf{out}}(\{r^*\})$, $\mathsf{PRF}_2(K_{id^*, \mathsf{out}}, r^*)$ is indistinguishable from random string.

Then, we change the value of y^* to $(r^*, \mathsf{PRF}_2(K_{id^*, \mathsf{out}}, r^*))$. Again indistinguishability follows from pseudorandomness property of punctured key.

1. Choose PRF key K at random for PRF_1.
2. Pick $(\mathsf{pk}_1, \mathsf{sk}_1) \leftarrow \mathsf{PKGen}(1^\lambda)$, $(\mathsf{pk}_2, \mathsf{sk}_2) \leftarrow \mathsf{PKGen}(1^\lambda)$.

3. Pick $(\mathsf{avk}, \mathsf{ask}) \leftarrow \mathsf{AuthGen}(1^\lambda)$ with respect to cover-free set system $\mathcal{T}$ and PRG.

4. On receiving a corrupt user's identity id, return the authentication as in real execution. That is, compute $t_{\mathsf{id}} \leftarrow \mathsf{AuthProve}(\mathsf{ask}, \mathsf{id})$ and send $(t_{\mathsf{id}}, \mathsf{pk}_1, \mathsf{pk}_2, \mathsf{crs})$.

5. Set $t_{\mathsf{id}^*} = \mathsf{AuthGen}(\mathsf{ask}, \mathsf{id}^*)$.

6. Set $\mathsf{flag}^* = 0$.

7. Let r^* be chosen randomly.

8. Choose a random PRF key $K_{\mathsf{id}^*,\mathsf{out}}$ for PRF_2.

9. Let x^* be the input. Let $m_1^* = (\mathsf{id}^* || x^* || t_{\mathsf{id}^*} || K_{\mathsf{id}^*,\mathsf{out}}(\{r^*\}) || \mathsf{flag}^*)$ and $m_2^* = (\mathsf{id}^* || x^* || t_{\mathsf{id}^*} || K_{\mathsf{id}^*,\mathsf{out}}(\{r^*\}) || \mathsf{flag}^*)$.

10. Compute c_1^*, c_2^* as follows: $c_1^* = \mathsf{PKEnc}(\mathsf{pk}_1, m_1^*; r_1)$, $c_2^* = \mathsf{PKEnc}(\mathsf{pk}_2, m_2^*; r_2)$.

11. Pick $(\mathsf{crs}, \tau) \leftarrow S_1(1^\lambda, \mathsf{stmt})$.

12. Compute $\pi^* = S_2(\mathsf{crs}, \tau, \mathsf{stmt})$.

13. Set $c^* = (c_1^*, c_2^*, \pi^*)$.

14. Let $y^* = (r^*, \mathsf{PRF}_2(K_{\mathsf{id}^*,\mathsf{out}}, r^*))$.

15. Let $P_{comp} = i\mathcal{O}(\mathrm{Compute})$.

16. Output $(P_{comp}, (\mathsf{id}^*, c^*))$ and the queries of other honest users.

Compute

Constants: $(\mathsf{id}^*, c^*, y^*)$, Secret key sk_1, puncturable PRF key $K(\{(\mathsf{id}^*, c^*)\})$, verification key avk and common reference string crs.
Input: Identity id and ciphertext $c = (c_1, c_2, \pi)$.

1. If $(\mathsf{id}, c) = (\mathsf{id}^*, c^*)$ output y^* and end.
2. If $\mathsf{NIZKVerify}(\mathsf{crs}, (c_1, c_2), \pi) = 0$, output $\perp$ and end.
3. Let $(\mathsf{id}' || x || t_{\mathsf{id}} || K_{\mathsf{id},\mathsf{out}} || \mathsf{flag}) = \mathsf{PKDec}(\mathsf{sk}_1, c_1)$. If $\mathsf{id} \neq \mathsf{id}'$, output $\perp$.
4. Compute $r = \mathsf{PRF}_1(K, (\mathsf{id}, c))$.
5. If $\mathsf{flag} = 1$, output $y = (r, \mathsf{PRF}_2(K_{\mathsf{id},\mathsf{out}}, r))$ and end.
6. Else if $\mathsf{flag} = 0$, and $\mathsf{Authverify}(\mathsf{avk}, \mathsf{id}, t_{\mathsf{id}}) = 1$, output $y = (r, \mathsf{PRF}_2(K_{\mathsf{id},\mathsf{out}}, r) \oplus F(\mathsf{id}, x))$ and end.
7. Output $y = \perp$ and end.

Fig. 8. Program Compute

$\mathsf{Hyb}_{i:5}$. In this hybrid, we change the value of flag^* to 1 instead of 0 and t_{id^*} to be a random string of appropriate length. We also set $x^* = 0^{\ell_{\mathsf{in}}}$. We also change back the key $K_{\mathsf{id}^*,\mathsf{out}}$ used in m_1^* and m_2^* to the original unpunctured key.

The indistinguishability follows via a sequence of hybrids using the two-key switching techniques. Note that here we crucially use that the fact that the program in the previous hybrid does not use x^* in computing the output on input c^*. Moreover, because of the initial "if" condition, there is no check on

flag^* or t_{id^*}. Hence, while switching keys for decryption, functional equivalence follows in a straight-forward manner.

1. Choose PRF key K at random for PRF_1.
2. Pick $(\mathsf{pk}_1, \mathsf{sk}_1) \leftarrow \mathsf{PKGen}(1^\lambda)$, $(\mathsf{pk}_2, \mathsf{sk}_2) \leftarrow \mathsf{PKGen}(1^\lambda)$.
3. Pick $(\mathsf{avk}, \mathsf{ask}) \leftarrow \mathsf{AuthGen}(1^\lambda)$ with respect to cover-free set system $\mathcal{T}$ and PRG.
4. On receiving a corrupt user's identity id, return the authentication as in real execution. That is, compute $t_{\mathsf{id}} \leftarrow \mathsf{AuthProve}(\mathsf{ask}, \mathsf{id})$ and send $(t_{\mathsf{id}}, \mathsf{pk}_1, \mathsf{pk}_2, \mathsf{crs})$.
5. Pick t_{id^*} to be a uniformly random string of appropriate length.
6. Set $\mathsf{flag}^* = 1$.
7. Let r^* be chosen randomly.
8. Choose a random PRF key $K_{\mathsf{id}^*, \mathsf{out}}$ for PRF_2.
9. Set $x^* = 0^{\ell_{\mathsf{in}}}$. Let $m_1^* = (\mathsf{id}^* || x^* || t_{\mathsf{id}^*} || K_{\mathsf{id}^*, \mathsf{out}} || \mathsf{flag}^*)$ and $m_2^* = (\mathsf{id}^* || x^* || t_{\mathsf{id}^*} || K_{\mathsf{id}^*, \mathsf{out}} || \mathsf{flag}^*)$.
10. Compute c_1^*, c_2^* as follows: $c_1^* = \mathsf{PKEnc}(\mathsf{pk}_1, m_1^*; r_1)$, $c_2^* = \mathsf{PKEnc}(\mathsf{pk}_2, m_2^*; r_2)$.
11. Pick $(\mathsf{crs}, \tau) \leftarrow S_1(1^\lambda, \mathsf{stmt})$.
12. Compute $\pi^* = S_2(\mathsf{crs}, \tau, \mathsf{stmt})$.
13. Set $c^* = (c_1^*, c_2^*, \pi^*)$.
14. Let $y^* = (r^*, \mathsf{PRF}_2(K_{\mathsf{id}^*, \mathsf{out}}, r^*))$.
15. Let $P_{comp} = i\mathcal{O}(\mathsf{Compute})$.
16. Output $(P_{comp}, (\mathsf{id}^*, c^*))$ and the queries of other honest users.

Compute

Constants: $(\mathsf{id}^*, c^*, y^*)$, Secret key sk_1, puncturable PRF key $K(\{(\mathsf{id}^*, c^*)\})$, verification key avk and common reference string crs.
Input: Identity id and ciphertext $c = (c_1, c_2, \pi)$.

1. If $(\mathsf{id}, c) = (\mathsf{id}^*, c^*)$ output y^* and end.
2. If $\mathsf{NIZKVerify}(\mathsf{crs}, (c_1, c_2), \pi) = 0$, output $\bot$ and end.
3. Let $(\mathsf{id}' || x || t_{\mathsf{id}} || K_{\mathsf{id}, \mathsf{out}} || \mathsf{flag}) = \mathsf{PKDec}(\mathsf{sk}_1, c_1)$ for appropriate length strings. If $\mathsf{id} \neq \mathsf{id}'$, output $\bot$ and end.
4. Compute $r = \mathsf{PRF}_1(K, (\mathsf{id}, c))$.
5. If $\mathsf{flag} = 1$, output $y = (r, \mathsf{PRF}_2(K_{\mathsf{id}, \mathsf{out}}, r))$ and end.
6. Else if $\mathsf{flag} = 0$, and $\mathsf{Authverify}(\mathsf{avk}, \mathsf{id}, t_{\mathsf{id}}) = 1$, output $y = (r, \mathsf{PRF}_2(K_{\mathsf{id}, \mathsf{out}}, r) \oplus F(\mathsf{id}, x))$ and end.
7. Output $y = \bot$ and end.

Fig. 9. Program Compute

$\mathsf{Hyb}_{i:6}$. In this sequence of hybrids, we revert back some of the changes we made. First, we again start generating the crs and the proof π^* honestly. The indistinguishability follows from the computational zero-knowledge property of the NIZK used.

Next, we set $r^* = \mathsf{PRF}_1(K, (\mathsf{id}^*, c^*))$ instead of random. The indistinguishability follows from the pseudorandomness property of the punctured PRF PRF_1.

Finally, we remove the initial "if" condition and the constants $(\mathsf{id}^*, c^*, y^*)$, and un-puncture the key K. The indistinguishability follows from the security of $i\mathcal{O}$.

1. Choose PRF key K at random for PRF_1.
2. Pick $(\mathsf{pk}_1, \mathsf{sk}_1) \leftarrow \mathsf{PKGen}(1^\lambda)$, $(\mathsf{pk}_2, \mathsf{sk}_2) \leftarrow \mathsf{PKGen}(1^\lambda)$.
3. Pick $(\mathsf{avk}, \mathsf{ask}) \leftarrow \mathsf{AuthGen}(1^\lambda)$ with respect to cover-free set system $\mathcal{T}$ and PRG.
4. On receiving a corrupt user's identity id, return the authentication as in real execution. That is, compute $t_{\mathsf{id}} \leftarrow \mathsf{AuthProve}(\mathsf{ask}, \mathsf{id})$ and send $(t_{\mathsf{id}}, \mathsf{pk}_1, \mathsf{pk}_2, \mathsf{crs})$.
5. Pick t_{id^*} to be a uniformly random string of appropriate length.
6. Set $\mathsf{flag}^* = 1$.
7. Choose a random PRF key $K_{\mathsf{id}^*, \mathsf{out}}$ for PRF_2.
8. Set $x^* = 0^{\ell_{\mathsf{in}}}$. Let $m_1^* = (\mathsf{id}^* || x^* || t_{\mathsf{id}^*} || K_{\mathsf{id}^*, \mathsf{out}} || \mathsf{flag}^*)$ and $m_2^* = (\mathsf{id}^* || x^* || t_{\mathsf{id}^*} || K_{\mathsf{id}^*, \mathsf{out}} || \mathsf{flag}^*)$.
9. Compute c_1^*, c_2^* as follows: $c_1^* = \mathsf{PKEnc}(\mathsf{pk}_1, m_1^*; r_1)$, $c_2^* = \mathsf{PKEnc}(\mathsf{pk}_2, m_2^*; r_2)$.
10. Pick $\mathsf{crs} \leftarrow \mathsf{NIZKSetup}(1^\lambda)$.
11. $\overline{\text{Compute } \pi^* = \mathsf{NIZKProve}(\mathsf{crs}, \mathsf{stmt}, (m_1^*, r_1, r_2)).}$
12. Set $c^* = (c_1^*, c_2^*, \pi^*)$.
13. Let $r^* = \mathsf{PRF}_1(K, (\mathsf{id}^*, c^*))$.
14. $\overline{\text{Let } y^* = (r^*, \mathsf{PRF}_2(K_{\mathsf{id}^*, \mathsf{out}}, r^*)).}$
15. Let $P_{comp} = i\mathcal{O}(\mathrm{Compute})$.
16. Output $(P_{comp}, (\mathsf{id}^*, c^*))$ and the queries of other honest users.

In this sequence of hybrids described above, we have shown that the view of the adversary is indistinguishable in the following two scenarios: 1) The honest user encodes his actual input x with $\mathsf{flag} = 0$ and a valid authentication t_{id}, and obtains output according to the function F on (id, x). 2) The honest user encodes $0^{\ell_{\mathsf{in}}}$ with $\mathsf{flag} = 1$ and uniformly random t_{id}, and receives encoding of 0 as output (without invoking the function F.)

Below we write the final hybrid obtained above as Hyb_1 as follows:

Hyb_1: This hybrid is same as $\mathsf{Hyb}_{m:6}$. In the hybrid $\mathsf{Hyb}_{m:6}$, all the user queries will have $\mathsf{flag} = 1$, t_{id} will be a random string, and input will be 0_{in}^ℓ. Hence, the program Compute will not invoke the function F for any of the honest users.

The underlined statement summarizes the main difference between Hyb_0 and Hyb_1. Since the program being obfuscated does not change between Hyb_0 and Hyb_1, we omit its description from here.

Compute

Constants: Secret key sk_1, <u>puncturable PRF key K</u>, verification key avk and common reference string crs.
Input: Identity id and ciphertext $c = (c_1, c_2, \pi)$.

1. If NIZKVerify(crs, $(c_1, c_2), \pi) = 0$, output $\perp$ and end.
2. Let $(id'||x||t_{id}||K_{id,out}||flag) = $ PKDec(sk_1, c_1). If id $\neq$ id', output $\perp$.
3. Compute $r = $ PRF$_1(K, (id, c))$.
4. If flag $= 1$, output $y = (r, $ PRF$_2(K_{id,out}, r))$ and end.
5. Else if flag $= 0$, and Authverify(avk, id, $t_{id}) = 1$, output $y = (r, $ PRF$_2(K_{id,out}, r) \oplus $ F(id, x)) and end.
6. Output $y = \perp$ and end.

Fig. 10. Program Compute

1. Choose PRF key K at random for PRF$_1$.
2. Pick $(pk_1, sk_1) \leftarrow$ PKGen(1^λ), $(pk_2, sk_2) \leftarrow$ PKGen(1^λ).
3. Pick (avk, ask) $\leftarrow$ AuthGen(1^λ) with respect to cover-free set system $\mathcal{T}$ and PRG.
4. Pick crs $\leftarrow$ NIZKSetup(1^λ).
5. Let $P_{comp} = i\mathcal{O}$(Compute).
6. On receiving a corrupt user's identity id, return the authentication as in real execution. That is, compute $t_{id} \leftarrow$ AuthProve(ask, id) and send $(t_{id}, pk_1, pk_2, crs)$ to the user.
7. For each of the honest users, t_{id} is set to a random string of appropriate length, flag is set to 1 and input is set to $0^{\ell_{in}}$. Ciphertexts (c_1, c_2) and proof π are generated honestly.
8. Output P_{comp} and queries of all honest users $id_1, \ldots, id_m$.

Hyb$_2$: We change the setup phase of authentication scheme to use FakeAuthGen instead of AuthGen. Let $\mathcal{I}$ denote the set of corrupt user identities. Note that $|\mathcal{I}| \leqslant k$ and set system $\mathcal{T}$ used in our scheme is a k-cover-free set system.

The two hybrids are indistinguishable by security properties of FakeAuthGen (see Section 2.5). Note that both hybrids do not depend on ask and need only the valid authentications for corrupt users.

1. Choose PRF key K at random for PRF$_1$.
2. Pick $(pk_1, sk_1) \leftarrow$ PKGen(1^λ), $(pk_2, sk_2) \leftarrow$ PKGen(1^λ).
3. Pick <u>(avk, ask) $\leftarrow$ FakeAuthGen($1^\lambda, \mathcal{I}$)</u> w.r.t. cover-free set system $\mathcal{T}$ and PRG.
4. Pick crs $\leftarrow$ NIZKSetup(1^λ).
5. Let $P_{comp} = i\mathcal{O}$(Compute).
6. On receiving a corrupt user's identity id, return the authentication as in real execution. That is, compute $t_{id} \leftarrow$ AuthProve(ask, id) and send

$(t_{id}, pk_1, pk_2, crs)$. As noted before, AuthProve still returns valid authentication for all users in $\mathcal{I}$.

7. For each of the honest users, t_{id} is set to a random string of appropriate length and flag is set to 1. Ciphertexts (c_1, c_2) and proof π is generated as in real execution.
8. Output P_{comp} and queries of all honest users $id_1, \ldots, id_m$.

Hyb_3: This is the most important hybrid, where we change the program from F to F. The two hybrids are indistinguishable by security of $i\mathcal{O}$. Note that in both hybrids the function is invoked iff the authentication of the user verifies under avk. In the both hybrids, this can happen only for corrupt users as there is no valid authentication for honest users. Finally, recall that the functions F and G are equivalent for corrupt users.

1. Choose PRF key K at random for PRF_1.
2. Pick $(pk_1, sk_1) \leftarrow PKGen(1^\lambda)$, $(pk_2, sk_2) \leftarrow PKGen(1^\lambda)$.
3. Pick $(avk, ask) \leftarrow FakeAuthGen(1^\lambda, \mathcal{I})$ w.r.t. cover-free set system $\mathcal{T}$ and PRG.
4. Pick $crs \leftarrow NIZKSetup(1^\lambda)$.
5. Let $P_{comp} = i\mathcal{O}(Compute)$.
6. On receiving a corrupt user's identity id, return the authentication as in real execution. That is, compute $t_{id} \leftarrow AuthProve(ask, id)$ and send $(t_{id}, pk_1, pk_2, crs)$.
7. For each of the honest users, t_{id} is set to a random string of appropriate length and flag is set to 1. Ciphertexts (c_1, c_2) and proof π is generated as in real execution.
8. Output P_{comp} and queries of all honest users $id_1, \ldots, id_m$.

Compute

Constants: Secret key sk_1, puncturable PRF key K, verification key avk and common reference string crs.
Input: Identity id and ciphertext $c = (c_1, c_2, \pi)$.

1. If $NIZKVerify(crs, (c_1, c_2), \pi) = 0$, output $\perp$ and end.
2. Let $(id'||x||t_{id}||K_{id,out}||flag) = PKDec(sk_1, c_1)$ for appropriate length strings. If $id \neq id'$, output $\perp$ and end.
3. Compute $r = PRF_1(K, (id, c))$.
4. If flag $= 1$, output $y = (r, PRF_2(K_{id,out}, r))$ and end.
5. Else if flag $= 0$, and $Authverify(avk, id, t_{id}) = 1$, output $y = (r, PRF_2(K_{id,out}, r) \oplus G(id, x))$ and end.
6. Output $y = \perp$ and end.

Fig. 11. Program Compute

Finally, using a similar sequence of hybrids we can move from Hyb_3 to a hybrid which corresponds to real execution using G and honest party inputs $x'_1, \ldots, x'_m$.

5   Our Secure Cloud Service Scheme with Cloud Inputs

In this section, we describe our modified scheme for service hosting on the cloud with cloud inputs. As before, we have three different parties: The provider who owns the service, the cloud where the service is hosted, and the users. Recall that we assume that the provider of the service is honest.

As before, let λ be the security parameter. Let k be the bound on the number of corrupt users.

Let $\mathcal{T}$ be a k-cover-free set system using a finite field $\mathbb{F}_q$ and polynomials of degee $d = (q-1)/k$ and $(\mathsf{AuthGen}, \mathsf{AuthProve}, \mathsf{Authverify})$ be the authentication scheme w.r.t. $\mathcal{T}$ as described in Section 2.5. As mentioned before, we use $q = k\lambda$, so that the number of sets/users is at least 2^λ. We interpret the user's identity id as the coefficients of a polynomial over $\mathbb{F}_q$ of degree at most d. Let the length of the identity be $\ell_{\mathsf{id}}:=(d+1)\lg q$ and length of the authentication be ℓ_{auth}. Note that in our scheme $\ell_{\mathsf{auth}} = 2\lambda q$.

Let $\mathsf{pke} = (\mathsf{PKGen}, \mathsf{PKEnc}, \mathsf{PKDec})$ be public key encryption scheme which accepts messages of length $\ell_e = (\ell_{\mathsf{id}} + \ell_{\mathsf{in}} + \ell_{\mathsf{auth}} + \ell_{\mathsf{kout}} + 1)$ and returns ciphertexts of length ℓ_c. Here ℓ_{in} is the length of the input of the user and ℓ_{kout} is the length of the key for PRF_2 described below.

Let $(\mathsf{NIZKSetup}, \mathsf{NIZKProve}, \mathsf{NIZKVerify})$ be the statistical simulation-sound non-interactive zero-knowledge proof system with simulator $(\mathsf{S}_1, \mathsf{S}_2)$. In our scheme we use the two-key paradigm along with statistically simulation-sound non-interactive zero-knowledge for non-malleability inspired from [6,15,17].

We will make use of two different family of puncturable PRFs. a) $\mathsf{PRF}_1(K, \cdot)$ that accepts inputs of length $(\ell_{\mathsf{id}} + \ell_c + \ell_z)$ and returns strings of length $\ell_r \geqslant (\ell_{\mathsf{id}} + \ell_c + \ell_z) + \lambda$. Here ℓ_z is the length of the cloud's input z. b) $\mathsf{PRF}_2(K_{\mathsf{id}}, \cdot)$ that accepts inputs of length ℓ_r and returns strings of length ℓ_{out}, where ℓ_{out} is the length of the output of program. Such PRFs exist by Theorem 3.

We put a lower bound on the length of output of PRF_1 because in the proof we would require that a random string of length ℓ_r does not lie in the image of $\mathsf{PRF}_1(K, \cdot)$.

Scheme Description. Consider an honest provider $\mathcal{H}$ who holds a function F which he wants to hosts on the cloud $\mathcal{C}$. Also, there will be a collection of users who will interact with the provider to obtain authentication which will enable them to run the program stored on the cloud. The provider does the following:

1. Chooses PRF key K at random for PRF_1.
2. Picks $(\mathsf{pk}_1, \mathsf{sk}_1) \leftarrow \mathsf{PKGen}(1^\lambda)$, $(\mathsf{pk}_2, \mathsf{sk}_2) \leftarrow \mathsf{PKGen}(1^\lambda)$.
3. Picks $(\mathsf{avk}, \mathsf{ask}) \leftarrow \mathsf{AuthGen}(1^\lambda)$ with respect to k-cover-free set system $\mathcal{T}$ and pseudorandom generator PRG.

4. Picks $\mathsf{crs} \leftarrow \mathsf{NIZKSetup}(1^\lambda)$.
5. Creates an indistinguishability obfuscation $P_{comp} = i\mathcal{O}(\text{Compute})$, where Compute is the same program as in Figure 1 with the following change: It takes an additional input z from the cloud along with identity id and ciphertext $c = (c_1, c_2, \pi)$ from the user. And while computing the output in Step 5 when $\mathsf{flag} = 0$ and user is authenticated as $y = (r, \mathsf{PRF}_2(K_{\mathsf{id,out}}, r) \oplus \mathsf{F}(\mathsf{id}, x, z))$ (using the cloud input z).
Here $\tilde{F} = P_{comp}$ and $\sigma = (\mathsf{ask}, \mathsf{pk}_1, \mathsf{pk}_2, \mathsf{crs})$.

Next, we describe the procedures SCSS.auth, SCSS.inp and SCSS.eval.

Procedure SCSS.auth: It takes as input user's id and secret state of the service provider $\sigma = (\mathsf{ask}, \mathsf{pk}_1, \mathsf{pk}_2, \mathsf{crs}))$. The provider computes $t_{\mathsf{id}} = \mathsf{AuthProve}(\mathsf{ask}, \mathsf{id})$ and sends back $\mathsf{auth}_{\mathsf{id}} = (t_{\mathsf{id}}, \mathsf{pk}_1, \mathsf{pk}_2, \mathsf{crs})$.

Procedure SCSS.inp$(1^\lambda, \mathsf{auth}_{\mathsf{id}} = (t_{\mathsf{id}}, \mathsf{pk}_1, \mathsf{pk}_2, \mathsf{crs}), x)$: The user chooses a key $K_{\mathsf{id,out}}$ for PRF_2. Let $m = (\mathsf{id}||x||t_{\mathsf{id}}||K_{\mathsf{id,out}}||0)$. It then computes $c_1 = \mathsf{PKEnc}(\mathsf{pk}_1, m; r_1)$, $c_2 = \mathsf{PKEnc}(\mathsf{pk}_2, m; r_2)$ and a SSS-NIZK proof π for

$$\exists m, t_1, t_2 \text{ s.t. } (c_1 = \mathsf{PKEnc}(\mathsf{pk}_1, m; t_1) \wedge c_2 = \mathsf{PKEnc}(\mathsf{pk}_2, m; t_2))$$

It outputs $\tilde{x} = (\mathsf{id}, c = (c_1, c_2, \pi))$ and $\alpha = K_{\mathsf{id,out}}$.

Procedure SCSS.eval$(\tilde{F} = P_{comp}, \tilde{x}, z)$: Let the cloud's input be z. Run $\tilde{F}$ on $(\tilde{x}, z)$ to obtain $\tilde{y}$. The user parses $\tilde{y}$ as $\tilde{y}_1, \tilde{y}_2$ and computes $y = \mathsf{PRF}_2(\alpha, \tilde{y}_1) \oplus \tilde{y}_2$.

Security Proof. For a formal proof that our scheme satisfies Theorem 2 i.e. it is a secure cloud service scheme with cloud inputs please refer to our full version.

References

1. Barak, B., Goldreich, O., Impagliazzo, R., Rudich, S., Sahai, A., Vadhan, S.P., Yang, K.: On the (Im)possibility of Obfuscating Programs. In: Kilian, J. (ed.) CRYPTO 2001. LNCS, vol. 2139, pp. 1–18. Springer, Heidelberg (2001)
2. Boneh, D., Waters, B.: Constrained Pseudorandom Functions and Their Applications. In: Sako, K., Sarkar, P. (eds.) ASIACRYPT 2013, Part II. LNCS, vol. 8270, pp. 280–300. Springer, Heidelberg (2013)
3. Boyle, E., Goldwasser, S., Ivan, I.: Functional Signatures and Pseudorandom Functions. In: Krawczyk, H. (ed.) PKC 2014. LNCS, vol. 8383, pp. 501–519. Springer, Heidelberg (2014)
4. Erdös, P., Frankl, P., Füredi, Z.: Families of finite sets in which no set is covered by the union of r others. Israel Journal of Mathematics **51**(1–2), 79–89 (1985)
5. Feige, U., Lapidot, D., Shamir, A.: Multiple noninteractive zero knowledge proofs under general assumptions. SIAM J. Comput. **29**(1), 1–28 (1999)
6. Garg, S., Gentry, C., Halevi, S., Raykova, M., Sahai, A., Waters, B.: Candidate indistinguishability obfuscation and functional encryption for all circuits. In: FOCS, pp. 40–49 (2013)
7. Gennaro, R., Gentry, C., Parno, B.: Non-interactive Verifiable Computing: Outsourcing Computation to Untrusted Workers. In: Rabin, T. (ed.) CRYPTO 2010. LNCS, vol. 6223, pp. 465–482. Springer, Heidelberg (2010)

8. Gentry, C., Halevi, S., Raykova, M., Wichs, D.: Outsourcing private ram computation. Cryptology ePrint Archive, Report 2014/148 (2014). http://eprint.iacr.org/

9. Goldreich, O., Goldwasser, S., Micali, S.: How to construct random functions (extended abstract). In: FOCS, pp. 464–479 (1984)

10. Goldwasser, S., Gordon, S.D., Goyal, V., Jain, A., Katz, J., Liu, F.-H., Sahai, A., Shi, E., Zhou, H.-S.: Multi-input Functional Encryption. In: Nguyen, P.Q., Oswald, E. (eds.) EUROCRYPT 2014. LNCS, vol. 8441, pp. 578–602. Springer, Heidelberg (2014)

11. Goldwasser, S., Kalai, Y.T., Rothblum, G.N.: Delegating computation: interactive proofs for muggles. In: STOC, pp. 113–122 (2008)

12. Kiayias, A., Papadopoulos, S., Triandopoulos, N., Zacharias, T.: Delegatable pseudorandom functions and applications. In: CCS, pp. 669–684 (2013)

13. Kumar, R., Rajagopalan, S., Sahai, A.: Coding Constructions for Blacklisting Problems without Computational Assumptions. In: Wiener, M. (ed.) CRYPTO 1999. LNCS, vol. 1666, pp. 609–623. Springer, Heidelberg (1999)

14. Micali, S.: CS proofs (extended abstracts). In: 35th Annual Symposium on Foundations of Computer Science, Santa Fe, New Mexico, USA, November 20-22, pp. 436–453 (1994)

15. Naor, M., Yung, M.: Public-key cryptosystems provably secure against chosen ciphertext attacks. In: STOC, pp. 427–437 (1990)

16. Parno, B., Howell, J., Gentry, C., Raykova, M.: Pinocchio: Nearly practical verifiable computation. In: SP, pp. 238–252 (2013)

17. Sahai, A.: Non-malleable non-interactive zero knowledge and adaptive chosen-ciphertext security. In: FOCS, pp. 543–553 (1999)

18. Sahai, A., Waters, B.: How to use indistinguishability obfuscation: deniable encryption, and more. In: STOC, pp. 475–484 (2014)

Obfuscation and E-Voting

How to Obfuscate Programs Directly

Joe Zimmerman[✉]

Stanford University, Stanford, USA
jzim@cs.stanford.edu

Abstract. We propose a new way to obfuscate programs, via composite-order multilinear maps. Our construction operates directly on straight-line programs (arithmetic circuits), rather than converting them to matrix branching programs as in other known approaches. This yields considerable efficiency improvements. For an NC^1 circuit of size s and depth d, with n inputs, we require only $O(d^2 s^2 + n^2)$ multilinear map operations to evaluate the obfuscated circuit—as compared with other known approaches, for which the number of operations is exponential in d. We prove virtual black-box (VBB) security for our construction in a generic model of multilinear maps of hidden composite order, extending previous models for the prime-order setting.

Our scheme works either with "noisy" multilinear maps, which can only evaluate expressions of degree λ^c for pre-specified constant c; or with "clean" multilinear maps, which can evaluate arbitrary expressions. With "noisy" maps, our new obfuscator applies only to NC^1 circuits, requiring the additional assumption of FHE in order to bootstrap to $P/poly$ (as in other obfuscation constructions). From "clean" multilinear maps, on the other hand (whose existence is still open), we present the first approach that would achieve obfuscation for $P/poly$ directly, without FHE.

Our construction is efficient enough that if "clean" multilinear maps were known, then general-purpose program obfuscation could become implementable in practice. Our results demonstrate that the question of "clean" multilinear maps is not a technicality, but a central open problem.

1   Introduction

Program obfuscation is the task of making code "unintelligible", so that the obfuscated code reveals nothing about the implementation beyond its functionality. Obfuscation has many practical applications, such as intellectual property protection and software watermarking, as well as applications to basic cryptographic primitives [DH76,BGI+01].

The theoretical study of obfuscation was initiated by Barak, Goldreich, Impagliazzo, Rudich, Sahai, Vadhan, and Yang [BGI+01]. In that work, the authors also showed that general-purpose program obfuscation could not achieve the natural definition of virtual black-box security (VBB), which led many to suspect that a useful general-purpose obfuscator was impossible. This view changed

© International Association for Cryptologic Research 2015
E. Oswald and M. Fischlin (Eds.): EUROCRYPT 2015, Part II, LNCS 9057, pp. 439–467, 2015.
DOI: 10.1007/978-3-662-46803-6_15

with the work of Garg, Gentry, Halevi, Raykova, Sahai, and Waters [GGH+13b], who proposed a general-purpose obfuscator based on the powerful primitive of *multilinear maps* [BS03], as constructed by Garg, Gentry, and Halevi [GGH13a], Coron, Lepoint, and Tibouchi [CLT13], and Gentry, Gorbunov, and Halevi [GGH14].

For their general-purpose obfuscator, Garg et al. [GGH+13b] proved the weaker notion of indistinguishability obfuscation ($i\mathcal{O}$) [BGI+01] in a generic model of encoded matrices. Subsequently it has been shown that in a generic model of multilinear maps, general-purpose obfuscation can even achieve VBB security [BR14, BGK+14], and that $i\mathcal{O}$ can be based on a single, instance-independent security assumption [GLSW14]. Sahai and Waters have also shown that even the weaker notion of $i\mathcal{O}$ has many cryptographic applications, via the technique of "punctured programs" [SW14]. Since then, obfuscation has become an extremely active area of study, and many other applications and complexity-theoretic implications have been explored; see [AGIS14] for an overview.

Even with known constructions and applications, however, general-purpose obfuscation is currently not feasible to implement in practice. The works of Ananth et al. [AGIS14] and Sahai and Zhandry [SZ14] investigate the question of optimizing obfuscation, and obtain significant improvements for some specific cases, but much work remains to be done. One major source of inefficiency is that in all previously known constructions, including those of [AGIS14, SZ14], obfuscation requires converting the input circuit to a matrix branching program, which incurs a considerable cost in performance.

1.1   Our Results

In this work, we propose a new way to construct obfuscation, which operates directly on straight-line programs (i.e., arithmetic circuits, Section 2.3), without converting them to matrix branching programs. The evaluation of an obfuscated circuit mirrors the structure of the original circuit.

Our construction is based on asymmetric composite-order multilinear maps [BS03, GGH13a, CLT13, GGH14]. It can operate either with "noisy" multilinear maps (such as the CLT construction), or with "clean" maps, for which there is still no known candidate. In the case of "noisy" multilinear maps, our construction (like others) is limited to NC^1, and requires FHE to bootstrap to P/poly. With "clean" multilinear maps, on the other hand, we show that we would be able to obfuscate P/poly directly, without the prohibitively expensive bootstrapping step via FHE. Indeed, if we knew how to construct "clean" multilinear maps, then our results in this work would *immediately* yield obfuscation for P/poly, with parameters that could be feasible in practice.

In addition to qualitatively new results, our techniques yield considerable performance improvements even for "noisy" multilinear maps. For instance, for circuits of size s and depth d with n inputs, we require only $O(d^2 s^2 + n^2)$ multilinear map elements and operations. All other known approaches require a number exponential in the circuit's depth, since every sub-circuit with fanout greater than 1 must be duplicated before converting the circuit to a matrix branching program.

Remark 1 (Cryptanalysis of CLT). For some time, it was believed that the CLT construction [CLT13], together with the modifications of [GLW14, App. B], provided a secure instantiation of a composite-order multilinear map. The obfuscation construction we develop in this work depends fundamentally on the composite-order setting, for which CLT has been the natural candidate instantiation.

However, subsequent to this work, there has been significant progress in the cryptanalysis of the CLT multilinear map. Generalizing the "zeroizing" attack of [GGH13a], Cheon, Han, Lee, Ryu, and Stehlé [CHL+14] have shown that given public encodings of a certain form, it is possible to factor the CLT modulus and thereby break the scheme. Further cryptanalysis showed that it does not help to rule out encodings of this particular form; variants of the Cheon et al. attack can be executed under much weaker hypotheses [GHMS14,BWZ14,CLT14].

In light of these attacks, it is not clear that composite-order multilinear maps can currently be instantiated. We are optimistic that new candidates will be discovered in the future, perhaps as variants of other known constructions [GGH13a, GGH14], and we await the development of suitable multilinear maps.

Perspective: towards implementable obfuscation. Currently, general-purpose obfuscation is not feasible to implement in practice. There have been two main obstacles to its implementation. The first is that, in known ("noisy") multilinear maps such as the GGH and CLT schemes, the noise—and hence the parameters—grow with the *degree* of the polynomial being computed over encoded elements; this limits us to NC^1 circuits, because the degree of a circuit may increase exponentially with its depth. The second obstacle is that, prior to this work, obfuscation required converting the input circuit to a matrix branching program, whose size in general is also exponential in the depth of the original circuit.

This work removes the second obstacle. In our construction, the number of multilinear map operations is polynomial in the circuit size; it is only the degree of multilinearity (and hence the noise growth in "noisy" multilinear maps) that restricts our construction to NC^1. If we could construct "clean" multilinear maps, then our results would immediately yield obfuscation for P/poly, with parameters that could be feasible in practice. In our view, our results indicate that constructing "clean" multilinear maps is one of the most fundamental open problems in cryptography.

Succinctness and keyed circuits. Our new approach is particularly effective for obfuscating *keyed* circuit families $(C(\cdot, \mathbf{y}))_{\mathbf{y} \in \{0,1\}^m}$ (Section 2.4), in which the circuit's structure C is public, and one only needs to hide a short secret key $\mathbf{y} \in \{0,1\}^m$ embedded in the circuit—as is common in many cryptographic applications. For example, for a keyed circuit $C : \{0,1\}^n \times \{0,1\}^m \to \{0,1\}$ of size s and depth d (with n inputs and key length m), our obfuscation consists of only $O(m + n^2)$ ring elements in the multilinear map, and evaluation requires $O(s + n^2)$ ring operations, with multilinearity degree $O(2^d + n^2)$.

Table 1. Performance for general (unkeyed) circuits of input length n, size s, and depth d. We always have $n, s < O(2^d)$, since the gates have fanin two; and in most applications we have $n, s \ll 2^d$. For moderately "narrow" circuits with $s < O(dn)$ and $d > 2 \lg n$, for example, we have $O(d^2 s^2 + n^2) = O(d^4 n^2) = o(2^d n)$. We present the cost here in terms of ring elements and ring operations. The concrete cost in bits and bit operations depends on the multilinear map (Section 2.8). For "clean" maps (whose existence is still open), the cost is just $\mathrm{poly}(\lambda)$. For "noisy" maps, the cost depends on the instantiation; e.g., for the CLT map [CLT13], the reader should multiply each row's obfuscation size and evaluation time by $O(\deg^{2+\varepsilon'}) \cdot \mathrm{poly}(\lambda)$, where deg is the corresponding multilinearity degree from the first column, and ε' is a small constant determined by the choice of the Θ parameter in composite-order CLT [GLW14, App. B].

	Degree of multilinearity	Obfuscation size (# ring elements)	Evaluation time (# ring operations)
Via Barrington [BR14, BGK+14]	$O(4^d n + n^2)$	$O(4^d n + n^2)$	$O(4^d n + n^2)$
[AGIS14]	$O(2^d n + n^2)$	$O(8^d n + n^2)$	$O(8^d n + n^2)$
[AGIS14] + [Gie01]	$O(2^{(1+\varepsilon)d} n + n^2)$	$O(2^{(1+\varepsilon)d} 4^{2/\varepsilon} n + n^2)$	$O(2^{(1+\varepsilon)d} 4^{2/\varepsilon} n + n^2)$
This work	$O(2^d n + n^2)$	$\mathbf{O(d^2 s^2 + n^2)}$	$\mathbf{O(d^2 s^2 + n^2)}$

For keyed circuits, we also define *succinct* obfuscation (Section 2.10), in which the obfuscation overhead size depends only on the input length n and the secret key length m, and is independent of the circuit size. Using our new techniques, along with the assumption that factoring is hard on average, we show that "clean" multilinear maps would imply *succinct* obfuscation for all of P/poly.

Of course, we can regard every circuit family as keyed, by viewing the original circuit as the secret key input to the universal circuit. In this case, succinctness means that the obfuscation overhead size depends only on the size of the part of the original circuit that the obfuscation needs to hide (as well as on the input length). However, the keyed model is especially natural, and we expect that in most applications it will find more use than general-purpose obfuscation.

New design spaces. When the obfuscator converts every circuit C to a matrix branching program, as in previously known approaches, it usually does not help to optimize the design of C itself. The depth of C determines the size of the resulting branching program,[1] but apart from that, every design strategy results in the same procedure to evaluate the obfuscated circuit $\mathcal{O}(C)$, and the same performance—namely, a series of matrix multiplications of encoded elements in the multilinear map.

By contrast, with our new techniques, the obfuscated program's evaluation mirrors the structure of the original arithmetic circuit. If these circuits are naturally keyed, as in most cryptographic applications, then the performance changes considerably with the design strategy, and we expose a rich new design space.

---

[1] In some cases, for Boolean formulas, the size of the branching program may depend on the formula's size [AGIS14].

The execution of any machine—say, a Turing machine or RAM—can be converted to a circuit with overhead at most polylogarithmic,[2] as long as the machine is already *oblivious* (Section 2.2)—i.e., its control flow does not depend on its input data. This means that any tools for designing efficient oblivious algorithms now apply to program obfuscation.

For example, to specialize our new construction to Boolean formulas, we use an efficient oblivious stack [HS66, PF79, MZ14] to evaluate the formulas in postfix order, and we rely on the Fast Fourier Transform (FFT) to reduce the degree of the resulting computation (see the full version [Zim14] for details). We believe that these applications are only the beginning, and we hope that this work will encourage further study of obfuscating *specific*, keyed circuit families. This goal is closely related to the design of efficient oblivious algorithms for specific problems, which is of independent interest in secure multi-party computation and other areas of cryptography. More broadly, while the existence of general-purpose obfuscation is an important theoretical result, we believe that its role in applications is actually quite limited; it is analogous to running all of our programs on a universal Turing machine.

VBB security in the generic model. Since obfuscation is such a powerful primitive, historically it has been difficult to prove constructions secure based on simple, falsifiable assumptions. In the first candidate construction for general-purpose obfuscation [GGH+13b], Garg et al. prove indistinguishability obfuscation ($i\mathcal{O}$) based on a meta-assumption which roughly asserts that the scheme is secure, which they validate in a generic model of generic (encoded) matrices. Brakerski and Rothblum [BR14] and Barak et al. [BGK+14] develop these results further, showing how to extend the obfuscation paradigm of [GGH+13b] to achieve the much stronger definition of *virtual black-box* (VBB) security in a very natural generic model of multilinear maps, similar to the generic group model [Sho97]. In this work, we also prove VBB security, in a generic model similar to that of [BR14, BGK+14], adapted to the setting of (hidden) composite order.

As observed by Brakerski and Rothblum [BR14], it is not clear how we should interpret a proof of VBB in a generic model, since we know that VBB security in the standard model is impossible for general circuit families [BGI+01]. However, as far as we know, it may be possible to achieve VBB obfuscation for many specific classes of circuits, even if not for the pathological examples in the negative results of [BGI+01]. We also do not know any (unconditional) negative results for $i\mathcal{O}$, and a proof of VBB in the generic model also implies $i\mathcal{O}$ in the generic model. Thus, it is plausible that our construction achieves $i\mathcal{O}$ for all circuits (or some intermediate definition, such as differing-inputs obfuscation [BGI+01, ABG+13, BCP14]), and a generic-model VBB proof serves as evidence of this as well.

More generally, a generic-model VBB proof shows that a scheme resists a wide class of "algebraic" attacks, and that any attack that breaks VBB security

---

[2] For instance, in some models there is overhead involved in decomposing word operations into bits.

must exploit some property of the concrete instantiation of multilinear maps.[3] As in the random oracle model, we know that no real primitive can actually instantiate the generic model in all cases [CGH98], and we view the negative result for VBB as another example of that paradigm. In this work, as in other works that rely on generic models [GGH+13b, BR14, BGK+14], we believe that a generic-model proof provides strong heuristic evidence that the corresponding (meta-)assumptions usually hold in the standard model. Of course, it would be even better to prove our construction secure based on a single (instance-independent) falsifiable assumption, as in the work of Gentry et al. [GLW14, GLSW14, GGHZ14]. We leave this as an important open problem for future work.

Extensions. We observe that our techniques can be naturally extended to *functional encryption* [O'N10, BSW11] (as well as its generalization, multi-input functional encryption [GGG+14]), enabling direct constructions that do not require the full machinery of obfuscation and NIZK proofs, and hence avoid their considerable performance cost. We now outline one approach to this extension; we leave the full development for future work. First we note that in our obfuscation construction, we give out an obfuscated *keyed* circuit, $\mathcal{O}(C(\cdot, \mathbf{y}))$, which acts much like the functional decryption key $f_{C(\cdot, \mathbf{y})}$ in a functional encryption scheme. The evaluator can select arbitrary inputs $\mathbf{x} \in \{0, 1\}^n$ of her choice, and use the obfuscated circuit to learn $C(\mathbf{x}, \mathbf{y})$. In functional encryption, however, the evaluator has an additional ability: she can "defer" the evaluation of $C(\mathbf{x}, \mathbf{y})$, by running $\mathsf{ct}_{\mathbf{x}} \leftarrow \mathsf{Enc}(\mathsf{pk}, \mathbf{x})$; then, roughly speaking, an adversary who obtains the value $\mathsf{ct}_{\mathbf{x}}$ learns nothing about $\mathbf{x}$, except those outputs $C(\mathbf{x}, \mathbf{y})$ for which the adversary has the corresponding keys $f_{C(\cdot, \mathbf{y})}$. So, to generalize our obfuscation construction to functional encryption, we need to enable the evaluator to "defer" an input $\mathbf{x}$ in this fashion. Since our construction already represents each input bit $x_1, \ldots, x_n \in \mathbf{x}$ as an encoded element in the multilinear map, this amounts to generating $\mathrm{poly}(\lambda)$ additional encoded elements, of which we can use a subset to "blind" an encoded input $\mathbf{x}$, constructing the ciphertext for the functional encryption scheme.

Another natural extension of our construction is to obfuscate circuits with *multi-bit output*,[4] $C : \{0, 1\}^n \times \{0, 1\}^m \to \{0, 1\}^\ell$ for $\ell > 1$. We defer the full details of this extension to the full version [Zim14]. At a high level, since our evaluation of an obfuscated circuit follows the structure of the original circuit, we can also reuse intermediate results for gates with fanout > 1, and we need not repeat the entire computation for each bit of the output (as we would in approaches based on Barrington's theorem). We remark that this extension is especially apt for algorithms such as block ciphers, which maintain and update

---

[3] Indeed, the negative result of [BGI+01] for VBB in the standard model is based on an attack in which an obfuscated circuit is evaluated on its own bit representation, which of course depends fundamentally on the concrete instantiation of multilinear maps.

[4] For simplicity, we restrict our discussion here to *keyed* circuit families (Section 2.4), as discussed above.

a small "working state" and read off a (multi-bit) output from that state at the end of the computation.

1.2 Our Techniques

We now give an overview of our techniques, and explain how they relate to other known approaches. To keep the presentation simple, we describe our techniques in terms of *keyed* arithmetic circuit families $C : \{0,1\}^n \times \{0,1\}^m \to \{0,1\}$, as described in Section 2.4. (We note that we can obtain keyed circuit families from various other machine models, including general Boolean circuits, by standard universal-program transformations; we defer the formal details to the full version [Zim14].)

Known approaches. All known constructions of general program obfuscation (including this work) are based on *multilinear maps* [BS03, GGH13a, CLT13, GGH14]. Multilinear maps, also known as graded multilinear maps or graded encodings [GGH13a, CLT13, GGH14], are a generalization of bilinear maps such as pairings over elliptic curves [Mil04, MOV93, Jou00, BF01]. Roughly speaking, a multilinear map lets us take a scalar x and produce an encoded version, $\hat{x} = [x]_S$, where $S \subseteq \mathcal{U}$ is a multi-set, called an *index set*, that indicates the level of the encoding $\hat{x}$ in a given hierarchy (namely, the subsets of $\mathcal{U}$ ordered by inclusion).[5] Elements can be added within the same index set, $[x]_S + [y]_S = [x+y]_S$; and elements can be multiplied, $[x]_S \cdot [y]_T = [xy]_{ST}$, as long as the resulting index set ST is still contained in $\mathcal{U}$. Finally, elements encoded at $\mathcal{U}$ itself can be zero-tested, to determine whether they encode the scalar 0.

Intuitively, multilinear maps seem like a perfect fit for program obfuscation. If we give out encoded versions of the secret key input $\mathbf{y} \in \{0,1\}^m$, then the evaluator can encode $\mathbf{x} \in \{0,1\}^m$ himself, use the multilinear map's arithmetic operations to evaluate C on the encoded elements, and zero-test the result to determine the output $C(\mathbf{x}, \mathbf{y}) \in \{0,1\}$. Unfortunately, unless we are extremely careful, the adversary can also evaluate other circuits $C'(\mathbf{x}, \mathbf{y}) \neq C(\mathbf{x}, \mathbf{y})$ on the encoded inputs—such as the circuit C' that ignores the input $\mathbf{x}$ and leaks a bit of the secret key $\mathbf{y}$. Previously known approaches [GGH+13b, BR14, BGK+14, AGIS14, GLSW14] solve this problem by "garbling" the program $C(\cdot, \mathbf{y})$, converting it to a randomized matrix branching program via Kilian's protocol [Kil88].

Structure of our scheme. In our construction, we do not convert the circuit $C(\cdot, \mathbf{y})$ to a matrix branching program. Rather, evaluation of the obfuscated circuit $\mathcal{O}(C(\cdot, \mathbf{y}))$ follows the structure of the original circuit C, performing C's operations on encoded versions of $\mathbf{x}, \mathbf{y}$ in the multilinear map (as depicted in Figure 1). To make sure the adversary evaluates the correct circuit, we make essential use of *composite-order* multilinear maps such as the CLT scheme [CLT13]. We encode scalars in $\mathbb{Z}_N$ for a composite modulus $N = N_{ev} N_{chk}$, and we view $\mathbb{Z}_N$ as a direct

---

[5] We describe here the case of *asymmetric* multilinear maps, since this is the one relevant to our constructions in this work.

product of the two rings $\mathbb{Z}_{N_{ev}}, \mathbb{Z}_{N_{chk}}$, defined by the Chinese Remainder Theorem. To emphasize this intuition, we write $[x_1, x_2]_S$ to refer to an encoding, at index set S of the value $x \in \mathbb{Z}_N$ such that $x \equiv x_1 \pmod{N_{ev}}$ and $x \equiv x_2 \pmod{N_{chk}}$. Evidently the multilinear map operations $(+, \times)$ operate componentwise on these pairs, and a value is zero only if both components are zero.

Now, in our construction, the second component of the direct product $(\mathbb{Z}_{N_{chk}})$ serves as a kind of "checksum" for the adversary's evaluation. When the adversary aims to learn the value of some other circuit $C'(x_1, \ldots, x_n, y_1, \ldots, y_m)$, he will be forced to evaluate the same polynomial in parallel (in the second component), on the uniformly random values $\alpha_1, \ldots, \alpha_n, \beta_1, \ldots, \beta_m$, as depicted in Figure 1. At the end of this procedure, we also provide a "check" encoding $\hat{C}^*$, whose $\mathbb{Z}_{N_{chk}}$ component is the *precomputed* value $C(\alpha_1, \ldots, \alpha_n, \beta_1, \ldots, \beta_m)$. The structure of our scheme ensures (roughly speaking) that the adversary can only perform a zero-test by subtracting off a multiple of this encoding $\hat{C}^*$. (For more details, we refer the reader to Construction 1.)

This design ensures that the adversary will learn nothing from evaluating the wrong circuit. Regardless of the inputs $\mathbf{x}, \mathbf{y}$, if the adversary evaluates an incorrect expression $C' \not\equiv C$, the result will not match our precomputed value $C(\alpha_1, \ldots, \alpha_n, \beta_1, \ldots, \beta_m)$ modulo N_{chk}, and hence the final subtraction will produce a nonzero value modulo $N = N_{ev}N_{chk}$ (so that the multilinear map's zero-test operation always returns "nonzero"). In essence, we have forced the adversary to run the Schwartz-Zippel identity-testing algorithm on his own chosen expression C', in parallel (componentwise) with its actual evaluation on $x_1, \ldots, x_n, y_1, \ldots, y_m$.

Enforcing consistency: index sets with multiplicity. In addition to making sure the adversary cannot evaluate the wrong circuit $C' \neq C$, we must also defend against "mix-and-match" attacks, in which the adversary evaluates the correct circuit C, but uses inconsistent values of input bits at different points in the evaluation. Since we do not convert every circuit to a branching program, it is not clear how to solve this problem with the index set constraint techniques of [BR14, BGK+14]. In our model, the adversary must be allowed plenty of flexibility in constructing his chosen query (since the honest evaluation follows the structure of the original circuit C, which is arbitrary), and yet the adversary must be able to complete all (and only) the consistent evaluations to the top-level index set $\mathcal{U}$.

Instead, we propose the following approach, depicted in Figure 1. We encode each input bit $(\hat{x}_{1,0}, \hat{x}_{1,1}, \hat{x}_{2,0}, \hat{x}_{2,1}, \ldots)$ at its own singleton index set $(X_{1,0}, X_{1,1}, X_{2,0}, X_{2,1}, \ldots)$. The adversary can evaluate whatever expressions he chooses, and the associated index sets will track the degree of the expression in each variable. Then, we give out "interlocking" elements $\hat{z}_{i,b}$ whose index sets contain $X_{i,1-b}^{\deg(x_i)}$ for each bit choice $b \in \{0, 1\}$ (where $\deg(x_i)$ is the degree of the variable x_i in the actual circuit C). By design of the index sets (Section 3), the adversary is forced to incorporate these elements $\hat{z}_{i,b}$ into any monomial that reaches the top level $\mathcal{U}$; but their index sets prevent the adversary from making any input-inconsistent choices within a given monomial.

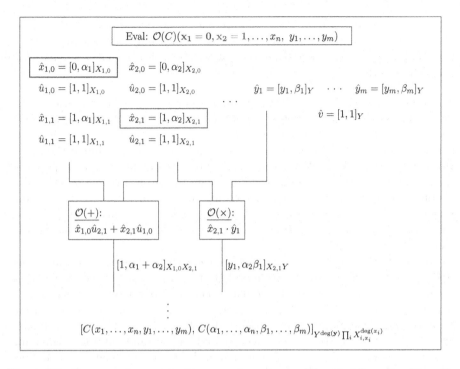

Fig. 1. The first step of our evaluation procedure, for an obfuscated (keyed) arithmetic circuit. First, we use the bits of the input string $\mathbf{x}$ (e.g., $x_1 = 1$, $x_2 = 0$, ..., x_n) to select the relevant input encodings $\hat{x}_{1,1}, \hat{x}_{2,0}, \ldots, \hat{x}_n$. We then run C directly on the encodings $\hat{x}_{1,1}, \hat{x}_{2,0}, \ldots, \hat{y}_1, \ldots, \hat{y}_m$, implementing C's arithmetic operations via the multilinear map, and multiplying by encodings of 1 to make index sets match. (Here $\deg(x_i)$ is the degree of C, as a multivariate polynomial, in the variable x_i; and similarly $\deg(\mathbf{y})$ is the total degree of C in the variables $y_1, \ldots, y_m$.)

Enforcing separability: componentwise blinding factors. Our "interlocking" elements $\hat{z}_{i,b}$ also contain additional blinding factors: $\delta_{i,b}$, in the evaluation component; and $\gamma_{i,b}$, in the "check" component (see Section 3 for details). Intuitively, we need the factors $\gamma_{i,b}$ to make sure that even if the adversary submits a "mixed" query that refers to more than one input string $\mathbf{x}$, the parts of the adversary's query that refer to different input strings are separated, each scaling a different γ monomial, so that they cannot cancel each other and thus the simulator can answer the zero-test query by addressing each consistent input independently.[6] The values $\delta_{i,b}$ are needed in the general case of arithmetic circuits (rather than just Boolean circuits), since there we may have integer outputs $C(\mathbf{x}, \mathbf{y}) \neq C(\mathbf{x}', \mathbf{y})$ such that neither $C(\mathbf{x}, \mathbf{y})$ nor $C(\mathbf{x}', \mathbf{y})$ is zero, and the adversary still should not be allowed to learn whether some specific linear combination of $C(\mathbf{x}, \mathbf{y})$ and $C(\mathbf{x}', \mathbf{y})$ is zero. Together with the design of the

---

[6] In this respect, the γ values in our construction play the same role as the scalar blinding factors in some other obfuscators (e.g., the α factors in [BGK+14]).

index sets described above, these blinding factors let us decompose the adversary's queries into independent subqueries each consistent with one input string $\mathbf{x} \in \{0,1\}^n$, which is essential for the construction of an efficient simulator in the VBB security proof.

Enforcing sequentiality: straddling sets and commitments. In order to achieve virtual black-box (VBB) security (in the generic model), our construction must also address the following subtle issue, raised in [BR14,BGK+14]. Roughly speaking, an efficient simulator in the generic model must examine the arithmetic expression z that the adversary evaluates via the multilinear map operations, and determine whether z would evaluate to zero in the real scheme. The simulator must make this decision based only on the information it receives from its own oracle $C(\cdot, \mathbf{y})$, which means that if the expression z includes terms from superpolynomially many possible inputs $\mathbf{x}$, then the simulator cannot necessarily answer the query efficiently.

We solve this problem by adapting an elegant technique of Barak et al. [BGK+14]. In that work, the authors describe a tool called *straddling sets*. A straddling set system consists of two partitions $\mathcal{S}_0, \mathcal{S}_1$ of the set $[n]$, each consisting of $O(n)$ subsets. The subsets are arranged so that once we choose a set from (say) the partition $\mathcal{S}_0$, we have committed to $\mathcal{S}_0$, and we cannot complete this set to form a full partition of $[n]$ except by adding all (and only) the remaining sets in the partition $\mathcal{S}_0$. The construction of [BGK+14] associates a straddling set system to each input bit $i \in \{1, \ldots, n\}$, for a total of $O(n^2)$ sets among all n partitions, and the index set of each encoded matrix includes a set from each of two different straddling set systems, indicating which of the corresponding two input bits the matrix selects (in the matrix branching program). Our use of straddling sets in this work is similar to their use in [BGK+14], with some adaptations to restrict which of our terms induce which straddling-set dependencies. We defer the full details to Section 3.

1.3   Related Work

As discussed above, our work builds on earlier constructions of program obfuscation [GGH+13b, CV13, BR14, BGK+14, AGIS14, GLSW14], but our new techniques differ in multiple ways—most notably, we obfuscate circuits directly, without converting them to branching programs.

The work of Gentry et al. [GLSW14] constructs indistinguishability obfuscation ($i\mathcal{O}$) from composite-order multilinear maps. In that work, extending the techniques of [GLW14], the authors show that $i\mathcal{O}$ can be based on a single, falsifiable assumption, independent of the particular circuit to be obfuscated. Previously it was only known how to prove $i\mathcal{O}$ in generic models of multilinear maps [GGH+13b, BR14, BGK+14], or from meta-assumptions that quantify over many circuits [PST14]. In [GLSW14], the emphasis is on the new assumption; the main construction is based on the standard paradigm of converting circuits to branching programs, as in [GGH+13b, BR14, BGK+14]. By contrast, our work proposes a new kind of construction, which avoids branching programs entirely;

while our security proof is given in a generic model similar to that of [BGK+14]. Thus, our work is largely orthogonal to that of [GLSW14]. As discussed above, we believe it may be possible to adapt our construction to base security on a single falsifiable assumption, as in [GLSW14], and we leave this as an important open problem for future work.

Our work is also complementary to that of Ananth et al. [AGIS14]. In that work, the authors give an obfuscation construction that is still based on matrix branching programs, as in [GGH+13b, BR14, BGK+14], but constructs those branching programs much more efficiently when the programs to be obfuscated are given as Boolean formulas. A key observation in [AGIS14] is that in order to evaluate a Boolean formula ϕ efficiently, we can simply test whether two specific vertices are connected in a directed graph related to ϕ. As the authors observe, this graph connectivity computation can be written as matrix multiplication, and thus it is well-suited to known approaches via matrix branching programs. More broadly, however, the graph connectivity computation is well-suited to program obfuscation *in general*—because the structure of matrix multiplication is independent of the input data (Section 2.2), and because it has relatively low degree as an arithmetic circuit. Indeed, the new obfuscator we develop in this work could also be run on the connectivity algorithms of [AGIS14]; and, as we show in the full version [Zim14, §4], for some parameter settings this would yield even better performance than running our obfuscator on a program that evaluates the formula ϕ directly (i.e., without converting it to a graph connectivity problem). The techniques we develop in this work expose a rich space of design choices for the computations that are *input* to the obfuscator, and the connectivity computation of [AGIS14] is an interesting example of one such design.

In concurrent and independent work, Applebaum and Brakerski [AB15] describe an obfuscator that is very similar to the simplified $i\mathcal{O}$ version of our construction [Zim14, Appendix A]. The construction of Applebaum and Brakerski only achieves the weaker notion of (generic-model) $i\mathcal{O}$, rather than (generic-model) VBB security as we achieve in our main construction [Zim14, §3]. Applebaum and Brakerski also give an extension that provides robustness in the stronger setting of low-level zero-test operations (see Remark 3 below), at the cost of n additional components in the composite-order encodings. We note that our construction in this work can also be extended to be robust in this stronger setting, at the cost of only 2 additional components, via the generic transformation of [BWZ14]. (Indeed, the zero-immunizing transformation of [BWZ14] applies to any scheme secure in the generic model of composite-order multilinear maps, and thus also improves the construction of Applebaum and Brakerski.)

2 Preliminaries

2.1 Conventions

For integers n, a, b, we denote by $[n]$ the set $\{1, \ldots, n\}$, and by $[a, b]$ the set $\{a, \ldots, b\}$. For a finite set S, we write $\mathsf{Uniform}(S)$ to mean the probability distribution that is uniform over the elements of S. For integers a, b, we write $\mathsf{Primes}[a, b]$ to mean the set of all prime numbers in $[a, b]$, and we overload this notation to refer to the distribution $\mathsf{Uniform}(\mathsf{Primes}[a, b])$. Following standard conventions of cryptography, we also define a variable λ, called the security parameter. We define a *negligible function* to be a function $\varepsilon(\lambda)$ that is $o(1/\lambda^c)$ for every $c > 0$, and we write $\mathsf{negl}(\lambda)$ to denote a negligible function of λ.

2.2 Oblivious Computation and the "Mux" Operation

A program is considered *data-oblivious*, or *oblivious*, if the sequence of primitive operations performed, as well as the identities of their operands (e.g., registers or memory locations in a RAM) is a deterministic function solely of the input length, and does not depend on the input. To make a program oblivious, there are many standard techniques. We now describe one such technique, known as "arithmetization" or "multiplexing" (abbreviated "mux"), which is involved in various compiler optimizations and static analyses of programs. The idea is very simple: whenever a program would call for input-dependent control flow, such as "if x then $y \leftarrow z$; else $y \leftarrow w$;", we remove the conditional, and replace every assignment statement in both branches with an arithmetized version: "$y \leftarrow x \cdot z + (1 - x) \cdot w$", also denoted "$y \leftarrow \mathsf{mux}(x, z, w)$".

2.3 Straight-Line Programs (Arithmetic Circuits)

In our obfuscation construction, we will find it natural to work with the computational model of straight-line programs over the integers. We say a straight-line program $P : \mathbb{Z}^n \to \mathbb{Z}$ computes a Boolean function $f : \{0, 1\}^n \to \{0, 1\}$ if for all $\mathbf{x} \in \{0, 1\}^n$, we have $f(\mathbf{x}) = 1 \Leftrightarrow P(\mathbf{x}) \neq 0$. When the context is clear, we abuse notation to write $P(\mathbf{x}) : \{0, 1\}^n \to \{0, 1\}$ to denote the Boolean function f that P computes. We note that straight-line programs are naturally identified with arithmetic circuits (fanin two, unbounded fanout). In this work, we will view straight-line programs and arithmetic circuits interchangeably.

The model of straight-line programs is extremely general. The execution of any machine—say, a Turing machine or RAM—can be expressed as a straight-line program over $\mathbb{Z}$, with overhead at most polylogarithmic,[7] provided that the machine is oblivious (Section 2.2). We also note that an arithmetic circuit $C : \{0, 1\}^n \to \{0, 1\}$ can be expressed as a formal multivariate polynomial in $\mathbb{Z}[x_1, \ldots, x_n]$ (perhaps after duplicating gates to account for fanout), and we will identify circuits with their corresponding polynomials. Although the multivariate polynomial for a given circuit C may be of exponential size, it can still be evaluated efficiently, and we can perform algebraic substitutions on it. We define the *degree* of an arithmetic circuit C in each input variable as the degree of its corresponding polynomial in that variable, and similarly for the total degree. Given a Boolean circuit C, evidently we can convert it into an

---

[7] For instance, in some models there is overhead involved in decomposing word operations into bits.

arithmetic circuit C' that computes the same function, with at most a constant factor overhead both in size and in depth. For the formal details, we refer the reader to the full version [Zim14].

2.4   Keyed Programs

In many cryptographic applications of obfuscation, we do not depend on hiding the entire structure of the obfuscated program from the adversary, but rather only need to hide a short secret key embedded in the program. We can formalize this notion as follows.

Definition 2.1 (Keyed Circuit Family). Let $C : \{0,1\}^n \times \{0,1\}^m \to \{0,1\}$ be an arithmetic circuit of size s and depth d, and for each $\mathbf{y} \in \{0,1\}^m$, define the function $f_{\mathbf{y}}(\mathbf{x}) = C(\mathbf{x}, \mathbf{y})$ for all inputs $\mathbf{x} \in \{0,1\}^n$. If $(C_{\mathbf{y}})_{\mathbf{y} \in \{0,1\}^m}$ is a family of arithmetic circuits such that each $C_{\mathbf{y}}$ computes $f_{\mathbf{y}}$, then we say that $(C_{\mathbf{y}})_{\mathbf{y} \in \{0,1\}^m}$ is a *keyed circuit family*, of size s and depth d, corresponding to the universal circuit C.

The model of "keyed" programs is especially natural for obfuscation, and we expect that in most cryptographic applications, it will find more use than general-purpose obfuscation. For theoretical purposes, however, we would still like to construct general-purpose obfuscation for large classes of circuits such as NC^1 or P/poly, for which the obfuscation must hide everything except the size of the circuit to be obfuscated. Thus, we make use of standard transformations from general circuit families to keyed circuit families, in which the secret key is the entire circuit to be obfuscated, and C is a universal circuit; we defer the formal details to the full version [Zim14]. We emphasize that these universal-circuit transformations are mainly for theoretical purposes. In practice, a much better approach would be to design, for each desired cryptographic application of obfuscation, a family of circuits that is already keyed with respect to the particular secret that needs to be hidden.

2.5   Composite-Order Multilinear Maps

Multilinear maps [BS03], also known as graded multilinear maps or graded encodings [GGH13a, CLT13, GGH14], are a generalization of bilinear maps such as pairings over elliptic curves [Mil04, MOV93, Jou00, BF01]. Intuitively, a multilinear map lets us take scalars x, y and produce corresponding encodings $\hat{x}, \hat{y}$ at any level of a given hierarchy, so that we can still perform arithmetic operations (e.g., $x + y, xy$) on the encoded representations, and yet it is hard to recover the original scalars x, y from encodings $\hat{x}, \hat{y}$. For example, in a symmetric bilinear map $e : \mathbb{G} \times \mathbb{G} \to \mathbb{G}_T$ (where g generates $\mathbb{G}$, and $e(g, g)$ generates $\mathbb{G}_T$), a scalar $x \in \mathbb{Z}$ can be encoded in $\mathbb{G}$ as g^x, or encoded in $\mathbb{G}_T$ as $e(g, g)^x$. The levels of the hierarchy here are $\mathbb{G}$ and $\mathbb{G}_T$, and the hierarchy's structure enforces constraints on the arithmetic operations that we can perform. For instance, via the group operation we can compute g^{x+y} (an encoding of $x+y$) from g^x and g^y (encodings of x and y), but to obtain an encoding of xy, we must increase the level in the hierarchy from $\mathbb{G}$ to $\mathbb{G}_T$, by computing the pairing $e(g^x, g^y) = e(g, g)^{xy}$.

In the case of symmetric bilinear maps, this hierarchical structure can be identified with the integers $0, 1, 2$ as indices, where the index 0 represents scalars, 1 represents elements of $\mathbb{G}$, and 2 represents elements of $\mathbb{G}_T$. Elements at the same index can be added together, while elements at arbitrary indices can be multiplied, but their indices add. For asymmetric bilinear maps, the more natural analogy is that of a subset lattice: specifically, a map $e : \mathbb{G}_1 \times \mathbb{G}_2 \to \mathbb{G}_T$ is identified with the subset lattice $\emptyset \subseteq \{A\}, \{B\} \subseteq \{A, B\}$, where $\emptyset$ corresponds to scalars, $\{A\}$ to $\mathbb{G}_1$, $\{B\}$ to $\mathbb{G}_2$, and $\{A, B\}$ to $\mathbb{G}_T$.

More generally, in the case of asymmetric multilinear maps, it is standard to work with general subset lattices, where the sets may contain elements with multiplicity. By convention, we will say that these sets are made up of *formal symbols*, denoted by capital letters (A, B, C), which serve the same role as formal variables in polynomials. Formally, we state the following definitions.

Definition 2.2 (Formal Symbol). A *formal symbol* is a bit string in $\{0, 1\}^*$, and distinct variables denote distinct bit strings. A *fresh* formal symbol is any bit string in $\{0, 1\}^*$ that has not already been assigned to another formal symbol.

Definition 2.3 (Index Sets). An *index set* is a multi-set of formal symbols called *indices*. The multiplicity of each index is written in binary, and so the degree of an set may be up to exponential in the size of its representation. By convention, for index sets we use set notation and product notation interchangeably, so that $A^3 B C^2$ represents $\{A, A, A, B, C, C\}$, and $A^3 B C^2 \cup ABC = A^4 B^2 C^3$.

Definition 2.4 (Composite-Order Multilinear Map ([BS03, GGH13a, CLT13, GLW14], adapted)). A *composite-order multilinear map* supports the following operations. Each operation (CM.Setup, CM.Add, CM.Mult, CM.ZeroTest, CM.Encode) is implemented by an efficient randomized algorithm.

- The setup procedure receives as input an index set $\mathcal{U}$ (Definition 2.3), which we refer to as the "top-level index set", as well as the security parameter λ (in unary), and an integer k indicating the number of components to generate for the modulus. It produces public parameters pp, secret parameters sp, and integers $N_1, \ldots, N_k$ as follows:

$$\mathsf{CM.Setup}(\mathcal{U}, 1^\lambda, k) \to (\mathsf{pp}, \mathsf{sp}, N_1, \ldots, N_k)$$

Each integer $N_1, \ldots, N_k$ is a product of $\mathrm{poly}(\lambda)$ primes, and each of these $k \cdot \mathrm{poly}(\lambda)$ primes is drawn independently from $\mathsf{Primes}[2^\lambda, 2^{\lambda+1}]$. We also define $N = \prod_{i \in [k]} N_i$, the overall modulus.[8]

---

[8] We remark here that our construction does not rely on the individual moduli $N_1, \ldots, N_k$ being composite, but we present the model in this full generality since it may be required in the chosen concrete instantiation, such as in the CLT multilinear map [CLT13].

- For each index set $\mathcal{S} \subseteq \mathcal{U}$, and each scalar $x \in \mathbb{Z}_N$, there is a set of strings $[x]_{\mathcal{S}} \subseteq \{0,1\}^*$, i.e., the set of all valid encodings of x at index set $\mathcal{S}$. [9] From here on, we will abuse notation to write $[x]_{\mathcal{S}}$ to stand for any element of $[x]_{\mathcal{S}}$ (i.e., any valid encoding of x at the index set $\mathcal{S}$).
- Elements at the same index set $\mathcal{S} \subseteq \mathcal{U}$ can be added, with the result also encoded at $\mathcal{S}$:

$$\mathsf{CM.Add}(\mathsf{pp},\ [x]_{\mathcal{S}},\ [y]_{\mathcal{S}}) \ \rightarrow\ [x+y]_{\mathcal{S}}$$

- Elements at two index sets $\mathcal{S}_1, \mathcal{S}_2$ can be multiplied, with the result encoded at the union of the two sets, as long as their union is still contained in $\mathcal{U}$:

$$\mathsf{CM.Mult}(\mathsf{pp},\ [x]_{\mathcal{S}_1},\ [y]_{\mathcal{S}_2}) \ \rightarrow\ \begin{cases} [xy]_{\mathcal{S}_1 \cup \mathcal{S}_2} & \text{if } \mathcal{S}_1 \cup \mathcal{S}_2 \subseteq \mathcal{U} \\ \bot & \text{otherwise} \end{cases}$$

- Elements at the top level $\mathcal{U}$ can be *zero-tested*:

$$\mathsf{CM.ZeroTest}(\mathsf{pp},\ [x]_{\mathcal{S}}) \ \rightarrow\ \begin{cases} \text{``zero''} & \text{if } \mathcal{S} = \mathcal{U} \text{ and } x = 0 \in \mathbb{Z}_N \\ \text{``nonzero''} & \text{otherwise} \end{cases}$$

- Using the secret parameters, one can generate a representation of a given scalar $x \in \mathbb{Z}$ at any index set $\mathcal{S} \subseteq \mathcal{U}$:

$$\mathsf{CM.Encode}(\mathsf{sp},\ x,\ \mathcal{S}) \ \rightarrow\ [x]_{\mathcal{S}}$$

- For the trivial index set $\mathcal{S} = \emptyset$, we specify that the valid encodings $[x]_{\emptyset}$ are just the integers congruent to x modulo N. (So, for instance, we can perform subtraction via $\mathsf{CM.Add}$, by scalar multiplication with -1.)

By convention (and by analogy to the setting of symmetric multilinear maps), we refer to the total degree of $\mathcal{U}$ as the *degree of multilinearity* of the map. When the context is clear, we also abuse notation to write, for encodings $\hat{a}, \hat{b}$, the expression $\hat{a} + \hat{b}$ to mean $\mathsf{CM.Add}(\mathsf{CM.pp}, \hat{a}, \hat{b})$; the expression $\hat{a}\hat{b}$ to mean $\mathsf{CM.Mult}(\mathsf{CM.pp}, \hat{a}, \hat{b})$; and likewise for other arithmetic expressions.

Features of composite order. By analogy to composite-order bilinear groups [BGN05], we would expect that composite-order multilinear maps would be significantly more powerful than their traditional prime-order analogs. Intuitively, this power is due to the fact that by encoding integers in $\mathbb{Z}_N$ for composite $N = N_1 \cdots N_k$, we implicitly encode a direct product, $\mathbb{Z}_{N_1} \times \ldots \times \mathbb{Z}_{N_k}$, as defined by the Chinese Remainder Theorem. Each of the k components can be used to store useful information, on which the ring operations act componentwise, and a value will pass the multilinear map's zero-test only if it encodes zero in *every*

---

[9] To be precise, we define $[x]_{\mathcal{S}} = \{\chi \in \{0,1\}^* : \mathsf{CM.IsEncoding}(\mathsf{pp}, \chi, x, \mathcal{S})\}$, where the predicate $\mathsf{CM.IsEncoding}$ is specified by the concrete instantiation of the multilinear map. The predicate $\mathsf{CM.IsEncoding}$ need not be efficiently decidable—and indeed, for the security of the multilinear map, it should not be.

component (i.e., modulo every N_i). Without knowing the factorization, however, the adversary cannot easily eliminate one component of an encoded value without eliminating them all. To better express this intuitive view, we introduce the following notation.

Remark 2 (Notation for Encodings of Direct Products). We use the notation $[x_1, x_2, \ldots, x_k]_S$ to refer to an encoding, at index set S, of the value $x \in \mathbb{Z}_N$ such that $x \equiv x_i \pmod{N_i}$ for each $i \in [k]$ (as determined by the Chinese Remainder Theorem).

2.6   The Generic Multilinear Map Model

To define security for composite-order multilinear maps, we will operate in a *generic model* of composite-order multilinear maps, which generalizes existing generic models for the prime-order case [GGH+13b, BR14, BGK+14]. This generic model is similar to the generic group model [Sho97]: intuitively, in the generic model, the only thing an adversary can do with ring elements is to apply the multilinear map operations.

More precisely, we say a scheme that uses multilinear maps is "secure in the generic model" if, for any concrete adversary breaking the real scheme, there is a generic adversary breaking a modified scheme in which the encoded ring elements are replaced by "handles" (concretely, fresh nonces), which the generic-model adversary can supply to a stateful oracle $\mathcal{M}$ (which performs the corresponding ring operations and zero-tests internally). For the complete exposition and formal definitions, we refer the reader to the full version [Zim14].

Remark 3 (Unique Encodings and Zero-Testing). In this work, as in [BGK+14], our generic model allows the adversary to zero-test *only* at the top-level index set $\mathcal{U}$. In candidate multilinear maps based on noisy encodings (e.g., [GGH13a, GGH14]), no weaknesses are known that would permit zero-testing outside $\mathcal{U}$. However, if in the future we discover multilinear maps for which this operation is possible—for instance, if elements have unique encodings—then our obfuscation construction would need to be modified for this setting. For such a modification, we refer the reader to the work of Boneh, Wu, and Zimmerman [BWZ14, §3], in which the authors show a generic transformation for composite-order multilinear maps that prevents the adversary from constructing nontrivial encodings of zero outside the top-level index set $\mathcal{U}$.

2.7   "Noisy" and "Clean" Multilinear Maps

The abstract definition of multilinear maps (Definition 2.4) is very natural, but we still do not know whether it can be instantiated. The breakthrough work of Garg et al. [GGH13a] showed the first candidate construction of an *approximate* or "noisy" variant of multilinear maps, in which the representation of each encoded ring element includes a random error term. When ring elements are added or multiplied, the resulting error term increases; eventually, the noise overwhelms the signal, and the zero-testing procedure no longer recovers the correct answer. Thus, unlike the "clean" multilinear maps of Definition 2.4, known "noisy" multilinear maps include an *a priori* restriction of the number and types of operations that can be performed.

In known multilinear map constructions [GGH13a, CLT13, GGH14], the noise restriction behaves as follows. Each encoded ring element carries a noise bound. The result of a fresh encoding operation (via CM.Encode) has a noise bound of $2^{f(\lambda)}$ (for some polynomial f pre-specified at setup); CM.Add results in a noise bound that grows with the sum of the bounds of its operands; and CM.Mult results in a noise bound that grows with the product. When the noise bound reaches $2^{g(\lambda)}$ (again for a pre-specified polynomial g), the zero-test operation always outputs $\perp$.

For our purposes in this work, we will model the noise restriction as stating that the multilinear map can only compute arithmetic expressions of *polynomial degree* (for a polynomial fixed at setup time)—or, equivalently, that the multiplicities of indices in the top-level index set $\mathcal{U}$ are presented in unary.

Definition 2.7 (**"Noisy" Composite-Order Multilinear Map**). A *noisy composite-order multilinear map* is defined as in Definition 2.4, except that the top-level index set $\mathcal{U}$ has its multiplicities presented in unary.

We note that Definition 2.7 considers only the noise growth due to multiplication operations, and disregards that of addition operations.[10] Technically, in order to instantiate this definition with the CLT multilinear map [CLT13], we would also need to specify that the ring operations may fail for computations with many additions and very few multiplications. However, our main theorems are unaffected by this restriction. In a broader sense, we also find that this simple definition in terms of multilinearity degree is more natural, and is better suited to other potential approaches to multilinear maps that may not incorporate noise terms in the same way as the approaches currently known.

2.8 Instantiation of Composite-Order Multilinear Maps

As discussed above in Remark 1, until very recently it was believed that the CLT scheme [CLT13] provided a secure instantiation of "noisy" composite-order multilinear maps. For completeness, we now briefly recount the structure of the CLT scheme. Fix a top-level index set $\mathcal{U} = A_1^{u_1} \cdots A_\ell^{u_\ell}$, where $A_1, \ldots, A_\ell$ are formal symbols. The CLT scheme generates an "inner" modulus $N = p_1 \ldots p_s$ and an "outer" modulus $N_{\text{outer}} = P_1 \ldots, P_s$ (for $s = \text{poly}(\lambda, \sum_i u_i)$), where

---

[10] More precisely, fix an arithmetic expression C of depth d and total degree r, and suppose we evaluate C on freshly encoded ring elements. The number of monomials in the expansion of C is at most 2^{dr}, so the noise bound of the resulting term is at most $2^{dr} \cdot (2^{f(\lambda)})^r$, and we will remain under the noise limit as long as $(d + f(\lambda))r < g(\lambda)$. In most cases of interest, we have $d \ll r$—in fact, if a constant fraction of the layers of C consist of multiplication gates, then $d = O(\lg r)$—and thus we can approximate the noise bound simply in terms of the degree.

$p_1, \ldots, p_s, P_1, \ldots, P_s$ are primes of bit-length poly $(\lambda, \sum_i u_i)$, and each P_i is much larger than p_i. For a more comprehensive exposition, we refer the reader to the full version [Zim14].

In order to use the CLT scheme as a composite-order multilinear map with inner modulus $N = N_1 \cdots N_k$, setting the parameters requires some care, since the scheme must remain secure even when the adversary sees encodings that are zero in one or more of the subrings $(\mathbb{Z}_{N_1}, \ldots, \mathbb{Z}_{N_k})$. Gentry et al. [GLW14] investigate this question, and conclude that if each modulus $N_1, \ldots, N_k$ is a product of many (i.e., poly(λ)) of the primes among $p_1, \ldots, p_s$, then the scheme resists obvious attacks along these lines. For the full analysis, we refer the reader to [GLW14, Appendix B].

Possible approaches for clean maps. While we know of some candidate strategies to instantiate "noisy" multilinear maps, instantiation of "clean" multilinear maps remains a central open problem. Current techniques for "noisy" maps [GGH13a, CLT13, GGH14] depend crucially on the noise to hide the encoded elements. Even if it is possible to extend these techniques, and thereby reduce the noise below quadratic in the multilinearity degree, it seems very unlikely that the noise can be made only *polylogarithmic* in the degree, as would be required for "clean" maps. However, the current approach via encodings with random noise is not necessarily the only possible route. The theory of bilinear maps [Mil04, MOV93, Jou00, BF01] does not incorporate noise terms at all, but rather relies on algebraic properties of pairings over elliptic curves. We believe that the most promising route to constructing "clean" multilinear maps is via structures that generalize these properties, such as abelian varieties. Some conditional negative results were presented by Boneh and Silverberg [BS03], but in general, the problem remains wide open.

2.9   Program Obfuscation

Our definition of VBB obfuscation is similar to the one studied in [BGK+14]. It is stronger than the original definition [BGI+01], in that we allow the adversary to output a string of arbitrary length, rather than just a single bit. In addition, the definition is parameterized over an ideal functionality (represented by a stateful oracle $\mathcal{M}$), to which both the obfuscator and the adversary have access. If $\mathcal{M}$ were the empty oracle, we would recover the usual definition of (strong) VBB obfuscation. In our setting, however, as in that of [BGK+14], the oracle $\mathcal{M}$ corresponds to our generic model of composite-order multilinear maps.

Definition 2.8 (Virtual Black-Box Obfuscation in an Idealized Model ([BGI+01, BGK+14])). Let $\mathcal{C} = (\mathcal{C}_\lambda)_{\lambda \in \mathbb{N}}$ be a family of Boolean circuits, and let $\mathcal{M}$ be a stateful oracle (possibly randomized). We say that a PPT machine $\mathcal{O}$ is a *virtual black-box obfuscator* for $\mathcal{C}$ in the $\mathcal{M}$-idealized model, if the following conditions are satisfied.

- Correctness: There is a negligible function ε such that for all $\lambda \in \mathbb{N}$, every circuit $C \in \mathcal{C}_\lambda$, every input $\mathbf{x}$ to C, and all possible random coins for $\mathcal{M}$, we have

$$\Pr[(\mathcal{O}^{\mathcal{M}}(1^\lambda, C))(\mathbf{x}) \neq C(\mathbf{x})] < \varepsilon(\lambda) \ .$$

- Virtual Black-Box: For every PPT adversary $\mathcal{A}$, there is a PPT simulator $\mathcal{S}$ such that for every PPT distinguisher D, there is a negligible function ε such that for all $C \in \mathcal{C}_\lambda$, we have

$$\left| \Pr[D(\mathcal{A}^{\mathcal{M}}(\mathcal{O}^{\mathcal{M}}(1^\lambda, C))) = 1] - \Pr[D(\mathcal{S}^C(1^\lambda, 1^{|C|})) = 1] \right| < \varepsilon(\lambda) \ ,$$

where the probability is over the coins of $D, \mathcal{A}, \mathcal{S}, \mathcal{O}$, and $\mathcal{M}$.

We extend Definition 2.8 in the standard way to entire circuit classes such as NC^1 and $\mathrm{P/poly}$; we defer the formal details to the full version [Zim14]. We also note that since we require the obfuscator $\mathcal{O}$ to be efficient, the output of $\mathcal{O}$ is a circuit of size $\mathrm{poly}(\lambda)$, and thus the *polynomial slowdown* property of [BGI+01] is immediate from the definition.

2.10   Keyed and Succinct Obfuscation

As discussed in Section 2.4, the model of "keyed" programs is especially natural for program obfuscation. We now state a modified definition of VBB obfuscation, suited to this setting.

Definition 2.9   (Keyed Virtual Black-Box Obfuscation). Fix a family of arithmetic circuits $\mathcal{C} = (C_\lambda)_{\lambda \in \mathbb{N}}$ (Section 2.3). For a stateful oracle $\mathcal{M}$ (possibly randomized), we say a pair of PPT algorithms $(\mathcal{O}, \mathcal{O}.\mathrm{Eval})$ is a *keyed virtual black-box obfuscator* for $\mathcal{C}$ in the $\mathcal{M}$-idealized model, if the following conditions are satisfied.

- Correctness: There is a negligible function ε such that the following holds. Fix $\lambda \in \mathbb{N}$ and an arithmetic circuit $C \in \mathcal{C}_\lambda$, where $C : \{0,1\}^n \times \{0,1\}^m \to \{0,1\}$. Then for every input $\mathbf{x} \in \{0,1\}^n$ and key $\mathbf{y} \in \{0,1\}^m$, and all possible random coins for $\mathcal{M}$, we have

$$\Pr[\tilde{C}_\mathbf{y} \leftarrow \mathcal{O}^{\mathcal{M}}(C, \mathbf{y}) \ ; \ \mathcal{O}.\mathrm{Eval}^{\mathcal{M}}(\tilde{C}_\mathbf{y}, C, \mathbf{x}) \neq C(\mathbf{x}, \mathbf{y})] < \varepsilon(\lambda) \ ,$$

where the probability is over the coins of $\mathcal{O}$.

- Virtual Black-Box: For every PPT adversary $\mathcal{A}$, there is a PPT simulator $\mathcal{S}$ such that for all PPT distinguishers D, and all $(C, n, m) \in \mathcal{C}$, we have

$$\left| \Pr[D(\mathcal{A}^{\mathcal{M}}(\mathcal{O}^{\mathcal{M}}(C, \mathbf{y})) = 1] - \Pr[D(\mathcal{S}^{C(\cdot, \mathbf{y})}(C)) = 1] \right| < \mathrm{negl}(|C|) \ ,$$

where the probability is over the coins of $D, \mathcal{A}, \mathcal{S}, \mathcal{O}$, and $\mathcal{M}$.

Intuitively, the definition of *keyed* program obfuscation separates the question of the *public* ("universal") circuit parameters from the size of the secret part of the circuit, which is to be obfuscated. It now makes sense to discuss *succinct* program obfuscation, in which the obfuscation size is independent of the public part of the circuit, and depends only on the secret key (and on the security parameter).

Definition 2.10 (Succinct Virtual Black-Box Obfuscation) The definition is the same as Definition 2.9, with the following additional requirement.

 – Succinctness: There exists a polynomial f such that for all $(C, n, m) \in C$ and all $\mathbf{y} \in \{0,1\}^m$, we have $|\mathcal{O}^{\mathcal{M}}(C, \mathbf{y})| \leq f(n, m, \lambda)$.

We also extend Definition 2.10 in the standard way to the classes P/poly and NC^1, just as in Definition 2.8.

2.11   Straddling Sets

Our obfuscator uses the multilinear map's index sets to enforce constraints on the adversary's evaluation. This requires careful design of the indices for each element. To simplify the presentation of our design, we now discuss some simple combinatorial properties that we use in our security proof.

An important building block is the notion of *straddling sets*, as described by Barak et al. [BGK+14]. Roughly speaking, an n-straddling set system consists of two partitions $\mathcal{S}_0, \mathcal{S}_1$ of the set $\{1, \ldots, n\}$, such that once we choose a set from (say) $\mathcal{S}_0$, we have committed to $\mathcal{S}_0$, and we cannot complete this set to form a full partition of $\{1, \ldots, n\}$ except by adding all (and only) the remaining sets in the partition $\mathcal{S}_0$. In fact, we require the following slightly stronger property.

Definition 2.11 (Straddling Set Systems ([BGK+14], adapted)) For $n \in \mathbb{N}$, an n-*straddling set system over a set* S consists of two partitions of $\mathcal{S}$, $\mathcal{S}_0 = (S_{0,1}, \ldots, S_{0,n})$ and $\mathcal{S}_1 = (S_{1,1}, \ldots, S_{1,n})$ with the following property. Fix $\mathcal{T} \subseteq \mathcal{S}$, and let T_0, T_1 be subsequences of $S_{0,1}, \ldots, S_{0,n}, S_{1,1}, \ldots, S_{1,n}$ such that each of T_0, T_1 is a partition of $\mathcal{T}$, and $T_0 \neq T_1$ (i.e., they are not the same subsequence). Then each of T_0, T_1 is one of the original partitions $\mathcal{S}_0, \mathcal{S}_1$, and $\mathcal{T} = \mathcal{S}$.

We note that the simple construction of straddling sets in [BGK+14] already satisfies our stronger definition. We defer the details to the full version [Zim14].

3   Construction

We now present our main obfuscation construction (Construction 1), which acts on keyed circuits (Section 2.4) as depicted in Figure 1. (We note that we can obtain keyed circuit families from various other machine models, including general Boolean circuits, by the transformations of Section 2.4.)

Construction 1 (Construction of Virtual Black-Box Obfuscation). Let $\mathsf{CM} = (\mathsf{CM.Setup}, \mathsf{CM.Add}, \mathsf{CM.Mult}, \mathsf{CM.ZeroTest}, \mathsf{CM.Encode})$ be a composite-order multilinear map (Definition 2.4). Fix an input $(C, \mathbf{y})$, where $\mathbf{y} \in \{0,1\}^m$, and $C : \{0,1\}^n \times \{0,1\}^m \to \{0,1\}$ is an arithmetic circuit (representing the keyed circuit $C_\mathbf{y}$, as in Section 2.4). Let d be the depth of the circuit C; let $\deg(\mathbf{y})$ be the total degree of C in all of the variables $y_1, \ldots, y_m$; and for each $i \in [n]$ let $\deg(x_i)$ be the degree of C in the variable x_i. For a security parameter $\lambda \in \mathbb{N}$ (represented in unary), the obfuscation procedure $\mathcal{O}(1^\lambda, C, \mathbf{y})$ operates as follows.

$\underline{\mathcal{O}(1^\lambda, C, \mathbf{y}):}$

1. For each $i \in [n]$, let $(S_{i,b,1}, \ldots, S_{i,b,n})_{b \in \{0,1\}}$ be an n-straddling set system (Definition 2.11) over a set $\mathcal{S}_i$ of $(2n - 1)$ fresh formal symbols. For each $b \in \{0,1\}$ and $i \in [n]$, define $\mathsf{BitCommit}_{i,b} = S_{i,b,i}$. For each $b_1, b_2 \in \{0,1\}$ and $i_1, i_2 \in [n]$ such that $i_1 < i_2$, define $\mathsf{BitFill}_{i_1,i_2,b_1,b_2} = S_{i_1,b_1,i_2} S_{i_2,b_2,i_1}$.

2. Construct the following index set of fresh formal symbols as the top-level index set:
$$\mathcal{U} = Y^{\deg(\mathbf{y})} \prod_{i \in [n]} (X_{i,0} X_{i,1})^{\deg(x_i)} Z_i W_i \mathcal{S}_i$$

3. Run $(\mathsf{CM.pp}, \mathsf{CM.sp}, N_{\mathrm{ev}}, N_{\mathrm{chk}}) \leftarrow \mathsf{CM.Setup}(\mathcal{U}, 1^{d+\lambda}, 2)$, indicating a security parameter of $d + \lambda$ for the multilinear map, and a modulus that decomposes into two factors $N = N_{\mathrm{ev}} N_{\mathrm{chk}}$.

4. For each $i \in [n]$, generate uniformly random values $\alpha_i, \gamma_{i,0}, \gamma_{i,1} \leftarrow \mathbb{Z}^*_{N_{\mathrm{chk}}}$ and $\delta_{i,0}, \delta_{i,1} \leftarrow \mathbb{Z}^*_{N_{\mathrm{ev}}}$. For each $j \in [m]$, generate a uniformly random value $\beta_j \leftarrow \mathbb{Z}^*_{N_{\mathrm{chk}}}$.

5. Compute the check value $C^* = C(\alpha_1, \ldots, \alpha_n, \beta_1, \ldots, \beta_m) \in \mathbb{Z}_{N_{\mathrm{chk}}}$.

6. Using $\mathsf{CM.Encode}(\mathsf{CM.sp}, \cdot)$, for $i \in [n]$, $j \in [m]$, and $b \in \{0,1\}$, generate the following encoded ring elements (using the notation of Remark 2):

$$\hat{x}_{i,b} = [b, \alpha_i]_{X_{i,b}} \qquad \hat{u}_{i,b} = [1, 1]_{X_{i,b}} \qquad \hat{y}_j = [y_j, \beta_j]_Y \qquad \hat{v} = [1, 1]_Y$$

$$\hat{z}_{i,b} = [\delta_{i,b}, \gamma_{i,b}]_{X_{i,1-b}^{\deg(x_i)} Z_i W_i \mathsf{BitCommit}_{i,b}} \qquad \hat{w}_{i,b} = [0, \gamma_{i,b}]_{W_i \mathsf{BitCommit}_{i,b}}$$

$$\hat{C}^* = [0, \ C^*]_{Y^{\deg(\mathbf{y})} \prod_{i \in [n]} (X_{i,0} X_{i,1})^{\deg(x_i)} Z_i}$$

For $b_1, b_2 \in \{0,1\}$ and each $i_1, i_2 \in [n]$ such that $i_1 < i_2$, generate the following encoded ring elements (using the notation of Remark 2):

$$\hat{s}_{i_1,i_2,b_1,b_2} = [1, 1]_{\mathsf{BitFill}_{i_1,i_2,b_1,b_2}}$$

For notational convenience, for each $i_2 < i_1 \in [n]$, we also define $\hat{s}_{i_2,i_1,b_2,b_1} = \hat{s}_{i_1,i_2,b_1,b_2}$. We refer to the elements $\hat{u}_{i,b}, \hat{v}, \hat{s}_{i_1,i_2,b_1,b_2}$ as *unit encodings*, since they each encode $1 \in \mathbb{Z}_N$, and they are incorporated solely for their effect on the index sets.

7. Output the values above, along with the public parameters of the multilinear map:

$$\mathcal{O}(1^{\lambda}, C, \mathbf{y}) = \Big(\mathsf{CM.pp}, \ (\hat{x}_{i,b}, \hat{u}_{i,b}, \hat{z}_{i,b}, \hat{w}_{i,b})_{i,b}, \ (\hat{y}_j)_j, \ \hat{v}, \ \hat{C}^*,$$

$$(\hat{s}_{i_1, i_2, b_1, b_2})_{i_1 < i_2 \in [n], b_1, b_2} \Big)$$

To evaluate the obfuscated program $\tilde{C}_{\mathbf{y}} = \mathcal{O}(1^{\lambda}, C, \mathbf{y})$ on an input $\mathbf{x} = x_1 \cdots x_n \in \{0,1\}^n$, the evaluation procedure $\mathcal{O}.\mathsf{Eval}(\tilde{C}_{\mathbf{y}}, C, \mathbf{x})$ operates as follows.

<u>$\mathcal{O}.\mathsf{Eval}(\tilde{C}_{\mathbf{y}}, C, \mathbf{x})$:</u>

1. Using the procedures $\mathsf{CM.Add}(\mathsf{CM.pp}, \cdot, \cdot)$ and $\mathsf{CM.Mult}(\mathsf{CM.pp}, \cdot, \cdot)$, along with the unit encodings $(\hat{u}_{i,x_i}, \hat{v})$, evaluate the circuit C on the encoded inputs $\hat{x}_{1,x_1}, \ldots, \hat{x}_{n,x_n}, \hat{y}_1, \ldots, \hat{y}_m$. In other words, substitute the values $\hat{x}_{1,x_1}, \ldots, \hat{y}_m$ for the corresponding input wires $x_{1,x_1}, \ldots, y_m$; and, for each gate in the circuit, substitute one of the following operations:
   - For a multiplication gate, on operands $[a]_S, [b]_T$, output $\mathsf{CM.Mult}(\mathsf{CM.pp}, [a]_S, [b]_T) = [ab]_{ST}$.
   - For an addition gate, we cannot substitute an invocation of $\mathsf{CM.Add}$ (since the index sets of the encoded operands need not match), so instead we substitute the following procedure (Figure 1, box "$\mathcal{O}(+)$"). Suppose the input values to the addition gate are the encoded elements $[a]_S, [b]_T$ for index sets $S, T \subseteq \mathcal{U}$. Using $\mathsf{CM.Mult}$, multiply each term $[a]_S, [b]_T$ by the powers of unit encodings $(\hat{u}_{i,x_i}, \hat{v})$ that are minimally necessary to raise the index set to $S \cup T$ for both resulting elements. Then, using $\mathsf{CM.Add}$, output the sum of the two elements.

   We note that the result of this procedure, for each sub-circuit of C, will be an encoding whose index set consists of factors corresponding to each input variable $(X_{i,b}, Y$, resp., for $\hat{x}_{i,b}, \hat{y}_j)$, raised to the power of the degree of the given sub-circuit in those variables. Thus in particular, at the end of the evaluation, the final term will be encoded at the index set $Y^{\deg(\mathbf{y})} \prod_{i \in [n]} X_{i,x_i}^{\deg(x_i)}$. We denote this final term $\hat{C}$ as follows:

$$\hat{C} = [C(x_1, \ldots, x_n, y_1, \ldots, y_m), C(\alpha_1, \ldots, \alpha_n, \beta_1, \ldots, \beta_m)]_{Y^{\deg(\mathbf{y})} \prod_i X_{i,x_i}^{\deg(x_i)}}$$

   (We remark that while we present simple algorithms here for clarity, there are many natural optimizations; for details, we refer the reader to the full version [Zim14, §4].)

2. Using the procedures $\mathsf{CM.Add}, \mathsf{CM.Mult}$, compute the unit encoding $\hat{\sigma} = \prod_{i_1 < i_2 \in [n]} \hat{s}_{i_1, i_2, x_{i_1}, x_{i_2}}$, and compute the following encoded element:

$$z = \left(\hat{C} \prod_{i \in [n]} \hat{z}_{i,x_i} - \hat{C}^* \prod_{i \in [n]} \hat{w}_{i,x_i} \right) \cdot \hat{\sigma}$$

3. Run CM.ZeroTest(CM.pp, z). If it outputs "zero", output 0; if "nonzero", output 1.

The correctness of Construction 1 is straightforward from the definitions of the multilinear map operations, and we defer the proof to the full version [Zim14].

Succinctness. In Construction 1, we instantiate the multilinear map with a security parameter of $d + \lambda$, rather than λ. As detailed in the full version [Zim14], this term reflects the bound from the Schwartz-Zippel identity testing algorithm. This is somewhat unsatisfying, since it prevents us from constructing *succinct* obfuscation (Definition 2.10), and intuitively it does not seem necessary to prove security. Indeed, it turns out that if we assume the hardness of factoring, then we can eliminate the extra term, by using a *computational* analog of the Schwartz-Zippel lemma (generalizing an elegant result of Boneh and Lipton [BL96]). We defer the details of this modification and its proof to the full version [Zim14]; here we just state the modified ("succinct") version of the construction.

Construction 2 **[Virtual Black-Box Obfuscation (Succinct Version)]**
Proceed as in Construction 1, except in step 3, provide 1^λ as the security parameter to CM.Setup, rather than $1^{d+\lambda}$.

Remark 4 (Indistinguishability Obfuscation) Our main result shows that Construction 1 achieves VBB obfuscation in the generic model of composite-order multilinear maps. However, we note that if we only need the weaker notion of *indistinguishability obfuscation* [BGI+01], then we can obtain better parameters by eliminating some of the encodings; notably, we avoid the $O(n^2)$ cost of the straddling-set encodings. For continuity, we defer the details of this modification to the full version [Zim14, Appendix A].

3.1 Main Theorems

We now state our main theorems, which show that our construction achieves VBB obfuscation in a generic model of composite-order multilinear maps. For space reasons, we defer the proofs of the main theorems to the full version [Zim14].

Our construction can be based either on "noisy" or on "clean" multilinear maps. Since we operate on circuits directly, unlike previous approaches which first convert them to branching programs, there is no *inherent* reason that our construction cannot be applied directly to all polynomial-size circuits. Indeed, assuming "clean" maps, we are able to prove VBB obfuscation for P/poly (in the generic model) directly, without the additional assumption of FHE as in the work of Garg et al. [GGH+13b]. Moreover, under the additional assumption that factoring integers is hard on average, we are also able to show that our construction (in its *succinct* variant, Construction 2) achieves *succinct* VBB obfuscation (Definition 2.10) for P/poly.

Theorem 3.2. *Suppose that factoring is hard on average. Then Construction 2 achieves* succinct *virtual black-box obfuscation for P/poly in the generic model of* clean *composite-order multilinear maps.*

For completeness, we also prove the non-succinct version of Theorem 3.2, since there we do not assume the hardness of factoring.[11]

Theorem 3.3. *Construction 1 (composed with a universal circuit simulation) achieves virtual black-box obfuscation for P/poly in the generic model of* clean *composite-order multilinear maps.*

Of course, it is still unknown how one might construct "clean" multilinear maps, and thus we prove separately that we achieve obfuscation for NC^1 given only "noisy" maps. As usual, we are unable to construct obfuscation for poly-size circuits directly from "noisy" maps, since the noise growth still increases with the degree (which is potentially exponential in the circuit depth). Still, we note that our construction is somewhat more general than the theorem suggests: even with "noisy" maps, our construction also works for *arithmetic* circuits whose depth is superlogarithmic but whose degree remains polynomial.

Theorem 3.4. *Construction 1 (composed with a universal circuit simulation) achieves virtual black-box obfuscation for NC^1 in the generic model of* noisy *composite-order multilinear maps.*

In the "noisy" case, we do not prove the corresponding theorem for *succinct* obfuscation, since in our definition (and in all known instantiations), the representation size of a ring element in a "noisy" multilinear map grows with the degree of multilinearity required. However, we remark that the analogous theorem would hold in the case of "noisy" multilinear maps whose representation size was nevertheless independent of the noise bound—the existence of such maps is also unknown.

4   Performance Analysis

We now discuss the asymptotic efficiency of our main construction. We give only a very brief summary here; for more details, we encourage the reader to follow the exposition in the full version [Zim14, §4].

First, we establish the basic performance parameters. It turns out that the time to evaluate an obfuscated circuit is dominated by the "raising" operations for addition gates, in which we multiply elements by unit encodings in order to make the index sets match. This fact dictates the overall optimization strategy; in the full version [Zim14] we give the details of two approaches ("cross-multiplication" and "pre-mixing"), which reduce this evaluation cost with

---

[11] We remark that this distinction is nontrivial: as far as we know, the existence of composite-order multilinear maps does not necessitate the hardness of factoring, even though the concrete instantiation via the CLT scheme [CLT13] would be trivially broken if factoring were easy.

different tradeoffs. Using the "cross-multiplication" optimization, for a keyed arithmetic circuit $C : \{0,1\}^n \times \{0,1\}^m \to \{0,1\}$ of size s and depth d, we find that the multilinearity degree required is $O(2^d + n^2)$, the (keyed) obfuscation size is $O(m + n^2)$ ring elements, and the evaluation time is $O(s + n^2)$ ring operations.[12] In particular, the number of ring elements depends only on the secret part of the circuit, i.e., the key $\mathbf{y} \in \{0,1\}^m$. Moreover, excluding the $O(n^2)$ operations that arise from straddling sets, the number of ring operations is proportional to the circuit size—reflecting the fact that our evaluation algorithm follows C's structure directly.

We also specialize our performance analysis to standard settings (both keyed and unkeyed), to provide a more direct comparison with other known approaches. For instance, for balanced Boolean formulas (unkeyed NC^1 circuits of depth d, with input length n bits), the multilinearity degree is only $\Theta(2^d n + n^2)$, and we require only $\Theta(2^d n + n^2)$ ring elements and operations—as compared with the standard approach via Barrington's theorem [GGH+13b, BR14, BGK+14], for which all three metrics are $\Theta(4^d n + n^2)$; or the parameterized approach of [AGIS14, Gie01], for which the degree is $\Theta(2^{(1+\varepsilon)d} n + n^2)$ and the other two parameters are $\Theta(2^{(1+\varepsilon)d} 4^{2/\varepsilon} n + n^2)$.

More generally, since our new obfuscator's evaluation mirrors the structure of the original circuit, we find that our techniques expose a rich new design space of algorithms that can be *input* to the obfuscator. For example, to specialize our construction to Boolean formulas, we use an efficient oblivious stack [HS66, PF79, MZ14] to evaluate the formulas in postfix order, and we rely on the Fast Fourier Transform (FFT) to reduce the degree of the resulting computation (as detailed in the full version [Zim14]). We feel that these applications are only the beginning, and we hope that this work will encourage further study of obfuscating *specific*, keyed circuit families.

5   Conclusions and Open Problems

We have proposed a new way to obfuscate programs, using composite-order multilinear maps. Our construction operates directly on straight-line programs (arithmetic circuits), rather than converting them to matrix branching programs, and thereby achieves considerable improvements in efficiency, as well as exposing a rich new design space of oblivious algorithms to serve as input to the obfuscator. Our results also yield the first known obfuscator (for keyed circuit families)

---

[12] We present the cost here in terms of ring elements and ring operations. The concrete cost in bits and bit operations depends on the multilinear map (Section 2.8). For "clean" maps (whose existence is still open), the cost is just $\mathrm{poly}(\lambda)$. For "noisy" maps, the cost depends on the instantiation; e.g., for the CLT map [CLT13], the reader should multiply every obfuscation size and evaluation time by $O(\deg^{2+\varepsilon'}) \cdot \mathrm{poly}(\lambda)$, where deg is the multilinearity degree required, and ε' is a small constant determined by the choice of the Θ parameter in composite-order CLT [GLW14, App. B].

in which the number of ring elements depends only on the lengths of the input and of the secret key.

Our results in this work highlight a number of open problems for further study. For one, our construction relies on the fact that the multilinear map has (hidden) composite order, in order to implement encodings of direct products via the Chinese Remainder Theorem. It is natural to wonder whether this property can be emulated using standard prime-order multilinear maps [GGH13a], via composite-to-prime-order transformations. While such transformations are known in some settings [GLW14, HHH+14], we are not aware of any transformations for *asymmetric* multilinear maps, in which we use index sets from arbitrary subset lattices with multiplicity (Section 2.5). We leave this as an interesting open problem for future work.

Another compelling line of research concerns the security assumptions and the applicability of the generic model. As Brakerski and Rothblum observe [BR14], no multilinear map can possibly instantiate the generic model perfectly, since we are able to use the generic model to construct VBB obfuscation, which we know is impossible for general circuit families [BGI+01]. Moreover, our results in this work highlight the fact that there are simple concrete examples of differences between the generic model and its instantiation via the CLT scheme—for instance, in one optimization based on the Fast Fourier Transform (detailed in the full version [Zim14, §4]), our computation is valid for CLT encodings but cannot be implemented in the generic model. While this particular difference is fortuitous, we are led to consider whether there are other algebraic properties that hold in the CLT scheme—and may, in fact, be compatible with concrete security assumptions, such as that of [GLW14]—yet which may indicate fundamental weaknesses in the generic model as it is used here and in [GGH+13b, BR14, BGK+14]. On the positive side, it would also be useful to avoid relying on the generic model entirely, instead proving $i\mathcal{O}$ for our construction based on concrete, instance-independent assumptions [GLW14, GLSW14]. We leave this as another important problem for future work.

The central open problem: "clean" multilinear maps. This work eliminates a key obstacle to implementing obfuscation in practice. Since we no longer depend on converting circuits to branching programs, our construction is efficient enough that if "clean" multilinear maps were known, then general-purpose obfuscation could become implementable in practice. Our results demonstrate that the question of "clean" multilinear maps is not a technicality, but a fundamental open problem.

Acknowledgments. The author is grateful to Dan Boneh, Amit Sahai, and David J. Wu for many helpful comments and discussions. This work was supported by an NSF Graduate Research Fellowship, the DARPA PROCEED program, a grant from ONR, and an IARPA project provided via DoI/NBC. Opinions, findings and conclusions or recommendations expressed in this material are those of the author and do not necessarily reflect the views of DARPA or IARPA.

References

[AB15] Applebaum, B., Brakerski, Z.: Obfuscating circuits via composite-order graded encoding. Cryptology ePrint Archive, Report 2015/025 (2015). http://eprint.iacr.org/

[ABG+13] Ananth, P., Boneh, D., Garg, S., Sahai, A., Zhandry, M.: Differing-inputs obfuscation and applications. Cryptology ePrint Archive, Report 2013/689 (2013). http://eprint.iacr.org/

[AGIS14] Ananth, P., Gupta, D., Ishai, Y., Sahai, A.: Optimizing obfuscation: Avoiding Barrington's theorem (2014). http://eprint.iacr.org/

[BCP14] Boyle, E., Chung, K.-M., Pass, R.: On extractability obfuscation. In: Lindell, Y. (ed.) TCC 2014. LNCS, vol. 8349, pp. 52–73. Springer, Heidelberg (2014)

[BF01] Boneh, D., Franklin, M.: Identity-based encryption from the Weil pairing. In: Kilian, J. (ed.) CRYPTO 2001. LNCS, vol. 2139, pp. 213–229. Springer, Heidelberg (2001)

[BGI+01] Barak, B., Goldreich, O., Impagliazzo, R., Rudich, S., Sahai, A., Vadhan, S.P., Yang, K.: On the (Im)possibility of obfuscating programs. In: Kilian, J. (ed.) CRYPTO 2001. LNCS, vol. 2139, pp. 1–18. Springer, Heidelberg (2001)

[BGK+14] Barak, B., Garg, S., Kalai, Y.T., Paneth, O., Sahai, A.: Protecting obfuscation against algebraic attacks. In: Nguyen, P.Q., Oswald, E. (eds.) EUROCRYPT 2014. LNCS, vol. 8441, pp. 221–238. Springer, Heidelberg (2014)

[BGN05] Boneh, D., Goh, E.-J., Nissim, K.: Evaluating 2-DNF formulas on ciphertexts. In: Kilian, J. (ed.) TCC 2005. LNCS, vol. 3378, pp. 325–341. Springer, Heidelberg (2005)

[BL96] Boneh, D., Lipton, R.J.: Algorithms for black-box fields and their application to cryptography. In: Koblitz, N. (ed.) CRYPTO 1996. LNCS, vol. 1109, pp. 283–297. Springer, Heidelberg (1996)

[BR14] Brakerski, Z., Rothblum, G.N.: Virtual black-box obfuscation for all circuits via generic graded encoding. In: Lindell, Y. (ed.) TCC 2014. LNCS, vol. 8349, pp. 1–25. Springer, Heidelberg (2014)

[BS03] Boneh, D., Silverberg, A.: Applications of multilinear forms to cryptography. Contemporary Mathematics **324**(1) (2003)

[BSW11] Boneh, D., Sahai, A., Waters, B.: Functional encryption: definitions and challenges. In: Ishai, Y. (ed.) TCC 2011. LNCS, vol. 6597, pp. 253–273. Springer, Heidelberg (2011)

[BWZ14] Boneh, D., Wu, D.J., Zimmerman, J.: Immunizing multilinear maps against zeroizing attacks. Cryptology ePrint Archive, Report 2014/930 (2014). http://eprint.iacr.org/

[CGH98] Canetti, R., Goldreich, O., Halevi, S.: The random oracle methodology, revisited (preliminary version). In: STOC (1998)

[CHL+14] Cheon, J.H., Han, K., Lee, C., Ryu, H., Stehle, D.: Cryptanalysis of the multilinear map over the integers. Cryptology ePrint Archive, Report 2014/906 (2014). http://eprint.iacr.org/

[CLT13] Coron, J.-S., Lepoint, T., Tibouchi, M.: Practical multilinear maps over the integers. In: Canetti, R., Garay, J.A. (eds.) CRYPTO 2013, Part I. LNCS, vol. 8042, pp. 476–493. Springer, Heidelberg (2013)

[CLT14] Coron, J-S., Lepoint, T., Tibouchi, M.: Cryptanalysis of two candidate fixes of multilinear maps over the integers. Cryptology ePrint Archive, Report 2014/975 (2014). http://eprint.iacr.org/

[CV13] Canetti, R., Vaikuntanathan, V.: Obfuscating branching programs using black-box pseudo-free groups. Cryptology ePrint Archive, Report 2013/500 (2013). http://eprint.iacr.org/

[DH76] Diffie, W., Hellman, M.E.: Multiuser cryptographic techniques. In: AFIPS National Computer Conference (1976)

[GGG+14] Goldwasser, S., Gordon, S.D., Goyal, V., Jain, A., Katz, J., Liu, F.-H., Sahai, A., Shi, E., Zhou, H.-S.: Multi-input functional encryption. In: Nguyen, P.Q., Oswald, E. (eds.) EUROCRYPT 2014. LNCS, vol. 8441, pp. 578–602. Springer, Heidelberg (2014)

[GGH13a] Garg, S., Gentry, C., Halevi, S.: Candidate multilinear maps from ideal lattices. In: Johansson, T., Nguyen, P.Q. (eds.) EUROCRYPT 2013. LNCS, vol. 7881, pp. 1–17. Springer, Heidelberg (2013)

[GGH+13b] Garg, S., Gentry, C., Halevi, S., Raykova, M., Sahai, A., Waters, B.: Candidate indistinguishability obfuscation and functional encryption for all circuits. In: FOCS (2013)

[GGH14] Gentry, C., Gorbunov, S., Halevi, S.: Graded multilinear maps from lattices. Cryptology ePrint Archive, Report 2014/645 (2014). http://eprint.iacr.org/

[GGHZ14] Garg, S., Gentry, C., Halevi, S., Zhandry, M.: Fully secure attribute based encryption from multilinear maps. Cryptology ePrint Archive, Report 2014/622 (2014). http://eprint.iacr.org/

[GHMS14] Gentry, C., Halevi, S., Maji, H.K., Sahai, A.: Zeroizing without zeroes: Cryptanalyzing multilinear maps without encodings of zero. Cryptology ePrint Archive, Report 2014/929 (2014). http://eprint.iacr.org/

[Gie01] Giel, O.: Branching program size is almost linear in formula size. J. Comput. Syst. Sci. **63**(2) (2001)

[GLSW14] Gentry, C., Lewko, A.B., Sahai, A., Waters, B.: Indistinguishability obfuscation from the multilinear subgroup elimination assumption. Cryptology ePrint Archive, Report 2014/309 (2014). http://eprint.iacr.org/

[GLW14] Gentry, C., Lewko, A., Waters, B.: Witness encryption from instance independent assumptions. In: Garay, J.A., Gennaro, R. (eds.) CRYPTO 2014, Part I. LNCS, vol. 8616, pp. 426–443. Springer, Heidelberg (2014)

[HHH+14] Herold, G., Hesse, J., Hofheinz, D., Ráfols, C., Rupp, A.: Polynomial spaces: a new framework for composite-to-prime-order transformations. In: Garay, J.A., Gennaro, R. (eds.) CRYPTO 2014, Part I. LNCS, vol. 8616, pp. 261–279. Springer, Heidelberg (2014)

[HS66] Hennie, F.C., Stearns, R.E.: Two-tape simulation of multitape Turing machines. J. ACM **13**(4) (1966)

[Jou00] Joux, A.: A one round protocol for tripartite Diffie-Hellman. In: ANTS, ANTS-IV, Springer-Verlag, London, UK (2000)

[Kil88] Kilian, J.: Founding cryptography on oblivious transfer. In: STOC (1988)

[Mil04] Miller, V.S.: The Weil pairing, and its efficient calculation. Journal of Cryptology **17**(4) (2004)

[MOV93] Menezes, A., Okamoto, T., Vanstone, S.A.: Reducing elliptic curve logarithms to logarithms in a finite field. IEEE Transactions on Information Theory **39**(5) (1993)

[MZ14] John, C.: Mitchell and Joe Zimmerman. Data-oblivious data structures. In: STACS (2014)

[O'N10] O'Neill, A.: Definitional issues in functional encryption. Cryptology ePrint Archive, Report 2010/556 (2010). http://eprint.iacr.org/

[PF79]   Pippenger, N., Fischer, M.J.: Relations among complexity measures. J. ACM **26**(2) (1979)

[PST14] Pass, R., Seth, K., Telang, S.: Indistinguishability obfuscation from semantically-secure multilinear encodings. In: Garay, J.A., Gennaro, R. (eds.) CRYPTO 2014, Part I. LNCS, vol. 8616, pp. 500–517. Springer, Heidelberg (2014)

[Sho97] Shoup, V.: Lower bounds for discrete logarithms and related problems. In: Fumy, W. (ed.) EUROCRYPT 1997. LNCS, vol. 1233, pp. 256–266. Springer, Heidelberg (1997)

[SW14]   Sahai, A., Waters, B.: How to use indistinguishability obfuscation: deniable encryption, and more. In: STOC (2014)

[SZ14]   Sahai, A., Zhandry, M.: Obfuscating low-rank matrix branching programs. Cryptology ePrint Archive, Report 2014/773 (2014). http://eprint.iacr.org/

[Zim14] Zimmerman, J.: How to obfuscate programs directly. Cryptology ePrint Archive, Report 2014/776 (2014). http://eprint.iacr.org/

End-to-End Verifiable Elections
in the Standard Model

Aggelos Kiayias$^{(\boxtimes)}$, Thomas Zacharias, and Bingsheng Zhang

Department of Informatics and Telecommunications, National and Kapodistrian
University of Athens, Athens, Greece
{aggelos,bzhang,thzacharias}@di.uoa.gr

Abstract. We present the cryptographic implementation of "DEMOS",
a new e-voting system that is *end-to-end verifiable* in the standard model,
i.e., without any additional "setup" assumption or access to a random
oracle (RO). Previously known end-to-end verifiable e-voting systems
required such additional assumptions (specifically, either the existence
of a "randomness beacon" or were only shown secure in the RO model).
In order to analyze our scheme, we also provide a modeling of end-to-
end verifiability as well as privacy and receipt-freeness that encompasses
previous definitions in the form of two concise attack games.

Our scheme satisfies end-to-end verifiability *information theoretically*
in the standard model and privacy/receipt-freeness under a computational assumption (subexponential Decisional Diffie Helman). In our construction, we utilize a number of techniques used for the first time in the
context of e-voting schemes that include utilizing randomness from bit-
fixing sources, zero-knowledge proofs with imperfect verifier randomness
and complexity leveraging.

1 Introduction

In an end-to-end (E2E) verifiable election system, voters have the ability to
verify that their vote was properly cast, recorded and tallied into the election
result. Intuitively, the security property that an E2E verifiable election intends
to capture is the ability of the voters to detect a malicious *election authority* that
tries to misrepresent the election outcome. E2E verifiability is a strong level of
security for election systems that has been widely accepted as a fundamental
requirement for their adoption, see e.g., [38].

In more details, E2E verifiability mandates that the voter can obtain a receipt
at the end of the ballot casting procedure that can allow her to verify that her
vote was (i) cast as intended, (ii) recorded as cast, and (iii) tallied as recorded.
Furthermore, any external third party should be able to verify that the election

A. Kiayias—Research was supported by ERC project CODAMODA.
A. Kiayias, T. Zacharias and B. Zhang—Research was supported by project FINER,
Greek Secretariat of Research and Technology funded under action "ARISTEIA 1."

E. Oswald and M. Fischlin (Eds.): EUROCRYPT 2015, Part II, LNCS 9057, pp. 468–498, 2015.
DOI: 10.1007/978-3-662-46803-6_16

procedure is executed properly. In fact, it is imperative that the receipts in an E2E system are delegatable i.e., the voter may delegate the task of verifiability to any interested third party, for instance an international organization of the voters' choosing that aggregates the task of verification. This requirement, as well as the fact that it should be infeasible for the voter to use her receipt as a proof of the way she voted (this is necessary to deter vote-selling/buying), make the design of end-to-end verifiable systems a challenging problem.

All known e-voting systems that offer E2E verifiability provide it under some setup assumption or in the random oracle (RO) model. Notably, E2E verifiability can be *argued* (note that it is never formally proven before) for Helios [1] in the RO model while for Remotegrity[1] [43] in the model where a trusted party (a "randomness beacon") provides a stream of unbiased and unpredictable random coins. More general approaches for defining auditable multiparty computation (MPC) have recently been proposed [3] and also rely on a setup assumption such as a CRS.

A critical shortcoming of using setup assumptions for establishing E2E verifiability in e-voting is the fact that the voters will be required to make a "leap of faith" and accept the setup assumption in order to accept the election result. This can be an unfortunate state of affairs: since the election authority (EA) cannot unequivocally convince the voters that the election is correct, then the election outcome can be always subject to dispute.

Our Results. Motivated by the above, we design a new e-voting system that we can prove E2E verifiable *information theoretically* in the standard model, i.e., without any setup assumption except the existence of a bulletin board (BB) which provides a consistent view of the election transcript. Our result is further strengthened by the fact that we make the absolute minimal assumptions on the computation capabilities of the voters: voters are merely modeled as finite state *transducers* and thus are incapable of performing any cryptographic operation during ballot-casting (note the auditing stage after the election would require the capability of cryptographic operations but they can be performed at any time, in the post-election stage).

To accomodate the analysis of our system we provide a model for E2E verifiability and voter privacy/receipt-freeness. Our model for E2E verifiability is inspired from input-indistinguishable computation of Micali, Pass and Rosen [35] since in their setting they are also faced with proving security for multiparty computation in the standard model (note however they do not deal with E2E verifiability/auditability in their setting). In our modeling, the election system involves three types of entities, the voters $V_1, \ldots, V_n$, the election authority (EA), and the bulletin board (BB) whose only role is to provide storage for the election transcript for the purpose of verification. Voters submit their votes by engaging in the ballot casting protocol to the EA and they are not allowed to

---

[1] Note that Remotegrity itself is only a "front-end" type of system. It will be E2E verifiable if combined with Scantegrity-II [14] as suggested by the authors of the paper.

interact with each other. Our definition of end-to-end verifiability considers a very powerful adversary that is computationally unbounded and *completely* controls the EA. On the other hand, BB is completely passive and is only writeable by the EA and readable by anyone. The definition is satisfied, if and only if the adversary is incapable of evading being detected when it manipulates the election result as long as a number of voters perform the verifiability procedure honestly. Voter privacy on the other hand, considers an adversary that has full access to all the the voters' receipts, views of the ballot casting protocol as well as it may control of a number of malicious voters. For any election tally, the adversary should be incapable of distinguishing the way honest voters vote.

Our construction cherry picks ideas put forth in previous works, specifically, code-voting and double ballots from [12,13], but also introduces a number of novel elements that enable us to prove E2E verifiability in the standard model. In order to achieve verifiability, our system utilizes a novel ZK proof for candidate encoding correctness and collects coins from the voters to form the challenge (specifically, a single random coin per voter). Given that the majority of voters cannot be assumed to be properly following the protocol, the sequence of voter contributed randomness is a particularly "weak source" that cannot be used for arguing the integrity of the election in a direct way — as we argue it is a very weak source akin to adaptive bit-fixing sources [34]. We then show (i) how it is possible to perform our ZK proof with a verifier that has imperfect randomness (just a min-entropy source), (ii) how to produce a (sufficiently long) sequence of min-entropy challenge from the random bits contributed by the voters. The tools that are important in our construction include a generalization of the Schwartz-Zippel lemma [41,44] for imperfect randomness and a suitable strategy for dividing the coins of the voters so that the entropy is not lost due to the adversarial strategy of the EA (who also controls a number of voters). Using these techniques we design a novel ZK protocol and we prove unconditionally end-to-end verifiability for our scheme. For voter privacy, we utilize complexity leveraging to construct a simulator that is capable of reducing a voter privacy attack to a subexponential DDH distinguisher and hence our system offers privacy and receipt-freeness under a computational assumption.

In summary, our e-voting system is the first construction achieving the properties E2E verifiability and voter privacy/receipt-freeness in the standard model. Furthermore, we prove E2E verifiability information theoretically assuming the voters are computationally restricted transducers that hence are incapable of performing any cryptographic operation during ballot casting. The only assumptions we make are subexponential Decisional Diffie Hellman assumption (for voter privacy/receipt-freeness) and a consistent bulletin board board. We remark that a consistent bulletin board can be easily seen to be a tight condition since without it, it is easy to verify that E2E verifiability of the election cannot be achieved: by controlling the BB, an adversarial EA can distribute voters to their own separate "islands" where within each one the voters will have their own verifiable view of an election result that can be - in reality - completely skewed. Implementing a consistent bulletin board is beyond our scope, however we note that it can be achieved in the standard model using Byzantine agrement (BA) (for BA, see e.g., [24]) by assuming secure channels between any pair of parties. In fact, recently, it is shown that one can achieve BA efficiently even without secure channels in a completely anonymous setting [25] hence removing the requirement for pairwise secure channels (but note that this latter work relies on proofs of work modeled in the RO model).

Why Previously Known Techniques Do Not Work. To motivate further our approach it is worth-while to emphasize in which way previous works fail to attain end-to-end verifiability in the standard model. Helios, culminates a long line of previous schemes that employ homomorphic type of voting [17,21] and utilizes the Benaloh challenge [5] as the fundamental mechanism to attain verifiability. Helios by design requires the voter to utilize a voter supporting device to prepare a ciphertext and after an indeterminate number of trials, the voter will cast the produced ciphertext. Such ciphertexts are to be homomorphically tallied and thus they should be accompanied by a proof of proper computation. While such proofs are easy to construct based on e.g., [19], they can only be argued interactively (which is insufficient in our setting since a corrupt EA together with a corrupt voter may cook up a malformed proof that is indistinguishable from a proper one) or using a NIZK [10]. This latter approach is taken in Helios where a RO-based NIZK is utilized. In case the RO is dropped in favor of a standard model NIZK, security would be impossible in our model as NIZK's require a common reference string (CRS) and this is unavailable in the standard model; if the CRS is setup by the EA then in case it is malicious it will know and exploit the trapdoor; on the other hand, the voters are not interacting with each other and hence cannot setup the CRS by employing an MPC protocol. It follows that obtaining E2E verifiability in the standard model is impossible to overcome for Helios or any other similar scheme. On the other hand, in the case of Remotegrity/Scantegrity n coins need to be obtained from the randomness beacon in order to prove the result correct. It is easy to verify that the system is insecure in terms of end-to-end verifiability in case the randomness beacon is biased. As before, the only parties active are the EA and the voters who cannot implement a randomness beacon that is required in the construction. In light of the above our construction offers a new paradigm in e-voting design: the randomness for the verification of the election can be collected distributively from the voters. Given that such randomness is by nature very weak (humans are very bad "randomness generators" and even worse malicious voters may collaborate with the election authority to cancel the honest voters' random bits) we show how suitable cryptographic techniques that deal with imperfect randomness can be employed to prove security.

Distributing the Election Authority. In our security model, we consider the EA as a single entity that is malicious in the verifiability game and honest in the privacy game. In practice one may want to distribute the EA to a number of "trustees" that collectively implement the EA functionality to improve the resiliency of the privacy property. While this is not a prime focus of our work (which centers on verifiability), it is feasible to design an efficient threshold protocol for implementing the EA. Note that our notion of voter privacy and receipt freeness can be easily extended to allow corrupted sub-authorities.

Other Required Properties of Election Systems. Our work by no means solves the complete set of desired requirements that are needed in an election system. Our voter-privacy definition implies receipt-freeness, i.e., provided that the voter receives the voter secret-key over an untappable channel[2], the voter cannot convince any third party about the way she voted. Nevertheless, this does not imply coercion resistance as the voter may still be forced to divulge the voter secret prior to her ballot-casting (this does not violate voter privacy - it just prevents the voter from actually using the system and enables the adversary to vote on the voter's behalf). There are techniques that can be used to increase coercion resistance for internet-voting (e.g., those of [16,28] and others) and they are compatible with our construction. We leave the integration of these techniques with information theoretic E2E verifiability for future work. Similarly, usability aspects are not within our current scope; nevertheless, we stress that we have implemented our scheme for 1-out-of-m elections and we have used it in real-world experiments[3].

Related Work. In [11], Chaum suggested for the first time that anonymous communication can lead to voting systems with *individual verifiability*, i.e., the voters can verify that their votes were counted correctly. In [40], Sako and Killian introduce explicitly the notion of *universal verifiability*, that is, the ability for anyone to verify that the election result derives from the cast votes. Universal verifiability is also defined by Juels, Catalano and Jakobsson in [28] in the computational model assuming a trusted setup. Kremer, Ryan and Smyth [30] introduced symbolic definitions for individual and universal verifiability in the context of applied pi calculus. A formal definition of universal verifiability is also provided by Chevallier-Mames et al. in [15].

End-to-end verifiability in the sense of cast-as-intended, recorded-as-cast, tallied-as-recorded was an outcome of the works of Chaum [13] and Neff [37]. The novelty was the generation of receipts that could be used for simple voter verification while achieving privacy. The term of E2E verifiability (more precisely, E2E integrity) also appeared in [18]. Marneffe, Pereira and Quisquater presented an ideal-world definition for election systems in [22] without explicitly considering verifiability as a property of the ideal world. In [38], Popoveniuc et al. proposed a definition of E2E verifiability via a list of properties.

Küsters, Truderung and Vogt [31] introduced symbolic and computational definitions of verifiability parameterized by a goal and an adversarial environment. In [33], the same authors showed that individual verifiability and universal

---

[2] An untappable channel enables the voter to deny the information that was transmitted in it. Physically distributing voter's secrets or using non-committing encryption [4] achieves untappability.

[3] For more information check our web-site http://www.demos-voting.org

verifiability are not sufficient to guarantee the "global" verifiability of an e-voting system. A number of other e-voting systems in the cryptographic setting that do not explicitly deal with E2E verifiability include [7,17,20,21].

Benaloh and Fischer [17] provided a computational definition of privacy as the property that any coalition of malicious voters cannot distinguish between any two vote assignments coming from a subset of honest voters that have the same partial tally. Receipt-freeness has been first studied by Benaloh and Tuinstra [6] and described as the property of an e-voting system to generate fake voter transcripts that are indistinguishable from genuine transcripts. Following this logic, in our voter privacy/receipt-freenes definition, we require simulation-based indistiguishability of the views of the voters when they engage in the ballot-casting stage. Chevallier-Mames et al. [15] introduced definitions for unconditional of privacy and receipt-freeness and showed incompatibility results of universal verifiability with each of these two properties.

Formal definitions for privacy and receipt-freeness have been proposed in the context of applied pi calculus [23] and the universal composability model [26,36]. Küsters, Truderung and Vogt [32], mention that simulation-based definitions are often too strong to show security for reasonable e-voting systems, due to their "yes or no" nature (the real and ideal setting are either indistinguishable or not). In [33], they measure the level of privacy of an e-voting system w.r.t. to the observation power the adversary has in a protocol run, via a definition which is close to the Dolev-Yao model.

In [8], Bernhard et al. proposed a game-based notion of ballot privacy and study the privacy of Helios. In their model, an adversary that chooses a fixed vote E, cannot distinguish a bulletin board that contains ballots for real votes from a bulletin board that contains ballots for E. Their definition was extended by Bernhard, Pereira and Warinschi [9] by allowing the adversary to statically corrupt election authorities. Both these definitions, although they imply a strong inditinguishability property, do not consider receipt-freeness. We note that our game-based definition captures both privacy and receipt-freeness while restricted to a single EA (and it can easily be extended by including a set of trustees that the adversary may corrupt).

As we have mentioned previously, modelling coercion resistance is out of the scope of this work. We refer the reader to [23,28,32,42] for formal definitions of coercion resistance in the cryptographic, symbolic and universal composability model.

Organization. In Section 2, we introduce the syntax and define the correctness, E2E verifibiality and voter privacy/receipt freeness of an e-voting system. In Section 3, we present at length the construction of our e-voting system, including a detailed description of all tools that are applied. In Section 4, we prove the E2E verifibiality and voter privacy/receipt freeness of our e-voting system in the security framework of Section 2.

2   E-voting Systems

2.1   Preliminaries

We use λ as the security parameter. Associated with an e-voting system, we also consider two other parameters, the number of voters n and number of candidates m which are both thought as polynomial functions of λ. Let Π be an e-voting system, where $\mathcal{P} = \{P_1, ..., P_m\}$ is the set of candidates and $\mathcal{V} = \{V_1, ..., V_n\}$ is the set of voters. We denote by $\mathcal{U} \subseteq 2^{\mathcal{P}}$ the collection of subsets of candidates that the voters are allowed to choose to vote for (which may include a "blank" option too). The candidate selection $\mathcal{U}_\ell$ of voter V_ℓ is an element in $\mathcal{U}$.

Let $\mathcal{P}^*$ be the set of vectors of candidate selections of arbitrary length. Let f be the *election evaluation function* from $\mathcal{P}^*$ to the set $\mathbb{Z}_+^m$ so that $f(\mathcal{U}_1, \ldots, \mathcal{U}_n)$ is equal to an m-vector whose i-th location is equal to the number of times P_i was chosen in the candidate selections $\mathcal{U}_1, \ldots, \mathcal{U}_n$.

The entities involved in an e-voting system Π, are the voters $V_1, \ldots, V_\ell$, the *election authority (EA)* and the *Bulletin Board (BB)*.

2.2   Syntax and Correctness

An e-voting system Π is a quintuple of algorithms and protocols $\langle$**Setup, Cast, Tally, Result, Verify**$\rangle$ specified as follows:

- The algorithm **Setup**$(1^\lambda, \mathcal{P}, \mathcal{V}, \mathcal{U})$ is executed by the EA and generates a master secret key msk, Π's public parameters Pub (which include $\mathcal{P}, \mathcal{V}, \mathcal{U}$) and the voters' secrets $s_1, \ldots, s_n$. EA has a state, st which is initialized as msk. In addition, it posts an initial public transcript $\tau = $ Pub on the BB.
- The interactive protocol **Cast** is between three parties, the voter V_ℓ, the BB and the EA. V_ℓ has input (Pub, $s_\ell, \mathcal{U}_\ell$), EA has input msk and BB has input τ. EA updates its state st and BB updates the public transcript τ. Upon successful termination, the voter V_ℓ receives a receipt α_ℓ. We denote by $view_\ell$ the view of the voter V_ℓ in the protocol **Cast**.
- The interactive protocol **Tally** with common input Pub is executed by the EA and the BB on inputs msk, τ respectively. Upon successful termination, the BB updates the public transcript τ.
- The algorithm **Result**(τ) outputs the result R_τ for the election or returns $\bot$ in case such result is undefined.
- The algorithm **Verify**(τ, α) outputs a value in $\{0, 1\}$, where α is a voter receipt (that corresponds to the voter's output from the **Cast** protocol).

Remark. In many election systems, the EA is implemented by more than a single authority. This means that **Setup** might be a protocol executed by those parties (as opposed to a standalone algorithm). However, from the point of view of E2E verifiability (where the system is considered malicious as a whole) this is completely immaterial. Hence, for simplicity in the syntax above we consider EA a single entity. In our construction the EA may also be distributed. We defer the details for how this may be done to the full version of the paper.

Definition 1 (Correctness). *The e-voting system Π has (perfect) correctness, if for any honest execution of Π that results in a public transcript τ where the voters $V_1, \ldots, V_n$ cast votes for options $\mathcal{U}_1, \ldots, \mathcal{U}_n$ and received receipts $\alpha_1, \ldots, \alpha_n$, it holds that*

$$\mathbf{Result}(\tau) = f(\mathcal{U}_1, \ldots, \mathcal{U}_n) \text{ and } \wedge_{\ell=1}^{n} (\mathbf{Verify}(\tau, \alpha_\ell) = 1).$$

2.3 E2E Verifiability

In order to define E2E verifiability formally, we introduce a suitable notation; given that candidate selections are elements of a set of m choices, we may encode them as m-bit strings, where the bit in the i-th position is 1 if and only if candidate P_i is selected. Further, we may aggregate the election results as the list with the number of votes each candidate has received, thus the output of the **Result** algorithm is a vector in $\mathbb{Z}_+^m$. In this case, a result is feasible if and only if the sum of all its coordinates is no greater than the number of voters.

In our formalization of the E2E verifiability, we postulate the existence of a *vote extractor* algorithm $\mathcal{E}$ (not necessarily running in polynomial-time) that explains the election transcript: namely, it receives input of the form (τ, A) where τ is an election transcript and $A = \{\alpha_\ell\}_{\ell \in \tilde{\mathcal{V}}}$ is a set of **Cast** protocol receipts. By $\tilde{\mathcal{V}}$, we denote the set of honest voters that voted successfully. Given such input, $\mathcal{E}$ will compute $n - |\tilde{\mathcal{V}}|$ vectors $\langle \mathcal{U}_\ell \rangle_{V_\ell \in \mathcal{V} \setminus \tilde{\mathcal{V}}}$ in $\{0,1\}^m$ (which correspond to the choices of all the voters outside of $\tilde{\mathcal{V}}$) that can be either a candidate selection if the voter has voted adversarially or a zero vector if the voter has not voted successfully; $\mathcal{E}$ returns the symbol $\bot$ in case such values cannot be defined. In the special case where all voters are honest and have voted successfully (i.e., $\tilde{\mathcal{V}} = \mathcal{V}$), $\mathcal{E}$ returns no value (outputs the empty set). The purpose of the $\mathcal{E}$ algorithm will be to capture the setting when the election transcript τ contains (in potentially encoded form) a set of well-formed actual votes.

Using the above notion, we will be capable to express the actual result encoded in an election transcript. Next, we want to formally express a measure of *deviation* from the actual election result (as such deviation is the objective of the adversary in an E2E verifiability attack). Some preliminary notions will be needed. In order to express formally the deviation the adversary aims at, it is natural to equip the space of results with a *metric*. We use the metric derived by the 1-norm, $\| \cdot \|_1$ scaled to half, i.e., $d_1 : \mathbb{Z}_+^m \times \mathbb{Z}_+^m \longrightarrow \mathbb{R}$ with $d_1(w, w') = \frac{1}{2} \cdot \|w - w'\|_1 = \frac{1}{2} \cdot \sum_{i=1}^{n} |w_i - w_i'|$ where w_i, w_i' is the i-th coordinate of w, w' respectively.

Consider $R \in \mathbb{Z}_+^m$ be the election results that correspond to the true voter intent of n voters, and $R' \in \mathbb{Z}_+^m$ be the published election results. Denote by $\max(\mathcal{U})$, the maximum cardinality of an element in $\mathcal{U}$. Two encodings of candidate selections are within $\max(\mathcal{U})$ distance, so intuitively, if the adversary wants to present R' as the result of the election, it may do that by manipulating the votes of at least $d_1(R, R')/\max(\mathcal{U})$ voters.

We define next the E2E Verifiability game, $G_{\text{E2E-Int}}^{\mathcal{A},\mathcal{E},d,\theta}$, between the adversary $\mathcal{A}$ and a challenger $\mathcal{C}$ using a voter extractor $\mathcal{E}$, that takes as input the security parameter, λ, the number of candidates, m and the number of voters, n.

Overview of the game $G_{\text{E2E-Ver}}^{\mathcal{A},\mathcal{E},d,\theta}(1^\lambda, m, n)$. The attack game is parameterized by d, which is the deviation amount (according to the metric $d_1(\cdot,\cdot)$) that the adversary wants to achieve and θ, the minimum number of voters that $\mathcal{A}$ must allow to vote honestly and terminate successfully. The adversary starts by selecting the voter and candidate identities for given parameters n, m. It also determines the allowed ways to vote as described by the set $\mathcal{U}$. The adversary fully controls the EA. The adversary manages the **Cast** protocol executions where it assumes the role of the EA. For each voter, the adversary may choose to corrupt it or to allow the challenger to play on its behalf. In the second case, the adversary provides the candidate selection that the honest voter will use in the **Cast** protocol. The adversary completes the execution of EA which results to the complete election transcript published in the BB. The adversary will win the game provided that all θ honest voters that completed the **Cast** protocol successfully will also audit the result successfully but the deviation of the tally is at least d; the adversary will also win in case the extractor fails to produce the candidate selection of the dishonest voters (but θ honest voters still verify correctly). The attack game is specified in detail in Figure 1.

Definition 2 (E2E-Verifiability). *Let $0 < \epsilon < 1$ and $n, m, d, \theta \in \mathbb{N}$ with $d > 0$ and $0 < \theta \leq n$. The election protocol Π w.r.t. the election function f achieves E2E verifiability with error ϵ, for a number of at least θ honest successful voters and tally deviation d if there exists a (not necessarily polynomial-time) vote-extractor $\mathcal{E}$ such that for any adversary $\mathcal{A}$:*

$$\Pr[G_{\text{E2E-Ver}}^{\mathcal{A},\mathcal{E},d,\theta}(1^\lambda, m, n) = 1] \leq \epsilon.$$

In plain words, Definition 2 suggests that an E2E verifiable e-voting system, provides an "official explanation" of adversarial votes via the vote extractor $\mathcal{E}$, such that if at least θ voters verify the result, then any adversary that attempts to manipulate the election tally (that includes the honest votes and the official explanation of the adversarial votes) by a shift of d votes will get caught except from some (supposedly small) probability ϵ.

Remark. In the only previous works [31,33] where end-to-end verifiability was considered at a "global level" as we do here, it was expressed with respect to a set of "good" runs γ of the e-voting protocol in the sense that a judge could test whether the protocol operated within the set γ. Even though sufficiently expressive, this formulation has the disadvantage that the set γ remains undetermined and thus the level of verifiability that is offered by the definition hinges on the proper definition of γ which may not be simple. Using our language the notion of a good run becomes explicit: a run of the e-voting protocol is good provided that the extractor $\mathcal{E}$ produces votes for the malicious voters which if they are

---

$E2E$ *Verifiability Game* $G_{\text{E2E}-\text{Ver}}^{\mathcal{A},\mathcal{E},d,\theta}(1^\lambda, m, n)$

1. $\mathcal{A}$ chooses a list of candidates $\mathcal{P} = \{P_1, ..., P_m\}$, a set of voters $\mathcal{V} = \{V_1, ..., V_n\}$ and the set of allowed candidate selections $\mathcal{U}$. It provides $\mathcal{C}$ with the sets $\mathcal{P}, \mathcal{V}, \mathcal{U}$ along with information Pub and voter credentials $\{s_\ell\}_{\ell \in [n]}$. Throughout the game, $\mathcal{C}$ plays the role of the BB.
2. The adversary $\mathcal{A}$ and the challenger $\mathcal{C}$ engages in an interaction where $\mathcal{A}$ schedules the **Cast** protocols of all voters. For each voter V_ℓ, $\mathcal{A}$ can either completely control the voter or allow $\mathcal{C}$ to operate on their behalf, in which case $\mathcal{A}$ provides a candidate selection $\mathcal{U}_\ell$ to $\mathcal{C}$. Then, $\mathcal{C}$ engages with the adversary $\mathcal{A}$ in the **Cast** protocol so that $\mathcal{A}$ plays the role of EA. Provided the protocol terminates successfully, $\mathcal{C}$ obtains the receipt α_ℓ on behalf of V_ℓ.

    Let $\tilde{\mathcal{V}}$ be the set of honest voters (i.e., those controlled by $\mathcal{C}$) that terminated successfully.
3. Finally, $\mathcal{A}$ posts the election transcript τ to the BB.

The game returns a bit which is 1 if and only if the following conditions hold true:

(i). $|\tilde{\mathcal{V}}| \geq \theta$, (i.e., at least θ honest voters terminated).
(ii). $\forall \ell \in [n]$: if $V_\ell \in \tilde{\mathcal{V}}$, then $\textbf{Verify}(\tau, \alpha_\ell) = 1$ (i.e., the voters in $\tilde{\mathcal{V}}$ verify their ballot successfully).

and either one of the following two conditions:

(iii-a). If $\perp \neq \langle \mathcal{U}_\ell \rangle_{V_\ell \in \mathcal{V} \setminus \tilde{\mathcal{V}}} \leftarrow \mathcal{E}(\tau, \{\alpha_\ell\}_{V_\ell \in \tilde{\mathcal{V}}})$,
then
$$d_1(\textbf{Result}(\tau), f(\langle \mathcal{U}_1, ..., \mathcal{U}_n \rangle)) \geq d.$$

(iii-b). $\perp \leftarrow \mathcal{E}(\tau, \{\alpha_\ell\}_{V_\ell \in \tilde{\mathcal{V}}})$.

Fig. 1. The E2E Verifiability Game between the challenger $\mathcal{C}$ and the adversary $\mathcal{A}$ using the vote extractor $\mathcal{E}$

added to the votes of the honest voters they produce a result that does not deviate from the published result according to the $d_1(\cdot, \cdot)$ metric. Note that our vote extractor may require super-polynomial time (in the same way that the set of good runs γ may have a membership test of super-polynomial complexity). We remark that the use of a super-polynomial extractor to define properly the inputs of the malicious participants and hence the soundness of a multiparty protocol is not novel to our work. For example see, Micali, Pass and Rosen [35] where they used a similar construct to prove security of their general multiparty computation protocol.

2.4   Voter Privacy (including Receipt-Freeness)

The definition of voter privacy concerns the actions that may be taken by the adversary to break the privacy and learn some information about the candidate selections of the honest voters. We specify the goal of the adversary in a very general way. In particular, for an attack against voter privacy to succeed, we ask that there is an election result, for which the adversary is capable of distinguishing how the honest voters voted while it has access to (i) the actual receipts that the voters obtained after ballot-casting as well as (ii) a set of protocol views that are consistent with all the honest voters' views in the **Cast** protocol instances they participated (and the adversary has observed).

Observe that any system that is secure against such an attack scenario would possess also "receipt-freeness", i.e., voters cannot prove how they voted by showing the receipt they obtain from the **Cast** protocol or even presenting their view in the **Cast** protocol. Given that in the privacy definition we allow the adversary to observe the view of the voter in the **Cast** protocol, we need to allow the voter to be able to "lie" about her view in this protocol (otherwise an attack could be trivially mounted). Note that this would require the voter input to the **Cast** protocol to be delivered via an untappable channel; in particular, the adversary should not have any side-channel information about the voter's secrets $s_1, \ldots, s_n$.

We formally define the voter privacy of an election via a *Voter Privacy/Receipt-freeness* game, denoted by $G_{t\text{-priv}}^{\mathcal{A},\mathcal{S}}$, that is played between an adversary $\mathcal{A}$ and a challenger $\mathcal{C}$, that takes as input the security parameter, λ, the number of voters, n, and the number of candidates, m, as described in Figure 2 and returns 1 or 0 depending on whether the adversary wins. An important feature of the game is the existence of an efficient "voter simulator" $\mathcal{S}$ that provides a simulated view of the voter in the **Cast** protocol. Intuitively, this simulator captures the way the voter can lie about her candidate selection in the **Cast** protocol in case she is coerced to present her view after she completes the ballot-casting procedure.

Overview of the Game $G_{t\text{-priv}}^{\mathcal{A},\mathcal{S}}(1^\lambda, n, m)$**.** The adversary starts by selecting the voters and candidates for given parameters n, m. It also determines the allowed ways to vote. The challenger flips a coin b (that will change its behavior during the course of the game) and will perform the **Setup** protocol. Subsequently, the adversary will schedule all **Cast** protocols selecting which voters it prefers to corrupt and which ones it prefers to allow to vote honestly. The adversary is allowed to corrupt at most t voters. The voters that remain uncorrupted are operated by the challenger and they are given two candidate selections to choose. The challenger will select which of the two candidate selections the voter will use in the **Cast** protocol according to the bit b. The adversary will also receive the receipt that is obtained by each voter as well as either the actual view of each voter during the **Cast** protocol, if $b = 0$, or a *simulated* view, if $b = 1$ (this addresses the receipt-freeness aspect). Upon completion of ballot-casting, the challenger executes the **Tally** protocol and posts the election result. Subsequently the adversary will attempt to guess b. The attack is successful provided that the adversary has corrupted up to t voters, the election tally is the same with respect to the two alternatives provided for each honest voter by the adversary and the adversary manages to guess the challenger's bit b. The game is presented in more detail in figure 2.

Voter Privacy/Receipt-freeness Game $G_{t\text{-priv}}^{\mathcal{A},\mathcal{S}}(1^\lambda, n, m)$

1. $\mathcal{A}$ on input $1^\lambda, n, m$, chooses a list of candidates $\mathcal{P} = \{P_1, ..., P_m\}$, a set of voters $\mathcal{V} = \{V_1, ..., V_n\}$, and the set of allowed candidate selections $\mathcal{U}$. It provides $\mathcal{C}$ the sets $\mathcal{P}$, $\mathcal{V}$, and $\mathcal{U}$.
2. $\mathcal{C}$ flips a coin $b \in \{0,1\}$ and performs the **Setup** protocol on input $(1^\lambda, \mathcal{P}, \mathcal{V}, \mathcal{U})$ to obtain $msk, s_1, \ldots, s_n, \text{Pub}$; it provides $\mathcal{A}$ with Pub.
3. The adversary $\mathcal{A}$ and the challenger $\mathcal{C}$ engage in an interaction where $\mathcal{A}$ schedules the **Cast** protocols of all voters which may run concurrently. For each voter $V_\ell \in \mathcal{V}$, the adversary chooses whether V_ℓ is corrupted:
   - If V_ℓ is corrupted, then $\mathcal{C}$ provides s_ℓ to $\mathcal{A}$, and then they engage in a **Cast** protocol where $\mathcal{A}$ plays the role of V_ℓ and $\mathcal{C}$ plays the role of EA and BB.
   - If V_ℓ is not corrupted, $\mathcal{A}$ provides two candidate selections $\langle \mathcal{U}_\ell^0, \mathcal{U}_\ell^1 \rangle$ to the challenger $\mathcal{C}$. $\mathcal{C}$ operates on V_ℓ's behalf, using $\mathcal{U}_\ell^b$ as the V_ℓ's input. The adversary $\mathcal{A}$ is allowed to observe the network trace of the **Cast** protocol where $\mathcal{C}$ plays the roles of V_ℓ, EA, and BB. When the **Cast** protocol terminates, the challenger $\mathcal{C}$ provides to $\mathcal{A}$: (i) the receipt α_ℓ that V_ℓ obtains from the protocol, and (ii) if $b = 0$, the current view of the internal state of the voter V_ℓ, $view_\ell$, that the challenger obtains from the **Cast** execution, or if $b = 1$, a simulated view of the internal state of V_ℓ produced by $\mathcal{S}(view_\ell)$.
4. $\mathcal{C}$ performs the **Tally** protocol playing the role of EA and BB. $\mathcal{A}$ is allowed to observe the network trace of that protocol.
5. Finally, $\mathcal{A}$ using all information collected above (including the contents of the BB) outputs a bit b^*.

Denote the set of corrupted voters as $\mathcal{V}_{\text{corr}}$ and the set of honest voters as $\tilde{\mathcal{V}} = \mathcal{V} \setminus \mathcal{V}_{\text{corr}}$. The game returns a bit which is 1 if and only if the following hold true:

(i). $b = b^*$ (i.e., the adversary guesses b correctly).
(ii). $|\mathcal{V}_{\text{corr}}| \leq t$ (i.e., the number of corrupted voters is bounded by t).
(iii). $f(\langle \mathcal{U}_\ell^0 \rangle_{V_\ell \in \tilde{\mathcal{V}}}) = f(\langle \mathcal{U}_\ell^1 \rangle_{V_\ell \in \tilde{\mathcal{V}}})$ (i.e., the election result w.r.t. the set of voters $\tilde{\mathcal{V}}$ does not leak b).

Fig. 2. The Voter-privacy/Receipt-freeness game

Definition 3 (Voter Privacy/Receipt-Freeness). *Let $n, m \in \mathbb{N}$. The e-voting system Π w.r.t. the election function f achieves voter privacy/receipt-freeness for at most t corrupted voters, if there is a PPT voter simulator $\mathcal{S}$ such that for any PPT adversary $\mathcal{A}$:*

$$\left| \Pr[G_{t\text{-priv}}^{\mathcal{A},\mathcal{S}}(1^\lambda, n, m) = 1] - 1/2 \right| = \mathsf{negl}(\lambda).$$

3   Presentation of Our e-Voting System

Our system has three stages, setup, ballot-casting and tallying, that parallel the operation of a Σ protocol. During setup stage, the EA produces a series of commitments and pre-audit data that correspond to a first move of a Σ protocol that will establish the validity of the commitments. During ballot-casting, voters engage with the EA in a protocol that will result in the recording of their votes, as well as in the submission of a random coin flip that will be used to produce the challenge for the Σ protocol. Voters will receive a receipt as their local output from the ballot-casting protocol that can be used for auditing the election result. In the third and final stage, the EA produces the tally of the election and completes the Σ protocol by publishing openings to commitments as well as other necessary information needed for verification. The verification step can take place at any time after the completion of the process using a collection of at least one receipt from the ballot-casting stage.

In our system, the voter implementation during the ballot-casting stage is expressed as a probabilistic transducer (see e.g., [27]) with a communication tape that has a number of states polynomial in the number of candidates m (and independent to other parameters such as n, λ). Given that such a machine is severely limited in the computational sense, in order to achieve ballot casting we utilize a code-voting approach (cf. [12]): the EA corresponds vote-codes to commitments posted in the BB, and voters cast their vote by simply sending to the EA the vote-code that they prefer. The commitments have an additive homomorphic property, hence it is possible to tally the result by homomorphically processing them and opening the resulting "tally commitment". The proof that we use in order to ensure verifiability is a conjunction of a cut-and-choose proof with a Σ proof that a committed value belongs to a set. The challenge needed for the Σ proof will be extracted by applying a suitable extraction mechanism to the coin flips of the voter transducers that are collected by the EA.

In Sections 3.1, 3.2, 3.3 and 3.4, we provide a detailed description of the tools that we apply for the construction of our system, i.e., (i) the homomorphic commitment scheme, (ii) a generalization of the Schwartz-Zippel lemma for imperfect randomness, (iii) the Σ protocol and (iv) the challenge extraction mechanism, respectively. We describe our e-voting system in Section 3.5 and prove its correctness in Section 3.6. For the better understanding of our system, we provide a toy example in Section 3.7.

3.1   Perfectly Binding Commitment

To achieve integrity against computationally unbounded adversaries, we have to use a perfectly binding commitment scheme. Moreover, our system requires such a commitment scheme to be additively homomorphic to facilitate the tally and audit process. In this work, we instantiate the commitment scheme with lifted ElGamal over elliptic curves. We use elliptic curve domain parameters $\mathsf{Param} := (p, a, b, g, q)$, generated by the curve generator $\mathcal{G}(1^\lambda)$, consisting of a prime p that specify the finite field $\mathbb{F}_p$, two elements $a, b \in \mathbb{F}_p$ that specify an elliptic curve $E(\mathbb{F}_p)$ defined by the equation: $E : y^2 = x^3 + ax + b \pmod{p}$, a base point $g = (x_g, y_g)$ on $E(\mathbb{F}_p)$, and a prime q which is the order of g. We denote the cyclic group generated by g as $\mathbb{G}$, and it is assumed that the DDH assumption holds over $\mathbb{G}$. More specifically, our commitment scheme consists of the following algorithms:

- Gen(Param, 1^λ): picks $x \leftarrow \mathbb{Z}_q$, sets $h := g^x$, and outputs ck $:= (\mathsf{Param}, h)$.
- $\mathsf{Com}_{\mathsf{ck}}(m; r)$: outputs $c := (g^r, g^m h^r)$.
- $\mathsf{Ver}_{\mathsf{ck}}(c; m; r)$: outputs accept if $c = (g^r, g^m h^r)$; otherwise, outputs reject.

It is obvious that the above commitment scheme is perfectly binding and computationally hiding under the DDH assumption, i.e. for any PPT adversary $\mathcal{A}$, we have that the advantage

$$\mathsf{Adv}_{\mathsf{hide}}(\mathcal{A}) := \left| \Pr \begin{bmatrix} \mathsf{Param} \leftarrow \mathcal{G}(1^\lambda); \mathsf{ck} \leftarrow \mathbb{Z}_q : \mathcal{A}(\mathsf{Param}, \mathsf{ck}); b \leftarrow \{0,1\}; \\ r \leftarrow \mathbb{Z}_q : \mathcal{A}(\mathsf{Com}_{\mathsf{ck}}(m_b; r)) = b \end{bmatrix} - 1/2 \right|$$

is negligible in λ. The commitment scheme is additively homomorphic. Namely,

$$\mathsf{Com}_{\mathsf{ck}}(m_1; r_1) \cdot \mathsf{Com}_{\mathsf{ck}}(m_2; r_2) = \mathsf{Com}_{\mathsf{ck}}(m_1 + m_2; r_1 + r_2).$$

3.2 Schwartz-Zippel (min-entropy variant)

We need a min-entropy variant of the Schwartz-Zippel lemma, to check the equality of two univariate polynomials f_1, f_2, i.e. test $f_1(x) - f_2(x) = 0$ for random $x \xleftarrow{D} \mathbb{Z}_q$. The probability that the test passes is at most $\frac{\max(d_1, d_2)}{2^\kappa}$ if $f_1 \neq f_2$, where d_i is the degree of f_i for $i \in \{1, 2\}$. We state the following lemma without proof (a proof will be provided in the full version).

Lemma 1 (min-entropy Schwartz-Zippel). *Let $f(x)$ be a non-zero univariate polynomial of degree d over $\mathbb{Z}_q$. Let D be a probability distribution on $\mathbb{Z}_q$ such that $H_\infty(D) \geq \kappa$. The probability of $f(x) = 0$ for a randomly chosen $x \xleftarrow{D} \mathbb{Z}_q$ is at most $\frac{d}{2^\kappa}$.*

3.3 A Σ Protocol for Candidate Encoding Correctness

In order to present the Σ protocol with clarity, we outline some necessary excerpts of the description of our system that will be explained in detail in Section 3.5.

Let $N = n+1$, where n is the number of voters. Each voter is given a ballot that consists of two equivalent parts that contain a list of m vote-codes corresponding to the list candidates $\{P_1, \ldots, P_m\}$. The voter will flip a coin to choose the part she is going to use for voting. At the **Setup** phase, each ballot is posted to the BB in committed form. Namely, it consists of two sets of commitments $E_{\ell, j}^{(a)}$ for $a \in \{0, 1\}, \ell = 1, \ldots, n, j = 1, \ldots, m$, and each set commits to a permutation of the encoded candidates, where candidate P_j is encoded as N^{j-1}.

We emphasize that it is not necessary to prove that each set of the commitments commits to a permutation of the encoded candidates $\{N^0, \ldots, N^{m-1}\}$ in an

1-out-of-m election. This is due to two facts: (i) EA will open one of the two sets of commitments according to the corresponding voter's coin a_ℓ (the set that corresponds to the unused ballot part); therefore, a malicious EA will be caught with probability $1/2$ by each honest voter if any of the committed sets is not a permutation of the encoded candidates or is an inconsistent permutation of the encoded candidates w.r.t. the one on the voter's ballot. (ii) Even if we ensure that the set of the commitments commits to a permutation of the encoded candidates, it does not imply that the permutation is consistent to the one on the voter's ballot. In an 1-out-of-m election, only one of the commitments will be used for tally, and thus proving that the set of the commitments commits to an unknown permutation of the encoded candidates can only provide the guarantee that the tallied commitment commits to an encoded candidate. Note that this guarantee is important; otherwise, given that we perform homomorphic tallying, it may be feasible for a cheating EA to introduce a large deviation to the actual tally result via a single inconsistent ballot; for instance, EA may commit to for some $j \in [m]$. Hence, we want the EA to show that each commitment commits to one of N^{j-1} for $j \in [m]$. [4] We can formalize the correctness of a single commitment problem as follows. Given commitments E, the prover wants to convince the verifier that he knows $r \in \mathbb{Z}_q$ such that $E = \mathsf{Com}_{\mathsf{ck}}(N^i; r)$ and $i \in [0, m-1]$. Let i, r be the prover's private input, and w.l.o.g. we assume m is a perfect power of 2. For general cases, say $2^{e-1} \geq m \geq 2^e$, we can show the conjunction $i \in [0, 2^e] \wedge (i + 2^e - m) \in [0, 2^e]$. Our Σ Protocol is described in Fig. 3.

Theorem 1. *Let $N > 0$ be a public integer. Given common input $E \in \mathbb{G} \times \mathbb{G}$, the protocol described in Fig. 3 is a Σ protocol for knowledge of $i \in \mathbb{N}, r \in \mathbb{Z}_q$ such that $E = \mathsf{Com}_{\mathsf{ck}}(N^i; r)$, $i \in [0, m-1]$ that is perfectly complete, statistically sound with soundness error $2^{-\kappa+1+\log\log m}$ when the verifier's challenge has min-entropy κ and computationally zero-knowledge with distinguishing advantage $\mathsf{Adv}_{\mathsf{zk}}(\mathcal{A}) \leq \log m \cdot \mathsf{Adv}_{\mathsf{hide}}(\mathcal{A})$ for any PPT adversary $\mathcal{A}$.*

Proof. It is straightforward to check that protocol in Fig. 3 achieves perfect completeness.

In terms of statistical soundness, the protocol verifies two facts. Namely, (i) $\{B_j\}_{j \in [0, \log m - 1]}$ commits to either 0 or 1, and (ii) E commits to $N^{\sum_{j=0}^{\log m - 1} b_j 2^j} = N^i$, where b_j is the opening of B_j. To check the first fact, for each committed b_j the protocol builds the degree 1 polynomial

$$g_1(X) = (1 - b_j)(b_j X + t) + c_0 = (1 - b_j)b_j X + c_0'$$

for some c_0 and c_0'. By min-entropy Schwartz-Zippel Lemma 1, if $H_\infty(\rho) \geq \kappa$ and $g_1(\rho) = 0$, the probability $\Pr[(1 - b_j)b_j \neq 0] \leq 2^{-\kappa}$. Hence, with at least

---

[4] For efficiency, EA is only required to show the commitments that are used for tally commit to valid encoded candidates. On the other hand, since EA cannot predicate which commitments are going to be used for tally before the election, she has to prepare all the Σ protocols in the **Setup** phase; whereas she is only required to complete those Σ protocols for the commitment that will be tallied in the **Tally** phase.

$P(i, r)$:

    Define b_j such that $i = \sum_{j=0}^{\log m-1} b_j 2^j$. Pick

    – $t_j, z_j, y_j, r_j, w_j, f_j \leftarrow \mathbb{Z}_q$ for $j \in [0, \log m - 1]$.

    Compute the following commitments:

    – For $j \in [0, \log m - 1]$,

        • $B_j = \mathsf{Com}_{\mathsf{ck}}(b_j; r_j)$; $T_j = \mathsf{Com}_{\mathsf{ck}}(t_j; z_j)$;

        • $Y_j = \mathsf{Com}_{\mathsf{ck}}((1 - b_j)t_j; y_j)$;

        • $W_j = \mathsf{Com}_{\mathsf{ck}}(w_j; f_j)$.

    Define A_j, a_j, r'_j such that $A_j = B_j^{N^{2^j}-1} \cdot \mathsf{Com}_{\mathsf{ck}}(1; 0) = \mathsf{Com}_{\mathsf{ck}}(a_j; r'_j)$, for $j \in$

    $[0, \log m-1]$. Define $\{\beta_j, \gamma_j\}_{j=0}^{\log m}$ such that $\prod_{j=0}^{\log m-1}(a_j X + w_j) = \sum_{j=0}^{\log m} \beta_j X^j$

    and $\prod_{j=0}^{\log m-1}(r'_j X + f_j) = \sum_{j=0}^{\log m} \gamma_j X^j$. (Note that for efficiency reasons, the

    prover needs to choose the $\{r_j\}_{j=0}^{\log m-1}$ such that $\gamma_{\log m} = r$ in previous step.)

    – For $j \in [0, \log m - 1]$, $D_j = \mathsf{Com}_{\mathsf{ck}}(\beta_j; \gamma_j)$.

> Return $\phi_1 = \{B_j, T_j, Y_j, W_j, D_j\}_{j=0}^{\log m-1}$ and
>
> $\mathrm{state}_\phi = \{t_j, z_j, y_j, r_j, b_j, w_j, f_j\}_{j=0}^{\log m-1}$.

$P \to V$: Send ϕ_1.

$V \to P$: | Send $\rho \leftarrow \mathbb{Z}_q$. |

$P(\mathrm{state}_\phi)$: Compute the following answers:

    – For $j \in [0, \log m - 1]$,

        • $t'_j = b_j \rho + t_j, z'_j = r_j \rho + z_j, y'_j = -y_j - r_j t'_j$;

        • $w'_j = a_j \rho + w_j, f'_j = r'_j \rho + f_j$;

> Set $\phi_2 = \{t'_j, z'_j, y'_j, w'_j, f'_j\}_{j=0}^{\log m-1}$.

$P \to V$: send ϕ_2

$V(E, \phi_1, \rho, \phi_2)$: Accept the proof (i.e. output accept) if and only if

    – For $j \in [0, \log m - 1]$,

        • $B_j^\rho \cdot T_j = \mathsf{Com}_{\mathsf{ck}}(t'_j, z'_j)$,

        • $(\mathsf{Com}_{\mathsf{ck}}(1; 0)/B_j)^{t'_j}/Y_j = \mathsf{Com}_{\mathsf{ck}}(0; y'_j)$;

        • $A_j^\rho \cdot W_j = \mathsf{Com}_{\mathsf{ck}}(w'_j, f'_j)$;

    – $E^{\rho^{\log m}} \prod_{j=0}^{\log m-1} D_j^{\rho^j} = \mathsf{Com}_{\mathsf{ck}}(\prod_{j=0}^{\log m-1} w'_j; \prod_{j=0}^{\log m-1} f'_j)$;

Fig. 3. The Σ Protocol for Ballot Correctness

$1 - 2^{-\kappa}$ probability $(1 - b_j)b_j = 0$, which implies $b_j \in \{0, 1\}$. To check the second fact, the protocol first computes $A_j = B_j^{N^{2^j}-1} \cdot \mathsf{Com}_{\mathsf{ck}}(1; 0)$ homomorphically. Let a_j be the opening of A_j. It is easy to see that $a_j = N^{2^j}$ if $b_j = 1$, $a_j = 1$ if $b_j = 0$, thus it holds that $a_j = b_j N^{2^j} + 1 - b_j = N^{b_j 2^j}$. So that the protocol just needs to verify that E commits to the product of a_j's. The verifier checks equality between two degree $\log m$ polynomials

$$g_2(X) = \prod_{j=0}^{\log m-1}(a_j X + w_j) = \sum_{j=0}^{\log m} \beta_j X^j \text{ and } g'_2(X) = u X^{\log m} + \sum_{j=0}^{\log m-1} \beta_j^* X^j$$

where u is the opening of E and β_j^* which is the opening of D_j and is provided by the (potentially malicious) prover. By min-entropy Schwartz-Zippel lemma, if $H_\infty(\rho) \geq \kappa$ and $g_2(\rho) = g_2'(\rho)$, the probability $\Pr[u = \beta_{\log m}] \geq 1 - \frac{\log m}{2^\kappa}$. Hence, we have $u = N^{\sum_{j=0}^{\log m - 1} b_j 2^j}$ with at least $1 - \frac{\log m}{2^\kappa}$ probability conditioned on the fact (i). Given that all $b_0, \ldots, b_{\log m - 1}$ need to be shown in $\{0, 1\}$ the entire proof is statistically sound with probability $(1 - 2^{-\kappa})^{\log m}(1 - \frac{\log m}{2^\kappa}) \geq 1 - \log m \cdot 2^{-\kappa+1}$.

Our protocol satisfies special soundness, i.e. there exists an extractor that can extract $i \in \mathbb{N}, r \in \mathbb{Z}_q$ if the prover is able to complete the protocol twice with the same ϕ_1 but two distinct challenges (we omit the construction of the extractor).

To show special honest verifier zero-knowledge property, we now construct a simulator that on input $\hat{\rho} \in \mathbb{Z}_q$ can output a transcript that is indistinguishable from the real one. The simulator randomly picks $b_0, \ldots, b_{\log m - 1} \leftarrow \{0, 1\}$ and generates $\{t_j, z_j, y_j, r_j, B_j, T_j, Y_j, t_j', z_j', y_j', w_j, f_j, W_j, w_j', f_j'\}_{j=0}^{\log m - 1}$ according to the protocol description. It then generates $\{D_j\}_{j=1}^{\log m - 1}$ according to the protocol and set

$$D_0 = \mathsf{Com}_{\mathsf{ck}}\left(\prod_{j=0}^{\log m - 1} w_j'; \prod_{j=0}^{\log m - 1} f_j' \right) / \left(E^{\hat{\rho}^{\log m}} \prod_{j=1}^{\log m - 1} D_j^{\hat{\rho}^j} \right) .$$

Subsequentely, the simulator sets $\hat{\phi}_1 = \{B_j, T_j, Y_j, W_j, D_j\}_{j=0}^{\log m - 1}$ and $\hat{\phi}_2 = \{t_j', z_j', y_j', w_j', f_j'\}_{j=0}^{\log m - 1}$, and it outputs $(\hat{\phi}_1, \hat{\rho}, \hat{\phi}_2)$. First of all, it is obvious that all the verification equations hold. Secondly, the distribution of all the variables in $\hat{\phi}_2$ are uniformly random, which is identical to that of a real transcript. Moreover, if the adversary can distinguish the simulated $\hat{\phi}_1$ from that of a real transcript, she must be able to distinguish at least one of the fake $\{B_j\}_{j=0}^{\log m - 1}$. By hybrid argument, we have for any PPT adversary $\mathcal{A}$, the advantage to distinguish the simulated proof is $\mathsf{Adv}_{\mathsf{zk}}(\mathcal{A}) \leq \log m \cdot \mathsf{Adv}_{\mathsf{hide}}(\mathcal{A})$. $\square$

3.4   Producing the Verifier's Challenges

The main difficulty in our setting is that we would like to extract the challenge of the Σ protocol from the voters' coins $\boldsymbol{a} = \langle a_1, \ldots, a_n \rangle \in \{0, 1\}^n$ using a deterministic algorithm. Recall that some of the voters might be malicious and colluding with the EA, so the entropy of the voters' coins is only contributed by the honest voters while the malicious voters' coins can depend on the honest ones. Note that the voters' coins should be ordered by their serial numbers, rather than their submission order. This is because in the latter case, the adversary can schedule the **Cast** protocols of all voters at will and as a result reduce the min-entropy of $\boldsymbol{a}$ to be at most $\log \theta$ where θ is the number of honest voters. Such level of entropy is insufficient to provide a sufficiently small verifiability error (that ideally drops exponentially with θ). For all the uncast ballots, we set their corresponding coins to 0 by default; therefore, $\boldsymbol{a}$ is always an n-bit source, regardless of the number of voters that complete the **Cast** protocol. We observe that the voters' coins $\boldsymbol{a}$ is a weaker source compared to a *non-oblivious bit-fixing source* [29], as the adversary is able to choose which bit(s) to fix during the coin flipping (source generation) process. On the other hand, if we restrict the adversary $\mathcal{A}$ in our verifiability game from being capable of scheduling **Cast** protocols freely and all voters have to submit their votes sequentially according to a pre-determined order in the ballot casting stage, the source $\boldsymbol{a}$ can be viewed as an *adaptive bit-fixing source* [34]; in such case, we can employ the deterministic extractor construction framework from [29] which applies a deterministic low influence function on segments of the source. The majority function is proven to be an optimal low influence function thus in this way we obtain a deterministic extractor that generates the challenge. However, this adversarial setting is not realistic in practice as ballot casting might be scheduled adversarially. Nevertheless, we emphasise that even using a non-oblivious bit-fixing source, Kamp and Zuckerman showed that at most n/ℓ bits can be extracted when ℓ out of n bits are fixed [29]. This result implies that if a deterministic extractor is used to generate $\Theta(\lambda)$ random bits, then this will restrict the percentage of corrupted voters to be below $\Theta(\frac{1}{\lambda})$ which might also be not a realistic expectation in practice. An alternative approach may use a condenser as opposed to an extractor. Randomized condensers with a small/constant seed space have been put forth see e.g. [2,39]; using such a tool one may iterate over all possible seeds and thus be assured that one of the seeds will allow the condenser to produce a sufficiently random challenge. For instance, Barak *et al.* [2] proposed a basic 2-bit seed condenser $\mathsf{con} : \{0,1\}^n \rightarrow (\{0,1\}^{n/3})^4$ such that for every δ-source X with $0 < \delta < 0.9$, at least one of the 4 output blocks of $\mathsf{con}(X)$ is a $(\delta + \Omega(\delta^2))$-source. Based on the composing lemma (Lemma 5.5 [2]), we can iteratively apply the condenser to achieve any desired constant rate. Given a c-coin condenser $\mathsf{Con} : \{0,1\}^n \mapsto (\{0,1\}^\ell)^c$, in order to produce a good challenge, by definition, it should hold that $c \cdot \ell > n$, which means that the condenser will produce c blocks, one of which is guaranteed to be sufficiently random. However as we observe below, we can utilize ZK amplification to obtain essentially the same result as with a c-coin condenser while sacrificing very little entropy from the weak source. We explain our technique next.

Let $\{0,1\}^{\ell_\Sigma}$ be the challenge space, where $\ell_\Sigma = \lfloor \log q \rfloor$ and q is the order of the underlying group used in the Σ protocol. Assume $n/k \le \ell_\Sigma$ for some $k \in \mathbb{Z}^+$. We evenly partition the voters' coins $\boldsymbol{a}$ into k blocks, denoted by $\boldsymbol{a}_1, \ldots, \boldsymbol{a}_k$. For each block $\boldsymbol{a}_i$, the EA should prove the correctness of the ballots using a separate Σ protocol with $\boldsymbol{a}_i$ as its challenge. The verifier only accepts the EA's proof if *all* the Σ protocols are valid. The theorem below shows that the soundness error of this k-times repeated Σ protocol drops exponentially with $\theta - k(\log \log m + 1)$.

Theorem 2. *Denote* $a = (a_1, \ldots, a_k)$, *and suppose* $H_\infty(a) = \theta$. *For all adversarial prover* $\mathcal{A}$, *we have that*

$$\epsilon(m, n, k, \theta) = \Pr \begin{bmatrix} \mathsf{ck} \leftarrow \mathsf{Gen}(\mathsf{Param}, 1^\lambda); (E, x, r, \{\phi_{1,i}\}_{i=1}^k) \leftarrow \mathcal{A}(\mathsf{Param}, \mathsf{ck}); \\ \{\phi_{2,i}\}_{i=1}^k \leftarrow \mathcal{A}(a_1, \ldots, a_k) : \mathsf{Ver}_{\mathsf{ck}}(E; x; r) = \mathsf{accept} \ \wedge \\ x \notin \{N^0, \ldots, N^{m-1}\} \ \wedge \ \forall i \in [k], V(E, \phi_{1,i}, a_i, \phi_{2,i}) = \mathsf{accept} \end{bmatrix}$$
$$\leq 2^{k \log \log m - \theta + k}.$$

Proof. See full version of this paper.   □

3.5   Description of our e-Voting System

The description of our e-voting system follows the syntax in Section 2.2. For simplicity, we present our system for *1-out-of-m elections*, i.e. $\mathcal{U} = \{\{P_1\}, \ldots, \{P_m\}\}$. The commitment scheme and the Σ-protocol that are applied in our system, are the ones presented at length in sections 3.1 and 3.3 respectively.

Setup$(1^\lambda, \mathcal{P} = \{P_1, \ldots, P_m\}, \mathcal{V} = \{V_1, \ldots, V_n\}, \mathcal{U} = \{\{P_1\}, \ldots, \{P_m\}\})$. Let (Gen, Com, Ver) be the PPT algorithms that constitute the perfectly binding, computationally hiding and additively homomorphic commitment scheme presented in Section 3.1. The EA runs Gen(Param, 1^λ) to generate the commitment key ck. Then, for $\ell \in [n]$, EA executes the following steps:

(i). It selects a unique label for the ℓ-th double ballot denoted by tag_ℓ.

(ii). It selects random permutations $\pi_\ell^{(0)}, \pi_\ell^{(1)}$ over $[m]$. The use of $\pi_\ell^{(0)}$ (reps. $\pi_\ell^{(1)}$) is to shuffle the order that the (vote-code, candidate) pairs in the part $s_\ell^{(0)}$ (resp. $s_\ell^{(1)}$) of the *double ballot* s_ℓ will be posted on the BB (in committed form), in order to support privacy.

(iii). For $j \in [m]$, it selects unique vote-codes $C_{\ell,j}^{(0)}, C_{\ell,j}^{(1)} \leftarrow \mathbb{Z}_q$, where q is the size of the group of the commitment scheme[5]. The vote-code $C_{\ell,j}^{(0)}$ (resp. $C_{\ell,j}^{(1)}$) is the one that will be associated with candidate P_j in part $s_\ell^{(0)}$ (resp. $s_\ell^{(1)}$) of s_ℓ.

(iv). For $a \in \{0, 1\}$, it prepares the ballot part $s_\ell^{(a)} = \left\{ \left(P_j, C_{\ell,j}^{(a)} \right) \right\}_{j \in [m]}$ and generates the ballot

$$\boxed{s_\ell = \left(\mathsf{tag}_\ell, s_\ell^{(0)}, s_\ell^{(1)} \right).}$$

(v). For $j \in [m]$, it computes $j' = \pi_\ell^{(a)}(j)$ and

---

[5] For simplicity in presentation, we commit to the vote-codes using the homomorphic commitment scheme of Section 3.1. We stress that since no arithmetic operations are executed in the vote-code commitments, we could use more efficient commitment schemes and in this case vote-codes may be drawn from a domain that is smaller than $\mathbb{Z}_q$ resulting in a more "user-friendly" interface.

- For $a \in \{0,1\}$ (where a indicates the part $s_\ell^{(a)}$ of s_ℓ), it chooses randomness $t_{\ell,j'}^{(a)} \leftarrow \mathbb{Z}_q$ and computes the *vote-code commitment* for $C_{\ell,j'}^{(a)}$:

$$\boxed{U_{\ell,j'}^{(a)} = \mathsf{Com}_{\mathsf{ck}}\left(C_{\ell,j'}^{(a)}; t_{\ell,j'}^{(a)}\right).}$$

- For $a \in \{0,1\}$, it chooses randomness $r_{\ell,j'}^{(a)} \leftarrow \mathbb{Z}_q$ and computes the *encoded candidate commitment* for $P_{j'}$:

$$\boxed{E_{\ell,j'}^{(a)} = \mathsf{Com}_{\mathsf{ck}}\left((n+1)^{j'-1}; r_{\ell,j'}^{(a)}\right),}$$

where $(n+1)^{j'-1}$ is the *encoding* of candidate $P_{j'}$. This encoding is selected to ensure the correctness of our system, as we show in Theorem 3.

- For $a \in \{0,1\}$, EA prepares *pre-audit data* $\phi_{1,\ell,j'}^{(a)}$ to be used for verifying that $E_{\ell,j'}^{(a)}$ is a commitment to a valid encoding from the set $\{(n+1)^0, \ldots, (n+1)^{m-1}\}$ at the verification phase. In addition, it maintains *prover state* $\mathsf{state}_{\phi,\ell,j'}^{(a)}$. Both $\phi_{1,\ell,j'}^{(a)}$ and $\mathsf{state}_{\phi,\ell,j'}^{(a)}$ are described in the Σ-protocol shown in Figure 3 (first move) of Section 3.3.

(vi). $\mathsf{Pub}_\ell = \left(\mathsf{tag}_\ell, \left\{(U_{\ell,j'}^{(a)}, E_{\ell,j'}^{(a)}, \phi_{1,\ell,j'}^{(a)})\right\}_{j\in[m]}^{a\in\{0,1\}}\right)$ is the public information w.r.t. s_ℓ. It is indexed by tag_ℓ and contains the ballot information for both parts in committed form, as well as the respective pre-audit data. The information that refers to the (vote-code, candidate) pair $(C_{\ell,j'}^{(a)}, P_{j'})$ is tabulated in the j-th location of the part that is associated with $s_\ell^{(a)}$.

The public information that EA generates is

$$\boxed{\mathsf{Pub} = (\mathsf{ck}, \mathcal{P}, \mathcal{U}, \{\mathsf{Pub}_\ell\}_{\ell\in[n]}).}$$

The secret key of EA is

$$\boxed{msk = \{\mathsf{Pub}_\ell, s_\ell, msk_\ell, \mathsf{state}_{\phi,\ell}\}_{\ell\in[n]},}$$

where we denote $msk_\ell = \left\{(C_{\ell,j}^{(a)}, t_{\ell,j}^{(a)}, \pi_\ell^{(a)}(j) = j', r_{\ell,j}^{(a)})\right\}_{j\in[m]}^{a\in\{0,1\}}$ and $\mathsf{state}_{\phi,\ell} = \left\{\mathsf{state}_{\phi,\ell,j'}^{(a)}\right\}_{j\in[m]}^{a\in\{0,1\}}$.

The **Cast** *protocol.* On input $(\mathsf{Pub}, s_\ell, \mathcal{U}_\ell)$, voter V_ℓ flips a coin $a_\ell \leftarrow \{0,1\}$ and picks part $s_\ell^{(a_\ell)}$ to vote and part $s_\ell^{(a_\ell)}$ for audit. Let P_{j_ℓ} be the candidate that V_ℓ is going to vote for, i.e., $\mathcal{U}_\ell = \{P_{j_\ell}\}$. Then, V_ℓ selects to submit $C_{\ell,j}^{(a_\ell)}$, which is the vote-code that corresponds to P_{j_ℓ} in part $s_\ell^{(a_\ell)}$. Next, V_ℓ casts the vote $\psi_\ell = \left(\mathsf{tag}_\ell, a_\ell, C_{\ell,j_\ell}^{(a_\ell)}\right)$. The EA receives the vote and updates its state st by appending ψ_ℓ. The receipt α_ℓ of V_ℓ is the vote ψ_ℓ and the part $s_\ell^{(1-a_\ell)}$ used for audit.

The **Tally**(Pub) *protocol.* Let $\tilde{\mathcal{V}}$ be the set of the voters that have voted successfully.

- For each $V_\ell \in \tilde{\mathcal{V}}$, the EA uses $(\text{tag}_\ell, a_\ell)$ from ψ_ℓ to recover the respective audit information $s_\ell^{(1-a_\ell)}$ from s_ℓ. Then, it sends to BB the list $\left\{ (\psi_\ell, s_\ell^{(1-a_\ell)}) \right\}_{V_\ell \in \tilde{\mathcal{V}}}$.
  It also opens all the vote-code commitments, $\left\{ U_{\ell,j}^{(a)} \right\}_{\ell \in [n], j \in [m]}^{a \in \{0,1\}}$, by sending the list of pairs $\left\{ (C_{\ell,j}^{(a)}, t_{\ell,j}^{(a)}) \right\}_{\ell \in [n], j \in [m]}^{a \in \{0,1\}}$ to the BB.
- The EA, for every ψ_ℓ corresponding to a $V_\ell \in \tilde{\mathcal{V}}$:
  - (i). locates the decommitted vote-code C_ℓ that matches the cast vote-code $C_{\ell,j_\ell}^{(a_\ell)}$. Then, it marks the vote-code $C_{\ell,j_\ell'}^{(a_\ell)}$ as 'voted' and adds the corresponding commitment $E_{\ell,j_\ell'}^{(a_\ell)}$ into the set $\mathbf{E}_{\text{tally}}$ (initially empty). Recall that $j_\ell' = \pi_\ell^{(a_\ell)}(j_\ell)$.
  - (ii). adds all the commitments $\{ E_{\ell,j}^{(1-a_\ell)} \}_{j \in [m]}$ that correspond to the vote-codes in $s_\ell^{(1-a_\ell)}$ into the set $\mathbf{E}_{\text{open}}$ (initially empty).

  When finalised, $\mathbf{E}_{\text{tally}}$ includes the collection of votes that will be counted (homomorphically) and $\mathbf{E}_{\text{open}}$ includes the information that will be used for verifying ballot correctness. After this happens, EA posts to the BB the list of marked vote-codes along with $\mathbf{E}_{\text{tally}}$ and $\mathbf{E}_{\text{open}}$.
- The EA produces and posts to the BB all the *verifier's challenges* $\{\rho_E\}_{E \in \mathbf{E}_{\text{tally}}}$ of the Σ-protocols for the validity of the commitments in $\mathbf{E}_{\text{tally}}$, as determined in Figure 3 (second move). The extraction of the challenges is done via the randomness contributed by the voters' coin-flips. The extraction method that is used is described in Section 3.4.
- The EA prepares and posts to the BB all the *post-audit data* $\{\phi_{2,E}\}_{E \in \mathbf{E}_{\text{tally}}}$ of the Σ-protocols for verifying the validity of the commitments in $\mathbf{E}_{\text{tally}}$, as determined in Figure 3 (third move). Thus, for each commitment in $\mathbf{E}_{\text{tally}}$ there is a triple of pre-audit data, challenge and post-audit data that form a *complete Σ proof* of a valid commitment to some encoded candidate.
- EA performs homomorphic tally by computing $E_{\text{sum}} = \prod_{E \in \mathbf{E}_{\text{tally}}} E$ and preparing (T, R) as the opening of E_{sum}. The additive homomorphic property implies that T is the election result encoded in the number system with base $N = n + 1$ and it is committed under randomness R, which is the sum of all the randomness used for the commitments in $\mathbf{E}_{\text{tally}}$. Next, EA opens all the commitments in $\mathbf{E}_{\text{open}}$. Let Open be the set of these openings. Finally, it sends Open, E_{sum} and (T, R) to the BB.
- In the end of the process, BB contains the list of the marked vote-codes, as well as

$$\text{Pub}, \left\{ (C_{\ell,j}^{(a)}, t_{\ell,j}^{(a)}) \right\}_{\ell \in [n], j \in [m]}^{a \in \{0,1\}}, (\mathbf{E}_{\text{tally}}, E_{\text{sum}}, (T, R)),$$

$$(\text{Open}, \mathbf{E}_{\text{open}}), \{\rho_E\}_{E \in \mathbf{E}_{\text{tally}}}, \{\phi_{2,E}\}_{E \in \mathbf{E}_{\text{tally}}}.$$

Result(τ). The election result R_τ is derived by the following decoding algorithm:

$$
\begin{array}{|l|}
\hline
\text{Set } X \leftarrow T; \\
\text{For } j = 1, \ldots, m: \\
\bullet\ x_j \leftarrow X \bmod (n+1); \\
\bullet\ X \leftarrow (X - x_j)/(n+1); \\
\text{Return } \langle x_1, \ldots, x_m \rangle; \\
\hline
\end{array}
$$

The correctness of the algorithm (and our system) is shown in Theorem 3.

Verify(τ, α). Initially, α is parsed as $\big(\mathsf{tag}, a, C, s^{(1-a)}\big)$. The algorithm returns 1 only if the following checks are valid:

(i). All committed information in τ is associated with n ballots indexed under different tags and no two vote-codes under the same tag are marked as 'voted'.

(ii). Let $\hat{C}$ be a vote-code that appears in part $\hat{s}^{(\hat{a})}$ of some ballot and has been marked as 'voted'. Then, only the committed information for the other part $\hat{s}^{(1-\hat{a})}$ of this ballot has been opened.

(iii). All the complete Σ proofs that are associated with commitments in $\mathbf{E}_{\mathsf{tally}}$ are valid.

(iv). $E_{\mathsf{sum}} = \prod_{E \in \mathbf{E}_{\mathsf{tally}}} E$.

(v). All the openings of the commitments are valid.

(vi). tag equals some tag_ℓ in τ for some $\ell \in [n]$ and it holds that $a = a_\ell$.

(vii). The vote-code that is marked as 'voted' and is associated to tag_ℓ is C where ℓ is as in item (vi).

(viii). The correspondence of candidate encodings to vote-codes revealed in the opening of the commitments $\{(U_{\ell,j}^{(1-a_\ell)}, E_{\ell,j}^{(1-a_\ell)})\}_{j \in [m]}$ where ℓ is as in item (vi), is equal to the one defined in $s^{(1-a)}$.

3.6   Correctness of Our e-Voting System

We prove the correctness of our system in the following theorem. In the remaining of the paper, we assume that $n \cdot (n+1)^{m-1} < q$.

Theorem 3. *Let q be the size of the group for the commitment scheme described in Section 3.1 and assume that $n \cdot (n+1)^{m-1} < q$. Then, the e-voting system described in Section 3.5 has perfect correctness.*

Proof. See full version of the paper. $\square$

3.7   Example of Our e-Voting System

For the better understanding of our e-voting system, we provide a toy example of a referendum where $P_1 = \text{YES}$, $P_2 = \text{NO}$ are the candidates and $\mathcal{V}$ consists of three voters V_1, V_2, V_3. Our goal is to familiarize the reader with the functionality of our system so, for simplicity, we deviate from the description in Section 3.5 by not including Σ-protocol proofs.

EA generates the vote-codes for the ballots s_1, s_2 and s_3 of V_1, V_2 and V_3 as

$$(C_{1,1}^{(0)} = 27935, C_{1,2}^{(0)} = 75218, C_{1,1}^{(1)} = 84439, C_{1,2}^{(1)} = 77396),$$
$$(C_{2,1}^{(0)} = 58729, C_{2,2}^{(0)} = 45343, C_{2,1}^{(1)} = 14582, C_{2,2}^{(1)} = 93484),$$
$$(C_{3,1}^{(0)} = 52658, C_{3,2}^{(0)} = 65864, C_{3,1}^{(1)} = 84373, C_{3,2}^{(1)} = 49251)$$

respectively. The double ballots s_1, s_2, s_3 are labelled by the tags $101, 102, 103$ respectively and are formed as follows:

101		102		103	
27935	YES	58729	YES	52658	YES
75218	NO	45343	NO	65864	NO
84439	YES	14582	YES	84373	YES
77396	NO	93484	NO	49251	NO

EA prepares the commitments to each vote-code and the encoding of the candidate that they correspond. The commitment for YES (resp. NO) is a commitment to $(3+1)^0 = 1$ (resp. $(3+1)^1 = 4$). Next, it chooses whether the commitments of the vote-code and candidate pairs are going to be ordered in the BB as they are in the ballot part, or swapped. For example, assume that for the ballot s_1, EA chooses to leave the order in ballot part (0) intact and to swap the pairs in ballot part (1). Then, the information posted in the BB for s_1 would have the following form:

101	
$\mathsf{Com}_{\mathsf{ck}}(27935; t_{1,1}^{(0)})$	$\mathsf{Com}_{\mathsf{ck}}(1; r_{1,1}^{(0)})$
$\mathsf{Com}_{\mathsf{ck}}(75218; t_{1,2}^{(0)})$	$\mathsf{Com}_{\mathsf{ck}}(4; r_{1,2}^{(0)})$
$\mathsf{Com}_{\mathsf{ck}}(77396; t_{1,2}^{(1)})$	$\mathsf{Com}_{\mathsf{ck}}(4; r_{1,2}^{(1)})$
$\mathsf{Com}_{\mathsf{ck}}(84439; t_{1,1}^{(1)})$	$\mathsf{Com}_{\mathsf{ck}}(1; r_{1,1}^{(1)})$

Suppose that V_1 votes for NO using ballot part (1), V_2 votes for YES using ballot part (1) and V_3 votes for YES using ballot part (0). Then, the votes cast by V_1, V_2 and V_3 are $(101, 1, 77396)$, $(102, 1, 14582)$ and $(103, 0, 52568)$ respectively. The receipts that the voters receive are

(101,1,77396)		(102, 1, 14582)		(103, 0, 52568)	
27935	YES	58729	YES	84373	YES
75218	NO	45343	NO	49251	NO

The coins that V_1, V_2 and V_3 have flipped, are $a_1 = 1, a_2 = 1$ and $a_3 = 0$ respectively. Hence, we get internal randomness, $(1,1,0)$, of 3 bits (which would be the "weak source" of randomness used for the extraction of the challenge of the Σ protocols). After the voting ends, EA opens the vote-code commitments, marks the cast vote-codes $77396, 14582$ and 52658 and includes the corresponding encoded candidate commitments $\mathsf{Com}_{\mathsf{ck}}(4; r_{1,2}^{(1)})$, $\mathsf{Com}_{\mathsf{ck}}(1; r_{2,1}^{(1)})$ and $\mathsf{Com}_{\mathsf{ck}}(1; r_{3,1}^{(0)})$ in the tally set. Next, EA performs homomorphic tally, by computing the product of the above encoded candidate commitments as

$$E_{\mathsf{sum}} = \mathsf{Com}_{\mathsf{ck}}(4; r_{1,2}^{(1)}) \cdot \mathsf{Com}_{\mathsf{ck}}(1; r_{2,1}^{(1)}) \cdot \mathsf{Com}_{\mathsf{ck}}(1; r_{3,1}^{(0)}) = \mathsf{Com}_{\mathsf{ck}}(6; r_{1,2}^{(1)} + r_{2,1}^{(1)} + r_{3,1}^{(0)}).$$

Then, EA publishes E_{sum}, along with the opening of E_{sum} at value $(6; r_{1,2}^{(1)} + r_{2,1}^{(1)} + r_{3,1}^{(0)})$. The result is derived by computing $x_1 = 6 \bmod 4 = 2$ and $x_2 = ((6 - x_1)/4) \bmod 4 = 1$, which is interpreted as two votes for YES and one for NO.

In the verification phase, the EA opens the commitments in the ballot parts that the voters selected for auditing. For example, V_1 would check the consistency of her receipt with audit information in the BB, as illustrated below

101			
27935	YES	$(1, r_{1,1}^{(0)})$	$\mathsf{Com}_{\mathsf{ck}}(1; r_{1,1}^{(0)})$
75218	NO	$(4, r_{1,2}^{(0)})$	$\mathsf{Com}_{\mathsf{ck}}(4; r_{1,2}^{(0)})$
77396	VOTED		$\mathsf{Com}_{\mathsf{ck}}(4; r_{1,2}^{(1)})$
84439			$\mathsf{Com}_{\mathsf{ck}}(1; r_{1,1}^{(1)})$

Encodings	
YES	1
NO	4

Observe that, as we will prove, the cut-and-choose verification that V_1 performs, does not reveal her vote even to a party that obtains her receipt. This is because the cast vote-code alone does not leak any information about the associated candidate, while the entirely opened auditing part only serves as a check that the correspondence of the vote-codes and candidates in this part has not been tampered with. Therefore, V_1 can delegate the task of verification to a third party, without compromising her privacy.

4   Security of Our e-Voting System

In this section, we prove the security of our system in the definitional framework presented in Sections 2.4 and 2.3.

4.1   E2E Verifiability of Our e-Voting System

We prove that our e-voting system achieves E2E verifiability information theoretically in the standard model. We follow the notation in Figure 1 and the description in 3.5.

Theorem 4. *Let n be the number of all voters and m be the number of candidates. Let q be the size of the group for the commitment scheme described in Section 3.1. The e-voting system described in 3.5 achieves E2E verifiability information theoretically with error $(1/2)^d + \epsilon(m, n, \lceil n/\lfloor \log q \rfloor \rceil, \theta - 1))$, where θ is the number of honest successful voters, d is the tally deviation that the adversary wants to achieve and $\epsilon(m, n, \lceil n/\lfloor \log q \rfloor \rceil, \theta - 1)$ is the soundness error of the Σ protocol performed by the EA given in Theorem 2.*

Proof. Without loss of generality (w.l.o.g.), we assume that in any adversarial execution as described in the E2E verifiability game $G_{\text{E2E}-\text{Ver}}^{\mathcal{A},\mathcal{E},d,\theta}(1^\lambda, m, n)$, exactly n ballots are tabulated on τ under n different tags vote-codes are marked as 'voted' correspond to different tags (if such deviations happen the transcript is immediately rejected). In the same spirit, we assume there is no double ballot that both parts have been opened and that all double ballots for honest voters in $\tilde{\mathcal{V}}$ are well-formed, otherwise they would not engage in the **Cast** protocol. Finally, we recall that the adversary cannot modify the history of the transcript since it does not have control over the BB. As a first step, we construct a vote extractor $\mathcal{E}$ for our system as follows:

Construction of the vote extractor. $\mathcal{E}$ has input τ and the set of receipts $\{\alpha_\ell\}_{V_\ell \in \tilde{\mathcal{V}}}$, where $\tilde{\mathcal{V}}$ is the set of the honest voters that voted successfully. Let $t \le |\tilde{\mathcal{V}}|$ be the number of different tags that appear in $\{\alpha_\ell\}_{V_\ell \in \tilde{\mathcal{V}}}$[6]. If **Result**$(\tau) = \bot$ (i.e., the transcript is not meaningful), then $\mathcal{E}$ outputs $\bot$. Otherwise, $\mathcal{E}$ (arbitrarily) arranges the voters in $\mathcal{V} \setminus \tilde{\mathcal{V}}$ and the tags not included in $\{\alpha_\ell\}_{V_\ell \in \tilde{\mathcal{V}}}$ as $\langle V_\ell^{\mathcal{E}} \rangle_{\ell \in [n - |\tilde{\mathcal{V}}|]}$ and $\langle \text{tag}_\ell^{\mathcal{E}} \rangle_{\ell \in [n-t]}$ respectively. Next, for every $\ell \in [n - |\tilde{\mathcal{V}}|]$:

1. If there is no marked as 'voted' vote-code that is associated with $\text{tag}_\ell^{\mathcal{E}}$, then $\mathcal{E}$ sets $\mathcal{U}_\ell^{\mathcal{E}} = \emptyset$ (encoded as the zero vector) which is interpreted as an abort for voter $V_\ell^{\mathcal{E}}$.

2. If there is a 'voted' vote-code $C_{\ell,j}^{(a)}$ that is associated with $\text{tag}_\ell^{\mathcal{E}}$, then $\mathcal{E}$ brute-force opens the respective encoded candidate commitment $E_{\ell,j}^{(a)}$ to a value Open_ℓ (recall the commitment is perfectly binding). If Open_ℓ is a valid encoding (i.e. $\text{Open}_\ell \in \{(n+1)^0, (n+1)^1, \ldots, (n+1)^{m-1}\}$) of a candidate $\mathcal{P}_\ell^{\mathcal{E}}$, then $\mathcal{E}$ sets $\mathcal{U}_\ell^{\mathcal{E}} = \{\mathcal{P}_\ell^{\mathcal{E}}\}$. Otherwise, it outputs $\bot$.

Finally, $\mathcal{E}$ outputs $\langle \mathcal{U}_\ell^{\mathcal{E}} \rangle_{V_\ell^{\mathcal{E}} \in \mathcal{V} \setminus \tilde{\mathcal{V}}}$. Note that if $t < |\tilde{\mathcal{V}}|$, then the remaining tags $\text{tag}_{n-|\tilde{\mathcal{V}}|+1}^{\mathcal{E}}, \ldots, \text{tag}_{n-t}^{\mathcal{E}}$ are ignored by $\mathcal{E}$.

Based on the above vote extractor, we will prove the E2E verifiability of our scheme. Assume an adversary $\mathcal{A}$ that wins the game $G_{\text{E2E}-\text{Ver}}^{\mathcal{A},\mathcal{E},d,\theta}(1^\lambda, m, n)$. Namely, $\mathcal{A}$ breaks E2E verifiability by allowing at least θ honest successful voters and

---

[6] This implies that the ballot audit for all voters in $\tilde{\mathcal{V}}$ focuses on a list of t tabulated ballots on the BB. Thus, an adversary may inject $|\tilde{\mathcal{V}}| - t$ ballots for candidate selections of its choice that will be counted in the final tally as if they were honest.

achieving tally deviation d. Since there is at least one honest voter that performs verification ($\theta > 0$), w.l.o.g. we assume that $\mathcal{A}$ always outputs meaningful transcripts.

Let F be the event that there exists a committed value in τ which is marked to be counted and invalid (i.e., it is in $\mathbf{E}_{\text{tally}}$ but it is not a commitment to some candidate encoding). Since condition (i) of $G_{\text{E2E-Ver}}^{\mathcal{A},\mathcal{E},d,\theta}(1^\lambda, m, n)$ holds, we have that there are at least θ honest voters. However, the soundness error of the Σ- protocol is going to be affected by the fact that the invalid commitment is in a specific ballot part. The min entropy of all the coins given the fact that the adversary knows the coin of the invalid commitment in order to win, is at least the min entropy of all the coins minus 1 bit (i.e., the entropy of that bit). Therefore, by applying Theorem 2 for min entropy equal to $\theta - 1$, we have that each Σ protocol has soundness error $\epsilon(m, n, \lceil n/\lfloor \log q \rfloor \rceil, \theta - 1)$. Hence, the probability that a committed value is invalid while verification accepts is no more than $\epsilon(m, n, \lceil n/\lfloor \log q \rfloor \rceil, \theta - 1)$. Since there is at least one honest voter that verifies, we conclude that

$$\Pr[G_{\text{E2E-Ver}}^{\mathcal{A},\mathcal{E},d,\theta}(1^\lambda, m, n) = 1 \wedge F] \leq \epsilon(m, n, \lceil n/\lfloor \log q \rfloor \rceil, \theta - 1). \tag{1}$$

Assume that F does not occur. Thus, all marked committed values in $\mathbf{E}_{\text{tally}}$ correspond to a valid candidate encoding. This implies that (a) the maximum deviation per marked commitment that $\mathcal{A}$ may achieve is 1 (the vote is counted for a candidate other than the intended one) and (b) $\mathcal{E}$ does not output $\perp$ (it returns a vector $\langle \mathcal{U}_\ell^{\mathcal{E}} \rangle_{V_\ell^{\mathcal{E}} \in \mathcal{V} \setminus \tilde{\nu}}$), so $\mathcal{A}$ wins because (i),(ii) and (iii-a) hold. The auditor can verify that E_{sum} is equal to the homomorphic commitment $\prod_{E \in \mathbf{E}_{\text{tally}}} E$. Due to the perfect binding of the commitment scheme, the tally $f(\langle \mathcal{U}_\ell^{\mathcal{E}} \rangle_{V_\ell^{\mathcal{E}} \in \mathcal{V} \setminus \tilde{\nu}})$ that $\mathcal{E}$ estimates as non-honest votes, is correctly included in the adversarial result that derives from the opening (T, R) of E_{sum}. Thus, the deviation from the intended result that $\mathcal{A}$ achieves, derives only by miscounting the honest votes. This may be achieved by $\mathcal{A}$ in two different possible ways:

1. **Modification attacks:** modify the committed information as compared with the one in an honest voter's ballot (e.g., alter the vote-code and candidate correspondence). The deviation achieved by this type of attack is at most 1.
2. **Clash attacks:** instruct r honest voters whose ballots are indexed under the same tag to vote so that the votes of any $r - 1$ out of these r voters are all different than some fixed $r - 1$ committed votes that are ignored by $\mathcal{E}$ (either cast by corrupted voters or initially injected in τ by $\mathcal{A}$). All r voters verify the correct counting of their votes by auditing the same information on the BB and hence miss the injected votes that produce the tally deviation. The deviation achieved by this type of attack is $r - 1$.

In the case where all ballot information is committed consistently on the BB without being deleted or replaced, the adversary can only perform a combination of these two attacks on the honest voters. Indeed, if all honestly cast votes are in one-to-one correspondence with the correct encoded candidate commitments, then the perfect binding property ensures that the opening of the homomorphic tally matches the intended result.

Let $\tilde{\mathcal{V}}_1, \ldots, \tilde{\mathcal{V}}_t$ be the partition of $\tilde{\mathcal{V}}$ s.t. each of these subsets consists of honest voters that their receipts (hence their ballots) are indexed under the same tag. These subsets are created adaptively, according to the strategy of $\mathcal{A}$, under the constraint that $|\tilde{\mathcal{V}}| \geq \theta$. Note that there are $|\tilde{\mathcal{V}}| - t$ ignored tags in vote extraction, while $\sum_{i \in [t]}(|\tilde{\mathcal{V}}_i| - 1) = |\tilde{\mathcal{V}}| - t$. This implies that the adversary can perform clash attacks in all these subsets, with maximum possible deviation. We will prove that given that F does not occur, the success probability of $\mathcal{A}$ is no more than $(1/2)^d$, whatever its strategy might be.

We observe that in order for $\mathcal{A}$ to win, all voters in $\mathcal{V}_i$ must have the same receipt, or else inconsistencies will cause verification to fail. To achieve this, $\mathcal{A}$ must instruct the voters from the same subset to vote so that they all cast the same vote-code (otherwise two marked vote-codes under the same tag should appear) and create the corresponding audit ballot part identically for each auditing voter. In detail, in order for $\mathcal{A}$ to win, the following must hold for each $\tilde{\mathcal{V}}_i$, $i \in [t]$:

1. There is a representative vote-code C_i that appears in part (a) of all the double ballots of the voters in $\tilde{\mathcal{V}}_i$. The voters must select this part to vote by casting C_i. Therefore, the coin-flippings of the auditing voters must be consistent, in the sense that they correspond to ballot parts that contain a consistent vote-code. There can be at most 2 consistent coin-flips (i.e., either all coins are flipped to 0 or all coins are flipped to 1). Thus, the probability of consistent coin-flipping in $\tilde{\mathcal{V}}_i$ is at most $2/2^{|\tilde{\mathcal{V}}_i|} = (1/2)^{|\tilde{\mathcal{V}}_i|-1}$. In addition, the ballot parts that will be used for auditing must contain the same information, up to a permutation of the vote-code and candidate pairs.

2. If $\mathcal{A}$ wants to achieve $|\tilde{\mathcal{V}}_i|$ deviation exploiting the voters in $\mathcal{V}_i$, then it must perform a modification attack in at least one voter V in $\tilde{\mathcal{V}}_i$. This is because if all voters' ballots are consistent to the corresponding committed information in τ, then by performing only a clash attack in $\tilde{\mathcal{V}}_i$, $\mathcal{A}$ can achieve deviation by at most $|\tilde{\mathcal{V}}_i| - 1$, as described above. However, the modification comes with a loss of $1/2$ success probability, since $\mathcal{A}$ must also guess which is the part that V is going to use for voting. Indeed, if V chooses to audit the modified part of the ballot, then she will detect the attack. Therefore, all voters in $\mathcal{V}_i$ must perform a consistent coin-flip that agrees with the coin-flip of V. It is straightforward that in case of a single modification attack this event happens with $1/2 \cdot (1/2)^{|\tilde{\mathcal{V}}_i|-1} = (1/2)^{|\tilde{\mathcal{V}}_i|}$ probability. Moreover, in case $\tilde{\mathcal{V}}_i \geq 2$, performing two modification attacks does not lead to any improvement in terms of probability or maximum deviation.

We note that the above arguments hold trivially, if $\tilde{\mathcal{V}}_i$ is a singleton. Let $\mathbf{X}$ be the set of subsets from $\{\tilde{\mathcal{V}}_1, \ldots, \tilde{\mathcal{V}}_t\}$ that $\mathcal{A}$ performs clash attacks and $\mathbf{Y}$ the collection that $\mathcal{A}$ performs a modification attack on at least one voter in each of the subsets. According to the previous arguments, we have the following cases:

(i) for each $\mathcal{V}_i \in \mathbf{X} \setminus \mathbf{Y}$ the maximum deviation is $|\tilde{\mathcal{V}}_i| - 1$, (ii) for each $\mathcal{V}_i \in \mathbf{Y} \setminus \mathbf{X}$ the maximum deviation is 1, (iii) for each $\mathcal{V}_i \in \mathbf{X} \cap \mathbf{Y}$ the maximum deviation is $|\tilde{\mathcal{V}}_i|$ and (iv) for each $\mathcal{V}_i \in \left\{ \tilde{\mathcal{V}}_1, \ldots, \tilde{\mathcal{V}}_t \right\} \setminus (\mathbf{X} \cup \mathbf{Y})$ the maximum deviation is 0. For brevity, let $x = |\mathbf{X}|$ and $y = |\mathbf{Y}|$. Therefore, we have that the tally deviation from the intended result that $\mathcal{A}$ achieves is at most

$$\sum_{\mathcal{V}_i \in \mathbf{X} \setminus \mathbf{Y}} (|\tilde{\mathcal{V}}_i| - 1) + \sum_{\mathcal{V}_i \in \mathbf{Y} \setminus \mathbf{X}} 1 + \sum_{\mathcal{V}_i \in \mathbf{X} \cap \mathbf{Y}} |\tilde{\mathcal{V}}_i| = \sum_{\mathcal{V}_i \in \mathbf{X}} |\tilde{\mathcal{V}}_i| - x + y \leq |\tilde{\mathcal{V}}| - x + y.$$

We will now upper bound the success probability of $\mathcal{A}$. Since $\{\tilde{\mathcal{V}}_1, \ldots, \tilde{\mathcal{V}}_t\}$ is a partition of $\tilde{\mathcal{V}}$, we have that $\mathcal{A}$ must not be detected by all the voters in all of these subsets. So,

$$\Pr[G_{\text{E2E-Ver}}^{\mathcal{A},\mathcal{E},d,\theta}(1^\lambda, m, n) = 1 | \neg F] \leq \prod_{\mathcal{V}_i \in \mathbf{Y}} (1/2)^{|\tilde{\mathcal{V}}_i|} \cdot \prod_{\mathcal{V}_i \in \{\tilde{\mathcal{V}}_1, \ldots, \tilde{\mathcal{V}}_t\} \setminus \mathbf{Y}} (1/2)^{|\tilde{\mathcal{V}}_i| - 1} =$$

$$= (1/2)^{\sum_{\mathcal{V}_i \in \mathbf{Y}} |\tilde{\mathcal{V}}_i| + \sum_{\mathcal{V}_i \in \{\tilde{\mathcal{V}}_1, \ldots, \tilde{\mathcal{V}}_t\} \setminus \mathbf{Y}} (|\tilde{\mathcal{V}}_i| - 1)} =$$

$$= (1/2)^{|\tilde{\mathcal{V}}| - (t - y)} \leq (1/2)^{|\tilde{\mathcal{V}}| - x + y},$$

because $x \leq t$. In order for $\mathcal{A}$ to win, it must hold that $|\tilde{\mathcal{V}}| - x + y \geq d$ (condition (iii-a) holds), therefore

$$\Pr[G_{\text{E2E-Ver}}^{\mathcal{A},\mathcal{E},d,\theta}(1^\lambda, m, n) = 1 \wedge \neg F] \leq \Pr[G_{\text{E2E-Ver}}^{\mathcal{A},\mathcal{E},d,\theta}(1^\lambda, m, n) = 1 | \neg F] \leq (1/2)^d. \tag{2}$$

By adding (1),(2) we conclude that

$$\Pr[G_{\text{E2E-Ver}}^{\mathcal{A},\mathcal{E},d,\theta}(1^\lambda, m, n) = 1] \leq (1/2)^d + \epsilon(m, n, \lceil n/\lfloor \log q \rfloor \rceil, \theta - 1). \qquad \square$$

Remark 1. Note that if the number of honest voters satisfies the bound $\theta = \Omega(n \log \log m / \log q + \lambda)$, then the overall soundness error of the repeated Σ protocol will be sufficiently small. For instance, in an election where there are $n = 1000$ voters and $m = 40$ candidates we can use a group with at least 500 bit prime order q. Assuming a number of $\theta = 50$ honest voters (5% of total) we can divide the 1000 voter's coins into two challenges with 500 bits each (i.e. $k = 2$). With these parameters the above theorem will have a verifiability error that is at most $2^{-43} + (1/2)^d$ where d is the tally deviation. We remark that in this setting no deterministic extractor would be able to provide sufficient entropy and hence our ZK amplification technique is crucial.

4.2   Voter Privacy/Receipt Freeness of Our e-Voting System

In order to show our scheme satisfies privacy, we utilize complexity leveraging. Specifically, the system security parameter is configured such that breaking the hiding property of the underlying commitment scheme is much harder than guessing the challenge of the Σ protocol; therefore, we can simulate the protocol's view by guessing the proof challenges without breaking the hiding property of the commitment scheme. Due to this proof technique, the number of corrupted voters t should be polynomially related to the security parameter λ in a certain way; while the total number of voters n can be any function that is $poly(\lambda)$ (as long as the correctness requirement is fulfilled, cf. theorem 3). We emphasize that given a specific n, our system can support privacy for any desired number of adversarial voters $t < n$ (as long as a suitably large security parameter λ is used).

Theorem 5. *Assume there exists a constant* $c, 0 < c < 1$ *such that for any* 2^{λ^c}-*time adversary* $\mathcal{A}$, *the advantage of breaking the hiding property of the commitment scheme is* $\mathsf{Adv}_{\mathsf{hide}}(\mathcal{A}) = \mathsf{negl}(\lambda)$. *Let* $t = \lambda^{c'}$ *for some constant* $c' < c$. *For any constant* $m \in \mathbb{N}$ *and* $n = poly(\lambda)$, *the e-voting system described in Section 3.5 achieves voter privacy/receipt-freeness for at most* t *corrupted voters.*

Proof. See full version of the paper. □

References

1. Adida, B.: Helios: Web-based open-audit voting. In: USENIX Security (2008)
2. Barak, B., Kindler, G., Shaltiel, R., Sudakov, B., Wigderson, A.: Simulating independence: New constructions of condensers, ramsey graphs, dispersers, and extractors. J. ACM **57**(4), 20:1–20:52 (2010)
3. Baum, C., Damgård, I., Orlandi, C.: Publicly auditable secure multi-party computation. In: Abdalla, M., De Prisco, R. (eds.) SCN 2014. LNCS, vol. 8642, pp. 175–196. Springer, Heidelberg (2014)
4. Beaver, D.: Plug and play encryption. In: Kaliski Jr., B.S. (ed.) CRYPTO 1997. LNCS, vol. 1294, pp. 75–89. Springer, Heidelberg (1997)
5. Benaloh, J.: Simple verifiable elections. USENIX (2006)
6. Benaloh, J.C., Tuinstra, D.: Receipt-free secret-ballot elections (extended abstract). In STOC (1994)
7. Benaloh, J.C., Yung, M.: Distributing the power of a government to enhance the privacy of voters (extended abstract). In: PODC (1986)
8. Bernhard, D., Cortier, V., Pereira, O., Smyth, B., Warinschi, B.: Adapting helios for provable ballot privacy. In: Atluri, V., Diaz, C. (eds.) ESORICS 2011. LNCS, vol. 6879, pp. 335–354. Springer, Heidelberg (2011)
9. Bernhard, D., Pereira, O., Warinschi, B.: How not to prove yourself: pitfalls of the fiat-shamir heuristic and applications to helios. In: Wang, X., Sako, K. (eds.) ASIACRYPT 2012. LNCS, vol. 7658, pp. 626–643. Springer, Heidelberg (2012)
10. Blum, M., Feldman, P., Micali, S.: Non-interactive zero-knowledge and its applications (extended abstract). In: STOC (1988)
11. Chaum, D.: Untraceable electronic mail, return addresses, and digital pseudonyms. Commun. ACM **24**(2), 84–88 (1981)
12. Chaum, D.: Surevote: technical overview. In: Proceedings of the Workshop on Trustworthy Elections, WOTE (2001)
13. Chaum, D.: Secret-ballot receipts: True voter-verifiable elections. IEEE Security & Privacy **2**(1), 38–47 (2004)

14. Chaum, D., Carback, R., Clark, J., Essex, A., Popoveniuc, S., Rivest, R.L., Ryan, P.Y.A., Shen, E., Sherman, A.T., Vora, P.L.: Scantegrity II: end-to-end verifiability by voters of optical scan elections through confirmation codes. IEEE TIFS **4**(4), 611–627 (2009)

15. Chevallier-Mames, B., Fouque, P.-A., Pointcheval, D., Stern, J., Traoré, J.: On some incompatible properties of voting schemes. In: Chaum, D., Jakobsson, M., Rivest, R.L., Ryan, P.Y.A., Benaloh, J., Kutylowski, M., Adida, B. (eds.) Towards Trustworthy Elections. LNCS, vol. 6000, pp. 191–199. Springer, Heidelberg (2010)

16. Clarkson, M.R., Chong, S., Myers, A.C.: Civitas: Toward a secure voting system. In: IEEE Symposium on Security and Privacy (2008)

17. Cohen, J.D., Fischer, M.J.: A robust and verifiable cryptographically secure election scheme (extended abstract). In: FOCS (1985)

18. United States Election Assistance Commission. Voluntary voting systems guidelines (2005)

19. Cramer, R., Damgård, I.B., Schoenmakers, B.: Proof of partial knowledge and simplified design of witness hiding protocols. In: Desmedt, Y.G. (ed.) CRYPTO 1994. LNCS, vol. 839, pp. 174–187. Springer, Heidelberg (1994)

20. Cramer, R., Franklin, M.K., Schoenmakers, B., Yung, M.: Multi-authority secret-ballot elections with linear work. In: Maurer, U.M. (ed.) EUROCRYPT 1996. LNCS, vol. 1070, pp. 72–83. Springer, Heidelberg (1996)

21. Cramer, R., Gennaro, R., Schoenmakers, B.: A secure and optimally efficient multi-authority election scheme. ETT **8**(5), 481–490 (1997)

22. de Marneffe, O., Pereira, O., Quisquater, J.-J.: Simulation-Based analysis of E2E voting systems. In: Frontiers of Electronic Voting (2007)

23. Delaune, S., Kremer, S., Ryan, M.: Verifying privacy-type properties of electronic voting protocols. J. of Computer Security **17**(4), 435–487 (2009)

24. Dolev, D., Fischer, M.J., Rob Fowler, T., Lynch, N.A., Raymond Strong, H.: An efficient algorithm for byzantine agreement without authentication. Information and Control **52**, 257–274 (1982)

25. Garay, J.A., Kiayias, A., Leonardos, N.: The bitcoin backbone protocol: analysis and applications. In: Oswald, E., Fischlin, M. (eds.) EUROCRYPT 2015, Part II. LNCS, pp. 281–310. Springer, Heidelberg (2015)

26. Groth, J.: Evaluating security of voting schemes in the universal composability framework. In: Jakobsson, M., Yung, M., Zhou, J. (eds.) ACNS 2004. LNCS, vol. 3089, pp. 46–60. Springer, Heidelberg (2004)

27. Gurari, E.M.: Introduction to the theory of computation. Computer Science Press (1989)

28. Juels, A., Catalano, D., Jakobsson, M.: Coercion-resistant electronic elections. IACR Cryptology ePrint Archive **2002**, 165 (2002)

29. Kamp, J., Zuckerman, D.: Deterministic extractors for bit-fixing sources and exposure-resilient cryptography. SIAM J. Comput. **36**(5), 1231–1247 (2006)

30. Kremer, S., Ryan, M., Smyth, B.: Election verifiability in electronic voting protocols. In: Gritzalis, D., Preneel, B., Theoharidou, M. (eds.) ESORICS 2010. LNCS, vol. 6345, pp. 389–404. Springer, Heidelberg (2010)

31. Küsters, R., Truderung, T., Vogt, A.: Accountability: Definition and relationship to verifiability. IACR Cryptology ePrint Archive **2010**, 236 (2010)

32. Küsters, R., Truderung, T., Vogt, A.: A game-based definition of coercion-resistance and its applications. In: CSF, pp. 122–136 (2010)

33. Küsters, R., Truderung, T., Vogt, A.: Verifiability, privacy, and coercion-resistance: new insights from a case study. In: IEEE Symposium on Security and Privacy, pp. 538–553. IEEE Computer Society (2011)

34. Lichtenstein, D., Linial, N., Saks, M.E.: Imperfect random sources and discrete controlled processes. In: STOC, pp. 169–177 (1987)
35. Micali, S., Pass, R., Rosen, A.: Input-indistinguishable computation. In: FOCS, pp. 367–378. IEEE Computer Society (2006)
36. Moran, T., Naor, M.: Receipt-Free universally-verifiable voting with everlasting privacy. In: Dwork, C. (ed.) CRYPTO 2006. LNCS, vol. 4117, pp. 373–392. Springer, Heidelberg (2006)
37. Andrew Neff, C.: Practical high certainty intent verification for encrypted votes. Votehere, Inc., whitepaper (2004)
38. Popoveniuc, S., Kelsey, J., Regenscheid, A., Voral, P.: Performance requirements for end-to-end verifiable elections. EVT/WOTE (2010)
39. Raz, R.: Extractors with weak random seeds. STOC (2005)
40. Sako, K., Kilian, J.: Receipt-Free mix-type voting scheme. In: Guillou, L.C., Quisquater, J.-J. (eds.) EUROCRYPT 1995. LNCS, vol. 921, pp. 393–403. Springer, Heidelberg (1995)
41. Schwartz, J.T.: Fast probabilistic algorithms for verification of polynomial identities. J. ACM 27(4), 701–717 (1980)
42. Unruh, D., Müller-Quade, J.: Universally composable incoercibility. IACR Cryptology ePrint Archive 2009, 520 (2009)
43. Zagórski, F., Carback, R.T., Chaum, D., Clark, J., Essex, A., Vora, P.L.: Remotegrity: design and use of an end-to-end verifiable remote voting system. In: Jacobson, M., Locasto, M., Mohassel, P., Safavi-Naini, R. (eds.) ACNS 2013. LNCS, vol. 7954, pp. 441–457. Springer, Heidelberg (2013)
44. Zippel, R.: Probabilistic algorithms for sparse polynomials. In: Ng, E.W. (ed.) EUROSAM 1979. LNCS, pp. 216–226. Springer, Heidelberg (1979)

Multi-Party Computations

Cryptographic Agents: Towards a Unified Theory of Computing on Encrypted Data

Shashank Agrawal[1]([✉]), Shweta Agrawal[2], and Manoj Prabhakaran[1]

[1] University of Illinois Urbana-Champaign, Champaign, USA
{sagrawl2,mmp}@illinois.edu
[2] Indian Institute of Technology Delhi, Delhi, India
shweta@cse.iitd.ac.in

Abstract. We provide a new framework of *cryptographic agents* that unifies various modern "cryptographic objects" — identity-based encryption, fully-homomorphic encryption, functional encryption, and various forms of obfuscation – similar to how the Universal Composition framework unifies various multi-party computation tasks like commitment, coin-tossing and zero-knowledge proofs. These cryptographic objects can all be cleanly modeled as *"schemata"* in our framework.

Highlights of our framework include the following:

- We use a new *indistinguishability preserving* (IND-PRE) definition of security that interpolates indistinguishability and simulation style definitions, which (often) sidesteps the known impossibilities for the latter. IND-PRE-security is parameterized by the choice of the "test" family, such that by choosing different test families, one can obtain different levels of security for the same primitive (including various standard definitions in the literature).
- We present a notion of *reduction* from one schema to another and a powerful *composition theorem* with respect to IND-PRE security. We show that obfuscation is a "complete" schema under this notion, under standard cryptographic assumptions. We also provide a stricter notion of reduction (Δ-reduction) that composes even when security is only with respect to certain restricted test families of importance.
- Last but not the least, our framework can be used to model abstractions like the generic group model and the random oracle model, letting one translate a general class of constructions in these heuristic models to constructions based on *standard model assumptions*.

We also illustrate how our framework can be applied to specific primitives like obfuscation and functional encryption. We relate our definitions to existing definitions and also give new constructions and reductions between different primitives.

S. Agrawal and M. Prabhakaran—Research supported in part by NSF grant 1228856.

E. Oswald and M. Fischlin (Eds.): EUROCRYPT 2015, Part II, LNCS 9057, pp. 501–531, 2015.
DOI: 10.1007/978-3-662-46803-6_17

1 Introduction

Over the last decade or so, thanks to remarkable breakthroughs in cryptographic techniques, a wave of "cryptographic objects" — identity-based encryption, fully-homomorphic encryption, functional encryption, and most recently, various forms of obfuscation — have opened up exciting new possibilities for computing on encrypted data. Initial foundational results on this front consisted of strong impossibility results. Breakthrough constructions, as they emerged, often used specialized security definitions which avoided such impossibility results. However, as these objects and their constructions have become numerous and complex, often building on each other, the connections among these disparate cryptographic objects — and among their disparate security definitions — have become increasingly confusing.

A case in point is functional encryption (FE) [80]. FE comes in numerous flavors — public key or symmetric [80,83], with or without function hiding [1, 22], public or private index [24], bounded or unbounded key [61,63,79]. Each flavor has several candidate security definitions — indistinguishability based [21,80], adaptive simulation based [24], non-adaptive simulation [76], unbounded simulation [6], fully-adaptive security [72], black-box/non black-box simulation [14] to name a few. In addition, FE can be constructed from obfuscation [52] and can be used to construct property preserving encryption [77], each of which have numerous security definitions of their own [10,18,66]. It is unclear how these definitions relate, particularly as primitives are composed, resulting in a landscape cluttered with similar yet different definitions, of different yet similar primitives.

The goal of this work is to provide a clean and unifying framework for diverse cryptographic objects and their various security definitions, equipped with powerful *reductions* and *composition theorems*. In our framework, security is parametrized by a family of "test" functions — by choosing the appropriate family, we are able to place known security definitions for a given object on the same canvas, enabling comparative analysis. Our framework is general enough to model abstractions like the generic group model, letting one translate a general class of constructions in these heuristic models to constructions based on *standard model assumptions*.

Why A Framework? A unifying framework like ours has significant potential for affecting the future course of development of the theory and practice of cryptographic objects. The most obvious impact is on the definitional aspects – both positive and negative results crucially hinge on the specifics of the definition. Our framework allows one to systematically explore different definitions obtained by instantiating each component in the framework differently. We can not only "rediscover" existing definitions in this way, but also discover new definitions, both stronger and weaker than the ones in the literature. As an example, we obtain a new notion of "adaptive differing-inputs obfuscation" that leads to significant simplifications in constructions using "differing-inputs obfuscation".

The framework offers a means to identify what is common to a variety of objects, to compare them against each other by reducing one to another, to build one from the other by using our composition theorems. In addition, one may more easily identify intermediate objects of appropriate functionality and security that can be used as part of a larger construction. Another important contribution of the framework is the ability to model computational assumptions suitable for these constructions at an appropriate level of abstraction [1].

Why a *New* Framework? One might wonder if an existing framework for secure multi-party computation (MPC) — like the Universal Composition (UC) framework — cannot be used, or repurposed, to handle cryptographic objects as well. While certain elements of these frameworks (like the real/ideal paradigm) are indeed relevant beyond MPC, there are several differences between MPC and cryptographic objects which complicates this approach (which indeed was the starting point for our framework). Firstly, there is a strict syntactic requirement on schemes implementing cryptographic objects — namely, that they are non-interactive — which is absent for MPC protocols; indeed, MPC frameworks typically do not impose any constraints on the number of rounds, let alone rule out interaction. Secondly, and more importantly, the security definition in general-purpose MPC frameworks typically follow a simulation paradigm[2]. Unfortunately, such a strong security requirement is well-known to be unrealizable — e.g., the "virtual black-box" definition of obfuscation is unrealizable [10]. To be relevant, it is very important that a framework for modeling obfuscation and other objects admits weaker security definitions.

Finally, a simple framework for cryptographic objects need not model various subtleties of protocol execution in a network that the MPC frameworks model. These considerations lead us to a bare-bones framework, which can model the basic security requirements of cryptographic objects (but little else).

Cryptographic Agents Framework. Our unifying framework, called the *Cryptographic Agents framework* models one or more (possibly randomized, stateful) objects that interact with each other, so that a user with access to their codes can only learn what it can learn from the output of these objects. As a running example, functional encryption schemes could be considered as consisting of "message agents" and "key agents."

---

[1] cf. in secure multi-party computation, the existence of a semi-honest OT protocol is a more appropriate assumption that the existence of an enhanced trapdoor one-way permutation

[2] One exception to this is the "input-indistinguishable computation" framework of Micali, Pass and Rosen for secure function evaluation of deterministic functions [74]. Unfortunately, this framework heavily relies on interactivity of protocols (an "implicit input" is defined by a transcript; but when a party interacts with an object it received, there is no well-defined transcript), and is unsuitable for modeling cryptographic objects.

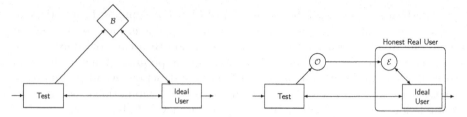

Fig. 1. The ideal world (on the left) and the real world with an honest user

To formalize the security requirement, we use a real-ideal paradigm, but at the same time rely on an indistinguishability notion (rather than a simulation-based security notion). We informally describe the framework below.

- **Ideal Execution.** The ideal world consists of two (adversarially designed) entities — a User and a Test — who can freely interact with each other. (See the left-hand side of Figure 1.) User is given access, via handles, to a collection of "agents" (interactive Turing Machines), maintained by $\mathcal{B}$ (a "blackbox"). User and Test are both allowed to add agents to the collection maintained by $\mathcal{B}$, but the class of agents that they can add are restricted by a *schema*.[3] The User can feed inputs to these agents, and also allow a set of them to interact with each other, in a "session." At the end of this interaction, the user obtains all the outputs from the session, and also additional handles to the agents with updated states.

  Example: In a schema capturing public-key functional encryption, there are two kinds of agents – "message agents" and "key agents." A message agent simply sends out (i.e., copies into its *communication tape*) an inbuilt message, every time it is invoked. A key agent reads a message from its incoming communication tape, applies an inbuilt function to it, and copies the result to its *output tape*. The user can add only message agents to the collection maintained by $\mathcal{B}$; Test can add key agents as well. Note that the outputs that the user receives from a session involving a message agent and a key agent is the output produced by the key agent (the message agent produces no output; it only communicates its message to the key agent). [4]

- **Real Execution.** The real execution also consists of two entities, the (real-world) user (or an adversary Adv) and Test. The latter is in fact the same as in the ideal world. But in the real world, when Test requests adding an agent to the collection of agents, the user is handed a cryptographically

---

[3] Here, a *schema* is analogous to a *functionality* in UC security. Thus different primitives like functional encryption and fully-homomorphic encryption are specified by different schemata.

[4] For functional encryption, neither inputs to agents nor their states are relevant, as the message and key agents have all the relevant information built in. However, obfuscation is most directly modeled by non-interactive agents that take an input, and modeling fully homomorphic encryption requires agents that maintain state.

generated object – a "cryptographic agent" – instead of a handle to this agent. The *correctness requirement* is that an honest user should be able to perform all the operations any User can in the ideal world (i.e., add new agents to the collection, and execute a session of agents, and thereby update their states) using an "execution" operation applied to the cryptographic agents. In Figure 1, $\mathcal{O}$ indicates the algorithm for encoding, and $\mathcal{E}$ indicates a procedure that applies an algorithm for session executions, as requested by the User. (However, an adversarial user Adv in the real world may analyze the cryptographic agents in anyway it wants.)

- **Security Definition.** We define IND-PRE (for indistinguishability preserving) security, which requires that *if* a Test is such that a certain piece of information about it (modeled as an input bit) remains hidden from every user in the ideal world, *then* that information should stay hidden from every user that interacts with Test in the real world as well. Note that we do not require that the view in the real world can be simulated in the ideal world. In the real world we require all entities to be computationally bounded. But in the *ideal* world, we may consider users that are computationally bounded or unbounded (possibly with a limit on the number of sessions it can invoke). Another variable in our definition is the family of tests: by default, we consider Tests that are PPT; but we may consider Tests from a family Γ, in which case the resulting security definition is termed Γ-IND-PRE security. These choices allow us to model different levels of security, which translate to various natural notions of security for specific schemata.

Our Contributions. Our main contribution is a new model of cryptographic computation, that unifies and extends primitives for computing on encrypted data such as obfuscation, functional encryption, fully homomorphic encryption, property preserving encryption, and such others. One can consider our framework analogous to the now-standard approach in secure multi-party computation (MPC) (e.g., following [39,58]) that uses *a common paradigm to abstract the security guarantees in a variety of different tasks* like commitments, zero-knowledge proofs, coin-flipping, oblivious-transfer, etc. While we anticipate several refinements and extensions to the framework presented here, we consider that, thanks to its simplicity, the current model already provides important insight about the "right" security notions for the primitives we capture, and opens up a wealth of new questions and connections for further investigation.

The list of technical results in this paper could be viewed in two parts: contributions to the foundational aspects of cryptographic objects, and contributions to specific objects of interest (mainly, obfuscation, functional encryption and assumptions related to (bi/multi-linear) groups). Some of our specific contributions to the foundational aspects of this area are as follows.

- We first define a general framework of cryptographic agents that can be instantiated for different primitives using different *schemata*. The resulting security definition, called Γ-IND-PRE-security is parameterized by a test family Γ.

For natural choices of Γ, these definitions tend to be not only stronger than standard definitions, but also easier to work with in larger constructions (see next). For some schemata, like obfuscation and functional encryption, choosing Γ to be the family of all PPT tests can lead to definitions that are known to be impossible to realize. But more restricted test families can be used to capture existing definitions (with candidate constructions) exactly: we identify Δ, Δ_{det} and Δ^* (defined later) as important test families that do this for obfuscation and/or functional encryption.

Δ-IND-PRE-security is of particular interest, because for each of the example primitives we consider in this paper — obfuscation, functional encryption, fully-homomorphic encryption and property-preserving encryption — Δ-IND-PRE-security for the corresponding schema implies the standard security definitions (that are not known to be impossible to realize) in the literature, and yet, is not known to be impossible to realize.

- We present a notion of reduction from one schema to another[5], and a composition theorem. This provides a modular means to build and analyze secure schemes for a complicated schema based on those for simpler schemata. Further, reduction provides a way to study, in abstract, relative complexity of different schemata: e.g., general purpose obfuscation turns out to be a "complete" schema under this notion.

- The notion of reduction mentioned above composes for Γ_{ppt}-IND-PRE-security where Γ_{ppt} is the class of all probabilistic polynomial time (PPT) tests. Unfortunately, obfuscation (and hence, any other complete schema) can be shown to be unrealizable under this definition. Hence, we present a more structured notion of reduction, called Δ-reduction, that composes with respect to Δ-IND-PRE-security as well.

These basic results have several important implications to specific primitives of interest. In this paper, we initiate the study of a few such primitives in our framework (and leave others to future work).

- **Functional Encryption.** Our framework provides a unified method to capture all variants of FE using just a few basic schemata by employing different test families. For concreteness, below we focus on public-key FE.
  - *Defining FE With and Without Function-Hiding.* Function-hiding (public-key) FE had proved difficult to define satisfactorily [1,22,23]. The IND-PRE framework provides a way to obtain a natural and general definition of this primitive. We present a simple schema $\Sigma_{\mathrm{FH\text{-}FE}}$ to capture the security guarantees of function-hiding FE; a similar schema Σ_{FE} captures FE without function-hiding.

---

[5] Our reduction uses a simulation-based security requirement. Thus, among other things, it also provides a means for capturing simulation-based security definition: we say that a scheme Π is a Γ-SIM-secure scheme for a schema Σ if Π reduces Σ to the null-schema.

- *Hierarchy of Security Requirements.* By using different test families, we obtain a hierarchy of security notions for FE (with and without function-hiding), Δ_{det}-IND-PRE $\Leftarrow \Delta$-IND-PRE $\Leftarrow$ IND-PRE $\Leftarrow$ SIM (see Footnote 5). Of these, Δ_{det}-IND-PRE security for FE without function-hiding is equivalent to the standard notion of security used currently [21,80]. The strongest one, SIM security, is impossible for general function families [6,14,24].
- *Constructions.* We present new constructions for Δ-IND-PRE secure FE (both with and without function hiding) for all polynomial-time computable functions. We also present an IND-PRE secure FE for the inner product functionality. Two of these constructions are in the form of reductions (a Δ-reduction to an obfuscation schema, and a (standard) reduction to a "bilinear generic group" schema, which are described below). Also, the first two constructions crucially rely on Δ-IND-PRE-security of obfuscation (i.e., adaptive differing-inputs obfuscation), thereby considerably simplifying the constructions and the analysis compared to those in recent work [8,28] which use (non-adaptive) differing-inputs obfuscation.

- **Obfuscation.** We study in detail, the various notions of obfuscation in the literature, and relate them to Γ-IND-PRE-security for various test families Γ. Our strongest definition of this form, which considers the family of all PPT tests, turns out to be impossible. Our definition is conceptually "weaker" than the virtual black-box simulation definition (in that it does not require a simulator), but the impossibility result of Barak et al. [10] continues to apply to this definition. To circumvent the impossibility, we identify three test families, Δ, Δ^* and Δ_{det}, such that Δ_{det}-IND-PRE-security is *equivalent* to indistinguishability obfuscation, Δ^*-IND-PRE-security is equivalent to differing inputs obfuscation, and Δ-IND-PRE-security implies both the above. We state a new definition for the security of obfuscation – *adaptive differing-inputs obfuscation* – which is equivalent Δ-IND-PRE-security. Informally, it is the same as differing inputs obfuscation, but an adversary is allowed to *interact* with the "sampler" (which samples two circuits one of which will be obfuscated and presented to the adversary as a challenge), even after it receives the obfuscation. Such a notion was independently introduced in [7].
- **Using the Generic Group in the Standard Model.** One can model random oracles and the generic group model as schemata. An assumption that such a schema has an IND-PRE-secure scheme is a standard model assumption, and to the best of our knowledge, not ruled out by the techniques in the literature. This is because, IND-PRE-security captures only certain indistinguishability guarantees of the generic group model, albeit in a broad manner (by considering arbitrary tests). Indeed, for random oracles, such an assumption is implied by (for instance) virtual black-box secure obfuscation of point-functions, a primitive that has plausible candidates in the literature. The generic group schema (as well as its bilinear version) is a highly versatile resource used in several constructions, including that of cryptographic objects that can be modeled as schemata. Such constructions can be consid-

ered as *reductions* to the generic group schema. Combined with our composition theorem, this creates a recipe for standard model constructions under a strong, but simple to state, computational assumption.

We give such an example for obtaining a standard model *function-hiding* public-key FE scheme for inner-product predicates (for which a satisfactory general security definition has also been lacking).

- **Other Primitives.** Our model is extremely flexible, and can easily capture most cryptographic objects for which an indistinguishability security notion is required. This includes witness encryption, functional witness encryption, fully homomorphic encryption (FHE), property-preserving encryption (PPE) etc. We discuss a couple of them – FHE and PPE – to illustrate this. We can model FHE using (stateful) cryptographic agents. The resulting security definition, even with the test family Δ_{det}, implies the standard definition in the literature, with the additional requirement that a ciphertext does not reveal how it was formed, even given the decryption key. For PPE, we show that an Δ_{det}-IND-PRE secure scheme for the PPE schema is in fact equivalent to a scheme that satisfies the standard definition of security for PPE.

Related Work. Here, we provide a short (non exhaustive) summary of related work on the objects that are studied in this paper.

Program Obfuscation. Program Obfuscation is the task of garbling a given program so that the input-output behavior is retained, but everything else about the program is hidden. The formal study of program obfuscation was initiated by Barak et al. [10] who showed that the strongest possible notion of security, called *virtual black box* security was impossible to achieve for general circuits. To address this, they defined weaker notions of security, such as *indistinguishability obfuscation* (denoted by I-Obf), which states that for two equivalent circuits C_0 and C_1, their obfuscations should be computationally indistinguishable. A related but stronger security notion defined by [10] was that of *differing input obfuscation* (denoted by DI-Obf), which further requires that an adversary who can distinguish between C_0 and C_1 can be used to *extract* an input on which the two circuits differ.

Despite these weakenings, the area of program obfuscation was plagued by impossibilities [62,67,71] for a long time, with few positive results, often for very specialized classes of functions [38,40,42,43,68,86]. This state of affairs, however, has improved significantly in recent times. We now have program obfuscators for complex functionalities such as conjunctions [32], d-CNF formulas [33], circuits [34,44,52] and even Turing machines [8], in weaker models of computation such as the generic graded encoding scheme model [8,32–34], the generic colored matrix model [52] and the idealized pseudo free group model [44].

These constructions are proven secure under different notions of security: virtual black box, I-Obf, DI-Obf. Alongside, several new applications have been developed for IP-Obf [81] and DI-Obf [8,28]. There is a growing research effort in exploring alternate notions of obfuscation [19,54].

Functional Encryption. Functional encryption generalizes public key encryption to allow fine grained access control on encrypted data. In functional encryption, a user can be provided with a secret key corresponding to a function f, denoted by SK_f. Given SK_f and ciphertext $\mathsf{CT}_x = \mathsf{Encrypt}(x)$, the user may run the decryption procedure to learn $f(x)$. Security of the system guarantees that nothing beyond $f(x)$ can be learned from CT_x and SK_f. Functional encryption systems traditionally focused on restricted classes of functions such as the identity function [3,4,21,27,46,47,56,82], membership checking [26], boolean formulas [16,65,70], inner product functions [5,69,70] and more recently, even regular languages [85]. Recent times saw constructions for more general classes of functions: Gorbunov et al. [64] and Garg et al. [53] provided the first constructions for an important subclass of FE called "public index FE" for all circuits, Goldwasser et al. [61] constructed succinct simulation-secure single-key FE scheme for all circuits, Garg et al. [52] constructed multi-key FE schemes for all circuits while Goldwasser et al. and Ananth et al. [8,60] constructed FE for Turing machines.

Fully homomorphic encryption. Fully homomorphic encryption allows a user to evaluate a circuit C on encrypted messages $\{\mathsf{CT}_i = \mathsf{Encrypt}(x_i)\}_{i \in [n]}$ so that $\mathsf{Decrypt}\big(C(\mathsf{CT}_1, \ldots, \mathsf{CT}_n)\big) = C(x_1, \ldots, x_n)$. Since the first breakthrough construction by Gentry [55], extensive research effort has been focused on providing improvements [30,31,35–37,49,57].

2   Preliminaries

To formalize the model of cryptographic agents, we shall use the standard notion of probabilistic interactive Turing Machines (ITM) with some modifications (see below). To avoid cumbersome formalism, we keep the description somewhat informal, but it is straightforward to fully formalize our model. We shall also not attempt to define the model in its most generality, for the sake of clarity.

In our case an ITM has separate tapes for input, output, incoming communication, outgoing communication, randomness and work-space.

Definition 1 (Agents and Family of Agents). *An agent is an interactive Turing Machine, with the following modifications:*

- *There is a special read-only parameter tape, which always consists of a security parameter κ, and possibly other parameters.*
- *There is an a priori restriction on the size of all the tapes other than the randomness tape (including input, communication and work tapes), as a function of the security parameter.*
- *There is a special blocking state such that if the machine enters such a state, it remains there if the input tape is empty. Similarly, there are blocking states which let the machine block if any combination of the communication tape and the input tape is empty.*

An agent family *is a maximal set of agents with the same program (i.e., state space and transition functions), but possibly different contents in their parameter tapes. We also allow an agent family to be the empty set* ∅.

We can allow *non-uniform agents* by allowing an additional advice tape. Our framework and basic results work in the uniform and non-uniform model equally well.

Note that an agent who enters a blocking state can move out of it if its configuration is changed by adding a message to its input tape and/or communication tape. However, if the agent enters a halting state, it will not move out of that state. An agent who never enters a blocking state is called a *non-reactive agent*. An agent who never reads or writes from a communication tape is called a *non-interactive agent*.

Definition 2 (Session). *A session maps a finite ordered set of agents, their configurations and inputs, to outputs and (updated) configurations of the same agents, as follows. The agents are initialized with the given inputs on their input tapes, and then executed together until they are deadlocked.*[6] *The result of applying the session is defined as the collection of outputs and configurations of the agents when the session terminates (if it terminates; if not, the result is left undefined).*

We shall be restricting ourselves to collections of agents such that sessions involving them are guaranteed to terminate. Note that we have defined a session to have only an initial set of inputs, so that the outcome of a session is well-defined (without the need to specify how further inputs would be chosen).

Next we define an important notion in our framework, namely that of an *ideal agent schema*, or simply, a schema. A schema plays the same role as a functionality does in the Universal Composition framework for secure multiparty computation. That is, it specifies what is legitimate for a user to do in a system. A schema defines the families of agents that a "user" and a "test" (or authority) are allowed to create.

Definition 3 (Ideal Agent Schema). *A (well-behaved) ideal agent schema* $\Sigma = (\mathcal{P}_{\mathsf{auth}}, \mathcal{P}_{\mathsf{user}})$ *(or simply schema) is a pair of agent families, such that there is a polynomial poly such that for any session of agents belonging to* $\mathcal{P}_{\mathsf{auth}} \cup \mathcal{P}_{\mathsf{user}}$ *(with any inputs and any configurations, with the same security parameter* κ*), the session terminates within* $\mathrm{poly}(\kappa, t)$ *steps, where* t *is the number of agents in the session.*

---

[6] More precisely, the first agent is executed till it enters a blocking or halting state, and then the second and so forth, in a round-robin fashion, until all the agents remain in blocking or halting states for a full round. After each execution of an agent, the contents of its outgoing communication tape are interpreted as an ordered sequence of messages to each of the other agents in the session (some or all of them possibly being empty messages), and copied over to the respective agents' incoming communication tapes.

Other Notation. If X and Y are a family of binary random variables (one for each value of κ), we write $X \approx Y$ if there is a negligible function negl such that $|\Pr[X = 1] - \Pr[Y = 1]| \leq \mathrm{negl}(\kappa)$. For two systems M and M', we say $M \approx M'$ if the two systems are indistinguishable to an interactive PPT distinguisher.

3 Defining Cryptographic Agents

In this section we define what it means for a cryptographic agent scheme to securely implement a given ideal agent schema. Intuitively, the security notion is of *indistinguishability preservation*: if two executions using an ideal schema are indistinguishable, we require them to remain indistinguishable when implemented using a cryptographic agent scheme. While it consists of several standard elements of security definitions, indistinguishability preservation as defined here is novel, and potentially of broader interest.

Ideal World. The ideal system for a schema Σ consists of two parties Test and User and a fixed third party $\mathcal{B}[\Sigma]$ (for "black-box"). All three parties are probabilistic polynomial time (PPT) ITMs, and have a security parameter κ built-in. We shall explicitly refer to their random-tapes as r, s and t. Test receives a "secret bit" b as input and User produces an output bit b'. The interaction between User, Test and $\mathcal{B}[\Sigma]$ can be summarized as follows:

- **Uploading agents.** Let $\Sigma = (\mathcal{P}_{\mathsf{auth}}, \mathcal{P}_{\mathsf{user}})$ where we associate $\mathcal{P}_{\mathsf{test}} := \mathcal{P}_{\mathsf{auth}} \cup \mathcal{P}_{\mathsf{user}}$ with Test and $\mathcal{P}_{\mathsf{user}}$ with User. Test and User can, at any point, choose an agent from its agent family and send it to $\mathcal{B}[\Sigma]$. More precisely, User can send a string to $\mathcal{B}[\Sigma]$, and $\mathcal{B}[\Sigma]$ will instantiate an agent $\mathcal{P}_{\mathsf{user}}$, with the given string (along with its own security parameter) as the contents of the parameter tape, and all other tapes being empty. Similarly, Test can send a string and a bit indicating whether it is a parameter for $\mathcal{P}_{\mathsf{auth}}$ or $\mathcal{P}_{\mathsf{user}}$, and it is used to instantiate an agent $\mathcal{P}_{\mathsf{auth}}$ or $\mathcal{P}_{\mathsf{user}}$, accordingly [7]. Whenever an agent is instantiated, $\mathcal{B}[\Sigma]$ sends a unique handle (a serial number) for that agent to User; the handle also indicates whether the agent belongs to $\mathcal{P}_{\mathsf{auth}}$ or $\mathcal{P}_{\mathsf{user}}$.
- **Request for Session Execution.** At any point in time, User may request an execution of a session, by sending an ordered tuple of handles $(h_1, \ldots, h_t)$ (from among all the handles obtained thus far from $\mathcal{B}[\Sigma]$) to specify the configurations of the agents in the session, along with their inputs. $\mathcal{B}[\Sigma]$ reports back the outputs from the session, and also gives new handles corresponding

---

[7] In fact, for convenience, we allow Test and User to specify multiple agents in a single message to $\mathcal{B}[\Sigma]$.

to the configurations of the agents when the session terminated.[8] If an agent halts in a session, no new handle is given for that agent.

Observe that only User receives any output from $\mathcal{B}[\Sigma]$; the communication between Test and $\mathcal{B}[\Sigma]$ is one-way. (See Figure 1.)

We define the random variable IDEAL⟨Test(b) | Σ | User⟩ to be the output of User in an execution of the above system, when Test gets b as input. We write IDEAL⟨Test | Σ | User⟩ in the case when the input to Test is a uniformly random bit. We also define TIME⟨Test | Σ | User⟩ as the maximum number of steps taken by Test (with a random input), $\mathcal{B}[\Sigma]$ and User in total.

Definition 4. *We say that* Test *is* hiding w.r.t. Σ *if* $\forall$ *PPT party* User,

$$\text{IDEAL}\langle\text{Test}(0) \mid \Sigma \mid \text{User}\rangle \approx \text{IDEAL}\langle\text{Test}(1) \mid \Sigma \mid \text{User}\rangle.$$

When the schema is understood, we shall refer to the property of being hiding w.r.t. a schema as simply being ideal-hiding.

Real World. A *cryptographic scheme* (or simply scheme) consists of a pair of (possibly stateful and randomized) programs $(\mathcal{O}, \mathcal{E})$, where $\mathcal{O}$ is an encoding procedure for agents in $\mathcal{P}_{\text{test}}$ and $\mathcal{E}$ is an execution procedure. The real world execution for a scheme $(\mathcal{O}, \mathcal{E})$ consists of Test, a user that we shall generally denote as Adv and the encoder $\mathcal{O}$. ($\mathcal{E}$ features as part of an honest user in the real world execution: see Figure 1.) Test remains the same as in the ideal world, except that instead of sending an agent to $\mathcal{B}[\Sigma]$, it sends it to the encoder $\mathcal{O}$. In turn, $\mathcal{O}$ encodes this agent and sends the resulting cryptographic agent to Adv.

We define the random variable REAL⟨Test(b) | $\mathcal{O}$ | Adv⟩ to be the output of Adv in an execution of the above system, when Test gets b as input; as before, we omit b from the notation to indicate a random bit. Also, as before, TIME⟨Test | $\mathcal{O}$ | User⟩ is the maximum number of steps taken by Test (with a random input), $\mathcal{O}$ and User in total.

Definition 5. *We say that* Test *is* hiding w.r.t. $\mathcal{O}$ *if* $\forall$ *PPT party* Adv,

$$\text{REAL}\langle\text{Test}(0) \mid \mathcal{O} \mid \text{Adv}\rangle \approx \text{REAL}\langle\text{Test}(1) \mid \mathcal{O} \mid \text{Adv}\rangle.$$

Note that REAL⟨Test | $\mathcal{O}$ | Adv⟩ = REAL⟨Test ∘ $\mathcal{O}$ | $\emptyset$ | Adv⟩ where $\emptyset$ stands for the null implementation. Thus, instead of saying Test is hiding w.r.t. $\mathcal{O}$, we shall sometimes say Test ∘ $\mathcal{O}$ is hiding (w.r.t. $\emptyset$). Also, when $\mathcal{O}$ is understood, we may simply say that Test is real-hiding.

---

[8] Note that if the same handle appears more than once in the tuple $(h_1, \ldots, h_t)$, it is interpreted as multiple agents with the same configuration (but possibly different inputs). Also note that after a session, the old handles for the agents are not invalidated; so a User can access a configuration of an agent any number of times, by using the same handle.

Syntactic Requirements on $(\mathcal{O}, \mathcal{E})$. $(\mathcal{O}, \mathcal{E})$ may or may not use a "setup" phase. In the latter case we call it a *setup-free cryptographic agent scheme*, and $\mathcal{O}$ is required to be a memory-less program that takes an agent $P \in \mathcal{P}_{\text{test}}$ as input and outputs a cryptographic agent that is sent to Adv. If the scheme has a setup phase, $\mathcal{O}$ consists of a triplet of memory-less programs $(\mathcal{O}_{\text{setup}}, \mathcal{O}_{\text{auth}}, \mathcal{O}_{\text{user}})$: in the real world execution, first $\mathcal{O}_{\text{setup}}$ is run to generate a secret-public key pair (MSK, MPK);[9] MPK is sent to Adv. Subsequently, when $\mathcal{O}$ receives an agent $P \in \mathcal{P}_{\text{auth}}$ it will invoke $\mathcal{O}_{\text{auth}}(P, \text{MSK})$, and when it receives an agent $P \in \mathcal{P}_{\text{user}}$, it will invoke $\mathcal{O}_{\text{user}}(P, \text{MPK})$, to obtain a cryptographic agent that is then sent to Adv.

$\mathcal{E}$ is required to be memoryless as well, except that when it gives a handle to a User, it can record a string against that handle, and later when User requests a session execution, $\mathcal{E}$ can access the string recorded for each handle in the session. There is a *compactness requirement* that the size of this string is *a priori* bounded (note that the state space of the ideal agents are also *a priori* bounded). If there is a setup phase, $\mathcal{E}$ can also access MPK each time it is invoked.

IND-PRE Security. Now we are ready to present the security definition of a cryptographic agent scheme $(\mathcal{O}, \mathcal{E})$ implementing a schema Σ. Below, the *honest real-world user*, corresponding to an ideal-world user User, is defined as the composite program $\mathcal{E} \circ$ User as shown in Figure 1.

Definition 6. *A cryptographic agent scheme* $\Pi = (\mathcal{O}, \mathcal{E})$ *is said to be a* Γ-IND-PRE-*secure scheme for a schema* Σ *if the following conditions hold.*

- *Correctness.* $\forall$ PPT User *and* $\forall$ Test $\in \Gamma$, IDEAL$\langle$Test $\mid \Sigma \mid$ User$\rangle \approx$ REAL$\langle$Test $\mid \mathcal{O} \mid \mathcal{E} \circ$ User$\rangle$. *If equality holds,* $(\mathcal{O}, \mathcal{E})$ *is said to have perfect correctness.*
- *Efficiency. There exists a polynomial* poly *such that,* $\forall$ PPT User, $\forall$Test $\in \Gamma$,

$$\text{TIME}\langle\text{Test} \mid \mathcal{O} \mid \mathcal{E} \circ \text{User}\rangle \leq \text{poly}(\text{TIME}\langle\text{Test} \mid \Sigma \mid \text{User}\rangle, \kappa).$$

- *Indistinguishability Preservation.* $\forall$Test $\in \Gamma$,

$$\text{Test } is \ hiding \ w.r.t. \ \Sigma \Rightarrow \text{Test } is \ hiding \ w.r.t. \ \mathcal{O}.$$

When Γ *is the family of all PPT tests – denoted by* Γ_{ppt}, *we simply say that* Π *is an* IND-PRE-*secure scheme for* Σ.

4 Reductions and Compositions

A fundamental question regarding (secure) computational models is that of reduction: which tasks can be reduced to which others. In the context of cryptographic agents, we ask which schemata can be reduced to which other schemata.

---

[9] For "master" secret and public-keys, following the terminology in some of our examples.

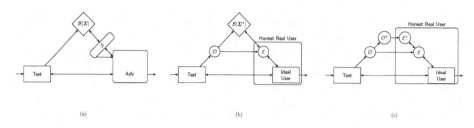

Fig. 2. $(\mathcal{O}, \mathcal{E})$ in (b) is a reduction from schema Σ to Σ^*. The security requirement is that no adversary Adv in the system (a) can distinguish that execution from an execution of the system in (b) (with Adv taking the place of honest real user). The correctness requirement is that the ideal User in (b) behaves the same as the ideal User interacting directly with $\mathcal{B}[\Sigma]$ (as in Figure 1(a)). (c) shows the composition of the hybrid scheme $(\mathcal{O}, \mathcal{E})^{\Sigma^*}$ with a scheme $(\mathcal{O}^*, \mathcal{E}^*)$ that IND-PRE-securely implements Σ^*.

We shall use a strong *simulation-based* notion of reduction. While a simulation-based security notion for general cryptographic agents or even just obfuscations (i.e., virtual black-box obfuscation) is too strong to exist, it is indeed possible to meet a simulation-based notion for reductions between schemata. This is *analogous to the situation in Universally Composable security*, where sweeping impossibility results exist for UC secure realizations in the plain model, but there is a rich structure of UC secure reductions among functionalities.

A *hybrid scheme* $(\mathcal{O}, \mathcal{E})^{\Sigma^*}$ is a cryptographic agent scheme in which $\mathcal{O}$ and $\mathcal{E}$ have access to $\mathcal{B}[\Sigma^*]$, as shown in Figure 2 (in the middle), where $\Sigma^* = (\mathcal{P}^*_{\text{auth}}, \mathcal{P}^*_{\text{user}})$. If $\mathcal{O}$ has a setup phase, we require that $\mathcal{O}_{\text{user}}$ uploads agents only in $\mathcal{P}^*_{\text{user}}$ (but $\mathcal{O}_{\text{auth}}$ can upload any agent in $\mathcal{P}^*_{\text{auth}} \cup \mathcal{P}^*_{\text{user}}$). In general, the honest user would be replaced by an adversarial user Adv. Note that the output bit of Adv in such a system is given by the random variable IDEAL$\langle$Test $\circ \mathcal{O} \mid \Sigma^* \mid$ Adv$\rangle$, where Test $\circ \mathcal{O}$ denotes the combination of Test and $\mathcal{O}$ as in Figure 2.

Definition 7 (Reduction). *We say that a (hybrid) cryptographic agent scheme* $\Pi = (\mathcal{O}, \mathcal{E})$ *reduces* Σ *to* Σ^* *with respect to* Γ, *if there exists a* PPT *simulator* $\mathcal{S}$ *such that* $\forall$ PPT User,

1. *Correctness:* $\forall$Test $\in \Gamma_{\text{ppt}}$, IDEAL$\langle$Test $\mid \Sigma \mid$ User$\rangle \approx$ IDEAL$\langle$Test$\circ\mathcal{O} \mid \Sigma^* \mid \mathcal{E}\circ$ User$\rangle$.
2. *Simulation:* $\forall$Test $\in \Gamma$, IDEAL$\langle$Test $\mid \Sigma \mid \mathcal{S} \circ$ User$\rangle \approx$ IDEAL$\langle$Test $\circ \mathcal{O} \mid \Sigma^* \mid$ User$\rangle$.

If $\Gamma = \Gamma_{\text{ppt}}$, *we simply say* Π *reduces* Σ *to* Σ^*. *If there exists a scheme that reduces* Σ *to* Σ^*, *then we say* Σ *reduces to* Σ^*. *(Note that correctness is required for all* PPT Test, *and not just in* Γ.)

Figure 2 illustrates a reduction. It also shows how such a reduction can be composed with an IND-PRE-secure scheme for Σ^*. Below, we shall use $(\mathcal{O}', \mathcal{E}') = (\mathcal{O} \circ \mathcal{O}^*, \mathcal{E}^* \circ \mathcal{E})$ to denote the composed scheme in Figure 2(c).[10]

Theorem 1 (Composition). *For any two schemata, Σ and Σ^*, if $(\mathcal{O}, \mathcal{E})$ reduces Σ to Σ^* and $(\mathcal{O}^*, \mathcal{E}^*)$ is an IND-PRE secure scheme for Σ^*, then $(\mathcal{O} \circ \mathcal{O}^*, \mathcal{E}^* \circ \mathcal{E})$ is an IND-PRE secure scheme for Σ.*

Proof sketch: Let $(\mathcal{O}', \mathcal{E}') = (\mathcal{O} \circ \mathcal{O}^*, \mathcal{E}^* \circ \mathcal{E})$. Also, let $\text{Test}' = \text{Test} \circ \mathcal{O}$ and $\text{User}' = \mathcal{E} \circ \text{User}$. To show correctness, note that for any User, we have

$$\text{REAL}\langle \text{Test} \mid \mathcal{O}' \mid \mathcal{E}' \circ \text{User} \rangle = \text{REAL}\langle \text{Test}' \mid \mathcal{O}^* \mid \mathcal{E}^* \circ \text{User}' \rangle$$

$$\overset{(a)}{\approx} \text{IDEAL}\langle \text{Test}' \mid \Sigma^* \mid \text{User}' \rangle$$

$$= \text{IDEAL}\langle \text{Test} \circ \mathcal{O} \mid \Sigma^* \mid \mathcal{E} \circ \text{User} \rangle$$

$$\overset{(b)}{\approx} \text{IDEAL}\langle \text{Test} \mid \Sigma \mid \text{User} \rangle$$

where (a) follows from the correctness guarantee of IND-PRE security of $(\mathcal{O}^*, \mathcal{E}^*)$, and (b) follows from the correctness guarantee of $(\mathcal{O}, \mathcal{E})$ being a reduction of Σ to Σ^*. (The other equalities are by regrouping the components in the system.)

It remains to prove that for all PPT Test, if Test is hiding w.r.t. Σ then Test is hiding w.r.t. $\mathcal{O}'$.

Firstly, we argue that Test is hiding w.r.t. $\Sigma \Rightarrow$ Test$'$ is hiding w.r.t. Σ^*. Suppose Test$'$ is not hiding w.r.t. Σ^*. This implies that there is some User such that $\text{IDEAL}\langle \text{Test}'(0) \mid \Sigma^* \mid \text{User} \rangle \not\approx \text{IDEAL}\langle \text{Test}'(1) \mid \Sigma^* \mid \text{User} \rangle$. But, by security of the reduction $(\mathcal{O}, \mathcal{E})$ of Σ to Σ^*, $\text{IDEAL}\langle \text{Test}'(b) \mid \Sigma^* \mid \text{User} \rangle \approx \text{IDEAL}\langle \text{Test}(b) \mid \Sigma \mid \mathcal{S} \circ \text{User} \rangle$, for $b = 0, 1$. Then, $\text{IDEAL}\langle \text{Test}(0) \mid \Sigma \mid \mathcal{S} \circ \text{User} \rangle \not\approx \text{IDEAL}\langle \text{Test}(1) \mid \Sigma \mid \mathcal{S} \circ \text{User} \rangle$, showing that Test is not hiding w.r.t. Σ. Thus we have,

$$\text{Test is hiding w.r.t. } \Sigma \Rightarrow \text{Test}' \text{ is hiding w.r.t. } \Sigma^*$$

$$\Rightarrow \text{Test}' \text{ is hiding w.r.t. } \mathcal{O}^*$$

$$\Rightarrow \text{Test is hiding w.r.t. } \mathcal{O}',$$

where the second implication is due to the fact that $(\mathcal{O}^*, \mathcal{E}^*)$ is an IND-PRE secure implementation of Σ^*, and the last implication follows by observing that for any Adv, we have $\text{REAL}\langle \text{Test}' \mid \mathcal{O}^* \mid \text{Adv} \rangle = \text{REAL}\langle \text{Test} \mid \mathcal{O}' \mid \text{Adv} \rangle$ (by regrouping the components). $\square$

Note that in the above proof, we invoked the security guarantee of $(\mathcal{O}^*, \mathcal{E}^*)$ only with respect to tests of the form $\text{Test} \circ \mathcal{O}$. Let $\Gamma \circ \mathcal{O} = \{\text{Test} \circ \mathcal{O} \mid \text{Test} \in \Gamma\}$. Then we have the following generalization.

---

[10] If $(\mathcal{O}, \mathcal{E})$ and $(\mathcal{O}^*, \mathcal{E}^*)$ have a setup phase, then it is implied that $\mathcal{O}'_{\text{auth}} = \mathcal{O}_{\text{auth}} \circ \mathcal{O}^*_{\text{auth}}$, $\mathcal{O}'_{\text{user}} = \mathcal{O}_{\text{user}} \circ \mathcal{O}^*_{\text{user}}$; invoking $\mathcal{O}'_{\text{setup}}$ invokes both $\mathcal{O}_{\text{setup}}$ and $\mathcal{O}^*_{\text{setup}}$, and may in addition invoke $\mathcal{O}^*_{\text{auth}}$ or $\mathcal{O}^*_{\text{user}}$.

Theorem 2 (Generalized Composition). *For any two schemata, Σ and Σ^*, if $(\mathcal{O}, \mathcal{E})$ reduces Σ to Σ^* and $(\mathcal{O}^*, \mathcal{E}^*)$ is a $(\Gamma \circ \mathcal{O})$-IND-PRE secure scheme for Σ^*, then $(\mathcal{O} \circ \mathcal{O}^*, \mathcal{E}^* \circ \mathcal{E})$ is a Γ-IND-PRE secure scheme for Σ.*

Theorem 3 (Transitivity of Reduction). *For any three schemata, $\Sigma_1, \Sigma_2, \Sigma_3$, if Σ_1 reduces to Σ_2 and Σ_2 reduces to Σ_3, then Σ_1 reduces to Σ_3.*

Proof sketch: If $\Pi_1 = (\mathcal{O}_1, \mathcal{E}_1)$ and $\Pi_2 = (\mathcal{O}_2, \mathcal{E}_2)$ are schemes that carry out the reduction of Σ_1 to Σ_2 and that of Σ_2 to Σ_3, respectively, we claim that the scheme $\Pi = (\mathcal{O}_1 \circ \mathcal{O}_2, \mathcal{E}_2 \circ \mathcal{E}_1)$ is a reduction of Σ_1 to Σ_3. The correctness of this reduction follows from the correctness of the given reductions. Further, if $\mathcal{S}_1$ and $\mathcal{S}_2$ are the simulators associated with the two reductions, we can define a simulator $\mathcal{S}$ for the composed reduction as $\mathcal{S}_2 \circ \mathcal{S}_1$. $\qquad\square$

5 Restricted Test Families: Δ, Δ^* and Δ_{det}

In order to capture various notions of security, we define various corresponding families of test functions. For some schemata of interest, such as obfuscation, there exist no IND-PRE secure schemes (see the full version [2] for details). Restricted test families are also useful to bypass these impossibilities.

We remark that one could define test families specifically adapted to the existing security definitions of various primitives, but our goal is to provide general test families *that apply meaningfully to all primitives*, and also, would support a composable notion of reduction. Towards this we propose the following sub-class of PPT tests, called Δ. Intuitively Δ is a set of tests that reveal everything about the agents it sends to the user except for one bit b. This exactly captures indistinguishability style definitions such as indistinguishability obfuscation, differing inputs obfuscation, indistinguishability style FE and such others.

We formalize this intuition as follows: for Test $\in \Delta$, each time Test sends an agent to $\mathcal{B}[\Sigma]$, it picks two agents (P_0, P_1). Both the agents are sent to User, and P_b is sent to $\mathcal{B}[\Sigma]$ (where b is the secret bit input to Test). Except for selecting the agent to be sent to $\mathcal{B}[\Sigma]$, Test is oblivious to the bit b. It will be convenient to represent Test(b) (for $b \in \{0,1\}$) as $\mathsf{D} \circ \mathsf{c} \circ \mathsf{s}(b)$, where D is a PPT party which communicates with User, and outputs pairs of the form (P_0, P_1) to c; c sends both the agents to User, and also forwards them to s; $\mathsf{s}(b)$ forwards P_b to $\mathcal{B}[\Sigma]$ (and sends nothing to User).

As we shall see, for both obfuscation and functional encryption, Δ-IND-PRE-security is indeed stronger than all the standard indistinguishability based security definitions in the literature.

But a drawback of restricting to a strict subset of all PPT tests is that the composition theorems (Theorem 1 and Theorem 3) do not hold any more. This is because, these composition theorems crucially relied on being able to define Test$' = $ Test $\circ \mathcal{O}$ as a member of the test family, where $\mathcal{O}$ was defined by the

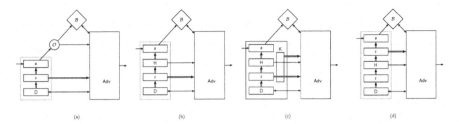

Fig. 3. Illustration of Δ and the extra requirements on Δ-reduction. (a) illustrates the structure of a test in Δ; the double-arrows indicate messages consisting of a pair of agents. The first condition on H is that (a) and (b) are indistinguishable to Adv: i.e., H can mimic the message from $\mathcal{O}$ without knowing the input bit to s. The second condition is that (c) and (d) are indistinguishable: i.e., K should be able to simulate the pairs of agents produced by H, based only on the input to H (copied by c to Adv) and the messages from H to Adv.

reduction (see Theorem 2). Nevertheless, as we shall see, analogous composition theorems do exist for Δ, if we enhance the definition of a reduction. At a high-level, we shall require $\mathcal{O}$ to have some natural additional properties that would let us convert Test $\circ$ $\mathcal{O}$ back to a test in Δ, if Test itself belongs to Δ.

Combining Machines: Some Notation. Before defining Δ-reduction and proving the related composition theorems, it will be convenient to introduce some additional notation. Note that the machines c and s above, as well as the program $\mathcal{O}$, have three communication ports (in addition to the secret bit that s receives): in terms of Figure 3, there is an input port below, an output port above and another output port on the right, to communicate with User. (D is also similar, except that it has no input port below, and on the right, it can interact with User by sending and receiving messages.) For such machines, we use $M_1 \circ M_2$ to denote connecting the output port above M_1 to the input port of M_2. The message from $M_1 \circ M_2$ to User is defined to consist of the pair of messages from M_1 and M_2 (formatted into a single message).

We shall also consider adding machines to the right of such a machine. Specifically, we use $M \,/\, K$ to denote modifying M using a machine K that takes as input the messages output by M to User (i.e., to its right), and to each such message may *append* an additional message of its own. Recall that for two systems M and M', we say $M \approx M'$ if the two systems are indistinguishable to an interactive PPT distinguisher. Using this notation, we define Δ-reduction.

Definition 8 (Δ-Reduction). *We say that a (hybrid) obfuscated agent scheme* $\Pi = (\mathcal{O}, \mathcal{E})$ Δ-*reduces* Σ *to* Σ^* *if*

1. *Π reduces Σ to Σ^* with respect to Δ (as in Definition 7), and*
2. *there exists PPT H and K such that*
   (a) *for all D such that D$\circ$c$\circ$s is hiding w.r.t. Σ, D$\circ$c$\circ$s$(b)\circ\mathcal{O} \approx$ D$\circ$c$\circ$H$\circ$s(b), for $b \in \{0,1\}$;*

(b) $\mathfrak{c} \circ \mathsf{H} \circ \mathfrak{c} \approx \mathfrak{c} \circ \mathsf{H} / \mathsf{K}$.

If there exists a scheme that Δ-reduces Σ to Σ^*, then we say Σ Δ-reduces to Σ^*.

Informally, condition (a) allows us to move $\mathcal{O}$ "below" $\mathfrak{s}(b)$: note that H will need to send any messages $\mathcal{O}$ used to send to User, without knowing b. Condition (b) requires that sending a copy of the pairs of agents output by H (by adding $\mathfrak{c}$ "above" H) is "safe": it can be simulated by K, which only sees the pair of agents that are given as input to H. Δ-reduction allows us to extend the composition theorem to Δ-IND-PRE security. We prove the following theorems in the full version of this paper [2].

Theorem 4 (Δ-Composition). *For any two schemata, Σ and Σ^*, if $(\mathcal{O}, \mathcal{E})$ Δ-reduces Σ to Σ^* and $(\mathcal{O}^*, \mathcal{E}^*)$ is a Δ-IND-PRE secure implementation of Σ^*, then $(\mathcal{O} \circ \mathcal{O}^*, \mathcal{E}^* \circ \mathcal{E})$ is a Δ-IND-PRE secure implementation of Σ.*

Theorem 5 (Transitivity of Δ-Reduction). *For any three schemata, Σ_1, Σ_2, Σ_3, if Σ_1 Δ-reduces to Σ_2 and Σ_2 Δ-reduces to Σ_3, then Σ_1 Δ-reduces to Σ_3.*

Other Restricted Test Families. We define two more restricted test families, Δ^* and Δ_{det}, which are of great interest for the obfuscation and functional encryption schemata. Both of these are subsets of Δ.

The family Δ_{det} simply consists of all deterministic tests in Δ. Equivalently, Δ_{det} is the class of all tests of the form $\mathsf{D} \circ \mathfrak{c} \circ \mathfrak{s}$, where D is a deterministic polynomial time party which communicates with User, and outputs pairs of the form (P_0, P_1) to $\mathfrak{c}$.

The family Δ^* consists of all tests in Δ which do not read any messages from User. Equivalently, Δ^* is the class of all tests of the form $\mathsf{D} \circ \mathfrak{c} \circ \mathfrak{s}$, where D is a PPT party which may send messages to User but does not accept any messages from User, and outputs pairs of the form (P_0, P_1) to $\mathfrak{c}$. As stated in the full version [2], the composition theorem for Δ, Theorem 4, extends to Δ^* as well.

6   Generic Group Schema

Our framework provides a method to convert a certain class of constructions — i.e., secure schemes for primitives that can be modeled as schemata — that are proven secure in heuristic models like the random oracle model [15] or the (bilinear) generic group model [73,84], into secure constructions in the standard model.

To be concrete, we consider the case of the generic group model. There are two important observations we make:

- Proving that a cryptographic scheme for a given schema Σ is secure in the generic group model typically amounts to a *reduction from Σ to a "generic group schema" Σ_{GG}.*
- The assumption that there is an IND-PRE-secure scheme Π_{GG} for Σ_{GG} is a standard-model assumption (that does not appear to be ruled out by known results or techniques).

Combined using the composition theorem (Theorem 1), these two observations yield a standard model construction for an IND-PRE-secure scheme for Σ.

Above, the generic group schema Σ_{GG} is defined in a natural way: the agents (all in $\mathcal{P}_{user}$, with $\mathcal{P}_{auth} = \emptyset$) are parametrized by elements of a large (say cyclic) group, and interact with each other to carry out group operations; the only output the agents produce for a user is the result of checking equality with another agent.

We formally state the assumption mentioned above:

Assumption 1 (Γ-Generic Group Agent Assumption). *There exists a Γ-IND-PRE-secure scheme for the generic group schema Σ_{GG}.*

Similarly, we put forward the *Γ-Bilinear* Generic Group Agent Assumption, where Σ_{GG} is replaced by Σ_{BGG} which has three groups (two source groups and a target group), and allows the bilinear pairing operation as well.

The most useful form of these assumptions (required by the composition theorem when used with the standard reduction) is when Γ is the set of all PPT tests. However, weaker forms of this assumption (like Δ-GGA assumption, or Δ^*-GGA assumption) are also useful, if a given construction could be viewed as a stronger form of reduction (like Δ-reduction).

While this assumption may appear too strong at first sight – given the impossibility results surrounding the generic group model – we argue that it is plausible. Firstly, observe that primitives that can be captured as schemata are somewhat restricted: primitives like zero knowledge that involve simulation based security, CCA secure encryption or non-committing encryption and such others do not have an interpretation as a secure schema. Secondly, IND-PRE security is weaker than simulation based security, and its achievability is not easily ruled out (see discussion in Section 10). Also we note that such an assumption already exists in the context of another popular idealized model: the random oracle model (ROM). Specifically, consider a natural definition of the random oracle schema, Σ_{RO}, in which the agents encode elements in a large set and interact with each other to carry out equality checks. Then, a Δ_{det}-IND-PRE-secure scheme for Σ_{RO} is equivalent to a point obfuscation scheme, which hides everything about the input except the output. The assumption that such a scheme exists is widely considered plausible, and has been the subject of prior research [38,40,42,86]. This fits into a broader theme of research that attempts to capture several features of the random oracle using standard model assumptions (e.g., [13,20]). The GGA assumption above can be seen as a similar approach to the generic group model, that captures only some of the security guarantees of the generic group model so that it becomes a plausible assumption in the standard model, yet is general enough to be of use in a broad class of applications.

One may wonder if we could use an even stronger assumption, by replacing the (bilinear) generic group schema Σ_{GG} or Σ_{BGG} by a multi-linear generic group schema Σ_{MGG}, which permits black box computation of multilinear map operations [25,51]. Interestingly, this assumption is provably false if we consider Γ to be Γ_{ppt}, since there exists a reduction of obfuscation schema Σ_{OBF} to Σ_{MGG} [9,34], and we have seen that there is no IND-PRE-secure scheme for Σ_{OBF}. On the other hand, for Γ being Δ or Δ^*, say, it remains a plausible assumption. Indeed, as mentioned earlier, Pass et al. introduced a computational assumption on multi-linear maps – called "semantic security" – and showed that the security of candidate constructions for indistinguishability obfuscation (aftersome modifications) can be based on semantically secure multi-linear groups [78]. We note that their assumption can be stated similar to Assumption 1, but using a multi-linear map schema and an appropriate test-family.

Falsifiability. Note that the above assumption as stated is not necessarily falsifiable, since there is no easy way to check that a given PPT test is hiding. However, it becomes falsifiable if instead of IND-PRE security, we used a modified notion of security IND-PRE', which requires that every test which is *efficiently provably* ideal-hiding is real-hiding. We note that IND-PRE' security suffices for all practical purposes as a security guarantee, and also suffices for the composition theorem. With this notion, to falsify the assumption, the adversary can (and must) provide a proof that a test is ideal-hiding and also exhibit a real world adversary who breaks its hiding when using the scheme.

7 Obfuscation Schema

In this section we define and study the obfuscation schema Σ_{OBF}. In the obfuscation schema, agents are deterministic, non-interactive and non-reactive: such an agent behaves as a simple Turing machine, that reads an input, produces an output and halts.

Definition. Below, we formally define the obfuscation schema. If $\mathcal{F}$ is a family of deterministic, non-interactive and non-reactive agents, we define

$$\Sigma_{\mathrm{OBF}(\mathcal{F})} := (\emptyset, \mathcal{F}).$$

That is, in the ideal execution User obtains handles for computing $\mathcal{F}$. We shall consider setup-free, IND-PRE secure implementations $(\mathcal{O}, \mathcal{E})$ of $\Sigma_{\mathrm{OBF}(\mathcal{F})}$.

A special case of $\Sigma_{\mathrm{OBF}(\mathcal{F})}$ corresponds to the case when $\mathcal{F}$ is the class of all functions that can be computed within a certain amount of time. More precisely, we can define the agent family $\mathcal{U}_s$ (for *universal* computation) to consist of agents of the following form: the parameter tape, which is at most $s(\kappa)$ bits long is taken to contain (in addition to κ) the description of an arbitrary binary circuit C; on input x, $\mathcal{U}_s$ will compute and output $C(x)$ (padding or truncating x as necessary). We define the "general" obfuscation schema

$$\Sigma_{\text{OBF}} := (\emptyset, \mathcal{P}_{\text{user}}^{\text{OBF}}) := \Sigma_{\text{OBF}(\mathcal{U}_s)},$$

for a given polynomial s. Here we have omitted s from the notation Σ_{OBF} and $\mathcal{P}_{\text{user}}^{\text{OBF}}$ for simplicity, but it is to be understood that whenever we refer to Σ_{OBF} some polynomial s is implied.

Completeness of Obfuscation. We show that Σ_{OBF} is a complete schema with respect to schematic reduction (Definition 7). That is, *every schema* (including possibly randomized, interactive, and stateful agents) can be reduced to Σ_{OBF}. We stress that this does not yield an IND-PRE-secure scheme for every schema (using composition), since there does not exist an IND-PRE-secure scheme for Σ_{OBF}, as described in the full version [2]. However, if there is, say, a hardware-based IND-PRE secure implementation of Σ_{OBF}, then this implementation can be used in a modular way to build an IND-PRE secure schema for any general functionality.

The reduction uses only standard cryptographic primitives: CCA secure public-key encryption and digital signatures. We present the full construction and proof in [2].

Relation to Existing Notions of Obfuscation. By using the test-families Δ_{det} and Δ^* in our framework, we can recover the notions of indistinguishability obfuscation and differing inputs obfuscation [10,11] exactly. We prove the following in the full version [2].

Lemma 1. *A set-up free Δ_{det}-IND-PRE-secure scheme for Σ_{OBF} (with perfect correctness) exists if and only if there exists an indistinguishability obfuscator.*

Lemma 2. *A set-up free Δ^*-IND-PRE-secure scheme for Σ_{OBF} (with perfect correctness) exists if and only if there exists a differing-inputs obfuscator.*

A Δ-IND-PRE secure scheme for Σ_{OBF} is a stronger notion than the above two notions of obfuscations (because Δ is a superset of Δ_{det} as well as Δ^*). One can give a definition of obfuscation in the traditional style, which exactly corresponds to this stronger notion. In the full version [2] we do exactly this, and term this adaptive differing inputs obfuscation. Independently, in [59] an equivalent definition appeared under the name of strong differing inputs obfuscation. Also, we note that we can model *Virtual Grey-Box Obfuscation* [17] in our framework, using an appropriate test-family and a statistical notion of hiding in Definition 4. This relies on an equivalence proven in [18] who give an indistinguishability based security definition for VGB security.

8   Functional Encryption

In this section, we present a schema Σ_{FE} for Functional Encryption. Although all variants of FE can [11] be captured as schemata secure against different families of test programs, we focus on adaptive secure, indistinguishability-based, public-key FE (with and without function-hiding). In Section 8.1 we introduce the schema Σ_{FE} for FE without function-hiding, and in Section 8.2 we introduce the schema $\Sigma_{\mathrm{FH\text{-}FE}}$ for function-hiding FE.

8.1   Functional Encryption Without Function Hiding

Public-key FE without function-hiding is the most well-studied variant of FE.
Definition. For a circuit family $\mathcal{C} = \{\mathcal{C}_\kappa\}$ and a message space $\mathcal{X} = \{\mathcal{X}_\kappa\}$, we define the schema $\Sigma_{\mathrm{FE}} = (\mathcal{P}_{\mathsf{auth}}^{\mathrm{FE}}, \mathcal{P}_{\mathsf{user}}^{\mathrm{FE}})$ as follows:

- $\mathcal{P}_{\mathsf{user}}^{\mathrm{FE}}$: An agent $P_x \in \mathcal{P}_{\mathsf{user}}^{\mathrm{FE}}$ simply sends x to the first agent in the session, where $x \in \mathcal{X}$ is a parameter of the agent, and halts. We will often refer to such an agent as a *message agent*.
- $\mathcal{P}_{\mathsf{auth}}^{\mathrm{FE}}$: An agent $P_C \in \mathcal{P}_{\mathsf{auth}}^{\mathrm{FE}}$, when invoked with input 0, outputs C (where $C \in \mathcal{C}$ is a parameter of the agent) and halts. If invoked with input 1, it reads a message $\tilde{x}$ from its incoming communication tape, writes $C(\tilde{x})$ on its output tape and halts. We will often refer to such an agent as a *function agent*.

Reducing Functional Encryption to Obfuscation. In a sequence of recent results [1,8,28,29,52,59], it was shown how to obtain various flavors of FE from various flavors of obfuscation. We investigate this connection in terms of schematic reducibility: can Σ_{FE} be reduced to Σ_{OBF}? For this reduction to translate to an IND-PRE-secure scheme for Σ_{FE}, we will need an IND-PRE-secure scheme for Σ_{OBF}, and a composition theorem.

Our main result in this section is a Δ-reduction of Σ_{FE} to Σ_{OBF}. Then, combined with a Δ-IND-PRE secure implementation of Σ_{OBF}, we obtain a Δ-IND-PRE secure implementation of Σ_{FE}, thanks to Theorem 4. [12]

Before explaining our reduction, we compare it with the results in [8,28,52]. At a high-level, these works could be seen as giving "$(\Gamma_{\mathrm{FE}}, \Gamma_{\mathrm{OBF}})$-reductions" from Σ_{FE} to Σ_{OBF} for some pair of test families Γ_{FE} and Γ_{OBF}, such that when it is composed with a Γ_{OBF}-IND-PRE-secure scheme for Σ_{OBF} one gets a Γ_{FE}-IND-PRE-secure scheme for Σ_{FE}. For example, in [52], $\Gamma_{\mathrm{OBF}} = \Delta_{\mathsf{det}}$

---

[11] Simulation-based definitions can be captured in terms of reduction to the null schema.

[12] Given a Δ^*-IND-PRE secure implementation of Σ_{OBF}, we could obtain a Δ^*-IND-PRE secure implementation of Σ_{FE} using the same reduction. This follows from the fact that the composition theorem for Δ, Theorem 4, extends to Δ^* as well. See the full version [2] for details.

(corresponding to indistinguishability obfuscation); there Γ_{FE} is a test-family that captures *selective-secure* functional encryption. We do not define such $(\Gamma_{\text{FE}}, \Gamma_{\text{OBF}})$-reductions formally in this work, as they are specific to the test-families used in [8,28,52]. Instead, we propose Δ-IND-PRE-security as a natural security notion for both obfuscation and functional encryption schemata, and provide a simpler Δ-reduction from Σ_{FE} to Σ_{OBF}.

Our Construction. We shall use a simple and natural functional encryption scheme: the key for a function f is simply a description of f with a signature on it; a ciphertext of a message m is an obfuscation of a program which when given as input a signed description of a function f, returns $f(m)$ if the signature verifies (and $\perp$ otherwise). Essentially the same construction was used in [28] as well, but they rely on "functional signatures" in which it is possible to derive keys for signing only messages satisfying an arbitrary relation. In our construction, we need only a standard digital signature scheme.

Below we describe our construction more formally, as a reduction from Σ_{FE} to Σ_{OBF} and prove that it is in fact a Δ-reduction. Let $\Sigma_{\text{FE}} = (\mathcal{P}_{\text{auth}}^{\text{FE}}, \mathcal{P}_{\text{user}}^{\text{FE}})$ and $\Sigma_{\text{OBF}} = (\emptyset, \mathcal{P}_{\text{user}}^{\text{OBF}})$. We shall only describe $\mathcal{O} = (\mathcal{O}_{\text{setup}}, \mathcal{O}_{\text{auth}}, \mathcal{O}_{\text{user}})$; $\mathcal{E}$ is naturally defined, and correctness is verified easily.

- $\mathcal{O}_{\text{setup}}$ picks a pair of signing and verification keys (SK, VK) for the signature scheme as (MSK, MPK).
- $\mathcal{O}_{\text{auth}}$, when given a function agent $P_f \in \mathcal{P}_{\text{auth}}^{\text{FE}}$, outputs (f, σ) to be sent to $\mathcal{E}$, where f is the parameter of P_f and σ is a signature on it.
- $\mathcal{O}_{\text{user}}$, when given an agent $P_m \in \mathcal{P}_{\text{user}}^{\text{FE}}$ as input, uploads an agent $P_{m,\text{MPK}} \in \mathcal{P}_{\text{user}}^{\text{OBF}}$ to $\mathcal{B}[\Sigma_{\text{OBF}}]$, which behaves as follows: on input (f, σ) $P_{m,\text{MPK}}$ verifies that σ is a valid signature on f with respect to the signature verification key MPK; if so, it outputs $f(m)$, and else $\perp$.

In the full version [2] we show that this is indeed a Δ reduction from Σ_{FE} to Σ_{OBF}.

Relation with Known Definitions. We examine the relation between IND-PRE-secure Functional Encryption with standard notions of security, such as indistinguishability based security. Firstly, we show that Δ_{det}-IND-PRE-secure is equivalent to indistinguishability secure FE.

Lemma 3. $\exists$ a Δ_{det}-IND-PRE-*secure scheme for* Σ_{FE} *iff* $\exists$ *an indistinguishability secure FE scheme.*

Note that an IND-PRE security implies Δ_{det}-IND-PRE security (for any schema). On the other hand, we show a strict separation between IND-PRE and Δ_{det}-IND-PRE security for FE.

Lemma 4. $\exists$ a Δ_{det}-IND-PRE *secure scheme for* Σ_{FE} *which is not an* IND-PRE *secure scheme for* Σ_{FE}.

We prove these results in the full version [2].

8.2   Function-Hiding Functional Encryption

Now we turn our attention to *function-hiding* FE (with public-keys). This a significantly more challenging problem, both in terms of construction and even in terms of definition [1,22,23]. The difficulty in definition stems from the public-key nature of the encryption which allows the adversary to evaluate the function encoded in a key on arbitrary inputs of its choice: hence a security definition cannot insist on indistinguishability between two arbitrary functions. In prior work, this is often handled by restricting the security definition to involve functions that are chosen from a restricted class of distributions, such that the adversary's queries cannot reveal anything about the functions so chosen. The definition arising from our framework naturally generalizes this, as the security requirement applies to all hiding tests and thereby removes the need of specifying *ad hoc* restrictions. We only need to specify a schema for function-hiding FE, and the rest of the security definition follows from the framework.

The definition of the schema corresponding to function-hiding FE, $\Sigma_{\text{FH-FE}} = (\mathcal{P}_{\text{auth}}^{\text{FH-FE}}, \mathcal{P}_{\text{user}}^{\text{FH-FE}})$, is identical to that of Σ_{FE}, except that a function agent $P_C \in \mathcal{P}_{\text{auth}}^{\text{FH-FE}}$ does not take any input, but always reads an input x from its communication tape and outputs $C(x)$. That is, the function agents do not reveal the function now.

Constructions. We present two constructions for function-hiding FE – an IND-PRE-secure scheme for the class of inner-product predicates, and a Δ-IND-PRE-secure scheme for all function families.

- The first construction is in fact an information-theoretic reduction of the schema $\Sigma_{\text{FH-FE(IP)}}$ (where IP denotes the class of inner-product predicates) to the schema Σ_{BGG}. Thus under the assumption that there is an IND-PRE secure scheme for Σ_{BGG}, we obtain a scheme for $\Sigma_{\text{FH-FE}}$, using Theorem 1. This construction is essentially the same as a construction in the recent work of [1], which was presented in the generic group model. Intuitively, the simulation based proof in [1] may be interpreted as a simulation based reduction from $\Sigma_{\text{FH-FE(IP)}}$ to Σ_{GG} satisfying Definition 7.
- The second construction is for general function-hiding FE: a Δ-IND-PRE-secure scheme for $\Sigma_{\text{FH-FE}}$, based on the assumption that a Δ-secure scheme for Σ_{OBF} exists. We mention that this construction is *not* a Δ-reduction. It relies on applying a signature to an obfuscation, and hence our framework cannot be used to model this as a black-box reduction (indeed, we cannot model the unforgeability requirement of signatures in our framework).

Further details of these constructions and their proofs are given in the full version [2].

9   Fully Homomorphic Encryption

In this section, we present a cryptographic agent schema Σ_{FHE} for Fully Homomorphic Encryption (FHE). This schema consists of *reactive agents* (i.e., agents which maintain state across invocations). For a message space $\mathcal{X} = \{\mathcal{X}\}_\kappa$ and a circuit family $\mathcal{F} = \{\mathcal{F}\}_\kappa$, we define the schema $\mathbb{P}_{\text{FHE}} = (\mathcal{P}_{\text{test}}^{\text{FHE}}, \mathcal{P}_{\text{user}}^{\text{FHE}})$ as follows:

- An agent $P^{\text{Msg}} \in \mathcal{P}_{\text{user}}^{\text{FHE}}$ is specified as follows: Its parameter tape consists of an initial value x. When invoked with an input C on its input tape, it reads a set of messages $x_2, x_3, \ldots, x_t$ from its communication tapes. Then it computes $C(x_1, .., x_t)$ where x_1 is its own value (either read from the work-tape, or if the work-tape is empty, from its parameter tape). Then it updates its work-tape with this value. When invoked without an input, it sends its message to the first program in the session.
- An agent $P^{\text{Dec}} \in \mathcal{P}_{\text{auth}}^{\text{FHE}}$ is defined as follows: when executed with an agent P^{Msg} it reads from its communication tape a single message from P^{Msg} and outputs it.[13]

In the full version [2] we show that a semantically secure FHE scheme $\mathbb{S}_{\text{FHE}} = (\text{Setup}, \text{Encrypt}, \text{Decrypt}, \text{Eval})$ can be naturally constructed from a Δ_{det}-IND-PRE secure scheme for Σ_{FHE}.

Other Examples. Several examples that we have not discussed, such as witness encryption and other flavors of FE, can also be naturally modeled as schemata. We present one more example — namely, property preserving encryption — in the full version [2], and leave the others to future work on these objects.

10   On Bypassing Impossibilities

An important aspect of our framework is that it provides a clean mechanism to tune the level of security for each primitive to a "sweet spot." The goal of such a definition is that it should imply prevalent achievable definitions while bypassing known impossibilities. The tuning is done by defining the family of tests, Γ with respect to which IND-PRE security is required. Below we discuss a few schemata and the definitions we recommend for them, based on what is known to be impossible.

Obfuscation. As we show in Section 7, an IND-PRE-secure scheme for Σ_{OBF} cannot exist. The impossibility proof relies on the fact that the test can upload an agent with (long) secrets in them. However, this argument stops applying when we restrict ourselves to tests in Δ: a test in Δ has the structure $\mathsf{D} \circ \mathsf{c} \circ \mathsf{s}$

---

[13] Note that there is no parameter to a $\mathcal{P}_{\text{auth}}$ agent as there is only one of its kind. However, we can allow a single schema to capture multiple FHE schemes with independent keys, in which case an index for the key would be the parameter for $\mathcal{P}_{\text{auth}}$ agents.

and c will reveal the agent to User. Note that then there could be at most one bit of uncertainty as to which agent was uploaded.

We point out that Δ-IND-PRE-security is much stronger than the prevalent notions of indistinguishability obfuscation and differing inputs obfuscation, introduced by Barak et al. [10]. Indeed, to the best of our knowledge, it would be the strongest definition of obfuscation known that can plausibly exist for all functions. We also observe that Δ-IND-PRE-secure obfuscation [14] is easier to use in constructions than differing-inputs obfuscation, as exemplified by our constructions in the full version [2].

Functional Encryption. Public-key function-hiding FE, as modeled by $\Sigma_{\text{FH-FE}}$, is a stronger primitive than obfuscation (for the same class of functions), as the latter can be easily reduced to the former. This means that there is no IND-PRE-secure scheme for $\Sigma_{\text{FH-FE}}$ for general functions. We again consider Δ-IND-PRE security as a sweet-spot for defining function-hiding functional encryption. Indeed, prior to this definition, arguably there was no satisfactory definition for this primitive. Standard indistinguishability based definitional approaches (which typically specify an explicit test that is ideal-hiding) run into the problem that if the user is allowed to evaluate a given function on any inputs of its choice, there is no one natural ideal-hiding test. Prior works have proposed different approaches to this problem: by restricting to only a specific test [22,23], or using a relaxed simulation-based definition [1,45]. Δ-IND-PRE security implies the definitions of Boneh et al. [22,23], but is in general incomparable with the simulation-based definitions in [1,45]. These latter definitions can be seen as using a test in the ideal world that allows the adversary to learn more information than in the real world. Our definition does not suffer from such information leakage.

For non-function-hiding FE (captured by the schema Σ_{FE}) too, there are many known impossibility results, when simulation-based security definitions are used [6,14,24]. At a high-level, these impossibilities followed a "compression" argument – the decryption of the challenge CT with the queried keys comprise a pseudorandom string R, but the adversary's key queries and challenge message are sequenced in such a way that to simulate its view, the simulator must somehow compress R significantly. These arguments do not apply to IND-PRE-security simply for the reason that there is no simulator implied by it. We do not have any candidate constructions for IND-PRE-secure scheme for Σ_{FE}, for general functions, but we leave open the possibility that it exists. We do however, provide a construction for a Δ-IND-PRE-secure scheme for Σ_{FE}, assuming one for Σ_{OBF}.

Generic Group and Random Oracle. It is well known that a proof of security in the generic group or the random oracle model provides only a heuristic security guarantee. Several works have shown that these oracles are "uninstantiable," and further there are uninstantiable primitives that can be implemented in the models with such oracles [12,41,48,50,75]. These results do not contradict

---

[14] or equivalently, adaptive differing-inputs obfuscation

Assumption 1, however, because the primitives in question, like non-commiting encryptions, zero-knowledge proofs and even signature schemes, do not fit into our framework of schemata. In other words, despite its generality, schemata can be used to model only certain kind of primitives, which seem insufficient to imply such separations between the generic group model and the standard model. As such, we propose Assumption 1, with $\Gamma = \Gamma_{\mathsf{ppt}}$, the family of all PPT tests, as an assumption worthy of investigation. However, the weaker assumption, with $\Gamma = \Delta$ suffices for our construction in the full version [2], if we settle for Δ-IND-PRE security for the resulting scheme.

References

1. Agrawal, S., Agrawal, S., Badrinarayanan, S., Kumarasubramanian, A., Prabhakaran, M., Sahai, A.: On the practical security of inner product functional encryption. To appear in PKC (2015)
2. Agrawal, S., Agrawal, S., Prabhakaran, M.: Cryptographic agents: Towards a unified theory of computing on encrypted data. Cryptology ePrint Archive, Report 2014/480 (2014). http://eprint.iacr.org/
3. Agrawal, S., Boneh, D., Boyen, X.: Efficient lattice (H)IBE in the standard model. In: Gilbert, H. (ed.) EUROCRYPT 2010. LNCS, vol. 6110, pp. 553–572. Springer, Heidelberg (2010)
4. Agrawal, S., Boneh, D., Boyen, X.: Lattice basis delegation in fixed dimension and shorter-ciphertext hierarchical IBE. In: Rabin, T. (ed.) CRYPTO 2010. LNCS, vol. 6223, pp. 98–115. Springer, Heidelberg (2010)
5. Agrawal, S., Freeman, D.M., Vaikuntanathan, V.: Functional encryption for inner product predicates from learning with errors. In: Lee, D.H., Wang, X. (eds.) ASIACRYPT 2011. LNCS, vol. 7073, pp. 21–40. Springer, Heidelberg (2011)
6. Agrawal, S., Gorbunov, S., Vaikuntanathan, V., Wee, H.: Functional encryption: new perspectives and lower bounds. In: Canetti, R., Garay, J.A. (eds.) CRYPTO 2013, Part II. LNCS, vol. 8043, pp. 500–518. Springer, Heidelberg (2013)
7. Alwen, J., Barbosa, M., Farshim, P., Gennaro, R., Gordon, S.D., Tessaro, S., Wilson, D.A.: On the relationship between functional encryption, obfuscation, and fully homomorphic encryption. In: Stam, M. (ed.) IMACC 2013. LNCS, vol. 8308, pp. 65–84. Springer, Heidelberg (2013)
8. Ananth, P., Boneh, D., Garg, S., Sahai, A., Zhandry, M.: Differing-inputs obfuscation and applications. Cryptology ePrint Archive (2013)
9. Barak, B., Garg, S., Kalai, Y.T., Paneth, O., Sahai, A.: Protecting obfuscation against algebraic attacks. In: Nguyen, P.Q., Oswald, E. (eds.) EUROCRYPT 2014. LNCS, vol. 8441, pp. 221–238. Springer, Heidelberg (2014)
10. Barak, B., Goldreich, O., Impagliazzo, R., Rudich, S., Sahai, A., Vadhan, S.P., Yang, K.: On the (Im)possibility of obfuscating programs. In: Kilian, J. (ed.) CRYPTO 2001. LNCS, vol. 2139, pp. 1–18. Springer, Heidelberg (2001)
11. Barak, B., Goldreich, O., Impagliazzo, R., Rudich, S., Sahai, A., Vadhan, S., Yang, K.: On the (im)possibility of obfuscating programs. J. ACM **59**(2), May 2012
12. Bellare, M., Boldyreva, A., Palacio, A.: An uninstantiable random-oracle-model scheme for a hybrid-encryption problem. In: Cachin, C., Camenisch, J.L. (eds.) EUROCRYPT 2004. LNCS, vol. 3027, pp. 171–188. Springer, Heidelberg (2004)
13. Bellare, M., Hoang, V.T., Keelveedhi, S.: Instantiating random oracles via UCEs. In: Canetti, R., Garay, J.A. (eds.) CRYPTO 2013, Part II. LNCS, vol. 8043, pp. 398–415. Springer, Heidelberg (2013)

14. Bellare, M., O'Neill, A.: Semantically-secure functional encryption: possibility results, impossibility results and the quest for a general definition. In: Abdalla, M., Nita-Rotaru, C., Dahab, R. (eds.) CANS 2013. LNCS, vol. 8257, pp. 218–234. Springer, Heidelberg (2013)

15. Bellare, M., Rogaway, P.: Random oracles are practical: A paradigm for designing efficient protocols. In: Proceedings of the First Annual Conference on Computer and Communications Security. ACM, November 1993

16. Bethencourt, J., Sahai, A., Waters, B.: Ciphertext-policy attribute-based encryption. In: IEEE Symposium on Security and Privacy, pp. 321–334 (2007)

17. Bitansky, N., Canetti, R.: On strong simulation and composable point obfuscation. In: Rabin, T. (ed.) CRYPTO 2010. LNCS, vol. 6223, pp. 520–537. Springer, Heidelberg (2010)

18. Bitansky, N., Canetti, R., Kalai, Y.T., Paneth, O.: On virtual grey box obfuscation for general circuits. In: Garay, J.A., Gennaro, R. (eds.) CRYPTO 2014, Part II. LNCS, vol. 8617, pp. 108–125. Springer, Heidelberg (2014)

19. Bitansky, N., Canetti, R., Paneth, O., Rosen, A.: Indistinguishability obfuscation vs. auxiliary-input extractable functions: One must fall. Cryptology ePrint Archive, Report 2013/641 (2013). http://eprint.iacr.org/

20. Boldyreva, A., Cash, D., Fischlin, M., Warinschi, B.: Foundations of non-malleable hash and one-way functions. In: Matsui, M. (ed.) ASIACRYPT 2009. LNCS, vol. 5912, pp. 524–541. Springer, Heidelberg (2009)

21. Boneh, D., Franklin, M.: Identity-based encryption from the weil pairing. In: Kilian, J. (ed.) CRYPTO 2001. LNCS, vol. 2139, pp. 213–229. Springer, Heidelberg (2001)

22. Boneh, D., Raghunathan, A., Segev, G.: Function-private identity-based encryption: hiding the function in functional encryption. In: Canetti, R., Garay, J.A. (eds.) CRYPTO 2013, Part II. LNCS, vol. 8043, pp. 461–478. Springer, Heidelberg (2013)

23. Boneh, D., Raghunathan, A., Segev, G.: Function-Private subspace-membership encryption and its applications. In: Sako, K., Sarkar, P. (eds.) ASIACRYPT 2013, Part I. LNCS, vol. 8269, pp. 255–275. Springer, Heidelberg (2013)

24. Boneh, D., Sahai, A., Waters, B.: Functional encryption: definitions and challenges. In: Ishai, Y. (ed.) TCC 2011. LNCS, vol. 6597, pp. 253–273. Springer, Heidelberg (2011)

25. Boneh, D., Silverberg, A.: Applications of multilinear forms to cryptography. IACR Cryptology ePrint Archive (2002)

26. Boneh, D., Waters, B.: Conjunctive, subset, and range queries on encrypted data. In: Vadhan, S.P. (ed.) TCC 2007. LNCS, vol. 4392, pp. 535–554. Springer, Heidelberg (2007)

27. Boyen, X., Waters, B.: Anonymous hierarchical identity-based encryption (without random oracles). In: Dwork, C. (ed.) CRYPTO 2006. LNCS, vol. 4117, pp. 290–307. Springer, Heidelberg (2006)

28. Boyle, E., Chung, K.-M., Pass, R.: On extractability obfuscation. In: Lindell, Y. (ed.) TCC 2014. LNCS, vol. 8349, pp. 52–73. Springer, Heidelberg (2014)

29. Boyle, E., Goldwasser, S., Ivan, I.: Functional signatures and pseudorandom functions. In: Krawczyk, H. (ed.) PKC 2014. LNCS, vol. 8383, pp. 501–519. Springer, Heidelberg (2014)

30. Brakerski, Z.: Fully homomorphic encryption without modulus switching from classical GapSVP. In: Safavi-Naini, R., Canetti, R. (eds.) CRYPTO 2012. LNCS, vol. 7417, pp. 868–886. Springer, Heidelberg (2012)

31. Brakerski, Z., Gentry, C., Vaikuntanathan, V.: (Leveled) fully homomorphic encryption without bootstrapping. In: ITCS (2012)
32. Brakerski, Z., Rothblum, G.N.: Obfuscating conjunctions. In: Canetti, R., Garay, J.A. (eds.) CRYPTO 2013, Part II. LNCS, vol. 8043, pp. 416–434. Springer, Heidelberg (2013)
33. Brakerski, Z., Rothblum, G.N.: Black-box obfuscation for d-cnfs. In: ITCS (2014)
34. Brakerski, Z., Rothblum, G.N.: Virtual black-box obfuscation for all circuits via generic graded encoding. In: Lindell, Y. (ed.) TCC 2014. LNCS, vol. 8349, pp. 1–25. Springer, Heidelberg (2014)
35. Brakerski, Z., Vaikuntanathan, V.: Fully homomorphic encryption from ring-LWE and security for key dependent messages. In: Rogaway, P. (ed.) CRYPTO 2011. LNCS, vol. 6841, pp. 505–524. Springer, Heidelberg (2011)
36. Brakerski, Z., Vaikuntanathan, V.: Efficient fully homomorphic encryption from (standard) LWE. In: FOCS (2011)
37. Brakerski, Z., Vaikuntanathan, V.: Lattice-based FHE as secure as PKE. In: ITCS (2014)
38. Canetti, R.: Towards realizing random oracles: hash functions that hide all partial information. In: Kaliski Jr., B.S. (ed.) CRYPTO 1997. LNCS, vol. 1294, pp. 455–469. Springer, Heidelberg (1997)
39. Canetti, R.: Universally composable security: a new paradigm for cryptographic protocols. In: Proceedings of the 42nd IEEE Symposium on Foundations of Computer Science, FOCS 2001 (2001)
40. Canetti, R., Dakdouk, R.R.: Obfuscating point functions with multibit output. In: Smart, N.P. (ed.) EUROCRYPT 2008. LNCS, vol. 4965, pp. 489–508. Springer, Heidelberg (2008)
41. Canetti, R., Goldreich, O., Halevi, S.: The random oracle methodology, revisited. In: STOC (1998)
42. Canetti, R., Micciancio, D., Reingold, O.: Perfectly one-way probabilistic hash functions (preliminary version). In: Proceedings of the Thirtieth Annual ACM Symposium on Theory of Computing, STOC 1998 (1998)
43. Canetti, R., Rothblum, G.N., Varia, M.: Obfuscation of hyperplane membership. In: Micciancio, D. (ed.) TCC 2010. LNCS, vol. 5978, pp. 72–89. Springer, Heidelberg (2010)
44. Canetti, R., Vaikuntanathan, V.: Obfuscating branching programs using black-box pseudo-free groups. Cryptology ePrint Archive, Report 2013/500 (2013). http://eprint.iacr.org/
45. Caro, A.D., Iovino, V.: On the power of rewinding simulators in functional encryption. Cryptology ePrint Archive, Report 2013/752 (2013). http://eprint.iacr.org/
46. Cash, D., Hofheinz, D., Kiltz, E., Peikert, C.: Bonsai trees, or how to delegate a lattice basis. In: Gilbert, H. (ed.) EUROCRYPT 2010. LNCS, vol. 6110, pp. 523–552. Springer, Heidelberg (2010)
47. Cocks, C.: An identity based encryption scheme based on quadratic residues. In: IMA Int. Conf., pp. 360–363 (2001)
48. Dent, A.W.: Adapting the weaknesses of the random oracle model to the generic group model. In: Zheng, Y. (ed.) ASIACRYPT 2002. LNCS, vol. 2501, pp. 100–109. Springer, Heidelberg (2002)
49. van Dijk, M., Gentry, C., Halevi, S., Vaikuntanathan, V.: Fully homomorphic encryption over the integers. In: Gilbert, H. (ed.) EUROCRYPT 2010. LNCS, vol. 6110, pp. 24–43. Springer, Heidelberg (2010)
50. Fischlin, M.: A note on security proofs in the generic model. In: Okamoto, T. (ed.) ASIACRYPT 2000. LNCS, vol. 1976, pp. 458–469. Springer, Heidelberg (2000)

51. Garg, S., Gentry, C., Halevi, S.: Candidate multilinear maps from ideal lattices. In: Johansson, T., Nguyen, P.Q. (eds.) EUROCRYPT 2013. LNCS, vol. 7881, pp. 1–17. Springer, Heidelberg (2013)

52. Garg, S., Gentry, C., Halevi, S., Raykova, M., Sahai, A., Waters, B.: Candidate indistinguishability obfuscation and functional encryption for all circuits. In: FOCS (2013)

53. Garg, S., Gentry, C., Halevi, S., Sahai, A., Waters, B.: Attribute-based encryption for circuits from multilinear maps. In: Canetti, R., Garay, J.A. (eds.) CRYPTO 2013, Part II. LNCS, vol. 8043, pp. 479–499. Springer, Heidelberg (2013)

54. Garg, S., Gentry, C., Halevi, S., Wichs, D.: On the implausibility of differing-inputs obfuscation and extractable witness encryption with auxiliary input (2014)

55. Gentry, C.: Fully homomorphic encryption using ideal lattices. In: STOC, pp. 169–178 (2009)

56. Gentry, C., Peikert, C., Vaikuntanathan, V.: Trapdoors for hard lattices and new cryptographic constructions. In: STOC (2008)

57. Gentry, C., Sahai, A., Waters, B.: Homomorphic encryption from learning with errors: conceptually-simpler, asymptotically-faster, attribute-based. In: Canetti, R., Garay, J.A. (eds.) CRYPTO 2013, Part I. LNCS, vol. 8042, pp. 75–92. Springer, Heidelberg (2013)

58. Goldreich, O., Micali, S., Wigderson, A.: How to play ANY mental game. In: STOC (1987)

59. Goldwasser, S., Gordon, S.D., Goyal, V., Jain, A., Katz, J., Liu, F.-H., Sahai, A., Shi, E., Zhou, H.-S.: Multi-input functional encryption. In: Nguyen, P.Q., Oswald, E. (eds.) EUROCRYPT 2014. LNCS, vol. 8441, pp. 578–602. Springer, Heidelberg (2014)

60. Goldwasser, S., Kalai, Y.T., Popa, R.A., Vaikuntanathan, V., Zeldovich, N.: How to run turing machines on encrypted data. In: Canetti, R., Garay, J.A. (eds.) CRYPTO 2013, Part II. LNCS, vol. 8043, pp. 536–553. Springer, Heidelberg (2013)

61. Goldwasser, S., Kalai, Y.T., Popa, R.A., Vaikuntanathan, V., Zeldovich, N.: Reusable garbled circuits and succinct functional encryption. In: STOC, pp. 555–564 (2013)

62. Goldwasser, S., Rothblum, G.N.: On best-possible obfuscation. In: Vadhan, S.P. (ed.) TCC 2007. LNCS, vol. 4392, pp. 194–213. Springer, Heidelberg (2007)

63. Gorbunov, S., Vaikuntanathan, V., Wee, H.: Functional encryption with bounded collusions via multi-party computation. In: Canetti, R., Safavi-Naini, R. (eds.) CRYPTO 2012. LNCS, vol. 7417, pp. 162–179. Springer, Heidelberg (2012)

64. Gorbunov, S., Vaikuntanathan, V., Wee, H.: Attribute based encryption for circuits. In: STOC (2013)

65. Goyal, V., Pandey, O., Sahai, A., Waters, B.: Attribute-based encryption for fine-grained access control of encrypted data. In: ACM Conference on Computer and Communications Security, pp. 89–98 (2006)

66. Hada, S.: Zero-knowledge and code obfuscation. In: Okamoto, T. (ed.) ASIACRYPT 2000. LNCS, vol. 1976, pp. 443–457. Springer, Heidelberg (2000)

67. Hofheinz, D., Malone-Lee, J., Stam, M.: Obfuscation for cryptographic purposes. In: Vadhan, S.P. (ed.) TCC 2007. LNCS, vol. 4392, pp. 214–232. Springer, Heidelberg (2007)

68. Hohenberger, S., Rothblum, G.N., Shelat, A., Vaikuntanathan, V.: Securely obfuscating re-encryption. In: Vadhan, S.P. (ed.) TCC 2007. LNCS, vol. 4392, pp. 233–252. Springer, Heidelberg (2007)

69. Katz, J., Sahai, A., Waters, B.: Predicate encryption supporting disjunctions, polynomial equations, and inner products. In: Smart, N.P. (ed.) EUROCRYPT 2008. LNCS, vol. 4965, pp. 146–162. Springer, Heidelberg (2008)

70. Lewko, A., Okamoto, T., Sahai, A., Takashima, K., Waters, B.: Fully secure functional encryption: attribute-based encryption and (hierarchical) inner product encryption. In: Gilbert, H. (ed.) EUROCRYPT 2010. LNCS, vol. 6110, pp. 62–91. Springer, Heidelberg (2010)

71. Lynn, B.Y.S., Prabhakaran, M., Sahai, A.: Positive results and techniques for obfuscation. In: Cachin, C., Camenisch, J.L. (eds.) EUROCRYPT 2004. LNCS, vol. 3027, pp. 20–39. Springer, Heidelberg (2004)

72. Matt, C., Maurer, U.: A constructive approach to functional encryption. Cryptology ePrint Archive, Report 2013/559 (2013). http://eprint.iacr.org/

73. Maurer, U.: Abstract models of computation in cryptography. In: IMA Int. Conf. (2005)

74. Micali, S., Pass, R., Rosen, A.: Input-indistinguishable computation. In: FOCS (2006)

75. Nielsen, J.B.: Separating random oracle proofs from complexity theoretic proofs: the non-committing encryption case. In: Yung, M. (ed.) CRYPTO 2002. LNCS, vol. 2442, pp. 111–126. Springer, Heidelberg (2002)

76. O'Neill, A.: Definitional issues in functional encryption. Cryptology ePrint Archive, Report 2010/556 (2010). http://eprint.iacr.org/

77. Pandey, O., Rouselakis, Y.: Property preserving symmetric encryption. In: Pointcheval, D., Johansson, T. (eds.) EUROCRYPT 2012. LNCS, vol. 7237, pp. 375–391. Springer, Heidelberg (2012)

78. Pass, R., Seth, K., Telang, S.: Indistinguishability obfuscation from semantically-secure multilinear encodings. In: Garay, J.A., Gennaro, R. (eds.) CRYPTO 2014, Part I. LNCS, vol. 8616, pp. 500–517. Springer, Heidelberg (2014)

79. Sahai, A., Seyalioglu, H.: Worry-free encryption: Functional encryption with public keys. In: CCS (2010)

80. Sahai, A., Waters, B.: Fuzzy identity-based encryption. In: Cramer, R. (ed.) EUROCRYPT 2005. LNCS, vol. 3494, pp. 457–473. Springer, Heidelberg (2005)

81. Sahai, A., Waters, B.: How to use indistinguishability obfuscation: Deniable encryption, and more. In: Crypto (2013)

82. Shamir, A.: Identity-based cryptosystems and signature schemes. In: Blakely, G.R., Chaum, D. (eds.) CRYPTO 1984. LNCS, vol. 196, pp. 47–53. Springer, Heidelberg (1985)

83. Shen, E., Shi, E., Waters, B.: Predicate privacy in encryption systems. In: Reingold, O. (ed.) TCC 2009. LNCS, vol. 5444, pp. 457–473. Springer, Heidelberg (2009)

84. Shoup, V.: Lower bounds for discrete logarithms and related problems. In: Fumy, W. (ed.) EUROCRYPT 1997. LNCS, vol. 1233, pp. 256–266. Springer, Heidelberg (1997)

85. Waters, B.: Functional encryption for regular languages. In: Safavi-Naini, R., Canetti, R. (eds.) CRYPTO 2012. LNCS, vol. 7417, pp. 218–235. Springer, Heidelberg (2012)

86. Wee, H.: On obfuscating point functions. In: STOC, pp. 523–532 (2005)

Executable Proofs, Input-Size Hiding Secure Computation and a New Ideal World

Melissa Chase[1][✉], Rafail Ostrovsky[2], and Ivan Visconti[3]

[1] Microsoft Research, Redmond, USA
melissac@microsoft.com
[2] UCLA, Los Angeles, USA
rafail@cs.ucla.edu
[3] University of Salerno, Fisciano, Italy
visconti@unisa.it

Abstract. In STOC 1987, Goldreich, Micali and Wigderson [GMW87] proved a fundamental result: it is possible to securely evaluate any function. Their security formulation consisted of transforming a real-world adversary into an ideal-world one and became a de facto standard for assessing security of protocols.

In this work we propose a new approach for the ideal world. Our new definition preserves the unconditional security of ideal-world executions and follows the spirit of the real/ideal world paradigm. Moreover we show that our definition is equivalent to that of [GMW87] when the input size is public, thus it is a strict generalization of [GMW87].

In addition, we prove that our new formulation is useful by showing that it allows the construction of protocols for input-size hiding secure two-party computation for any two-party functionality under standard assumptions and secure against malicious adversaries. More precisely we show that in our model, in addition to securely evaluating every two-party functionality, one can also protect the input-size privacy of one of the two players. Such an input-size hiding property is not implied by the standard definitions for two-party computation and is not satisfied by known constructions for secure computation. This positively answers a question posed by [LNO13] and [CV12]. Finally, we show that obtaining such a security notion under a more standard definition (one with a more traditional ideal world) would imply a scheme for "proofs of polynomial work", a primitive that seems unlikely to exist under standard assumptions.

Along the way, we will introduce the notion of "executable proof", which will be used in our ideal-world formulation and may be of independent interest.

Keywords: Secure computation · Ideal world · Input-size hiding · Proofs of work · FHE · PCP of proximity

1 Introduction

Goldreich, Micali and Wigderson proved in [GMW87] that secure computation is possible for any function, as long as there is a majority of honest players. They

© International Association for Cryptologic Research 2015
E. Oswald and M. Fischlin (Eds.): EUROCRYPT 2015, Part II, LNCS 9057, pp. 532–560, 2015.
DOI: 10.1007/978-3-662-46803-6_18

provided a compiler that on input a circuit computing the function produces a protocol that parties can run to obtain the correct output without revealing any additional information.

Following this result, a long line of works ([GMW87],[GL91],[MR92],[Bea92], [Can05]) developed what is now considered the de facto standard for proving security of a protocol. This notion, which we will refer to as the real/ideal-world paradigm, consists of showing that for any attack that can be carried out by a real-world adversary $\mathcal{A}$ during the execution of the protocol there is a corresponding attack which could be carried out by the ideal-world adversary Sim. Since the setting where Sim works is secure by definition, the real-world protocol must be secure against $\mathcal{A}$.

We note that for general functionalities, the real/ideal world is the only way we know to meaningfully capture security against arbitrarily malicious adversaries. In what follows, we will use *secure* to mean secure against malicious parties, unless otherwise stated, and we will focus, as in [GMW87] on the stand-alone setting.

Beyond the standard real/ideal-world definition. The real/ideal-world paradigm has long been the main measure to evaluate what can and can not be securely computed. The difficulties (and sometimes impossibilities) of proving security under the traditional real/ideal-world formulation have been considered an inherent price to pay for a solid security notion. This has motivated a variety of alternative definitions circumventing such difficulties/impossibilities by explicitly decreasing the security guaranteed by the standard real/ideal world definition. Examples of weaker security notions are those involving trusted third parties, set-up assumptions, superpolynomial-time simulation and so on. This motivates the following question:

Open problem 1: Are there other ways of defining the ideal/real world which would capture all the desirable properties mentioned above, but which might allow us to circumvent some difficulties and impossibilities of the traditional definition?

1.1 A Case Study: Hiding the Input Size

In 2003 Micali, Rabin and Kilian [MRK03] identified an important limitation of the traditional real/ideal-world paradigm. They noticed that in the real world there are interesting cases where a player would like to protect the *size* of his input. This seems increasingly relevant in today's world of big data: one might imagine settings where the number or sensor readings, the size of the customer database, the quantity of user profiles collected, or the total amount of information stored in an advertising database might be considered extremely private or confidential information.

[MRK03] models input-size hiding by saying that the protocol must hide the party's input in a setting where there is no fixed upper bound on the size of the input: although of course honest parties will run on polynomial-length inputs, there is no limit on what those polynomials may be. This guarantees that nothing is revealed about the input size, and has the additional advantage that it requires protocols where parties' efficiency does not depend on an upper bound, but only on the size of *their actual input* and the complexity of the functionality for that input.[1] As discussed by [MRK03], known previous results do not allow one to obtain such security (e.g., the [GMW87] compiler inherently reveals the size of the input).

Previous work on input-size hiding. Micali et al. explored the case of a player P_0 holding a set Φ of polynomial but unrestricted size (i.e., not upperbounded by any fixed polynomial) and another player P_1 holding an element x. Their function f always outputs x to P_0 and outputs 1 to P_1 if $x \in \Phi$ and 0 otherwise. They gave a game-based solution called "Zero-Knowledge Sets" (ZK sets or ZKS), but achieving standard simulation-based security remained an open problem.

There have been a few other works in this direction. [IP07] studied the evaluation of branching programs as another interesting application of input-size hiding secure computation. Their solution to the above problem in the setting of secure two-party computation (2PC) is round efficient, however it does not provide input-size hiding by the above definition (the length of the program that corresponds to the input of P_0 is bounded), and they do not achieve simulation-based security. More recently, [ACT11] focused on achieving input-size hiding set intersection and obtained an efficient scheme. Their solution only addresses semi-honest adversaries, and security is proved in the random oracle model. [CV12] proposed a construction that satisfies a modified real/ideal-world definition specifically for the set membership functionality studied in [MRK03]; we will discuss below some of the challenges in extending this to cover general functionalities. The importance in practice of input-size hiding secure computation was considered in [CFT13] where the authors presented an efficient protocol for size and position hiding private substring matching[2].

Very recently, [LNO13] discussed the case of general functionalities, but again their constructions are limited to the case of semi-honest adversaries. This leads to the obvious question:

Open problem 2: Is it possible to construct input-size hiding protocols for general functionalities that are secure against malicious adversaries, or is revealing the size of players' inputs inherent in any general 2PC that achieves security against malicious adversaries?

Our variant of input-size hiding. Lindell et al. [LNO13] also provide a general definition of input-size hiding secure computation, essentially extending the

---

[1] It also has advantages in terms of concrete security in that it results in protocols where the efficiency of the simulator depends only on the complexity of the adversary (and not on some assumed upper bound on its input size).

[2] In this type of protocol the first party could for instance run on input a digitized genome while the second party could run on input a set of DNA markers. The goal in such an use of the protocol is to securely check whether the genome matches the markers, without revealing any additional information, not even the number of markers.

real/ideal-world paradigm in the natural way, and a classification of different types of input-size hiding. Here we will focus on the case where the output size is fixed, and where only one party wants to hide the size of his input. For example, consider the setting where one party wants to run a set of proprietary computations on each element of another party's large private database, and obtain some aggregate results. If the computations can be described in fixed size but the size of the database is private, then our results apply.

As noted by Ishai and Paskin in [IP07] and formally proven in [LNO13] there exist some interesting functionalities for which two-sided input-size hiding is not possible, and similar cases where it is impossible to hide the size of the players' output. Thus, given that we want to achieve results for general functionalities, we restrict ourselves to the one-sided input-size hiding, fixed output-size setting.

We stress that in this work we do not aim to construct protocols for functionalities that work on superpolynomial-sized inputs but only protocols that work for any polynomial-sized input, without a fixed polynomial upper bound on the possible input size.

1.2   Limitations of the Real/Ideal-World Paradigm in the Input-Size Hiding Setting

Why input-size hiding secure 2PC is so tough to achieve. We first begin by recalling the [LNO13] semi-honest input-size hiding protocol, again restricting to the case where only one party's input size is hidden (say P_0) and where the output size is fixed and known. The protocol proceeds roughly as follows: First P_1 generates an FHE key pair and sends the public key along with an encryption of his input x_1 to P_0. Then P_0 uses his input x_0 and the FHE evaluation to evaluate $f(x_0, x_1)$. He sends the result back to P_1, who decrypts and outputs the result.[3] The result is secure in the semi-honest model as long as the FHE is semantically secure and circuit private.

We can immediately see that this protocol is not secure against a malicious $P_0^\star$, since there is no guarantee that the ciphertexts that $P_0^\star$ returns corresponds to $f(x_0, \cdot)$ for some valid x_0. Instead $P_0^\star$ could return an incorrect ciphertext to influence P_1's output or to choose his input conditioned on x_1. More fundamentally, if we consider the real/ideal-world paradigm (which as we noted above is the only way we know to accurately capture security against malicious adversaries for general functionalities), we see that the simulator needs to be able to extract an input x_0 to send to the functionality.

Traditionally, this problem is solved by requiring that the malicious party includes a proof of knowledge (PoK) of his input. In the input-size hiding setting, we could imagine using an input-size hiding PoK where the proof does not reveal the size of the witness (although as we will discuss later, these are not so easy

---

[3] For simplicity we consider the case where only P_1 receives output, but similar issues occur in the setting where only P_0 receives output, or where both parties receive input.

to achieve). The simulator could then extract from this PoK and send the result to the functionality.

However, here we run into trouble: Recall that the protocol cannot fix any polynomial upper bound on the length of the prover's input (otherwise it would not really be input-size hiding). Now, suppose that an adversary $P_0^\star$ decides to run the protocol using a superpolynomial-length input. Note that using a superpolynomial-length input does not necessarily mean that the adversary must be superpolynomial; it may be that the adversary is working with a compact representation a much longer input. And suppose that the adversary can find a way to efficiently run the protocol and generate a proof given only this short representation. Then finding a corresponding polynomial-time ideal-world adversary will be impossible: this ideal adversary would have to send the functionality an equivalent input (of superpolynomial size!) and this would require superpolynomial time. (Concretely think of the set membership function; if the set Φ chosen by $P_0^\star$ consists of all k-bit strings such that the last bit is 0, then $P_0^\star$ has in mind an input of exponential size, and thus efficiently extracting this input will be impossible. Notice that $P_0^\star$ could still be efficient because it is possible to represent that huge set as a small circuit.)

We could of course simply assume that we can design a PoK or more generally a protocol which an honest party can run on any polynomial-sized input, but for which no polynomial-time adversary can execute the protocol on *any* superpolynomial input. However, we argue that this seems inherently non-standard: essentially, we would be assuming an object which is easy on any polynomial-sized input but becomes computationally infeasible as soon as the input is even slightly superpolynomial. This is therefore the inherent major difficulty. Even if $P_0^\star$ is guaranteed to be efficient (polynomial time), we have no way of guaranteeing that the *input that $P_0^\star$ is implicitly using* is of polynomial size.

Formalizing the limitation of the real/ideal-world definition w.r.t. hiding the input size. Lindell et al. [LNO13] conjectured that their construction (which is shown to be secure against semi-honest adversaries) could be augmented with a "proof of work" in order to be secure against malicious adversaries; essentially the idea was to solve the problem described above by requiring the adversary to prove that the size of his input is polynomial. Unfortunately currently there is no candidate construction for proofs of work under standard assumptions; moreover, as we just mentioned, non-standard assumptions seem inherent, in that a proof of work makes an assumption on the abilities of a polynomial-time adversary on a problem instance that is only guaranteed to be superpolynomial (rather than exponential). This prompts the following question.

Open problem 3: is it possible to achieve input-size hiding secure 2PC for all functionalities in the traditional real/ideal world without relying on proofs of work?

In Section 2.1, we formalize this notion of proofs of work, which we refer to as a proof of polynomial work or PPW. On the positive side, this seems to capture the intuition for what [LNO13] use in their proposed extension to security against malicious adversaries. On the other hand, as we have discussed, these proofs of work seem inherently to require non-standard assumptions. This then presents the next open question:

Open problem 4: How can we meaningfully define input-size hiding secure 2PC if we are interested in constructions under standard assumptions?

1.3   A New Ideal World

Given the above limitations, we take a step back and consider what we need from our security definition. The traditional real/ideal-world paradigm has three key features: 1) In the ideal world it is clear from inspection what functionality is provided and what an adversary can learn or influence. Indeed, players are simply required to send their inputs to a trusted functionality $\mathcal{F}$ that will then evaluate the function and distribute the outputs to the players. This guarantees that even if P_0 is corrupted[4]: a) the output is correct and consistent with some valid input x_0, b) P_0's choice of input x_0 cannot depend on P_1's input x_1, and c) P_0 cannot cause a selective failure, i.e. P_0 cannot cause the protocol to fail conditioned on the input chosen by P_1. 2) In the ideal world, security holds unconditionally. Again, this is important because we want it to be obvious that the ideal world provides the desired security. 3) The ideal world is efficient (i.e., the ideal functionality $\mathcal{F}$ and the ideal adversary Sim are polynomial time). This is crucial when we want to use secure computation as a part of a larger protocol: if a protocol achieves a real/ideal-world definition, then we can argue that we could replace it with $\mathcal{F}$ and Sim. However if $\mathcal{F}$ and Sim are inefficient, then the resulting game will not be polynomial time, and any reductions to standard hardness assumptions will fail.

Our key observation then is that in order to enforce these properties the functionality does not actually need to receive P_0's input x_0. Instead it only needs a) to ensure that x_0 is fixed and independent of x_1, and b) an efficient way to compute $f(x_0, x_1)$ consistently with x_0.

The new ideal world. This leads to the following relaxation of the ideal world. Instead of requiring P_0 to send his input directly, we instead require P_0 to send an *implicit representation* of his input. The only requirement on this representation is that it must uniquely define the party's true input x_0.[5] We will use $\mathsf{Rep}(x_0)$ to denote some implicit representation corresponding to x_0. (Our ideal world will take the specification of this representation as a parameter; the definition will require that there exist a valid representation under which the real and ideal worlds are identical.)

Then in order to allow the functionality to compute P_1's output, the ideal P_0 will also send a circuit C describing how to compute the output given any input x_1 from P_1. Finally, we require that this circuit C on input x_1 produce not

---

[4] We use corrupt P_0 as an example: clearly the analogous properties also hold if P_1 is corrupt.

[5] For our ideal world to be realizable, it must hold that any polynomial-sized input has a polynomial-sized representation.

only the output $f(x_0, x_1)$, but also some evidence that this output is correctly computed according to x_1 and the input defined by $\mathsf{Rep}(x_0)$. Intuitively, because P_0 sends $\mathsf{Rep}(x_0)$, this guarantees that x_0 is fixed and independent of x_1, and because C provides evidence that its output is correct, we are guaranteed that (if the evidence is valid), the output provided to P_1 is indeed $f(x_0, x_1)$. Finally, we note that the only way for P_0 to cause a selective failure is for $C(x_1)$ to output invalid evidence - in all other cases the functionality will send to P_1 a valid output.

That leaves two issues to resolve: 1) how to formalize this "evidence", and 2) what happens if $C(x_1)$ produces evidence that is invalid.

Executable proofs. Ignoring the implicit input for a moment, we might consider an ideal world which works as follows: $\mathcal{F}$ receives from one of the parties P_0 not only the input x_0 but also a circuit C. Then, instead of computing the output directly, $\mathcal{F}$, having obtained input x_1 from P_1, runs $C(x_1)$ to obtain (y, w), where w is an NP witness for the statement $y = f(x_0, x_1)$. $\mathcal{F}$ verifies w and outputs y to P_1 iff the verification succeeds.[6] Clearly this is equivalent to the traditional notion of security because the NP witness *unconditionally* guarantees that $\mathcal{F}$ produces the correct output.

Now, what if we want $\mathcal{F}$ to be able to verify statements which may not be in NP? [7]

We might want to consider cases where, rather than an NP-witness, $\mathcal{F}$ is given *some other kind of proof*. As long as the proof is unconditionally sound and efficiently verifiable we still have a meaningful notion of security. If we want to consider more general languages, we might imagine providing $\mathcal{F}$ with a PCP to verify instead of an NP witness. Because PCPs are unconditionally sound, this would still satisfy the first property. However, even if they can be verified efficiently, the PCPs for the language could still be exponentially long while as argued above, we want our ideal parties and $\mathcal{F}$ to run in polynomial time, so it might be impossible for the ideal party to output an entire PCP. Thus we introduce the notion of an "executable proof". This is a new concept of proof that has similarities with classical proofs, interactive proofs and PCPs. However executable proofs differ from the above concepts since they focus on a giving to a verifier the capability of checking the veracity of a statement (potentially not in NP) by running a circuit (i.e., an executable proof) locally.

In particular we will make use of *executable PCPs*. An executable PCP is a circuit which on input i produces the ith bit of a PCP (i.e., a circuit representation of a PCP). Given a description of such a circuit, $\mathcal{F}$ can run the PCP

---

[6] Addressing the case where verification fails is somewhat more subtle. See below for more discussion.

[7] For example in the context of input-size hiding protocols, as discussed above, we might consider the case where $\mathcal{F}$ is given only a compact representation of x_0 while the actual x_0 may be of superpolynomial length. In this case it may be that verifying $f(x_0, x_1) = y$ given only x_1 and the representation of x_0 is not in NP. (Note that in this case a witness that includes the explicit x_0 would have superpolynomial length, and so would not be a valid NP witness.)

verifier to unconditionally verify the statement. If the circuit representation is polynomial sized, this verification is efficient.

The nice point here compared to just using a witness for the statement is that the description of the executable PCP can be much shorter than a standard witness (it essentially depends on the complexity of describing the given witness); this will play a fundamental role in our constructions.

Ideal Errors. We solve the second issue by slightly modifying the notion of real/ideal-world executions. In the ideal world $\mathcal{F}$ will verify the proof π and then complete the protocol only if the proof was accepting. If π failed in convincing $\mathcal{F}$, then $\mathcal{F}$ will send P_1 a special message "ideal error", indicating that the ideal input was invalid. Finally, our definition for secure computation will require that the real-world execution never produce this "ideal error" as output of P_1.[8] This guarantees that in any secure realization any real world adversary must have a corresponding ideal world adversary who causes this error to occur in the output of the ideal P_1 only with negligible probability. (This is because any ideal world execution in which the ideal honest player P_1 outputs such an error with non-negligible probability would be instantly distinguishable from the real world where such an output for P_1 cannot appear by definition).

We stress that the flow of data follows the standard notion of the real/ideal paradigm where players send data to $\mathcal{F}$ first, and then $\mathcal{F}$ performs a computation and sends outputs (waiting for the approval of $\mathcal{A}$ for fairness reasons) to players. By the unconditional soundness of the proof given by π, it is clear that the adversary is committed to an input and the output is consistent with that input (as long as "ideal error" does not occur). And finally, our ideal adversary runs in polynomial time, and the implicit input and the circuit C are produced by the ideal adversary; this means that $\mathcal{F}$ will also run in polynomial time[9]. Thus, our new formulation has all the desirable properties mentioned above. As a sanity check, we note that our definition is equivalent to the traditional real/ideal-world definition in the case where the input lengths are fixed known polynomials.

1.4   Constructing Input-Size Hiding Under the New Definition

Finally, we show that our new definition is realizable. We show a protocol that satisfies our input-size hiding secure 2PC and that builds on top of several recent advanced tools, and follows the outline from the semi-honest construction of [LNO13] described above. Roughly, we will use fully homomorphic encryption (FHE) as in [LNO13] so that the adversary P_0 can evaluate the function given only an encryption of P_1's input, which will give privacy for P_1. To guarantee

---

[8] Technically we can guarantee this by requiring that the real execution replaces any "ideal error" in its output by $\perp$.

[9] To see this note that a polynomial time adversary must produce polynomial sized circuits for the ideal input and the circuit C, $\mathcal{F}$'s operation consists of evaluating the circuit C and running a polynomial time verification algorithm on the proof produced by C, and polynomial sized circuits can always be evaluated in polynomial time and produce polynomial length output.

that the adversary P_0 must behave correctly we will require that P_0 commit to (via an input-size hiding commitment) and prove knowledge of his input before receiving the ciphertext from P_1. However, in designing this proof of knowledge, we are faced with the issue discussed above of extracting a potentially very long input from a short proof of knowledge. To address this we will use a special proof of knowledge introduced by [CV12] called a "universal argument of quasi knowledge" (UAQK) that has short communication complexity and provides a (non-black box) extractor that outputs a *short* "implicit" representation of the witness. Therefore the issue of efficiently extracting from an adversary that has in mind a very large input is solved by extracting a small implicit representation of this input. Looking ahead to the proof, it is this implicit represent that will be used as Rep in the ideal world. After applying the FHE evaluation to compute an encryption of $f(x_0, x_1)$, P_0 is required to give a UAQK to prove knowledge of a *PCP of proximity* proving that her work on ciphertexts was done correctly. With a PCP of proximity, a verifier can verify the proof while accessing only selected bits of the statement and proof. Again looking ahead, the simulator will use the code of an adversary P_0 and the extractor of the UAQK to generate a circuit which can output single bits of the PCP of proximity; such a circuit is used to instantiate the executable PCP in the ideal world. Here the use of PCPs of proximity is critical since they allow us to verify proofs by reading only small parts of statements and proofs. (This allows the functionality to verify correctness of the claimed output given only an implicit representation of P_0's input.)

Concretely, our protocol can be instantiated by assuming FHE and CRHFs, this proves that our notion can be achieved under standard assumptions, avoiding random oracles [BR93, CGH98], non-black-box extraction assumptions [Dam92] (see [Nao03] about their non-falsifiability), superpolynomial-time simulation, and proofs of work.

1.5   Short Summary of Our Results

In this work we embark on the challenging task of defining and achieving input-size hiding security against malicious adversaries under a simulation-based definition, following the spirit of [GMW87]. In Section 2.2 we give a new definition of an ideal world that has all the desirable properties of the real/ideal paradigm mentioned above, *and* allows us to capture input-size hiding, thus answering the last open question. We pair this result with another contribution: in Section 2.1 we show that achieving input-size hiding secure 2PC under the standard real/ideal-world formulation implies the existence of proofs of work. This solves the third problem and gives evidence of the power of our new formulation. Finally, in order to show that our size definition *is* realizable under standard assumptions, in Section 3 we provide a construction which can be instantiated under FHE and CRHFs. Thus we also provide a solution to the second open problem. All together these results provide an answer to our first question: a demonstration of how considering a modified security model can still give meaningful security while allowing us to circumvent impossibility results inherent in the traditional definitions.

1.6   Discussion

Other variations on the ideal world. One obvious alternative would be to simply allow for an unbounded functionality $\mathcal{F}$: $\mathcal{F}$ could then extract the entire (potentially exponentially long) input from the implicit input C, and then compute the appropriate output. However, our aim here is a definition giving guarantees *as close as possible to standard secure 2PC* and, as mentioned above, one crucial property of secure 2PC is that the functionality is efficient.

We compare our variation of the ideal world with the simulation-with-aborts definition used for fairness issues. Simulation-with-aborts is a simple variation of [GMW87] and *must* be used in light of an impossibility result. However it introduces a security weakness in the ideal world that is reflected in the real world. While our variation is somewhat less straightforward, it can be used to achieve a stronger security notion under standard assumptions. Our variation applied to the simulation-with-aborts definition, does not introduce any additional security drawback that can be reflected in real-world protocols. Moreover, it allows us to capture input-size hiding, and as we will see, it has the indisputable benefit that it can be realized under standard assumptions.

Timing attacks: input-size hiding is relevant also in practice. While input-size hiding computation may be theoretically interesting, one might ask whether it makes sense in practice. As already pointed out in [IP07, CV12], any protocol may be vulnerable to a basic timing attack in which an adversary can guess the size of the honest player's input purely based on the time he takes to perform each computation.

We note, however, that there are many practical scenarios where such attacks are not applicable. Indeed, in order to mount such an attack the adversary needs to be able to accurately estimate the resources of the other player; in many cases this may be difficult. Furthermore, in many applications a player may have time for preprocessing or access to large clusters (as in computations that are run only infrequently, or protocols involving cloud computing companies). Since the adversary will not know how much precomputation/parallelization has been used, it cannot conclude much about the size of the honest party's input. For example, the standard protocols for ZK sets allow for preprocessing: all computation that depends of the size of the input can be performed before any interaction occurs. We note that our definition does not preclude the existence of protocols for interesting functionalities that make use of precomputation/parallelization to prevent these basic timing attacks.

Comparison with [CV12]. Chase and Visconti [CV12] made a first step in this direction by defining and realizing a real/ideal-world notion for a functionality modeling ZK sets called "secure database commitment". The solution of [CV12] is based on two key ideas: 1) defining a modified ideal world; 2) simulating by relying on a new tool that implements a special form of proof of knowledge with short communication complexity. More specifically, they define an ideal world where (roughly) player P_0 sends $\mathcal{F}$ a circuit C which implicitly defines a set, while player P_1 directly sends its input x. $\mathcal{F}$ will then compute $(x, y = C(x))$ and send x to P_0 and y to P_1. This ideal world is still perfectly secure because any circuit C uniquely defines a set (i.e., the set of all strings on which the circuit outputs 1).

Given this ideal world, they are still faced with the issue discussed above of extracting a potentially very long input from a short proof of knowledge. This was the original motivation for the introduction of UAQKs: The issue of efficiently extracting from an adversary that has in mind a very large input is solved by extracting a small implicit representation of this input. [CV12] then shows how to construct an ad-hoc circuit that can be sent by Sim to $\mathcal{F}$ from such an implicit representation.

Unfortunately, while the result of [CV12] solves the problem left open by [MRK03], their solution does not extend to other functionalities. One limitation of the approach in [CV12] is that it gives input-size privacy and input privacy for P_0 but no input privacy at all for P_1. This is appropriate for the functionality they consider, but obviously undesirable in general. The more significant issue, however, is that in the "secure database commitment" functionality the correctness of P_0's input (the input whose size must be hidden) can be verified simply by inspection. Indeed $\mathcal{F}$ can simply check that the provided circuit C has k input wires and only one output wire. This means that for every k-bit string x, C decides the membership or non-membership of x with respect to the unique set that is implicitly defined by C itself. Note that C both defines P_0's input set and efficiently computes the set membership functionality. The obvious question then is whether this approach can be generalized.

Unfortunately for other functionalities the above approach fails spectacularly. The first issue is the possibility that P_0 might send a circuit C whose behavior is not consistent with any valid input. For example, consider the function $f(\Phi, x)$ that outputs the number of elements of Φ that are greater than x. Now, if an adversary P_0 sends a circuit C which is supposed to compute $f(\Phi, \cdot)$ to the functionality, there is no way for the functionality to verify that this circuit C does compute such a function. For example, it is possible that $C(x) > C(x')$ when $x' < x$, which clearly can not be consistent with any set Φ. Thus, a functionality $\mathcal{F}$ which simply receives a circuit C from $\mathcal{A} = P_0^\star$, and sends $C(x)$ to P_1, would be clearly insecure. A second issue involves $P_0^\star$ learning P_1's input. Indeed, consider a circuit C that on input x_1 instead of giving in output $(y_0, y_1) = f(x_0, x_1)$ (i.e., y_0 for P_0 and y_1 for P_1) outputs (x_1, y_1). In this case P_1 would get the correct output, but $P_0^\star$ manages to learn P_1's private input. A third issue is that of *selective failure*, in which $P_0^\star$ can adaptively corrupt P_1's output depending on P_1's input. For example, $P_0^\star$ could compute a circuit that depending on the input x_1 will output a value that is not in the output space of the function; $\mathcal{F}$ might send this invalid output to P_1 or send an error message, but in both cases P_1's reaction would allow $P_0^\star$ to learn something about his input. Notice that the 1st and 3rd issues above also apply in case only P_1 receives an output, while the 2nd issue also applies when only $P_0^\star$ receives an output.

Our work avoids these issues by including the executable proof and an "ideal error" in the ideal world. A valid executable proof guarantees that the functionality will only output a result if it does correspond to $f(x_0, x_1)$ for the specified x_0. The "ideal error" will guarantee that if C ever produces and invalid executable proof then the two worlds are clearly distinguishable; this holds because in the ideal world the functionality sends "ideal error" to P_1 while by definition "ideal error" can not appear as output of P_1 in the real world.

1.7   Open Problems and Future Work

We observe that there are several new ideas here that might be interesting for future study. First, executable PCPs: what languages have polynomial-sized executable PCPs? Note that an efficient executable PCP is different from a PCP with efficient prover - the latter would require that the PCP be of polynomial length, whereas the PCP represented by an efficient executable PCP might be exponentially long; we only require that each bit be efficiently computable.

Our new ideal world also presents several interesting questions. First there is the use of executable PCPs (or more generally, any type of unconditionally sound proofs) in the ideal world: might this allow us to avoid some of the impossibility results in secure computation? Similarly, we propose an ideal world in which $\mathcal{F}$ only receives an implicit representation, evaluates a program produced by one of the parties to obtain the output, and then merely verifies that the result is correct. Again, one might ask whether this gives more power than the traditional ideal world where $\mathcal{F}$ receives the explicit input and computes the output itself.

We also introduce the idea of proofs of polynomial work (PPW) and show one possible application. Other interesting questions would be to look at possible constructions of PPW, or to formally show that PPW requires non-standard assumptions, or to consider other applications where PPW could be useful. One could also consider how to achieve input-size hiding using superpolynomial-time simulation.

We only study the simplest possible world here - we do not for example address the problem of composition, or of obtaining efficient protocols or those that would allow for preprocessing or parallelization. Finally, we leave the question of addressing the case of hiding the input-size of both players (at least for some functionalities) for future research.

2   Secure 2-Party Computation and Proofs of Work

2.1   Input-Size Hiding and Proofs of Polynomial Work

We now show that when the standard ideal world is considered, input-size hiding is hard to achieve under standard assumptions since it implies some form of proof of work that we call proof of polynomial work. There have been many works studying proofs of work, going back to [DN92]. However, as far as we know our notion is not captured by any of the previous definitions.

Roughly, for security parameter k, a PPW is a protocol between P,V where P and V take as input a number n represented as a k-bit string. For honest players we expect n to be polynomial in k. For any polynomial time $\mathcal{A}$ playing as P we want a polynomial upper bound for the n's on which he can cause V to accept. Intuitively this means that if $\mathcal{A}$ can convince V to accept an n, we know that it is bounded by a polynomial (i.e., there exists a polynomial p such that V will reject any $n > p(k)$).

Definition 1. *A proof of polynomial work (PPW) is a pair (P,V) such that the following two properties hold: 1) (correctness) there exist fixed polynomials* poly *and* poly' *such that the running time of P and V for security parameter k and input $n < 2^k$, is respectively* poly(n) *and* poly'(k), *and the output of V is 1. 2) (security) for every polynomial-time adversary $\mathcal{A}$, there exists a polynomial p and a negligible function μ such that for sufficiently large k, for any $n \geq p(k)$, V on input n, interacting with $\mathcal{A}$ outputs 1 with probability at most $\mu(k)$.*

Theorem 1. *One-sided input-size hiding secure 2PC (secure with respect to the standard ideal world) implies the existence of a proof of polynomial work.*

Proof. First, consider a PPW with a somewhat weaker security property, which only guarantees that $\mathcal{A}$ succeeds on $n \geq p(k)$ with probability at most $1/2 + \mu(k)$ for some negligible function μ. Note that given a PPW with this weak security property, we could easily construct a PPW with the above property just by sequential composition. Thus, we focus here on showing that input-size hiding with a standard ideal/real-world security definition would imply a weak PPW.

We now show how to construct a weak PPW (P,V) by starting from a protocol for input-size hiding secure 2PC (P_0, P_1). Consider the functionality $\mathcal{F}$ that receives a set of integers from P_0 and an integer n from P_1 and proceeds as follows: if the set is the list of numbers from 1 to n, then $\mathcal{F}$ outputs 1 to P_1, otherwise it outputs $\bot$ to P_1. Now, suppose we had a protocol for $\mathcal{F}$ that hides the size of P_0's input under the standard simulation-based definition of secure 2PC. If there exists an input-size hiding 2PC protocol for $\mathcal{F}$ then we obtain the following PPW (P,V): P plays as P_0 on input $\Phi = \{1,\ldots,n\}$ and wants to make V running on input n output 1; both parties use security parameter k. By efficiency of the 2PC we have that if n is represented as a k-bit strong, then V runs in time polynomial in k and P runs in time polynomial in n. And clearly by observation honest $V(n)$ outputs 1 when interacting with honest $P(n)$. Therefore correctness is satisfied.

We then consider security. Suppose for contradiction that the weak PPW property does not hold. Then there exists a polynomial-time adversary $\mathcal{A}$ such that for all polynomials p and all negligible functions μ, there are infinitely many k such that on some $n > p(k)$ (where n is represented as a k-bit string), $\mathcal{A}$ causes $V(n)$ to output 1 with probability greater than $1/2 + \mu(k)$.

2PC guarantees that for any $\mathcal{A}$ there is a 2PC simulator and a negligible function μ' such that for all sufficiently large k, for all inputs n represented as

k-bit strings, the real and ideal executions can be distinguished with probability at most $1/2 + \mu'$.

Let p' be the running time of the 2PC simulator for $\mathcal{A}$, let $p = 2p'$, consider $\mu = 2\mu'$, and let D be the 2PC distinguisher that outputs 1 if $V(n)$ outputs 1, and a random guess otherwise. Note that the simulator is assumed to have expected running time $p'(k) = p(k)/2$, so with probability at least $1/2$, it will run in time at most $p(k)$. However, in order to cause $V(n)$ to output 1 it must output the set $\{1, \ldots, n\}$ which requires at least n time. Thus, for $n > p(k)$, in the ideal game $V(n)$ outputs 1 with probability at most $1/2$.

Now, if the weak PPW property does not hold, as explained above there are infinitely many k such that on some $n > p(k)$, $\mathcal{A}$ causes $V(n)$ to output 1 with probability greater than $1/2 + 2\mu'(k)$. For every such n, D clearly succeeds in distinguishing real and ideal executions with probability greater than $1/2 + \mu'(k)$. However, by 2PC security as we have said before, for all sufficiently long n, D must have advantage at most $1/2 + \mu'(k)$. Thus, we have reached a contradiction.

We do not have any candidate constructions based on standard assumptions, and in fact this seems difficult. We could of course construct them by direct relying on some number-theoretic assumptions, but this would require strong generic-group assumptions.

2.2 Our New Definition: A New Ideal World

We give a new general formulation for 2-party computation; we will show later that under this formulation we can achieve 1-side input-size hiding secure computation for any functionality.

First let us informally review the standard ideal-world for secure 2PC of an efficient function $f = (f_0(\cdot, \cdot), f_1(\cdot, \cdot))$, considering the simulation-with-aborts variation. An ideal-world player P_b for $b \in \{0, 1\}$ sends his input x_b to a functionality $\mathcal{F}$ and gets as output $f_b(x_0, x_1)$. An adversary P_b^* after getting her output, can decide whether P_{1-b} should receive his output or not. The communication is always through $\mathcal{F}$.

In this work we consider the setting of *static* inputs and corruptions (e.g., inputs of both parties are specified before the execution of any protocol and the adversary corrupts one of the two players before the protocol starts). Furthermore, we consider secure computation protocols with *aborts* and no *fairness*. This notion is well studied in literature [Gol04]. More specifically, the adversary can abort at any point and the adversary can decide when (if at all) the honest parties will receive their output as computed by the function.

Before presenting our new definition, we will discuss a few necessary concepts.

Input sizes. In the discussion and definition below we will assume w.l.o.g. that P_0 is the party who wishes to hide the size of his input. We use k to denote the security parameter. Honest P_0's input length is assumed to be $\mathsf{poly}(k)$ for some polynomial poly, although this polynomial is not fixed by the protocol or known to P_1. The input of P_1 is then of a fixed length, so w.l.o.g. we assume it is a k-bit string; we also assume that the output of the function f is always a k-bit string.

All parties (honest and malicious) run in time polynomial in k. As discussed in Section 1, we want our ideal functionality $\mathcal{F}$ to run in time polynomial in the size of the messages it receives from the parties; since the ideal parties are polynomial time (in k), the functionality will be as well (this polynomial may depend on the adversary). Throughout the discussion, unless otherwise specified "polynomial" means a polynomial in the security parameter k which may depend on $P_0^\star$.

Implicit representation of data. As discussed in Section 1, we will consider an ideal world in which one party only submits an implicit representation of this input. The only properties that we require for our definition is that this representation be efficiently computable for any polynomial-size input, and that the input is uniquely defined by its implicit representation. More formally, we say that an implicit representation is defined by a potentially unbounded function Decode : $\{0,1\}^* \rightarrow \{0,1\}^*$, which maps each implicit representation back to an input string, and an efficiently computable injective function Rep : $\{0,1\}^* \rightarrow \{0,1\}^*$ which computes an implicit representation of each input. We require that for all $x \in \{0,1\}^*$, Decode(Rep(x)) $= x$, and for any string x we refer to Rep(x) as an implicit representation of the explicit string x.

One implicit representation which we will use often is the circuit representation, by which we mean a circuit that when queried on input i outputs the i-th bit of the explicit string.[10] This representation can be of much shorter size (depending on the data), even potentially logarithmic in the length of the string. As an example, consider the 2^k-bit string s where all odd positions are 0s while all even positions are 1s. Clearly, one can construct a circuit of size $O(k)$ (therefore of size logarithmic in the size of s) that on input i outputs the i-th bit of s. Given a circuit representation s' of a string s, we denote by $s'(i)$ the i-th bit of the underlying explicit string.

Ideal errors. As discussed in Section 1, our formulation is based on an ideal-world experiment whose output clearly specifies whether the computation has been performed correctly or whether something went wrong. Therefore, the honest player's output will be either (this is the good case) the canonical output corresponding to an element in the range of the function, or (this is the bad case) a special message **ideal error** that does not belong to the output space of the function. The ideal-world adversary in standard 2PC is allowed to stop the delivery of the output to the honest player, (to avoid fairness impossibility results proved in [Cle86]), but will not be allowed to stop delivery of the **ideal error** message. (This **ideal error** represents a failure that should never happen in a secure real-world implementation, and we need it to be visible in the output of the ideal-world experiment.) This is similar to the way that ideal world inconsistencies are handled in UC definitions (see for example $\mathcal{F}_{SIG}$ in [Can03][11]).

---

[10] To make this formally injective we can define all invalid circuits to be implicit representations of 0.

[11] That functionality outputs an error and halts, which also makes the two games clearly distinguishable (the functionality never produces output for the honest party). We chose to make this explicit by defining the ideal error, but it has the same effect.

We require by definition that `ideal error` does not occur in the real world. A real protocol is considered to be secure for a function f if: 1) for all real-world adversaries there exists an ideal-world adversary such that the executions in the real and ideal worlds are indistinguishable: 2) the honest parties in the real world execution do not ever output `ideal error`.[12]

This means that for every real-world adversary, there must be an ideal-world adversary that causes the ideal honest party to output `ideal error` with at most negligible probability, but produces the same execution output (i.e., adversary's view and honest player output). This is because any ideal adversary that causes `ideal error` with non-negligible probability would make the two executions clearly distinguishable.

Our ideal error helps to define security because it characterizes the "bad" events of our ideal world; combining this with the fact that the real-world protocol never produces an ideal error and with the fact that any adversary of the real-world can be simulated in the ideal world, we get the desired security guarantees.

Special unconditionally sound proofs: executable PCPs. Our ideal functionality will be parameterized by an unconditionally sound proof system. We will say that a protocol satisfies input-size hiding for a given function if there exists an unconditionally sound proof system such that (for all adversaries there exists a simulator such that) the executions of the ideal and real worlds are indistinguishable. The only requirements we will make on this proof system are that it be unconditionally sound, with negligible soundness error, and that verification time be polynomial in the size of the proof. This does mean that we have some cryptographic tools in the ideal model, however the unconditional soundness means that security of the ideal model is not based on any computational assumption. As discussed in the intro, the ideal P_0 will send to the functionality a circuit C which computes both the output and a proof; this proof will allow the functionality to verify correctness of that output in polynomial time (since the ideal-world adversary is polynomial time, this proof will have polynomial size). We require unconditionally sound proofs so that in the ideal world correctness holds unconditionally. Computational assumptions may risk the basic guarantee that the functionality be trivially secure.

When we prove security of our size-hiding protocol, we will instantiate the proofs in the ideal world with *executable PCPs*. An executable PCP for language L is defined by a probabilistic polynomial-time verifier V, and satisfies perfect completeness ($\forall x \in L$, $\exists \pi$ such that $\Pr[V(x, \pi) = 1] = 1$) and unconditional soundness ($\forall x \notin L, \forall \pi, \Pr[V(x, \pi) = 1]$ is negligible in the length of x), where the probabilities are over V's random coins. Equivalently, we can view it as a circuit version of a PCP: the prover sends the verifier a circuit "computing" the PCP. In order to verify the PCP, the verifier will run the circuit on inputs corresponding to his PCP queries; the circuit's output will be viewed as the corresponding bit

---

[12] This can be enforced by requiring that a real-world experiment checks whether the honest party outputs `ideal error`, and if so replaces this output with $\bot$.

of the PCP; hence the name "executable PCP". (We will equivalently use the term executable proof.) We emphasize that the soundness is unconditional, so as argued above, we can use it in the ideal world. We will denote by EX_π a scheme implementing an executable proof, and by π an individual proof that can be verified by $\mathcal{F}$.

Functionalities. In 2PC, the output computed by the functionality $\mathcal{F}$ is a function $f(x_0, x_1)$ of the inputs x_0 and x_1 received from P_0 and P_1; traditionally f is described by a circuit. This means that the size (or at least an upperbound) of inputs and outputs is fixed as specified by the domain and range of f. For instance, if f is the set intersection function, we have that the domain of f fixes a bound on the number of elements in each player's set. Instead, in our setting we want honest players to have inputs of unrestricted length, because any fixed polynomial bound inherently reveals some information about the size of the inputs. For every input length there should be a different function for implementing the *same* functionality. We need therefore a concise formalization of a functionality that corresponds to a family of functions accommodating different input lengths.

The natural way to formalize this consists of describing the functionality as a deterministic efficient machine M, than on input a pair $(1^i, 1^j)$ outputs the circuit $C_{f_{i,j}}$. For each i, j, such a circuit describes the function $f_{i,j}$ that has the appropriate domain to accommodate inputs of size i and j. (Note that we will assume throughout that the length of the output is always bounded and independent of i and j.) We will focus here on the case of hiding the size of the input of only one player, so we will only need to consider families indexed by a single size parameter (i.e., $M(1^i), C_{f_i}$ and f_i). We denote by f the family of functions.

On using circuits instead of Turing machines. Circuits have the advantage that any circuit produced by a polynomial time machine will run in polynomial time on all inputs; using them for implicit input makes clear that the functionality is efficient. Using circuits for the functions $f_{i,j}$ is arbitrary but closer to other 2PC work.

Putting this together. We follow the outline suggested in Section 1. Formally, we require P_0 to send to $\mathcal{F}$ an implicit representation $\bar{x}_0$ of its input x_0, and a circuit C that for any input x outputs the pair $((y_0, y_1), \pi)$ where $(y_0, y_1) = f(x_0, x)$. Here π is a proof that can be used by $\mathcal{F}$ to check unconditionally that (y_0, y_1) is correct according to f, x and $\bar{x}_0$. $\mathcal{F}$ will therefore check the correctness of the proof given by π. If π convinces $\mathcal{F}$, then y_0 is sent to P_0 and y_1 is sent to P_1, keeping in mind that in this case output delivery to an honest player is conditioned on the approval of the adversary. If instead $\mathcal{F}$ is not convinced by π, then $\mathcal{F}$ does not send any output to P_0 and sends `ideal error` to P_1, without waiting for P_0's approval.

Execution in the ideal world. We now describe an ideal execution with a PPT adversary Sim who has auxiliary input z and controls one of the parties. The PPT trusted third party that computes $f = \{f_i\}_{i \in \mathcal{N}}$ will be denoted by $\mathcal{F}$. Without loss of generality, let P_0 be the player interested in keeping the size of his input private. We will first describe the execution in the setting in which the adversary Sim controls P_1, then follow with the setting in which the adversary controls P_0.

1. *Inputs:* Sim receives as input x_1 and auxiliary input z, party P_0 receives as input x_0 and constructs a triple $(i, \bar{x}_0, C)$, where $i = |x_0|$, $\bar{x}_0$ is an implicit representation of x_0, C as described above computes $f_{|x_0|}(x_0, \cdot)$ and the executable PCP.

2. *P_0 sends input to trusted party:* upon activation, P_0 sends $(i, \bar{x}_0, C)$ to $\mathcal{F}$.

3. Sim *sends input to $\mathcal{F}$ and receives output:* whenever Sim wishes, it may send a message x_1' to $\mathcal{F}$, for any x_1' of its choice. Upon receiving this message, $\mathcal{F}$ computes $((y_0, y_1), \pi) = C(x_1')$, verifies π, and sends y_1 to Sim. (Once an output has already been sent to Sim, all further input messages are ignored by $\mathcal{F}$.)

4. Sim *instructs $\mathcal{F}$ to answer P_0:* when Sim sends a message of the type end to $\mathcal{F}$, $\mathcal{F}$ sends y_0 to P_0. If inputs have not yet been received by $\mathcal{F}$, then $\mathcal{F}$ ignores message end.

5. *Outputs:* P_0 always outputs y_0 that it received from $\mathcal{F}$. Sim may output an arbitrary (probabilistic polynomial-time computable) function of its auxiliary input z, the initial input x_1, and the output obtained from $\mathcal{F}$.

The ideal execution of $f = \{f_i\}_{i \in \mathcal{N}}$ using implicit representation Rep and an executable PCP EX_π (with security parameter k, initial inputs (x_0, x_1) and auxiliary input z to Sim), denoted by
$\text{IDEAL}_{f, \text{Sim}, \text{Rep}, EX_\pi}(k, x_0, x_1, z)$ is the output pair of P_0 and Sim from the above execution. We now consider the case in which the adversary Sim corrupts P_0 while P_1 is honest.

1. *Inputs:* P_1 receives as input x_1, Sim receives as input x_0 and auxiliary input z.

2. *P_1 sends input to $\mathcal{F}$:* upon activation P_1 sends x_1 to $\mathcal{F}$.

3. Sim *sends input to $\mathcal{F}$ and receives output:* whenever Sim wishes, it may send a message $(i', \bar{x}_0', C')$ to $\mathcal{F}$. Upon receiving this message, $\mathcal{F}$ computes $((y_0, y_1), \pi) = C'(x_1)$. $\mathcal{F}$ then verifies π to check unconditionally that the pair (y_0, y_1) corresponds to $f_{i'}(x_0', x_1)$ where x_0' is the explicit representation of $\bar{x}_0'$ and $i' = |x_0'|$. If the proof given by π is not accepting, $\mathcal{F}$ sends ideal error to P_1. If the proof given by π is accepting, $\mathcal{F}$ sends y_0 to Sim. (Once output has been sent to either P_1 or Sim, all further input messages are ignored by $\mathcal{F}$.)

4. Sim *instructs $\mathcal{F}$ to answer P_1:* when Sim sends a message of the type end to $\mathcal{F}$, $\mathcal{F}$ sends y_1 to P_1. If inputs have not yet been received by $\mathcal{F}$ or ideal error was sent to P_1, $\mathcal{F}$ ignores message end.

5. *Outputs:* P_1 outputs whatever it received from $\mathcal{F}$ (i.e., **ideal error** or y_1). Sim may output an arbitrary (probabilistic polynomial-time computable) function of its auxiliary input z, the initial input x_0, and the output y_0 obtained from $\mathcal{F}$.

The ideal execution of $f = \{f_i\}_{i \in k}$ using implicit representation Rep and an executable PCP EX_π (with security parameter k, initial inputs (x_0, x_1) and auxiliary input z to Sim), denoted by $\text{IDEAL}_{f,\text{Sim},\text{Rep},EX_\pi}(k, x_0, x_1, z)$ is the output pair of Sim and P_1 from the above execution.

Execution in the real world. We next consider the real world in which a real two-party protocol is executed (and there exists no trusted third party). Formally, a two-party protocol $\Pi = (\Pi_0, \Pi_1)$ is defined by two sets of instructions Π_0 and Π_1 for parties P_0 and P_1, respectively. A protocol is said to be polynomial time if the running times of both Π_0 and Π_1 are bounded by fixed polynomials in the security parameter k and in the size of the corresponding inputs.

Let f be as above and let Π be a PPT two-party protocol for computing f. In addition, assume that a non-uniform PPT adversary (with non-uniform input z) controls either P_0 or P_1. We describe the case in which the party P_1 is corrupted, and therefore we will denote it as $\mathcal{A} = P_1^\star$. The setting in which party P_0 is corrupted proceeds in a similar manner. The adversary $\mathcal{A} = P_1^\star$ on input x_1 starts by activating P_0, who uses his input x_0 and follows the protocol instructions Π_0 while the adversary $\mathcal{A} = P_1^\star$ follows any arbitrary polynomial time strategy. Upon the conclusion of this execution P_0 writes its output from the execution on its output-tape while the adversary $\mathcal{A} = P_1^\star$ may output any arbitrary polynomial time function of its view of the computation. To enforce the condition that **ideal error** never occurs in the output of the real execution we require that if **ideal error** does occur in the output of the honest party, the real-world execution will replace it with $\perp$. The real-world execution of Π (with security parameter k, initial inputs (x_0, x_1), and auxiliary input z to the adversary $\mathcal{A} = P_1^\star$), denoted by $\text{REAL}_{\Pi,P_1^\star}(k, x_0, x_1, z)$, is defined as the output pair of P_0 and $\mathcal{A} = P_1^\star$, resulting from the above process.

Security as emulation of real-world attacks in the ideal world. We can now define security of protocols. Loosely speaking, a 2-party protocol Π is 1-sided input-size secure if there exist Rep and EX_π such that for every real-world PPT adversary $\mathcal{A} = P^\star$, there exists an ideal-world PPT adversary Sim such that for all pairs of initial inputs (x_0, x_1), the outcome of the ideal execution using Rep and EX_π with adversary Sim is computationally indistinguishable from the outcome of a real protocol execution with $\mathcal{A} = P^\star$. We now present a formal definition.

Definition 2. *Let f and Π be as above. Π is said to securely compute f if there exists an executable PCP EX_π and an implicit representation Rep such that for every $b \in \{0, 1\}$ and every real-world non-uniform PPT adversary $\mathcal{A} = P^\star$ controlling party P_b there exists an ideal-world non-uniform probabilistic expected* *polynomial-time adversary* Sim *controlling P_b such that*

$$\{\text{IDEAL}_{f,\text{Sim},\text{Rep},EX_\pi}(k,x_0,x_1,z)\}_{k\in\mathcal{N};z\in\{0,1\}^*;x_0\in\{0,1\}^{\text{poly}(k)};x_1\in\{0,1\}^k} \approx$$

$$\{\text{REAL}_{\Pi,P^*}(k,x_0,x_1,z)\}_{k\in\mathcal{N};z\in\{0,1\}^*;x_0\in\{0,1\}^{\text{poly}(k)};x_1\in\{0,1\}^k}.$$

A sanity check. We note that our definition implies standard 2PC (with NBB simulator) when the input size is a fixed polynomial: in that case the implicit input is equivalent to explicit input (one can efficiently extract all the bits) and the unconditional proofs ensure the correctness.

Discussion. This definition has all the desirable properties mentioned in Section 1. First, it is clear that no information is revealed to the adversary beside the output y_b. Moreover, as long as `ideal error` does not occur, it is clear by unconditional soundness of EX_π that the output is indeed equal to $f(x_0, x_1)$ for the input implicitly defined by $\bar{x}_0$. (Again, since the real protocol cannot output `ideal error`, any attack on a real protocol translates into an ideal attack in which `ideal error` does not occur.) We obtain the second property (unconditional security) directly because EX_π is unconditionally sound. The third property follows because the ideal adversary must be efficient, and $\mathcal{F}$ just runs the circuit received from Sim. (Efficient algorithms cannot produce inefficient circuits.)

3   Realizing Input-Size Hiding Secure 2-Party Computation

Here we show that input-size hiding is possible. We begin by introducing the tools that are used in our construction. Then we give an informal description of our protocol, followed by a more formal specification.

Special commitment schemes. We will require a special type of commitment scheme that we call "size hiding", which will allow the sender to commit to a string and later to open only some bits of the string, in such a way that the commitment (and opening) does not reveal the size of the committed message. We will denote it by (Gen, Com, Dec, Ver) where Gen is run by the receiver to generate parameters[13], Com commits to a string whose length is not a priori bounded, Dec reveals a bit of the committed string and Ver verifies the opening of a bit. A size-hiding commitment scheme can be constructed by using any commitment scheme along with a Merkle tree. One can also use a zero-knowledge[14] set scheme [MRK03]. For more details see the full version.

Error-correcting codes. We will use error-correcting codes (ECC) with constant distance. See the full version.

---

[13] Note that this is a 2-message commitment rather than a CRS-model commitment, so the hiding properties must hold even against adversarially chosen parameters.

[14] Actually indistinguishability as discussed in [CDV06] is sufficient here.

ZKUAQKs. We use the standard definitions (see the full version) of interactive proof systems, zero knowledge (ZK) and proofs of knowledge. We also use zero-knowledge universal arguments of quasi knowledge (ZKUAQKs) as introduced by [CV12]. In the full version we give the definitions introduced in previous work for zero knowledge for interactive arguments, for the proof of knowledge property for a universal argument (UA) and for quasi-knowledge for universal arguments. Informally, a universal argument of quasi knowledge (UAQK) is a universal argument with a special proof of knowledge property. Being a universal argument, it can be used to prove that a machine on input a certain string produces a certain output in a given number of steps T. The communication complexity and the running time of the verifier do not depend on T, which means that one can have a polynomial-time verifier even when T and the witness used by the prover are superpolynomial in the size of the statement. The special proof of knowledge property guarantees that for any polynomial time adversarial prover there always exists an extractor that runs in expected polynomial time and outputs bits of a valid witness. Moreover if the success probability of the prover is non-negligible, then for any polynomially computable set of indexes Φ, the extractor queried on each input $i \in \Phi$ with overwhelming probability outputs the i-th bit of a valid witness.

[CV12] gives a constant-round construction of a ZKUAQK based on the existence of CRHFs, building on the zero-knowledge universal argument of [Bar04]. (Since a universal argument is an interactive argument, the definition of a ZKUAQK is simply a UAQK which also satisfies the ZK property.) Indeed by plugging the zero-knowledge UA of [Bar04] in the witness indistinguishable UAQK of [CV12] (this works since ZK implies WI) we have that the quasi knowledge property follows directly. To see the ZK property, note that in the protocol in [CV12] the prover runs a ZK verifier, sends some commitments, and runs several ZK proofs sequentially. Thus, a simulator can easily run such steps by making use of the the simulator for the ZK proofs and sending commitments of random messages. Zero knowledge therefore follows from sequential composition of the ZK property of the UA [Bar04], and from the hiding property of the commitment.

Fully homomorphic encryption [Gen09]. A fully homomorphic encryption (FHE) scheme is a semantically secure encryption scheme (KeyGen, Enc, Dec) augmented with an additional algorithm Eval that allows for computations over encrypted ciphertexts. See the full version for details.

Probabilistic checkable proofs of proximity. A "PCP of proximity" (PCPP) proof [BSGH+06] is a relaxation of a standard PCP, that only verifies that the input is close to an element of the language. It has the property that the PCP verifier needs only the description of the Turing machine $\mathcal{M}$ deciding the language and oracle access to bits of the input (x_0, x_1) of $\mathcal{M}$ and to bits of the PCP proof π. See the full version for details.

3.1   High-Level Overview of the Protocol

Here we describe a protocol which provides size-hiding for P_0 for functions in which only P_1 receives output. See the full version for protocols which allow either or both parties to receive output. At a high level, our protocol follows the outline described in Section 1 and consists of the following 3 steps:

1st Part. In the first part, P_1 sends to P_0 parameters for a size-hiding string commitment scheme. Then P_0 uses this scheme in order to send to P_1 the commitment com of its input x_0 expanded by means of an error correcting code. P_0 then proves "quasi knowledge" of the committed value. This is done by using a ZKUAQK and ends the first part. The above first part of the protocol implements the idea of P_0 committing to its input along with a zero knowledge argument of "quasi knowledge". Looking ahead the simulator will use this argument to extract from $P_0^\star$ a reliable implicit representation of the committed input. The ECC guarantees that the explicit input will be well defined and correct even if the extracted circuit is incorrect in a few positions. (Recall that quasi knowledge allows the extracted circuits to be incorrect on any negligible fraction of the positions.)

2nd Part. In the second part of the protocol, P_1 sends the public key for FHE. This key will later be used by P_0 to perform the correct computation on encrypted data. P_1 also proves (in ZK) knowledge of the corresponding secret key, and then sends an encryption e of its input x_1. Intuitively, the ciphertext e combined with the proof of knowledge of the secret key guarantees that P_1 "knows" his input. Looking ahead to the proof, this is useful because it will allow the simulator to decrypt e and extract $P_1^\star$'s input. This ends this part of the protocol, which focuses on P_1 committing to its input in a way that is both extractable and usable to perform computations over encrypted data.

3rd Part. P_0 uses the FHE evaluation algorithm and the ciphertext e received from P_1 in order to compute the encryption e' of P_1's output according to the function f with inputs x_0 and x_1. Then e' is sent to P_1. P_0 also computes a PCPP proof π proving that e' has been correctly computed by applying the function $f(x_0, \cdot)$ to e. Then P_0 proves by means of a ZKUAQK, "quasi knowledge" of a value x_0 that is committed (after ECC expansion) in com and of a PCPP proof π as described above corresponding to that x_0. Finally, P_1 decrypts e' therefore obtaining its output. This part of the protocol thereby focuses on P_0 computing P_1's output e' and sending it to P_1, and proving with a ZKUAQK that e' was computed correctly and there is a PCPP proof confirming it. Here, circuit privacy of the encryption scheme guarantees that P_1 learns nothing about P_0's input. "Quasi knowledge" of the ZKUAQK allows the simulator to obtain from $P_1^\star$ a circuit representation of a PCPP. Very roughly, the PCPP properties allow the functionality to verify that e' is correct given only this circuit representation of the PCPP and the implicit representation of x_0 that we extracted in step 1. This is possible because the verifier a of PCPP (i.e., the functionality, in our case) only needs access to few bits of the the PCP proof and only part of the statement.

3.2   Our Protocol for Input-Size Hiding Secure 2PC

We now give a specification of our protocol. For function family $\{f_i\}$ defined by circuit $M(\cdot)$, our protocol appears in Fig. 1 and uses the following ingredients, as defined above. (For extensions, see the full version.)

▷ A circuit private FHE scheme (KeyGen, Enc, Dec, Eval).

▷ A size-hiding string commitment scheme (Gen, Com, Dec, Ver).

▷ An error correcting code (ECC, ECCDec) with polynomial expansion and constant distance δ.

▷ A PCPP (Prove$_{\mathsf{PCPP}}$, Verify$_{\mathsf{PCPP}}$) with proximity parameter δ for the following pair language: $((i, e, e', \mathsf{pk}), x') \in \mathcal{L}_{\mathsf{PCPP}}$ if there exists randomness r' and input x such that $e' \leftarrow \mathsf{Eval}(\mathsf{pk}, C, e, r') \wedge x' = \mathsf{ECC}(x) \wedge i = |x| \wedge f_i$ is as defined by $M \wedge C$ is the circuit for $f_i(x, \cdot)$.

▷ A ZKPoK (P$_{\mathsf{POK}}$, V$_{\mathsf{POK}}$) for the following relation: $(\mathsf{pk}, \sigma) \in R_3$ iff $(\mathsf{pk}, \mathsf{sk}) \leftarrow \mathsf{KeyGen}(\sigma)$.

▷ A ZKUAQK (Prover$_{\mathsf{UAQK}}$, Verifier$_{\mathsf{UAQK}}$) for the following relations.

  R_1: accept $((\mathsf{com}, \eta), (i, x', x, \mathsf{dec}))$ iff $\mathsf{Ver}(\eta, \mathsf{com}, \mathsf{dec}, x') = 1 \wedge x' = \mathsf{ECC}(x) \wedge |x| = i)$. (By $\mathsf{Ver}(\eta, \mathsf{com}, \mathsf{dec}, x') = 1$, we mean that verification succeeds on all bits of x'.) We denote by L_1 the corresponding language.

  R_2: accept $((\mathsf{com}, \eta, e, e', \mathsf{pk}), (i, \mathsf{dec}, x', r', x, r'', \pi))$ iff $\mathsf{Ver}(\eta, \mathsf{com}, \mathsf{dec}, x') = 1$ and $\pi = \mathsf{Prove}_{\mathsf{PCPP}}(((i, e, e', \mathsf{pk}), x'), (r', x); r'')$ is an honestly generated proof for $((i, e, e', \mathsf{pk}), x')) \in \mathcal{L}_{\mathsf{PCPP}}$ (generated using randomness r''). We denote by L_2 the corresponding language.

Theorem 2. *The protocol in Fig. 1 securely computes function family f defined by M, under Definition 2 (i.e., for one-sided size-hiding secure 2-party computation).*

Here we give the main ideas for the proof. For more details, see the full version.

First, we need to describe an implicit representation and an executable PCP scheme that we will use for the ideal execution.

The implicit representation. In the ideal model we require that the implicit representation uniquely determines the explicit input, i.e. there must exist some (potentially inefficient) decoding algorithm Decode that maps every implicit representation x' to some explicit input. In our construction, this will consist of taking an implicit circuit representation x', extracting all the bits of the corresponding string $\tilde{x}$ by evaluating x' on $1, \ldots i'$, where i' is the length of an encoding under ECC of a string of length i, and then running the ECC decoding algorithm $\mathsf{ECCDec}(\tilde{x})$ to produce x. $\mathsf{Rep}(x)$ simply outputs a circuit representation of $\mathsf{ECC}(x)$.

The executable PCP. The ideal world requires an executable PCP for checking membership of a statement in the language: $(i, x'_0, y, x_1) \in \mathcal{L}_{\mathsf{Ideal}}(\mathsf{Decode})$ if there exists x_0 such that $\mathsf{Decode}(x'_0) = x_0, \wedge |x_0| = i \wedge y = f_i(x_0, x_1)$. The executable PCP EX_π will be instantiated through a circuit representation of a PCPP proof. Indeed proofs given by a PCPP are unconditionally sound but of size polynomial in the length of the witness and this could be too long. However, a circuit representation of a PCPP proof can have short size and still can be

Players: P_0 and P_1 with private inputs x_0 and x_1 respectively.

Common input: the description of the machine $\mathcal{M}$ describing the function family $f = \{f_i\}_{i \in \mathcal{N}}$.

1. $P_1 \to P_0$: P_1 picks random coins σ, runs $\eta \leftarrow \mathsf{Gen}(\sigma)$ and send η to P_0.
2. $P_0 \to P_1$: P_0 computes $(\mathsf{com}, \mathsf{dec}) = \mathsf{Com}(\eta, x_0' = \mathsf{ECC}(x_0), \mathbf{r})$ with random coins $\mathbf{r}$ and sends com to P_1.
3. $P_0 \leftrightarrow P_1$: P_0 and P_1 run the ZKUAQK $\langle \mathsf{Prover}_{\mathsf{UAQK}}((\mathsf{com}, \eta), (|x_0|, x_0', x_0, \mathsf{dec}))$, $\mathsf{Verifier}_{\mathsf{UAQK}}((\mathsf{com}, \eta)) \rangle$ for language L_1 to prove quasi knowledge of an opening to com that can be correctly decoded. P_1 aborts if $\mathsf{Verifier}_{\mathsf{UAQK}}$ rejects.
4. $P_1 \to P_0$: P_1 chooses random coins σ' and runs $(\mathsf{pk}, \mathsf{sk}) \leftarrow \mathsf{KeyGen}(\sigma')$. P_1 sends pk to P_0.
5. $P_1 \leftrightarrow P_0$: P_1 and P_0 run the ZKPoK $\langle \mathsf{P}_{\mathsf{POK}}(\mathsf{pk}, \sigma'), \mathsf{V}_{\mathsf{POK}}(\mathsf{pk}) \rangle$ to prove knowledge of the coins used to generate pk. P_0 aborts if $\mathsf{V}_{\mathsf{POK}}$ does not accept.
6. $P_1 \to P_0$: P_1 picks random coins r_e and computes $e \leftarrow \mathsf{Enc}(\mathsf{pk}, x_1, r_e)$. P_1 sends e to P_0.
7. $P_0 \to P_1$: P_0 computes the circuit C for $f_{|x_0|}(x_0, \cdot)$, chooses a sufficiently long random string r' and then computes $e' \leftarrow \mathsf{Eval}(\mathsf{pk}, C, e, r')$. P_0 sends e' to P_1.
8. $P_0 \leftrightarrow P_1$: P_0 runs $\pi \leftarrow \mathsf{Prove}_{\mathsf{PCPP}}((|x_0|, e, e', \mathsf{pk}, x_0'), (r', x_0); r'')$ after picking random coins r'', thereby generating a PCPP π showing that e' is correctly computed from e, pk and x_0 such that $x_0' = \mathsf{ECC}(x_0)$. Then P_0 and P_1 run the ZKUAQK $\langle \mathsf{Prover}_{\mathsf{UAQK}}((\mathsf{com}, \eta, e, e', \mathsf{pk}), (|x_0|, \mathsf{dec}, x_0', r', x_0, r'', \pi))$, $\mathsf{Verifier}_{\mathsf{UAQK}}(\mathsf{com}, \eta, e, e', \mathsf{pk}) \rangle$ for language L_2 to prove quasi knowledge of an opening x_0', dec to com and of a PCPP proof π computed with randomness r'' showing that e' is correctly computed with randomness r' and inputs e, pk and x_0 such that $x_0' = \mathsf{ECC}(x_0)$. P_1 aborts if $\mathsf{Verifier}_{\mathsf{UAQK}}$ rejects.
9. P_1: P_1 runs $y = \mathsf{Dec}(\mathsf{sk}, e')$ and outputs y.

Fig. 1. A secure protocol for with input-size hiding for P_0 and output for P_1

easily used to unconditionally verify the validity of the intended statement since it can be executed a polynomial number (independent of the witness size) of times to obtain the bits of the PCPP proof needed by the PCPP verifier. In fact, the proof system that we use will be somewhat more involved: the proof will include additional values σ, e, e', x_0'' as well as the circuit representing the PCPP $C_{\pi'}$. Formally, we can define the required executable proof by defining its verification algorithm.

The verifier $\mathsf{Verify}((i, x_0', y, x_1), \bar{\pi})$ for the executable proof proceeds as follows (recall that (i, x_0', C) will be the input received from the player that aims to hide the size of his inputs, and $(y, \bar{\pi})$ is the output of $C(x_1)$)

1. Parse $\bar{\pi} = (\sigma, e, e', x_0'', C_{\pi'})$, and view both x_0' and x_0'' as circuit representations of i'-bit strings (again, i' is the length of an encoded string of length i using ECC). If $\bar{\pi}$ cannot be parsed this way, output 0.
2. Choose k random locations $i_1, \ldots, i_k \in \{0, \ldots, i'-1\}$, and halt and output 0 if $x_0'(i) \neq x_0''(i)$ for any $i \in i_1, \ldots, i_k$.

3. Compute $(\mathsf{pk}, \mathsf{sk}) \leftarrow \mathsf{KeyGen}(\sigma)$, and halt and output 0 if $\mathsf{Dec}(\mathsf{sk}, e) \neq x_1$ or $\mathsf{Dec}(\mathsf{sk}, e') \neq y$.
4. Run the PCPP verifier $\mathsf{Verify}_{\mathsf{PCPP}}((i, e, e', \mathsf{pk}), x_0')$ for language $\mathcal{L}_{\mathsf{PCPP}}$, to obtain index sets I_π, I_z and decision circuit D. Compute $x_0'(j)$ on each index $j \in I_z$ and compute $C_{\pi'}(j)$ on each index $j \in I_\pi'$; call the resulting list of bits X. Finally output the result of $D(X)$.

Note that an honest prover when given x_0 can efficiently generate an accepting proof for each valid x_1, y. Note also that PCPP proofs require the verifier to access only a few bits of the statement and the proof in order to be convinced, so we obtain an efficient verifier.

Lemma 1. *The above proof system is unconditionally sound for the language* $\mathcal{L}_{\mathsf{Ideal}}(\mathsf{Decode})$.

Proof. The soundness of the PCPP guarantees that x_0' is close to a valid codeword. Then we have that if $\mathsf{ECCDec}(x_0') \neq \mathsf{ECCDec}(x_0'')$ then the probability that we sample k random positions without finding any difference among x_0' and x_0'' is negligible. Then, by soundness of the PCPP, if the verifier accepts, we know that with all but negligible probability $e' \leftarrow \mathsf{Eval}(\mathsf{pk}, C, e, r')$ for some r', where C is the circuit for $f_i(\mathsf{ECCDec}(x_0'), \cdot)$ and $i = |x_0|$. Finally, the verifier will generate $(\mathsf{pk}, \mathsf{sk}) \leftarrow \mathsf{KeyGen}(\sigma)$ and check that $x_1 = \mathsf{Dec}(\mathsf{sk}, e)$ and $y = \mathsf{Dec}(\mathsf{sk}, e')$. By the circuit privacy property, we then get that the distribution of e' is statistically close to $\mathsf{Enc}(\mathsf{pk}, C(x_1))$ and if we let $x_0 = \mathsf{ECCDec}(x_0'') = \mathsf{ECCDec}(x_0')$, this means that $\mathsf{Dec}(\mathsf{sk}, e') = C(x_1) = f_i(x_0, x_1) = y$ as desired.

Security with Corrupt P_1. Now we are ready to sketch the proof of security for the case where P_1 is corrupt. For any real-world adversary P_1^*, we will show an ideal-world adversary Sim such that the ideal and real-world outputs are indistinguishable. Sim will simulate P_1^* internally. It receives parameters for the commitment scheme from P_1^* in step 1, commits to 0 in step 2, and runs the ZK simulator for the UAQK with P_1^* in step 3. In step 4, it receives pk, and in step 5 it runs the PoK extractor to extract σ'. Then in step 6 it receives e and computes $(\mathsf{pk}, \mathsf{sk}) \leftarrow \mathsf{KeyGen}(\sigma')$, and $x_1 = \mathsf{Dec}(\mathsf{sk}, e)$. It sends x_1 to the functionality and receives y. In step 7, it sends $e' = \mathsf{Enc}(\mathsf{pk}, y)$, and in step 8 it runs the ZK simulator for the UAQK.

We argue that the ideal-world output with this simulator is indistinguishable from the real-world output with P_1^* through a series of games. We define Game 0 to be the real game, and then proceed as follows:

- Game 1: UAQK Simulator. This is identical to the real game except that in steps 3 and 8, P_0 uses the ZK simulator. (This is indistinguishable by the Zero Knowledge property of the ZKUAQK.)
- Game 2: Simulated commitment. This is identical to game 1 except that in step 2 P_0 forms a commitment to 0. (This is indistinguishable by hiding property of the commitment scheme.)

- Game 3: Extracting σ'. This is identical to game 2 except that in step 5 P_0 uses the PoK extractor to extract σ', and aborts if $\mathsf{KeyGen}(\sigma') = (\mathsf{pk}', \mathsf{sk}')$ such that $\mathsf{pk}' \neq \mathsf{pk}$. (This is indistinguishable by the PoK property.)
- Game 4: Decrypting e. This is identical to game 3 except that in step 7 P_0 computes $x_1 = \mathsf{Dec}(\mathsf{sk}, e)$ and then sends $e' = \mathsf{Enc}(\mathsf{pk}, f_{|x_0|}(x_0, x_1))$. (This is indistinguishable by the circuit privacy property of the FHE scheme.)
- Game 5: Ideal Game. The only difference is that in Game 4 P_0 computes $f_{|x_0|}(x_0, x_1)$ and encrypts it, while in the ideal game Sim sends x_1 to the ideal functionality, receives $y = f_{|x_0|}(x_0, x_1)$, and encrypts that, so the two games are identical.

Corrupt P_0. Finally we consider the case when party P_0 is corrupted. For any real world adversary $\mathcal{A}$, we will show an ideal-world adversary Sim such that the ideal and real-world outputs are indistinguishable. Here we present the intuition behind the proof. (For a more detailed treatment, see the full version.)

At a high level the idea is that the simulator will use the extractor for the UAQK in step 3 to construct an implicit representation x_0' of x_0. Then, for C it will construct a circuit which on input x_1 1) continues to run $\mathcal{A}$ with an honest P_1 using input x_1 in steps 4-7, 2) decrypts the ciphertext e' received in step 7 to obtain y, and 3) uses the extractor for the UAQK in step 8 to construct an implicit representation of the statistically sound proof (in particular of x_0'' and the PCPP π'). Finally, in order to ensure that the protocol is aborted with the same probability in both worlds, the simulator will first run $\mathcal{A}$ once with honest P_1; it will rewind to step 3 and construct x_0' and C as described above only if this first run is successful. Since the simulator does not know x_1, it will instead use $x_1 = 0$ for this run, and we will argue that the result will be indistinguishable. *The ideal world never produces* ideal error *except with negligible probability.* Recall that to verify the proof π produced by $C(x_1)$, the functionality will have to check several things: 1) that x_0' and x_0'' are close, 2) that e, e' decrypt to x_1 and y, and 3) that the PCPP π' verifies for the statement $(i, e, e', \mathsf{pk}), x_0''$.

Thus, we need only show that these three checks will succeed. The argument goes as follows. First, we argue that x_0'' extracted in step 8 must be very close to x_0' extracted in step 3. If not, we could use the UAQK extractors to extract some pair of bits that differ along with a pair of valid openings for those bits, and thus produce a contradiction to the binding property. The second check is clearly satisfied by the way that e and y are computed. Finally, the quasi-knowledge property of the UAQK implies that almost all of the bits of the extracted PCPP will be correct, so the verification should succeed with all but negligible probability.

P_1's output in the two games is indistinguishable given that the functionality does not send ideal error. The issue here is that the functionality will run the circuit C to obtain P_1's output, which is essentially like rewinding and rerunning steps 4-8 of the protocol. (This is an issue because Sim will produce its ideal output using $\mathcal{A}$'s initial run, so we need to make sure that P_1's output is still consistent with this initial run.) Thus, we have to argue that rewinding to step 4 can not change P_1's output. Above, we argued that C produces a valid proof

that $y = f_{|x_0|}(x_0, x_1)$ where x_0 is as defined by the decoding of the implicit string produced by the UAQK extractor in step 3. Similarly, we can argue that if we extract from the UAQK in the first run-through, we can also produce a valid proof that y produced in that run is also equal to $y = f_{|x_0|}(x_0, x_1)$ for the same x_0. Finally, by the unconditional soundness of the proof described in Section 3.2, we conclude that P_1's output y will be the same in both games.

The adversary's output in the two games is indistinguishable. The main difference is that in the real game, $\mathcal{A}$ is interacting with P_1 whose input is x_1, while in the ideal game, Sim's output is what $\mathcal{A}$ produces when run with P_1 whose input is 0. This follows fairly directly from semantic security. Note that we also need zero knowledge to ensure that the proof in step 5 does not reveal anything about sk or x_1.

A technical issue. There is one technical issue that occurs because we are building on UAQKs. The issue is that for our simulator to work, we need to ensure that the UAQK extractors run in polynomial time, and succeed with overwhelming probability. By definition, we are guaranteed that from a prover with success probability p, a UAQK extractor will run in time $1/p$ and successfully extract a witness with overwhelming probability assuming p is non-negligible. Here, we need to ensure that the UAQK is given a prover that succeeds with non-negligible probability. (Unless we have a real world adversary that aborts with all but negligible probability - in that case our simulator will also abort with all but negligible probability.) The issue is that that the adversary's probability of aborting may depend on the random coins that P_1 uses up until that point, and in particular on the randomness used in forming the key pair pk, sk and the encryption e. Recall that our simulator uses the first run, with $e = \mathsf{Enc}(\mathsf{pk}, 0, \cdot)$ to determine whether to abort, and then rewinds and gives the ideal functionality a circuit that extracts from a prover who is sent $e = \mathsf{Enc}(\mathsf{pk}, x_1, \cdot)$ (under a fresh public key). It is possible that for some values of e, $\mathcal{A}$ always aborts; we may get unlucky and in the first run get an e on which $\mathcal{A}$ successfully completes the protocol (so we continue and form C), and then when C is run it ends up with an e for which $\mathcal{A}$ aborts with high probability thus causing the extractor to fail and the circuit C to not produce a valid proof π. However, if there is a non-negligible probability with which $\mathcal{A}$ does not abort on the first run, then there must be a non-negligible chance that it will produce valid proofs on the rewinding as well. (This follows from semantic security because the only difference in the runs is the value encrypted in e.) Thus, we will rewind many times, find one on which $\mathcal{A}$ does produce valid proofs, and extract from that run. To determine how many times to rewind (so that we can argue that at least one will be successful but the process still runs in expected polynomial time), we will use estimation techniques from [CV12]. For a more detailed proof see the full version.

Acknowledgments. Research supported in part by MIUR Project PRIN "GenData 2020", NSF grants CCF-0916574; IIS-1065276; CCF-1016540; CNS-1118126; CNS-1136174; US-Israel BSF grant 2008411, OKAWA Foundation Research Award, IBM Faculty Research Award, Xerox Faculty Research Award, B. John Garrick Foundation Award, Teradata Research Award, and Lockheed-Martin Corporation Research Award. This material is also based upon work supported by the Defense Advanced Research Projects Agency through the U.S. Office of Naval Research under Contract N00014-11-1-0392. The views expressed are those of the author and do not reflect the official policy or position of the Department of Defense or the U.S. Government.

References

[ACT11] Ateniese, G., De Cristofaro, E., Tsudik, G.: (If) size matters: size-hiding private set intersection. In: Catalano, D., Fazio, N., Gennaro, R., Nicolosi, A. (eds.) PKC 2011. LNCS, vol. 6571, pp. 156–173. Springer, Heidelberg (2011)

[Bar04] Barak, B.: Non-black-box techniques in cryptography. Ph.D Thesis (2004)

[Bea92] Beaver, D.: Foundations of secure interactive computing. In: Feigenbaum, J. (ed.) CRYPTO 1991. LNCS, vol. 576, pp. 377–391. Springer, Heidelberg (1992)

[BR93] Bellare, M., Rogaway, P.: Random oracles are practical: a paradigm for designing efficient protocols. In: ACM Conference on Computer and Communications Security, pp. 62–73. ACM (1993)

[BSGH+06] Ben-Sasson, E., Goldreich, O., Harsha, P., Sudan, M., Vadhan, S.P.: Robust pcps of proximity, shorter pcps, and applications to coding. SIAM J. Comput. 36(4), 889–974 (2006)

[Can03] Canetti, R.: Universally composable signatures, certification and authentication. Cryptology ePrint Archive, Report 2003/239 (2003). http:// eprint.iacr.org/

[Can05] Canetti, R.: Universally composable security: a new paradigm for cryptographic protocols. Cryptology ePrint Archive, Report 2000/67 (version 13 Dec 2005) (2005). http://eprint.iacr.org/2000/067/20051214:064128

[CDV06] Catalano, D., Dodis, Y., Visconti, I.: Mercurial commitments: minimal assumptions and efficient constructions. In: Halevi, S., Rabin, T. (eds.) TCC 2006. LNCS, vol. 3876, pp. 120–144. Springer, Heidelberg (2006)

[CFT13] De Cristofaro, E., Faber, S., Tsudik, G.: Secure genomic testing with size- and position-hiding private substring matching. In: Proceedings of the 12th annual ACM Workshop on Privacy in the Electronic Society, WPES 2013, Berlin, Germany, November 4, 2013, pp. 107–118 (2013)

[CGH98] Canetti, R., Goldreich, O., Halevi, S.: The random oracle methodology, revisited (preliminary version). In: Vitter, J.S. (ed.), Proceedings of the Thirtieth Annual ACM Symposium on the Theory of Computing, Dallas, Texas, USA, 23–26 May, 1998, pp. 209–218. ACM (1998)

[Cle86] Cleve, R.: Limits on the security of coin flips when half the processors are faulty (extended abstract). In: STOC, pp. 364–369. ACM (1986)

[CV12] Chase, M., Visconti, I.: Secure database commitments and universal arguments of quasi knowledge. In: Safavi-Naini, R., Canetti, R. (eds.) CRYPTO 2012. LNCS, vol. 7417, pp. 236–254. Springer, Heidelberg (2012)

[Dam92] Damgård, I.B.: Towards practical public key systems secure against chosen ciphertext attacks. In: Feigenbaum, J. (ed.) CRYPTO 1991. LNCS, vol. 576, pp. 445–456. Springer, Heidelberg (1992)

[DN92] Dwork, C., Naor, M.: Pricing via processing or combatting junk mail. In: Brickell, E.F. (ed.) CRYPTO 1992. LNCS, vol. 740, pp. 139–147. Springer, Heidelberg (1993)

[Gen09] Gentry, C.: Fully homomorphic encryption using ideal lattices. In: STOC, pp. 169–178. ACM (2009)

[GL91] Goldwasser, S., Levin, L.A.: Fair computation of general functions in presence of immoral majority. In: Menezes, A., Vanstone, S.A. (eds.) CRYPTO 1990. LNCS, vol. 537, pp. 77–93. Springer, Heidelberg (1991)

[GMW87] Goldreich, O., Micali, S., Wigderson, A.: How to play any mental game or a completeness theorem for protocols with honest majority. In: STOC, pp. 218–229. ACM (1987)

[Gol04] Goldreich, O.: Foundations of cryptography, vol. 2: Basic applications (2004)

[IP07] Ishai, Y., Paskin, A.: Evaluating branching programs on encrypted data. In: Vadhan, S.P. (ed.) TCC 2007. LNCS, vol. 4392, pp. 575–594. Springer, Heidelberg (2007)

[LNO13] Lindell, Y., Nissim, K., Orlandi, C.: Hiding the input-size in secure two-party computation. In: Sako, K., Sarkar, P. (eds.) ASIACRYPT 2013, Part II. LNCS, vol. 8270, pp. 421–440. Springer, Heidelberg (2013)

[MR92] Micali, S., Rogaway, P.: Secure computation. In: Feigenbaum, J. (ed.) CRYPTO 1991. LNCS, vol. 576, pp. 392–404. Springer, Heidelberg (1992)

[MRK03] Micali, S., Rabin, M.O., Kilian, J.: Zero-knowledge sets. In: FOCS, pp. 80–91. IEEE Computer Society (2003)

[Nao03] Naor, M.: On cryptographic assumptions and challenges. In: Boneh, D. (ed.) CRYPTO 2003. LNCS, vol. 2729, pp. 96–109. Springer, Heidelberg (2003)

Encryption

Semantically Secure Order-Revealing Encryption: Multi-input Functional Encryption Without Obfuscation

Dan Boneh[1]([✉]), Kevin Lewi[1], Mariana Raykova[2], Amit Sahai[3],
Mark Zhandry[1], and Joe Zimmerman[1]

[1] Stanford University, Stanford, US
dabo@cs.stanford.edu
[2] SRI International, Menlo Park, US
[3] Computer Science, UCLA and Center for Encrypted Functionalities,
Los Angeles, US

Abstract. Deciding "greater-than" relations among data items just given their encryptions is at the heart of search algorithms on encrypted data, most notably, non-interactive binary search on encrypted data. Order-preserving encryption provides one solution, but provably provides only limited security guarantees. Two-input functional encryption is another approach, but requires the full power of obfuscation machinery and is currently not implementable.

We construct the first implementable encryption system supporting greater-than comparisons on encrypted data that provides the "best-possible" semantic security. In our scheme there is a public algorithm that given two ciphertexts as input, reveals the order of the corresponding plaintexts and nothing else. Our constructions are inspired by obfuscation techniques, but do not use obfuscation. For example, to compare two 16-bit encrypted values (e.g., salaries or age) we only need a 9-way multilinear map. More generally, comparing k-bit values requires only a $(k/2+1)$-way multilinear map. The required degree of multilinearity can be further reduced, but at the cost of increasing ciphertext size.

Beyond comparisons, our results give an implementable secret-key multi-input functional encryption scheme for functionalities that can be expressed as (generalized) branching programs of polynomial length and width. Comparisons are a special case of this class, where for k-bit inputs the branching program is of length $k + 1$ and width 4.

1 Introduction

Functional encryption [BSW11] is a public-key encryption system that supports "partial" decryption keys: decrypting a ciphertext $c = E(\mathsf{pk}, m)$ using a key sk_f reveals $f(m)$ and nothing else. Multi-input functional encryption [GGG+14] is a generalization of functional encryption where the key sk_f acts on ℓ ciphertexts $c_1 = E(\mathsf{pk}, m_1), \dots, c_\ell = E(\mathsf{pk}, m_\ell)$ to reveal $f(m_1, \dots, m_\ell)$ and nothing else.

© International Association for Cryptologic Research 2015
E. Oswald and M. Fischlin (Eds.): EUROCRYPT 2015, Part II, LNCS 9057, pp. 563–594, 2015.
DOI: 10.1007/978-3-662-46803-6_19

Existing constructions for general multi-input functional encryption are based on obfuscation and thus are not currently feasible to implement, even for simple functionalities.

In this paper we present a construction for *secret-key* multi-input functional encryption from multilinear maps. By restricting our attention to the secret-key setting, we are able to achieve a much more efficient construction, without the full machinery of obfuscation and NIZK proofs.

For concreteness, in the introduction we present our results as they apply to a specific application called *order-revealing encryption* [AKS+04, BCL+09, BCO11]. The paper body presents the results in their full generality, namely as a *secret-key* multi-input functional encryption scheme.

1.1   Order-Revealing Encryption

Definition. A secret-key encryption scheme is *order-revealing*[1] [BCO11] if there is a public procedure that takes two *encrypted* plaintexts as input and reports their lexicographic ordering. This procedure, which we call the order-revealing algorithm, requires no secrets and can be evaluated by anyone. More precisely, an order-revealing scheme is a tuple (G, E, D) of algorithms. Algorithm G outputs a pair $(\mathsf{sk}, \mathsf{comp})$ where sk is a secret encryption key and $\mathsf{comp}(\cdot, \cdot)$ is an efficient deterministic algorithm that takes two ciphertexts as input and outputs either '$<$' or '$\geq$'. Algorithms $E(\mathsf{sk}, m)$ and $D(\mathsf{sk}, c)$ are standard encryption/decryption algorithms where $m \in \{0, \dots, B\}$ for some B. In addition to the standard correctness of decryption we also require that for all $(\mathsf{sk}, \mathsf{comp})$ output by G and for all plaintexts m_0, m_1 we have:

$$m_0 < m_1 \quad \implies \quad \Pr[\mathsf{comp}(\, E(\mathsf{sk}, m_0)\,,\, E(\mathsf{sk}, m_1)\,) ='\!<'] = 1$$
$$m_0 \geq m_1 \quad \implies \quad \Pr[\mathsf{comp}(\, E(\mathsf{sk}, m_0)\,,\, E(\mathsf{sk}, m_1)\,) ='\!\geq'] = 1$$

An order-revealing encryption scheme is secure if a ciphertext reveals nothing about the corresponding plaintext beyond its lexicographic relation relative to other ciphertexts. This is defined using a simple variant of the standard semantic security game [GM82]: the adversary is given algorithm $\mathsf{comp}(\cdot, \cdot)$ and access to a "left-right-oracle" $\mathcal{O}(\cdot, \cdot)$ that on input (m_0, m_1) returns $E(\mathsf{sk}, m_b)$ for some $b \in \{0, 1\}$ chosen at the beginning of the game. After adaptively querying the oracle $\mathcal{O}$ the adversary outputs a guess b' and wins the game if $b = b'$. Let $(m_0^{(0)}, m_1^{(0)}), \dots, (m_0^{(q)}, m_1^{(q)})$ be the adversary's queries to $\mathcal{O}$. To ensure that the adversary cannot use algorithm $\mathsf{comp}(\cdot, \cdot)$ to trivially win the game we require that the relative ordering of messages on the left is the same as the relative ordering on the right, namely for all $0 \leq i, j \leq q$:

$$m_0^{(i)} < m_0^{(j)} \quad \iff \quad m_1^{(i)} < m_1^{(j)}$$

The scheme is secure if the adversary cannot win this game with non-negligible advantage. We refer to this notion as *best-possible semantic security*. We give a complete (and more general) definition in Section 3.

---

[1] In [BCO11] order revealing encryption was called "efficiently-orderable encryption."

Note that a *public-key* order-revealing encryption scheme is impossible: if an adversary has unrestricted access to the encryption algorithm, he can use the encryption algorithm and the order-revealing algorithm $\mathsf{comp}(\cdot, \cdot)$ to decrypt any ciphertext using binary search without the secret key.

Applications. Order-revealing encryption (ORE) is motivated by the problem of answering range queries on a remote encrypted database [AKS+04, BCL+09]. Consider a remote database holding encrypted pairs (name, salary). The data owner wishes to retrieve all records with a salary greater than t. If salaries are encrypted using an ORE then the database can sort all records on its own from lowest salary to highest. This sorting can be done even when records are inserted sequentially into the database (perhaps by multiple users who share the secret encryption key) and requires no interaction with the data owner(s). To issue the range query the data owner sends the encryption of t under the ORE key. In response, the database first uses binary search on the encrypted salaries to locate the smallest encrypted record R with a salary greater then t and then simply sends all records to the "right" of R back to the user. Thus, for a database of n records, the database's work is $O(\log n)$ and requires only one round of interaction with the client, as in the case of a cleartext database. Security of the ORE ensures that the database learns nothing beyond the relative ordering of records and queries.

Alternate Approaches. Before describing our construction we briefly survey a few alternate constructions for answering range queries on a remote encrypted database.

Boldyreva et al. [BCL+09, BCO11] describe an elegant primitive called Order Preserving Encryption (OPE) where encryption preserves the relative ordering of plaintexts. Comparing encrypted data is then done by simply comparing the corresponding ciphertexts. However, OPE leaks information about the relative distances of plaintexts. Recent work of Malkin et al. [MTY13] constructs an OPE scheme with a partial security guarantee, hiding the low-order bits of plaintexts, but still does not achieve best-possible semantic security. Indeed, Boldyreva et al. [BCL+09] prove that no OPE scheme can possibly achieve best-possible semantic security. In ORE, unlike OPE, comparisons are done with a dedicated algorithm $\mathsf{comp}(\cdot, \cdot)$ which is the reason best-possible semantic security can be achieved.

A very different approach to answering range queries on encrypted data uses garbled RAMs [LO13, GHL+14]. With garbled RAMs the database can answer range queries without learning any information about the data, but answering the range queries requires more rounds of interaction per query and the database's work is higher than with ORE.

Other approaches to answering range queries are based on public-key predicate encryption [BW07, SBC+07, KSW08] and require a linear scan through the database. With ORE, range queries can be answered in logarithmic time in the size of the database. We also mention a result of Popa et al. [PLZ13] who describe an interactive protocol for answering range queries. Interaction is used to maintain a sorted data structure at the database by offloading some comparisons to the client. Finally, we note that ORE is a special case of secret-key two-input functional encryption [GGG+14].

1.2   Order Revealing Encryption: Our Construction

Our construction begins with a simple automaton for the comparison function on two inputs that we represent as a low-width matrix branching program. We encrypt ciphertexts in a way such that given two independently-created ciphertexts, anyone can run the comparison branching program to reveal the relative ordering of the corresponding plaintexts. While our encryption scheme applies to any multi-input functionality expressed as a matrix branching program (see Section 2.2), for the rest of this section we use the two-input comparison automaton and its branching program as a concrete example to illustrate the construction.

The Comparison Automaton and Branching Program. Fig. 1 shows a five-state automaton A that computes the ordering of two inputs $x = x_1 x_2 \cdots x_n$ and $y = y_1 y_2 \ldots y_n$ in $\{0,1\}^n$ when the input is processed in an interleaved order (of the form $x_1 y_1 x_2 y_2 \cdots x_n y_n$). From this automaton we derive four 5×5 matrices $\mathbf{X}_0, \mathbf{X}_1, \mathbf{Y}_0, \mathbf{Y}_1$, where each is the adjacency matrix of a subgraph of A: for $b \in \{0,1\}$, the matrix $\mathbf{X}_b$ is the adjacency matrix of the subgraph consisting only of the b-transitions used by input bits of x, and the matrix $\mathbf{Y}_b$ is the adjacency matrix of the subgraph consisting only of the b-transitions used by input bits of y. Note that these matrices are not invertible because of the sink states in the automaton. This introduces additional challenges in the security proof; however, we are able to handle branching programs with non-invertible matrices using recent results of Sahai and Zhandry [SZ14].

Let $\mathbf{e}_i$ be the 5-vector containing 1 in position i and zero elsewhere. Then the product $\mathbf{e}_1^{\mathsf{T}} \cdot \prod_{i=1}^{n} (\mathbf{X}_{x_i} \mathbf{Y}_{y_i})$ results in a vector with a single "1" in three possible locations (corresponding to either the "$x > y$", "$x < y$", or "=" final states), and the location of the "1" determines the result of the comparison operation on x and y. Hence, the matrices $\mathbf{X}_0, \mathbf{X}_1, \mathbf{Y}_0, \mathbf{Y}_1$ form a matrix branching program for the two-input comparison function. In the full version we show that a simple reordering of the inputs reduces the matrix program length to only $n+1$ matrices each of dimension 4×4, but for simplicity we ignore this optimization here.

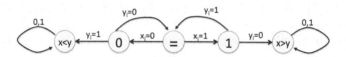

Fig. 1. The 5-state comparison automaton on inputs $x, y \in \{0,1\}^n$ where '=' is the start state. Input bits are processed in an interleaved order $x_1 \, y_1 \, x_2 \, y_2 \ldots$

The ORE Encryption Scheme. Fix a prime q. The setup algorithm G uniformly samples $2n - 1$ invertible matrices $\mathbf{R}_1, \ldots, \mathbf{R}_{2n-1}$ from $\mathrm{GL}_5(\mathbb{Z}_q)$. These matrices form the secret encryption key sk. During encryption these matrices will be used to randomize the matrices of the comparison branching program using Kilian's randomization technique [Kil88]. We define two additional vectors $\mathbf{R}_0 := \mathbf{e}_1^{\mathsf{T}}$ and $\mathbf{R}_{2n} := \mathbf{e}_5$. The secret key also contains the parameters for an asymmetric multilinear map [GGH13a] with $2n$ indices (i.e., of degree $2n$). We divide the $2n$ indices into two disjoint size-n sets $\mathcal{U}_1$ and $\mathcal{U}_2$.

The encryption algorithm encrypts a plaintext $x = x_1 x_2 \cdots x_n \in \{0,1\}^n$ as follows. It first samples a partition $(S_1, \ldots, S_n)$ of $\mathcal{U}_1$ and a partition $(T_1, \ldots, T_n)$ of $\mathcal{U}_2$. These partitions are sampled at random from a family of partitions we call an "exclusive partition family." They must satisfy a specific combinatorial property needed to prevent certain "mix-and-match" attacks where the attacker tries to run the comparison algorithm on improperly formed ciphertexts. We define and construct these partition families in Section 2.5. They are a generalization of the "straddling sets" used in Barak et al. [BGK+14].

Next, the encryption algorithm samples random scalars $\alpha_1, \ldots, \alpha_{2n} \in \mathbb{Z}_q^*$ and constructs the 5×5 matrices

$$\hat{\mathbf{X}}_i = \alpha_i \cdot (\mathbf{R}_{2i-2} \, \mathbf{X}_{x_i} \, \mathbf{R}_{2i-1}^{-1}) \qquad \text{and} \qquad \hat{\mathbf{Y}}_i = \alpha_{n+i} \cdot (\mathbf{R}_{2i-1} \, \mathbf{Y}_{x_i} \, \mathbf{R}_{2i}^{-1})$$

for $i \in [n]$ where we define $\mathbf{R}_{2n}^{-1} := \mathbf{e}_5$. Recall that the matrices $\mathbf{R}_i$ are taken from the secret key and the matrices $\mathbf{X}_0, \mathbf{X}_1$ and $\mathbf{Y}_0, \mathbf{Y}_1$ are the matrices in the comparison branching program. Because $\mathbf{R}_0$ and $\mathbf{R}_{2n}$ are vectors, so are $\hat{\mathbf{X}}_0$ and $\hat{\mathbf{Y}}_n$. All other ciphertext components are square matrices.

Finally, for $i \in [n]$ the encryption algorithm encodes the entries of $\hat{\mathbf{X}}_i$ under the index set S_i of the multilinear map, and encodes the entries of $\hat{\mathbf{Y}}_i$ under the index set T_i. The resulting $2n$ encoded 5×5 matrices $(\{\hat{\mathbf{X}}_i\}_{i=1}^n, \{\hat{\mathbf{Y}}_j\}_{j=1}^n)$ are output as the encryption of $x \in \{0,1\}^n$.

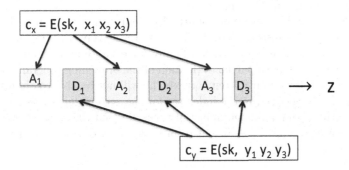

Fig. 2. The order-revealing algorithm applied to encryptions of $x_1 x_2 x_3$ and $y_1 y_2 y_3$

The Order-Revealing Algorithm. Given two independently-created cipher-texts c_x and c_y corresponding to plaintexts x and y, the order-revealing algorithm computes the interleaved product of the matrices in the left half of c_x with the matrices in the right half of c_y. In other words, if $c_x = (\{\mathbf{A}_i\}_{i=1}^n, \{\mathbf{B}_j\}_{j=1}^n)$ and $c_y = (\{\mathbf{C}_i\}_{i=1}^n, \{\mathbf{D}_j\}_{j=1}^n)$ then $z = \mathbf{A}_1\mathbf{D}_1\mathbf{A}_2\mathbf{D}_2 \cdots \mathbf{A}_n\mathbf{D}_n$, as shown in Fig. 2. We compute z using the multilinear map and the result is a single group element (a scalar) because $\mathbf{A}_1$ and $\mathbf{D}_n$ are vectors. Finally, the algorithm zero-tests z and the outcome reveals the ordering of x and y. Zero-testing this z is possible because it is an encoding of an element under the full $2n$ index set, by the structure of the partitions.

To verify that the final zero-test correctly reveals the ordering of x and y, observe that the scalar z expands to the quantity

$$\left(\mathbf{e}_1^\mathsf{T} \mathbf{X}_{x_1} \mathbf{R}_1^{-1}\right) \left(\mathbf{R}_1 \mathbf{Y}_{y_1} \mathbf{R}_2^{-1}\right) \cdots \left(\mathbf{R}_{2n-2}\mathbf{X}_{x_n} \mathbf{R}_{2n-1}^{-1}\right) \left(\mathbf{R}_{2n-1}\mathbf{Y}_{y_n}\mathbf{e}_5\right) \qquad (1)$$

Hence, z takes on a non-zero value if and only if the comparison automaton terminates in the state "$x < y$". Note that we omitted the scalars α_i in the expansion (1) for ease of exposition. Their presence causes z to be either 0 or non-zero, as opposed to 0 or 1.

Security. We prove the security of a generalization of this construction in the generic multilinear map model [GGH+13b, BR14, BGK+14]. The use of Kilian's randomization technique in the encryption key restricts the adversary's ability to manipulate ciphertext components in an elementary manner, such as by computing products of matrices out of order. Also, the use of the random scalars $\alpha_1, \ldots, \alpha_{2n}$ prevents the adversary from correlating multiple encryptions of plaintexts which share the same bit pattern. However, there is still a large domain of attacks that the adversary could potentially take advantage of. For example, an adversary can combine components from multiple ciphertexts to look for relations, or he can compare the results of partial evaluations of the branching program on different inputs.

In order to handle these types of attacks, we use the combinatorial structure provided by our exclusive partition families. Intuitively, the use of a random partition from an exclusive partition family for each ciphertext ensures that if the adversary computes a partial evaluation of the branching program, or tries to mix components from multiple ciphertexts, he will not be able to obtain a group element which is encoded in the index set for the zero-tester, as required by the generic multilinear map model. In fact, it turns out that the use of these exclusive partition families is indeed sufficient to prove security of the construction in the generic model.

Performance. Our basic construction requires a $(2n+2)$-way multilinear map to evaluate comparisons on n-bit numbers. However, simple optimizations, including re-ordering of the matrices in the branching program, enables us to shrink the total length of the comparison branching program to only $(n + 1)$ matrices each of dimension 4×4 (see Section 2.2 for details). Consequently, we only need an $(n + 1)$-way multilinear map to evaluate comparisons on n-bit numbers. The secret encryption key contains $16n$ elements in $\mathbb{Z}_q$, and each ciphertext is $16n - 8$ encoded group elements. We can further reduce the required degree of multilinearity by a factor of $\log_2 B$ by representing messages in base-B (instead of base-2) and modifying the comparison automaton to compare one base-B digit per step. This shortens the length of the branching program (and therefore the degree of multilinearity) by a factor of $\log_2 B$, but at the cost of increasing the number of states in the automaton by a factor of B and consequently increasing the number of group elements in the ciphertext by a factor of approximately $B^2 / \log_2 B$. For example, moving to base $B = 4$ gives multilinearity $(n/2 + 1)$, with ciphertexts requiring $18n - 24$ group elements.

Concretely, for $n = 16$ bits, we can use a 9-linear map giving ciphertexts of 264 group elements. While this scheme is still too inefficient for practical use, the construction *can* be implemented and provides an important step towards more realistic ORE schemes. This is in contrast to the immense number of levels of multilinearity required to obtain ORE from obfuscation-based constructions.

Generalizing to Multi-input Functional Encryption. While we used order-revealing encryption (ORE) as an example application, our construction is more general: it gives a secret-key multi-input functional encryption where the degree of multilinearity needed for decrypting with a key sk_f depends on the length of the branching program representing f. In fact, every matrix in the branching program can depend on *all* the bits of one of the inputs to f and this can be used to shrink the length of the branching program. We refer to these as *generalized branching programs* and define them precisely in the next section.

Our base multi-input functional encryption scheme supports a single function f (such as comparison) fixed a-priori during initial key generation. This function f defines the branching program relative to which all encryptions are computed. This apparent single-function limitation is easily removed using universal circuits: the functionality fixed a-priori is a universal circuit U that takes as input the description of a function f and its inputs $x_1, \ldots, x_n$ and outputs $f(x_1, \ldots, x_n)$. Now, a functional encryption "key" sk_f for a function f is simply the encryption of f under our encryption scheme. Given sk_f and the encryptions of $x_1, \ldots, x_n$ the functionality for the universal circuit U can be used to compute $f(x_1, \ldots, x_n)$ in the clear.

1.3   Other Related Work

Multi-input functional encryption was introduced by Goldwasser et al. [GGG+14], who gave constructions based on indistinguishability obfuscation [BGI+01, GGH+13b] and differing-inputs obfuscation [BGI+01, BCP14, ABG+13].

Our construction of multi-input functional encryption is inspired by obfuscation techniques [GGH+13b, BBC+14, AGI+14], but does not use obfuscation.

Instead we build multi-input functional encryption directly from multilinear maps. Several other results use obfuscation techniques to obtain more efficient constructions directly from multilinear maps. Zhandry [Zha14] showed how to construct n-way Diffie-Hellman key exchange without trusted setup, a result that was previously known only using obfuscation [BZ14]. Concurrently with this work, Garg et al. [GGH+14] showed how to construct single-input functional encryption from multilinear maps; however, their motivation was to obtain security proofs from concrete assumptions, rather than efficiency. The constructions in this paper are considerably more efficient (we make use of a much smaller number of matrices), but our security proof is in the generic multilinear map model.

Single-input functional encryption [BSW11] has been traditionally defined in the public-key settings and studied extensively [O'N10, GVW12, AGV+13, BO13, CIJ+13, GGH+13b, GKP+13, BCP14]. In this paper, however, we focus on secret-key (multi-input) functional encryption, which is sufficient for data processing on a remote encrypted database, including order-revealing encryption. Focusing on the secret-key setting enables us to give a simple construction from multilinear maps. Single-input *secret-key* functional encryption was previously explored for the inner-product functionality by Shen et al. [SSW09] and more generally by Goldwasser et al. [GKP+13]. Brakerski and Segev [BS14] recently showed how to convert any secret-key functional encryption scheme into one where secret keys do not reveal their functionality.

2   Preliminaries

2.1   Conventions

For an integer n, we write $[n]$ to denote the set $\{1, \ldots, n\}$. For a finite set S, we write $\mathsf{Uniform}(S)$ to denote the probability distribution that is uniform over the elements of S. When working with vectors in $\mathbb{Z}^n$ for some integer n, for each $i \in [n]$ we write $\mathbf{e}_i$ to denote the ith unit column vector, i.e., the vector $(x_1, x_2, \ldots, x_n)^{\mathsf{T}}$ such that $x_i = 1$ and, for all $i' \neq i \in [n]$, we have $x_{i'} = 0$. We write $\mathrm{GL}_w(\mathbb{Z}_q)$ to represent the set of all $w \times w$ invertible matrices over $\mathbb{Z}_q$.

2.2   Matrix Branching Programs (MBPs)

In this section, we define a variant of matrix branching programs for which our main construction applies. These generalized matrix branching programs are a sequence of efficiently computable Boolean circuits that turn a given multivariate input into a matrix.

Definition 2.1 (Generalized Matrix Branching Program). Let $\mathcal{X} \subset \{0,1\}^*$ be a set of possible input strings, and let $f : \mathcal{X}^m \to \{0,1\}$ be a multi-input function. A *generalized matrix branching program* P of length ℓ and width w, over $\mathbb{Z}_q$ for a prime q, is a tuple of the form

$$P = (\, q,\ m,\ d,\ \mathsf{inp},\ (\mathcal{M}_1,\ \ldots,\ \mathcal{M}_\ell)\,),$$

where for each $j \in [\ell]$, the function $\mathcal{M}_j : \mathcal{X} \to \mathbb{Z}_q^{w \times w}$ is computable by an efficient deterministic algorithm. The value inp is a lookup table of the form

$$\mathsf{inp} = (\mathsf{inp}(1), \ldots, \mathsf{inp}(\ell)),$$

where for each $j \in [\ell]$, we have $\mathsf{inp}(j) \in [m]$. The branching program takes m inputs and we say that at step j it *inspects* input number $\mathsf{inp}(j) \in [m]$. To simplify notation, we require the branching program to inspect each of its m input variables exactly d times[2] (so that the length of the program, ℓ, is precisely md). We also introduce the following shorthand notations:

- For a branching program step $j \in [\ell]$, input slot $i \in [m]$, and sub-index $h \in [d]$, we write $j = \mathsf{inp}.\mathsf{j}(i, h)$ to signify that j is the step in which the program inspects input slot i for the hth time.
- For a branching program step $j \in [\ell]$ and sub-index $h \in [d]$, we write $h = \mathsf{inp}.\mathsf{h}(j)$ to signify that j is the step in which the program inspects the corresponding input slot $\mathsf{inp}(j)$ for the hth time.

We say that P *computes* the function f if, for all inputs $\mathbf{x} = (x^{(1)}, \ldots, x^{(m)}) \in \mathcal{X}^m$,

$$\left(\prod_{j \in [\ell]} \mathcal{M}_j(x^{(\mathsf{inp}(j))}) \right)[1, 1] = 0 \quad \Longleftrightarrow \quad f(\mathbf{x}) = 1.$$

Since every program P computes a unique function f, we also write $P(\mathbf{x})$ to denote $f(\mathbf{x})$.

Following Sahai and Zhandry [SZ14], we also define the notion of a *non-shortcutting* matrix branching program.

Definition 2.2 (Shortcuts in Matrix Branching Programs [SZ14]). A branching program has a *shortcut* on input $\mathbf{x} = (x^{(1)}, \ldots, x^{(m)}) \in \mathcal{X}^m$ if either:

$$\left(\prod_{j \in [\ell]} \mathcal{M}_j(x^{(\mathsf{inp}(j))}) \right) \cdot \mathbf{e}_1 = \mathbf{0}_{w \times 1} \qquad \text{or} \qquad \mathbf{e}_1^{\mathsf{T}} \cdot \left(\prod_{j \in [\ell]} \mathcal{M}_j(x^{(\mathsf{inp}(j))}) \right) = \mathbf{0}_{1 \times w}$$

In such a case, it is possible to determine that $f(\mathbf{x}) = 1$ without carrying out the entire matrix product. We say that a branching program is *non-shortcutting* if, for all inputs $\mathbf{x}$, it has no shortcuts on $\mathbf{x}$. We require that every generalized matrix branching program is non-shortcutting.

---

[2] We note that this assumption is without loss of generality, since given any program of length ℓ that does not satisfy this condition, we can construct a new program whose value of d is the original program's value of ℓ, and pad the program with dummy matrix functions that always return the identity matrix regardless of their input string. (Alternatively, for practical applications, it is also easy to adapt the techniques we describe to the general case, albeit at the expense of cumbersome notation.).

We note that there are multiple ways to obtain a generalized matrix branching program from a circuit, or from a time-bounded Turing machine or RAM. Barrington's theorem [Bar86] shows how to convert a Boolean circuit of depth d into a matrix branching program of length $O(4^d)$ and width 5. The work of Ananth, Gupta, Ishai, and Sahai [AGI+14] takes a different approach to obtain MBPs for Boolean formulas that avoids the complexity of Barrington's construction. They construct a layered automaton for any Boolean formula which consists of several states including a starting state and an accepting state together with edges denoting the transitions between states based on the input bit values. Given such an automaton representation, a formula can be evaluated by counting the number of paths between the starting and the accepting state. Ananth et al. show that a Boolean formula of size s can be converted into a layered graph-based branching program with $O(s)$ layers with matrices of size $O(s^2)$. Thus, the size of the resulting MBP is $O(s^3)$. Subsequently, Sahai and Zhandry [SZ14] improve the conversion, giving MBP's of length $O(s)$ and size $O(s(\log_2 s)^2)$. Our approach follows the general method of computing automata with generalized MBPs, but we observe that for some problems such as comparing two-bit strings, we can directly construct extremely efficient automata that do not use the general translation from formulas to automata.

For more details, we refer the reader to the full version.

2.3 Randomized Matrix Branching Programs

In our construction, as in obfuscation constructions that use MBPs [GGH+13b, BGK+14, BR14, AGI+14], we must make sure that the adversary always evaluates the MBP by multiplying together one matrix selection for each step $j \in [\ell]$. In particular, we must ensure that partial matrix products, which omit some steps, will not reveal any information about the program.

The main ingredient we need here is the MBP randomization technique of Kilian [Kil88], in which we pre- and post-multiply each matrix in the MBP by matching, invertible random "blinding" matrices $\mathbf{R}_0, \ldots, \mathbf{R}_\ell$. Intuitively, the resulting randomized MBP fixes the order in which the randomized MBP matrices can be multiplied, i.e., requiring one matrix for each step in the original MBP. Any other product will also contain at least one random "blinding" matrix, rendering the result useless to the adversary.

In addition, we combine Kilian's randomization technique with "bookend vectors" $\hat{\mathbf{s}}, \hat{\mathbf{t}}$, as introduced in [GGH+13b], which further restrict the adversary to projecting a single scalar entry of the matrix product resulting from the MBP evaluation (namely, the entry at position [1,1]). Testing whether this scalar is zero suffices to determine the Boolean output of the program, while preventing the adversary from learning extra information by testing other matrix entries.

We now present the details of the randomized MBP construction.

Definition 2.3 (Randomized MBPs ([Kil88], adapted)). *We define an efficient randomized procedure* MBPRand, *such that, for a given generalized matrix branching program*

$$P = (\ q,\ m,\ d,\ \mathsf{inp},\ (\mathcal{M}_1,\ \ldots,\ \mathcal{M}_\ell)\ ),$$

the procedure $\mathsf{MBPRand}(P)$ *outputs a tuple* $\hat{P}$ *of the form*

$$\hat{P} = \left(\ q,\ m,\ d,\ \mathsf{inp},\ (\hat{\mathcal{M}}_1,\ \ldots,\ \hat{\mathcal{M}}_\ell),\ \hat{\mathbf{s}},\ \hat{\mathbf{t}}\ \right),$$

where, for each $j \in [\ell]$, *the function* $\hat{\mathcal{M}}_j : \mathcal{X} \rightarrow \mathbb{Z}_q^{w \times w}$ *is represented, like* $\mathcal{M}_j$, *as a Boolean circuit; and* $\hat{\mathbf{s}}$ *and* $\hat{\mathbf{t}}$ *are vectors in* $\mathbb{Z}_q^w$.

The procedure $\mathsf{MBPRand}$ *operates as follows. It samples* $(\ell + 1)$ *invertible matrices* $\mathbf{R}_0, \ldots, \mathbf{R}_\ell$ *uniformly at random from* $\mathrm{GL}_w(\mathbb{Z}_q)$. *It computes the values*

$$\hat{\mathbf{s}} = \mathbf{e}_1^{\mathsf{T}} \mathbf{R}_0^{-1} \qquad and \qquad \hat{\mathbf{t}} = \mathbf{R}_\ell \mathbf{e}_1,$$

and, for each $j \in [\ell]$, *the function* $\hat{\mathcal{M}}_j$ *defined as*

$$\hat{\mathcal{M}}_j(x) = \mathbf{R}_{j-1}^{-1} \mathcal{M}_j(x)\, \mathbf{R}_j.$$

Finally, it outputs the tuple

$$\hat{P} = \left(\ q,\ m,\ d,\ \mathsf{inp},\ (\hat{\mathcal{M}}_1,\ \ldots,\ \hat{\mathcal{M}}_\ell),\ \hat{\mathbf{s}},\ \hat{\mathbf{t}}\ \right).$$

To evaluate a randomized MBP $\hat{P}$ on an input $\mathbf{x} = (x^{(1)}, \ldots, x^{(m)})$, we run each (randomized) matrix function $\hat{\mathbf{M}}_j$ on the indicated input string $x^{(\mathsf{inp}(j))}$, producing a randomized matrix $\hat{\mathbf{M}}_j$. We write $\mathsf{MBPSelect}(\hat{P}, \mathbf{x})$ to denote the sequence of randomized matrices and bookend vectors $(\hat{\mathbf{s}}, \hat{\mathbf{M}}_1, \ldots, \hat{\mathbf{M}}_\ell, \hat{\mathbf{t}})$, and to evaluate the program, we multiply all of these randomized matrices and vectors together. Formally, we define the following procedures.

Definition 2.4 (Evaluation for Randomized MBPs ([Kil88], adapted)).
Fix a generalized matrix branching program P *and a vector of inputs* $\mathbf{x} = (x^{(1)}, \ldots, x^{(m)}) \in \mathcal{X}^m$, *and suppose that*

$$\hat{P} = \left(\ q,\ m,\ d,\ \mathsf{inp},\ (\hat{\mathcal{M}}_1,\ \ldots,\ \hat{\mathcal{M}}_\ell),\ \hat{\mathbf{s}},\ \hat{\mathbf{t}}\ \right) \ \leftarrow\ \mathsf{MBPRand}(P).$$

For each $j \in [\ell]$, *we define* $\hat{\mathbf{M}}_j = \hat{\mathcal{M}}_j(x^{(\mathsf{inp}(j))})$, *and we define*

$$\mathsf{MBPSelect}(\hat{P}, \mathbf{x}) = \left(\hat{\mathbf{s}}^{\mathsf{T}},\ \hat{\mathbf{M}}_1, \ldots, \hat{\mathbf{M}}_\ell,\ \hat{\mathbf{t}}\right).$$

Finally, we define

$$\mathsf{MBPEval}\left(\hat{\mathbf{s}}^{\mathsf{T}},\ \hat{\mathbf{M}}_1, \ldots, \hat{\mathbf{M}}_\ell,\ \hat{\mathbf{t}}\right)\ =\ \hat{\mathbf{s}}^{\mathsf{T}} \left(\prod_{j \in \ell} \hat{\mathbf{M}}_j\right) \hat{\mathbf{t}}.$$

Given the above definitions, the proof of the following lemma follows immediately.

Lemma 2.5 (Correctness for Randomized MBPs). *Fix a generalized matrix branching program P, and a vector of inputs $\mathbf{x} = (x^{(1)}, \ldots, x^{(m)}) \in \mathcal{X}^m$. Then,*

$$\mathsf{MBPEval}(\mathsf{MBPSelect}(\hat{P}, \mathbf{x})) = 0 \quad \Longleftrightarrow \quad f(\mathbf{x}) = 1.$$

Ordinarily, for MBPs derived from Barrington's theorem [Bar86], we would also be able to state a simulation theorem, showing that the output distribution $\mathsf{MBPSelect}(\hat{P}, \mathbf{x})$ depends only the output of the original program, $P(\mathbf{x})$. In our construction, however, we obtain much more efficient programs by other techniques , and the matrices $\mathcal{M}_j(x)$ in these programs do not always have full rank. Indeed, the kernel of each matrix may depend on the input vector $\mathbf{x}$, and as a result, the output distributions $\mathsf{MBPSelect}(\hat{P}, \cdot)$ may be noticeably different for different inputs $\mathbf{x}_0, \mathbf{x}_1$, even if the outputs of the program, $P(\mathbf{x}_0) = P(\mathbf{x}_1)$, are ultimately identical.

Instead of constructing a simulator, we rely on a weaker property that is still strong enough to prove security of our main construction. Specifically, we show that even though the distributions $\mathsf{MBPSelect}(\hat{P}, \mathbf{x}_0)$ and $\mathsf{MBPSelect}(\hat{P}, \mathbf{x}_1)$ may differ, they cannot be distinguished by a certain weak family of tests; in our construction (Section 4), we will show that these are the only tests an adversary can possibly perform in our security model. To define such a family of tests, we refer to the following definition of Sahai and Zhandry [SZ14].

Definition 2.6 (Allowable Tests [SZ14]). *Let $p : \mathbb{Z}_q^{2w+w^2\ell} \to \mathbb{Z}_q$ be a multilinear (multivariate) polynomial over the entries of $\hat{\mathbf{s}}, \hat{\mathbf{t}} \in \mathbb{Z}_q^w$ and $\hat{\mathbf{M}}_1, \ldots, \hat{\mathbf{M}}_\ell \in \mathbb{Z}_q^{w \times w}$ (as formal variables). We say p is an allowable test polynomial if each monomial in the expansion of p contains at most one entry of each vector $\hat{\mathbf{s}}, \hat{\mathbf{t}}$ and matrix $\hat{\mathbf{M}}_1, \ldots, \hat{\mathbf{M}}_\ell$.*

Lemma 2.7 (Security for Randomized MBPs). *Fix a non-shortcutting generalized matrix branching program P (over $\mathbb{Z}_q$, for $q > 2^\lambda$), two input vectors $\mathbf{x}_0, \mathbf{x}_1$ such that $P(\mathbf{x}_0) = P(\mathbf{x}_1)$, and an allowable test polynomial p (Def. 2.6). Then either*

$$\Pr\left[\hat{P} \leftarrow \mathsf{MBPRand}(P) \ ; \ p(\mathsf{MBPSelect}(\hat{P}, \mathbf{x}_b)) = 0\right] = 1$$

for both bits $b \in \{0, 1\}$, or,

$$\Pr\left[\hat{P} \leftarrow \mathsf{MBPRand}(P) \ ; \ p(\mathsf{MBPSelect}(\hat{P}, \mathbf{x}_b)) = 0\right] < \mathsf{negl}(\lambda)$$

for both bits $b \in \{0, 1\}$.

Lemma 2.7 follows immediately from the results of Sahai and Zhandry [SZ14]; we defer the formal treatment to the full version.

2.4   Multilinear Maps

Multilinear maps [BS03], also known as graded encodings, or graded multilinear maps [GGH13a, CLT13], are a generalization of bilinear maps such as pairings over elliptic curves [Mil04, MOV93, Jou00, BF01]. Roughly speaking, a multilinear map lets us take a scalar $x \in \mathbb{F}_q$ and produce an encoded version, $\hat{x} = [x]_S$, where $S \subseteq \mathcal{U}$ is a finite set, called an *index set*, that indicates the level of the encoding $\hat{x}$ in a given hierarchy (namely, the subsets of $\mathcal{U}$ ordered by inclusion).[3]

By convention, we will say that these index sets are made up of *formal symbols*, denoted by capital letters (A, B, C), which serve the same role as formal variables in polynomials. To be fully precise, we state the following definitions.

Definition 2.8 (Formal Symbol). A *formal symbol* is a bit string in $\{0, 1\}^*$, and distinct variables denote distinct bit strings. A *fresh* formal symbol is any bit string in $\{0, 1\}^*$ that has not already been assigned to another formal symbol.

Definition 2.9 (Index Sets). An *index set* is a set of formal symbols called *indices*. By convention, for index sets we use set notation and product notation interchangeably, so that ABC represents $\{A, B, C\}$, and $ABC \cup D = ABCD$.

Definition 2.10 (Multilinear Map ([BS03, GGH13a, CLT13])). A multilinear map over prime-order finite fields supports the following operations. Each of the operations (MM.Setup, MM.Add, MM.Mult, MM.ZeroTest, MM.Encode) is implemented by an efficient randomized algorithm.

- The setup procedure receives as input an index set $\mathcal{U}$ (Definition 2.9), which we refer to as the "top-level index set", as well as the security parameter λ (in unary). It produces public parameters pp (which include an $O(\lambda)$-bit prime q), and secret evaluation parameters sk:

$$\mathsf{MM.Setup}(\mathcal{U}, \ 1^\lambda) \ \rightarrow \ (\mathsf{pp}, \ \mathsf{sk})$$

- For each index set $S \subseteq \mathcal{U}$, and each scalar $x \in \mathbb{Z}_q$, there is a set of strings $[x]_S \subseteq \{0, 1\}^*$, i.e., the set of all valid encodings of x at index set S. [4] From here on, we will abuse notation to write $[x]_S$ to stand for any element of $[x]_S$ (i.e., any valid encoding of x at the index set S).

- Elements at the same index set $S \subseteq \mathcal{U}$ can be added, with the result also encoded at S:

$$\mathsf{MM.Add}(\mathsf{pp}, \ [x]_S, \ [y]_S) \ \rightarrow \ [x + y]_S$$

---

[3] We describe here the case of *asymmetric* multilinear maps, since this is the one relevant to our constructions in this work.

[4] To be more precise, we define $[x]_S = \{\chi \in \{0, 1\}^* : \mathsf{MM.IsEncoding}(\mathsf{pp}, \chi, x, S)\}$, where the predicate MM.IsEncoding is specified by the concrete instantiation of the multilinear map. In general, the predicate MM.IsEncoding is not necessarily efficiently decidable—and indeed, for the security of the multilinear map, it should not be.

- Elements at two index sets S_1, S_2 can be multiplied, with the result encoded at the union of the two sets, as long as their union is still contained in $\mathcal{U}$:

$$\text{MM.Mult}(\text{pp}, [x]_{S_1}, [y]_{S_2}) \rightarrow \begin{cases} [xy]_{S_1 \cup S_2} & \text{if } S_1 \cup S_2 \subseteq \mathcal{U} \\ \bot & \text{otherwise} \end{cases}$$

- Elements at the top level $\mathcal{U}$ can be *zero-tested*:

$$\text{MM.ZeroTest}(\text{pp}, [x]_S) \rightarrow \begin{cases} \text{"zero"} & \text{if } S = \mathcal{U} \text{ and } x = 0 \in \mathbb{Z}_q \\ \text{"nonzero"} & \text{otherwise} \end{cases}$$

- Using the secret parameters, one can generate a representation of a given scalar $x \in \mathbb{Z}_q$ at any index set $S \subseteq \mathcal{U}$:

$$\text{MM.Encode}(\text{sp}, x, S) \rightarrow [x]_S$$

- For the trivial index set $S = \emptyset$, we specify that the only valid encoding of $[x]_\emptyset$ is just the scalar $x \in \mathbb{F}_q$. (So, for instance, we can perform subtraction via MM.Add, by scalar multiplication with -1.)

By convention, we refer to the cardinality of $\mathcal{U}$ as the *degree of multilinearity* of the map.[5] Technically, known instantiations of multilinear maps [GGH13a, CLT13] are only approximate, and have a "noise" term that restricts the degree of multilinearity to a pre-specified polynomial in the security parameter. However, this restriction will not affect our results in this work, and to keep the presentation simple we do not model the restriction formally.

When the context is clear, we also abuse notation to write, for encoded elements $\hat{a}, \hat{b}$, the expression $\hat{a} + \hat{b}$ to mean MM.Add(MM.pp, $\hat{a}, \hat{b}$); the expression $\hat{a}\hat{b}$ to mean MM.Mult(MM.pp, $\hat{a}, \hat{b}$); and likewise for other arithmetic expressions.

The Generic Multilinear Map Model. To define security, we will operate in the generic multilinear map model (also known as the *generic graded encoding model* [GGH+13b, BR14, BGK+14]). This model is very similar to the generic group model [Sho97]—intuitively, in this model, the only operations an adversary can use with encoded elements are the operations of the multilinear map. More precisely, we say a scheme that uses multilinear maps is secure in the generic multilinear map model if, for any concrete adversary breaking the real scheme, there is an ideal adversary breaking a modified scheme in which each concrete encoded element is replaced by a "handle" (concretely, a fresh nonce), mapped to the actual encoded scalar in a table unavailable to the adversary.

---

[5] In some cases, when we optimize a construction that uses multilinear maps, we find that we never need to encode elements of a given singleton index set. Thus in general, for constructions that are optimized in this way, we relax the definition of multilinearity degree to refer to the total number of sequential multiplications that must be performed on any encoded elements in the construction.

Each multilinear map operation is replaced by an oracle query that takes two handles and returns another fresh handle (creating a new table entry), except for the zero-test oracle query, which, when given a handle, returns "zero" if the corresponding scalar in the table is zero, and "nonzero" otherwise. We defer the formal definitions to the full version.

2.5 Exclusive Partition Families

Even though the randomized MBPs of Section 2.3 impose certain restrictions on how their matrices can be multiplied together to remove the randomizing factors, this alone does not prevent an adversary from learning more information than just the outputs of honest evaluations on the MBP. The issue is that the adversary may execute "mix-and-match" attacks, using encoded matrices from multiple ciphertexts in the same evaluation. Our construction will use the multilinear map's index sets to enforce constraints on the adversary's evaluation, ruling out this kind of attack. As with the "straddling sets" technique of Barak et al. [BGK+14], in order to use index sets to enforce this restriction, we need to design these index sets with some combinatorial properties in mind.

In more detail, suppose U is the top-level index set in the multilinear map, and $\mathcal{F}$ is some family of partitions of U. Intuitively, whenever we *intend* terms to be multiplied together (e.g., because they are matrix elements from a consistent choice of ciphertexts), the index sets of those terms will partition U, so that the product of the encoded elements can legally be zero-tested. We will design the partition family $\mathcal{F}$ so that our intended partitions (those in $\mathcal{F}$) are the only partitions of U that the adversary can possibly construct given the index sets of the terms we provide, thereby ruling out "mix-and-match" attacks.

Formally, we define the following:

Definition 2.11 (Partition). *The collection of sets $P = \{S_1, \ldots, S_d\}$ is a partition of a set U if $S_1 \cup \cdots \cup S_d = U$; each S_i is a nonempty subset of U; and $S_i \cap S_j = \emptyset$ for each $i \neq j$.*

Definition 2.12 (Exclusive Partition Family). *Fix a set U, and a family $\mathcal{F}$ of partitions of U, where we write the N partitions in the family $\mathcal{F}$ as the rows of the matrix:*

$$\begin{pmatrix} S_{1,1} & S_{1,2} & \cdots & S_{1,d} \\ \vdots & \vdots & \ddots & \vdots \\ S_{N,1} & S_{N,2} & \cdots & S_{N,d} \end{pmatrix}$$

We say that $\mathcal{F}$ is an (N, d)-exclusive partition family of U if the only partitions of U that can be formed from sets in $\mathcal{F}$ are precisely the rows of the matrix. (Formally: for all $(i_1, j_1), \ldots, (i_m, j_m) \in [N] \times [d]$, the collection $P = \{S_{i_1,j_1}, \ldots, S_{i_m,j_m}\}$ is a partition of U if and only if $i_1 = \ldots = i_m$ and $\{j_1, \ldots, j_m\} = [d]$.)

We say that an exclusive partition family $\mathcal{F}$ is *explicit* if there is an efficient deterministic algorithm which, when given $i \in [N], j \in [d]$, outputs the elements of $S_{i,j}$ (i.e., outputs the index of each element in some canonical ordering of the elements of U). We note that if $\mathcal{F}$ is explicit, then it is also easy to sample a partition $(S_{i,1}, \ldots, S_{i,d})$ uniformly over all of the partitions in $\mathcal{F}$, simply by choosing uniform $i \leftarrow [N]$. To simplify notation, we write this sampling procedure as $(S_{i,1}, \ldots, S_{i,d}) \overset{\$}{\leftarrow} \mathcal{F}$.

Construction 2.13 $((2^\lambda, d)$-**Exclusive Partition Families**). Let $d, \lambda > 0$ be integers, and let U be a set of size $(1 + (d-1)(\lambda+1))$. Denote the elements of U as

$$U = \{\, a_1, a_2, \ldots, a_d, \quad b_{2,1}, \ldots, b_{2,\lambda}, \quad \ldots, \quad b_{d,1}, \ldots, b_{d,\lambda} \,\},$$

and identify an index $i \in [2^\lambda]$ with the string $\rho(i) \in \{0,1\}^\lambda$ that forms the binary representation of $(i-1)$. Define

$$S_{i,1} = \{a_1\} \cup \bigcup_{j \in \{2,\ldots,d\}} \{b_{j,k} : \rho(i)_k = 1\}$$

and for each $j \in \{2, \ldots, d\}$, define

$$S_{i,j} = \{a_j\} \cup \{b_{j,k} : \rho(i)_k = 0\}.$$

Finally, define the family $\mathcal{F}(d,\lambda) = ((S_{1,1}, \ldots, S_{1,d}), \ldots, (S_{N,1}, \ldots, S_{N,d}))$.

Lemma 2.14 $((2^\lambda, d)$-**Exclusive Partition Families**). *For integers $d, \lambda > 0$, the family $\mathcal{F}(d,\lambda)$ defined by Construction 2.13 is an explicit $(2^\lambda, d)$-exclusive partition family.*

Proof. By construction, each $(S_{i,1}, \ldots, S_{i,d})$ is a partition of U consisting of d sets, and the elements of each set are efficiently computable. Now, suppose that for some choice of sets $(i_1, j_1), \ldots, (i_m, j_m) \in [N] \times [d]$, the collection $P = \{S_{i_1,j_1}, \ldots, S_{i_m,j_m}\}$ is a partition of U. Then there exists some $r^* \in [m]$ such that the set $S_{i_{r^*}, j_{r^*}}$ contains a_1. The only such sets are of the form:

$$S_{i_{r^*}, j_{r^*}} = S_{i_{r^*}, 1} = \{a_1\} \cup \bigcup_{j \in \{2,\ldots,d\}} \{b_{j,k} : \rho(i_{r^*})_k = 1\}$$

Assume for sake of contradiction that for some $r \in [m]$, $i_r \neq i_{r^*}$. We cannot have $j_r = 1$, since this would cover the element a_1 twice: once by $S_{i_{r^*}, j_{r^*}}$, and once by S_{i_r, j_r}. Thus $j_r \in \{2, \ldots, d\}$, and the set S_{i_r, j_r} is of the form:

$$S_{i_r, j_r} = \{a_{j_r}\} \cup \{b_{j_r,k} : \rho(i_r)_k = 0\}$$

But for each $k \in [\lambda]$, the only sets that contain $b_{j_r,k}$ also contain either a_1 or a_{j_r}, and we already have $a_1 \in S_{i^*,1}$ and $a_{j_r} \in S_{i_r, j_r}$ covered by the putative partition P. Hence the only elements $b_{j_r,k}$ that are covered by P are those of the form $\{b_{j,k} : \rho(i_{r^*})_k = 1\}$ and $\{b_{j,k} : \rho(i_r)_k = 0\}$. Since by assumption $i_r \neq i_{r^*}$, the strings $\rho(i_r), \rho(i_{r^*})$ differ on some bit $k^* \in [\lambda]$. If $\rho(i_{r^*})_{k^*} = 0$ and

$\rho(i_r)_k = 1$, then P fails to cover b_{j_r,k^*}, while if $\rho(i_{r^*})_{k^*} = 1$ and $\rho(i_r)_k = 0$, then P covers b_{j_r,k^*} twice. In either case P is not a partition of U, contradicting our assumption. So we conclude that $i_{r^*} = i_1 = \ldots = i_m$, and thus $\mathcal{F}$ is an explicit $(2^\lambda, d)$-exclusive partition family.

We also observe that our definition of exclusive partition families generalizes the *straddling set systems* of Barak et al. [BGK+14]. Indeed, for any integer $d > 0$, a straddling set system $\mathbb{S}_d$ (as defined in [BGK+14]) is a $(2, d)$-exclusive partition family.

3   Secret-Key Multi-Input Functional Encryption (SK-MIFE)

We now discuss the definition of secret-key multi-input functional encryption (SK-MIFE), which is a special case of the definition of multi-input functional encryption (MIFE) in [GGG+14].

In fact we will specialize this definition further, to the case of SK-MIFE with a *single* function evaluation key (1SK-MIFE). We note that it is straightforward to construct ordinary SK-MIFE (enabling multiple function keys) from 1SK-MIFE, as follows. We can set the single functionality in 1SK-MIFE to be a universal branching program, $U(f, x_1, \ldots, x_n)$, which takes as one of its inputs the function f to be evaluated. In this SK-MIFE scheme, the key to evaluate a particular function f will be the 1SK-MIFE encryption 1SK-MIFE.Enc(sk, 1, f) (for input slot 1 in the universal program U).

We also note that 1SK-MIFE already covers the application of order-revealing encryption (ORE), since here we only want to enable a single function on MIFE ciphertexts: namely, the comparison function. As we will see below, working with 1SK-MIFE enables us to achieve a much more efficient construction. Thus, we will restrict our attention to 1SK-MIFE here.

3.1   Definitions

A single-key, secret-key multi-input functional encryption (1SK-MIFE) scheme

$$\Pi = (1\text{SK-MIFE.Setup}, \ 1\text{SK-MIFE.Enc}, \ 1\text{SK-MIFE.Dec})$$

supports the following operations. Each operation is implemented by a randomized algorithm, which (with all but negligible probability) runs in time polynomial in its input length and the security parameter λ.

- The setup procedure takes as input a security parameter λ and a program P, given as an m-input matrix branching program (Section 2.2) over $\mathbb{Z}_q$ for some prime $q > 2^\lambda$. The setup procedure outputs an evaluation key ek and a secret key sk.

$$1\text{SK-MIFE.Setup}(\lambda, P) \ \rightarrow \ (\text{ek}, \ \text{sk})$$

- The encryption procedure takes as input a secret key sk, an input variable index $i \in [m]$, and an input $x \in \mathcal{X}$, and outputs a ciphertext ct.

$$1\text{SK-MIFE.Enc}(\text{sk}, i, x) \rightarrow \text{ct}$$

- The decryption procedure takes as input an evaluation key ek and ciphertexts $\text{ct}^{(1)}, \ldots, \text{ct}^{(m)}$, and outputs a computation result $b \in \{0, 1\}$.

$$1\text{SK-MIFE.Dec}(\text{ek}, \text{ct}^{(1)}, \ldots, \text{ct}^{(m)}) \rightarrow b$$

Definition 3.1 (1SK-MIFE Correctness). *A 1SK-MIFE scheme Π is correct if for any uniform multi-input matrix branching program P, and any inputs $x^{(1)}, \ldots, x^{(m)} \in \mathcal{X}$, if $(\text{ek}, \text{sk}) \leftarrow 1\text{SK-MIFE.Setup}(\lambda, P)$ and for each $i \in [m]$ it is the case that $\text{ct}^{(i)} \leftarrow 1\text{SK-MIFE.Enc}(\text{sk}, i, x^{(i)})$, then,*

$$1\text{SK-MIFE.Dec}(\text{ek}, \text{ct}^{(1)}, \ldots, \text{ct}^{(m)}) \rightarrow P(x^{(1)}, \ldots, x^{(m)}).$$

Security. It is clearly impossible to achieve (standard) semantic security for 1SK-MIFE, since by design, our scheme must leak some information about the plaintexts—namely, the result of evaluating the 1SK-MIFE program P on every possible choice of query plaintext tuple. Our goal, then, is best-possible semantic security, in which we leak *only* this information. In this respect, our security definition is similar to IND-OCPA in the special case of order-preserving (or order-revealing) encryption [BCL+09], but of course we must generalize it for 1SK-MIFE. Our definition is also similar to the indistinguishability-based definitions of (general) multi-input functional encryption given by Goldwasser et al. [GGG+14]. We now present the formal details.

Definition 3.2 (1SK-MIFE Security Game). *Fix a generalized matrix branching program P (to be used in the 1SK-MIFE scheme). For an adversary $\mathcal{A}$, and for each "world" bit $b \in \{0, 1\}$, we define the experiment $\text{Expt}_{P,Q,b}^{1\text{SK-MIFE}}(\mathcal{A})$, parameterized over a number of queries Q:*

Experiment $\text{Expt}_{P,Q,b}^{1\text{SK-MIFE}}(\mathcal{A})$:

1. $\mathcal{A}$ *receives an evaluation key* ek, *where* $(\text{ek}, \text{sk}) \leftarrow 1\text{SK-MIFE.Setup}(\lambda, P)$.
2. $\mathcal{A}$ *makes Q adaptive queries to a left-or-right encryption oracle, as follows. For each $t \in [Q]$, the adversary sends* $\text{query}_t = (i_t, x_{t,0}, x_{t,1})$, *and is given a ciphertext* $\text{ct}_t \leftarrow 1\text{SK-MIFE.Enc}(\text{sk}, i_t, x_{t,b})$.
3. $\mathcal{A}$ *outputs a bit* $b' \in \{0, 1\}$, *which is the output of the experiment.*

Definition 3.3 (Input-Consistent Queries). *In an execution trace of the experiment $\text{Expt}_{P,Q,b}^{1\text{SK-MIFE}}(\mathcal{A})$ (Definition 3.2), let $t_1, \ldots, t_m \in [Q]$ be time steps in the adversary's query sequence, such that for every input slot index $i \in [m]$, we have $\text{query}_{t_i}[1] = i$ (i.e., at time t_1, the adversary queried for input slot 1; at time t_2, the adversary queried for input slot 2; and so on). Then we say the query time sequence $\tau = (t_1, \ldots, t_m)$ is input-consistent. Furthermore, for each world bit $b \in \{0, 1\}$, we say that such an input-consistent sequence τ selects the vector of inputs $\mathbf{x}_{\tau,b} = (x_{t_1,b}, \ldots, x_{t_m,b})$.*

Definition 3.4 (Execution Trace). *Fix an adversary $\mathcal{A}$ in the generic multilinear map model. We define the* execution trace *of the experiment $\mathsf{Expt}^{\mathsf{1SK\text{-}MIFE}}_{P,Q,b}(\mathcal{A})$ to be the sequence of all oracle query-response pairs, both between $\mathcal{A}$ and the challenger and between $\mathcal{A}$ and the multilinear map oracle.*

Definition 3.5 (Admissibility of Execution Traces). *An execution trace of the experiment $\mathsf{Expt}^{\mathsf{1SK\text{-}MIFE}}_{P,Q,b}(\mathcal{A})$ is* admissible *if the Q adaptive queries made by the adversary satisfy the following condition: for every input-consistent query time sequence $\boldsymbol{\tau} \in [Q]^m$, letting $\mathbf{x}_{\tau,b}$ denote the vector of inputs selected by $\boldsymbol{\tau}$ in world b, we have $P(\mathbf{x}_{\tau,0}) = P(\mathbf{x}_{\tau,1})$.*

We note that admissibility can be checked, for any given execution trace, in time $O([Q]^m) \cdot \mathrm{poly}(\lambda, |P|))$, simply by testing the condition every possible sequence $\boldsymbol{\tau}$. Thus, if m is a constant—e.g., for order-revealing encryption, where the arity of the comparison program is $m = 2$—then admissibility can be checked in polynomial time. For general programs P, the arity m may be $\omega(1)$, in which case admissibility may not be efficiently checkable. Nevertheless, we can still define IND-security the same way.

Definition 3.6 (IND-security for 1SK-MIFE). *A 1SK-MIFE scheme Π is Q-IND-secure if, for all generalized matrix branching programs P, and all efficient adversaries $\mathcal{A}$, the quantity*

$$\mathsf{Adv}^{\mathsf{1SK\text{-}MIFE}}_{P,Q}(\mathcal{A}) = |W_0 - W_1|$$

is negligible, where for each world bit $b \in \{0,1\}$ we define

$$W_b = \Pr\left[\mathsf{Expt}^{\mathsf{1SK\text{-}MIFE}}_{P,Q,b}(\mathcal{A}) \text{ outputs } 1 \text{ and yields an admissible execution trace}\right].$$

Application to Order-Revealing Encryption. Our motivating application of 1SK-MIFE is order-revealing encryption (ORE). In this case, the program P is a matrix branching program for the comparison function, which takes two bit strings $x, y \in \{0,1\}^n$ representing numbers in binary, and returns 1 if $x \le y$. The 1SK-MIFE evaluation key ek then fills the role of the comparison algorithm in ORE.

Strictly speaking, in addition to the comparison algorithm, ORE requires that someone who holds the secret key can also decrypt each ciphertext, revealing the original string $x \in \{0,1\}^n$. We can accomplish this by including, along with the 1SK-MIFE ciphertext, another encryption of x under an ordinary (semantically-secure) symmetric encryption scheme, and including this scheme's secret key as part of the key in ORE.

4 Our 1SK-MIFE Construction

Consider an m-input generalized matrix branching program (MBP) of length ℓ. We construct a 1SK-MIFE for the function computed by this MBP. To encrypt an input $x \in \mathcal{X}$ we construct the set of matrices obtained by considering the input $(x, \ldots, x) \in \mathcal{X}^m$ to the MBP. We randomize each matrix in the branching program as in Section 2.3 by using a randomizing matrix taken from the secret key. These randomizing matrices $\mathbf{R}_i$ are fixed at key generation time and used for all encryptions. The encryption procedure then chooses random scalars $\alpha_1, \ldots, \alpha_\ell$ and, more importantly, chooses random index sets for a multilinear map with which to encode each of the matrices (these index sets are chosen from an *exclusive partition family* which, as we will see, have the properties needed for correctness and security). The encryptor encodes each randomized matrix using its assigned index set and outputs the set of encoded matrices as the encryption of x. Now, to compute the MBP function given m independently-created ciphertexts we can select appropriate encoded matrices from each ciphertext and compute their product using the multilinear map, as done in the ORE example in Section 1. We then zero-test the result to learn the output of the function in the clear.

The challenge with this approach is to guarantee that any meaningful evaluation has to use all of the matrices in a set of m ciphertexts and no other elements. In other words, the difficulty in the security proof lies in preventing attacks that evaluate the decryption function by mixing matrices from different encryptions for the same input position. We resolve this issue by relying on exclusive partition families from Definition 2.12. For each input position i that determines d matrices in the generalized MBP, we construct a $(2^\lambda, d)$-exclusive partition family $\mathcal{F}^{(i)}$. To encrypt a message for that position, we sample at random a partition $(S_1^{(i)}, \ldots, S_d^{(i)})$ from the family $\mathcal{F}^{(i)}$ and use the sets from the partition as the index sets for encoded matrices included in the encryption. The properties of the exclusive partition families guarantee that MBP evaluations using matrices from ciphertexts generated by sampling different partitions from $\mathcal{F}^{(i)}$ will fail because the result will not be encoded with respect to the index set for the zero-tester.

We now describe the formal construction for the above intuition.

Construction 4.1   (1SK-MIFE). The 1SK-MIFE construction consists of the following procedures:

- 1SK-MIFE.Setup(λ, P):
  The setup procedure receives as input a security parameter λ and a generalized matrix branching program $P : \mathcal{X}^m \to \{0, 1\}$ of the form

$$P = (\ q,\ m,\ d,\ \mathsf{inp},\ (\mathcal{M}_1,\ \ldots,\ \mathcal{M}_\ell)\ ),$$

  as described in Section 2.2, where $\mathcal{X} \subset \{0, 1\}^*$ is a space of possible input strings, each $\mathcal{M}_j : \mathcal{X} \to \mathrm{GL}_w(\mathbb{Z}_q)$ is expressed as a Boolean circuit, and $\ell = md$.
  For each input variable index $i \in [m]$, let $\mathcal{F}^{(i)}$ be a $(2^\lambda, d)$-exclusive partition family (Lemma 2.14) over a set $\mathcal{U}_i$ of $O(d\lambda)$ fresh formal indices (Section 2.4),

and let A_s, A_t also be fresh formal indices. The setup procedure forms a top-level universe of indices

$$\mathcal{U} = A_s A_t \prod_{i \in [m]} \mathcal{U}_i,$$

and generates corresponding parameters for a multilinear map

$$(\text{MM.pp, MM.sp}) \leftarrow \text{MM.Setup}(\mathcal{U}, q).$$

Then, it randomizes P via the method of Definition 2.3, producing a randomized program $\hat{P}$ as

$$\hat{P} = \text{MBPRand}(P) = \left(q, \; m, \; n, \; \text{inp}, \; (\hat{\mathcal{M}}_1, \; \ldots, \; \hat{\mathcal{M}}_\ell), \; \hat{\mathbf{s}}, \; \hat{\mathbf{t}} \right).$$

Finally, it outputs the evaluation key ek and the secret key sk:

$$\text{ek} = \left(\text{MM.pp}, \; P, \; [\hat{\mathbf{s}}]_{A_s}, \; [\hat{\mathbf{t}}]_{A_t} \right) \qquad \text{sk} = (\text{MM.sp}, \hat{P})$$

(using MM.Encode(MM.sp, $\cdot, \cdot$) to generate fresh encoded elements $[\hat{\mathbf{s}}]_{A_s}, [\hat{\mathbf{t}}]_{A_t}$).

- 1SK-MIFE.Enc(sk, i, x):
The encryption procedure receives as input the secret key sk $= (\text{MM.sp}, \hat{P})$, an input variable index $i \in [m]$, and a plaintext $x \in \mathcal{X}$ (to be encrypted to the ith input slot of the branching program).
Let $\mathcal{F}^{(i)}$ be a $(2^\lambda, d)$-exclusive partition family (Lemma 2.14) over $\mathcal{U}_i$, as defined in 1SK-MIFE.Setup above. The encryption procedure samples a partition uniformly at random from the family $\mathcal{F}^{(i)}$ of the form

$$\left(S_1^{(i)}, \; \ldots, \; S_d^{(i)} \right) \xleftarrow{\$} \mathcal{F}^{(i)}.$$

The procedure also chooses scalars $\alpha_1, \ldots, \alpha_d \leftarrow \mathbb{Z}_q^*$ uniformly at random. Finally, for each $h \in [d]$, the procedure generates the following fresh encoded elements (using MM.Encode(MM.sp, $\cdot, \cdot$)):

$$\text{ct}_h := \left[\alpha_h \, \hat{\mathcal{M}}_{\text{inp.j}(i,h)}(x) \right]_{S_h^{(i)}},$$

and outputs the ciphertext ct $= (\text{ct}_1, \ldots, \text{ct}_d)$.

- 1SK-MIFE.Dec(ek, $\text{ct}^{(1)}, \ldots, \text{ct}^{(m)}$): The decryption procedure receives as input the public parameters ek $= (\text{MM.pp}, P, [\hat{\mathbf{s}}]_{A_s}, [\hat{\mathbf{t}}]_{A_t})$, along with m ciphertexts $\text{ct}^{(1)}, \ldots, \text{ct}^{(m)}$. Each ciphertext is parsed as

$$\text{ct}^{(i)} = (\text{ct}_1^{(i)}, \ldots, \text{ct}_d^{(i)}) = \left(\hat{\mathbf{C}}_1^{(i)}, \; \ldots \; \hat{\mathbf{C}}_d^{(i)} \right),$$

where the entries of the matrices $\hat{\mathbf{C}}_h^{(i)}$ are encoded elements in the multilinear map. Then, using the multilinear map operations (MM.Add, MM.Mult), it computes

$$z = [\hat{\mathbf{s}}]_{A_s} \cdot \left(\prod_{j \in [\ell]} \hat{\mathbf{C}}_{\mathsf{inp}.h(j)}^{(\mathsf{inp}(j))} \right) \cdot [\hat{\mathbf{t}}]_{A_t} .$$

Using the operation MM.ZeroTest, the procedure tests whether z encodes zero in $\mathbb{F}_q$, and outputs 1 if so, and 0 otherwise.

Functional correctness follows from the definition of Construction 4.1, along with the correctness of the multilinear map procedures. Formally, we state the following theorem.

Theorem 4.2. *Construction 4.1 is correct (Definition 3.1).*

To prove Theorem 4.2, we first show that for a given evaluation on m honestly-generated ciphertexts, all of the index sets "match up" for each $i \in [m]$, so that the result z is a valid zero-test query; this follows from the properties of exclusive partition families (Definition 2.12). Then, we show that the actual value of z corresponds to the execution of the original program; this follows by correctness of the randomization procedure MBPRand (Definition 2.3).

Proof. Fix a multi-input matrix branching program P, a security parameter λ, and a tuple of plaintext inputs $\mathbf{x} = (x^{(1)}, \ldots, x^{(m)})$. Let $(\mathsf{ek}, \mathsf{sk}) \leftarrow \text{1SK-MIFE.Setup}(\lambda, P)$, and suppose that for each $i \in [m]$, we have $\mathsf{ct}^{(i)} \leftarrow \text{1SK-MIFE.Enc}(\mathsf{sk}, i, x^{(i)})$. Then we claim that $\text{1SK-MIFE.Dec}(\mathsf{sk}, x^{(1)}, \ldots, x^{(m)}) \rightarrow P(\mathbf{x})$.

To begin, we write:

$$\mathsf{ct}^{(i)} = (\hat{\mathbf{M}}_1^{(i)}, \ldots, \hat{\mathbf{M}}_d^{(i)}),$$

where the entries of the each matrix $\hat{\mathbf{M}}_h^{(i)}$ are encoded elements in the multilinear map. Note that 1SK-MIFE.Dec outputs the result of zero-testing the following encoded element:

$$z = [\hat{\mathbf{s}}]_{A_s} \cdot \left(\prod_{j \in [\ell]} \hat{\mathbf{M}}_{\mathsf{inp}.h(j)}^{(\mathsf{inp}(j))} \right) \cdot [\hat{\mathbf{t}}]_{A_t}$$

Hence, for correctness, it suffices to show that for honestly constructed ciphertexts, z is a valid (non-$\perp$) encoded element at the top-level index set $\mathcal{U}$, and that z's value in $\mathbb{Z}_q$ is zero precisely when P evaluates to 1 on $\mathbf{x}$.

By definition, for any $j \in [\ell]$, we have $j = \mathsf{inp}.j(\mathsf{inp}(j), \mathsf{inp}.h(j))$ (Section 2.2). Thus by construction of 1SK-MIFE.Enc:

$$z = [\hat{\mathbf{s}}]_{A_s} \cdot \left(\prod_{j \in [\ell]} \left[\alpha_j' \, \hat{\mathcal{M}}_j(x^{(\mathsf{inp}(j))}) \right]_{S_{\mathsf{inp}.h(j)}^{(\mathsf{inp}(j))}} \right) \cdot [\hat{\mathbf{t}}]_{A_t} ,$$

for some $\alpha'_j \in \mathbb{Z}_q^*$ chosen by 1SK-MIFE.Enc on some input. Now, note that

$$\left\{ S_{\text{inp.}h(j)}^{(\text{inp}(j))} : j \in [\ell] \right\} \;=\; \left\{ S_h^{(i)} : i \in [m], h \in [d] \right\}. \tag{2}$$

Since for each $i \in [m]$, the tuple $(S_h^{(\text{inp}(j))})_{h \in [d]}$ is a partition of $\mathcal{U}_i$ (Lemma 2.14), we conclude that the right-hand side of (2) is a partition of $(\mathcal{U} \setminus (A_s \cup A_t))$, and thus so is the left-hand side. Hence each MM.Mult operation performed by the functional decryption procedure is valid, and the result z is an element of $\mathbb{Z}_q$ encoded at the top-level universe $\mathcal{U}$.

It only remains to establish that z encodes zero precisely when the program evaluates to 1 on the corresponding inputs. We have that

$$z \;=\; \left[\left(\prod_{j \in [\ell]} \alpha'_j \right) \hat{\mathbf{s}} \cdot \left(\prod_{j \in [\ell]} \hat{\mathcal{M}}_j(x^{(\text{inp}(j))}) \right) \cdot \hat{\mathbf{t}} \right]_{\mathcal{U}},$$

and hence, by the correctness of the randomized encoding (Lemma 2.5),

$$z \;=\; \left[\left(\prod_{j \in [\ell]} \alpha'_j \right) \cdot \left(\prod_{j \in [\ell]} \mathcal{M}_j(x^{(\text{inp}(j))}) \right) [1, 1] \right]_{\mathcal{U}}.$$

Since each $\alpha'_j \in \mathbb{Z}_q^*$ is invertible, z encodes zero if and only if

$$\left(\prod_{j \in [\ell]} \mathcal{M}_j(x^{(\text{inp}(j))}) \right) [1, 1] = 0,$$

so by the definition of the branching program, we conclude that

$$z = 0 \quad \Longleftrightarrow \quad P(\mathbf{x}) = 1.$$

Remark 4.3. As written, Construction 4.1 requires an $(\ell + 2)$-way multilinear map to support the computation of z in 1SK-MIFE.Dec. However, we note that we could optimize the construction so that 1SK-MIFE.Enc pre-multiplies the vectors $\hat{\mathbf{s}}$ and $\hat{\mathbf{t}}$ with the first and last matrices, respectively, $\hat{C}_{\text{inp.}h(1)}^{(\text{inp}(1))}, \hat{C}_{\text{inp.}h(\ell)}^{(\text{inp}(\ell))}, \ldots$. This would enable us to reduce the degree of the computation from $(\ell + 2)$ to ℓ (and hence obtain better parameters for the multilinear map); in the special case of order-revealing encryption, we have $\ell = k + 1$, and thus we reduce the degree required from $(k + 3)$ to $(k + 1)$. For simplicity, however, we present the construction without this optimization.

Remark 4.4 (Multi-Bit Output). For simplicity, we present our SK-MIFE construction only for functions that output a single bit. However, the construction can easily be extended to functions with multi-bit output in a number of ways.

First, if a given generalized branching program already outputs k bits[6], then we can output the same k bits via the techniques of Sahai and Zhandry, replacing the bookend vectors $\hat{s}, \hat{t}$ by randomized diagonal matrices as described in [SZ14]. This transformation yields multi-bit output at essentially no additional performance cost. Alternatively, for arbitrary programs (not represented efficiently as multi-bit branching programs *a priori*), we can also simply run k copies of our scheme in parallel, supporting multi-bit output at the cost of a factor k loss in efficiency.

4.1   Security Proof

Our main theorem states that the construction above indeed yields a secure 1SK-MIFE scheme.

Theorem 4.5 (1SK-MIFE Security).   *The 1SK-MIFE construction of Section 4 is* poly(λ)*-IND-secure in the generic multilinear map model.*

Before proving Theorem 4.5, we first give a few relevant definitions and lemmas. Our proof techniques in this section are similar to those in related works that use the generic multilinear map model [BR14, BGK+14].

Remark 4.6 (Queries Referring to Formal Polynomials).   Formally, the generic multilinear map model is defined in terms of oracle queries on "handles" (nonces). In any particular security game, however, it is usually more intuitive to regard each oracle query as a formal polynomial. The formal variables are specified in terms of the expressions initially supplied to the MM.Encode procedure (as appropriate to the security game), and the adversary can construct new polynomials by making oracle queries for the generic-model ring operations MM.Add, MM.Mult. Rather than operating on a handle, then, we can think of each valid MM.ZeroTest query as *referring* to a formal polynomial encoded at the top-level universe $\mathcal{U}$. The result of the query is "zero" precisely if the given polynomial evaluates to zero, when its variables are instantiated with the *real* joint distribution over their values in $\mathbb{Z}_q$, generated as in the actual security game. For precise definitions, we refer the reader to the full version.

Structure Lemmas.   Our 1SK-MIFE construction uses index sets to enforce constraints on the adversary's evaluation (as depicted in Fig. 3). The purpose of these constraints is to prevent the adversary from constructing zero-test queries that are inconsistent—i.e., use encodings that "mix and match" elements of different ciphertexts. To show that our design indeed prevents these undesired queries, we first state and prove a few simple definitions and "structure lemmas", showing that all valid query polynomials have a certain form.

---

[6] In such a branching program, the output is determined by the upper left $k_1 \times k_2$ submatrix ($k = k_1 k_2$) of the final matrix product, as opposed to just the upper left entry. The output of the program is the $k_1 \times k_2$ Boolean matrix indicating which entries in the submatrix are 0.

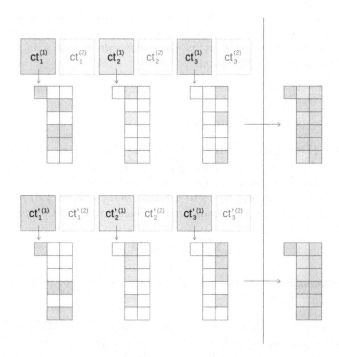

Fig. 3. The matrices of two 1SK-MIFE ciphertexts, $\mathsf{ct} = (\mathsf{ct}_1^{(1)}, \mathsf{ct}_2^{(1)}, \mathsf{ct}_3^{(1)})$ and $\mathsf{ct}' = (\mathsf{ct}_1'^{(1)}, \mathsf{ct}_2'^{(1)}, \mathsf{ct}_3'^{(1)})$ (both encrypted to slot 1), with the index set of each matrix depicted below it. Since the index sets are defined by two different elements of the same exclusive partition family, the adversary cannot "mix and match" elements from the two ciphertexts.

Definition 4.7 (Query-Consistent Polynomials). *For an execution trace of the experiment* $\mathsf{Expt}_{P,Q,b}^{\mathsf{1SK\text{-}MIFE}}(\mathcal{A})$ *in the generic multilinear map model, consider any input-consistent sequence* $\tau = (t_1, \dots, t_m)$ *of query times (Definition 3.3). By definition of the encryption procedure, the corresponding ciphertexts for those query times are encoded elements that refer to formal polynomials (Remark 4.6) of the form* $\mathsf{ct}_{t_i,h} = \alpha_{t_i,h}\hat{\mathbf{M}}_{t_i,h}$, *where* $\alpha_{t_i,h}$ *is a scalar and* $\hat{\mathbf{M}}_{t_i,h}$ *is a* $w \times w$ *matrix. We now define the formal polynomial*

$$\alpha_\tau = \prod_{i\in[m],\ h\in[d]} \alpha_{t_i,h}$$

(intuitively, the α *coefficient that would be present, for a given query sequence* τ, *in an honest evaluation of the program), as well as the tuple of formal polynomials*

$$\hat{\mathbf{M}}|_\tau = \left(\hat{\mathbf{M}}_{t_{\mathsf{inp}(1)},\mathsf{inp.h}(1)}, \dots, \hat{\mathbf{M}}_{t_{\mathsf{inp}(\ell)},\mathsf{inp.h}(\ell)}\right)$$

(intuitively, the matrices whose entries would be involved in an honest evaluation of the program). Finally, we say that a formal polynomial $z_{\tau,b}$ *is consistent with*

the query sequence τ if it can be expressed as a polynomial in the entries of the correct vectors and matrices $(\hat{\mathbf{s}},\ \hat{\mathbf{M}}|_\tau,\ \text{and}\ \hat{\mathbf{t}})$, scaled by the correct blinding coefficient, α_τ. More precisely, z_τ is consistent with τ if it is identically equal to a formal polynomial of the form

$$z_\tau = \alpha_\tau \cdot p_\tau(\hat{\mathbf{s}},\ \hat{\mathbf{M}}|_\tau,\ \hat{\mathbf{t}})$$

for some polynomial p_τ of degree $\mathrm{poly}(\lambda)$.

Lemma 4.8 (Decomposition of Zero-Test Queries). *Fix any efficient adversary $\mathcal{A}$. In the experiment $\mathsf{Expt}_{P,Q,b}^{\mathsf{1SK\text{-}MIFE}}(\mathcal{A})$, with all but negligible probability, every* $\mathsf{MM.ZeroTest}$ *query made by $\mathcal{A}$ that is valid (i.e., whose handle is at the top-level universe $\mathcal{U}$), refers to a polynomial (Remark 4.6) formally equal to a sum of (potentially exponentially many) query-consistent polynomials of the form*

$$z = \sum_\tau \alpha_\tau \cdot p_\tau(\hat{\mathbf{s}},\ \hat{\mathbf{M}}|_\tau,\ \hat{\mathbf{t}}),$$

and each polynomial p_τ is allowable (Definition 2.6) and consistent with a query sequence τ (Definition 4.7).

Proof. Consider any valid formal polynomial z submitted to $\mathsf{MM.ZeroTest}$. First, we expand the polynomial z into a sum of monomials (for purposes of analysis, not by the scheme), and collect like terms with respect to the α variables. Each term in the resulting expression must be encoded at the top-level universe $\mathcal{U}$, since some valid zero-testing handle refers to their sum. This means, in particular, that the index set of each term must contain a partition of every $\mathcal{U}_i$.

The only variables available to the adversary whose index sets contain elements of $\mathcal{U}_i$ are the ciphertexts $\mathsf{ct}_{t,h}$ generated during time steps $t \in \mathcal{T}^{(i)}$, where $\mathcal{T}^{(i)}$ is the set of all times at which the adversary made chosen-plaintext queries for input slot i. For these time steps, we will assume that the partitions selected by the challenger:

$$\left(P_t = (S_{t,1}^{(i)}, \ldots, S_{t,d}^{(i)}) : t \in \mathcal{T}^{(i)}\right)$$

are distinct, since each is drawn independently uniform from a family of size 2^λ, regardless of the adversary's queries, and thus by the birthday bound a collision occurs with negligible probability.

This implies that the index sets $S_{t,h}^{(i)}$ are distinct elements of the exclusive partition family $\mathcal{F}_{i_t}$, and thus by Lemma 2.14, for each $i \in [m]$, the only monomials whose index sets can cover each $\mathcal{U}_i$ all share the same value of the partition P_t (and hence of t), and thus are precisely products of one element from each component of the same query ciphertext, ct_{t_i}. Finally, for each $h \in [d]$, we note that the hth term of each such ciphertext contains precisely the factors $\alpha_{t_i,h}$ and $\mathbf{M}_{t_i,h}$. Thus, letting $\tau = (t_1, \ldots, t_m) \subseteq [Q]$, we conclude that such monomials have precisely a leading factor of α_τ, while the remaining factors are drawn from $\mathbf{M}|_\tau$, as desired. We observe that each such monomial (and hence their sum, p_τ) must be allowable (Definition 2.6), since all entries of each vector and matrix

$\hat{s}, \hat{M}|_\tau, \hat{t}$ are encoded at the same index set, and thus the monomial can only include one factor from each. Finally, the degree of the polynomial p_τ must be at most $\text{poly}(\lambda)$, since the index set of any formal polynomial grows with its degree, and the size of any valid index set is bounded by the size of the top-level universe $\mathcal{U}$.

We are now ready to present the main proof of Theorem 4.5.

4.2   Proof of Theorem 4.5

Proof. Fix an efficient adversary $\mathcal{A}$ for the experiment $\text{Expt}^{\text{1SK-MIFE}}_{P,\text{poly}(\lambda),b}(\mathcal{A})$ in the generic graded encoding model. We will show that for every admissible trace π in the experiment (Definition 3.5), except for failure events of negligible probability, the probability that the experiment yields the trace π when $b = 0$ differs by a negligible amount from the probability that it yields the trace π when $b = 1$. It then follows immediately that $\text{Adv}^{\text{1SK-MIFE}}_{P,Q}(\mathcal{A}) = |W_0 - W_1|$ is negligible, as desired.

First, we note that in any trace π, the only responses sent to $\mathcal{A}$ are either (a) handles in the multilinear map, via MM.Encode, from the public parameters and from ciphertexts generated for chosen-plaintext queries; (b) handles in the multilinear map, via MM.Add, MM.Mult, from queries to the generic map oracle $\mathcal{M}$; or else (c) answers to MM.ZeroTest queries on handles in the multilinear map. Since in the generic model the handles for (a) and (b) are uniform independent nonces, their distribution clearly does not depend on b. Thus, our task reduces to showing that for each MM.ZeroTest query, the probability of each response ("zero", "nonzero") differs by a negligible amount between the cases $b = 0$ and $b = 1$. The claim will then follow by a union bound, since $\mathcal{A}$ (being efficient) can make only polynomially many oracle queries.[7]

Fix a valid MM.ZeroTest query, which refers to a formal multivariate polynomial z (Remark 4.6). By Lemma 4.8, z is identically equal to a polynomial of the form

$$\sum_\tau \alpha_\tau \cdot p_\tau(\hat{s}, \ \hat{M}|_\tau, \ \hat{t}) \ ,$$

where each polynomial p_τ is allowable (Definition 2.6) and consistent with the query sequence τ (Definition 4.7). For each bit $b \in \{0, 1\}$, let $\mathbf{x}_{\tau,b} = (x_{t_1,b}, \dots, x_{t_m,b})$ be the chosen-plaintext queries corresponding to τ in the adversary's execution trace up to the point of query z. Since by assumption the execution trace is admissible (Definition 3.5), we have $P(\mathbf{x}_{\tau,0}) = P(\mathbf{x}_{\tau,1})$. By Lemma 2.7, we now conclude that each formal polynomial p_τ, when evaluated on the real distribution of values in $\mathbb{Z}_q$ from the oracle's table, is either zero with probability

---

[7] Technically, we must also show that the distribution of the values in the oracle's table, conditioned on each possible subsequence of past oracle query-response pairs (assuming no failure events), has negligible statistical distance from its prior distribution from MM.Setup; this follows by a standard conditional probability argument, given that the probability of each failure event is negligible.

1 for both values of $b \in \{0, 1\}$, or else is nonzero with all but negligible probability for both values of $b \in \{0, 1\}$. We consider the following cases:

- Suppose that for all τ in the formal sum for z, the polynomial p_τ evaluates to zero on its argument's entire support. In this case, the entire query z will evaluate to zero always, regardless of the value of b.
- Suppose that for some τ^* in the formal sum for z, the polynomial p_{τ^*} evaluates to zero negligibly often, regardless of the value of b (and consider the lexicographically first such τ^*, without loss of generality). Then for both values of b, when the query z is instantiated with the real distribution of all values except the α variables, p_{τ^*} evaluates to a polynomial function of the α variables which, with all but negligible probability, is not identically zero. Since the distribution over the α variables is statistically close to independently uniform over $\mathbb{Z}_q$, the Schwartz-Zippel lemma implies that the entire query z will evaluate to a nonzero value regardless of the value of b, except for failure events with negligible probability.

Thus, for each MM.ZeroTest query, the probability that the answer is "zero" differs by a negligible amount between the cases $b = 0$ and $b = 1$, as desired.

5   Extensions

Stateful Encryption. In the construction of Section 4, since encryption is required to be stateless, we need to generate a fresh partition for each encryption (and rely on the birthday bound to prevent collisions). However, in many applications of SK-MIFE, it may be reasonable to modify the encryption procedure to be stateful. For instance, suppose a client is encrypting an entire database to be stored on a remote server (and later queried according to the functions for which we reveal MIFE evaluation keys). Here the client may know the contents of the entire database in advance, or may be able to retain local state between interactions with the server. In either case, if the maximum number of database elements N is known in advance, then we can simply replace the $(2^\lambda, d)$-exclusive partition families in the construction (Section 4) with $(2^{\lceil \log N \rceil}, d)$-exclusive partition families, and instead of sampling a partition index uniformly at random for each encryption, use the partitions in order: the ith partition for the ith encryption operation, for each $i \in [N]$.

6   Conclusions

We presented a secret-key multi-input functional encryption scheme for functionalities that can be captured by a *generalized* branching programs of polynomial length and width. An interesting functionality in this family is *comparison* which enables comparisons of symmetrically encrypted data. We refer to this specific functionality as order-revealing encryption (ORE). ORE can be used to answer range queries on symmetrically encrypted data in one round and in logarithmic time in the size of the database.

Our construction is inspired by obfuscation techniques, but does not use obfuscation. Instead it is built directly from multilinear maps and is substantially simpler than current obfuscation-based schemes. While the resulting order-revealing encryption (ORE) scheme is still too inefficient for practical use, it provides a first step towards building usable ORE systems. We hope that future work will further improve the efficiency of ORE and, more generally, the efficiency of secret-key multi-input functional encryption.

Acknowledgments. This work was supported by NSF, the DARPA PROCEED program, a grant from ONR, and by a Google faculty scholarship. Opinions, findings and conclusions or recommendations expressed in this material are those of the author(s) and do not necessarily reflect the views of DARPA.

Research supported in part from a DARPA/ONR PROCEED award, NSF Frontier Award 1413955, NSF grants 1228984, 1136174, 1118096, and 1065276, a Xerox Faculty Research Award, a Google Faculty Research Award, an equipment grant from Intel, and an Okawa Foundation Research Grant. This material is based upon work supported by the Defense Advanced Research Projects Agency through the U.S. Office of Naval Research under Contract N00014-11-1-0389. The views expressed are those of the author(s) and do not reflect the official policy or position of the Department of Defense, the National Science Foundation, or the U.S. Government.

References

[ABG+13] Ananth, P., Boneh, D., Garg, S., Sahai, A., Zhandry, M.: Differing-inputs obfuscation and applications. IACR Cryptology ePrint Archive 2013, 689 (2013)

[AGI+14] Ananth, P., Gupta, D., Ishai, Y., Sahai, A.: Optimizing obfuscation: Avoiding barrington's theorem. IACR Cryptology ePrint Archive 2014, 222 (2014)

[AGV+13] Agrawal, S., Gorbunov, S., Vaikuntanathan, V., Wee, H.: Functional encryption: new perspectives and lower bounds. In: Canetti, R., Garay, J.A. (eds.) CRYPTO 2013, Part II. LNCS, vol. 8043, pp. 500–518. Springer, Heidelberg (2013)

[AKS+04] Agrawal, R., Kiernan, J., Srikant, R., Xu, Y.: Order preserving encryption for numeric data (2004)

[Bar86]   Barrington, D.A.: Bounded-width polynomial-size branching programs recognize exactly those languages in NC1. In: Proceedings, 18th ACM STOC, pp. 1–5 (1986)

[BBC+14] Barak, B., Bitansky, N., Canetti, R., Kalai, Y.T., Paneth, O., Sahai, A.: Obfuscation for evasive functions. In: Lindell, Y. (ed.) TCC 2014. LNCS, vol. 8349, pp. 26–51. Springer, Heidelberg (2014)

[BCL+09] Boldyreva, A., Chenette, N., Lee, Y., O'Neill, A.: Order-preserving symmetric encryption. In: Joux, A. (ed.) EUROCRYPT 2009. LNCS, vol. 5479, pp. 224–241. Springer, Heidelberg (2009)

[BCO11] Boldyreva, A., Chenette, N., O'Neill, A.: Order-preserving encryption revisited: improved security analysis and alternative solutions. In: Rogaway, P. (ed.) CRYPTO 2011. LNCS, vol. 6841, pp. 578–595. Springer, Heidelberg (2011)

[BCP14] Boyle, E., Chung, K.-M., Pass, R.: On extractability obfuscation. In: Lindell, Y. (ed.) TCC 2014. LNCS, vol. 8349, pp. 52–73. Springer, Heidelberg (2014)

[BF01] Boneh, D., Franklin, M.: Identity-based encryption from the weil pairing. In: Kilian, J. (ed.) CRYPTO 2001. LNCS, vol. 2139, pp. 213–229. Springer, Heidelberg (2001)

[BGI+01] Barak, B., Goldreich, O., Impagliazzo, R., Rudich, S., Sahai, A., Vadhan, S.P., Yang, K.: On the (im)possibility of obfuscating programs. In: Kilian, J. (ed.) CRYPTO 2001. LNCS, vol. 2139, pp. 1–18. Springer, Heidelberg (2001)

[BGK+14] Barak, B., Garg, S., Kalai, Y.T., Paneth, O., Sahai, A.: protecting obfuscation against algebraic attacks. In: Nguyen, P.Q., Oswald, E. (eds.) EUROCRYPT 2014. LNCS, vol. 8441, pp. 221–238. Springer, Heidelberg (2014)

[BO13] Bellare, M., O'Neill, A.: Semantically-secure functional encryption: possibility results, impossibility results and the quest for a general definition. In: Abdalla, M., Nita-Rotaru, C., Dahab, R. (eds.) CANS 2013. LNCS, vol. 8257, pp. 218–234. Springer, Heidelberg (2013)

[BR14] Brakerski, Z., Rothblum, G.N.: Virtual black-box obfuscation for all circuits via generic graded encoding. In: Lindell, Y. (ed.) TCC 2014. LNCS, vol. 8349, pp. 1–25. Springer, Heidelberg (2014)

[BS03] Boneh, D., Silverberg, A.: Applications of multilinear forms to cryptography. Contemporary Mathematics 324(1), 71–90 (2003)

[BS14] Brakerski, Z., Segev, G.: Function-private functional encryption in the private-key setting. Cryptology ePrint Archive, Report 2014/550, 2014. http://eprint.iacr.org/

[BSW11] Boneh, D., Sahai, A., Waters, B.: Functional encryption: definitions and challenges. In: Ishai, Y. (ed.) TCC 2011. LNCS, vol. 6597, pp. 253–273. Springer, Heidelberg (2011)

[BW07] Boneh, D., Waters, B.: Conjunctive, subset, and range queries on encrypted data. In: Vadhan, S.P. (ed.) TCC 2007. LNCS, vol. 4392, pp. 535–554. Springer, Heidelberg (2007)

[BZ14] Boneh, D., Zhandry, M.: Multiparty key exchange, efficient traitor tracing, and more from indistinguishability obfuscation. In: Garay, J.A., Gennaro, R. (eds.) CRYPTO 2014, Part I. LNCS, vol. 8616, pp. 480–499. Springer, Heidelberg (2014)

[CIJ+13] De Caro, A., Iovino, V., Jain, A., O'Neill, A., Paneth, O., Persiano, G.: On the achievability of simulation-based security for functional encryption. In: Canetti, R., Garay, J.A. (eds.) CRYPTO 2013, Part II. LNCS, vol. 8043, pp. 519–535. Springer, Heidelberg (2013)

[CLT13] Coron, J.-S., Lepoint, T., Tibouchi, M.: Practical multilinear maps over the integers. In: Canetti, R., Garay, J.A. (eds.) CRYPTO 2013, Part I. LNCS, vol. 8042, pp. 476–493. Springer, Heidelberg (2013)

[GGG+14] Goldwasser, S., Gordon, S.D., Goyal, V., Jain, A., Katz, J., Liu, F.-H., Sahai, A., Shi, E., Zhou, H.-S.: Multi-input functional encryption. In: Nguyen, P.Q., Oswald, E. (eds.) EUROCRYPT 2014. LNCS, vol. 8441, pp. 578–602. Springer, Heidelberg (2014)

[GGH13a] Garg, S., Gentry, C., Halevi, S.: Candidate multilinear maps from ideal lattices. In: Johansson, T., Nguyen, P.Q. (eds.) EUROCRYPT 2013. LNCS, vol. 7881, pp. 1–17. Springer, Heidelberg (2013)

[GGH+13b] Garg, S., Gentry, C., Halevi, S., Raykova, M., Sahai, A., Waters, B.: Candidate indistinguishability obfuscation and functional encryption for all circuits. Cryptology ePrint Archive, Report 2013/451, 2013. http:// eprint.iacr.org/

[GGH+14] Garg, S., Gentry, C., Halevi, S., Zhandry, M.: Fully secure functional encryption without obfuscation. Cryptology ePrint Archive, Report 2014/666 (2014). http://eprint.iacr.org/

[GHL+14] Gentry, C., Halevi, S., Lu, S., Ostrovsky, R., Raykova, M., Wichs, D.: Garbled RAM revisited. In: Nguyen, P.Q., Oswald, E. (eds.) EURO-CRYPT 2014. LNCS, vol. 8441, pp. 405–422. Springer, Heidelberg (2014)

[GKP+13] Goldwasser, S., Kalai, Y.T., Popa, R.A., Vaikuntanathan, V., Zeldovich, N.: Reusable garbled circuits and succinct functional encryption. In: STOC (2013)

[GM82] Goldwasser, S., Micali, S.: Probabilistic encryption and how to play mental poker keeping secret all partial information. In: STOC, pp. 365–377 (1982)

[GVW12] Gorbunov, S., Vaikuntanathan, V., Wee, H.: Functional encryption with bounded collusions via multi-party computation. In: Safavi-Naini, R., Canetti, R. (eds.) CRYPTO 2012. LNCS, vol. 7417, pp. 162–179. Springer, Heidelberg (2012)

[Jou00] Joux, A.: A one round protocol for tripartite diffie-hellman. In: Proceedings of the 4th International Symposium on Algorithmic Number Theory, pp. 385–394 (2000)

[Kil88] Kilian, J.: Founding cryptography on oblivious transfer. In: STOC (1988)

[KSW08] Katz, J., Sahai, A., Waters, B.: Predicate encryption supporting disjunctions, polynomial equations, and inner products. In: Smart, N.P. (ed.) EUROCRYPT 2008. LNCS, vol. 4965, pp. 146–162. Springer, Heidelberg (2008)

[LO13] Lu, S., Ostrovsky, R.: How to garble RAM programs? In: Johansson, T., Nguyen, P.Q. (eds.) EUROCRYPT 2013. LNCS, vol. 7881, pp. 719–734. Springer, Heidelberg (2013)

[Mil04] Miller, V.J.: The Weil pairing, and its efficient calculation. Journal of Cryptology (2004)

[MOV93] Menezes, A., Okamoto, T., Vanstone, S.A.: Reducing elliptic curve logarithms to logarithms in a finite field. IEEE Transactions on Information Theory 39(5), 1639–1646 (1993)

[MTY13] Malkin, T., Teranishi, I., Yung, M.: Order-preserving encryption secure beyond one-wayness. IACR Cryptology ePrint Archive 2013, 409 (2013)

[O'N10] O'Neill, A.: Definitional issues in functional encryption. Cryptology ePrint Archive, Report 2010/556 (2010). http://eprint.iacr.org/

[PLZ13] Popa, R.A., Li, F.H., Zeldovich, N.: An ideal-security protocol for order-preserving encoding. In: S&P, pp. 463–477 (2013)

[SBC+07] Shi, E., Bethencourt, J., Chan, H.T., Song, D.X., Perrig, A.: Multi-dimensional range query over encrypted data. In: S&P, pp. 350–364 (2007)

[Sho97] Shoup, V.: Lower bounds for discrete logarithms and related problems. In: Fumy, W. (ed.) EUROCRYPT 1997. LNCS, vol. 1233, pp. 256–266. Springer, Heidelberg (1997)

[SSW09] Shen, E., Shi, E., Waters, B.: Predicate privacy in encryption systems. In: Reingold, O. (ed.) TCC 2009. LNCS, vol. 5444, pp. 457–473. Springer, Heidelberg (2009)

[SZ14] Sahai, A., Zhandry, M.: Obfuscating low-rank matrix branching programs. Cryptology ePrint Archive, Report 2014/773 (2014). http://eprint.iacr.org/

[Zha14] Zhandry, M.: How to avoid obfuscation using witness PRFs. Cryptology ePrint Archive, Report 2014/301 (2014). http://eprint.iacr.org/

Improved Dual System ABE in Prime-Order Groups via Predicate Encodings

Jie Chen[1]([⊠]), Romain Gay[2], and Hoeteck Wee[2]

[1] East China Normal University, Shanghai, China
s080001@e.ntu.edu.sg
[2] ENS, Paris, France
{rgay,wee}@di.ens.fr

Abstract. We present a modular framework for the design of efficient adaptively secure attribute-based encryption (ABE) schemes for a large class of predicates under the standard k-Lin assumption in prime-order groups; this is the first uniform treatment of dual system ABE across different predicates and across both composite and prime-order groups. Via this framework, we obtain concrete efficiency improvements for several ABE schemes. Our framework has three novel components over prior works: (i) new techniques for simulating composite-order groups in prime-order ones, (ii) a refinement of prior encodings framework for dual system ABE in composite-order groups, (iii) an extension to weakly attribute-hiding predicate encryption (which includes anonymous identity-based encryption as a special case).

1 Introduction

Attribute-based encryption (ABE) [15,27] is a new paradigm for public-key encryption that enables fine-grained access control for encrypted data. In ABE, ciphertexts are associated with descriptive values x in addition to a plaintext, secret keys are associated with values y, and a secret key decrypts the ciphertext if and only if $\mathsf{P}(x, y) = 1$ for some boolean predicate P. Here, y together with P may express an arbitrarily complex access policy, which is in stark contrast to traditional public-key encryption, where access is all or nothing. The simplest example of ABE is that of identity-based encryption (IBE) [5,12,28] where P

J. Chen—Shanghai Key Laboratory of Multidimensional Information Processing and Shanghai Key Lab of Trustworthy Computing. Supported by the National Natural Science Foundation of China (Grant Nos. 61472142, 61321064, 61172085), Science and Technology Commission of Shanghai Municipality (Grant Nos. 14YF1404200, 13JC1403500).

R. Gay—Supported in part by ANR-14-CE28-0003 (Project EnBiD).

H. Wee—CNRS, INRIA and Columbia University. Supported in part by ANR-14-CE28-0003 (Project EnBiD), NSF Award CNS-1445424, the Alexander von Humboldt Foundation and a Google Faculty Research Award.

ⓒ International Association for Cryptologic Research 2015
E. Oswald and M. Fischlin (Eds.): EUROCRYPT 2015, Part II, LNCS 9057, pp. 595–624, 2015.
DOI: 10.1007/978-3-662-46803-6_20

corresponds to equality. The security requirement for ABE enforces resilience to collusion attacks, namely any group of users holding secret keys for different values learns nothing about the plaintext if none of them is individually authorized to decrypt the ciphertext. This should hold even if the adversary *adaptively* decides which secret keys to ask for.

ABE in Prime-Order Groups. The goal of this work is to obtain efficient adaptively secure ABE for a large class of predicates. We now have a fairly good understanding of how to obtain such schemes in composite-order bilinear groups, thanks to Waters' powerful *dual system encryption methodology* [30] and recent unifying frameworks in [2,31] for the design of dual system ABE schemes. However, these latter frameworks only work in composite-order bilinear groups, for which group operations and especially pairing computations are prohibitively slow. In practice, prime-order bilinear groups are preferable [16] as they admit not only more efficient but also more compact instantiations. To mitigate the gap between ease of theoretical design and practical efficiency, a series of works studied techniques for converting cryptosystems relying on composite-order groups to cryptosystems based on prime-order groups [10,11,14,20,23,24], largely in the context of dual system ABE. In addition, we have direct constructions of dual system prime-order hierarchical identity-based encryption (HIBE) schemes in [3,18] that bypass a conversion from composite-order groups, but the techniques in these constructions do not seem to naturally extend beyond (H)IBE. Furthermore, the prior constructions rely on fairly distinct techniques, and efficiency improvements in one construction do not necessarily translate to a different construction and a different predicate. In short, prior works fall short of providing a unifying and modular framework for the design of efficient dual system ABE schemes in prime-order groups that work for a large class of predicates (c.f. Fig. 1).

1.1   Our Contributions

We present a modular framework for the design of efficient dual system ABE schemes for a large class of predicates under the standard k-Lin assumption in prime-order groups; this is the first uniform treatment of dual system ABE across different predicates *and* across both composite and prime-order groups. Via this framework, we obtain concrete efficiency improvements for several ABE schemes. Our framework has three novel components over prior works: (i) new techniques for simulating composite-order groups in prime-order ones, (ii) a refinement of the encodings framework for dual system ABE for composite-order groups in [2,31], (iii) an extension to weakly attribute-hiding predicate encryption [6,19] (which includes anonymous IBE as a special case). The last two components answer the open problems left in [2,31].

New Techniques for Simulating Composite-Order Groups. The starting point of our construction is simply a simpler choice of basis. Fix a bilinear

	compact HIBE	boolean formula	k-Lin	anonymous IBE	weakly-AH ZIPE
DPVS [11, 20, 23, 24]	no	yes	yes	yes	yes
sparse DPVS [26]	yes	?	?	yes	yes
QANIZK [18]	yes	?	yes	yes	?
dual system groups [10]	yes	?	yes	?	?
MAC-to-(H)IBE [3]	yes	?	yes	yes	?
this work	yes	yes	yes	yes	yes

Fig. 1. Summary of previous approaches for building efficient dual system (H)IBE and ABE in prime-order groups. The first column refers to HIBE with constant-size ciphertexts; the second refers to KP/CP-ABE for boolean formula. The third column refers to instantiations from the general k-Lin assumption. The last two columns address extensions to stronger notions of security like anonymity and weakly attribute-hiding (AH) inner product encryption (ZIPE). Additional discussion is provided in Sect. 1.2.

group (G_1, G_2, G_T) with $e : G_1 \times G_2 \to G_T$ of prime order p. We pick random matrices $(\mathbf{A}, \mathbf{B}) \leftarrow_R \mathbb{Z}_p^{(k+1) \times k}$, along with random vectors $\mathbf{a}^\perp, \mathbf{b}^\perp \in \mathbb{Z}_p^{k+1}$ so that $\mathbf{a}^{\perp\top} \mathbf{A} = \mathbf{b}^{\perp\top} \mathbf{B} = \mathbf{0}$, and we assume $\mathbf{a}^{\perp\top} \mathbf{b}^\perp \neq 0$. Observe that[1]

$$([\mathbf{A}]_1, [\mathbf{b}^\perp]_1) := (g_1^{\mathbf{A}}, g_1^{\mathbf{b}^\perp}) \in G_1^{(k+1) \times k} \times G_1^{k+1}$$

forms a basis for G_1^{k+1}. Similarly,

$$([\mathbf{B}]_2, [\mathbf{a}^\perp]_2) := (g_2^{\mathbf{B}}, g_2^{\mathbf{a}^\perp}) \in G_2^{(k+1) \times k} \times G_2^{k+1}$$

forms a basis for G_2^{k+1}. In the context of dual system encryption, we use $[\mathbf{A}]_1$ as a basis for normal components in the ciphertext space, and $[\mathbf{b}^\perp]_1$ as a basis for semi-functional components. Similarly, we use $[\mathbf{B}]_2$ as a basis for normal components in the secret key space, and $[\mathbf{a}^\perp]_2$ as a basis for semi-functional components. Indistinguishability for elements with and without random semi-functional components follow readily from the k-Lin assumption. Moreover, we have an orthogonality property given by $\mathbf{a}^{\perp\top} \mathbf{A} = \mathbf{b}^{\perp\top} \mathbf{B} = \mathbf{0}$, which tells us that the normal and semi-functional components in different spaces cancel out.

We can then randomize this basis by choosing $\mathbf{W} \in \mathbb{Z}_p^{(k+1) \times (k+1)}$ uniformly at random and using $([\mathbf{W}^\top \mathbf{A}]_1, [\mathbf{W}^\top \mathbf{b}^\perp]_1)$ for G_1^{k+1} and $([\mathbf{W}\mathbf{B}]_2, [\mathbf{W}\mathbf{a}^\perp]_2)$ for G_2^{k+1}. For decryption correctness, we will exploit the following "associative" property when the new basis interacts with the original one, namely:

$$e([\mathbf{A}]_1, [\mathbf{W}\mathbf{B}]_2) = e([\mathbf{W}^\top \mathbf{A}]_1, [\mathbf{B}]_2) \qquad (1)$$

where we define the pairing operation on matrices via

$$e([\mathbf{M}]_1, [\mathbf{M}']_2) := e(g_1, g_2)^{\mathbf{M}^\top \mathbf{M}'}.$$

---

[1] Following [13], we use the implicit representation notation for group elements, as explained in Sect. 4.1.

Observe that $\mathbf{W}$ has one unit of residual entropy given $(\mathbf{W}^\top \mathbf{A}, \mathbf{WB})$. This will be crucial for carrying out the information-theoretic argument in the proof of ABE security via the dual system encryption methodology [2,30,31].

We note that prior transformations in prime-order groups in [14,20,23,24] try to simulate all of the structure in composite-order groups (e.g. orthogonality). We simulate less structure (associativity, c.f. Eqn. (1)), thus leading to better concrete efficiency. However, when combined with the existing encodings framework for dual system ABE schemes in composite-order groups, we cannot even guarantee ABE decryption correctness. We compensate for less structure while simulating composite-order groups by imposing more structure to the encodings, which we can achieve without increasing the size of the encodings. We will exploit the additional structure in the encodings for correctness and for security. We now proceed to describe our encodings framework for ABE.

Modular Approach for ABE. We begin with the observation that the prior composite-order ABE schemes in [2,31] (generalizing [21,22]) may be modified so that master public key, secret key and ciphertext are of the form:

$$
\begin{aligned}
\mathsf{mpk} &:= \left(g_1, \ g_1^{\mathbf{w}}, \ e(g_1, g_1)^\alpha \right) \\
\mathsf{sk}_y &:= \left(g_1^r, \ g_1^{\mathsf{kE}(y,\alpha)+r\cdot\mathsf{rE}(y,\mathbf{w})} \right) \\
\mathsf{ct}_x &:= \left(g_1^s, \ g_1^{s\cdot\mathsf{sE}(x,\mathbf{w})}, \ e(g_1,g_1)^{\alpha s}\cdot m \right)
\end{aligned}
\tag{2}
$$

Here, g_1 is a generator of order p_1 where the underlying composite group order is the product of three primes p_1, p_2, p_3 (for simplicity we consider the case of a symmetric bilinear group); $\mathbf{w}$ is a vector of length n; and $\mathsf{kE}, \mathsf{rE}, \mathsf{sE}$ are a triple of deterministic "encoding" functions that depend on the underlying predicate P (we refer to these functions as key encoding, receiver encoding and sender encoding respectively.) Syntactically, this is already a refinement of the prior frameworks in [2,31] which associates a single function with sk_y given by

$$
(y, \alpha, \mathbf{w}, r) \mapsto \left(r, \ \mathsf{kE}(y,\alpha) + r\cdot\mathsf{rE}(y,\mathbf{w}) \right)
\tag{3}
$$

in the exponent. The prior frameworks allow for instance for kE to be randomized. With the refinement in place, we can now specify the restricted α-reconstruction property used for correctness:

(restricted α-reconstruction.) For every x, y for which $\mathsf{P}(x,y) = 1$, there is a linear map L_{xy} such that for all α, r,

$$
L_{xy}\left(\mathsf{kE}(y,\alpha) + r\cdot\mathsf{rE}(y,\mathbf{w}), \ r\cdot\mathsf{sE}(x,\mathbf{w}) \right) = \alpha.
$$

This means that we can recover $e(g_1,g_1)^{\alpha s}$ given

$$
e(g_1^s, g_1^{\mathsf{kE}(y,\alpha)+r\cdot\mathsf{rE}(y,\mathbf{w})}) \quad \text{and} \quad e(g_1^{s\cdot\mathsf{sE}(x,\mathbf{w})}, g_1^r),
$$

upon which we can decrypt the ciphertext. Observe that we only need to pair the first component g_1^s of ct_x with the second component of sk_y and the second component of ct_x with the first component g_1^r of sk_y. Correctness now relies on a so-called *associativity property* [10], namely that for all i and all w_i:

$$e(g_1^s, g_1^{w_i r}) = e(g_1^{w_i s}, g_1^r) \tag{4}$$

To translate the scheme to prime-order groups, we carry out the following substitution:

$$w_i \mapsto \mathbf{W}_i \in \mathbb{Z}_p^{(k+1) \times (k+1)}, \qquad s \mapsto \mathbf{s} \in \mathbb{Z}_p^k, \qquad r \mapsto \mathbf{r} \in \mathbb{Z}_p^k$$
$$g_1^s \mapsto [\mathbf{As}]_1, \qquad\qquad g_1^r \mapsto [\mathbf{Br}]_2$$
$$g_1^{w_i s} \mapsto [\mathbf{W}_i^\top \mathbf{As}]_1, \qquad g_1^{w_i r} \mapsto [\mathbf{W}_i \mathbf{Br}]_2$$

Using (1), we have

$$e([\mathbf{As}]_1, [\mathbf{W}_i \mathbf{Br}]_2) = e([\mathbf{W}_i^\top \mathbf{As}]_1, [\mathbf{Br}]_2)$$

which is exactly what we used in composite-order groups in (4). In fact, a stronger "pairwise associativity" property holds in composite-order groups, namely for all i, j and all w_i, w_j:

$$e(g_1^{w_j s}, g_1^{w_i r}) = e(g_1^{w_i s}, g_1^{w_j r})$$

which is not satisfied by our prime-order techniques since $\mathbf{W}_i$ and $\mathbf{W}_j$ do not commute. Restricted α-reconstruction means that we do not need to pair $g_1^{w_j s}$ with $g_1^{w_i r}$ during decryption, and thus the associativity property already suffices for decryption correctness. For maximal modularity, we describe our compiler using the framework of dual system groups introduced in [10], which allows us to simultaneously capture prime-order and composite-order groups.

Next, we specify the privacy property which we use in the proof of ABE security:

(α-**privacy.**) For every x, y for which $\mathsf{P}(x, y) = 0$, α is perfectly hidden given

$$\mathsf{sE}(x, \mathbf{w}), \quad \mathsf{kE}(y, \alpha) + \mathsf{rE}(y, \mathbf{w})$$

where $\mathbf{w} \leftarrow_{\mathrm{R}} \mathbb{Z}_p^n$.

We stress that the privacy requirement only needs to hold in a private-key setting where the adversary does not see $\mathbf{w}$ and in a one-time setting where the adversary only gets a single copy of $\mathsf{sE}(x, \mathbf{w}), \mathsf{kE}(y, \alpha) + \mathsf{rE}(y, \mathbf{w})$. As pointed out in [31], the dual system encryption methodology can be used to boost security in a private-key, one-time, non-adaptive setting as given by α-privacy to a full-fledged public-key, many-time, adaptive setting as is required for ABE security. One novelty in this work over [2,31] lies in carrying this out over prime-order bilinear groups. In the proof, we exploit the fact that the key sk_y leaks no information about $\mathbf{w}$ when $r = 0$ (c.f. Eqn. (2)). This way, we can ensure that in each step in the proof of security, at most one secret key leaks information about $\mathbf{w}$ in the semi-functional space. This is important since α-privacy only holds when $\mathbf{w}$ is used once. We also introduce new attribute-hiding privacy requirements for encodings in this work (c.f. Sect. 7.2).

New Encodings. For many predicates, the prior encodings in [2,31] satisfy the new refinement trivially. In addition, we introduce a number of new encodings:

- For KP-ABE for boolean formula, the prior encoding corresponding to the secret key in [2,31] is given by

$$(r, \alpha_1 + rw_1, \ldots, \alpha_\ell + rw_\ell)$$

where $(\alpha_1, \ldots, \alpha_\ell)$ are random shares of α using a linear secret-sharing scheme and fresh randomness for each secret key. This does not satisfy the syntactic refinement captured in Eqn. (3). In our scheme, we use

$$(r, \alpha_1' + r(w_1 + v_1), \ldots, \alpha_\ell' + r(w_\ell + v_\ell))$$

where $(\alpha_1', \ldots, \alpha_\ell')$ are *deterministically* derived from α using the secret-sharing scheme with randomness fixed to 0 and $(v_1, \ldots, v_\ell)$ are *random* shares of 0. In the ensuing KP-ABE scheme, we use the same $v_1, \ldots, v_\ell$ across all secret keys whereas prior constructions use fresh randomness for secret-sharing for each key. In addition, we obtain an analogous construction for CP-ABE. Here, we avoid having to consider randomized sender encodings as in [2,31]. The final encodings have the same sizes as the prior ones, while satisfying the new refinement requirement. Moreover, by using associativity (c.f. Eqn. (4)), we reduce the number of pairings for the decryption to a constant and avoid exponentiations in the target group at the cost of cheaper exponentiations in the source groups.

- We extend the encodings for KP-ABE and CP-ABE to arithmetic branching programs, based on the selectively secure KP-ABE for arithmetic branching programs in [17]. Combined with our generic framework, we obtain the first adaptively secure KP-ABE and CP-ABE for arithmetic branching programs.

- We also present a new encoding for broadcast encryption with n users where both the receiver and sender encoding have sublinear $O(\sqrt{n})$ length and a simple encoding for large universe fuzzy IBE.

Achieving Weak Attribute-Hiding. In a weakly attribute-hiding scheme, we need to guarantee the privacy of the ciphertext attribute x against collusions that are not authorized to decrypt the challenge ciphertext. To achieve this property, we require additional properties from the underlying encoding and the underlying group structure (extending ideas from [1,3,25]). We use the fact that for any vector $\mathbf{c} \in \mathbb{Z}_p^{k+1}$ outside the span of $\mathbf{A}$, the vector $\mathbf{W}^\top \mathbf{c}$ is uniformly random given $\mathbf{W}^\top \mathbf{A}$, where $\mathbf{W}$ is a uniformly random matrix. We can then use $\mathbf{W}^\top \mathbf{c}$ to information-theoretically blind the attribute in the challenge ciphertext. For this to work, we need to make sure that the semi-functional secret keys do not leak any *additional* information about $\mathbf{WB}$.

New ABE Schemes. We describe several concrete new ABE schemes obtained via our new framework (c.f. Fig. 2). Specifically, we obtain:

functionality	improvements
KP-ABE boolean formula	50 % savings in SK size, faster Dec
CP-ABE boolean formula	50 % savings in CT size, faster Dec
KP-ABE arithmetic formula	first adaptively secure scheme
CP-ABE arithmetic formula	first adaptively secure scheme
NIPE	25-50 % savings in SK and CT size and in Dec time
weakly attribute-hiding ZIPE	25 % savings in SK and CT size and in Dec time

Fig. 2. Summary of efficiency improvements in our new ABE schemes. Here, SK, CT, and Dec stand for secret key, ciphertext, and decryption respectively.

- ABE schemes for the inner product and non-zero inner product predicates with a 25 % improvement in secret key and ciphertext sizes and decryption time, improving upon previous constructions in [26];
- a key-policy ABE scheme for boolean formula with a 50 % improvement in secret key size and faster decryption and an analogous result for ciphertext-policy ABE, improving upon previous constructions in [20,25];
- the first adaptively secure key-policy and ciphertext-policy ABE schemes for arithmetic formula and branching programs without an exponential security loss, improving upon previous constructions in [8,17].

Along the way, we also generalize several previous constructions for $k = 2$ to general k with $k = 1$ being particularly relevant for practical efficiency. More generally, the parameters of our schemes under k-Lin is $k + 1$ times those of the best composite-order schemes based on subgroup assumptions: this achieves a "seemingly best-possible" composite-to-prime-order transformation where each composite element is simulated using $k + 1$ prime-order elements.

Finally, our prime-order ABE schemes are simpler to describe than prior schemes as they share the same structure as existing composite-order schemes. In particular, we obtain the following anonymous IBE scheme:

$$\mathsf{mpk} = [\mathbf{A}, \mathbf{W}_0^\top \mathbf{A}, \mathbf{W}_1^\top \mathbf{A}]_1, [\mathbf{k}^\top \mathbf{A}]_T$$

$$\mathsf{sk}_{\mathsf{id}} = [\mathbf{Br}, \mathbf{k} + (\mathbf{W}_0 + \mathsf{id} \cdot \mathbf{W}_1)\mathbf{Br}]_2 \in G_2^{2(k+1)}$$

$$\mathsf{ct}_{\mathsf{id}} = [\mathbf{As}, (\mathbf{W}_0 + \mathsf{id} \cdot \mathbf{W}_1)^\top \mathbf{As}]_1, [\mathbf{k}^\top \mathbf{As}]_T \cdot m \in G_1^{2(k+1)} \times G_T$$

where $\mathbf{A}, \mathbf{B} \in \mathbb{Z}_p^{(k+1) \times k}$, $\mathbf{W}_0, \mathbf{W}_1 \in \mathbb{Z}_p^{(k+1) \times (k+1)}$, $\mathbf{s}, \mathbf{r} \in \mathbb{Z}_p^k$, $\mathbf{k} \in \mathbb{Z}_p^{k+1}$. This scheme extends naturally to a non-anonymous BBG-style compact HIBE [7] (this is not the case for the prime-order IBE schemes in [11,20]).

1.2 Discussion

Comparison with Prior Works. A summary of the prior approaches for obtaining efficient adaptively secure efficient dual system (H)IBE and ABE is presented in Fig. 1. The most general technique we have for simulating composite-order groups in prime-order ones are those based on "dual pairing vector spaces" (DPVS) [11, 20, 23, 24]. However, these techniques do not preserve the asymptotic efficiency of the underlying schemes; in particular, applying them to the composite-order compact HIBE schemes in [21] blows up the ciphertext size from constant to linear. The sparse DPVS technique [26, 29] uses subgroups of sparse matrices with mostly zero entries to overcome this limitation; however, they substantially limit the generality of the DPVS technique: the structure of these matrices now depend on the predicate and the composite-order scheme (to preserve efficiency), and the analysis for correctness, efficiency and security are more involved. The constructions in [10] fail to extend to boolean formula due to the need for additional randomness for secret-sharing, and also do not extend to yield anonymous IBE. The direct constructions in [3, 18] that bypass a conversion from composite-order groups do not seem to naturally extend beyond (H)IBE: the former uses tag-based languages where tags correspond to identities, and the latter relies on the notion of message authentication codes where messages correspond to identities. In particular, we do not know analogues of these constructions for either the inner product predicate or CP/KP-ABE for boolean formula.

As noted earlier, another novel contribution in this work over prior unifying frameworks in [2, 31] (generalizing [21, 22]) for composite-order groups lies in realizing the weakly-attribute guarantee. This is particularly challenging in composite-order groups for two reasons: (i) there is an explicit anonymity attack on the Lewko-Waters IBE [21] in composite-order group and (ii) the attribute in the semi-functional ciphertext is leaked in the G_{p_1}-component. Interestingly, we are still able to show that our prime-order analog of the Lewko-Waters IBE is anonymous.

Organization. We recall the definition of an attribute-based encryption scheme in Sect. 2. We recall the notion of dual system groups in Sect. 3 and describe our instantiations in Sect. 4. We describe our notion of predicate encodings in Sect. 5. We present our generic ABE construction in Sect. 6. We handle weakly attribute-hiding predicate encryption in Sect. 7. We defer instantiations of predicate encodings and all other details to the full version of this paper.

2   Preliminaries

Notation. We denote by $s \leftarrow_R S$ the fact that s is picked uniformly at random from a finite set S. By PPT, we denote a probabilistic polynomial-time algorithm. Throughout this paper, we use 1^λ as the security parameter. We use $\cdot$ to denote multiplication as well as component-wise multiplication.

2.1   Attribute-Based Encryption

An attribute-based encryption (ABE) scheme for a predicate $P(\cdot, \cdot)$ consists of four algorithms (Setup, Enc, KeyGen, Dec):

Setup$(1^\lambda, \mathcal{X}, \mathcal{Y}, \mathcal{M}) \to (\mathsf{mpk}, \mathsf{msk})$. The setup algorithm gets as input the security parameter λ, the attribute universe $\mathcal{X}$, the predicate universe $\mathcal{Y}$, the message space $\mathcal{M}$ and outputs the public parameter mpk, and the master key msk.

Enc$(\mathsf{mpk}, x, m) \to \mathsf{ct}_x$. The encryption algorithm gets as input mpk, an attribute $x \in \mathcal{X}$ and a message $m \in \mathcal{M}$. It outputs a ciphertext ct_x. Note that x is public given ct_x.

KeyGen$(\mathsf{mpk}, \mathsf{msk}, y) \to \mathsf{sk}_y$. The key generation algorithm gets as input msk and a value $y \in \mathcal{Y}$. It outputs a secret key sk_y. Note that y is public given sk_y.

Dec$(\mathsf{mpk}, \mathsf{sk}_y, \mathsf{ct}_x) \to m$. The decryption algorithm gets as input sk_y and ct_x such that $\mathsf{P}(x, y) = 1$. It outputs a message m.

Correctness. We require that for all $(x, y) \in \mathcal{X} \times \mathcal{Y}$ such that $\mathsf{P}(x, y) = 1$ and all $m \in \mathcal{M}$,
$$\Pr[\mathsf{Dec}(\mathsf{mpk}, \mathsf{sk}_y, \mathsf{Enc}(\mathsf{mpk}, x, m)) = m] = 1,$$
where the probability is taken over $(\mathsf{mpk}, \mathsf{msk}) \leftarrow \mathsf{Setup}(1^\lambda, \mathcal{X}, \mathcal{Y}, \mathcal{M})$, $\mathsf{sk}_y \leftarrow$ KeyGen$(\mathsf{mpk}, \mathsf{msk}, y)$, and the coins of Enc.

Security Definition. For a stateful adversary $\mathcal{A}$, we define the advantage function
$$\mathsf{Adv}_{\mathcal{A}}^{\mathrm{ABE}}(\lambda) := \Pr \left[b = b' : \begin{array}{l} (\mathsf{mpk}, \mathsf{msk}) \leftarrow \mathsf{Setup}(1^\lambda, \mathcal{X}, \mathcal{Y}, \mathcal{M}); \\ (x^*, m_0, m_1) \leftarrow \mathcal{A}^{\mathsf{KeyGen}(\mathsf{msk}, \cdot)}(\mathsf{mpk}); \\ b \leftarrow_{\mathrm{R}} \{0, 1\}; \mathsf{ct}_{x^*} \leftarrow \mathsf{Enc}(\mathsf{mpk}, x^*, m_b); \\ b' \leftarrow \mathcal{A}^{\mathsf{KeyGen}(\mathsf{msk}, \cdot)}(\mathsf{ct}_{x^*}) \end{array} \right] - \frac{1}{2}$$

with the restriction that all queries y that $\mathcal{A}$ makes to KeyGen$(\mathsf{msk}, \cdot)$ satisfies $\mathsf{P}(x^*, y) = 0$ (that is, sk_y does not decrypt ct_{x^*}). An ABE scheme is *adaptively secure* if for all PPT adversaries $\mathcal{A}$, the advantage $\mathsf{Adv}_{\mathcal{A}}^{\mathrm{ABE}}(\lambda)$ is a negligible function in λ.

3   Dual System Groups

This section is largely adapted from [10].

3.1   Overview

Dual system groups contain a triple of abelian groups $(\mathbb{G}, \mathbb{H}, \mathbb{G}_T)$ and a non-degenerate bilinear map $e : \mathbb{G} \times \mathbb{H} \to \mathbb{G}_T$. For concreteness, we may think of $(\mathbb{G}, \mathbb{H}, \mathbb{G}_T)$ as composite-order bilinear groups. Dual system groups take as input a parameter 1^n (think of n as the universe size in KP-ABE) and satisfy the following properties:

(**subgroup indistinguishability.**) There are two computationally indistinguishable ways to sample correlated $(n + 1)$-tuples from $\mathbb{G}^{n+1}$: the "normal" distribution, and a higher-entropy distribution with "semi-functional components". We sample the normal distribution using SampG and the semi-functional components using $\widehat{\mathsf{SampG}}$. An analogous property holds for $\mathbb{H}^{n+1}$, with algorithms SampH and $\widehat{\mathsf{SampH}}$ respectively, with an important distinction in the auxiliary input provided to the distinguisher. For concreteness, think in terms of symmetric bilinear groups of composite order N where

$$\mathsf{SampG} \to (g_1^s, g_1^{s\mathbf{w}}) \in G_N^{n+1} \quad \text{and} \quad \mathsf{SampH} \to (g_1^r, g_1^{r\mathbf{w}}) \in G_N^{n+1}$$

$$\widehat{\mathsf{SampG}} \to (g_2^s, g_2^{s\mathbf{w}}) \in G_N^{n+1} \quad \text{and} \quad \widehat{\mathsf{SampH}} \to (g_2^r, g_2^{r\mathbf{w}}) \in G_N^{n+1}$$

Here, N is the product of three primes p_1, p_2, p_3; g_1, g_2 are generators of order p_1, p_2; and $g_1^{\mathbf{w}} \in G_N^n$ is part of the public parameters.

(**associativity.**) For all $(g_0, g_1, \ldots, g_n) \in \mathbb{G}^{n+1}$ and all $(h_0, h_1, \ldots, h_n) \in \mathbb{H}^{n+1}$ drawn from the respective normal distributions according to SampG and SampH, we have that for all $i = 1, \ldots, n$,

$$e(g_0, h_i) = e(g_i, h_0).$$

We require this property for correctness (c.f. Eqn. (4)).

(**right subgroup $\mathbb{H}$.**) There is some distinguished element $h^* \in \mathbb{H}$, which generates the semi-functional components in $\mathbb{H}$. It is convenient to think of h^* as being orthogonal to the normal distribution over $\mathbb{G}$ (c.f. orthogonality). On the other hand, we require that h^* is *not* orthogonal to the semi-functional components in $\mathbb{G}$ (c.f. non-degeneracy), so that we get a random value when we decrypt a semi-functional ciphertext with a semi-functional key.

(**parameter-hiding.**) Both normal distributions can be efficiently sampled given the public parameters; on the other hand, given only the public parameters, the higher-entropy distributions contain n "units" of information-theoretic entropy (in the semi-functional component), one unit for each of the n elements in the $(n + 1)$-tuple apart from the first. In the formal statement, the hidden entropy is captured by n random exponents $(u_1, \ldots, u_n)$ shared across $\mathbb{G}$ and $\mathbb{H}$. It is crucial here that we use the same u_i in $\mathbb{G}$ and in $\mathbb{H}$, so that decryption succeeds with nominally semi-functional objects.

3.2   Definitions

Syntax. Dual system groups consist of six randomized algorithms given by (SampP, SampGT, SampG, SampH) along with $(\widehat{\mathsf{SampG}}, \widehat{\mathsf{SampH}})$:

SampP$(1^\lambda, 1^n)$: On input $(1^\lambda, 1^n)$, output public and secret parameters $(\mathsf{pp}, \mathsf{sp})$, where:

- pp contains a prime p of length $\Omega(\lambda)$, a triple of abelian groups $(\mathbb{G}, \mathbb{H}, \mathbb{G}_T)$, a non-degenerate bilinear map $e : \mathbb{G} \times \mathbb{H} \to \mathbb{G}_T$, a linear map μ defined on $\mathbb{H}$, along with some additional parameters used by SampG, SampH;
- the groups $(\mathbb{G}, \mathbb{H}, \mathbb{G}_T)$ are $\mathbb{Z}_p$-modules where $\mathbb{Z}_p$ acts on $\mathbb{G}, \mathbb{H}, \mathbb{G}_T$ via exponentiation;
- given pp, we can uniformly sample from $\mathbb{H}$;
- sp contains $h^* \in \mathbb{H}$ (where $h^* \neq 1$), along with some additional parameters used by $\widehat{\mathsf{SampG}}, \widehat{\mathsf{SampH}}$;

SampGT : $\mathrm{Im}(\mu) \to \mathbb{G}_T$. (As a concrete example, suppose $\mu : \mathbb{H} \to \mathbb{G}_T$ and $\mathrm{Im}(\mu) = \mathbb{G}_T$.)

SampG(pp): Output $\mathbf{g} \in \mathbb{G}^{n+1}$.

SampH(pp): Output $\mathbf{h} \in \mathbb{H}^{n+1}$.

$\widehat{\mathsf{SampG}}$(pp, sp): Output $\hat{\mathbf{g}} \in \mathbb{G}^{n+1}$.

$\widehat{\mathsf{SampH}}$(pp, sp): Output $\hat{\mathbf{h}} \in \mathbb{H}^{n+1}$.

The first four algorithms are used in the actual scheme, whereas the last two algorithms are used only in the proofs of security. We define SampG_0 to denote the first group element in the output of SampG, and we define $\widehat{\mathsf{SampG}}_0, \widehat{\mathsf{SampH}}_0$ analogously.

Remark 1. Given a $\mathbb{Z}_p$-linear function $L : \mathbb{Z}_p^n \to \mathbb{Z}_p$ given by $(w_1, \ldots, w_n) \mapsto a_1 w_1 + \cdots + a_n w_n$ (where $a_1, \ldots, a_n \in \mathbb{Z}_p$ are fixed constants), L acts on $\mathbb{Z}_p$-modules $\mathbb{G}^n, \mathbb{H}^n, \mathbb{G}_T^n$ in the natural way. For instance, $L : \mathbb{G}^n \to \mathbb{G}$ is given by $(g_1, \ldots, g_n) \mapsto g_1^{a_1} \cdots g_n^{a_n}$. This extends also to general $\mathbb{Z}_p$-linear functions $L : \mathbb{Z}_p^n \to \mathbb{Z}_p^m$ coordinate-wise.

Correctness. The requirements for correctness are as follows:

(projective.) For all $h \in \mathbb{H}$ and all coin tosses s, we have $\mathsf{SampGT}(\mu(h); s) = e(\mathsf{SampG}_0(\mathsf{pp}; s), h)$.

(associative.) For all $(g_0, g_1, \ldots, g_n) \leftarrow \mathsf{SampG}(\mathsf{pp})$ and $(h_0, h_1, \ldots, h_n) \leftarrow \mathsf{SampH}(\mathsf{pp})$ and for all $i = 1, \ldots, n$, we have $e(g_0, h_i) = e(g_i, h_0)$.

($\mathbb{H}$-subgroup.) The output of SampH(pp) is the uniform distribution over a subgroup of $\mathbb{H}^{n+1}$.

Security. The requirements for security are as follows:

(orthogonality.) $\mu(h^*) = 1$.

(non-degeneracy.) For all $\hat{h}_0 \leftarrow \widehat{\mathsf{SampH}}_0(\mathsf{pp}, \mathsf{sp})$, h^* lies in the group generated by $\hat{h}_0$. For all $\hat{g}_0 \leftarrow \widehat{\mathsf{SampG}}_0(\mathsf{pp}, \mathsf{sp})$, we have $e(\hat{g}_0, h^*)^\alpha$ is identically distributed to the uniform distribution over $\mathbb{G}_T$, where $\alpha \leftarrow_{\mathrm{R}} \mathbb{Z}_p$.

(left subgroup indistinguishability.) For any adversary $\mathcal{A}$, we define the advantage function:

$$\mathsf{Adv}_{\mathcal{A}}^{\mathsf{LS}}(\lambda) := \left| \Pr[\, \mathcal{A}(\mathsf{pp}, \boxed{\mathbf{g}}) = 1 \,] - \Pr[\, \mathcal{A}(\mathsf{pp}, \boxed{\mathbf{g} \cdot \hat{\mathbf{g}}}) = 1 \,] \right|$$

where $(\mathsf{pp}, \mathsf{sp}) \leftarrow \mathsf{SampP}(1^\lambda, 1^n)$, $\mathbf{g} \leftarrow \mathsf{SampG}(\mathsf{pp})$, $\hat{\mathbf{g}} \leftarrow \widehat{\mathsf{SampG}}(\mathsf{pp}, \mathsf{sp})$.

(right subgroup indistinguishability.) For any adversary $\mathcal{A}$, we define the advantage function:

$$\mathsf{Adv}_{\mathcal{A}}^{\mathsf{RS}}(\lambda) := \left| \Pr[\, \mathcal{A}(\mathsf{pp}, h^*, \mathbf{g} \cdot \hat{\mathbf{g}}, \boxed{\mathbf{h}}) = 1 \,] - \Pr[\, \mathcal{A}(\mathsf{pp}, h^*, \mathbf{g} \cdot \hat{\mathbf{g}}, \boxed{\mathbf{h} \cdot \hat{\mathbf{h}}}) = 1 \,] \right|$$

where $(\mathsf{pp}, \mathsf{sp}) \leftarrow \mathsf{SampP}(1^\lambda, 1^n)$, $\mathbf{g} \leftarrow \mathsf{SampG}(\mathsf{pp})$, $\hat{\mathbf{g}} \leftarrow \widehat{\mathsf{SampG}}(\mathsf{pp}, \mathsf{sp})$, $\mathbf{h} \leftarrow \mathsf{SampH}(\mathsf{pp})$, $\hat{\mathbf{h}} \leftarrow \widehat{\mathsf{SampH}}(\mathsf{pp}, \mathsf{sp})$.

(parameter-hiding.) The following distributions are identically distributed

$$\{\mathsf{pp}, h^*, \boxed{\hat{\mathbf{g}}, \hat{\mathbf{h}}}\} \quad \text{and} \quad \{\mathsf{pp}, h^*, \boxed{\hat{\mathbf{g}} \cdot \hat{\mathbf{g}}', \hat{\mathbf{h}} \cdot \hat{\mathbf{h}}'}\}$$

where

$$(\mathsf{pp}, \mathsf{sp}) \leftarrow \mathsf{SampP}(1^\lambda, 1^n); \qquad u_1, \ldots, u_n \leftarrow_{\mathrm{R}} \mathbb{Z}_p;$$

$$\hat{\mathbf{g}} = (\hat{g}_0, \ldots) \leftarrow \widehat{\mathsf{SampG}}(\mathsf{pp}, \mathsf{sp}); \quad \hat{\mathbf{h}} = (\hat{h}_0, \ldots) \leftarrow \widehat{\mathsf{SampH}}(\mathsf{pp}, \mathsf{sp});$$

$$\hat{\mathbf{g}}' := (1, \hat{g}_0^{u_1}, \ldots, \hat{g}_0^{u_n}) \in \mathbb{G}^{n+1}; \quad \hat{\mathbf{h}}' := (1, \hat{h}_0^{u_1}, \ldots, \hat{h}_0^{u_n}) \in \mathbb{H}^{n+1}.$$

4 Instantiations of DSG from k-Lin

We present a new instantiation of dual system groups under the k-Lin assumption, inspired by the constructions in [3,10].

Overview. The prior construction of DSG [10] (building upon [11,20,24,25]) starts with a random $\mathbf{B} \leftarrow_{\mathrm{R}} \mathsf{GL}_{k+1}(\mathbb{Z}_p)$ and defines $\mathbf{B}^* := (\mathbf{B}^\top)^{-1}$ so that $\mathbf{B}^\top \mathbf{B}^*$ is the identity matrix; then uses $\mathbf{B}$ for $\mathsf{SampG}, \widehat{\mathsf{SampG}}$ and $\mathbf{B}^*$ for $\mathsf{SampH}, \widehat{\mathsf{SampH}}$. In our construction, we may start with any pair of matrices $\mathbf{A}, \mathbf{B}$ in $\mathbb{Z}_p^{(k+1) \times k}$ of full rank:

- In addition, we pick $\mathbf{a}^\perp, \mathbf{b}^\perp$ so that $\mathbf{a}^{\perp\top}\mathbf{A} = \mathbf{b}^{\perp\top}\mathbf{B} = \mathbf{0}$ and $\mathbf{a}^{\perp\top}\mathbf{b}^\perp \neq 0$; we then use $(\mathbf{A}, \mathbf{b}^\perp)$ for $\mathsf{SampG}, \widehat{\mathsf{SampG}}$ and $(\mathbf{B}, \mathbf{a}^\perp)$ for $\mathsf{SampH}, \widehat{\mathsf{SampH}}$.
- We achieve randomization as follows: again, pick a random $\mathbf{W} \leftarrow_{\mathrm{R}} \mathbb{Z}_p^{(k+1) \times (k+1)}$ and replace $(\mathbf{A}, \mathbf{B})$ with $(\mathbf{W}^\top \mathbf{A}, \mathbf{W}\mathbf{B})$. The associativity property follows from the equation:

$$(\mathbf{W}^\top \mathbf{A})^\top \mathbf{B} = \mathbf{A}^\top (\mathbf{W}\mathbf{B})$$

Interestingly, the prior construction in [10] randomizes by multiplying a random $\mathbf{W}$ on the right, whereas our construction multiplies a random $\mathbf{W}$ on the left. Together with the fact that we no longer require the fact that $\mathbf{B}^\top \mathbf{B}^*$ is the identity, we substantially simplify the proof of subgroup indistinguishability.

4.1 Cryptographic Assumptions

We follow the notation and algebraic framework for Diffie-Hellman-like assumptions in [13].

Prime-Order Bilinear Groups. A generator $\mathcal{G}$ takes as input a security parameter λ and outputs a description $(p, G_1, G_2, G_T, g_1, g_2, e)$, where p is a prime of $\Theta(\lambda)$ bits; G_1, G_2 and G_T are cyclic groups of order p; g_1, g_2 are generators of G_1 and G_2 respectively; and $e : G_1 \times G_2 \rightarrow G_T$ is a non-degenerate bilinear map. Given $a \in \mathbb{Z}_p$, we use $[a]_1$ to denote g_1^a, $[a]_2$ to denote g_2^a, $[a]_T$ to denote $e(g_1, g_2)^a$. This extends to vectors and matrices in the obvious way. We define $e([\mathbf{A}]_1, [\mathbf{B}]_2) := [\mathbf{A}^\top \mathbf{B}]_T$.

Linear Assumption. Let $\mathcal{D}_k$ be an efficiently samplable distribution of matrices $(\mathbf{A}, \mathbf{a}^\perp)$ over $\mathbb{Z}_p^{(k+1) \times k} \times \mathbb{Z}_p^{k+1}$ so that $\mathbf{A}^\top \mathbf{a}^\perp = \mathbf{0}$ and $\mathbf{a}^\perp \neq \mathbf{0}$. In particular, we consider the distribution generated as follows: pick $a_1, \ldots, a_k \leftarrow_{\mathrm{R}} \mathbb{Z}_p^*$ and set

$$\mathbf{A} := \begin{pmatrix} a_1 & & & \\ & a_2 & & \\ & & \ddots & \\ & & & a_k \\ 1 & 1 & \cdots & 1 \end{pmatrix} \in \mathbb{Z}_p^{(k+1) \times k} \quad \text{and} \quad \mathbf{a}^\perp := \begin{pmatrix} a_1^{-1} \\ a_2^{-1} \\ \vdots \\ a_k^{-1} \\ -1 \end{pmatrix} \in \mathbb{Z}_p^{(k+1)}.$$

This distribution captures the k-linear assumption, which stipulates that

$$([\mathbf{A}], [\mathbf{As}]) \approx_c ([\mathbf{A}], [\mathbf{z}])$$

where $\mathbf{s} \leftarrow_{\mathrm{R}} \mathbb{Z}_p^k, \mathbf{z} \leftarrow_{\mathrm{R}} \mathbb{Z}_p^{k+1}$ in both G_1 and G_2.

Assumption 1 (k-Lin: the k-linear assumption in G_1) *For any adversary $\mathcal{A}$, we define the advantage function:*

$$\mathsf{Adv}_{\mathcal{A}}^{k\text{-Lin}} := \big| \Pr[\mathcal{A}((p, G_1, G_2, G_T, g_1, g_2, e); [\mathbf{A}]_1, [\mathbf{As}]_1) = 1]$$
$$- \Pr[\mathcal{A}((p, G_1, G_2, G_T, g_1, g_2, e); [\mathbf{A}]_1, [\mathbf{z}]_1) = 1] \big|$$

where $(p, G_1, G_2, G_T, g_1, g_2, e) \leftarrow \mathcal{G}(1^\lambda)$, $(\mathbf{A}, \mathbf{a}^\perp) \leftarrow \mathcal{D}_k$, $\mathbf{s} \leftarrow_{\mathrm{R}} \mathbb{Z}_p^k$, $\mathbf{z} \leftarrow_{\mathrm{R}} \mathbb{Z}_p^{k+1}$.

We will slightly abuse notation and also use $\mathsf{Adv}_{\mathcal{A}}^{k\text{-Lin}}$ to denote the corresponding advantage function for G_2.

Basis Lemma. The following structural lemma tells us that if we pick random $(\mathbf{A}, \mathbf{a}^\perp), (\mathbf{B}, \mathbf{b}^\perp) \leftarrow \mathcal{D}_k$, then with overwhelming probability, both $(\mathbf{A}, \mathbf{b}^\perp)$ and $(\mathbf{B}, \mathbf{a}^\perp)$ form a basis for $\mathbb{Z}_p^{k+1}$ and $\mathbf{a}^\perp, \mathbf{b}^\perp$ are not orthogonal. We will assume henceforth that this property always holds.

Lemma 1 (Basis Lemma). *With probability $1 - 1/p$ over $(\mathbf{A}, \mathbf{a}^\perp), (\mathbf{B}, \mathbf{b}^\perp) \leftarrow \mathcal{D}_k$, it holds that:*

$$\left(\mathbf{a}^\perp \notin span(\mathbf{B})\right) \wedge \left(\mathbf{b}^\perp \notin span(\mathbf{A})\right) \wedge \left(\mathbf{a}^{\perp\top} \mathbf{b}^\perp \neq 0\right).$$

Proof. It is easy to see that if $\mathbf{a}^{\perp\top} \mathbf{b}^\perp \neq 0$, then

$$\left(\mathbf{a}^\perp \notin span(\mathbf{B})\right) \quad \text{and} \quad \left(\mathbf{b}^\perp \notin span(\mathbf{A})\right)$$

since every vector in $span(\mathbf{A})$ is orthogonal to $\mathbf{a}^\perp$ and every vector in $span(\mathbf{B})$ is orthogonal to $\mathbf{b}^\perp$. Observe that $\mathbf{a}^{\perp\top} \mathbf{b}^\perp = 1 + \sum_{i=1}^{d} (a_i b_i)^{-1}$ and

$$\Pr\left[1 + \sum_{i=1}^{d} (a_i b_i)^{-1} \neq 0 : a_1, b_1, \ldots, a_k, b_k \leftarrow_{\text{R}} \mathbb{Z}_p^*\right] = 1 - 1/p.$$

The lemma then follows readily. □

Remark 2. Observe that Lemma 1 is not particular to the k-Lin distribution, since a similar proof works for any example of matrix distribution $\mathcal{D}_k$ presented in [13], namely $\mathcal{U}_{k+1,k}$, k-Casc, k-SCasc and k-ILin [13, Section 3.4].

4.2   Construction

Our construction is as follows:

SampP$(1^\lambda, 1^n)$: On input $(1^\lambda, 1^n)$, do:

- run $(p, G_1, G_2, G_T, g_1, g_2, e) \leftarrow \mathcal{G}(1^\lambda)$, where $\mathcal{G}(1^\lambda)$ is an asymmetric prime-order group generator;
- define $(\mathbb{G}, \mathbb{H}, \mathbb{G}_T, e) := (G_1^{k+1}, G_2^{k+1}, G_T, e)$;
- sample $(\mathbf{A}, \mathbf{a}^\perp), (\mathbf{B}, \mathbf{b}^\perp) \leftarrow \mathcal{D}_k$, along with $\mathbf{W}_1, \ldots, \mathbf{W}_n \leftarrow_{\text{R}} \mathbb{Z}_p^{(k+1)\times(k+1)}$;
- define $\mu : G_2^{k+1} \to G_T^k$ by $\mu([\mathbf{k}]_2) = [\mathbf{A}^\top \mathbf{k}]_T$;
- set $h^* := [\mathbf{a}^\perp]_2$.

Output

$$\mathsf{pp} := \left((p, \mathbb{G}, \mathbb{H}, \mathbb{G}_T, e); \begin{array}{l} [\mathbf{A}]_1, [\mathbf{W}_1^\top \mathbf{A}]_1, \ldots, [\mathbf{W}_n^\top \mathbf{A}]_1 \\ [\mathbf{B}]_2, [\mathbf{W}_1 \mathbf{B}]_2, \ldots, [\mathbf{W}_n \mathbf{B}]_2 \end{array} \right);$$

$$\mathsf{sp} := \left(\mathbf{a}^\perp, \mathbf{b}^\perp, \mathbf{W}_1, \ldots, \mathbf{W}_n \right).$$

SampGT$([\mathbf{p}]_T)$: Pick $\mathbf{s} \leftarrow_{\text{R}} \mathbb{Z}_p^k$ and output $[\mathbf{s}^\top \mathbf{p}]_T \in G_T$.

SampG(pp): Pick $\mathbf{s} \leftarrow_{\text{R}} \mathbb{Z}_p^k$ and output

$$\left([\mathbf{As}]_1, [\mathbf{W}_1^\top \mathbf{As}]_1, \ldots, [\mathbf{W}_n^\top \mathbf{As}]_1\right) \in (G_1^{k+1})^{n+1}.$$

$\mathsf{SampH}(\mathsf{pp})$: Pick $\mathbf{r} \leftarrow_{\mathrm{R}} \mathbb{Z}_p^k$ and output

$$\left([\mathbf{Br}]_2, [\mathbf{W}_1\mathbf{Br}]_2, \ldots, [\mathbf{W}_n\mathbf{Br}]_2 \right) \in (G_2^{k+1})^{n+1}.$$

$\widehat{\mathsf{SampG}}(\mathsf{pp}, \mathsf{sp})$: Pick $\hat{s} \leftarrow_{\mathrm{R}} \mathbb{Z}_p^*$ and output

$$\left([\mathbf{b}^{\perp}\hat{s}]_1, [\mathbf{W}_1^{\top}\mathbf{b}^{\perp}\hat{s}]_1, \ldots, [\mathbf{W}_n^{\top}\mathbf{b}^{\perp}\hat{s}]_1 \right) \in (G_1^{k+1})^{n+1}.$$

$\widehat{\mathsf{SampH}}(\mathsf{pp}, \mathsf{sp})$: Pick $\hat{r} \leftarrow_{\mathrm{R}} \mathbb{Z}_p^*$ and output

$$\left([\mathbf{a}^{\perp}\hat{r}]_2, [\mathbf{W}_1\mathbf{a}^{\perp}\hat{r}]_2, \ldots, [\mathbf{W}_n\mathbf{a}^{\perp}\hat{r}]_2 \right) \in (G_2^{k+1})^{n+1}.$$

Correctness. We check correctness properties as follows:

(projective.) This follows readily from the fact that for all $\mathbf{k} \in \mathbb{Z}_p^{k+1}, \mathbf{s} \in \mathbb{Z}_p^k$:

$$(\mathbf{As})^{\top}\mathbf{k} = (\mathbf{A}^{\top}\mathbf{k})^{\top}\mathbf{s}.$$

(associative.) This follows readily from the fact that for all $\mathbf{s} \in \mathbb{Z}_p^k, \mathbf{r} \in \mathbb{Z}_p^k, \mathbf{W}_i \in \mathbb{Z}_p^{(k+1) \times (k+1)}$:

$$(\mathbf{W}_i^{\top}\mathbf{As})^{\top}(\mathbf{Br}) = (\mathbf{As})^{\top}(\mathbf{W}_i\mathbf{Br}).$$

($\mathbb{H}$-subgroup.) This follows readily from the fact that $\mathbb{Z}_p^k$ is an additive group.

Security. We check security properties as follows:

(orthogonality.) This follows readily from $\mathbf{A}^{\top}\mathbf{a}^{\perp} = \mathbf{0}$.

(non-degeneracy.) This follows readily from $\mathbf{b}^{\perp^{\top}}\mathbf{a}^{\perp} \neq 0$.

We establish left subgroup indistinguishability, right subgroup indistinguishability, and parameter-hiding in the next three lemmas. The left and right subgroup indistinguishability relies on the k-Lin assumption in prime-order groups, whereas parameter-hiding is unconditional.

Lemma 2 (Left Subgroup Indistinguishability from k-Lin). *For any adversary $\mathcal{A}$, there exists an adversary $\mathcal{B}$ such that:*

$$\mathsf{Adv}_{\mathcal{A}}^{\mathrm{LS}}(\lambda) \leq \mathsf{Adv}_{\mathcal{B}}^{k\text{-Lin}} + 2/p$$

and $\mathsf{Time}(\mathcal{B}) \approx \mathsf{Time}(\mathcal{A}) + k^2 \cdot \mathrm{poly}(\lambda, n)$ *where* $\mathrm{poly}(\lambda, n)$ *is independent of* $\mathsf{Time}(\mathcal{A})$.

The proof is a simpler case of the proof of Lemma 3, we omit it here.

Lemma 3 (Right Subgroup Indistinguishability from k-Lin). *For any adversary $\mathcal{A}$, there exists an adversary $\mathcal{B}$ such that:*

$$\mathsf{Adv}^{\mathrm{RS}}_{\mathcal{A}}(\lambda) \leq \mathsf{Adv}^{k\text{-Lin}}_{\mathcal{B}} + 2/p$$

and $\mathsf{Time}(\mathcal{B}) \approx \mathsf{Time}(\mathcal{A}) + k^2 \cdot \mathrm{poly}(\lambda, n)$ *where* $\mathrm{poly}(\lambda, n)$ *is independent of* $\mathsf{Time}(\mathcal{A})$.

We may rewrite the corresponding advantage function as:

$$\mathsf{Adv}^{\mathrm{RS}}_{\mathcal{A}}(\lambda) := \left| \Pr[\, \mathcal{A}(\mathsf{pp}, h^*, \mathbf{g} \cdot \hat{\mathbf{g}}, \mathbf{h}) = 1 \,] - \Pr[\, \mathcal{A}(\mathsf{pp}, h^*, \mathbf{g} \cdot \hat{\mathbf{g}}, \mathbf{h} \cdot \hat{\mathbf{h}}) = 1 \,] \right|$$

where

$$(\mathsf{pp}, \mathsf{sp}) \leftarrow \mathsf{SampP}(1^\lambda, 1^n); \quad \mathbf{s}, \mathbf{r} \leftarrow_{\mathrm{R}} \mathbb{Z}_p^k; \; \hat{s}, \hat{r} \leftarrow_{\mathrm{R}} \mathbb{Z}_p^*; \quad h^* := \left[\mathbf{a}^\perp \right]_2;$$

$$\mathbf{g} \cdot \hat{\mathbf{g}} := \left(\left[\mathbf{As} + \mathbf{b}^\perp \hat{s} \right]_1, \left[\mathbf{W}_1^\top (\mathbf{As} + \mathbf{b}^\perp \hat{s}) \right]_1, \ldots, \left[\mathbf{W}_n^\top (\mathbf{As} + \mathbf{b}^\perp \hat{s}) \right]_1 \right);$$

$$\mathbf{h} := \left(\left[\mathbf{Br} \right]_2, \left[\mathbf{W}_1 \mathbf{Br} \right]_2, \ldots, \left[\mathbf{W}_n \mathbf{Br} \right]_2 \right);$$

$$\mathbf{h} \cdot \hat{\mathbf{h}} := \left(\left[\mathbf{Br} + \mathbf{a}^\perp \hat{r} \right]_2, \left[\mathbf{W}_1 (\mathbf{Br} + \mathbf{a}^\perp \hat{r}) \right]_2, \ldots, \left[\mathbf{W}_n (\mathbf{Br} + \mathbf{a}^\perp \hat{r}) \right]_2 \right).$$

Proof. The adversary $\mathcal{B}$ samples $(\mathbf{A}, \mathbf{a}^\perp) \leftarrow \mathcal{D}_k$ along with $\mathbf{W}_1, \ldots, \mathbf{W}_n \leftarrow_{\mathrm{R}} \mathbb{Z}_p^{(k+1) \times (k+1)}$. Recall that $(\mathbf{B}, \mathbf{a}^\perp)$ is a basis for $\mathbb{Z}_p^{k+1}$, so $\{ \mathbf{Br} + \mathbf{a}^\perp \hat{r} : \mathbf{r} \leftarrow_{\mathrm{R}} \mathbb{Z}_p^k, \hat{r} \leftarrow_{\mathrm{R}} \mathbb{Z}_p^* \}$ is statistically close to the uniform distribution. Adversary $\mathcal{B}$ then gets as input

$$\left(\, (p, G_1, G_2, G_T, g_1, g_2, e), [\mathbf{B}]_2, \left[\mathbf{Br} + \mathbf{a}^\perp \hat{r} \right]_2 \right)$$

where either $\hat{r} = 0$ or $\hat{r} \leftarrow_{\mathrm{R}} \mathbb{Z}_p^*$, and proceeds as follows:

Simulating pp, h^*. Output

$$\begin{array}{llll} [\mathbf{A}]_1, & [\mathbf{W}_1^\top \mathbf{A}]_1, & \ldots, & [\mathbf{W}_n^\top \mathbf{A}]_1 \\ [\mathbf{B}]_2, & [\mathbf{W}_1 \mathbf{B}]_2, & \ldots, & [\mathbf{W}_n \mathbf{B}]_2 \end{array} \quad \text{and} \quad \left[\mathbf{a}^\perp \right]_2$$

Simulating $\left[\mathbf{As} + \mathbf{b}^\perp \hat{s} \right]_1, \left[\mathbf{W}_i^\top (\mathbf{As} + \mathbf{b}^\perp \hat{s}) \right]_1$. Note that $\mathcal{B}$ does not know $\mathbf{b}^\perp$. Instead, $\mathcal{B}$ samples $\tilde{\mathbf{s}} \leftarrow_{\mathrm{R}} \mathbb{Z}_p^{k+1}$ and outputs

$$[\tilde{\mathbf{s}}]_1, [\mathbf{W}_1^\top \tilde{\mathbf{s}}]_1, \ldots, [\mathbf{W}_n^\top \tilde{\mathbf{s}}]_1.$$

Observe that $\mathbf{As} + \mathbf{b}^\perp \hat{s}$ is statistically close to the uniform vector $\tilde{\mathbf{s}}$ as long as $\mathbf{b}^\perp \notin \mathrm{span}(\mathbf{A})$ and $\hat{s} \leftarrow_{\mathrm{R}} \mathbb{Z}_p$.

Simulating the Challenge. Upon receiving a k-Lin challenge, $\mathcal{B}$ outputs

$$\left[\mathbf{Br} + \mathbf{a}^\perp \hat{r} \right]_2, \left[\mathbf{W}_1 (\mathbf{Br} + \mathbf{a}^\perp \hat{r}) \right]_2, \ldots, \left[\mathbf{W}_n (\mathbf{Br} + \mathbf{a}^\perp \hat{r}) \right]_2$$

where either $\hat{r} = 0$ or $\hat{r} \leftarrow_{\mathrm{R}} \mathbb{Z}_p$.

Observe that:

- if $\hat{r} = 0$, then we can write the output challenge as

$$[\mathbf{Br}]_2, \ [\mathbf{W}_1\mathbf{Br}]_2, \ \ldots, \ [\mathbf{W}_n\mathbf{Br}]_2.$$

which equals $\mathbf{h}$; we obtain the left distribution in the statement of the lemma;
- if $\hat{r} \leftarrow_R \mathbb{Z}_p$, then we can write the output challenge as

$$[\mathbf{Br} + \mathbf{a}^\perp\hat{r}]_2, \ [\mathbf{W}_1(\mathbf{Br} + \mathbf{a}^\perp\hat{r})]_2, \ \ldots, \ [\mathbf{W}_n(\mathbf{Br} + \mathbf{a}^\perp\hat{r})]_2.$$

which equals $\mathbf{h} \cdot \hat{\mathbf{h}}$; we obtain the right distribution in the statement of the lemma.

Typically, we sample $\hat{s}, \hat{r} \leftarrow_R \mathbb{Z}_p^*$ for $\widehat{\mathsf{SampG}}(\mathsf{pp}, \mathsf{sp})$ and $\widehat{\mathsf{SampH}}(\mathsf{pp}, \mathsf{sp})$; this yields a $2/p$ negligible difference in the advantage. The lemma then follows readily. $\square$

Lemma 4 (Parameter-Hiding). *The following distributions are identically distributed*

$$\left\{ pp, [\mathbf{a}^\perp]_2, \begin{array}{l} [\mathbf{b}^\perp\hat{s}]_1, \ [\mathbf{W}_1^\top\mathbf{b}^\perp\hat{s}]_1, \ \ldots, \ [\mathbf{W}_n^\top\mathbf{b}^\perp\hat{s}]_1 \\ [\mathbf{a}^\perp\hat{r}]_2, \ [\mathbf{W}_1\mathbf{a}^\perp\hat{r}]_2, \ \ldots, \ [\mathbf{W}_n\mathbf{a}^\perp\hat{r}]_2 \end{array} \right\} \quad and$$

$$\left\{ pp, [\mathbf{a}^\perp]_2, \begin{array}{l} [\mathbf{b}^\perp\hat{s}]_1, \ [(\mathbf{W}_1^\top\mathbf{b}^\perp + u_1\mathbf{b}^\perp)\hat{s}]_1, \ \ldots, \ [(\mathbf{W}_n^\top\mathbf{b}^\perp + u_n\mathbf{b}^\perp)\hat{s}]_1 \\ [\mathbf{a}^\perp\hat{r}]_2, \ [(\mathbf{W}_1\mathbf{a}^\perp + u_1\mathbf{a}^\perp)\hat{r}]_2, \ \ldots, \ [(\mathbf{W}_n\mathbf{a}^\perp + u_n\mathbf{a}^\perp)\hat{r}]_2 \end{array} \right\}$$

where $(pp, sp) \leftarrow \mathsf{SampP}(1^\lambda, 1^n)$, $\hat{s}, \hat{r} \leftarrow_R \mathbb{Z}_p^*$ *and* $u_1, \ldots, u_n \leftarrow_R \mathbb{Z}_p$.

Proof. Fix $g_1, g_2, (\mathbf{A}, \mathbf{a}^\perp), (\mathbf{B}, \mathbf{b}^\perp), \hat{s}, \hat{r}$; that is, we prove that the statement holds for all $g_1, g_2, (\mathbf{A}, \mathbf{a}^\perp), (\mathbf{B}, \mathbf{b}^\perp), \hat{s}, \hat{r}$. Set $\mathbf{V} := \mathbf{a}^\perp\mathbf{b}^{\perp\top} \in \mathbb{Z}_p^{(k+1)\times(k+1)}$ which satisfies the following properties:

$$\mathbf{V}^\top\mathbf{A} = \mathbf{0} \quad and \quad \mathbf{VB} = \mathbf{0} \tag{5}$$

$$\mathbf{Va}^\perp = (\mathbf{a}^{\perp\top}\mathbf{b}^\perp)\mathbf{a}^\perp \quad and \quad \mathbf{V}^\top\mathbf{b}^\perp = (\mathbf{a}^{\perp\top}\mathbf{b}^\perp)\mathbf{b}^\perp \tag{6}$$

Eqn. (6) basically says that $\mathbf{a}^\perp$ and $\mathbf{b}^\perp$ are the respective eigenvectors of $\mathbf{V}$ and $\mathbf{V}^\top$. Now, consider the following "change of variables" in the first distribution, namely, replace

$$\mathbf{W}_i \ \text{with} \ \mathbf{W}_i + u_i(\mathbf{a}^{\perp\top}\mathbf{b}^\perp)^{-1}\mathbf{V}, \ i = 1, \ldots, n.$$

Clearly, this does not change the first distribution. Now, observe that

$$\left[(\mathbf{W}_i + u_i(\mathbf{a}^{\perp\top}\mathbf{b}^\perp)^{-1}\mathbf{V})^\top\mathbf{A}\right]_1 = [\mathbf{W}_i^\top\mathbf{A}]_1;$$

$$\left[(\mathbf{W}_i + u_i(\mathbf{a}^{\perp\top}\mathbf{b}^\perp)^{-1}\mathbf{V})\mathbf{B}\right]_2 = [\mathbf{W}_i\mathbf{B}]_2$$

where we use (5) in the last equalities. That is, pp remains unchanged. In addition, we have

$$\left[(\mathbf{W}_i + u_i(\mathbf{a}^{\perp^\top}\mathbf{b}^\perp)^{-1}\mathbf{V})^\top\mathbf{b}^\perp\right]_1 = \left[\mathbf{W}_i^\top\mathbf{b}^\perp + u_i\mathbf{b}^\perp\right]_1;$$

$$\left[(\mathbf{W}_i + u_i(\mathbf{a}^{\perp^\top}\mathbf{b}^\perp)^{-1}\mathbf{V})\mathbf{a}^\perp\right]_2 = \left[\mathbf{W}_i\mathbf{a}^\perp + u_i\mathbf{a}^\perp\right]_2$$

where we use (6) in the last equalities. Indeed, this is exactly the second distribution.   □

5   Predicate Encodings

In this section, we describe a refinement of the predicate encodings from [2,31] which we use in this work. We refer to Sect. 1.1 for an overview of the refinement.

Predicate Encodings. Fix a predicate $P : \mathcal{X} \times \mathcal{Y} \rightarrow \{0,1\}$. A $\mathbb{Z}_p$-*bilinear predicate encoding* for P is a tuple of deterministic algorithms (sE, rE, kE, sD, rD) satisfying the following properties:

(linearity.) For all $(x,y) \in \mathcal{X} \times \mathcal{Y}$, the functions $sE(x,\cdot)$, $rE(y,\cdot)$, $kE(y,\cdot)$, $sD(x,y,\cdot)$, $rD(x,y,\cdot)$ are $\mathbb{Z}_p$-linear.

(restricted α-reconstruction.) For all $(x,y) \in \mathcal{X} \times \mathcal{Y}$ such that $P(x,y) = 1$ and for all $\mathbf{w} \in \mathcal{W}$:

$$sD(x,y,sE(x,\mathbf{w})) = rD(x,y,rE(y,\mathbf{w})) \quad \text{and} \quad rD(x,y,kE(y,\alpha)) = \alpha.$$

(α-privacy.) For all $(x,y) \in \mathcal{X} \times \mathcal{Y}$ such that $P(x,y) = 0$, and for all $\alpha \in \mathbb{Z}_p$, the joint distribution $\{sE(x,\mathbf{w}), kE(y,\alpha) + rE(y,\mathbf{w})\}$ *perfectly* hides α. That is, for all $\alpha \in \mathbb{Z}_p$, the following joint distributions[2] are *identically* distributed:

$$\{x,y,\alpha,sE(x,\mathbf{w}),kE(y,\alpha)+rE(y,\mathbf{w})\} \quad \text{and} \quad \{x,y,\alpha,sE(x,\mathbf{w}),rE(y,\mathbf{w})\}$$

where the randomness is taken over $\mathbf{w} \leftarrow_R \mathcal{W}$.

Remark 3. Given a predicate encoding as defined above, we can construct an encoding (rE', sE') which achieves the notion in [2,31] by considering:

$$sE' = sE \quad \text{and} \quad rE'(y,\alpha,\mathbf{w},r) = (r, kE(y,\alpha) + r \cdot rE(y,\mathbf{w})).$$

Note that rE' leaks no information about $\mathbf{w}$ when $r = 0$ which trivially yields the $\mathbf{w}$-hiding property in [31] (aka parameter-hiding in [2]). Here, we use the fact that kE does not depend on $\mathbf{w}$.

---

[2] Note that since $kE(y,\cdot)$ is $\mathbb{Z}_p$-linear, we have $kE(y,0) + rE(y,\mathbf{w}) = rE(y,\mathbf{w})$.

Example: Equality. Fix a prime integer p. Consider the equality predicate where $\mathcal{X} = \mathcal{Y} = \mathbb{Z}_p$ and $P(x, y) = 1$ iff $x = y$. The following is a predicate encoding for equality used in [4,21]:

$$\mathsf{sE}(x, (w_1, w_2)) := w_1 + w_2 x \quad \mathsf{rE}(y, (w_1, w_2)) := w_1 + w_2 y \quad \mathsf{kE}(y, \alpha) := \alpha$$

$$\mathsf{sD}(x, y, c) = c \qquad\qquad \mathsf{rD}(x, y, k) = k$$

When $x = y$, $w_1 + w_2 x = w_1 + w_2 y$ and we can reconstruct α. For α-privacy, we exploit the fact that $(w_1 + w_2 x, w_1 + w_2 y)$ are pairwise independent when $x \neq y$.

6   ABE from Dual System Groups and Predicate Encodings

Starting from a predicate encoding for P, we construct an ABE for P using dual system groups. We refer to Sect. 1.1 for an overview of the scheme, which is of the form:

$$\mathsf{mpk} := \left(g_1, \; g_1^{\mathbf{w}}, \; e(g_1, g_1)^{\alpha} \right)$$

$$\mathsf{sk}_y := \left(g_1^r, \; g_1^{\mathsf{kE}(y, \alpha) + r \cdot \mathsf{rE}(y, \mathbf{w})} \right)$$

$$\mathsf{ct}_x := \left(g_1^s, \; g_1^{s \cdot \mathsf{sE}(x, \mathbf{w})}, \; e(g_1, g_1)^{\alpha s} \cdot m \right)$$

We will generate mpk using $\mathsf{SampP}(1^\lambda, 1^n)$, where $\mathbf{w} \in \mathbb{Z}_p^n$. We will use $\mathsf{SampG}(\mathsf{pp})$ to generate the terms $(g_1^s, g_1^{s\mathbf{w}})$ in the ciphertext, from which we can compute $(g_1^s, g_1^{s \cdot \mathsf{sE}(x, \mathbf{w})})$ by linearity of $\mathsf{sE}(x, \cdot)$. Similarly, we use $\mathsf{SampH}(\mathsf{pp})$ to generate the terms $(g_1^r, g_1^{r\mathbf{w}})$ in the secret key, from which we can compute $(g_1^r, g_1^{r \cdot \mathsf{rE}(y, \mathbf{w})})$. We replace g_1^α with $\mathsf{msk} \leftarrow_{\mathrm{R}} \mathbb{H}$.

6.1   Construction

$\mathsf{Setup}(1^\lambda, 1^n)$: On input $(1^\lambda, 1^n)$, first sample

$$(\mathsf{pp}, \mathsf{sp}) \leftarrow \mathsf{SampP}(1^\lambda, 1^n).$$

Pick $\mathsf{msk} \leftarrow_{\mathrm{R}} \mathbb{H}$ and output the master public and secret key pair

$$\mathsf{mpk} := (\, \mathsf{pp}, \; \mu(\mathsf{msk}) \,) \quad \text{and} \quad \mathsf{msk}.$$

$\mathsf{Enc}(\mathsf{mpk}, x, m)$: On input $x \in \mathcal{X}$ and $m \in \mathbb{G}_T$, sample

$$(g_0, g_1, \ldots, g_n) \leftarrow \mathsf{SampG}(\mathsf{pp}; s), \; g_T' \leftarrow \mathsf{SampGT}(\mu(\mathsf{msk}); s)$$

and output[3]

$$\mathsf{ct}_x := (\, C_0 := g_0, \; \mathbf{C}_1 := \mathsf{sE}(x, (g_1, \ldots, g_n)), \; C' := g_T' \cdot m \,).$$

---

[3] See Remark 1 for an explanation of the function $\mathsf{sE}(x, (g_1, \ldots, g_n))$.

KeyGen(mpk, msk, y): On input $y \in \mathcal{Y}$, sample

$$(h_0, h_1, \ldots, h_n) \leftarrow \mathsf{SampH}(\mathsf{pp})$$

and output

$$\mathsf{sk}_y := (\ K_0 := h_0,\ \mathbf{K}_1 := \mathsf{kE}(y, \mathsf{msk}) \cdot \mathsf{rE}(y, (h_1, \ldots, h_n))\ ).$$

Dec(mpk, sk_y, ct_x): Compute

$$e(g_0, \mathsf{msk}) \leftarrow e(C_0, \mathsf{rD}(x, y, \mathbf{K}_1)) / e(\mathsf{sD}(x, y, \mathbf{C}_1), K_0)$$

and recover the message as

$$m \leftarrow C' \cdot e(g_0, \mathsf{msk})^{-1} \in \mathbb{G}_T.$$

Correctness. For all $(x, y) \in \mathcal{X} \times \mathcal{Y}$ such that $\mathsf{P}(x, y) = 1$, we have

$$
\begin{aligned}
&e(C_0, \mathsf{rD}(x, y, \mathbf{K}_1)) \\
&= e(g_0, \mathsf{rD}(x, y, \mathsf{rE}(y, (h_1, \ldots, h_n)))) \cdot e(g_0, \mathsf{rD}(x, y, \mathsf{kE}(y, \mathsf{msk}))) \\
&= e(g_0, \mathsf{rD}(x, y, \mathsf{rE}(y, (h_1, \ldots, h_n)))) \cdot e(g_0, \mathsf{msk}) \\
&= \mathsf{rD}(x, y, \mathsf{rE}(y, (e(g_0, h_1), \ldots, e(g_0, h_n)))) \cdot e(g_0, \mathsf{msk}) \\
&= \mathsf{rD}(x, y, \mathsf{rE}(y, (e(g_1, h_0), \ldots, e(g_n, h_0)))) \cdot e(g_0, \mathsf{msk}) \\
&= \mathsf{sD}(x, y, \mathsf{sE}(x, (e(g_1, h_0), \ldots, e(g_n, h_0)))) \cdot e(g_0, \mathsf{msk}) \\
&= e(\mathsf{sD}(x, y, \mathsf{sE}(x(g_1, \ldots, g_n))), h_0) \cdot e(g_0, \mathsf{msk}) \\
&= e(\mathsf{sD}(x, y, \mathbf{C}_1), K_0) \cdot e(g_0, \mathsf{msk})
\end{aligned}
$$

In line 2, we use linearity of $\mathsf{rD}(x, y, \cdot)$ and $e(g_0, \cdot)$. In line 3 and line 6, we use α-reconstruction. In line 4 and line 7, we use the fact that the functions $e(g_0, \cdot)$, $e(\cdot, h_0)$ and $\mathsf{sD}(x, y, \mathsf{sE}(y, \cdot))$ commute with linear functions. That is, given a $\mathbb{Z}_p$-linear function $L : \mathbb{Z}_p^n \rightarrow \mathbb{Z}_p$ given by $(w_1, \ldots, w_n) \mapsto a_1 w_1 + \cdots + a_n w_n$, we have:

$$
\begin{aligned}
e(g_0, L(h_1, \ldots, h_n)) &= e(g_0, h_1^{a_1} \cdots h_n^{a_n}) \\
&= e(g_0, h_1)^{a_1} \cdots e(g_0, h_n)^{a_n} \\
&= L(e(g_0, h_1), \ldots, e(g_0, h_n))
\end{aligned}
$$

In line 5, we use associativity in DSG. Finally, by *projective*, $g_T' = e(g_0, \mathsf{msk})$. Correctness follows readily.

game	ciphertext $(C_0, \mathbf{C}_1, C')$	secret key $(K_0, \mathbf{K}_1)$	justification
0	$(1, \mathbf{1}, 1)$	$(1, (h^*)^{\mathsf{kE}(y,0)} \cdot \mathbf{1})$	$\mathbf{1} = (h^*)^{\mathsf{kE}(y,0)}$
1	$\boxed{(\hat{g}_0, \mathsf{sE}(x, \hat{\mathbf{g}}), e(\hat{g}_0, \mathsf{msk}))}$	$(1, (h^*)^{\mathsf{kE}(y,0)} \cdot \mathbf{1})$	left subgroup ind
2.i.1	$(\hat{g}_0, \mathsf{sE}(x, \hat{\mathbf{g}}), e(\hat{g}_0, \mathsf{msk}))$	$(\boxed{\hat{h}_0}, (h^*)^{\mathsf{kE}(y,0)} \cdot \boxed{\mathsf{rE}(y, \hat{\mathbf{h}})})$	right subgroup ind
2.i.2	$(\hat{g}_0, \mathsf{sE}(x, \hat{\mathbf{g}}), e(\hat{g}_0, \mathsf{msk}))$	$(\hat{h}_0, \boxed{(h^*)^{\mathsf{kE}(y,\alpha)}} \cdot \mathsf{rE}(y, \hat{\mathbf{h}}))$	α-privacy
2.i.3	$(\hat{g}_0, \mathsf{sE}(x, \hat{\mathbf{g}}), e(\hat{g}_0, \mathsf{msk}))$	$(\boxed{1}, (h^*)^{\mathsf{kE}(y,\alpha)} \cdot \boxed{\mathbf{1}})$	right subgroup ind
3	$(\hat{g}_0, \mathsf{sE}(x, \hat{\mathbf{g}}), \boxed{\text{random}})$	$(1, (h^*)^{\mathsf{kE}(y,\alpha)} \cdot \mathbf{1})$	

Fig. 3. Sequence of games in the "semi-functional" space. We omitted the normal components: those sampled using $\mathsf{SampG}, \mathsf{SampH}$, and we omitted $e(g_0, \mathsf{msk}) \cdot m$ in C' and $\mathsf{kE}(y, \mathsf{msk})$ in sk_y. We drew a box to highlight the differences between each game and the preceding one, and games $2.i.\text{x}$ refer to the i'th secret key. The semi-functional components of the keys transition from $(h^*)^{\mathsf{kE}(y,0)}$ to $(h^*)^{\mathsf{kE}(y,\alpha)}$. For the final transition, we use the fact that $e(\hat{g}_0, \mathsf{msk})$ is statistically random given $\mathsf{msk} \cdot (h^*)^\alpha$.

6.2 Proof of Security

We prove the following theorem:

Theorem 1. *Under the left and right subgroup indistinguishability (described in Sect. 3), the ABE scheme described in Sect. 6.1 is adaptively secure (in the sense of Definition 2.1). More precisely, for any adversary $\mathcal{A}$ that makes at most q key queries against the ABE scheme, there exist adversaries $\mathcal{B}_1, \mathcal{B}_2, \mathcal{B}_3$ such that:*

$$\mathsf{Adv}_{\mathcal{A}}^{\mathrm{ABE}}(\lambda) \leq \mathsf{Adv}_{\mathcal{B}_1}^{\mathrm{LS}}(\lambda) + q \cdot \mathsf{Adv}_{\mathcal{B}_2}^{\mathrm{RS}}(\lambda) + q \cdot \mathsf{Adv}_{\mathcal{B}_3}^{\mathrm{RS}}(\lambda)$$

and

$$\max\{\mathsf{Time}(\mathcal{B}_1), \mathsf{Time}(\mathcal{B}_2), \mathsf{Time}(\mathcal{B}_3)\} \approx \mathsf{Time}(\mathcal{A}) + q \cdot \mathrm{poly}(\lambda, n)$$

where $\mathrm{poly}(\lambda, n)$ *is independent of* $\mathsf{Time}(\mathcal{A})$.

The proof follows via a series of games, analogous to that in [10,21,30,31], and outlined in Fig. 3. We first define two auxiliary algorithms and then the semi-functional distributions, upon which we can describe the games.

Auxiliary Algorithms. We consider the following algorithms:

$\widehat{\mathsf{Enc}}(\mathsf{pp}, x, m; \mathsf{msk}, \mathbf{t})$: On input $x \in \mathcal{X}$, $m \in \mathbb{G}_T$, and $\mathbf{t} := (T_0, T_1, \ldots, T_n) \in \mathbb{G}^{n+1}$, output

$$\mathsf{ct}_x := (\, T_0, \; \mathsf{sE}(x, (T_1, \ldots, T_n)), \; e(T_0, \mathsf{msk}) \cdot m \,).$$

$\widehat{\mathsf{KeyGen}}(\mathsf{pp}, \mathsf{msk}', y; \mathbf{t})$: On input $\mathsf{msk}' \in \mathbb{H}$, $y \in \mathcal{Y}$, and $\mathbf{t} := (T_0, T_1, \ldots, T_n) \in \mathbb{H}^{n+1}$, output

$$\mathsf{sk}_y := (\, T_0, \; \mathsf{kE}(y, \mathsf{msk}') \cdot \mathsf{rE}(y, (T_1, \ldots, T_n)) \,).$$

In all the proofs and figures that follow, we denote $\mathsf{sE}(x, (T_1, \ldots, T_n))$ by $\mathsf{sE}(x, \mathbf{t})$ for notational convenience, and we define $\mathsf{rE}(y, \mathbf{t})$ analogously.

Auxiliary Distributions.

Semi-functional Master Secret Key.

$$\widehat{\mathsf{msk}} := \mathsf{msk} \cdot (h^*)^\alpha,$$

where $\boxed{\alpha \leftarrow_{\mathrm{R}} \mathbb{Z}_p}$.

Semi-functional Ciphertext.

$$\widehat{\mathsf{Enc}}(\mathsf{pp}, x, m; \mathsf{msk}, \boxed{\mathbf{g} \cdot \hat{\mathbf{g}}}),$$

where $\boxed{\mathbf{g} \leftarrow \mathsf{SampG}(\mathsf{pp}) \text{ and } \hat{\mathbf{g}} \leftarrow \widehat{\mathsf{SampG}}(\mathsf{pp}, \mathsf{sp})}$.

Pseudo-normal Secret Key.

$$\widehat{\mathsf{KeyGen}}(\mathsf{pp}, \mathsf{msk}, y; \boxed{\mathbf{h} \cdot \hat{\mathbf{h}}}),$$

where fresh $\boxed{\mathbf{h} \leftarrow \mathsf{SampH}(\mathsf{pp}) \text{ and } \hat{\mathbf{h}} \leftarrow \widehat{\mathsf{SampH}}(\mathsf{pp}, \mathsf{sp})}$ are chosen for each secret key.

Pseudo-SF Secret Key.

$$\widehat{\mathsf{KeyGen}}(\mathsf{pp}, \boxed{\widehat{\mathsf{msk}}}, y; \mathbf{h} \cdot \hat{\mathbf{h}}),$$

where fresh $\mathbf{h} \leftarrow \mathsf{SampH}(\mathsf{pp})$ and $\hat{\mathbf{h}} \leftarrow \widehat{\mathsf{SampH}}(\mathsf{pp}, \mathsf{sp})$ are chosen for each secret key.

Semi-functional Secret Key.

$$\widehat{\mathsf{KeyGen}}(\mathsf{pp}, \widehat{\mathsf{msk}}, y; \boxed{\mathbf{h}}),$$

where a fresh $\boxed{\mathbf{h} \leftarrow \mathsf{SampH}(\mathsf{pp})}$ is chosen for each secret key. We note that the semi-functional key generation algorithm is identical to the normal key generation except that it replaces msk with $\widehat{\mathsf{msk}}$ as input.

Game Sequence. We present a series of games. We write $\mathsf{Adv}_{\mathrm{xxx}}(\lambda)$ to denote the advantage of $\mathcal{A}$ in $\mathsf{Game}_{\mathrm{xxx}}$.

- Game_0: is the real security game (c.f. Sect. 2.1).
- Game_1: is the same as Game_0 except that the challenge ciphertext is semi-functional.
- $\mathsf{Game}_{2,i,1}$ for i from 1 to q, $\mathsf{Game}_{2,i,1}$ is the same as Game_1 except that the first $i-1$ keys are semi-functional, the last $q-i$ keys are normal while the i'th key is pseudo-normal.

- $\mathsf{Game}_{2,i,2}$ for i from 1 to q, $\mathsf{Game}_{2,i,2}$ is the same as Game_1 except that the first $i - 1$ keys are semi-functional, the last $q - i$ keys are normal while the i'th key is pseudo-SF.

- $\mathsf{Game}_{2,i,3}$ for i from 1 to q, $\mathsf{Game}_{2,i,3}$ is the same as Game_1 except that the first i keys are semi-functional, the last $q - i$ keys are normal.

- Game_3: is the same as $\mathsf{Game}_{2,q,3}$, except that the challenge ciphertext is a semi-functional encryption of a random message in $\mathbb{G}_T$.

In Game_3, the view of the adversary is statistically independent of the challenge bit b. Hence, $\mathsf{Adv}_3(\lambda) = 0$. We complete the proof by establishing the following sequence of lemmas. We omit the proofs of lemmas 5, 6, 8, 9 as they are the same as those of lemmas 1, 2, 5, 6 in [10, Section 4].

Lemma 5 (Normal to SF Ciphertext: Game_0 to Game_1). *For any adversary $\mathcal{A}$ that makes at most q key queries, there exists an adversary $\mathcal{B}_1$ such that*

$$|\mathsf{Adv}_0(\lambda) - \mathsf{Adv}_1(\lambda)| \leq \mathsf{Adv}_{\mathcal{B}_1}^{\mathrm{LS}}(\lambda)$$

and $\mathsf{Time}(\mathcal{B}_1) \approx \mathsf{Time}(\mathcal{A}) + q \cdot \mathrm{poly}(\lambda, n)$ where $\mathrm{poly}(\lambda, n)$ is independent of $\mathsf{Time}(\mathcal{A})$.

Lemma 6 (Normal to Pseudo-Normal Keys: $\mathsf{Game}_{2,i-1,3}$ to $\mathsf{Game}_{2,i,1}$). *For $i = 1, \ldots, q$, for any adversary $\mathcal{A}$ that makes at most q key queries, there exists an adversary $\mathcal{B}_2$ such that*

$$|\mathsf{Adv}_{2,i-1,3}(\lambda) - \mathsf{Adv}_{2,i,1}(\lambda)| \leq \mathsf{Adv}_{\mathcal{B}_2}^{\mathrm{RS}}(\lambda)$$

and $\mathsf{Time}(\mathcal{B}_2) \approx \mathsf{Time}(\mathcal{A}) + q \cdot \mathrm{poly}(\lambda, n)$ where $\mathrm{poly}(\lambda, n)$ is independent of $\mathsf{Time}(\mathcal{A})$. (We note that $\mathsf{Game}_{2,0,3}$ is identical to Game_1.)

Lemma 7 (Pseudo-Normal to Pseudo-SF Keys: $\mathsf{Game}_{2,i,1}$ to $\mathsf{Game}_{2,i,2}$). *For $i = 1, \ldots, q$, we have*

$$|\mathsf{Adv}_{2,i,1}(\lambda) - \mathsf{Adv}_{2,i,2}(\lambda)| = 0.$$

Proof. Observe that the only difference between $\mathsf{Game}_{2,i,1}$ and $\mathsf{Game}_{2,i,2}$ lies in that we replace msk in $\mathsf{Game}_{2,i,1}$ with $\widehat{\mathsf{msk}}$ in $\mathsf{Game}_{2,i,2}$ as input for the i'th secret key query, where $\mathsf{msk} \leftarrow_{\mathrm{R}} \mathbb{H}$, $\alpha \leftarrow_{\mathrm{R}} \mathbb{Z}_p$ and $\widehat{\mathsf{msk}} := \mathsf{msk} \cdot (h^*)^{\alpha}$. Thus, it suffices to establish the following:

Claim. or all α, all $x \in \mathcal{X}$ and $y \in \mathcal{Y}$, where $\mathsf{P}(x, y) = 0$, the following distributions are identically distributed:

$$\{\mathsf{pp}, \mathsf{msk}, (h^*)^{\alpha}, \widehat{\mathsf{Enc}}(\mathsf{pp}, x, m_{\beta}; \mathsf{msk}, \mathbf{g} \cdot \hat{\mathbf{g}}), \widehat{\mathsf{KeyGen}}(\mathsf{pp}, \boxed{\mathsf{msk}}, y; \mathbf{h} \cdot \hat{\mathbf{h}})\} \quad \text{and}$$

$$\{\mathsf{pp}, \mathsf{msk}, (h^*)^{\alpha}, \widehat{\mathsf{Enc}}(\mathsf{pp}, x, m_{\beta}; \mathsf{msk}, \mathbf{g} \cdot \hat{\mathbf{g}}), \widehat{\mathsf{KeyGen}}(\mathsf{pp}, \boxed{\mathsf{msk} \cdot (h^*)^{\alpha}}, y; \mathbf{h} \cdot \hat{\mathbf{h}})\}.$$

We defer the proof of the claim for now, and first explain how the lemma follows from the claim. Given $(\mathsf{pp}, \mathsf{msk}, (h^*)^\alpha)$, we can output $\mathsf{mpk} := (\mathsf{pp}, \mu(\mathsf{msk}))$ and generate the first $i-1$ semi-functional secret keys, and the remaining $q-i$ normal secret keys using

$$\widehat{\mathsf{KeyGen}}(\mathsf{pp}, \mathsf{msk} \cdot (h^*)^\alpha, y; \mathsf{SampH}(\mathsf{pp})) \quad \text{and} \quad \widehat{\mathsf{KeyGen}}(\mathsf{pp}, \mathsf{msk}, y; \mathsf{SampH}(\mathsf{pp}))$$

respectively.

This would in turn imply that $\mathsf{Game}_{2,i,1}$ and $\mathsf{Game}_{2,i,2}$ are statistically indistinguishable. We note that this holds even if the adversary chooses y adaptively after seeing the challenge ciphertext ct_{x^*}, or if the challenge x^* is chosen after the adversary sees sk_y. $\square$

Proof (of Claim). By linearity, we have:

$$\widehat{\mathsf{Enc}}(\mathsf{pp}, x, m_\beta; \mathsf{msk}, \mathbf{g} \cdot \hat{\mathbf{g}}) = \widehat{\mathsf{Enc}}(\mathsf{pp}, x, m_\beta; \mathsf{msk}, \mathbf{g}) \cdot \widehat{\mathsf{Enc}}(\mathsf{pp}, x, 1; \mathsf{msk}, \hat{\mathbf{g}})$$

$$\widehat{\mathsf{KeyGen}}(\mathsf{pp}, \mathsf{msk}, y; \mathbf{h} \cdot \hat{\mathbf{h}}) = \widehat{\mathsf{KeyGen}}(\mathsf{pp}, \mathsf{msk}, y; \mathbf{h}) \cdot \widehat{\mathsf{KeyGen}}(\mathsf{pp}, 1, y; \hat{\mathbf{h}})$$

$$\widehat{\mathsf{KeyGen}}(\mathsf{pp}, \mathsf{msk} \cdot (h^*)^\alpha, y; \mathbf{h} \cdot \hat{\mathbf{h}}) = \widehat{\mathsf{KeyGen}}(\mathsf{pp}, \mathsf{msk}, y; \mathbf{h}) \cdot \widehat{\mathsf{KeyGen}}(\mathsf{pp}, (h^*)^\alpha, y; \hat{\mathbf{h}})$$

Therefore, it suffices to show that:

$$\{\mathsf{pp}, \mathsf{msk}, (h^*)^\alpha, \widehat{\mathsf{Enc}}(\mathsf{pp}, x, 1; \mathsf{msk}, \hat{\mathbf{g}}), \widehat{\mathsf{KeyGen}}(\mathsf{pp}, \boxed{1}, y; \hat{\mathbf{h}})\} \quad \text{and}$$

$$\{\mathsf{pp}, \mathsf{msk}, (h^*)^\alpha, \widehat{\mathsf{Enc}}(\mathsf{pp}, x, 1; \mathsf{msk}, \hat{\mathbf{g}}), \widehat{\mathsf{KeyGen}}(\mathsf{pp}, \boxed{(h^*)^\alpha}, y; \hat{\mathbf{h}})\}$$

are identically distributed.

By parameter-hiding, we may replace $(\mathsf{pp}, h^*, \boxed{\hat{\mathbf{g}}, \hat{\mathbf{h}}})$ with $(\mathsf{pp}, h^*, \boxed{\hat{\mathbf{g}} \cdot \hat{\mathbf{g}}', \hat{\mathbf{h}} \cdot \hat{\mathbf{h}}'})$, which means it suffices to show that:

$$\{\mathsf{pp}, \mathsf{msk}, (h^*)^\alpha, \widehat{\mathsf{Enc}}(\mathsf{pp}, x, 1; \mathsf{msk}, \hat{\mathbf{g}} \cdot \hat{\mathbf{g}}'), \widehat{\mathsf{KeyGen}}(\mathsf{pp}, \boxed{1}, y; \hat{\mathbf{h}} \cdot \hat{\mathbf{h}}')\} \quad \text{and}$$

$$\{\mathsf{pp}, \mathsf{msk}, (h^*)^\alpha, \widehat{\mathsf{Enc}}(\mathsf{pp}, x, 1; \mathsf{msk}, \hat{\mathbf{g}} \cdot \hat{\mathbf{g}}'), \widehat{\mathsf{KeyGen}}(\mathsf{pp}, \boxed{(h^*)^\alpha}, y; \hat{\mathbf{h}} \cdot \hat{\mathbf{h}}')\}$$

are identically distributed. At this point, we expand the expressions for $\widehat{\mathsf{Enc}}$ and $\widehat{\mathsf{KeyGen}}$:

$$\widehat{\mathsf{Enc}}(\mathsf{pp}, x, 1; \mathsf{msk}, \hat{\mathbf{g}} \cdot \hat{\mathbf{g}}') = (\hat{g}_0, \mathsf{sE}(x, \hat{\mathbf{g}}) \cdot \mathsf{sE}(x, \hat{\mathbf{g}}'), e(\hat{g}_0, \mathsf{msk}))$$

$$= (\hat{g}_0, \mathsf{sE}(x, \hat{\mathbf{g}}) \cdot \hat{g}_0^{\mathsf{sE}(x, \mathbf{u})}, e(\hat{g}_0, \mathsf{msk}))$$

where $\mathbf{u}$ denotes the vector $\mathbf{u} := (u_1, \ldots, u_n)$ and thus $\mathsf{sE}(x, \hat{\mathbf{g}}') = \mathsf{sE}(x, \hat{g}_0^{\mathbf{u}}) = \hat{g}_0^{\mathsf{sE}(x, \mathbf{u})}$;

$$\widehat{\mathsf{KeyGen}}(\mathsf{pp}, 1, y; \hat{\mathbf{h}} \cdot \hat{\mathbf{h}}') = (\hat{h}_0, \mathsf{rE}(y, \hat{\mathbf{h}}) \cdot \hat{h}_0^{\mathsf{rE}(y, \mathbf{u})})$$

$$\widehat{\mathsf{KeyGen}}(\mathsf{pp}, (h^*)^\alpha, y; \hat{\mathbf{h}} \cdot \hat{\mathbf{h}}') = (\hat{h}_0, \mathsf{kE}(y, (h^*)^\alpha) \cdot \mathsf{rE}(y, \hat{\mathbf{h}}) \cdot \hat{h}_0^{\mathsf{rE}(y, \mathbf{u})})$$

Since h^* lies in the group generated by $\hat{h}_0$, we have $\mathsf{kE}(y, (h^*)^\alpha) = \mathsf{kE}(y, (h_0)^{\alpha'}) = \hat{h}_0^{\mathsf{kE}(y,\alpha')}$ for some $\alpha' \in \mathbb{Z}_p$; the claim then follows readily from α'-privacy, that is, $\mathsf{rE}(y, \mathbf{u})$ and $\mathsf{kE}(y, \alpha') + \mathsf{rE}(y, \mathbf{u})$ are identically distributed. $\qquad\square$

Lemma 8 (Pseudo-SF to SF Keys: $\mathsf{Game}_{2,i,2}$ to $\mathsf{Game}_{2,i,3}$). *For $i = 1, \ldots, q$, for any adversary $\mathcal{A}$ that makes at most q key queries, there exists an adversary $\mathcal{B}_3$ such that*

$$|\mathsf{Adv}_{2,i,2}(\lambda) - \mathsf{Adv}_{2,i,3}(\lambda)| \leq \mathsf{Adv}_{\mathcal{B}_3}^{\mathrm{RS}}(\lambda)$$

and $\mathsf{Time}(\mathcal{B}_3) \approx \mathsf{Time}(\mathcal{A}) + q \cdot \mathrm{poly}(\lambda, n)$ where $\mathrm{poly}(\lambda, n)$ is independent of $\mathsf{Time}(\mathcal{A})$.

Lemma 9 (Final Transition: $\mathsf{Game}_{2,q,3}$ to Game_3). *For any adversary $\mathcal{A}$, we have*

$$|\mathsf{Adv}_{2,q,3}(\lambda) - \mathsf{Adv}_3(\lambda)| = 0.$$

7 Extension to Weakly Attribute-Hiding

We present an extension of our framework to weakly attribute-hiding predicate encryption [6,19]. A predicate encryption scheme has the same syntax as an ABE in Sect. 2.1 except the attribute x on the ciphertext is not public; for security, we require in addition that x remains hidden from the adversary.

7.1 Security Definition

For a stateful adversary $\mathcal{A}$, we define the advantage function

$$\mathsf{Adv}_{\mathcal{A}}^{\mathrm{PE}}(\lambda) := \Pr\left[b = b' : \begin{array}{l} (\mathsf{mpk}, \mathsf{msk}) \leftarrow \mathsf{Setup}(1^\lambda, \mathcal{X}, \mathcal{Y}, \mathcal{M}); \\ (x_0^*, x_1^*, m_0, m_1) \leftarrow \mathcal{A}^{\mathsf{KeyGen}(\mathsf{msk}, \cdot)}(\mathsf{mpk}); \\ b \leftarrow_{\mathrm{R}} \{0, 1\}; \mathsf{ct}_{x_b^*} \leftarrow \mathsf{Enc}(\mathsf{mpk}, x_b^*, m_b); \\ b' \leftarrow \mathcal{A}^{\mathsf{KeyGen}(\mathsf{msk}, \cdot)}(\mathsf{ct}_{x_b^*}) \end{array} \right] - \frac{1}{2}$$

with the restriction that all queries y that $\mathcal{A}$ makes to $\mathsf{KeyGen}(\mathsf{msk}, \cdot)$ satisfies $\mathsf{P}(x_0^*, y) = \mathsf{P}(x_1^*, y) = 0$ (that is, sk_y does not decrypt the challenge ciphertext). A predicate encryption scheme is *adaptively secure and weakly attribute-hiding* if for all PPT adversaries $\mathcal{A}$, the advantage $\mathsf{Adv}_{\mathcal{A}}^{\mathrm{PE}}(\lambda)$ is a negligible function in λ.[4]

---

[4] In a fully attribute-hiding scheme, the adversary is also allowed key queries y for which $\mathsf{P}(x_0^*, y) = \mathsf{P}(x_1^*, y) = 1$, in which case the challenge messages m_0, m_1 must be equal.

7.2   Attribute-Hiding Encodings

We say that a $\mathbb{Z}_p$-bilinear predicate encoding (c.f. Section 5) for $\mathsf{P} : \mathcal{X} \times \mathcal{Y} \to \{0, 1\}$ is *attribute-hiding* if it satisfies the following additional properties:

(x-oblivious α-reconstruction.) $\mathsf{sD}(x, y, \cdot)$ and $\mathsf{rD}(x, y, \cdot)$ are independent of x.

(attribute-hiding.) For all $(x, y) \in \mathcal{X} \times \mathcal{Y}$ such that $\mathsf{P}(x, y) = 0$, the joint distribution of $\{\mathsf{sE}(x, \mathbf{w}), \mathsf{rE}(y, \mathbf{w})\}$ is uniformly random. That is, the following distributions are *identically* distributed:

$$\big\{x, y, \mathsf{sE}(x, \mathbf{w}), \mathsf{rE}(y, \mathbf{w})\big\} \quad \text{and} \quad \big\{x, y, \mathbf{v}\big\}$$

where the randomness is taken over $\mathbf{w} \leftarrow_{\mathrm{R}} \mathcal{W}$ and $\mathbf{v} \leftarrow_{\mathrm{R}} \mathbb{Z}_p^{|\mathsf{sE}(\cdot)| + |\mathsf{rE}(\cdot)|}$.

7.3   Attribute-Hiding Dual System Groups

Recall from the introduction in Sect. 1.1 that to realize weakly attribute-hiding predicate encryption, we will use the fact that for any vector $\mathbf{c} \in \mathbb{Z}_p^{k+1}$ outside the span of $\mathbf{A}$, the vector $\mathbf{W}^\top \mathbf{c} \in \mathbb{Z}_p^{k+1}$ is uniformly random given $\mathbf{W}^\top \mathbf{A} \in \mathbb{Z}_p^{(k+1) \times k}$, provided $\mathbf{WB}$ remains hidden. We can then use $\mathbf{W}^\top \mathbf{c}$ to completely blind the attribute in the challenge ciphertext. We also need to make sure that the semi-functional secret keys do not leak any *additional* information about $\mathbf{WB}$. The former is captured by $\mathbb{G}$-uniformity, and the latter by $\mathbb{H}$-hiding. In particular, the secret keys in the predicate encryption scheme satisfy the following properties:

– the distribution of normal secret keys is completely determined given $\mathbf{B}, \mathbf{W}_1\mathbf{B}, \dots, \mathbf{W}_n\mathbf{B}$ and leaks no *additional* information about $\mathbf{W}_1, \dots, \mathbf{W}_n$;
– the distribution of semi-functional secret keys is completely determined given $\mathbf{A}, \mathbf{W}_1^\top\mathbf{A}, \dots, \mathbf{W}_n^\top\mathbf{A}$ and leaks no *additional* information about $\mathbf{W}_1, \dots, \mathbf{W}_n$.

Additional properties. We assume that pp in dual system groups has a $\mathsf{pp}_{\mathbb{G}}$-component which is sufficient to run SampG. We then require dual system groups to satisfy the following additional properties.

($\mathbb{H}$-hiding) There is an (inefficient) randomized procedure SampH^* that given $\mathsf{pp}_{\mathbb{G}}$ and h^*, outputs a distribution identical to that of

$$\mathbf{h} \cdot (h^*)^{(0, \mathbf{v})}$$

where $\mathbf{h} \leftarrow \mathsf{SampH}(\mathsf{pp})$, $\mathbf{v} \leftarrow_{\mathrm{R}} \mathbb{Z}_p^n$.

($\mathbb{G}$-uniformity) The following distributions are identically distributed

$$\left\{ \mathsf{pp}_{\mathbb{G}}, h^*, \boxed{\mathbf{g} \cdot \hat{\mathbf{g}}} \right\} \quad \text{and} \quad \left\{ \mathsf{pp}_{\mathbb{G}}, h^*, \boxed{\mathbf{g}'} \right\}$$

where $(\mathsf{pp}, \mathsf{sp}) \leftarrow \mathsf{SampP}(1^\lambda, 1^n)$, $\mathbf{g} = (g_0, \dots) \leftarrow \mathsf{SampG}(\mathsf{pp})$, $\hat{\mathbf{g}} = (\hat{g}_0, \dots) \leftarrow \widehat{\mathsf{SampG}}(\mathsf{pp}, \mathsf{sp})$, $\mathbf{g}' \leftarrow_{\mathrm{R}} \{g_0\hat{g}_0\} \times \mathbb{G}^n$.

In the full version of this paper, we show that our instantiations satisfy the additional attribute-hiding requirements when $\mathsf{pp}_{\mathbb{G}}$ is defined to be:

$$\mathsf{pp}_{\mathbb{G}} := (\ (p, \mathbb{G}, \mathbb{H}, \mathbb{G}_T, e); [\mathbf{A}]_1, [\mathbf{W}_1^{\top}\mathbf{A}]_1, \ldots, [\mathbf{W}_n^{\top}\mathbf{A}]_1, [\mathbf{B}]_2\ ).$$

7.4 Weakly Attribute-Hiding PE

Starting from an attribute-hiding encoding and an attribute-hiding dual system group, we can construct a predicate encryption scheme as described in Sect. 6.1, with the following modification: we put $\mathsf{pp}_{\mathbb{G}}$ instead of pp in mpk (which suffices for SampG and Enc). We show that the ensuing scheme is weakly attribute-hiding:

Theorem 2. *Under the left and right subgroup indistinguishability (described in Sect. 3), the predicate encryption scheme described above is adaptively secure and weakly attribute-hiding (in the sense of Definition 7.1). More precisely, for any adversary $\mathcal{A}$ that makes at most q key queries against the predicate encryption scheme, there exist adversaries $\mathcal{B}_1, \mathcal{B}_2, \mathcal{B}_3$ such that:*

$$\mathsf{Adv}_{\mathcal{A}}^{\mathrm{PE}}(\lambda) \leq \mathsf{Adv}_{\mathcal{B}_1}^{\mathrm{LS}}(\lambda) + q \cdot \mathsf{Adv}_{\mathcal{B}_2}^{\mathrm{RS}}(\lambda) + q \cdot \mathsf{Adv}_{\mathcal{B}_3}^{\mathrm{RS}}(\lambda)$$

and

$$\max\{\mathsf{Time}(\mathcal{B}_1), \mathsf{Time}(\mathcal{B}_2), \mathsf{Time}(\mathcal{B}_3)\} \approx \mathsf{Time}(\mathcal{A}) + q \cdot \mathrm{poly}(\lambda, n)$$

where $\mathrm{poly}(\lambda, n)$ is independent of $\mathsf{Time}(\mathcal{A})$.

The proof follows via a series of games, outlined in Fig. 4.

Auxiliary Distributions. The auxiliary algorithms and distributions are the same as in Sect. 6.2 with the following modifications: (1) pseudo-SF and semi-functional secret keys have additional h^*-components, (2) $\widehat{\mathsf{Enc}}$ and $\widehat{\mathsf{KeyGen}}$ get as input $\mathsf{pp}_{\mathbb{G}}$ instead of pp (neither algorithm needs to run SampH).

Pseudo-SF Secret Key.

$$\widehat{\mathsf{KeyGen}}(\mathsf{pp}_{\mathbb{G}}, \boxed{\widehat{\mathsf{msk}}}, y; \boxed{\mathbf{h} \cdot \hat{\mathbf{h}} \cdot (h^*)^{(0,\mathbf{v})}}),$$

where fresh $\boxed{\mathbf{h} \leftarrow \mathsf{SampH}(\mathsf{pp}), \hat{\mathbf{h}} \leftarrow \widehat{\mathsf{SampH}}(\mathsf{pp}, \mathsf{sp}), \text{ and } \mathbf{v} \leftarrow_{\mathrm{R}} \mathbb{Z}_p^n}$ are chosen for each secret key.

Semi-functional Secret Key.

$$\widehat{\mathsf{KeyGen}}(\mathsf{pp}_{\mathbb{G}}, \widehat{\mathsf{msk}}, y; \boxed{\mathbf{h} \cdot (h^*)^{(0,\mathbf{v})}}),$$

where a fresh $\boxed{\mathbf{h} \leftarrow \mathsf{SampH}(\mathsf{pp}) \text{ and } \mathbf{v} \leftarrow_{\mathrm{R}} \mathbb{Z}_p^n}$ are chosen for each secret key.

game	ciphertext $(C_0, \mathbf{C}_1, C')$	secret key $(K_0, \mathbf{K}_1)$	justification
0	$(1, \mathbf{1}, 1)$	$(1, (h^*)^{\mathsf{kE}(y,0)} \cdot \mathbf{1})$	$\mathbf{1} = (h^*)^{\mathsf{kE}(y,0)}$
1	$\boxed{(\hat{g}_0, \mathsf{sE}(x, \hat{\mathbf{g}}), e(\hat{g}_0, \mathsf{msk}))}$	$(1, (h^*)^{\mathsf{kE}(y,0)} \cdot \mathbf{1})$	left subgroup ind
2.i.1	$(\hat{g}_0, \mathsf{sE}(x, \hat{\mathbf{g}}), e(\hat{g}_0, \mathsf{msk}))$	$(\boxed{\hat{h}_0}, (h^*)^{\mathsf{kE}(y,0)} \cdot \boxed{\mathsf{rE}(y, \hat{\mathbf{h}})})$	right subgroup ind
2.i.2	$(\hat{g}_0, \mathsf{sE}(x, \hat{\mathbf{g}}), e(\hat{g}_0, \mathsf{msk}))$	$(\hat{h}_0, \boxed{(h^*)^{\mathsf{kE}(y,\alpha)+\mathsf{rE}(y,\mathbf{v}_i)}} \cdot \mathsf{rE}(y, \hat{\mathbf{h}}))$	AH encoding
2.i.3	$(\hat{g}_0, \mathsf{sE}(x, \hat{\mathbf{g}}), e(\hat{g}_0, \mathsf{msk}))$	$(\boxed{1}, (h^*)^{\mathsf{kE}(y,\alpha)+\mathsf{rE}(y,\mathbf{v}_i)} \cdot \boxed{\mathbf{1}})$	right subgroup ind
3	$(\hat{g}_0, \mathsf{sE}(x, \hat{\mathbf{g}}), \boxed{\text{random}})$	$(1, (h^*)^{\mathsf{kE}(y,\alpha)+\mathsf{rE}(y,\mathbf{v}_i)} \cdot \mathbf{1})$	AH encoding
4	$(\hat{g}_0, \boxed{\text{random}}, \text{random})$	$(1, (h^*)^{\mathsf{kE}(y,\alpha)+\mathsf{rE}(y,\mathbf{v}_i)} \cdot \mathbf{1})$	AH encoding
			$\mathbb{H}$-hiding
			$\mathbb{G}$-uniformity

Fig. 4. Sequence of games in the "semi-functional" space for weakly attribute-hiding PE. We omitted the normal components: those sampled using $\mathsf{SampG}, \mathsf{SampH}$, and we omitted $e(g_0, \mathsf{msk}) \cdot m$ in C' and $\mathsf{kE}(y, \mathsf{msk})$ in sk_y. We drew a box to highlight the differences between each game and the preceding one, and games $2.i.x$ refer to the i'th secret key. The semi-functional components of the keys transition from $(h^*)^{\mathsf{kE}(y,0)}$ to $(h^*)^{\mathsf{kE}(y,\alpha)+\mathsf{rE}(y,\mathbf{v}_i)}$, with a fresh $\mathbf{v}_i \leftarrow_{\mathrm{R}} \mathbb{Z}_p^n$ for the i'th key. In the penultimate transition, we use the fact that $e(\hat{g}_0, \mathsf{msk})$ is statistically random given $\mathsf{msk} \cdot (h^*)^\alpha$. In the final transition, we use the fact that $\mathbf{C}_1$ (including normal components) is statistically random.

Game Sequence. We proceed exactly as in Sect. 6.2 with the same auxiliary algorithms but with the following modifications: (1) the distributions of pseudo-SF and semi-functional secret keys have additional h^*-components, (2) the challenge ciphertext uses the attribute x_b^* as defined in the security experiment, and (3) we append an extra game Game_4 where we switch x_b^* to random at the end:

- Game_0: is the real security game (c.f. Sect. 7.1).
- The descriptions of Game_1, $\mathsf{Game}_{2,i,1}$, $\mathsf{Game}_{2,i,2}$, $\mathsf{Game}_{2,i,3}$, and Game_3 are identical to those in Sect. 6.2, we omit them here.
- Game_4: is the same as Game_3, except we replace x_b^* in the challenge ciphertext with a random attribute $x^* \leftarrow_{\mathrm{R}} \mathcal{X}$.

In Game_4, the view of the adversary is statistically independent of the challenge bit b. Hence, $\mathsf{Adv}_4(\lambda) = 0$. We defer the proofs to the full version of this paper.

Acknowledgments. We thank Eike Kiltz and Jiaxin Pan for insightful discussions, and the anonymous reviewers for helpful feedback on the write-up.

References

1. Agrawal, S., Freeman, D.M., Vaikuntanathan, V.: Functional encryption for inner product predicates from learning with errors. In: Lee, D.H., Wang, X. (eds.) ASI-ACRYPT 2011. LNCS, vol. 7073, pp. 21–40. Springer, Heidelberg (2011)
2. Attrapadung, N.: Dual system encryption via doubly selective security: framework, fully secure functional encryption for regular languages, and more. In: Nguyen, P.Q., Oswald, E. (eds.) EUROCRYPT 2014. LNCS, vol. 8441, pp. 557–577. Springer, Heidelberg (2014)
3. Blazy, O., Kiltz, E., Pan, J.: (Hierarchical) identity-based encryption from affine message authentication. In: Garay, J.A., Gennaro, R. (eds.) CRYPTO 2014, Part I. LNCS, vol. 8616, pp. 408–425. Springer, Heidelberg (2014)
4. Boneh, D., Boyen, X.: Efficient selective-ID secure identity-based encryption without random oracles. In: Cachin, C., Camenisch, J.L. (eds.) EUROCRYPT 2004. LNCS, vol. 3027, pp. 223–238. Springer, Heidelberg (2004)
5. Boneh, D., Franklin, M.K.: Identity-based encryption from the Weil pairing. SIAM J. Comput. 32(3), 586–615 (2003)
6. Boneh, D., Waters, B.: Conjunctive, subset, and range queries on encrypted data. In: Vadhan, S.P. (ed.) TCC 2007. LNCS, vol. 4392, pp. 535–554. Springer, Heidelberg (2007), Also Cryptology ePrint Archive, Report 2006/287
7. Boneh, D., Boyen, X., Goh, E.-J.: Hierarchical identity based encryption with constant size ciphertext. In: Cramer, R. (ed.) EUROCRYPT 2005. LNCS, vol. 3494, pp. 440–456. Springer, Heidelberg (2005)
8. Boneh, D., Gentry, C., Gorbunov, S., Halevi, S., Nikolaenko, V., Segev, G., Vaikuntanathan, V., Vinayagamurthy, D.: Fully key-homomorphic encryption, arithmetic circuit ABE and compact garbled circuits. In: Nguyen, P.Q., Oswald, E. (eds.) EUROCRYPT 2014. LNCS, vol. 8441, pp. 533–556. Springer, Heidelberg (2014)
9. Chen, J., Wee, H.: Fully, (almost) tightly secure IBE and dual system groups. In: Canetti, R., Garay, J.A. (eds.) CRYPTO 2013, Part II. LNCS, vol. 8043, pp. 435–460. Springer, Heidelberg (2013)
10. Chen, J., Wee, H.: Dual system groups and its applications - compact HIBE and more. IACR Cryptology ePrint Archive, Report 2014/265 (2014), Preliminary version in [9]
11. Chen, J., Lim, H.W., Ling, S., Wang, H., Wee, H.: Shorter IBE and signatures via asymmetric pairings. In: Abdalla, M., Lange, T. (eds.) Pairing 2012. LNCS, vol. 7708, pp. 122–140. Springer, Heidelberg (2013)
12. Cocks, C.: An identity based encryption scheme based on quadratic residues. In: Honary, B. (ed.) Cryptography and Coding 2001. LNCS, vol. 2260, p. 360. Springer, Heidelberg (2001)
13. Escala, A., Herold, G., Kiltz, E., Ràfols, C., Villar, J.: An algebraic framework for Diffie-Hellman assumptions. In: Canetti, R., Garay, J.A. (eds.) CRYPTO 2013, Part II. LNCS, vol. 8043, pp. 129–147. Springer, Heidelberg (2013)
14. Freeman, D.M.: Converting pairing-based cryptosystems from composite-order groups to prime-order groups. In: Gilbert, H. (ed.) EUROCRYPT 2010. LNCS, vol. 6110, pp. 44–61. Springer, Heidelberg (2010)
15. Goyal, V., Pandey, O., Sahai, A., Waters, B.: Attribute-based encryption for fine-grained access control of encrypted data. In: ACM Conference on Computer and Communications Security, pp. 89–98 (2006)
16. Guillevic, A.: Comparing the pairing efficiency over composite-order and prime-order elliptic curves. In: Jacobson, M., Locasto, M., Mohassel, P., Safavi-Naini, R. (eds.) ACNS 2013. LNCS, vol. 7954, pp. 357–372. Springer, Heidelberg (2013)

17. Ishai, Y., Wee, H.: Partial garbling schemes and their applications. In: Esparza, J., Fraigniaud, P., Husfeldt, T., Koutsoupias, E. (eds.) ICALP 2014. LNCS, vol. 8572, pp. 650–662. Springer, Heidelberg (2014)

18. Jutla, C.S., Roy, A.: Shorter quasi-adaptive NIZK proofs for linear subspaces. In: Sako, K., Sarkar, P. (eds.) ASIACRYPT 2013, Part I. LNCS, vol. 8269, pp. 1–20. Springer, Heidelberg (2013)

19. Katz, J., Sahai, A., Waters, B.: Predicate encryption supporting disjunctions, polynomial equations, and inner products. In: Smart, N.P. (ed.) EUROCRYPT 2008. LNCS, vol. 4965, pp. 146–162. Springer, Heidelberg (2008)

20. Lewko, A.: Tools for simulating features of composite order bilinear groups in the prime order setting. In: Pointcheval, D., Johansson, T. (eds.) EUROCRYPT 2012. LNCS, vol. 7237, pp. 318–335. Springer, Heidelberg (2012)

21. Lewko, A., Waters, B.: New techniques for dual system encryption and fully secure HIBE with short ciphertexts. In: Micciancio, D. (ed.) TCC 2010. LNCS, vol. 5978, pp. 455–479. Springer, Heidelberg (2010)

22. Lewko, A., Okamoto, T., Sahai, A., Takashima, K., Waters, B.: Fully secure functional encryption: attribute-based encryption and (hierarchical) inner product encryption. In: Gilbert, H. (ed.) EUROCRYPT 2010. LNCS, vol. 6110, pp. 62–91. Springer, Heidelberg (2010)

23. Okamoto, T., Takashima, K.: Homomorphic encryption and signatures from vector decomposition. In: Galbraith, S.D., Paterson, K.G. (eds.) Pairing 2008. LNCS, vol. 5209, pp. 57–74. Springer, Heidelberg (2008)

24. Okamoto, T., Takashima, K.: Hierarchical predicate encryption for inner-products. In: Matsui, M. (ed.) ASIACRYPT 2009. LNCS, vol. 5912, pp. 214–231. Springer, Heidelberg (2009)

25. Okamoto, T., Takashima, K.: Fully secure functional encryption with general relations from the decisional linear assumption. In: Rabin, T. (ed.) CRYPTO 2010. LNCS, vol. 6223, pp. 191–208. Springer, Heidelberg (2010)

26. Okamoto, T., Takashima, K.: Achieving short ciphertexts or short secret-keys for adaptively secure general inner-product encryption. In: Lin, D., Tsudik, G., Wang, X. (eds.) CANS 2011. LNCS, vol. 7092, pp. 138–159. Springer, Heidelberg (2011), Also, Cryptology ePrint Archive, Report 2011/648

27. Sahai, A., Waters, B.: Fuzzy identity-based encryption. In: Cramer, R. (ed.) EURO-CRYPT 2005. LNCS, vol. 3494, pp. 457–473. Springer, Heidelberg (2005)

28. Shamir, A.: Identity-Based cryptosystems and signature schemes. In: Blakely, G.R., Chaum, D. (eds.) CRYPTO 1984. LNCS, vol. 196, pp. 47–53. Springer, Heidelberg (1985)

29. Takashima, K.: Expressive attribute-based encryption with constant-size ciphertexts from the decisional linear assumption. In: Abdalla, M., De Prisco, R. (eds.) SCN 2014. LNCS, vol. 8642, pp. 298–317. Springer, Heidelberg (2014)

30. Waters, B.: Dual system encryption: realizing fully secure IBE and HIBE under simple assumptions. In: Halevi, S. (ed.) CRYPTO 2009. LNCS, vol. 5677, pp. 619–636. Springer, Heidelberg (2009)

31. Wee, H.: Dual system encryption via predicate encodings. In: Lindell, Y. (ed.) TCC 2014. LNCS, vol. 8349, pp. 616–637. Springer, Heidelberg (2014)

Resistant Protocols

Resisting Randomness Subversion: Fast Deterministic and Hedged Public-Key Encryption in the Standard Model

Mihir Bellare[1]([✉]) and Viet Tung Hoang[2,3]

[1] Department of Computer Science and Engineering,
University of California San Diego, San Diego, USA
`mihir@eng.ucsd.edu`
[2] Department of Computer Science, Georgetown University,
Washington, DC, USA
[3] Department of Computer Science, University of Maryland,
College Park, USA

Abstract. This paper provides the first *efficient, standard-model, fully-secure* schemes for some related and challenging forms of public-key encryption (PKE), namely deterministic and hedged PKE. These forms of PKE defend against subversion of random number generators, an end given new urgency by recent revelations on the nature and extent of such subversion. We resolve the (recognized) technical challenges in reaching these goals via a new paradigm that combines UCEs (universal computational extractors) with LTDFs (lossy trapdoor functions). Crucially, we rely only on a weak form of UCE, namely security for statistically (rather than computationally) unpredictable sources. We then define and achieve unique-ciphertext PKE as a way to defend against implementation subversion via algorithm-substitution attacks.

1 Introduction

Recent revelations about the prevalence of mass-surveillance and subversion raise new challenges for cryptography. This paper is concerned with subversion of public-key encryption (PKE). We first consider randomness-subversion attacks, namely ones that undermine randomness-generation processes. Forms of PKE resisting these have in fact already been defined, namely deterministic public-key encryption (D-PKE) [3] and hedged public-key encryption (H-PKE) [4]. However, good schemes —we mean efficient ones providing full security in the standard model— are not only lacking but a recognized challenge [53]. With the new impetus and urgency arising from the subversion perspective, we revisit these goals to provide such schemes. We achieve our ends via a new PKE paradigm in which universal computational extractors (UCEs) [8] —of the weaker ilk requiring only statistical rather than computational unpredictability— are combined with lossy trapdoor functions (LTDFs) [48].

We then turn to defending against subversion of encryption implementations via algorithm-substitution attacks [12,56]. Here we follow [12] to define the

© International Association for Cryptologic Research 2015
E. Oswald and M. Fischlin (Eds.): EUROCRYPT 2015, Part II, LNCS 9057, pp. 627–656, 2015.
DOI: 10.1007/978-3-662-46803-6_21

new goal of unique ciphertext public-key encryption (U-PKE) and then reach it generically and efficiently from D-PKE.

Deterministic PKE. Technically, conceptually and historically, D-PKE is the core goal in this domain, and we begin there. The encryption algorithm of a D-PKE scheme takes public encryption key ek and message m to deterministically return a ciphertext c. We use the IND formalization of [6] which they show equivalent to the PRIV formalization of [3]. These formalizations capture the best possible privacy, namely semantic security for unpredictable messages that do not depend on the public key.

The core IND requirement asks for privacy when messages are individually unpredictable but may be arbitrarily correlated. We call this *full IND security* for emphasis. Full security is important in practice. For example, I might upload an encrypted file, then make a small edit to the file, re-encrypt and re-upload, so that the messages underlying the successive ciphertexts are very similar. It is thus the desired goal.

The EwH —encrypt with hash— D-PKE scheme of [3] encrypts message m under a (any) randomized IND-CPA scheme RE with the coins set to a hash of m. When the hash function is a random oracle, they showed EwH achieves full IND security. Achieving full IND security in the standard model however seemed out of reach. Many standard-model D-PKE schemes, using sophisticated techniques [6,11,17,19,30,33,49], have been proposed, but the security they achieve is not full. They only achieve security for *block sources*, where each message is assumed unpredictable *even given prior ones*, which is not realistic in practice.

The elusiveness of full security in the standard model was explained by Wichs [53], who showed that it could not be achieved under any single-stage assumption. To achieve full security one thus needs a multi-stage assumption. However most assumptions are single stage and it was not immediately clear what would even be a candidate for a suitable multi-stage assumption.

Such a candidate emerged with the UCE class of assumptions of security for hash functions of BHK1 [8]. The latter showed that the RO in EwH could be securely instantiated with a function family H that is $\mathsf{UCE}[\mathcal{S}^{\mathrm{cup}}]$ —UCE-secure for *computationally* unpredictable sources— to yield a standard model, fully IND secure D-PKE scheme. Unfortunately, soon after, Brzuska, Farshim and Mittelbach (BFM) [21] showed that $\mathsf{UCE}[\mathcal{S}^{\mathrm{cup}}]$-security is not achievable if indistinguishability obfuscation (iO) [2,34,35] is possible. BFM [21] and BHK1 [8] independently proposed to instead use $\mathsf{UCE}[\mathcal{S}^{\mathrm{sup}}]$— UCE-security for *statistically* unpredictable sources. BFM [21] give some evidence that their attacks will not extend to $\mathsf{UCE}[\mathcal{S}^{\mathrm{sup}}]$ and that this assumption is weaker.

This raises several questions. Can one show that the scheme EwH is secure under $\mathsf{UCE}[\mathcal{S}^{\mathrm{sup}}]$? If not, can one provide a new, different D-PKE scheme that achieves full IND-security under $\mathsf{UCE}[\mathcal{S}^{\mathrm{sup}}]$?

Results for D-PKE. Our first result is negative. We show that if iO is possible then the RO in EwH is not universally instantiable. In more detail, given *any* family of functions H —in particular a $\mathsf{UCE}[\mathcal{S}^{\mathrm{sup}}]$ one— we build a (pathological and H-dependent) randomized PKE scheme RE such that (1) RE is IND-CPA secure, but (2) An attack shows that the D-PKE scheme EwH[H, RE] given by the EwH transform is not IND-secure. The starting point is ideas of BFM [21], but several new ideas are needed, including several applications of a variable-output-length PRF to allocate randomness for the iO and a base PKE scheme in such a way that both (1) and (2) are possible. We note that the same negative result was obtained independently and concurrently by [22]. A general framework to obtain RO un-instantiability results via iO is given in [38] but it applies to single-stage games and thus doesn't yield a result for D-PKE.

Let H be a UCE[$\mathcal{S}^{\mathrm{sup}}$] function family. Then our negative result rules out showing an analogue of BHK1 [8], namely that EwH[H, RE] is fully IND secure for *any* IND-CPA RE. But there is a loophole, namely that the negative result does not preclude showing this for a *particular* choice of RE. We exploit this loophole to arrive at the desired goal of a fully IND secure D-PKE scheme under UCE[$\mathcal{S}^{\mathrm{sup}}$], as follows. We take the ROM BR93 PKE scheme [13], instantiate its trapdoor function with a *lossy* trapdoor function (LTDF) [32,48], and instantiate its RO with H, to get a standard-model PKE scheme RE. Next, we take the D-PKE scheme EwH[H, RE], which has two uses of H, under two independent keys. Our D-PKE scheme DE1 is obtained by implementing these two uses of H with a single key. We prove that DE1 is fully IND secure assuming the LTDF is secure and H is UCE[$\mathcal{S}^{\mathrm{sup}}$]. We remark that using a single H key is important to prove security under UCE[$\mathcal{S}^{\mathrm{sup}}$], not just an efficiency optimization.

The connection of LTDFs to D-PKE was first made by Boldyreva, Fehr and O'Neill (BFO) [17]. Their LTDF-based D-PKE schemes however only achieve security for block sources, not full IND security. The block source restriction seems quite inherent in their methods, and indeed due to Wichs [53] we do not expect to achieve fully IND secure D-PKE using LTDFs alone. Our approach combines LTDFs with UCE[$\mathcal{S}^{\mathrm{sup}}$] to surmount this obstacle.

DE1 is the first D-PKE scheme that is fully IND secure in the standard model. Beyond that, however, it has the following important practical attributes: it is competitive on short messages, very fast on long messages, and supports variable-length messages directly. These practical attributes are a first for standard-model D-PKE schemes.

LTDFs and UCE[$\mathcal{S}^{\mathrm{sup}}$] are a productive and (in retrospect) natural match. Intuitively, LTDFs allow us to move to a game with information-theoretic guarantees, at which point it becomes possible to exploit UCE under statistical unpredictability. We view DE1 as a relatively simple illustration of the power of the UCE+LTDF method. H-PKE brings new challenges, which we surmount via non-trivial extensions of the basic method. We believe the UCE+LTDF method will have applications beyond this as well.

Hedged PKE. The encryption algorithm of a H-PKE scheme takes public encryption key ek, message m and randomness r to deterministically return a ciphertext c. The H-IND requirement of BBNRSS [4] has two parts: (1) standard IND-CPA security if r is good, meaning uniform and independent across encryptions, and (2) semantic security of m if the pair (m, r) is unpredictable and does not depend on the public key. This second requirement is formalized as indistinguishability under chosen-distribution attack (IND-CDA) [4].

H-IND-secure PKE aims to provide the best possible privacy in the face of untrusted randomness. If the randomness is good, it does as well as standard IND-CPA encryption. But, whereas schemes providing only IND-CPA can fail spectacularly under poor randomness [4,20,46], H-IND PKE will not. It will compensate for poor randomness by also exploiting any available entropy in the message, protecting the latter as long as the message and randomness *together* are unpredictable. This is as good as it can get, since if the message-randomness pair is predictable, trial re-encryption on candidate pairs will recover the message underlying a target ciphertext. IND-CDA is an extension of IND that coincides with the latter if the randomness has no entropy at all.

In practice the most desirable form of IND-CDA is, again, full, meaning privacy when message-randomness pairs, although individually unpredictable, may be arbitrarily correlated. By full H-IND, we mean IND-CPA plus full IND-CDA. In the ROM, fully H-IND PKE is achieved by an extension of EwH called REwH that encrypts m under an IND-CPA scheme with the coins set to the hash of $m \parallel r$ [4]. In the standard model, things are more difficult. Providing a fully IND-CDA PKE scheme is harder than providing a fully IND D-PKE scheme because the unpredictability pertains to (m, r) not just m and also, more importantly, because IND-CDA is formalized in [4] as an *adaptive* requirement. Additionally, while IND-CPA is easy in isolation, it is *not* in combination with IND-CDA. The reason is subtle, namely that IND-CDA breaks when m depends on the public key, but IND-CPA must remain secure in this case. This butting of heads of the IND-CPA and IND-CDA conditions doubles the challenge of achieving fully H-IND PKE compared to fully IND D-PKE.

These technical difficulties are reflected in the landscape of standard-model schemes, where fully H-IND PKE has not been achieved under *any* assumption. BBNRSS [4] build standard-model H-IND PKE schemes by composition of standard-model D-PKE and IND-CPA schemes, and also directly via anonymous LTDFs, but these schemes achieve IND-CDA only for block sources. (The latter now means that message-randomness pairs are assumed to be unpredictable even given prior ones.) It is instructive that full H-IND PKE has not even been achieved under $\mathsf{UCE}[\mathcal{S}^{\mathrm{cup}}]$. To elaborate, recall that BHK1 [8] showed that $\mathsf{UCE}[\mathcal{S}^{\mathrm{cup}}]$-instantiating the RO in EwH results in a fully IND secure standard-model D-PKE scheme. We can correspondingly $\mathsf{UCE}[\mathcal{S}^{\mathrm{cup}}]$-instantiate the RO in REwH. But, even if the resulting scheme can be shown fully IND-CDA, there seems no reason it is IND-CPA. The reason is the difficulty alluded to above. Namely, a UCE hash function may not provide security on messages that are a function of the hashing key, but the latter is part of the public key and IND-CPA requires security for messages depending on the public key.

But the bar for us is even higher: due to the BFM attacks [21] on $\mathsf{UCE}[\mathcal{S}^{\mathrm{cup}}]$, we want to use the weaker $\mathsf{UCE}[\mathcal{S}^{\mathrm{sup}}]$ assumption, just as we did for DE1. We thus face at least two difficulties. The first is to achieve full IND-CDA under $\mathsf{UCE}[\mathcal{S}^{\mathrm{sup}}]$. Here the main challenge is handling adaptivity. But beyond that the fundamental above-mentioned difficulty of achieving IND-CPA in the same scheme remains, because no form of UCE guarantees security for messages that depend on the hashing key.

Results for H-PKE. We surmount the technical difficulties discussed above to provide the first standard-model, fully H-IND PKE schemes. We specify three schemes, HE1, HE2 and HE3. All efficiently achieve our security goals, the second and third handle variable-length messages, and the third further adds better concrete security.

Recall that we obtained DE1 as $\mathsf{EwH}[\mathsf{H}, \mathsf{BR93}[\mathsf{LT}, \mathsf{H}]]$, where H is $\mathsf{UCE}[\mathcal{S}^{\mathsf{sup}}]$ and LT is a LTDF. A natural idea is to similarly get H-PKE as $\mathsf{REwH}[\mathsf{H}, \mathsf{BR93}[\mathsf{LT}, \mathsf{H}]]$. (In both cases we use one hash key rather than two.) We are able to show this achieves full IND-CDA. This is significant since handling adaptivity required anonymous LTDFs in [4] which we do not need. But we then hit the problem above, namely $\mathsf{UCE}[\mathcal{S}^{\mathsf{sup}}]$ security of H may not be enough to provide IND-CPA. We resolve this by building a *particular*, suitable $\mathsf{UCE}[\mathcal{S}^{\mathsf{sup}}]$ family H. We first build a particular family U of AU (almost universal) hash functions and then obtain H by applying the AU-then-Hash transform of BHK2 [9] to a fixed-input-length $\mathsf{UCE}[\mathcal{S}^{\mathsf{sup}}]$ family $\overline{\mathsf{H}}$ and our U. We refer to the resulting PKE scheme as HE1. We are able to show that it is full IND-CDA as well as IND-CPA assuming $\mathsf{UCE}[\mathcal{S}^{\mathsf{sup}}]$ security of $\overline{\mathsf{H}}$ and security of the LTDF.

This achieves, for the first time, the security goal of fully H-IND PKE in the standard model, which we consider already significant. But in terms of practicality, HE1 is not ideal because it can only handle fixed-length messages. HE2 efficiently encrypts variable and arbitrary length messages while retaining full H-IND security. It uses a variable-output-length PRF in addition to the primitives used by HE1. Finally, HE3 exploits some combinatorial techniques to obtain better security bounds, as a result of which it offers security for lower values of the message min-entropy than the other schemes.

Speed. Our D-PKE and H-PKE schemes are the first to achieve full security in the standard model, which we believe is a significant theoretical contribution. However, beyond that, they have important practical attributes, expanded on below and in Section 5.

It is well known that asymmetric primitives are orders of magnitude less efficient than symmetric ones. Central to making standard IND-CPA encryption efficient is hybrid encryption as represented by the KEM-DEM paradigm [25]. Encryption generates a random asymmetrically-protected per-message symmetric key and then symmetrically encrypts the message under the latter, leading to cheap encryption of long messages. But for standard model D-PKE and H-PKE the hybrid encryption paradigm breaks down, because, with the constraint of being deterministic or not trusting the randomness, it is not clear how to even pick the per-message key. This difficulty is recognized and seems quite fundamental and hard to bypass. As a result, prior standard-model D-PKE and H-PKE schemes fix the message length and rely only on asymmetric operations. Their cost in asymmetric operations becomes exorbitant on long messages and they also cannot encrypt variable-length messages.

Our methods break these efficiency bottlenecks to recover hybrid-encryption like performance. Our DE1, HE2 and HE3 schemes handle messages of variable and arbitrary length, and the asymmetric cost is fixed independent of the message length, so that we pay only in hashing as the message length grows. Placing us in a particularly good position to exploit this is the speed of UCE[$\mathcal{S}^{\mathrm{sup}}$] functions. Direct constructions based on HMAC-SHA-256 [8,45] are already efficient, but in fact still more efficient and even parallelizable constructions are given in BHK2 [9], along with software implementations and cost comparisons. Meanwhile LTDFs can be efficiently instantiated in a variety of ways [32,40,43,48], making the asymmetric component competitive. This leads overall to performance comparable to existing IND-CPA schemes while providing protection against randomness subversion.

In practice concrete security is important to know how to set parameters. Good bounds are important so that one may use smaller parameters. (The cost of the asymmetric operations is usually cubic in the key length so cutting the latter by one-half yields a factor eight speedup.) For this reason we not only state in our theorems the concrete security bounds of the reductions but also try to obtain good ones.

Unique-Ciphertext PKE. In an algorithm-substitution attack (ASA) [12,56], the prescribed encryption algorithm is replaced with a malicious one that may attempt to leak information about the message to "big brother" based on a shared key. BPR [12] formalize the attacker goal in an ASA as compromising privacy without detection. BPR [12] and ACMPS [1] indicate that randomized encryption will be subject to successful attack. In the symmetric setting, BPR [12] show that ASAs can be protected against by a form of deterministic encryption they call unique-ciphertext symmetric encryption.

We analogously define unique-ciphertext PKE. U-PKE requires that for every key pair (ek, dk) and message m, there is at most one ciphertext c that decrypts to m under dk. A U-PKE scheme is thus deterministic, but not every D-PKE scheme is U-PKE. For example, appending to a D-PKE ciphertext a zero bit ignored by decryption leaves D-PKE intact but violates U-PKE. In Section 6 we show however how to achieve U-PKE in a simple and generic way from D-PKE. Combining this with our efficient D-PKE scheme above yields efficient U-PKE, allowing us to better defend against ASAs.

Discussion and Related Work. In a world of subversion, there are no panaceas. As with BPR [12], our goals are deliberately restricted in scope. We aim to provide better (not perfect) security in the face of some (not all) subversion threats. Thus, we restrict attention to randomness-subversion attacks and algorithm-substitution attacks. We assume that key-generation, being one-time, can leverage good randomness.

We might view IND-CPA as the optimistic view (the randomness is excellent, use it), D-PKE as the pessimistic view (the randomness may be bad so, to be safe, ignore it) and H-IND PKE as the pragmatic view (I don't know how good the randomness is but I will just get the best out of it that I can). We would expect the extent and nature of randomness subversion to vary rather than be ubiquitous and total, in part because subversion will aim to evade detection. In this light H-IND PKE emerges as the best defense in the face of randomness subversion.

Failures of randomness-generation processes [24, 28, 29, 39, 41, 44] have in the past been attributed to error. Now we know better, namely that some should be attributed to subversion. This makes practical defenses more urgent and increases the motivation for work like ours that delivers such defenses.

At SXSW 2014, Snowden said "... we know that the encryption algorithms we are using today work ... it is the random number generators that are attacked as opposed to the encryption algorithms themselves ... ". We aim, in some sense, to turn this on its head. We suggest that the encryption algorithms *don't* work because they are not robust in the face of poor randomness. We pursue practical hedged encryption as a counter-measure.

We do not expect or aim to maintain, under subversion, the high level of security we can achieve in its absence. Security will unavoidably degrade. Our goal with H-IND PKE is for it to degrade as little as possible rather than disappear. This philosophy sets us apart from most of the related work on randomness subversion we will discuss in the next paragraph, which either aims to understand under what limitations on the class of attacks one can achieve the same security one would under perfect randomness, or shows that such security is not possible.

Yilek [55] studies randomness-reset attacks, where the randomness is uniform but the adversary can force its re-use across different encryptions. Paterson, Schuldt and Sibborn [47] introduce related-randomness attacks, where encryption is under adversary-specified functions of some initial uniform randomness, providing negative results, as well as positive results for some classes of attacks. Birrell, Chung, Pass and Telang [15] and Hemenway and Ostrovsky [40] study the encryption of randomness-dependent messages. Austrin, Chung, Mahmoody, Pass and Seth [1] show that encryption is insecure under even quite weak adversarial tampering of randomness. Authenticated key-exchange with bad randomness is studied in [31,54]. Negative results for cryptography with imperfect randomness are provided by [18,26,27]. Kamara and Katz [42] study symmetric encryption providing semantic security under good coins in the face of chosen-plaintext attacks involving bad coins.

Ristenpart and Yilek [50] study the use of H-IND PKE in real systems. Brakerski and Segev [19] study D-PKE security in the presence of auxiliary information about messages. Raghunathan, Segev and Vadhan [49] study security of D-PKE when the message may depend on the public key. Vergnaud and Xiao [52] study IND-CDA when the message and randomness may depend on the public key. In the symmetric setting, Rogaway and Shrimpton's misuse-resistant authenticated encryption [51] represents a form of hedging.

2 Preliminaries

We review basic notation and definitions including games, function families, VOL PRFs, LTDFs and UCE.

By $\lambda \in \mathbb{N}$ we denote the security parameter and by 1^λ its unary representation. We denote the number of coordinates of a vector $\mathbf{x}$ by $|\mathbf{x}|$, and the length of a string $x \in \{0,1\}^*$ by $|x|$. Algorithms are randomized unless otherwise indicated. Running time is worst case. "PT" stands for "polynomial-time," whether for randomized algorithms or deterministic ones. If A is an algorithm, we let $y \leftarrow A(x_1, \ldots; r)$ denote running A with randomness r on inputs $x_1, \ldots$ and assigning the output to y. We let $y \leftarrow_\$ A(x_1, \ldots)$ be the resulting of picking r at random and letting $y \leftarrow A(x_1, \ldots; r)$. We let $[A(x_1, \ldots)]$ denote the set of all possible outputs of A when invoked with inputs $x_1, \ldots$.

We use the code based game playing framework of [14]. (See Fig. 1 for an example.) By $G^A(\lambda)$ we denote the event that the execution of game G with adversary A and security parameter λ results in output true, the game output being what is returned by GAME.

For concrete security assessments, we adopt the notation of [10]. Let the *number of queries* of A to an oracle PROC be the function $\mathbf{Q}_A^{\text{PROC}}$ that on input λ returns the maximum number of queries that A makes to PROC when executed with security parameter λ, the maximum over all coins and all possible replies to queries to all oracles of A. Time assessments are simplified by the convention that running time is that of the game rather than merely the adversary, and we let $\mathbf{T}(G^{A_1, A_2, \cdots})$ denote the function of λ that returns the maximum execution time of game G with adversaries $A_1, A_2, \ldots$ and security parameter λ, the maximum over all coins, and the time being all inclusive, meaning the time taken by game procedures to compute replies is included.

Function Families. Our syntax for function families follows [8], in particular allowing variable output lengths. This is important in our applications to encrypt messages of variable length, which in turn is important in practice. A family of functions H specifies the following. On input the unary representation 1^λ of the security parameter $\lambda \in \mathbb{N}$, key generation algorithm H.Kg returns a key $hk \in \{0,1\}^{\text{H.kl}(\lambda)}$, where H.kl: $\mathbb{N} \to \mathbb{N}$ is the key length function associated to H. The deterministic, PT evaluation algorithm H.Ev takes 1^λ, key hk an input $x \in \{0,1\}^*$ with $|x| \in \text{H.IL}(\lambda)$, and a unary encoding 1^ℓ of an output length $\ell \in \text{H.OL}(\lambda)$ to return $\text{H.Ev}(1^\lambda, hk, x, 1^\ell) \in \{0,1\}^\ell$. Here H.IL is the input-length function associated to H, so that $\text{H.IL}(\lambda) \subseteq \mathbb{N}$ is the set of allowed input lengths, and similarly H.OL is the output-length function associated to H, so that $\text{H.OL}(\lambda) \subseteq \mathbb{N}$ is the set of allowed output lengths. The latter allows us to cover functions of variable output length. If H has fixed input length then let H.il denote the function such that $\text{H.IL}(\lambda) = \{\text{H.il}(\lambda)\}$ for every $\lambda \in \mathbb{N}$. If H has fixed output length, define H.ol likewise.

Variable Output Length PRFs. A variable output length (VOL) PRF is a function family F such that F.Kg returns a uniformly distributed key in $\{0,1\}^{\text{F.kl}}$ and $\text{Adv}_{F,A}^{\text{prf}}(\lambda) = 2\Pr[\text{PRF}_F^A(\lambda)] - 1$ is negligible for every PT adversary A, where

GAME $\mathrm{CPA}^A_{\mathsf{PKE}}(\lambda)$	GAME $\mathrm{PRF}^A_{\mathsf{F}}(\lambda)$	GAME $\mathrm{Lossy}^A_{\mathsf{LT}}(\lambda)$
$(ek, dk) \leftarrow_\$ \mathsf{PKE.Kg}(1^\lambda)$	$b \leftarrow_\$ \{0,1\}$; $fk \leftarrow_\$ \{0,1\}^{\mathsf{F.kl}(\lambda)}$	$(ek, dk) \leftarrow_\$ \mathsf{LT.EKg}(1^\lambda)$
$b \leftarrow_\$ \{0,1\}$	$b' \leftarrow_\$ A^{\mathrm{RR}}(1^\lambda)$	$lk \leftarrow_\$ \mathsf{LT.LKg}(1^\lambda)$
$(m_0, m_1, ,) \leftarrow_\$ A(1^\lambda, ek)$	Return $(b = b')$	$b \leftarrow_\$ \{0,1\}$
$c \leftarrow_\$ \mathsf{PKE.Enc}(ek, m_b)$		If $b = 1$ then $K \leftarrow ek$
$b' \leftarrow_\$ A(1^\lambda, t, c)$	$\underline{\mathrm{RR}(x, 1^\ell)}$	Else $K \leftarrow lk$
Return $(b = b')$	If $b = 1$ then	$b' \leftarrow A(1^\lambda, K)$
	$\quad y \leftarrow \mathsf{F.Ev}(1^\lambda, fk, x, 1^\ell)$	Return $(b' = b)$
	Else $y \leftarrow_\$ \{0,1\}^\ell$	
	Return y	

Fig. 1. Left: Game CPA defining IND-CPA security of a PKE scheme PKE. **Middle:** Game PRF defining the PRF security of a variable-output-length function family F. **Right:** Game Lossy defining the security of a lossy trapdoor function LT.

game $\mathrm{PRF}^A_{\mathsf{F}}$ is defined in the middle panel of Fig. 1. In this game the adversary is given an oracle RR that either implements a random oracle or $\mathsf{F.Ev}(1^\lambda, fk, \cdot, \cdot)$, where $fk \leftarrow_\$ \{0,1\}^{\mathsf{F.kl}(\lambda)}$ is a random key. We assume that A doesn't repeat a prior RR query, and any RR query $(x, 1^\ell)$ must satisfy $x \in \mathsf{F.IL}(\lambda)$ and $\ell \in \mathsf{F.OL}(\lambda)$. This extends [36] to VOL families. A practical construction of a VOL PRF from a blockcipher is given in [16].

Public-Key Encryption. A PKE scheme PKE defines PT algorithms PKE.Kg, PKE.Enc, PKE.Dec, the last deterministic. Algorithm PKE.Kg takes as input 1^λ and outputs a public encryption key $ek \in \{0,1\}^{\mathsf{PKE.ekl}(\lambda)}$ and a secret decryption key dk, where $\mathsf{PKE.ekl}: \mathbb{N} \to \mathbb{N}$ is the public-key length of PKE. Algorithm PKE.Enc takes as input $1^\lambda, ek$ and a message m with $|m| \in \mathsf{PKE.IL}(\lambda)$ to return a ciphertext c, where PKE.IL is the input-length function associated to PKE, so that $\mathsf{PKE.IL}(\lambda) \subseteq \mathbb{N}$ is the set of allowed input (message) lengths. Algorithm PKE.Dec takes $1^\lambda, dk, c$ and outputs $m \in \{0,1\}^* \cup \{\bot\}$. Correctness requires that $\mathsf{PKE.Dec}(1^\lambda, dk, c) = m$ for all $\lambda \in \mathbb{N}$, all $(ek, dk) \in [\mathsf{PKE.Kg}(1^\lambda)]$ all m with $|m| \in \mathsf{PKE.IL}(\lambda)$ and all $c \in [\mathsf{PKE.Enc}(1^\lambda, ek, m)]$. Scheme PKE is IND-CPA secure [37] if $\mathsf{Adv}^{\mathrm{ind\text{-}cpa}}_{\mathsf{PKE},A}(\lambda) = 2[\mathrm{CPA}^A_{\mathsf{PKE}}(\lambda)] - 1$ is negligible for every PT adversary A, where game CPA is defined in the left panel of Fig. 1. We require that the messages m_0, m_1 output by A have the same length $|m_0| = |m_1| \in \mathsf{PKE.IL}(\lambda)$. Let $\mathsf{PKE.rl}: \mathbb{N} \to \mathbb{N}$ denote the randomness-length function of PKE, meaning $\mathsf{PKE.Enc}(1^\lambda, \cdot, \cdot)$ draws its coins at random from $\{0,1\}^{\mathsf{PKE.rl}(\lambda)}$. We say that PKE has input length $\mathsf{PKE.il}: \mathbb{N} \to \mathbb{N}$ if $\mathsf{PKE.IL}(\lambda) = \{\mathsf{PKE.il}(\lambda)\}$ for all $\lambda \in \mathbb{N}$, and refer to this as a PKE scheme that only allows fixed length messages. Our goal will be to allow variable and arbitrary-length messages, ideally $\mathsf{PKE.IL}(\cdot) = \mathbb{N}$, but at least some large subset thereof.

Lossy Trapdoor Functions. A lossy trapdoor function [48] LT specifies PT algorithms LT.EKg, LT.LKg, LT.Ev, LT.Inv, the last two deterministic, as well as an input length $\mathsf{LT.il}: \mathbb{N} \to \mathbb{N}$ and an output length $\mathsf{LT.ol}: \mathbb{N} \to \mathbb{N}$. Key-generation algorithm LT.EKg takes 1^λ and returns an "injective" key ek and a

Game $\mathrm{UCE}_{\mathsf{H}}^{S,D}(\lambda)$	$\mathrm{HASH}(x, 1^\ell)$
$b \leftarrow\!\!{\scriptstyle\$} \{0,1\}$; $hk \leftarrow\!\!{\scriptstyle\$} \mathsf{H.Kg}(1^\lambda)$	If $T[x, \ell] = \bot$ then
$L \leftarrow\!\!{\scriptstyle\$} S^{\mathrm{HASH}}(1^\lambda)$; $b' \leftarrow\!\!{\scriptstyle\$} D(1^\lambda, hk, L)$	If $b = 0$ then $T[x, \ell] \leftarrow\!\!{\scriptstyle\$} \{0,1\}^\ell$
Return $(b' = b)$	Else $T[x, \ell] \leftarrow \mathsf{H.Ev}(1^\lambda, hk, x, 1^\ell)$
	Return $T[x, \ell]$
Game $\mathrm{Pred}_S^P(\lambda)$	$\mathrm{HASH}(x, 1^\ell)$
$Q \leftarrow \emptyset$; $L \leftarrow\!\!{\scriptstyle\$} S^{\mathrm{HASH}}(1^\lambda)$; $Q' \leftarrow\!\!{\scriptstyle\$} P(1^\lambda, L)$	If $T[x, \ell] = \bot$ then $T[x, \ell] \leftarrow\!\!{\scriptstyle\$} \{0,1\}^\ell$
Return $(Q' \cap Q \neq \emptyset)$	$Q \leftarrow Q \cup \{x\}$; Return $T[x, \ell]$
Game $\mathrm{Reset}_S^R(\lambda)$	$\mathrm{HASH}(x, 1^\ell)$
$\mathsf{Dom} \leftarrow \emptyset$; $L \leftarrow\!\!{\scriptstyle\$} S^{\mathrm{HASH}}(1^\lambda)$; $b \leftarrow\!\!{\scriptstyle\$} \{0,1\}$	If $T[x, \ell] = \bot$ then $T[x, \ell] \leftarrow\!\!{\scriptstyle\$} \{0,1\}^\ell$
If $b = 0$ then // reset the array T	$\mathsf{Dom} \leftarrow \mathsf{Dom} \cup \{(x, \ell)\}$; Return $T[x, \ell]$
For all $(x, \ell) \in \mathsf{Dom}$ do	
$\quad T[x, \ell] \leftarrow\!\!{\scriptstyle\$} \{0,1\}^\ell$	
$b' \leftarrow R^{\mathrm{HASH}}(1^\lambda, L)$; Return $(b' = b)$	

Fig. 2. Games UCE **(top),** Pred **(middle), and** Reset **(bottom) to define UCE security**

decryption key dk. Evaluation algorithm LT.Ev takes 1^λ, ek and $x \in \{0,1\}^{\mathsf{LT.il}(\lambda)}$ to return an $\mathsf{LT.ol}(\lambda)$-bit string. Inversion algorithm LT.Inv takes 1^λ, dk and $y \in \{0,1\}^{\mathsf{LT.ol}(\lambda)}$ to return a $\mathsf{LT.il}(\lambda)$-bit string. The *correctness requirement* demands that $\mathsf{LT.Inv}(1^\lambda, dk, \mathsf{LT.Ev}(1^\lambda, ek, x)) = x$ for every $\lambda \in \mathbb{N}$, every $(ek, dk) \in [\mathsf{LT.EKg}(1^\lambda)]$ and every $x \in \{0,1\}^{\mathsf{LT.il}(\lambda)}$. Algorithm LT.LKg, given 1^λ, returns a "lossy" key lk. Let $\tau : \mathbb{N} \to \mathbb{N}$ be a function such that $2^{-\tau(\cdot)}$ is negligible. We say that LT is τ-lossy if the size of the set $\{\mathsf{LT.Ev}(1^\lambda, lk, x) \mid x \in \{0,1\}^{\mathsf{LT.il}(\lambda)}\}$ is at most $2^{\mathsf{LT.il}(\lambda) - \tau(\lambda)}$ for every $\lambda \in \mathbb{N}$ and every $lk \in [\mathsf{LT.LKg}(1^\lambda)]$. Security of an LTDF demands two things. First, lossy and injective keys are indistinguishable. Formally, $\mathsf{Adv}_{\mathsf{LT},A}^{\mathsf{ltdf}}(\lambda) = 2 \Pr[\mathrm{Lossy}_{\mathsf{LT}}^A(\cdot)] - 1$ must be negligible for every PT adversary A, where game Lossy is defined in the right panel of Fig. 1. Second, LTDF is τ-lossy for some τ such that $2^{-\tau(\cdot)}$ is negligible. To simplify concrete security analyses, we assume that LT.LKg's worst-case running time is at most that of LT.EKg.

There are by now many constructions of LTDFs known [32,40,43,48]. As an example, RSA is shown to be lossy [43] under the Φ-hiding assumption of [23]. For a 2048-bit modulus, one may choose $\tau = 430$ for 80-bit security.

UCE. We recall the Universal Computational Extractor (UCE) framework of BHK1 [8]. Let H be a family of functions as defined above. Let S be an adversary called the *source* and D an adversary called the *distinguisher*. We associate to them and H the game $\mathrm{UCE}_{\mathsf{H}}^{S,D}(\lambda)$ at the left panel of Fig. 2. The source has access to an oracle HASH and we require that any query $(x, 1^\ell)$ made to this oracle satisfy $|x| \in \mathsf{H.IL}(\lambda)$ and $\ell \in \mathsf{H.OL}(\lambda)$. When the challenge bit b is 1 (the "real" case) the oracle responds via H.Ev under a key hk that is chosen by the game and *not* given to the source. When $b = 0$ (the "random" case) it responds as a random oracle. The source then leaks a string L to its accomplice distinguisher.

The latter *does* get the key hk as input and must now return its guess $b' \in \{0, 1\}$ for b. The game returns true iff $b' = b$, and the uce-advantage of (S, D) is defined for $\lambda \in \mathbb{N}$ via $\mathsf{Adv}^{\mathsf{uce}}_{\mathsf{H}, S, D}(\lambda) = 2 \Pr[\mathrm{UCE}^{S,D}_{\mathsf{H}}(\lambda)] - 1$. If $\mathcal{S}$ is a class (set) of sources, we say that H is $\mathrm{UCE}[\mathcal{S}]$-secure if $\mathsf{Adv}^{\mathsf{uce}}_{\mathsf{H}, S, D}(\cdot)$ is negligible for all sources $S \in \mathcal{S}$ and all PT distinguishers D. Trivial attacks from [8] show that $\mathrm{UCE}[\mathcal{S}]$-security is not achievable if $\mathcal{S}$ is the class of all PT sources. To obtain meaningful notions of security, BHK1 [8] impose restrictions on the source. There are many ways to do this; below we'll focus on what they call statistically unpredictable and reset-secure sources.

A source is unpredictable if it is hard to guess the source's HASH queries even given the leakage, in the *random case* of UCE game. Formally, let S be a source and P an adversary called a predictor. Consider game $\mathrm{Pred}^P_S(\lambda)$ in the middle panel of Fig. 2. Given the leakage, P outputs a set Q'; we require that $|Q'|$ is polynomially bounded. The predictor wins if this set contains a HASH-query of the source. For $\lambda \in \mathbb{N}$ we let $\mathsf{Adv}^{\mathsf{pred}}_{S,P}(\lambda) = \Pr[\mathrm{Pred}^P_S(\lambda)]$. We say that S is statistically unpredictable if $\mathsf{Adv}^{\mathsf{pred}}_{S,P}(\cdot)$ is negligible for all (even computationally unbounded) predictors P. We say that H is $\mathrm{UCE}[\mathcal{S}^{\mathsf{sup}}]$-secure if $\mathsf{Adv}^{\mathsf{uce}}_{\mathsf{H}, S, D}(\cdot)$ is negligible for all statistically unpredictable PT sources and all PT distinguishers.

The second restriction on sources from [8] is reset security. Let S be a source and R an adversary called a reset adversary. The source again is executed with its HASH being a random oracle. The reset adversary is either given access to the same random oracle or to an *independent* one. The requirement is that it should not be able to tell which. Consider game $\mathrm{Reset}^R_S(\lambda)$ at the right panel of Fig. 2; we require that R make only polynomial number of queries to HASH. For $\lambda \in \mathbb{N}$ we let $\mathsf{Adv}^{\mathsf{reset}}_{S,R}(\lambda) = 2 \Pr[\mathrm{Reset}^R_S(\lambda)] - 1$. We say S is statistically reset-secure if $\mathsf{Adv}^{\mathsf{reset}}_{S,R}(\cdot)$ is negligible for all reset adversaries R. We say that H is $\mathrm{UCE}[\mathcal{S}^{\mathsf{srs}}]$-secure if $\mathsf{Adv}^{\mathsf{uce}}_{\mathsf{H}, S, D}(\cdot)$ is negligible for all statistically reset-secure PT sources and all PT distinguishers.

BHK1 [8] show that $\mathrm{UCE}[\mathcal{S}^{\mathsf{srs}}]$-security of H implies $\mathrm{UCE}[\mathcal{S}^{\mathsf{sup}}]$-security of H. BFM [21] show that if indistinguishability obfuscation for all circuits is possible then $\mathrm{UCE}[\mathcal{S}^{\mathsf{cup}}]$ —UCE for *computationally* unpredictable sources— is not achievable in the standard model. However $\mathrm{UCE}[\mathcal{S}^{\mathsf{sup}}]$ and $\mathrm{UCE}[\mathcal{S}^{\mathsf{srs}}]$ are not subject to their attack and emerge as weaker and plausible assumptions. Moving to the statistical versions was independently suggested by BHK1 [8] and BFM [21]. These statistical assumptions will be the basis of our constructs.

While $\mathrm{UCE}[\mathcal{S}^{\mathsf{sup}}]$ and $\mathrm{UCE}[\mathcal{S}^{\mathsf{srs}}]$ may seem like strong assumptions, we know that multi-stage assumptions are necessary to reach our goals [53]. There are very few candidate multi-stage assumptions and amongst them the ones we use are the more plausible.

$\mathrm{UCE}[\mathcal{S}^{\mathsf{sup}}]$ and $\mathrm{UCE}[\mathcal{S}^{\mathsf{srs}}]$ families may be efficiently instantiated via HMAC-SHA-256 [8,45] or super-efficiently via [9], which we will exploit for efficient schemes.

GAME $\text{IND}_{\text{DE}}^{A}(\lambda)$

$b \leftarrow_\$ \{0,1\}$; $(ek, dk) \leftarrow_\$ \text{DE.Kg}(1^\lambda)$; $(\mathbf{m}_0, \mathbf{m}_1) \leftarrow_\$ A_1(1^\lambda)$
For $i = 1$ to $|\mathbf{m}_0|$ do $\mathbf{c}[i] \leftarrow_\$ \text{DE.Enc}(1^\lambda, ek, \mathbf{m}_b[i])$
$b' \leftarrow_\$ A_2(1^\lambda, ek, \mathbf{c})$; Return $(b = b')$

$\text{DE.Kg}(1^\lambda)$

$(ek, dk) \leftarrow_\$ \text{RE.Kg}(1^\lambda)$; $hk \leftarrow_\$ \text{H.Kg}(1^\lambda)$
Return $((ek, hk), dk)$

$\text{DE.Enc}(1^\lambda, (ek, hk), m)$

$r \leftarrow \text{H.Ev}(1^\lambda, hk, ek \,\|\, m, 1^{\text{RE.rl}(\lambda)})$
$c \leftarrow \text{RE.Enc}(1^\lambda, ek, m; r)$; Return c

$\text{DE.Dec}(1^\lambda, dk, c)$

$m \leftarrow \text{RE.Dec}(1^\lambda, dk, c)$; Return m

GAME $\text{IO}_{\text{G}}^{A}(\lambda)$

$(C_0, C_1, t) \leftarrow_\$ A(1^\lambda)$; $b \leftarrow_\$ \{0,1\}$; $P \leftarrow_\$ \text{G.Ob}(1^\lambda, C_b)$
$b' \leftarrow_\$ A(t, P)$; Return $(b = b')$

Fig. 3. Top: Game defining IND security of D-PKE scheme DE. **Middle:** D-PKE scheme DE = EwH[H, RE]. **Bottom:** Game defining iO security of an indistinguishability obfuscator G.

3   Efficient, Fully IND Secure D-PKE

This section begins with a negative result —that assuming iO the random oracle (RO) in EwH is not *universally* instantiable— and then provides a complementary positive result —that there is a *particular* instantiation of the RO and IND-CPA scheme in EwH that results in a fully IND secure D-PKE scheme. The latter, which is the main result of this section, showcases our UCE+LTDF method and brings a new D-PKE scheme with two attributes: (1) On the theoretical front, it is the first D-PKE scheme shown *fully* IND secure in the standard model, and (2) On the practical front, it encrypts variable-input length messages and achieves hybrid-encryption like efficiency on long messages.

D-PKE and EwH. We say that a PKE scheme DE is a deterministic public-key encryption (D-PKE) [3] if the encryption algorithm DE.Enc is deterministic. We use the IND formalization of security of BFOR [6], which they show equivalent to the PRIV formalization of [3]. Game IND defining the IND notion is shown in the left panel of Fig. 3. An IND adversary $A = (A_1, A_2)$ is a pair of PT algorithms, where A_1 on input 1^λ returns a pair of message vectors $(\mathbf{m}_0, \mathbf{m}_1)$. We require that (i) there be a polynomial v such that $|\mathbf{m}_0| = |\mathbf{m}_1| \le v(\lambda)$ and $|\mathbf{m}_0[i]| = |\mathbf{m}_1[i]| \in \text{DE.IL}(\lambda)$, for every $i \le |\mathbf{m}_0|$, and (ii) messages $\mathbf{m}_0[1], \ldots, \mathbf{m}_0[|\mathbf{m}_0|]$ are distinct and also messages $\mathbf{m}_1[1], \ldots, \mathbf{m}_1[|\mathbf{m}_1|]$ are distinct. The guessing probability $\text{Guess}_A(\cdot)$ of A is the function that on input $\lambda \in \mathbb{N}$ returns the maximum, over all b, m, i, of $\Pr[\mathbf{m}_b[i] = m]$, the probability over $(\mathbf{m}_0, \mathbf{m}_1) \leftarrow_\$ A_1(1^\lambda)$. We say that A has *high min-entropy* if $\text{Guess}_A(\cdot)$ is negligible. We let $\text{Adv}^{\text{ind}}_{\text{DE},A}(\lambda) = 2\Pr[\text{IND}^A_{\text{DE}}(\lambda)] - 1$ and say that DE is IND-secure if $\text{Adv}^{\text{ind}}_{\text{DE},A}(\cdot)$ is negligible for all PT A of high min-entropy.

We stress that this definition captures *full* security because the messages in the message vectors may be arbitrarily correlated. This is what is needed in practice. In contrast, security for block sources [17] requires that each message in each vector has high min entropy even given prior ones. This is often not true in practice and security only for block sources is quite weak, yet prior standard-model schemes have only been able to achieve this.

EwH [3] is a simple and natural transform that takes a family of functions H and a randomized PKE scheme RE to return the D-PKE scheme DE = EwH[H, RE] whose algorithms are shown in the middle panel of Fig. 3. We let DE.IL = RE.IL. We require that $\text{RE.rl}(\lambda) \in \text{H.OL}(\lambda)$ and $\text{RE.ekl}(\lambda) + \ell \in \text{H.IL}(\lambda)$ for all $\lambda \in \mathbb{N}$ and all $\ell \in \text{RE.IL}(\lambda)$.

Indistinguishability Obfuscation. We recall the definition of [34], which extends that of [2] to allow auxiliary information. We say that circuits C_0 and C_1 are *functionally equivalent*, denoted $C_0 \equiv C_1$, if they have the same size, the same number n of inputs, and $C_0(x) = C_1(x)$ for every input $x \in \{0,1\}^n$. An indistinguishability obfuscator (iO) G defines PT algorithms G.Ob, G.Ev and a randomness length function G.rl: $\mathbb{N} \to \mathbb{N}$. Algorithm G.Ob takes as input 1^λ and a circuit C, and outputs a string P using randomness of length $\text{G.rl}(\lambda)$. Deterministic algorithm G.Ev takes as input strings P, x and returns $y \in \{0,1\}^* \cup \{\bot\}$. We require that for any circuit C, any input x for C any $\lambda \in \mathbb{N}$, and any $P \in [\text{G.Ob}(1^\lambda, C)]$, it holds that $\text{G.Ev}(P, x) = C(x)$. An adversary A is *well-formed* if $\Pr[C_0 \not\equiv C_1 : (C_0, C_1, t) \leftarrow_s A(1^\lambda)]$ is negligible. We say that G is iO-secure if $\text{Adv}^{\text{io}}_{\text{G},A}(\lambda) = 2\Pr[\text{IO}^A_{\text{G}}(\lambda)] - 1$ is negligible for every PT well-formed adversary A, where game IO is defined at the right panel of Fig. 3.

Implausibility of Universal Instantiation of EwH. BBO [3] showed that if H is implemented via a RO then EwH[H, RE] is IND-secure for *any* IND-CPA RE. A basic theoretical and practical question is whether the RO in this result can be securely instantiated. The most desirable instantiation is *universal*, by which we mean there is a function family H such that EwH[H, RE] is IND-secure for any IND-CPA RE. Here we show that if iO exists then there is no such universal instantiation. Given any function family H we build an IND-CPA PKE scheme RE such that EwH[H, RE] is not IND-secure. We stress that this does not preclude providing specific H, RE such that EwH[H, RE] is IND-secure, and indeed it is in this way that we will later obtain our positive result.

Our findings strengthen, and are consistent with, prior work. BHK1 [8] showed that a UCE[$\mathcal{S}^{\text{cup}}$] family will provide a universal instantiation of EwH, but UCE[$\mathcal{S}^{\text{cup}}$] is ruled out under iO by BFM [21], so there is no contradiction. However, following BFM, it remained possible that some other class of function families might be able to universally instantiate EwH. Under iO, we rule this out.

Circuit $C_{1^\lambda, x, y}(hk)$

// Input length is $H.kl(\lambda)$, and output length is $|x|$

$r \leftarrow H.Ev(1^\lambda, hk, x, 1^{H.ol(\lambda)})$; $fk \leftarrow r[1, F.kl(\lambda)]$

$u \leftarrow F.Ev(1^\lambda, fk, 0^{F.il(\lambda)}, 1^{F.kl(\lambda)+\lambda})$

If $y = u$ then return x

Return $0^{|x|}$

$RE.Enc(1^\lambda, ek, m; r)$

$fk \leftarrow r[1, F.kl(\lambda)]$; $y \leftarrow F.Ev(1^\lambda, fk, 0^{F.il(\lambda)}, 1^{F.kl(\lambda)+\lambda})$

$r_1 \leftarrow F.Ev(1^\lambda, fk, 0 \| 1^{F.il(\lambda)-1}, 1^{G.rl(\lambda)})$; $r_2 \leftarrow F.Ev(1^\lambda, fk, 1^{F.il(\lambda)}, 1^{\overline{RE}.rl(\lambda)})$

$x \leftarrow ek \| m$; $P \leftarrow G.Ob(1^\lambda, C_{1^\lambda, x, y}; r_1)$; $c' \leftarrow \overline{RE}.Enc(1^\lambda, ek, m; r_2)$

$c \leftarrow (c', P)$; Return c

$RE.Dec(1^\lambda, dk, c)$

$(c', P) \leftarrow c$; Return $\overline{RE}.Dec(1^\lambda, dk, c')$

Fig. 4. Middle, Bottom: Encryption and decryption algorithm of the counter-example PKE scheme RE for Proposition 1. **Top:** Circuit constructed and obfuscated in RE.Enc.

We let H be a function family with input length H.il and output length H.ol. We will build the counter-example PKE scheme RE from H and the following auxiliary primitives: an arbitrary, base IND-CPA scheme $\overline{RE}$, a VOL PRF F and an iO scheme G. The result is as follows.

Proposition 1. *Let* H *be a function family with input length* H.il *and output length* H.ol. *Let* F *be a VOL PRF with* F.IL = F.OL = $\mathbb{N}$. *Assume* F.kl $\leq$ H.ol. *Let* $\overline{RE}$ *be an IND-CPA PKE scheme with fixed input length* $\overline{RE}$.il *and public key length* $\overline{RE}$.pkl *satisfying* $\overline{RE}$.il + $\overline{RE}$.pkl = H.il. *Let* G *be an iO-secure iO scheme. Define PKE scheme* RE *as follows. Let* RE.il = $\overline{RE}$.il. *Let* RE.Kg = $\overline{RE}$.Kg. *Let the encryption and decryption algorithms of* RE *be as shown in Fig. 4. Then (1)* EwH[H, RE] *is not IND-secure, but (2)* RE *is IND-CPA secure.* ∎

The proof of Proposition 1 is in [7]. Here we will sketch the ideas. An encryption $c = (c', P)$ of a message m under RE with public key ek will have two parts. The first, c', is an encryption of m under $\overline{RE}$ with ek. The second, P, is an obfuscated circuit that will (1) help attack DE = EwH[H, RE] yet (2) not compromise IND-CPA security of RE. The question is how to construct RE to ensure *both* properties. (Ensuring either alone is trivial.)

The starting idea, inspired by BFM [21], is to have RE.Enc, given $1^\lambda, ek, m$ and coins r, create the following circuit:

$$C_{1^\lambda, ek, m, r}(hk) : \text{If } H(1^\lambda, hk, ek\|m, 1^{RE.rl(\lambda)}) = r \text{ then return } m \text{ else return } 0^{|m|}.$$

The input to the circuit is a key hk for H, and the hardwired values $1^\lambda, ek, m, r$ are the inputs to the algorithm RE.Enc that creates the circuit. Now RE.Enc lets P be an obfuscation of this circuit. Pretend for now that the obfuscation process

DE1.Kg(1^λ)
$(ek, dk) \leftarrow\!\!{\scriptstyle\$}\ \mathsf{LT.EKg}(1^\lambda);\ hk \leftarrow\!\!{\scriptstyle\$}\ \mathsf{H.Kg}(1^\lambda);\ \text{Return}\ ((ek, hk), (dk, hk))$

DE1.Enc($1^\lambda, (ek, hk), m$)
$r \leftarrow \mathsf{H.Ev}(1^\lambda, hk, m, 1^{\mathsf{LT.il}(\lambda)})\ ;\ trap \leftarrow \mathsf{LT.Ev}(1^\lambda, ek, r)$ $c \leftarrow m \oplus \mathsf{H.Ev}(1^\lambda, hk, r, 1^{|m|})\ ;\ \text{Return}\ (trap, c)$

DE1.Dec($1^\lambda, (dk, hk), (trap, c)$)
$r \leftarrow \mathsf{LT.Inv}(1^\lambda, dk, trap)\ ;\ \text{Return}\ c \oplus \mathsf{H.Ev}(1^\lambda, hk, r, 1^{|c|})$

Fig. 5. The algorithms of our DE1 D-PKE scheme

is deterministic, which of course is not true, and also that no coins are used to create c', which is also not true. Under these assumptions, if an attacker has an EwH ciphertext $(c', P) = \mathsf{DE.Enc}(1^\lambda, (ek, hk), m)$, and also has the public key (ek, hk) of DE, then it can run P on hk which, due to the structure of EwH and the construction of $C_{1^\lambda, ek, m, r}$, returns m, breaking the IND-security of DE. But there are a number of difficulties. One is that there seems no reason that this RE retains IND-CPA security assuming only iO security of the obfuscation. Another is that the obfuscation and $\overline{\mathsf{RE}}$ are randomized, and RE has to provide coins for both from r yet be able to create P to allow the attack when r is produced via the hash in EwH.

We will use the VOL PRF F to allocate pseudorandom coins for the obfuscation process and $\overline{\mathsf{RE}}$. The key for F will be a prefix $fk \leftarrow r[1, \mathsf{F.kl}(\lambda)]$ of the coins r provided to RE.Enc. Recall that in our definition of a VOL PRF, the key generation always samples $fk \leftarrow\!\!{\scriptstyle\$}\ \{0, 1\}^{\mathsf{F.kl}(\lambda)}$, so if r is truly random then we give F a correctly generated key. Instead of hardwiring r to the circuit, we hardwire $y \leftarrow \mathsf{F.Ev}(1^\lambda, fk, 0^{\mathsf{F.il}(\lambda)}, 1^\ell)$ for an appropriate ℓ. We also hardwire $x = ek\|m$ rather than ek, m separately. Our circuit $C_{1^\lambda, x, y}$ is shown in the left panel of Fig. 4. We need (1) an attack on $\mathsf{DE} = \mathsf{EwH}[\mathsf{H}, \mathsf{RE}]$ and (2) a proof that RE is IND-CPA. For (1) our claim is that if $C_{1^\lambda, ek\|m, y}$ is produced by RE.Enc within DE then $C_{1^\lambda, ek\|m, y}(hk)$ will return $ek\|m$, and thus running an obfuscation P of $C_{1^\lambda, ek\|m, y}$ on hk will return the same. For (2), r is truly random so $C_{1^\lambda, ek\|m, y}$ as produced during encryption is indistinguishable from $C_{1^\lambda, ek\|m, u}$ with u a random ℓ-bit string, by PRF security of F. To use iO security, we want that when u is random the probability that there exists a $\mathsf{H.kl}(\lambda)$-bit z such that $C_{1^\lambda, ek\|m, u}(z) \neq 0^{|ek\,\|\,m|}$ is negligible. This is established via a counting argument which relies on having set ℓ to be large enough. See [7] for details.

The DE1 Scheme. We now provide our positive result on D-PKE, namely an efficient, fully IND standard model scheme under $\mathsf{UCE}[\mathcal{S}^{\mathsf{sup}}]$. Let H be a $\mathsf{UCE}[\mathcal{S}^{\mathsf{sup}}]$ function family with $\mathsf{H.IL}(\cdot) = \mathsf{H.OL}(\cdot) = \mathbb{N}$. From the above we know that $\mathsf{EwH}[\mathsf{H}, \mathsf{RE}]$ will not be IND for all IND-CPA RE. We consider instead a particular choice of IND-CPA RE. Recall that BR93 [13] present a simple TDF-based PKE scheme proven IND-CPA in the ROM. We instantiate their TDF with a LTDF and then instantiate the RO with H to get a standard-model

PKE scheme we denote $\mathsf{RE} = \mathsf{BR93}[\mathsf{LT},\mathsf{H}]$. We now consider the standard-model D-PKE scheme $\mathsf{EwH}[\mathsf{H},\mathsf{RE}]$. In this scheme, H is used twice, with two independent keys. Our final $\mathsf{DE1}$ D-PKE scheme is obtained by using the same key for both invocations of H. The algorithms of this scheme are shown in Fig. 5. Importantly, $\mathsf{DE1.IL}(\cdot) = \mathsf{H.OL}(\cdot) = \mathbb{N}$, meaning we can encrypt messages of arbitrary and varying length. We note that using a single H key is not only an optimization in key size but also avoids using multi-key variants of UCE [8] and is important to prove security under $\mathsf{UCE}[\mathcal{S}^{\mathrm{sup}}]$. The following says that $\mathsf{DE1}$ is IND-secure.

Theorem 2. *Let* LT *be a lossy trapdoor function and* H *a* $\mathsf{UCE}[\mathcal{S}^{\mathrm{sup}}]$ *function family with* $\mathsf{H.IL}(\cdot) = \mathsf{H.OL}(\cdot) = \mathbb{N}$. *Let* $\mathsf{DE1}$ *be constructed as in Fig. 5. Then*

Asymptotic result: $\mathsf{DE1}$ *is IND-secure.*

Concrete result: Let A *be an adversary and* P *a predictor. We can construct an adversary* B, *a source* S, *and a distinguisher* D *such that*

$$\mathsf{Adv}^{\mathrm{ind}}_{\mathsf{DE1},A}(\cdot) \leq 2\mathsf{Adv}^{\mathrm{ltdf}}_{\mathsf{LT},B}(\cdot) + 2\mathsf{Adv}^{\mathrm{uce}}_{\mathsf{H},S,D}(\cdot) + \frac{3v^2}{2^{\mathsf{LT.il}}} \tag{1}$$

$$\mathsf{Adv}^{\mathrm{pred}}_{S,P}(\cdot) \leq \frac{1.5v^2}{2^{\mathsf{LT.il}}} + qv \cdot \mathsf{Guess}_A(\cdot) + \frac{qv}{2^\tau} \tag{2}$$

where q *is the maximum of the size of* P*'s output in the execution of* Pred^P_S, v *is the maximum of the size of* A*'s message vector in the execution of* $\mathrm{IND}^A_{\mathsf{DE}}$, *and* τ *is the lossiness of* LT. *Furthermore,* $\mathbf{T}(\mathsf{UCE}^{S,D}_{\mathsf{H}}) \leq \mathbf{T}(\mathrm{IND}^A_{\mathsf{DE1}})$; $\mathbf{Q}^{\mathrm{HASH}}_S \leq v$; *and* $\mathbf{T}(\mathsf{Lossy}^B_{\mathsf{LT}}) \leq \mathbf{T}(\mathrm{IND}^A_{\mathsf{DE1}})$. ∎

The proof is in [7]. Here we discuss some of the ideas. To construct a source S and a distinguisher D, a naive method is to let them run A to simulate game $\mathrm{IND}^A_{\mathsf{DE1}}$. However this won't produce a statistically unpredictable source. The key idea is to let our source generate a *lossy* key lk. instead of an injective key ek as in game $\mathrm{IND}^A_{\mathsf{DE1}}$. The statistical unpredictability of S then follows from the lossiness of LT, as represented by (2). On the other hand, game $\mathsf{UCE}^{S,D}_{\mathsf{H}}$ for challenge bit $b = 1$ no longer coincides with game $\mathrm{IND}^A_{\mathsf{DE1}}$. Still, this gap can be bounded by constructing B attacking LT, so that (1) holds.

In Section 5 we discuss how, under appropriate instantiations of the $\mathsf{UCE}[\mathcal{S}^{\mathrm{sup}}]$ family, $\mathsf{DE1}$ is extremely efficient compared to prior standard-model D-PKE schemes.

BFOR [6] originally defined an IND adversary as a triple (A_0, A_1, A_2), where A_0 specifies state information that is passed on to A_1, A_2. Results from [5] indicate this is important to ensure that security in the standard model implies security in the ROM. For notational simplicity, here we omit A_0. Our construction and proof work for the original IND definition with the following modification. One first needs to redefine Guess_A as the conditional min-entropy of the messages, given the state, and then include the state as a part of the leakage of S.

GAME $\text{CDA}_{\mathsf{HE}}^A(\lambda)$
$(ek, dk) \leftarrow\!\!\text{\tiny\$}\ \mathsf{HE.Kg}(1^\lambda)\ ;\ b \leftarrow\!\!\text{\tiny\$}\ \{0,1\}\ ;\ ,\ \ \leftarrow\!\!\text{\tiny\$}\ A_2^{\mathrm{LR}}(1^\lambda)$
$b' \leftarrow\!\!\text{\tiny\$}\ A_2(,\ , ek)\ ;\ \text{Return}\ (b = b')$

$\underline{\mathrm{LR}(d)}$
$(\mathbf{m}_0, \mathbf{m}_1, \mathbf{r}) \leftarrow\!\!\text{\tiny\$}\ A_1(1^\lambda, d)$
For $i = 1$ to $|\mathbf{r}|$ do $\mathbf{c}[i] \leftarrow \mathsf{HE.Enc}(1^\lambda, ek, \mathbf{m}_b[i]; \mathbf{r}[i])$
Return $\mathbf{c}$

Fig. 6. Game defining IND-CDA security of PKE scheme HE

4 Fully Secure Hedged PKE

In this section we provide the first fully H-IND PKE schemes in the standard model. Additionally our schemes are efficient. HE1 is our base scheme encrypting fixed-length messages; HE2 encrypts variable-length messages; HE3 has a tighter security analysis. Our schemes provide pragmatic and effective defense against subversion of encryption randomness.

Hedged PKE. To achieve standard IND-CPA security, PKE schemes demand truly random coins. Many well-known PKE schemes fail spectacularly, allowing message recovery from the ciphertext, if the latter is created with even somewhat weak coins [4, 20, 46]. BBNRSS [4] introduce security under chosen-distribution attack (IND-CDA) to provide meaningful security when bad randomness is used. A secure hedged PKE scheme must provide IND-CPA security when the coins are truly random, and fall back to IND-CDA security when bad coins are provided. Formally, for a PKE scheme HE, we say that HE is H-IND secure if (1) HE is IND-CPA secure, and (2) HE is IND-CDA secure. Game CDA defining the IND-CDA notion is given in Fig. 6. An IND-CDA adversary $A = (A_1, A_2)$ is a pair of algorithms. In the first part of the attack, A_2 can adaptively query oracle LR, each query taking a distribution-specifier string d and returning a challenge ciphertext vector $\mathbf{c}$. In this phase A_2 does not get ek. Once this stage ends, it gets ek and must then render its decision. Algorithm A_1 defines a distribution over triples $(\mathbf{m}_0, \mathbf{m}_1, \mathbf{r})$ that is a function of d. We require that (i) there be a polynomial v such that $|\mathbf{m}_0| = |\mathbf{m}_1| = |\mathbf{r}| \leq v(\lambda)$, (ii) $|\mathbf{m}_0[i]| = |\mathbf{m}_1[i]| \in \mathsf{HE.IL}(\lambda)$ and $|\mathbf{r}[i]| = \mathsf{HE.rl}(\lambda)$ for every $i \leq |\mathbf{r}|$, and (iii) for each $b \in \{0,1\}$ the $|\mathbf{r}|$ pairs $(\mathbf{m}_b[i], \mathbf{r}[i])$ are distinct, where $1 \leq i \leq |\mathbf{r}|$. Let $\text{Guess}_A(\cdot)$ be the function that on input $\lambda \in \mathbb{N}$ returns the maximum, over all b, i, m, r, d, of $\Pr[(\mathbf{m}_b[i], \mathbf{r}[i]) = (m, r)]$, the probability over $(\mathbf{m}_0, \mathbf{m}_1, \mathbf{r}) \leftarrow\!\!\text{\tiny\$}\ A_1(1^\lambda, d)$. We say that A has high min-entropy if $\text{Guess}_A(\cdot)$ is negligible. We say that HE is IND-CDA-secure if $\text{Adv}_{\mathsf{HE},A}^{\mathsf{cda}}(\cdot) = 2\Pr[\text{CDA}_{\mathsf{HE}}^A(\cdot)] - 1$ is negligible for every PT adversary A of high min-entropy. We stress that this captures full IND-CDA since the messages in the message vectors may be arbitrarily correlated.

The HE1 Scheme. Recall we obtained our D-PKE scheme DE1 via a BR93-based instantiation of EwH. In analogy it is natural to try to obtain an H-

$\mathsf{Hedge}[\mathsf{H},\mathsf{LT}].\mathsf{Kg}(1^\lambda)$	$\mathsf{Hedge}[\mathsf{H},\mathsf{LT}].\mathsf{Enc}(1^\lambda,(ek,hk),m;r)$
$hk \leftarrow_\$ \mathsf{H}.\mathsf{Kg}(1^\lambda)$	$x \leftarrow \mathsf{H}.\mathsf{Ev}(1^\lambda, hk, r \parallel m, 1^{\mathsf{LT.il}(\lambda)})$
$(ek, dk) \leftarrow_\$ \mathsf{LT}.\mathsf{EKg}(1^\lambda)$	$trap \leftarrow \mathsf{LT}.\mathsf{Ev}(1^\lambda, ek, x)$
Return $((ek, hk), (dk, hk))$	$c \leftarrow \mathsf{H}.\mathsf{Ev}(1^\lambda, hk, x, 1^{|m|}) \oplus m$
	Return $(trap, c)$
	$\mathsf{Hedge}[\mathsf{H},\mathsf{LT}].\mathsf{Dec}(1^\lambda, (dk, hk), (trap, c))$
	$x \leftarrow \mathsf{LT}.\mathsf{Inv}(1^\lambda, dk, trap)$
	$m \leftarrow \mathsf{H}.\mathsf{Ev}(1^\lambda, hk, x, 1^{|c|}) \oplus c$; Return m

$\mathsf{H}.\mathsf{Kg}(1^\lambda)$	$\mathsf{H}.\mathsf{Ev}(1^\lambda, hk, x, 1^\ell)$
$uk \leftarrow_\$ \mathsf{U}.\mathsf{Kg}(1^\lambda)$; $\overline{hk} \leftarrow_\$ \overline{\mathsf{H}}.\mathsf{Kg}(\lambda)$	$(\overline{hk}, uk) \leftarrow hk$; $u \leftarrow \mathsf{U}.\mathsf{Ev}(1^\lambda, uk, x)$
$hk \leftarrow (\overline{hk}, uk)$; Return hk	$y \leftarrow \overline{\mathsf{H}}.\mathsf{Ev}(1^\lambda, \overline{hk}, u, 1^\ell)$; Return y

$\mathsf{U}.\mathsf{Kg}(1^\lambda)$	$\mathsf{U}.\mathsf{Ev}(1^\lambda, (\overline{uk}, rk), x)$
$\overline{uk} \leftarrow_\$ \overline{\mathsf{U}}.\mathsf{Kg}(1^\lambda)$	If $|x| < \mathsf{U}.\mathsf{ol}(\lambda)$ then
$mk \leftarrow_\$ \{0,1\}^{\mathsf{U}.\mathsf{ol}(\lambda)}$	Return $mk \oplus (x \parallel 10^{\mathsf{U}.\mathsf{ol}(\lambda)-|x|})$
$rk \leftarrow_\$ \mathrm{GF}(2^{\mathsf{U}.\mathsf{ol}(\lambda)}) \backslash \{0^{\mathsf{U}.\mathsf{ol}(\lambda)}\}$	$x_1 \leftarrow x[1, \mathsf{U}.\mathsf{ol}(\lambda)]$; $x_2 \leftarrow x[\mathsf{U}.\mathsf{ol}(\lambda)+1, |x|]$
Return $(\overline{uk}, rk, mk)$	$y \leftarrow \overline{\mathsf{U}}.\mathsf{Ev}(1^\lambda, \overline{uk}, x_2) \oplus (x_1 \times rk)$
	Return y

Fig. 7. Top: The PKE scheme $\mathsf{Hedge}[\mathsf{H}, \mathsf{LT}]$ associated to function family H and LTDF LT. **Middle:** The $\mathsf{H} = \mathsf{AU}\text{-}\mathsf{then}\text{-}\mathsf{Hash}[\mathsf{U}, \overline{\mathsf{H}}]$ VIL $\mathsf{UCE}[\mathcal{S}^{\mathrm{sup}}]$ family built from an AU hash U and a FIL $\mathsf{UCE}[\mathcal{S}^{\mathrm{sup}}]$ family $\overline{\mathsf{H}}$. **Bottom:** The $\mathsf{U} = \mathsf{Hash}\text{-}\mathsf{then}\text{-}\mathsf{Mask}[\overline{\mathsf{U}}]$ AU family built from an AU family $\overline{\mathsf{U}}$. The operator $\times$ is multiplication in the finite field $\mathrm{GF}(2^{\mathsf{U}.\mathsf{ol}(\lambda)})$ and the string $0^{\mathsf{U}.\mathsf{ol}(\lambda)}$ encodes the zero element of $\mathrm{GF}(2^{\mathsf{U}.\mathsf{ol}(\lambda)})$. **HE1:** Our HE1 PKE scheme is obtained from an LTDF LT, a FIL $\mathsf{UCE}[\mathcal{S}^{\mathrm{sup}}]$ family $\overline{\mathsf{H}}$ and an AU family $\overline{\mathsf{U}}$ as $\mathsf{HE1} = \mathsf{Hedge}[\mathsf{H}, \mathsf{LT}]$ with $\mathsf{H} = \mathsf{AU}\text{-}\mathsf{then}\text{-}\mathsf{Hash}[\mathsf{U}, \overline{\mathsf{H}}]$ and $\mathsf{U} = \mathsf{Hash}\text{-}\mathsf{then}\text{-}\mathsf{Mask}[\overline{\mathsf{U}}]$.

IND scheme via a similar BR93-based instantiation of the REwH transform of BBNRSS [4]. This results in the candidate scheme $\mathsf{Hedge}[\mathsf{H}, \mathsf{LT}]$, associated to a function family H and LTDF LT, whose algorithms are shown in the left panel of Fig. 7. Here $\mathsf{Hedge}[\mathsf{H}, \mathsf{LT}].\mathsf{IL}(\cdot) = \mathsf{H}.\mathsf{OL}(\cdot)$, meaning we can encrypt messages of length matching the allowed output lengths of H.

We first ask if one can show IND-CDA security of $\mathsf{Hedge}[\mathsf{H}, \mathsf{LT}]$ assuming $\mathsf{UCE}[\mathcal{S}^{\mathrm{sup}}]$ security of H. This involves two new difficulties relative to Theorem 2. The first, more minor, is the presence of the randomness. The second is more major, namely that the IND-CDA notion is adaptive. To address this, BBNRSS [4] needed quite involved techniques including anonymous LTDFs and an adaptive LHL, and yet only achieved security for block sources, not the full IND-CDA security that we target. However we are able to show that $\mathsf{Hedge}[\mathsf{H}, \mathsf{LT}]$ does achieve (full) IND-CDA assuming only that LT is a (standard) LTDF and H is $\mathsf{UCE}[\mathcal{S}^{\mathrm{sup}}]$.

But recall that H-IND requires also that $\mathsf{Hedge}[\mathsf{H}, \mathsf{LT}]$ is IND-CPA. But it is quite unclear why this would be true under $\mathsf{UCE}[\mathcal{S}^{\mathrm{sup}}]$ security of H. The reason is that UCE guarantees nothing for inputs depending on hk but messages in

IND-CPA can depend on the public key, which contains hk. This difficulty is quite fundamental and at first seemed impossible to circumvent within the UCE framework. We resolve it by using a *particular* UCE[$\mathcal{S}^{\mathrm{sup}}$] family H. Let $\overline{\mathsf{H}}$ be a fixed input length UCE[$\mathcal{S}^{\mathrm{sup}}$] family. Recall that the AU-then-Hash transform of BHK2 [10] takes an AU (almost universal) family U and $\overline{\mathsf{H}}$ to return a variable input length family $\mathsf{H} = \mathsf{AU\text{-}then\text{-}Hash}[\mathsf{U}, \overline{\mathsf{H}}]$ that they show is itself UCE[$\mathcal{S}^{\mathrm{sup}}$]. We will take an (arbitrary) AU family $\overline{\mathsf{U}}$ and construct another, special AU family $\mathsf{U} = \mathsf{Hash\text{-}then\text{-}Mask}[\overline{\mathsf{U}}]$ via a transform called Hash-then-Mask that we introduce. Then our UCE[$\mathcal{S}^{\mathrm{sup}}$] family is $\mathsf{H} = \mathsf{AU\text{-}then\text{-}Hash}[\mathsf{U}, \overline{\mathsf{H}}]$. With this choice we will be able to show that $\mathsf{HE1} = \mathsf{Hedge}[\mathsf{H}, \mathsf{LT}]$ —this is our scheme— is IND-CPA. In conjunction with our prior claim, HE1 is then H-IND as desired.

We now detail this. We recall some definitions from BHK2 [9]. Let V be a fixed output length (FOL) function family. Let $\lambda, m \in \mathbb{N}$. Let

$$\mathbf{Coll1}_{\mathsf{V}}(\lambda, m) = \max\left\{ \Pr[y = \mathsf{V.Ev}(1^\lambda, vk, x)] : |y| = \mathsf{V.ol}(\lambda) \text{ and } |x| \le m \right\}$$

$$\mathbf{Coll2}_{\mathsf{V}}(\lambda, m_0, m_1) = \max\left\{ \Pr[\mathsf{V.Ev}(1^\lambda, vk, x_0) = \mathsf{V.Ev}(1^\lambda, vk, x_1)] : \right.$$
$$\left. |x_0| \le m_0, |x_1| \le m_1 \text{ and } x_0 \ne x_1 \right\}$$

$$\mathbf{Coll}_{\mathsf{V}}(\lambda, m_0, m_1) = \max\left\{ \mathbf{Coll2}_{\mathsf{V}}(\lambda, m_0, m_1), \mathbf{Coll1}_{\mathsf{V}}(\lambda, \min\{m_0, m_1\}) \right\} .$$

In the first and second equations, the probability is over $vk \leftarrow\!\!\text{\$}\, \mathsf{V.Kg}(1^\lambda)$. A FOL family V is *almost universal* (AU) if for all polynomials $M_0, M_1 \colon \mathbb{N} \to \mathbb{N}$ the function f_{M_0, M_1} is negligible, where for $\lambda \in \mathbb{N}$ we let $f_{M_0, M_1}(\lambda) = \mathbf{Coll}_{\mathsf{V}}(\lambda, M_0(\lambda), M_1(\lambda))$.

Now let $\overline{\mathsf{U}}$ be a (FOL) AU family having $\overline{\mathsf{U}}.\mathsf{IL} = \mathbb{N}$. We introduce a transform called Hash-then-Mask that given $\overline{\mathsf{U}}$ returns the family $\mathsf{U} = \mathsf{Hash\text{-}then\text{-}Mask}[\overline{\mathsf{U}}]$ defined in the right panel of Fig. 7. It has $\mathsf{U.ol} = \overline{\mathsf{U}}.\mathsf{ol}$ and $\mathsf{U.IL} = \mathbb{N}$. Lemma 3 below shows that U is itself an AU family.

Lemma 3. *Let $\overline{\mathsf{U}}$ be a (FOL) AU hash of $\overline{\mathsf{U}}.\mathsf{IL} = \mathbb{N}$. Let $\mathsf{U} = \mathsf{Hash\text{-}then\text{-}Mask}[\overline{\mathsf{U}}]$. Then for any $\lambda, m, m' \in \mathbb{N}$ we have (a) $\mathbf{Coll1}_{\mathsf{U}}(\lambda, m) \le \mathbf{Coll1}_{\overline{\mathsf{U}}}(\lambda, m) + 2^{-\overline{\mathsf{U}}.\mathsf{ol}(\lambda)}$ and (b) $\mathbf{Coll2}_{\mathsf{U}}(\lambda, m, m') \le \mathbf{Coll2}_{\overline{\mathsf{U}}}(\lambda, m, m') + 2/2^{\overline{\mathsf{U}}.\mathsf{ol}(\lambda)}$.* ∎

The proof of Lemma 3 is in [7]. Note that BHK2 [9] provide an extremely fast construction of an AU family $\overline{\mathsf{U}}$, running at 0.4 cycles per byte. Our Hash-then-Mask does not degrade speed much, and thus the family $\mathsf{U} = \mathsf{Hash\text{-}then\text{-}Mask}[\overline{\mathsf{U}}]$ used in our scheme is also fast.

Now let $\overline{\mathsf{H}}$ be a function family with FIL $\overline{\mathsf{H}}.\mathsf{il}$ and with $\overline{\mathsf{H}}.\mathsf{OL} = \mathbb{N}$. Let U be a FOL AU function family with $\mathsf{U.ol} = \overline{\mathsf{H}}.\mathsf{il}$ and with $\mathsf{U.IL} = \overline{\mathsf{H}}.\mathsf{OL} = \mathbb{N}$. The AU-then-Hash transform of BHK2 [9] takes $\mathsf{U}, \overline{\mathsf{H}}$ and returns the family $\mathsf{H} = \mathsf{AU\text{-}then\text{-}Hash}[\mathsf{U}, \overline{\mathsf{H}}]$ shown in the middle panel of Fig. 7. It has $\mathsf{H.OL} = \mathsf{H.IL} = \mathbb{N}$. BHK2 [9] show that if $\overline{\mathsf{H}}$ is UCE[$\mathcal{S}^{\mathrm{sup}}$] then so is H.

We are finally ready to define our HE1 scheme. Let $\overline{\mathsf{H}}$ be a function family with FIL $\overline{\mathsf{H}}.\mathsf{il}$ and with $\overline{\mathsf{H}}.\mathsf{OL} = \mathbb{N}$. Let $\overline{\mathsf{U}}$ be a (FOL) AU family having $\overline{\mathsf{U}}.\mathsf{IL} = \mathbb{N}$. Let LT be an LTDF. Let $\ell\colon \mathbb{N} \to \mathbb{N}$ be a polynomial. Then let $\mathsf{HE1} = \mathsf{Hedge}[\mathsf{H}, \mathsf{LT}]$ with $\mathsf{H} = \mathsf{AU\text{-}then\text{-}Hash}[\mathsf{U}, \overline{\mathsf{H}}]$ and $\mathsf{U} = \mathsf{Hash\text{-}then\text{-}Mask}[\overline{\mathsf{U}}]$. A subtle point is that we set $\mathsf{HE1}.\mathsf{il} = \ell$, meaning HE1 is restricted to encrypt messages of length ℓ.

Why this is needed is not evident from the scheme description but will be needed in the proof of security. We also set $\mathsf{HE1.rl} = \overline{\mathsf{U}}.\mathsf{ol}$. Theorem 4 below shows that HE1 is H-IND secure. The concrete security statements refer to

$$\mathsf{Adv}_{\mathsf{U}}^{\mathsf{coll}}(\lambda, p, \sigma)$$

$$= \max \left\{ \sum_{i=1}^{k} \sum_{j=1}^{k'} \mathbf{Coll}_{\mathsf{U}}(\lambda, m_i, m_j') : k \right\} \leq p, k' \leq p, \sum_{i=1}^{k} m_i \leq \sigma, \sum_{i=1}^{k'} m_i' \leq \sigma.$$

Theorem 4. *Let $\overline{\mathsf{H}}$ be a $\mathsf{UCE}[\mathcal{S}^{\mathrm{sup}}]$ function family with FIL $\overline{\mathsf{H}}.\mathsf{il}$ and with $\overline{\mathsf{H}}.\mathsf{OL} = \mathbb{N}$. Let $\overline{\mathsf{U}}$ be a (FOL) AU family having $\overline{\mathsf{U}}.\mathsf{IL} = \mathbb{N}$. Let LT be an LTDF. Let $\ell\colon \mathbb{N} \to \mathbb{N}$ be a polynomial. Let HE1 be defined from $\overline{\mathsf{H}}, \overline{\mathsf{U}}, \mathsf{LT}, \ell$ as above.*

Asymptotic result: *HE1 is H-IND secure.*

Concrete IND-CPA result: *Let A be an adversary and $\overline{P}$ be a predictor. We can construct a source $\overline{S}$, a distinguisher $\overline{D}$ and an adversary B such that*

$$\mathsf{Adv}_{\mathsf{HE1},A}^{\mathsf{ind-cpa}}(\cdot) \leq 2\mathsf{Adv}_{\overline{\mathsf{H}},\overline{S},\overline{D}}^{\mathsf{uce}}(\cdot) + 2\mathsf{Adv}_{\mathsf{LT},B}^{\mathsf{ltdf}}(\cdot) + 2^{1-\overline{\mathsf{U}}.\mathsf{ol}}$$

$$\mathsf{Adv}_{\overline{S},\overline{P}}^{\mathsf{pred}}(\cdot) \leq \frac{\sqrt{q}}{2^{\tau/2}} + \sqrt{q \cdot \mathbf{Coll2}_{\overline{\mathsf{U}}}(\cdot, \mathsf{LT.il})} + \frac{2\sqrt{q}}{2^{\overline{\mathsf{U}}.\mathsf{ol}/2}}$$

where q is the maximum of the size of $\overline{P}$'s output in the execution of $\mathrm{Pred}_{\overline{S}}^{\overline{P}}$ and τ is the lossiness of LT. Furthermore, $\mathbf{T}(\mathrm{Lossy}_{\mathsf{LT}}^B), \mathbf{T}(\mathrm{UCE}_{\overline{\mathsf{H}}}^{\overline{S},\overline{D}})$; and $\mathbf{Q}_S^{\mathrm{HASH}} = 2$.

Concrete IND-CDA result: *Let A be an adversary and $\overline{P}$ be a predictor. We can construct a source $\overline{S}$, a distinguisher $\overline{D}$ and an adversary B such that*

$$\mathsf{Adv}_{\mathsf{HE1},A}^{\mathsf{cda}}(\cdot) \leq 2\mathsf{Adv}_{\mathsf{LT},B}^{\mathsf{ltdf}}(\cdot) + 2\mathsf{Adv}_{\overline{\mathsf{H}},\overline{S},\overline{D}}^{\mathsf{uce}}(\cdot) + 2\mathsf{Adv}_{\mathsf{U}}^{\mathsf{coll}}(\cdot, 2p, s) +$$

$$3p^2 \cdot \mathrm{Guess}_A(\cdot) + \frac{19p^2}{2^{\min\{\overline{\mathsf{U}}.\mathsf{ol},\mathsf{LT.il}\}}}$$

$$\mathsf{Adv}_{\overline{S},\overline{P}}^{\mathsf{pred}}(\cdot) \leq \sqrt{2q \cdot \mathsf{Adv}_{\mathsf{U}}^{\mathsf{coll}}(\cdot, 2p, s)} + 2p\sqrt{q \cdot \mathrm{Guess}_A(\cdot)} + \frac{6p\sqrt{q}}{2^{\min\{\overline{\mathsf{U}}.\mathsf{ol},\tau\}/2}}$$

where p is the maximum of the total number of messages that A produces in the execution of $\mathrm{CDA}_{\mathsf{HE1}}^A$, $s = p \cdot (\overline{\mathsf{U}}.\mathsf{ol} + \mathsf{LT.il} + \ell)$, q is the maximum of the size of $\overline{P}$'s output in the execution of $\mathrm{Pred}_{\overline{S}}^{\overline{P}}$, and τ is the lossiness of LT. Moreover, $\mathbf{T}(\mathrm{Lossy}_{\mathsf{LT}}^B), \mathbf{T}(\mathrm{UCE}_{\overline{\mathsf{H}}}^{\overline{S},\overline{D}}) \leq \mathbf{T}(\mathrm{CDA}_{\mathsf{HE1}}^A)$; and $\mathbf{Q}_{\overline{S}}^{\mathrm{HASH}} \leq 2p$.   ∎

The proof of Theorem 4 is in [7]. Here we discuss some of the ideas. For IND-CPA security, recall that the adversary A makes only a single LR query. The transform Hash-then-Mask ensures that, for any string m, if r is a random $\overline{\mathsf{U}}.\mathsf{ol}(\lambda)$-bit string and $uk \leftarrow_\$ \mathsf{U.Kg}(1^\lambda)$ then $u \leftarrow \mathsf{U}(1^\lambda, uk, r \,\|\, m)$ is also uniformly random, independent of m. Therefore, one doesn't need to know m to sample $r \leftarrow_\$ \{0, 1\}^{\overline{\mathsf{U}}.\mathsf{ol}(\lambda)}$

HE2.Enc$(1^\lambda, (ek, hk), m; r)$	HE2.Dec$(1^\lambda, (dk, hk), (trap, c))$
$x \leftarrow$ H.Ev$(1^\lambda, hk, r \parallel m, 1^{\text{LT.il}(\lambda)})$	$x \leftarrow$ LT.Inv$(1^\lambda, dk, trap)$
$trap \leftarrow$ LT.Ev$(1^\lambda, ek, x)$	$seed \leftarrow$ H.Ev$(1^\lambda, hk, x, 1^{\text{F.kl}(\lambda)+\overline{U}.\text{ol}(\lambda)})$
$seed \leftarrow$ H.Ev$(1^\lambda, hk, x, 1^{\text{F.kl}(\lambda)+\overline{U}.\text{ol}(\lambda)})$	$y \leftarrow seed[1, \overline{U}.\text{ol}(\lambda)]$
$y \leftarrow seed[1, \overline{U}.\text{ol}(\lambda)]$	$fk \leftarrow seed[\overline{U}.\text{ol}(\lambda) + 1, \lvert seed \rvert]$
$fk \leftarrow seed[\overline{U}.\text{ol}(\lambda) + 1, \lvert seed \rvert]$	$mask \leftarrow$ F.Ev$(1^\lambda, fk, 0^{\text{F.il}(\lambda)}, 1^{\lvert c \rvert})$
$mask \leftarrow$ F.Ev$(1^\lambda, fk, 0^{\text{F.il}(\lambda)}, 1^{\lvert m \rvert})$	$m \leftarrow$ H.Ev$(1^\lambda, hk, y, 1^{\lvert c \rvert}) \oplus mask \oplus c$
$c \leftarrow$ H.Ev$(1^\lambda, hk, y, 1^{\lvert m \rvert}) \oplus mask \oplus m$	Return m
Return $(trap, c)$	

Fig. 8. Encryption and decryption algorithms of HE2, where $\overline{U}$ is an AU family, $\overline{H}$ is a FIL UCE$[\mathcal{S}^{\text{sup}}]$ family, F is a VOL PRF, LT is a LTDF. Here U = Hash-then-Mask$[\overline{U}]$ and H = AU-then-Hash$[U, \overline{H}]$.

and compute $x \leftarrow$ H.Ev$(1^\lambda, hk, r \parallel m, 1^{\text{LT.il}(\lambda)})$, because one can instead sample $u \leftarrow_\$ \{0,1\}^{\overline{U}.\text{ol}(\lambda)}$ and compute $x \leftarrow \overline{H}.Ev(1^\lambda, \overline{hk}, u, 1^{\text{LT.il}(\lambda)})$. The source will leak H.Ev$(1^\lambda, hk, x, 1^{\lvert m \rvert})$ so that the distinguisher can run A to get m and xor the two strings to complete the ciphertext. Still, computing H.Ev$(1^\lambda, hk, x, 1^{\lvert m \rvert})$ requires knowing $\lvert m \rvert$; it's why HE1 can only handle fixed-length messages. For IND-CDA security, we can actually prove that Hedge$[H, LT]$ is IND-CDA secure for *any* UCE$[\mathcal{S}^{\text{sup}}]$ H. The source will run A_1 and the first phase of A_2 to create the ciphertexts via the HASH oracle. Note that during the first phase, A_2 only receives what the source sees, and therefore doesn't get to learn the hash key hk. UCE then allows us to switch to a game in which the adversary has to fight an RO-based scheme, and thus its adaptivity is futile. Moreover, it can only specify *distributions*, and thus despite the adaptivity, the chance that the source repeats a HASH query is about $p^2 \cdot \text{Guess}_A$. We again exploit the lossiness of LT to allow statistical unpredictability.

The HE2 Scheme. With HE1 we reach our goal of the first fully H-IND secure PKE scheme in the standard model. Additionally it is more efficient than prior standard-model schemes that only achieved non-full security. However, like prior standard-model schemes, it is FIL, meaning only encrypts messages of a fixed length. We now provide the HE2 scheme that retains the security properties of HE1 but additionally can encrypt messages of variable and arbitrary length. Furthermore it can do this with hybrid-encryption like performance, meaning the asymmetric cost is fixed as message length grows.

The additional tool that we need is a VOL PRF F —this means F.OL$(\cdot) = \mathbb{N}$— such that $\lambda \in$ F.IL(λ) for every $\lambda \in \mathbb{N}$. As before let $\overline{H}$ be a function family with FIL $\overline{H}.$il and with $\overline{H}.$OL$(\cdot) = \mathbb{N}$. Let $\overline{U}$ be a (FOL) AU family having $\overline{U}.$IL$(\cdot) = \mathbb{N}$. Let LT be an LTDF. Let U = Hash-then-Mask$[\overline{U}]$ and H = AU-then-Hash$[U, \overline{H}]$. The encryption and decryption algorithms of HE2 are specified in Fig. 8. The key-generation algorithm HE2.Kg is the same as HE1.Kg. We let HE2.rl = $\overline{U}.$ol. But this time HE2.IL$(\cdot) = \mathbb{N}$, meaning we can encrypt messages of any length. Theorem 5 below formally confirms that HE2 is H-IND secure.

Theorem 5. *Let* F *be a PRF with* $F.OL(\cdot) = \mathbb{N}$ *and* $\lambda \in F.IL(\lambda)$ *for every* $\lambda \in \mathbb{N}$. *Let* $\overline{H}$ *be a* UCE[$\mathcal{S}^{\mathrm{sup}}$] *function family with FIL* $\overline{H}.il$ *and with* $\overline{H}.OL(\cdot) = \mathbb{N}$. *Let* $\overline{U}$ *be a (FOL) AU family having* $\overline{U}.IL(\cdot) = \mathbb{N}$. *Let* LT *be an LTDF. Let* HE2 *be defined from* $F, \overline{H}, \overline{U}, LT$ *as above.*

Asymptotic result: HE2 *is H-IND secure.*

Concrete IND-CPA result: Let A *be an adversary and* $\overline{P}$ *be a predictor. We can construct a source* $\overline{S}$, *a distinguisher* $\overline{D}$, *adversaries* B *and* C *such that*

$$\mathsf{Adv}^{\mathrm{ind\text{-}cpa}}_{\mathsf{HE2},A}(\cdot) \le 2\mathsf{Adv}^{\mathrm{uce}}_{\overline{H},\overline{S},\overline{D}}(\cdot) + 2\mathsf{Adv}^{\mathrm{ltdf}}_{\mathsf{LT},B}(\cdot) + 2\mathsf{Adv}^{\mathrm{prf}}_{\mathsf{F},C}(\cdot) + 2^{1-\overline{U}.\mathrm{ol}}$$

$$\mathsf{Adv}^{\mathrm{pred}}_{\overline{S},\overline{P}}(\cdot) \le \frac{\sqrt{q}}{2^{\tau/2}} + \sqrt{q \cdot \mathbf{Coll2}_{\overline{U}}(\cdot, \mathsf{LT}.\mathrm{il})} + \frac{2\sqrt{q}}{2^{\overline{U}.\mathrm{ol}/2}}$$

where q *is the maximum of the size of* $\overline{P}$'s *output in the execution of* $\mathrm{Pred}^{\overline{P}}_{\overline{S}}$ *and* τ *is the lossiness of* LT. *Furthermore,* $\mathbf{T}(\mathrm{Lossy}^B_{\mathsf{LT}}), \mathbf{T}(\mathrm{UCE}^{\overline{S},\overline{D}}_{\overline{H}}), \mathbf{T}(\mathrm{PRF}^C_{\mathsf{F}}) \le \mathbf{T}(\mathrm{CPA}^A_{\mathsf{HE3}}); \mathbf{Q}^{\mathrm{RR}}_C = 1;$ *and* $\mathbf{Q}^{\mathrm{HASH}}_S = 2$.

Concrete IND-CDA result: Let A *be an adversary and* $\overline{P}$ *be a predictor. We can construct a source* $\overline{S}$, *a distinguisher* $\overline{D}$, *adversary* B *such that*

$$\mathsf{Adv}^{\mathrm{cda}}_{\mathsf{HE},A}(\cdot) \le 2\mathsf{Adv}^{\mathrm{ltdf}}_{\mathsf{LT},B}(\cdot) + 2\mathsf{Adv}^{\mathrm{uce}}_{\overline{H},\overline{S},\overline{D}}(\cdot) + 2\mathsf{Adv}^{\mathrm{coll}}_{\overline{U}}(\cdot, 3p, s) +$$

$$5p^2 \cdot \mathrm{Guess}_A(\cdot) + \frac{44p^2}{2^{\min\{\overline{U}.\mathrm{ol},\mathsf{LT}.\mathrm{il}\}}}$$

$$\mathsf{Adv}^{\mathrm{pred}}_{\overline{S},\overline{P}}(\cdot) \le \sqrt{2q\mathsf{Adv}^{\mathrm{coll}}_{\overline{U}}(\cdot, 3p, s)} + 2.5p\sqrt{q \cdot \mathrm{Guess}_A(\cdot)} + \frac{9.5p\sqrt{q}}{2^{\min\{\overline{U}.\mathrm{ol},\tau\}/2}}$$

where p *is the maximum of the total number of messages that* A *produces in the execution of* $\mathrm{CDA}^A_{\mathsf{HE2}}$, s *is* $3p \cdot \max\{\overline{U}.\mathrm{ol}, \mathsf{LT}.\mathrm{il}\}$ *plus the maximum of the total length of messages that* A *produces in the execution of* $\mathrm{CDA}^A_{\mathsf{HE2}}$, q *is the maximum of the size of* $\overline{P}$'s *output in the execution of* $\mathrm{Pred}^{\overline{P}}_{\overline{S}}$, *and* τ *is the lossiness of* LT. *In addition,* $\mathbf{T}(\mathrm{Lossy}^B_{\mathsf{LT}}), \mathbf{T}(\mathrm{UCE}^{\overline{S},\overline{D}}_{\overline{H}}) \le \mathbf{T}(\mathrm{CDA}^A_{\mathsf{HE2}});$ *and* $\mathbf{Q}^{\mathrm{HASH}}_{\overline{S}} \le 3p$. ∎

The proof of Theorem 5 is in [7]. Here we give some intuition about why HE2 can securely handle variable-length messages. We'll only discuss the IND-CPA case, in which the message length may depend on the public key. The source will be responsible for producing a PRF key fk, whose length is independent of the public key, and will leak it along with some other information. The UCE security is only used to ensure that fk looks random to the distinguisher. The task of generating the two pads $F.Ev(1^\lambda, fk, 0^{F.il(\lambda)}, 1^{|m|})$ and $H.Ev(1^\lambda, hk, y, 1^{|m|})$ is left to the distinguisher who runs A to get m. Note that the distinguisher always creates $H.Ev(1^\lambda, hk, y, 1^{|m|})$ regardless of the challenge bit of game UCE. We then use the PRF security of F to ensure that the first pad looks random to A. Consequently, in the string $(trap, c)$ that A receives, the first component is independent of the message, and the second component is indistinguishable from a random string.

The HE3 Scheme. Consider the $p\sqrt{q \cdot \mathrm{Guess}_A(\cdot)}$ term in the concrete bound for IND-CDA security in Theorem 5. This is worse than the "optimal" bound $p(q + p) \cdot \mathrm{Guess}_A(\cdot)$ if one uses a random oracle. Why does this gap matter? Asymptotically, we know that $\mathrm{Guess}_A(\cdot)$ is negligible, and hence this entire term is negligible too, under either of the two bounds. But concretely, the first bound means that we must have more min-entropy in the messages to get security. This is not desirable in practice. For example if we encrypt passwords, their min-entropy may be borderline. Thus it would be desirable to have a better bound. Moreover, it would also be desirable to give a simple construction based on a *generic* UCE-secure hash. We achieve both goals with our HE3 scheme.

The only ingredients we need this time are a PRF F (with fixed input length F.il and $\mathsf{F.OL}(\cdot) = \mathbb{N}$), a UCE[$\mathcal{S}^{\mathrm{srs}}$] family H (with $\mathsf{H.IL}(\cdot) = \mathsf{H.OL}(\cdot) = \mathbb{N}$) and a LTDF LT. We let $\rho \colon \mathbb{N} \to \mathbb{N}$ be a polynomial that is a parameter of the scheme. The encryption and decryption algorithms of HE3 are shown in Fig. 9 and the key-generation algorithm HE3.Kg is the same as HE1.Kg. We let HE3.rl $= \rho$. We also let $\mathsf{HE3.IL}(\cdot) = \mathbb{N}$, meaning the scheme encrypts variable and arbitrary length messages. While the scheme is quite simple it's challenging to find an analysis to match the desired bound $p(q + p) \cdot \mathrm{Guess}_A(\cdot)$ for the reset-advantage in the IND-CDA setting. A naive analysis will end up in an inferior bound $q^2 p \cdot \mathrm{Guess}_A(\cdot)$. Let $(m_1, r_1), \ldots, (m_p, r_p)$ be the message-coin pairs specified by A's IND-CDA queries. The reset adversary R is given a random oracle RO that on input (x, ℓ), returns a random string of length ℓ. Let Bad be the event that R queries $y \leftarrow \mathsf{RO}(m_k, \rho(\lambda))$ and then queries $\mathsf{RO}(y \oplus r_k, \mathsf{F.kl}(\lambda) + \lambda)$ for some $k \leq p$. For HE3 to be IND-CDA secure, Bad must not occur. Suppose the reset adversary R queries $\mathsf{RO}(x_1, \rho(\lambda)), \ldots, \mathsf{RO}(x_{\lfloor q/2 \rfloor}, \rho(\lambda))$, and then queries $\mathsf{RO}(z_1, \mathsf{F.kl}(\lambda) + \lambda), \ldots, \mathsf{RO}(z_{\lfloor q/2 \rfloor}, \mathsf{F.kl}(\lambda) + \lambda)$. If there are $i, j \leq \lfloor q/2 \rfloor$ and $k \leq p$ such that $x_i = m_k$ and $\mathsf{RO}(x_i, \rho(\lambda)) \oplus z_j = r_k$ then Bad occurs. This seems to happen with probability $\frac{q^2 p}{4} \mathrm{Guess}_A(\cdot)$, because R can *adaptively* choose z_j after seeing $\mathsf{RO}(x_1, \rho(\lambda)), \ldots, \mathsf{RO}(x_{\lfloor q/2 \rfloor}, \rho(\lambda))$.

To tackle this problem, we exploit a combinatorial technique on the coin length ρ—a parameter that we fully control. From Lemma 6 below, the chance that Bad occurs is at most $qp \cdot \mathrm{Guess}_A(\cdot) + q^2 p \cdot 2^{-\rho(\lambda)/3}$. If ρ is large enough, say $\rho(\lambda) \geq 4.5\lambda$ for every $\lambda \in \mathbb{N}$, then this matches the optimal bound. The proof of Lemma 6 is in [7].

Lemma 6. *Let U, V be random variables over $\{0,1\}^*$ and $\{0,1\}^\ell$, respectively. Assume that the maximum, over all u, v, of $\Pr[(U, V) = (u, v)]$, is at most ϵ. Let RO be a random oracle and let $W = \mathsf{RO}(U, \ell) \oplus V$. For any adversary A that makes at most q queries to RO, the probability that the first component of one of A's RO queries is W is at most $q\epsilon + q^2 \cdot 2^{-\ell/3}$.* ∎

Theorem 7 below confirms that HE3 is H-IND secure with very good concrete security bounds. While UCE[$\mathcal{S}^{\mathrm{sup}}$] is enough for IND-CPA security, IND-CDA requires the stronger UCE[$\mathcal{S}^{\mathrm{srs}}$] assumption. The proof is in [7].

Theorem 7. *Let F be a PRF with $\mathsf{F.OL}(\cdot) = \mathbb{N}$ and fixed input length F.il. Let H be a UCE[$\mathcal{S}^{\mathrm{srs}}$] function family with $\mathsf{H.IL}(\cdot) = \mathsf{H.OL}(\cdot) = \mathbb{N}$. Let LT be an LTDF*

$\mathsf{HE3.Enc}(1^\lambda, (ek, hk), m; r)$	$\mathsf{HE3.Dec}(1^\lambda, (dk, hk), (trap, c))$
$w \leftarrow \mathsf{H.Ev}(1^\lambda, hk, m, 1^{\lvert r \rvert}) \oplus r$	$x \leftarrow \mathsf{LT.Inv}(1^\lambda, dk, trap)$
$x \leftarrow \mathsf{H.Ev}(1^\lambda, hk, w, 1^{\mathsf{LT.il}(\lambda)})$	$seed \leftarrow \mathsf{H.Ev}(1^\lambda, hk, x, 1^{\mathsf{F.kl}(\lambda)+\lambda})$
$trap \leftarrow \mathsf{LT.Ev}(1^\lambda, ek, x)$	$y \leftarrow seed[1, \lambda]\,;\ fk \leftarrow seed[\lambda+1, \lvert seed \rvert]$
$seed \leftarrow \mathsf{H.Ev}(1^\lambda, hk, x, 1^{\mathsf{F.kl}(\lambda)+\lambda})$	$mask \leftarrow \mathsf{F.Ev}(1^\lambda, fk, 0^{\mathsf{F.il}(\lambda)}, 1^{\lvert c \rvert})$
$y \leftarrow seed[1, \lambda]\,;\ fk \leftarrow seed[\lambda+1, \lvert seed \rvert]$	$m \leftarrow \mathsf{H.Ev}(1^\lambda, hk, y, 1^{\lvert c \rvert}) \oplus mask \oplus c$
$mask \leftarrow \mathsf{F.Ev}(1^\lambda, fk, 0^{\mathsf{F.il}(\lambda)}, 1^{\lvert m \rvert})$	Return m
$c \leftarrow \mathsf{H.Ev}(1^\lambda, hk, y, 1^{\lvert m \rvert}) \oplus mask \oplus m$	
Return $(trap, c)$	

Fig. 9. Encryption and decryption algorithms of HE3, where H is a $\mathsf{UCE}[\mathcal{S}^{\mathrm{srs}}]$ family, F is a VOL PRF and LT is a LTDF

such that $\mathsf{LT.il}(\lambda) \geq \lambda$ *for all* $\lambda \in \mathbb{N}$. *Let* $\rho \colon \mathbb{N} \to \mathbb{N}$ *be a polynomial such that* $\rho(\lambda) \geq \lambda$ *for all* $\lambda \in \mathbb{N}$. *Let* HE3 *be defined from* F, H, LT, ρ *as above.*

Asymptotic result: HE3 *is H-IND secure.*

Concrete IND-CPA result: Let A be an adversary and P be a predictor. We can construct a source S, a distinguisher D, adversaries B and C such that

$$\mathsf{Adv}^{\mathsf{ind\text{-}cpa}}_{\mathsf{HE3}, A}(\cdot) \leq 2\mathsf{Adv}^{\mathsf{uce}}_{\mathsf{H}, S, D}(\cdot) + 2\mathsf{Adv}^{\mathsf{ltdf}}_{\mathsf{LT}, B}(\cdot) + 2\mathsf{Adv}^{\mathsf{prf}}_{\mathsf{F}, C}(\cdot) + 2^{1-\rho}$$

$$\mathsf{Adv}^{\mathsf{pred}}_{S, P}(\cdot) \leq \frac{2q}{2^\rho} + \frac{q}{2^\tau}$$

where q is the maximum of the size of P's output in the execution of Pred^P_S and τ is the lossiness of LT. *Furthermore,* $\mathbf{T}(\mathrm{Lossy}^B_{\mathsf{LT}})$, $\mathbf{T}(\mathrm{UCE}^{S,D}_{\mathsf{H}})$, $\mathbf{T}(\mathrm{PRF}^C_{\mathsf{F}}) \leq \mathbf{T}(\mathrm{CPA}^A_{\mathsf{HE3}})$; $\mathbf{Q}^{\mathrm{RR}}_C = 1$; *and* $\mathbf{Q}^{\mathrm{HASH}}_S = 2$.

Concrete IND-CDA result: Let A be an adversary and R be a predictor. We can construct a source S, a distinguisher D, adversary B such that

$$\mathsf{Adv}^{\mathsf{cda}}_{\mathsf{HE}, A}(\lambda) \leq 2\mathsf{Adv}^{\mathsf{ltdf}}_{\mathsf{LT}, B}(\lambda) + 2\mathsf{Adv}^{\mathsf{uce}}_{\mathsf{H}, S, D}(\lambda) + p^2 \cdot \mathrm{Guess}_A(\lambda) +$$

$$\frac{8p^2}{2^\lambda} + \frac{12p^2}{2^{\min\{\tau(\lambda), \rho(\lambda)\}}}$$

$$\mathsf{Adv}^{\mathsf{reset}}_{S, R}(\lambda) \leq p(p+q) \cdot \mathrm{Guess}_A(\lambda) + \frac{5p^2}{2^\lambda} + \frac{6.5p^2}{2^{\min\{\tau(\lambda), \rho(\lambda)\}}} + \frac{pq^2}{2^{\rho(\lambda)/3}}$$

where p is the maximum of the total number of messages that A produces in the execution of $\mathrm{CDA}^A_{\mathsf{HE3}}$, $q = \mathbf{Q}^{\mathrm{HASH}}_R$, and τ is the lossiness of LT. *Furthermore,* $\mathbf{T}(\mathrm{Lossy}^B_{\mathsf{LT}})$, $\mathbf{T}(\mathrm{UCE}^{S,D}_{\mathsf{H}}) \leq \mathbf{T}(\mathrm{CDA}^A_{\mathsf{HE3}})$; *and* $\mathbf{Q}^{\mathrm{HASH}}_S \leq 3p$. ∎

5   Efficiency and Comparisons with Prior Schemes

Our schemes improve on prior work on both the theoretical and practical fronts. On the theoretical front, DE1 is the first standard-model D-PKE scheme that is *fully* IND secure and HE1, HE2, HE3 are the first standard-model PKE schemes achieving full H-IND, meaning IND-CPA plus *full* IND-CDA. Prior standard-model D-PKE (resp. PKE) schemes only achieved IND (resp. IND-CDA) for block sources, which assumes messages (resp. message-randomness pairs) are unpredictable even given prior ones, which is unlikely to be true in applications.

On the practical front, prior standard-model schemes fix a message length, create keys depending on it, and use only asymmetric operations, making them inflexible and inefficient. Our schemes handle variable input length messages with hybrid-encryption like efficiency, meaning the asymmetric cost is fixed and one pays only in hashing as message length grows. Exploiting fast instantiations of UCE[$\mathcal{S}^{\mathrm{sup}}$] and UCE[$\mathcal{S}^{\mathrm{srs}}$] functions [9,45], this yields high performance.

To elaborate, recall that asymmetric primitives are orders of magnitude more expensive than symmetric ones. Crucial to making IND-CPA PKE efficient is the hybrid encryption paradigm as represented by the KEM-DEM framework [25]. Here, PKE.Enc($1^\lambda, ek, m$) uses its coins to generate a random symmetric key K along with an encapsulation c_a of K under ek, and returns ciphertext (c_a, c_s) where c_s is a symmetric encryption of m under K. The asymmetric cost is thus fixed regardless of message length and is amortized out for long messages. Ideally, we would like a similar generic hybrid encryption paradigm for D-PKE and H-PKE. But, despite interest and search, this has not been found. The reason in part is the apparently crucial use of randomness in the choice of K. As a result, prior standard-model D-PKE and H-PKE schemes have used only asymmetric operations. This has resulted not only in fixed message lengths but in costs that are exorbitant for long messages.

Our methods and schemes change this. Although we do not provide a generic hybrid encryption paradigm for these domains, our DE1, HE2 and HE3 schemes achieve hybrid-encryption like performance, meaning the asymmetric cost is fixed regardless of message length, and one pays only in symmetric operations — in our case this means hashing via the UCE[$\mathcal{S}^{\mathrm{sup}}$] or UCE[$\mathcal{S}^{\mathrm{srs}}$] functions— as the message length grows.

To capitalize on this for performance, good and careful instantiation of the UCE hash functions is needed. We need UCE functions H that are both VIL —variable input length, H.IL($\cdot$) = $\mathbb{N}$— and VOL —variable output length, H.OL($\cdot$) = $\mathbb{N}$. We now discuss how best to obtain these.

A simple instantiation of a UCE family is based on HMAC-SHA-256, as suggested in [8] and justified in [45]. While this yields a VIL family, it is FOL (fixed output length). A method to turn FOL UCE families into VOL ones is given in [8], but is slow. A better and faster transform is provided in [7]. With this we get UCE[$\mathcal{S}^{\mathrm{sup}}$] and UCE[$\mathcal{S}^{\mathrm{srs}}$] families with very good performance. These suffice for DE1, HE1 and HE3.

But one can do even better. BHK2 [9] provide a fast FIL, VOL UCE[$\mathcal{S}^{\mathrm{sup}}$] function $\overline{\mathsf{H}}$ based on AES. They also provide a fast AU family $\overline{\mathsf{U}}$. Applying their AU-then-Hash transform will return a VIL, VOL UCE[$\mathcal{S}^{\mathrm{sup}}$] family H that is significantly faster than the HMAC-SHA-256 based instantiation. This suffices for DE1 and HE1.

UE.Kg(1^λ)	UE.Enc($1^\lambda, ek, m$)	UE.Dec($1^\lambda, (ek, dk), c$)
$(ek, dk) \twoheadleftarrow\!\!\$ \ \mathsf{DE.Kg}(1^\lambda)$	$c \leftarrow \mathsf{DE.Enc}(ek, m)$	$m \leftarrow \mathsf{DE.Dec}(dk, c)$
Return $(ek, (ek, dk))$	Return c	If $m \neq \perp$ then
		$\quad c' \leftarrow \mathsf{DE.Enc}(ek, m)$
		$\quad$ If $c' \neq c$ then return $\perp$
		Return m

Fig. 10. U-PKE scheme UE = UniqueCtx[DE] constructed from D-PKE scheme DE

Recall HE2 needs a UCE[$\mathcal{S}^{\mathrm{sup}}$] family H of a special form, but it is based on AU-then-Hash and thus amenable to an efficient instantiation. Start again from $\overline{\mathsf{H}}, \overline{\mathsf{U}}$ from BHK2 as above. This time turn $\overline{\mathsf{U}}$ into U via our Hash-then-Mask transform —this preserves performance— and apply AU-then-Hash to this to get H. This UCE[$\mathcal{S}^{\mathrm{sup}}$] family is again exceptionally fast and of the special form required for HE2.

6   Unique-Ciphertext PKE

In an algorithm-substitution attack (ASA) [12], the prescribed encryption algorithm is replaced with a subverted one that may attempt to leak information about the message to "big brother." The latter and the subverted algorithm may even share a key based on which they communicate. BPR [12] formalize the attacker goal in an ASA as compromising privacy while evading detection, the latter meaning that subverted ciphertexts are indistinguishable from real ones even given the decryption key. They focus on the symmetric setting. They give attacks showing that randomized, stateless schemes will succumb to attack. They show however that security against ASAs may be achieved by what they call unique ciphertext symmetric encryption schemes.

BPR [12] initiate the study of ASAs for PKE. Continuing that theme, we define unique ciphertext PKE. We say that a PKE scheme PKE has unique ciphertexts, or is a U-PKE scheme, if for every $\lambda \in \mathbb{N}$, every $(ek, dk) \in [\mathsf{PKE.Kg}(1^\lambda)]$, and every message m, there is at most one ciphertext $c \in \{0, 1\}^*$ such that $\mathsf{PKE.Dec}(1^\lambda, dk, c) \neq \perp$. Coupled with correctness, this means that for every $\lambda \in \mathbb{N}$, every $(ek, dk) \in [\mathsf{PKE.Kg}(1^\lambda)]$ and every $m \in \{0, 1\}^*$ with $|m| \in \mathsf{PKE.IL}(\lambda)$ the set $[\mathsf{PKE.Enc}(1^\lambda, ek, m)]$ has size exactly one. The latter means that a unique ciphertext scheme is deterministic, meaning a D-PKE scheme.

We now ask how to design a U-PKE scheme. The natural thought is that any D-PKE scheme is a U-PKE scheme. This is not true. As an example, take any IND D-PKE scheme, and modify it so that encryption pre-pends a bit to the ciphertext that is ignored by decryption. This is still an IND D-PKE scheme, but it does not have unique ciphertexts, because if c is the encryption of m under $1^\lambda, ek$ in the starting D-PKE scheme then both $0 \| c$ and $1 \| c$ are valid ciphertexts in the new D-PKE scheme.

However, we show that one can transform any given D-PKE scheme DE into a U-PKE scheme UE. The U-PKE public key is the same as the D-PKE one, but the secret key is the pair (ek, dk) consisting of the D-PKE public key and matching secret key. Encryption is as in D-PKE. U-PKE decryption of ciphertext c first recovers the candidate message m via D-PKE decryption of c under dk and then checks that re-encrypting m under ek yields c, rejecting otherwise. $\mathsf{UE} = \mathsf{UniqueCtx}[\mathsf{DE}]$ is is formally specified in Fig. 10.

The security requirement for U-PKE contains to be IND, meaning a U-PKE scheme is treated just as a D-PKE scheme in the context of security. Applying our $\mathsf{UniqueCtx}$ to $\mathsf{DE1}$ thus yields a very efficient IND U-PKE scheme.

In the symmetric setting, unique-ciphertext encryption could be stateful and thus attain IND-CPA type security [12]. Here, a synchronized state is shared between sender and receiver. In the PKE setting, however, it is does not seem practical to assume that the sender and receiver share a synchronized state. Indeed, this would go against the spirit of public-key cryptography. As a consequence, for the benefit of unique ciphertexts, security must drop compared to IND-CPA, meaning we pay in security to protect against ASAs.

Acknowledgments. Bellare is supported in part by NSF grants CNS-1116800 and CNS-1228890. Hoang is supported in part by NSF grant 1223623. Part of the work was done when Hoang was working at UCSD, supported in part by NSF grants CNS-1116800 and CNS-1228890.

References

1. Austrin, P., Chung, K.-M., Mahmoody, M., Pass, R., Seth, K.: On the impossibility of cryptography with tamperable randomness. In: Garay, J.A., Gennaro, R. (eds.) CRYPTO 2014, Part I. LNCS, vol. 8616, pp. 462–479. Springer, Heidelberg (2014)
2. Barak, B., Goldreich, O., Impagliazzo, R., Rudich, S., Sahai, A., Vadhan, S.P., Yang, K.: On the (im)possibility of obfuscating programs. In: Kilian, J. (ed.) CRYPTO 2001. LNCS, vol. 2139, pp. 1–18. Springer, Heidelberg (2001)
3. Bellare, M., Boldyreva, A., O'Neill, A.: Deterministic and efficiently searchable encryption. In: Menezes, A. (ed.) CRYPTO 2007. LNCS, vol. 4622, pp. 535–552. Springer, Heidelberg (2007)
4. Bellare, M., Brakerski, Z., Naor, M., Ristenpart, T., Segev, G., Shacham, H., Yilek, S.: Hedged public-key encryption: How to protect against bad randomness. In: Matsui, M. (ed.) ASIACRYPT 2009. LNCS, vol. 5912, pp. 232–249. Springer, Heidelberg (2009)
5. Bellare, M., Dowsley, R., Keelveedhi, S.: How secure is deterministic encryption? In: Public-Key Cryptography-PKC 2015. Springer (2015)
6. Bellare, M., Fischlin, M., O'Neill, A., Ristenpart, T.: Deterministic encryption: Definitional equivalences and constructions without random oracles. In: Wagner, D. (ed.) CRYPTO 2008. LNCS, vol. 5157, pp. 360–378. Springer, Heidelberg (2008)
7. Bellare, M., Hoang, V.T.: Resisting randomness subversion: Fast deterministic and hedged public-key encryption in the standard model. Cryptology ePrint Archive, Report 2014/786 (2014)
8. Bellare, M., Hoang, V.T., Keelveedhi, S.: Instantiating random oracles via UCEs. Cryptology ePrint Archive, Report 2013/424 (2013). Preliminary version in CRYPTO 2013

9. Bellare, M., Hoang, V.T., Keelveedhi, S.: Cryptography from compression functions: The UCE bridge to the ROM. In: Garay, J.A., Gennaro, R. (eds.) CRYPTO 2014, Part I. LNCS, vol. 8616, pp. 169–187. Springer, Heidelberg (2014)

10. Bellare, M., Hoang, V.T., Keelveedhi, S.: Cryptography from compression functions: The UCE bridge to the ROM. In: Garay, J.A., Gennaro, R. (eds.) CRYPTO 2014, Part I. LNCS, vol. 8616, pp. 169–187. Springer, Heidelberg (2014)

11. Bellare, M., Kiltz, E., Peikert, C., Waters, B.: Identity-based (lossy) trapdoor functions and applications. In: Pointcheval, D., Johansson, T. (eds.) EUROCRYPT 2012. LNCS, vol. 7237, pp. 228–245. Springer, Heidelberg (2012)

12. Bellare, M., Paterson, K.G., Rogaway, P.: Security of symmetric encryption against mass surveillance. In: Garay, J.A., Gennaro, R. (eds.) CRYPTO 2014, Part I. LNCS, vol. 8616, pp. 1–19. Springer, Heidelberg (2014)

13. Bellare, M., Rogaway, P.: Random oracles are practical: A paradigm for designing efficient protocols. In: Ashby, V. (ed.) ACM CCS 1993, pp. 62–73. ACM Press, November 1993

14. Bellare, M., Rogaway, P.: The security of triple encryption and a framework for code-based game-playing proofs. In: Vaudenay, S. (ed.) EUROCRYPT 2006. LNCS, vol. 4004, pp. 409–426. Springer, Heidelberg (2006)

15. Birrell, E., Chung, K.-M., Pass, R., Telang, S.: Randomness-dependent message security. In: Sahai, A. (ed.) TCC 2013. LNCS, vol. 7785, pp. 700–720. Springer, Heidelberg (2013)

16. Boldyreva, A., Chenette, N., Lee, Y., O'Neill, A.: Order-preserving symmetric encryption. In: Joux, A. (ed.) EUROCRYPT 2009. LNCS, vol. 5479, pp. 224–241. Springer, Heidelberg (2009)

17. Boldyreva, A., Fehr, S., O'Neill, A.: On notions of security for deterministic encryption, and efficient constructions without random oracles. In: Wagner, D. (ed.) CRYPTO 2008. LNCS, vol. 5157, pp. 335–359. Springer, Heidelberg (2008)

18. Bosley, C., Dodis, Y.: Does privacy require true randomness? In: Vadhan, S.P. (ed.) TCC 2007. LNCS, vol. 4392, pp. 1–20. Springer, Heidelberg (2007)

19. Brakerski, Z., Segev, G.: Better security for deterministic public-key encryption: The auxiliary-input setting. In: Rogaway, P. (ed.) CRYPTO 2011. LNCS, vol. 6841, pp. 543–560. Springer, Heidelberg (2011)

20. Brown, D.R.L.: A weak-randomizer attack on RSA-OAEP with e = 3. Cryptology ePrint Archive, Report 2005/189 (2005). http://eprint.iacr.org/2005/189

21. Brzuska, C., Farshim, P., Mittelbach, A.: Indistinguishability obfuscation and UCEs: The case of computationally unpredictable sources. In: Garay, J.A., Gennaro, R. (eds.) CRYPTO 2014, Part I. LNCS, vol. 8616, pp. 188–205. Springer, Heidelberg (2014)

22. Brzuska, C., Farshim, P., Mittelbach, A.: Random oracle uninstantiability from indistinguishability obfuscation. Cryptology ePrint Archive, Report 2014/867 (2014). http://eprint.iacr.org/2014/867

23. Cachin, C., Micali, S., Stadler, M.A.: Computationally private information retrieval with polylogarithmic communication. In: Stern, J. (ed.) EUROCRYPT 1999. LNCS, vol. 1592, pp. 402–414. Springer, Heidelberg (1999)

24. Checkoway, S., Niederhagen, R., Everspaugh, A., Green, M., Lange, T., Ristenpart, T., Bernstein, D.J., Maskiewicz, J., Shacham, H., Fredrikson, M.: On the practical exploitability of dual EC in TLS implementations. In: Proceedings of the 23rd USENIX Security Symposium, pp. 319–335, August 2014

25. Cramer, R., Shoup, V.: Design and analysis of practical public-key encryption schemes secure against adaptive chosen ciphertext attack. SIAM Journal on Computing 33(1), 167–226 (2003)

26. Dodis, Y., López-Alt, A., Mironov, I., Vadhan, S.: Differential privacy with imperfect randomness. In: Safavi-Naini, R., Canetti, R. (eds.) CRYPTO 2012. LNCS, vol. 7417, pp. 497–516. Springer, Heidelberg (2012)

27. Dodis, Y., Ong, S.J., Prabhakaran, M., Sahai, A.: On the (im)possibility of cryptography with imperfect randomness. In: 45th FOCS, pp. 196–205. IEEE Computer Society Press, October 2004

28. Dodis, Y., Pointcheval, D., Ruhault, S., Vergnaud, D., Wichs, D.: Security analysis of pseudo-random number generators with input: /dev/random is not robust. Cryptology ePrint Archive, Report 2013/338 (2013). http://eprint.iacr.org/2013/338

29. Dorrendorf, L., Gutterman, Z., Pinkas, B.: Cryptanalysis of the windows random number generator. In: Ning, P., di Vimercati, S.D.C., Syverson, P.F. (eds.) ACM CCS 2007, pp. 476–485. ACM Press, October 2007

30. Escala, A., Herranz, J., Libert, B., Ràfols, C.: Identity-based lossy trapdoor functions: new definitions, hierarchical extensions, and implications. In: Krawczyk, H. (ed.) PKC 2014. LNCS, vol. 8383, pp. 239–256. Springer, Heidelberg (2014)

31. Feltz, M., Cremers, C.: On the limits of authenticated key exchange security with an application to bad randomness. Cryptology ePrint Archive, Report 2014/369 (2014). http://eprint.iacr.org/2014/369

32. Freeman, D.M., Goldreich, O., Kiltz, E., Rosen, A., Segev, G.: More constructions of lossy and correlation-secure trapdoor functions. Journal of Cryptology 26(1), 39–74 (2013)

33. Fuller, B., O'Neill, A., Reyzin, L.: A unified approach to deterministic encryption: new constructions and a connection to computational entropy. In: Cramer, R. (ed.) TCC 2012. LNCS, vol. 7194, pp. 582–599. Springer, Heidelberg (2012)

34. Garg, S., Gentry, C., Halevi, S., Raykova, M., Sahai, A., Waters, B.: Candidate indistinguishability obfuscation and functional encryption for all circuits. In: 54th FOCS, pp. 40–49. IEEE Computer Society Press, October 2013

35. Gentry, C., Lewko, A., Sahai, A., Waters, B.: Indistinguishability obfuscation from the multilinear subgroup elimination assumption. Cryptology ePrint Archive, Report 2014/309 (2014). http://eprint.iacr.org/2014/309

36. Goldreich, O., Goldwasser, S., Micali, S.: How to construct random functions. Journal of the ACM 33(4), 792–807 (1986)

37. Goldwasser, S., Micali, S.: Probabilistic encryption. Journal of Computer and System Sciences 28(2), 270–299 (1984)

38. Green, M.D., Katz, J., Malozemoff, A.J., Zhou, H.-S.: A unified approach to idealized model separations via indistinguishability obfuscation. Cryptology ePrint Archive, Report 2014/863 (2014). http://eprint.iacr.org/2014/863

39. Gutterman, Z., Pinkas, B., Reinman, T.: Analysis of the linux random number generator. In: 2006 IEEE Symposium on Security and Privacy, pp. 371–385. IEEE Computer Society Press, May 2006

40. Hemenway, B., Ostrovsky, R.: Building lossy trapdoor functions from lossy encryption. In: Sako, K., Sarkar, P. (eds.) ASIACRYPT 2013, Part II. LNCS, vol. 8270, pp. 241–260. Springer, Heidelberg (2013)

41. Heninger, N., Durumeric, Z., Wustrow, E., Halderman, J.A.: Mining your Ps and Qs: Detection of widespread weak keys in network devices. In: Proceedings of the 21st USENIX Security Symposium, pp. 205–220, August 2012

42. Kamara, S., Katz, J.: How to encrypt with a malicious random number generator. In: Nyberg, K. (ed.) FSE 2008. LNCS, vol. 5086, pp. 303–315. Springer, Heidelberg (2008)

43. Kiltz, E., O'Neill, A., Smith, A.: Instantiability of RSA-OAEP under chosen-plaintext attack. In: Rabin, T. (ed.) CRYPTO 2010. LNCS, vol. 6223, pp. 295–313. Springer, Heidelberg (2010)

44. Lenstra, A.K., Hughes, J.P., Augier, M., Bos, J.W., Kleinjung, T., Wachter, C.: Public keys. In: Safavi-Naini, R., Canetti, R. (eds.) CRYPTO 2012. LNCS, vol. 7417, pp. 626–642. Springer, Heidelberg (2012)

45. Mittelbach, A.: Salvaging indifferentiability in a multi-stage setting. In: Nguyen, P.Q., Oswald, E. (eds.) EUROCRYPT 2014. LNCS, vol. 8441, pp. 603–621. Springer, Heidelberg (2014)

46. Ouafi, K., Vaudenay, S.: Smashing SQUASH-0. In: Joux, A. (ed.) EUROCRYPT 2009. LNCS, vol. 5479, pp. 300–312. Springer, Heidelberg (2009)

47. Paterson, K.G., Schuldt, J.C.N., Sibborn, D.L.: Related randomness attacks for public key encryption. In: Krawczyk, H. (ed.) PKC 2014. LNCS, vol. 8383, pp. 465–482. Springer, Heidelberg (2014)

48. Peikert, C., Waters, B.: Lossy trapdoor functions and their applications. In: Ladner, R.E., Dwork, C., (eds.) 40th ACM STOC, pp. 187–196. ACM Press, May 2008

49. Raghunathan, A., Segev, G., Vadhan, S.: Deterministic public-key encryption for adaptively chosen plaintext distributions. In: Johansson, T., Nguyen, P.Q. (eds.) EUROCRYPT 2013. LNCS, vol. 7881, pp. 93–110. Springer, Heidelberg (2013)

50. Ristenpart, T., Yilek, S.: When good randomness goes bad: Virtual machine reset vulnerabilities and hedging deployed cryptography. In: NDSS 2010. The Internet Society, February / March 2010

51. Rogaway, P., Shrimpton, T.: A provable-security treatment of the key-wrap problem. In: Vaudenay, S. (ed.) EUROCRYPT 2006. LNCS, vol. 4004, pp. 373–390. Springer, Heidelberg (2006)

52. Vergnaud, D., Xiao, D.: Public-key encryption with weak randomness: Security against strong chosen distribution attacks. Cryptology ePrint Archive, Report 2013/681 (2013). http://eprint.iacr.org/2013/681

53. Wichs, D.: Barriers in cryptography with weak, correlated and leaky sources. In: Kleinberg, R.D. (ed.). In: ITCS 2013, pp. 111–126. ACM, January 2013

54. Yang, G., Duan, S., Wong, D.S., Tan, C.H., Wang, H.: Authenticated key exchange under bad randomness. Cryptology ePrint Archive, Report 2011/688 (2011). http://eprint.iacr.org/2011/688

55. Yilek, S.: Resettable public-key encryption: How to encrypt on a virtual machine. In: Pieprzyk, J. (ed.) CT-RSA 2010. LNCS, vol. 5985, pp. 41–56. Springer, Heidelberg (2010)

56. Young, A., Yung, M.: Kleptography: Using cryptography against cryptography. In: Fumy, W. (ed.) EUROCRYPT 1997. LNCS, vol. 1233, pp. 62–74. Springer, Heidelberg (1997)

Cryptographic Reverse Firewalls

Ilya Mironov[1]($\boxtimes$) and Noah Stephens-Davidowitz[2]

[1] Google, Menlo Park, US
mironov@gmail.com
[2] Department of Computer Science, New York University, New York, US
noahsd@gmail.com

Abstract. Recent revelations by Edward Snowden [3,20,27] show that a user's own hardware and software can be used against her in various ways (e.g., to leak her private information). And, a series of recent announcements has shown that widespread implementations of cryptographic software often contain serious bugs that cripple security (e.g., [12–14,22]). This motivates us to consider the following (seemingly absurd) question: *How can we guarantee a user's security when she may be using a malfunctioning or arbitrarily compromised machine?* To that end, we introduce the notion of a *cryptographic reverse firewall* (RF). Such a machine sits between the user's computer and the outside world, potentially modifying the messages that she sends and receives as she engages in a cryptographic protocol.

A good reverse firewall accomplishes three things: (1) it *maintains functionality*, so that if the user's computer is working correctly, the RF will not break the functionality of the underlying protocol; (2) it *preserves security*, so that regardless of how the user's machine behaves, the presence of the RF will provide the same security guarantees as the properly implemented protocol; and (3) it *resists exfiltration*, so that regardless of how the user's machine behaves, the presence of the RF will prevent the machine from leaking any information to the outside world. Importantly, we do not model the firewall as a trusted party. It does not share any secrets with the user, and the protocol should be both secure and functional without the firewall (when the protocol's implementation is correct).

Our security definition for reverse firewalls depends on the security notion(s) of the underlying protocol. As such, our model generalizes much prior work (e.g., [5,7,26,32]) and provides a general framework for building cryptographic schemes that remain secure when run on compromised machine. It is also a modern take on a line of work that received considerable attention in the 80s and 90s (e.g., [7,9,11,15,16,30,31]).

We show that our definition is achievable by constructing a private function evaluation protocol with a secure reverse firewall for each party. Along the way, we design an oblivious transfer protocol that also has a secure RF for each party, and a rerandomizable garbled circuit that is both more efficient and more secure than previous constructions. Finally, we show how to convert *any* protocol into a protocol with an exfiltration-resistant reverse firewall for all parties. (In other words, we provide a generic way to prevent a tampered machine from leaking information to an eavesdropper via *any* protocol.)

Most of this work was done in Microsoft Research.

© International Association for Cryptologic Research 2015
E. Oswald and M. Fischlin (Eds.): EUROCRYPT 2015, Part II, LNCS 9057, pp. 657–686, 2015.
DOI: 10.1007/978-3-662-46803-6_22

1   Introduction

Recent revelations of Edward Snowden show that powerful actors will go to remarkable lengths to obtain secret information. In particular, the National Security Agency has engineered a backdoor into a public cryptographic standard [3,27] and intercepted hardware as it was being delivered to customers in order to tamper with it [20]. Meanwhile, multiple serious flaws have been uncovered in widely used implementations of cryptographic protocols, leaving many users vulnerable to simple but devastating attacks (e.g., [12–14,22]). The extreme complexity of modern cryptographic implementations makes it extremely difficult for experts (let alone the typical user) to detect such vulnerabilities, even when they are introduced innocently. Attackers that deliberately insert such vulnerabilities into hardware and software can make this even harder by using cryptographic methods to cover their tracks.

So, facing the disturbing (and quite real) possibility of a compromise that reaches inside one's communication platform, we consider the following seemingly paradoxical question: *Can we design cryptographic protocols that achieve meaningful security when the adversary may arbitrarily tamper with the victim's computer?*

To resolve this question, we present a strong and general notion of security in the presence of an active tampering adversary and show how to instantiate powerful cryptographic primitives in this model. Of course, if Alice's computer simply chooses to replace her first message to Bob in some protocol with, for example, her secret business plans, we cannot hope to guarantee her security without some sort of help. Inverting the metaphor from network security, we propose and investigate the power of a (cryptographic) reverse firewall—an entity whose role is to protect cryptographic schemes and protocols from insider attacks. Informally, a cryptographic reverse firewall (RF) is a machine run by a third party (e.g., a security contractor hired by Alice's employer) that sits somewhere between Alice and the outside world and prevents Alice's computer from compromising her security by potentially modifying the messages that it sends and receives. In contrast to the standard firewall, the focus of a reverse firewall is on the inside of the perimeter. In particular, one important goal of reverse firewall is prevention of exfiltration attacks. Our primary contribution is the definition of reverse firewalls and the additional level of security that they bring to cryptographic protocols.

More specifically, we define three desirable properties of reverse firewalls. First, a reverse firewall should *maintain functionality*. I.e., if Alice's computer is behaving as it should, then the RF should not break the underlying functionality of the protocol. Second, a reverse firewall should *preserve security*. I.e., if the protocol without the RF present provides some security guarantee when Alice's computer behaves as it should, then the protocol *with* the RF present should provide this same security guarantee *regardless of how Alice's computer behaves*. Finally, a reverse firewall should *resist exfiltration*. Intuitively, an RF is exfiltration-resistant if Alice's tampered implementation cannot leak any information to the outside world through the firewall.

We defer much of the discussion of our definition to Section 2, where we introduce it formally. We emphasize, however, that the reverse firewall is *not* a trusted third party, and we do not rely solely on it for security. If Alice's implementation of the protocol is correct, then the protocol should be secure and functional without the firewall. In other words, we ask that the firewall *preserves* security, not that it *provides* it. In addition, the RF only has access to Alice's incoming and outgoing messages and any public parameters—not to Alice's state or input or any shared secrets. In effect, we place no more trust in the reverse firewall than we do in the communication medium. (We additionally require that firewalls be "stackable," so that one party may have arbitrarily many firewalls. Security is then guaranteed if just one of the firewalls is implemented correctly—or if Alice's own implementation is correct.)

Note that our security definition is quite strong, as it imagines the adversary "living inside of our computer." Consider, for example, a secure coin-flipping protocol in which Alice wishes to agree on a fair coin toss with Bob. Informally, the protocol is secure for Alice in the standard setting (i.e., without reverse firewalls) if Bob cannot bias the resulting coin toss alone. In our setting, we imagine both parties *working together* to bias the coin toss in Bob's favor. (Bob is adversarial as always, and in our setting, Bob may have also tampered with Alice's computer so that it is effectively "on Bob's side.") The only defense against this attack is a reverse firewall that can modify the messages that Alice sends and receives but must do so in a way that does not break the protocol when Alice and Bob are honest. (And, again, it must do so without access to any privileged information.)

In spite of this strength, we show that security in this model is achievable for very strong primitives. Indeed, we construct a two-round private function evaluation protocol that is secure in this model (Section 4). In particular, *each* party in this protocol has a corresponding secure reverse firewall. In other words, we show a relatively simple protocol that allows Alice and Bob to jointly and securely compute any circuit with the remarkable property that a reverse firewall can guarantee Alice's security even when Bob has tampered with her computer, and vice versa. This immediately shows that a very large class of two-party primitives can be realized securely in this model. The main ingredients for this protocol are an oblivious transfer scheme that itself has a secure reverse firewall for each party (Section 3) and a rerandomizable version of Yao's garbled circuit (Section 4.1). Our oblivious transfer protocol is a modified version of the Naor-Pinkas/Aiello-Ishai-Reingold protocol [1,25]. Our rerandomizable garbled circuit is significantly more efficient than the construction of Gentry et al. [19], and it achieves a stronger notion of rerandomizability. (See Section 1.1 for further comparison.)

Finally, in Section 5, we show a generic construction that can convert *any* protocol into a protocol with the same functionality that has an exfiltration-resistant reverse firewall. In other words, we provide a generic way to prevent a tampered machine from leaking information to an eavesdropper via any protocol. So, for the important special case in which Alice is primarily concerned with passive eavesdroppers, we show that *any* multiparty functionality can be implemented in our model.

Our protocols are described in full in terms of basic group operations, and we avoid using "heavy machinery" like non-interactive zero-knowledge proofs in our constructions. In particular, this means that our protocols are relatively simple and efficient and that the security of our constructions follows from relatively weak complexity-theoretic assumptions (namely, the slight variants of the decisional Diffie-Hellman assumption presented in Appendix A).

1.1   Related Work

In this section we give a summary of related prior work, starting with the most directly comparable and recent literature. Given the size and the scope of existing work dealing with various models of insider attacks and mitigation strategies, our focus is on the similarities and differences between our work and prior art rather than a comprehensive review of all previous approaches.

Algorithm-substitution Attacks. Motivated by the potential threat of powerful adversaries subverting implementations of cryptographic algorithms, Bellare, Paterson, and Rogaway recently proposed a formalization of the notion of resilience of symmetric encryption schemes to algorithm-substitution attacks (ASA) [5]. They observe that modern standards for symmetric encryption crucially rely on sender-chosen randomness to attain acceptable security levels. Since these standards do not include any mechanisms for ensuring that randomness used in the encryption stage is unbiased, they effectively enable a communication channel, which a corrupt implementation may use to leak information to an external party.

Bellare et al. define a general framework for ASA security, identifying two adversarial goals—avoiding detection and conducting surveillance. They cast several algorithm-substitution attacks against symmetric-key encryption in this framework, showing that widely deployed secure communication protocols, such as SSL/TLS, IPsec, and SSH, are vulnerable to these attacks. Furthermore, they present a universal, essentially undetectable attack effective against any stateless, randomized symmetric-key encryption scheme.

On the positive (defensive) side, Bellare et al. advocate using stateful, deterministic encryption schemes with unique ciphertexts as a counter-ASA measure. They construct a provably ASA-resilient encryption scheme based on the encode-then-encipher paradigm, and prove that all nonce-based schemes satisfying a natural non-degeneracy condition can be converted into stateful schemes with unique ciphertexts by choosing their nonces sequentially.

Our work extends Bellare et al. in several directions. First, we include in our treatment arbitrary two- and multi-party protocols, as opposed to just symmetric-key encryption. Second, we shift our objective from developing primitives that are ASA-resilient by design to constructing protocols that are reverse-firewall-ready. Bellare et al. only achieve security against adversaries that do not break the functionality of the encryption scheme ("functionality-maintaining adversaries" in our terminology). By making a stronger assumption—availability of an uncorrupted reverse firewall—we are able to achieve stronger security guarantees, such as security against tampered implementations that break functionality.

Our results and techniques can be viewed as complementary. Whereas Bellare et al. make a strong case for suppressing "freedom of choice" in cryptographic primitives, we demonstrate that additional randomness can be injected by an intermediary in some protocols to achieve stronger security guarantees for a much wider range of primitives.

Collusion-free Protocols and Mediated Collusion-free Protocols. Informally, Lepinski, Micali, and shelat say that a multi-party protocol is collusion-free if the parties cannot communicate information about their private inputs to each other via the protocol [23]. For example, a collusion-free protocol for the game of poker allows parties to play a hand of poker, but it does not allow them to communicate information about their cards to other players during the hand.

This notion resembles our definition of exfiltration resistance in that it disallows subliminal communication via the protocol, but the two notions are incomparable. On one hand, the definition of Lepinski et al. is much stronger than ours because it does not allow the use of a third-party reverse firewall to prevent subliminal communication. On the other hand, it is much weaker because it specifies what information parties are not allowed to communicate. Indeed, their constructions involve a setup phase that is conducted before the parties are given their inputs, and the authors observe that this setup phase can be used as a subliminal channel. So, in our model, their protocols are completely insecure. Their constructions also require strong physical assumptions to ensure verifiable determinism.

To avoid the need for the setup phase and physical assumptions, Alwen, shelat, and Visconti introduce the mediated model for collusion-free protocols [2]. In this model, all communication between the parties is routed through a mediator. Intuitively, the mediator rerandomizes the parties' messages in much the same way that our reverse firewalls do. However, the mediator is much more powerful than a reverse firewall in that (1) it intercepts all parties' messages and (2) it may exchange messages with the parties in any order. In contrast, our firewall modifies the messages sent and received by a single party in an online fashion, and we require our protocols to work without the firewall present. Because Alwen et al. give the mediator this additional power, they must explicitly model security against the mediator as a separate property of the protocol. In contrast, we get security "against the firewall" for free, as a natural consequence of the security of the underlying protocol. Their security definition is also stronger in the sense that it includes a strong notion of secure multi-party computation. While our notion of security preservation allows for such security, we intentionally do not require it in general.

Subliminal Channels and Divertible Protocols. A long series of works explored the idea of subliminal channels in various cryptosystems (e.g., [7, 9, 11, 15, 16, 30, 31]). Simmons [30] introduced the notion by showing subliminal channels in various signature and authentication schemes. The underlying theme of this work is a story in which two prisoners, Alice and Bob, wish to communicate in some sanctioned way through the prison's warden (e.g., Alice wishes to tell Bob in some authenticated manner that she has not been harmed). The warden wishes to remove any subliminal messages from this communication (e.g., to prevent Alice from communicating escape plans to Bob). The warden in this story is quite similar to our reverse firewall, and the notion of a subliminal-free channel is closely related to our notion of exfiltration resistance. Because of the wide body of work with a variety of definitions, results, and applications, we focus on a small portion that is most related to our work—divertible protocols.

Intuitively, a protocol is divertible if a warden sitting between Alice and Bob can rerandomize the messages of both parties so that (1) neither party is aware of the warden's existence and (2) neither party can distinguish between an interaction with a dishonest party with the warden in the middle and an interaction with an honest party. Okamoto and Ohta provided the first definition of divertibility for zero-knowledge proofs [26] (based on earlier definitions of subliminal-free zero-knowledge proofs), and Burmester et al. showed that all languages in NP have a divertible zero-knowledge proof [9,10]. These simple and elegant constructions immediately provide zero-knowledge proofs with reverse firewalls for all languages in NP.

Blaze, Bleumer, and Strauss showed how to generalize and strengthen the definition of divertibility to apply to any two-party cryptographic protocol [7]. Indeed, their prescient definition comes close to our notion of a protocol with an exfiltration-resistant reverse firewall. We highlight three primary differences between their work and ours.

1. In our terminology, Blaze et al. consider only exfiltration resistance and not security preservation. In some applications (e.g., zero-knowledge proofs), the two properties are equivalent, but in many important applications (such as those that we consider in the sequel), the two properties are very different. (See Section 2.3 for further discussion of the distinction between these two properties.)

2. Blaze et al. implicitly assume that any dishonest version of the prover still provides valid proofs. (In our language, tampered provers must "maintain functionality.") This assumption is necessary for the prover of zero-knowledge proofs, but in general we can and should do better.

3. They consider only synchronous protocols with two parties and one warden. We consider asynchronous multi-party protocols in which each party may have its own firewall. By separating the warden into multiple firewalls and moving away from the synchronous model, our definition becomes much stronger, as our firewalls do not have the benefit of seeing all messages from all parties sent during a round before deciding how to modify them. (Indeed, Blaze et al. provide an example of a simple divertible key-agreement protocol. However, this protocol is *not* secure in our model because it crucially relies on the synchronous model of communication for its security.) We also find our more modular model to be more natural in our modern context, in which different parties may have different security needs.

Divertible protocols also differ from protocols with reverse firewalls in a number of more subtle ways. For example, Blaze et al. require that the warden is undetectable to either party. The protocols presented in the sequel achieve this notion of "transparency", but we intentionally do not require it as part of our definition.

In short, divertible protocols and subliminal-free channels were founded on a story that predates the concerns that motivate our work. Our more modern story, in which Alice and Bob (who need not be prisoners!) are concerned that their computers have been corrupted, leads naturally to our more general definition.

Kleptography. Young and Yung identified an important subclass of insider threats against cryptographic schemes, which they called *kleptographic attacks* [32]. The goal of a kleptographic attack is to leak a secret to an adversary who planted a malicious implementation of a cryptographic system on a victim's computer. The attack is asymmetric—the compromised implementation may carry the attacker's public key, but a private key is necessary in order to read from the subliminal channel. A secure kleptographic attack is undetectable as long as the system is accessed as a black box, and while it may be identified if one reverse engineers the implementation, this will only expose the attacker's public key. In particular, if multiple systems run the same compromised software stack, a successful reverse engineering effort of one such system will not help in breaching the security of others.

The (now withdrawn) NIST-standardized Dual Elliptic Curve Determnistic Random Bit Generator (Dual_EC_DRBG) is an example of a mechanism with a potential kleptographic backdoor [8,29].

Our adversarial model is a relaxation of the kleptographic attacker. We consider the possibility that the adversary may not worry about detection and is not concerned about a split-key solution.

Rerandomizable Garbled Circuits. Gentry, Halevi, and Vaikuntanathan construct a rerandomizable version of Yao's garbled circuit in order to build an "i-hop" homomorphic encryption scheme [19]. Their construction is quite elegant, and its security is based on a slightly weaker assumption than ours (pure decisional Diffie-Hellman, as opposed to the slight variants presented in Appendix A). But, it does not work in our context. Informally, their circuit is rerandomizable when constructed honestly, but the rerandomization of a dishonestly constructed circuit can easily be distinguished from a freshly garbled circuit. (With negligible probability, even the honest implementation can create circuits that in some sense "cannot be rerandomized.") In our context, in which we consider the possibility that the garbled circuit was constructed by a corrupted algorithm, this is a fatal flaw. We thus construct a new garbling scheme that can be rerandomized in a much stronger sense.

Our scheme (presented in Section 4) is also substantially more efficient than that of Gentry et al. The size of a single gate in their circuit is $O(\lambda^2)$ group elements, where λ is the security parameter, whereas our gates require only a constant number of group elements. As a consequence, our rerandomizable garbling scheme (which uses a trick inspired by Prabhakaran and Rosulek [28]) also implies a significantly more efficient implementation of i-hop homomorphic encryption.

Combiners. An alternative defense against untrusted implementations of a cryptographic primitive is to *combine* multiple implementations of the same primitive in some way so that the combined primitive will be secure if a suitably large subset of the initial primitives are secure. This idea is quite common in the literature, and it was formalized by Harnik et al., who show that many primitives have elegant robust combiners [21].

Combiners solve a slightly different problem than reverse firewalls. Firewalls guarantee security when a user's system has been arbitrarily compromised, while combiners provide security only when the user already has access to at least one secure implementation of a primitive (and a secure implementation of the combiner itself!). Intuitively, combiners are applicable when multiple implementations of the same primitive exist that either (1) may have bugs in them or (2) rely on different unproven assumptions. In contrast, reverse firewalls work even when our implementations have been intentionally compromised.

2   Cryptographic Reverse Firewalls

We now present our general definition of a cryptographic reverse firewall that can be applied to a large class of primitives. This requires us first to define a cryptographic protocol in a (very general) way that suits our purposes. We note, however, that we describe the concrete schemes presented in the sequel in simpler terms. So, this level of generality is not necessary to understand the rest of the paper.

2.1   Cryptographic protocols

Definition 1 (Cryptographic protocol). *A cryptographic protocol $\mathcal{P}$ defines an interaction between stateful parties $(P_1, \ldots, P_\ell)$. First, a setup procedure $\mathsf{setup}(1^\lambda)$ is run, where λ is the security parameter. It returns a starting state for each party $(\sigma_{P_i})_{i=1}^\ell$, which we call their respective* input; *public parameters ρ; and a schedule of messages.[1] The parties proceed to send messages to each other according to the schedule. Each party has an associated* next *message algorithm $\mathsf{next}_{P_i}(\sigma_{P_i})$ that is called when it must output a message and a message receipt algorithm $\mathsf{receive}_{P_i}(\sigma_{P_i}, m)$ that is called upon receipt of a message to update the party's state. After the protocol is finished, each party runs its* output *algorithm $\mathsf{output}_{P_i}(\sigma_{P_i})$ and returns the result.*

---

[1] Note that we only consider protocols in which the message schedule is fixed by setup. Formally, this schedule determines the number of messages that a party must receive from each other party before sending each message. (E.g., Alice will send her second message after she has received three messages from Bob, two from Carol, and one from David.) We omit explicit reference to this schedule in the sequel as it will always be clear.

We identify the protocol with its parties and setup procedure, $\mathcal{P} = ($setup, $(P_i)_{i=1}^{\ell}$), and we identify the parties with the algorithms that define them, $P_i = ($receive$_{P_i}$, next$_{P_i}$, output$_{P_i})$. A complete record of all messages sent during a run of the protocol is a transcript $\mathcal{T}$.

We call a run of a protocol a run with input I *if the parties' respective input and the public parameters are set to the values represented by I. We assume implicitly that the input I satisfies certain* validity *requirements.*

A protocol must satisfy functionality requirements $\mathcal{F}$, *which place constraints on the output of the parties for particular input I, and* security requirements $\mathcal{S}$, *which place constraints on the message distribution conditioned on specific input I. For our purposes, it will often be convenient to assign to each security requirement $\mathcal{S}$ a specific party who "is concerned with $\mathcal{S}$." For a party P, we say that a protocol is* secure for P *if all of P's security requirements are met.*

For example, a one-out-of-two oblivious transfer (OT) protocol is a protocol between a sender, Alice, and a receiver, Bob. Alice's input is a pair of messages m_0, m_1, and Bob's input is a bit b. The protocol is functional if Bob's output is m_b. It is secure for Bob if for any valid messages m_0, m_1, no efficient algorithm playing the role of Alice can predict b with non-negligible advantage after the protocol is complete. (I.e., Alice is *oblivious* to Bob's bit b.) Intuitively, the protocol is secure for Alice if no efficient algorithm playing the role of Bob can "learn any information" other than m_0 or m_1 (but not both!).

Below, we list some terminology and notation that will be useful in the next section.

Definition 2 (Protocols and parties). *For a protocol $\mathcal{P} = ($setup$, (P_i)_{i=1}^{\ell})$ satisfying functionality $\mathcal{F}$, input I, party P, index j, and index set $J \subseteq \{1, \ldots, \ell\}$,*

1. $\mathcal{T} \leftarrow \mathcal{P}(I)$ *denotes setting the variable $\mathcal{T}$ to the transcript obtained by a run of $\mathcal{P}$ with input I;*
2. $\mathcal{P}_{P_j \Rightarrow P}$ *is the protocol obtained by replacing party P_j with P in the protocol $\mathcal{P}$;*
3. $\mathcal{P}_{J \Rightarrow P}$ *is the protocol obtained by replacing all of the parties $\{P_j\}_{j \in J}$ with a single implementation of P in $\mathcal{P}$ (i.e., the parties $\{P_j\}_{j \in J}$ "collapse" into a single party P that has a single state σ_P);*
4. *if any party sends the special symbol $\perp$ as a message at any time, then the protocol immediately ends and, by definition, functionality has been violated; and*
5. P *maintains $\mathcal{F}$ for P_j in $\mathcal{P}$ if $\mathcal{P}_{P_j \Rightarrow P}$ satisfies $\mathcal{F}$ with all but negligible probability over the random coins of the parties and* setup *procedure of $\mathcal{P}$ for any fixed input.*

When $\mathcal{F}$, P_j, and $\mathcal{P}$ are clear, we simply say that P maintains functionality.

2.2 Cryptographic Reverse Firewalls

Definition 3 (Cryptographic reverse firewall). *A* cryptographic reverse firewall *(RF) is a stateful algorithm $\mathcal{W}$ that takes as input its state and a* *message and outputs an updated state and message. For simplicity, we do not write the state of $\mathcal{W}$ explicitly.*

For a party $P = (\mathsf{receive}, \mathsf{next}, \mathsf{output})$ and reverse firewall $\mathcal{W}$, the composed party is defined as

$$\mathcal{W} \circ P := (\mathsf{receive}_{\mathcal{W} \circ P}(\sigma, m) = \mathsf{receive}_P(\sigma, \mathcal{W}(m)),$$
$$\mathsf{next}_{\mathcal{W} \circ P}(\sigma) = \mathcal{W}(\mathsf{next}_P(\sigma)),$$
$$\mathsf{output}_{\mathcal{W} \circ P}(\sigma) = \mathsf{output}_P(\sigma)) .$$

When the composed party engages in a protocol, the state of $\mathcal{W}$ is initialized to the public parameters ρ. If $\mathcal{W}$ is meant to be composed with a party P, we call it a reverse firewall for P.

Intuitively, an RF simply modifies Alice's incoming and outgoing messages. Alice of course does not want a reverse firewall to ruin her protocol's functionality when her internal implementation is correct. Indeed, we want something more than this. Alice's employer may wish to deploy multiple reverse firewalls (one internal firewall managed by its network administrators, one provided by a security contractor, another by networking equipment vendor, etc.), and we do not want such "stacking" of firewalls to break functionality. The definition below captures this.

Definition 4 (Functionality-maintaining RFs). *For any reverse firewall $\mathcal{W}$ and any party P, let $\mathcal{W}^1 \circ P = \mathcal{W} \circ P$, and for $k \geq 2$, let $\mathcal{W}^k \circ P = \mathcal{W} \circ (\mathcal{W}^{k-1} \circ P)$.*

For a protocol $\mathcal{P}$ that satisfies some functionality requirements $\mathcal{F}$, we say that a reverse firewall $\mathcal{W}$ maintains $\mathcal{F}$ for P_j in $\mathcal{P}$ if $\mathcal{W}^k \circ P_j$ maintains $\mathcal{F}$ for P_j in $\mathcal{P}$ for any polynomially bounded $k \geq 1$. When $\mathcal{F}$, P_j, and $\mathcal{P}$ are clear, we simply say that $\mathcal{W}$ maintains functionality.

We emphasize that we are interested in reverse firewalls that *maintain* the functionality of an already functional protocol—protocols that do not function without the firewall are not nearly as interesting. We also note that the reverse firewalls described in the sequel actually achieve much stronger properties. In particular, they are all "transparent", so that the behavior of $\mathcal{W} \circ P$ is identical to the behavior of P if P is the honest implementation. And, $\mathcal{W} \circ P$ is functionality maintaining whenever P is (and not just when P is an honest implementation). While these properties seem desirable for many applications, we do not wish to exclude from our definitions firewalls that, for example, append a signature to each message that they send.

More interestingly, we would like a reverse firewall to protect Alice from an adversary that may have tampered with her computer. To that end, we ask that the firewall *preserves* the security properties of the underlying protocol. So, we are only interested in protocols that are already secure without the firewall present. Since this definition depends on the security properties of the underlying protocol, it provides a general framework for the study of arbitrary cryptographic primitives in this model. Our strongest notion of security imagines a completely adversarial algorithm replacing Alice's implementation of the protocol and requires that security is still preserved even in this setting. Our weaker notion only considers tampered implementations that maintain functionality.

Definition 5 (Security-preserving RFs). *For a protocol* $\mathcal{P} = (\text{setup}, (\text{next}_{P_i}, \text{receive}_{P_i}, \text{output}_{P_i})_{i=1}^{\ell})$ *that satisfies some security requirements* $\mathcal{S}$ *and functionality* $\mathcal{F}$ *and a reverse firewall* $\mathcal{W}$,

1. $\mathcal{W}$ *strongly preserves* $\mathcal{S}$ *for* P_j *in* $\mathcal{P}$ *if the protocol* $\mathcal{P}_{P_j \Rightarrow \mathcal{W} \circ P_{\mathcal{A}}^*}$ *satisfies* $\mathcal{S}$ *for any probabilistic polynomial-time* $P_{\mathcal{A}}^*$; *and*
2. $\mathcal{W}$ *weakly preserves* $\mathcal{S}$ *for* P_j *in* $\mathcal{P}$ *against* $\mathcal{F}$-*maintaining adversaries if the protocol* $\mathcal{P}_{P_j \Rightarrow \mathcal{W} \circ P_{\mathcal{A}}^*}$ *satisfies* $\mathcal{S}$ *for any probabilistic polynomial-time* $P_{\mathcal{A}}^*$ *that maintains functionality* $\mathcal{F}$.

When $\mathcal{S}$, P_j, $\mathcal{P}$ *and* $\mathcal{F}$ *are clear, we simply say that* $\mathcal{W}$ *strongly preserves security or weakly preserves security respectively.*

One type of attack that particularly concerns us is *exfiltration*, in which Alice's corrupted computer attempts to leak some private information (e.g., secret business plans) to an adversary who has control over some (possibly empty) list of other parties J. We call security against such an attack *exfiltration resistance*, and we define it in terms of the game $\text{LEAK}(\mathcal{P}, P_j, J, \lambda)$, presented in Figure 1. Intuitively, the game LEAK asks the adversary to distinguish between a tampered implementation of party P_j and an honest implementation. An exfiltration-resistant reverse firewall therefore prevents an adversary from even learning whether Alice's computer has been compromised—let alone her secret business plans.

$$
\begin{array}{l}
\textbf{proc. } \text{LEAK}(\mathcal{P}, P_j, J, \mathcal{W}, \lambda) \\
(\sigma_{\mathcal{A}}, P_{\mathcal{A}}^*, P_{\mathcal{B}}^*, I) \leftarrow \mathcal{A}(1^\lambda) \\
b \xleftarrow{\$} \{0, 1\} \\
\text{IF } b = 1, P^* \leftarrow \mathcal{W} \circ P_{\mathcal{A}}^* \\
\text{ELSE, } P^* \leftarrow \mathcal{W} \circ P_j \\
T^* \leftarrow \mathcal{P}_{P_j \Rightarrow P^*, J \Rightarrow P_{\mathcal{B}^*}}(I) \\
b^* \leftarrow \mathcal{A}(\sigma_{\mathcal{A}}, T^*, \sigma_{P_{\mathcal{B}}^*}) \\
\text{OUTPUT } (b = b^*)
\end{array}
$$

Fig. 1. $\text{LEAK}(\mathcal{P}, P_j, J, \lambda)$, the exfiltration resistance security game for a reverse firewall $\mathcal{W}$ for party P_j in protocol $\mathcal{P}$ with corrupted parties J and security parameter λ. (Formally, the adversary represents a party by a collection of three (possibly randomized) circuits that implement the relevant functions receive, next, and output.)

Definition 6 (Exfiltration-resistant RFs). *For a protocol* $\mathcal{P}$ *satisfying functionality* $\mathcal{F}$ *and a reverse firewall* $\mathcal{W}$,

1. $\mathcal{W}$ *is* $(\mathcal{P}, P_j, J)$-*strongly exfiltration-resistant if no PPT adversary* $\mathcal{A}$ *achieves advantage that is non-negligible in the security parameter* λ *in the game* $\text{LEAK}(\mathcal{P}, P_j, J, \mathcal{W}, \lambda)$; *and*

2. $\mathcal{W}$ *is* $(\mathcal{P}, P_j, J)$*-weakly exfiltration-resistant against* $\mathcal{F}$*-maintaining adversaries if no PPT adversary* $\mathcal{A}$ *achieves advantage that is non-negligible in the security parameter* λ *in the game* $\mathsf{LEAK}(\mathcal{P}, P_j, J, \mathcal{W}, \lambda)$ *provided that the adversary's output* $P_{\mathcal{A}}^*$ *maintains* $\mathcal{F}$ *for* P_j.

When P_j, $\mathcal{P}$, *and* $\mathcal{F}$ *are clear, we simply say that* $\mathcal{W}$ *is* strongly exfiltration-resistant against J *or* weakly exfiltration-resistant against J *respectively. In the special case when* J *is empty, we say that* $\mathcal{W}$ *is* exfiltration-resistant against eavesdroppers.

This brings us to our strongest security notion.

Definition 7 (Robust RFs). *A cryptographic reverse firewall* $\mathcal{W}$ *is* robust *for a party* P_j *in* $\mathcal{P}$ *with functionality requirements* $\mathcal{F}$ *and security requirements* $\mathcal{S}$ *if it is* $\mathcal{F}$*-maintaining, strongly* $\mathcal{S}$*-preserving, and strongly exfiltration-resistant against the collection of all parties other than* P_j *in* $\mathcal{P}$. *We often simply say that* $\mathcal{W}$ *is* robust *when* P_j, $\mathcal{P}$, $\mathcal{F}$, *and* $\mathcal{S}$ *are clear.*

2.3   Discussion of the Definitions

The newly introduced terminology for security of reverse firewalls and a new type of adversary facilitates accurate and tight characterization of security guarantees offered by schemes in the sequel. Before we proceed to constructions, some analysis of the new notions is in order.

The Relationship Between Exfiltration-resistant and Security-preserving Firewalls. For many natural notions of security, exfiltration resistance and security preservation are equivalent. For example, a reverse firewall preserves the semantic security of an encryption scheme if and only if it is exfiltration-resistant against an eavesdropper. However, for notions of security that do not promise privacy, a security-preserving firewall is not necessarily exfiltration-resistant. For example, a reverse firewall may preserve the binding property of a commitment scheme, but it may still allow information to leak out of a compromised machine. Even when a security requirement does imply some type of privacy, a firewall that preserves it may not be exfiltration-resistant. Consider the hiding property of a commitment scheme, which guarantees privacy during the initial (commitment) phase, but it certainly does not prevent information from leaking during the opening phase. In fact, it is relatively easy to construct reverse firewalls that strongly preserve the hiding property of commitment schemes (just use a rerandomizable commitment scheme), but it is provably impossible to construct a strongly exfiltration-resistant reverse firewall for the sender against the receiver in any commitment scheme! (Loosely speaking, the functionality of a commitment scheme allows the sender to communicate a message to the receiver. So, a reverse firewall cannot hope to simultaneously maintain functionality and prevent the sender from leaking information to the receiver.)

On the other hand, it may seem at first that an exfiltration-resistant reverse firewall always preserves security, since interaction with such an RF composed with an adversarially chosen circuit is, by definition, indistinguishable from interaction with an honest implementation. (Technically, we ask that the RF composed with an adversarially chosen circuit is indistinguishable from *the RF composed with* an honest implementation.) However, this is not always the case. For example, if security requirements are simulation-based or consider adversaries who have access to oracles or are computationally unbounded, then an exfiltration-resistant firewall may not preserve security.

Functionality-maintaining Adversaries.   Intuitively, our weaker security notions exclude the "more conspicuous" adversaries whose tampered circuit would be noticed by honest parties participating in the protocol with non-negligible probability. However, even our weakest adversaries may behave arbitrarily some negligible fraction of the time against honest parties. This distinction can be quite important in the context of security definitions that allow for the corruption of other players in the protocol. For example, consider an oblivious transfer protocol in which Bob's first message is uniformly random over some large set (as is the case in Section 3). A tampered implementation of Alice in this protocol may respond to one specific such message by, say, encoding the XOR of both of Alice's inputs into its response to Bob. Such an implementation can still be functionality-maintaining because this event rarely happens when Bob behaves honestly. But, the security definition of oblivious transfer requires that an adversary playing the role of Bob should not be able to learn the XOR of the inputs.

So, any reverse firewall that even *weakly* preserves Alice's security in such a model must somehow address this issue. In Section 3, we approach it by composing a firewall for Alice that only works against tampered implementations that *always* maintain functionality with a firewall that is exfiltration-resistant *for Bob against Alice*. (The composed firewall is still serving Alice's security—Bob's outputs are randomized for her protection, not his.) We expect this approach to be useful in future work.

Timing and Scheduling Issues.   Our model does not explicitly account for the timing of messages. In practice, message timing is a natural channel, and a tampered implementation could, of course, use this to leak information and compromise Alice's security. So, any reverse firewall in the real world must account for this (e.g., by fixing the time between when it receives a message and when it forwards Alice's response). As the above discussion shows, in some cases, it might be necessary for the firewall to control the timing of both outgoing *and* incoming messages. In a protocol with more than two parties, this issue naturally becomes more complicated. In such cases, protocol designers should consider the relative timing of messages from multiple parties' perspectives and the order in which Alice receives messages from various parties.

3   Oblivious Transfer

Naor and Pinkas and, independently, Aiello, Ishai, and Reingold developed very similar OT protocols whose security reduces immediately to DDH [1,25]. We present a version of this protocol that is suitable for our setting. In particular, Alice's input is a pair of elements (m_0, m_1) in some group G of order p in which DDH is hard, and Bob's input is a bit b. Alice and Bob then engage in the protocol shown in Figure 2.

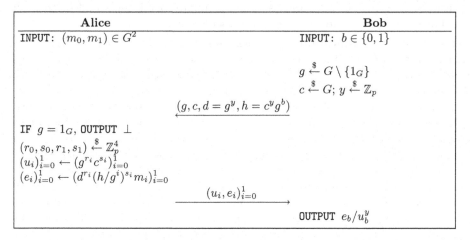

Fig. 2. A version of Naor-Pinkas/Aiello-Ishai-Reingold protocol for oblivious transfer

Proposition 1. *The protocol shown in Figure 2 is correct and secure for both parties if DDH is hard in G.*

Proof. Let $x = \log_g c$, which is well defined since $g \neq 1_G$ and G is cyclic. Correctness follows from the fact that $u_b^y = g^{s_b x y + r_b y} = (h/g^b)^{s_b} d^{r_b}$. Bob's security follows immediately from the DDH assumption in G.

To prove security for Alice, we note that if $(g, c, d, h) \neq (g, g^x, g^y, g^{xy+b})$ for some $x, y \in \mathbb{Z}_p$ and $b \in \{0, 1\}$, then (u_b, e_b) is uniformly random. Indeed, note that

$$\log_g u_b = r_b + x \cdot s_b,$$
$$\log_g (e_b/m_b) = y \cdot r_b + (\log_g h - b) \cdot s_b.$$

It follows that u_b and e_b are distributed uniformly and independently unless $\log_g h - b = xy$. This allows us to construct, for any (not necessarily efficient) adversary $\mathcal{B}$ playing the role of Bob, an (inefficient) simulator $S_\mathcal{B}$ with access to the ideal functionality $\mathcal{F}$ that behaves as follows on input b.

1. $(\sigma, g, c, d, h) \leftarrow \mathcal{B}()$.
2. $(m_0, m_1) \xleftarrow{\$} G^2$.
3. If $(g, c, d, h) = (g, g^x, g^y, g^{xy+b})$ for $b \in \{0, 1\}$, set $m_b \leftarrow \mathcal{F}(b)$.
4. $(r_0, r_1, s_0, s_1) \xleftarrow{\$} \mathbb{Z}_p$.

5. $(u_i, e_i)_{i=0}^1 \leftarrow (g^{r_i} c^{s_i}, d^{r_i} (h/g^i)^{s_i} m_i)_{i=0}^1$.
6. Output $\mathcal{B}(\sigma, u_0, e_0, u_1, e_1)$.

It should be clear that the simulator's "message" $(u_i, e_i)_{i=0}^1$ is distributed identically to the message that $\mathcal{B}$ receives from Alice in the real protocol, and the result follows. $\qquad\square$

We present reverse firewalls for both parties in our variant of the Naor-Pinkas/Aiello-Ishai-Reingold protocol and show that they are secure. Bob's reverse firewall is shown in Figure 3, and Alice's is shown in Figure 4. Alice's firewall by itself strongly prevents leaks against eavesdroppers. In order for it to weakly maintain security, it must be composed with Bob's firewall.

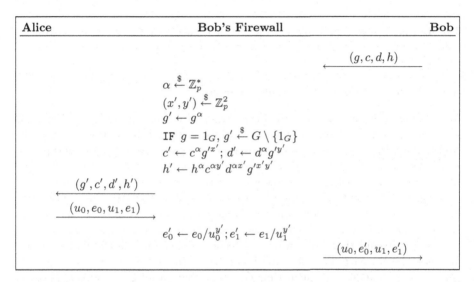

Fig. 3. Bob's reverse firewall for the protocol shown in Figure 2

In the full version of the paper [24], we prove the following theorem.

Theorem 2. *Bob's reverse firewall $\mathcal{W}_\mathsf{B}$ shown in Figure 3 maintains correctness and is robust if the chosen-base DDH with a hint game is hard in G.*

Alice's reverse firewall $\mathcal{W}_\mathsf{A}$ shown in Figure 4 maintains correctness and is strongly exfiltration-resistant against an eavesdropper if DDH is hard in G. The composed firewall $\mathcal{W}_\mathsf{B} \circ \mathcal{W}_\mathsf{A}$ also weakly preserves security against Bob.

4 Private Function Evaluation

We now construct a private function evaluation scheme based on the oblivious transfer protocol from Section 3 and a version of Yao's garbled circuit. We assume that the reader is familiar with garbled circuits and this type of construction (see, for example, [4]). Our key technical tool is a rerandomizable garbled circuit based on ElGamal encryption [17], which may be of independent interest.

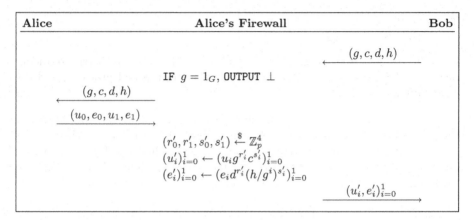

Fig. 4. Alice's reverse firewall for the protocol shown in Figure 2. It is strongly exfiltration-resistant, and it weakly preserves security when it is composed with the firewall shown in Figure 3.

4.1 A Rerandomizable Garbled Circuit

We wish to use the homomorphic properties and rerandomizability of ElGamal encryption to make a rerandomizable garbled circuit. But, a subtlety immediately arises: Yao's garbled circuit construction makes heavy use of encryptions of private keys (which can be used to decrypt more encryptions of private keys, etc.). However, in ElGamal encryption, private keys are elements in $\mathbb{Z}_p$ but messages are elements of a group G of order p in which DDH is hard. Our construction requires an efficient injective homomorphism from the key space to the message space. But, since DDH is easy in $\mathbb{Z}_p$, such a map cannot exist.

To get around this issue, we use a technique inspired by Prabhakaran and Rosulek [28]. In particular, for circuits of depth D, we need groups $G_1, \ldots, G_D$ of prime order $|G_d| = p_d$ such that G_d is a subgroup of $\mathbb{Z}_{p_{d+1}}^*$ and p_{d+1}/p_d is polynomially bounded[2] for $d < D$. In particular, this means that, given $g \in G_d$ and $h \in G_{d+1}$, the operation h^g is well-defined, and elements from G_d can therefore serve as private keys for ElGamal encryption over G_{d+1}.

Formally we say that a vertex z is at depth d in a circuit layout $\mathcal{L}$ if the longest path from an input vertex to z has length $d - 1$, and we write $\mathsf{depth}(z) = d$. For ease of presentation, we assume that all edges in the circuit layout $\mathcal{L}$ are between vertices of adjacent depths (i.e., edges do not "skip levels") and that all output vertices have maximal depth D. With this simplification, we can use the group G_d to garble vertices at depth d. (Note that this restriction is not necessary, and the garbling scheme generalizes naturally to handle arbitrary circuits.)

---

[2] In practice, such chains of primes can be found efficiently. Indeed, the sequence defined by starting at $q_1 = 2$ and setting q_{i+1} to be the minimal prime with $q_{i+1} \equiv 1$ mod q_i is suitable. There are 497 primes in this sequence between 2^{1024} and 2^{6144}. The ratios between successive primes in this specific chain are conjectured to remain polynomially bounded in the length of the primes, and other chains with this property are conjectured to be abundant. See, for example, [18].

Our garbling scheme for a circuit $\mathcal{C}$ is shown in Figure 5, and a schematic illustration of gate evaluation is provided in Figure 6. Alice can use the function Garble to garble a circuit $\mathcal{C}$ (represented by a collection of gate functions (f_z)), yielding a collection of ciphertexts (A_z) and *input tags* $(T_z^{(b)})_{z \in \mathcal{I}, b \in \{0,1\}}$. Given a collection of ciphertexts (A_z) and input tags $(T_z^{(x_z)})_{z \in \mathcal{I}}$ corresponding to some input x, Bob can use the function Eval to compute $\mathcal{C}(x)$.

In particular, Garble assigns two tags $T_z^{(0)}$ and $T_z^{(1)}$ to each vertex z, which represent the vertex taking the value 0 and 1 respectively. $T_z^{(b)}$ is a uniformly random group element for all vertices that are not output gates, while the tags of output gates are simply encodings g_D^b of output bits. Intuitively, we want Bob to "only be able to learn" the tag corresponding to the value that each gate takes when $\mathcal{C}$ is evaluated on his input.

The function Garble represents each non-input gate z by A_z, a collection of ElGamal ciphertexts. The ciphertexts are encrypted under one of four private keys, each of which is the *product* of a tag from the gate's left parent $T_{L(z)}^{(b_L)}$ and a tag from the gate's right parent $T_{R(z)}^{(b_R)}$. The ciphertexts contain encryptions under the private key $T_{L(z)}^{(b_L)} \cdot T_{R(z)}^{(b_R)}$ of the tag $T_z^{f_z(b_L, b_R)}$ corresponding to the gate's output on some input (b_L, b_R). The ciphertexts are arranged randomly in the collection so that their order does not reveal any information about the circuit. So that Bob can know *which* ciphertext he should decrypt at each gate, together with each encrypted tag we also include a second ciphertext that encrypts a location bit τ (under the same key). Bob can then use the two location bits from a gate's left and right parent to know which ciphertext C_{τ_L, τ_R} to decrypt at the current gate.

The output of Garble is a collection of tags and location bits $(T_z^{(b)}, \tau_z^{(b)})_{z \in \mathcal{I}, b \in \{0,1\}}$ for the input vertices together with the ciphertexts $(A_z)_{z \in V \setminus \mathcal{I}}$. The function Eval takes as input the ciphertexts (A_z) and the tags and location bits corresponding to some input x, $(T_z^{(x_z)}, \tau_z^{(x_z)})$, and it outputs $\mathcal{C}(x)$.

4.2 PFE from Garbled Circuits and OT

With the garbling scheme from Figure 5 and the oblivious transfer scheme from Section 3, we can build a private function evaluation protocol, which we present in Figure 7. We note that the protocol can be optimized so that Bob sends his oblivious transfer messages in one batch. With this optimization, the protocol requires only two messages. (Bob sends (g_1, c) and his oblivious transfer requests in a single message. Alice then sends her responses to the oblivious transfer requests and the garbled circuit, also in a single message.) The proof of security as well as the reverse firewalls and their corresponding proofs of security can be naturally modified to accommodate this change.

We prove the following proposition in the full version of the paper.

proc. Garble($\mathcal{C} = (f_z), g_1$)
FOR $d = 2, \ldots, D$,
$\quad g_d \xleftarrow{\$} G_d \setminus \{1_{G_d}\}$
FOR z in V,
$\quad b_z^* \xleftarrow{\$} \{0, 1\}$
$\quad$ IF $z \in \mathcal{O}$,
$\quad\quad (T_z^{(0)}, T_z^{(1)}) \leftarrow (1_{G_D}, g_D)$
$\quad$ ELSE,
$\quad\quad d \leftarrow \mathsf{depth}(z)$
$\quad\quad (T_z^{(0)}, T_z^{(1)}) \xleftarrow{\$} G_d^2$
FOR z in $V \setminus \mathcal{I}$,
$\quad A_z \xleftarrow{\$} \mathsf{GarbleGate}(z)$
FOR z in $\mathcal{I}$,
$\quad \tau_z^{(0)} \leftarrow b_z^*; \tau_z^{(1)} \leftarrow 1 \oplus b_z^*$
OUTPUT $((T_z^{(b)}, \tau_z^{(b)}), (A_z), (g_d))$

proc. GarbleGate(z)
$d \leftarrow \mathsf{depth}(z)$
FOR (b_L, b_R) in $\{0, 1\}^2$,
$\quad k \leftarrow T_{L(z)}^{(b_L)} \cdot T_{R(z)}^{(b_R)}$
$\quad \tau_L = b_L \oplus b_{L(z)}^*$
$\quad \tau_R = b_R \oplus b_{R(z)}^*$
$\quad \eta \leftarrow (\tau_L, \tau_R)$
$\quad h_\eta \leftarrow g_d^k$
$\quad b \leftarrow f_z(b_L, b_R)$
$\quad (r, s) \xleftarrow{\$} \mathbb{Z}_{p_d}^2$
$\quad (u_\eta, e_\eta) \leftarrow (g_d^r, h_\eta^r T_z^{(b)})$
$\quad \tau \leftarrow b \oplus b_z^*$
$\quad (v_\eta, w_\eta) \leftarrow (g_d^s, h_\eta^s g_d^\tau)$
OUTPUT $(h_\eta, u_\eta, e_\eta, v_\eta, w_\eta)$

proc. Eval($(T_z, \tau_z), (A_z), (g_d)_{d=1}^D$)
FOR $d = 1, \ldots, D$,
$\quad$ IF $g_d = 1_{G_D}$, OUTPUT $\perp$
FOR z in $V \setminus \mathcal{I}$,
$\quad (T_z, \tau_z) \leftarrow \mathsf{EvalGate}(z)$
FOR z in $\mathcal{O}$,
$\quad$ IF $T_z \notin \{1_{G_D}, g_D\}$, OUTPUT $\perp$
OUTPUT $(\log_{g_D} T_z)_{z \in \mathcal{O}}$

proc. EvalGate(z)
$k \leftarrow T_{L(z)} \cdot T_{R(z)}$
$d \leftarrow \mathsf{depth}(z)$
PARSE $(h_\eta, u_\eta, e_\eta, v_\eta, w_\eta) \leftarrow A_z$
$\eta \leftarrow (\tau_{L(z)}, \tau_{R(z)})$
IF $h_\eta \neq g_d^k$, OUTPUT $\perp$
$(T_z, B_z) \leftarrow (e_\eta / u_\eta^k, w_\eta / v_\eta^k)$
IF $B_z \notin \{1_{G_d}, g_d\}$, OUTPUT $\perp$
OUTPUT $(T_z, \log_{g_d} B_z)$

Fig. 5. Our garbled circuit scheme with input circuit $\mathcal{C}$ of depth D and a publicly known layout. (We assume for simplicity that all edges in the circuit are from vertices of depth d to vertices of depth $d+1$ and that all output vertices have maximal depth.)

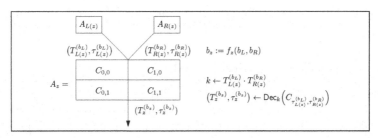

Fig. 6. A schematic representation of the evaluation of a single gate. The bits b_L, b_R, and b_z are not known to the evaluation algorithm.

Proposition 3. *The private function evaluation protocol shown in Figure 7 is correct and secure for both Alice and Bob if DDH is hard in the (G_i).*

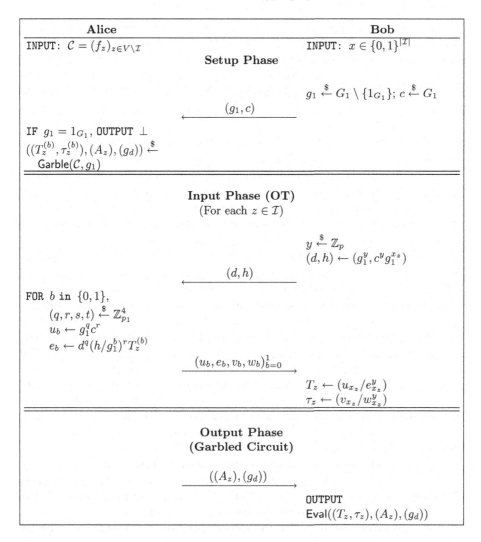

Fig. 7. A private function evaluation protocol using our oblivious transfer protocol from Section 3 and our garbled circuit scheme shown in Figure 5. (See Figure 5 for the functions Garble and Eval.)

4.3 Reverse Firewalls for PFE

Bob's reverse firewall is very similar to his reverse firewall for the oblivious transfer protocol in Section 3 (see full version for details). Alice's reverse firewall is shown in Figure 8. It makes use of a function $\mathsf{Rerand}_{\mathsf{Garble}}$ that rerandomizes garbled circuits. This procedure is rather complicated because our garbled circuits necessarily have many moving parts: location bits τ; the ordering of the ciphertexts, which is determined by the location bits; tags T; the keys, which are products of the tags; and the randomness used to encrypt the tags and location bits. Our task is to rerandomize all of this without breaking functionality. Below, we describe the intuition behind the rerandomization procedure.

Ideally, in order to rerandomize the tags in the garbled circuit, we would simply use the malleability of ElGamal to multiply each tag $T_z^{(b)}$ by a uniformly random mask $\mathcal{R}_z^{(b)}$. But (as Gentry et al. observe in a similar context [19]), the firewall cannot know which tags are used to generate which keys—so maintaining consistency between tags and keys would not be possible with this approach. We can, however, multiply *both* $T_z^{(0)}$ and $T_z^{(1)}$ by a single uniformly random mask $\mathcal{R}_z$ (i.e., we can multiply all the corresponding ciphertexts by $\mathcal{R}_z$). Since we apply this operation to both tags, we can easily maintain consistency (after noting that an ElGamal encryption under a private key k can be easily converted into an encryption under $k \cdot k'$ without knowing k). But, we need a second degree of freedom per gate (otherwise, $T_z^{(0)}/T_z^{(1)}$ would remain unchanged).

We find our solution in the location bits. In particular, for each ciphertext $(h, u, e, v, w) = (h,\ g^r,\ h^r T,\ g^s,\ h^s g^\tau)$, we use the homomorphic property of ElGamal encryption to multiply the tag T by $g^{\beta_z \tau}$ for uniformly random β_z. Since the location bit τ encodes which ciphertexts will be encrypted under a key generated from T, we do not need to know which tags correspond to which keys to maintain consistency between the tags and keys—we just need to know that whichever tag had a corresponding location bit $\tau = 1$ was multiplied by g^{β_z}. The complete mask is therefore $\mathcal{R}_z g^{\beta_z \tau}$ for the appropriate value of τ. (Of course, a tampered implementation playing the role of Alice may not produce ciphertexts of the correct form $(h, g^r, h^r T, g^s, h^s g^\tau)$ where τ is a bit. Our rerandomization algorithm will still multiply each key of the children of the node z by the mask $\mathcal{R}_z g^{\beta_z \tau}$ for the appropriate value of τ. This rerandomization of *keys* is what makes the scheme secure.)

We also need a way to rerandomize the location bits themselves. Recall that the location bits τ are encrypted as $(v, w) = (g^s, h^s g^\tau)$. In order to rerandomize them, we note that $(v^{-1}, w^{-1}g) = (g^{-s}, h^{-s}g^{1-\tau})$ is an encryption of $\tau \oplus 1$. We can therefore flip the location bits without knowing their values.

To maintain consistency with the rerandomization of the oblivious transfer rounds, $\mathsf{Rerand}_{\mathsf{Garble}}$ takes as input the masks that should be used to rerandomize the input tags. In particular, the procedure takes as input a collection of garbled gates $(A_z)_{z \in V \setminus \mathcal{I}}$, group elements $(g_d)_{d=1}^D$, and masks for the input vertices $(\mathcal{R}_z, \beta_z, b_z^*)_{z \in \mathcal{I}}$, and it outputs new ciphertexts (A_z') and new group elements (g_d'). The masks $\mathcal{R}_z$ and β_z are used to mask tags as described above, and the bit b_z^* determines whether the location bits $\tau_z^{(b)}$ should be flipped. (The masks for non-input vertices are selected uniformly at random by the rerandomization procedure.)

In the full version of the paper, we prove the following theorem.

Theorem 4. *The reverse firewall for Bob is robust if the DDH with a hint game is hard in G_1.*

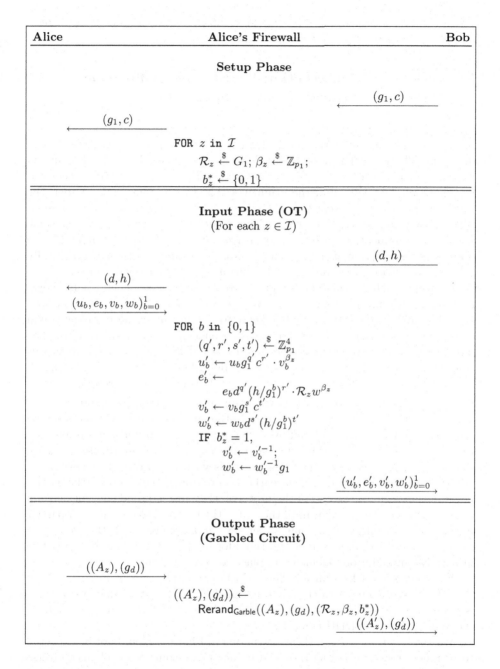

Fig. 8. Alice's firewall for the private function evaluation protocol shown in Figure 7. See the full version of the paper for the formal definition of $\mathsf{Rerand}_{\mathsf{Garble}}$.

The reverse firewall for Alice shown in Figure 8 maintains correctness, weakly preserves Alice's security, and is strongly exfiltration-resistant against an eavesdropper if non-uniform DDH is hard in the (G_d).

5   A Generic Construction for Strong Exfiltration Resistance Against Eavesdroppers

We now show that *any* protocol can be converted into a protocol that has a reverse firewall for each party that is strongly exfiltration-resistant against eavesdroppers. The resulting protocol will have at most one additional (broadcast) message per party (or fewer than two additional messages per party in the non-broadcast model). For all of the primitives that we consider in this paper, the resulting protocol will also satisfy the same security requirements as the original protocol. We cannot say that the resulting protocol will always satisfy the same security requirements for arbitrary primitives because security requirements are quite a general notion. For example, a security requirement could specifically ask that a protocol does *not* have an exfiltration-resistant reverse firewall.

In order to achieve this, the key idea is to use a public-key encryption scheme that is rerandomizable and has a *rerandomizable key*. I.e., a reverse firewall should be able to convert any public key into a uniformly random public key in such a way that it can also convert messages encrypted under the resulting key into messages encrypted under the original key. ElGamal encryption has this property (as we observe in Section 4), so we describe the scheme using ElGamal.

In particular, we interpret all messages as elements in some group G of order p in which DDH is hard. Each party computes $g \xleftarrow{\$} G \setminus \{1_G\}$ and $x \xleftarrow{\$} \mathbb{Z}_p$ and sends the message $(g, h = g^x)$ to all other parties. All future messages m sent to a party are then replaced by ciphertexts encrypted under her public key $(u = g^r, e = h^r m)$. Each time any party receives an encrypted message (u, e), she decrypts it $m = e/u^x$ and then proceeds with the protocol as normal. In addition, to prevent leakage due to early termination of the protocol, the parties never output $\perp$ until the end of the protocol; they instead send encryptions of a special message $m_\perp$ and wait until the end of the protocol to output $\perp$. A party's reverse firewall simply rerandomizes her keys and ciphertexts. If the party ever sends a message that is not of the right form, the firewall simply sends two uniformly random group elements in place of an encryption.

We show such a firewall for Alice in the two-party case in Figure 9. Note that Bob can implement essentially the same firewall. The fact that this firewall is strongly exfiltration-resistant against eavesdroppers follows immediately from the assumption that DDH is hard in G.

We note that, in general, the construction in Figure 9 should not be expected to "compose well" with other reverse firewalls. I.e., if some protocol has a reverse firewall that preserves Alice's security but is not exfiltration-resistant, we cannot necessarily apply the above transformation and obtain a protocol with a reverse firewall that *both* preserves Alice's security and is exfiltration-resistant, as it will not be possible for an efficient firewall to compute arbitrary functions on

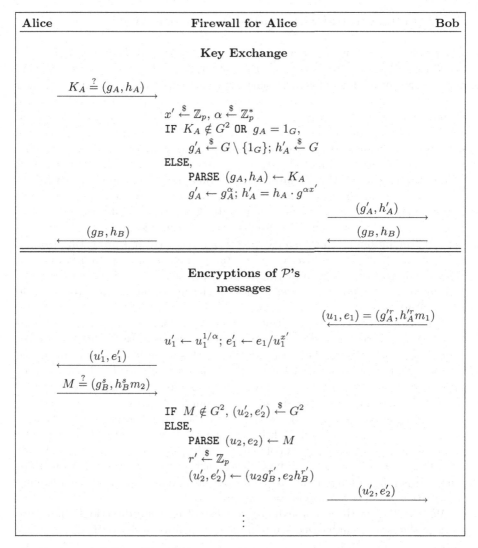

Fig. 9. A reverse firewall for Alice in a modified arbitrary two-party protocol $\mathcal{P}$. Two messages are added to the protocol in which the parties exchange public keys. They then follow the specification of $\mathcal{P}$, replacing messages m_i with ciphertexts $(g^r, h^r m_i)$. Bob has a similar reverse firewall.

the messages if they are encrypted. Even a very simple operation like equality testing (e.g., testing whether a message is some specific element) cannot be done efficiently if the message is encrypted under a semantically secure scheme. So, in general, one may need to choose between strongly exfiltration-resistant firewalls and firewalls that preserve security.

6   Conclusion and Directions for Future Work

The revelations of Edward Snowden [3,20,27] highlight a different kind of threat posed by sophisticated adversaries—the potential hijacking of a user's own software or hardware for subversive purposes. A compromised machine engaged in a cryptographic protocol may (perhaps selectively) fail to protect security or enable a covert communication channel through which the attacker can leak sensitive information or coordinate its activities. Standard solutions such as testing, auditing, or monitoring cannot in general ensure security since the attacker may use cryptographic methods to cover its tracks (aided by the complexity of modern protocols and the ubiquitous use of randomness in communications).

To counter the threat of insider attacks, we propose the concept of a (cryptographic) reverse firewall, whose role is to backstop the security of some underlying cryptographic scheme. We discuss several desirable properties of reverse firewalls (maintaining functionality, preserving security, and protecting against exfiltration attacks) and two types of tampering (arbitrary tampering and functionality-maintaining tampering). The generality of our definition provides a framework for studying insider attacks and counter-measures across a wide range of primitives.

Our main technical contribution is a protocol for private function evaluation based on Yao's garbled circuits and oblivious transfer that admits a reverse firewall for both parties. The instantiation of this remarkably strong primitive in a way that remains secure even when the user's computer has been compromised shows the power of reverse firewalls as a tool for protecting against insider attacks. In addition, our rerandomizable garbling scheme is more efficient and is secure against a stronger adversary than the scheme proposed by Gentry et al. [19] (though we rely on slightly stronger number-theoretic assumptions).

We also show that *any* protocol can be easily converted into a protocol with an exfiltration-resistant reverse firewall for each party (and the same functionality). This provides a generic way to prevent a tampered machine from leaking information to an eavesdropper via any protocol.

We conclude with a (non-exhaustive!) list of exciting directions for future work in the newly emphasized study of defense against insider attacks:

1. The most obvious direction for future work is simply the instantiation of more primitives in this framework. While this work includes an instantiation of private function evaluation (which can be used to instantiate many more primitives), there is still much more to study. For example, can we achieve stronger notions of security for two party computation? (We prove a relatively restricted notion of security for private function evaluation.) How efficiently (and under what assumptions) can we instantiate simpler primitives in this model? What can we achieve in the multi-party case? What about other primitives that are not implied by PFE (such as authenticated key agreement)?

2. We hope that future work on reverse firewalls develops a comprehensive collection of composable, efficient, modular protocols with secure reverse

firewalls. The "holy grail" would be a full characterization of functionalities and security properties for which reverse firewalls exist.
3. More generally, we hope to see a systematic study of defensive mechanisms against deliberate insider attacks. The legitimate targets of these attacks include software libraries, hardware platforms, communication channels, standards, protocols, sources of entropy, system parameters, and the choice of constants.

A   Groups and Hardness Assumptions

Definition 8 (Family of groups). *We say that* $\mathbb{G} = (G_i)_{i=1}^{\infty}$ *is an efficiently computable family of groups if there is some probabilistic polynomial-time algorithm* setup *such that* setup(1^λ) *outputs a representation of a group* G_i *with all group elements represented by* poly(λ) *bits, a polynomial-size circuit that outputs a uniformly random group element on random input, the order of the group, and a polynomial-size circuit that computes the group operation over* G_i.

Throughout this paper, whenever we refer to a group G with certain properties, we implicitly define a family of groups $\mathbb{G}$ with these properties and assume that $G \xleftarrow{\$} $ setup(1^λ), where λ is the security parameter. We assume that all algorithms have access to the group description. We write 1_G to denote the identity element in G. When we speak of negligible probabilities, polynomial-time algorithms, etc., we mean probabilities that are negligible in the security parameter λ, algorithms whose running time is polynomial in the security parameter, etc. We sometimes need to work with more than one group at a time, so we extend these notions in the natural way to a collection of groups.

Definition 9 (Decisional Diffie-Hellman). *Let* G *be a group of order* p. *Then, we say that* decisional Diffie-Hellman *(DDH) is hard in* G *if no probabilistic polynomial-time algorithm* $\mathcal{A}$ *can distinguish between* (g, g^x, g^y, g^{xy}), *where* $g \xleftarrow{\$} G$, $(x, y) \xleftarrow{\$} \mathbb{Z}_p^2$, *and* $(g_1, g_2, g_3, g_4) \xleftarrow{\$} G^4$.

We will need a slight variant of the DDH assumption, which we call *DDH with a hint*.

Definition 10 (DDH with a hint). *We say that* DDH with a hint *is hard in* G *if no probabilistic polynomial-time adversary* $\mathcal{A}$ *has non-negligible advantage in the following game.*

1. $(\sigma, g, c, d) \xleftarrow{\$} \mathcal{A}(1^\lambda)$, *with* $(g, c, d) \in G^3$.
2. *Sample* $b \xleftarrow{\$} \{0, 1\}$ *and* $(x, y) \xleftarrow{\$} \mathbb{Z}_p^2$.
3. *If* $b = 1$, *set* $z \leftarrow xy$. *Otherwise, set* $z \xleftarrow{\$} \mathbb{Z}_p$.
4. $b^* \xleftarrow{\$} \mathcal{A}(\sigma, (g^x, g^y, g^z, c^x, d^y))$.
5. $\mathcal{A}$ *wins if and only if* $b = b^*$.

It will also be convenient to define two hardness assumptions that are implied by DDH.

Definition 11 (Subgroup DDH). *Let G be a group of order p and $\hat{G}$ be a subgroup of $\mathbb{Z}_p^*$. We say that $\hat{G}$-subgroup DDH is hard in G if no probabilistic polynomial-time algorithm $\mathcal{A}$ can distinguish between (g, g^x, g^y, g^{xy}), where $g \xleftarrow{\$} G$, $(x, y) \xleftarrow{\$} \hat{G}^2$, and $(g_1, g_2, g_3, g_4) \xleftarrow{\$} G^4$.*

Lemma 1. *Let G be a group of order p and $\hat{G}$ be a subgroup of $\mathbb{Z}_p^*$. If DDH is hard in G and $|G|/|\hat{G}|$ is polynomially bounded, then $\hat{G}$-subgroup DDH is hard in G.*

Proof. Fix some probabilistic polynomial-time adversary $\mathcal{A}$ in the DDH game, and let $g \xleftarrow{\$} G$. Consider the cosets of $\hat{G}$ in $\mathbb{Z}_p^*$. In particular, we can associate to each pair of cosets (C_i, C_j) an advantage

$$P_{C_i, C_j} := \Pr_{(x,y) \xleftarrow{\$} C_i \times C_j} [\mathcal{A}(g, g^x, g^y, g^{xy}) = 1] - \Pr_{(x,y,z) \xleftarrow{\$} C_i \times C_j \times \mathbb{Z}_p} [\mathcal{A}(g, g^x, g^y, g^z) = 1].$$

Suppose that $\mathcal{A}$ has non-negligible advantage in the $\hat{G}$-subgroup DDH game. Then, there is some constant k such that $P_{\hat{G}, \hat{G}} > \lambda^{-k}$. Let $I = |G|/|\hat{G}|$ be the index of $\hat{G}$ over G, and recall that I is polynomially bounded. By the pigeonhole principle, there must be some interval between 0 and λ^{-k} of length $1/(2\lambda^k I^2)$ such that none of the values P_{C_i, C_j} is in this interval. So, by the Chernoff bound, for each (C_i, C_j), we can run $\mathcal{A}$, say, $100\lambda^{3k} I^5$ times to classify P_{C_i, C_j} as either greater than the midpoint of this interval or less than it, failing with only negligible probability. Indeed, given (g, g^x) for unknown x in coset $C(x)$ and any coset C_j, we can classify $P_{C(x), C_j}$ by running $\mathcal{A}$ a total of $100\lambda^{3k} I^5$ times on input of the form $(g, g^{\alpha x}, g^y, g^{\alpha xy})$ and input of the form $(g, g^{\alpha x}, g^y, g^z)$ for $z \xleftarrow{\$} \mathbb{Z}_p$, $\alpha \xleftarrow{\$} \hat{G}$, and $y \xleftarrow{\$} C_j$ and comparing the results. Similarly, given (g, g^y), we can classify $P_{C_i, C(y)}$.

Finally, we claim that given (g, g^x, g^y), we can classify $P_{C(x), C(y)}$. We do this by first classifying all of the P_{C_i, C_j}. We then divide the C_i into left equivalence classes such that for two elements C_i and C_k in the same equivalence class, P_{C_i, C_j} has the same classification as P_{C_k, C_j} for all C_j. We similarly divide the C_j into right equivalence classes. Finally, using the idea outlined above, we can identify the left equivalence class of $C(x)$ and the right equivalence class of $C(y)$. We can then categorize $P_{C(x), C(y)}$ by finding the unique category that "matches" these equivalence classes.

So, an adversary $\mathcal{A}'$ in the DDH game can, on input (g, g^x, g^y, g^z), first categorize $P_{C(x), C(y)}$. If $P_{C(x), C(y)}$ is greater than the midpoint of the interval, it outputs $\mathcal{A}(g, g^x, g^y, g^z)$. Otherwise, it flips a coin and outputs the result. Since $P_{\hat{G}, \hat{G}} > \lambda^{-k}$, it follows that with probability at least $|\hat{G}|/|G| = 1/\text{poly}(\lambda)$, we have that $P_{C(x), C(y)}$ is larger than the midpoint. The result follows. ☐

Definition 12 (k-DDH and subgroup k-DDH). *Let G be a group of order p. For $k \geq 2$, we say that k-DDH is hard in G if no probabilistic polynomial-time algorithm $\mathcal{A}$ can distinguish between $(g, (g^{x_i})_{i=1}^k, (g^{x_i x_j})_{1 \leq i < j \leq k})$ and $(g_i^*)_{i=1}^\ell$ with $\ell = k(k+1)/2 + 1$, where $g \xleftarrow{\$} G$, $(x_i) \xleftarrow{\$} \mathbb{Z}_p^k$, and $(g_i^*) \xleftarrow{\$} G^\ell$.*

Let G be a group of order p, $\hat{G}$ be a subgroup of $\mathbb{Z}_p^*$, and $k \geq 2$. We say that $\hat{G}$-subgroup k-DDH is hard in G if no probabilistic polynomial-time algorithm $\mathcal{A}$ can distinguish between $(g, (g^{x_i})_{i=1}^k, (g^{x_i x_j})_{1 \leq i < j \leq k})$ and $(g_i^*)_{i=1}^\ell$, where $g \xleftarrow{\$} G$, $(x_i) \xleftarrow{\$} \hat{G}^k$, and $(g_i^*) \xleftarrow{\$} G^\ell$.

Lemma 2. *Let G be a group of order p. If DDH is hard in G, then k-DDH is hard in G for any polynomially bounded k.*

Let $\hat{G}$ be a subgroup of $\mathbb{Z}_p^*$. If DDH is hard in G and $|G|/|\hat{G}|$ is polynomially bounded, then $\hat{G}$-subgroup k-DDH is hard in G for any polynomially bounded k.

Proof. For $i = 0, \ldots, (k^2 - k)/2$, let **Game** i be the game of distinguishing between a uniformly random tuple $(g_1^*, \ldots, g_\ell^*) \xleftarrow{\$} G^\ell$ and a tuple of the form $(g, (g^{x_i})_{i=1}^k, (g^{x_i x_j})_{1 \leq i < j \leq k})$ with the last i elements changed to a uniformly random element. It follows from the assumption that DDH is hard in G that no adversary can have non-negligibly larger advantage in **Game** i than in **Game** $i+1$. The result follows by noting that **Game 0** is the k-DDH game and that no adversary can have any advantage in **Game** $(k^2 - k)/2$. The second claim follows analogously to the proof of Lemma 1. □

We will also require a non-uniform version of DDH.

Definition 13 (Non-uniform decisional Diffie-Hellman). *Let G be a group of order p. We say that non-uniform decisional Diffie-Hellman is hard in G if no probabilistic polynomial-time algorithm $\mathcal{A}$ with auxiliary information $\mathsf{aux} = \mathsf{aux}(G)$ can distinguish between (g, g^x, g^y, g^{xy}), where $g \xleftarrow{\$} G$, $(x, y) \xleftarrow{\$} \mathbb{Z}_p^2$, and $(g_1, g_2, g_3, g_4) \xleftarrow{\$} G^4$. Note that aux does not need to be efficiently computable.*

We similarly extend the definitions of $\hat{G}$-subgroup DDH, k-DDH, and $\hat{G}$-subgroup k-DDH to the non-uniform setting. Finally, one more definition will be useful.

Definition 14 (Chosen-bases $\hat{G}$-subgroup k-DDH). *Let G be a group of order p, $\hat{G}$ be a subgroup of $\mathbb{Z}_p^*$, and $k \geq 2$. We say that chosen-bases $\hat{G}$-subgroup k-DDH is hard in G if no probabilistic polynomial-time algorithm $\mathcal{A}$ has non-negligible advantage in the following game.*

1. *$(\sigma, (g_i)_{i=1}^k, (h_{i,j})_{1 \leq i < j \leq k}) \xleftarrow{\$} \mathcal{A}(1^\lambda)$, with $g_i, h_{i,j} \in G \setminus \{1_G\}$.*
2. *Sample $b \xleftarrow{\$} \{0,1\}$, $(x_i)_{i=1}^k \xleftarrow{\$} \mathbb{Z}_p^k$, and $(g_i^*)_{i=1}^\ell \xleftarrow{\$} G^\ell$, where $\ell = (k^2 + k)/2$.*
3. *If $b = 0$, $b^* \xleftarrow{\$} \mathcal{A}(\sigma, (g_i^{x_i})_{i=1}^k, (h_{i,j}^{x_i x_j})_{i<j})$. Otherwise, $b^* \xleftarrow{\$} \mathcal{A}(\sigma, (g_i^*))$.*
4. *$\mathcal{A}$ wins if and only if $b = b^*$.*

Lemma 3. *Let G be a group of order p, and let $\hat{G}$ be a subgroup of $\mathbb{Z}_p^*$. If non-uniform DDH is hard in G and $|G|/|\hat{G}|$ is polynomially bounded, then chosen-bases $\hat{G}$-subgroup k-DDH is hard in G for any polynomially bounded k.*

Proof. We first note that the natural non-uniform analogue of Lemma 2 holds by an essentially identical proof. In particular, it suffices to show that chosen-bases $\hat{G}$-subgroup k-DDH is hard in G if non-uniform $\hat{G}$-subgroup k-DDH is hard in G.

Let $\mathcal{A}$ be an adversary in the chosen-bases $\hat{G}$-subgroup k-DDH game in G. Note that $\mathcal{A}$ may not be deterministic, but we can fix the output of $\mathcal{A}$, $(\sigma, (g_i)_{i=1}^k, (h_{i,j})_{1 \le i < j \le k}) \overset{\$}{\leftarrow} \mathcal{A}(1^\lambda)$, such that the advantage of $\mathcal{A}$ with this fixed output is maximal. Let $\mathsf{aux} = (\sigma, (\log_{g_1}(g_i))_{i=1}^k, (\log_{g_1}(h_{i,j}))_{1 \le i < j \le k})$.

We then build $\mathcal{A}'$, an adversary in the non-uniform $\hat{G}$-subgroup k-DDH in G as follows. $\mathcal{A}'$ receives auxiliary input $(\sigma, (\log_{g_1}(g_i))_{i=1}^k, (\log_{g_1}(h_{i,j}))_{1 \le i < j \le k})$ and challenge $((g_i^*)_{i=1}^k, (h_{i,j}^*))$. For each i, j, it sets $g_i' \leftarrow g_i^{* \log_{g_1} g_i}$ and $h_{i,j}' \leftarrow h_{i,j}^{* \log_{g_1}(h_{i,j})}$. It then returns $\mathcal{A}(\sigma, (g_i'), (h_{i,j}'))$.

It should be clear that the view of $\mathcal{A}$ is identical to its view in the $\hat{G}$-subgroup k-DDH game in G. $\qquad\square$

References

1. Aiello, W., Ishai, Y., Reingold, O.: Priced oblivious transfer: how to sell digital goods. In: Pfitzmann, B. (ed.) EUROCRYPT 2001. LNCS, vol. 2045, pp. 119–135. Springer, Heidelberg (2001)
2. Alwen, J., Shelat, A., Visconti, I.: Collusion-free protocols in the mediated model. In: Wagner, D. (ed.) CRYPTO 2008. LNCS, vol. 5157, pp. 497–514. Springer, Heidelberg (2008)
3. Ball, J., Borger, J., Greenwald, G.: Revealed: how US and UK spy agencies defeat internet privacy and security. Guardian Weekly, September 2013
4. Bellare, M., Hoang, V.T., Rogaway, P.: Foundations of garbled circuits. In: Proceedings of the 2012 ACM Conference on Computer and Communications Security, CCS 2012, pp. 784–796. ACM, New York (2012)
5. Bellare, M., Paterson, K.G., Rogaway, P.: Security of symmetric encryption against mass surveillance. In: Garay, J.A., Gennaro, R. (eds.) CRYPTO 2014, Part I. LNCS, vol. 8616, pp. 1–19. Springer, Heidelberg (2014)
6. Bellare, M., Paterson, K.G., Rogaway, P.: Security of symmetric encryption against mass surveillance. Cryptology ePrint Archive, Report 2014/438 (2014). http://eprint.iacr.org/
7. Blaze, M., Bleumer, G., Strauss, M.J.: Divertible protocols and atomic proxy cryptography. In: Nyberg, K. (ed.) EUROCRYPT 1998. LNCS, vol. 1403, pp. 127–144. Springer, Heidelberg (1998)
8. Brown, D., Vanstone, S.: Elliptic curve random number generation, US Patent App. 11/336,814, August 16 (2007)

9. Burmester, M., Desmedt, Y.G.: All languages in NP have divertible zero-knowledge proofs and arguments under cryptographic assumptions. In: Damgård, I.B. (ed.) EUROCRYPT 1990. LNCS, vol. 473, pp. 1–10. Springer, Heidelberg (1991)

10. Burmester, M., Desmedt, Y., Itoh, T., Sakurai, K., Shizuya, H.: Divertible and subliminal-free zero-knowledge proofs for languages. J. Cryptology **12**, 197–223 (1999)

11. Burmester, M., Desmedt, Y., Itoh, T., Sakurai, K., Shizuya, H., Yung, M.: A progress report on subliminal-free channels. In: Anderson, R. (ed.) Information Hiding. LNCS, vol. 1174, pp. 157–168. Springer, Berlin Heidelberg (1996)

12. Vulnerability summary for CVE-2014-1260 ('Heartbleed'), April 2014. http://cve.mitre.org/cgi-bin/cvename.cgi?name=CVE-2014-1260

13. Vulnerability summary for CVE-2014-1266 ('goto fail'), February 2014. http://cve.mitre.org/cgi-bin/cvename.cgi?name=CVE-2014-1266

14. Vulnerability summary for CVE-2014-6271 ('Shellshock'), September 2014. http://cve.mitre.org/cgi-bin/cvename.cgi?name=CVE-2014-6271

15. Desmedt, Y.: Subliminal-free sharing schemes. In: Proceedings of the 1994 IEEE international symposium on information theory, p. 490, June 1994

16. Desmedt, Y.G.: Abuses in cryptography and how to fight them. In: Goldwasser, S. (ed.) CRYPTO 1988. LNCS, vol. 403, pp. 375–389. Springer, Heidelberg (1990)

17. ElGamal, Taher: A public key cryptosystem and a signature scheme based on discrete logarithms. In: Robert Blakley, George, Chaum, David (eds.) CRYPT 2004. LNCS, vol. 196, pp. 10–18. Springer, New York (1985)

18. Ford, K., Konyagin, S.V., Luca, F.: Prime chains and Pratt trees. Geometric and Functional Analysis **20**(5), 1231–1258 (2010)

19. Gentry, C., Halevi, S., Vaikuntanathan, V.: i-Hop homomorphic encryption and rerandomizable yao circuits. In: Rabin, T. (ed.) CRYPTO 2010. LNCS, vol. 6223, pp. 155–172. Springer, Heidelberg (2010)

20. Greenwald, G.: No Place to Hide: Edward Snowden, the NSA, and the U.S. Surveillance State. Metropolitan Books, May 2014

21. Harnik, D., Kilian, J., Naor, M., Reingold, O., Rosen, A.: On robust combiners for oblivious transfer and other primitives. In: Cramer, R. (ed.) EUROCRYPT 2005. LNCS, vol. 3494, pp. 96–113. Springer, Heidelberg (2005)

22. Lenstra, A.K., Hughes, J.P., Augier, M., Bos, J.W., Kleinjung, T., Wachter, C.: Public keys. In: Safavi-Naini, R., Canetti, R. (eds.) CRYPTO 2012. LNCS, vol. 7417, pp. 626–642. Springer, Heidelberg (2012)

23. Lepinksi, M., Micali, S., Shelat, A.: Collusion-free protocols. In: Proceedings of the Thirty-seventh Annual ACM Symposium on Theory of Computing, STOC 2005, pp. 543–552. ACM, New York (2005)

24. Mironov, I., Stephens-Davidowitz, N.: Cryptographic reverse firewalls. Cryptology ePrint Archive, Report 2014/758, full version (2014). http://eprint.iacr.org/

25. Naor, M., Pinkas, B.: Efficient oblivious transfer protocols. In: Proceedings of the Twelfth Annual ACM-SIAM Symposium on Discrete Algorithms, SODA 2001, pp. 448–457. Society for Industrial and Applied Mathematics, Philadelphia (2001)

26. Okamoto, T., Ohta, K.: Divertible zero knowledge interactive proofs and commutative random self-reducibility. In: Quisquater, J.-J., Vandewalle, J. (eds.) EUROCRYPT 1989. LNCS, vol. 434, pp. 134–149. Springer, Heidelberg (1990)

27. Perlroth, N., Larson, J., Shane, S.: N.S.A. able to foil basic safeguards of privacy on Web. The New York Times, September 2013

28. Prabhakaran, M., Rosulek, M.: Rerandomizable RCCA encryption. In: Menezes, A. (ed.) CRYPTO 2007. LNCS, vol. 4622, pp. 517–534. Springer, Heidelberg (2007)
29. Shumow, D., Ferguson, N.: On the possibility of a back door in the NIST SP800-90 Dual Ec Prng. CRYPTO Rump Session (2007)
30. Simmons, G.: The prisoners' problem and the subliminal channel. In: Chaum, D. (ed.) Advances in Cryptology, pp. 51–67. Springer, US (1984)
31. Simmons, G.J.: The subliminal channel and digital signatures. In: Beth, T., Cot, N., Ingemarsson, I. (eds.) EUROCRYPT 1984. LNCS, vol. 209, pp. 364–378. Springer, Heidelberg (1985)
32. Young, A., Yung, M.: The dark side of "Black-Box" cryptography, or: should we trust capstone? In: Koblitz, N. (ed.) CRYPTO 1996. LNCS, vol. 1109, pp. 89–103. Springer, Heidelberg (1996)

Key Exchange

Mind the Gap: Modular Machine-Checked Proofs of One-Round Key Exchange Protocols

Gilles Barthe[1], Juan Manuel Crespo[1,2], Yassine Lakhnech[3],
and Benedikt Schmidt[1(✉)]

[1] IMDEA Software Institute, Madrid, Spain
{gilles.barthe,benedikt.schmidt}@imdea.org
[2] FireEye Germany, Dresden, Germany
juanmanuel.crespo@fireeye.com
[3] University of Grenoble and VERIMAG, Grenoble, France
yassine.lakhnech@imag.fr

Abstract. Using EasyCrypt, we formalize a new modular security proof for one-round authenticated key exchange protocols in the random oracle model. Our proof improves earlier work by Kudla and Paterson (ASIACRYPT 2005) in three significant ways: we consider a stronger adversary model, we provide support tailored to protocols that utilize the Naxos trick, and we support proofs under the Computational DH assumption not relying on Gap oracles. Furthermore, our modular proof can be used to obtain concrete security proofs for protocols with or without adversarial key registration. We use this support to investigate, still using EasyCrypt, the connection between proofs without Gap assumptions and adversarial key registration. For the case of honestly generated keys, we obtain the first proofs of the Naxos and Nets protocols under the Computational DH assumption. For the case of adversarial key registration, we obtain machine-checked and modular variants of the well-known proofs for Naxos, Nets, and Naxos+.

Keywords: Provable security · Security protocols · EasyCrypt · Key exchange · Interactive theorem proving

1 Introduction

Cryptographic protocols, like TLS, SSH, and VPNs, are one of the main building blocks of the Internet. At the heart of these protocols lies a key exchange protocol, which allows two parties to establish a shared session key used for building a secure channel. Traditionally, key exchange has often been realized using key transport protocols. Here, one participant generates the session key and uses public key encryption and signatures to transport it to the peer. Since this approach usually uses a longterm public key for encryption, it lacks resilience against leakage of the corresponding secret key, either through cryptanalysis or coercion. Concretely, if an adversary obtains the longterm secrets of a participant, he can obtain all his session keys. Resilience against such attacks is called

© International Association for Cryptologic Research 2015
E. Oswald and M. Fischlin (Eds.): EUROCRYPT 2015, Part II, LNCS 9057, pp. 689–718, 2015.
DOI: 10.1007/978-3-662-46803-6_23

forward secrecy [24]. While long known in the cryptographic community, forward secrecy has recently come under public light following revelations about mass surveillance and implementation bugs such as Heartbleed. As a consequence, we expect that the ongoing shift from key transport protocols to key agreement protocols that achieve forward secrecy will accelerate; for instance, there is consensus to deprecate RSA key transport in TLS 1.3.

One solution to achieve forward secrecy is to use protocols that use an ephemeral Diffie-Hellman (DH) exchange. Since the ephemeral DH exchange uses fresh exponents for each session, protocols using them can provide forward secrecy. In order to provide authentication, most popular protocols such as TLS and SSH sign the exchanged DH messages. Theoretically, key agreement protocols based on signed DH are well understood and allow for relatively straightforward proofs of the classical security properties and forward secrecy [10,18]. In practice, their usage in real-world protocols poses additional problems and there is a large body of work on analyzing the security of the combined channel establishment protocol [13,27,32].

Nevertheless, the use of signatures has several disadvantages. First, standardization and implementation must include a signature scheme which might not be required otherwise. Second, the use of signatures might compromise deniability [30]. Third, signing and verification time might be a bottleneck. Furthermore, several realistic attacks are still possible for one-round versions of such protocols. For example, leakage of session randomness can lead to the compromise of future sessions in signed DH protocols [31, Section1.6].

To address these deficiencies, implicitly authenticated key exchange (IAKE) protocols have been introduced in [40]. Such protocols enhance an ephemeral DH exchange with static DH keys that are only used in the key computation. Many protocols of this type have been proposed, such as HQMV [31], Naxos [36], and Nets [38], and they often surpass signature-based protocols in terms of performance and security. For example, the HMQV protocol, which is a hashed variant of the MQV [37] protocol, adds authentication to the ephemeral Diffie-Hellman protocol at a very low cost if Shamir's trick [25] is used for multi-exponentiation. Prominent instances of deployed systems based on such protocols include the EMV [17] chip based payment system, which uses a custom protocol and Blackberry phones, which use the elliptic curve version of MQV [37]. One of the main adversary models for IAKE protocols is the extended Canetti-Krawczyk (eCK) model [36], which provides very strong security guarantees such as (weak) perfect forward secrecy and session key secrecy even in the case where the session's randomness is leaked.

However, a number of concerns with the provable security of this class of protocols remain. First, only some of them achieve efficient designs and tight reductions under standard assumptions such as computational DH (CDH). Instead, known proofs of efficient protocols often use the Forking Lemma (and therefore give non-tight reductions), or strong assumptions such as Gap-CDH [43]. Second, and probably more importantly, the security definitions for key exchange protocols are an order of magnitude more complex than standard definitions for most cryptographic primitives, such as IND-CCA. This results in long proofs that few people understand or check for flaws. Unsurprisingly, numerous attacks have been discovered on key exchange protocols [28,31,41,42], even on those claimed provably secure. This second problem is not exclusive to key exchange protocols. In fact, two approaches have been developed to tame the complexity of cryptographic proofs in the computational model.

The first approach is to develop generic results that can be applied to many concrete instances. While genericity does not eliminate the possibility of flaws, it allows to build a reduced corpus of results on which the security of protocols depends, and gives greater incentive to examine their proofs carefully. One popular class of generic results in cryptography are protocol transformations. If a protocol Π is secure with respect to an adversary model $\mathcal{M}$, then Π can be transformed into a (more complicated) protocol Π' that is secure with respect to a stronger adversary model $\mathcal{M}'$. For key exchange, this approach was pioneered by Bellare, Canetti, and Krawczyk [8] and other transformations have been proposed by Kudla and Paterson [33], Cremers and Feltz [23], and Boyd et al. [16]. However, existing transformations have several drawbacks, in particular: the transformation in [8] cannot be applied to many protocols of interest; the transformations in [16,23] assume that the initial protocol is already secure in the eCK model; and the transformation in [33] only supports proofs under Gap assumptions, predates the eCK model and is only applicable to weaker security models.

The second approach is to build machine-checked, independently verifiable proofs of security; this approach has been suggested notably by Halevi [26], and more recently by Hales[1] in the context of verifying the absence of trapdoors in NIST standards. Assuming that the verification tool is correct, one can gain trust in a formal proof simply by checking the definitions it uses and the theorem statement, since the tool ensures the correctness of the reasoning steps. There are two mature tools to perform machine-checked cryptographic proofs in the computational model: CryptoVerif [14] and EasyCrypt [5,6]. CryptoVerif is an automatic prover in the computational model and has been applied to cryptographic constructions such as the Full Domain Hash signature scheme, Kerberos, and the One-Encryption Key Exchange. EasyCrypt is a toolset for the construction and verification of game-based cryptographic proofs and has mostly been applied to cryptographic primitives, such as the Cramer-Shoup encryption scheme, and the OAEP padding scheme. So far neither of these tools have been used to obtain machine-checked proofs of modern key exchange protocols with respect to their intended security definitions.

Both approaches are complementary. Indeed, machine-checked proofs make *checking proofs* efficient, but they also significantly increase the cost of *building proofs*. As a consequence, generic results are ideal targets for machine-checked proofs, for two reasons. First, the cost of building proofs for generic results is justified by their multiple applications. Second, the level of abstraction required

---

[1]   https://jiggerwit.wordpress.com/2013/11/04/formalizing-nist-standards/

to obtain generic proofs combined with the explicit tracking of assumptions in machine-checked proofs often provides new insights.

Contributions

We develop a new generic proof of security for key-exchange protocols, and instantiate it to obtain security proofs for known protocols with respect to different adversary models and hardness assumptions. In the cases of Naxos and Nets, we show that it is possible to obtain a CDH proof (without GAP) if static keys are honestly generated. We also formalize our generic proof and its instantiations using EasyCrypt. We elaborate on these points below.

Generic Proof for eCK Security. We consider the class of one-round Diffie-Hellman protocols defined in the random oracle model where the session key is the output of a hash function. We reduce eCK-security of a key exchange protocol in this class to a condition on the key computation function and four simple games, in which the adversary can access at most one oracle. For protocols that employ the Naxos trick and use $h(x, a)$ as the exponent of the DH message, we provide an even simpler reduction with three games.

Concretely, we structure our generic proof in terms of protocol transformations and different versions of the security game. We are interested in eCK security. As proof tools, we also use three additional security games:

- eCK: Adversary must distinguish the session key of a fresh test session from random key.
- eCK^{nt}: Variant of eCK where adversary must provide the actor's static secret key as input to the ephemeral reveal oracle.
- CSK: Simplified game for protocols that do not use the Naxos trick where adversary must compute session key of test session (4 cases).
- CSK^{nt}: Simplified game for protocols that use the Naxos trick where adversary must compute session key of test session (3 cases).

We then define protocol transformations T^{nt} (use Naxos trick) and T^{hsk} (hash session key) and prove that the following implications hold for all protocols Π:

$$\Pi \text{ is } eCK^{nt}\text{-secure} \implies T^{nt}(\Pi) \text{ is } eCK\text{-secure}$$
$$\Pi \text{ is } CSK^{nt}\text{-secure} \implies T^{hsk}(\Pi) \text{ is } eCK^{nt}\text{-secure}$$
$$\Pi \text{ is } CSK\text{-secure} \implies T^{hsk}(\Pi) \text{ is } eCK\text{-secure}$$

As an example, consider the Naxos protocol which uses the Naxos trick and hashes its session key. We first define the "core" of Naxos and call it $Naxos^{core}$. Since it holds that $Naxos = T^{hsk}(T^{nt}(Naxos^{core}))$, it suffices to prove that $Naxos^{core}$ is CSK^{nt}-secure to obtain that Naxos is eCK-secure. While the original eCK security definition consists of a game with seven oracles where the winning condition contains a complicated freshness condition, the CSK^{nt} game has a very simple winning condition and only provides a decision oracle that allows the adversary to confirm session key guesses.

Protocol	Existing Proof	Our Proofs	EasyCrypt
Naxos [36]	eCK/Gap-CDH	eCK$_{kr}$/Gap-CDH, eCK$_{nkr}$/CDH	yes
Nets [38]	eCK$_{kr}$/Gap-CDH	eCK$_{kr}$/Gap-CDH, eCK$_{nkr}$/CDH	yes
Naxos+ [39]	eCK$_{kr}$/Gap-CDH	eCK$_{kr}$/CDH	yes
HMQV [31]*	CK$_{HMQV}$/Gap-CDH+KEA1	eCK$_{kr}$/Gap-CDH	no

Fig. 1. Obtained proofs for Key Exchange Protocols (*see explanation, nt=non-tight)

To compare different models of key distribution, we support two versions of the eCK model: The eCK$_{nkr}$ model where all static keys are honestly generated and the eCK$_{kr}$ model that allows the adversary to adaptively register arbitrary public keys for dishonest parties without providing a proof of possession. The original eCK model [36] sits in between our two versions. The adversary can register arbitrary public keys for dishonest parties *before* activating the first session, i.e., the registered public keys can depend on public keys of honest parties, but not on protocol messages, as, for example, required for Kaliski's attack [28] on MQV.

Our proof improves [33] in several ways: it uses the stronger eCK adversary model (with and without adversarial key registration); it supports proofs under standard assumptions (whereas the proof from [33] requires Gap assumptions), and; it exploits the Naxos trick resulting in simpler proof obligations for protocols that use it.

Concrete Proofs. We instantiate the generic proof to obtain security proofs for existing protocols; in all cases, the proofs of the simplified games are short by the standards of machine-checked proofs. Our results are summarized in Figure 1. Concretely, we prove that:

- Naxos and Nets are secure in the eCK model under the CDH assumption if keys are honestly generated. If we allow arbitrary adversarial key registration, we require the Gap-CDH assumption as in the original proof.
- The Naxos variant Naxos+ [39] is secure in the eCK model with arbitrary adversarial key registration under the CDH assumption. Here we obtain a similar result to the original proof using our generic proof method.
- A version of HMQV is secure in the eCK model under the Gap-CDH assumption. The version we analyze includes the identities and exchanged message in the input of the key derivation hash. The proof does not need KEA1 (knowledge of exponent assumption).

EasyCrypt Formalization. We have formalized all models, our generic proof for protocols using the Naxos trick, and the proofs for Nets, Naxos, and Naxos+ in EasyCrypt. Our formalization constitutes the biggest case study developed with the tool so far; e.g. the generic proof for protocols using the Naxos trick takes about 30,000 lines of code, including game definitions (about 50 of them), specifications, and proofs. On the other hand, the instantiation of the proof for concrete protocols is short and takes less than 1,000 lines each. Our formalization also includes several reusable libraries that deal with random oracles, Twin DH, and common proof techniques such as plug and pray, that we discuss in Section 2.3.

Future Work

There are several directions for future work, including:

1. Automation and synthesis. The next logical step of this work is to *extend* our library of high-level principles to reason about AKE proofs in the random oracle model and provide more automation to simplify their application. These high-level principles will serve as a useful basis for future formalizations in Easy-Crypt (beyond AKE), but will also make it faster to extend the current proof to support new features. They could also serve as a basis for fully automated proof methods and allow for the use of synthesis to generate secure protocols, following [3].

2. Extensions. We plan to strengthen our results in different directions. Possible extensions include adversary models with a more precise model of the CA [16], adversary models that allow reveal of different parts of state, and models of weak randomness. Moreover, we are also interested in using our framework to analyze larger protocols that use AKE as a subprotocol. This will be valuable to evaluate existing [45] and future proposals for secure transport-layer protocols.

3. Implementations. Our model provides a precise specification of the protocol. Using the techniques from [2], we intend to carry the security proof to executable implementations.

Related Work

There is a vast body of literature on key-exchange protocols and on their associated security models; for a comparison between some existing models we refer to [20,22,34]. In addition to Naxos+, which we already mentioned, there are other protocols that achieve eCK-security under the CDH assumption, e.g., by Kim, Fujioka, and Ustaoglu [29] or by Pan and Wang [44].

There has been extensive work on the formal verification of key exchange protocols, see for instance the recent survey [15]. A significant amount of work is carried in the symbolic model, a high-level model which idealizes the treatment of cryptographic primitives. This level of abstraction makes the symbolic model amenable to automated analysis, and many tools have been developed for proving protocol security. Recent results focusing on DH-based key exchange protocols include [7], [35] and [46]. Over the last decade, many results on computational soundness results [1,21] have shown that under certain conditions, protocols deemed secure in the symbolic model remain secure in the computational model. Another related line of research (see, e.g., [12]) deals with the verification of implementations of security protocols such as TLS in the computational model.

2   Background

In this section, we give some background on notation, authenticated key exchange protocols, and EasyCrypt.

2.1   Notation

A^* denotes the set of all sequences with elements taken from A. For two sequences s_1 and s_2, we use $S_1 +\!\!+ S_2$ to denote their concatenation. We use $s_1 \xleftarrow{+\!\!+} s_2$ as a shorthand for the assignment $s_1 \leftarrow s_1 +\!\!+ s_2$. In the special case of bitstrings b_1 and b_2, we also use $b_1 \| b_2$ to denote their concatenation.

We use $A \rightharpoonup B$ to denote the set of partial functions from A to B. If f is a (partial) function, we define $f[a := b]$ as the function $x \mapsto if\ x = a\ then\ b\ else\ f(x)$. In games, we use $f[a] \leftarrow b$ as a shorthand for $f \leftarrow f[a := b]$ (update f at key a). For a finite set A, we use $x \xleftarrow{\$} A$ to denote that x is uniformly sampled from A.

We use $\mathbb{G}$ to denote a cyclic group of prime order p with generator g. We use $\mathbb{F}_p$ to denote the field of integers modulo p. We use $\mathsf{dlog}(Y)$ to denote the discrete logarithm of Y with respect to the basis g. We define $\mathsf{dh}(X, Y) \doteq X^{\mathsf{dlog}(Y)}$ and $\mathsf{ddh}(X, Y, Z) \doteq (\mathsf{dh}(X, Y) = Z)$. Based on the previous definitions, we define the following cryptographic assumptions. The challenger for DLOG gives $X \xleftarrow{\$} \mathbb{G}$ to the adversary who must return $\mathsf{dlog}(X)$. The challenger for CDH gives $X, Y \xleftarrow{\$} \mathbb{G}$ to the adversary who must return $\mathsf{dh}(X, Y)$. For SCDH, the adversary is given the same challenge, but must return a set containing $\mathsf{dh}(X, Y)$. We also define Gap versions [43] of these assumptions where the adversary is given access to an oracle that returns $\mathsf{ddh}(X, Y, Z)$ for arbitrary $X, Y, Z \in \mathbb{G}$.

2.2   One-Round Authenticated Key Exchange Protocols

In the following, we focus on one-round key exchange protocols. We believe most of our results can be extended to a more general notion of protocol. Further note that our results are not restricted to DH-based protocols and the formal definitions in Section 3.1 will generalize some of the notions we introduce informally in this section.

Figure 2 shows the computations and exchanged messages for a typical DH-based key exchange protocol. We assume a protocol consists of three components. First, there is a protocol component for key generation, which we show in the first line. Here, a participant $\hat{A}$ samples the *static secret key* a and computes the corresponding *static public key* A. Second, there is a component responsible for the distribution of the static public keys. We ignore the details for now and just assume that an agent can obtain the public key of another agent.

Finally, there is a component responsible for establishing the session key. This component consists of an *initiator role* and a *responder role*. If an agent $\hat{A}$ executes an instance of the initiator (resp. responder) role with the goal of establishing a session key with $\hat{B}$, we call this execution a session with *role* initiator (resp. responder), *actor* $\hat{A}$, and *peer* $\hat{B}$.

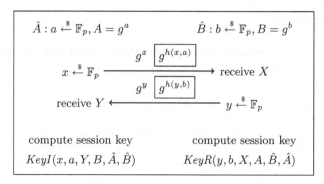

Fig. 2. Generic two pass protocol. Protocols using the Naxos trick use boxed messages.

When the initiator role is activated with actor $\hat{A}$ and peer $\hat{B}$, it first generates an *ephemeral secret key* x, computes the *ephemeral public key* X, sends it to $\hat{B}$, and waits for a reply. When the responder $\hat{B}$ is activated with a received message from $\hat{A}$, he stores the received message as X, generates y and Y in the same way as the initiator, sends Y to $\hat{A}$, and computes the *session key* using the *KeyR* function. When the initiator is activated with the received message, he computes the session key using *KeyI*.

We can define the HMQV protocol by using *KeyI/KeyR* that compute the key as $H(\sigma)$ for $\sigma = \mathsf{dh}(X,Y)\,\mathsf{dh}(X,B)^e\,\mathsf{dh}(A,Y)^d\,\mathsf{dh}(A,B)^{de}$, $e = \bar{h}(X,\hat{B})$, and $d = \bar{h}(Y,\hat{A})$. We can define the Naxos and Nets protocols by using the boxed expressions from Figure 2 to compute X and Y. These protocols both utilize the Naxos trick which combines the static and the ephemeral secret using the hash function h to obtain the exponent of ephemeral public key. Since the hash output is never stored and recomputed when required, these protocols are analyzed with respect to possible leakage of x or a, but leakage of $h(x,a)$ is not considered. The Naxos protocol defines the session key as $H(\sigma)$ for $\sigma = \mathsf{dh}(A,Y)\,\|$ $\mathsf{dh}(X,B)\,\|\,\mathsf{dh}(X,Y)\,\|\,\hat{A}\,\|\,\hat{B}$. The Nets protocol defines the session key as $H(\sigma)$ for $\sigma = \mathsf{dh}(X,Y)\,\mathsf{dh}(X,B)\,\mathsf{dh}(A,Y)\,\mathsf{dh}(A,B)\,\|\,\mathsf{dh}(X,Y)\,\|\,\hat{A}\,\|\,\hat{B}\,\|\,X\,\|\,Y$. The Naxos+ protocol extends the Naxos protocols with the additional group element $\mathsf{dh}(A,B)$, i.e., the session key is defined as $H(\sigma)$ for $\sigma = \mathsf{dh}(A,Y)\,\|\,\mathsf{dh}(X,B)\,\|$ $\mathsf{dh}(X,Y)\,\|\,\mathsf{dh}(A,B)\,\|\,\hat{A}\,\|\,\hat{B}$.

Informally, the security notion expected of such protocols is the following. If $\hat{A}$ completes a session with (honest) peer $\hat{B}$, then the session string computed by $\hat{A}$ is indistinguishable from a random bitstring for everyone except $\hat{B}$. It has been shown by Canetti and Krawczyk [18] that this is sufficient to establish a secure channel between $\hat{A}$ and $\hat{B}$. The secure channel can then be used for key confirmation. Recent adversary models like eCK build on this definition, but also allow for many scenarios where the adversary learns additional information such as ephemeral secret keys, static secret keys, or session keys. The eCK-model guarantees resilience against Unknown Key Share Attacks, Key Compromise Impersonation Resilience, and Weak Perfect Forward Secrecy, which we discuss at the end of Section 3.1.

2.3   EasyCrypt

EasyCrypt [5,6] is a machine-checked framework for building and verifying security proofs of cryptographic constructions. EasyCrypt follows the code-based, game-based approach to reductionist arguments: a proof consists of a series of probabilistic programs with adversarial code, called games, and of probabilistic claims relating the probability of one or more events in one or more games. However, EasyCrypt adopts a foundational approach, meaning that probabilistic claims, and the overall security statement, must all be justified to the last detail by means of elementary rules. Leveraging the state of the art in program verification, all probabilistic claims are proved using a probabilistic Relational Hoare Logic (pRHL), which generalizes Relational Hoare Logic [11] to a probabilistic setting. pRHL is a program logic whose judgments are of the form

$$\{\Phi\}c_1 \sim c_2\{\Psi\}$$

where c_1 and c_2 are games and Φ and Ψ are relations on program states. The rules of pRHL allow to derive valid judgments, where a judgment as above is valid if for every initial memories m_1 and m_2 that are related by Φ, the output sub-distributions obtained by executing c_1 on m_1 and c_2 on m_2 respectively are related by $\Psi^{\#}$, where $\#$ is an operator that lifts relations on states to relations on sub-distributions over states. The definition of $\#$ is inspired from probabilistic process algebra. For suitable choices of Ψ, this implies inequalities of the form

$$\Pr[c_1, m_1 : E_1] \leq \Pr[c_2, m_2 : E_2]$$

which are typical in game-based proofs, i.e., the probability of event E_1 after executing c_1 in initial memory m_1 is upper-bounded by the probability of event E_2 after executing c_2 in m_2.

Although pRHL captures common patterns of reasoning in cryptographic proofs, there is an impedance mismatch between cryptographic practice and proofs built using pRHL; in particular, pRHL lacks mechanisms to instantiate previous results, and to apply high-level principles in proofs. To make matters precise, consider for instance the reduction of SCDH to CDH: using pRHL, one can prove that any instance of SCDH can be reduced to CDH, but one cannot perform the proof once and for all, and reuse the result. Fortunately, EasyCrypt now features a module system; the module system combines the power of module systems, as they exist in functional programming languages, with a system of capabilities that is used to restrict access to oracles or fragments of memories, as required in cryptography. The module system can be used for performing successive reductions locally, as often featured in pen-and-paper proofs. Module systems are essential to formalize complex proofs such as the ones considered here; indeed, previous attempts to carry out the generic proof without the module system were unsuccessful, because the adversary was carried explicitly throughout the proof, making reasoning unwieldy.

Additionally, the module system allows to prove general principles once and for all, and to carry out proofs simply by applying high-level principles. In our formalization underlying this paper, we make extensive use of the following principles:

- lazy and eager sampling: this is used to switch back and forth between an implementation of a random function in which images are sampled on demand (lazily), or during initialization of the game (eagerly);
- plug and pray: if some event Φ happens for some $0 \leq i < n$, randomly sample a value j in this range and consider the event $\Phi \wedge i = j$ instead of Φ; and
- adversary prescience: this is used to provide an upper bound to the probability that an adversary guesses an unused value in the range of a random function

3   Model and Generic Proof

In this section, we first introduce our generic protocol model and our versions of the eCK model with and without adversarial key registration. Afterwards, we present our generic proof for protocols that employ the Naxos trick.

3.1   eCK$_{kr}$ Security and eCK$_{nkr}$ Security

We assume given a set ID of agent identities. We also define the set Role $= \{\mathcal{I}, \mathcal{R}\}$ and the function $(\cdot)^\star$: Role $\to$ Role such that $\mathcal{I}^\star = \mathcal{R}$ and $\mathcal{R}^\star = \mathcal{I}$.

Generic Protocol Model. A protocol definition consists of instantiations for the types and functions given in the first column of Figure 3. These types and functions are instantiated as follows:

- The sequence $H_1 : \mathsf{I}_1 \to \mathsf{O}_1, \dots, H_k : \mathsf{I}_k \to \mathsf{O}_k$ defines the types of hash functions used by the protocol.
- Sk defines the type of static secret keys, Pk defines the type of static public keys, Esk defines the type of ephemeral secret keys, Epk defines the type of ephemeral public keys, and Key defines the type of session keys.
- The function Pk defines how the static public key is computed from the static secret key and the function Epk defines how the ephemeral public key is computed from the ephemeral secret key and the static secret key.
- The functions $KeyI$ and $KeyR$ define how the session key is computed from the actor's secret data, the peer's public data, and the participants' identities. We use partial functions to capture failure, e.g., if a subgroup element check fails for one of the arguments.

We keep the distributions according to which the static and ephemeral secret keys are sampled implicit and assume they are uniformly sampled unless otherwise stated. The functions Epk, $KeyI$, and $KeyR$ can use the hash functions H_i. See Figure 3 for the Naxos^{core} instantiation of the generic model. In the next section, we will demonstrate how Naxos^{core} can be transformed into Naxos.

Types/Functions	Naxos^{core}	Naxos $= \mathcal{T}^{\mathsf{hsk}}(\mathcal{T}^{\mathsf{nt}}(\mathsf{Naxos}^{core}))$
Hash functions	$\emptyset$	$H: \mathbb{G}^3 \times \mathsf{ID}^2 \to \{0,1\}^l, h: \mathbb{F}_p^2 \to \mathbb{F}_p$
Sk, Pk, Esk, Epk, Key	$\mathbb{F}_p, \mathbb{G}, \mathbb{F}_p, \mathbb{G}, \mathbb{G}^3 \times \mathsf{ID}^2$	$\mathbb{F}_p, \mathbb{G}, \mathbb{F}_p, \mathbb{G}, \{0,1\}^l$
$Pk: \mathsf{Sk} \to \mathsf{Pk}$ $Epk: \mathsf{Esk} \times \mathsf{Sk} \to \mathsf{Epk}$	$a \mapsto g^a$ $(x, \_) \mapsto g^x$	$a \mapsto g^a$ $(x, a) \mapsto g^{h(x,a)}$
$KeyI: \mathsf{Esk} \times \mathsf{Sk} \times \mathsf{Epk}$ $\times \mathsf{Pk} \times \mathsf{ID} \times \mathsf{ID} \to \mathsf{Key}_\perp$	$(x,a,Y,B,\hat{A},\hat{B}) \mapsto$ $Y^a \,\|\, B^x \,\|\, Y^x \,\|\, \hat{A} \,\|\, \hat{B}$	$(x,a,Y,B,\hat{A},\hat{B}) \mapsto$ $H(Y^a \,\|\, B^{h(x,a)} \,\|\, Y^{h(x,a)} \,\|\, \hat{A} \,\|\, \hat{B})$
$KeyR: \mathsf{Esk} \times \mathsf{Sk} \times \mathsf{Epk}$ $\times \mathsf{Pk} \times \mathsf{ID} \times \mathsf{ID} \to \mathsf{Key}_\perp$	$(y,b,X,A,\hat{B},\hat{A}) \mapsto$ $A^y \,\|\, X^b \,\|\, X^y \,\|\, \hat{A} \,\|\, \hat{B}$	$(x,a,Y,B,\hat{B},\hat{A}) \mapsto$ $H(A^{h(y,b)} \,\|\, X^b \,\|\, X^{h(y,b)} \,\|\, \hat{A} \,\|\, \hat{B})$

Fig. 3. Generic Protocol Model with Naxos^{core} instantiation and transformation

Protocol Transformations. We define two transformations $\mathcal{T}^{\mathsf{hsk}}$ and $\mathcal{T}^{\mathsf{nt}}$. The first transformation $\mathcal{T}^{\mathsf{hsk}}$ modifies a protocol to hash the session key. The second transformation $\mathcal{T}^{\mathsf{nt}}$ modifies a protocol to utilize the Naxos trick. Figure 3 demonstrates how the Naxos protocol can be obtained by applying the two transformations to Naxos^{core}. We assume $\mathcal{T}^{\mathsf{hsk}}$ is implicitly parameterized by a positive integer l defining the size of the hash function output.

Given a protocol Π using hash functions $\boldsymbol{H}$, defining types Sk, Pk, Esk, Epk, Key, and defining functions Pk, Epk, $KeyI$, $KeyR$, the transformed protocols $\mathcal{T}^{\mathsf{hsk}}(\Pi)$ and $\mathcal{T}^{\mathsf{nt}}(\Pi)$ are defined as follows. We obtain $\mathcal{T}^{\mathsf{hsk}}(\Pi)$ from Π by adding a hash function $H: \mathsf{Key} \to \{0,1\}^l$ to $\boldsymbol{H}$, changing the type Key to $\{0,1\}^l$, redefining $KeyI$ in terms of the original $KeyI$ as $ki \mapsto H(KeyI(ki))$, and redefining $KeyR$ analogously. We obtain $\mathcal{T}^{\mathsf{nt}}(\Pi)$ from Π by adding a hash function $h: \mathsf{Esk} \times \mathsf{Sk} \to \mathsf{Esk}$ to $\boldsymbol{H}$ and redefining Epk in terms of the original Epk as $(x,a) \mapsto Epk(h(x,a),a)$. We also redefine the key computation to use $h(x,a)$ instead of x. Note that the original Epk usually ignores its second input and a is therefore only used as input to h in the computation of the ephemeral public key. We denote the composition of $\mathcal{T}^{\mathsf{nt}}$ and $\mathcal{T}^{\mathsf{hsk}}$ with $\mathcal{T}^{\mathsf{nt,hsk}}$.

Security Experiments. To define the games eCK$_{\mathsf{kr}}$ and eCK$_{\mathsf{nkr}}$ (with and without adversarial key registration), we first define the type St for the state of protocol sessions and the type Ev for the events required to express the security definition. We define St as Role $\times$ Esk $\times$ Epk $\times$ ID $\times$ ID $\times$ Epk$_\perp$ $\times$ Key$_\perp$. We define Ev as the data type generated by the constructors

EphRev : Epk $\to$ Ev, KeyRev : Epk $\to$ Ev, StaticRev : ID $\to$ Ev,

Accept : Role $\times$ Epk $\times$ ID $\times$ ID $\times$ Epk $\to$ Ev, and Dishonest : ID $\to$ Ev,

The main procedure of the games eCK$_{\mathsf{kr},\Pi}(\mathcal{A})$ and eCK$_{\mathsf{nkr},\Pi}(\mathcal{A})$ is given in the first column of Figure 4. We assume that the adversary $\mathcal{A}$ consists of the two procedures $\mathcal{A}_1$ and $\mathcal{A}_2$ sharing state. In the games, the adversary is provided with access to the oracles defined in the second column of Figure 4 and with random oracle access using wrappers $H_1^{\mathcal{A}}, \ldots, H_k^{\mathcal{A}}$. The oracles *establishHonest* and *establishDishonest* (only in $\mathsf{eCK}_{kr,\Pi}$) allow the adversary to establish honest agents for which the keys are sampled and dishonest agents where the public key can be chosen. For honest agents, the adversary can control the execution of initiator and responder sessions using $init_1$, $init_2$, and *resp*. Dishonest agents can be used as peers of protocol sessions, but cannot be used as actors since the static secret key is required to execute the protocol. The remaining oracles allow the adversary to reveal static secrets, ephemeral secrets, and session keys.

The adversary wins if he can distinguish the session key of the test session from a random session key and the test session is fresh, i.e., he did not perform forbidden reveal queries. The freshness condition is formalized using the *fresh* predicate given in Figure 5. We use the ephemeral public key to identify a session for session key reveals and ephemeral reveals.

Discussion. In eCK_{kr}, we allow the actor of the test session to execute sessions with dishonest users, but the actor and peer of the test session itself must be honest. In both eCK_{kr} and eCK_{nkr}, we disallow $\hat{A} = \hat{B}$ because many deployed protocols disallow this case or use distinct keys for different roles. It would be possible to lift this limitation at the cost of additional proof obligations for users of the generic proof.

The freshness condition captures Unknown Key Share Attacks because if $\hat{A}$ establishes a key with $\hat{B}$, but $\hat{B}$ believes that he shares this key with $\hat{C} \neq \hat{A}$, then there are two non-matching sessions with the same session key and one of them can be revealed. It captures Key Compromise Impersonation because leakage of the actors static secret key is allowed for the test session. It also captures Weak Perfect Forward Secrecy because for all sessions where the adversary is passive (there is a matching session), reveals for all ephemeral secrets, except for those of the test session and its matching session, and for all static secrets are allowed. The stronger notion of Perfect Forward Secrecy requires changes to the freshness condition and we leave such an extension of our results open for future work.

In our definition of Naxos, we use the type $\mathbb{G}$ for ephemeral and static public keys. This models an implementation ensuring that these values are elements of $\mathbb{G}$. It is also possible to use a "larger type" and explicitly model the required checks using failure in the key computation functions.

3.2   Generic Proof

Before presenting our generic proof, we define three properties of core protocols:

(P1) The functions Pk and Epk are injective.

(P2) $KeyI(x, a, Y, B, \hat{A}, \hat{B})$ is efficiently computable from $KeyR(x, a, Y, B, \hat{A}, \hat{B})$.

(P3) If two distinct sessions $(X, Y, \hat{A}, \hat{B}, r)$ and $(X', Y', \hat{A}', \hat{B}', r')$ compute the same session key, then $(X, Y, \hat{A}, \hat{B}) = (Y', X', \hat{B}', \hat{A}')$ and $\{r, r'\} = \{\mathcal{I}, \mathcal{R}\}$.

We assume the second property for simplicity. For core protocols, which we consider here, it usually suffices to reorder the key string elements to obtain

Game:	Oracles (eCK$_\mathsf{nkr}$ does not include *establishDishonest*):	
var evs : Ev* = [] var ses : Nat $\rightharpoonup$ St = $\emptyset$ var sks : ID $\rightharpoonup$ Sk = $\emptyset$ var pks : ID $\rightharpoonup$ Pk = $\emptyset$ var i : Nat = 0 $t \leftarrow \mathcal{A}_1()$ $(r,\_,X,\hat{A},\hat{B},Y,k)$ $\quad \leftarrow ses[t]$ $b \xleftarrow{\$} \{0,1\}$ $k' \xleftarrow{\$} \mathsf{Key}$ $b' \leftarrow \mathcal{A}_2(b\,?\,k:k')$ $t \leftarrow (r,X,\hat{A},\hat{B},Y)$ return $\quad b = b' \wedge \mathit{fresh}_{evs}(t)$	$init_1(\hat{A},\hat{B}) : \mathsf{Epk} =$ $\quad i \leftarrow i+1$ $\quad a \leftarrow sks[\hat{A}]$ $\quad$ if $a = \bot \vee \hat{A} = \hat{B}$ then $\qquad$ return $\bot$ $\quad x \xleftarrow{\$} \mathsf{Esk};\ X \leftarrow Epk(x,a)$ $\quad ses[i] \leftarrow (\mathcal{I},x,X,\hat{A},\hat{B},\bot,\bot)$ $\quad$ return (i,X) $init_2(i,Y) =$ $\quad (\mathcal{I},x,X,\hat{A},\hat{B},\bar{Y},\_) \leftarrow ses[i]$ $\quad$ if $\bar{Y} \neq \bot$ then return $\bot$ $\quad a \leftarrow sks[\hat{A}];\ B \leftarrow pks[\hat{B}]$ $\quad k \leftarrow KeyI(x,a,Y,B,\hat{A},\hat{B})$ $\quad ses[i] \leftarrow (\mathcal{I},x,X,\hat{A},\hat{B},Y,k)$ $\quad$ if $k = \bot$ then return $\bot$ $\quad evs \xleftarrow{+\!+} \mathsf{Accept}(\mathcal{I},X,\hat{A},\hat{B},Y)$ $resp(\hat{B},\hat{A},X) : \mathsf{Epk} =$ $\quad i \leftarrow i+1$ $\quad$ if $\hat{A} = \hat{B}$ then return $\bot$ $\quad b \leftarrow sks[\hat{B}];\ A \leftarrow pks[\hat{A}]$ $\quad y \xleftarrow{\$} \mathsf{Esk};\ Y \leftarrow Epk(y,b)$ $\quad k \leftarrow KeyR(y,b,X,A,\hat{B},\hat{A})$ $\quad$ if $k = \bot$ then return $\bot$ $\quad ses[i] \leftarrow (\mathcal{R},y,Y,\hat{B},\hat{A},X,k)$ $\quad evs \xleftarrow{+\!+} \mathsf{Accept}(\mathcal{R},Y,\hat{B},\hat{A},X)$ $\quad$ return (i,Y)	$establishHonest(\hat{A}) : \mathsf{Pk} =$ $\quad$ if $pks[\hat{A}] \neq \bot$ then $\qquad$ return $\bot$ $\quad sks[\hat{A}] \xleftarrow{\$} \mathsf{Sk}$ $\quad pks[\hat{A}] \leftarrow Pk(sks[\hat{A}])$ $\quad$ return $pks[\hat{A}]$ $establishDishonest(\hat{A},A) =$ $\quad$ if $pks[\hat{A}] \neq \bot$ then $\qquad$ return $\bot$ $\quad pks[\hat{A}] \leftarrow A$ $\quad evs \xleftarrow{+\!+} \mathsf{Dishonest}(\hat{A})$ $staticRev(\hat{A}) : \mathsf{Sk} =$ $\quad evs \xleftarrow{+\!+} \mathsf{StaticRev}(\hat{A})$ $\quad$ return $sks[\hat{A}]$ $ephRev(i) : \mathsf{Esk} =$ $\quad (\_,x,X,\_,\_,\_,\_) \leftarrow ses[i]$ $\quad evs \xleftarrow{+\!+} \mathsf{EphRev}(X)$ $\quad$ return x $keyRev(i) : \mathsf{Key} =$ $\quad (\_,\_,X,\_,\_,\_,k) \leftarrow ses[i]$ $\quad evs \xleftarrow{+\!+} \mathsf{KeyRev}(X)$ $\quad$ return k

Fig. 4. Games $\mathsf{eCK}_{\mathsf{kr},\Pi}(\mathcal{A})$ and $\mathsf{eCK}_{\mathsf{nkr},\Pi}(\mathcal{A})$ for $\mathcal{A} = (\mathcal{A}_1,\mathcal{A}_2)$ and protocol Π

$KeyI(ki)$ from $KeyR(ki)$. The third property is called strong partnering in [33] and ensures key independence.

Exploiting the Naxos Technique. We exploit that for protocols $\mathcal{T}^{\mathsf{nt}}(\Pi)$ using the Naxos technique, both x and a are required to learn the secret input $h(x,a)$ of Epk. This is a consequence of the fact that the value $h(x,a)$ cannot be revealed by the adversary in the eCK model. This decision is motivated by the assumption that honest agents executing the protocol never store the value $h(x,a)$. We can therefore prove security of Π in a restricted $\mathsf{eCK}^{\mathsf{nt}}$ game to obtain eCK-security of $\mathcal{T}^{\mathsf{nt}}(\Pi)$. For $m \in \{\mathsf{kr},\mathsf{nkr}\}$, we obtain $\mathsf{eCK}^{\mathsf{nt}}_m$ from eCK_m

---

$fresh_{evs}(r, X, \hat{A}, \hat{B}, Y) \doteq$

> There is no session key reveal for t, not both ephemeral and static reveal for t,
> $\mathsf{KeyRev}(X) \notin evs \land \neg(\mathsf{EphRev}(X) \in evs \land \mathsf{StaticRev}(\hat{A}) \in evs)$
> and the adversary did not register $\hat{A}$'s or $\hat{B}$'s public keys.

$\land \; \mathsf{Dishonest}(\hat{A}) \notin evs \land \mathsf{Dishonest}(\hat{B}) \notin evs$

> If there is a matching session t', then

$\land \; (\mathsf{Accept}(r^\star, Y, \hat{B}, \hat{A}, X) \in evs \implies$

>> there is no key reveal for t' and not both ephemeral and static reveal for t'.

$\quad (\mathsf{KeyRev}(Y) \notin evs \land \neg(\mathsf{EphRev}(Y) \in evs \land \mathsf{StaticRev}(\hat{B}) \in evs)))$

> If there is no matching session, then there is no static reveal for B.

$\land \; (\mathsf{Accept}(r^\star, Y, \hat{B}, \hat{A}, X) \notin evs \implies \mathsf{StaticRev}(\hat{B}) \notin evs)$

Fig. 5. Freshness condition for a trace evs and a test session $t = (r, X, \hat{A}, \hat{B}, Y)$

by replacing $ephRev$ with $ephRev^{nt}$ as defined below:

$$ephRev^{nt}(i, a) : \mathsf{Esk} =$$
$$(\_, x, X, \hat{A}, \_, \_, \_) \leftarrow ses[i]$$
$$\text{if } a \neq sks[\hat{A}] \text{ then return } \bot$$
$$evs \overset{+\!+}{\leftarrow} \mathsf{EphRev}(X)$$
$$\text{return } x$$

Informally, our reduction exploits that x for Π in eCK^{nt} corresponds to $h(x, a)$ for $T^{nt}(\Pi)$ in eCK and a query $ephRev^{nt}(i, a)$ in eCK^{nt} corresponds to the sequence of queries $x \leftarrow ephRev(i); h^{\mathcal{A}}(x, a)$ in eCK.

To state our lemma, we define $\mathcal{A}$ to be a (q_{se}, q_{ag}, q_H) eCK_m (or eCK^{nt}_m) adversary if $\mathcal{A}$ activates at most q_{se} sessions involving at most q_{ag} agents and performs at most q_{H_i} queries to the random oracle $H^{\mathcal{A}}_i$. We use q_h to denote the number of queries to the random oracle $h^{\mathcal{A}}$ introduced by the T^{nt} transformation.

Lemma 1. *Let* $m \in \{\mathsf{kr}, \mathsf{nkr}\}$, Π *be a protocol, and* $\mathcal{A}$ *a* (q_{se}, q_{ag}, q_H) eCK_m *adversary. Then there is a* (q_{se}, q_{ag}, q_H) eCK^{nt}_m *adversary* $\mathcal{B}$ *such that*

$$\Pr\left[\mathsf{eCK}_{m, T^{nt}(\Pi)}(\mathcal{A}) = 1\right] \leq \Pr\left[\mathsf{eCK}^{nt}_{m, \Pi}(\mathcal{B}) = 1\right] + \epsilon_{T^{nt}}$$

where $\epsilon_{T^{nt}} = 2 q_h \, q_{se}/|\mathsf{Esk}| + q^2_{se}/2\,|\mathsf{Esk}|$. *Furthermore, the adversary* $\mathcal{B}$ *runs in time at most* $\mathcal{O}(q_h \, t_{Pk} + t_{\mathcal{A}})$ *where* t_{Pk} *is the time required to compute* Pk.

In our EasyCrypt formalization, we explicitly construct the simulator $\mathcal{S}$ sketched in the proof below and prove the probability statement for $\mathcal{B} = \mathcal{S}(\mathcal{A})$.

Proof (Sketch). After bounding the probability of collisions for ephemeral secrets and bounding the probability of the adversary querying $h^{\mathcal{A}}(x, *)$ for an ephemeral secret x before revealing it, we define a simulator $\mathcal{B}$ that calls $\mathcal{A}$ and handles queries as follows: On queries $init_1$ and $resp$, $\mathcal{B}$ updates a mapping from the

$G_{1,m}^{hsk,nt}$ (a secret):	$G_{2,m}^{hsk,nt}$ (x, b secret):	$G_3^{hsk,nt}$ (x, y secret):
$a \xleftarrow{\$} Sk;\quad A \leftarrow Pk(a)$	$x \xleftarrow{\$} Esk;\quad X \leftarrow Epk(x)$	$x \xleftarrow{\$} Esk;\ X \leftarrow Epk(x)$
$z \xleftarrow{\$} Esk^{q_{se}};\ Z \leftarrow Epk(z)$	$b \xleftarrow{\$} Sk;\quad B \leftarrow Pk(b)$	$y \xleftarrow{\$} Esk;\ Y \leftarrow Epk(y)$
$c \xleftarrow{\$} Sk^{q_{ag}-1}$	$z \xleftarrow{\$} Esk^{q_{se}-1};\ Z \leftarrow Epk(z)$	$c \xleftarrow{\$} Sk^{q_{ag}}$
$a' \leftarrow \mathcal{B}_1(A, \mathbf{Z}, \mathbf{c})$	$c \xleftarrow{\$} Sk^{q_{ag}-1}$	$(i, j, \hat{A}, \hat{B}, S) \leftarrow \mathcal{B}_3(X, Y, \mathbf{c})$
return $(a = a')$	$(i, Y, \hat{A}, \hat{B}, S) \leftarrow \mathcal{B}_2(X, B, \mathbf{c}, \mathbf{Z})$	$C \leftarrow Pk(c_j)$
	$k \leftarrow KeyI(x, c_i, Y, B, \hat{A}, \hat{B})$	$k \leftarrow KeyI(x, c_i, Y, C, \hat{A}, \hat{B})$
	return $(k \in S \wedge k \neq \bot)$	return $(k \in S \wedge k \neq \bot)$
$eqS^{kr}(i, Y, \underline{C}, \hat{A}, \hat{C}, k) =$	$eqS^{kr}(j, W, \underline{C}, \hat{B}, \hat{C}, k) =$	
$\quad ki \leftarrow (z_i, a, Y, \underline{C}, \hat{A}, \hat{C})$	$\quad ki \leftarrow (z_j, b, W, \underline{C}, \hat{B}, \hat{C})$	
$\quad$ return $(k = KeyI(ki))$	$\quad$ return $(k = KeyI(ki))$	
$eqS^{nkr}(i, Y, \underline{j}, \hat{A}, \hat{C}, k) =$	$eqS^{nkr}(j, W, \underline{u}, \hat{B}, \hat{C}, k) =$	
$\quad C \leftarrow Pk(\underline{c_j})$	$\quad C = Pk(\underline{c_u})$	
$\quad ki \leftarrow (z_i, a, Y, \underline{C}, \hat{A}, \hat{C})$	$\quad ki \leftarrow (z_j, b, W, \underline{C}, \hat{B}, \hat{C})$	
$\quad$ return $(k = KeyI(ki))$	$\quad$ return $(k = KeyI(ki))$	

Fig. 6. Games defining $\mathsf{CSK}_{kr,\Pi}^{nt}(\mathcal{B})$ and $\mathsf{CSK}_{nkr,\Pi}^{nt}(\mathcal{B})$ for $\mathcal{B} = (\mathcal{B}_1, \mathcal{B}_2, \mathcal{B}_3)$ with alternative eqS-oracle definitions for kr and nkr

session index i of the started session to the public key A_i of i's actor. For queries $ephRev(i)$, $\mathcal{B}$ samples and stores the value $\bar{x}_i$ ensuring that there are no collisions and that answers are consistent, i.e., $\mathcal{B}$ simulates the ephemeral secrets in $\mathsf{eCK}_{m,\mathcal{T}^{nt}(\Pi)}$. On query $h^{\mathcal{A}}(z, c)$, $\mathcal{B}$ checks if there is an i such that $z = \bar{x}_i$ and $Pk(c) = A_i$ (which implies $a_i = c$, i.e., c is equal to the static secret key of the i-th session) and returns $ephRev^{nt}(i, a_i)$ if the check succeeds and $h(z, c)$ otherwise. All other queries are just forwarded. In the reduction, the ephemeral secrets x_i in $\mathsf{eCK}_{m,\Pi}^{nt}$ correspond to hash values $h(x_i, a_i)$ in $\mathsf{eCK}_{m,\mathcal{T}^{nt}(\Pi)}$. $\square$

Exploiting the Hashing of the Session Key. The CSK_{nkr}^{nt} and CSK_{kr}^{nt} models for protocols that employ the Naxos technique are defined by the three games given in Figure 6. The winning conditions state that the adversary must compute certain keys. They result from case distinctions where we show that the adversary cannot win unless he queries these keys to $ephRev^{nt}$ or the random oracle H. We first describe the games and then explain how they are used in the reduction.

$G_{1,m}^{hsk,nt}$: The adversary is given a static public key A, a vector $\mathbf{Z}$ of ephemeral public keys, and a vector $\mathbf{c}$ of static secret keys. To win, he must return the static secret key a for A. He is given access to a decision oracle that returns 1 if the given k is the session key for a session with session data $(z_i, a, , Y, C, \hat{A}, \hat{C})$ where z_i must be an element of $\mathbf{z}$, a is fixed, and $\hat{A}$, $\hat{C}$, and Y can be arbitrary. For $m = kr$, C can be arbitrary. For $m = nkr$, C must be an element of $Pk(\mathbf{c})$ reflecting that keys are honestly generated.

$G_{2,m}^{hsk,nt}$: The adversary is given an ephemeral public key X, a static public key B, a vector $\mathbf{Z}$ of ephemeral public keys, and a vector $\mathbf{c}$ of static secret keys. He chooses a static secret key c_i from $\mathbf{c}$, an arbitrary ephemeral public key Y, and arbitrary agent identities $\hat{A}$ and $\hat{B}$. To win, he must return a set S that contains the session key for $(x, c_i, Y, B, \hat{A}, \hat{B})$. He is provided with access to a decision oracle that returns 1 if the given k is the session key for a session with session data $(z_j, b, W, C, \hat{B}, \hat{C})$ where z_j must be an element of $\mathbf{z}$, b is fixed, and W, $\hat{B}$, and $\hat{C}$ can be arbitrary. For $m = \mathsf{kr}$, the static public key C of the peer can be arbitrary. For $m = \mathsf{nkr}$, C must be an element of $Pk(\mathbf{c})$.

$G_3^{\mathsf{hsk,nt}}$: The adversary is given ephemeral public keys X, Y and a vector $\mathbf{c}$ of static secret keys. He chooses static secret keys c_i, c_j in $\mathbf{c}$ and arbitrary $\hat{A}$, $\hat{B}$. To win, he must return a set S that contains the session key for $(x, c_i, Y, Pk(c_j), \hat{A}, \hat{B})$.

In the reduction, we use $G_{1,m}^{\mathsf{hsk,nt}}$ to handle the case where the adversary queries $ephRev^{\mathsf{nt}}(i, a)$ without revealing the static secret a for some $\hat{A}$. For the remaining cases, we know that the ephemeral secret x of the test session must be secret. We use $G_{2,m}^{\mathsf{hsk,nt}}$ to handle the case where the static secret b of the test session's peer remains unrevealed and $G_3^{\mathsf{hsk,nt}}$ to handle the case where b is revealed and there is a matching session with unrevealed ephemeral secret y. The eqS oracle in $G_{1,m}^{\mathsf{hsk,nt}}$ is used to synchronize queries to $H^{\mathcal{A}}$ and $keyRev$ for $\hat{A}$'s sessions. Analogously, eqS in $G_2^{\mathsf{hsk,nt}}$ is used for $\hat{B}$'s sessions. We can now state our main theorem using q_h (resp. q_H) to denote the number of queries to the oracle introduced by $\mathcal{T}^{\mathsf{nt}}$ (resp. $\mathcal{T}^{\mathsf{hsk}}$).

Theorem 1. *Let $m \in \{\mathsf{kr}, \mathsf{nkr}\}$ and Π be a protocol satisfying properties* **P1**–**P3**. *Let $\mathcal{A}$ be a (q_{se}, q_{ag}, q_H) eCK_m adversary. Then there are $\mathsf{CSK}_m^{\mathsf{nt}}$ adversaries $\mathcal{B}_1$–$\mathcal{B}_3$ such that*

$$2\Pr\left[\mathsf{eCK}_{m,\mathcal{T}^{\mathsf{nt,hsk}}(\Pi)}(\mathcal{A}) = 1\right] - 1$$
$$\leq \delta_1 \Pr\left[G_{1,m,\Pi}^{\mathsf{hsk,nt}}(\mathcal{B}_1) = 1\right] + \delta_2 \Pr\left[G_{2,m,\Pi}^{\mathsf{hsk,nt}}(\mathcal{B}_2) = 1\right]$$
$$+ \delta_3 \Pr\left[G_{3,\Pi}^{\mathsf{hsk,nt}}(\mathcal{B}_3) = 1\right] + \epsilon_{\mathcal{T}^{\mathsf{nt,hsk}}}$$

for $\epsilon_{\mathcal{T}^{\mathsf{nt,hsk}}} = (2\,q_h\,q_{se} + 2\,q_{se}^2)/|\mathsf{Esk}|$, $\delta_1 = q_{ag}$, $\delta_2 = q_{ag}\,q_{se}$, and $\delta_3 = q_{se}^2$. Furthermore, the adversaries $\mathcal{B}_1$ and $\mathcal{B}_2$ perform at most $q_H\,q_{se}$ queries to eqS and the adversaries $\mathcal{B}_2$ and $\mathcal{B}_3$ return sets of size at most $2\,q_H$. The adversaries $\mathcal{B}_1$–$\mathcal{B}_3$ run in time at most $\mathcal{O}((q_h + q_{ag})\,t_{Pk} + q_{se}\,t_{proto} + q_{se}\,q_H + t_{\mathcal{A}})$ where t_{proto} denotes the time to execute a protocol session.

Proof (Sketch). We first apply Lemma 1. Then it remains to prove that $\mathsf{CSK}_m^{\mathsf{nt}}$-security of Π implies $\mathsf{eCK}_m^{\mathsf{nt}}$-security of $\mathcal{T}^{\mathsf{hsk}}(\Pi)$. Let σ denote the input to H used to compute the session key of the test session. We first bound the probability that the adversary wins without querying σ to $H_{\mathcal{A}}$ by $1/2$. First, note that he cannot reveal a session key with hash input σ since condition **P3** for Π implies that the corresponding session is either a matching session or the test session itself (up to collisions of ephemeral secrets and guessing of unused ephemeral

Game:	Oracles:
var $evs : \mathsf{Ev}^* = [\,]$ var $sks : \mathsf{ID} \rightharpoonup \mathsf{Sk} = \emptyset$ var $pks : \mathsf{ID} \rightharpoonup \mathsf{Pk} = \emptyset$ var $ses : \mathsf{Nat} \rightharpoonup \mathsf{St} = \emptyset$ var $i : \mathsf{Nat} = 0$ $(S,t) \leftarrow \mathcal{A}_1()$ $(r,\_,X,\hat{A},\hat{B},Y,k) \leftarrow ses[t]$ $ts \leftarrow (r,X,\hat{A},\hat{B},Y)$ return $(k \in S \wedge k \neq \perp \wedge \mathit{fresh}_{evs}(ts))$	Replace $keyRev$ and $h^{\mathcal{A}}$ with eqS. Keep other oracles. $eqS(i,k) : \mathsf{Key} =$ $(r,\_,X,\hat{A},\hat{B},Y,k') \leftarrow ses[i]$ $evs \leftarrow^{+\!+} \mathsf{KeyRev}(r,X,\hat{A},\hat{B},Y)$ return $(k = k')$

Fig. 7. Intermediate game GI used in reductions (eCK^{nt} to CSK^{nt} and eCK to CSK)

secrets). He therefore receives a key that is sampled independently of his view for both values of b and cannot do better than guessing b in this case.

We now proceed by bounding the probability of $\sigma \in Q_H \wedge \mathit{fresh}_{evs}(sid)$ in eCK$^{\mathsf{nt}}_{m,\mathcal{T}^{\mathsf{hsk}}(\Pi)}$ where $sid = (r,X,\hat{A},\hat{B},Y)$ and Q_H is the set of values queried to H by the adversary. Our goal is to perform a reduction to the intermediate game $GI_{m,\Pi}$ shown in Figure 7. The simulator will use the eqS oracle in $GI_{m,\Pi}$ to simulate the oracles $H^{\mathcal{A}}$ and $keyRev$ and return (t, Q_H). The eqS oracle is used to synchronize values returned in $keyRev$ and H, but it cannot be used for the call to H for σ in the main body. We therefore perform a sequence of steps that includes enforcing a (monotonous version of) freshness to remove this call before performing the reduction.

To obtain the three games $G^{\mathsf{hsk,nt}}_{1,m,\Pi}$, $G^{\mathsf{hsk,nt}}_{2,m,\Pi}$, and $G^{\mathsf{hsk,nt}}_{3,\Pi}$ from $GI_{m,\Pi}$, we perform two case distinctions followed by one reduction for each case. The first case distinction is for the event that the adversary queries $\mathsf{EphRev}(i,a)$ without performing $\mathsf{StaticRev}(\hat{A})$ and revealing a beforehand. To bound this probability, we first guess $\hat{A}$ and then perform a reduction to $G^{\mathsf{hsk,nt}}_{1,m,\Pi}$. Since the adversary can reveal all secrets except for a and the ephemeral secret keys of $\hat{A}$, the simulator receives the static secret keys $\boldsymbol{c}$ of the other agents, the ephemeral public keys of $\hat{A}$'s sessions, and A. The simulator samples all other values himself and can simulate all oracles on its own, except for eqS where the provided oracle is used for $\hat{A}$'s sessions. If $m = \mathsf{nkr}$, all keys are honestly generated and for all queries to eqS, the static public key of the peer is equal to $Pk(c)$ for some $c \in \boldsymbol{c}$. If $m = \mathsf{kr}$, the static public key of the peer can be arbitrary.

Before performing the second case distinction, we guess the test session. Since there is no ephemeral reveal without a previous static reveal, the test session's ephemeral secret x cannot be revealed. We now perform a case distinction if the adversary reveals the static secret key b of the peer $\hat{B}$ of the test session. If not, then we know that x, b, and the ephemeral secret keys of $\hat{B}$'s sessions are secret. To perform the reduction to $G^{\mathsf{hsk,nt}}_{2,m,\Pi}$, we guess $\hat{B}$ and define a simulator that receives X, B, the static secret keys $\boldsymbol{c}$ of all agents except $\hat{B}$, and the ephemeral public keys of $\hat{B}$'s sessions. The simulator samples all other values himself and

Game G_{2DDH}:	Game G:
$x \xleftarrow{\$} \mathbb{F}_p;\ X \leftarrow g^x$	$x \xleftarrow{\$} \mathbb{F}_p;\ X \leftarrow g^x$
$\boldsymbol{y} \xleftarrow{\$} \mathbb{F}_p^n;\ \boldsymbol{Y} \leftarrow g^{\boldsymbol{y}}$	$z \xleftarrow{\$} \mathbb{F}_p;\ Z \leftarrow g^z$
$z \xleftarrow{\$} \mathbb{F}_p;\ Z \leftarrow g^z$	$t \leftarrow \mathcal{B}(X, Z)$
$t \leftarrow \mathcal{A}^{\text{2DDH}}(X, \boldsymbol{Y}, Z)$	return $\phi(X, Z, t)$
return $\phi(X, Z, t)$	
$\text{2DDH}(i, \hat{Z}, U, V) = $ return	
$\quad \text{ddh}(X, \hat{Z}, U) \wedge \text{ddh}(Y_i, \hat{Z}, U)$	

Fig. 8. Twin DDH games G_{2DDH} and G

can simulate all oracles on its own, except for eqS where the provided oracle is used for $\hat{B}$'s sessions. Like in the previous case, the static public key of the peer is equal to $Pk(c)$ for some $c \in \boldsymbol{c}$ if $m = \text{nkr}$ and arbitrary otherwise.

In the last case, there is a static reveal for the peer $\hat{B}$ of the test session. Hence, there must be a matching session with ephemeral secret key y and the only other value that cannot be revealed is x. We guess the matching session and since eqS queries for the test session and the matching session are forbidden, the simulator for $G_{3,\Pi}^{\text{hsk,nt}}$ can simulate the eqS oracle on its own in this case.   □

4   Trapdoor Test, Twin DH, and (S)CDH

To minimize the EasyCrypt proof effort, we first prove a generalized version of the Twin DH Assumption from [19]. We use this result for the protocol proofs and to obtain a tighter reduction from CDH to SCDH based on Shoup's self corrector [47].

Twin DH. In the original Twin DH assumption, the adversary is given challenges $X, Y, Z \in \mathbb{G}$ and has to compute the group elements $(\text{dh}(X, Z), \text{dh}(Y, Z))$ given oracle access to

$$\text{2DDH}(\hat{Z}, U, V) \doteq (\text{ddh}(X, \hat{Z}, U) \wedge \text{ddh}(Y, \hat{Z}, V)).$$

The value Y is called the "twin" of X and the assumption can be seen as a "twin version" of the Strong DH assumption, which is a variant of Gap CDH where the first input of the DDH oracle is fixed. In contrast to these two assumptions, Twin DH follows from CDH in all groups since the 2DDH oracle can be simulated using the trapdoor test.

Our generalization uses n twins $Y_1, \ldots, Y_n$ of X instead of a single twin and consequently provides a 2DDH oracle that can be used with all twins X, Y_i. Concretely, for a predicate ϕ, we define the two games G_{2DDH} and G given in Figure 8 and prove the following lemma for which the proof can be found in Appendix A.

Lemma 2. *Let $\mathcal{A}$ be a G_{2DDH} adversary that performs at most q queries to* 2DDH. *Then there exists a G adversary $\mathcal{B}$ such that*

$$\Pr\left[G_{2DDH}(\mathcal{A}) = 1\right] \leq \Pr\left[G(\mathcal{B}) = 1\right] + q/p.$$

Moreover, $\mathcal{B}$ runs in time $\mathcal{O}(T_{\mathcal{A}} + q\,t_{\mathbb{G}} + n\,t_{\mathbb{G}})$ where $t_{\mathbb{G}}$ denotes the time required to perform a group operation such as exponentiation or division.

We define the following reductions as instantiations of this lemma:
- CDH_{2DDH} to CDH for $\phi(X, Z, U) \doteq \mathsf{dh}(X, Z) = U$.
- DLOG_{2DDH} to DLOG for $\phi(X, Z, x') \doteq X = g^{x'}$.
- SCDH_{2DDH} to SCDH for $\phi(X, Z, S) \doteq \mathsf{dh}(X, Z) \in S$.

An efficient reduction from SCDH to CDH. We have formalized the proof following the approach outlined by Cash et al. in [19]. Note that our proof critically relies on the possibility to relate the probability that an adversary who is called twice wins both times to the probability for a single win. Support for this type of reasoning is a recent extension to EasyCrypt. The proof can be found in Appendix A.

Theorem 2. *Let $\mathcal{A}$ be an SCDH adversary that returns a set of size at most m. Then there exists a CDH adversary $\mathcal{B}$ such that*

$$\Pr\left[\mathsf{SCDH}(\mathcal{A}) = 1\right] \leq \sqrt{\Pr\left[\mathsf{CDH}(\mathcal{B}) = 1\right]} + m^2/q.$$

Furthermore, the adversary $\mathcal{B}$ runs in time $\mathcal{O}(T_{\mathcal{A}} + m^2\,t_{\mathbb{G}})$.

5   Case Studies

We first present the application of our generic proof to the Naxos and Naxos+ protocols. Afterwards, we present our proofs for the Nets protocol.

5.1   Proofs for Naxos and Naxos$^+$

We first prove that Naxos is secure in our eCK_{nkr} model with honestly generated keys under the CDH assumption. In the proof, we discuss why it does not generalize to the eCK_{kr} model with adversarial key registration. Afterwards, we describe two ways to obtain a proof in the eCK_{kr} model from the instantiation of our generic proof. First, the proof can be performed with respect to the Gap-CDH assumption. Second, the protocol can be extended with an additional group element in the key yielding the Naxos+ protocol [39] which was proved secure under the CDH assumption in a model similar to eCK_{kr}.

eCK$_{nkr}$-security of Naxos Under the CDH Assumption. The following theorem states that Naxos is secure in our model without adversarial key registration if the CDH problem is hard.

Theorem 3. *Let $\mathcal{A}$ be a (q_{se}, q_{ag}, q_H) eCK$_{nkr}$ adversary. Then there exist adversaries $\mathcal{C}_1$, $\mathcal{C}_2$, and $\mathcal{C}_3$ such that*

$$2\Pr\left[\mathsf{eCK}_{nkr,Naxos}(\mathcal{A}) = 1\right] - 1 \leq \quad \delta_1\left(\Pr\left[\mathsf{DLOG}(\mathcal{C}_1) = 1\right] + q_H\,q_{se}/p\right)$$

$$+ \delta_2\left(\sqrt{\Pr\left[\mathsf{CDH}(\mathcal{C}_2) = 1\right] + 4\,q_H^2/p} + q_H\,q_{se}/p\right)$$

$$+ \delta_3\left(\sqrt{\Pr\left[\mathsf{CDH}(\mathcal{C}_3) = 1\right] + 4\,q_H^2/p}\right) + \epsilon_{\mathcal{T}^{nt,hsk}}$$

where δ_1, δ_2, δ_3, and $\epsilon_{\mathcal{T}^{nt,hsk}}$ are defined as in Theorem 1. Furthermore, $\mathcal{C}_1$, $\mathcal{C}_2$, and $\mathcal{C}_3$ run in time at most $\mathcal{O}(n\,t_{\mathbb{G}} + t_{\mathcal{A}})$ where $n = \max\{q_h, q_{ag}, q_H\,q_{se}, q_H^2\}$.

Proof. he definition of Naxos^{core} is given in Figure 3. It is easy to check that Naxos^{core} satisfies **P1–P3** and Naxos $= \mathcal{T}^{nt,hsk}(\text{Naxos}^{core})$. We can therefore apply Theorem 1 to reduce eCK$_{nkr}$-security of Naxos to CSK$_{nkr}^{nt}$-security of Naxos^{core}. This step accounts for the loss of $\epsilon_{\mathcal{T}^{nt,hsk}}$ and yields adversaries $\mathcal{B}_1$–$\mathcal{B}_3$ that return sets of size at most $2\,q_H$ and perform at most $q_H\,q_{se}$ queries to eqS. In the next step, we will define $\mathcal{C}_1$, $\mathcal{C}_2$, and $\mathcal{C}_3$ and prove that the inequalities

$$\Pr\left[G_{1,nkr}^{hsk,nt}(\mathcal{B}_1) = 1\right] \leq \Pr\left[\mathsf{DLOG}(\mathcal{C}_1) = 1\right] + q_H\,q_{se}/p$$

$$\Pr\left[G_{2,nkr}^{hsk,nt}(\mathcal{B}_2) = 1\right] \leq \sqrt{\Pr\left[\mathsf{CDH}(\mathcal{C}_2) = 1\right] + 4\,q_H^2/p} + q_H\,q_{se}/p$$

$$\Pr\left[G_{3,nkr}^{hsk,nt}(\mathcal{B}_3) = 1\right] \leq \sqrt{\Pr\left[\mathsf{CDH}(\mathcal{C}_3) = 1\right] + 4\,q_H^2/p}$$

hold where $G_{i,nkr}^{hsk,nt}$ denotes the corresponding CSK$_{nkr}^{nt}$ game instantiated with Naxos^{core}.

Game $G_{1,nkr}^{hsk,nt}$. Instantiating with Naxos^{core} yields:

$$a \xleftarrow{\$} \mathbb{F}_p;\quad A \leftarrow g^a$$
$$z \xleftarrow{\$} \mathbb{F}_p^{q_{se}};\quad Z \leftarrow g^z$$
$$c \xleftarrow{\$} \mathbb{F}_p^{q_{ag}-1}$$
$$a' \leftarrow \mathcal{B}_1(A, Z, c)$$
$$\text{return } (a = a')$$

$$eqS(i, Y, j, \hat{A}, \hat{C}, k) =$$
$$\text{return } k = (\mathsf{dh}(A, Y) \,\|\, Z_i^{c_j} \,\|\, \mathsf{dh}(Z_i, Y) \,\|\, \hat{A} \,\|\, \hat{C})$$

Since we perform a reduction to DLOG$_{2DDH}$ in the first step, we have already rewritten eqS such that it does not use a and z. Before continuing, we rename DLOG$_{2DDH}$ such that X becomes A, Y becomes Z, and Z becomes R. Our DLOG$_{2DDH}$ adversary $\mathcal{C}_1'$ then receives the DLOG-challenge A, the twins Z of A, and the value R which is unused in DLOG. $\mathcal{C}'_1$ samples c, calls $\mathcal{B}_1$ with $(A, \mathbf{Z}, c)$, and returns $\mathcal{B}_1$'s return value, which is equal to $\mathsf{dlog}(A)$ whenever $\mathcal{B}_1$ wins. $\mathcal{C}'_1$ uses the following implementation to simulate eqS:

$$eqS(i, Y, j, \hat{A}, \hat{C}, k) =$$
$$(U_1 \| U_2 \| U_3 \| \hat{D} \| \hat{E}) \leftarrow k$$
$$d \leftarrow \mathsf{2DDH}(i, U_1, U_3)$$
$$\mathsf{return} \ (d \wedge U_2 = Z_i^{c_j} \wedge \hat{D} = \hat{A} \wedge \hat{E} = \hat{C})$$

Since the original eqS returns 1 if and only if $U_1 = \mathsf{dh}(A, Y)$ and $U_3 = \mathsf{dh}(Z_i, Y)$ (which corresponds to the 2DDH result) and the remaining equalities hold, the simulation is perfect. We can now apply Lemma 2 to obtain a reduction to DLOG for an adversary $\mathcal{C}_1$.

While this reasoning step is valid in the $\mathsf{eCK}_{\mathsf{kr}}$ model, it does not work in the $\mathsf{eCK}_{\mathsf{kr}}$ model since the adversary can register arbitrary static public keys. Hence, the eqS oracle takes $C \in \mathsf{Pk}$ instead of an index j into c. In this case, we cannot check if $U_2 = \mathsf{dh}(Z_i, C)$ by performing the test $U_2 = Z_i^{c_j}$ in the implementation of eqS for the simulator.

Game $G_{2,\mathsf{nkr}}^{\mathsf{hsk},\mathsf{nt}}$. Instantiating with Naxos^{core} yields:

$$x \stackrel{\$}{\leftarrow} \mathbb{F}_p; \qquad X \leftarrow g^x$$
$$b \stackrel{\$}{\leftarrow} \mathbb{F}_p; \qquad B \leftarrow g^b$$
$$\mathbf{z} \stackrel{\$}{\leftarrow} \mathbb{F}_p^{q_{se}-1}; \ \mathbf{Z} \leftarrow g^{\mathbf{z}}$$
$$\mathbf{c} \stackrel{\$}{\leftarrow} \mathbb{F}_p^{q_{ag}-1}$$
$$(i, Y, \hat{A}, \hat{B}, S) \leftarrow \mathcal{B}_2(X, B, \mathbf{c}, \mathbf{Z})$$
$$\mathsf{return} \ (Y^{c_i} \| \mathsf{dh}(B, X) \| \mathsf{dh}(X, Y) \| \hat{A} \| \hat{B}) \in S$$

$$eqS(j, W, u, \hat{B}, \hat{C}, k) =$$
$$\mathsf{return} \ k = (\mathsf{dh}(B, W) \| Z_j^{c_u} \| \mathsf{dh}(Z_j, W) \| \hat{B} \| \hat{C})$$

For this game, we perform the reduction in three steps. The first reduction is to $\mathsf{SCDH}_{\mathsf{2DDH}}$ for which we define the adversary $\mathcal{C}'_2$. Then we use Lemma 2 to get rid of the 2DDH oracle and finally Theorem 2 to transform the SCDH adversary into a CDH adversary which yields the adversary $\mathcal{B}_2$. Before continuing, we rename $\mathsf{SCDH}_{\mathsf{2DDH}}$ such that X becomes B, $\mathbf{Y}$ becomes $\mathbf{Z}$, and Y becomes X. The CDH challenge is therefore B, X and $\mathbf{Z}$ is the vector of twins of B for which the 2DDH oracle can be used.

We define the $\mathsf{SCDH}_{\mathsf{2DDH}}$ adversary $\mathcal{C}'_2$ as follows. $\mathcal{C}'_2$ gets $B, \mathbf{Z}, X$ as input, samples $\mathbf{c}$, calls $\mathcal{B}_2$ with these values, and gets $(i, Y, \hat{A}, \hat{B}, S)$. To transform S into a set that contains $\mathsf{dh}(B, X)$ whenever $\mathcal{B}_2$ wins, $\mathcal{C}'_2$ applies the function $(U_1 \| U_2 \| U_3 \| \hat{A} \| \hat{B}) \mapsto U_2$. To (perfectly) simulate the orginal eqS, $\mathcal{C}'_2$ uses the implementation

$$eqS(j, W, u, \hat{B}, \hat{C}, k) =$$
$$(U_1 \| U_2 \| U_3 \| \hat{D} \| \hat{E}) \leftarrow k$$
$$d \leftarrow \mathsf{2DDH}(i, U_1, U_3)$$
$$\mathsf{return} \ (d \wedge U_2 = Z_j^{c_u} \wedge \hat{D} = \hat{B} \wedge \hat{E} = \hat{C}).$$

Since the adversary can register arbitrary static public keys in the $\mathsf{eCK_{kr}}$ model, the eqS oracle in the kr version of this game takes $C \in \mathsf{Pk}$ instead of an index u into $\mathbf{c}$. In this case, we cannot check if $U_2 = \mathsf{dh}(Z_j, C)$ by performing the test $U_2 = Z_j^{c_u}$ in the implementation of eqS for the simulator.

Game $G_{3,\mathsf{nkr}}^{\mathsf{hsk,nt}}$. Instantiating with Naxos^{core} yields:

$$x \xleftarrow{\$} \mathbb{F}_p; X \leftarrow g^x$$
$$y \xleftarrow{\$} \mathbb{F}_p; Y \leftarrow g^y$$
$$\mathbf{c} \xleftarrow{\$} \mathsf{Sk}^{q_{ag}}$$
$$(i, j, \hat{A}, \hat{B}, S) \leftarrow \mathcal{B}_3(X, Y, \mathbf{c})$$
$$\text{return } (Y^{c_i} \| X^{c_j} \| \mathsf{dh}(X, Y) \| \hat{A} \| \hat{B}) \in S$$

We can directly perform a reduction to SCDH and then use Theorem 2 to obtain a reduction to CDH. For the reduction to SCDH, we use the function $(U_1 \| U_2 \| U_3 \| \hat{D} \| \hat{E}) \mapsto U_3$ to transform S into a set that contains $\mathsf{dh}(X, Y)$. This case directly generalizes to $\mathsf{eCK_{kr}}$ since the third game is identical in this case.   □

$\mathsf{eCK_{kr}}$-security of Naxos and Naxos+. In the previous proof, we have pointed out where the proof breaks down in the $\mathsf{eCK_{kr}}$ model. We will now describe how to adapt the proof to (1) prove $\mathsf{eCK_{kr}}$-security of Naxos under the Gap-CDH assumption and (2) prove $\mathsf{eCK_{kr}}$-security of Naxos+ under the CDH assumption.

For the proof with respect to Gap-CDH, we can deal with all the problematic cases by calling the DDH oracle with the right input, e.g., with $\mathsf{DDH}(Z_i, C, U_2)$ for the first game. Note that there is no need for the twinning technique at all in this case and our generic proof can be instantiated in a very similar way to the original Naxos proof.

The $\mathsf{Naxos+}^{core}$ protocol can be obtained from the Naxos^{core} protocol by adding the additional group element $\mathsf{dh}(A, B)$ to the key. Concretely, we define

$$\mathsf{Key} = \mathbb{G}^4 \times \mathsf{ID}^2,$$
$$\mathsf{KeyI}(x, a, Y, B, \hat{A}, \hat{B}) = Y^a \| B^x \| Y^x \| B^a \| \hat{A} \| \hat{B}, \text{ and}$$
$$\mathsf{KeyR}(y, b, X, A, \hat{B}, \hat{A}) = A^y \| X^b \| X^y \| A^b \| \hat{A} \| \hat{B}.$$

The additional group element is only required to simulate the eqS oracle. Everything else, in particular the case **Game** $G_3^{\mathsf{hsk,nt}}$, can be trivially adapted.

Game $G_{1,\mathsf{kr}}^{\mathsf{hsk,nt}}$. For Naxos+, we must simulate the following eqS oracle (we underline the differences to the Naxos version):

$$eqS(i, Y, \underline{C}, \hat{A}, \hat{C}, k) =$$
$$\text{return } k = (\mathsf{dh}(A, Y) \| \underline{\mathsf{dh}(Z_i, C)} \| \mathsf{dh}(Z_i, Y) \| \underline{\mathsf{dh}(A, C)} \| \hat{A} \| \hat{C})$$

By using the 2DDH oracle for the group elements 1&3 and 2&4, we obtain the following implementation of eqS.

$$eqS(i, Y, j, \hat{A}, \hat{C}, k) =$$
$$(U_1 \| U_2 \| U_3 \| U_4 \| \hat{D} \| \hat{E}) \leftarrow k$$
$$d_1 \leftarrow 2\mathsf{DDH}(i, U_1, U_3)$$
$$d_2 \leftarrow 2\mathsf{DDH}(i, U_2, U_4)$$
$$\mathsf{return}\ (d_1 \wedge d_2 \wedge \hat{D} = \hat{A} \wedge \hat{E} = \hat{C})$$

The simulation is perfect because the 2DDH calls returns 1 if and only if $U_1 = \mathsf{dh}(A, Y) \wedge U_3 = \mathsf{dh}(Z_i, Y)$ and $U_4 = \mathsf{dh}(A, C) \wedge U_2 = \mathsf{dh}(Z_i, C)$.

Game $G_{2,\mathsf{kr}}^{\mathsf{hsk},\mathsf{nt}}$. For Naxos+, we must simulate the following eqS oracle

$$eqS(j, W, \underline{C}, \hat{B}, \hat{C}, k) =$$
$$\mathsf{return}\ k = (\mathsf{dh}(B, W) \| \underline{\mathsf{dh}(Z_j, C)} \| \mathsf{dh}(Z_j, W) \| \underline{\mathsf{dh}(B, C)} \| \hat{B} \| \hat{C})$$

By using the 2DDH oracle first for the group elements 1 and 3 and then using the oracle in a second call for the group elements 2 and 4, we obtain the following implementation of eqS.

$$eqS(i, Y, j, \hat{A}, \hat{C}, k) =$$
$$(U_1 \| U_2 \| U_3 \| U_4 \| \hat{D} \| \hat{E}) \leftarrow k$$
$$d_1 \leftarrow 2\mathsf{DDH}(i, U_1, U_3)$$
$$d_2 \leftarrow 2\mathsf{DDH}(i, U_4, U_2)$$
$$\mathsf{return}\ (d_1 \wedge d_2 \wedge \hat{D} = \hat{A} \wedge \hat{E} = \hat{C})$$

The simulation is perfect because the first 2DDH calls returns 1 iff $U_1 = \mathsf{dh}(B, W) \wedge U_3 = \mathsf{dh}(Z_j, W)$ and the second call returns 1 iff $U_4 = \mathsf{dh}(B, C) \wedge U_2 = \mathsf{dh}(Z_j, C)$.

5.2 Proofs for Nets

The proofs for Nets are structured very similarly to the corresponding Naxos proofs and yield similar bounds. We therefore summarize the required changes in this section and refer to our EasyCrypt formalization for details.

The proof that Nets is secure in our $\mathsf{eCK}_{\mathsf{nkr}}$ model with honestly generated keys under the CDH assumption is follows the corresponding proof for Naxos. The only significant difference is how the 2DDH oracle is used to simulate the eqS oracles in the first and second games. Whereas the Naxos protocol uses the concatenation of three group elements in the key, Nets uses the concatenation of two group elements $U_1 \| U_2$ where $U_1 = \mathsf{dh}(A, B)\,\mathsf{dh}(A, Y)\,\mathsf{dh}(X, B)\,\mathsf{dh}(X, Y)$ and $U_2 = cdh(X, Y)$. Computing the right queries to 2DDH for simulating eqS requires divisions. Concretely, the first game uses $2\mathsf{DDH}(U_1/A^{c_j}\, Z_i^{c_j}\, U_2, U_2)$ and the second game uses $2\mathsf{DDH}(U_1/B^{c_j}\, Z_i^{c_j}\, U_2, U_2)$.

To prove $\mathsf{eCK}_{\mathsf{kr}}$-security under the Gap-CDH assumption, it is again possible to closely follow the original proof and use the DDH oracle to simulate eqS.

G_1^{hsk} $(a, b$ secret, poss. no matching):	G_2^{hsk} $(x, b$ secret, poss. no matching):

$a, b \xleftarrow{\$} \text{Sk}; \ A \leftarrow Pk(a); \ B \leftarrow Pk(b)$
 $z \xleftarrow{\$} \text{Esk}^{q_{se}}$
 $(i, Y, \hat{A}, \hat{B}, S) \leftarrow \mathcal{A}(z, A, B)$
 $k \leftarrow KeyI(z_i, a, Y, B, \hat{A}, \hat{B})$
 return $(k \in S \wedge k \neq \bot)$
 	
 $eqS(i, C, W, D, \hat{C}, \hat{D}, k) =$
    if $C \notin \{A, B\}$ then return $\bot$
    if $C = A$ then $c \leftarrow a$ else $c \leftarrow b$
    return $KeyI(z_i, c, W, D, \hat{C}, \hat{D}) = k$
	$x \xleftarrow{\$} \text{Esk}; \ X \leftarrow Epk(X)$
	 $b \xleftarrow{\$} \text{Sk}; \ B \leftarrow Pk(b)$
	 $z \xleftarrow{\$} \text{Esk}^{q_{se}-1}$
	 $c \xleftarrow{\$} \text{Sk}^{q_{ag}-1}$
	 $(i, Y, \hat{A}, \hat{B}, S) \leftarrow \mathcal{A}(c, z, X, B)$
	 $k \leftarrow KeyI(x, c_i, Y, B, \hat{A}, \hat{B})$
	 return $(k \in S \wedge k \neq \bot)$
	
	 $eqS(i, W, D, \hat{B}, \hat{D}, k) =$
	    return $KeyI(z_i, b, W, D, \hat{B}, \hat{D}) = k$

G_3^{hsk} $(a, y$ secret):	G_4^{hsk} $(x, y$ secret):
$a \xleftarrow{\$} \text{Sk}; \ A \leftarrow Pk(a)$ $y \xleftarrow{\$} \text{Esk}; \ Y \leftarrow Epk(y)$ $z \xleftarrow{\$} \text{Esk}^{q_{se}-1}; \ c \xleftarrow{\$} \text{Sk}^{q_{ag}-1}$ $(i, j, \hat{A}, \hat{B}, S) \leftarrow \mathcal{A}(c, z, A, Y)$ $k \leftarrow KeyI(z_i, a, Y, Pk(c_j), \hat{A}, \hat{B})$ return $(k \in S \wedge k \neq \bot)$ $eqS(i, W, D, \hat{A}, \hat{D}, k) =$ return $KeyI(z_i, a, W, D, \hat{A}, \hat{D}) = k$	$x \xleftarrow{\$} \text{Esk}; \ X \leftarrow Epk(x)$ $y \xleftarrow{\$} \text{Esk}; \ Y \leftarrow Epk(y)$ $c \xleftarrow{\$} \text{Sk}^{q_{ag}}$ $(i, j, \hat{A}, \hat{B}, S) \leftarrow \mathcal{A}(c, X, Y)$ $k \leftarrow KeyI(x, c_i, Y, Pk(c_j), \hat{A}, \hat{B})$ return $(k \in S \wedge k \neq \bot)$

Fig. 9. Games defining CSK_{kr}

6 Protocols Without Naxos Trick

In this section, we describe our generic proof for protocols that do no utilize the Naxos trick and its application to a version of HMQV. The results of this section have not been formalized in EasyCrypt and we leave this open for future work.

6.1 Model and Generic Proof

We prove a reduction from the eCK_{kr} model to the CSK_{kr} model defined by the games given in Figure 9.

Theorem 4. *Let Π be a protocol that satisfies* **P1–P3**. *For all efficient adversaries that win the* $\text{eCK}_{\text{kr}, \mathcal{T}^{\text{hsk}}(\Pi)}$ *game with non-negligible probability, there exists an efficient adversary that wins one of the* $\text{CSK}_{\text{kr}, \Pi}$ *games with non-negligible probability .*

The proof is analogous to the proof of Theorem 1 and appears in the full version of the paper [4]. The proof performs a different case distinction with respect to the reveal queries performed by the adversary than the proof of Theorem 1.

6.2 eCK$_{kr}$-security of mHMQV Under the Gap-CDH Assumption

We first define our (modified version) mHMQV^{core} as follows. We use $Pk(a) = g^a$ and $Epk(x, a) = g^x$ for ephemeral and static key computation. Using the hash function $\bar{h} : \mathbb{G} \rightarrow \mathbb{F}_p$, we define the session keys:

$$KeyI(x, a, Y, B, \hat{A}, \hat{B}) = (YB^{\bar{h}(Y)})^{x+a\,\bar{h}(X)} \parallel \hat{A} \parallel \hat{B} \parallel X \parallel Y$$

$$KeyR(y, b, X, A, \hat{B}, \hat{A}) = (XA^{\bar{h}(X)})^{y+b\,\bar{h}(Y)} \parallel \hat{A} \parallel \hat{B} \parallel X \parallel Y$$

We instantiate the types using $\mathbb{G}$ for group elements and $\mathbb{F}_p$ for exponents. We then define mHMQV as $T^{hsk}(\text{mHMQV}^{core})$. A similar version of HMQV has been proposed in the original paper [31, Remark 9.1] for compatibility between the variants with one, two, and three passes. We slightly deviate from the original definition by removing the identities from $\bar{h}$'s input (like in MQV) and including $\hat{A}$, $\hat{B}$, X and Y as input to the key derivation hash. Including additional session data in the hash is considered a prudent engineering principle [16] because it ensures agreement on this data. Second, it allows us to apply our generic proof directly since the resulting protocol satisfies **P3**. To make the protocol symmetric, it would be possible to sort the tuples $\hat{A}, X$ and $\hat{B}, Y$ to determine the order of these elements. We prove the following theorem for mHMQV.

Theorem 5. *If there is an efficient adversary that wins the* eCK$'_{\text{mHMQV}}$ *game with non-negligible probability, then there is an efficient adversary that wins the Gap-CDH game with non-negligible probability.*

Proof (Sketch). Since mHMQV^{core} satisfies **P1–P3**, we can apply Theorem 4 and prove CSK$_{kr}$-security of mHMQV^{core}. As in the Nets proof, we ignore the public part $\hat{A} \parallel \hat{B} \parallel X \parallel Y$ in our discussion of winning conditions and eqS. Before discussing the individual games, we note that under the Gap-CDH assumption which provides a DDH-oracle, it is possible to simulate the eqS oracle in all of the games since at least the secret key z_i is always known. To simulate eqS queries, e.g., in G_1^{hsk}, it suffices to compute

$$W^{z_i}\,\mathsf{dh}(C, W)^{\bar{h}(g^{z_i})}\,D^{z_i\,\bar{h}(W)}\,\mathsf{dh}(C, D)^{\bar{h}(g^{z_i})\,\bar{h}(W)} = k$$

for z_i in $\boldsymbol{z}$, $C \in \{A, B\}$, and W, D, k arbitrary. To achieve this, the DDH oracle can be used to check

$$\mathsf{dh}(C, W^{\bar{h}(g^{z_i})}D^{\bar{h}(g^{z_i})\,\bar{h}(W)}) = \frac{k}{W^{z_i}\,E^{z_i\,\bar{h}(W)}}.$$

For game G_1^{hsk}, we perform a reduction to Gap-CDH using the Forking Lemma. We know there exists an adversary $\mathcal{A}$ such that for the CDH challenge A, B and uniformly sampled $\boldsymbol{z}$, the call $\mathcal{A}(\boldsymbol{z}, A, B)$ returns i, Y, and a set S that contains

$$Y^{z_i}\,\mathsf{dh}(A, Y)^{\bar{h}(Z_i)}\,B^{z_i\,\bar{h}(Y)}\,\mathsf{dh}(A, B)^{\bar{h}(Z_i)\,\bar{h}(Y)}$$

with non-negligible probability. To apply the Forking Lemma from [9], we use $\mathcal{A}$ to define a randomized algorithm $\mathcal{B}$ that returns $v \in [q_{\bar{h}}]$, $\mathsf{dh}(A, Y)\,\mathsf{dh}(A, B)^{\bar{h}(Y)}$, and Y such that Y is the v-th query to $\bar{h}$ with non-negligible probability. First, $\mathcal{B}$ guesses v, then it calls $\mathcal{A}$ with the CDH challenge A, B and uniformly sampled z. $\mathcal{B}$ then computes the result from $\mathcal{A}$'s return values i, Y, S as follows. If Y is not the v-th query, $\mathcal{B}$ returns $\perp$. Otherwise, $\mathcal{B}$ divides all elements of S by $Y^{z_i} B^{z_i \bar{h}(Y)}$, exponentiates the result with $1/\bar{h}(g^{z_i})$, and uses the DDH-oracle to search for U with $\mathsf{ddh}(A, Y B^{\bar{h}(Y)}, U)$. If there is no such value, $\mathcal{B}$ returns $\perp$. Otherwise, $\mathcal{B}$ returns $v, Y, \mathsf{dh}(A, Y) \, \mathsf{dh}(A, B)^{\bar{h}(Y)}$. The Forking Lemma yields a randomized algorithm $\mathcal{C}$ from $\mathcal{B}$ that returns

$$Y, \mathsf{dh}(A, Y) \, \mathsf{dh}(A, B)^e, \mathsf{dh}(A, Y) \, \mathsf{dh}(A, B)^{e'}$$

with $e \neq e'$ with non-negligible probability. Intuitively, the algorithm first calls $\mathcal{B}$ to obtain $v, Y, \mathsf{dh}(A, Y) \, \mathsf{dh}(A, B)^e$ for $e = \bar{h}(Y)$. Then, it calls $\mathcal{B}$ again using the same randomness, but resampling the values returned by $\bar{h}$ for all query-indices greater or equal than v, i.e., $e' = \bar{h}(Y)$ is the first value that differs. We can then compute

$$\mathsf{dh}(A, B) = \left(\frac{\mathsf{dh}(A, Y) \, \mathsf{dh}(A, B)^e}{\mathsf{dh}(A, Y) \, \mathsf{dh}(A, B)^{e'}} \right)^{\frac{1}{e - e'}}.$$

For game G_2^{hsk}, we also reduce to Gap-CDH. We know there exists an adversary $\mathcal{A}$ such that for the CDH challenge X, B and uniformly sampled c and z, the call $\mathcal{A}(c, z, X, B)$ returns i, Y, and a set S that contains

$$\mathsf{dh}(X, Y) \, Y^{c_i \bar{h}(X)} \, \mathsf{dh}(X, B)^{\bar{h}(Y)} \, B^{c_i \, \bar{h}(X) \, \bar{h}(Y)}$$

with non-negligible probability. Using a similar approach as before, we can obtain an algorithm that returns the group element $\mathsf{dh}(X, Y) \, \mathsf{dh}(X, B)^e$ and the group element $\mathsf{dh}(X, Y) \, \mathsf{dh}(X, B)^{e'}$ for $e \neq e'$ with non-negligible probability. We can then compute $\mathsf{dh}(X, B)$ like in the previous case.

For G_3^{hsk}, the reduction to Gap-CDH is simpler than the previous two cases since we know two secret keys instead of only one. We can call $\mathcal{A}$ with randomly sampled c, z, and a CDH challenge A, Y. Since $\mathcal{A}$ returns i, j, and a set S that contains

$$Y^{z_i} \, \mathsf{dh}(A, Y)^{\bar{h}(g^{z_i})} \, g^{z_i \, c_j \, \bar{h}(Y)} \, A^{c_j \, \bar{h}(g^{z_i}) \, \bar{h}(Y)}$$

with non-negligible probability, we can then use the DDH oracle to find $\mathsf{dh}(A, Y)$. For G_4^{hsk}, we can perform a similar reduction to Gap-CDH for the CDH challenge X, Y. $\qquad\square$

Acknowledgments. We thank the anonymous reviewers for their valuable comments and suggestions. We also thank François Dupressoir, Benjamin Grégoire, César Kunz, and Pierre-Yves Strub for their help and the development of EasyCrypt features required to build the proof. This work is supported in part by ONR grant N00014-12-1-0914, Madrid regional project S2009TIC-1465 PROMETIDOS, and Spanish projects TIN2009-14599 DESAFIOS 10, and TIN2012-39391-C04-01 Strongsoft. The research of Schmidt has received funds from the European Commission's Seventh Framework Programme Marie Curie Cofund Action AMAROUT II (grant no. 291803).

A   Proofs For Twin DH and (S)CDH

In this appendix, we present the proofs for Lemma 2 and Theorem 2.

Proof (of Lemma 2). We define $\mathcal{B}$ as

$$\mathcal{B}(Z, Y) \doteq$$
$$r \xleftarrow{\$} \mathbb{F}_p^n;\ s \xleftarrow{\$} \mathbb{F}_p^n;\ Y_1 \leftarrow g^{s_1}/X^{r_1};\ \ldots;\ Y_n \leftarrow g^{s_n}/X^{r_n}$$
$$\text{return } \mathcal{A}^{\text{2DDH}}(X, Y, Z)$$

and note that the distribution on (X, Y, Z) is the same as in G_{2DDH}. To simulate the 2DDH oracle, $\mathcal{B}$ uses the test $U^{r_i}V = \hat{Z}^{s_i}$ instead of $\text{ddh}(X, \hat{Z}, U) \wedge \text{ddh}(Y_i, \hat{Z}, V)$. The probability that these tests do not agree is at most $1/p$. Since the adversary can perform q queries to 2DDH, the probability of distinguishing the simulator is at most q/p.   □

Proof (Theorem 2). We first prove that

$$\Pr\left[\text{SCDH}(\mathcal{A}) = 1\right] = \sqrt{\Pr\left[\text{CDH}_{\text{2DDH}}(\mathcal{B}) = 1\right]}$$

where $n = 1$ for CDH_{2DDH}, i.e., there is only one twin. To achieve this, we define:

$$\mathcal{B}(X, Y, Z) \doteq u \xleftarrow{\$} \mathbb{F}_p^*;\ S_1 \leftarrow \mathcal{A}(X, Z);\ S_2 \leftarrow \mathcal{A}(Y, Z^u)$$
$$\text{foreach } (Z_1, Z_2) \in S_1 \times S_2:$$
$$\text{if } \text{2DDH}(Z, Z_1, Z_2^{1/u}) \text{ then return } Z_1$$

Since $\mathcal{B}$ wins whenever $\mathcal{A}$ wins both times, $\mathcal{B}$'s winning probability is equal to the square of $\mathcal{A}$'s winning probability. We then conclude the proof by applying Lemma 2 and observing that the given simulator calls the 2DDH oracle at most m^2 times.   □

References

1. Abadi, M., Rogaway, P.: Reconciling two views of cryptography (the computational soundness of formal encryption). Journal of Cryptology **15**(2), 103–127 (2002)
2. Almeida, J.B., Barbosa, M., Barthe, G., Dupressoir, F.: Certified computer-aided cryptography: efficient provably secure machine code from high-level implementations. In: Sadeghi, A.-R., Gligor, V.D., Yung, M. (eds.) ACM CCS 13: 20th Conference on Computer and Communications Security, pp. 1217–1230. ACM Press, November 2013
3. Barthe, G., Crespo, J.M., Grégoire, B., Kunz, C., Lakhnech, Y., Schmidt, B., Béguelin, S.Z.: Fully automated analysis of padding-based encryption in the computational model. In: Sadeghi, A.-R., Gligor, V.D., Yung, M. (eds.) ACM CCS 13: 20th Conference on Computer and Communications Security, pp. 1247–1260. ACM Press, November 2013
4. Barthe, G., Crespo, J.M., Lakhnech, Y., Schmidt, B.: Mind the gap: Modular machine-checked proofs of one-round key exchange protocols. Cryptology ePrint Archive 2015, (2015). http://eprint.iacr.org/

5. Barthe, G., Dupressoir, F., Grégoire, B., Kunz, C., Schmidt, B., Strub, P.-Y.: EasyCrypt: A Tutorial. In: Aldini, A., Lopez, J., Martinelli, F. (eds.) FOSAD VII. LNCS, vol. 8604, pp. 146–166. Springer, Heidelberg (2014)
6. Barthe, G., Grégoire, B., Heraud, S., Béguelin, S.Z.: Computer-aided security proofs for the working cryptographer. In: Rogaway, P. (ed.) CRYPTO 2011. LNCS, vol. 6841, pp. 71–90. Springer, Heidelberg (2011)
7. Basin, D., Cremers, C.: Modeling and analyzing security in the presence of compromising adversaries. In: Gritzalis, D., Preneel, B., Theoharidou, M. (eds.) ESORICS 2010. LNCS, vol. 6345, pp. 340–356. Springer, Heidelberg (2010)
8. Bellare, M., Canetti, R., Krawczyk, H.: A modular approach to the design and analysis of authentication and key exchange protocols (extended abstract). In: 30th Annual ACM Symposium on Theory of Computing, pp. 419–428. ACM Press, May 1998
9. Bellare, M., Neven, G.: Multi-signatures in the plain public-key model and a general forking lemma. In: Juels, A., Wright, R.N., Vimercati, S. (eds.) ACM CCS 06: 13th Conference on Computer and Communications Security, pp. 390–399. ACM Press, October / November 2006
10. Bellare, M., Rogaway, P.: Entity authentication and key distribution. In: Stinson, D.R. (ed.) CRYPTO 1993. LNCS, vol. 773, pp. 232–249. Springer, Heidelberg (1994)
11. Benton, N.: Simple relational correctness proofs for static analyses and program transformations. In: 31st ACM SIGPLAN-SIGACT Symposium on Principles of Programming Languages, POPL 2004, pp. 14–25. ACM, New York (2004)
12. Bhargavan, K., Fournet, C., Kohlweiss, M., Pironti, A., Strub, P.: Implementing tls with verified cryptographic security. In: 2013 IEEE Symposium on Security and Privacy (SP), pp. 445–459. IEEE (2013)
13. Bhargavan, K., Fournet, C., Kohlweiss, M., Pironti, A., Strub, P.-Y., Zanella-Béguelin, S.: Proving the TLS handshake secure (as it is). In: Garay, J.A., Gennaro, R. (eds.) CRYPTO 2014, Part II. LNCS, vol. 8617, pp. 235–255. Springer, Heidelberg (2014)
14. Blanchet, B.: A computationally sound mechanized prover for security protocols. In: 2006 IEEE Symposium on Security and Privacy, pp. 140–154. IEEE Computer Society Press, May 2006
15. Blanchet, B.: Security protocol verification: Symbolic and computational models. In: Degano, P., Guttman, J.D. (eds.) Principles of Security and Trust. LNCS, vol. 7215, pp. 3–29. Springer, Heidelberg (2012)
16. Boyd, C., Cremers, C., Feltz, M., Paterson, K.G., Poettering, B., Stebila, D.: ASICS: Authenticated key exchange security incorporating certification systems. In: Crampton, J., Jajodia, S., Mayes, K. (eds.) ESORICS 2013. LNCS, vol. 8134, pp. 381–399. Springer, Heidelberg (2013)
17. Brzuska, C., Smart, N.P., Warinschi, B., Watson, G.J.: An analysis of the EMV channel establishment protocol. In: Sadeghi, A.-R., Gligor, V.D., Yung, M. (eds.) ACM CCS 13: 20th Conference on Computer and Communications Security, pp. 373–386. ACM Press, November 2013
18. Canetti, R., Krawczyk, H.: Analysis of key-exchange protocols and their use for building secure channels. In: Pfitzmann, B. (ed.) EUROCRYPT 2001. LNCS, vol. 2045, p. 453. Springer, Heidelberg (2001)
19. Cash, D.M., Kiltz, E., Shoup, V.: The twin Diffie-Hellman problem and applications. In: Smart, N.P. (ed.) EUROCRYPT 2008. LNCS, vol. 4965, pp. 127–145. Springer, Heidelberg (2008)

20. Choo, K.-K.R., Boyd, C., Hitchcock, Y.: Examining indistinguishability-based proof models for key establishment protocols. In: Roy, B. (ed.) ASIACRYPT 2005. LNCS, vol. 3788, pp. 585–604. Springer, Heidelberg (2005)

21. Cortier, V., Kremer, S., Warinschi, B.: A survey of symbolic methods in computational analysis of cryptographic systems. Journal of Automated Reasoning **46**(3–4), 225–259 (2011)

22. Cremers, C.J.: Formally and practically relating the ck, ck-hmqv, and eck security models for authenticated key exchange. Cryptology ePrint Archive, Report 2009/253, (2009). http://eprint.iacr.org/

23. Cremers, C., Feltz, M.: Beyond eCK: Perfect forward secrecy under actor compromise and ephemeral-key reveal. In: Foresti, S., Yung, M., Martinelli, F. (eds.) ESORICS 2012. LNCS, vol. 7459, pp. 734–751. Springer, Heidelberg (2012)

24. Diffie, W., van Oorschot, P.C., Wiener, M.J.: Authentication and authenticated key exchanges. Des. Codes Cryptography **2**(2), 107–125 (1992)

25. El Gamal, Taher: A Public Key Cryptosystem and a Signature Scheme Based on Discrete Logarithms. In: Blakely, G.R., Chaum, David (eds.) CRYPTO 1984. LNCS, vol. 196, pp. 10–18. Springer, Heidelberg (1985)

26. Halevi, S.: A plausible approach to computer-aided cryptographic proofs. Cryptology ePrint Archive, Report 2005/181, (2005). http://eprint.iacr.org/2005/181

27. Jager, T., Kohlar, F., Schäge, S., Schwenk, J.: On the security of TLS-DHE in the standard model. In: Safavi-Naini, R., Canetti, R. (eds.) CRYPTO 2012. LNCS, vol. 7417, pp. 273–293. Springer, Heidelberg (2012)

28. Kaliski Jr., B.S.: An unknown key-share attack on the MQV key agreement protocol. ACM Transactions on Information and System Security (TISSEC) **4**(3), 275–288 (2001)

29. Kim, M., Fujioka, A., Ustaoğlu, B.: Strongly secure authenticated key exchange without naxos' approach. In: Takagi, T., Mambo, M. (eds.) IWSEC 2009. LNCS, vol. 5824, pp. 174–191. Springer, Heidelberg (2009)

30. Krawczyk, H.: SIGMA: The 'SIGn-and-MAc' approach to authenticated diffie-hellman and its use in the IKE protocols. In: Boneh, D. (ed.) CRYPTO 2003. LNCS, vol. 2729, pp. 400–425. Springer, Heidelberg (2003)

31. Krawczyk, H.: HMQV: A high-performance secure Diffie-Hellman protocol. In: Shoup, V. (ed.) CRYPTO 2005. LNCS, vol. 3621, pp. 546–566. Springer, Heidelberg (2005)

32. Krawczyk, H., Paterson, K.G., Wee, H.: On the security of the TLS protocol: A systematic analysis. In: Canetti, R., Garay, J.A. (eds.) CRYPTO 2013, Part I. LNCS, vol. 8042, pp. 429–448. Springer, Heidelberg (2013)

33. Kudla, C., Paterson, K.G.: Modular security proofs for key agreement protocols. In: Roy, B. (ed.) ASIACRYPT 2005. LNCS, vol. 3788, pp. 549–565. Springer, Heidelberg (2005)

34. Kudla, C.J.: Special Signature Schemes and Key Agreement Protocols. PhD thesis, University of London (2006)

35. Küsters, R., Truderung, T.: Using ProVerif to analyze protocols with Diffie-Hellman exponentiation. In: Computer Security Foundations Symposium (CSF), pp. 157–171. IEEE (2009)

36. LaMacchia, B.A., Lauter, K., Mityagin, A.: Stronger security of authenticated key exchange. In: Susilo, W., Liu, J.K., Mu, Y. (eds.) ProvSec 2007. LNCS, vol. 4784, pp. 1–16. Springer, Heidelberg (2007)

37. Law, L., Menezes, A., Qu, M., Solinas, J., Vanstone, S.: An efficient protocol for authenticated key agreement. Designs, Codes and Cryptography **28**(2), 119–134 (2003)

38. Lee, J., Park, C.S.: An efficient authenticated key exchange protocol with a tight security reduction. IACR Cryptology ePrint Archive **2008**, 345 (2008)
39. Lee, J., Park, J.H.: Authenticated key exchange secure under the computational diffie-hellman assumption. Cryptology ePrint Archive, Report 2008/344, (2008). http://eprint.iacr.org/
40. Matsumoto, T., Takashima, Y.: On seeking smart public-key-distribution systems. IEICE TRANSACTIONS (1976–1990) **69**, 99–106 (1986)
41. Menezes, A.: Another look at HMQV. Mathematical Cryptology JMC **1**(1), 47–64 (2007)
42. Menezes, A., Ustaoglu, B.: On the importance of public-key validation in the MQV and HMQV key agreement protocols. In: Barua, R., Lange, T. (eds.) INDOCRYPT 2006. LNCS, vol. 4329, pp. 133–147. Springer, Heidelberg (2006)
43. Okamoto, T., Pointcheval, D.: The gap-problems: A new class of problems for the security of cryptographic schemes. In: Kim, K. (ed.) PKC 2001: 4th International Workshop on Theory and Practice in Public Key Cryptography. Lecture Notes in Computer Science, vol. 1992, pp. 104–118. Springer, Feb. (2001)
44. Pan, J., Wang, L.: Tmqv: a strongly eck-secure diffie-hellman protocol without gap assumption. In: Boyen, X., Chen, X. (eds.) ProvSec 2011. LNCS, vol. 6980, pp. 380–388. Springer, Heidelberg (2011)
45. Petullo, W.M., Zhang, X., Solworth, J.A., Bernstein, D.J., Lange, T.: MinimaLT: minimal-latency networking through better security. In: Sadeghi, A.-R., Gligor, V.D., Yung, M. (eds.) ACM CCS 13: 20th Conference on Computer and Communications Security, pp. 425–438. ACM Press, November 2013
46. Schmidt, B., Meier, S., Cremers, C., Basin, D.: Automated analysis of Diffie-Hellman protocols and advanced security properties. In: Computer Security Foundations Symposium (CSF), pp. 78–94. IEEE (2012)
47. Shoup, V.: Lower bounds for discrete logarithms and related problems. In: Fumy, W. (ed.) EUROCRYPT 1997. LNCS, vol. 1233, pp. 256–266. Springer, Heidelberg (1997)

Authenticated Key Exchange from Ideal Lattices

Jiang Zhang[1], Zhenfeng Zhang[1(✉)], Jintai Ding[2,3(✉)],
Michael Snook[3], and Özgür Dagdelen[4]

[1] Trusted Computing and Information Assurance Laboratory, SKLCS,
Institute of Software, Chinese Academy of Sciences, Beijing, China
jiangzhang09@gmail.com, zfzhang@tca.iscas.ac.cn
[2] Heshi Inc., Shixenze, China
[3] Department of Mathematical Sciences, University of Cincinnati, Cincinnati, USA
jintai.ding@gmail.com, snookml@mail.uc.edu
[4] Technische Universität Darmstadt, Darmstadt, Germany
oezguer.dagdelen@cased.de

Abstract. In this paper, we present a practical and provably secure two-pass authenticated key exchange protocol over ideal lattices, which is conceptually simple and has similarities to the Diffie-Hellman based protocols such as HMQV (CRYPTO 2005) and OAKE (CCS 2013). Our method does not involve other cryptographic primitives—in particular, it does not use signatures—which simplifies the protocol and enables us to base the security directly on the hardness of the ring learning with errors problem. The security is proven in the Bellare-Rogaway model with weak perfect forward secrecy in the random oracle model. We also give a one-pass variant of our two-pass protocol, which might be appealing in specific applications. Several concrete choices of parameters are provided, and a proof-of-concept implementation shows that our protocols are indeed practical.

1 Introduction

Key Exchange (KE) is a fundamental cryptographic primitive, allowing two parties to securely generate a common secret key over an insecure network. Because symmetric cryptographic tools (*e.g.,* AES) are reliant on both parties having a shared key in order to securely transmit data, KE is one of the most used cryptographic tools in building secure communication protocols (*e.g.,* SSL/TLS, IPSec, SSH). Following the introduction of the Diffie-Hellman (DH) protocol [1], cryptographers have devised a wide selection of KE protocols with various use-cases. One such class is Authenticated Key Exchange (AKE), which enables each party to verify the other's identity so that an adversary cannot impersonate an honest party in the conversation.

For an AKE protocol, each party has a pair of *static keys*: a *static secret key* and a corresponding *static public key*. The static public key is certified to belong to its owner using a public-key or ID-based infrastructure. During an execution of the protocol, each party generates a pair of ephemeral keys—an

© International Association for Cryptologic Research 2015
E. Oswald and M. Fischlin (Eds.): EUROCRYPT 2015, Part II, LNCS 9057, pp. 719–751, 2015.
DOI: 10.1007/978-3-662-46803-6_24

ephemeral secret key and an *ephemeral public key*—and sends the *ephemeral public key* to the other party. Then, these keys are used along with the transcripts of the session to create a shared *session state*, which is then passed to a *key derivation function* to obtain a common session key. Intuitively, such a protocol is secure if no efficient adversary is able to extract any information about the session key from the publicly exchanged messages. More formally, Bellare and Rogaway [2] introduced an indistinguishability-based security model for AKE, the BR model, which captures key authentication such as *implicit mutual key authentication* and *confidentiality of agreed session keys*. The most prominent alternatives stem from Canetti and Krawczyk [3] and LaMacchia *et al.* [4], that also account for scenarios in which the adversary is able to obtain information about a static secret key or a session state other than the state of the target session. In practice, AKE protocols are usually required to have a property, Perfect Forward Secrecy (PFS), that an adversary cannot compromise session keys after a completed session, even if it obtains the parties' static secret keys (*e.g.*, via the Heartbleed attack[1]). As shown in [5], no two-pass *implicit* AKE protocol based on public-key authentication can achieve PFS (but this may not be true for two-pass AKEs with *explicit* authentication [6]). Thus, the notion of weak PFS (wPFS) is usually considered for two-pass implicit AKE protocols, which states that the session key of an honestly run session remains private if the static keys are compromised after the session is finished [5].

One approach for achieving authentication in KE protocols is to explicitly authenticate the exchanged messages between the involved parties by using some cryptographic primitives (*e.g.*, signatures, or MACs), which usually incurs additional computation and communication overheads with respect to the basic KE protocol, and complicates the understanding of the KE protocol. This includes several well-known protocols such as IKE [7,8], SIGMA [9], SSL [10], TLS [11–15], as well as the standard in German electronic identity cards, namely EAC [16], and the standardized protocols OPACITY [17] and PLAID [18]. Another line of designing AKEs follows the idea of MTI [19] and MQV [20],[2] which aims at providing implicit authentication by directly utilizing the algebraic structure of DH problems (*e.g.*, HMQV [5] and OAKE [26]). All the above AKEs are based on classic hard problems, such as factoring, the RSA problem, or the computational/decisional DH problem. Since these hard problems are vulnerable to quantum computers [27] and as we are moving into the era of quantum computing, it is very appealing to find other counterparts based on problems believed to be resistant to quantum attacks. For instance, post-quantum AKE is considered of high priority by NIST [28]. Due to the potential benefits of lattice-based constructions such as asymptotic efficiency, conceptual simplicity, and worst-case hardness assumptions, it makes perfect sense to build lattice-based AKEs.

---

[1] http://heartbleed.com/

[2] Note that MQV has been widely standardized by ANS [21,22], ISO/IEC [23] and IEEE [24], and recommended by NIST and NSA Suite B [25].

1.1   Our Contribution

In this paper, we propose an efficient AKE protocol based on the Ring Learning With Errors (Ring-LWE), which in turn is as hard as some lattice problems (*e.g.,* SIVP) in the worst case on ideal lattices [29,30]. Our method avoids introducing extra cryptographic primitives, thus simplifying the design and reducing overhead. In particular, the parties are not required to either encrypt any messages with the other's public key, nor sign any of their own messages during key exchange. Furthermore, by having the key exchange as a self-contained system, we reduce the security assumptions needed, and are able to directly rely on the hardness of Ring-LWE in the random oracle model.

By utilizing many useful properties of Ring-LWE problems and discrete Gaussian distributions, we establish an approach to combine both the static and ephemeral public/secret keys, in a manner similar to HMQV [5]. Thus, our protocol not only enjoys many nice properties of HMQV such as two-pass messages, implicit key authentication, high efficiency, and without using any explicit entity authentication techniques (*e.g.,* signatures), but also has many properties of lattice-based cryptography, such as asymptotic efficiency, conceptual simplicity, worst-case hardness assumption, as well as resistance to quantum computer attacks. However, there are also several shortcomings inherited from lattice-based cryptography, such as "handling of noises" and large public/secret keys. Besides, unlike HMQV which works on "nicely-behaved" cyclic groups, the security of our protocol cannot be proven in the CK model [3] due to the underlying noise-based algebraic structures. Fortunately, we prove the security in the BR model (adapted to the public-key setting [31]), which is the most common model considered as it is usually strong enough for many practical applications and it comes with composability [32]. In addition, our protocol achieves the weak PFS property, which is known as the best PFS notion achievable by two-pass AKEs with implicit authentication [5].

As MQV [20] and HMQV [5], we also present a one-pass variant of our basic protocol (*i.e.,* only a single message is needed to derive a shared session key), which might be useful in client-server based applications. Finally, we select concrete choices of parameters and construct a proof-of-concept implementation to examine the efficiency of our protocols. Though the implementation has not undergone any real optimization, the performance results already indicate that our protocols are practical.

Besides, we note that none of the techniques we use prevents us from instantiating our AKE protocol based on standard lattices. One just has to keep in mind that key sizes and performance eventually become worse.

1.2   Techniques, and Relation to HMQV

Our AKE protocol is inspired by HMQV [5], which makes our protocol share some similarities to HMQV. However, there are also many differences between our protocol and HMQV due to the different underlying algebraic structures. To better illustrate the similarities and differences between our AKE protocol and HMQV, we first briefly recall the HMQV protocol [5]. Let $\mathbb{G}$ be a cyclic group with generator $g \in \mathbb{G}$. Let $(P_i = g^{s_i}, s_i)$ and $(P_j = g^{s_j}, s_j)$ be the static public/secret key pairs of party i and party j, respectively. During the protocol, both parties exchange ephemeral public keys, $i.e.$, party i sends $X_i = g^{r_i}$ to party j, and party j sends $Y_j = g^{r_j}$ to party i. Then, both parties compute the same key material $k_i = (P_j^d Y_j)^{s_i c + r_i} = g^{(s_i c + r_i)(s_j d + r_j)} = (P_i^c X_i)^{s_j d + r_j} = k_j$ where $c = H_1(j, X)$ and $d = H_1(i, Y)$ are computed by using a function H_1, and use it as input of a key derivation function H_2 to generate a common session key, $i.e.$, $\mathrm{sk}_i = H_2(k_i) = H_2(k_j) = \mathrm{sk}_j$.

As mentioned above, HMQV has many nice properties such as only two-pass messages, implicit key authentication, high efficiency, and without using any explicit entity authentication techniques ($e.g.$, signatures). Our main goal is to construct a lattice-based counterpart such that it not only enjoys all those nice properties of HMQV, but also belongs to post-quantum cryptography, $i.e.$, the underlying hardness assumption is believed to hold even against quantum computer. However, such a task is highly non-trivial since the success of HMQV greatly relies on the nice properties of cyclic groups such as commutativity ($i.e.$, $(g^a)^b = (g^b)^a$) and perfect (and public) randomization ($i.e.$ g^a can be perfectly randomized by computing $g^a g^r$ with a uniformly chosen r at random).

Fortunately, as noticed in [33–35], the Ring-LWE problem supports some kind of "approximate" commutativity, and can be used to build a passive-secure key exchange protocol. Specifically, let R_q be a ring, and χ be a Gaussian distribution over R_q. Then, given two Ring-LWE tuples with both secret and errors choosen from χ, $e.g.$, $(a, b_1 = as_1 + e_1)$ and $(a, b_2 = as_2 + e_2)$ for randomly chosen $a \leftarrow_r R_q, s_1, s_2, e_1, e_2 \leftarrow_r \chi$, the approximate equation $s_1 b_2 \approx s_1 a s_2 \approx s_2 b_1$ holds with overwhelming probability for proper parameters. By the same observation, we construct an AKE protocol (as illustrated in Fig. 1), where both the static and ephemeral public keys are actually Ring-LWE elements corresponding to a globally public element $a \in R_q$. In order to overcome the inability of "approximate" commutativity, our protocol has to send a signal information w_j computed by using a function Cha [33]. Combining this with another useful function Mod_2, both parties are able to compute the same key material $\sigma_i = \sigma_j$ (from the approximately equal values k_i and k_j) with a guarantee that $\sigma_j = \mathsf{Mod}_2(k_j, w_j)$ has high min-entropy even conditioned on the partial information $w_j = \mathsf{Cha}(k_j)$ of k_j (thus it can be used to derive a uniform session key sk_j).

However, the strategy of sending out the information $w_j = \mathsf{Cha}(k_j)$ inherently brings an undesired byproduct. Specifically, unlike HMQV, the security of our AKE protocol cannot be proven in the CK model which allows the adversaries to obtain the session state ($e.g.$, k_i at party i or k_j at party j) via $session$ $state$ $reveal$ queries. This is because in a traditional definition of session identifier that consists of all the exchanged messages, the two "different" sessions with identifiers $\mathrm{sid} = (i, j, x_i, y_j, w_j)$ and $\mathrm{sid}' = (i, j, x_i, y_j, w_j')$ have the same session state, $i.e.$, k_i at party i.[3] This also means that we cannot directly use

---

[3] This problem might not exist if one consider a different definition of session identifier, $e.g.$, the one that was uniquely determined at the beginning of the protocol execution.

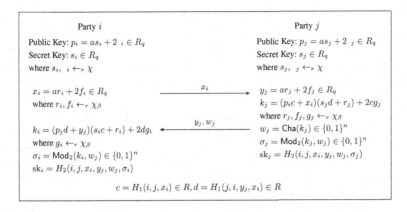

Fig. 1. Our AKE protocol from Ring-LWE

$\sigma_i = \sigma_j$ as the session key, because the binding between the value of σ_i and the session identifier (especially for the signal part w_j) is too loose. In particular, the fact that $\sigma_i = \mathsf{Mod}_2(k_i, w_j)$ corresponding to sid is simply a shift of $\sigma_i' = \mathsf{Mod}_2(k_i, w_j')$ corresponding to sid'(by the definition of the Mod_2 function), may potentially help the adversary distinguish σ_i with the knowledge of σ_i'. We prevent the adversary from utilizing this weakness by setting the session key as the output of the hash function H_2 (modeled as a random oracle) which tightly binds the session identifier sid and the key material σ_i (i.e., $\mathsf{sk}_i = H_2(\mathsf{sid}, \sigma_i)$). Our technique works due to another useful property of Mod_2, which guarantees that $\sigma_i = \mathsf{Mod}_2(k_i, w_j)$ preserves the high min-entropy property of k_i for any w_j (and thus is enough to generate a secure session key by using a good randomness extractor H_2, e.g., a random oracle).[4]

In order to finally get a security proof of our AKE protocol in the BR model with weakly perfect forward secrecy, we have to make use of the following property of Gaussian distributions, namely some kind of "public randomization". Specifically, let χ_α and χ_β be two Gaussian distributions with standard deviation α and β, respectively. Then, the sum of the two distributions is still a Gaussian distribution χ_γ with standard deviation $\gamma = \sqrt{\alpha^2 + \beta^2}$. In particular, if $\beta \gg \alpha$ (e.g., $\beta/\alpha = 2^{\omega(\log \kappa)}$ for some security parameter κ), we have that the distribution χ_γ is statistically close to χ_β. This technique is also known as "noise flooding" and has been applied, for instance, in proving robustness of the LWE assumption [36]. The security proof of our protocol is based on the observation that such a technique allows to statistically hide the distribution of

---

[4] We remark that this is also the reason why the nice reconciliation mechanism in [34] cannot be used in our protocol. Specifically, it is unclear whether the reconciliation function $\mathsf{rec}(\cdot, \cdot)$ in [34] could also preserve the high min-entropy property of the first input (i.e., which might not be uniformly random) for any (maliciously chosen) second input.

χ_α in a bigger distribution χ_β, and for now let us keep it in mind that a large distribution will be used to hide a small one.

To better illustrate our technique, we take party j as an example, $i.e.$, the one who combines his static and ephemeral secret keys by computing $\hat{r}_j = s_j d + r_j$ where $d = H_1(j, i, y_j, x_i)$. We notice that the value $\hat{r}_j$ actually behaves like a "signature" on the messages that party j knows so far. In other words, it should be difficult to compute $\hat{r}_j$ if we do not know the corresponding "signing key" s_j. Indeed, this combination is necessary to provide the implicit entity authentication. However, it also poses an obstacle to getting a security proof since the simulator may also be unaware of s_j. Fortunately, if the randomness r_j is chosen from a big enough Gaussian distribution, then the value $\hat{r}_j$ almost obliterates all information of s_j. More specifically, the simulator can directly choose $\hat{r}_j$ such that $\hat{r}_j = s_j d + r_j$ for some unknown r_j by computing $y_j = (a\hat{r}_j + 2\hat{f}_j) - p_j d$, and programming the random oracle $d = H_1(j, i, y_j, x_i)$ correspondingly. The properties of Gaussian distributions and the random oracle H_1 implies that y_j has almost identical distribution as in the real run of the protocol. Now, we check the randomness of $k_j = (p_i c + x_i)\hat{r}_j + 2cg_j$. Note that for the test session, we can always guarantee that at least one of the pair (p_i, x_i) is honestly generated (and thus is computationally indistinguishable from uniformly distributed element under the Ring-LWE assumption), or else there is no "secrecy" to protect if both p_i and x_i are chosen by the adversary. That is, $p_i c + x_i$ is always random if c is invertible in R_q. Again, by programming $c = H_1(i, j, x_i)$, the simulator can actually replace $p_i c + x_i$ with $\hat{x}_i = cu_i$ for a uniformly distributed ring element u_i. In this case, we have that $k_j = \hat{x}_i \hat{r}_j + 2cg_j = c(u_i \hat{r}_j + 2g_j)$ should be computationally indistinguishable from a uniformly distributed element under the Ring-LWE assumption. In other words, when proving the security one can replace k_j with a uniformly distributed element to derive a high min-entropy key material σ_j by using the Mod_2 function as required.

Unfortunately, directly using "noise flooding" has a significant drawback, $i.e.$, the requirement of a super-polynomially large standard deviation β, which may lead to a nightmare for practical performance due to a super-polynomially large modulus q for correctness and a very large ring dimension n for the hardness of the underlying Ring-LWE problems. Fortunately, we can reduce the big cost by further employing the rejection sampling technique [37]. Rejection sampling is a crucial technique in signature schemes to make the distribution of signatures independent of the signing key, and has been applied in many other lattice-based signature schemes [38–41].

In our case the combination of the static and ephemeral secret keys, $\hat{r}_j = s_j d + r_j$, at party j is essentially a signature on all the public messages under party j's public key (we again take party j as an example, but note that similar analysis also holds for party i). Thus, we can freely use the rejection sampling technique to relax the requirement on a super-polynomially large β. In other words, we can use a much smaller β, but require party j to use r_j if $\hat{r}_j = s_j d + r_j$ follows the distribution χ_β, and to resample a new r_j otherwise. We note that by deploying rejection sampling in our AKE it is the first time that rejection

Table 1. Comparison of lattice-based AKEs (CCA† means CCA-security with high min-entropy keys [43], and EUF-CMA means existential unforgeability under chosen message attacks)

Protocols	KEM/PKE	Signature	Message-pass	Model	RO?	Num. of R_q
FSXY12 [43]	CCA†	-	2-pass	CK	×	$\gg 7$
FSXY13 [44]	OW-CCA	-	2-pass	CK	$\sqrt{}$	7
Peikert14 [34]	CPA	EUF-CMA	3-pass	SK-security	$\sqrt{}$	> 2 *
BCNS14 [35]	CPA	EUF-CMA	4-pass	ACCE	$\sqrt{}$	2 for KEM **
Ours	-	-	2-pass	BR with wPFS	$\sqrt{}$	2

  * The actual number of ring elements depends on the choice of the concrete lattice-based signatures.
 ** Since the protocol uses traditional signatures to provide authentication, it does not contain any other ring elements.

sampling is used beyond signature schemes in lattice-based cryptography. As for signatures, rejection sampling is done locally, and thus will not affect the interaction between the two parties, $i.e.$, two-pass messages. Even though the computational performance of each execution might become worse with certain (small) probability (due to rejection and repeated sampling), the average computational cost is much better than the setting of using a super-polynomially large β.

1.3 Related Work, Comparison and Discussion

In the past few years, many cryptographers have put effort into constructing different kinds of KE protocols from lattices. At Asiacrypt 2009, Katz and Vaikuntanathan [42] proposed the first password-based authenticated key exchange protocol that can be proven secure based on the LWE assumption. Ding $et\ al.$ [33] elegantly constructed a passive-secure KE protocol on (Ring-)LWE by using a nice error-removing technique with a signal message. Like the standard DH protocol, the protocol in [33] could not provide authentication—it is not an AKE protocol—and is thus vulnerable to man-in-the-middle attacks. This motivates us to design an efficient AKE protocol on (ideal) lattices, especially an MQV-style one with implicit authentication.

Since the work of Katz et al. [42], there are four papers focusing on designing AKEs from lattices [34,35,43,44]. At a high level, all of them are following generic transformations from key encapsulation mechanisms (KEM) to AKEs. Concretely, Fujioka $et\ al.$ [43] proposed a generic construction of AKE from KEMs, which can be proven secure in the CK model. Informally, they showed that if there is a CCA-secure KEM with high min-entropy keys and a family of pseudorandom functions (PRF), then there is a secure AKE protocol in the standard model. Thus, by using existing lattice-based CCA-secure KEMs such as [45,46], it is possible to construct lattice-based AKE protocols in the standard model. However, as the authors commented, their construction was just of theoretic interest due to huge public keys and the lack of an efficient and direct construction of PRFs from (Ring-)LWE. Later, the paper [44] tried to get a practical AKE protocol by improving the efficiency of the generic framework in [43], and showed that one-way CCA-secure KEMs were enough to get AKEs in the random oracle model. The two protocols in [43,44] share some similarities such as having two-pass messages, and involving three encryptions (*i.e.*, two encryptions under each party's static public key and one encryption under an ephemeral public key). However, the use of the random oracle heuristic makes the protocol in [44] more efficient than that in [43]. Specifically, the protocol in [44] requires exchanging seven ring elements when instantiated with the CPA-secure encryption from Ring-LWE [29] by first transforming it into a CCA-secure one with the Fujisaki-Okamoto transformation.

Recently, Peikert [34] presented an efficient KEM based on Ring-LWE, which was then transformed into an AKE protocol by using the same structure as SIGMA [9]. Similar to the SIGMA protocol, the resulting protocol had three-pass messages and was proven SK-secure [47] in the random oracle model. For the computation overheads, Peikert's protocol involved one KEM, two signatures and two MACs. By treating the KEM in [34] as a DH-like KE protocol, Bos *et al.* [35] integrated it into the Transport Layer Security (TLS) protocol by directly using signatures to provide explicit authentication. Actually, the authors used traditional digital signatures such as RSA and ECDSA, and thus their protocol was not a pure post-quantum AKE. As for the security, the protocol in [35] was proven secure in the authenticated and confidential channel establishment (ACCE) security model [48] (which is based on the BR model, but has many differences to capture entity authentication and channel security).

Due to the lack of concrete security analysis and parameter choices in the literature, we only give a theoretical comparison of lattice-based AKEs in Table 1. In summary, our protocol only has two-pass messages (about two ring elements) and does not use signatures/MACs at all, and its security relies on the hardness of Ring-LWE in the random oracle model. To the best of our knowledge there is not a single post-quantum authenticated key exchange protocol (until this work) which directly relies on a quantum-hard computational problem and does not make use of explicit cryptographic primitives except hash functions.

1.4   On the Quantum Hardness of Our AKE Protocol

We call our AKE protocol post-quantum as our protocol relies merely on the Ring-LWE assumption, which is believed to hold even in presence of polynomial-time quantum computers. However, we emphasize that it does not mean necessarily that our scheme is quantum resistant. This may sound confusing and controversial in the beginning; that is why we clarify this issue in the following. While the underlying assumption may give the impression that our scheme is quantum secure, our security analysis makes use of rewinding the adversary, which is generally hard to apply to a quantum algorithm (exceptions can be found in [49,50]). Moreover, our proof is done in the random oracle model. In [51], Boneh et al. introduced the quantum random oracle model, and show that proofs in this augmented model are more realistic when considering quantum adversaries. In fact, many well-known transformations proven secure in the classical random oracle model cannot be (easily) proven secure against quantum algorithms, such as the Fiat-Shamir transform [52,53]. Moreover, it is not clear whether the security models for key exchange are appropriate when considering quantum adversaries. An update of security models (in general) may necessary when considering quantum adversaries (see [54,55]). Therefore, we do not claim that our scheme is quantum resistant, but believe it is a big step forward.

2 Preliminaries

2.1 Notation

Let κ be the natural security parameter, and all quantities are implicitly dependent on κ. Let $\text{poly}(\kappa)$ denote an unspecified function $f(\kappa) = O(\kappa^c)$ for some constant c. The function log denotes the natural logarithm. We use standard notation O, ω to classify the growth of functions. If $f(\kappa) = O(g(\kappa) \cdot \log^c \kappa)$, we denote $f(\kappa) = \tilde{O}(g(\kappa))$. We say a function $f(\kappa)$ is negligible if for every $c > 0$, there exists a N such that $f(\kappa) < 1/\kappa^c$ for all $\kappa > N$. We use $\text{negl}(\kappa)$ to denote a negligible function of κ, and we say a probability is overwhelming if it is $1 - \text{negl}(\kappa)$.

The set of real numbers (integers) is denoted by $\mathbb{R}$ ($\mathbb{Z}$, resp.). We use $\leftarrow_r$ to denote randomly choosing an element from some distribution (or the uniform distribution over some finite set). Vectors are in column form and denoted by bold lower-case letters (e.g., $\mathbf{x}$). The ℓ_2 and ℓ_∞ norms we designate by $\|\cdot\|$ and $\|\cdot\|_\infty$. The ring of polynomials over $\mathbb{Z}$ ($\mathbb{Z}_q = \mathbb{Z}/q\mathbb{Z}$, resp.) we denote by $\mathbb{Z}[x]$ ($\mathbb{Z}_q[x]$, resp.).

Let X be a distribution over finite set S. The min-entropy of X is defined as

$$H_\infty(X) = -\log(\max_{s \in S} \Pr[X = s]).$$

Intuitively, the min-entropy says that if we (privately) choose x from X at random, then no (unbounded) algorithm can guess the value of x correctly with probability greater than $2^{-H_\infty(X)}$.

2.2 Security Model for AKE

We now recall the Bellare-Rogaway security model [2,31], restricted to the case of two-pass AKE protocol.

Sessions. We fix a positive integer N to be the maximum number of honest parties that use the AKE protocol. Each party is uniquely identified by an integer i in $\{1, 2, \ldots, N\}$, and has a static key pair consisting of a static secret key sk_i and static public key pk_i, which is signed by a Certificate Authority (CA). A single run of the protocol is called a *session*. A session is activated at a party by an incoming message of the form (Π, I, i, j) or the form (Π, R, j, i, X_i), where Π is a protocol identifier; I and R are role identifiers; i and j are party identifiers. If party i receives a message of the form (Π, I, i, j), we say that i is the session initiator. Party i then outputs the response X_i intended for party j. If party j receives a message of the form (Π, R, j, i, X_i), we say that j is the session responder; party j then outputs a response Y_j to party i. After exchanging these messages, both parties compute a session key.

If a session is activated at party i with i being the initiator, we associate with it a *session identifier* sid $= (\Pi, I, i, j, X_i)$ or sid $= (\Pi, I, i, j, X_i, Y_j)$. Similarly, if a session is activated at party j with j being the responder, the session identifier has the form sid $= (\Pi, R, j, i, X_i, Y_j)$. For a session identifier sid $= (\Pi, *, i, j, *[, *])$, the third coordinate—that is, the first party identifier—is called the owner of the session; the other party is called the peer of the session. A session is said to be *completed* when its owner computes a session key. The *matching session* of sid $= (\Pi, I, i, j, X_i, Y_j)$ is the session with identifier $\widetilde{\text{sid}} = (\Pi, R, j, i, X_i, Y_j)$ and vice versa.

Adversarial Capabilities. We model the adversary $\mathcal{A}$ as a probabilistic polynomial time (PPT) Turing machine with full control over all communication channels between parties, including control over session activations. In particular, $\mathcal{A}$ can intercept all messages, read them all, and remove or modify any desired messages as well as inject its own messages. We also suppose $\mathcal{A}$ is capable of obtaining hidden information about the parties, including static secret keys and session keys to model potential leakage of them in genuine protocol executions. These abilities are formalized by providing $\mathcal{A}$ with the following oracles (we split the Send query as in [3] into Send_0, Send_1 and Send_2 queries for the case of two-pass protocols):

- $\mathsf{Send}_0(\Pi, I, i, j)$: $\mathcal{A}$ activates party i as an initiator. The oracle returns a message X_i intended for party j.
- $\mathsf{Send}_1(\Pi, R, j, i, X_i)$: $\mathcal{A}$ activates party j as a responder using message X_i. The oracle returns a message Y_j intended for party i.
- $\mathsf{Send}_2(\Pi, R, i, j, X_i, Y_j)$: $\mathcal{A}$ sends party i the message Y_j to complete a session previously activated with a $\mathsf{Send}_0(\Pi, I, i, j)$ query that returned X_i.
- $\mathsf{SessionKeyReveal}(\text{sid})$: The oracle returns the session key associated with the session sid if it has been generated.
- $\mathsf{Corrupt}(i)$: The oracle returns the static secret key belonging to party i. A party whose key is given to $\mathcal{A}$ in this way is called *dishonest*; a party not compromised in this way is called *honest*.
- $\mathsf{Test}(\text{sid}^*)$: The oracle chooses a bit $b \leftarrow_r \{0, 1\}$. If $b = 0$, it returns a key chosen uniformly at random; if $b = 1$, it returns the session key associated with sid^*. Note that we impose some restrictions on this query. We only allow $\mathcal{A}$ to query this oracle once, and only on a fresh (see Definition 1) session sid^*.

Definition 1 (Freshness).   *Let* $\text{sid}^* = (\Pi, I, i^*, j^*, X_i, Y_j)$ *or* $(\Pi, R, j^*, i^*, X_i, Y_j)$ *be a completed session with initiator party* i^* *and responder party* j^*. *If the* *matching session exists, denote it* $\widetilde{\text{sid}}^*$. *We say that* sid* *is fresh if the following conditions hold:*

- $\mathcal{A}$ *has not made a* SessionKeyReveal *query on* sid*.
- $\mathcal{A}$ *has not made a* SessionKeyReveal *query on* $\widetilde{\text{sid}}^*$ *(if it exists).*
- *Neither party* i* *nor* j* *is dishonest if* $\widetilde{\text{sid}}^*$ *does not exist. I.e.,* $\mathcal{A}$ *has not made a* Corrupt *query on either of them.*

Recall that in the original BR model [2], no corruption query is allowed. In the above freshness definition, we allow the adversary to corrupt both parties of sid* if the matching session exists, *i.e.*, the adversary can obtain the parties' secret key in advance and then passively eavesdrops the session sid* (and thus $\widetilde{\text{sid}}^*$). We remark that this seems to be stronger than what is needed for capturing wPFS [5], where the adversary is only allowed to corrupt a party after an honest session sid* (and thus $\widetilde{\text{sid}}^*$) has been completed.

Security Game. The security of a two-pass AKE protocol is defined in terms of the following game. The adversary $\mathcal{A}$ makes any sequence of queries to the oracles above, so long as only one Test query is made on a fresh session, as mentioned above. The game ends when $\mathcal{A}$ outputs a guess b' for b. We say $\mathcal{A}$ wins the game if its guess is correct, so that $b' = b$. The advantage of $\mathcal{A}$, $\mathbf{Adv}_{\Pi,\mathcal{A}}$, is defined as $|\Pr[b' = b] - 1/2|$.

Definition 2 (Security). *We say that an AKE protocol Π is secure if the following conditions hold:*

- *If two honest parties complete matching sessions then they compute the same session key with overwhelming probability.*
- *For any PPT adversary $\mathcal{A}$, the advantage $\mathbf{Adv}_{\Pi,\mathcal{A}}$ is negligible.*

2.3   The Gaussian Distributions and Rejection Sampling

For any positive real $\alpha \in \mathbb{R}$, and vectors $\mathbf{c} \in \mathbb{R}^m$, the continuous Gaussian distribution over $\mathbb{R}^m$ with standard deviation α centered at $\mathbf{v}$ is defined by the probability function $\rho_{\alpha,\mathbf{c}}(\mathbf{x}) = (\frac{1}{\sqrt{2\pi\alpha^2}})^m \exp\left(\frac{-\|\mathbf{x}-\mathbf{v}\|^2}{2\alpha^2}\right)$. For integer vectors $\mathbf{c} \in \mathbb{R}^n$, let $\rho_{\alpha,\mathbf{c}}(\mathbb{Z}^m) = \sum_{\mathbf{x}\in\mathbb{Z}^m} \rho_{\alpha,\mathbf{c}}(\mathbf{x})$. Then, we define the discrete Gaussian distribution over $\mathbb{Z}^m$ as $D_{\mathbb{Z}^m,\alpha,\mathbf{c}}(\mathbf{x}) = \frac{\rho_{\alpha,\mathbf{c}}(\mathbf{x})}{\rho_{\alpha,\mathbf{c}}(\mathbb{Z}^m)}$, where $\mathbf{x} \in \mathbb{Z}^m$. The subscripts s and $\mathbf{c}$ are taken to be 1 and $\mathbf{0}$ (respectively) when omitted. The following lemma says that for large enough α, almost all the samples from $D_{\mathbb{Z}^m,\alpha}$ are small.

Lemma 1 ([56]). *Letting real $\alpha = \omega(\sqrt{\log m})$, constant $\eta > 1/\sqrt{2\pi}$, then we have that* $\Pr_{\mathbf{x}\leftarrow_r D_{\mathbb{Z}^m,\alpha}}[\|\mathbf{x}\| > \eta \cdot \alpha\sqrt{m}] \le \frac{1}{2}D^n$, *where $D = \eta\sqrt{2\pi e} \cdot e^{-\pi\cdot\eta^2}$. In particular, we have* $\Pr_{\mathbf{x}\leftarrow_r D_{\mathbb{Z}^m,\alpha}}[\|\mathbf{x}\| > \alpha\sqrt{m}] \le 2^{-m+1}$.

Now, we recall rejection sampling in Theorem 1 from [37], which will be used in the security proof of our AKE protocol.

Theorem 1 (Rejection Sampling [37]). *Let V be a subset of $\mathbb{Z}^m$ in which all the elements have norms less than T, $\alpha = \omega(T\sqrt{\log m})$ be a real, and $\psi : V \to \mathbb{R}$ be a probability distribution. Then there exists a constant $M = O(1)$ such that the distribution of the following algorithm Samp_1 :*

1: $\mathbf{c} \leftarrow_r \psi$
2: $\mathbf{z} \leftarrow_r D_{\mathbb{Z}^m, \alpha, \mathbf{c}}$
3: *output* $(\mathbf{z}, \mathbf{c})$ *with probability* $\min\left(\frac{D_{\mathbb{Z}^m, \alpha}(\mathbf{z})}{MD_{\mathbb{Z}^m, \alpha, \mathbf{c}}(\mathbf{z})}, 1\right)$.

is within statistical distance $\frac{2^{-\omega(\log m)}}{M}$ from the distribution of the following algorithm Samp_2 :

1: $\mathbf{c} \leftarrow_r \psi$
2: $\mathbf{z} \leftarrow_r D_{\mathbb{Z}^m, \alpha}$
3: *output* $(\mathbf{z}, \mathbf{c})$ *with probability* $1/M$.

Moreover, the probability that Samp_1 outputs something is at least $\frac{1-2^{-\omega(\log m)}}{M}$. More concretely, if $\alpha = \tau T$ for any positive τ, then $M = e^{12/\tau + 1/(2\tau^2)}$ and the output of algorithm Samp_1 is within statistical distance $\frac{2^{-100}}{M}$ of the output of Samp_2, and the probability that $\mathcal{A}$ outputs something is at least $\frac{1-2^{-100}}{M}$.

2.4   Ring Learning with Errors

Let the integer n be a power of 2, and consider the ring $R = \mathbb{Z}[x]/(x^n + 1)$. For any positive integer q, we define the ring $R_q = \mathbb{Z}_q[x]/(x^n + 1)$ analogously. For any polynomial $y(x)$ in R (or R_q), we identify y with its coefficient vector in $\mathbb{Z}^n$ (or $\mathbb{Z}_q^n$). Then, we define the norm of a polynomial to be the (Euclidean) norm of its coefficient vector.

Lemma 2. *For any $s, t \in R$, we have $\|s \cdot t\| \le \sqrt{n} \cdot \|s\| \cdot \|t\|$ and $\|s \cdot t\|_\infty \le n \cdot \|s\|_\infty \cdot \|t\|_\infty$.*

The discrete Gaussian distribution over the ring R can be naturally defined as the distribution of ring elements whose coefficient vectors are distributed according to the discrete Gaussian distribution over $\mathbb{Z}^n$, e.g., $D_{\mathbb{Z}^n, \alpha}$ for some positive real α. Letting χ_α be the discrete Gaussian distribution over $\mathbb{Z}^n$ with standard deviation α centered at $\mathbf{0}$, i.e., $\chi_\alpha := D_{\mathbb{Z}^n, \alpha}$, we now adopt the following notational convention: since bold-face letters denote vectors, $\mathbf{x} \leftarrow_r \chi_\alpha$ means we sample the vector $\mathbf{x}$ from the distribution χ_α; for normal weight variables (e.g., $y \leftarrow_r \chi_\alpha$) we sample an element of R whose coefficient vector is distributed according to χ_α.

Now we come to the statement of the Ring-LWE assumption; we will use a special case detailed in [29]. Let R_q be defined as above, and $s \leftarrow_r R_q$. We define A_{s, χ_α} to be the distribution of the pair $(a, as + x) \in R_q \times R_q$, where $a \leftarrow_r R_q$ is uniformly chosen and $x \leftarrow_r \chi_\alpha$ is independent of a.

Definition 3 (Ring-LWE Assumption). *Let R_q and χ_α be defined as above, and $s \leftarrow_r R_q$. The Ring-LWE assumption $RLWE_{q,\alpha}$ states that it is hard for any PPT algorithm to distinguish A_{s,χ_α} from the uniform distribution on $R_q \times R_q$ with only polynomially many samples.*

The following lemma says that the hardness of the Ring-LWE assumption can be reduced to some hard lattice problems such as the Shortest Independent Vectors Problem (SIVP) over ideal lattices.

Proposition 1 (A special case of [29]). *Let n be a power of 2, α be a real number in $(0,1)$, and q be a prime such that $q \bmod 2n = 1$ and $\alpha q > \omega(\sqrt{\log n})$. Define $R_q = \mathbb{Z}_q[x]/\langle x^n + 1 \rangle$ as above. Then, there exists a polynomial time quantum reduction from $\tilde{O}(\sqrt{n}/\alpha)$-SIVP in the worst case to average-case $RLWE_{q,\beta}$ with ℓ samples, where $\beta = \alpha q \cdot (n\ell/\log(n\ell))^{1/4}$.*

It has been proven that the Ring-LWE assumption still holds even if the secret s is chosen according to the error distribution χ_β rather than uniformly [29, 57]. This variant is known as the *normal form*, and is preferable for controlling the size of the error term [58,59]. The underlying Ring-LWE assumption also holds when scaling the error by a constant t relatively prime to q [58], *i.e.*, using the pair $(a_i, a_i s + t x_i)$ rather than $(a_i, a_i s + x_i)$. Several lattice-based cryptographic schemes have been constructed based on this variant [58,59]. In our case, we will fix $t = 2$. Besides, recall that the $RLWE_{q,\beta}$ assumption guarantees that for some prior fixed (but randomly chosen) s, the tuple $(a, as + 2x)$ is computationally indistinguishable from the uniform distribution over $R_q \times R_q$ if $a \leftarrow_r R_q$ and $x \leftarrow \chi_\beta$. In this paper, we will use a matrix form of the ring-LWE assumption. Formally, let $B_{\chi_\beta,\ell_1,\ell_2}$ be the distribution of $(\mathbf{a}, \mathbf{B} = (b_{i,j})) \in R_q^{\ell_1} \times R_q^{\ell_1 \times \ell_2}$, where $\mathbf{a} = (a_0, \ldots, a_{\ell_1-1}) \leftarrow_r R_q^{\ell_1}$, $\mathbf{s} = (s_0, \ldots, s_{\ell_2-1}) \leftarrow_r R_q^{\ell_2}$, $e_{i,j} \leftarrow_r \chi_\beta$, and $b_{i,j} = a_i s_j + 2e_{i,j}$ for $i \in \{0, \ldots, \ell_1 - 1\}$ and $j \in \{0, \ldots, \ell_2 - 1\}$. For polynomially bounded ℓ_1 and ℓ_2, one can show that the distribution of $B_{\chi_\beta,\ell_1,\ell_2}$ is pseudorandom based on the $RLWE_{q,\beta}$ assumption [45].

3 Authenticated Key Exchange from Ring-LWE

We now introduce some notations. For an odd prime $q > 2$, take $\mathbb{Z}_q = \{-\frac{q-1}{2}, \ldots, \frac{q-1}{2}\}$ and define the subset $E := \{-\lfloor \frac{q}{4} \rfloor, \ldots, \lfloor \frac{q}{4} \rfloor\}$ as the middle half of $\mathbb{Z}_q$. We also define Cha to be the characteristic function of *the complement of E*, so $\mathsf{Cha}(v) = 0$ if $v \in E$ and 1 otherwise. Obviously, for any v in $\mathbb{Z}_q$, $v + \mathsf{Cha}(v) \cdot \frac{q-1}{2} \bmod q$ belongs to E. We define an auxiliary modular function, $\mathsf{Mod}_2 \colon \mathbb{Z}_q \times \{0,1\} \to \{0,1\}$ as $\mathsf{Mod}_2(v, b) = (v + b \cdot \frac{q-1}{2}) \bmod q \bmod 2$.

In the following lemma, we show that given the bit $b = \mathsf{Cha}(v)$, and a value $w = v + 2e$ with sufficiently small e, one can recover $\mathsf{Mod}_2(v, \mathsf{Cha}(v))$. In particular, we have $\mathsf{Mod}_2(v, b) = \mathsf{Mod}_2(w, b)$.

Lemma 3. *Let q be an odd prime, $v \in \mathbb{Z}_q$ and $e \in \mathbb{Z}_q$ such that $|e| < q/8$. Then, for $w = v + 2e$, we have $\mathsf{Mod}_2(v, \mathsf{Cha}(v)) = \mathsf{Mod}_2(w, \mathsf{Cha}(v))$.*

Proof. Note that $w + \mathsf{Cha}(v)\frac{q-1}{2} \bmod q = v + \mathsf{Cha}(v)\frac{q-1}{2} + 2e \bmod q$. Now, $v + \mathsf{Cha}(v)\frac{q-1}{2} \bmod q$ is in E as we stated above; that is, $-\lfloor\frac{q}{4}\rfloor \le v + \mathsf{Cha}(v)\frac{q-1}{2} \bmod q \le \lfloor\frac{q}{4}\rfloor$. Thus, since $-q/8 < e < q/8$, we have $-\lfloor\frac{q}{2}\rfloor \le v + \mathsf{Cha}(v)\frac{q-1}{2} \bmod q + 2e \le \lfloor\frac{q}{2}\rfloor$. Therefore, we have $v + \mathsf{Cha}(v)\frac{q-1}{2} \bmod q + 2e = v + \mathsf{Cha}(v)\frac{q-1}{2} + 2e \bmod q = w + \mathsf{Cha}(v)\frac{q-1}{2} \bmod q$. Thus, $\mathsf{Mod}_2(w, \mathsf{Cha}(v)) = \mathsf{Mod}_2(v, \mathsf{Cha}(v))$.

Now, we extend the two functions Cha and Mod_2 to ring R_q by applying them coefficient-wise to ring elements. Namely, for ring element $v = (v_0, \ldots, v_{n-1}) \in R_q$ and binary-vector $\mathbf{b} = (b_0, \ldots, b_{n-1}) \in \{0,1\}^n$, define $\widetilde{\mathsf{Cha}}(v) = (\mathsf{Cha}(v_0), \ldots, \mathsf{Cha}(v_{n-1}))$ and $\widetilde{\mathsf{Mod}_2}(v, \mathbf{b}) = (\mathsf{Mod}_2(v_0, b_0), \ldots, \mathsf{Mod}_2(v_{n-1}, b_{n-1}))$. For simplicity, we slightly abuse the notations and still use Cha (resp. Mod_2) to denote $\widetilde{\mathsf{Cha}}$ (resp. $\widetilde{\mathsf{Mod}_2}$). Clearly, the result in Lemma 3 still holds when extending to ring elements.

In our AKE protocol, the two involved parties will use Cha and Mod_2 to derive a common key material. Concretely, the responder will publicly send the result of Cha on his own secret ring element to the initiator in order to compute a shared key material from two "close" ring elements (by applying the Mod_2 function). Ideally, for a uniformly chosen element v from R_q at random, we hope that the output of $\mathsf{Mod}_2(v, \mathsf{Cha}(v))$ is uniformly distributed $\{0,1\}^n$. However, this can never happen when q is an odd prime. Fortunately, we can show that the output of $\mathsf{Mod}_2(v, \mathsf{Cha}(v))$ conditioned on $\mathsf{Cha}(v)$ has high min-entropy, and thus can be used to extract an (almost) uniformly distributed session key. Actually, we can prove a stronger result.

Lemma 4. *Let q be any odd prime and R_q be the ring defined above. Then, for any $\mathbf{b} \in \{0,1\}^n$ and any $v' \in R_q$, the output distribution of $\mathsf{Mod}_2(v+v', \mathbf{b})$ given $\mathsf{Cha}(v)$ has min-entropy at least $-n\log(\frac{1}{2} + \frac{1}{|E|-1})$, where v is uniformly chosen from R_q at random. In particular, when $q > 203$, we have $-n\log(\frac{1}{2} + \frac{1}{|E|-1}) > 0.97n$.*

Proof. Since each coefficient of v is independently and uniformly chosen from $\mathbb{Z}_q$ at random, we can simplify the proof by focusing on the first coefficient of v. Formally, letting $v = (v_0, \ldots, v_{n-1})$, $v' = (v'_0, \ldots, v'_{n-1})$ and $\mathbf{b} = (b_0, \ldots, b_{n-1})$, we condition on $\mathsf{Cha}(v_0)$:

- If $\mathsf{Cha}(v_0) = 0$, then $v_0 + v'_0 + b_0 \cdot \frac{q-1}{2}$ is uniformly distributed over $v'_0 + b_0 \cdot \frac{q-1}{2} + E \bmod q$. This shifted set has $(q+1)/2$ elements, which are either consecutive integers—if the shift is small enough—or two sets of consecutive integers—if the shift is large enough to cause wrap-around. Thus, we must distinguish a few cases:
  - If $|E|$ is even and no wrap-around occurs, then the result of $\mathsf{Mod}_2(v_0 + v'_0, b_0)$ is clearly uniform on $\{0,1\}$. Hence, the result of $\mathsf{Mod}_2(v_0 + v'_0, b_0)$ has no bias.
  - If $|E|$ is odd and no wrap-around occurs, then the result of $\mathsf{Mod}_2(v_0 + v'_0, b_0)$ has a bias $\frac{1}{2|E|}$ over $\{0,1\}$. In other words, the $\mathsf{Mod}_2(v_0 + v'_0, b_0)$ will output either 0 or 1 with probability exactly $\frac{1}{2} + \frac{1}{2|E|}$.

- If $|E|$ is odd and wrap-around does occur, then the set $v_0' + b_0 \cdot \frac{q-1}{2} + E \bmod q$ splits into two parts, one with an even number of elements, and one with an odd number of elements. This leads to the same situation as with no wrap-around.
- If $|E|$ is even and wrap-around occurs, then our sample space is split into either two even-sized sets, or two odd sized sets. If both are even, then once again the result of $\mathsf{Mod}_2(v_0 + v_0', b_0)$ is uniform. If both are odd, it is easy to calculate that the result of $\mathsf{Mod}_2(v_0 + v_0', b_0)$ has a bias with probability $\frac{1}{|E|}$ over $\{0,1\}$.

- If $\mathsf{Cha}(v_0) = 1$, $v_0 + v_0' + b_0 \cdot \frac{q-1}{2}$ is uniformly distributed over $v_0' + b_0 \cdot \frac{q-1}{2} + \tilde{E}$, where $\tilde{E} = \mathbb{Z}_q \setminus E$. Now $|\tilde{E}| = |E| - 1$, so by splitting into the same cases as $\mathsf{Cha}(v_0) = 0$, the result of $\mathsf{Mod}_2(v_0 + v_0', b)$ has a bias with probability $\frac{1}{|E|-1}$ over $\{0,1\}$.

In all, we have that the result of $\mathsf{Mod}_2(v_0 + v_0', b_0)$ conditioned on $\mathsf{Cha}(v_0)$ has min-entropy at least $-\log(\frac{1}{2} + \frac{1}{|E|-1})$. Since the bits in the result of $\mathsf{Mod}_2(v + v', \mathbf{b})$ are independent, we have that given $\mathsf{Cha}(v)$, the min-entropy $H_\infty(\mathsf{Mod}_2(v + v', \mathbf{b})) \geq -n\log(\frac{1}{2} + \frac{1}{|E|-1})$. This completes the first claim. The second claim directly follows from the fact that $-\log(\frac{1}{2} + \frac{1}{|E|-1}) > -\log(0.51) > 0.97$ when $q > 203$. □

Remark 1 (On Uniformly Distributed Keys). It is known that randomness extractors can be used to obtain an almost uniformly distributed key from a biased bit-string with high min-entropy [60–64]. In practice, as recommended by NIST [65], one can actually use the standard cryptographic hash functions such as SHA-2 to derive a uniformly distributed key if the source string has at least 2κ min-entropy, where κ is the length of the cryptographic hash function.

3.1   The Protocol

We now describe our protocol in detail. Let n be a power of 2, and q be an odd prime such that $q \bmod 2n = 1$. Take $R = \mathbb{Z}[x]/(x^n + 1)$ and $R_q = \mathbb{Z}_q[x]/(x^n + 1)$ as above. For any positive $\gamma \in \mathbb{R}$, let $H_1 \colon \{0,1\}^* \to \chi_\gamma = D_{\mathbb{Z}^n, \gamma}$ be a hash function that always outputs invertible elements in R_q.[5] Let $H_2 \colon \{0,1\}^* \to \{0,1\}^\kappa$ be the key derivation function, where κ is the bit-length of the final shared key. We model both functions as random oracles [67]. Let χ_α, χ_β be two discrete Gaussian distributions with parameters $\alpha, \beta \in \mathbb{R}^+$. Let $a \in R_q$ be the global public parameter uniformly chosen from R_q at random, and M be a constant determined by Theorem 1. Let $p_i = as_i + 2e_i \in R_q$ be party i's static public key, where (s_i, e_i) is the corresponding static secret key; both s_i and e_i are taken

---

[5] In practice, one can first use a hash function (*e.g.*, SHA-2) to obtain a uniformly random string, and then use it to sample from $D_{\mathbb{Z}^n, \gamma}$. The algorithm outputs a sample only if it is invertible in R_q, otherwise, it tries another sample and repeats. By Lemma 10 in [66], we can have a good probability to sample an invertible element in each trial for an appropriate choice of γ.

from the distribution χ_α. Similarly, party j has static public key $p_j = as_j + 2e_j$ and static secret key (s_j, e_j).

Initiation. Party i proceeds as follows:

1. Sample $r_i, f_i \leftarrow_r \chi_\beta$ and compute $x_i = ar_i + 2f_i$;
2. Compute $c = H_1(i, j, x_i)$, $\hat{r}_i = s_i c + r_i$ and $\hat{f}_i = e_i c + f_i$;
3. Go to step 4 with probability $\min\left(\frac{D_{\mathbb{Z}^{2n}, \beta}(\mathbf{z})}{M D_{\mathbb{Z}^{2n}, \beta, \mathbf{z}_1}(\mathbf{z})}, 1\right)$, where $\mathbf{z} \in \mathbb{Z}^{2n}$ is the coefficient vector of $\hat{r}_i$ concatenated with the coefficient vector of $\hat{f}_i$, and $\mathbf{z}_1 \in \mathbb{Z}^{2n}$ is the coefficient vector of $s_i c$ concatenated with the coefficient vector of $e_i c$; otherwise go back to step 1;
4. Send x_i to party j.

Response. After receiving x_i from party i, party j proceeds as follows:

1′. Sample $r_j, f_j \leftarrow_r \chi_\beta$ and compute $y_j = ar_j + 2f_j$;
2′. Compute $d = H_1(j, i, y_j, x_i)$, $\hat{r}_j = s_j d + r_j$ and $\hat{f}_j = e_j d + f_j$;
3′. Go to step 4′ with probability $\min\left(\frac{D_{\mathbb{Z}^{2n}, \beta}(\mathbf{z})}{M D_{\mathbb{Z}^{2n}, \beta, \mathbf{z}_1}(\mathbf{z})}, 1\right)$, where $\mathbf{z} \in \mathbb{Z}^{2n}$ is the coefficient vector of $\hat{r}_j$ concatenated with the coefficient vector of $\hat{f}_j$, and $\mathbf{z}_1 \in \mathbb{Z}^{2n}$ is the coefficient vector of $s_j d$ concatenated with the coefficient vector of $e_j d$; otherwise go back to step 1′;
4′. Sample $g_j \leftarrow_r \chi_\beta$, compute $k_j = (p_i c + x_i)\hat{r}_j + 2cg_j$ where $c = H_1(i, j, x_i)$;
5′. Compute $w_j = \mathsf{Cha}(k_j) \in \{0, 1\}^n$ and send (y_j, w_j) to party i;
6′. Compute $\sigma_j = \mathsf{Mod}_2(k_j, w_j)$ and derive the session key $\mathrm{sk}_j = H_2(i, j, x_i, y_j, w_j, \sigma_j)$.

Finish. Party i receives the pair (y_j, w_j) from party j, and proceeds as follows:

5. Sample $g_i \leftarrow_r \chi_\beta$ and compute $k_i = (p_j d + y_j)\hat{r}_i + 2dg_i$ with $d = H_1(j, i, y_j, x_i)$;
6. Compute $\sigma_i = \mathsf{Mod}_2(k_i, w_j)$ and derive the session key $\mathrm{sk}_i = H_2(i, j, x_i, y_j, w_j, \sigma_i)$.

Remark 2. Deploying our protocol practically in a large scale requires the support of a PKI with a trusted Certificate Authority (CA). In this setting, all the system parameters (such as a) will be generated by the CA like other PKI-based protocols.

In the above protocol, both parties will make use of rejection sampling, *i.e.,* they will repeat the first three steps with certain probability. By Theorem 1, the probability that each party will repeat the steps is about $1 - \frac{1}{M}$ for some constant M and appropriately chosen β. Thus, one can hope that both parties will send something to each other after an averaged M times repetitions of the first three steps. Next, we will show that once they send something to each other, both parties will finally compute a shared session key.

3.2 Correctness

To show the correctness of our AKE protocol, *i.e.,* that both parties compute the same session key $\mathrm{sk}_i = \mathrm{sk}_j$, it suffices to show that $\sigma_i = \sigma_j$. Since σ_i and

σ_j are both the output of Mod_2 with $\mathsf{Cha}(k_j)$ as the second argument, we need only to show that k_i and k_j are sufficiently close by Lemma 3. Note that the two parties will compute k_i and k_j as follows:

$$
\begin{aligned}
k_i &= (p_j d + y_j)\hat{r}_i + 2dg_i \\
&= a(s_j d + r_j)\hat{r}_i + 2(e_j d + f_j)\hat{r}_i \\
&\quad + 2dg_i \\
&= a\hat{r}_i\hat{r}_j + 2\widetilde{g}_i
\end{aligned}
\qquad
\begin{aligned}
k_j &= (p_i c + x_i)\hat{r}_j + 2cg_j \\
&= a(s_i c + r_i)\hat{r}_j + 2(e_i c + f_i)\hat{r}_j \\
&\quad + 2cg_j \\
&= a\hat{r}_i\hat{r}_j + 2\widetilde{g}_j
\end{aligned}
$$

where $\widetilde{g}_i = \hat{f}_j\hat{r}_i + dg_i$, and $\widetilde{g}_j = \hat{f}_i\hat{r}_j + cg_j$. Then $k_i = k_j + 2(\widetilde{g}_i - \widetilde{g}_j)$, and we have $\sigma_i = \sigma_j$ if $\|\widetilde{g}_i - \widetilde{g}_j\|_\infty < q/8$ by Lemma 3.

4   Security

Theorem 2. *Let n be a power of 2 satisfying $0.97n \geq 2\kappa$, prime $q > 203$ satisfying $q = 1 \bmod 2n$, real $\beta = \omega(\alpha\gamma n\sqrt{n\log n})$ and let H_1, H_2 be random oracles. Then, if $RLWE_{q,\alpha}$ is hard, the proposed AKE is secure with respect to Definition 2.*

The intuition behind our proof is quite simple. Since the public element a and the public key of each party (e.g., $p_i = as_i + 2e_i$) actually consist of a $\mathrm{RLWE}_{q,\alpha}$ tuple with Gaussian parameter α (scaled by 2), the parties' static public keys are computationally indistinguishable from uniformly distributed elements in R_q under the Ring-LWE assumption. Similarly, both the exchanged elements x_i and y_j are also computationally indistinguishable from uniformly distributed elements in R_q under the $\mathrm{RLWE}_{q,\beta}$ assumption.

Without loss of generality, we take party j as an example to check the distribution of the session key. Note that if k_j is uniformly distributed over R_q, we have $\sigma_j \in \{0,1\}^n$ has high min-entropy (i.e., $0.97n > 2\kappa$) even conditioned on w_j by Lemma 4. Since H_2 is a random oracle, we have that sk_j is uniformly distributed over $\{0,1\}^\kappa$ as expected. Now, let us check the distribution of $k_j = (p_i c + x_i)(s_j d + r_j) + 2cg_j$. As one can imagine, we want to establish the randomness of k_j based on pseudorandomness of "Ring-LWE samples" with public element $\hat{a}_j = c^{-1}(p_i c + x_i) = p_i + c^{-1}x_i$, the secret $\hat{s}_j = s_j d + r_j$, as well as the error term $2g_j$ (thus we have $k_j = c(\hat{a}_j\hat{s}_j + 2g_j)$). Actually, k_j is pseudorandom due to the following fact: 1) c is invertible in R_q; 2) $\hat{a}_j$ is uniformly distributed over R_q whenever p_i or x_i is uniform, and 3) $\hat{s}_j$ has distribution statistically close to χ_β by the strategy of rejection sampling in Theorem 1. In other words, $\hat{a}_j\hat{s}_j + 2g_j$ is statistically close to a $\mathrm{RLWE}_{q,\beta}$ sample, and thus is pseudorandom.

Formally, let N be the maximum number of parties, and m be maximum number of sessions for each party. We distinguish the following five types of adversaries:

Type I: $\mathsf{sid}^* = (\Pi, I, i^*, j^*, x_{i^*}, (y_{j^*}, w_{j^*}))$ is the test session, and y_{j^*} is output by a session activated at party j by a $\mathsf{Send}_1(\Pi, R, j^*, i^*, x_{i^*})$ query.

Type II: $\text{sid}^* = (\Pi, I, i^*, j^*, x_{i^*}, (y_{j^*}, w_{j^*}))$ is the test session, and y_{j^*} is **not** output by a session activated at party j^* by a $\text{Send}_1(\Pi, R, j^*, i^*, x_{i^*})$ query.

Type III: $\text{sid}^* = (\Pi, R, j^*, i^*, x_{i^*}, (y_{j^*}, w_{j^*}))$ is the test session, and x_{i^*} is **not** output by a session activated at party i^* by a $\text{Send}_0(\Pi, I, i^*, j^*)$ query.

Type IV: $\text{sid}^* = (\Pi, R, j^*, i^*, x_{i^*}, (y_{j^*}, w_{j^*}))$ is the test session, and x_{i^*} is output by a session activated at party i^* by a $\text{Send}_0(\Pi, I, i^*, j^*)$ query, but i^* either never completes the session, or i^* completes it with exact y_{j^*}.

Type V: $\text{sid}^* = (\Pi, R, j^*, i^*, x_{i^*}, (y_{j^*}, w_{j^*}))$ is the test session, and x_{i^*} is output by a session activated at party i^* by a $\text{Send}_0(\Pi, I, i^*, j^*)$ query, but i^* completes the session with another $y'_j \neq y_{j^*}$.

The five types of adversaries give a complete partition of all the adversaries. The weak perfect forward secrecy (wPFS) is captured by allowing **Type I** and **Type IV** adversaries to obtain the static secret keys of both party i^* and j^* by using Corrupt queries. Since sid^* definitely has no matching session for **Type II**, **Type III**, and **Type V** adversaries, no corruption to either party i^* or party j^* is allowed by Definition 1. The security proofs for the five types of adversaries are similar, except the forking lemma [68] is involved for **Type II**, **Type III**, and **Type V** adversaries by using the assumption that H_1 is a random oracle. Informally, the adversary must first "commit" x_i (y_j, resp.) before seeing c (d, resp.), thus it cannot determine the value $p_i c + x_i$ or $p_j d + y_i$ in advance (but the simulator can set the values by programming H_1 when it tries to embed Ring-LWE instances with respect to either $p_i c + x_i$ or $p_j d + y_i$ as discussed before).

For space reason, we only give the security proof for **Type I** adversaries in Lemma 5, and defer the proofs for other types of adversaries to the full version.

Lemma 5. *Let n be a power of 2 satisfying $0.97n \geq 2\kappa$, prime $q > 203$ satisfying $q = 1 \mod 2n$, real $\beta = \omega(\alpha\gamma n\sqrt{n\log n})$. Then, if $RLWE_{q,\alpha}$ is hard, the proposed AKE is secure against any PPT **Type I** adversary $\mathcal{A}$ in the random oracle model.*

*In particular, if there is a PPT **Type I** adversary $\mathcal{A}$ breaking our protocol with non-negligible advantage ϵ, then there is a PPT algorithm $\mathcal{B}$ solving $RLWE_{q,\alpha}$ with advantage at least $\frac{\epsilon}{m^2 N^2} - \text{negl}(\kappa)$.*

Proof. We prove this lemma via a sequence of games $G_{1,l}$ for $0 \leq l \leq 7$, where the first game $G_{1,0}$ is almost the same as the real one except that the simulator randomly guesses the test session at the beginning of the game and aborts the simulation if the guess is wrong, while the last game $G_{1,7}$ is a fake one with randomly and independently chosen session key for the test session (thus the adversary can only win the game with negligible advantage). The security is established by showing that any two consecutive games are computationally indistinguishable. **Bold fonts** are used to highlight the changes of each game with respect to its previous game.

Game $G_{1,0}$. $\mathcal{S}$ chooses $i^*, j^* \leftarrow_r \{1, \ldots, N\}$, $s_{i^*}, s_{j^*} \leftarrow_r \{1, \ldots, m\}$, and hopes that the adversary will use $\text{sid}^* = (\Pi, I, i^*, j^*, x_{i^*}, (y_{j^*}, w_{j^*}))$ as the test session, where x_{i^*} is output by the s_{i^*}-th session of party i^*, and y_{j^*} is output by the $s_{j^*}^*$-th session of party j^* activated by a $\mathsf{Send}_1(\Pi, R, j^*, i^*, x_{i^*})$ query. Then, $\mathcal{S}$ chooses $a \leftarrow_r R_q$, generates static public keys for all parties (by choosing $s_i, e_i \leftarrow_r \chi_\alpha$), and simulates the security game for $\mathcal{A}$. Specifically, $\mathcal{S}$ maintains two tables L_1, L_2 for the random oracles H_1, H_2, respectively, and answers the queries from $\mathcal{A}$ as follows:

- $H_1(in)$: If there does not exist a tuple (in, out) in L_1, choose an invertible element $out \in \chi_\gamma$ at random, and add (in, out) into L_1. Then, return out to $\mathcal{A}$.
- $H_2(in)$ queries: If there does not exist a tuple (in, out) in L_2, choose a vector $out \leftarrow_r \{0,1\}^\kappa$, and add (in, out) into L_2. Then, return out to $\mathcal{A}$.
- $\mathsf{Send}_0(\Pi, I, i, j)$: $\mathcal{A}$ activates a new session of i with intended party j, $\mathcal{S}$ proceeds as follows:
  1. Sample $r_i, f_i \leftarrow_r \chi_\beta$ and compute $x_i = ar_i + 2f_i$;
  2. Compute $c = H_1(i, j, x_i)$, $\hat{r}_i = s_i c + r_i$ and $\hat{f}_i = e_i c + f_i$;
  3. Go to step 4 with probability $\min\left(\frac{D_{\mathbb{Z}^{2n},\beta}(\mathbf{z})}{MD_{\mathbb{Z}^{2n},\beta,\mathbf{z}_1}(\mathbf{z})}, 1\right)$, where $\mathbf{z} \in \mathbb{Z}^{2n}$ is the coefficient vector of $\hat{r}_i$ concatenated with the coefficient vector of $\hat{f}_i$, and $\mathbf{z}_1 \in \mathbb{Z}^{2n}$ is the coefficient vector of $s_i c$ concatenated with the coefficient vector of $e_i c$; otherwise go back to step 1;
  4. Return x_i to $\mathcal{A}$;
- $\mathsf{Send}_1(\Pi, R, j, i, x_i)$: $\mathcal{S}$ proceeds as follows:
  1'. Sample $r_j, f_j \leftarrow_r \chi_\beta$ and compute $y_j = ar_j + 2f_j$;
  2'. Compute $d = H_1(j, i, y_j, x_i)$, $\hat{r}_j = s_j d + r_j$ and $\hat{f}_j = e_j d + f_j$;
  3'. Go to step 4' with probability $\min\left(\frac{D_{\mathbb{Z}^{2n},\beta}(\mathbf{z})}{MD_{\mathbb{Z}^{2n},\beta,\mathbf{z}_1}(\mathbf{z})}, 1\right)$, where $\mathbf{z} \in \mathbb{Z}^{2n}$ is the coefficient vector of $\hat{r}_j$ concatenated with the coefficient vector of $\hat{f}_j$, and $\mathbf{z}_1 \in \mathbb{Z}^{2n}$ is the coefficient vector of $s_j d$ concatenated with the coefficient vector of $e_j d$; otherwise go back to step 1';
  4'. Sample $g_j \leftarrow_r \chi_\beta$, compute $k_j = (p_i c + x_i)\hat{r}_j + 2c g_j$ where $c = H_1(i, j, x_i)$;
  5'. Compute $w_j = \mathsf{Cha}(k_j) \in \{0,1\}^n$ and return (y_j, w_j) to $\mathcal{A}$;
  6'. Compute $\sigma_j = \mathsf{Mod}_2(k_j, w_j)$ and derive the session key $\mathrm{sk}_j = H_2(i, j, x_i, y_j, w_j, \sigma_j)$.
- $\mathsf{Send}_2(\Pi, I, i, j, x_i, (y_j, w_j))$: $\mathcal{S}$ computes k_i and sk_i as follows:
  5. Sample $g_i \leftarrow_r \chi_\beta$ and compute $k_i = (p_j d + y_j)\hat{r}_i + 2 d g_i$ where $d = H_1(j, i, y_j, x_i)$;
  6. Compute $\sigma_i = \mathsf{Mod}_2(k_i, w_j)$ and derive the session key $\mathrm{sk}_i = H_2(i, j, x_i, y_j, w_j, \sigma_i)$.
- $\mathsf{SessionKeyReveal}(\mathrm{sid})$: Let $\mathrm{sid} = (\Pi, *, i, *, *, *, *)$, $\mathcal{S}$ returns sk_i if the session key of sid has been generated.
- $\mathsf{Corrupt}(i)$: Return the static secret key s_i of i to $\mathcal{A}$.
- $\mathsf{Test}(\mathrm{sid})$: Let $\mathrm{sid} = (\Pi, I, i, j, x_i, (y_j, w_j))$, $\mathcal{S}$ aborts if $(i, j) \neq (i^*, j^*)$, or x_i and y_j are not output by the s_{i^*}-th session of party i^* and the $s_{j^*}^*$-th session of party j^*, respectively. Else, $\mathcal{S}$ chooses $b \leftarrow_r \{0,1\}$, returns $\mathrm{sk}_i' \leftarrow_r \{0,1\}^\kappa$ if $b = 0$. Otherwise, return the session key sk_i of sid.

Claim 1. *The probability that* S *will not abort in* $G_{1,0}$ *is at least* $\frac{1}{m^2 N^2}$.

Proof. This claim directly follows from the fact that S randomly chooses $i^*, j^* \leftarrow_r \{1, \ldots, N\}$ and $s_{i^*}, s_j^* \leftarrow_r \{1, \ldots, m\}$ independently from the view of $\mathcal{A}$. □

Game $G_{1,1}$. S behaves almost the same as in $G_{1,0}$ except in the following case:

- Send$_1(\Pi, R, j, i, x_i)$: If $(i, j) \neq (i^*, j^*)$, or it is not the s_j^*-th session of j^*, S answers the query as in Game $G_{1,0}$. Otherwise, it proceeds as follows:

  1'. Sample $r_j, f_j \leftarrow_r \chi_\beta$ and compute $y_j = ar_j + 2f_j$;

  2'. **Sample an invertible element** $d \leftarrow_r \chi_\gamma$, and compute $\hat{r}_j = s_j d + r_j$, $\hat{f}_j = e_j d + f_j$;

  3'. Go to step 4' with probability $\min\left(\frac{D_{\mathbb{Z}^{2n},\beta}(\mathbf{z})}{M D_{\mathbb{Z}^{2n},\beta,\mathbf{z}_1}(\mathbf{z})}, 1\right)$, where $\mathbf{z} \in \mathbb{Z}^{2n}$ is the coefficient vector of $\hat{r}_j$ concatenated with the coefficient vector of $\hat{f}_j$, and $\mathbf{z}_1 \in \mathbb{Z}^{2n}$ is the coefficient vector of $s_j d$ concatenated with the coefficient vector of $e_j d$; otherwise go back to step 1';

  4'. **Abort if there is a tuple** $((j, i, y_j, x_i), *)$ **in** L_1. **Else, add** $((j, i, y_j, x_i), d)$ **into** L_1. Then, sample $g_j \leftarrow_r \chi_\beta$ and compute $k_j = (p_i c + x_i)\hat{r}_j + 2cg_j$ where $c = H_1(i, j, x_i)$;

  5'. Compute $w_j = \mathsf{Cha}(k_j) \in \{0, 1\}^n$ and return (y_j, w_j) to $\mathcal{A}$;

  6'. Compute $\sigma_j = \mathsf{Mod}_2(k_j, w_j)$ and derive the session key $\mathsf{sk}_j = H_2(i, j, x_i, y_j, w_j, \sigma_j)$.

Let $F_{1,l}$ be the event that $\mathcal{A}$ outputs a guess b' that equals to b in Game $G_{1,l}$.

Claim 2. *If* $RLWE_{q,\beta}$ *is hard, then* $\Pr[F_{1,l}] = \Pr[F_{1,0}] - \mathrm{negl}(\kappa)$.

Proof. Since H_1 is a random oracle, Game $G_{1,0}$ and Game $G_{1,1}$ are identical if the adversary $\mathcal{A}$ does not make a H_1 query $((j, i, y_j, x_i), *)$ before S generates y_j. Thus, the claim follows if the probability that $\mathcal{A}$ makes such a query in both Games is negligible. Actually, if $\mathcal{A}$ can make the query before seeing y_j with non-negligible probability, we can construct an algorithm $\mathcal{B}$ that breaks the RLWE$_{q,\beta}$ assumption.

Formally, after given a ring-LWE challenge tuple $(u, \mathbf{b}) \in R_q \times R_q^\ell$ in matrix form for some polynomially bounded ℓ, $\mathcal{B}$ sets $a = u$ and behaves like in Game $G_{1,0}$ until $\mathcal{B}$ has to generate y_j for the s_j^*-th session of j^* intended for party i^*. Instead of generating a fresh y_j, $\mathcal{B}$ simply sets y_j as the first unused elements in $\mathbf{b} = (b_0, \ldots, b_{\ell-1})$, and checks if there is a tuple $((j, i, y_j, x_i), *)$ in L_1. If yes, it returns 1 and aborts, else it returns 0 and aborts.

It is easy to check that $\mathcal{A}$ has the same view as in $G_{1,0}$ and $G_{1,1}$ until the point that $\mathcal{B}$ has to compute y_j. Moreover, if $\mathbf{b} = (b_0 = ur_0 + 2f_0, \ldots, b_{\ell-1} = ur_{\ell-1} + 2f_{\ell-1})$ for some randomly choose $r_{\ell'}, f_{\ell'} \leftarrow_r \chi_\beta$ where $\ell' \in \{0, 1, \ldots, \ell - 1\}$, we have the probability that $\mathcal{A}$ will make the H_1 query with (j, i, y_j, x_i) is non-negligible by assumption. While if $\mathbf{b}$ is uniformly distributed over R_q^ℓ, we have the probability that $\mathcal{A}$ will make the H_1 query with (j, i, y_j, x_i) is negligible. This shows that $\mathcal{B}$ can be used to solve Ring-LWE assumption by interacting with $\mathcal{A}$. □

Game $G_{1,2}$. $\mathcal{S}$ behaves almost the same as in $G_{1,1}$ except in the following case:

- $\mathsf{Send}_1(\Pi, R, j, i, x_i)$: If $(i,j) \neq (i^*, j^*)$, or it is not the s_j^*-th session of j^*, $\mathcal{S}$ answers the query as in Game $G_{1,1}$. Otherwise, it proceeds as follows:
  1'. Sample an invertible element $d \leftarrow_r \chi_\gamma$, and **choose $\mathbf{z} \leftarrow_r D_{\mathbb{Z}^{2n}, \beta}$**;
  2'. **Parse $\mathbf{z}$ as two ring elements $\hat{r}_j, \hat{f}_j \in R_q$, and define** $y_j = a\hat{r}_j + 2\hat{f}_j - p_j d$;
  3'. **Go to step 4' with probability $1/M$; otherwise go back to step 1'**;
  4'. Abort if there is a tuple $((j, i, y_j, x_i), *)$ in L_1. Else, add $((j, i, y_j, x_i), d)$ into L_1. Then, sample $g_j \leftarrow_r \chi_\beta$ and compute $k_j = (p_i c + x_i)\hat{r}_j + 2cg_j$ where $c = H_1(i, j, x_i)$;
  5'. Compute $w_j = \mathsf{Cha}(k_j) \in \{0,1\}^n$ and return (y_j, w_j) to $\mathcal{A}$;
  6'. Compute $\sigma_j = \mathsf{Mod}_2(k_j, w_j)$ and derive the session key $\mathsf{sk}_j = H_2(i, j, x_i, y_j, w_j, \sigma_j)$.

Claim 3. *If $\beta = \omega(\alpha \gamma n \sqrt{n \log n})$, then $\Pr[F_{1,2}] = \Pr[F_{1,1}] - \mathsf{negl}(\kappa)$.*

Proof. By Lemma 1 and Lemma 2, we have that both $\|s_j d\| \leq \alpha \gamma n \sqrt{n}$ and $\|e_j d\| \leq \alpha \gamma n \sqrt{n}$ (in Game $G_{1,1}$) hold with overwhelming probability. This means that $\beta = \omega(\alpha \gamma n \sqrt{n \log n})$ satisfies the requirement in Theorem 1, and thus the distribution of $(d, \mathbf{z})$ in Game $G_{1,2}$ is statistically close to that in $G_{1,1}$. The claim follows from the fact that the equation $y_j = a\hat{r}_j + 2\hat{f}_j - p_j d$ holds in both Game $G_{1,1}$ and $G_{1,2}$. $\quad\square$

Game $G_{1,3}$. $\mathcal{S}$ behaves almost the same as in $G_{1,2}$, except for the following case:

- $\mathsf{Send}_0(\Pi, I, i, j)$: If $(i,j) \neq (i^*, j^*)$, or it is not the s_{i^*}-th session of i^*, $\mathcal{S}$ answers as in Game $G_{1,2}$. Otherwise, it proceeds as follows:
  1. Sample $r_i, f_i \leftarrow_r \chi_\beta$ and compute $x_i = ar_i + 2f_i$;
  2. **Sample an invertible element $c \leftarrow_r \chi_\gamma$, and compute $\hat{r}_i = s_i c + r_i$, $\hat{f}_i = e_i c + f_i$;**
  3. Go to step 4 with probability $\min\left(\frac{D_{\mathbb{Z}^{2n}, \beta}(\mathbf{z})}{M D_{\mathbb{Z}^{2n}, \beta, \mathbf{z}_1}(\mathbf{z})}, 1\right)$, where $\mathbf{z} \in \mathbb{Z}^{2n}$ is the coefficient vector of $\hat{r}_i$ concatenated with the coefficient vector of $\hat{f}_i$, and $\mathbf{z}_1 \in \mathbb{Z}^{2n}$ is the coefficient vector of $s_i c$ concatenated with the coefficient vector of $e_i c$; otherwise go back to step 1;
  4. **Abort if there is a tuple $((i, j, x_i), *)$ in L_1. Else, add $((i, j, x_i), c)$** into L_1. Return x_i to $\mathcal{A}$.

Claim 4. *If $RLWE_{q,\beta}$ is hard, then $\Pr[F_{1,3}] = \Pr[F_{1,2}] - \mathsf{negl}(\kappa)$.*

Proof. The proof is similar to the proof of Claim 2, we omit the details. $\quad\square$

Game $G_{1,4}$. $\mathcal{S}$ behaves almost the same as in $G_{1,3}$ except for the following case:

- $\mathsf{Send}_0(\Pi, I, i, j)$: If $(i,j) \neq (i^*, j^*)$, or it is not the s_{i^*}-th session of i^*, $\mathcal{S}$ answers as in Game $G_{1,3}$. Otherwise, it proceeds as follows:
  1. Sample an invertible element $c \leftarrow_r \chi_\gamma$, and **choose $\mathbf{z} \leftarrow_r D_{\mathbb{Z}^{2n}, \beta}$**;
  2. **Parse $\mathbf{z}$ as two ring elements $\hat{r}_i, \hat{f}_i \in R_q$, and define** $x_i = a\hat{r}_i + 2\hat{f}_i - p_i c$;

3. **Go to step 4 with probability** $1/M$; **otherwise go back to step 1**;
4. Abort if there is a tuple $((i,j,x_i),*)$ in L_1. Else, add $((i,j,x_i),c)$ into L_1. Return x_i to $\mathcal{A}$.

Claim 5. *If* $\beta = \omega(\alpha\gamma n\sqrt{n\log n})$, *then* $\Pr[F_{1,4}] = \Pr[F_{1,3}] - \text{negl}(\kappa)$.

Proof. The proof is similar to the proof of Claim 3, we omit the details. $\square$

Game $G_{1,5}$. $\mathcal{S}$ behaves almost the same as in $G_{1,4}$ except for the following case:

- $\mathsf{Send}_2(\Pi, I, i, j, x_i, (y_j, w_j))$: If $(i,j) \neq (i^*, j^*)$, or it is not the s_{i^*}-th session of i^*, $\mathcal{S}$ behaves as in Game $G_{1,4}$. Otherwise, if (y_j, w_j) is output by the s_j^*-th session of party j^*, $\mathcal{S}$ **sets** $\text{sk}_i = \text{sk}_j$, where sk_j is the session key of $\text{sid} = (\Pi, R, j, i, x_i, (y_j, w_j))$. Else, $\mathcal{S}$ samples $g_i \leftarrow_r \chi_\beta$ and computes $k_i = (p_j d + y_j)\hat{r}_i + 2dg_i$ where $d = H_1(j, i, y_j, x_i)$. Finally, it computes $\sigma_i = \text{Mod}_2(k_i, w_j)$ and derives the session key $\text{sk}_i = H_2(i, j, x_i, y_j, w_j, \sigma_i)$.

Claim 6. $\Pr[F_{1,5}] = \Pr[F_{1,4}] - \text{negl}(\kappa)$.

Proof. This claim follows since $G_{1,5}$ is just a conceptual change of $G_{1,4}$ by the correctness of the protocol. $\square$

Game $G_{1,6}$. $\mathcal{S}$ behaves almost the same as in $G_{1,5}$ except in the following case:

- $\mathsf{Send}_0(\Pi, I, i, j)$: If $(i,j) \neq (i^*, j^*)$, or it is not the s_{i^*}-th session of i^*, $\mathcal{S}$ answers as in Game $G_{1,5}$. Otherwise, it proceeds as follows:
  1. Sample an invertible element $c \leftarrow_r \chi_\gamma$, and **choose** $\hat{x}_i \leftarrow_r R_q$;
  2. **Define** $x_i = \hat{x}_i - p_i c$;
  3. Go to step 4 with probability $1/M$; otherwise go back to step 1;
  4. Abort if there is a tuple $((i,j,x_i),*)$ in L_1. Else, add $((i,j,x_i),c)$ into L_1. Return x_i to $\mathcal{A}$.
- $\mathsf{Send}_2(\Pi, I, i, j, x_i, (y_j, w_j))$: If $(i,j) \neq (i^*, j^*)$, or it is not the s_{i^*}-th session of i^*, or (y_j, w_j) is output by the s_j^*-th session of party j^*, $\mathcal{S}$ behaves the same as in $G_{1,5}$. Otherwise, it proceeds as follows:
  5. **Randomly choose** $k_i \leftarrow_r R_q$;
  6. Compute $\sigma_i = \text{Mod}_2(k_i, w_j)$ and derive the session key $\text{sk}_i = H_2(i, j, x_i, y_j, w_j, \sigma_i)$.

Note that in Game $G_{1,6}$, we have made two changes: 1) The term $a\hat{r}_i + 2\hat{f}_i$ in Game $G_{1,5}$ is replaced by a uniformly chosen element $\hat{x} \in R_q$ at random; 2) The value $k_i = (p_j d + y_j)\hat{r}_i + 2dg_i$ in Game $G_{1,5}$ is replaced by a uniformly chosen string $k_i \leftarrow_r R_q$, when (y_j, w_j') is output by the s_j^*-th session of party j^* but $w_j \neq w_j'$. In the following, we will employ the "deferred analysis" proof technique in [69], which informally allows us to proceed the security games by patiently postponing some tough probability analysis to a later game. Specially, for $\ell = 5, 6, 7$, denote $Q_{1,l}$ as the event in Game $G_{1,\ell}$ that 1) (y_j, w_j') is output by the s_j^*-th session of party j^* but $w_j \neq w_j'$; and 2) $\mathcal{A}$ makes a query to H_2 that is exactly used to generate the session key sk_i for the s_{i^*}-th session of party i^*, *i.e.*, $\mathrm{sk}_i = H_2(i, j, x_i, y_j, w_j, \sigma_i)$ for $\sigma_i = \mathsf{Mod}_2(k_i, w_j)$. Ideally, if $Q_{1,5}$ does not happen, then the adversary cannot distinguish whether a correctly computed k_i or a randomly chosen one is used (since H_2 is a random oracle, and the adversary gains no information about k_i even if it obtains the session key sk_i). However, we cannot prove the claim immediately due to technical reason. Instead, we will show that $\Pr[Q_{1,5}] \approx \Pr[Q_{1,6}] \approx \Pr[Q_{1,7}]$ and $\Pr[Q_{1,7}]$ is negligible in κ.

Claim 7. *If $RLWE_{q,\beta}$ is hard, $\Pr[Q_{1,6}] = \Pr[Q_{1,5}] - \mathrm{negl}(\kappa)$, and $\Pr[F_{1,6}|\neg Q_{1,6}] = \Pr[F_{1,5}|\neg Q_{1,5}] - \mathrm{negl}(\kappa)$.*

Proof. Note that H_2 is a random oracle, the event $Q_{1,5}$ is independent from the distribution of the corresponding sk_i. Namely, no matter whether or not $\mathcal{A}$ obtains sk_i, $\Pr[Q_{1,5}]$ is the same, which also holds for $\Pr[Q_{1,6}]$. In addition, under the $RLWE_{q,\beta}$ assumption, we have $\hat{x}_i = a\hat{r}_i + 2\hat{f}_i$ in $G_{1,5}$ is computationally indistinguishable from uniform distribution over R_q, and thus the public information (*i.e.*, static public keys and public transcripts) in $G_{1,5}$ and $G_{1,6}$ is computationally indistinguishable. In particular, the view of the adversary $\mathcal{A}$ before $Q_{1,\ell}$ happens for $\ell = 5, 6$ is computationally indistinguishable, which implies that $\Pr[Q_{1,6}] = \Pr[Q_{1,5}] - \mathrm{negl}(\kappa)$. Besides, if $Q_{1,l}$ for $l = 5, 6$ does not happen, the distribution of sk_i is the same in both games. In other words, $\Pr[F_{1,6}|\neg Q_{1,6}] = \Pr[F_{1,5}|\neg Q_{1,5}] - \mathrm{negl}(\kappa)$. □

Game $G_{1,7}$. $\mathcal{S}$ behaves almost the same as in $G_{1,6}$ except in the following case:

- $\mathsf{Send}_1(\Pi, R, j, i, x_i)$: If $(i, j) \neq (i^*, j^*)$, or it is not the s_j^*-th session of j^*, $\mathcal{S}$ answers the query as in Game $G_{1,6}$. Otherwise, it proceeds as follows:
  - $1'$. Sample an invertible element $d \leftarrow_r \chi_\gamma$, and **choose** $\hat{y}_j \leftarrow_r R_q$;
  - $2'$. **Define** $y_j = \hat{y}_j - p_j d$;
  - $3'$. Go to step $4'$ with probability $1/M$; otherwise go back to step $1'$;
  - $4'$. Abort if there is a tuple $((j, i, y_j, x_i), *)$ in L_1. Else, add $((j, i, y_j, x_i), d)$ into L_1. Then, the simulator $\mathcal{S}$ **uniformly chooses** $k_j \leftarrow_r R_q$ **at random**;
  - $5'$. Compute $w_j = \mathsf{Cha}(k_j) \in \{0, 1\}^n$ and return (y_j, w_j) to $\mathcal{A}$;
  - $6'$. Compute $\sigma_j = \mathsf{Mod}_2(k_j, w_j)$ and derive the session key $\mathrm{sk}_j = H_2(i, j, x_i, y_j, w_j, \sigma_j)$.

Claim 8. *Let n be a power of 2, prime $q > 203$ satisfying $q = 1 \mod 2n$, $\beta = \omega(\alpha\gamma n\sqrt{n \log n})$. Then, if $RLWE_{q,\beta}$ is hard, Game $G_{1,6}$ and $G_{1,7}$ are computationally indistinguishable. In particular, we have $\Pr[Q_{1,7}] = \Pr[Q_{1,6}] - \mathrm{negl}(\kappa)$, and $\Pr[F_{1,7}|\neg Q_{1,7}] = \Pr[F_{1,6}|\neg Q_{1,6}] - \mathrm{negl}(\kappa)$.*

Proof. Assume there is an adversary that distinguishes Game $G_{1,6}$ and $G_{1,7}$, we now construct a distinguisher $\mathcal{D}$ that solves the Ring-LWE problem. Specifically, let $(\mathbf{u} = (u_0, \ldots, u_{\ell-1}), \mathbf{B}) \in R_q^\ell \times R_q^{\ell \times \ell}$ be a challenge Ring-LWE tuple in matrix form for some polynomially bounded ℓ, $\mathcal{D}$ first sets public parameter $a = u_0$. Then, it randomly chooses invertible elements $\mathbf{v} = (v_1, \ldots, v_{\ell-1}) \leftarrow \chi_\gamma^{\ell-1}$, and compute $\hat{\mathbf{u}} = (v_1 \cdot u_1, \ldots, v_{\ell-1}u_{\ell-1})$. Finally, $\mathcal{D}$ behaves the same as $\mathcal{S}$ in Game $G_{1,6}$, except for the following cases:

- $\text{Send}_0(\Pi, I, i, j)$: If $(i,j) \neq (i^*, j^*)$, or it is not the s_{i^*}-th session of i^*, $\mathcal{S}$ answers as in Game $G_{1,6}$. Otherwise, it proceeds as follows:
  1. **Set c and $\hat{x}_i$ be the first unused element in $\mathbf{v}$ and $\hat{\mathbf{u}}$, respectively**;
  2. Define $x_i = \hat{x}_i - p_i c$;
  3. Go to step 4 with probability $1/M$; otherwise go back to step 1;
  4. Abort if there is a tuple $((i,j,x_i), *)$ in L_1. Else, add $((i,j,x_i), c)$ into L_1. Return x_i to $\mathcal{A}$.
- $\text{Send}_1(\Pi, R, j, i, x_i)$: If $(i,j) \neq (i^*, j^*)$, or it is not the s_j^*-th session of j^*, $\mathcal{S}$ answers the query as in Game $G_{1,6}$. Otherwise, it proceeds as follows:
  1'. Sample an invertible element $d \leftarrow_r \chi_\gamma$, and **set $\hat{y}_j$ be the first unused element in $\mathbf{b}_0 = (b_{0,0}, \ldots, b_{0,\ell-1})$**;
  2'. Define $y_j = \hat{y}_j - p_j d$;
  3'. Go to step 4' with probability $1/M$; otherwise go back to step 1';
  4'. Abort if there is a tuple $((j,i,y_j,x_i), *)$ in L_1. Else, add $((j,i,y_j,x_i), d)$ into L_1. Then, let $\ell_1 \geq 1$ be the index that $\hat{x}_i$ appears in $\hat{\mathbf{u}}$, and $\ell_2 \geq 0$ be the index that $\hat{y}_j$ appears in $\mathbf{b}_0$, the simulator $\mathcal{S}$ **sets $k_j = cb_{\ell_1, \ell_2}$**;
  5'. Compute $w_j = \text{Cha}(k_j) \in \{0,1\}^n$ and return (y_j, w_j) to $\mathcal{A}$;
  6'. Compute $\sigma_j = \text{Mod}_2(k_j, w_j)$ and derive the session key $\text{sk}_j = H_2(i, j, x_i, y_j, w_j, \sigma_j)$.

Since $\mathbf{v}$ is randomly and independently chosen from $\chi_\gamma^{\ell-1}$, the distribution of c is identical to that in Game $G_{1,6}$ and Game $G_{1,7}$. Besides, since each v_i is invertible in R_q, we have $\hat{\mathbf{u}}$ is uniformly distributed over $R_q^{\ell-1}$, which shows that the distribution of $\hat{x}_i$ is identical to that in Game $G_{1,6}$ and Game $G_{1,7}$. Moreover, if $(\mathbf{u}, \mathbf{B}) \in R_q^\ell \times R_q^{\ell \times \ell}$ is a Ring-LWE challenge tuple in matrix form, we have $\hat{y}_j = u_0 s_{\ell_2} + 2e_{0,\ell_2}$ and $k_j = cb_{\ell_1,\ell_2} = cu_{\ell_1} s_{\ell_2} + 2ce_{\ell_1,\ell_2} = \hat{x}_i s_{\ell_2} + 2ce_{\ell_1,\ell_2} = (x_i + p_i c)s_{\ell_2} + 2ce_{\ell_1,\ell_2}$ for some randomly chosen $s_{\ell_2}, e_{0,\ell_2}, e_{\ell_1,\ell_2} \leftarrow_r \chi_\beta$. This shows that the view of $\mathcal{A}$ is the same as in Game $G_{1,6}$. While if $(\mathbf{u}, \mathbf{B}) \in R_q^\ell \times R_q^{\ell \times \ell}$ is uniformly distributed over $R_q^\ell \times R_q^{\ell \times \ell}$, we have both $\hat{y}_j$ and $k_j = cb_{\ell_1,\ell_2}$ are uniformly distributed over R_q (since c is invertible). Thus, the view of $\mathcal{A}$ is the same as in $G_{1,7}$. In all, we have shown that $\mathcal{D}$ can be used to break Ring-LWE assumption if $\mathcal{A}$ can distinguish Game $G_{1,6}$ and $G_{1,7}$. $\qquad\square$

Claim 9. *If $0.97n > 2\kappa$, we have $\Pr[Q_{1,7}] = \text{negl}(\kappa)$*

Proof. Let $k_{i,\ell}$ be the element "computed" by $\mathcal{S}$ for the s_i^*-th session at party i^* in Games $G_{1,\ell}$, and $k_{j,\ell}$ be the element "computed" by $\mathcal{S}$ for the s_j^*-th session at party j^*. By the correctness of the protocol, we have that $k_{i,5} = k_{j,5} + \hat{g}$ for some $\hat{g}$ with small coefficients in $G_{1,5}$. Since we have proven that the view of the adversary before $Q_{1,\ell}$ happens in Game $G_{1,5}$, $G_{1,6}$ and $G_{1,7}$ is computationally indistinguishable, the equation $k_{i,7} = k_{j,7} + \hat{g}'$ should still hold for some $\hat{g}'$ with small coefficients in the adversary's view until $Q_{1,7}$ happens in $G_{1,7}$. Let (y_j, w_j) be output by the s_j^*-th session of party $j = j^*$, and (y_j, w_j') be the message that is used to complete the test session (*i.e.*, the s_{i^*}-th session of party $i = i^*$). Note that $k_{j,7}$ is randomly chosen from R_q, and the adversary can only obtain the information of $k_{j,7}$ from the public w_j, the dependence of $\hat{g}$ on k_j should be totally determined by the information of w_j. Thus, we have that

$\sigma'_i = \mathsf{Mod}_2(k_i, w'_j) = \mathsf{Mod}_2(k_j + \hat{g}', w'_j)$ conditioned on w_j has high min-entropy by Lemma 4. In other words, the probability that the adversary makes a query $H_2(i, j, x_i, y_j, w'_j, \sigma'_i)$ is at most $2^{-0.97n} + \mathsf{negl}(\kappa)$, which is negligible in κ.   □

Claim 10. $\Pr[F_{1,7} | \neg Q_{1,7}] = 1/2 + \mathsf{negl}(\kappa)$

Proof. Let (y_j, w_j) be output by the s_j^*-th session of party $j = j^*$, (y_j, w'_j) be the message that is used to complete the test session (*i.e.*, the s_{i^*}-th session of party $i = i^*$). We distinguish the following two cases:

- $w_j = w'_j$: In this case, we have $\mathsf{sk}_i = \mathsf{sk}_j = H_2(i, j, x_i, y_j, w_j, \sigma_i)$, where $\sigma_i = \sigma_j = \mathsf{Mod}_2(k_j, w_j)$. Note that in $G_{1,7}$, k_j is randomly chosen from the uniform distribution over R_q, we have that $\sigma_j \in \{0, 1\}^n$ (conditioned on w_j) has min-entropy at least $0.97n$ by Lemma 4. Thus, the probability that $\mathcal{A}$ has made a H_2 query with σ_i is less than $2^{-0.97n} + \mathsf{negl}(\kappa)$.
- $w_j \neq w'_j$: By assumption that $Q_{1,7}$ does not happen, we have that $\mathcal{A}$ will never make a H_2 query with σ_i.

The probability that $\mathcal{A}$ has made a H_2 query with σ_i is negligible. This claim follows from the fact that if the adversary does not make a query with σ_i exactly, the distribution of sk_i is uniform over $\{0, 1\}^\kappa$ due to the random oracle property of H_2, *i.e.*, $\Pr[F_{1,7} | \neg Q_{1,7}] = 1/2 + \mathsf{negl}(\kappa)$.   □

Combining the claims 1~10, we have that Lemma 5 follows.

5   One-Pass Protocol from Ring-LWE

As MQV [20] and HMQV [5], our AKE protocol has a one-pass variant, which only consists of a single message from one party to the other. Let $a \in R_q$ be the global public parameter uniformly chosen from R_q at random, and M be a constant. Let $p_i = as_i + 2e_i \in R_q$ be party i's static public key, where (s_i, e_i) is the corresponding static secret key; both s_i and e_i are taken from the distribution χ_α. Similarly, party j has static public key $p_j = as_j + 2e_j$ and static secret key (s_j, e_j). The other parameters and notations used here are the same as that in Section 3.

Initiation. Party i proceeds as follows:

1. Sample $r_i, f_i \leftarrow_r \chi_\beta$ and compute $x_i = ar_i + 2f_i$;
2. Compute $c = H_1(i, j, x_i)$, $\hat{r}_i = s_i c + r_i$ and $\hat{f}_i = e_i c + f_i$;
3. Go to step 4 with probability $\min\left(\frac{D_{\mathbb{Z}^{2n}, \beta}(\mathbf{z})}{M D_{\mathbb{Z}^{2n}, \beta, \mathbf{z}_1}(\mathbf{z})}, 1\right)$, where $\mathbf{z} \in \mathbb{Z}^{2n}$ is the coefficient vector of $\hat{r}_i$ concatenated with the coefficient vector of $\hat{f}_i$, and $\mathbf{z}_1 \in \mathbb{Z}^{2n}$ is the coefficient vector of $s_i c$ concatenated with the coefficient vector of $e_i c$; otherwise go back to step 1;
4. Sample $g_i \leftarrow_r \chi_\beta$ and compute $k_i = p_j \hat{r}_i + 2g_i$ where $c = H_1(i, j, x_i)$;
5. Compute $w_i = \mathsf{Cha}(k_i) \in \{0, 1\}^n$ and send (y_i, w_i) to party j;
6. Compute $\sigma_i = \mathsf{Mod}_2(k_i, w_i)$, and derive the session key $\mathsf{sk}_i = H_2(i, j, x_i, w_i, \sigma_i)$.

Finish. Party j receives the pair (x_i, w_i) from party i, and proceeds as follows:

1′. Sample $g_j \leftarrow_r \chi_\alpha$, compute $k_j = (p_i c + x_i)s_j + 2cg_j$ where $c = H_1(i, j, x_i)$;
2′. Compute $\sigma_j = \mathsf{Mod}_2(k_j, w_i)$ and derive the session key $\mathrm{sk}_j = H_2(i, j, x_i, w_i, \sigma_j)$.

The correctness of the protocol simply follows from the fact that $k_i = p_j \hat{r}_i + 2g_i = (as_j + 2e_j)(s_i c + r_i) + 2g_i \approx a(s_i c + r_i)s_j + 2(e_i c + f_i)s_j + 2cg_j = k_j$. The security of the protocol cannot be proven in the BR model with party corruption, since the one-pass protocol inherently can not provide wPFS due to the lack of messages from the receiver j. Besides, the protocol cannot prevent a replay attack without additional measures like keeping a state or using synchronized time. However, we can prove its security in a weak model similar to [5] which avoids the (above) inherent insufficiencies for one-pass protocols. Since the proof is parallel to the two-pass one, we omit the details.

Finally, we remark that the one-pass protocol can essentially be used as a KEM, and can be transformed into a CCA-secure encryption scheme in the random oracle model by combining it with a CPA-secure symmetric-key encryption scheme together with a MAC algorithm in a standard way (where both keys are derived from the session key in the one-pass protocol). The resulting encryption has two interesting properties: 1) it allows the receiver to verify the sender's identity, but no one else can verify it (since only the receiver can compute the session key, *i.e.*, it provides some kind of sender authentication); 2) the sender can deny having created such a ciphertext, because the receiver can also create such a ciphertext by itself (*i.e.*, it is a deniable encryption).

6   Concrete Parameters and Timings

In this section, we present concrete choices of parameters, and the timings in a proof-of-concept implementation. Our selection of parameters for our AKE protocols can be found in Table 2. Those parameters were chosen such that the correctness property is satisfied with high probability and with the choice of different levels of security.

For the correctness of our two-pass protocol, the error term must be bounded by $\|\tilde{g}_i - \tilde{g}_j\|_\infty < q/8$. Note that $\tilde{g}_i = (e_j d + f_j)(s_i c + r_i) + dg_i$, and $\tilde{g}_j = (e_i c + f_i)(s_j d + r_j) + cg_j$, where $e_i, e_j \leftarrow_r \chi_\alpha$, $c, d \leftarrow_r \chi_\gamma$, and $f_i, f_j, r_i, r_j, g_i, g_j \leftarrow_r \chi_\beta$. Due to the symmetry, we only estimate the size of $\|\tilde{g}_i\|_\infty$. At this point, we use the following fact about the product of two Gaussian distributed random values (as stated in [35]). Let $x \in R$ and $y \in R$ be two polynomials whose coefficients are distributed according to a discrete Gaussian distribution with standard deviation σ and τ, respectively. The individual coefficients of the product xy are then (approximately) normally distributed around zero with standard deviation $\sigma \tau \sqrt{n}$ where n is the degree of the polynomial.

In our case, it means that we have $\|(e_j d + f_j)(s_i c + r_i)\|_\infty \leq 6\beta^2 \sqrt{n}$ and $\|dg_i\|_\infty \leq 6\gamma\beta\sqrt{n}$ with overwhelming probability (since erfc(6) is about 2^{-55}). Note that the distributions of $e_j d + f_j$ and $s_i c + r_i$ are both according to χ_β since we use rejection sampling in the protocol. Now, to choose an appropriate β

Table 2. Choices of parameters (The bound 6α with $\mathrm{erfc}(6) \approx 2^{-55}$ is used to estimate the size of secret keys)

Protocol	Choice of Parameters	n	Security	α	τ	$\log \beta$	$\log q$ (bits)	Size (KB)			
								pk	sk (expt.)	init. msg	resp. msg
Two-pass	I_1	1024	80 bits	3.397	12	16.1	45	5.625	1.5	5.625	5.75
	I_2		75 bits	3.397	24	17.1	47	5.875	1.5	5.875	6.0
	II_1	2048	230 bits	3.397	12	17.1	47	11.75	3.0	11.75	12.0
	II_2		210 bits	3.397	36	18.7	50	12.50	3.0	12.50	12.75
One-pass	III_1	1024	160 bits	3.397	12	16.1	30	3.75	1.5	3.875	-
	III_2		140 bits	3.397	36	17.7	32	4.0	1.5	4.125	-
	IV_1	2048	360 bits	3.397	12	17.1	32	8.0	3.0	8.25	-
	IV_2		350 bits	3.397	36	18.7	33	8.25	3.0	8.5	-

we set $\eta = 1/2$ in Lemma 1 such that $\|e_j d\|, \|s_i c\| \leq 1/2\alpha\gamma n$ with probability at most $2 \cdot 0.943^{-n}$. Hence, for $n \geq 1024$, we get a potential decryption error with only a probability about 2^{-87}. In order to make the rejection sampling work, it is sufficient to set $\beta \geq \tau \cdot 1/2\alpha\gamma n = 1/2\tau\alpha\gamma n$ for some constant τ (which is much better than the worst-case bound $\beta = \omega(\alpha\gamma\sqrt{n \log n})$ in Theorem 1). For instance, if $\tau = 12$, we have an expect number of rejection sampling about $M = 2.72$ and a statistical distance about $\frac{2^{-100}}{M}$ by Theorem 1. For such a choice of β, we can safely assume that $\|\tilde{g}_i\|_\infty \leq 6\beta^2\sqrt{n} + 6\gamma\beta\sqrt{n} \leq 7\beta^2\sqrt{n}$. Thus, it is enough to set $16 \cdot 7\beta^2\sqrt{n} < q$ for correctness of the protocol in Section 3.

Though the Ring-LWE problem enjoys a worst-case connection to some hard problems (*e.g.*, SIVP [29]) on ideal lattices, the connection as summarized in Proposition 1 seems less powerful to estimate the actual security for concrete choices of parameters. In order to assess the concrete security of our parameters, we use the approach of [70], which investigates the two most efficient ways to solve the underlying (Ring-)LWE problem, namely the embedding and decoding attacks. As opposed to [70], the decoding attack is more efficient against our instances because the Ring-LWE case with $m \geq 2n$ is close to the optimal attack dimension for the corresponding attacks. The decoding attack first uses a lattice reduction algorithm, such as BKZ [71] / BKZ 2.0 [72] and then applies a decoding algorithm like the ones in [73–75]. Finally, the closest vector is returned as the error polynomial, and the secret polynomial is recovered.

As recommended in [74,76], it is enough to set the Gaussian parameter $\alpha \geq 3.2$ so that the discrete Gaussian $D_{\mathbb{Z}^n,\alpha}$ approximates the continuous Gaussian D_α extremely well.[6] In our experiment, we fix $\alpha = 3.397$ for a better performance of the Gaussian sampling algorithm in [39]. As for the choices of γ, we set $\gamma = \alpha$ for simplicity (actually such a choice in our experiments works very well: no rejection happened in 1000 hash evaluations). In Table 2, we set all other parameters β, n, q for our two-pass protocol to satisfy the correctness condition. We also give the parameter choices of our one-pass protocol (in this case, we

---

[6] Only α is considered because $\beta \gg \alpha$, and the (Ring-)LWE problem becomes harder as α grows bigger (for a fixed modulus q).

can save a factor of β in q due to the asymmetry). Note that n is required to be a power of 2 in our protocol (*i.e.*, it is very sparsely distributed[7]). We present several candidate choices of parameters for $n = 1024, 2048$, and estimate the sizes of public keys, secret keys, and communication overheads in Table 2.

Table 3. Timings of proof-of-concept implementations in ms

Protocol	Parameters	τ	Initiation	Response	Finish	Protocol	Parameters	τ	Initiation	Finish
Two-pass	I_1	12	22.05 ms	30.61 ms	4.35 ms	One-pass	III_1	12	26.17 ms	3.64 ms
	I_2	24	14.26 ms	19.18 ms	4.41 ms		III_2	36	14.57 ms	3.70 ms
	II_1	12	49.77 ms	60.31 ms	9.44 ms		IV_1	12	53.78 ms	7.75 ms
	II_2	36	25.40 ms	36.96 ms	9.59 ms		IV_2	36	32.28 ms	7.94 ms

We have implemented our AKE protocol by using the NTL library compiled with the option NTL_GMP_LIP = on (*i.e.*, building NTL using the GNU Multi-Precision package). The implementations are written in C++ without any parallel computations or multi-thread programming techniques. The program is run on a Dell Optiplex 780 computer with Ubuntu 12.04 TLS 64-bit system, a 2.83GHz Intel Core 2 Quad CPU and 3.8GB RAM. We use an n-dimensional Fast Fourier Transform (FFT) for the multiplications of two ring elements [78,79], and the CDT algorithm [80] as a tool for hashing to $D_{\mathbb{Z}^n, \gamma}$ and sampling from $D_{\mathbb{Z}^n, \alpha}$, but the DDLL algorithm [39] for sampling from $D_{\mathbb{Z}^n, \beta}$ (because the CDT algorithm has to store large precomputed values for a big β). In Table 3, we present the average timings of each operation (in millisecond, ms) for 1000 executions. Since our protocols also allow some precomputations like sampling Gaussian distributions offline, the timings can be greatly reduced if this is considered in practice. Finally, we note that our implementation has not undergone any real optimization, and it can be much improved in practice.

7   Conclusions and Open Problems

In this paper, a two-pass AKE and its one-pass variant are proposed. Both protocols are carefully built upon on the algebraic structure of (Ring-)LWE problems and several recent developments in lattice-based cryptography, and are proven secure based on the hardness of Ring-LWE in the random oracle model. However, the literature shows that the use of random oracle is delicate for proving quantum resistance [51]. It is of great interest to investigate the quantum security of our protocol, or to design an efficient protocol without the random oracle heuristic (and the need of rewinding).

---

[7] We remark such a choice of n is not necessary, but it gives a simple analysis and implementation. In practice, one might use the techniques for Ring-LWE cryptography in [77] to give a tighter choice of parameters for desired security levels.

Acknowledgments. Jiang Zhang and Zhenfeng Zhang are supported by China's 973 program (No. 2013CB338003) and the National Natural Science Foundation of China (No. 61170278, 91118006). Jintai Ding is partially supported by the Charles Phelps Taft fund. Özgür Dagdelen is supported by the German Federal Ministry of Education and Research (BMBF) within EC-SPRIDE and by the DFG as part of project P1 within the CRC 1119 CROSSING. We would like to thank Johannes Buchmann, Lily Chen, Oded Regev, Adi Shamir, Tsuyoshi Takagi and Xiang Xie for useful discussions, and the anonymous reviewers of EUROCRYPT 2015 for helpful comments and suggestions.

References

1. Diffie, W., Hellman, M.: New directions in cryptography. IEEE Transactions on Information Theory **22**, 644–654 (1976)
2. Bellare, M., Rogaway, P.: Entity authentication and key distribution. In: Stinson, D.R. (ed.) CRYPTO 1993. LNCS, vol. 773, pp. 232–249. Springer, Heidelberg (1994)
3. Canetti, R., Krawczyk, H.: Analysis of key-exchange protocols and their use for building secure channels. In: Pfitzmann, B. (ed.) EUROCRYPT 2001. LNCS, vol. 2045, pp. 453–474. Springer, Heidelberg (2001)
4. LaMacchia, B.A., Lauter, K., Mityagin, A.: Stronger security of authenticated key exchange. In: Susilo, W., Liu, J.K., Mu, Y. (eds.) ProvSec 2007. LNCS, vol. 4784, pp. 1–16. Springer, Heidelberg (2007)
5. Krawczyk, H.: HMQV: a high-performance secure diffie-hellman protocol. In: Shoup, V. (ed.) CRYPTO 2005. LNCS, vol. 3621, pp. 546–566. Springer, Heidelberg (2005)
6. Cremers, C., Feltz, M.: Beyond eCK: perfect forward secrecy under actor compromise and ephemeral-key reveal. In: Foresti, S., Yung, M., Martinelli, F. (eds.) ESORICS 2012. LNCS, vol. 7459, pp. 734–751. Springer, Heidelberg (2012)
7. Harkins, D., Carrel, D., et al.: The internet key exchange (IKE). Technical report, RFC 2409, November 1998
8. Kaufman, C., Hoffman, P., Nir, Y., Eronen, P.: Internet key exchange protocol version 2 (IKEv2). Technical report, RFC 5996, September 2010
9. Krawczyk, H.: SIGMA: the 'SIGn-and-MAc' approach to authenticated diffie-hellman and its use in the IKE protocols. In: Boneh, D. (ed.) CRYPTO 2003. LNCS, vol. 2729, pp. 400–425. Springer, Heidelberg (2003)
10. Freier, A.: The SSL protocol version 3.0 (1996). http://wp.netscape.com/eng/ssl3/draft302.txt
11. Dierks, T.: The transport layer security (TLS) protocol version 1.2 (2008)
12. Krawczyk, H., Paterson, K.G., Wee, H.: On the security of the TLS protocol: a systematic analysis. In: Canetti, R., Garay, J.A. (eds.) CRYPTO 2013, Part I. LNCS, vol. 8042, pp. 429–448. Springer, Heidelberg (2013)
13. Mavrogiannopoulos, N., Vercauteren, F., Velichkov, V., Preneel, B.: A cross-protocol attack on the TLS protocol. In: CCS, pp. 62–72 (2012)
14. Giesen, F., Kohlar, F., Stebila, D.: On the security of TLS renegotiation. In: CCS, pp. 87–398 (2013)
15. Brzuska, C., Fischlin, M., Smart, N.P., Warinschi, B., Williams, S.C.: Less is more: relaxed yet composable security notions for key exchange. Int. J. Inf. Sec. **12**, 267–297 (2013)

16. Dagdelen, Ö., Fischlin, M.: Security analysis of the extended access control protocol for machine readable travel documents. In: Burmester, M., Tsudik, G., Magliveras, S., Ilić, I. (eds.) ISC 2010. LNCS, vol. 6531, pp. 54–68. Springer, Heidelberg (2011)

17. Dagdelen, Ö., Fischlin, M., Gagliardoni, T., Marson, G.A., Mittelbach, A., Onete, C.: A cryptographic analysis of OPACITY. In: Crampton, J., Jajodia, S., Mayes, K. (eds.) ESORICS 2013. LNCS, vol. 8134, pp. 345–362. Springer, Heidelberg (2013)

18. Degabriele, J.P., Fehr, V., Fischlin, M., Gagliardoni, T., Günther, F., Marson, G.A., Mittelbach, A., Paterson, K.G.: Unpicking PLAID. In: Chen, L., Mitchell, C. (eds.) SSR 2014. LNCS, vol. 8893, pp. 1–25. Springer, Heidelberg (2014)

19. Matsumoto, T., Takashima, Y.: On seeking smart public-key-distribution systems. IEICE Transactions (1976–1990) **69**, 99–106 (1986)

20. Menezes, A., Qu, M., Vanstone, S.: Some new key agreement protocols providing mutual implicit authentication. In: SAC, pp. 22–32 (1995)

21. ANS X9.42-2001: Public key cryptography for the financial services industry: Agreement of symmetric keys using discrete logarithm cryptography (2001)

22. ANS X9.63-2001: Public key cryptography for the financial services industry: Key agreement and key transport using elliptic curve cryptography (2001)

23. ISO/IEC: 11770–3:2008 information technology - security techniques - key management - part 3: Mechanisms using asymmetric techniques (2008)

24. IEEE 1363: IEEE std 1363–2000: Standard specifications for public key cryptography. IEEE, August 2000

25. Barker, E., Chen, L., Roginsky, A., Smid, M.: Recommendation for pair-wise key establishment schemes using discrete logarithm cryptography. NIST Special Publication **800**, 56A (2013)

26. Yao, A.C.C., Zhao, Y.: OAKE: A new family of implicitly authenticated Diffie-Hellman protocols. In: CCS, pp. 1113–1128 (2013)

27. Shor, P.: Polynomial-time algorithms for prime factorization and discrete logarithms on a quantum computer. SIAM Journal on Computing **26**, 1484–1509 (1997)

28. Chen, L.: Practical impacts on qutumn computing. In: Quantum-Safe-Crypto Workshop at the European Telecommunications Standards Institute (2013). http://docbox.etsi.org/Workshop/2013/201309_CRYPTO/S05_DEPLOYMENT/NIST_CHEN.pdf.

29. Lyubashevsky, V., Peikert, C., Regev, O.: On ideal lattices and learning with errors over rings. In: Gilbert, H. (ed.) EUROCRYPT 2010. LNCS, vol. 6110, pp. 1–23. Springer, Heidelberg (2010)

30. Ducas, L., Durmus, A.: Ring-LWE in polynomial rings. In: PKC, pp. 34–51 (2012)

31. Blake-Wilson, S., Johnson, D., Menezes, A.: Key agreement protocols and their security analysis. In: Proceedings of the 6th IMA International Conference on Cryptography and Coding, Springer-Verlag, London, UK, pp. 30–45 (1997)

32. Brzuska, C., Fischlin, M., Warinschi, B., Williams, S.C.: Composability of Bellare-Rogaway key exchange protocols. In: CCS, pp. 51–62 (2011)

33. Ding, J., Xie, X., Lin, X.: A simple provably secure key exchange scheme based on the learning with errors problem. Cryptology ePrint Archive, Report 2012/688 (2012)

34. Peikert, C.: Lattice cryptography for the internet. In: Mosca, M. (ed.) PQCrypto 2014. LNCS, vol. 8772, pp. 197–219. Springer, Heidelberg (2014)

35. Bos, J.W., Costello, C., Naehrig, M., Stebila, D.: Post-quantum key exchange for the TLS protocol from the ring learning with errors problem. Cryptology ePrint Archive, Report 2014/599 (2014)

36. Goldwasser, S., Kalai, Y.T., Peikert, C., Vaikuntanathan, V.: Robustness of the learning with errors assumption. In: Innovations in Computer Science, pp. 230–240 (2010)

37. Lyubashevsky, V.: Lattice signatures without trapdoors. In: Pointcheval, D., Johansson, T. (eds.) EUROCRYPT 2012. LNCS, vol. 7237, pp. 738–755. Springer, Heidelberg (2012)

38. Güneysu, T., Lyubashevsky, V., Pöppelmann, T.: Practical lattice-based cryptography: a signature scheme for embedded systems. In: Prouff, E., Schaumont, P. (eds.) CHES 2012. LNCS, vol. 7428, pp. 530–547. Springer, Heidelberg (2012)

39. Ducas, L., Durmus, A., Lepoint, T., Lyubashevsky, V.: Lattice signatures and bimodal gaussians. In: Canetti, R., Garay, J.A. (eds.) CRYPTO 2013, Part I. LNCS, vol. 8042, pp. 40–56. Springer, Heidelberg (2013)

40. Bai, S., Galbraith, S.D.: An improved compression technique for signatures based on learning with errors. In: Benaloh, J. (ed.) CT-RSA 2014. LNCS, vol. 8366, pp. 28–47. Springer, Heidelberg (2014)

41. Hoffstein, J., Pipher, J., Schanck, J.M., Silverman, J.H., Whyte, W.: Practical signatures from the partial fourier recovery problem. In: Boureanu, I., Owesarski, P., Vaudenay, S. (eds.) ACNS 2014. LNCS, vol. 8479, pp. 476–493. Springer, Heidelberg (2014)

42. Katz, J., Vaikuntanathan, V.: Smooth projective hashing and password-based authenticated key exchange from lattices. In: Matsui, M. (ed.) ASIACRYPT 2009. LNCS, vol. 5912, pp. 636–652. Springer, Heidelberg (2009)

43. Fujioka, A., Suzuki, K., Xagawa, K., Yoneyama, K.: Strongly secure authenticated key exchange from factoring, codes, and lattices. In: PKC, pp. 467–484 (2012)

44. Fujioka, A., Suzuki, K., Xagawa, K., Yoneyama, K.: Practical and post-quantum authenticated key exchange from one-way secure key encapsulation mechanism. In: ASIACCS, pp. 83–94 (2013)

45. Peikert, C., Waters, B.: Lossy trapdoor functions and their applications. In: STOC, pp. 187–196 (2008)

46. Peikert, C.: Public-key cryptosystems from the worst-case shortest vector problem: extended abstract. In: STOC, pp. 333–342 (2009)

47. Canetti, R., Krawczyk, H.: Security analysis of IKE's signature-based key-exchange protocol. In: Yung, M. (ed.) CRYPTO 2002. LNCS, vol. 2442, pp. 143–161. Springer, Heidelberg (2002)

48. Jager, T., Kohlar, F., Schäge, S., Schwenk, J.: On the security of TLS-DHE in the standard model. In: Safavi-Naini, R., Canetti, R. (eds.) CRYPTO 2012. LNCS, vol. 7417, pp. 273–293. Springer, Heidelberg (2012)

49. Watrous, J.: Zero-knowledge against quantum attacks. SIAM J. Comput. **39**, 25–58 (2009)

50. Unruh, D.: Quantum proofs of knowledge. In: Pointcheval, D., Johansson, T. (eds.) EUROCRYPT 2012. LNCS, vol. 7237, pp. 135–152. Springer, Heidelberg (2012)

51. Boneh, D., Dagdelen, Ö., Fischlin, M., Lehmann, A., Schaffner, C., Zhandry, M.: Random oracles in a quantum world. In: Lee, D.H., Wang, X. (eds.) ASIACRYPT 2011. LNCS, vol. 7073, pp. 41–69. Springer, Heidelberg (2011)

52. Dagdelen, Ö., Fischlin, M., Gagliardoni, T.: The fiat–shamir transformation in a quantum world. In: Sako, K., Sarkar, P. (eds.) ASIACRYPT 2013, Part II. LNCS, vol. 8270, pp. 62–81. Springer, Heidelberg (2013)

53. Ambainis, A., Rosmanis, A., Unruh, D.: Quantum attacks on classical proof systems (the hardness of quantum rewinding). In: FOCS 2014, pp. 474–483. IEEE (2014)
54. Boneh, D., Zhandry, M.: Secure signatures and chosen ciphertext security in a quantum computing world. In: Canetti, R., Garay, J.A. (eds.) CRYPTO 2013, Part II. LNCS, vol. 8043, pp. 361–379. Springer, Heidelberg (2013)
55. Song, F.: A note on quantum security for post-quantum cryptography. In: Mosca, M. (ed.) PQCrypto 2014. LNCS, vol. 8772, pp. 246–265. Springer, Heidelberg (2014)
56. Micciancio, D., Regev, O.: Worst-case to average-case reductions based on gaussian measures. SIAM J. Comput. **37**, 267–302 (2007)
57. Applebaum, B., Cash, D., Peikert, C., Sahai, A.: Fast cryptographic primitives and circular-secure encryption based on hard learning problems. In: Halevi, S. (ed.) CRYPTO 2009. LNCS, vol. 5677, pp. 595–618. Springer, Heidelberg (2009)
58. Brakerski, Z., Vaikuntanathan, V.: Fully homomorphic encryption from ring-LWE and security for key dependent messages. In: Rogaway, P. (ed.) CRYPTO 2011. LNCS, vol. 6841, pp. 505–524. Springer, Heidelberg (2011)
59. Brakerski, Z., Gentry, C., Vaikuntanathan, V.: Fully homomorphic encryption without bootstrapping. In: ITCS, Innovations in Theoretical Computer Science, pp. 309–325 (2012)
60. Chor, B., Goldreich, O.: Unbiased bits from sources of weak randomness and probabilistic communication complexity. In: FOCS, pp. 429–442 (1985)
61. Trevisan, L., Vadhan, S.: Extracting randomness from samplable distributions. In: FOCS, pp. 32–42 (2000)
62. Trevisan, L.: Extractors and pseudorandom generators. J. ACM **48**, 860–879 (2001)
63. Dodis, Y., Gennaro, R., Håstad, J., Krawczyk, H., Rabin, T.: Randomness extraction and key derivation using the CBC, cascade and HMAC modes. In: Franklin, M. (ed.) CRYPTO 2004. LNCS, vol. 3152, pp. 494–510. Springer, Heidelberg (2004)
64. Barak, B., Impagliazzo, R., Wigderson, A.: Extracting randomness using few independent sources. SIAM Journal on Computing **36**, 1095–1118 (2006)
65. Barker, E., Roginsky, A.: Recommendation for the entropy sources used for random bit generation. Draft NIST Special Publication 800–90B, August 2012
66. Stehlé, D., Steinfeld, R.: Making NTRU as secure as worst-case problems over ideal lattices. In: Paterson, K.G. (ed.) EUROCRYPT 2011. LNCS, vol. 6632, pp. 27–47. Springer, Heidelberg (2011)
67. Bellare, M., Rogaway, P.: Random oracles are practical: a paradigm for designing efficient protocols. In: CCS, pp. 62–73 (1993)
68. Bellare, M., Neven, G.: Multi-signatures in the plain public-key model and a general forking lemma. In: CCS, pp. 390–399 (2006)
69. Gennaro, R., Shoup, V.: A note on an encryption scheme of Kurosawa and Desmedt. Cryptology ePrint Archive, Report 2004/194 (2004)
70. Dagdelen, O., Bansarkhani, R.E., Göpfert, F., Güneysu, T., Oder, T., Pöppelmann, T., Sánchez, A.H., Schwabe, P.: High-speed signatures from standard lattices. In: LATINCRYPT (2014)
71. Schnorr, C., Euchner, M.: Lattice basis reduction: Improved practical algorithms and solving subset sum problems. Mathematical Programming **66**, 181–199 (1994)
72. Chen, Y., Nguyen, P.Q.: BKZ 2.0: better lattice security estimates. In: Lee, D.H., Wang, X. (eds.) ASIACRYPT 2011. LNCS, vol. 7073, pp. 1–20. Springer, Heidelberg (2011)

73. Babai, L.: On Lovász' lattice reduction and the nearest lattice point problem. Combinatorica **6**, 1–13 (1986)
74. Lindner, R., Peikert, C.: Better key sizes (and attacks) for LWE-based encryption. In: Kiayias, A. (ed.) CT-RSA 2011. LNCS, vol. 6558, pp. 319–339. Springer, Heidelberg (2011)
75. Liu, M., Nguyen, P.Q.: Solving BDD by enumeration: an update. In: Dawson, E. (ed.) CT-RSA 2013. LNCS, vol. 7779, pp. 293–309. Springer, Heidelberg (2013)
76. Gentry, C., Halevi, S., Smart, N.P.: Homomorphic evaluation of the AES circuit. In: Safavi-Naini, R., Canetti, R. (eds.) CRYPTO 2012. LNCS, vol. 7417, pp. 850–867. Springer, Heidelberg (2012)
77. Lyubashevsky, V., Peikert, C., Regev, O.: A toolkit for ring-LWE cryptography. In: Johansson, T., Nguyen, P.Q. (eds.) EUROCRYPT 2013. LNCS, vol. 7881, pp. 35–54. Springer, Heidelberg (2013)
78. Cormen, T.H., Leiserson, C.E., Rivest, R.L., Stein, C., et al.: Introduction to algorithms, vol. 2. MIT press, Cambridge (2001)
79. Lyubashevsky, V., Micciancio, D., Peikert, C., Rosen, A.: SWIFFT: a modest proposal for FFT hashing. In: Nyberg, K. (ed.) FSE 2008. LNCS, vol. 5086, pp. 54–72. Springer, Heidelberg (2008)
80. Peikert, C.: An efficient and parallel gaussian sampler for lattices. In: Rabin, T. (ed.) CRYPTO 2010. LNCS, vol. 6223, pp. 80–97. Springer, Heidelberg (2010)

Quantum Cryptography

Non-Interactive Zero-Knowledge Proofs in the Quantum Random Oracle Model

Dominique Unruh[(✉)]

University of Tartu, Tartu, Estonia
unruh@ut.ee

Abstract. We present a construction for non-interactive zero-knowledge proofs of knowledge in the random oracle model from general sigma-protocols. Our construction is secure against quantum adversaries. Prior constructions (by Fiat-Shamir and by Fischlin) are only known to be secure against classical adversaries, and Ambainis, Rosmanis, Unruh (FOCS 2014) gave evidence that those constructions might not be secure against quantum adversaries in general.

To prove security of our constructions, we additionally develop new techniques for adaptively programming the quantum random oracle.

1 Introduction

Classical NIZK Proofs. Zero-knowledge proofs are a vital tool in modern cryptography. Traditional zero-knowledge proofs (e.g., [12]) are interactive protocols, this makes them cumbersome to use in many situations. To circumvent this problem, non-interactive zero-knowledge (NIZK) proofs were introduced [4]. NIZK proofs circumvent the necessity for interaction by introducing a CRS, which is a publicly known value that needs to be chosen by a trusted third party. The ease of use of NIZK proofs comes at a cost, though: generally, NIZK proofs will be less efficient and based on stronger assumptions than their interactive counterparts. So-called sigma protocols (a certain class of three move interactive proofs, see below) exist for a wide variety of problems and admit very generic operations for efficiently constructing more complex ones [6,8] (e.g., the "or" of two sigma protocols). In contrast, efficient NIZK proofs using a CRS exist only for specific languages (most notably related to bilinear groups, using Groth-Sahai proofs [14]). To alleviate this, Fiat and Shamir [10] introduced so-called Fiat-Shamir proofs that are NIZK proofs in the random oracle model.[1] Those can transform any sigma protocol into a NIZK proof. (In fact the construction is even a proof *of knowledge*, but we will ignore this distinction for the moment.) The Fiat-Shamir construction (or variations of it) has been used in a number

---

[1] [10] originally introduced them as a heuristic construction for signatures schemes (with a security proof in the random oracle model by [15]). However, the construction can be seen as a NIZK proof of knowledge in the random oracle model.

© International Association for Cryptologic Research 2015
E. Oswald and M. Fischlin (Eds.): EUROCRYPT 2015, Part II, LNCS 9057, pp. 755–784, 2015.
DOI: 10.1007/978-3-662-46803-6_25

of notable protocols, e.g., Direct Anonymous Attestation [5] and the Helios voting system [1]. A second construction of NIZK proofs in the random oracle model was proposed by Fischlin [11]. Fischlin's construction is less efficient than Fiat-Shamir (and imposes an additional condition on the sigma protocol, called "unique responses"), but it avoids certain technical difficulties that Fiat-Shamir has (Fischlin's construction does not need rewinding).

Quantum NIZK Proofs. However, if we want security against quantum adversaries, the situation becomes worse. Groth-Sahai proofs are not secure because they are based on hardness assumptions in bilinear groups that can be broken by Shor's algorithm [17]. And Ambainis, Rosmanis, and Unruh [2] show that the Fiat-Shamir construction is not secure in general, at least relative to a specific oracle. Although this does not exclude that Fiat-Shamir is still secure without oracle, it at least makes a proof of security less likely – at the least, such a security proof would be non-relativizing, while all known proof techniques that deal with rewinding in the quantum case [18,22] are relativizing. Similarly, [2] also shows Fischlin's scheme to be insecure in general (relative to an oracle). Of course, even if Fiat-Shamir and Fischlin's construction are insecure in general, for certain specific sigma-protocols, Fiat-Shamir or Fischlin could still be secure. (Recall that both constructions take an *arbitrary* sigma-protocol and convert it into a NIZK proof.) In fact, Dagdelen, Fischlin, and Gagliardoni [7] show that for a specific class of sigma-protocols (with so-called "oblivious commitments"), a *variant* of Fiat-Shamir is secure[2]. However, sigma-protocols with oblivious commitments are themselves already NIZK proofs in the CRS model.[3] (This is not immediately obvious from the definition presented in [7], but we show this fact in Section A.) Also, sigma-protocols with oblivious commitments are not closed under disjunction and similar operations (at least not using the constructions from [6]), thus losing one of the main advantages of sigma-protocols for efficient protocol design. Hence sigma-protocols with oblivious commitments are a much stronger assumption than just normal sigma-protocols; we lose one of the main advantages of the classical Fiat-Shamir construction: the ability to transform *arbitrary* sigma-protocols into NIZK proofs. Summarizing, prior to this paper, no generic quantum-secure construction was known to transform sigma-protocols into NIZK proofs or NIZK proofs of knowledge in the random oracle model. ([7] left this explicitly as an open problem.)

Our Contribution. We present a NIZK proof system in the random oracle model, secure against quantum adversaries. Our construction takes any sigma protocol (that has the standard properties "honest verifier zero-knowledge" (HVZK) and "special soundness") and transforms it into a non-interactive proof. The resulting proof is a zero-knowledge proof of knowledge (secure

---

[2] Security is shown for Fiat-Shamir as a signature scheme, but the proof technique most likely also works for Fiat-Shamir as a NIZK proof of knowledge.

[3] This observation does not trivialize the construction from [7] because a sigma-protocol with oblivious commitments is a *non-adaptive single-theorem* NIZK proof in the CRS model while the construction from [7] yields an *adaptive multi-theorem* NIZK proof in the random oracle model. See Section A.

against polynomial-time quantum adversaries) with the extra property of "online extractability". This property guarantees that the witness from a proof can be extracted without rewinding. (Fischlin's scheme also has this property in the classical setting, but not Fiat-Shamir.) Furthermore the scheme is non-malleable, more precisely simulation-sound. That is, given a proof for one statement, it is not possible to create a proof for a related statement. This property is, e.g., important if we wish to construct a signature-scheme from the NIZK proof.

As an application we show how to use our proof system to get strongly unforgeable signatures in the quantum random oracle model from any sigma protocol (assuming a generator for hard instances).

In order to prove the security, we additionally develop a result on random oracle programming in the quantum setting (see the full version [19]) which is a strengthening of a lemma from [20,21] to the adaptive case. It allows us to reduce the probability that the adversary notices that a random oracle has been reprogrammed to the probability of said adversary querying the oracle at the programmed location. (This would be relatively trivial in a classical setting but becomes non-trivial if the adversary can query in superposition.) For space reasons, in the main body of this paper, we only state two special cases of this result (Corollaries 6 and 7).

Further Related Work. Dagdelen, Fischlin, and Gagliardoni [7] show the impossibility of proving the quantum security of Fiat-Shamir using a reduction that does not perform quantum rewinding.[4] Ambainis, Rosmanis, and Unruh [2] show the quantum insecurity of Fiat-Shamir and Fischlin's scheme relative to an oracle (and therefore the impossibility of a relativizing proof, even with quantum rewinding). Faust, Kohlweiss, Marson, and Venturi [9] show that Fiat-Shamir is zero-knowledge and simulation-sound extractable (not simulation-sound online-extractable) in the classical setting under the additional assumption of "unique responses" (a.k.a. computational strict soundness). Fischlin [11] shows that Fischlin's construction is zero-knowledge and online-extractable (not simulation-sound online-extractable) in the classical setting assuming unique responses.

Difficulties with Fiat-Shamir and Fischlin. In order to understand our protocol construction, we first explain why Fiat-Shamir and Fischlin's scheme are difficult to prove secure in the quantum setting. A sigma-protocol consists of three messages $com, ch, resp$ where the "commitment" com is chosen by the prover, the "challenge" ch is chosen uniformly at random by the verifier, and the "response" $resp$ is computed by the prover depending on ch. Given a sigma-protocol, and a random oracle H, the Fiat-Shamir construction produces the commitment com, computes the challenge $ch := H(com)$, and computes a response $resp$ for that challenge. The proof is then $\pi := (com, ch, resp)$, and the verifier checks whether it is a valid execution of the sigma-protocol, and whether $ch = H(com)$. How do we prove that Fiat-Shamir is a proof (or a proof of knowledge)? (The zero-knowledge property is less interesting for the present discussion, so we skip it.) Very roughly, given a malicious prover P, we

---

[4] I.e., a reduction that cannot apply the inverse of the unitary describing the adversary.

first execute P to get $(com, ch, resp)$. Then we rewind P to the oracle query $H(com)$ that returned ch. We then change ("program") the random oracle such that $H(com) := ch'$ for some random $ch' \neq ch$. And then we then continue the execution of P with the modified oracle H. Then P will output a new triple $(com', ch', resp')$. And since com was determined before the point of rewinding, we have $com = com'$. (This is a vague intuition. But the "forking lemma" [15] guarantees that this actually works with sufficiently large probability.) Then we can use a property of sigma-protocols called "special soundness". It states: given valid sigma-protocol interactions $(com, ch, resp), (com, ch', resp')$, one can efficiently compute a witness for the statement being proven. Thus we have constructed an extractor that, given a (successful) malicious prover P, finds a witness. This implies that Fiat-Shamir is a proof of knowledge.

What happens if we try and translate this proof idea into the quantum setting? First of all, rewinding is difficult in the quantum setting. We can rewind P by applying the inverse unitary transformation $P^\dagger$ to reconstruct an earlier state of P. However, if we measure the output of P before rewinding, this disturbs the state, and the rewinding will return to an undefined earlier state. In some situations this can be avoided by showing that the output that is measured contains little information about the state and thus does not disturb the state too much [18], but it is not clear how to do that in the case of Fiat-Shamir. (The output $(com, ch, resp)$ may contain a lot of entropy due to com, ch, even if we require $resp$ to be unique.)

Even if we have solved the problem of rewinding, we face a second problem. We wish to reprogram the random oracle at the input where it is being queried. Classically, the input of a random oracle query is a well-defined notion. In the quantum setting, though, the query input may be in superposition, and we cannot measure the input because this would disturb the state.

So when trying to prove Fiat-Shamir secure, we face two problems to which we do not have a solution: rewinding, and determining the input to an oracle query.

We now turn to Fischlin's scheme. Fischlin's scheme was introduced in the classical case to avoid the rewinding used in Fiat-Shamir. (There are certain reasons why even classically, rewinding leads to problems, see [11].) Here the prover is supposed to send a valid triple $(com, ch, resp)$ such that $H(com, ch, resp) \bmod 2^b = 0$ for a certain parameter b. (This is an oversimplification but good enough for explaining the difficulties.) By choosing b large enough, a prover can only find triples $(com, ch, resp)$ with $H(com, ch, resp) \bmod 2^b = 0$ by trying out several such triples. Thus, if we inspect the list of all query inputs to H, we will find several different valid triples $(com, ch, resp)$. In particular, there will be two triples $(com, ch, resp)$ and $(com', ch', resp')$ with $com = com'$. (Due to the oversimplified presentation here, the reader will have to take on trust that we can achieve $com = com'$, see [11] for a full analysis.) Again using special soundness, we can extract a witness from these two triples. So Fischlin's scheme is a proof of knowledge with the extra benefit that the extractor can extract without rewinding, just by looking at the oracle queries ("online-extraction").

What happens if we try to show the security of Fischlin's scheme in the quantum setting? Then we again face the problem that there is no well-defined notion of "the list of query inputs". If we measure the query inputs, this disturbs the malicious prover. If we do not measure the query inputs, they are not well-defined.

The problems with Fiat-Shamir and Fischlin seem not to be just limitations of our proof techniques, [2] shows that relative to some oracle, Fiat-Shamir and Fischlin actually become insecure.

Our Protocol. So both in Fiat-Shamir and in Fischlin's scheme we face the challenge that it is difficult to get the query inputs made by the malicious prover. Nevertheless, in our construction we will still try to extract the query inputs, but with a twist: Assume for a moment that the random oracle G is a permutation. Then, given $G(x)$ it is, at least in principle, possible to extract x. Can we use this idea to save Fischlin's scheme? No, because in Fischlin's scheme we need the inputs to queries whose outputs we never learn; inverting G will not help. So in our scheme, for any query input x we want to learn, we need to include $G(x)$ in the output. Basically, we sent $(com, G(resp_1), \ldots, G(resp_n))$ where the $resp_j$ are the responses for com given different challenges ch_j. Then, by inverting two of the G, we can get two triples $(com, ch, resp)$ and $(com, ch', resp')$ which allows us to extract the witness. However, so far we have not made sure that the malicious prover indeed puts valid responses into the queries. He could simply send random values instead of $G(resp_j)$. To avoid this, we use a cut-and-choose technique similar to what is done in Fiat-Shamir: We first produce a number of proofs $(com_i, G(resp_{i,1}), \ldots, G(resp_{i,n}))$. Then we hash all of them with a second random oracle H (not a permutation). The result of the hashing indicates for each com_i which of the $resp_{i,j}$ should be revealed. A malicious prover who succeeds in this will have to include valid responses in at least a large fraction of the $G(resp_{i,j})$. Thus by inverting G, we can find two valid triples $(com, ch, resp)$ and $(com, ch', resp')$ if the malicious prover's proof passes verification. The full protocol is described in Figure 1.

We have not discussed yet: What if G is not a permutation (a random function will usually not be a permutation)? And how to efficiently invert G? The answer to the first is: as long as domain and range of G are the same, G is indistinguishable from a random permutation [24]. So although the real protocol execution uses a G that is a random function, in an execution with the extractor, we simply feed a random permutation to the prover. To answer the second, we need to slightly change our approach (but not the protocol): Zhandry [23] shows that a random function is indistinguishable from a $2q$-wise independent function (where q is the number of oracle queries performed). Random polynomials of degree $\leq 2q - 1$ over a finite field are $2q$-wise independent.[5] So if,

---

[4] The values h_{i,J_i} could be omitted since they can be recomputed as $h_{i,J_i} = G(resp_{i,J_i})$. We include them to keep the notation simple.

[5] Proof: Fix distinct $x_1, \ldots, x_{2q}$. For any $a_1, \ldots, a_{2q}$ there exists exactly one polynomial of degree $\leq 2q - 1$ with $\forall i. f(x_i) = a_i$ (by interpolation). Hence, for uniformly random f of degree $\leq 2q - 1$, the tuple $(f(x_1), \ldots, f(x_{2q}))$ equals each $(a_1, \ldots a_{2q})$ with the same probability. Hence $(f(x_1), \ldots, f(x_{2q}))$ is uniformly distributed, so f is $2q$-wise independent by definition.

P_{OE}:

Input: (x, w) with $(x, w) \in R$
// Create $t \cdot m$ proofs $\quad (com_i, ch_{i,j}, resp_{i,j})$
for $i = 1$ **to** t **do** $\quad com_i \leftarrow P_{\Sigma}^1(x, w)$ $\quad$ **for** $j = 1$ **to** m **do** $\quad\quad ch_{i,j} \xleftarrow{\$} N_{ch} \setminus \{ch_{i,1}, \ldots, ch_{i,j-1}\}$ $\quad\quad resp_{i,j} \leftarrow P_{\Sigma}^2(ch_{i,j})$
// Commit to responses
for $i = 1$ **to** t **do** $\quad$ **for** $j = 1$ **to** m **do** $\quad\quad h_{i,j} := G(resp_{i,j})$
// Get challenge by hashing $J_1 \| \ldots \| J_t :=$ $H(x, (com_i)_i, (ch_{i,j})_{i,j}, (h_{i,j})_{i,j})$
// Return proof (only some responses)   **return** $\pi := ((com_i)_i, (ch_{i,j})_{i,j}, (h_{i,j})_{i,j}, (resp_{i,J_i})_i)$ [5]

V_{OE}:

Input: (x, π) with $\pi =$ $\quad\quad ((com_i)_i, (ch_{i,j})_{i,j}, (h_{i,j})_{i,j}, (resp_i)_i)$
$J_1 \| \ldots \| J_t :=$ $H(x, (com_i)_i, (ch_{i,j})_{i,j}, (h_{i,j})_{i,j})$
for $i = 1$ **to** t **do** $\quad$ check $ch_{i,1}, \ldots, ch_{i,m}$ pairwise $\quad$ distinct
for $i = 1$ **to** t **do** $\quad$ check $\quad V_{\Sigma}(x, com_i, ch_{i,J_i}, resp_i) = 1$
for $i = 1$ **to** t **do** $\quad$ check $h_{i,J_i} = G(resp_i)$.
if all checks succeed **then** $\quad$ **return** 1

Fig. 1. Prover $P_{OE}^{G,H}(x, w)$ (left) and verifier $V_{OE}^{G,H}(x, \pi)$ (right) from Definition 8. The missing notation will be introduced in Section 2.2.

during extraction, we replace G not by a random permutation, but by a random polynomial, we can efficiently invert G. (The preimage will not be unique, but the number of possible preimage will be small enough so that we can scan through all of them.) This shows that our protocol is online-extractable: the extractor simply replaces G by a random polynomial, inverts all $G(resp_{i,j})$, searches for two valid triples $(com, ch, resp)$ and $(com, ch', resp')$, and computes the witness. The formal description of the extractor is given in Section 3.2. Our scheme is then online-extractable.

Of course, we also need that the resulting scheme is zero-knowledge. The construction of the simulator is quite standard: To be able to create simulated proofs $com_i, ch_{i,j}, resp_{i,j}$, the simulator needs to know in advance which of the $G(resp_{i,j})$ he has to reveal. Since the choice which to reveal is determined by the result of hashing the proofs using H, the simulator first picks the value that H should return, creates the proofs using the knowledge of that value, and later programs H to return the chosen value. In a classical setting, it is quite easy to see that this simulator works correctly. In the quantum setting, we need to work harder: we need to generalize a lemma from [20] that shows that the adversary does not notice when we program the random oracle.

To prove that our scheme is not just online-extractable, but simulation-sound online-extractable, the same ideas as above can be used, we just need to be careful to show that proofs produced by the simulator cannot be transformed into new

	length of proof			computation	
	commitments	challenges	responses	commitments	responses
Our scheme	t	tm	tm	t	tm
Fiat-Shamir	1	0	1	1	1
Fischlin	r	r	r	r	$2^t r$

Fig. 2. Complexity of our scheme, Fiat-Shamir, and Fischlin. Our parameters t, m must satisfy that $t \log m$ is superlogarithmic. The parameters t, r of Fischlin must satisfy that there exists some b such that br and 2^{t-b} are both superlogarithmic.

valid proofs without changing them completely. This turns out to follow from the collision-resistance of G (Lemma 11).

Efficiency Comparison with Fiat-Shamir and Fischlin. In Figure 2, we show both the communication complexity (length of proof) and the computational complexity (in terms of invocations of the prover of the sigma-protocol) of our scheme, and for comparison of Fiat-Shamir and Fischlin. Notice, however, that a fair comparison of the efficiency is impossible, because the schemes have incomparable parameters. If we pick $m = 2$, our scheme and Fischlin's scheme seem comparable both in communication and computational complexity. But the resulting parameters might not lead to the same security level. For a fair comparison, we would need to pick parameters with comparable security level, but for that, we need to know the reduction used in the security proofs of the schemes that we compare. But Fiat-Shamir and Fischlin have no security proof in the quantum setting. Even Fiat-Shamir might, given a sufficiently bad security reduction, be less efficient than our scheme if the reduction forces the security parameter of the underlying Σ-protocol up. (Although this seems unlikely.)

The runtime of our extractor (which in the end affects the concrete security level when our protocol is used as a subprotocol) is quadratic in the number of adversary queries. This is dominated by the time for inverting a polynomial of degree q. A different implementation of the oracle G (e.g., a strong pseudorandom permutation) might get rid of this factor altogether. Finding a suitable candidate is an open problem.

Organization. In Section 2 we introduce the main security notions used in this paper: those of non-interactive proof systems in the random oracle model (Section 2.1) and those of sigma-protocols (Section 2.2). In Section 3 we introduce and prove secure our NIZK proof system. In Section 4 we illustrate the use of our results and construct a signature scheme in the random oracle model from sigma-protocols. In Section A we discuss sigma-protocols with oblivious commitments and their relation to the CRS model. The proofs of our results on adaptive random oracle programming are given in the full version [19].

1.1 Preliminaries

By $x \leftarrow A(y)$ we denote the (quantum or classical) algorithm A executed with (classical) input y, and its (classical) output assigned to x. We write $x \leftarrow A^H(y)$

if A has access to an oracle H. We stress that A may query the random oracle H in superposition. By $x \xleftarrow{\$} M$ we denote that x is uniformly randomly chosen from the set M. $\Pr[P : G]$ refers to the probability that the predicate P holds true when the free variables in P are assigned according to the program (game) in G. All algorithms implicitly depend on a security parameter η that we never write. If we say a quantity is *negligible* or *overwhelming*, we mean that it is in $o(\eta^c)$ or $1 - o(\eta^c)$ for all $c > 0$ where η denote the security parameter. A *polynomial-time* algorithm is a *classical* one that runs in polynomial-time in its input length and the security parameter, and a *quantum-polynomial-time* algorithm is a *quantum* algorithm that runs in polynomial-time in input and security parameter.

With $\{0,1\}^n$ we denote the bitstrings of length n, with $\{0,1\}^{\leq n}$ the bitstrings of length at most n, and with $\{0,1\}^*$ those of any length. $(M \to N)$ refers to the set of all functions from M to N. $a\|b$ is the concatenation of bitstrings a and b. $GF(2^n)$ is a finite field of size 2^n, and $GF(2^n)[X]$ is the set of polynomials over that field. ∂p refers to the degree of the polynomial p. The *collision entropy* of a random variable X is $-\log\Pr[X = X']$ where X' is independent of X and has the same distribution. The *min-entropy* is $\min_x(-\log\Pr[X = x])$. A family of functions F is called *q-wise-independent* if for any distinct $x_1, \ldots, x_q$ and for $f \xleftarrow{\$} F$, $f(x_1), \ldots, f(x_q)$ are independently uniformly distributed. $E[X]$ is the expected value of the random variable X.

$TD(\rho, \rho')$ denotes the trace distance between two density operators.

2   Security Notions

In the following we present the security notions used in this work. All security notions capture security against quantum adversaries. To make the notions strongest possible, we formulate them with respect to quantum adversaries, but classical honest parties (and classical simulators and extractors).

2.1   Non-Interactive Proof Systems

In the following, we assume a fixed efficiently decidable relation R on bitstrings, defining the language of our proof systems. That is, a *statement* x is in the language iff there exists a *witness* w with $(x, w) \in R$. We also assume a distribution ROdist on functions, modeling the distributions of our random oracle. (E.g., for a random oracle $H : \{0,1\}^* \to \{0,1\}^n$, ROdist would be the uniform distribution on $\{0,1\}^* \to \{0,1\}^n$.)

A *non-interactive proof system* consists of two polynomial-time oracle algorithms $P(x, w), V(x, \pi)$. (The argument π of V represents the proof produced by P.) We require that $P^H(x, w) = \bot$ whenever $(x, w) \notin R$ and that $V^H(x, \pi) \in \{0, 1\}$. Inputs and outputs of P and V are classical.

Definition 1 (Completeness). (P, V) *is* complete *iff for any quantum-polynomial-time oracle algorithm A, the following is negligible:*

$$\Pr[(x, w) \in R \wedge ok = 0 : H \leftarrow \mathsf{ROdist}, (x, w) \leftarrow A^H(),$$
$$\pi \leftarrow P^H(x, w), ok \leftarrow V^H(x, \pi)].$$

Zero-knowledge. We now turn to the zero-knowledge property. Zero-knowledge means that an adversary cannot distinguish between real proofs and proofs produced by a simulator (that has no access to the witness). In the random oracle model, we furthermore allow the simulator to control the random oracle. Classically, this means in particular that the simulator learns the input for each query, and can decide on the response adaptively. In the quantum setting, this is not possible: since the random oracle can be queried in superposition, measuring its input would disturb the state of the adversary. We chose an alternative route here: the simulator is allowed to output a circuit that represents the function computed by the random oracle. And he is allowed to update that circuit whenever he is invoked. However, the simulator is *not* invoked upon a random oracle query. (This makes the definition only stronger.) We now proceed to the formal definition:

A *simulator* is a pair of classical algorithms (S_{init}, S_P). S_{init} outputs a circuit H describing a classical function which represents the initial (simulated) random oracle. The stateful algorithm $S_P(x)$ returns a proof π. Additionally S_P is given access to the description H and may replace it with a different description (i.e., it can program the random oracle).

Definition 2 (Zero-knowledge). *Given a simulator (S_{init}, S_P), the oracle $S'_P(x, w)$ does: If $(x, w) \notin R$, return $\bot$. Else return $S_P(x)$. (The purpose of S'_P is merely to serve as an interface for the adversary who expects a prover taking two arguments x, w.)*

A non-interactive proof system (P, V) is zero-knowledge iff there is a polynomial-time simulator (S_{init}, S_P) such that for every quantum-polynomial-time oracle algorithm A, the following is negligible:

$$\left| \Pr[b = 1 : H \leftarrow \mathsf{ROdist}, b \leftarrow A^{H,P}()] - \Pr[b = 1 : H \leftarrow S_{init}(), b \leftarrow A^{H,S'_P}()] \right|.$$
(1)

We assume that both S_{init} and S_P have access to and may depend on a polynomial upper bound on the runtime of A.

The reason why we allow the simulator to know an upper bound of the runtime of the adversary is that we use the technique of [23] of using q-wise independent hash functions to mimic random functions. This approach requires that we know upper bounds on the number and size of A's queries; the runtime of A provides such bounds.

Online-extractability. We will now define online-extractability. Online-extractable proofs are a specific form of proofs of knowledge where extraction is supposed to work by only looking at the proofs generated by the adversary and at the oracle queries performed by him. Unfortunately, in the quantum setting, it is not possible to generate (or even define) the list of oracle queries because doing so would imply measuring the oracle input, which would disturb the adversary's state. So, different from the classical definition in [11], we do not give the extractor the power to see the oracle queries. Is it then possible at all for the extractor to extract? Yes, because we allow the extractor to see the description of the random oracle H that was produced by the simulator S_{init}. If the simulator produces suitable circuit descriptions, those descriptions may help the extractor to extract in a way that would not be possible with oracle access alone. We now proceed to the formal definition:

An *extractor* is an algorithm $E(H, x, \pi)$ where H is assumed to be a description of the random oracle, x a statement and π a proof of x. E is supposed to output a witness. Inputs and outputs of E are classical.

Definition 3 (Online extractability). *A non-interactive proof system (P, V) is online extractable with respect to S_{init} iff there is a polynomial-time extractor E such that for any quantum-polynomial-time oracle algorithm A, we have that*

$$\Pr[ok = 1 \wedge (x, w) \notin R : H \leftarrow S_{init}(), (x, \pi) \leftarrow A^H(),$$
$$ok \leftarrow V^H(x, \pi), w \leftarrow E(H, x, \pi)]$$

is negligible. We assume that both S_{init} and E have access to and may depend on a polynomial upper bound on the runtime of A.

Online-extractability intuitively implies that it is not possible for an adversary to produce a proof for a statement for which he does not know a witness (because the extractor can extract a witness from what the adversary produces). However, it does not exclude that the adversary can take one proof π_1 for one statement x_1 and transform it into a valid proof for another statement x_2 (even without knowing a witness for x_2), as long as a witness for x_2 could efficiently be computed from a witness for x_1. This problem is usually referred to as malleability.

To avoid malleability, one definitional approach is simulation-soundness [13, 16]. The idea is that extraction of a witness from the adversary-generated proof should be successful even if the adversary has access to simulated proofs (as long as the adversary generated proof does not equal one of the simulated proofs). Adapting this idea to online-extractability, we get:

Definition 4 (Simulation-sound online-extractability). *A non-interactive proof system (P, V) is simulation-sound online-extractable with respect to simulator (S_{init}, S_P) iff there is a polynomial-time extractor E such that for any quantum-polynomial-time oracle algorithm A, we have that*

$$\Pr[ok = 1 \wedge (x, \pi) \notin simproofs \wedge (x, w) \notin R :$$
$$H \leftarrow S_{init}(), (x, \pi) \leftarrow A^{H, S_P}(), ok \leftarrow V^H(x, \pi), w \leftarrow E(H, x, \pi)]$$

is negligible. Here simproofs is the set of all proofs returned by S_P (together with the corresponding statements).

We assume that S_{init}, S_P, and E have access to and may depend on a polynomial upper bound on the runtime of A.

Notice that A^{H, S_P} gets access to S_P, not to S'_P. That is, A can even create simulated proofs of statements where he does not know the witness.

2.2 Sigma Protocols

We now introduce sigma protocols. The notions in this section are standard, all we do to adopt them to the quantum setting is to make the adversary quantum-polynomial-time. Note that the definitions are formulated without the random oracle, we only use the random oracle for constructing a NIZK proof out of the sigma protocol.

A *sigma protocol* for a relation R is a three message proof system. It is described by the domains $N,, N_{ch}, N_{resp}$ of the messages (where $|N_{ch}| \geq 2$), a polynomial-time prover (P_1, P_2) and a deterministic polynomial-time verifier V. The first message from the prover is $com \leftarrow P_1(x, w)$ and is called the *commitment* , the uniformly random reply from the verifier is $ch \overset{\$}{\leftarrow} N_{ch}$ (called *challenge*), and the prover answers with $resp \leftarrow P_2(ch)$ (the *response*). We assume P_1, P_2 to share state. Finally $V(x, com, ch, resp)$ outputs whether the verifier accepts.

Definition 5 (Properties of sigma protocols). *Let $(N,, N_{ch}, N_{resp}, P_1, P_2, V)$ be a sigma protocol. We define:*

- **Completeness:** *For any quantum-polynomial-time algorithm A, the following is negligible:*

$$\Pr[(x, w) \in R \land ok = 0 : (x, w) \leftarrow A, com \leftarrow P_1(x, w), ch \overset{\$}{\leftarrow} N_{ch},$$
$$resp \leftarrow P_2(ch), ok \leftarrow V(x, com, ch, resp)]$$

- **Computational special soundness:** *There is a polynomial-time algorithm E_Σ such that for any quantum-polynomial-time A, the following is negligible:*

$$\Pr[(x, w) \notin R \land ch \neq ch' \land ok = ok' = 1 : (x, com, ch, resp, ch', resp') \leftarrow A(),$$
$$ok \leftarrow V(x, com, ch, resp), ok' \leftarrow V(x, com, ch', resp'),$$
$$w \leftarrow E_\Sigma(x, com, ch, resp, ch', resp')].$$

- **Honest-verifier zero-knowledge (HVZK):** *There is a polynomial-time algorithm S_Σ (the simulator) such that for any stateful quantum-polynomial-time algorithm A the following is negligible for all $(x, w) \in R$:*

$$\Big|\ \Pr[b = 1 : (x, w) \leftarrow A(), com \leftarrow P_1(x, w), ch \overset{\$}{\leftarrow} N_{ch}, resp \leftarrow P_2(ch),$$
$$b \leftarrow A(com, ch, resp)]$$
$$- \Pr[b = 1 : (x, w) \leftarrow A(), (com, ch, resp) \leftarrow S(x), b \leftarrow A(com, ch, resp)]\Big|$$

Note that the above are the standard conditions expected from sigma-protocols in the classical setting. In contrast, for a sigma-protocol to be a *quantum* proof of knowledge, a much more restrictive condition is required, strict soundness [2,18]. Interestingly, this condition is not needed for our protocol to be quantum secure.

2.3   Random Oracle Programming

For space reasons, we just state here the two special cases of our random oracle programming theorem that we will be using (in the proof of Theorem 10). For details, refer to the full version [19].

Corollary 6. *Let M, N be finite sets and $H : M \to N$ be the random oracle. Let A_0, A_C, A_2 be algorithms, where A_0^H makes at most q queries to H, A_C is classical, and the output of A_C is in M and has collision-entropy at least k given A_C's initial state. A_0, A_C, A_2 may share state.*
Then

$$\left| \Pr[b = 1 : H \xleftarrow{\$} (M \to N), A_0^H(), x \leftarrow A_C(), B := H(x), b \leftarrow A_2^H(B)] \right.$$
$$\left. - \Pr[b = 1 : H \xleftarrow{\$} (M \to N), A_0^H(), x \leftarrow A_C(), B \xleftarrow{\$} N, H(x) := B, b \leftarrow A_2^H(B)] \right|$$
$$\leq (4 + \sqrt{2})\sqrt{q}\, 2^{-k/4}.$$

Corollary 7. *Let M, N be finite sets and $H : M \to N$ be the random oracle. Let A_0, A_1 be algorithms that perform at most q_0, q_1 oracle queries, respectively, and that may share state. Let A_C be a classical algorithm that may access (the classical part of) the final state of A_0. (But A_1 does not access A_C's state.) Assume that the output of A_C has min-entropy at least k given its initial state. Then*

$$\left| \Pr[b = 1 : H \xleftarrow{\$} (M \to N), A_0^H(), x \leftarrow A_C(), B := H(x), b \leftarrow A_1^H(B)] \right.$$
$$\left. - \Pr[b = 1 : H \xleftarrow{\$} (M \to N), A_0^H(), x \leftarrow A_C(), B \xleftarrow{\$} N, b \leftarrow A_1^H(B)] \right|$$
$$\leq (4 + \sqrt{2})\sqrt{q_0}\, 2^{-k/4} + 2q_1 2^{-k/2}.$$

3   Online-Extractable NIZK Proofs

In the following, we assume a sigma protocol $\Sigma = (N,, N_{ch}, N_{resp}, P_\Sigma^1, P_\Sigma^2, V_\Sigma)$
   for a relation R. Assume that $N_{resp} = \{0,1\}^{\ell_{resp}}$ for some ℓ_{resp}.[6] We use this sigma protocol to construct the following non-interactive proof system:

Definition 8 (Online-extractable proof system (P_{OE}, V_{OE})). *The proof system (P_{OE}, V_{OE}) is parametrized by polynomially-bounded integers t, m where m is a power of 2 with $2 \leq m \leq |N_{ch}|$.*
   We use random oracles $H : \{0,1\}^* \to \{1, \ldots, m\}^t$ and $G : N_{resp} \to N_{resp}$.[7]
Prover and verifier are defined in Figure 1.

---

[6] Any N_{resp} can be efficiently embedded in a set of fixed length bitstrings $\{0,1\}^{\ell_{resp}}$ (there is no need for this embedding to be surjective). So any sigma protocol can be transformed to have $N_{resp} = \{0,1\}^{\ell_{resp}}$ for some ℓ_{resp}.

[7] The definitions from Section 2.1 are formulated with respect to only a single random oracle with distribution ROdist. Having two oracles, however, can be encoded in that framework by letting ROdist be the uniform distribution over pairs of functions with the respective domains/ranges.

$S_{P_{OE}}$:

Input: x
for $i = 1$ **to** t **do**
$\quad J_i \xleftarrow{\$} \{1, \dots, m\};$
$\quad (com_i, ch_{i,J_i}, resp_{i,J_i}) \leftarrow S_{\Sigma}(x)$
$\quad$ **for** $j = 1$ **to** m **except** $j = J_i$ **do**
$\quad\quad ch_{i,j} \xleftarrow{\$}$
$\quad\quad N_{ch} \setminus \{ch_{i,J_i}, ch_{i,1}, \dots, ch_{i,j-1}\}$
for $i = 1$ **to** t **do**
$\quad h_{i,J_i} := G(resp_{i,J_i})$
$\quad$ **for** $j = 1$ **to** m **except** $j = J_i$ **do**
$\quad\quad h_{i,j} \xleftarrow{\$} N_{resp}$
$H(x, (com_i)_i, (ch_{i,j})_{i,j}, (h_{i,j})_{i,j}) := J_1 \| \dots \| J_t$
return $\pi :=$
$\quad ((com_i)_i, (ch_{i,j})_{i,j}, (h_{i,j})_{i,j}, (resp_{i,J_i})_i)$

S_{init}^{OE}:

Parameters: upper bounds q_G, q_H on the number of queries to G and H; upper bound ℓ on the length of the inputs to H; embedding ι_ℓ
$p_G \xleftarrow{\$} GF(2^{\ell_{resp}})[X]$ with $\partial p_G \leq 2q_G - 1$
$p_H \xleftarrow{\$} GF(2^{\ell^*})[X]$ with $\partial p_H \leq 2q_H - 1$
// Construct circuits G, H:
$G(x) := p_G(x)$ **for** $x \in \{0,1\}^{\ell_{resp}}$
$H(x) := p_H(\iota_\ell(x))_{1 \dots t \log m}$
$\quad\quad\quad\quad$ **for** $x \in \{0,1\}^{\leq \ell}$
return descriptions of G, H

Fig. 3. The simulator $(S_{P_{OE}}, S_{init}^{OE})$ for (P_{OE}, V_{OE}). S_{Σ} is the simulator for $(P_{\Sigma}^1, P_{\Sigma}^2, V_{\Sigma})$, cf. Definition 5. $H(x) := y$ means the description of H is replaced by a new description with $H(x) = y$. Bounds q_G, q_H, ℓ include calls made by the adversary and by P_{OE}. Such bounds are known because the runtime of A is known to the simulator (cf. Definition 2). ι_ℓ is an arbitrary efficiently computable and invertible injection $\iota_\ell : \{0,1\}^{\leq \ell} \to \{0,1\}^{\ell^*}$ for some $\ell^* \geq t \log m$. $p_H(\iota_\ell(x))_{1 \dots t \log m}$ denotes $p_H(\iota_\ell(x))$ truncated to the first $t \log m$ bits. We assume that $GF(2^{\ell_{resp}}) = \{0,1\}^{\ell_{resp}}$ and $GF(2^{\ell^*}) = \{0,1\}^{\ell^*}$; such a representation can be found in polynomial-time [3].

Lemma 9 (Completeness). *If Σ is complete, (P_{OE}, V_{OE}) is complete.*

Proof. Since Σ is complete, $V_{\Sigma}(x, com_i, ch_{i,j}, resp_{i,j}) = 1$ for all i, j with overwhelming probability. Then all checks performed by V_{OE} succeed by construction of P_{OE}. $\qquad\square$

3.1 Zero-Knowledge

Theorem 10 (Zero-knowledge). *Assume that Σ is HVZK, and that the response of P_{Σ}^2 has superlogarithmic min-entropy (given its initial state and its input ch).*[8]

Let κ' be a lower bound on the collision-entropy of the tuple $((com_i)_i, (ch_{i,j})_{i,j}, (h_{i,j})_{i,j})$ produced by P_{OE} (given its initial state and the oracle G, H). Assume that κ' is superlogarithmic.[9]

Then (V_{OE}, P_{OE}) is zero-knowledge with the simulator $(S_{init}^{OE}, S_{P_{OE}})$ from Figure 3.

---

[8] We can always transform a sigma protocol into one with responses with superlogarithmic min-entropy by adding some random bits to the responses.

[9] This can always be achieved by adding random bits to the commitments.

Proof. We prove this using a sequence of games. We start with the real model (first term of (1)) and transform it into the ideal model (second term of (1)) step by step, never changing $\Pr[b = 1]$ by more than a negligible amount. In each game, new code lines are marked with $\boxed{\text{new}}$ and changed ones with $\boxed{\text{chg}}$ (removed ones are simply crossed out).

Let ROdist be the uniform distribution on pairs of functions G, H (with the respective domains and ranges as in Definition 8). Then the first term of (1) becomes:

Game 1. (Real model) $G, H \xleftarrow{\$} \text{ROdist}, b \leftarrow A^{G,H,P_{OE}}$.

We now modify the prover. Instead of getting $J_1, \ldots, J_t$ from the random oracle H, he chooses $J_1, \ldots, J_t$ at random and programs the random oracle H to return those values $J_1, \ldots, J_t$.

Game 2. $G, H \xleftarrow{\$} \text{ROdist}, b \leftarrow A^{G,H,P}$ *with the following prover P:*

$$
\begin{array}{ll}
& \quad \vdots \\
& \textbf{for } i = 1 \textbf{ to } t \textbf{ do} \\
\boxed{\text{new}} & \quad J_i \leftarrow \{1, \ldots, m\} \\
& \quad com_i \leftarrow P_\Sigma^1(x, w) \\
& \quad \vdots \\
& \sout{J_1\|\ldots\|J_t := H(x, (com_i)_i, (ch_{i,j})_{i,j}, (h_{i,j})_{i,j})} \\
\boxed{\text{chg}} & H(x, (com_i)_i, (ch_{i,j})_{i,j}, (h_{i,j})_{i,j}) := J_1\|\ldots\|J_t \\
& \quad \vdots
\end{array}
$$

By assumption the argument $(x, (com_i)_i, (ch_{i,j})_{i,j}, (h_{i,j})_{i,j})$ to H has superlogarithmic collision-entropy κ' (given the state at the beginning of the corresponding invocation of P_{OE}). Thus from Corollary 6 we get (using a standard hybrid argument) that $|\Pr[b = 1 : \text{Game 1}] - \Pr[b = 1 : \text{Game 2}]|$ is negligible.

Next, we change the order in which the prover produces the subproofs $(com_i, ch_{i,j}, resp_{i,j})$: For each i, the $(com_i, ch_{i,j}, resp_{i,j})$ with $j = J_i$ is produced first.

Game 3. $G, H \xleftarrow{\$} \text{ROdist}, b \leftarrow A^{G,H,P}$ *with the P as follows:*

$$
\begin{array}{ll}
& \quad \vdots \\
& \textbf{for } i = 1 \textbf{ to } t \textbf{ do} \\
& \quad J_i \leftarrow \{1, \ldots, m\}; \ com_i \leftarrow P_\Sigma^1(x, w) \\
\boxed{\text{new}} & \quad ch_{i,J_i} \xleftarrow{\$} N_{ch}; \ resp_{i,J_i} \leftarrow P_\Sigma^2(ch_{i,J_i}) \\
\boxed{\text{chg}} & \quad \textbf{for } j = 1 \textbf{ to } m \textbf{ except } j = J_i \textbf{ do} \\
\boxed{\text{chg}} & \quad\quad ch_{i,j} \xleftarrow{\$} N_{ch} \setminus \{ch_{i,J_i}, ch_{i,1}, \ldots, ch_{i,j-1}\} \\
& \quad\quad resp_{i,j} \leftarrow P_\Sigma^2(ch_{i,j}) \\
& \quad \vdots
\end{array}
$$

Obviously, changing the order of the P_Σ^2-invocations does not change anything because P_Σ^2 has no side effects. At a first glance, it seems that the values $ch_{i,j}$ are chosen according to different distributions in both games, but in fact in both games $(ch_{i,1}, \ldots, ch_{i,m})$ are uniformly distributed conditioned on being pairwise distinct. Thus $\Pr[b = 1 : \text{Game } 2] = \Pr[b = 1 : \text{Game } 3]$.

Now we change how the $h_{i,j}$ are constructed. Those $h_{i,j}$ that are never opened are picked at random.

Game 4. $G, H \xleftarrow{\$} \text{ROdist}, b \leftarrow A^{G,H,P}$ *with the P as follows:*

	$\vdots$
	for $i = 1$ **to** t **do**
$\boxed{\text{new}}$	$\quad h_{i,J_i} := G(resp_{i,J_i})$
$\boxed{\text{chg}}$	$\quad$ **for** $j = 1$ **to** m **except** $j = J_i$ **do**
$\boxed{\text{chg}}$	$\quad\quad h_{i,j} \xleftarrow{\$} N_{resp}$
	$\vdots$

Note that the argument $resp_{i,j}$ to G has superlogarithmic min-entropy (given the value of all variables when $G(resp_{i,j})$ is invoked) since we assume that the responses of P_Σ^2 have superlogarithmic min-entropy. Thus from Corollary 7 we get (using a standard hybrid argument) that $|\Pr[b = 1 : \text{Game } 3] - \Pr[b = 1 : \text{Game } 4]|$ is negligible. (H in the corollary is G here, and A_C in the corollary is P_Σ^2 here.)

Now we omit the computation of the values $resp_{i,j}$ that are not used:

Game 5. $G, H \xleftarrow{\$} \text{ROdist}, b \leftarrow A^{G,H,P}$ *with the P as follows:*

$\vdots$
for $j = 1$ **to** m **except** $j = J_i$ **do**
$\quad ch_{i,j} \xleftarrow{\$} N_{ch} \setminus \{ch_{i,J_i}, ch_{i,1}, \ldots, ch_{i,j-1}\}$
$\quad \cancel{resp_{i,j} \leftarrow P_\Sigma^2(ch_{i,j})}$
$\vdots$

We now replace the honestly generated proof $(com_i, ch_{i,J_i}, resp_{i,J_i})$ by one produced by the simulator S_Σ (from Definition 5).

Game 6. $G, H \xleftarrow{\$} \text{ROdist}, b \leftarrow A^{G,H,P}$ *with the P as follows:*

	$\vdots$
	for $i = 1$ **to** t **do**
	$\quad J_i \leftarrow \{1, \ldots, m\};\ \cancel{com_i \leftarrow P_\Sigma^1(x,w)}$
	$\quad \cancel{ch_{i,J_i} \xleftarrow{\$} N_{ch};\ resp_{i,J_i} \leftarrow P_\Sigma^2(ch_{i,J_i})}$
$\boxed{\text{new}}$	$\quad (com_i, ch_{i,J_i}, resp_{i,J_i}) \leftarrow S_\Sigma(x)$
	$\vdots$

Since Σ is HVZK by assumption, $|\Pr[b = 1 : \text{Game } 5] - \Pr[b = 1 : \text{Game } 6]|$ is negligible.

Note that P as defined in Game 6 does not use the witness w any more. Thus we can replace P by a simulator that depends only on the statement x. That simulator $S_{P_{OE}}$ is given in Figure 3.

Game 7. $G, H \xleftarrow{\$} \text{ROdist}, b \leftarrow A^{G,H,S'_{P_{OE}}}$ *for* $S_{P_{OE}}$ *from Figure 3. (Recall that* $S'_{P_{OE}}$ *is defined in terms of* $S_{P_{OE}}$, *see Definition 2.)*

From the definition of $S_{P_{OE}}$ in Figure 3 we immediately get $\Pr[b = 1 : \text{Game } 6] = \Pr[b = 1 : \text{Game } 7]$.

Finally, we replace ROdist by oracles as chosen by S_{init}^{OE} from Figure 3. (In general, any construction of S_{init}^{OE} would do for the proof of the zero-knowledge property, as long as it returns G, H that are indistinguishable from random. However, in the proof of extractability we use that G is constructed in this specific way.)

Game 8. $G, H \xleftarrow{\$} S_{init}^{OE}, b \leftarrow A^{G,H,S'_{P_{OE}}}$ *for* $(S_{init}^{OE}, S_{P_{OE}})$ *from Figure 3.*

For the following argument, we introduce the following abbreviation: Given distributions on functions H, H', by $H \approx_{q,\ell} H'$ we denote that H and H' are perfectly indistinguishable by any quantum algorithm making at most q queries and making no queries with input longer than ℓ. We omit q or ℓ if $q = \infty$ or $\ell = \infty$. Let $p_G, p_H, \ell, \iota_\ell, \ell^*$ be as defined in Figure 3.

Let G_R denote the function $G : N_{resp} \to N_{resp}$ as chosen by ROdist, and let G_S denote the function $G = p_G$ chosen by S_{init}^{OE}. It is easy to see that a uniformly random polynomial p of degree $\leq 2q - 1$ is $2q$-wise independent. [23] shows that a $2q$-wise independent function is perfectly indistinguishable from a random function by an adversary performing at most q queries (the queries may be in superposition). Then $G_R \approx_{q_G} G_S$.

Similarly, let H_R and H_S denote $H : \{0,1\}^* \to \{0,1\}^{t \log m}$ as chosen by ROdist or S_{init}^{OE}, respectively. Then $p_H \approx_{2q_H} H'$ for a uniformly random function $H' : \{0,1\}^{\ell^*} \to \{0,1\}^{\ell^*}$. Hence $p_H \circ \iota_\ell \approx_{q_H} H' \circ \iota_\ell \approx H''$ for uniformly random $H'' : \{0,1\}^{\leq \ell} \to \{0,1\}^{\ell^*}$. Hence $H_S = (p_H \circ \iota_\ell)_{1...t \log m} \approx_{q_H} (H'')_{1...t \log m}$ where $H_{1...t \log m}$ means H with its output restricted to the first $t \log m$ bits.[10] And $H'' \approx_\ell H_3$ for uniformly random $H_3 : \{0,1\}^* \to \{0,1\}^{\ell^*}$. Thus $H_S \approx_{q_H} (H'')_{1...t \log m} \approx_\ell (H_3)_{1...t \log m} \approx H_R$, hence $H_S \approx_{q_H, \ell} H_R$.

Since q_H and q_G are upper bounds on the number of queries to H and G and ℓ bounds input length of the H-queries made by A, $G_R \approx_{q_G} G_S$ and $H_S \approx_{q_H, \ell} H_R$ imply that A cannot distinguish the oracles G_R, H_R produced by ROdist from the oracles G_S, H_S produced by S_{init}^{OE}. Thus $\Pr[b = 1 : \text{Game } 7] = \Pr[b = 1 : \text{Game } 8]$.

---

[10] Notice that to see this, we need to be able to implement $(H'')_{1...t \log m}$ using a single oracle query to H''. This can be done by initializing the output qubits of H'' that shall be ignored with $|+\rangle$, see [24, Section 3.2].

$E_{P_{OE}}$:

Input: $G = p_G, H, x, \pi =$
$\quad ((com_i), (ch_{i,j}), (h_{i,j}), (resp_i))$
$J_1 \| \ldots \| J_t := H(x, (com_i)_i, (ch_{i,j})_{i,j}, (h_{i,j})_{i,j})$
for $i = 1$ **to** t **do**
$\quad$ **for** $j = 1$ **to** m **except** J_i **do**
$\quad\quad$ **for each** $resp' \in p_G^{-1}(h_{i,j})$ **do**
$\quad\quad\quad$ **if** $V_\Sigma(x, com_i, ch_{i,j}, resp') = 1$ **then**
$\quad\quad\quad\quad$ **return**
$\quad\quad\quad\quad\quad E_\Sigma(x, com_i, ch_{i,J_i}, resp_i, ch_{i,j}, resp')$

V_Σ and E_Σ are verifier and extractor of the sigma protocol Σ. $p_G^{-1}(h)$ is the set of preimages of h under p_G. Since p_G is a polynomial over $\mathrm{GF}(2^{\ell_{resp}})$ of degree $\leq 2q$, the set $p_G^{-1}(h)$ is polynomial-time computable, namely in time $O(q^2 \ell_{resp}^2)$ [3].

Fig. 4. The extractor $E_{P_{OE}}$ for (P_{OE}, V_{OE})

Summarizing, we have that $\left| \Pr[b = 1 : \text{Game 1}] - \Pr[b = 1 : \text{Game 8}] \right|$ is negligible. Since Game7 are the games in (1), it follows that (P_{OE}, V_{OE}) is zero-knowledge. $\qquad\square$

3.2 Online Extractability

We now proceed to prove that (P_{OE}, V_{OE}) is simulation-sound online-extractable using the extractor $E_{P_{OE}}$ from Figure 4.

To analyze $E_{P_{OE}}$, we define a number of random variables and events that can occur in the execution of the simulation-soundness game (Definition 4). Remember, the game in question is $G, H \leftarrow S_{init}^{OE}, (x, \pi) \leftarrow A^{G,H,S_{P_{OE}}}, ok \leftarrow V_{OE}^{G,H}(x, \pi), w \leftarrow E_{P_{OE}}(H, x, \pi)$, and $simproofs$ is the set of all proofs returned by $S_{P_{OE}}$ (together with the corresponding statements).

- H_0: Let H_0 denote the initial value of H as returned by S_{init}^{OE}. (H can change during the game because $S_{P_{OE}}$ programs it, see Figure 3. On the other hand, G does not change.)
- H_1: Let H_1 denote to the final value of H (as used by V_{OE} for computing ok).
- ShouldEx: $ok = 1$ and $(x, \pi) \notin simproofs$. (I.e., in this case the extractor should find a witness.)
- ExFail: $ok = 1$ and $(x, \pi) \notin simproofs$ and $(x, w) \notin R$. (ExFail represents a successful attack.)
- MallSim: $ok = 1$ and $(x, \pi) \notin simproofs$ and $(x, \pi^*) \in simproofs$ for some $\pi^* = ((com_i)_i, (ch_{i,j})_{i,j}, (h_{i,j})_{i,j}, (resp_i^*)_i)$ where $((com_i)_i, (ch_{i,j})_{i,j}, (h_{i,j})_{i,j}, (resp_i)_i) := \pi$. (In other words, the adversary produces a valid proof that differs from one of the simulator generated proofs (for the same statement x) only in the $resp$-components).
- We call a triple $(com, ch, resp)$ Σ-valid iff $V_\Sigma(x, com, ch, resp) = 1$ (x will always be clear from the context). If R is a set, we call (com, ch, R) set-valid iff there is a $resp \in R$ such that $(com, ch, resp)$ is Σ-valid. And Σ-invalid and set-invalid are the negations of Σ-valid and set-valid.

The following technical lemma establishes that an adversary with access to the simulator $S_{P_{OE}}$ cannot produce a new valid proof by just changing the *resp*-components of a simulated proof. This will cover one of the attack scenarios covered in the proof of simulation-sound online-extractability below.

Lemma 11 (Non-malleability). *Let κ be a lower bound on the collision-entropy of the tuple $\big((com_i)_i, (ch_{i,j})_{i,j}, (h_{i,j})_{i,j}\big)$ produced by $S_{P_{OE}}$ (given its initial state and the oracle G, H). Let q_G be an upper bound for the number of queries to G made by A and $S_{P_{OE}}$ and V_{OE} together. Let n be an upper bound on the number of invocations of $S_{P_{OE}}$.*

Then $\Pr[\mathsf{MallSim}] \leq \frac{n(n+1)}{2} 2^{-\kappa} + O\big((q_G + 1)^3 2^{-\ell_{resp}}\big)$.

Proof. First, since G is chosen as a polynomial of degree $2q_G - 1$ and is thus $2q_G$-wise independent, by [23] G is perfectly indistinguishable from a uniformly random G within q_G queries. Thus, for the proof of this lemma, we can assume that G is a uniformly random function.

In the definition of MallSim, since $ok = 1$, we have that π is accepted by V_{OE}. In particular, this implies that $G(resp_i) = h_{i,J_i}$ for all i by definition of V_{OE}. And $J_1\|\ldots\|J_t = H_1(x, \pi_{half})$ where $\pi_{half} := \big((com_i)_i, (ch_{i,j})_{i,j}, (h_{i,j})_{i,j}\big)$ is π without the *resp*-components. Furthermore, by construction of $S_{P_{OE}}$, we have that π^* satisfies: $G(resp_i^*) = h_{i,J_i^*}$ for all i and $J_1^*\|\ldots\|J_t^* = H^*(x, \pi_{half})$ where H^* denotes the value of H directly after $S_{P_{OE}}$ output π^*. (I.e., H^* might differ from H_1 if further invocations of $S_{P_{OE}}$ programmed H further.) But if $H_1(x, \pi_{half}) = H^*(x, \pi_{half})$, then $J_i = J_i^*$ for all i, and thus $G(resp_i) = G(resp_i^*)$ for all i. And since $\pi \notin simproofs$ and $\pi^* \in simproofs$ by definition of MallSim, we have that $resp_i \neq resp_i^*$ for some i.

Thus

$$\Pr[\mathsf{MallSim}] \leq \Pr[H_1(x, \pi_{half}) \neq H^*(x, \pi_{half})]$$
$$+ \Pr[\exists i : G(resp_i) = G(resp_i^*) \wedge resp_i \neq resp_i^*].$$

If we have $H_1(x, \pi_{half}) \neq H^*(x, \pi_{half})$, this implies that $S_{P_{OE}}$ reprogrammed H after producing π^*. This implies in particular that in two invocations of $S_{P_{OE}}$, the same tuple $\pi_{half} = \big((com_i)_i, (ch_{i,j})_{i,j}, (h_{i,j})_{i,j}\big)$ was chosen. This happens with probability at most $\frac{n(n+1)}{2} 2^{-\kappa}$ because each such tuple has collision-entropy at least κ.

Finally, since G is a random function that is queried at most q_G times, $\Pr[\exists i : G(resp_i) = G(resp_i^*) \wedge resp_i \neq resp_i^*] \in O\big((q_G + 1)^3 2^{-\ell_{resp}}\big)$ by [24, Theorem 3.1] (collision-resistance of the random oracle).

Thus $\Pr[\mathsf{MallSim}] \leq \frac{n(n+1)}{2} 2^{-\kappa} + O\big((q_G + 1)^3 2^{-\ell_{resp}}\big)$. $\square$

The following lemma states that, if H is uniformly random, the adversary cannot produce a valid proof (conditions (i),(ii)) from which is it not possible to extract a second response for one of the com_i by inverting G (condition (iii)). This lemma already implies online-extractability, because it implies that the extractor $E_{P_{OE}}$ will get a commitment com_i with two valid responses. However, it does not go the full way to showing simulation-sound online-extractability yet, because in that setting, the adversary has access to $S_{P_{OE}}$ which reprograms the random oracle H, so H cannot be treated as a random function.

Lemma 12. *Let G be an arbitrarily distributed function, and let H_0 : $\{0,1\}^{\leq \ell} \rightarrow \{0,1\}^{t \log m}$ be uniformly random (and independent of G). Then it is hard to find x and $\pi = \big((com_i), (ch_{i,j}), (h_{i,j}), (resp_i)\big)$ such that:*
(i) $h_{i,J_i} = G(resp_i)$ for all i with
$$J_1 \| \dots \| J_t := H_0(x, (com_i)_i, (ch_{i,j})_{i,j}, (h_{i,j})_{i,j}).$$
(ii) $(com_i, ch_{i,J_i}, resp_i)$ is Σ-valid for all i.
(iii) $(com_i, ch_{i,j}, G^{-1}(h_{i,j}))$ is set-invalid for all i and j with $j \neq J_i$.
More precisely, if A^{G,H_0} makes at most q_H queries to H_0, it outputs (x, π) with these properties with probability at most $2(q_H + 1)2^{-(t \log m)/2}$.

Proof. Without loss of generality, we can assume that G is a fixed function and that A knows that function. Thus in the following, we only provide oracle access to H_0 to A.

For any given value of H_0, we call a tuple $\big(x, (com_i), (ch_{i,j}), (h_{i,j})\big)$ an H_0-*solution* iff:

for each i, j, we have that $(com_i, ch_{i,j}, G^{-1}(h_{i,j}))$ is set-valid iff $j = J_i$
where $J_1 \| \dots \| J_t := H_0(x, (com_i)_i, (ch_{i,j})_{i,j}, (h_{i,j})_{i,j})$.

(The name "H_0-solution" derives from the fact that we are trying to solve an equation in terms of H_0.)

It is easy to see that if x and $\pi = \big((com_i), (ch_{i,j}), (h_{i,j}), (resp_i)\big)$ satisfies (i)–(iii), then $\big(x, (com_i), (ch_{i,j}), (h_{i,j})\big)$ is an H_0-solution. (Note for the case $j = J_i$ that $h_{i,J_i} = G(resp_i)$ implies $resp_i \in G^{-1}(h_{i,j})$. With the Σ-validity of $(com_i, ch_{i,J_i}, resp_i)$ this implies the set-validity of $(com_i, ch_{i,j}, G^{-1}(h_{i,j}))$.)

Thus it is sufficient to prove that $A^{H_0}()$ making at most q_H queries outputs an H_0-solution with probability at most $2(q_H+1)2^{-(t \log m)/2}$. Fix such an adversary A^{H_0}; denote the probability that it outputs an H_0-solution (for uniformly random H_0) with μ.

We call $\big(x, (com_i), (ch_{i,j}), (h_{i,j})\big)$ a *candidate* iff for each i, there is exactly one J_i^* such that $(com_i, ch_{i,J_i^*}, G^{-1}(h_{i,J_i^*}))$ is set-valid. Notice that a non-candidate can never be an H_0-solution. (This justifies the name "candidate", those are candidates for being an H_0-solution, awaiting a test-call to H_0.)

For any given candidate c, for uniformly random H_0, the probability that c is an H_0-solution is $2^{-t \log m}$. (Namely c is an H_0-solution iff all $J_i = J_i^*$ for all i, i.e., there is exactly one output of $H_0(c) \in \{0,1\}^{t \log m}$ that makes c an H_0-solution.)

Let Cand denote the set of all candidates. Let $F : \mathsf{Cand} \rightarrow \{0,1\}$ be a random function with all $F(c)$ i.i.d. with $\Pr[F(c) = 1] = 2^{-t \log m}$.

Given F, we construct $H_F : \{0,1\}^* \rightarrow \{0,1\}^{t \log m}$ as follows:
- For each $c \notin \mathsf{Cand}$, assign a uniformly random $y \in \{0,1\}^{t \log m}$ to $H_F(c)$.
- For each $c \in \mathsf{Cand}$ with $F(c) = 1$, let $H_F(c) := J_1^* \| \dots \| J_t^*$ where $J_1^*, \dots, J_t^*$ are as in the definition of candidates.

- For each $c \in$ Cand with $F(c) = 0$, assign a uniformly random $y \in \{0,1\}^{t \log m} \setminus \{J_1^* \| \ldots \| J_t^*\}$ to $H_F(c)$.

Since $F(c) = 1$ with probability $2^{-t \log m}$, $H_F(c)$ is uniformly distributed over $\{0,1\}^{t \log m}$ for $c \in$ Cand. Thus H_F is a uniformly random function.

Since $A^{H_0}()$ outputs an H_0-solution with probability μ and H_F has the same distribution as H_0, $A^{H_F}()$ outputs an H_F-solution c with probability μ. Since an H_F-solution c must be a candidate, we have $c \in$ Cand. And c can only be an H_F-solution if $H_F(c) = J_1^* \| \ldots \| J_t^*$, i.e., if $F(c) = 1$. Thus $A^{H_F}()$ returns some c with $F(c) = 1$ with probability μ.

However, to explicitly construct H_F, A^{H_F} needs to query all values of F, so the number of F-queries is not bounded by q_H. However, A^{H_F} can be simulated by the following algorithm S^F:

- Pick uniformly random $H_1 : \{0,1\}^{\leq \ell} \to \{0,1\}^{t \log m}$. Set $H_2(c) := J_1^* \| \ldots \| J_t^*$ for all $c \in$ Cand. For all $c \in$ Cand, let $H_3(c) := y$ for uniformly random $y \in \{0,1\}^{t \log m} \setminus \{J_1^* \| \ldots \| J_t^*\}$.
- Let $H_F'(c) := H_1(c)$ if $c \notin$ Cand, let $H_F'(c) := H_2(c)$ if $c \in$ Cand and $F(c) = 1$, let $H_F'(c) := H_3(c)$ if $c \in$ Cand and $F(c) = 0$.
- Run $A^{H_F'}()$.

The function H_F' constructed by S has the same distribution as H_F (given the same F). Thus S outputs c with $F(c) = 1$ with probability μ. Furthermore, no F-queries are needed to construct H_1, H_2, H_3, and a single F-query is needed for each H_F'-query performed by A^{H_F}. Thus S performs at most q_H F-queries. Using the hardness of search in a random function (see the full version [19]), we get $\mu \leq 2(q_H + 1)2^{-(t \log m)/2}$. □

Theorem 13 (Simulation-sound online-extractability). *Assume that Σ has special soundness. Let κ be a lower bound on the collision-entropy of the tuple $\big((com_i)_i, (ch_{i,j})_{i,j}, (h_{i,j})_{i,j}\big)$ produced by $S_{P_{OE}}$ (given its input and the oracles G, H). Assume that $t \log m$ and κ and ℓ_{resp} are superlogarithmic.*

Then (V_{OE}, P_{OE}) is simulation-sound online-extractable with extractor $E_{P_{OE}}$ from Figure 4 and with respect to the simulator $(S_{P_{OE}}, S_{init}^{OE})$ from figure 3.

A concrete bound μ on the success probability is given in (6) below.

Proof. Given $\pi = \big((com_i)_i, (ch_{i,j})_{i,j}, (h_{i,j})_{i,j}, (resp_i)_i\big)$, let $\pi_{half} := \big((com_i)_i, (ch_{i,j})_{i,j}, (h_{i,j})_{i,j}\big)$, i.e., π without the $resp$-components.

Fix an adversary A for the game in Definition 4. Assume A, $S_{P_{OE}}$, V_{OE} together perform at most q_G queries to G and q_H queries to H, and that at most n instances of $S_{P_{OE}}$ are invoked.

Let $\mathsf{Ev}_{(i)}$, $\mathsf{Ev}_{(ii)}$, $\mathsf{Ev}_{(iii)}$ denote the events that conditions (i), (ii), (iii) from Lemma 12 are satisfied.

Assume that $\mathsf{ShouldEx} \wedge \neg\mathsf{MallSim} \wedge \neg\mathsf{Ev}_{(iii)}$ occurs. Intuitively, this means that we are in a situation we the extractor should extract ($\mathsf{ShouldEx}$), but cannot do so ($\neg\mathsf{Ev}_{(iii)}$), and the adversary managed to bring this situation about without using simulator generated proofs, i.e. without using malleability ($\neg\mathsf{MallSim}$). Since we exclude malleability attacks by Lemma 11, this is basically the only case we will need to worry about.

The event ShouldEx by definition entails $ok = 1$ and $(x, \pi) \notin simproofs$. Furthermore, $\neg$MallSim then implies that for all $(x^*, \pi^*) \in simproofs$, we have that $(x^*, \pi^*_{half}) \neq (x, \pi_{half})$. In an invocation $\pi^* \leftarrow S_{P_{OE}}(x^*)$, $S_{P_{OE}}$ only reprograms H at position $H(x^*, \pi^*_{half})$, hence $H(x, \pi_{half})$ is never reprogrammed. Thus $H_0(x, \pi_{half}) = H_1(x, \pi_{half})$. Furthermore $ok = 1$ implies by definition of V_{OE} (and the fact that H_1 denotes H at the time of invocation of V_{OE}): $(com_i, ch_{i,J_i}, resp_i)$ is Σ-valid for all i and $h_{i,J_i} = G(resp_i)$ for all i, where $J_1 \| \dots \| J_t := H_1(x, \pi_{half})$. Since $H_0(x, \pi_{half}) = H_1(x, \pi_{half})$, we have $J_1 \| \dots \| J_t = H_0(x, \pi_{half})$ as well. And $\neg$Ev$_{(iii)}$ implies that $(com_i, ch_{i,j}, G^{-1}(h_{i,j}))$ is set-valid for some i, j with $j \neq J_i$. Thus by construction, $E_{P_{OE}}$ outputs $w := E_{\Sigma}(x, com_i, ch_{i,J_i}, resp_i, ch_{i,j}, resp')$ for some $resp' \in G^{-1}(h_{i,j})$ such that $(com_i, ch_{i,j}, resp')$ is Σ-valid. Furthermore, $ok = 1$ implies by definition of V_{OE} that $ch_{i,1}, \dots, ch_{i,t}$ are pairwise distinct, in particular $ch_{i,j} \neq ch_{i,J_i}$. And $ok = 1$ implies that $(com_i, ch_{i,J_i}, resp_i)$ is Σ-valid. On such inputs, the special soundness of E_{Σ} (cf. Definition 5) implies that $(x, w) \in R$ with probability at least $1 - \varepsilon_{sound}$ for negligible ε_{sound}. Thus

$$\Pr[\text{ShouldEx} \wedge (x, w) \in R \wedge \neg\text{MallSim} \wedge \neg\text{Ev}_{(iii)}]$$
$$\geq \Pr[\text{ShouldEx} \wedge \neg\text{MallSim} \wedge \neg\text{Ev}_{(iii)}] - \varepsilon_{sound}. \quad (2)$$

Then since ExFail $\iff$ ShouldEx $\wedge (x, w) \notin R$,

$$\Pr[\text{ExFail} \wedge \neg\text{MallSim} \wedge \neg\text{Ev}_{(iii)}]$$
$$= \Pr[\text{ShouldEx} \wedge \neg\text{MallSim} \wedge \neg\text{Ev}_{(iii)}]$$
$$- \Pr[\text{ShouldEx} \wedge (x, w) \in R \wedge \neg\text{MallSim} \wedge \neg\text{Ev}_{(iii)}] \overset{(2)}{\leq} \varepsilon_{sound}. \quad (3)$$

Then

$$\Pr[\text{ExFail} \wedge \neg\text{MallSim}]$$
$$= \Pr[\text{ExFail} \wedge \neg\text{MallSim} \wedge \text{Ev}_{(iii)}] + \Pr[\text{ExFail} \wedge \neg\text{MallSim} \wedge \neg\text{Ev}_{(iii)}]$$
$$\overset{(3)}{\leq} \Pr[\text{ExFail} \wedge \neg\text{MallSim} \wedge \text{Ev}_{(iii)}] + \varepsilon_{sound}. \quad (4)$$

Assume ExFail $\wedge \neg$MallSim. As seen above (in the case ShouldEx $\wedge \neg$MallSim $\wedge \neg$Ev$_{(iii)}$), this implies that $H_0(x, \pi_{half}) = H_1(x, \pi_{half})$ and that $(com_i, ch_{i,J_i}, resp_i)$ is Σ-valid for all i and $h_{i,J_i} = G(resp_i)$ for all i, where $J_1 \| \dots \| J_t := H_1(x, \pi_{half})$. This immediately implies Ev$_{(i)}$ and Ev$_{(ii)}$. Thus

$$\Pr[\text{ExFail} \wedge \neg\text{MallSim}] \overset{(4)}{\leq} \Pr[\text{ExFail} \wedge \neg\text{MallSim} \wedge \text{Ev}_{(iii)}] + \varepsilon_{sound}$$
$$\overset{(*)}{=} \Pr[\text{ExFail} \wedge \neg\text{MallSim} \wedge \text{Ev}_{(i)} \wedge \text{Ev}_{(ii)} \wedge \text{Ev}_{(iii)}] + \varepsilon_{sound}$$
$$\leq \Pr[\text{Ev}_{(i)} \wedge \text{Ev}_{(ii)} \wedge \text{Ev}_{(iii)}] + \varepsilon_{sound} \quad (5)$$

where $(*)$ uses ExFail $\wedge \neg$MallSim $\Rightarrow$ Ev$_{(i)} \wedge$ Ev$_{(ii)}$.

As already seen in the proof of Theorem 10, $H = H_0$ as chosen by S_{init}^{OE} is perfectly indistinguishable from a uniformly random $H_0 : \{0, 1\}^{\leq \ell} \to \{0, 1\}^{t \log m}$

using only q_H queries. Thus we can apply Lemma 12, and get $\Pr[\mathsf{Ev}_{(i)} \wedge \mathsf{Ev}_{(ii)} \wedge \mathsf{Ev}_{(iii)}] \le 2(q_H+1)2^{-(t\log m)/2}$.

And by Lemma 11, we have $\Pr[\mathsf{MallSim}] \le \frac{n(n+1)}{2}2^{-\kappa} + O\big((q_G+1)^3 2^{-\ell_{resp}}\big)$. We have

$$\Pr[\mathsf{ExFail}] \le \Pr[\mathsf{ExFail} \wedge \neg\mathsf{MallSim}] + \Pr[\mathsf{MallSim}]$$

$$\overset{(5)}{\le} \Pr[\mathsf{Ev}_{(i)} \wedge \mathsf{Ev}_{(ii)} \wedge \mathsf{Ev}_{(iii)}] + \varepsilon_{sound} + \Pr[\mathsf{MallSim}]$$

$$\le 2(q_H+1)2^{-(t\log m)/2} + \varepsilon_{sound} + \frac{n(n+1)}{2}2^{-\kappa} + O\big((q_G+1)^3 2^{-\ell_{resp}}\big) =: \mu.$$

$$(6)$$

Since the adversary A is polynomial-time, q_H, q_G, n are polynomially-bounded. Furthermore $t\log m$ and κ and ℓ_{resp} are superlogarithmic by assumption. Thus μ is negligible. And since ExFail is the probability that the adversary wins in Definition 4, it follows that (P_{OE}, V_{OE}) is simulation-sound online-extractable. □

Corollary 14. *If there is a sigma-protocol Σ that is complete and HVZK and has special soundness, then there exists a non-interactive zero-knowledge proof system with simulation-sound online extractability in the random oracle model.*

Proof. Without loss of generality, we can assume that the commitments and the responses of Σ have at least superlogarithmic collision-entropy κ'. (This can always be achieved without losing completeness, HVZK, or special soundness by adding κ' random bits to the commitments and the responses of Σ.) This also implies that ℓ_{resp} is superlogarithmic. And it implies that the tuples $\big((com_i)_i, (chi_{i,j})_{i,j}, (h_{i,j})_{i,j}, (resp_i)_i\big)$ produced by P_{OE} have superlogarithmic collision-entropy $\ge \kappa'$.

Fix polynomially-bounded t, m such that m is a power of two with $2 \le m \le |N_{resp}|$ and such that $t\log m$ is superlogarithmic. (E.g., t superlogarithmic and $m = 2$.) and let (V_{OE}, P_{OE}) be as in Definition 8 (with parameters t, m).

Then by Theorem 10, (V_{OE}, P_{OE}) is zero-knowledge.

The collision-entropy κ of the tuples $\big((com_i)_i, (chi_{i,j})_{i,j}, (h_{i,j})_{i,j}, (resp_i)_i\big)$ produced by $S_{P_{OE}}$ is superlogarithmic. (Otherwise one could distinguish between P_{OE} and $S_{P_{OE}}$ by invoking it twice with the same argument and checking if they result in the same tuple.)

Then by Theorem 13, (V_{OE}, P_{OE}) is simulation-sound online-extractable. □

4   Signatures

A typical application of non-interactive zero-knowledge proofs of knowledge are signature schemes. E.g., the Fiat-Shamir construction [10] was originally described as a signature scheme. As a litmus test whether our security definitions (Definition 2 and Definition 4) are reasonable in the quantum setting, we demonstrate how to construct signatures from non-interactive simulation-sound online-extractable zero-knowledge protocols (in particular the protocol (P_{OE}, V_{OE}) from Definition 8). The construction is standard, and the proof simple, but we believe that such a sanity check for the definitions is necessary, because sometimes a definition is perfectly reasonable in the classical setting while its natural quantum counterpart is almost useless. (An example is the classical definition of "computationally binding commitments" which was shown to imply almost no security in the quantum setting [2].)

The basic idea of the construction is that to sign a message m, one needs to show the knowledge of one's secret key. Thus, we need a relation R between public and secret keys, and we need an algorithm G to generate public/secret key pairs such that it is hard to guess the secret key. The following definition formalizes this:

Definition 15 (Hard instance generators). *We call an algorithm G a hard instance generator for a relation R iff*
- $\Pr[(p, s) \in R : (p, s) \leftarrow G()]$ *is overwhelming and*
- *for any polynomial-time A, $\Pr[(p, s') \in R : (p, s) \leftarrow G(), s' \leftarrow A(p)]$ is negligible.*

An example of a hard instance generator would be: $R := \{(p, s) : p = f(s)\}$ for a one-way function f, and G picks s uniformly from the domain of f, sets $p := f(s)$, and returns (p, s).

Now a signature is just a proof of knowledge of the secret key. That is, the statement is the public key, and the witness is the secret key. However, a signature should be bound to a particular message. For this, we include the message m in the statement that is proven. That is, the statement that is proven consists of a public key and a message, but the message is ignored when determining whether a given statement has a witness or not. (In the definition below, this is formalized by considering an extended relation R'.) The simulation-soundness of the proof system will then guarantee that a proof/signature with respect to one message cannot be transformed into a proof/signature with respect to another message because this would mean changing the statement.

A signature scheme consists of a key generation algorithm $(pk, sk) \leftarrow KeyGen()$. The secret key sk is used to sign a message m using the signing algorithm $\sigma \leftarrow Sign(sk, m)$ to get a signature σ. And the signature is valid iff $Verify(pk, \sigma, m) = 1$.

Definition 16 (Signatures from non-interactive proofs). *Let G be a hard instance generator for a relation R. Let $R' := \{((p, m), s) : (p, s) \in R\}$. Let (P, V) be a non-interactive proof system for R' (in the random oracle model). Then we construct the signature scheme $(KeyGen, Sign, Verify)$ as follows:*
- *$KeyGen()$: Pick $(p, s) \leftarrow G()$. Let $pk := p$, $sk := (p, s)$. Return (pk, sk).*
- *$Sign(sk, m)$ with $sk = (p, s)$: Run $\sigma \leftarrow P(x, w)$ with $x := (p, m)$ and $w := s$. Return σ.*
- *$Verify(pk, \sigma, m)$ with $pk = y$: Run $ok \leftarrow V(x, \sigma)$ with $x := (p, m)$. Return ok.*

Notice that if we use the scheme (P_{OE}, V_{OE}) from Definition 8, we do not need to explicitly find a sigma-protocol for the relation R'. This is because an HVZK sigma protocol with special soundness for R will automatically also be an HVZK sigma protocol with special soundness for R'. Thus, the only effect of considering the relation R' is that in P_{OE}, the message m will be additionally included in the hash query $H(x, (com_i), (ch_i), (h_{i,j}))$ as part of $x = (p, m)$.

Definition 17 (Strong unforgeability). *A signature scheme (KeyGen, Sign, Verify) is* strongly unforgeable *iff for all polynomial-time adversaries A,*

$$\Pr[ok = 1 \wedge (m^*, \sigma^*) \notin Q : H \leftarrow \mathsf{ROdist}, (pk, sk) \leftarrow KeyGen(),$$
$$(\sigma^*, m^*) \leftarrow A^{H,\mathbf{Sig}}(pk), ok \leftarrow Verify(pk, \sigma^*, m^*)]$$

is negligible. Here **Sig** *is a classical oracle that upon classical input m returns Sign(sk, m). (But queries to H are quantum.) And Q is the list of all queries made to* **Sig**. *(I.e., when* **Sig**(m) *returns* σ, (m, σ) *is added to the list Q.)*

If we replace $(m^*, \sigma^*) \notin Q$ *by* $\forall \sigma. (m^*, \sigma) \notin Q$, *we say the signature scheme is* unforgeable.

Theorem 18 (Unforgeability). *If* (P, V) *is zero-knowledge and has simulation-sound online-extractability, then the signature scheme (KeyGen, Sign, Verify) from Definition 16 is strongly unforgeable.*

Proof. Fix a quantum-polynomial-time adversary A. We need to show that the following probability P_1 is negligible.

$$P_1 := \Pr[ok = 1 \wedge (m^*, \sigma^*) \notin Q : H \leftarrow \mathsf{ROdist}, (pk, sk) \leftarrow KeyGen(),$$
$$(\sigma^*, m^*) \leftarrow A^{H,\mathbf{Sig}}(pk), ok \leftarrow Verify(pk, \sigma^*, m^*)]$$

By definition of the signature scheme,

$$P_1 = \Pr[ok = 1 \wedge (m^*, \sigma^*) \notin Q : H \leftarrow \mathsf{ROdist}, (p, s) \leftarrow G(),$$
$$(\sigma^*, m^*) \leftarrow A^{H,\mathbf{Sig}}(p), ok \leftarrow V((p, m^*), \sigma^*)]$$

And **Sig**(m) returns the proof $P((p, m), s)$. And G is the hard instance generator used in the construction of the signature scheme.

Since G is a hard instance generator, we have that $(p, s) \in R$ with overwhelming probability. Thus, with overwhelming probability, for all m, $((p, m), s) \in R'$. Thus, with overwhelming probability, **Sig** invokes $P((p, m), s)$ only with $((p, m), s) \in R'$. Since (P, V) is zero-knowledge (Definition 2), we can replace $H \leftarrow \mathsf{ROdist}$ by $H \leftarrow S_{init}()$ and $P((p, m), s)$ by $S_P((p, m))$ where (S_{init}, S_P) is the simulator for (P, V). That is, $|P_1 - P_2|$ is negligible where:

$$P_2 := \Pr[ok = 1 \wedge (m^*, \sigma^*) \notin Q : H \leftarrow S_{init}(), (p, s) \leftarrow G(),$$
$$(\sigma^*, m^*) \leftarrow A^{H,\mathbf{Sig}'}(p), ok \leftarrow V((p, m^*), \sigma^*)]$$

and **Sig'**(m) returns $S_P((p, m))$.

Let E be the extractor whose existence is guaranteed by the simulation-sound online-extractability of (P, V), see Definition 4. Consider the following game $\mathbf{G}$:

$$\mathbf{G} \quad := \quad H \leftarrow S_{init}(), (p, s) \leftarrow G(), (\sigma^*, m^*) \leftarrow A^{H, \mathbf{Sig}'}(p),$$
$$ok \leftarrow V((p, m^*), \sigma^*), s' \leftarrow E(H, (p, m^*), \sigma^*).$$

That is, we perform the same operations as in P_2, except that we additionally try to extract a witness for the statement (p, m^*). Since the output of E is simply ignored, $\Pr[ok = 1 \ \wedge \ (m^*, \sigma^*) \notin Q : \mathbf{G}] = P_2$.

Let *simproofs* denote the list of queries made to S_P, i.e., whenever $\mathbf{Sig}'(m)$ queries $S_P((p, m))$ resulting in proof/signature σ, (p, m, σ) is appended to *simproofs*. Note that whenever some (p, m, σ) is appended to *simproofs*, (m, σ) is appended to Q. Thus $(m^*, \sigma^*) \notin Q$ implies $(p, m^*, \sigma^*) \notin$ *simproofs*.

Since (P, V) is simulation-sound online-extractable, $P_3 := \Pr[ok = 1 \ \wedge \ (p, m^*, \sigma^*) \notin$ *simproofs* $\wedge \ ((p, m^*), s') \notin R' : \mathbf{G}]$ is negligible.

Since $(m^*, \sigma^*) \notin Q$ implies $(p, m^*, \sigma^*) \notin$ *simproofs*, and $((p, m^*), s') \in R'$ iff $(p, s') \in R$, we have $P_3 \geq P_4$ with $P_4 := \Pr[ok = 1 \wedge (m^*, \sigma^*) \notin Q \wedge (p, s') \notin R : \mathbf{G}]$. Hence P_4 is negligible.

And since G is a hard instance generator and s is never given to any algorithm in $\mathbf{G}$, $P_5 := \Pr[ok = 1 \wedge (m^*, \sigma^*) \notin Q \wedge (p, s') \in R : \mathbf{G}]$ is negligible.

Thus $P_2 = P_4 + P_5$ is negligible. And since $|P_1 - P_2|$ is negligible, P_1 is negligible. Since this holds for any quantum-polynomial-time A, the signature scheme is strongly unforgeable. □

Note that this proof is exactly as it would have been in the classical case (even though the adversary A was quantum). This is due to the fact that simulation-sound online-extractability as defined in Definition 4 allows us to extract a witness in a non-invasive way: we do not need to operate in any way on the quantum state of the adversary (be it by measuring or by rewinding); we get the witness purely by inspecting the classical proof/signature σ^*. This avoids the usual problem of disturbing the quantum state while trying to extract a witness.

Acknowledgments. We thank Marc Fischlin and Tommaso Gagliardoni for valuable discussions and the initial motivation for this work. This work was supported by the Estonian ICT program 2011-2015 (3.2.1201.13-0022), the European Union through the European Regional Development Fund through the sub-measure "Supporting the development of R&D of info and communication technology", by the European Social Fund's Doctoral Studies and Internationalisation Programme DoRa, by the Estonian Centre of Excellence in Computer Science, EXCS.

A   Sigma-Protocols with Oblivious Commitments

In this section we review the definition of sigma-protocols with oblivious commitments [7] and explain why they directly imply NIZK proofs in the CRS model.

Definition 19 (Sigma-protocols with oblivious commitments, following [7]). *A sigma-protocol* $\Sigma = (N, , N_{ch}, N_{resp}, P_{\Sigma}^1, P_{\Sigma}^2, V_{\Sigma})$ *has oblivious commitments if* P_{Σ}^1 *simply chooses and return a uniformly random bitstring from* $N, .$[11]

In other words, in a sigma-protocol with oblivious commitments, the first message (the commitment) is uniformly random. (While normally, we only require the second message to be uniformly random.)

Note that [7] defines oblivious commitments slightly differently: the prover does not have to send a uniformly random commitment. Instead, given its commitment, it should be efficiently feasible to find randomness that leads to that commitment. But [7] points out that that definition is equivalent to what we wrote in Definition 19 (in the sense that a protocol satisfying one definition can easily be transformed into one satisfying the other). Furthermore, [7] actually assumes Definition 19 in their construction, so we give and discuss that definition here. [7] proves (restated using the language from our paper):

Theorem 20 (Fiat-Shamir-like signatures, [7]). *Assume a hard instance generator* G *and a sigma-protocol* Σ *with oblivious commitments, completeness, special-soundness, and HVZK.*

Then there is an unforgeable signature scheme (build in an efficient way from G *and* Σ*).*

The actual construction used [7] is not Fiat-Shamir, but only inspired by Fiat-Shamir. The crucial difference is that the commitments are not chosen by the prover, but instead are hash values output by the random oracle (the same way as the challenges are output by the random oracle in normal Fiat-Shamir).

At the first glance this theorem might seem unrelated to the problem of constructing NIZK proofs. However, their proof of unforgeability implicitly proves the existence of an extractor (though not of a simulation-sound extractor) because it works by extracting two sigma-protocol executions and then computing a witness from those.

Note however that the proof from [7] does not show that their construction is zero-knowledge. Yet, we conjecture that with the random oracle programming techniques presented here, one can show that their construction is zero-knowledge using a proof similar to ours.

Relation to CRS NIZK Proofs. We now argue why sigma-protocols with oblivious commitments are quite a strong assumption. Namely, they are by themselves (without any use of a random oracle) already NIZK proofs of knowledge in the CRS model.

Given a sigma-protocol $\Sigma = (N, , N_{ch}, N_{resp}, P_{\Sigma}^1, P_{\Sigma}^2, V_{\Sigma})$ with oblivious commitments, we construct a proof system $\Pi_{\Sigma} = (CRS, P, V)$ in the CRS model as

---

[11] We stress that P_{Σ}^1 needs to directly output its randomness. For example, if P_{Σ}^1 produces $com := f(r)$ with random r using a one-way permutation f, then P_{Σ}^1 does not have oblivious commitments, even though com is uniformly distributed. (Because P_{Σ}^1 additionally produces a preimage of com under f.)

follows: The CRS crs is uniformly random from the set $crs := N_, \times N_{ch}$. The prover $P(crs, x, w)$ splits $crs =: (com, ch)$, runs $P_\Sigma^1(x, w)$ with the randomness that would yield com (this is possible because in a sigma-protocol with oblivious commitments, P_Σ^1 just outputs its randomness), and runs $resp \leftarrow P_\Sigma^2(ch)$. The proof is $\pi := resp$. The verifier $V(crs, x, \pi)$ splits $crs =: (com, ch)$ and $resp := \pi$ and runs $V_\Sigma(x, com, ch, resp)$ and accepts if V_Σ accepts.

We now show that (P, V) is both zero-knowledge and a proof of knowledge in the CRS model.

Definition 21 (Zero-knowledge in the CRS model). *A non-interactive protocol (CRS, P, V) is* (single-theorem, non-adaptive) *zero-knowledge in the CRS model for relation R iff there exists a polynomial-time simulator S such that for any quantum-polynomial-time adversary (A_1, A_2), the following is negligible:*

$$\big| \Pr[(x, w) \in R \wedge b = 1 : (x, w) \leftarrow A_1(), \ crs \xleftarrow{\$} CRS, \ \pi \leftarrow P(crs, x, w),$$
$$b \leftarrow A_2(crs, \pi)]$$
$$- \Pr[(x, w) \in R \wedge b = 1 : (x, w) \leftarrow A_1(), \ crs, \pi \xleftarrow{\$} S(x), \ b \leftarrow A_2(crs, \pi)] \big|$$

Notice that we have chosen the variant of zero-knowledge that is usually called single-theorem, non-adaptive zero-knowledge. That is, given one CRS, one is allowed to produce only a single proof. And the statement x that is to be proven may not depend on the CRS.

Lemma 22. *If Σ is a zero-knowledge sigma-protocol with oblivious commitments, then Π_Σ is zero-knowledge in the CRS model.*

Proof. Let $S(x)$ be a simulator that runs $(com, ch, resp) := S_\Sigma(x)$ where S_Σ is the simulator of the sigma-protocol (see Definition 5). Then S computes $crs := (com, ch)$ and $\pi := resp$ and returns (crs, π). Note that $crs = (com, ch) \xleftarrow{\$} CRS = N_, \times N_{ch}$ yields the same distribution of (com, ch) as $com \leftarrow P_\Sigma^1(x)$, $ch \xleftarrow{\$} N_{ch}$. Together with the fact that Σ is zero-knowledge, one easily sees that the probability difference in Definition 21 is negligible for quantum-polynomial-time (A_1, A_2). $\square$

Definition 23 (Proofs of knowledge in the CRS model). *A non-interactive protocol (CRS, P, V) is a* (single-theorem, non-adaptive) *proof of knowledge in the CRS model for relation R iff there exists a polynomial-time extractor (E_1, E_2) such that the output of E_1 is quantum-computationally indistinguishable from $crs \xleftarrow{\$} CRS$, and such that for any quantum-polynomial-time adversary (A_1, A_2), the following probability is negligible:*

$$\Pr[ok = 1 \wedge (x, w) \notin R : x \leftarrow A_1(), crs \leftarrow E_1(x), \pi \leftarrow A_2(crs), w \leftarrow E_2(\pi)]. \quad (7)$$

Note that again, we have defined a weak form of proofs of knowledge: single-theorem and non-adaptive.

Lemma 24. *Let Σ be a sigma-protocol with oblivious commitments. Assume that Σ is zero-knowledge with the following extra properties: for $(com, ch, resp) \leftarrow S_\Sigma(x)$, (com, ch) is quantum-computationally indistinguishable from uniform, and $V_\Sigma(com, ch, resp) = 1$ with overwhelming probability.[12]*
Then Π_Σ is a proof of knowledge in the CRS model.

Proof.   Let $E_1(x)$ run the simulator $(com, ch, resp) \leftarrow S_\Sigma(x)$ of the sigma-protocol Σ. Then E_1 picks $ch' \stackrel{\$}{\leftarrow} N_{ch} \setminus ch$. Then E_1 outputs $crs := (com, ch')$.

Since (com, ch) chosen as $(com, ch, resp) \leftarrow S_\Sigma(x)$ is indistinguishable from uniform, so is (com, ch') as chosen by E_1. Thus $crs = (com, ch')$ as picked by $E_1(x)$ is quantum-computationally indistinguishable from $crs \stackrel{\$}{\leftarrow} CRS = N_, \times N_{ch}$.

The second part of the extractor, $E_2(\pi)$, sets $resp' := \pi$. This yields two executions of the sigma-protocol: $(com, ch, resp)$ and $(com, ch', resp')$ with $ch \neq ch'$. Then E_2 runs $w \leftarrow E_\Sigma(x, com, ch, resp, ch', resp')$ (the extractor of Σ) to get a witness w and returns that witness.

The first execution $(com, ch, resp)$ is valid (i.e., V_Σ accepts it) with overwhelming probability, since $(com, ch, resp)$ was produced by the simulator and thus passes verification with overwhelming probability (by assumption in the lemma). If additionally the second execution $(com, ch', resp')$ is valid (i.e., if $ok = 1$ in (7)), then E_Σ returns a correct witness with overwhelming probability (i.e., $(x, w) \in R$). Thus the case $ok = 1 \wedge (x, w) \notin R$ occurs with negligible probability, hence the probability in (7) is negligible.   □

Summarizing, a sigma-protocol with oblivious commitments is already a NIZK proof of knowledge in the CRS model in itself. Hence sigma-protocols with oblivious commitments seem to be a much stronger assumption that just sigma-protocols. (At least we are not aware of any generic construction, classical or quantum, that transforms a sigma-protocols into a NIZK proof/proof of knowledge in the CRS model, without using random oracles.)

One may ask why the fact that sigma-protocols with oblivious commitments are already NIZK proofs of knowledge does not trivialize the construction from [7] since it converts a NIZK proof of knowledge into a NIZK proof of knowledge. The crucial point is that sigma-protocols with oblivious commitments are only *single-theorem non-adaptive* NIZK proofs. So one can interpret the construction from [7] as a way of strengthening a specific kind of NIZK proofs to become

---

[12] At the first glance, those properties already follow from zero-knowledge and completeness of Σ. However, zero-knowledge and completeness do not apply when there exists no witness for x. So we need to explicitly require those conditions to also hold when x has no witness.

Note that the proof in [7] does not need these conditions because in their setting, the statement x is the honestly generated public key of the signature scheme, and thus always has a witness. If, however, one would adapt their proof to show that their construction is actually a NIZK proof of knowledge, those conditions would be needed for the same reasons as in our proof of Lemma 24.

multi-theorem adaptive ones.[13] (Actually, seen like this, their construction becomes a very natural one: the statement is hashed using the random oracle, and the hash is used as a CRS for the proof.)

Sigma-protocols with Oblivious Commitments and Efficient Protocols. One major advantage of sigma-protocols is that they allow for very efficient constructions of sigma-protocols for complex relations from simpler ones [6,8]. For example, given sigma-protocols for two relations R_1, R_2, it is possible to build a sigma-protocol for the disjunction $R := \{((x_1, x_2), w) : (x_1, w) \in R_1 \vee (x_2, w) \in R_2\}$. Unfortunately, even when starting with sigma-protocols with oblivious commitments for R_1, R_2, the resulting sigma-protocol for R will not have oblivious commitments any more. This is because the protocol for R sends a commitment (com_1, com_2) where com_1 is generated by the prover of R_1, and com_2 by the simulator of R_2 (or vice versa). Since given the output of the simulator, it is in general hard to determine its randomness, it will not be possible to find the randomness that lead to com_2. Hence the protocol does not have oblivious commitments.

References

1. Adida, B.: Helios: web-based open-audit voting. In: van Oorschot, P.C. (ed.) USENIX Security Symposium 2008, pp. 335–348. USENIX (2008). http://www.usenix.org/events/sec08/tech/full_papers/adida/adida.pdf
2. Ambainis, A., Rosmanis, A., Unruh, D.: Quantum attacks on classical proof systems (the hardness of quantum rewinding). In: FOCS 2014, pp. 474–483. IEEE, October 2014
3. Ben-Or, M.: Probabilistic algorithms in finite fields. In: FOCS 1981, pp. 394–398. IEEE (1981)
4. Blum, M., Feldman, P., Micali, S.: Non-interactive zero-knowledge and its applications. In: Proceedings of the Twentieth Annual ACM Symposium on Theory of Computing, STOC 1988, pp. 103–112. ACM, New York (1988)
5. Brickell, E., Camenisch, J., Chen, L.: Direct anonymous attestation. In: ACM CCS 2004, pp. 132–145. ACM, New York (2004)
6. Cramer, R., Damgård, I.B., Schoenmakers, B.: Proof of partial knowledge and simplified design of witness hiding protocols. In: Desmedt, Y.G. (ed.) CRYPTO 1994. LNCS, vol. 839, pp. 174–187. Springer, Heidelberg (1994)
7. Dagdelen, Ö., Fischlin, M., Gagliardoni, T.: The fiat–shamir transformation in a quantum world. In: Sako, K., Sarkar, P. (eds.) ASIACRYPT 2013, Part II. LNCS, vol. 8270, pp. 62–81. Springer, Heidelberg (2013)
8. Damgård, I.: On σ-protocols. Course notes for "Cryptologic Protocol Theory" (2010). http://www.cs.au.dk/~ivan/Sigma.pdf, http://www.webcitation.org/6O9USFecZ (Retrieved March 17, 2014)
9. Faust, S., Kohlweiss, M., Marson, G.A., Venturi, D.: On the non-malleability of the fiat-shamir transform. In: Galbraith, S., Nandi, M. (eds.) INDOCRYPT 2012. LNCS, vol. 7668, pp. 60–79. Springer, Heidelberg (2012)

---

[13] Assuming that their construction can indeed be proven secure as a NIZK proof of knowledge in the random oracle model.

10. Fiat, A., Shamir, A.: How to prove yourself: practical solutions to identification and signature problems. In: Odlyzko, A.M. (ed.) CRYPTO 1986. LNCS, vol. 263, pp. 186–194. Springer, Heidelberg (1987)

11. Fischlin, M.: Communication-efficient non-interactive proofs of knowledge with online extractors. In: Shoup, V. (ed.) CRYPTO 2005. LNCS, vol. 3621, pp. 152–168. Springer, Heidelberg (2005)

12. Goldreich, O., Micali, S., Wigderson, A.: Proofs that yield nothing but their validity or all languages in NP have zero-knowledge proof systems. J ACM 38(3), 690–728 (1991)

13. Groth, J.: Simulation-sound NIZK proofs for a practical language and constant size group signatures. In: Lai, X., Chen, K. (eds.) ASIACRYPT 2006. LNCS, vol. 4284, pp. 444–459. Springer, Heidelberg (2006)

14. Groth, J., Sahai, A.: Efficient non-interactive proof systems for bilinear groups. In: Smart, N.P. (ed.) EUROCRYPT 2008. LNCS, vol. 4965, pp. 415–432. Springer, Heidelberg (2008)

15. Pointcheval, D., Stern, J.: Security proofs for signature schemes. In: Maurer, U.M. (ed.) EUROCRYPT 1996. LNCS, vol. 1070, pp. 387–398. Springer, Heidelberg (1996)

16. A. Sahai. Non-malleable non-interactive zero knowledge and adaptive chosen-ciphertext security. In: FOCS 1999, pp. 543–553. IEEE (1999)

17. Shor, P.W.: Algorithms for quantum computation: discrete logarithms and factoring. In: FOCS 1994, pp. 124–134. IEEE (1994)

18. Unruh, D.: Quantum proofs of knowledge. In: Pointcheval, D., Johansson, T. (eds.) EUROCRYPT 2012. LNCS, vol. 7237, pp. 135–152. Springer, Heidelberg (2012)

19. Unruh, D.: Non-interactive zero-knowledge proofs in the quantum random oracle model. IACR ePrint 2014/587 (2014). Full version of this paper

20. Unruh, D.: Quantum position verification in the random oracle model. In: Crypto 2014, LNCS. Springer, February 2014. To appear, preprint on IACR ePrint 2014/118

21. Unruh, D.: Revocable quantum timed-release encryption. In: Nguyen, P.Q., Oswald, E. (eds.) EUROCRYPT 2014. LNCS, vol. 8441, pp. 129–146. Springer, Heidelberg (2014)

22. Watrous, J.: Zero-knowledge against quantum attacks. SIAM J. Comput. 39(1), 25–58 (2009)

23. Zhandry, M.: Secure identity-based encryption in the quantum random oracle model. In: Safavi-Naini, R., Canetti, R. (eds.) CRYPTO 2012. LNCS, vol. 7417, pp. 758–775. Springer, Heidelberg (2012)

24. Zhandry, M.: A note on the quantum collision and set equality problems, Dec. 2013. arXiv:1312.1027v3 [cs.CC]

Privacy Amplification in the Isolated Qubits Model

Yi-Kai Liu[(⊠)]

Applied and Computational Mathematics Division,
National Institute of Standards and Technology,
Gaithersburg, MD, USA
yi-kai.liu@nist.gov

Abstract. Isolated qubits are a special class of quantum devices, which can be used to implement tamper-resistant cryptographic hardware such as one-time memories (OTM's). Unfortunately, these OTM constructions leak some information, and standard methods for privacy amplification cannot be applied here, because the adversary has advance knowledge of the hash function that the honest parties will use.

In this paper we show a stronger form of privacy amplification that solves this problem, using a *fixed* hash function that is secure against all possible adversaries in the isolated qubits model. This allows us to construct single-bit OTM's which only leak an exponentially small amount of information.

We then study a natural generalization of the isolated qubits model, where the adversary is allowed to perform a polynomially-bounded number of entangling gates, in addition to unbounded local operations and classical communication (LOCC). We show that our technique for privacy amplification is also secure in this setting.

1 Introduction

Can one build tamper-resistant cryptographic hardware whose security is based on the laws of quantum mechanics? This is a natural question, as there are many unusual phenomena in quantum mechanics, such as the impossibility of cloning an unknown quantum state, which seem relevant to cryptography. However, despite these encouraging signs, it turns out that many common cryptographic functionalities, such as bit commitment and oblivious transfer (with information-theoretic security), *cannot* be implemented in a quantum world [1–4].

Recently, there has been progress using a different approach to this problem, called the "isolated qubits model" [5,6]. Isolated qubits are qubits with long coherence times, which can only be accessed using single-qubit gates and measurements; entangling operations are forbidden. Thus, in the isolated qubits model, one assumes an additional restriction on what the adversary can do. Formally, the adversary is only allowed to perform local operations and classical communication, or LOCC, where "local operations" are operations on single qubits, and "classical communication" refers to communication between the

© International Association for Cryptologic Research 2015
E. Oswald and M. Fischlin (Eds.): EUROCRYPT 2015, Part II, LNCS 9057, pp. 785–814, 2015.
DOI: 10.1007/978-3-662-46803-6_26

qubits. (Likewise, honest parties are also restricted to LOCC. Furthermore, while the adversary can perform an unbounded number of operations, all honest parties must run in polynomial time.) Isolated qubits can be viewed as special-purpose quantum devices, which can implement functionalities such as oblivious transfer that are not possible using quantum mechanics alone. Isolated qubits could conceivably be implemented using solid-state nuclear spins, such as quantum dots or nitrogen vacancy centers [7,8].

Using isolated qubits, there are natural candidate constructions that lead to a variety of tamper-resistant cryptographic hardware. The first step is to construct *one-time memories* (OTM's) [5]. Intuitively, a one-time memory is a device that does non-interactive oblivious transfer, i.e., Alice programs the device with two messages s and t, then gives the device to Bob, who can choose to read either s or t (but not both).

Using one-time memories, one can then construct *one-time programs* [9–12], which are useful for program obfuscation, access control and copy protection. A one-time program is a program that can be run only once, and hides its internal state. More precisely, Alice chooses some circuit C, compiles it into a one-time program, and gives it to Bob; Bob then chooses an input x, runs the one-time program, and learns the output of the computation $C(x)$; but Bob learns nothing else, and cannot run the program on another input.

Unfortunately it is not yet possible to prove the security of these one-time programs in the isolated qubits model. This is because the proof of security for the one-time memories in [5] is not strong enough — it allows some extra information to *leak* to the adversary, which can cause problems when the one-time memories are used as part of a larger construction.

In this paper we address the issue of information leakage, by developing a privacy amplification technique that works in the isolated qubits model. By combining this privacy amplification technique with the leaky one-time memories from [5], we obtain new one-time memories that only leak an exponentially small amount of information. These new one-time memories store single bits rather than strings, but these can also be plugged into known constructions for one-time programs [10]. This removes one of the main obstacles to constructing provably-secure one-time programs.

1.1 Privacy Amplification

The candidate construction for one-time memories in [5] was proven to satisfy a "leaky" definition of security, where up to a constant fraction of the bits of the messages could be leaked to the adversary. This notion of security was not as strong as one would have liked, but on the positive side, the adversary's uncertainty was expressed in terms of the smoothed min-entropy, which suggested that the leakage problem might be addressed using some kind of privacy amplification.

However, there is an obstacle to using privacy amplification with our one-time memories. Usually, in privacy amplification, the adversary has partial information about some string s (while the honest parties have complete knowledge of s). Then the honest parties choose a random seed q, and apply a hash function F_q to produce a shorter string $F_q(s)$, which will be almost completely unknown to the adversary. This works provided that the random seed q is chosen independent of the adversary's actions.

But in the case of our one-time memories, all the information needed to decode the messages — including the random seed q — must be provided at the beginning, before the adversary decides how to attack the OTM (i.e., what measurement to perform on the qubits). Thus the adversary's attack can depend on q, and so standard methods of privacy amplification may not be secure.

We show a variant of privacy amplification which uses a *fixed* hash function F (without a random seed), and is secure in the isolated qubits model. Intuitively, this relies on two ideas. First, we use a stronger family of hash functions, namely r-wise independent functions, where r grows polynomially in the security parameter k. These r-wise independent functions can be computed efficiently, but they behave more like truly random functions, in that they satisfy large-deviation bounds, similar to Hoeffding's inequality [13–15].

Second, we exploit the fact that the only way for the adversary to learn about s is by performing LOCC measurements on the qubits that encode s. Rather than considering all possible LOCC measurement strategies, which are represented by decision trees, we consider all possible LOCC measurement outcomes, which are represented by POVM elements.[1] Due to the LOCC restriction, these POVM elements are tensor products of single-qubit operators. So there are not too many of them. Say we discretize the set of possible measurement outcomes, with some fixed resolution.[2] Then the number of LOCC measurement outcomes grows exponentially with the number of qubits; this is in contrast with the number of *entangled* measurement outcomes, which grows doubly-exponentially with the number of qubits. Hence we can use a union bound over the set of all LOCC measurement outcomes.

We do privacy amplification as follows. We first choose a hash function F from an r-wise independent family. We then fix F permanently, and announce it to the adversary. We claim that, with high probability over the choice of F, this privacy amplification scheme will be secure against *all* possible LOCC adversaries, i.e., every adversary who uses LOCC measurements and gains at most partial information about the string s, will still have very little information about $F(s)$.

The proof uses a covering argument over the set of all LOCC measurement outcomes. First, fix some particular LOCC measurement outcome M. Let S be the random variable representing the string s, and suppose the hash function F outputs a single bit $F(S)$. One can calculate the bias of the bit $F(S)$, conditioned on having observed outcome M, as follows:

$$\mathbb{E}_S((-1)^{F(S)} \mid M) = \sum_s (-1)^{F(s)} \Pr(S = s \mid M). \tag{1}$$

(Here $\mathbb{E}_S$ denotes the expectation value obtained by averaging over S.)

---

[1] POVM elements are defined in Section 2.2, but we do not require these formal definitions here.

[2] Formally, we consider an ε-net, as defined in Section 2.1.

We want to show that $\mathbb{E}_S((-1)^{F(S)} \mid M)$ is small. Note that $\mathbb{E}_S((-1)^{F(S)} \mid M)$ is a linear combination of terms $(-1)^{F(s)}$, where each $F(s)$ is a random variable describing the initial choice of the hash function F. We can use Hoeffding-like inequalities to show that, with high probability over the choice of F, $\mathbb{E}_S((-1)^{F(S)} \mid M)$ is sharply concentrated around 0. This will work provided that $\sum_s \Pr(S = s \mid M)^2$ is small, which follows since the Renyi entropy $H_2(S|M)$ (or the smoothed min-entropy $H_\infty^\varepsilon(S|M)$) are large, which holds since the adversary has at most partial information about S. Thus, one can conclude that, for a fixed LOCC measurement outcome M, with high probability over the choice of F, $\mathbb{E}_S((-1)^{F(S)} \mid M)$ is small, i.e., privacy amplification succeeds.

Finally, one uses the union bound over all LOCC measurement outcomes M. This shows that, with high probability over the choice of F, for all LOCC measurement outcomes M, privacy amplification succeeds. This completes the proof.

The above sketch shows privacy amplification for a single string s, but a similar technique can be applied to an OTM that stores two strings s and t. Here one applies two hash functions F and G, which output a pair of bits $F(s)$ and $G(t)$. Now there is an additional complication, since the adversary has the possibility of learning information about the *correlations* between $F(s)$ and $G(t)$. To address this issue, one needs to bound the quantity

$$\mathbb{E}_{ST}((-1)^{F(S)+G(T)} \mid M) = \sum_{st}(-1)^{F(s)}(-1)^{G(t)}\Pr(S = s, T = t \mid M). \quad (2)$$

This is a quadratic function of the random variables $(-1)^{F(s)}$ and $(-1)^{G(t)}$, describing the initial choices of the hash functions F and G. This can be bounded using the Hanson-Wright inequality [17,18], adapted for r-wise independent variables using the techniques of [14,15].

Formally, this shows a reduction from an almost-perfect single-bit OTM to a leaky string-OTM. (That is, given an OTM that stores two strings and leaks a constant fraction of the information, one can construct an OTM that stores two bits and leaks an exponentially small amount of information.) By combining with the results of [5], we get almost-perfect single-bit OTM's in the isolated qubits model.

1.2   Beyond the Isolated Qubits Model

Next, we study a generalization of the isolated qubits model, where the adversary is allowed to perform a polynomially-bounded number of 2-qubit entangling gates, in addition to unbounded LOCC operations. More precisely, this model is specified by a constant $c \geq 0$, and a "depth" parameter d, which can grow with the security parameter k, as long as $d \leq k^c$; then this model allows the adversary to apply quantum circuits of depth d containing 2-qubit gates combined with unbounded LOCC operations. (Honest parties are still restricted to polynomial-time LOCC.) This model may be a more accurate description of real solid-state qubits, where one can perform noisy entangling gates, but the accumulation of noise makes it difficult to entangle large numbers of qubits at once.

It is an interesting open problem to construct OTM's that are secure in this model. We show that our reduction from almost-perfect single-bit OTM's to leaky string-OTM's still works in this setting. More precisely, for any constant $c \geq 0$, and any depth $d \leq k^c$, we show a variant of our reduction, whose efficiency is polynomial in d, that remains secure in this depth-d model. The proof uses the same ideas as before.

Unfortunately, the leaky string-OTM's from [5] are not known to be secure in this setting. Nonetheless we believe it should be possible to construct leaky string-OTM's in this depth-d model, for at least some super-constant values of d, for the following intuitive reason: in order to break the leaky string-OTM's from [5], one has to break a particular version of Wiesner's conjugate coding scheme [19], and this requires running a classical decoding algorithm on a quantum superposition of inputs, which requires applying a quantum circuit with a certain minimum number of entangling gates.

1.3   Discussion

Related Work: This paper builds on recent work on non-interactive one-time memories in the isolated qubits model [5,6]. Some similar ideas have been investigated in connection with other cryptographic tasks, such as bit commitment, quantum money and password-based identification [20–22]. There is also a related line of work on LOCC state discrimination, involving "nonlocality without entanglement" and data-hiding states [23–26].

Deterministic privacy amplification has also been studied for other cryptographic tasks, such as secret key distribution based on causality constraints [27]. Our results can also be compared to earlier work on deterministic extractors for special classes of random sources, as well as exposure-resilient cryptography and leakage-resilient cryptography [28–30], [31,32]. However, these earlier works considered classical adversaries, with various kinds of restrictions; our result, with a quantum adversary restricted to (unbounded) LOCC operations, seems to be new.

Open Problems: The overall goal of this work is to construct one-time programs whose security is based on the properties of realistic physical devices. One-time memories and the isolated qubits model are useful steps along the way to achieving this goal, but there remain several open problems.

First, can one prove that these one-time memories satisfy a sufficiently strong notion of security, so that they can be composed to build one-time programs? Privacy amplification is helpful, but there may be other issues that affect the security of more complicated protocols, such as the adversary's ability to wait until later stages of the protocol before performing any measurements.

Second, can one modify the isolated qubits model so that it matches more closely the properties of real solid-state qubits, e.g., by allowing a limited number of entangling operations? Our model involving bounded-depth quantum circuits is one step in this direction.

2   Preliminaries

2.1   Notation, ε-nets

For any two matrices A and B, we write $A \preceq B$ if and only if $B - A$ is positive semidefinite. We let $\|A\|$ denote the operator norm, $\|A\|_{\mathrm{tr}}$ denote the trace norm, and $\|A\|_F$ denote the Frobenius norm. For any vector v, we let $\|v\|_p$ denote the ℓ_p norm of v. For any two probability densities P and Q, we let $\|P - Q\|_1$ denote the ℓ_1 distance between them.

We write $\Pr[\mathcal{E}]$ to denote the probability of an event $\mathcal{E}$. We write $\mathbb{E}[X]$ to denote the expectation value of a random variable X. In some cases we write $\Pr_X[\cdot]$ or $\mathbb{E}_X[\cdot]$ to emphasize that we are considering probabilities associated with a random variable X. We write $P_{X|Y}$ to denote a probability density function $P_{X|Y}(x|y) = \Pr[X = x \mid Y = y]$. In some cases we abuse this notation, e.g., if $\mathcal{E}$ is an event, we write $P_{\mathcal{E}X|Y}(x|y) = \Pr[\mathcal{E}, X = x \mid Y = y]$. Also, if $\mathcal{E}$ is an event, we let $1_{\mathcal{E}}$ be the indicator random variable for $\mathcal{E}$, which equals 1 when the event $\mathcal{E}$ happens, and equals 0 otherwise.

Suppose E is a subset of some normed space, with norm $\|\cdot\|$. Let $\varepsilon > 0$. We say that $\tilde{E}$ is an ε-net for E if $\tilde{E} \subset E$, and for every $x \in E$, there exists some $y \in \tilde{E}$ such that $\|x - y\| \leq \varepsilon$.

2.2   Quantum Measurements

A quantum state is described by a *density matrix* $\rho \in \mathbb{C}^{d \times d}$ with $\rho \succeq 0$ and $\mathrm{tr}(\rho) = 1$. A quantum measurement can be described by a *completely-positive trace-preserving map* $\mathcal{E} : \mathbb{C}^{d \times d} \to \mathbb{C}^{d \times d}$, which can be written in the form $\mathcal{E}(\rho) = \sum_i K_i \rho K_i^{\dagger}$, where the $K_i \in \mathbb{C}^{d \times d}$ are called *Kraus operators* and $\sum_i K_i^{\dagger} K_i = I$. Given a state ρ, the measurement returns outcome i with probability $\mathrm{tr}(K_i \rho K_i^{\dagger})$, in which case the post-measurement state is given by $K_i \rho K_i^{\dagger} / \mathrm{tr}(K_i \rho K_i^{\dagger})$.

A measurement outcome can also be described by a *POVM element*,[3] that is, a matrix $M \in \mathbb{C}^{d \times d}$ with $0 \preceq M \preceq I$. Given a state ρ, the probability that a measurement returns outcome M is given by $\mathrm{tr}(M\rho)$. (In the example in the previous paragraph, the outcome i is described by the POVM element $K_i^{\dagger} K_i$.)

2.3   LOCC and Separable Measurements

In the isolated qubits model, qubits are only accessible via *local operations and classical communication* (LOCC), that is, one can perform single-qubit quantum operations, and use classical information (obtained by measuring one qubit) to choose what operation to perform on another qubit. LOCC strategies can thus be represented by decision trees, where each vertex corresponds to a single-qubit operation, and each edge corresponds to a possible (classical) outcome of that operation [5,6].

---

[3] POVM refers to positive operator-valued measure, though we will not need to use this concept here.

A measurement on m qubits is called *separable* if it can be written in the form $\mathcal{E}$: $\rho \mapsto \sum_i K_i \rho K_i^\dagger$, where each operator K_i is a tensor product of m single-qubit operators, $K_i = K_{i,1} \otimes K_{i,2} \otimes \cdots \otimes K_{i,m}$. It is easy to see that any LOCC measurement is separable [34].

2.4   Smoothed Min-entropy

We recall the definition of the smoothed conditional min-entropy:

$$H_\infty^\varepsilon(X|Y) = \max_{\mathcal{E}:\, \Pr(\mathcal{E}) \geq 1-\varepsilon} \; \min_{x,y} \Big[-\lg\big[P_{\mathcal{E}X|Y}(x|y) \big] \Big], \tag{3}$$

where the maximization is over all events $\mathcal{E}$ (defined by the conditional probabilities $P_{\mathcal{E}|XY}$) such that $\Pr(\mathcal{E}) \geq 1 - \varepsilon$. Note that a lower-bound of the form $H_\infty^\varepsilon(X|Y) \geq h$ implies that there exists an event $\mathcal{E}$ with $\Pr(\mathcal{E}) \geq 1 - \varepsilon$ such that, for all x and y, $\Pr[\mathcal{E}, X = x|Y = y] \leq 2^{-h}$.

We will need the following "entropy splitting lemma," which appeared in [33]. Intuitively, this says that if X_0 and X_1 together have min-entropy at least α, then at least one of them (indicated by the random variable C) must have min-entropy at least $\alpha/2$.

Proposition 2.1. *Let $\varepsilon \geq 0$, and let X_0, X_1 and Z be random variables (which may be over different alphabets) such that $H_\infty^\varepsilon(X_0, X_1 \,|\, Z) \geq \alpha$. Then there exists a random variable C taking values in $\{0, 1\}$ such that*

$$H_\infty^{\varepsilon+\varepsilon'}(X_{1-C} \,|\, Z, C) \geq \tfrac{1}{2}\alpha - 1 - \lg(\tfrac{1}{\varepsilon'}) \qquad \text{(for any } \varepsilon' > 0). \tag{4}$$

2.5   Leaky String-OTM's

The main result from [5] was a construction of a leaky string-OTM (which stores two strings, and leaks at most a constant fraction of the information) in the isolated qubits model. Here we state this result using slightly different language — in particular, we state the result in terms of "δ-non-negligible" measurement outcomes, whereas in [5] this terminology was used in the proof but not in the statement of the theorem.

Definition 2.1. *For any quantum state $\rho \in \mathbb{C}^{d \times d}$, and any $\delta > 0$, we say that a measurement outcome (POVM element) $M \in \mathbb{C}^{d \times d}$ is δ-non-negligible if $\text{tr}(M\rho) \geq \delta \,\text{tr}(M)/d$.*

Intuitively, these are the only measurement outcomes we need to consider in our security proof, as the total probability contributed by all the other "δ-negligible" measurement outcomes is never more than δ. To see this, consider any measurement, which can be described by a collection of POVM elements $\{M_z \mid z = 1, 2, \ldots\}$ such that $\sum_z M_z = I$. Say we perform this measurement on some state ρ, and let Z be the random variable representing the outcome of the measurement (so Z takes values $M_1, M_2, \ldots$). Then the total probability of observing a δ-negligible measurement outcome is at most δ:

Pr[outcome Z is δ-negligible]

$$= \sum_{z \,:\, M_z \text{ is } \delta\text{-negl.}} \mathrm{tr}(M_z \rho) < \sum_{z \,:\, M_z \text{ is } \delta\text{-negl.}} \delta \, \mathrm{tr}(M_z)/d \leq \delta. \quad (5)$$

We now restate the main result from [5]:

Theorem 2.1. *For any $k \geq 2$, and for any small constant $0 < \mu \ll 1$, there exists an OTM construction that stores two messages $s, t \in \{0,1\}^\ell$, where $\ell = \Theta(k^2)$, and has the following properties:*

1. *Correctness and efficiency: there are honest strategies for programming the OTM with messages s and t, and for reading either s or t, using only LOCC operations, and time polynomial in k.*
2. *"Leaky" security: Let $\delta_0 > 0$ be any constant, and set $\delta = 2^{-\delta_0 k}$. Suppose the messages s and t are chosen independently and uniformly at random in $\{0,1\}^\ell$. For any LOCC adversary, and any separable[4] measurement outcome M that is δ-non-negligible, we have the following security bound:*

$$H_\infty^\varepsilon(S, T \mid Z = M) \geq \left(\tfrac{1}{2} - \mu\right) \ell - \delta_0 k. \quad (6)$$

Here S and T are the random variables describing the two messages, Z is the random variable representing the adversary's measurement outcome, and we have $\varepsilon \leq \exp(-\Omega(k))$.

2.6   Ideal Bit-OTM's

We now define security for an "ideal" OTM that stores two bits $a_0, a_1 \in \{0,1\}$. Note that there is a subtle point with defining security: while the OTM should hide at least one of the messages (a_0, a_1), which one remains hidden may depend on the adversary's actions in a complicated way. Our definition of security asserts that, conditioned on the adversary's measurement outcome, there exists a binary random variable C that indicates which of the two messages remains hidden. (For example, C appears naturally when one uses the entropy splitting lemma, Prop. 2.1.) Formally, we let A_0 and A_1 be random variables representing the two messages. Our security definition asserts that the message A_C is nearly uniformly distributed, even given knowledge of the other message A_{1-C}, the value of C, and the adversary's measurement outcome.

Definition 2.2. *We say that a single-bit OTM construction is secure if the following holds: Let $k \geq 1$ be a security parameter. Suppose the OTM is programmed with two messages $a_0, a_1 \in \{0,1\}$ chosen uniformly at random. Consider any LOCC adversary, and let Z be the random variable representing the results of*

---

[4] Note that this includes LOCC measurement outcomes as a special case.

the adversary's measurements. Then there exists a random variable C, which takes values in $\{0, 1\}$, such that:

$$\|P_{A_C A_{1-C} C Z} - U_{A_C} \times P_{A_{1-C} C Z}\|_1 \leq 2^{-\Omega(k)}, \tag{7}$$

where $P_{A_C A_{1-C} C Z}$ denotes the probability density on the random variables (A_C, A_{1-C}, C, Z), $P_{A_{1-C} C Z}$ denotes the marginal probability density on (A_{1-C}, C, Z), and U denotes the uniform distribution on $\{0, 1\}$.

We remark that this security guarantee involves the adversary's measurement outcome Z, which is *classical* rather than quantum information. While this may seem like an artificial restriction on the adversary, we argue that it is simply a natural consequence of the isolated qubits model. By definition, the adversary is unable to perform any entangling operations on the isolated qubits contained in the OTM; thus the only way the adversary can access those qubits is by performing a measurement, and converting the quantum state into a classical measurement outcome.

2.7 t-Wise Independent Hash Functions

Let $\mathcal{H}$ be a collection of functions h that map $\{1, \ldots, N\}$ to $\{1, \ldots, M\}$. Let $t \geq 1$ be an integer. Let H be a function chosen uniformly at random from $\mathcal{H}$; then this defines a collection of random variables $\{H(x) \mid x = 1, \ldots, N\}$. We say that $\mathcal{H}$ is *t-wise independent* if for all subsets $S \subset \{1, \ldots, N\}$ of size $|S| \leq t$, the random variables $\{H(x) \mid x \in S\}$ are independent and uniformly distributed in $\{1, \ldots, M\}$.

We will use the fact that there exist efficient constructions for t-wise independent hash functions, which run in time polynomial in t, $\log N$ and $\log M$; see [13] for details.

Proposition 2.2. *For all integers $n \geq 1$, $m \geq 1$ and $t \geq 1$, there exist families of t-wise independent functions $\mathcal{H} = \{h : \{0, 1\}^n \to \{0, 1\}^m\}$, such that sampling a random function in $\mathcal{H}$ takes $t \cdot \max\{n, m\}$ random bits, and evaluating a function in $\mathcal{H}$ takes time $\mathrm{poly}(n, m, t)$.*

We will use the following large-deviation bound for sums of t-wise independent random variables. This is a slight variant of results in [14] (see also [15]); we sketch the proof in the full version of the paper [16].

Proposition 2.3. *Let $t \geq 2$ be an even integer, and let $\mathcal{H}$ be a family of t-wise independent functions that map $\{1, \ldots, N\}$ to $\{0, 1\}$. Fix some constants $a_1, \ldots, a_N \in \mathbb{R}$. Let H be a function chosen uniformly at random from $\mathcal{H}$, and define the random variable*

$$Y = \sum_{x=1}^{N} (-1)^{H(x)} a_x. \tag{8}$$

Then $\mathbb{E} Y = 0$, *and we have the following large-deviation bound: for any* $\lambda > 0$,

$$\Pr(|Y| \geq \lambda) \leq 2e^{1/(6t)} \sqrt{\pi t} \left(\frac{vt}{e\lambda^2} \right)^{t/2}, \tag{9}$$

where $v = \sum_{x=1}^{N} a_x^2$.

We will also use a large-deviation bound for quadratic functions of $2t$-wise independent random variables. This is based on the Hanson-Wright inequality [17] (see also [18] for a more modern, slightly stronger result), partially derandomized using the techniques of [14] (see also [15]). We sketch the proof in the full version of the paper [16].

Proposition 2.4. *Let* $t \geq 2$ *be an even integer, and let* $\mathcal{H}$ *be a family of* $2t$-*wise independent functions that map* $\{1, \ldots, N\}$ *to* $\{0, 1\}$. *Let* $A \in \mathbb{R}^{N \times N}$ *be a symmetric matrix,* $A^T = A$. *Let* H *be a function chosen uniformly at random from* $\mathcal{H}$, *and define the random variable*

$$S = \sum_{x,y=1}^{N} A_{xy} \left((-1)^{H(x)} (-1)^{H(y)} - \delta_{xy} \right), \tag{10}$$

where δ_{xy} *equals 1 if* $x = y$, *and equals 0 otherwise.*

Then $\mathbb{E} S = 0$, *and we have the following large-deviation bound: for any* $\lambda > 0$,

$$\Pr(|S| \geq \lambda) \leq 4e^{1/(6t)} \sqrt{\pi t} \left(\frac{4\|\widetilde{A}\|_F^2 t}{e\lambda^2} \right)^{t/2} + 4e^{1/(12t)} \sqrt{2\pi t} \left(\frac{8\|\widetilde{A}\| t}{e\lambda} \right)^t, \tag{11}$$

where $\widetilde{A} \in \mathbb{R}^{N \times N}$ *is the entry-wise absolute value of* A, *that is,* $\widetilde{A}_{xy} = |A_{xy}|$.

3 Privacy Amplification for One-Time Memories Using Isolated Qubits

Our main result is a reduction from "ideal" one-time memories to "leaky" one-time memories, in the isolated qubits model. More precisely, we assume the existence of a "leaky" one-time memory $\mathcal{D}$ that stores two strings $s, t \in \{0, 1\}^\ell$, and leaks any constant fraction of the bits of (s, t). (Such leaky OTM's were constructed previously in [5].) We then construct an "ideal" one-time memory $\mathcal{D}'$ that stores two bits $a_0, a_1 \in \{0, 1\}$, and leaks an exponentially small amount of information about either a_0 or a_1 (so that at least one of the bits (a_0, a_1) remains almost completely hidden).

Our construction makes use of two functions $F, G : \{0, 1\}^\ell \to \{0, 1\}$, which are chosen from an r-wise independent random ensemble. (We will specify the value of r later, in the statement of Theorem 3.1.) Once the functions F and G have been chosen, they are fixed permanently, and they become part of the public description of the one-time memory $\mathcal{D}'$. (In particular, the adversary may attack $\mathcal{D}'$ using LOCC strategies that depend on F and G. We show that with high probability over the choice of F and G, $\mathcal{D}'$ is secure against all such attacks.)

We define the "ideal" one-time memory $\mathcal{D}'$ to have the following behavior. First, one can program $\mathcal{D}'$ with two messages $a_0, a_1 \in \{0,1\}$. $\mathcal{D}'$ implements this functionality in the following way:

1. Choose $s \in F^{-1}(a_0)$ and $t \in G^{-1}(a_1)$ uniformly at random, e.g., using rejection sampling.[5]
2. Program a "leaky" one-time memory $\mathcal{D}$ with the messages s and t, and return $\mathcal{D}$.

Given the device $\mathcal{D}'$, an honest user can retrieve either a_0 or a_1 as follows:

1. Read either s or t from the device $\mathcal{D}$, as appropriate.
2. Compute either $a_0 = F(s)$ or $a_1 = G(t)$, as appropriate.

We now prove the correctness and security of these "ideal" one-time memories $\mathcal{D}'$.

Theorem 3.1. *Fix some constants $k_0 \geq 1$, $\theta \geq 1$, $\delta_0 > 0$, $\alpha > 0$ and $\varepsilon_0 > 0$.*

Suppose we have a family of devices $\mathcal{D} = \{\mathcal{D}_k \mid k \geq k_0\}$, indexed by a security parameter $k \geq k_0$. Suppose these devices $\mathcal{D}_k$ are "leaky" string-OTM's in the isolated qubits model, in the sense of Theorem 2.1. More precisely, suppose that for all $k \geq k_0$,

1. *The device $\mathcal{D}_k$ stores two messages $s, t \in \{0,1\}^{\ell}$, where $\ell \geq k$.*
2. *The device $\mathcal{D}_k$ uses m qubits, where $k \leq m \leq k^{\theta}$.*
3. *Correctness and efficiency: there are honest strategies for programming the device $\mathcal{D}_k$ with messages s and t, and for reading either s or t, using only LOCC operations, and time polynomial in k.*
4. *"Leaky" security: Suppose the device $\mathcal{D}_k$ is programmed with two messages (s,t) chosen uniformly at random. Consider any LOCC adversary, and let Z be the random variable representing the result of the adversary's measurement. Let M be any separable measurement outcome that is δ-non-negligible, where $\delta = 2^{-\delta_0 k}$. Then we have:*

$$H_{\infty}^{\varepsilon}(S, T | Z = M) \geq \alpha k, \tag{12}$$

where $\varepsilon \leq 2^{-\varepsilon_0 k}$.

Now let $\mathcal{D}' = \{\mathcal{D}'_k \mid k \geq k_0\}$ be the family of devices constructed above, using r-wise independent random functions F and G, with

$$r = 4(\gamma + 1)k^{2\theta}. \tag{13}$$

(This choice of r is motivated by the union bound, see equation (33). Here γ is some universal constant, see equation (29).)

---

[5] Choose $s, t \in \{0,1\}^{\ell}$ uniformly at random, and repeat until one gets s and t that satisfy $F(s) = a_0$ and $G(t) = a_1$.

Then these devices $\mathcal{D}'_k$ are "ideal" OTM's in the isolated qubits model, in the sense of Definition 2.2. More precisely, for all $k \geq k_0$, with probability $\geq 1 - e^{-\Omega(k^{2\theta})}$ (over the choice of F and G), the following statements hold:

1. *The device $\mathcal{D}'_k$ stores two messages $a_0, a_1 \in \{0, 1\}$.*
2. *The device $\mathcal{D}'_k$ uses m qubits, where $k \leq m \leq k^\theta$.*
3. *Correctness and efficiency: there are honest strategies for programming the device $\mathcal{D}'_k$ with messages a_0 and a_1, and for reading either a_0 or a_1, using only LOCC operations, and time polynomial in k.*
4. *"Ideal" security: Suppose the device $\mathcal{D}'_k$ is programmed with two messages (a_0, a_1) chosen uniformly at random. Consider any LOCC adversary, and let Z be the random variable representing the results of the adversary's measurements. Then there exists a random variable C, which takes values in $\{0, 1\}$, such that:*

$$\|P_{A_C A_{1-C} C Z} - U_{A_C} \times P_{A_{1-C} C Z}\|_1$$
$$\leq 4 \cdot 2^{-\delta_0 k} + 2 \cdot 2^{-\varepsilon_0 k} + 2 \cdot 2^{-(\alpha/8)k} + 4(r+1) \cdot 2^{-(\alpha/6)k} \qquad (14)$$
$$\leq 2^{-\Omega(k)},$$

where $P_{A_C A_{1-C} C Z}$ denotes the probability density on the random variables (A_C, A_{1-C}, C, Z), $P_{A_{1-C} C Z}$ denotes the marginal probability density on (A_{1-C}, C, Z), and U denotes the uniform distribution on $\{0, 1\}$.

By taking the leaky string-OTM's constructed in [5] (see Theorem 2.1), and applying the above reduction, we obtain ideal OTM's in the isolated qubits model:

Corollary 3.1. *There exist ideal OTM's in the isolated qubits model, in the sense of Definition 2.2.*

3.1   Overview of the Proof

We now prove Theorem 3.1. It is easy to see that the devices $\mathcal{D}'_k$ behave correctly. To prove that the devices $\mathcal{D}'_k$ are secure, we will use a covering argument over the set of all separable measurement outcomes that can be observed by an LOCC adversary.

We emphasize that we will be covering the set of all measurement outcomes, which are represented by POVM elements M, and *not* the set of all LOCC adversaries, which are represented by the random variables Z. To see why this is sufficient to prove security, note that for any two adversaries (represented by random variables Z and Z') that can observe the same measurement outcome M, the events $Z = M$ and $Z' = M$ are identically distributed.

In the following argument, whenever we consider a particular measurement outcome M, we will also implicitly fix some adversary (represented by a random variable Z) that is capable of observing that outcome M. We say that the scheme is "secure at M" if the scheme is secure when the adversary observes outcome M (i.e., when the event $Z = M$ occurs).

First, we will show that for any (fixed) separable measurement outcome M, with high probability (over the choice of the random functions F and G used to construct $\mathcal{D}'_k$), the scheme is secure at M. Next, we will construct an ε-net $\widetilde{W}$ for the set of all separable measurement outcomes, and show that with high probability (over F and G), the scheme is secure at all points $\widetilde{M} \in \widetilde{W}$ simultaneously. Finally, we will show that any separable measurement outcome M can be approximated by a measurement outcome $\widetilde{M} \in \widetilde{W}$, such that security at $\widetilde{M}$ implies security at M.

We set the parameters in the following way: the last part of the argument (approximating M by $\widetilde{M} \in \widetilde{W}$) determines how small we must choose ε when constructing the ε-net $\widetilde{W}$; this determines the cardinality of $\widetilde{W}$, which affects the union bound; this determines how large we must choose r when choosing the r-wise independent random functions F and G.

We now show the details:

Part 1: We begin with the following lemma, which describes what happens when we fix a particular measurement outcome M. We assume that M is separable and δ-non-negligible; then the security guarantee for the leaky string-OTM (equation (12)) implies that:

$$H_\infty^\varepsilon(S, T | Z = M) \geq \alpha k. \tag{15}$$

The lemma introduces a random variable C that indicates which of the two messages A_0 and A_1 remains unknown to the adversary; call this message A_C. In addition, the lemma introduces an event $\mathcal{E}$ that "smooths" the distribution, by excluding some low-probability failure events. We then define a quantity $Q_c(M)$ that measures the bias of the message A_C, smoothed by $\mathcal{E}$ and conditioned on $C = c$ and $Z = M$. Similarly, we define a quantity $R_c(M)$ that measures the correlations between the messages A_0 and A_1, smoothed by $\mathcal{E}$ and conditioned on $C = c$ and $Z = M$. The lemma shows that, with high probability (over F and G), $Q_c(M)$ and $R_c(M)$ are small.

Lemma 3.1. *Fix any measurement outcome M such that $H_\infty^\varepsilon(S, T | Z = M) \geq \alpha k$. Define $\eta = 2^{-\eta_0 k}$ where $\eta_0 = \alpha/8$. Then there exists a random variable C, taking values in $\{0, 1\}$, and there exists an event $\mathcal{E}$, occurring with probability $\Pr(\mathcal{E} | Z = M) \geq 1 - \varepsilon - \eta$, such that the following statement holds: Say we define, for all $c \in \{0, 1\}$,*

$$\begin{aligned} Q_c(M) &= \mathbb{E}(1_\mathcal{E} \cdot (-1)^{A_C} \,|\, C = c, Z = M) \\ &= \Pr(\mathcal{E}, A_C = 0 \,|\, C = c, Z = M) - \Pr(\mathcal{E}, A_C = 1 \,|\, C = c, Z = M), \end{aligned} \tag{16}$$

which is a random variable depending on F and G. Then for all $c \in \{0, 1\}$, and all $\lambda > 0$,

$$\Pr_{FG}(|Q_c(M)| \geq \lambda) \leq 2e^{1/(6r)} \sqrt{\pi r} \left(\frac{2^{-(\alpha/3)k} r}{e \lambda^2} \right)^{r/2}. \tag{17}$$

In addition, say we define, for all $c \in \{0, 1\}$,

$$R_c(M) = \mathbb{E}(1_\mathcal{E} \cdot (-1)^{A_0 + A_1} \,|\, C = c, Z = M), \tag{18}$$

which is a random variable depending on F and G. Then for all $c \in \{0,1\}$, and all $\lambda > 0$,

$$\Pr_{FG}(|R_c(M)| \geq \lambda) \leq 8e^{1/(3r)}\sqrt{\pi r}\left(\frac{8 \cdot 2^{-(\alpha/3)k}r^2}{e^2\lambda^2}\right)^{r/4}. \qquad (19)$$

We will prove this lemma in Section 3.2. This lemma is useful for the following reason: when $Q_c(M)$ and $R_c(M)$ are small, this implies security of the devices $\mathcal{D}'_k$ in the case where the adversary observes measurement outcome M. We now state this observation more precisely:

Lemma 3.2. *Fix any measurement outcome M, and any $c \in \{0,1\}$. Suppose that $|Q_c(M)| \leq \varepsilon_1$ and $|R_c(M)| \leq \varepsilon_2$. Then*

$$\|P_{A_C A_{1-C}\mathcal{E}|C=c,Z=M} - U_{A_C} \times P_{A_{1-C}\mathcal{E}|C=c,Z=M}\|_1 \leq \varepsilon_1 + \varepsilon_2, \qquad (20)$$

where $P_{A_C A_{1-C}\mathcal{E}|C=c,Z=M}$ is the probability density

$$P_{A_C A_{1-C}\mathcal{E}|C=c,Z=M}(a, a') = \Pr(A_C = a, A_{1-C} = a', \mathcal{E} \mid C = c, Z = M), \qquad (21)$$

and U denotes the uniform distribution on $\{0,1\}$.

We now prove Lemma 3.2. We can represent the probability density $P_{A_C A_{1-C}\mathcal{E}|C=c,Z=M}$ as a vector $\boldsymbol{p} \in \mathbb{R}^2 \otimes \mathbb{R}^2$, whose entries are given by $p_{aa'} = P_{A_C A_{1-C}\mathcal{E}|C=c,Z=M}(a, a')$. Now define vectors $\boldsymbol{u} = \frac{1}{2}(1,1)$ and $\boldsymbol{d} = \frac{1}{2}(1,-1)$, which form an orthogonal basis for $\mathbb{R}^2$. Then we can write $\boldsymbol{p}$ in this basis:

$$\boldsymbol{p} = \alpha_{00}\boldsymbol{u} \otimes \boldsymbol{u} + \alpha_{01}\boldsymbol{u} \otimes \boldsymbol{d} + \alpha_{10}\boldsymbol{d} \otimes \boldsymbol{u} + \alpha_{11}\boldsymbol{d} \otimes \boldsymbol{d}, \qquad (22)$$

for some coefficients $\alpha_{00}, \alpha_{01}, \alpha_{10}, \alpha_{11} \in \mathbb{R}$. We can write $Q_c(M)$ and $R_c(M)$ as follows:

$$Q_c(M) = 4(\boldsymbol{d} \otimes \boldsymbol{u})^T \boldsymbol{p} = \alpha_{10}, \qquad (23)$$

$$R_c(M) = 4(\boldsymbol{d} \otimes \boldsymbol{d})^T \boldsymbol{p} = \alpha_{11}, \qquad (24)$$

hence we know that $|\alpha_{10}| \leq \varepsilon_1$ and $|\alpha_{11}| \leq \varepsilon_2$. Finally, note that the probability density $U_{A_C} \times P_{A_{1-C}\mathcal{E}|C=c,Z=M}$ is represented by the following vector (call it $\boldsymbol{q}$):

$$\boldsymbol{q} = \boldsymbol{u} \otimes \left(2(\boldsymbol{u}^T \otimes I)\boldsymbol{p}\right) = \alpha_{00}\boldsymbol{u} \otimes \boldsymbol{u} + \alpha_{01}\boldsymbol{u} \otimes \boldsymbol{d}. \qquad (25)$$

We can combine these facts to bound the ℓ_1 distance between $\boldsymbol{p}$ and $\boldsymbol{q}$:

$$\|\boldsymbol{p} - \boldsymbol{q}\|_1 \leq |\alpha_{10}|\|\boldsymbol{d} \otimes \boldsymbol{u}\|_1 + |\alpha_{11}|\|\boldsymbol{d} \otimes \boldsymbol{d}\|_1 \leq \varepsilon_1 + \varepsilon_2. \qquad (26)$$

This proves Lemma 3.2.

Part 2: We let W denote the set of all separable measurement outcomes, and we construct an ε-net $\widetilde{W}$ for W. Specifically, we define W as follows:

$$W = \{M \in (\mathbb{C}^{2\times 2})^{\otimes m} \mid M = \bigotimes_{i=1}^m M_i, \, 0 \preceq M_i \preceq I\}. \qquad (27)$$

Lemma 3.3. *For any $0 < \mu \leq 1$, there exists a set $\widetilde{W} \subset W$, of cardinality $|\widetilde{W}| \leq (\frac{9m}{\mu})^{4m}$, which is a μ-net for W with respect to the operator norm $\|\cdot\|$.*

We will prove this lemma in Section 3.3. Now, we will use the union bound to show that, with high probability, for all $\widetilde{M} \in \widetilde{W}$, $Q_c(\widetilde{M})$ is small simultaneously. First, we use Lemma 3.3, and we set

$$\mu = 2^{-(\alpha/6)k} \cdot \frac{\delta^4}{4^m} \tag{28}$$

(this choice is motivated by equation (37) below — we choose μ small enough that the μ-net gives a good approximation of any measurement outcome). Also, recall that $k \leq m \leq k^\theta$. Then the cardinality of $\widetilde{W}$ is bounded by

$$\begin{aligned}
|\widetilde{W}| &\leq \left(9m \cdot 2^{(\alpha/6)k} \cdot \frac{4^m}{\delta^4}\right)^{4m} \\
&= (9m \cdot 2^{(\alpha/6)k+4\delta_0 k+2m})^{4m} \\
&\leq 2^{\gamma k^{2\theta}},
\end{aligned} \tag{29}$$

for all sufficiently large k; here γ is some universal constant. Next, we use Lemma 3.1, and we set

$$\lambda = 2^{-(\alpha/6)k} \cdot 2r; \tag{30}$$

then we have that

$$\Pr_{FG}(|Q_c(M)| \geq \lambda) \leq 2e^{1/(6r)}\sqrt{\pi r}(4er)^{-r/2}, \tag{31}$$

$$\Pr_{FG}(|R_c(M)| \geq \lambda) \leq 8e^{1/(3r)}\sqrt{\pi r}(e^2/2)^{-r/4}. \tag{32}$$

Finally, we use the union bound, and we set r sufficiently large (see equation (13)); then we have that

$$\begin{aligned}
\Pr_{FG}\Big(\exists \widetilde{M} &\in \widetilde{W}, \exists c \in \{0,1\}, \text{ s.t. } \widetilde{M} \text{ is } \delta\text{-non-negligible, and} \\
&\max\{|Q_c(\widetilde{M})|, |R_c(\widetilde{M})|\} \geq \lambda\Big) \\
&\leq 2 \cdot 2^{\gamma k^{2\theta}} \cdot \left(2e^{1/(6r)}\sqrt{\pi r}(4er)^{-r/2} + 8e^{1/(3r)}\sqrt{\pi r}(e^2/2)^{-r/4}\right) \\
&\leq e^{-\Omega(k^{2\theta})}.
\end{aligned} \tag{33}$$

Hence, with high probability (over F and G), we have that:

$$\forall \widetilde{M} \in \widetilde{W}, \forall c \in \{0,1\}, (\widetilde{M} \text{ is } \delta\text{-non-negligible}) \Rightarrow$$
$$\max\{|Q_c(\widetilde{M})|, |R_c(\widetilde{M})|\} \leq \lambda. \tag{34}$$

Also, note that $\lambda \leq 2^{-\Omega(k)}$. Via Lemma 3.2, this implies that the device $\mathcal{D}'_k$ is secure in the case where the adversary observes any of the measurement outcomes in the set $\widetilde{W}$.

Part 3: We state two lemmas that describe how an arbitrary measurement outcome M can be approximated by another measurement outcome $\widetilde{M}$. (Implicitly, we fix some adversary that is capable of observing outcome M, and some other adversary that is capable of observing $\widetilde{M}$. We let these adversaries be represented by random variables Z and $\widetilde{Z}$.)

Roughly speaking, the first lemma shows that if M is 2δ-non-negligible, then $\widetilde{M}$ is δ-non-negligible.

Lemma 3.4. *Suppose that* $M, \widetilde{M} \in (\mathbb{C}^{2\times2})^{\otimes m}$, *and* $0 \preceq M \preceq I$, *and* $0 \preceq \widetilde{M} \preceq I$. *Suppose that* M *is* 2δ-*non-negligible, where* $0 < \delta \leq \frac{1}{2}$, *and* $\mathrm{tr}(M) \geq 1$. *Suppose that* $\widetilde{M}$ *satisfies* $\|M - \widetilde{M}\| \leq \mu$, *where* $\mu \leq \frac{2}{3}\delta \cdot 2^{-m}$. *Then* $\widetilde{M}$ *is* δ-*non-negligible.*

The second lemma shows that, if the quantities $Q_c(\widetilde{M})$ and $R_c(\widetilde{M})$ are defined in terms of a random variable $\widetilde{C}$ and an event $\widetilde{\mathcal{E}}$ (as in equations (16) and (18)), then we can also define the quantities $Q_c(M)$ and $R_c(M)$ (by choosing C and $\mathcal{E}$ in an appropriate way), so that $Q_c(M) \approx Q_c(\widetilde{M})$ and $R_c(M) \approx R_c(\widetilde{M})$.

Lemma 3.5. *Suppose that* $M, \widetilde{M} \in (\mathbb{C}^{2\times2})^{\otimes m}$, *and* $0 \preceq M \preceq I$, *and* $0 \preceq \widetilde{M} \preceq I$. *Suppose that* M *is* 2δ-*non-negligible, where* $0 < \delta \leq \frac{1}{2}$, *and* $\|M\| = 1$. *Suppose that* $\widetilde{M}$ *satisfies* $\|M - \widetilde{M}\| \leq \mu$, *where* $\mu \leq \frac{1}{2}$, *and* $\widetilde{M}$ *is* δ-*non-negligible.*

Suppose there exists a random variable $\widetilde{C}$, *taking values in* $\{0,1\}$, *and there exists an event* $\widetilde{\mathcal{E}}$, *occurring with probability* $\Pr(\widetilde{\mathcal{E}}|\widetilde{Z} = \widetilde{M})$; *and let* $Q_c(\widetilde{M})$ *and* $R_c(\widetilde{M})$ *be defined in terms of* $\widetilde{C}$ *and* $\widetilde{\mathcal{E}}$, *as shown in equations (16) and (18).*

Let $0 < \tau \leq \frac{1}{2}$. *Then there exists a random variable* C, *taking values in* $\{0,1\}$, *and there exists an event* $\mathcal{E}$, *occurring with probability* $\Pr(\mathcal{E}|Z = M) \geq \Pr(\widetilde{\mathcal{E}}|\widetilde{Z} = \widetilde{M}) - \tau$, *such that if* $Q_c(M)$ *and* $R_c(M)$ *are defined in terms of* C *and* $\mathcal{E}$, *then the following statements hold:*

1. *For every* $c \in \{0,1\}$, *either* $Q_c(M) = 0$, *or we have:*

$$|Q_c(M) - Q_c(\widetilde{M})| \leq 2\mu\left(\frac{2^m}{\tau\delta}\right)^2. \tag{35}$$

2. *For every* $c \in \{0,1\}$, *either* $R_c(M) = 0$, *or we have:*

$$|R_c(M) - R_c(\widetilde{M})| \leq 2\mu\left(\frac{2^m}{\tau\delta}\right)^2. \tag{36}$$

We will prove these two lemmas in Section 3.4. Using these lemmas, we now show that the device $\mathcal{D}'_k$ is secure, when the adversary observes *any* separable measurement outcome $M \in W$ that is 2δ-non-negligible.

Without loss of generality, suppose that $\|M\| = 1$. (To see this, note that without loss of generality, we can assume $M \neq 0$. We can then multiply M by a scalar factor, as long as $0 \preceq M \preceq I$, without changing the distributions of the other variables conditioned on $Z = M$. Also note that the δ-non-negligibility of M is invariant under this scaling, see Definition 2.1.) Note that this implies $\mathrm{tr}(M) \geq 1$.

Let $\widetilde{M} \in \widetilde{W}$ be the nearest point in the μ-net $\widetilde{W}$; so we have $\|M - \widetilde{M}\| \leq \mu$, where μ is set according to equation (28). By Lemma 3.4, $\widetilde{M}$ is δ-non-negligible. By equation (34), we get that for all $c \in \{0,1\}$, $|Q_c(\widetilde{M})| \leq \lambda$ and $|R_c(\widetilde{M})| \leq \lambda$, where $\lambda = 2^{-(\alpha/6)k} \cdot 2r$.

Using Lemma 3.5, and setting $\tau = \delta$, we get that for every $c \in \{0,1\}$, either $Q_c(M) = 0$, or

$$|Q_c(M) - Q_c(\widetilde{M})| \leq 2\mu \cdot \frac{4^m}{\delta^4} = 2 \cdot 2^{-(\alpha/6)k}, \tag{37}$$

and likewise, either $R_c(M) = 0$, or $|R_c(M) - R_c(\widetilde{M})| \leq 2 \cdot 2^{-(\alpha/6)k}$. So we conclude that for all $c \in \{0,1\}$,

$$|Q_c(M)| \leq 2^{-(\alpha/6)k} \cdot 2(r+1), \tag{38}$$

$$|R_c(M)| \leq 2^{-(\alpha/6)k} \cdot 2(r+1). \tag{39}$$

Using Lemma 3.2, we get that the device $\mathcal{D}'_k$ is secure, for all separable 2δ-non-negligible measurement outcomes $M \in W$ that the adversary may observe:

$$\|P_{A_C A_{1-C} \mathcal{E} | C=c, Z=M} - U_{A_C} \times P_{A_{1-C} \mathcal{E} | C=c, Z=M}\|_1$$
$$\leq 2^{-(\alpha/6)k} \cdot 4(r+1) \leq 2^{-\Omega(k)}. \tag{40}$$

We can write this security guarantee in a more convenient form. Consider any LOCC adversary, and let Z be the random variable representing the results of the adversary's measurements. We can write:[6]

$$\|P_{A_C A_{1-C} C Z} - U_{A_C} \times P_{A_{1-C} C Z}\|_1$$
$$\leq \sum_M \Pr(Z = M) \|P_{A_C A_{1-C} C | Z=M} - U_{A_C} \times P_{A_{1-C} C | Z=M}\|_1$$
$$\leq 4\delta + \sum_{M \,:\, M \text{ is } 2\delta\text{-non-negl.}} \Pr(Z = M) \cdot$$
$$\|P_{A_C A_{1-C} C | Z=M} - U_{A_C} \times P_{A_{1-C} C | Z=M}\|_1$$
$$\leq 4\delta + \sum_{M \,:\, M \text{ is } 2\delta\text{-non-negl.}} \Pr(Z = M) \cdot$$
$$\left(2(\varepsilon + \eta) + \|P_{\mathcal{E} A_C A_{1-C} C | Z=M} - U_{A_C} \times P_{\mathcal{E} A_{1-C} C | Z=M}\|_1 \right)$$
$$\leq 4\delta + 2(\varepsilon + \eta) + \sum_{M \,:\, M \text{ is } 2\delta\text{-non-negl.}} \Pr(Z = M) \sum_c \Pr(C = c | Z = M) \cdot$$
$$\|P_{\mathcal{E} A_C A_{1-C} | C=c, Z=M} - U_{A_C} \times P_{\mathcal{E} A_{1-C} | C=c, Z=M}\|_1$$

---

[6] There is a minor technicality involving the definition of the random variable C. We have already defined C whenever $Z = M$, for any δ-non-negligible separable measurement outcome M. We now need to define C in cases where $Z = M$ and M is δ-negligible. In these cases we simply define C in an arbitrary way.

$$\leq 4\delta + 2(\varepsilon + \eta) + 2^{-(\alpha/6)k} \cdot 4(r+1)$$

$$\leq 4 \cdot 2^{-\delta_0 k} + 2 \cdot 2^{-\varepsilon_0 k} + 2 \cdot 2^{-(\alpha/8)k} + 4(r+1) \cdot 2^{-(\alpha/6)k} \qquad (41)$$

$$\leq 2^{-\Omega(k)},$$

where we used the fact that $\sum_{M \,:\, M \text{ is } 2\delta\text{-negl.}} \Pr(Z = M) \leq 2\delta$ (see equation (5)), the fact that $\Pr(\neg\mathcal{E}|Z = M) \leq \varepsilon + \eta$ (see Lemma 3.1), the security bound from equation (40), and finally the definitions of δ, ε and η (see Theorem 3.1 and Lemma 3.1). This completes the proof of Theorem 3.1. $\qquad\square$

3.2   Security at a Single Point M

We now prove Lemma 3.1. We are given that $H_\infty^\varepsilon(S, T|Z = M) \geq \alpha k$. We will use the entropy splitting lemma (Prop. 2.1). For notational convenience, we define σ_c to be a function that takes two arguments, and returns the first argument if $c = 0$ and the second argument if $c = 1$, that is,

$$\sigma_c(s,t) = \begin{cases} s & \text{if } c = 0, \\ t & \text{if } c = 1. \end{cases} \qquad (42)$$

Setting $\eta = 2^{-\eta_0 k}$ and $\eta_0 = \alpha/8$, we get that there exists a random variable C, taking values in $\{0, 1\}$, such that:

$$H_\infty^{\varepsilon+\eta}(\sigma_C(S,T)\,|\,C, Z = M) \geq (\alpha/2)k - 1 - \eta_0 k \geq (\alpha/3)k. \qquad (43)$$

Using the definition of the smoothed conditional min-entropy, we get that there exists an event $\mathcal{E}$, occurring with probability $\Pr(\mathcal{E}\,|\,Z = M) \geq 1 - \varepsilon - \eta$, such that for all $c \in \{0, 1\}$, and all $s \in \{0, 1\}^\ell$, $\Pr(\mathcal{E}, \sigma_c(S, T) = s\,|\,C = c, Z = M) \leq 2^{-(\alpha/3)k}$. In particular, this implies that

$$\sum_{s \in \{0,1\}^\ell} \Pr(\mathcal{E}, \sigma_c(S,T) = s\,|\,C = c, Z = M)^2 \leq 2^{-(\alpha/3)k}. \qquad (44)$$

We now proceed to bound the quantity $Q_c(M)$. We consider the case where $c = 0$ (the $c = 1$ case is similar). In this case, we can write

$$Q_0(M) = \sum_{s \in \{0,1\}^\ell} (-1)^{F(s)} \Pr(\mathcal{E}, S = s\,|\,C = 0, Z = M). \qquad (45)$$

Since F is an r-wise independent random function, we can apply the large deviation bound in Prop. 2.3 (making use of equation (44)). This proves equation (17).

Finally, we will bound the quantity $R_c(M)$. We consider the case where $c = 0$ (the $c = 1$ case is similar). In this case, we can write

$$R_0(M) = \sum_{s,t \in \{0,1\}^\ell} (-1)^{F(s)+G(t)} \Pr(\mathcal{E}, S = s, T = t\,|\,C = 0, Z = M). \qquad (46)$$

We will bound this using Prop. 2.4. To this end, we define a function $H : \{0,1\} \times \{0,1\}^\ell \to \{0,1\}$, which returns the following values:

$$H(i,s) = \begin{cases} F(s) & \text{if } i = 0 \\ G(s) & \text{if } i = 1. \end{cases} \tag{47}$$

We define a matrix $A \in \mathbb{R}^{(2 \cdot 2^\ell) \times (2 \cdot 2^\ell)}$, whose entries are indexed by $\{0,1\} \times \{0,1\}^\ell$, and have the following values:

$$A_{(i,s),(j,t)} = \begin{cases} \frac{1}{2} \Pr(\mathcal{E}, S = s, T = t \mid C = 0, Z = M) & \text{if } (i,j) = (0,1) \\ \frac{1}{2} \Pr(\mathcal{E}, S = t, T = s \mid C = 0, Z = M) & \text{if } (i,j) = (1,0) \\ 0 & \text{otherwise.} \end{cases} \tag{48}$$

A straightforward calculation then shows that $R_0(M)$ can be written in the form

$$R_0(M) = \sum_{(i,s),(j,t)} A_{(i,s),(j,t)} \left((-1)^{H(i,s)} (-1)^{H(j,t)} - \delta_{(i,s),(j,t)} \right). \tag{49}$$

Since F and G are r-wise independent random functions, we can apply Prop. 2.4, setting $t = r/2$.[7] We will use the following bounds on $\widetilde{A}$:

$$\begin{aligned} \left\| \widetilde{A} \right\|^2 \leq \left\| \widetilde{A} \right\|_F^2 &= \sum_{(i,s),(j,t)} A^2_{(i,s),(j,t)} \\ &= \tfrac{1}{2} \sum_{s,t} \Pr(\mathcal{E}, S = s, T = t \mid C = 0, Z = M)^2 \\ &\leq \tfrac{1}{2} \sum_s \left(\sum_t \Pr(\mathcal{E}, S = s, T = t \mid C = 0, Z = M) \right)^2 \\ &= \tfrac{1}{2} \sum_s \Pr(\mathcal{E}, S = s \mid C = 0, Z = M)^2 \\ &\leq \tfrac{1}{2} \cdot 2^{-(\alpha/3)k}, \end{aligned} \tag{50}$$

where in the last line we used equation (44). We substitute into Prop. 2.4; this proves equation (19). This completes the proof of Lemma 3.1. $\qquad\square$

3.3   Constructing an ε-net

We now prove Lemma 3.3. First, consider the set

$$V = \{ X \in \mathbb{C}^{2 \times 2} \mid \|X\|_{\ell_\infty} \leq \sqrt{2}, \, X^\dagger = X \}, \tag{51}$$

where $\|\cdot\|_{\ell_\infty}$ denotes the ℓ_∞ norm, viewing each 2×2 matrix as a 4-dimensional vector. Let $\delta > 0$ (we will choose a specific value for δ later). It is easy to see

---

[7] The careful reader will notice that one can actually use Prop. 2.4 with $t = r$, and thereby prove a stronger bound. The argument of Prop. 2.4 still goes through, because $R_0(M)$ is *bilinear* in the random variables $F(s)$ and $G(t)$, and these two groups of random variables are chosen independently of each other.

that there exists a δ-net $\widetilde{V}$ for V, with respect to the ℓ_∞ norm, with cardinality $|\widetilde{V}| \leq (\frac{2}{\delta} + 1)^4$. (For instance, one can describe each point in V using 4 real parameters, and choose a grid with spacing $\delta\sqrt{2}$.)

Next, consider the set of single-qubit POVM elements:

$$U = \{X \in \mathbb{C}^{2\times 2} \mid 0 \preceq X \preceq I\}. \tag{52}$$

Note that $U \subset V$, since $\|X\|_{\ell_\infty} \leq \|X\|_F \leq \sqrt{2}\|X\|$. We will construct a 4δ-net $\widetilde{U}$ for U, by "rounding" each point in $\widetilde{V}$ into U. Define a function $r : V \to U$ that maps each point in V to the nearest point in U with respect to the ℓ_∞ norm, that is,

$$r(X) = \arg\min_{Y \in U} \|X - Y\|_{\ell_\infty}. \tag{53}$$

Let $\widetilde{U}$ be the image of $\widetilde{V}$ under this map, that is, $\widetilde{U} = \{r(X) \mid X \in \widetilde{V}\}$. Note that $|\widetilde{U}| \leq |\widetilde{V}|$.

It is easy to see that $\widetilde{U}$ is a 2δ-net for U, with respect to the ℓ_∞ norm. (This follows because, for any $X \in U$, there exists some $Y \in \widetilde{V}$ such that $\|X - Y\|_{\ell_\infty} \leq \delta$, and we know that $r(Y) \in \widetilde{U}$ and $\|Y - r(Y)\|_{\ell_\infty} \leq \delta$.) This implies that $\widetilde{U}$ is a 4δ-net for U, with respect to the operator norm $\|\cdot\|$. (This follows because $\|X\| \leq \|X\|_F \leq 2\|X\|_{\ell_\infty}$.)

We are now ready to consider the set W. We can write W in the form

$$W = \{M \mid M = \bigotimes_{i=1}^{m} M_i, \ M_i \in U\}. \tag{54}$$

We then define $\widetilde{W} = \{M \mid M = \bigotimes_{i=1}^{m} M_i, \ M_i \in \widetilde{U}\}$. Note that $\widetilde{W}$ has cardinality $|\widetilde{W}| \leq |\widetilde{U}|^m$.

We claim that $\widetilde{W}$ is a $4m\delta$-net for W, with respect to the operator norm $\|\cdot\|$. To see this, consider any $M \in W$, and construct some $\widetilde{M} \in \widetilde{W}$ that approximates it, as follows. M can be written in the form $M = \bigotimes_{i=1}^{m} M_i$. For each M_i, there is a point $\widetilde{M_i} \in \widetilde{U}$ within distance $\|M_i - \widetilde{M_i}\| \leq 4\delta$. We then let $\widetilde{M} = \bigotimes_{i=1}^{m} \widetilde{M_i}$.

We upper-bound the distance $\|M - \widetilde{M}\|$ as follows, by defining a sequence of intermediate steps, and using the triangle inequality. For all $s = 0, 1, 2, \ldots, m$, define $M^{(s)} = (\widetilde{M_1} \otimes \cdots \otimes \widetilde{M_s}) \otimes (M_{s+1} \otimes \cdots \otimes M_m)$. Then we have that $M = M^{(0)}$, $\widetilde{M} = M^{(m)}$, and

$$\|M - \widetilde{M}\| \leq \sum_{s=0}^{m-1} \|M^{(s)} - M^{(s+1)}\|$$

$$= \sum_{s=0}^{m-1} \left\| (\widetilde{M_1} \otimes \cdots \otimes \widetilde{M_s}) \otimes (M_{s+1} - \widetilde{M_{s+1}}) \right. \tag{55}$$

$$\left. \otimes (M_{s+2} \otimes \cdots \otimes M_m) \right\|$$

$$\leq 4m\delta,$$

where we used the fact that $\|A \otimes B\| = \|A\| \, \|B\|$.

Finally, we set $\delta = \mu/(4m)$. Then $\widetilde{W}$ is a μ-net for W, with respect to the operator norm $\|\cdot\|$. The cardinality of $\widetilde{W}$ is $|\widetilde{W}| \leq (\frac{2}{\delta} + 1)^{4m} = (\frac{8m}{\mu} + 1)^{4m} \leq (\frac{9m}{\mu})^{4m}$, provided that $\mu \leq 1$. This proves Lemma 3.3. $\qquad\square$

3.4 Continuity Arguments

We now prove Lemma 3.4. Since M is 2δ-non-negligible (with respect to some quantum state ρ), we have $\Pr(M) = \operatorname{tr}(M\rho) \geq 2\delta \cdot 2^{-m} \operatorname{tr}(M)$. Since $\|M - \widetilde{M}\| \leq \mu$, and $\operatorname{tr}(M) \geq 1$, we can write

$$
\begin{aligned}
\Pr(\widetilde{M}) = \operatorname{tr}(\widetilde{M}\rho) &\geq \operatorname{tr}(M\rho) - \mu \\
&\geq 2\delta \cdot 2^{-m} \operatorname{tr}(M) - \mu \\
&\geq \delta \cdot 2^{-m} \operatorname{tr}(M) + \delta \cdot 2^{-m} - \mu \\
&\geq \delta \cdot 2^{-m} \operatorname{tr}(\widetilde{M}) - \delta \cdot \mu + \delta \cdot 2^{-m} - \mu \\
&= \delta \cdot 2^{-m} \operatorname{tr}(\widetilde{M}) + \delta \cdot 2^{-m} - (1 + \delta)\mu.
\end{aligned}
\tag{56}
$$

Since $\mu \leq \frac{2}{3}\delta \cdot 2^{-m}$, and $\delta \leq \frac{1}{2}$, we have $(1+\delta)\mu \leq \delta \cdot 2^{-m}$. By plugging into the above equation, we see that $\widetilde{M}$ is δ-non-negligible. This proves Lemma 3.4. $\quad\square$

We now prove Lemma 3.5. By assumption, there is a random variable $\widetilde{C}$, which is defined by the probabilities $\Pr(\widetilde{C} = c \mid \widetilde{Z} = \widetilde{M}, S = s, T = t)$; and there is an event $\widetilde{\mathcal{E}}$, which is defined by the probabilities $\Pr(\widetilde{\mathcal{E}} \mid \widetilde{C} = c, \widetilde{Z} = \widetilde{M}, S = s, T = t)$. Also, let ρ_{st} be the quantum state used to encode messages (s, t), i.e., this is the state of the one-time memory, conditioned on $S = s$ and $T = t$.

We start by writing $Q_c(\widetilde{M})$ and $R_c(\widetilde{M})$ in a more explicit form. First consider $Q_0(\widetilde{M})$, and note that $A_0 = F(S)$. We can write $Q_0(\widetilde{M})$ in the form:

$$
\begin{aligned}
Q_0(\widetilde{M}) &= \left(\frac{1}{\Pr(\widetilde{C} = 0, \widetilde{Z} = \widetilde{M})} \right) \cdot \\
&\quad \sum_{s,t \in \{0,1\}^\ell} (-1)^{F(s)} \Pr(\widetilde{\mathcal{E}}, S = s, T = t, \widetilde{C} = 0, \widetilde{Z} = \widetilde{M}) \\
&= \left(\frac{1}{\Pr(\widetilde{C} = 0, \widetilde{Z} = \widetilde{M})} \right) \cdot \\
&\quad \sum_{s,t \in \{0,1\}^\ell} (-1)^{F(s)} \Pr(\widetilde{\mathcal{E}}, \widetilde{C} = 0 \mid \widetilde{Z} = \widetilde{M}, S = s, T = t) \operatorname{tr}(\widetilde{M}\rho_{st}) 4^{-\ell} \\
&= \left(\frac{1}{\Pr(\widetilde{C} = 0, \widetilde{Z} = \widetilde{M})} \right) \operatorname{tr}(\widetilde{M}\nu_0),
\end{aligned}
\tag{57}
$$

where we define the matrix $\nu_0 \in (\mathbb{C}^{2\times 2})^{\otimes m}$ as follows:

$$\nu_0 = 4^{-\ell} \sum_{s,t\in\{0,1\}^\ell} (-1)^{F(s)} \Pr(\widetilde{\mathcal{E}}, \widetilde{C} = 0 \,|\, \widetilde{Z} = \widetilde{M}, S = s, T = t)\, \rho_{st}. \tag{58}$$

Note that $\|\nu_0\|_{\mathrm{tr}} \le 1$. In addition, we can write $\Pr(\widetilde{C} = 0, \widetilde{Z} = \widetilde{M})$ in the form:

$$\begin{aligned}
\Pr(&\widetilde{C} = 0, \widetilde{Z} = \widetilde{M}) \\
&= \sum_{s,t\in\{0,1\}^\ell} \Pr(\widetilde{C} = 0, \widetilde{Z} = \widetilde{M}, S = s, T = t) \\
&= \sum_{s,t\in\{0,1\}^\ell} \Pr(\widetilde{C} = 0 \,|\, \widetilde{Z} = \widetilde{M}, S = s, T = t)\, \mathrm{tr}(\widetilde{M}\rho_{st})\, 4^{-\ell} \\
&= \mathrm{tr}(\widetilde{M}\xi_0),
\end{aligned} \tag{59}$$

where we define the matrix $\xi_0 \in (\mathbb{C}^{2\times 2})^{\otimes m}$ as follows:

$$\xi_0 = 4^{-\ell} \sum_{s,t\in\{0,1\}^\ell} \Pr(\widetilde{C} = 0 \,|\, \widetilde{Z} = \widetilde{M}, S = s, T = t)\, \rho_{st}. \tag{60}$$

Also, note that $\|\xi_0\|_{\mathrm{tr}} \le 1$. We can also write similar expressions for $Q_1(\widetilde{M})$, $R_0(\widetilde{M})$ and $R_1(\widetilde{M})$. We can summarize this as follows:

$$Q_c(\widetilde{M}) = \frac{\mathrm{tr}(\widetilde{M}\nu_c)}{\mathrm{tr}(\widetilde{M}\xi_c)}, \qquad R_c(\widetilde{M}) = \frac{\mathrm{tr}(\widetilde{M}\theta_c)}{\mathrm{tr}(\widetilde{M}\xi_c)}, \tag{61}$$

where $\nu_c, \theta_c, \xi_c \in (\mathbb{C}^{2\times 2})^{\otimes m}$ satisfy $\|\nu_c\|_{\mathrm{tr}} \le 1$, $\|\theta_c\|_{\mathrm{tr}} \le 1$ and $\|\xi_c\|_{\mathrm{tr}} \le 1$.

We now consider the measurement outcome M. We will construct a random variable C and an event $\mathcal{E}$, which will allow us to define the quantities $Q_c(M)$ and $R_c(M)$. Roughly speaking, C and $\mathcal{E}$ (conditioned on $Z = M$) will behave similarly to $\widetilde{C}$ and $\widetilde{\mathcal{E}}$ (conditioned on $\widetilde{Z} = \widetilde{M}$). However, if there exists some $c \in \{0,1\}$ for which the probability $\Pr(C = c \,|\, Z = M)$ is unusually small, then we will define $\mathcal{E}$ to exclude this event, in order to avoid situations where $Q_c(M)$ "blows up" because the denominator is very small.

Formally, we construct the random variable C and the event $\mathcal{E}$ by specifying the following probabilities (for all $c \in \{0,1\}$ and $s,t \in \{0,1\}^\ell$):

$$\begin{aligned}
\Pr(C = c \,|\, &Z = M, S = s, T = t) \\
&= \Pr(\widetilde{C} = c \,|\, \widetilde{Z} = \widetilde{M}, S = s, T = t),
\end{aligned} \tag{62}$$

$$\begin{aligned}
\Pr(\mathcal{E} \,|\, &C = c, Z = M, S = s, T = t) \\
&= \begin{cases} 0 & \text{if } \Pr(C = c \,|\, Z = M) < \tau, \\ \Pr(\widetilde{\mathcal{E}} \,|\, \widetilde{C} = c, \widetilde{Z} = \widetilde{M}, S = s, T = t) & \text{otherwise.} \end{cases}
\end{aligned} \tag{63}$$

We now show that $\Pr(\mathcal{E} \,|\, Z = M) \ge \Pr(\widetilde{\mathcal{E}} \,|\, \widetilde{Z} = \widetilde{M}) - \tau$. Let us say that $c \in \{0,1\}$ is "bad" if $\Pr(C = c \,|\, Z = M) < \tau$. There are two possible values, 0 and 1, and at most one of them can be bad. If neither one is bad, then $\Pr(\mathcal{E} \mid Z = M) = \Pr(\widetilde{\mathcal{E}} \mid \widetilde{Z} = \widetilde{M})$. If one particular value (say 0) is bad, then we have:

$$
\begin{aligned}
\Pr(&\mathcal{E} \mid Z = M) \\
&\geq \Pr(\mathcal{E} \mid C = 1, \, Z = M) \Pr(C = 1 \mid Z = M) \\
&= \Pr(\widetilde{\mathcal{E}} \mid \widetilde{C} = 1, \, \widetilde{Z} = \widetilde{M}) \Pr(\widetilde{C} = 1 \mid \widetilde{Z} = \widetilde{M}) \\
&= \Pr(\widetilde{\mathcal{E}} \mid \widetilde{Z} = \widetilde{M}) - \Pr(\widetilde{\mathcal{E}} \mid \widetilde{C} = 0, \, \widetilde{Z} = \widetilde{M}) \Pr(\widetilde{C} = 0 \mid \widetilde{Z} = \widetilde{M}) \\
&> \Pr(\widetilde{\mathcal{E}} \mid \widetilde{Z} = \widetilde{M}) - \tau.
\end{aligned}
\tag{64}
$$

We now define $Q_c(M)$ in terms of C and $\mathcal{E}$, using equation (16). Note that if c is bad, then $\Pr(\mathcal{E} \mid C = c, Z = M) = 0$, which implies $Q_c(M) = 0$.

We will show that if c is not bad, then $Q_c(M) \approx Q_c(\widetilde{M})$. When c is not bad, the events $C = c$ and $\mathcal{E}$ (conditioned on the events $Z = M$, $S = s$ and $T = t$) have exactly the same probabilities as the events $\widetilde{C} = c$ and $\widetilde{\mathcal{E}}$ (conditioned on the events $\widetilde{Z} = \widetilde{M}$, $S = s$ and $T = t$). So we can write $Q_c(M)$ in the form

$$
Q_c(M) = \frac{\operatorname{tr}(M\nu_c)}{\operatorname{tr}(M\xi_c)},
\tag{65}
$$

where ν_c and ξ_c are the *same* matrices used to express $Q_c(\widetilde{M})$ in equation (61). In addition, we can lower-bound $\operatorname{tr}(M\xi_c)$ and $\operatorname{tr}(\widetilde{M}\xi_c)$ as follows:

$$
\operatorname{tr}(M\xi_c) = \Pr(C = c, M) \geq \tau \Pr(M)
\tag{66}
$$

$$
\geq \tau \cdot 2\delta \cdot 2^{-m} \operatorname{tr}(M) \geq \tau \cdot 2\delta \cdot 2^{-m} \|M\|
\tag{67}
$$

$$
\geq \tau \cdot 2\delta \cdot 2^{-m},
\tag{68}
$$

$$
\operatorname{tr}(\widetilde{M}\xi_c) = \Pr(\widetilde{C} = c, \widetilde{M}) \geq \tau \Pr(\widetilde{M})
\tag{69}
$$

$$
\geq \tau\delta \cdot 2^{-m} \operatorname{tr}(\widetilde{M}) \geq \tau\delta \cdot 2^{-m} \|\widetilde{M}\|
\tag{70}
$$

$$
\geq \tau\delta \cdot 2^{-m}(1 - \mu) \geq \tau\delta \cdot 2^{-m} \cdot \tfrac{1}{2}.
\tag{71}
$$

Now we can write $Q_c(M) - Q_c(\widetilde{M})$ as follows:

$$
Q_c(M) - Q_c(\widetilde{M}) = \frac{\operatorname{tr}((M - \widetilde{M})\nu_c)}{\operatorname{tr}(M\xi_c)} + \operatorname{tr}(\widetilde{M}\nu_c) \frac{\operatorname{tr}((\widetilde{M} - M)\xi_c)}{\operatorname{tr}(M\xi_c)\operatorname{tr}(\widetilde{M}\xi_c)}.
\tag{72}
$$

We can then upper-bound this quantity:

$$
\begin{aligned}
|Q_c(M) &- Q_c(\widetilde{M})| \\
&\leq \frac{\mu}{\tau \cdot 2\delta \cdot 2^{-m}} + (1 + \mu)\frac{\mu}{\tau \cdot 2\delta \cdot 2^{-m} \cdot \tau\delta \cdot 2^{-m} \cdot \frac{1}{2}} \\
&= \frac{\mu}{\tau \cdot 2\delta \cdot 2^{-m}}\left(1 + \frac{(1 + \mu)}{\tau\delta \cdot 2^{-m} \cdot \frac{1}{2}}\right) \\
&\leq 2\mu\left(\frac{2^m}{\tau\delta}\right)^2.
\end{aligned}
\tag{73}
$$

Similarly, we define $R_c(M)$ in terms of C and $\mathcal{E}$, using equation (18). Using the same argument as above, we see that if c is bad, then $R_c(M) = 0$, and if c is not bad, then $R_c(M) \approx R_c(\widetilde{M})$. This completes the proof of Lemma 3.5. $\square$

4   Beyond the Isolated Qubits Model

We now describe a class of adversaries who can perform a polynomial number of 2-qubit entangling operations, in addition to unbounded LOCC. In particular, we will choose some "depth" parameter d (which may grow polynomially with the security parameter k), and we will consider adversaries who can apply quantum circuits whose depth is bounded by d. These kinds of attacks may be feasible in real physical systems, where one can perform noisy entangling gates. Intuitively, one may expect that the noise will accumulate when the adversary applies a long sequence of entangling gates; so it is easier for the adversary to apply shallow (low-depth) quantum circuits.

We will then show that our privacy amplification result for one-time memories (Theorem 3.1) still holds against these depth-d adversaries, where d can grow polynomially in k, and the privacy amplification technique now runs in time polynomial in d.

First, we will need a few definitions. Let $\mathcal{E} : \rho \mapsto \sum_i K_i \rho K_i^\dagger$ be a generalized quantum measurement. We say that $\mathcal{E}$ is 2-local if every Kraus operator K_i can be written as a tensor product of 2-qubit operators (where different Kraus operators K_i may arrange the qubits into pairs in different ways). As a simple example, if $\mathcal{E}_1, \mathcal{E}_2, \ldots, \mathcal{E}_\ell$ are 2-qubit quantum measurements, then $\mathcal{E}_1 \otimes \mathcal{E}_2 \otimes \cdots \otimes \mathcal{E}_\ell$ is a 2-local quantum measurement on 2ℓ qubits.

Note that 2-local measurements can be viewed as a generalization of separable measurements, in the following sense. First, if $\mathcal{E}$ is separable, then $\mathcal{E}$ is 2-local. Also, if $\mathcal{E}_1$ and $\mathcal{E}_2$ are separable, and $\mathcal{F}$ is 2-local, then $\mathcal{E}_2 \circ \mathcal{F} \circ \mathcal{E}_1$ is 2-local. Thus any 2-local measurement can include a separable measurement (and in particular, an LOCC measurement) "for free."

We say that an adversary is 2-local with depth d if it performs a measurement of the form $\mathcal{E} = \mathcal{E}_d \circ \mathcal{E}_{d-1} \circ \cdots \circ \mathcal{E}_1$, where $\mathcal{E}_1, \mathcal{E}_2, \ldots, \mathcal{E}_d$ are 2-local measurements. That is, the adversary first performs the measurement $\mathcal{E}_1$, obtains a classical measurement outcome i_1, then performs the measurement $\mathcal{E}_2$, obtains a classical measurement outcome i_2, and so on; after the final measurement $\mathcal{E}_d$, the post-measurement quantum state is discarded.

We say that the corresponding POVM element $M_{i_1,i_2,\ldots,i_d}$ is 2-local with depth d. We can write it in the following form:

$$M_{i_1,i_2,\ldots,i_d} = (K_{1,i_1}^\dagger K_{2,i_2}^\dagger \cdots K_{d,i_d}^\dagger)(K_{d,i_d} \cdots K_{2,i_2} K_{1,i_1}), \qquad (74)$$

where the K_{a,i_a} denote the Kraus operators of the measurement $\mathcal{E}_a$, that is, $\mathcal{E}_a(\rho) = \sum_{i_a} K_{a,i_a} \rho K_{a,i_a}^\dagger$, and each K_{a,i_a} can be written as a tensor product of 2-qubit operators.

We now extend our privacy amplification result for one-time memories (Theorem 3.1) to the case of 2-local depth-d adversaries.

Theorem 4.1. *Fix some constant $\varphi \geq 0$.*

Suppose that $\mathcal{D}$ is a family of "leaky" string-OTM's, as described in Theorem 3.1, but with a stronger security guarantee, which holds for all measurement outcomes that are 2-local with depth $d \leq k^\varphi$ (rather than for all separable measurement outcomes).

Now construct a new family of devices $\mathcal{D}'$, as described in Theorem 3.1, but where we set the parameter r (for the r-wise independent random functions F and G) as follows:

$$r = 4(\gamma + 1)k^{2\theta + \varphi}. \tag{75}$$

Then these devices $\mathcal{D}'$ are "ideal" OTM's, as described in Theorem 3.1, but again with a stronger security guarantee, which holds for all measurement outcomes that are 2-local with depth $d \leq k^\varphi$ (rather than for all separable measurement outcomes).

Thus, if one could construct "leaky" string-OTM's that were secure against 2-local depth-d adversaries, then one would immediately get "ideal" bit-OTM's in this setting. Unfortunately, the leaky string-OTM's from [5] are not known to be secure in this setting, and so we leave this as an open problem.

4.1   Overview of the Proof

We prove Theorem 4.1 using the same approach as for Theorem 3.1. Most of the argument is unchanged; the key difference is in Lemma 3.3, where we now want to construct an ε-net for the set of all 2-local depth-d measurement outcomes (rather than the set of all separable measurement outcomes).

Let Λ be the set of all 2-local depth-d measurement outcomes:

$$\Lambda = \{M \in (\mathbb{C}^{2\times2})^{\otimes m} \mid M = (K_1^\dagger \cdots K_d^\dagger)(K_d \cdots K_1), \\ \text{where } K_1, \ldots, K_d \in L\}, \tag{76}$$

where L is the set of all operators $K \in (\mathbb{C}^{2\times2})^{\otimes m}$ that can be written as tensor products of 2-qubit operators having operator norm at most 1. We will construct an ε-net for Λ, using the following lemma:

Lemma 4.1. *For any $0 < \mu \leq 1$, there exists a set $\widetilde{\Lambda} \subset \Lambda$, of cardinality $|\widetilde{\Lambda}| \leq \left(\frac{24dm^{17/16}}{\mu}\right)^{16md}$, which is a μ-net for Λ with respect to the operator norm $\|\cdot\|$.*

We will prove this lemma in Section 4.2. Now, we set

$$\mu = 2^{-(\alpha/6)k} \cdot \frac{\delta^4}{4^m} \tag{77}$$

(the same as in the proof of Theorem 3.1). Also, recall that $k \leq m \leq k^\theta$, and $d \leq k^\varphi$. Then the cardinality of $\widetilde{\Lambda}$ is bounded by

$$|\widetilde{\Lambda}| \leq \left(24dm^{17/16} \cdot 2^{(\alpha/6)k} \cdot \frac{4^m}{\delta^4}\right)^{16md}$$

$$= \left(24dm^{17/16} \cdot 2^{(\alpha/6)k+4\delta_0 k+2m}\right)^{16md}$$
$$\leq 2^{\gamma k^{2\theta+\varphi}}, \tag{78}$$

for all sufficiently large k; here γ is some universal constant. This bound plays the role of equation (29) in the proof of Theorem 3.1.

One then continues with the same argument as in Theorem 3.1: one uses the union bound over the set $\widetilde{\Lambda}$, while setting the parameter r sufficiently large (see equation (75)). This gives a result similar to equation (33).

The rest of the proof is the same as for Theorem 3.1. This completes the proof of Theorem 4.1. □

4.2   Constructing an ε-net

We now prove Lemma 4.1. First, consider the set

$$V = \{X \in \mathbb{C}^{4\times 4} \mid \|X\|_{\ell_\infty} \leq 2\}. \tag{79}$$

Let $\delta > 0$ (we will choose a specific value for δ later). It is easy to see that there exists a δ-net $\widetilde{V}$ for V, with respect to the ℓ_∞ norm, with cardinality $|\widetilde{V}| \leq (\frac{2\sqrt{2}}{\delta}+1)^{32}$. (For instance, one can describe each point in V with 32 real parameters, and choose a grid with spacing $\delta\sqrt{2}$.)

Next, consider the set of 2-qubit Kraus operators:

$$U = \{X \in \mathbb{C}^{4\times 4} \mid \|X\| \leq 1\}. \tag{80}$$

Note that $U \subset V$, since $\|X\|_{\ell_\infty} \leq \|X\|_F \leq 2\|X\|$. We will construct an 8δ-net $\widetilde{U}$ for U, by taking the points in $\widetilde{V}$ and "rounding" them into U. Define a function $r : V \to U$ that maps each point in V to the nearest point in U with respect to the ℓ_∞ norm, that is,

$$r(X) = \arg\min_{Y \in U} \|X - Y\|_{\ell_\infty}. \tag{81}$$

Let $\widetilde{U}$ be the image of $\widetilde{V}$ under this map, that is, $\widetilde{U} = \{r(X) \mid X \in \widetilde{V}\}$. Note that $|\widetilde{U}| \leq |\widetilde{V}|$.

It is easy to see that $\widetilde{U}$ is a 2δ-net for U, with respect to the ℓ_∞ norm. (This follows because, for any $X \in U$, there exists some $Y \in \widetilde{V}$ such that $\|X - Y\|_{\ell_\infty} \leq \delta$, and we know that $r(Y) \in \widetilde{U}$ and $\|Y - r(Y)\|_{\ell_\infty} \leq \delta$.) This implies that $\widetilde{U}$ is an 8δ-net for U, with respect to the operator norm $\|\cdot\|$. (This follows because $\|X\| \leq \|X\|_F \leq 4\|X\|_{\ell_\infty}$.)

Next, we let L be the set of all operators $K \in (\mathbb{C}^{2\times 2})^{\otimes m}$ that can be written as tensor products of 2-qubit operators in U. We then define $\widetilde{L}$ to be the set of all operators $K \in (\mathbb{C}^{2\times 2})^{\otimes m}$ that can be written as tensor products of 2-qubit operators in $\widetilde{U}$. Note that $\widetilde{L}$ has cardinality $|\widetilde{L}| \leq m! |\widetilde{U}|^{m/2}$, since every operator

$K \in \widetilde{L}$ can be written in the form $\bigotimes_{j=1}^{m/2} K_j$ (where $K_j \in \widetilde{U}$) conjugated with a permutation of the qubits. (For simplicity, let us assume that m is even.)

We claim that $\widetilde{L}$ is a $4m\delta$-net for L, with respect to the operator norm $\|\cdot\|$. To see this, consider any $K \in L$, and construct some $\widetilde{K} \in \widetilde{L}$ that approximates it as follows. First, relabel the qubits so that K can be written in the form $K = \bigotimes_{j=1}^{m/2} K_j$ (where $K_j \in U$). For each K_j, there is a point $\widetilde{K}_j \in \widetilde{U}$ within distance $\|K_j - \widetilde{K}_j\| \le 8\delta$. We then define $\widetilde{K} = \bigotimes_{j=1}^{m/2} \widetilde{K}_j$.

We upper-bound the distance $\|K - \widetilde{K}\|$ as follows, by defining a sequence of intermediate steps, and using the triangle inequality. For all $s = 0, 1, 2, \ldots, m/2$, define $K^{(s)} = (\widetilde{K}_1 \otimes \cdots \otimes \widetilde{K}_s) \otimes (K_{s+1} \otimes \cdots \otimes K_{m/2})$. Then we have that $K = K^{(0)}$, $\widetilde{K} = K^{(m/2)}$, and

$$
\begin{aligned}
\|K - \widetilde{K}\| &\le \sum_{s=0}^{m/2-1} \|K^{(s)} - K^{(s+1)}\| \\
&= \sum_{s=0}^{m/2-1} \big\| (\widetilde{K}_1 \otimes \cdots \otimes \widetilde{K}_s) \otimes (K_{s+1} - \widetilde{K}_{s+1}) \\
&\qquad\qquad\qquad\qquad \otimes (K_{s+2} \otimes \cdots \otimes K_{m/2}) \big\| \\
&\le (m/2)\, 8\delta = 4m\delta,
\end{aligned}
\tag{82}
$$

where we used the fact that $\|A \otimes B\| = \|A\| \, \|B\|$.

Finally, we consider the set Λ of all 2-local depth-d measurement outcomes:

$$
\begin{aligned}
\Lambda = \{M \in (\mathbb{C}^{2\times 2})^{\otimes m} \mid M = (K_1^\dagger \cdots K_d^\dagger)(K_d \cdots K_1), \\
\text{where } K_1, \ldots, K_d \in L\}.
\end{aligned}
\tag{83}
$$

We then define the set $\widetilde{\Lambda}$ as follows:

$$
\begin{aligned}
\widetilde{\Lambda} = \{M \in (\mathbb{C}^{2\times 2})^{\otimes m} \mid M = (K_1^\dagger \cdots K_d^\dagger)(K_d \cdots K_1), \\
\text{where } K_1, \ldots, K_d \in \widetilde{L}\}.
\end{aligned}
\tag{84}
$$

Note that $\widetilde{\Lambda}$ has cardinality $|\widetilde{\Lambda}| \le |\widetilde{L}|^d$.

We claim that $\widetilde{\Lambda}$ is an $8dm\delta$-net for Λ, with respect to the operator norm $\|\cdot\|$. To see this, consider any $M \in \Lambda$, and construct some $\widetilde{M} \in \widetilde{\Lambda}$ that approximates it as follows. M can be written in the form $M = (K_1^\dagger \cdots K_d^\dagger)(K_d \cdots K_1)$ (where $K_j \in L$). For each K_j, there is a point $\widetilde{K}_j \in \widetilde{L}$ within distance $\|K_j - \widetilde{K}_j\| \le 4m\delta$. We then let $\widetilde{M} = (\widetilde{K}_1^\dagger \cdots \widetilde{K}_d^\dagger)(\widetilde{K}_d \cdots \widetilde{K}_1)$.

We upper-bound the distance $\|M - \widetilde{M}\|$ as follows, by defining a sequence of intermediate steps, and using the triangle inequality. For all $s = 0, 1, 2, \ldots, 2d$, define $M^{(s)}$ to be an operator of the form $(K_1^\dagger \cdots K_d^\dagger) \cdot (K_d \cdots K_1)$, where the first s factors (reading from left to right) have tilde's, and the remaining $2d - s$ factors do not have tilde's. Then we have that $M = M^{(0)}$, $\widetilde{M} = M^{(2d)}$, and

$$\|M - \widetilde{M}\| \leq \sum_{s=0}^{2d-1} \|M^{(s)} - M^{(s+1)}\|$$

$$= \sum_{s=0}^{d-1} \|(\widetilde{K}_1^\dagger \cdots \widetilde{K}_s^\dagger)(K_{s+1}^\dagger - \widetilde{K}_{s+1}^\dagger)(K_{s+2}^\dagger \cdots K_d^\dagger)(K_d \cdots K_1)\|$$

$$+ \sum_{s=d}^{2d-1} \|(\widetilde{K}_1^\dagger \cdots \widetilde{K}_d^\dagger)(\widetilde{K}_d \cdots \widetilde{K}_{2d-s+1})(K_{2d-s} - \widetilde{K}_{2d-s}) \cdot$$

$$(K_{2d-s-1} \cdots K_1)\| \tag{85}$$

$$\leq 2d \cdot 4m\delta = 8dm\delta,$$

where we used the fact that $\|AB\| \leq \|A\| \|B\|$.

Finally, we set $\delta = \mu/(8dm)$. Then $\widetilde{\Lambda}$ is a μ-net for Λ, with respect to the operator norm $\|\cdot\|$. The cardinality of $\widetilde{\Lambda}$ is

$$|\widetilde{\Lambda}| \leq |\widetilde{L}|^d \leq (m!)^d |\widetilde{U}|^{md/2}$$

$$\leq (m!)^d \left(\tfrac{2\sqrt{2}}{\delta} + 1\right)^{16md}$$

$$\leq m^{md} \left(\tfrac{16\sqrt{2}dm}{\mu} + 1\right)^{16md} \tag{86}$$

$$\leq \left(\tfrac{24dm^{17/16}}{\mu}\right)^{16md},$$

provided that $\mu \leq 1$. This proves Lemma 4.1. □

References

1. Lo, H.-K., Chau, H.F.: Is quantum bit commitment really possible? Phys. Rev. Lett. **78**, 3410 (1997)
2. Lo, H.-K.: Insecurity of quantum secure computations. Phys. Rev. A **56**(2), 1154–1162 (1997)
3. Mayers, D.: Unconditionally secure quantum bit commitment is impossible. Phys. Rev. Lett. **78**, 3414–3417 (1997)
4. Buhrman, H., Christandl, M., Schaffner, C.: Complete Insecurity of Quantum Protocols for Classical Two-Party Computation. Phys. Rev. Lett. **109**, 160501 (2012)
5. Liu, Y.-K.: Single-Shot Security for One-Time Memories in the Isolated Qubits Model. In: Garay, J.A., Gennaro, R. (eds.) CRYPTO 2014, Part II. LNCS, vol. 8617, pp. 19–36. Springer, Heidelberg (2014)
6. Liu, Y.-K.: Building one-time memories from isolated qubits. ITCS, pp. 269–286 (2014)
7. Saeedi, K., et al.: Room-Temperature Quantum Bit Storage Exceeding 39 Minutes Using Ionized Donors in Silicon-28. Science **342**(6160), 830–833 (2013)
8. Dreau, A., et al.: Single-Shot Readout of Multiple Nuclear Spin Qubits in Diamond under Ambient Conditions. Phys. Rev. Lett. **110**, 060502 (2013)

9. Goldwasser, S., Kalai, Y.T., Rothblum, G.N.: One-Time Programs. In: Wagner, D. (ed.) CRYPTO 2008. LNCS, vol. 5157, pp. 39–56. Springer, Heidelberg (2008)

10. Goyal, V., Ishai, Y., Sahai, A., Venkatesan, R., Wadia, A.: Founding Cryptography on Tamper-Proof Hardware Tokens. In: Micciancio, D. (ed.) TCC 2010. LNCS, vol. 5978, pp. 308–326. Springer, Heidelberg (2010)

11. Bellare, M., Hoang, V.T., Rogaway, P.: Adaptively Secure Garbling with Applications to One-Time Programs and Secure Outsourcing. In: Wang, X., Sako, K. (eds.) ASIACRYPT 2012. LNCS, vol. 7658, pp. 134–153. Springer, Heidelberg (2012)

12. Broadbent, A., Gutoski, G., Stebila, D.: Quantum one-time programs. In: Canetti, R., Garay, J.A. (eds.) CRYPTO 2013, Part II. LNCS, vol. 8043, pp. 344–360. Springer, Heidelberg (2013)

13. Vadhan, S.P.: Pseudorandomness. Foundations and Trends in Theoretical Computer Science $\mathbf{7}(13)$, 1–336 (2011)

14. Bellare, M., Rompel, J.: Randomness-Efficient Oblivious Sampling. FOCS, 276–287 (1994)

15. Schmidt, J.P., Siegel, A., Srinivasan, A.: Chernoff-Hoeffding Bounds for Applications with Limited Independence. SIAM J. Discrete Math. $\mathbf{8}(2)$, 223–250 (1995)

16. Liu, Y.-K.: Privacy amplification in the isolated qubits model. Arxiv:1410.3918

17. Hanson, D.L., Wright, F.T.: A Bound on Tail Probabilities for Quadratic Forms in Independent Random Variables. Ann. Math. Stat. $\mathbf{42}(3)$, 1079–1083 (1971)

18. Rudelson, M., Vershynin, R.: Hanson-Wright inequality and sub-gaussian concentration. Electronic Communications in Probability $\mathbf{18}$, 1–9 (2013)

19. Wiesner, S.: Conjugate coding. ACM SIGACT News $\mathbf{15}(1)$, 78–88 (1983). original manuscript written circa 1970

20. Salvail, L.: Quantum Bit Commitment from a Physical Assumption. In: Krawczyk, H. (ed.) CRYPTO 1998. LNCS, vol. 1462, pp. 338–353. Springer, Heidelberg (1998)

21. Pastawski, F., Yao, N.Y., Jiang, L., Lukin, M.D., Cirac, J.I.: Unforgeable Noise-Tolerant Quantum Tokens. Proc. Nat. Acad. Sci. $\mathbf{109}$, 16079–16082 (2012)

22. Bouman, N.J., Fehr, S., González-Guillén, C., Schaffner, C.: An All-But-One Entropic Uncertainty Relation, and Application to Password-Based Identification. In: Kawano, Y. (ed.) TQC 2012. LNCS, vol. 7582, pp. 29–44. Springer, Heidelberg (2012)

23. Bennett, C.H., DiVincenzo, D.P., Fuchs, C.A., Mor, T., Rains, E., Shor, P.W., Smolin, J.A., Wootters, W.K.: Quantum nonlocality without entanglement. Phys. Rev. A $\mathbf{59}$, 1070–1091 (1999)

24. Childs, A.M., Leung, D., Mancinska, L., Ozols, M.: A framework for bounding nonlocality of state discrimination. arXiv:1206.5822

25. DiVincenzo, D.P., Leung, D.W., Terhal, B.M.: Quantum Data Hiding. IEEE Trans. Inf. Theory $\mathbf{48}(3)$, 580–599 (2002)

26. Eggeling, T., Werner, R.F.: Hiding Classical Data in Multipartite Quantum States. Phys. Rev. Lett. $\mathbf{89}$, 097905 (2002)

27. Masanes, L.: Universally Composable Privacy Amplification from Causality Constraints. Phys. Rev. Lett. $\mathbf{102}$, 140501 (2009)

28. Trevisan, L., Vadhan, S.P.: Extracting Randomness from Samplable Distributions. FOCS, 32–42 (2000)

29. Kamp, J., Zuckerman, D.: Deterministic Extractors for Bit-Fixing Sources and Exposure-Resilient Cryptography. SIAM J. Comput. $\mathbf{36}(5)$, 1231–1247 (2006)

30. Gabizon, A.: Deterministic Extraction from Weak Random Sources, Springer-Verlag (2011)

31. Akavia, A., Goldwasser, S., Vaikuntanathan, V.: Simultaneous Hardcore Bits and Cryptography against Memory Attacks. In: Reingold, O. (ed.) TCC 2009. LNCS, vol. 5444, pp. 474–495. Springer, Heidelberg (2009)
32. Naor, M., Segev, G.: Public-Key Cryptosystems Resilient to Key Leakage. In: Halevi, S. (ed.) CRYPTO 2009. LNCS, vol. 5677, pp. 18–35. Springer, Heidelberg (2009)
33. Damgård, I.B., Fehr, S., Renner, R.S., Salvail, L., Schaffner, C.: A Tight High-Order Entropic Quantum Uncertainty Relation with Applications. In: Menezes, A. (ed.) CRYPTO 2007. LNCS, vol. 4622, pp. 360–378. Springer, Heidelberg (2007)
34. Horodecki, R., Horodecki, P., Horodecki, M., Horodecki, K.: Quantum Entanglement. Rev. Mod. Phys. **81**, 865–942 (2009)

Discrete Logarithms

Generic Hardness of the Multiple Discrete Logarithm Problem

Aaram Yun[✉]

Ulsan National Institute of Science and Technology (UNIST),
Ulsan, Republic of Korea
aaramyun@unist.ac.kr

Abstract. We study generic hardness of the multiple discrete logarithm problem, where the solver has to solve n instances of the discrete logarithm problem simultaneously. There are known generic algorithms which perform $O(\sqrt{np})$ group operations, where p is the group order, but no generic lower bound was known other than the trivial bound. In this paper we prove the tight generic lower bound, showing that the previously known algorithms are asymptotically optimal. We establish the lower bound by studying hardness of a related computational problem which we call the search-by-hyperplane-queries problem, which may be of independent interest.

Keywords: Multiple discrete logarithm · Search-by-hyperplane-queries · Generic group model

1 Introduction

Multiple Discrete Logarithm Problem. Let G be a cyclic group of order p, where p is prime, and let g be a generator of G. Then the Discrete Logarithm (DL) problem is defined as follows: given (G, p, g, g^α) for a uniform random $\alpha \xleftarrow{\$} \mathbb{Z}_p$, find out α.

Similarly, the Multiple Discrete Logarithm (MDL) problem is defined as follows: given $(G, p, g, g^{\alpha_1}, \ldots, g^{\alpha_n})$, for independently chosen uniform random elements $\alpha_1, \ldots, \alpha_n \xleftarrow{\$} \mathbb{Z}_p$, find out $\vec{\alpha} = (\alpha_1, \ldots, \alpha_n)$.

The discrete logarithm problem (and related variants like the Diffie-Hellman problem) is used for many cryptographic constructions and its hardness was studied widely. On the other hand, as far as we know, there are no cryptographic constructions whose security is based on the multiple discrete logarithm problem.

Still, the multiple discrete logarithm problem is relevant in the context of standard curves in the elliptic curve cryptography. Since generating good elliptic curves is rather computationally expensive, some standards like NIST's FIPS 186 [1] recommend using a few standard curves to instantiate cryptographic schemes. Hence, in such a setting, we naturally have to consider the multiple discrete logarithm problem. Hitchcock et al. [7] analyzed efficiency of algorithms

© International Association for Cryptologic Research 2015
E. Oswald and M. Fischlin (Eds.): EUROCRYPT 2015, Part II, LNCS 9057, pp. 817–836, 2015.
DOI: 10.1007/978-3-662-46803-6_27

solving the multiple discrete logarithm problem to see how using such a standard curve affects security.

Moreover, some cryptographic constructions *require* a user to solve 'small' discrete logarithm problems: either the group order p is small, or the exponent α is chosen from a small subset $I \subseteq \mathbb{Z}_p$. One such example is the Boneh-Goh-Nissim homomorphic encryption [5], where in order to decrypt a ciphertext, a user has to first compute g^m from the given ciphertext and then solve the discrete logarithm to recover the message m. Another example is the Maurer-Yacobi identity-based encryption [10]. Their construction uses a *trapdoor discrete logarithm group*, where the discrete logarithm problem is feasible to a user who has the trapdoor information, while hard for those who do not. They achieve this by using a composite-order group, and then the trapdoor information is the factorization of the group order. A user who has the factorization can solve DL on small groups so the discrete logarithm problem is feasible, but an adversary has to solve the DL problem in a large group. For these cases, efficient algorithms for solving DL is crucial, and for example, Lee, Cheon, and Hong [9] and Bernstein and Lange [2] showed how to speed up the solution of the discrete logarithm problem via precomputation. When considered as a whole, these become algorithms for solving the multiple discrete logarithm problem.

Generic Group Model. In general, hardness of a cryptographic problem based on a group does not depend solely on the isomorphism class of the underlying group. For example, while we believe that, if we carefully choose an elliptic curve and a subgroup G of prime order p on it, then the discrete logarithm problem on G would be difficult, we also know that the same problem is trivial on the additive group $\mathbb{Z}_p$ which is nonetheless isomorphic to G. What is important is how the same isomorphism class is encoded to a concrete 'representation'. When $\xi : \mathbb{Z}_p \to \{0,1\}^t$ is an injective function, we say that ξ is an *encoding* of the group $\mathbb{Z}_p$. In such a case, we may define $G := \xi(\mathbb{Z}_p)$, and make G into a group by giving G the unique group structure induced from the bijection $\xi : \mathbb{Z}_p \xrightarrow{\sim} G$. Conversely, we can see that any concrete cyclic group with prime order p should come from such an encoding $\xi : \mathbb{Z}_p \to \{0,1\}^t$ together with functions $\mu : \{0,1\}^t \times \{0,1\}^t \to \{0,1\}^t$, $\iota : \{0,1\}^t \to \{0,1\}^t$ such that $\mu|_{G \times G}$ and $\iota|_G$ give multiplication and inversion on G, respectively.

Also, a sophisticated algorithm may analyze and exploit structures of such an encoding to solve group-based computational problems. Naturally, such an algorithm is specific to that particular encoding. On the other hand, there are many 'generic' algorithms which are agnostic to the particular encoding used. One such example is the Baby-Step-Giant-Step algorithm for solving the discrete logarithm problem: BSGS algorithm does not assume anything about the group encoding, except that it is indeed a group encoding, therefore it works for any cyclic group, even though better algorithms exist for some specific groups.

'Generic hardness' of a cryptographic problem, that is, hardness against such generic algorithms, was studied for many group-based cryptographic problems. While a proof of generic hardness cannot really replace serious cryptanalysis for such a problem, at least it serves as a sanity check, in the sense that if a problem can be solved efficiently even by a generic algorithm, certainly one cannot base cryptographic constructions on such an easy problem. Also, for example on elliptic curves, so far no better non-generic algorithms are known.

To analyze such generic algorithms, the generic group model was proposed by Nechaev and Shoup [11,12]. In the generic group model, to ensure that a generic algorithm cannot exploit the encoding of a group, a *random encoding*, an encoding $\xi : \mathbb{Z}_p \to \{0,1\}^t$ which is uniform randomly chosen from the set of all injections $\mathbb{Z}_p \hookrightarrow \{0,1\}^t$, is used. Since in such a case we cannot expect any efficient algorithms for group laws, the group laws are given by oracles: the algorithm makes oracle queries by giving encodings of group elements like $\xi(\alpha), \xi(\beta)$, and the oracle returns the result of multiplication or division of these elements in encoded form. In the generic group model, we consider the query complexity of an algorithm to measure its efficiency.

Generic Algorithms for DL and MDL Problems. Shoup [12] analyzed generic hardness of the discrete logarithm problem. He showed that any generic DL solver which makes at most q queries to the group law oracles has the success probability at most $O(q^2/p)$. In other words, any generic DL solver with some constant success probability should make at least $\Omega(\sqrt{p})$ queries.

As explained before, there are generic algorithms for DL with asymptotically tight matching upper bounds. The Baby-Step-Giant-Step algorithm is an example, and Pollard's rho algorithm is another. Both algorithms perform $O(\sqrt{p})$ group operations. And this gives us a trivial generic algorithm for solving MDL: simply repeat such an asymptotically optimal generic algorithm n times, where n is the total number of DL instances. The total complexity would be $O(n\sqrt{p})$.

In fact, there is a better generic algorithm for MDL. Kuhn and Struik [8] extended Pollard's rho to a generic algorithm solving MDL. Their algorithm performs $O(\sqrt{np})$ group operations.

On the other hand, as far as we know, precise generic hardness of MDL is not known. Clearly, solving n DL instances would be at least as hard as solving one single DL instance, therefore Shoup's lower bound $\Omega(\sqrt{p})$ applies here. Kuhn and Struik [8] conjectured that the tight lower bound would be $\Omega(\sqrt{np})$, but this has never been proved yet. This means that even the highly improbable possibility of a generic algorithm solving n DL instances within $O(\sqrt{p})$, independent of n, is not yet eliminated!

Perhaps one reason for this situation might be that, most of the previous results on generic hardness of cryptographic problems were based solely on the standard technique also originated from Shoup [12]: instead of choosing the hidden exponents (for example, $\alpha_1, \ldots, \alpha_n$ in the MDL) at the beginning, the game is modified so that the exponents are chosen at the *end* of the game, and all responses to the group law queries are made with respect to polynomials of those exponents, where the undetermined exponents are considered as unknown variables. In this modified game, usually it is straightforward to show that the solver has only small probability of winning. The proof also has to analyze the difference between the two games, but when the number of queries is not too large, it is possible to show that the difference is again small, by using the Schwartz-Zippel lemma. In other words, this technique formalizes the following intuition: as long as the number of queries is not too large, interesting things rarely happen, not much useful information is revealed to the solver, and the solver cannot perform well. Despite the simplicity and genericity, this technique was highly effective, being able to establish asymptotically tight lower bounds for problems like the discrete logarithm problem [12], the Diffie-Hellman problem [12], the strong Diffie-Hellman problem [3], the decision linear problem [4], and many others.

On the other hand, for the situation of MDL, we do consider cases where the solver makes queries *more* than the Shoup bound $\sqrt{p}$. Therefore, a solver *does* obtain some nontrivial information, and Shoup's technique breaks down. In order to establish a nontrivial lower bound for MDL, a more careful analysis of the problem is needed.

In this paper, we show that the conjecture of Kuhn and Struik is indeed correct: any generic algorithm solving MDL with constant success probability should make at least $\Omega(\sqrt{np})$ queries to the group law oracles.

Search-by-Hyperplane-Queries Problem. To circumvent the limitation of Shoup's technique, we establish the generic lower bound of MDL by analyzing a closely related problem, which we call Search-by-Hyperplane-Queries (SHQ) problem. In the SHQ problem, a uniform random point $\vec{\alpha} = (\alpha_1, \ldots, \alpha_n)$ of the n-dimensional affine space $\mathbb{Z}_p^n$ is hidden, and the goal of the solver is to find the point $\vec{\alpha}$. Of course, the success probability of any unaided solver is at most $1/p^n$. Therefore, we allow any solver to make adaptive *hyperplane queries*. Recall that an affine hyperplane $H \subseteq \mathbb{Z}_p^n$ can be described by an equation of form $a_1 X_1 + \cdots + a_n X_n = b$, where $a_1, \ldots, a_n, b \in \mathbb{Z}_p$. A hyperplane query is asked by specifying a hyperplane H via the coefficients $a_1, \ldots, a_n, b$, and the intended meaning of the query is 'is $\vec{\alpha} \in H$?' A SHQ solver may make a series of adaptive hyperplane queries, and use the information gained by such queries to find the hidden point $\vec{\alpha}$.

We are going to show that any SHQ solver which makes at most q hyperplane queries has success probability at most $O((eq/np)^n)$, where e is the base of the natural logarithm. Therefore, any SHQ solver with some constant success probability should make $\Omega(np)$ queries. Then, we are going to show that this lower bound for the SHQ problem implies the $\Omega(\sqrt{np})$ lower bound for the MDL problem.

Since the SHQ problem looks interesting by itself, we also analyze the worst-case version of the SHQ problem, and show that any worst-case SHQ solver has to make at least $n(p-1)$ queries. This is a tight lower bound; there is a corresponding solver realizing the bound. Moreover, we also analyze another variant of the worst-case version where a solver is allowed to output a list L which contains the correct answer $\vec{\alpha}$, instead of uniquely identifying the correct solution. We again establish a tight lower bound for this version.

2 Multiple Discrete Logarithm Problem in the Generic Group Model

2.1 Generic Group Model

Let p be a prime number, and let $\xi : \mathbb{Z}_p \to \{0,1\}^t$ be a *random encoding* of $\mathbb{Z}_p$, that is, a uniform randomly chosen function among all injective functions of form $\mathbb{Z}_p \to \{0,1\}^t$ for some t satisfying $t \geq \log_2 p$. We define the *group law oracle* μ as the oracle satisfying the following:

$$\mu(b, \xi(\alpha), \xi(\beta)) = \xi(\alpha + (-1)^b \beta \bmod p),$$

where $b \in \{0,1\}$ is a bit indicating whether multiplication or division is intended.

In the *generic group model*, we consider the generic algorithm, which is a probabilistic algorithm A to which is initially given a list of group elements $\xi(\beta_1), \ldots, \xi(\beta_k)$, encoded by the random encoding ξ. Also, while running, the algorithm A can make group law queries to the oracle μ. Finally A halts with an output. Note that ξ is never explicitly given to A, but only implicitly via the initial input and the group law oracles.

2.2 Multiple Discrete Logarithm Problem

Let G be a cyclic group of order p, where p is prime, and let g be a generator of G. Also, let n be an integer. We require that $n = o(p)$: formally, we consider a family of such numbers, so that there is a main parameter λ, and both n and p are functions of λ, and $n(\lambda)/p(\lambda) \to 0$, as $\lambda \to \infty$.

Then we may define the *Multiple Discrete Logarithm (MDL) problem* as:

Given $(G, p, g, g^{\alpha_1}, \ldots, g^{\alpha_n})$, find out $(\alpha_1, \ldots, \alpha_n)$, where $\alpha_1, \ldots, \alpha_n \xleftarrow{\$} \mathbb{Z}_p$ are independently chosen uniform random elements.

We consider the MDL problem in the generic group model. Hence, for a generic algorithm A, we define $\mathbf{Adv}_{p,n}^{\mathsf{mdl}}(A)$, the *advantage* of A in solving the MDL problem as

$$\mathbf{Adv}_{p,n}^{\mathsf{mdl}}(A) = \mathbf{Pr}[A^\mu(p, \xi(1), \xi(\alpha_1), \ldots, \xi(\alpha_n)) = (\alpha_1, \ldots, \alpha_n)],$$

where the probability is over the random choice of ξ, $\alpha_1, \ldots, \alpha_n$, and the internal randomness of A.

For any generic MDL solver A, let us say that A *solves MDL with constant advantage* if there exists some constant $c > 0$ such that

$$\mathbf{Adv}_{p,n}^{\mathsf{mdl}}(A) \geq c,$$

for any value of the parameter λ.

Remark 1. We remark that the condition $n = o(p)$ we impose here is rather natural. It is reasonable to assume that n, the number of DL instances in consideration, is polynomially bounded, so $n = o(p)$ holds if p is exponentially large. But the condition is much less demanding than that. It may hold even when p is not exponentially large in comparision with n, for example, when $n = \Theta(\lambda)$ and $p = \Theta(\lambda^2)$, or when $n = \Theta(1)$ and $p = \Theta(\lambda)$.

Remark 2. While we may extend our examination of MDL solvers to include those with non-negligible success probability, that would complicate the relationship between n, p, and the number of queries, since a solver may make trade-offs between the number of queries and the success probability. In fact, we may amplify any such non-negligible probability to a constant probability with slowdown by at most a polynomial factor. So, 'standardizing' this trade-off by insisting some constant success probability is reasonable, and this approach is adopted by many authors, including Shoup [12].

3   Search-by-Hyperplane-Queries Problem

In this section, we describe the Search-by-Hyperplane-Queries (SHQ) problem. Let p be a prime number and $\mathbb{Z}_p^n$ be the n-dimensional affine space over the finite field $\mathbb{Z}_p$. As in the MDL problem, we assume that $n = o(p)$.[1]

Let $X_1, \ldots, X_n$ be the canonical coordinate functions of $\mathbb{Z}_p^n$. Then, an affine hyperplane H in $\mathbb{Z}_p^n$ can be written by a formula of form $a_1 X_1 + \cdots + a_n X_n = b$ for some $a_1, \ldots, a_n, b \in \mathbb{Z}_p$, with $a_i \neq 0$ for some i. Sometimes we represent such a hyperplane H by the linear expression $a_1 X_1 + \cdots + a_n X_n - b$, or even simply by the tuple $(a_1, \ldots, a_n, b)$.

Let $\vec{\alpha} \in \mathbb{Z}_p^n$ be a point in the affine space. We define

$$\mathsf{H}(\vec{\alpha}, H) := \begin{cases} 1 & \text{if } \vec{\alpha} \in H, \\ 0 & \text{otherwise.} \end{cases}$$

The SHQ problem is as follows: pick a uniform random point $\vec{\alpha}$ of $\mathbb{Z}_p^n$. The goal of the problem is to correctly guess the hidden point $\vec{\alpha}$. Without anything else, the probability of correct guess is p^{-n}. Therefore, up to some q adaptive hyperplane queries are allowed: a solver for this problem is allowed to submit up to q hyperplane queries $H_1, \ldots, H_q$ adaptively, and for each such query, the result $\mathsf{H}(\vec{\alpha}, H_i)$ is given. In other words, the solver is given the hyperplane query oracle $\mathsf{H}(\vec{\alpha}, \cdot)$.

For a SHQ solver A, we define $\mathbf{Adv}_{p,n}^{\mathsf{shq}}(A)$, the advantage of A in solving SHQ, as

$$\mathbf{Adv}_{p,n}^{\mathsf{shq}}(A) = \mathbf{Pr}[A^{\mathsf{H}(\vec{\alpha}, \cdot)}(p, n) = \vec{\alpha}],$$

where the probability is over the random choice of $\vec{\alpha}$ and the internal randomness of A.

---

[1] In fact, for SHQ we only require $p^{-n} = o(1)$, which is implied by the given condition.

For any SHQ solver A, let us say that A *solves SHQ with constant advantage* if there exists some constant $c > 0$ such that

$$\mathbf{Adv}_{p,n}^{\mathsf{shq}}(A) \geq c,$$

for any value of the parameter λ.

Worst-Case SHQ. We may also consider the worst-case version of the SHQ problem: instead of searching for the uniform randomly chosen $\vec{\alpha}$ with constant advantage, the worst-case SHQ problem is to find any instance $\vec{\alpha} \in \mathbb{Z}_p^n$. Formally, we say that a generic algorithm A *solves SHQ in the worst case within q queries*, if for any $\vec{\alpha} \in \mathbb{Z}_p^n$, $A^{\mathsf{H}(\vec{\alpha}, \cdot)}(p, n)$ always outputs $\vec{\alpha}$ after at most q queries.

Example 1 (Brute-force solver). Here we exhibit a very simple, 'brute-force' SHQ solver. We identify $\mathbb{Z}_p$ with $\{0, 1, \ldots, p-1\}$, and consider hyperplanes of form $X_i = j$, where $i = 1, \ldots, n$, and $j = 1, \ldots, p-1$. There are total $n(p-1)$ such hyperplanes, and we see that non-adaptive hyperplane queries for these $q := n(p-1)$ hyperplanes are enough to correctly find any $\vec{\alpha}$: let $\vec{\alpha} = (\alpha_1, \ldots, \alpha_n)$. For any i, if $\mathsf{H}(\vec{\alpha}, X_i = j) = 1$ for some $j = 1, \ldots, p-1$, then $\alpha_i = j$. On the other hand, if $\mathsf{H}(\vec{\alpha}, X_i = j) = 0$ for all $j = 1, \ldots, p-1$, then clearly $\alpha_i = 0$. So in this way the brute-force solver completely determines all coordinates of $\vec{\alpha}$.

While the above brute-force solver looks very trivial, it turns out that it is actually optimal, by Theorem 2 at Section 5.

4   Relationship Between the Two Problems

In this section, we show that MDL and SHQ are closely related, and any hardness result for SHQ immediately produces a hardness result for MDL.

Theorem 1. *Let A be any generic MDL solver which makes at most q queries. Then, using A, it is possible to construct a SHQ solver B which makes at most $(q+n)(q+n+1)/2$ queries, and satisfying*

$$\mathbf{Adv}_{p,n}^{\mathsf{shq}}(B) \geq \mathbf{Adv}_{p,n}^{\mathsf{mdl}}(A).$$

Proof. We describe how B works. First B receives (p, n) as the input, and B also has access to the oracle $\mathsf{H}(\vec{\alpha}, \cdot)$, for a uniform randomly chosen $\vec{\alpha} = (\alpha_1, \ldots, \alpha_n) \xleftarrow{\$} \mathbb{Z}_p^n$. For convenience, let us define $\alpha_0 := 1$. The solver B has to simulate a random encoding $\xi : \mathbb{Z}_p \to \{0, 1\}^t$ for A. To do this, B maintains two sequences, $\{s_i\}_i$ and $\{L_i\}_i$, where $s_i \in \{0, 1\}^t$ are random bitstrings generated by B and given to A as simulated output of the encoding function ξ, and L_i are linear functions of form $L_i(X_1, \ldots, X_n) = a_1 X_1 + \cdots + a_n X_n + b \in \mathbb{Z}_p[X_1, \ldots, X_n]$. The idea is to simulate the random encoding ξ, by pretending $s_i = \xi(L_i(\vec{\alpha}))$ for $(s_i, L_i) \in T$.

- Initialization: Here B prepares the simulation of the initial input to A: B chooses $s_0 \xleftarrow{\$} \{0,1\}^t$, and defines $L_0 := 1$. Next, B chooses $s_1, \ldots, s_n$ recursively as follows: when choosing s_i, if there is some $j < i$ with $\mathsf{H}(\vec{\alpha}, X_i = X_j) = 1$ then B picks smallest such j and defines $s_i := s_j$. Otherwise, B chooses $s_i \xleftarrow{\$} \{0,1\}^t \setminus \{s_0, \ldots, s_{i-1}\}$. And, L_i is defined as X_i. Let ctr be n. Finally, B runs $A(p, s_0, s_1, s_2, \ldots, s_n)$.
- Queries: when A makes a query[2] $\mu(b, s_i, s_j)$ for some $0 \le i, j \le ctr$ and $b \in \{0,1\}$, B increments $ctr \leftarrow ctr+1$, then defines s_{ctr} and L_{ctr} as follows: L_{ctr} is simply defined as $L_i + (-1)^b L_j$. Now, if there is $k < ctr$ with $\mathsf{H}(\vec{\alpha}, L_{ctr} = L_k) = 1$, then B picks the smallest such k and defines $s_{ctr} := s_k$. Otherwise, B randomly picks $s_{ctr} \xleftarrow{\$} \{0,1\}^t \setminus \{s_0, \ldots, s_{ctr-1}\}$. Finally, B returns s_{ctr} as the answer to the query.
- Output: eventually, A halts with output $\vec{\beta} = (\beta_1, \ldots, \beta_n) \in \mathbb{Z}_p^n$. B then also outputs $\vec{\beta}$ and halts.

Now, let us analyze the SHQ solver B. At the initialization phase, B can choose s_i after making i hyperplane queries; so B makes $1 + \cdots + n = n(n+1)/2$ hyperplane queries up to this point. Similarly, to determine s_{ctr}, B has to make ctr hyperplane queries. In total, the number of hyperplane queries B makes is bounded by

$$\frac{n(n+1)}{2} + \sum_{ctr=n+1}^{n+q} ctr = \frac{n(n+1)}{2} + nq + \frac{q(q+1)}{2}$$
$$= \frac{n^2 + n + q^2 + q + 2nq}{2}$$
$$= \frac{(q+n)(q+n+1)}{2}.$$

Next we have to show that

$$\mathbf{Adv}_{p,n}^{\mathsf{shq}}(B) \ge \mathbf{Adv}_{p,n}^{\mathsf{mdl}}(A).$$

In fact, we will show that $\mathbf{Adv}_{p,n}^{\mathsf{shq}}(B) = \mathbf{Adv}_{p,n}^{\mathsf{mdl}}(A)$. For this, we need only to show that the simulated input $(p, s_0, s_1, \ldots, s_n)$ given to A has the same distribution as in the original generic MDL problem, and also the simulated group law oracle has the same distribution as in the original generic MDL problem. Let $\xi : \mathbb{Z}_p \to \{0,1\}^t$ be a random encoding, and let $s_i' := \xi(\alpha_i)$ for $i = 0, 1, \ldots, n$, and let $s_{n+1}', s_{n+2}', \ldots$ be the sequence of bitstrings which would be given as the answers to the oracle queries made by A, when A is engaged in the real MDL game with ξ. Finally, let $\alpha_i := \xi^{-1}(s_i')$ for $i = n+1, n+2, \ldots$. Then, we need only to show the following: the random variables s_{ctr} and s_{ctr}' are identically distributed for any $ctr \in \{1, \ldots, q+n\}$, conditioned on the event that

$$s_i = s_i' \text{ and } \alpha_i = L_i(\vec{\alpha}), \quad \text{for all } i = 0, 1, 2, \ldots, ctr - 1.$$

---

[2] Here we may assume that μ never makes group law queries using bitstrings outside of s_i, because B may ensure that A can guess bitstrings in $\xi(\mathbb{Z}_p)$ only with negligible probability, by sufficiently enlarging the bit length t.

Let us prove this only for $ctr > n$: the case for $s_0, \ldots, s_n$ can be done similarly. Suppose that the group law query of A is $\mu(b, s_i, s_j)$ when determining the bitstring s_{ctr}. Then, s'_{ctr} is easy to compute: $s'_i = \xi(\alpha_i), s'_j = \xi(\alpha_j)$, so $s'_{ctr} = \xi(\alpha_i + (-1)^b \alpha_j)$. Also, $\alpha_{ctr} = \xi^{-1}(s'_{ctr}) = \alpha_i + (-1)^b \alpha_j = L_i(\vec{\alpha}) + (-1)^b L_j(\vec{\alpha}) = (L_i + (-1)^b L_j)(\vec{\alpha}) = L_{ctr}(\vec{\alpha})$. We need to compare this s'_{ctr} with s_{ctr} computed by the algorithm B.

- When there is no $k < ctr$ with $H(\vec{\alpha}, L_{ctr} = L_k) = 1$: in this case, we have $s_{ctr} \xleftarrow{\$} \{0,1\}^t \setminus \{s_0, \ldots, s_{ctr-1}\}$. But, this means that $L_{ctr}(\vec{\alpha}) \neq L_k(\vec{\alpha})$, that is, $\alpha_{ctr} \neq \alpha_k$ for $k = 0, \ldots, ctr - 1$. So $s'_i = \xi(\alpha_{ctr})$ is uniformly distributed on $\{0,1\}^t \setminus \{\xi(\alpha_0), \ldots, \xi(\alpha_{ctr-1})\}$. Since $s_i = s'_i = \xi(\alpha_i)$ by assumption, we see that s_{ctr} and s'_{ctr} are identically distributed in this case.
- Otherwise: let k be the smallest index such that $H(\vec{\alpha}, L_{ctr} = L_k) = 1$. Then s_{ctr} is defined to be s_k. On the other hand, this means that $L_{ctr}(\vec{\alpha}) = L_k(\vec{\alpha})$, in other words $\alpha_{ctr} = \alpha_k$, so $s'_{ctr} = \xi(\alpha_{ctr}) = \xi(\alpha_k) = s'_k$. Since we have $s_k = s'_k$ by assumption, we see that s_{ctr} and s_k are in fact the same in this case.

Hence, in both cases, we see that s_{ctr} and s'_{ctr} are identically distributed. Therefore the theorem follows.   □

5   Query Complexity of the SHQ Problem

In this section, we analyze the complexity of the SHQ problem. In fact, we are going to analyze both the worst-case version and the average-case version.

5.1   Useless Queries

One crucial notion that we are going to use is that of useless queries. Let us define a hyperplane query H useless, if it is possible to know that the return value $H(\vec{\alpha}, H)$ should be 1 before making the query, based on the return values for the previous hyperplane queries made: for example, if the solver A previously made a query H and received the answer $H(\vec{\alpha}, H) = 1$, then making the same query H again will definitely give the same answer 1. Another example is that, if A previously made $p - 1$ queries $X_1 = j$ for $j = 1, \ldots, p - 1$ and received answer $H(\vec{\alpha}, X_1 = j) = 0$ for all $j = 1, \ldots, p - 1$, then A can deduce that $H(\vec{\alpha}, X_1 = 0) = 1$, so the hyperplane query $X_1 = 0$ is useless. In general, suppose so far A made $q = r + s$ hyperplane queries $H_1, \ldots, H_r, H'_1, \ldots, H'_s$, and assume that $H(\vec{\alpha}, H_i) = 1$ for $i = 1, \ldots, r$, and $H(\vec{\alpha}, H'_j) = 0$ for $j = 1, \ldots, s$. Then the information given by the answers to the queries is exactly

$$\vec{\alpha} \in \bigcap_{i=1}^{r} H_i \setminus \bigcup_{j=1}^{s} H'_j.$$

Hence, we may formally define a hyperplane query H made at this point as useless if

$$\bigcap_{i=1}^{r} H_i \setminus \bigcup_{j=1}^{s} H'_j \subseteq H.$$

If a query H is not useless, we call it *useful*.

Note that it is possible to determine if H is useless or not algorithmically. Since we only consider the query complexity of solvers, this does not even have to be efficient.

Remark 3. While it is possible to extend the definition of useless queries to include all queries which are destined to return 0 as the answer, we choose not to. This is because later we want to force a solver to make exactly q useful queries. So if a solver does not make enough queries, then we modify it to make additional useful queries. In fact, we modify a solver to make additional queries which are destined to return 0, which would all be useful according to our current definition.

5.2   Worst-Case SHQ

Theorem 2. *Any worst-case SHQ solver should make at least $n(p-1)$ queries.*

Proof. Let A be a worst-case SHQ solver. We show that, without loss of generality, we may assume that A never asks useless queries. Suppose that A is a solver which may ask useless queries. Then, we construct a solver B as follows: B runs A internally, and eventually outputs A's output. When A asks a hyperplane query H, B first determines if it is useless or not. If it is useless, then B replies with 1. If it is useful, then B makes the same oracle query, receives the answer bit b, and returns the same bit b to the solver A. So, B is a worst-case SHQ solver which makes no more queries than A, and B also does not make any useless queries. If we show this theorem for B, then the result for A immediately follows.

Now, let A be a worst-case SHQ solver which never makes useless queries. Suppose that A makes at most q queries, and $q < n(p-1)$. Let $H_1, H_2, \ldots, H_q$ be the affine hyperplanes queried by A, represented by linear equations: let

$$H_i(X_1, \ldots, X_n) = a_{i1}X_1 + \cdots + a_{in}X_n - b_i.$$

Then we show that $|\cup_{i=1}^{q} H_i| \leq p^n - 2$. First, we cannot have that $|\cup_{i=1}^{q} H_i| = p^n$; in this case, we have $\cup_{i=1}^{q} H_i = \mathbb{Z}_p^n$, so

$$\mathbb{Z}_p^n \setminus \bigcup_{i=1}^{q-1} H_i \subseteq H_q,$$

which shows that the last query H_q is useless.

Next, suppose that $|\cup_{i=1}^{q} H_i| = p^n - 1$. Let $\mathbb{Z}_p^n \setminus \cup_{i=1}^{q} H_i$, which is a singleton, be $\{\vec{\beta} = (\beta_1, \ldots, \beta_n)\}$.

Then, we define $F \in \mathbb{Z}_p[X_1, \ldots, X_n]$ as

$$F(X_1, \ldots, X_n) := \prod_{i=1}^{q} (a_{i1}(X_1 + \beta_1) + \cdots + a_{in}(X_n + \beta_n) - b_i).$$

We can easily see that $\deg(F) = q < n(p-1)$, $F(\vec{0}) \neq 0$, and $F(\vec{x}) = 0$ for any $\vec{x} \neq \vec{0}$, which contradicts Theorem 1.8 of Bruen [6], which we quote as Theorem 3 below.

Therefore, whenever $q < n(p-1)$, there should be at least two points $\vec{\beta} \neq \vec{\gamma} \in \mathbb{Z}_p^n$ which are not on $\cup_{i=1}^{q} H_i$. This allows us to use the standard adversary argument against A: for any such SHQ solver A, whenever A asks a hyperplane query H, answer with 0. In the end, if A outputs $\vec{\beta}$, pretend that $\vec{\alpha} = \vec{\gamma}$, and if A outputs any point other than $\vec{\beta}$, pretend that $\vec{\alpha} = \vec{\beta}$. This shows that A in general does not solve the worst-case SHQ problem. Therefore, q should be at least $n(p-1)$ if A is any worst-case SHQ solver. □

Theorem 3 (Theorem 1.8 of [6]). *Let F in $\mathbb{Z}_p[X_1, \ldots, X_n]$ satisfy the following conditions.*

1. $F(\vec{0}) \neq 0$
2. $F(\vec{x}) = 0$ if $\vec{x} \neq \vec{0}$

Then $\deg(F) \geq n(p-1)$.

For the proof of Theorem 3, we refer to [6].

5.3   Worst-Case SHQ with Uncertainty

Theorem 2 shows that the brute-force SHQ solver given in Example 1 is actually optimal in that, if any algorithm A makes at most $q < n(p-1)$ queries, then A is not a worst-case SHQ solver: there are instances where A cannot find the correct answer.

Therefore, if an algorithm A makes at most $q < n(p-1)$ queries, then the best A could do might be to output a list L which contains the correct solution $\vec{\alpha}$, instead of uniquely identifying the correct solution. For such an algorithm, let us call $|L|$ the *uncertainty*. We call an algorithm A as the *worst-case SHQ solver with uncertainty level u*, if A always outputs a list L containing the correct solution $\vec{\alpha}$, and $|L| \leq u$.

The solver in Example 1 can easily be modified to output such a list, even when $q < n(p-1)$: let $q = r(p-1) + s$ for some $r, s \in \mathbb{Z}$ with $0 \leq s < p-1$. the solver makes $r(p-1)$ hyperplane queries of form $\mathsf{H}(\vec{\alpha}, X_i = j)$ for $i = 1, \ldots, r$, $j = 1, \ldots, p-1$, to completely determine $\alpha_1, \ldots, \alpha_r$, and makes additional s queries of form $\mathsf{H}(\vec{\alpha}, X_{r+1} = j)$ for $j = 1, \ldots, s$. If $\mathsf{H}(\vec{\alpha}, X_{r+1} = j) = 1$ for some j, then the brute-force solver knows $\alpha_1, \ldots, \alpha_r, \alpha_{r+1}$, and so it outputs the list L consisting of points $(\alpha_1, \ldots, \alpha_{r+1}, \beta_{r+2}, \ldots, \beta_n)$, for $(\beta_{r+2}, \ldots, \beta_n) \in \mathbb{Z}_p^{n-r-1}$. On the other hand, if none of the s queries return 0, then it outputs the list L consisting of points

$$(\alpha_1, \ldots, \alpha_r, \gamma, \beta_{r+2}, \ldots, \beta_n),$$

where $\gamma \notin \{1, \ldots, s\}$ and $(\beta_{r+2}, \ldots, \beta_n) \in \mathbb{Z}_p^{n-r-1}$. Therefore, $|L| \leq (p - s)p^{n-r-1}$ in both cases. So, the brute-force SHQ solver can be considered as a worst-case SHQ solver with uncertainty level $u = (p - s)p^{n-r-1}$. The question is, can we find a SHQ solver with the same q but smaller uncertainty level?

We show that the brute-force solver is still optimal even in this context:

Theorem 4. *Let A be a worst-case SHQ solver with uncertainty level u. Suppose A makes at most q hyperplane queries, and let $q = r(p-1)+s$ with $0 \leq s < p-1$. Then, u should be at least $(p - s)p^{n-r-1}$.*

Proof. Again we may assume that A never makes useless queries. Let $H_1, H_2, \ldots, H_q$ be the affine hyperplanes queried by A, represented by linear equations: let

$$H_i(X_1, \ldots, X_n) = a_{i1}X_1 + \cdots + a_{in}X_n - b_i.$$

Then, we simply define $F \in \mathbb{Z}_p[X_1, \ldots, X_n]$ as

$$F(X_1, \ldots, X_n) := \prod_{i=1}^{q} H_i(X_1, \ldots, X_n).$$

Let $Z(F) \subseteq \mathbb{Z}_p^n$ be the set of $\vec{\beta} \in \mathbb{Z}_p^n$ such that $F(\vec{\beta}) = 0$. Clearly, $Z(F) = \cup_{i=1}^{q}H_i$. Since A never makes useless queries, $\cup_{i=1}^{q}H_i \neq \mathbb{Z}_p^n$, as in Theorem 2. Then, by Theorem 3.6 of Sorensen [13] which we quote as Theorem 5 below, we have

$$\left| \bigcup_{i=1}^{q} H_i \right| \leq p^n - (p - s)p^{n-r-1}.$$

Now, suppose that A is a solver with uncertainty level $u < (p - s)p^{n-r-1}$. Then, we can use the standard adversary argument as follows: for any query H_i of A, reply with 0. Let L be the final output of A. Since $|\cup H_i| \leq p^n - (p-s)p^{n-r-1}$ and $|L| < (p - s)p^{n-r-1}$, we have

$$\left| L \cup \bigcup_{i=1}^{q} H_i \right| < p^n,$$

hence there exists some $\vec{\alpha} \in \mathbb{Z}_p^n$ such that $\vec{\alpha} \notin L \cup (\cup_i H_i)$. This shows that with respect to this particular $\vec{\alpha}$, the answer 0 to all the queries was consistent, and despite this $\vec{\alpha} \notin L$, contradicting that A is a worst-case solver with uncertainty level u. Therefore, for any such solver A, u should be at least $(p - s)p^{n-r-1}$. □

The proof of Theorem 4 relies on the following Theorem 5, which estimates the number of rational points on codimension-1 algebraic sets.

Theorem 5 (Theorem 3.6 of [13]). *Let $F \in \mathbb{Z}_p[X_1, \ldots, X_n]$ be a polynomial of degree q, with $q \leq n(p-1)$. Let $q = r(p-1)+s$, $0 \leq s < p-1$, and let $|Z(F)|$ denote the number of zeros of F in $\mathbb{Z}_p^n$. Then,*

$$|Z(F)| = p^n$$

or

$$|Z(F)| \leq p^n - (p - s)p^{n-r-1}.$$

For the proof of Theorem 5, we refer to [13].

5.4   Average-Case SHQ

Now let us return to the average-case SHQ, which is related to MDL.

Theorem 6. *Let A be any SHQ solver which makes at most q hyperplane queries. Then,*

$$\mathbf{Adv}_{p,n}^{\mathsf{shq}}(A) \leq \frac{1}{p^n} \sum_{i=0}^{n} \binom{q}{i}.$$

Proof. Let A be a SHQ solver which makes at most q hyperplane queries. We are going to argue that we may safely assume that A satisfies certain properties.

First, using essentially the same argument as in Theorem 2, WLOG we may assume that A never makes useless queries.

Second, we may also assume that A makes exactly q (useful) queries: if A is a SHQ solver never making useless queries, then we define a SHQ solver B as follows: B initializes a counter $ctr \leftarrow 0$, runs A internally, and whenever A makes a query H, then B makes the same query, receives the answer bit b, then returns the bit b to the solver A, and increments the counter: $ctr \leftarrow ctr + 1$. Eventually, A will halt with an output $\vec{\alpha}'$. Since ctr counts the number of hyperplane queries made by A, we have $ctr \leq q$. Then B makes $q - ctr$ additional hyperplane queries which are not useless as follows: in case there was at least one hyperplane query H made by A with 0 as the answer, all of the $q - ctr$ remaining queries made by B will be H: surely this query is not useless, for the answer should be 0. On the other hand, in case there was at least one hyperplane query H made by A with 1 as the answer, let us write H as $H(X_1, \ldots, X_n) = a_1 X_1 + \cdots + a_n X_n - b$. Then, let H_0 be the corresponding linear hyperplane defined by $H_0(X_1, \ldots, X_n) = a_1 X_1 + \cdots + a_n X_n$. Clearly, $H_0 \neq \mathbb{Z}_p^n$, so there exists a vector $\vec{v} \in \mathbb{Z}_p^n$ satisfying $\vec{v} \notin H_0$. In fact, we may easily find such a $\vec{v}$: since $(a_1, \ldots, a_n) \neq \vec{0}$, WLOG we may assume $a_1 \neq 0$. Then, $\vec{v} := (a_1, 0, 0, \ldots, 0)$ is such an example. Now, let H' be the hyperplane $H + \vec{v}$, which is a parallel translation of H by $\vec{v}$. We may show that $\mathsf{H}(\vec{\alpha}, H') = 0$: suppose not, then $\vec{\alpha} \in H' = H + \vec{v}$, and $\vec{\alpha} \in H$ by assumption. Then, from these two we may conclude that $\vec{v} \in H_0$, which contradicts the construction of $\vec{v}$. Therefore, in this case B makes $q - ctr$ queries, all of them H'. Again these queries are not useless. Finally, B halts with the answer $\vec{\alpha}'$, which was the output of A.

By the construction, B makes exactly q useful queries, but since the output of B is identical to that of A, we have $\mathbf{Adv}_{p,n}^{\mathsf{shq}}(B) = \mathbf{Adv}_{p,n}^{\mathsf{shq}}(A)$. So, if we prove this theorem for B, the theorem for A clearly follows.

Therefore, now assume that our SHQ solver A makes exactly q useful queries. In general, A may be probabilistic, consuming finite but unbounded number of random bits. Therefore, let us write $A^{\mathsf{H}(\vec{\alpha}, \cdot)}(p, n; \vec{r})$ as the output of the algorithm A with input p, n, while having access to the oracle $\mathsf{H}(\vec{\alpha}, \cdot)$ and when the randomness used is $\vec{r} = (r_1, r_2, r_3, \ldots) \in \{0, 1\}^\infty$.

Then we observe that, once $\vec{\alpha}$, $\vec{r}$, and the algorithm A are fixed, the queries made by A and the corresponding answers are also fixed. More precisely, let $H_1, \ldots, H_q$ be the hyperplane queries made by A with some fixed $\vec{\alpha}$, $\vec{r}$, and let $b_1, \ldots, b_q$ be the answer bits: $b_i = \mathsf{H}(\vec{\alpha}, H_i)$. Let us define $\vec{H} := (H_1, \ldots, H_q)$ and

$\vec{b} := (b_1, \ldots, b_q)$. Then, in fact, we can see that A, $\vec{r}$, and $\vec{b}$ completely determine $\vec{H}$, and A, $\vec{r}$, and $\vec{\alpha}$ completely determine $\vec{b}$. So we use the following notation: $\vec{H} = \mathcal{H}_{\vec{r}}^{(A)}(\vec{b})$, $\vec{b} = \mathcal{B}_{\vec{r}}^{(A)}(\vec{\alpha})$. Sometimes we just write $\mathcal{H}(\vec{b})$, $\mathcal{B}(\vec{\alpha})$ to simplify notation, when the context is clear.

Moreover, we see that the output $A^{H(\vec{\alpha}, \cdot)}(p, n; \vec{r})$ of the algorithm A is completely determined by A, $\vec{r}$, and the vector $\vec{b}$. So we may write $A^{H(\vec{\alpha}, \cdot)}(p, n; \vec{r})$ as $\mathcal{A}_{\vec{r}}(\vec{b})$. Again, sometimes we just write $\mathcal{A}(\vec{b})$, suppressing $\vec{r}$. For a randomly chosen $\vec{\alpha}$, since the output $\mathcal{A}_{\vec{r}}(\vec{b})$ is determined by $\vec{b} = \mathcal{B}(\vec{\alpha})$, which is in turn determined by $\vec{\alpha}$, we may write $A^{H(\vec{\alpha}, \cdot)}(p, n; \vec{r}) = \mathcal{A}(\mathcal{B}(\vec{\alpha}))$.

Now, let us fix the randomness $\vec{r}$, and let us compute the advantage of A, which is $\mathbf{Pr}[A^{H(\vec{\boldsymbol{\alpha}}, \cdot)}(p, n; \vec{r}) = \vec{\boldsymbol{\alpha}}]$, where the probability is only over the random choice of $\vec{\boldsymbol{\alpha}}$. Here, to emphasize that it is a random variable, we used the bold typeface to write $\vec{\boldsymbol{\alpha}}$. We then have

$$\mathbf{Pr}[A^{H(\vec{\boldsymbol{\alpha}}, \cdot)}(p, n; \vec{r}) = \vec{\boldsymbol{\alpha}}] = \mathbf{Pr}[\mathcal{A}(\mathcal{B}(\vec{\boldsymbol{\alpha}})) = \vec{\boldsymbol{\alpha}}]$$
$$= \sum_{\vec{\alpha}} \mathbf{Pr}[\vec{\boldsymbol{\alpha}} = \vec{\alpha}] \cdot \mathbf{Pr}[\mathcal{A}(\mathcal{B}(\vec{\boldsymbol{\alpha}})) = \vec{\boldsymbol{\alpha}} \mid \vec{\boldsymbol{\alpha}} = \vec{\alpha}]$$
$$= \frac{1}{p^n} \sum_{\vec{\alpha}} \mathbf{Pr}[\mathcal{A}(\mathcal{B}(\vec{\alpha})) = \vec{\alpha}],$$

where $\vec{\boldsymbol{\alpha}}$ is a random variable with uniform distribution on $\mathbb{Z}_p^n$, and $\vec{\alpha}$ is used for possible concrete values of $\vec{\boldsymbol{\alpha}}$. Note that $\mathbf{Pr}[\mathcal{A}(\mathcal{B}(\vec{\alpha})) = \vec{\alpha}]$ should be either 0 or 1, for any $\vec{\alpha}$, because all randomness is fixed: we have $\mathbf{Pr}[\mathcal{A}(\mathcal{B}(\vec{\alpha})) = \vec{\alpha}] = 1$ iff $\mathcal{A}(\mathcal{B}(\vec{\alpha})) = \vec{\alpha}$. Continuing,

$$\mathbf{Pr}[A^{H(\vec{\boldsymbol{\alpha}}, \cdot)}(p, n; \vec{r}) = \vec{\boldsymbol{\alpha}}] = \frac{1}{p^n} \sum_{\vec{\alpha}} \mathbf{Pr}[\mathcal{A}(\mathcal{B}(\vec{\alpha})) = \vec{\alpha}],$$
$$= \frac{1}{p^n} \sum_{\vec{b}} \sum_{\vec{\alpha}: \mathcal{B}(\vec{\alpha}) = \vec{b}} \mathbf{Pr}[\mathcal{A}(\mathcal{B}(\vec{\alpha})) = \vec{\alpha}],$$
$$= \frac{1}{p^n} \sum_{\vec{b}} \sum_{\vec{\alpha}: \mathcal{B}(\vec{\alpha}) = \vec{b}} \mathbf{Pr}[\mathcal{A}(\vec{b}) = \vec{\alpha}],$$

We can see that, in the above, for any $\vec{b}$,

$$\sum_{\vec{\alpha}: \mathcal{B}(\vec{\alpha}) = \vec{b}} \mathbf{Pr}[\mathcal{A}(\vec{b}) = \vec{\alpha}] \leq 1,$$

where the sum is over all $\vec{\alpha}$ satisfying $\mathcal{B}(\vec{\alpha}) = \vec{b}$. Indeed, the only $\vec{\alpha}$ which can possibly make $\mathbf{Pr}[\mathcal{A}(\vec{b}) = \vec{\alpha}] = 1$ is $\vec{\alpha} = \mathcal{A}(\vec{b})$, so if $\mathcal{B}(\mathcal{A}(\vec{b})) = \vec{b}$, then the above value is 1, and if $\mathcal{B}(\mathcal{A}(\vec{b})) \neq \vec{b}$ then the above value is 0.

Therefore, we see that

$$\mathbf{Pr}[A^{\mathsf{H}(\vec{\alpha},\cdot)}(p,n;\vec{r}) = \vec{\alpha}] \le \frac{1}{p^n} \sum_{\vec{b}} 1$$

$$= \frac{\text{the number of all possible } \vec{b}\text{'s}}{p^n}.$$

Any $\vec{b} = \mathcal{B}(\alpha)$ is a bitstring of length q, and moreover, in any such $\vec{b}$, 1 cannot occur more than n times. This is because we assumed that the algorithm A never makes useless queries; suppose $H_1, \ldots, H_m$ are hyperplane queries made by A with 1 as the answer. Then, all of these hyperplanes intersect ($\vec{\alpha}$ is on all of them). Moreover, due to the fact that all these queries were useful, we have

$$H_1 \cap \cdots \cap H_i \nsubseteq H_{i+1},$$

for all $i = 1, 2, \ldots, m-1$. But then each additional hyperplane should decrement the dimension of the intersection by 1, so there can be at most n such hyperplanes, and there can be at most n 1s in any $\vec{b}$. Hence we have,

$$\mathbf{Pr}[A^{\mathsf{H}(\vec{\alpha},\cdot)}(p,n;\vec{r}) = \vec{\alpha}] \le \frac{1}{p^n} \sum_{i=0}^{n} \binom{q}{i}.$$

Finally, the theorem is satisfied for general A, because when conditioned on any randomness $\vec{r}$, the success probability is bounded by the same upper bound $p^{-n} \sum_{i=0}^{n} \binom{q}{i}$. □

Corollary 1. *Let A be any SHQ solver which makes at most q hyperplane queries. Then,*

$$\mathbf{Adv}_{p,n}^{\mathsf{shq}}(A) \le \frac{1}{p^n} + \frac{1}{2}\left(\frac{eq}{np}\right)^n.$$

Proof. The proof follows from Theorem 6 and the following Theorem 7. □

Remark 4. If we write q as $q = np\delta$ for some δ, then Corollary 1 says that the advantage of the solver A is bounded by $p^{-n} + (e\delta)^n/2$. Since we assume that $n = o(p)$, certainly $p^{-n} \le n/p = o(1)$. Now we want to show that $\delta = \Omega(1)$. Suppose not. Then we may find an increasing sequence $\{\lambda_i\}$ of values of the parameter λ such that $\delta(\lambda_i) \to 0$ as $i \to 0$. Then, $e\delta(\lambda_i) < 1$ eventually, and then $(e\delta(\lambda_i))^n/2 \le e\delta(\lambda_i)/2 \to 0$ as $i \to 0$. Therefore, this contradicts that A solves SHQ with constant advantage. This shows that if A solves SHQ with constant advantage, then $\delta = q/np = \Omega(1)$. In short, a SHQ solver with constant advantage should make $\Omega(np)$ queries.

Theorem 7. *We have*

$$\sum_{i=1}^{n} \binom{q}{i} \le \frac{1}{2}\left(\frac{eq}{n}\right)^n$$

for any positive integers q, n satisfying $1 \le n \le q$.

The proof of Theorem 7 is in Appendix A.

6   Conclusion

6.1   Generic Hardness of MDL

By combining the results so far, we obtain the following corollary:

Corollary 2. *Let A be any generic MDL solver which makes at most q queries. Then,*

$$\mathbf{Adv}_{p,n}^{\mathsf{mdl}}(A) \leq \frac{1}{p^n} + \frac{1}{2}\left(\frac{e(q+n+1)^2}{2np}\right)^n.$$

Proof. This follows directly from Theorem 1 and Corollary 1.   □

Let us write $q = \sqrt{np}\delta$ for some δ. Then, the upper bound of $\mathbf{Adv}_{p,n}^{\mathsf{mdl}}(A)$ in Corollary 2 can be expanded as

$$\frac{1}{p^n} + \frac{1}{2}\left(\frac{e(\sqrt{np}\delta + n + 1)^2}{2np}\right)^n$$
$$= \frac{1}{p^n} + \frac{1}{2}\left(\frac{e\delta^2}{2} + e\delta\sqrt{\frac{n}{p}} + \frac{e\delta}{\sqrt{np}} + \frac{en}{2p} + \frac{e}{p} + \frac{e}{2np}\right)^n.$$

Suppose that A solves MDL with constant advantage. Then we can see that $\delta = \Omega(1)$: suppose not, then we may assume that we can find an increasing sequence $\{\lambda_i\}$ of values of the parameter λ such that $\delta(\lambda_i) \to 0$ as $i \to 0$. Then, $\delta(\lambda_i)$ is eventually bounded by $\sqrt{1/e}$, and since we assume that $n = o(p)$, we have

$$\frac{e\delta(\lambda_i)^2}{2} + e\delta(\lambda_i)\sqrt{\frac{n(\lambda_i)}{p(\lambda_i)}} + \frac{e\delta(\lambda_i)}{\sqrt{n(\lambda_i)p(\lambda_i)}} + \frac{en(\lambda_i)}{2p(\lambda_i)} + \frac{e}{p(\lambda_i)} + \frac{e}{2n(\lambda_i)p(\lambda_i)} \to 0,$$

as $i \to 0$. Therefore,

$$\frac{1}{p(\lambda_i)^{n(\lambda_i)}} + \frac{1}{2}\left(\frac{e(\sqrt{n(\lambda_i)p(\lambda_i)}\delta + n(\lambda_i) + 1)^2}{2n(\lambda_i)p(\lambda_i)}\right)^n \to 0,$$

as $i \to 0$, contradicting that A has constant advantage. Hence, we conclude that $\delta = q/\sqrt{np} = \Omega(1)$. Therefore, if a generic MDL solver has constant advantage, then it should make $\Omega(\sqrt{np})$ queries. This affirmatively settles Kuhn and Struik's conjecture [8].

6.2   Interval-MDL

We may also consider Interval-MDL, where instead of the exponents $\alpha_1, \ldots, \alpha_n$ are chosen from the whole group $\mathbb{Z}_p$, they are chosen from an interval $\{0, 1, \ldots, l-1\} \subseteq \mathbb{Z}_p$ of size l. For example, Boneh-Goh-Nissim homomorphic encryption [5] requires solving DL for exponents chosen from such an interval, and Bernstein and Lange [2] suggested preprocessing methods to speed up such computations.

We remark that with trivial modifications, all of our results (except those about the worst-case SHQ problems) also apply to Interval-MDL and the corresponding Interval-SHQ: in the upper bounds for advantages, simply replace the group order p with the interval size l. For example, the bound in Corollary 2 becomes

$$\frac{1}{l^n} + \frac{1}{2}\left(\frac{e(q+n+1)^2}{2nl}\right)^n,$$

and a generic Interval-MDL solver with constant advantage should make $\Omega(\sqrt{nl})$ queries, assuming $n = o(l)$. This is because our proof techniques, especially that of Theorem 6, work equally well for the interval version. For that matter, the size-l subset does not even have to be an interval: any subset of size l would do.

Acknowledgments. This research was supported by Basic Science Research Program through the National Research Foundation of Korea (NRF) funded by the Ministry of Education (No. 2011-0025127).

A Proof of Theorem 7

Before proving Theorem 7, we need a technical lemma:

Lemma 1. *Suppose that $q \geq 5$ and $2 \leq n \leq q - 3$. Then,*

$$q\sum_{i=1}^{n}\binom{q}{i} \geq (n+1)\sum_{i=1}^{n+1}\binom{q}{i}. \tag{1}$$

Proof. Letting $S := \sum_{i=1}^{n}\binom{q}{i}$, we may write the inequality (1) as

$$qS \geq (n+1)\left(S + \binom{q}{n+1}\right). \tag{2}$$

This can be simplified as

$$\frac{n+1}{q-n-1}\binom{q}{n+1} \leq S. \tag{3}$$

But,

$$\begin{aligned}
\frac{n+1}{q-n-1}\binom{q}{n+1} &= \frac{n+1}{q-n-1} \cdot \frac{q!}{(n+1)!(q-n-1)!} \\
&= \frac{q-n}{q-n-1} \cdot \frac{q!}{n!(q-n)!} \tag{4} \\
&= \frac{q-n}{q-n-1}\binom{q}{n}.
\end{aligned}$$

So, the inequality (1) is equivalent to

$$\left(1 + \frac{1}{q-n-1}\right)\binom{q}{n} \leq \sum_{i=1}^{n}\binom{q}{i}, \tag{5}$$

which in turn is equivalent to

$$\frac{1}{q-n-1}\binom{q}{n} \le \sum_{i=1}^{n-1}\binom{q}{i}. \tag{6}$$

So let us prove this inequality (6).

Consider the function $f(n) := (n-1)(q-1-n)$. As a function of n, this is a quadratic concave function with $f(1) = f(q-1) = 0$. Since we assume $2 \le n \le q-3$, we have $f(n) \ge \min(f(2), f(q-3))$. Since $f(2) = q-3 \ge 2$ and $f(q-3) = 2(q-4) \ge 2$, we have

$$(n-1)(q-1-n) \ge 2, \tag{7}$$

for any $n = 2, \ldots, q-3$. Simple calculation shows that this is equivalent to

$$\frac{1}{(q-n-1)n} \le \frac{1}{q-n+1}. \tag{8}$$

Then,

$$
\begin{aligned}
\frac{1}{q-n-1}\binom{q}{n} &= \frac{1}{(q-n-1)n} \cdot n\binom{q}{n} \\
&\le \frac{1}{q-n+1} \cdot n\binom{q}{n} \\
&\le \frac{n}{q-n+1} \cdot \frac{q!}{n!(q-n)!} = \frac{q!}{(n-1)!(q-n+1)!} \\
&= \binom{q}{n-1} \le \sum_{i=1}^{n-1}\binom{q}{i}.
\end{aligned}
\tag{9}
$$

$\square$

Now we are ready to prove Theorem 7:

Theorem 7. *We have*

$$\sum_{i=1}^{n}\binom{q}{i} \le \frac{1}{2}\left(\frac{eq}{n}\right)^n \tag{10}$$

for any positive integers q, n satisfying $1 \le n \le q$.

Proof. The proof is based on case analysis. First, we prove the inequality when $q \ge 5$ and $1 \le n \le q-2$.

From Lemma 1, we have

$$q\sum_{i=1}^{n}\binom{q}{i} \ge (n+1)\sum_{i=1}^{n+1}\binom{q}{i}, \tag{11}$$

for $q \ge 5$ and $2 \le n \le q-3$.

Then, since $e \ge (1+1/n)^n$, we have

$$eq\sum_{i=1}^{n}\binom{q}{i} \ge \left(1+\frac{1}{n}\right)^n (n+1)\sum_{i=1}^{n+1}\binom{q}{i}, \tag{12}$$

which is equivalent to

$$\left(\frac{n}{eq}\right)^n \sum_{i=1}^{n} \binom{q}{i} \geq \left(\frac{n+1}{eq}\right)^{n+1} \sum_{i=1}^{n+1} \binom{q}{i}. \tag{13}$$

Also, when $n = 1$, the above inequality (13) is

$$\frac{1}{eq} \binom{q}{1} \geq \left(\frac{2}{eq}\right)^2 \sum_{i=1}^{2} \binom{q}{i}, \tag{14}$$

which is equivalent to

$$\frac{e}{2} \geq 1 + \frac{1}{q}, \tag{15}$$

which is certainly satisfied when $q \geq 5$. So,

$$\left(\frac{n}{eq}\right)^n \sum_{i=1}^{n} \binom{q}{i} \tag{16}$$

is a decreasing function for $n \in \{1, 2, \ldots, q-2\}$. Then, for any $n = 1, 2, \ldots, q-2$, we have

$$\left(\frac{n}{eq}\right)^n \sum_{i=1}^{n} \binom{q}{i} \leq \left(\frac{1}{eq}\right)^1 \sum_{i=1}^{1} \binom{q}{i} = \frac{1}{e} \leq \frac{1}{2}, \tag{17}$$

proving the inequality (10) when $q \geq 5$ and $1 \leq n \leq q - 2$.

Therefore, we need to handle the remaining cases: when $q \leq 4$, or when $n = q - 1, q$.

– Case $n = q$: Then the inequality (10) is equivalent to

$$2^q - 1 \leq \frac{1}{2} \left(\frac{eq}{q}\right)^q = \frac{e^q}{2}. \tag{18}$$

This holds when $2^q \leq e^q/2$, which can be written as $q/(q+1) \geq \log 2 \approx 0.693\cdots$. So this inequality holds when $q \geq 3$; then $q/(q+1) \geq 0.75 > \log 2$. We can also check that $2^q - 1 \leq e^q/2$ holds for $q = 1, 2$ separately.

– Case $n = q - 1$: Then the inequality (10) is equivalent to

$$2^q - 2 \leq \left(\frac{q}{q-1}\right)^{q-1} \frac{e^{q-1}}{2}. \tag{19}$$

Since the right-hand side is greater than $e^{q-1}/2$, the inequality is satisfied if $2^q - 2 \leq e^{q-1}/2$. First, we can check that $2^q \leq e^{q-1}/2$ holds if $q \geq 6$. And we can also separately check the inequality (19) for $q = 2, \ldots, 5$. This finishes this case.

– Case $q \leq 4$: Here, we need only to show that the inequality (10) holds when $n = 1$ or 2 (of course when $n \leq q$). This is because, when $q = 1, 2$, then $n = 1, 2$ cases cover all possibilities. Also, when $q = 3, 4$, then $n = 1, 2$, and $n = q - 1, q$ cases cover all possibilities. Hence,

− Case $n = 1$: Then the inequality (10) is equivalent to

$$q \le \frac{1}{2} \left(\frac{eq}{1} \right), \tag{20}$$

which holds trivially, since $e \ge 2$.
− Case $n = 2$: Then the inequality (10) is equivalent to

$$q + \frac{q(q-1)}{2} = \frac{q(q+1)}{2} \le \frac{1}{2} \left(\frac{eq}{2} \right)^2. \tag{21}$$

Simplifying, we get

$$\frac{1}{q} \le \frac{e^2}{4} - 1 \approx 0.847 \cdots, \tag{22}$$

which holds for $q \ge 2$.   □

References

1. Digital signature standard (DSS). NIST (National Institute of Standards and Technology) FIPS, 186–4 (2013)
2. Bernstein, D.J., Lange, T.: Computing small discrete logarithms faster. In: Galbraith, S., Nandi, M. (eds.) INDOCRYPT 2012. LNCS, vol. 7668, pp. 317–338. Springer, Heidelberg (2012)
3. Boneh, D., Boyen, X.: Short signatures without random oracles and the SDH assumption in bilinear groups. J. Cryptol. **21**(2), 149–177 (2008)
4. Boneh, D., Boyen, X., Shacham, H.: Short group signatures. In: Franklin, M. (ed.) CRYPTO 2004. LNCS, vol. 3152, pp. 41–55. Springer, Heidelberg (2004)
5. Boneh, D., Goh, E.-J., Nissim, K.: Evaluating 2-DNF formulas on ciphertexts. In: Kilian, J. (ed.) TCC 2005. LNCS, vol. 3378, pp. 325–341. Springer, Heidelberg (2005)
6. Bruen, A.A.: Polynomial multiplicities over finite fields and intersection sets. Journal of Combinatorial Theory, Series A **60**(1), 19–33 (1992)
7. Hitchcock, Y., Montague, P., Carter, G., Dawson, E.: The efficiency of solving multiple discrete logarithm problems and the implications for the security of fixed elliptic curves. International Journal of Information Security **3**(2), 86–98 (2004)
8. Kuhn, F., Struik, R.: Random walks revisited: Extensions of Pollard's Rho algorithm for computing multiple discrete logarithms. In: Vaudenay, S., Youssef, A.M. (eds.) SAC 2001. LNCS, vol. 2259, p. 212. Springer, Heidelberg (2001)
9. Lee, H.T., Cheon, J.H., Hong, J.: Accelerating ID-based encryption based on trapdoor DL using pre-computation. Cryptology ePrint Archive, Report 2011/187 (2011). http://eprint.iacr.org/2011/187
10. Maurer, U.M., Yacobi, Y.: A non-interactive public-key distribution system. Designs, Codes and Cryptography **9**(3), 305–316 (1996)
11. Nechaev, V.I.: Complexity of a determinate algorithm for the discrete logarithm. Mathematical Notes **55**(2), 165–172 (1994)
12. Shoup, V.: Lower bounds for discrete logarithms and related problems. In: Fumy, W. (ed.) EUROCRYPT 1997. LNCS, vol. 1233, pp. 256–266. Springer, Heidelberg (1997)
13. Sørensen, A.B.: On the number of rational points on codimension-1 algebraic sets in $P^n(F_q)$. Discrete Mathematics **135**(1–3), 321–334 (1994)

Author Index

Printed in the United States
By Bookmasters